THE HAMMOND WORLD ATLAS

SUPERIOR EDITION

HAMMOND INCORPORATED
MAPLEWOOD, NEW JERSEY New York Chicago

Hammond Publications Advisory Board

PRINTED IN THE UNITED STATES OF AMERICA

Library of Congress Cataloging in Publication Data
Hammond Incorporated.
Hammond world atlas.
1. Atlases. I. Title.
G1019.H556 1976 912 76-20417
ISBN 0-8437-1620-7

Contents

GAZETTEER-INDEX OF THE WORLD

This alphabetical list of grand divisions, countries, states, colonial possessions, etc., gives area, population, capital or chief town, and index references and page numbers on which they are shown on the largest scale. The index reference shows the square on the respective map in which the name of the entry may be located.

Country	Area (Sq. Miles)	Population	Capital or Chief Town	Index Ref.	Plate No.
Afars and Issas, Terr. of the	8,498	125,050	Djibouti	P 9	38
*Afghanistan	250,000	17,078,263	Kabul	A 2	34
Africa	11,682,000	345,000,000	....	....	38-39
Alabama, U.S.A.	51,609	3,444,165	Montgomery	....	50
Alaska, U.S.A.	586,412	302,173	Juneau	....	53
*Albania	11,100	2,126,000	Tiranë	B 3	29
Alberta, Canada	255,285	1,614,000	Edmonton	E 5	43
*Algeria	919,515	13,547,000	Algiers	F 6	38
American Samoa	76	27,769	Pago Pago	K 7	41
Andorra	175	19,000	Andorra la Vella	G 1	27
Angola	481,351	5,430,000	Luanda	K14	39
Antarctica	5,500,000	....		E 9	17
Antigua	171	63,000	St. Johns	G 3	48
*Argentina	1,072,070	23,983,000	Buenos Aires	....	47
Arizona, U.S.A.	113,909	1,772,482	Phoenix	....	54
Arkansas, U.S.A.	53,104	1,923,295	Little Rock	....	59
Ascension	34	1,486	Georgetown	D13	39
Asia	17,032,000	2,043,997,000	....	....	32
*Australia	2,967,741	12,630,000	Canberra	....	40
*Austria	32,374	7,419,341	Vienna	B 3	29
*Bahamas	5,382	197,000	Nassau	C 1	48
*Bahrain	231	207,000	Manama	G 4	33
*Bangladesh	55,126	70,000,000	Dacca	F 3	34
*Barbados	166	253,620	Bridgetown	G 4	48
*Belgium	11,779	9,660,154	Brussels	....	24
Belize	8,867	122,000	Belmopan	B 1	48
*Benin	43,483	3,029,000	Porto-Novo	G10	38
Bermuda	21	52,000	Hamilton	G 2	48
*Bhutan	18,000	770,000	Thimphu	G 3	34
*Bolivia	424,163	4,804,000	La Paz, Sucre	G 7	46
*Botswana	219,815	629,000	Gaborone	L16	39
*Brazil	3,284,426	90,840,000	Brasília	....	46-47
British Columbia, Canada	366,255	2,161,000	Victoria	D 5	43
British Indian Ocean Terr.	30	1,000	Victoria (Seychelles)	L10	32
Brunei	2,226	130,000	Bandar Seri Begawan	E 4	36
*Bulgaria	42,829	8,501,000	Sofia	D 3	29
*Burma	261,789	27,000,000	Rangoon	B 2	35
*Burundi	10,747	3,475,000	Bujumbura	M12	39
California, U.S.A.	158,693	19,953,134	Sacramento	....	60
*Cambodia	70,898	6,701,000	Phnom Penh	E 4	35
*Cameroon	183,568	5,836,000	Yaoundé	J10	38
*Canada	3,851,809	21,489,000	Ottawa	....	43
Canal Zone	647	44,650	Balboa Heights	E 3	48
*Cape Verde	1,557	285,000	Praia	H 5	17
Cayman Islands	100	10,652	Georgetown	B 3	48
*Central African Republic	240,534	1,518,000	Bangui	K10	38
Central America	197,559	18,900,000	....	....	48
*Ceylon (Sri Lanka)	25,332	12,300,000	Colombo	E 7	34
*Chad	495,752	3,869,000	N'Djamena	K 8	38
Channel Islands	75	117,000	....	E 6	23
*Chile	292,257	8,834,820	Santiago	....	47
*China (mainland)	3,691,506	740,000,000	Peking	....	37
China (Taiwan)	13,948	14,577,000	Taipei	K 7	37
*Colombia	439,513	21,117,000	Bogotá	F 3	46
Colorado, U.S.A.	102,247	2,207,259	Denver	....	65
*Comoro Islands	863	275,000	Moroni	P14	39
*Congo	132,046	915,000	Brazzaville	J12	39
Connecticut, U.S.A.	5,009	3,032,217	Hartford	....	66
Cook Islands	93	20,000	Avarua	K 7	41
*Costa Rica	19,575	1,800,000	San José	C 3	48
*Cuba	42,827	8,553,395	Havana	B 2	48
*Cyprus	3,473	649,000	Nicosia	C 3	33
*Czechoslovakia	49,370	14,497,000	Prague	C 1	29
Delaware, U.S.A.	2,057	548,104	Dover	....	101
*Denmark	16,625	4,910,000	Copenhagen	B 3	24
District of Columbia, U.S.A.	67	756,510	Washington	F 5	100
Dominica	290	70,302	Roseau	G 4	48
*Dominican Republic	18,704	4,011,589	Santo Domingo	D 3	48
*Ecuador	109,483	6,144,000	Quito	E 4	46
*Egypt	386,100	33,329,000	Cairo	M 6	38
*El Salvador	8,260	3,418,455	San Salvador	B 2	48
England, U.K.	50,327	46,102,300	London	F 5	23
*Equatorial Guinea	10,831	305,100	Malabo	H11	39
*Ethiopia	471,776	24,764,000	Addis Ababa	O 9	38
Europe	4,063,000	644,574,000	....	....	22
Faerøe Islands, Den.	540	38,000	Tórshavn	D 2	22
Falkland Islands	4,618	2,000	Stanley	H14	47
*Fiji	7,015	519,000	Suva	H 7	41
*Finland	130,128	4,706,000	Helsinki	E 2	24
Florida, U.S.A.	58,560	6,789,443	Tallahassee	....	68
*France	212,841	50,770,000	Paris	....	26
French Guiana	35,135	48,000	Cayenne	K 3	46
French Polynesia	1,544	109,000	Papeete	M 7	41
*Gabon	103,346	500,000	Libreville	J12	39
*Gambia	4,003	357,000	Banjul	C 9	38
Georgia, U.S.A.	58,876	4,589,575	Atlanta	....	72
*Germany, East (German Democratic Republic)	41,814	17,117,000	Berlin	....	25
*Germany, West (Federal Republic of)	95,959	61,194,600	Bonn	....	25
*Ghana	91,843	8,545,561	Accra	F10	38
Gibraltar	2	27,000	Gibraltar	D 4	27
Gilbert Is.	(land) 290	47,922	Bairiki	H 5	41
*Great Britain and Northern Ireland (United Kingdom)	94,214	55,534,000	London	....	23
*Greece	50,548	8,838,000	Athens	C 4	29
Greenland	840,000	47,000	Godthåb	P 2	42
*Grenada	133	96,000	St. George's	F 4	48
Guadeloupe and Dependencies	687	324,000	Basse-Terre	F 3	48
Guam	209	86,926	Agaña	E 4	41
*Guatemala	42,042	5,200,000	Guatemala	B 2	48
*Guinea	94,925	3,890,000	Conakry	D 9	38
*Guinea-Bissau	13,948	517,000	Bissau	C 9	38
*Guyana	83,000	763,000	Georgetown	J 2	46
*Haiti	10,694	4,867,190	Port-au-Prince	D 3	48
Hawaii, U.S.A.	6,450	769,913	Honolulu	....	75
*Holland (Netherlands)	13,958	13,077,000	Amsterdam, The Hague	....	24
*Honduras	43,277	2,495,000	Tegucigalpa	C 2	48
Hong Kong	398	4,089,000	Victoria	J 7	37
*Hungary	35,915	10,315,597	Budapest	E 3	29
*Iceland	39,768	203,000	Reykjavík	C 2	22
Idaho, U.S.A.	83,557	713,008	Boise	....	76
Illinois, U.S.A.	56,400	11,113,976	Springfield	....	78
*India	1,269,339	586,266,000	New Delhi	....	34
Indiana, U.S.A.	36,291	5,193,669	Indianapolis	....	83
*Indonesia	763,264	119,572,000	Djakarta	....	36
Iowa, U.S.A.	56,290	2,825,041	Des Moines	....	84
*Iran	636,293	28,448,000	Tehran	G 3	33
*Iraq	167,924	9,431,000	Baghdad	E 3	33
*Ireland	26,600	2,944,000	Dublin	B 4	23
Isle of Man, U.K.	227	50,000	Douglas	D 3	23
*Israel	7,993	2,911,000	Jerusalem	....	31
*Italy	116,303	54,504,000	Rome	....	28
*Ivory Coast	124,503	4,800,000	Abidjan	E10	38
*Jamaica	4,411	1,972,000	Kingston	C 3	48
*Japan	143,662	104,665,171	Tokyo	....	36
*Jordan	37,297	2,300,000	Amman	....	31
Kansas, U.S.A.	82,264	2,249,071	Topeka	....	88
Kentucky, U.S.A.	40,395	3,219,311	Frankfort	....	93
*Kenya	224,902	10,880,200	Nairobi	O11	39
Korea, North	46,540	13,300,000	P'yŏngyang	C 2	36
Korea, South	38,452	31,683,000	Seoul	C 3	36
*Kuwait	6,177	733,196	Al Kuwait	F 4	33
*Laos	90,428	2,900,000	Vientiane	E 3	35
*Lebanon	4,015	2,800,000	Beirut	C 3	33
*Lesotho	11,716	930,000	Maseru	M17	39
*Liberia	43,000	1,200,000	Monrovia	E10	38
*Libya	679,359	1,900,000	Tripoli	J 6	38
Liechtenstein	61	21,000	Vaduz	E 1	27
Louisiana, U.S.A.	48,523	3,643,180	Baton Rouge	....	95
*Luxembourg	999	339,000	Luxembourg	H 8	24

***Members of the United Nations**

GAZETTEER-INDEX OF THE WORLD

Country	Area (Sq. Miles)	Population	Capital or Chief Town	Index Ref.	Plate No.
Macao	6.2	292,000	Macao	H 7	37
*Madagascar	226,657	7,011,563	Tananarive	R16	39
Maine, U.S.A.	33,215	993,663	Augusta	....	98
*Malawi	45,747	4,900,000	Lilongwe	N14	39
Malaya, Malaysia	50,670	9,000,000	Kuala Lumpur	D 7	35
*Malaysia	128,308	10,583,000	Kuala Lumpur	E 5	36
*Maldives	115	110,770	Male	L 9	32
*Mali	463,948	4,929,000	Bamako	F 8	38
*Malta	122	321,000	Valletta	E 7	28
Manitoba, Canada	251,000	979,000	Winnipeg	G 3	43
Martinique	425	332,000	Fort-de-France	G 4	48
Maryland, U.S.A.	10,577	3,922,399	Annapolis	....	101
Massachusetts, U.S.A.	8,257	5,689,170	Boston	....	104
*Mauritania	397,954	1,140,000	Nouakchott	D 8	38
*Mauritius	787	823,000	Port Louis	S19	39
*Mexico	761,601	48,313,438	Mexico City	....	42
Michigan, U.S.A.	58,216	8,875,083	Lansing	....	106
Midway Islands	2	2,356	....	H 3	41
Minnesota, U.S.A.	84,068	3,805,069	St. Paul	....	110
Mississippi, U.S.A.	47,716	2,216,912	Jackson	....	112
Missouri, U.S.A.	69,686	4,677,399	Jefferson City	....	117
Monaco	368 acres	23,035	Monaco	G 6	26
*Mongolia	604,090	1,300,000	Ulan Bator	F 2	37
Montana, U.S.A.	147,138	694,409	Helena	....	118
Montserrat	38	12,300	Plymouth	G 3	48
*Morocco	172,413	15,577,000	Rabat	E 5	38
*Mozambique	308,641	9,029,000	Maputo	N16	39
Nauru	8.2	7,000	Yaren dist.	G 6	41
Nebraska, U.S.A.	77,227	1,483,791	Lincoln	....	121
*Nepal	54,362	10,845,000	Kathmandu	E 3	34
*Netherlands	13,958	13,077,000	Amsterdam, The Hague	....	24
Netherlands Antilles	390	220,000	Willemstad	D 4	48
Nevada, U.S.A.	110,540	488,738	Carson City	....	122
New Brunswick, Canada	28,354	624,000	Fredericton	K 6	43
New Caledonia & Dependencies	8,548	100,579	Nouméa	F 8	41
Newfoundland, Canada	156,185	520,000	St. John's	L 6	43
New Hampshire, U.S.A.	9,304	737,681	Concord	....	124
New Hebrides	5,700	80,000	Vila	G 7	41
New Jersey, U.S.A.	7,836	7,168,164	Trenton	....	129
New Mexico, U.S.A.	121,666	1,016,000	Santa Fe	....	130
New York, U.S.A.	49,576	18,241,266	Albany	....	132
*New Zealand	103,736	2,815,000	Wellington	M 7	4[illegible]
*Nicaragua	45,698	1,984,000	Managua	C 2	48
*Niger	489,189	4,016,000	Niamey	H 8	38
*Nigeria	356,669	66,174,000	Lagos	H10	38
Niue	100	5,323	Alofi	K 7	41
North America	9,363,000	314,000,000	....	....	42
North Carolina, U.S.A.	52,586	5,082,059	Raleigh	....	137
North Dakota, U.S.A.	70,665	617,761	Bismarck	....	138
Northern Ireland, U.K.	5,459	1,512,500	Belfast	C 3	23
Northwest Territories, Canada	1,304,903	34,000	Yellowknife	E 3	43
*Norway	125,181	3,893,000	Oslo	B 2	24
Nova Scotia, Canada	21,425	767,000	Halifax	K 7	43
Ohio, U.S.A.	41,222	10,652,017	Columbus	....	140
Oklahoma, U.S.A.	69,919	2,559,253	Oklahoma City	....	145
*Oman	82,000	565,000	Muscat	G 6	33
Ontario, Canada	412,582	7,707,000	Toronto	G 5	43
Oregon, U.S.A.	96,981	2,091,385	Salem	....	146
Pacific Islands, U.S. Trust Terr. of the	687	98,009	Tanapag	E,F 5	41
*Pakistan	310,403	60,000,000	Islamabad	B 3	34
*Panama	29,209	1,425,343	Panamá	D 3	48
*Papua New Guinea	183,540	2,563,610	Port Moresby	E 6	41
*Paraguay	157,047	2,314,000	Asunción	J 6	46, 47
Pennsylvania, U.S.A.	45,333	11,793,909	Harrisburg	....	150
*Persia (Iran)	636,293	28,448,000	Tehran	G 3	33
*Peru	496,222	13,586,300	Lima	E 5	46
*Philippines	115,707	39,079,000	Quezon City	H 4	36
Pitcairn Islands	18	80	Adamstown	O 8	41
*Poland	120,702	32,889,000	Warsaw	....	31
*Portugal	35,510	9,560,000	Lisbon	....	27
Portuguese Timor	5,762	590,000	Dili	H 7	36
Prince Edward Island, Canada	2,18[illegible]	110,000	Charlottetown	K 6	43
Puerto Rico	3,43[illegible]	2,689,932	San Juan	E 3	48
*Qatar	4,247	140,000	Doha	G 4	33
Québec, Canada	594,860	6,023,000	Québec	J 5	43
Réunion	969	436,000	St-Denis	R20	39
Rhode Island, U.S.A.	1,214	949,723	Providence	....	104
Rhodesia	150,332	5,310,000	Salisbury	L15	39
*Rumania	91,699	20,394,000	Bucharest	D 2	29
*Rwanda	10,169	3,500,000	Kigali	N12	39
Sabah, Malaysia	29,388	633,000	Kota Kinabalu	F 4	36
St. Christopher-Nevis-Anguilla	138	56,000	Basseterre	F 3	48
St. Helena	47	6,462	Jamestown	E15	39
St. Lucia	238	110,000	Castries	G 4	48
St-Pierre and Miquelon	93.5	5,235	St-Pierre	L 6	43
St. Vincent	150	95,000	Kingstown	F 4	48
San Marino	23.4	19,000	San Marino	D 3	28
*São Tomé e Príncipe	372	79,000	São Tomé	F11	39
Sarawak, Malaysia	48,250	950,000	Kuching	E 5	36
Saskatchewan, Canada	251,700	933,000	Regina	F 5	43
*Saudi Arabia	920,000	7,200,000	Riyadh, Mecca	E 4	33
Scotland, U.K.	30,411	5,194,000	Edinburgh	D 2	23
*Senegal	75,750	3,780,000	Dakar	D 9	38
Seychelles	145	55,000	Victoria	J10	32
*Siam (Thailand)	198,455	35,448,000	Bangkok	D 3	35
*Sierra Leone	27,925	2,512,000	Freetown	C10	38
*Singapore	225	2,034,000	Singapore	E 7	35
Solomon Islands	10,983	161,525	Honiara	G 6	41
*Somalia	246,200	2,730,000	Mogadishu	R10	38
*South Africa	471,663	21,282,000	Cape Town, Pretoria	L18	39
South America	6,875,000	186,000,000	....	....	47-48
South Carolina, U.S.A.	31,055	2,590,516	Columbia	....	152
South Dakota, U.S.A.	77,047	666,257	Pierre	....	154
South-West Africa	317,838	615.000	Windhoek	K16	39
*Spain	194,896	33,290,000	Madrid	....	27
Spanish Sahara	102,702	63,000	El Aaiún	D 7	38
*Sri Lanka	25,332	12,300,000	Colombo	E 7	34
*Sudan	967,495	15,312,000	Khartoum	M 9	38
*Surinam	55,144	389,000	Paramaribo	J 3	46
*Swaziland	6,704	411,879	Mbabane	N17	39
*Sweden	173,665	7,978,000	Stockholm	C 2	24
Switzerland	15,941	6,230,000	Bern	....	27
*Syria	71,498	5,866,000	Damascus	D 2	33
*Tanzania	362,819	12,896,000	Dar es Salaam	N13	39
Tennessee, U.S.A.	42,244	3,924,164	Nashville	....	93
Texas, U.S.A.	267,339	11,196,730	Austin	....	158
*Thailand	198,455	35,448,000	Bangkok	D 3	35
*Togo	21,853	2,004,711	Lomé	G10	38
Tokelau Islands	3.9	2,000	Fakaofo	J 6	41
Tonga	270	83,000	Nuku'alofa	J 7	41
*Trinidad and Tobago	1,980	1,040,000	Port of Spain	G 5	48
Tristan da Cunha	40	269	Edinburgh	H 7	17
*Tunisia	63,378	5,027,000	Tunis	H 5	38
*Turkey	301,381	34,375,000	Ankara	C 2	33
Turks and Caicos Is.	166	6,000	Cockburn Town	D 2	48
Tuvalu	(land) 10	5,890	Fongafale	H 6	41
*Uganda	92,674	9,764,000	Kampala	N11	39
*Ukrainian S.S.R., U.S.S.R.	232,046	47,136,000	Kiev	C 5	30
*Union of Soviet Socialist Republics	8,649,498	241,748,000	Moscow	....	30
*United Arab Emirates	32,278	179,126	Abu Dhabi	G 5	33
*United Kingdom	94,214	55,534,000	London	....	23
*United States of America, land	3,536,855	203,235,298	Washington, D.C.	....	44-45
land and water	3,615,123				
*Upper Volta	105,841	5,330,000	Ouagadougou	F 9	38
*Uruguay	72,172	2,900,000	Montevideo	J10	47
Utah, U.S.A.	84,916	1,059,273	Salt Lake City	....	160
Vatican City	109 acres	1,000	....	C 4	28
*Venezuela	352,143	10,398,907	Caracas	G 2	46
Vermont, U.S.A.	9,609	444,732	Montpelier	....	124
Vietnam, North	61,293	21,340,000	Hanoi	E 3	35
Vietnam, South	66,897	16,543,434	Saigon	F 4	35
Virginia, U.S.A.	40,817	4,648,494	Richmond	....	163
Virgin Islands, British	59	10,484	Road Town	F 3	48
Virgin Islands, U.S.A.	132	63,200	Charlotte Amalie	F 3	48
Wake Island, U.S.A.	2.5	1,097	....	H 4	41
Wales (incl. Monmouthshire), U.K.	8,017	2,724,540	Cardiff	E 4	23
Wallis and Futuna	106	8,546	Matautu	J 7	41
Washington, U.S.A.	68,192	3,409,169	Olympia	....	166
Western Samoa	1,133	139,810	Apia	J 7	41
West Virginia, U.S.A.	24,181	1,744,237	Charlestown	....	168
*White Russian S.S.R. (Byelorussian S.S.R.), U.S.S.R.	80,154	9,003,000	Minsk	C 4	30
Wisconsin, U.S.A.	56,154	4,417,933	Madison	....	173
World	57,491,000	3,632,000,000	....	....	17
Wyoming, U.S.A.	97,914	332,416	Cheyenne	....	174
*Yemen Arab Republic	75,000	5,000,000	San'a	E 7	33
*Yemen, Peoples Dem. Rep. of	111,075	1,220,000	Aden	F 7	33
*Yugoslavia	98,766	20,586,000	Belgrade	B 2	29
Yukon Territory, Canada	207,076	17,000	Whitehorse	C 3	43
*Zaire	905,563	21,637,876	Kinshasa	L12	39
*Zambia	290,586	4,056,995	Lusaka	M14	39

Introduction to the Maps and Indexes

The following notes have been added to aid the reader in making the best use of this atlas. Though he may be familiar with maps and map indexes, the publisher believes that a quick review of the material below will add to his enjoyment of this reference work.

Arrangement — The Plan of the Atlas. The sequence of maps in this American-designed atlas is international in arrangement. Units on outer space and the world as a whole are followed by pages devoted to Europe and its countries. Following the maps of the European continent and its countries, the geographic sequence plan proceeds as follows: Asia, Africa, the Pacific and Australia, North America and South America. Special maps on world climate patterns and major resources next appear and the map collection closes with detailed state maps of the United States.

Political Maps of Continents, Countries and States — The Primary Reference Tool. The basic maps in this collection are the political maps. It is our feeling that the reader is likely to refer to political maps more often than to any other kind of map when confronted by such questions as — Where? How big? What is it near? Answering these common queries is the function of political maps. Each political map stresses *political* phenomena — countries, internal political divisions, boundaries, cities and towns. The major political unit or units, shown on the map, are banded in distinctive colors for easy identification and delineation. First-order political subdivisions (states, provinces, counties on the state maps) are shown, scale permitting.

The reader is advised to make use of the *legend* appearing under the title on each political map. Map *symbols,* the special "language" of maps, are explained in the legend. Each variety of dot, circle, star or interrupted line has a special meaning which should be clearly understood by the user so that he may interpret the map data correctly.

Each country has been portrayed at a *scale* commensurate with its political, areal, economic or tourist importance. In certain cases, a whole map unit may be devoted to a single nation if that nation is considered to be of prime interest to most atlas users. In other cases, several nations will be shown on a single map if, as separate entities, they are of lesser relative importance. Areas of dense settlement and important significance within a country have been enlarged and portrayed in inset maps inserted on the margins of the main map. The reader is advised to refer to the linear or "bar" scale appearing on each map or map inset in order to ascertain the basic scale of the map or to determine the distance between points.

The *projection* system used for each map is noted near the title of the map. Map projections are the special graphic systems used by cartographers to render the curved three-dimensional surface of the globe on a flat surface. Optimum map projections determined by the attributes of the area have been used by the publishers for each map in the atlas.

A word here as to the choice of place names on the maps. Throughout the atlas names appear, with a few exceptions, in their local official spellings. However, conventional Anglicized spellings are used for major geographical divisions and for towns and topographic features for which English forms exist; i.e., "Spain" instead of "España" or "Munich" instead of "München." Names of this type are normally followed by the local official spelling in parentheses.

Names of cities and towns in the United States follow the forms listed in the *Directory of Post Offices* of the United States Postal Service. Domestic physical names follow the decisions of the Board on Geographic Names, U.S. Department of the Interior, and of various state geographic name boards.

It is the belief of the publishers that the boundaries shown in a general reference atlas should reflect current geographic and political realities. This policy has been followed consistently in the atlas. The presentation of *de facto* boundaries in cases of territorial dispute between various nations does not imply the political endorsement of such boundaries by the publisher, but simply the honest representation of boundaries as they exist at the time of the printing of the atlas maps.

Special Purpose Maps. These maps deal with vital topics of world geography — global climate patterns, resource distribution, demography and major political groupings. The dynamic changes and movements of weather phenomena are brought out clearly on the pressure and winds, ocean currents, temperature and rainfall maps. The world resource maps portray the world's leading producers of mineral and agricultural commodities by means of symbols proportionate to the yield of each major producing country. The population distribution and political associations maps illustrate important facets of human geography.

Accompanying each state map are relief and economic maps of the area. The purpose of the relief map is to illustrate the surface configuration (TOPOGRAPHY) of the region. A shading technique in color simulates the relative ruggedness of the terrain — plains, plateaus, valleys, hills and mountains. The economic maps allow one to determine the basic agricultural, industrial and resource activities and patterns of the state's economy. Color bands express broad categories of *dominant land use,* such as cereal belts, forest lands, livestock range lands or nonagricultural wastes. Red commodity names, on the other hand, pinpoint the areas of production of *specific* crops, i.e., wheat, cotton, sugar beets, etc. Major mineral occurrences are denoted by standard letter symbols appearing in blue. The products of each important industrial area are listed in boxes at the margin of the map.

Indexes — Pinpointing a Location. A comprehensive index of world cities and towns appears on pages 9 through 16. If you are unfamiliar with the location of a particular urban place and wish to find its position within the confines of the subject area of the map, consult this index as your first step. The name of the feature sought will be found in its proper alphabetical sequence with its map page number and a key reference letter-number combination corresponding to its location on the map. After noting the key reference letter-number combination for the place name, turn to the map. The place name will be found within the square formed by the two lines of latitude and the two lines of longitude which enclose the co-ordinates — i.e., the marginal letters and numbers. The following diagram illustrates the system of indexing.

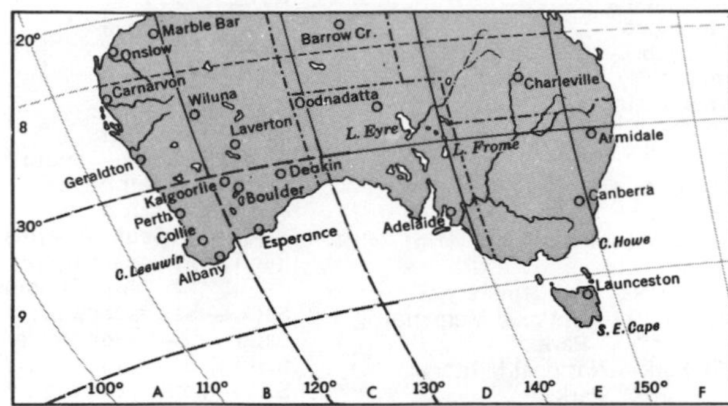

Accompanying the index entries for cities and towns are *population figures* for the particular entries. The population figures have been taken from the latest official censuses and estimates of the various nations. The Gazetteer-Index of the World on the preceding pages provides a quick reference index for countries and other important areas. This Gazetteer-Index provides a conveniently arranged statistical comparison contained in two pages.

Each state map is accompanied by a comprehensive index of the place names appearing on the map; population figures for cities, towns, counties and the state as a whole are provided. All index entries for cities and towns in the United States are preceded by a five-digit postal ZIP code number applying to the community. This useful feature permits the reader to address his mail so that it will be routed and delivered more efficiently and quickly by the U.S. Postal Service. A dagger (†) designates those places that do not possess a post office. The ZIP code number listed in such cases refers to that of the nearest post office. An asterisk (*) marks those larger cities which are divided into multiple ZIP code areas. Using the single ZIP code number listed in such cases will direct your letter to the proper city with dispatch. However, if the precise ZIP code number of the address within the city is needed, it is suggested that the reader refer to the latest National ZIP Code Directory at his local post office. This detailed guide lists every street in a multiple ZIP code city with the proper ZIP code for the street.

The publishers have tried to make this work the most comprehensive and useful atlas available, and it is hoped that it will prove a valuable reference work. Any constructive suggestions from the reader will be welcomed.

Sources and Acknowledgments

A multitude of sources goes into the making of a large-scale reference work such as this. To list them all would take many pages and would consume space better devoted to the maps and reference materials themselves. However, certain general sources were very useful in preparing this work and are listed below.

STATISTICAL OFFICE OF THE UNITED NATIONS.
Demographic Yearbook. New York. Issued annually.

STATISTICAL OFFICE OF THE UNITED NATIONS.
Statistical Yearbook. New York. Issued annually.

THE GEOGRAPHER, U.S. DEPARTMENT OF STATE.
International Boundary Study papers. Washington. Various dates.

THE GEOGRAPHER, U.S. DEPARTMENT OF STATE.
Geographic Notes. Washington. Various dates.

UNITED STATES BOARD ON GEOGRAPHIC NAMES.
Decisions on Geographic Names in the United States. Washington. Various dates.

UNITED STATES BOARD ON GEOGRAPHIC NAMES.
Official Standard Names Gazetteers. Washington. Various dates.

CANADIAN PERMANENT COMMITTEE ON GEOGRAPHICAL NAMES.
Gazetteer of Canada series. Ottawa. Various dates.

UNITED STATES POSTAL SERVICE.
Directory of Post Offices. Washington. 1970.

UNITED STATES POSTAL SERVICE.
National Zip Code Directory. Washington. 1970-1971.

UNITED STATES POSTAL SERVICE.
Postal Bulletin. Washington. Issued weekly.

UNITED STATES DEPARTMENT OF THE INTERIOR. BUREAU OF MINES.
Minerals Yearbook. 4 vols. Washington. Various dates.

UNITED STATES GEOLOGICAL SURVEY.
Elevations and distances in the United States. Washington. 1969.

UNITED STATES DEPARTMENT OF COMMERCE. JOINT PUBLICATIONS RESEARCH SERVICE.
JPRS reports dealing with foreign geography. Washington. Various dates.

CARTACTUAL.
Cartactual — Topical Map Service. Budapest. Issued bi-monthly.

AMERICAN GEOGRAPHICAL SOCIETY.
Focus. New York. Issued ten times a year.

A sample list of sources used for <u>specific</u> countries follows:

Algeria
COMMISSARIAT NATIONAL AU RECENSEMENT DE LA POPULATION.
Résultats Préliminaires du Recensement Général de la Population Effectué en 1966. Oran.

Barbados
BARBADOS STATISTICAL SERVICE.
1970 Census. St. Michael.

Chile
INSTITUTO NACIONAL DE ESTADÍSTICAS.
XIV Censo Nacional de Población y III de Vivienda. 1970. Santiago.

Dominican Republic
OFICINA NACIONAL DE ESTADÍSTICA.
Censo Nacional de Población y Habitación. 9 y 10 Enero de 1970. Santo Domingo.

France
INSTITUT NATIONAL DE LA STATISTIQUE ET DES ÉTUDES ÉCONOMIQUES.
Recensement de 1968. Population de la France. Paris.

Ghana
CENSUS OFFICE.
1970 Population Census of Ghana. Accra

Iran
IRANIAN STATISTICAL CENTER.
National Census of Population and Housing, 1966. Tehran.

Ireland
THE CENTRAL STATISTICS OFFICE.
Census of Population of Ireland 1966. Dublin.

Kenya
MINISTRY OF ECONOMIC PLANNING AND DEVELOPMENT. STATISTICS DIVISION.
Provisional Results of the 1969 Population Census. Nairobi.

Kuwait
MINISTRY OF GUIDANCE & INFORMATION.
Population Census 1970. Kuwait.

Mexico
DIRECCIÓN GENERAL DE ESTADÍSTICA.
IX Censo General de Población 1970. México, D.F.

New Caledonia
INSTITUT NATIONAL DE LA STATISTIQUE ET DES ÉTUDES ÉCONOMIQUES (France).
Recensement de 1969. Paris.

Panama
DIRECCIÓN DE ESTADÍSTICA Y CENSO.
Censos Nacionales de 1970. Panamá.

Rhodesia
CENTRAL STATISTICAL OFFICE.
1969 Population Censuses. Salisbury.

Tanzania
CENTRAL STATISTICAL BUREAU.
1967 Population Census. Dar es Salaam.

Togo
DIRECTION DE LA STATISTIQUE.
Résultats Provisoires du Recensement Général de la Population 1970. Lomé.

U.S.S.R.
CENTRAL STATISTICAL ADMINISTRATION.
Preliminary Results of the All-Union Census of Population 1970. Moscow.

United States
BUREAU OF THE CENSUS.
1970 Census of Population. Washington.

CORPS OF ENGINEERS.
Reservoir status lists and maps. Various districts.

Zaire
MINISTÈRE DE L'INTÉRIEUR ET DES AFFAIRES COUTUMIÈRES.
Recensement Général de la Population 1970. Kinshasa.

Zambia
CENTRAL STATISTICAL OFFICE.
Population and Housing Census — 1969. Lusaka.

Glossary of Abbreviations

A

A. A. F. — Army Air Field
Acad. — Academy
A. C. T. — Australian Capital Territory
adm. — administration; administrative
adm. city-co. — administrative city-county
A. F. B. — Air Force Base
Afgh., Afghan. — Afghanistan
Afr. — Africa
A. & I. — Terr. of the Afars and Issas
Ala. — Alabama
Alb. — Albania
Alg. — Algeria
Alta. — Alberta
Amer. — American
Amer. Samoa — American Samoa
And. — Andorra
Ant. — Antarctica
Ar. — Arabia
arch. — archipelago
Arg. — Argentina
Ariz. — Arizona
Ark. — Arkansas
A. S. S. R. — Autonomous Soviet Socialist Republic
Austr., Austral. — Australian, Australia
aut. — autonomous
Aut. Obl. — Autonomous Oblast
aut. prov. — autonomous province

B

B. — bay
Bah. — Bahamas
Barb. — Barbados
Battlef. — Battlefield
Bch. — Beach
Belg. — Belgium
Berm. — Bermuda
Bol. — Bolivia
Bots. — Botswana
Br. — Branch
Br. — British
Braz. — Brazil
Br. Col. — British Columbia
Br. Ind. Oc. Terr. — British Indian Ocean Territory
Bulg. — Bulgaria

C

C. — cape
Calif. — California
can. — canal
cap. — capital
Cent. Afr. Rep. — Central African Republic
Cent. Amer. — Central America
C. G. Sta. — Coast Guard Station
C. H. — Court House
chan. — channel
Chan. Is. — Channel Islands
Chem. Ctr. — Chemical Center
co. — county
C. of G. H. — Cape of Good Hope
Col. — Colombia
Colo. — Colorado
comm. — commissary
Conn. — Connecticut
cont. — continent
cord. — cordillera (mountain range)
C. Rica — Costa Rica
C. S. — County Seat
C. Verde — Cape Verde
Cy. — City
C. Z. — Canal Zone
Czech. — Czechoslovakia

D

D. C. — District of Columbia
Del. — Delaware
Dem. — Democratic
Den. — Denmark
depr. — depression
dept. — department
des. — desert
dist., dist's — district, districts
div. — division
Dom. Rep. — Dominican Republic
dry riv. — dry river

E

E. — East
Ec., Ecua. — Ecuador
E. Ger. — East Germany
elec. div. — electoral division
El Salv. — El Salvador
Eng. — England
Eq. Guin. — Equatorial Guinea
escarp. — escarpment
est. — estuary
Eth. — Ethiopia

F

Falk. Is. — Falkland Islands
Fin. — Finland
Fk., Fks. — Fork, Forks
Fla. — Florida
for. — forest
Fr. — France, French
Fr. Gui. — French Guiana
Fr. Poly. — French Polynesia
Ft. — Fort

G

G. — gulf
Ga. — Georgia
Game Res. — Game Reserve
Ger. — Germany
geys. — geyser
Gibr. — Gibraltar
Gilb. Is. — Gilbert Islands
glac. — glacier
gov. — governorate
Gr. — Group
Greenl. — Greenland
Gt. Brit. — Great Britain
Guad. — Guadeloupe
Guat. — Guatemala
Guy. — Guyana

H

har., harb., hbr. — harbor
hd. — head
highl. — highland, highlands
Hist. — Historic, Historical
Hond. — Honduras
Hts. — Heights
Hung. — Hungary

I

i., isl., — island, isle
Ice., Icel. — Iceland
Ida. — Idaho
Ill. — Illinois
Ind. — Indiana
ind. city — independent city
Indon. — Indonesia
Ind. Res. — Indian Reservation
int. div. — internal division
inten. — intendency
interm. str. — intermittent stream
Int'l — International
Ire. — Ireland
is., isls. — islands
Isr. — Israel
isth. — isthmus

J

Jam. — Jamaica
Jct. — Junction

K

Kans. — Kansas
Ky. — Kentucky

L

L. — Lake, Loch, Lough
La. — Louisiana
Lab. — Laboratory
lag. — lagoon
Ld. — Land
Leb. — Lebanon
Les. — Lesotho
Liecht. — Liechtenstein
Lux. — Luxembourg

M

Madag. — Madagascar
Man. — Manitoba
Mart. — Martinique
Mass. — Massachusetts
Maur. — Mauritania
Md. — Maryland
met. area — metropolitan area
Mex. — Mexico
Mich. — Michigan
Minn. — Minnesota
Miss. — Mississippi
Mo. — Missouri
Mon. — Monument
Mong. — Mongolia
Mont. — Montana
Mor. — Morocco
Moz., Mozamb. — Mozambique
mt. — mount
mtn. — mountain

N

N., No. — North, Northern
N. Amer. — North America
N. A. S. — Naval Air Station
Nat'l — National
Nat'l Cem. — National Cemetery
Nat'l Mem. Park — National Memorial Park
Nat'l Mil. Park — National Military Park
Nat'l Pkwy. — National Parkway
Nav. Base — Naval Base
Nav. Sta. — Naval Station
N. B., N. Br. — New Brunswick
N. C. — North Carolina
N. Dak. — North Dakota
Nebr. — Nebraska
Neth. — Netherlands
Neth. Ant. — Netherlands Antilles
Nev. — Nevada
New Cal. — New Caledonia
Newf. — Newfoundland
New Hebr. — New Hebrides
N. H. — New Hampshire
Nic. — Nicaragua
N. Ire. — Northern Ireland
N. J. — New Jersey
N. Mex. — New Mexico
Nor. — Norway, Norwegian
No. Terr. — Northern Territory (Australia)
N. S. — Nova Scotia
N. S. W. — New South Wales
N. W. T. — Northwest Territories (Canada)
N. Y. — New York
N. Z. — New Zealand

O

Obl. — Oblast
O. F. S. — Orange Free State
Okla. — Oklahoma
Okr. — Okrug
Ont. — Ontario
Ord. Depot — Ordnance Depot
Oreg. — Oregon

P

Pa. — Pennsylvania
Pac. — Pacific
Pac. Is. — Pacific Islands, Territory of the
Pak. — Pakistan
Pan. — Panama
Par. — Paraguay
par. — parish
passg. — passage
P.D.R. Yemen — Peoples Democratic Republic of Yemen
P. E. I. — Prince Edward Island
pen. — peninsula
Phil., Phil. Is. — Philippines
Pk. — Park
pk. — peak
plat. — plateau
P. N. G. — Papua New Guinea
Port. — Portugal, Portuguese
P. Rico — Puerto Rico
pref. — prefecture
prom. — promontory
prov. — province, provincial
prov. dist. — provincial district
pt. — point

Q

Que. — Québec
Queens. — Queensland

R

R. — River
ra. — range
Rec., Recr. — Recreation, Recreational
reg. — region
Rep. — Republic
res. — reservoir
Res. — Reservation, Reserve
Rhod. — Rhodesia
R. I. — Rhode Island
riv. — river
Rum. — Rumania

S

S. — South
Sa. — Sierra, Serra
S. Afr., S. Africa — South Africa
salt dep. — salt deposit
salt des. — salt desert
S. Amer. — South America
São T. & Pr. — São Tomé and Príncipe
Sask. — Saskatchewan
Saudi Ar. — Saudi Arabia
S. Aust., S. Austral. — South Australia
S. C. — South Carolina
Scot. — Scotland
Sd. — Sound
S. Dak. — South Dakota
Sen. — Senegal
sen. dist. — senatorial district
Seych. — Seychelles
S. F. S. R. — Soviet Federated Socialist Republic
Sing. — Singapore
S. Leone — Sierra Leone
S. Marino — San Marino
Sol. Is. — Solomon Islands
Sp. — Spanish
Spr., Sprs. — Spring, Springs
S. S. R. — Soviet Socialist Republic
St., Ste. — Saint, Sainte
Sta. — Station
St. Chr.-N.-A. — Saint Christopher-Nevis-Anguilla
St. P. & M. — Saint Pierre and Miquelon
str., strs. — strait, straits
Sur. — Surinam
S. W. Afr. — South-West Africa
Swaz. — Swaziland
Switz. — Switzerland

T

Tanz. — Tanzania
Tas. — Tasmania
Tenn. — Tennessee
terr., terrs. — territory, territories
Tex. — Texas
Thai. — Thailand
Trin. & Tob. — Trinidad and Tobago
Tun. — Tunisia
twp. — township

U

U. A. E. — United Arab Emirates
U. K. — United Kingdom
Upp. Volta — Upper Volta
urb. area — urban area
Urug. — Uruguay
U. S. — United States
U. S. S. R. — Union of Soviet Socialist Republics

V

Va. — Virginia
Vall. — Valley
Ven., Venez. — Venezuela
V. I. (Br.) — Virgin Islands (British)
V. I. (U. S.) — Virgin Islands (U. S.)
Vic. — Victoria
Vill. — Village
vol. — volcano
Vt. — Vermont

W

W. — West, Western
Wash. — Washington
W. Aust., W. Austral. — Western Australia
W. Ger. — West Germany
Wis. — Wisconsin
W. Samoa — Western Samoa
W. Va. — West Virginia
Wyo. — Wyoming

Y

Yugo. — Yugoslavia
Yukon — Yukon Territory

Index of Principal Cities of the World

This alphabetical list of cities and towns gives statistics of population based on the latest official census reports or most recent reliable estimates. Each line begins with the name of a place, followed by the name of the country or state, the population, the index reference and plate number. This index reference gives the location of the city or town name on the accompanying map plates. The name is found within the square formed by the two lines of latitude or longitude which enclose each of the co-ordinates—i.e. the marginal letters and numbers. In the case of maps consisting entirely of insets, the name is found near the intersection point of imaginary lines connecting the co-ordinates.

Where space on the map has not permitted giving the complete form of a name, the extended form is shown in the index. Where a place may be known under different names or by various spellings of the same name, the different forms have been included, to a large extent, in the index. Where an alternative spelling in parentheses is shown on the map itself, the first name gives the local official form, the conventional form following in parentheses.

* Capitals of countries, states and provinces. † Population figure includes suburbs or subdivision.

Aachen, W. Germany, 177,642 ......A 3 25
Abadan, Iran, 262,962 ......E 3 33
Abbeville, France, 23,770 ......D 2 26
Abécher, Chad, 19,650 ......L 9 38
Åbenrå, Denmark, 15,101 ......B 3 24
Abeokuta, Nigeria, 217,201 ......G10 38
Aberdare, Wales, 38,210 ......E 5 23
Aberdeen, Scotland, 181,089 ......E 2 23
Abidjan,* Ivory Coast, 180,000 ......E10 38
Abilene, Tex., 89,653 ......E 5 158
Abu Dhabi,* United Arab Emirates, 22,000 ......F 5 33
Acámbaro, Mexico, †80,259 ......E 4 42
Acapulco, Mexico, †234,866 ......E 5 42
Accra,* Ghana, 337,828 ......G10 38
Acre, Israel, 28,100 ......C 2 31
Adana, Turkey, 289,919 ......C 2 33
Adapazarı, Turkey, 86,124 ......B 1 33
Addis Ababa,* Ethiopia, 644,120......O10 38
Adelaide,* S. Australia, Australia, †727,916 ......D 7 40
Aden,* Peoples Dem. Rep. of Yemen, 150,000 ......E 7 33
Afyon, Turkey, 44,026 ......B 2 33
Agaña,* Guam, 2,131 ......E 4 41
Agra, India, 594,858 ......C 3 34
Agrigento, Sicily, Italy, 46,947 ......D 6 28
Aguascalientes, Mexico, †222,105..D 4 42
Ahmadabad, India, 1,588,378 ......C 4 34
Ahmadnagar, India, 117,215 ......C 5 34
Ahwaz, Iran, 206,375 ......E 3 33
Aix, France, 74,948 ......F 6 26
Aix-les-Bains, France, 20,594 ......G 5 26
Aizuwakamatsu, Japan, 104,000......F 2 36
Ajaccio, France, 38,776 ......B 7 26
Ajmer, India, 262,480 ......C 3 34
Akashi, Japan, 187,000 ......E 4 36
Akita, Japan, 233,000 ......E 3 36
Akola, India, 168,454 ......D 4 34
Akron, Ohio, 275,425 ......G 3 140
Aktyubinsk, U.S.S.R., 150,000 ......F 4 30
Alameda, Calif., 70,968 ......J 2 60
Albacete, Spain, 61,635 ......F 3 27
Albany, Ga., 72,623 ......D 7 72
Albany,* N.Y., 115,781 ......N 5 133
Albi, France, 38,867 ......E 6 26
Ålborg, Denmark, 82,871 ......B 3 24
Albuquerque, N. Mex., 243,751......C 3 130
Aldridge-Brownhills, England, 87,530 ......G 3 23
Alençon, France, 30,368 ......D 3 26
Aleppo, Syria, 566,770 ......C 2 33
Alessandria, Italy, 65,908 ......B 2 28
Alexandria, Egypt, 1,803,900 ......M 5 38
Alexandria, La., 41,557 ......E 4 94
Alexandria, Va., 110,938 ......P 3 163
Algeciras, Spain, 51,096 ......D 4 27
Algiers,* Algeria, 943,142 ......G 4 38
Alhambra, Calif., 62,125 ......C10 60
Alicante, Spain, 103,289 ......F 3 27
Aligarh, India, 254,008 ......D 3 34
Aliquippa, Pa., 22,277 ......B 4 150
Alkmaar, Netherlands, †52,091 ......E 2 24
Al Kuwait,* Kuwait, 80,008 ......E 4 33
Allahabad, India, 493,524 ......E 3 34
Allentown, Pa., 109,527 ......L 4 151
Alleppey, India, 160,064 ......D 7 34
Alma-Ata, U.S.S.R., 730,000 ......H 5 30
Almelo, Netherlands, †58,941......J 3 24
Almería, Spain, 76,643 ......E 4 27
Alor Star, Malaysia, 52,915 ......D 6 35
Alton, Ill., 39,700 ......A 6 78
Altoona, Pa., 63,115 ......F 4 150
Amagasaki, Japan, 532,000 ......E 4 36
'Amara, Iraq, 64,847 ......E 3 33
Amarillo, Tex., 127,010 ......C 2 158
Ambala, India, 83,649 ......D 2 34

Ambato, Ecuador, 53,372 ......E 4 46
Amboina, Indon., †70,000 ......H 6 36
Amersfoort, Netherlands, †78,189..F 3 24
Amiens, France, 116,107 ......E 3 26
Amman,* Jordan, 330,220 ......D 4 31
Amoy, China, 308,000 ......J 7 37
Amravati, India, 193,636 ......D 4 34
Amritsar, India, 432,663 ......C 2 34
Amsterdam,* Neth., 831,463 ......E 3 24
Amsterdam, N.Y., 25,524 ......M 5 133
Anaheim, Calif., 166,408 ......D11 60
Ancona, Italy, 77,748 ......D 3 28
Anchorage, Alaska, 48,081 ......J 2 52
Anderlecht, Belgium, 103,832 ......D 6 24
Anderson, Ind., 70,787 ......F 4 83
Andizhan, U.S.S.R., 188,000 ......H 5 30
Andorra la Vella,* Andorra, 2,250 ......G 1 27
Andria, Italy, 69,499 ......F 4 28
Angarsk, U.S.S.R., 204,000 ......L 4 30
Angers, France, 127,415 ......C 4 26
Ankara,* Turkey, 905,660 ......B 2 33
Anking, China, 129,000 ......J 5 37
Annaba, Algeria, 152,006 ......H 4 38
An Najaf, Iraq, 128,096 ......D 3 33
Annapolis,* Md., 30,095 ......M 5 101
Ann Arbor, Mich., 99,797 ......F 6 106
An Nasiriya, Iraq, 60,405 ......E 3 33
Annecy, France, 53,361 ......G 5 26
Anniston, Ala., 31,533 ......G 3 50
Anshan, China, 833,000 ......K 3 37
Antâkya, Turkey, 57,855 ......C 2 33
Antalya, Turkey, 71,833 ......B 2 33
Antibes, France, 47,393 ......G 6 26
Antofagasta, Chile, †126,252 ......F 8 47
Antung, China, 370,000 ......K 3 37
Antwerp, Belgium, 234,099 ......D 5 24
Anyang, China, 153,000 ......H 4 37
Anzhero-Sudzhensk, U.S.S.R., 106,000 ......J 4 30
Aomori, Japan, 252,000 ......F 2 36
Apeldoorn, Netherlands, 123,628 ..G 3 24
Apia,* Western Samoa, 27,000 ......J 7 41
Appleton, Wis., 57,143 ......J 7 173
'Aqaba, Jordan, 8,908 ......D 5 31
Aracaju, Brazil, 179,512 ......N 6 46
Araçatuba, Brazil, 85,660 ......K 8 46
Arad, Rumania, 132,757 ......C 2 29
Arak, Iran, 71,925 ......E 3 33
Araraquara, Brazil, 82,607 ......L 8 46
Archangel, U.S.S.R., 343,000 ......E 3 30
Ardebil, Iran, 83,596 ......E 2 33
Arequipa, Peru, 194,700 ......F 7 46
Argenteuil, France, 87,106 ......A 1 26
Århus, Denmark, 117,266 ......B 3 24
Arica, Chile, †92,394 ......F 7 46
Arles, France, 33,575 ......F 6 26
Arlington, Texas, 89,723 ......F 2 158
Arlington, Va., 174,284 ......O 3 163
Armavir, U.S.S.R., 146,000 ......E 5 30
Armentières, France, 24,460 ......E 2 26
Arnhem, Netherlands, 132,531 ......H 4 24
Arras, France, 48,494 ......E 2 26
Asahikawa, Japan, 293,000 ......F 2 36
Asansol, India, 157,388 ......F 4 34
Aschaffenburg, W. Germany, 56,236 ......C 4 25
Asheville, N.C., 57,681 ......D 3 136
Ashkhabad, U.S.S.R., 253,000......F 6 30
Ashland, Ky., 29,245 ......R 4 93
Asmara, Ethiopia, 190,500 ......O 9 38
Asnières, France, 79,942 ......A 1 26
Asti, Italy, 44,455 ......B 2 28
Astrakhan', U.S.S.R., 411,000......E 5 30
Asunción,* Paraguay, †411,500......J 9 47
Aswân, Egypt, 127,700 ......N 7 38
Asyût, Egypt, 154,100 ......N 6 38

Athens,* Greece, 627,564 ......D 4 29
Atlanta,* Ga., 497,421 ......D 3 72
Atlantic City, N.J., 47,859 ......E 5 129
Aubervilliers, France, 73,559 ......B 1 26
Auburn, N.Y., 34,599 ......G 5 132
Auckland, New Zealand, 152,200....L 5 40
Augsburg, W. Germany, 214,376....D 4 25
Augusta, Ga., 59,864 ......J 4 72
Augusta,* Maine, 21,945 ......D 7 98
Aurangabad, India, 150,514 ......C 5 34
Aurora, Colo., 74,974 ......K 3 65
Aurora, Ill., 74,812 ......E 2 78
Austin,* Tex., 251,808 ......G 7 158
Avellaneda, Argentina, †329,626....O12 47
Avignon, France, 78,871 ......F 6 26
Ayacucho, Peru, 28,500 ......F 6 46
Ayr, Scotland, 47,635 ......D 3 23
Bacău, Rumania, 73,481 ......D 2 29
Bacolod, Philippines, 156,900 ......G 3 36
Badalona, Spain, 90,655 ......H 2 27
Baden-Baden, W. Germany, 38,852 ......C 4 25
Baghdad,* Iraq, 1,028,083 ......E 3 33
Baguio, Philippines, 58,000 ......G 2 36
Bahia (Salvador), Brazil, 998,258 ......N 6 46
Bahía Blanca, Arg., †150,354 ......H11 47
Baia Mare, Rumania, 62,769 ......C 2 29
Baile Átha Cliath (Dublin), *Ireland, 537,448 ......C 4 23
Bakersfield, Calif., 69,515 ......F 8 60
Baku, U.S.S.R., 1,261,000 ......F 5 30
Balıkesir, Turkey, 69,341 ......A 2 33
Balikpapan, Indon., 113,000 ......F 6 36
Baltimore, Md., 905,759 ......M 3 101
Bamako,* Mali, 88,500 ......E 9 38
Bamberg, W. Germany, 68,713 ......D 4 25
Bandar Seri Begawan, *Brunei, 37,000 ......E 4 36
Bandjarmasin, Indon., 264,000 ......E 6 36
Bandung, Indon., †1,006,000 ......H 2 36
Bangalore, India, †1,648,232 ......C 6 34
Bangkok,* Thailand, 1,299,528 ......D 4 35
Bangor, Maine, 33,168 ......F 6 98
Bangui,* Central African Rep., †240,000 ......K10 38
Banja Luka, Yugoslavia, 55,000 ......B 2 29
Banjul,* Gambia, 31,800 ......C 9 38
Baranovichi, U.S.S.R., 102,000 ......C 4 30
Barcelona, Spain, 1,555,564 ......H 2 27
Barcelona, Venezuela, 42,379 ......H 2 46
Bareilly, India, 299,629 ......D 3 34
Bari, Italy, 293,963 ......F 4 28
Barking, England, 167,960 ......C 5 23
Barletta, Italy, 67,419 ......F 4 28
Barnagore, India, 131,431 ......F 1 34
Barnaul, U.S.S.R., 439,000 ......J 4 30
Barnet, England, 314,530 ......B 5 23
Barnsley, England, 74,880 ......F 4 23
Baroda, India, 467,422 ......C 4 34
Barquisimeto, Venezuela, 280,086..F 2 46
Barranquilla, Colombia, 816,706 ....F 1 46
Barrow-in-Furness, Eng., 63,460....E 3 23
Basel, Switz., 213,000 ......C 1 27
Basildon, England, 122,760 ......G 5 23
Basra, Iraq, 313,327 ......E 3 33
Bassein, Burma, 77,905 ......B 3 35
Basse-Terre,* Guadeloupe, 16,000 ......F 4 48
Basseterre,* St. Christopher, 15,726 ......F 3 48
Bath, England, 84,760 ......E 5 23
Baton Rouge,* La., 165,963 ......K 2 95
Battle Creek, Mich., 38,931 ......D 6 106
Baurú, Brazil, 120,178 ......L 8 46
Bay City, Mich., 49,449 ......F 5 106
Bayonne, France, 39,761 ......C 6 26

Bayonne, N.J., 72,743 ......B 2 129
Bayreuth, W. Germany, 63,387 ......D 4 25
Beaumont, Tex., 117,548 ......K 7 158
Bebington, England, 57,060 ......F 2 23
Bedford, England, 68,650 ......F 4 23
Beersheba, Israel, 51,600 ......B 5 31
Beira, Mozambique, †58,235 ......O15 39
Beirut,* Lebanon, 700,000 ......C 3 33
Békéscsaba, Hungary, 53,000 ......F 3 29
Belém, Brazil, 565,097 ......L 4 46
Belfast,* Northern Ireland, United Kingdom, 360,400 ......D 3 23
Belfort, France, 53,001 ......G 4 26
Belgaum, India, †213,830 ......D 5 34
Belgorod, U.S.S.R., 151,000 ......D 4 30
Belgrade,* Yugoslavia, 745,000 ......C 2 29
Belize City, Belize, 37,000 ......B 1 48
Bellary, India, 125,127 ......D 5 34
Belleville, Ill., 41,699 ......B 6 78
Belleville, N.J., 34,722 ......B 2 129
Bellingham, Wash., 39,375 ......C 2 166
Belmopan,* Belize, 1,500 ......B 1 48
Belo Horizonte, Brazil, 1,106,722 ......M 7 46
Beloit, Wis., 35,729 ......H10 173
Benares (Varanasi), India, 560,296 ......E 3 34
Bene Beraq, Israel, 51,700 ......B 3 31
Benghazi, Libya, 137,295 ......K 5 38
Benin City, Nigeria, 116,774 ......H10 38
Beni Suef, Egypt, 78,829 ......N 6 38
Beograd (Belgrade),* Yugoslavia, 745,000 ......C 2 29
Beppu, Japan, 144,000 ......C 4 36
Berezniki, U.S.S.R., 145,000 ......F 4 30
Bergamo, Italy, 110,666 ......B 2 28
Bergen, Norway, †270,000 ......A 2 24
Berhampur, India, 117,635 ......F 5 34
Berkeley, Calif., 116,716 ......J 2 60
Berlin,* East Germany, 1,084,000 ......F 4 25
Berlin, West Germany, 2,134,256 ......F 4 25
Bern,* Switzerland, 166,800 ......C 2 27
Berwyn, Ill., 52,502 ......B 2 78
Besançon, France, 107,939 ......G 4 26
Bethesda, Md., 71,621 ......E 4 100
Bethlehem, Pa., 72,686 ......M 4 151
Beverly, Mass., 38,348 ......E 5 104
Beverly Hills, Calif., 33,416 ......C10 60
Bexley, England, 215,610 ......C 5 23
Béziers, France, 74,517 ......E 6 26
Bhagalpur, India, 172,700 ......F 4 34
Bhatpara, India, 205,303 ......F 1 34
Bhavnagar, India, 226,072 ......C 4 34
Bhilai, India, 174,557 ......E 4 34
Bhopal, India, 309,285 ......D 4 34
Białystok, Poland, 149,000 ......F 2 31
Biarritz, France, 26,628 ......C 6 26
Biel, Switzerland, 67,800 ......C 1 27
Bielefeld, W. Germany, 169,347......C 2 25
Bielsko-Biała, Poland, 84,000 ......D 4 31
Bihar, India, 100,052 ......F 3 34
Bijapur, India, 103,308 ......D 5 34
Bikaner, India, 188,598 ......C 3 34
Bilaspur, India, 130,804 ......E 4 34
Bilbao, Spain, 293,939 ......E 1 27
Binghamton, N.Y., 64,123 ......J 6 132
Birkenhead, England, 141,950......E 4 23
Birmingham, Ala., 300,910 ......D 3 50
Birmingham, England, 1,086,400....E 4 23
Biskra, Algeria, 59,275 ......H 5 38
Bismarck,* N. Dak., 34,703 ......J 6 138
Bissau,* Guinea-Bissau, 60,000 ......D 9 38
Bitola, Yugoslavia, 52,000 ......C 3 29
Biysk, U.S.S.R., 186,000 ......J 4 30
Bizerte, Tunisia, 51,700 ......J 4 38

Blackburn, England, 100,010 ....E 4 23
Blackpool, England, 146,700 ....E 4 23
Blagoveshchensk, U.S.S.R., 128,000 ....N 4 30
Blantyre, Malawi, 109,461 ....N15 39
Blida, Algeria, 99,238 ....G 4 38
Bloemfontein,* Orange Free State, South Africa, 146,200 ....L17 39
Bloomfield, N.J., 52,029 ....B 2 129
Bloomington, Ill., 39,992 ....D 3 78
Bloomington, Minn., 81,970 ....G 6 110
Blumenau, Brazil, 85,942 ....L 9 47
Bobo-Dioulasso, Upper Volta, 56,100 ....F 9 38
Bobruysk, U.S.S.R., 138,000 ....C 4 30
Bochum, W. Germany, 346,886......B 3 25
Bogor, Indon., 172,000 ....H 2 36
Bogotá,* Colombia, 2,037,904 ....F 3 46
Boise,* Idaho, 74,990 ....B 6 76
Bologna, Italy, 443,178 ....C 2 28
Bolton, England, 152,500 ....E 4 23
Bolzano, Italy, 84,685 ....C 1 28
Bombay, India, 5,968,546 ....B 9 34
Bonn,* W. Germany, 299,376........B 3 25
Bootle, England, 79,950 ....F 2 23
Borås, Sweden, 70,238 ....C 3 24
Bordeaux, France, 263,808 ....C 5 26
Boston,* Mass., 641,071 ....D 7 104
Bottrop, W. Germany, 108,161 ....B 3 25
Bouaké, Ivory Coast, 100,000 ....F10 38
Boulogne-Billancourt, France, 108,846 ....A 2 26
Boulogne-sur-Mer, France, 49,064 ....D 2 26
Bourges, France, 67,137 ....E 4 26
Bournemouth, England, 149,820 ....F 5 23
Bradford, England, 293,210 ....F 4 23
Braga, Portugal, 40,977 ....B 2 27
Brăila, Rumania, 147,495 ....D 2 29
Brandenburg, E. Germany, 90,753 ....E 2 25
Brasília,* Brazil, 272,002 ....L 7 46
Brașov, Rumania, 175,264 ....D 2 29
Bratislava, Czechoslovakia, 278,835 ....D 2 29
Bratsk, U.S.S.R., 155,000 ....L 4 30
Brazzaville,* Congo, 160,000 ....J12 39
Breda, Netherlands, 121,209 ....E 4 24
Bremen, W. Germany, 227,184 ....C 2 25
Bremerhaven, W. Germany, 148,793 ....C 2 25
Brent, England, 281,530 ....B 5 23
Brentwood, England, 58,250 ....C 5 23
Brescia, Italy, 140,518 ....C 2 28
Brest, France, 150,696 ....A 3 26
Bridgeport, Conn., 156,542 .... C 4 66
Bridgetown,* Barbados, 12,430 ....G 4 48
Brighton, England, 163,600 ....F 5 23
Brindisi, Italy, 63,480 ....G 4 28
Brisbane,* Queensland, Australia, 656,222 ....J 5 40
Bristol, Conn., 55,487 ....D 2 66
Bristol, England, 427,230 ....E 5 23
Brno, Czechoslovakia, 333,831 ......D 2 29
Brockton, Mass., 89,040 ....K 4 104
Bromley, England, 303,550 ....B 5 23
Brooklyn, N.Y., 2,602,012 ....N 9 133
Bruges, Belgium, 52,249 ....B 5 24
Brunswick, W. Germany, 225,168 ....D 2 25
Brussels (Bruxelles),* Belgium, †1,073,111 ....D 6 24
Bryansk, U.S.S.R., 318,000 ....D 4 30
Bucaramanga, Colombia, 279,703 ....F 2 46
Bucharest (București),* Rumania, 1,431,993 ....D 2 29
Budapest,* Hungary, 1,990,000 .....E 3 29
Buenaventura, Colombia, 113,301 ....E 3 46
Buenos Aires,* Argentina, 3,549,000 ....O11 47
Buga, Colombia, 65,535 ....E 3 46
Buffalo, N.Y., 462,768 ....B 5 132
Bujumbura,* Burundi, 90,000 ......N12 39
Bukavu, Zaire, 134,861 ....M12 39
Bukittinggi, Indon., 62,000 ....B 6 36
Bulawayo, Rhodesia, 245,590 ....M16 39
Burbank, Calif., 88,871 ....C10 60
Burdwan, India, 144,970 ....F 4 34
Burgas, Bulgaria, 122,212 ....D 3 29
Burgos, Spain, 79,810 ....E 1 27
Burhanpur, India, 105,349 ....D 4 34
Burlington, Iowa, 32,366 ....L 7 85
Burlington, Vt., 38,633 ....A 3 124
Burnley, England, 76,610 ....E 4 23
Bursa, Turkey, 211,644 ....A 1 33
Burujird, Iran, 71,476 ....E 3 33
Bury, England, 67,070 ....G 2 23
Busto Arsizio, Italy, 58,483 ....B 2 28
Butte, Mont., 23,368 ....D 5 118
Buzău, Rumania, 56,380 ....D 2 29
Bydgoszcz, Poland, 264,400 ....D 2 31
Bytom, Poland, 191,000 ....B 4 31
Cabanatuan, Philippines, 80,000....G 2 36
Cádiz, Spain, 117,871 ....C 4 27
Caen, France, 106,790 ....C 3 26
Cagayan de Oro, Philippines, 78,000 ....G 4 36
Cagliari, Sardinia, Italy, 172,925 ....B 5 28
Caguas, Puerto Rico, 62,807 ....G 1 48
Cairo,* Egypt, 4,219,853 ....N 5 38
Calais, France, 70,153 ....D 2 26
Calcutta, India, 7,040,345 ....F 4 34
Calgary, Alberta, Canada 403,319 ....E 5 43
Cali, Colombia, 820,809 ....E 3 46
Calicut (Kozhikode), India, 333,980 ....C 6 34
Callao, Peru, 335,400 ....E 6 46
Caltanissetta, Sicily, Italy, 51,699 ....D 6 28
Camagüey, Cuba, 178,600 ....B 2 48
Cambridge, England, 100,200 ....G 4 23
Cambridge, Mass., 100,361 ....D 7 104
Camden, England, 228,080 ....B 5 23
Camden, N.J., 102,551 ....B 3 129
Campeche, Mexico, †81,147 ....G 4 42
Campinas, Brazil, 328,629 ....L 8 47
Campo Grande, Brazil, 130,792 ....K 8 46
Campos, Brazil, 153,310 ....M 8 46
Canberra,* Australia, 92,308 ...... H 7 40
Candia (Iráklion), Crete, Greece, 63,458 ....D 5 29
Cannes, France, 66,590 ....G 6 26
Canterbury, England, 33,140 ....G 5 23
Can Tho, South Vietnam, 92,132 E 5 35
Canton, China, 1,867,000 ....H 7 37
Canton, Ohio, 110,053 ....H 4 140
Cape Coast, Ghana, 41,230 ....F11 38
Cape Town,* Cape of Good Hope, *South Africa, 625,000 ....K18 39
Cap-Haïtien, Haiti, 30,000 ....D 3 48
Caracas,* Venezuela, 786,710 ....G 1 46
Carcassonne, France, 40,580 ....E 6 26
Cárdenas, Cuba, 67,400 ....B 2 48
Cardiff, Wales, 285,860 ....E 5 23
Carlisle, England, 71,090 ....E 3 23
Carrara, Italy, 37,386 ....C 2 28
Carson City,* Nev., 15,468 ....B 3 122
Cartagena, Colombia, 229,040 ....E 1 46
Cartagena, Spain, 42,424 ....F 4 27
Caruaru, Brazil, 101,006 ....N 5 46
Casablanca, Morocco, 1,320,000 ....E 5 38
Castellón de la Plana, Spain, 52,868 ....G 3 27
Castries,* St. Lucia, 4,353 ....G 4 48
Catania, Sicily, Italy, 358,700 ....E 6 28
Cayenne,* Fr. Guiana, 19,668 ......K 2 46
Ceará (Fortaleza), Brazil, 520,175 ....N 4 46
Cebu, Philippines, 332,100 ....G 3 36
Cedar Rapids, Iowa, 110,642 ....K 5 85
České Budějovice, Czechoslovakia, 70,000 ....C 2 29
Ceuta, Spain, 88,000 ....D 5 27
Châlons-sur-Marne, France, 48,558 ....F 3 26
Chambéry, France, 49,858 ....F 5 26
Champigny-sur-Marne, France, 70,353 ....C 2 26
Chandigarh, India, 218,807 ....D 2 34
Changchih, China, 180,000 ....H 4 37
Changchow, China, 300,000 ....J 5 37
Changchun, China, 988,000 ....K 3 37
Changsha, China, 709,000 ....H 6 37
Charleroi, Belgium, 24,895 ....D 7 24
Charleston, S.C., 66,945 ....G 6 152
Charleston,* W. Va., 71,505 ....C 6 168
Charleville-Mézières, France, 55,230 ....F 3 26
Charlotte, N.C., 241,178 ....H 4 136
Charlotte Amalie, St. Thomas, *Virgin Islands (U.S.), 12,372 ....F 3 48
Charlottetown,* Prince Edward I., Canada, 19,133 ....K 6 43
Chartres, France, 34,128 ....D 3 26
Chatham, England, 55,460 ....G 5 23
Chattanooga, Tenn., 119,082 ....K10 93
Cheadle and Gatley, England, 57,290 ....G 2 23
Cheboksary, U.S.S.R., 216,000 .....E 4 30
Chefoo, China, 140,000 ....K 4 37
Chelmsford, England, 56,900 ....G 5 23
Chelsea, Mass., 30,625 ....D 6 104
Cheltenham, England, 76,000........F 5 23
Chelyabinsk, U.S.S.R., 874,000 ....G 4 30
Chemnitz (Karl-Marx-Stadt), E. Germany, 295,443 ....E 3 25
Chengchow, China, 785,000 ....H 5 37
Chengtu, China, 1,135,000 ....F 5 37
Cherbourg, France, 37,933 ....C 3 26
Cheremkhovo, U.S.S.R., 109,000....L 4 30
Cherepovets, U.S.S.R., 189,000 ....D 4 30
Chernigov, U.S.S.R., 159,000 ....D 4 30
Chernovtsy, U.S.S.R., 187,000 ......C 5 30
Chesapeake, Va., 89,580 ....R 7 163
Chester, England, 60,880 ....E 4 23
Chester, Pa., 56,331 ....L 7 151
Chesterfield, England, 70,420 ....F 4 23
Cheyenne,* Wyo., 40,914 ....H 4 175
Chiai, China, 191,074 ....K 7 37
Chiba, Japan, 407,000 ....H 2 36
Chicago, Ill., 3,369,359 ....B 2 78
Chiclayo, Peru, 140,800 ....E 5 46
Chicopee, Mass., 66,676 ....D 4 104
Chiengmai, Thailand, 65,600 ....C 3 35
Chihuahua, Mexico, †363,850 ....D 2 42
Chillán, Chile, †102,361 ....F11 47
Chimbote, Peru, 102,800 ....E 5 46
Chimkent, U.S.S.R., 247,000 ....G 5 30
Chinchow, China, 400,000 ....J 3 37
Chinkiang, China, 190,000 ....J 5 37
Chinwangtao, China, 210,000 ....K 4 37
Chita, U.S.S.R., 242,000 ....M 4 30
Chittagong, Bangladesh, 364,205 ....G 4 34
Chorzów, Poland, 153,100 ....B 4 31
Christchurch, New Zealand, 165,000 ....L 7 40
Christiansted, St. Croix, Virgin Islands (U.S.), 2,966 ....H 2 48
Chuchow, China, 190,000 ....H 6 37
Chungking, China, 2,165,000 ....G 6 37
Chur, Switzerland, 29,100 ....E 2 27
Cicero, Ill., 67,058 ....B 2 78
Ciénaga, Colombia, 142,893 ....F 1 46
Cienfuegos, Cuba, 91,800 ....B 2 48
Cincinnati, Ohio, 452,524 ....B 9 140
Ciudad Bolívar, Venez., 63,266 .....H 2 46
Ciudad Guayana, Venezuela, 127,681 ....H 2 46
Ciudad Juárez, Mexico, †436,054....C 1 42
Clarksburg, W. Va., 24,864 ....F 4 168
Clermont-Ferrand, France, 124,531 ....E 5 26
Cleveland, Ohio, 750,879 ....H 9 140
Cleveland Heights, Ohio, 60,767.....J 9 140
Clifton, N.J., 82,084 ....B 2 129
Clinton, Iowa, 34,719 ....N 5 85
Cluj, Rumania, 193,375 ....C 2 29
Coatbridge, Scotland, 52,804 ....E 3 23
Cochabamba, Bolivia, 157,000 ......G 7 46
Cochin, India, 438,420 ....D 6 34
Coimbatore, India, 353,469 ....D 6 34
Coimbra, Portugal, 46,313 ....B 2 27
Colchester, England, 75,210 ....G 5 23
Colmar, France, 58,623 ....G 3 26
Cologne, W. Germany, 866,308 ....B 3 25
Colombes, France, 80,224 ....A 1 26
Colombo,* Sri Lanka, 551,200 ....D 7 34
Colón, Panama, 67,641 ....D 3 48
Colorado Springs, Colo., 135,060 ....K 5 65
Columbia,* S.C., 113,542 ....F 4 152
Columbus, Ga., 155,028 ....C 6 72
Columbus,* Ohio, 540,025 ....E 6 140
Como, Italy, 64,301 ....B 2 28
Compiègne, France, 28,881 ....E 3 26
Compton, Calif., 78,611 ....C11 60
Conakry,* Guinea, 43,000 ....D10 38
Concepción, Chile, †189,929 ....F11 47
Concord, Calif., 85,164 ....K 1 60
Concord,* N.H., 30,022 ....D 5 124
Concordia, Argentina, 56,654 ....J10 47
Constanța, Rumania, 165,245 ....E 2 29
Constantine, Algeria, 243,558 ......H 4 38
Copenhagen,* Denmark, 643,262....C 3 24
Coquimbo, Chile, †55,360 ....F10 47
Córdoba, Argentina, †589,153 ....G10 47
Córdoba, Spain, 167,808 ....D 4 27
Corinth, Greece, 15,892 ....C 4 29
Cork, Ireland, 77,980 ....B 5 23
Corpus Christi, Tex., 204,525 ....G10 158
Corrientes, Argentina, 97,507 ....J 9 47
Cosenza, Italy, 70,201 ....F 5 28
Costa Mesa, Calif., 72,660 ....D11 60
Cotonou, Benin, 120,000 ....G10 38
Cottbus, E. Germany, 75,541 ....F 3 25
Council Bluffs, Iowa, 60,348 ....B 6 84
Courbevoie, France, 57,998 ....A 2 26
Coventry, England, 335,650............F 4 23
Covington, Ky., 52,535 ....S 2 93
Coyoacán, Mexico, †338,850 ....F 1 42
Cracow, Poland, 540,200 ....E 3 31
Craiova, Rumania, 166,249 ....C 2 29
Cranston, R.I., 74,287 ....J 5 104
Cremona, Italy, 64,775 ....B 2 28
Croydon, England, 327,130 ....B 6 23
Csepel, Hungary, 86,287 ....E 3 29
Cúcuta, Colombia, 207,091 ....F 2 46
Cuddalore, India, 101,345 ....E 6 34
Cuenca, Ecuador, 60,402 ....E 4 46
Cuiabá, Brazil, 83,621 ....J 7 46
Culiacán, Mexico, †358,812 ....C 3 42
Cumaná, Venezuela, 69,937 ....H 1 46
Cumberland, Md., 29,724 ....D 2 100
Curitiba, Brazil, 483,038 ....L 9 47
Cuttack, India, 198,405 ....F 4 34
Cuzco, Peru, 108,900 ....F 6 46
Czestochowa, Poland, 179,400 ......D 3 31
Dabrowa Górnicza, Poland, 60,100 ....C 4 31
Dacca,* Bangladesh, 556,712 ....G 4 34
Dairen, China, 766,400 ....K 4 37
Dakar,* Senegal, 550,000 ....C 9 38
Da Lat, S. Vietnam, 83,992 ....F 5 35
Dallas, Tex., 844,401 ....H 2 158
Damascus,* Syria, 789,840 ....C 3 33
Damietta, Egypt, 71,780 ....N 5 38
Da Nang, S. Vietnam, 363,343 ....E 3 35
Danville, Ill., 42,570 ....F 3 78
Danville, Va., 46,391 ....K 7 163
Darbhanga, India, 132,129 ....F 3 34
Dar es Salaam,* Tanzania, 272,821 ....P13 39
Darjeeling, India, 42,662..................F 3 34
Darlington, England, 84,700 ....F 3 23
Darmstadt, W. Ger., 141,075 ....C 4 25
Darwin,* Northern Territory, Australia, 18,042 ....E 2 40
Davangere, India, 121,018 ....D 6 34
Davao, Philippines, 337,000 ....H 4 36
Davenport, Iowa, 98,469 ....M 5 85
Dayton, Ohio, 243,601 ....B 6 140
Dearborn, Mich., 104,199 ....B 7 106
Debrecen, Hungary, 160,000 ....F 3 29
Decatur, Ill., 90,397 ....E 4 78
Dehra Dun, India, 170,187 ....D 2 34
Deir ez Zor, Syria, 60,335 ....C 2 33
Delft, Netherlands, 83,698 ....D 3 24
Delhi, India, 3,279,955 ....D 3 34
Delmenhorst, W. Ger., 63,685 ....C 2 25
Den Helder, Netherlands, †60,612 ....E 2 24
Denizli, Turkey, 64,331 ....A 2 33
Denver,* Colo., 514,678 ....K 3 65
Derby, England, 221,240 ....F 4 23
Des Moines,* Iowa, 201,404 ....G 5 84
Dessau, E. Germany, 95,682 ....E 3 25
Detmold, W. Ger., 64,473 ....C 3 25
Detroit, Mich., 1,513,601 ....B 7 106
Deurne, Belgium, 75,819 ....E 5 24
Deventer, Netherlands, †65,319 ......H 3 24
Dhulia, India, 137,089 ....C 4 34
Diégo-Suarez, Malagasy Rep., 40,237 ....R14 39
Dieppe, France, 29,829 ....D 3 26
Dijon, France, 143,120 ....F 4 26

Dili,* Port. Timor, †52,158 ....H 7 36
Dindigul, India, 127,406 ....D 6 34
Diyarbakir, Turkey, 475,916 ....C 2 33
Dizful, Iran, 84,499 ....E 3 33
Djakarta,* Indonesia, 3,429,000 ....H 1 36
Djambi, Indon., 139,000 ....C 6 36
Djibouti,* Terr. of the Afars and Issas, 41,200 ....P 9 38
Djokjakarta, Indonesia, 385,000 ....J 2 36
Dnepropetrovsk, U.S.S.R., 863,000 ....D 5 30
Dobrich (Tolbukhin), Bulg., 55,111 ....D 2 29
Doha,* Qatar, 45,000 ....F 4 33
Doncaster, England, 84,050 ....F 4 23
Donetsk, U.S.S.R., 879,000 ....D 5 30
Dordrecht, Netherlands, †88,699 ....E 4 24
Dortmund, W. Ger., 648,883 ....B 3 25
Douai, France, 47,347 ....E 2 26
Douala, Cameroon, 230,000 ....J10 38
Douglas,* Isle of Man, 20,385 ....D 3 23
Dover,* Del., 17,488 ....R 4 101
Dover, England, 35,640 ....G 5 23
Drammen, Norway, 47,261 ....A 1 24
Dresden, E. Germany, 449,848 ....E 3 25
Dubai, U.A.E., †65,000 ....F 4 33
Dublin,* Ireland, 537,448 ....C 4 23
Dubuque, Iowa, 62,309 ....M 3 85
Dudley, England, 181,380 ....G 3 23
Duisburg, W. Germany, 457,891 ....B 3 25
Duluth, Minn., 100,578 ....G 4 110
Dundalk, Md., 85,377 ....N 3 101
Dundee, Scotland, 181,950 ....E 2 23
Dunedin, New Zealand, 77,800 ....L 7 40
Dunkirk (Dunkerque), France, 26,038 ....E 2 26
Dún Laoghaire, Ire., 47,792 ....C 4 23
Durango, Mexico, †192,934 ....D 3 42
Durban, Natal, S. Africa, 662,900 ....N17 39
Durham, N.C., 95,438 ....M 2 137
Durrës (Durazzo), Alb., 47,900 ....B 3 29
Dushanbe, U.S.S.R., 374,000 ....G 6 30
Düsseldorf, W. Ger., 680,806 ....B 3 25
Dzerzhinsk, U.S.S.R., 221,000 ....E 4 30
Dzhambul, U.S.S.R., 188,000 ....H 5 30
Ealing, England, 297,910 ....B 5 23
Eastbourne, England, 69,290 ....G 5 23
East Chicago, Ind., 46,982 ....C 1 83
East Cleveland, Ohio, 39,600 ....H 9 140
Easton, Pa., 30,256 ....M 4 151
East Orange, N.J., 75,471 ....B 2 129
East St. Louis, Ill., 69,996 ....B 6 78
East London, Cape of Good Hope, S. Africa, 134,100 ....M18 39
Eau Claire, Wis., 44,619 ....D 6 173
Ede, Netherlands, †71,952 ....G 3 24
Edinburgh,* Scotland, United Kingdom, 465,421 ....E 3 23
Edirne, Turkey, 46,091 ....A 1 33
Edmonton,* Alberta, Canada, 438,152 ....E 5 43
Eindhoven, Netherlands, 188,631 ....F 5 24
Eisenach, E. Germany, 50,234 ....D 3 25
El Aaiún,* Sp. Sahara, 10,000 ....D 6 38
Elath, Israel, 7,000 ....D 5 31
Elâzığ, Turkey, 78,605 ....C 2 33
Elbląg, Poland, 86,700 ....D 1 31
El Faiyûm, Egypt, 133,800 ....M 6 38
El Ferrol, Spain, 62,010 ....B 1 27
Elgin, Ill., 55,691 ....E 1 78
El Iskandariya (Alexandria), Egypt, 1,803,900 ....M 5 38
Elizabeth, N.J., 112,654 ....B 2 129
Elkhart, Ind., 43,152 ....F 1 83
Ellesmere Port, Eng., 56,750 ....F 2 23
El Minya, Egypt, 112,800 ....M 6 38
Elmira, N.Y., 39,945 ....G 6 132
El Paso, Tex., 322,261 ....A10 158
El Qâhira (Cairo),* Egypt, 4,219,853 ....N 5 38
Eluru, India, 127,047 ....E 5 34
Elyria, Ohio, 53,427 ....F 3 140
Emden, W. Germany, 48,313 ....B 2 25
Emmen, Netherlands, †79,707 ....J 2 24
Enfield, England, 265,600 ....B 5 23
Engel's, U.S.S.R., 130,000 ....E 4 30
Enid, Okla., 44,986 ....L 2 145
Enschede, Netherlands, 139,245 ....J 3 24
Ensenada, Mexico, †113,320 ....A 1 42
Epsom and Ewell, Eng., 72,190 ....B 6 23
Erbil, Iraq, 90,320 ....D 2 33
Erfurt, E. Germany, 193,745 ....D 3 25
Erie, Pa., 129,231 ....B 1 150
Erivan, U.S.S.R., 767,000 ....E 6 30
Erlangen, W. Germany, 85,727 ....D 4 25
Erzurum, Turkey, 105,317 ....D 2 33
Esbjerg, Denmark, 62,952 ....B 3 24
Esher, England, 63,190 ....B 6 23
Eskilstuna, Sweden, 65,580 ....C 3 24
Eskişehir, Turkey, 173,882 ....B 2 33
Essen, W. Germany, 704,769 ....B 3 25
Esslingen, W. Germany, 86,497 ....C 4 25
Euclid, Ohio, 71,552 ....J 9 140
Eugene, Oreg., 78,389 ....D 3 146
Evanston, Ill., 79,808 ....B 1 78
Evansville, Ind., 138,764 ....C 9 83
Everett, Mass., 42,485 ....D 6 104
Everett, Wash., 53,622 ....C 3 166
Exeter, England, 92,880 ....E 5 23
Fairbanks, Alaska, 14,771 ....J 2 53
Faizabad, India, 102,794 ....F 3 34
Fall River, Mass., 96,898 ....K 6 104
Famagusta, Cyprus, 38,000 ....B 2 33
Fareham, England, 79,740 ....F 5 23
Fargo, N. Dak., 53,365 ....S 6 139
Fatehgarh, India, 103,282 ....D 3 34
Ferrara, Italy, 90,419 ....C 2 28
Fez, Morocco, 280,000 ....F 5 38
Firenze (Florence), Italy, 413,455 ....C 3 28
Firozabad, India, 133,945 ....D 3 34
Fitchburg, Mass., 43,343 ....G 2 104
Fiume (Rijeka), Yugoslavia, 108,000 ....A 2 29
Flensburg, W. Germany, 96,778 ....C 1 25
Flint, Mich., 193,317 ....F 6 106
Florence, Italy, 413,455 ....C 3 28
Florianópolis, Brazil, 115,665 ....L 9 46
Foggia, Italy, 108,682 ....E 4 28
Folkestone, England, 45,270 ....G 5 23
Fond du Lac, Wis., 35,515 ....K 8 173
Foochow, China, 623,000 ....J 6 37
Forest, Belgium, 55,799 ....D 6 24
Forlì, Italy, 65,376 ....D 2 28
Fortaleza, Brazil, 520,175 ....N 4 46
Fort-de-France,* Martinique, 100,000 ....G 4 48
Fort Lauderdale, Fla., 139,590 ....B 4 68
Fort Wayne, Ind., 178,021 ....G 2 83
Fort Worth, Tex., 393,476 ....E 2 158
Franca, Brazil, 86,852 ....L 8 46
Frankfort,* Ky., 21,902 ....M 4 93
Frankfurt am Main, W. Germany, 660,410 ....C 3 25
Frankfurt an der Oder, E. Germany, 58,866 ....F 2 25
Fredericton,* New Brunswick, Canada, 24,254 ....K 6 43
Freetown,* Sierra Leone, 170,600 ....D10 38
Freiburg, W. Germany, 165,960 ....B 5 25
Fremantle, W. Australia, Australia, 25,284 ....B 2 40
Fremont, Calif., 100,869 ....K 2 60
Fresno, Calif., 165,972 ....F 7 60
Fribourg, Switzerland, 38,500 ....C 2 27
Frunze, U.S.S.R., 431,000 ....H 5 30
Fukui, Japan, 193,000 ....D 3 36
Fukuoka, Japan, 812,000 ....C 4 36
Fukushima, Japan, 225,000 ....F 3 36
Fukuyama, Japan, 233,000 ....D 4 36
Fullerton, Calif., 85,987 ....D11 60
Funabashi, Japan, 281,000 ....H 2 36
Funchal,* Madeira, Portugal, 43,301 ....A 2 27
Fürth, W. Germany, 94,310 ....D 4 25
Fushun, China, 1,019,000 ....K 3 37
Fusin, China, 290,000 ....K 3 37
Gabès, Tunisia, 32,300 ....H 5 38
Gaborone,* Botswana, 18,000 ....L16 39
Gadag, India, 95,381 ....D 5 34
Gadsden, Ala., 53,928 ....G 2 50
Galaţi, Rumania, 160,097 ....D 2 29
Galesburg, Ill., 36,290 ....C 3 78
Galle, Sri Lanka, 64,942 ....D 7 34
Galveston, Tex., 61,809 ....L 3 158
Galway, Ireland, 22,028 ....B 4 23
Gander, Newfoundland, Canada, 7,748 ....L 6 43
Garden Grove, Calif., 121,371 ....D11 60
Garden Reach, India, 155,520 ....F 2 34
Garfield, N.J., 30,797 ....B 2 129
Garland, Texas, 81,437 ....H 1 158
Gary, Ind., 175,415 ....C 1 83
Gateshead, England, 100,060 ....F 3 23
Gauhati, India, 122,981 ....G 3 34
Gävle, Sweden, 60,868 ....C 2 24
Gaya, India, 179,826 ....F 4 34
Gaza, Egypt, 87,793 ....B 3 33
Gaziantep, Turkey, 160,152 ....C 2 33
Gdańsk, Poland, 333,500 ....D 1 31
Gdynia, Poland, 171,900 ....D 1 31
Gelsenkirchen, W. Germany, 348,620 ....B 3 25
Geneva, Switzerland, 169,500 ....B 2 27
Genoa (Genova), Italy, 747,794 ....B 2 28
Georgetown,* Cayman Is., 4,106 ....A 3 48
Georgetown,* Guyana, 97,190 ....J 2 46
Georgetown (Penang), Malaysia, 234,903 ....C 6 35
Gera, E. Germany, 109,989 ....E 3 25
Germiston, Transvaal, S. Africa, 189,600 ....M17 39
Ghent (Gent), Belgium, 153,301 ....C 5 24
Gibraltar,* Gibraltar, 27,000 ....D 4 27
Giessen, W. Germany, 74,731 ....C 3 25
Gifu, Japan, 398,000 ....E 4 36
Gijón, Spain, 92,020 ....D 1 27
Glasgow, Scotland, 927,948 ....D 3 23
Glendale, Calif., 132,752 ....C10 60
Gliwice, Poland, 164,900 ....A 4 31
Gloucester, England, 90,530 ....E 5 23
Godthaab,* Greenland, 7,166 ....N 3 42
Goiânia, Brazil, 362,152 ....L 7 46
Gomel', U.S.S.R., 272,000 ....D 4 30
Gómez Palacio, Mexico, 135,743 ....D 3 42
Gonaïves, Haiti, †99,140 ....D 3 48
Gondar, Ethiopia, 24,673 ....O 9 38
Gorakhpur, India, 230,701 ....E 3 34
Gorizia, Italy, 35,307 ....D 2 28
Gor'kiy, U.S.S.R., 1,170,000 ....E 4 30
Görlitz, E. Germany, 88,632 ....F 3 25
Gorontalo, Indon., 88,000 ....G 5 36
Gorzów Wielkopolski, Poland, 69,700 ....B 2 31
Gosport, England, 76,160 ....F 5 23
Göteborg, Sweden, 444,131 ....B 3 24
Gotha, E. Germany, 57,692 ....D 3 25
Göttingen, W. Ger., 115,227 ....D 3 25
Gottwaldov, Czechoslovakia, 63,000 ....D 2 29
Grahamstown, Cape of Good Hope, S. Africa, 37,600 ....M18 39
Granada, Nicaragua, 28,507 ....C 3 48
Granada, Spain, 150,186 ....E 4 27
Grand Rapids, Mich., 197,649 ....D 5 106
Gravenhage, 's (The Hague), *Netherlands, 550,613 ....D 3 24
Gravesend, England, 55,310 ....G 5 23
Graz, Austria, 253,000 ....C 3 29
Great Falls, Mont., 60,091 ....F 3 118
Great Yarmouth, England, 50,760 ....G 4 23
Green Bay, Wis., 87,809 ....K 6 173
Greenock, Scotland, 70,267 ....A 2 23
Greensboro, N.C., 144,076 ....K 2 137
Greenville, S.C., 61,436 ....C 2 152
Greenwich, England, 228,030 ....B 5 23
Grenoble, France, 161,230 ....F 5 26
Grimsby, England, 96,500 ....F 4 23
Grodno, U.S.S.R., 132,000 ....C 4 30
Groningen, Netherlands, 168,843 ....H 1 24
Groznyy, U.S.S.R., 341,000 ....E 5 30
Grudziądz, Poland, 73,700 ....D 2 31
Guadalajara, Mexico, †1,196,218 ....D 4 42
Guanajuato, Mexico, †65,258 ....E 4 42
Guantánamo, Cuba, 135,100 ....C 2 48
Guatemala,* Guatemala, 700,000 ....B 2 48
Guayaquil, Ecuador, 738,591 ....D 4 46
Guelph, Ontario, Canada, 60,087 ....H 7 43
Gulbarga, India, 145,630 ....D 5 34
Guntur, India, 269,941 ....E 5 34
Gütersloh, W. Germany, 76,343 ....C 3 25
Gwalior, India, 406,755 ....D 3 34
Győr, Hungary, 81,000 ....D 3 29
Haarlem, Netherlands, 172,235 ....D 3 24
Hachinohe, Japan, 209,000 ....F 2 36
Hachioji, Japan, 229,000 ....H 2 36
Hackensack, N.J., 36,008 ....B 2 129
Hackney, England, 238,530 ....B 5 23
Hagen, W. Germany, 203,048 ....B 3 25
Hagerstown, Md., 35,862 ....G 2 100
Hague, The,* Neth., 550,613 ....D 3 24
Haifa, Israel, 212,200 ....B 2 31
Haiphong, N. Vietnam, 182,496 ....E 2 35
Hakodate, Japan, 249,000 ....F 2 36
Haleb (Aleppo), Syria, 566,770 ....C 2 33
Halifax,* Nova Scotia, Canada, 122,035 ....K 7 43
Halifax, England, 93,570 ....G 1 23
Halle, E. Germany, 263,928 ....D 3 25
Hälsingborg, Sweden, 80,801 ....C 3 24
Hama, Syria, 390,084 ....C 2 33
Hamadan, Iran, 124,167 ....E 3 33
Hamamatsu, Japan, 420,000 ....E 4 36
Hamburg, W. Ger., 1,817,122 ....D 2 25
Hameln, W. Germany, 47,114 ....C 2 25
Hamilton,* Bermuda, 3,000 ....G 3 48
Hamilton, Ontario, Canada, 309,173 ....H 7 43
Hamilton, New Zealand, 67,700 ....L 6 40
Hamilton, Ohio, 67,865 ....A 7 140
Hamm, W. Germany, 84,302 ....B 3 25
Hammersmith, England, 192,810 ....B 5 23
Hammond, Ind., 107,888 ....B 1 83
Hampton, Va., 120,779 ....R 6 163
Hamtramck, Mich., 27,245 ....B 6 106
Hangchow, China, 794,000 ....J 5 37
Hannover, W. Germany, 517,783 ....C 2 25
Hanoi,* N. Vietnam, 414,620 ....E 2 35
Harar, Ethiopia, 40,499 ....P10 38
Harbin, China, 1,595,000 ....L 2 37
Haringey, England, 242,300 ....B 5 23
Harrisburg,* Pa., 68,061 ....J 5 150
Harrogate, England, 62,680 ....F 4 23
Harrow, England, 207,700 ....B 5 23
Hartford,* Conn., 158,017 ....E 1 66
Haverhill, Mass., 46,120 ....K 1 104
Hastings, England, 69,020 ....G 5 23
Havana,* Cuba, 1,008,500 ....A 2 48
Havering, England, 252,860 ....C 5 23
Hayward, Calif., 93,058 ....K 2 60
Hazleton, Pa., 30,426 ....L 4 151
Hebron, Jordan, 38,309 ....C 4 31
Heerlen, Netherlands, †75,147 ....G 6 24
Heidelberg, W. Germany, 121,929 ....C 4 25
Heilbronn, W. Germany, 99,440 ....C 4 25
Helena,* Mont., 22,730 ....E 4 118
Helsingör, Denmark, 29,775 ....B 3 24
Helsinki,* Finland, 531,286 ....D 2 24
Hemel Hempstead, Eng., 66,200 ....F 5 23
Hengelo, Netherlands, †69,618 ....J 3 24
Hengyang, China, 240,000 ....H 6 37
Henzada, Burma, 61,972 ....B 3 35
Herat, Afghanistan, 71,563 ....A 2 34
Hereford, England, 47,170 ....E 4 23
Herford, W. Germany, 67,267 ....C 2 25
Hermosillo, Mexico, †206,663 ....B 2 42
Herne, W. Germany, 100,798 ....B 3 25
Hertogenbosch, 's, Netherlands, †81,574 ....G 4 24
Hialeah, Fla., 102,452 ....B 4 68
Highland Park, Mich., 35,444 ....B 6 106
High Point, N.C., 63,259 ....J 3 137
High Wycombe, Eng., 57,360 ....F 5 23
Hildesheim, W. Germany, 95,926 ....D 2 25
Hilla, Iraq, 84,717 ....D 3 33
Hillingdon, Eng., 237,050 ....B 5 23
Hilversum, Netherlands, 99,792 ....F 3 24
Himeji, Japan, 403,000 ....D 4 36
Hiroshima, Japan, 542,000 ....C 4 36
Hobart,* Tasmania, Australia, 53,257 ....H 7 40
Hoboken, N.J., 45,380 ....C 2 129
Hodeida, Yemen Arab Rep., 40,000 ....D 7 33
Hódmezővásárhely, Hung., 53,000 ....F 3 29
Hof, W. Germany, 54,805 ....D 3 25
Hofei, China, 360,000 ....J 5 37
Hofuf, Saudi Arabia, 83,000 ....E 4 33
Hoihow, China, 402,000 ....H 7 37
Hokang, China, 200,000 ....M 2 37
Holguín, Cuba, 100,500 ....C 2 48
Hollywood, Fla., 85,047 ....B 4 68
Holon, Israel, 55,200 ....B 3 31

Limerick, Ireland, 50,786 B 4 23
Limoges, France, 127,605 D 5 26
Limón, Costa Rica, 30,676 D 3 48
Linares, Chile, †61,011 F11 47
Linares, Spain, 50,527 E 3 27
Lincoln, England, 75,570 F 4 23
Lincoln,* Nebr., 149,518 H 4 121
Linköping, Sweden, 77,881 C 3 24
Linz, Austria, 205,762 C 2 29
Lipetsk, U.S.S.R., 290,000 E 4 30
Lisbon (Lisboa),* Port., 828,000 A 1 27
Little Rock,* Ark., 132,483 F 4 59
Liverpool, England, 677,450 F 2 23
Livingstone, Zambia, †43,000 L15 39
Livonia, Mich., 110,109 F 6 106
Livorno (Leghorn), Italy, 152,517 C 3 28
Ljubljana, Yugoslavia, 183,000 A 2 29
Llanelly, Wales, 27,570 D 5 23
Łódź, Poland, 750,400 D 3 31
Logroño, Spain, 58,545 E 1 27
Lomas de Zamora, Arg., †275,219 012 47
Lomé,* Togo, 90,600 G10 38
London, Ontario, Canada, 223,222 H 7 43
London,* England,* United Kingdom, 7,703,410 B 5 23
Londonderry, Northern Ireland, 55,000 C 3 23
Long Beach, Calif., 358,633 C11 60
Lorain, Ohio, 78,185 F 3 140
Lorient, France, 66,023 B 4 26
Los Alamos, N. Mex., 11,310 C 3 130
Los Angeles, Calif., 2,809,596 C10 60
Louisville, Ky., 361,958 K 4 93
Lourdes, France, 17,627 C 6 26
Louvain, Belgium, 32,125 E 6 24
Lowell, Mass., 94,239 J 2 104
Lower Hutt, New Zealand, 58,700 L 6 40
Loyang, China, 500,000 H 5 37
Luanda,* Angola, 400,000 J13 39
Lubbock, Tex., 149,101 C 4 158
Lübeck, W. Germany, 242,191 D 2 25
Lublin, Poland, 211,900 F 3 31
Lubumbashi, Zaire, 318,000 M14 39
Lucca, Italy, 45,398 C 3 28
Lucerne, Switzerland, 73,000 D 1 27
Lucknow, India, 750,512 E 3 34
Lüdenscheid, W. Ger., 80,096 B 3 25
Ludhiana, India, 401,124 D 2 34
Ludwigsburg, W. Ger., 79,538 C 4 25
Ludwigshafen, W. Ger., 174,698 C 4 25
Luleå, Sweden, 36,428 D 2 24
Lund, Sweden, 50,494 C 3 24
Lüneburg, W. Ger., 59,944 D 2 25
Lünen, W. Germany, 72,195 B 3 25
Lusaka,* Zambia, †238,200 M15 39
Lüshun (Port Arthur), China, 126,000 K 4 37
Lüta, China, 1,590,000 K 4 37
Luton, England, 156,690 F 5 23
Luxembourg,* Lux., 77,458 H 8 24
L'vov, U.S.S.R., 553,000 C 4 30
Lyallpur, Pakistan, 425,248 C 2 34
Lynchburg, Va., 54,083 K 6 163
Lynn, Mass., 90,294 D 6 104
Lyon, France, 524,500 F 5 26
Maastricht, Netherlands, †93,927 G 6 24
Macao,* Macao, 262,000 H 7 37
Maceió, Brazil, 242,867 N 5 46
Machida, Japan, 154,000 H 2 36
Macon, Ga., 122,423 E 5 72
Madison,* Wis., 172,007 H 9 173
Madiun, Indon., 152,000 J 2 36
Madras, India, 2,470,288 E 6 34
Madrid,* Spain, 2,850,631 F 4 27
Madurai, India, 548,298 D 7 34
Maebashi, Japan, 225,000 E 3 36
Magdeburg, E. Ger., 268,269 D 2 25
Magelang, Indon., 119,000 J 2 36
Magnitogorsk, U.S.S.R., 364,000 G 4 30
Maidstone, England, 67,400 G 5 23
Maiduguri, Nigeria, 139,965 J 9 38
Mainz, W. Germany, 176,720 C 4 25
Majunga, Madagascar, 47,654 R15 39
Makhachkala, U.S.S.R., 186,000 E 5 30
Malabo,* Equat. Guinea, †37,237 H11 38
Malacca, Malaysia, 69,848 D 7 35
Málaga, Spain, 259,245 D 4 27
Malang, Indon., 419,000 K 2 36
Malatya, Turkey, 104,428 C 2 33
Malden, Mass., 56,127 D 6 104
Male,* Maldives, 13,336 C 8 34
Malegaon, India, 191,784 C 4 34
Malines, Belgium, 65,728 E 5 24
Malmö, Sweden, 256,064 C 3 24
Manado, Indon., 160,000 G 5 36
Managua,* Nicaragua, 262,047 C 2 48
Manama,* Bahrain, 79,098 E 4 33
Manaus, Brazil, 284,118 H 4 46
Manchester, England, 593,770 G 2 23
Manchester, N.H., 87,754 E 6 124
Mandalay, Burma, 195,348 C 2 35
Mangalore, India, 171,759 C 6 34
Manila, Philippines, 1,499,000 G 3 36
Manisa, Turkey, 69,711 A 2 33
Manizales, Colombia, 267,543 E 2 46
Mannheim, W. Ger., 330,920 C 4 25
Mansfield, England, 56,210 F 4 23
Mansfield, Ohio, 55,047 F 4 140
Mantua, Italy, 55,806 C 2 28
Manzanillo, Cuba, 91,200 C 2 48
Manzanillo, Mexico, †46,170 D 4 42
Maputo,* Mozambique, 65,716 N17 39
Maracaibo, Venezuela, 625,101 F 1 46
Maracay, Venezuela, 185,655 G 1 46
Maraş, Turkey, 63,284 C 2 33
Marburg, W. Germany, 51,382 C 3 25
Mar del Plata, Arg., 141,886 J11 47
Margate, England, 49,080 G 5 23
Marianao, Cuba, 454,700 A 2 48
Maribor, Yugoslavia, 89,000 A 2 29
Marília, Brazil, 73,165 K 8 46
Marion, Ind., 39,607 F 3 83
Marion, Ohio, 38,646 D 4 140
Marl, W. Germany, 75,779 B 3 25
Marrakech, Morocco, 295,000 E 5 38
Marseille, France, 880,527 F 6 26
Maseru,* Lesotho, 18,797 M17 39
Mason City, Iowa, 30,379 G 2 84
Massa, Italy, 46,992 C 2 28
Massawa, Ethiopia, 25,000 O 8 38
Massillon, Ohio, 32,539 G 4 140
Masulipatnam, India, 112,636 E 5 34
Matamoros, Mexico, †182,887 F 3 42
Matanzas, Cuba, 84,100 B 2 48
Mathura, India, 131,813 D 3 34
Matsue, Japan, 115,000 D 4 36
Matsumoto, Japan, 159,000 E 3 36
Matsuyama, Japan, 310,000 D 4 36
Maturín, Venezuela, 54,362 H 2 46
Mayagüez, Puerto Rico, 69,485 F 1 48
Maykop, U.S.S.R., 111,000 D 5 30
Maywood, Ill., 29,019 A 2 78
Mazatlán, Mexico, †171,835 C 3 42
Mbabane,* Swaziland, 13,803 N17 39
Mecca,* Saudi Arabia, 185,000 C 5 33
Mechelen (Malines), Belgium, 65,728 E 5 24
McKeesport, Pa., 37,977 C 7 150
Medan, Indonesia, 590,000 B 5 36
Medellín, Colombia, 967,825 E 2 46
Medford, Mass., 64,397 C 6 104
Medina, Saudi Arabia, 72,000 D 5 33
Meerut, India, 271,325 D 3 34
Meissen, E. Germany, 47,166 E 3 25
Meknès, Morocco, 235,000 E 5 38
Melbourne,* Victoria, Australia, †2,110,168 L 2 40
Melilla, Spain, 77,000 F 4 38
Melrose, Mass., 33,180 D 6 104
Memphis, Tenn., 623,530 B10 92
Mendoza, Argentina, 109,122 G10 47
Menton, France, 23,401 G 6 26
Mérida, Mexico, †253,856 G 4 42
Mérida, Venezuela, 46,339 F 2 46
Meriden, Conn., 55,959 D 2 66
Meridian, Miss., 45,083 G 6 112
Merseburg, E. Ger., 55,562 D 3 25
Mersin, Turkey, 86,692 B 2 33
Merthyr Tydfil, Wales, 56,360 E 5 23
Merton, England, 183,570 B 5 23
Meshed, Iran, 409,616 H 2 33
Messina, Sicily, Italy, 202,095 E 5 28
Mestre, Italy, 138,822 D 2 28
Metairie, La., 136,477 O 4 95
Metz, France, 105,533 G 3 26
Mexicali, Mexico, †390,411 A 1 42
Mexico City,* Mexico, †3,025,564 F 1 42
Miami, Fla., 334,859 B 5 68
Miami Beach, Fla., 87,072 C 5 68
Michigan City, Ind., 39,369 C 1 83
Middleton, Eng., 57,510 G 2 23
Middletown, Conn., 36,924 E 2 66
Middletown, Ohio, 48,767 A 6 140
Milan, Italy, 1,573,009 B 2 28
Milwaukee, Wis., 717,372 M 1 173
Minneapolis, Minn., 434,400 E 5 110
Minsk, U.S.S.R., 907,000 C 4 30
Mirzapur, India, 105,920 E 4 34
Mishawaka, Ind., 35,517 E 1 83
Miskolc, Hungary, 180,000 F 2 29
Mito, Japan, 167,000 F 3 36
Miyakonojo, Japan, 121,000 C 5 36
Miyazaki, Japan, 212,000 C 5 36
Mobile, Ala., 190,026 C 9 50
Modena, Italy, 107,814 C 2 28
Mogadishu,* Somalia, 170,000 R11 39
Mogilev, U.S.S.R., 202,000 D 4 30
Molfetta, Italy, 61,226 F 4 28
Moline, Ill., 46,237 C 2 78
Mombasa, Kenya, 234,400 P12 39
Monaco,* Monaco, 1,649 G 6 26
Mönchengladbach, W. Germany, 152,172 B 3 25
Moncton, New Brunswick, Canada, 47,891 K 6 43
Monghyr, India, 102,462 F 3 34
Monroe, La., 56,374 F 2 95
Monrovia,* Liberia, †100,000 D10 38
Mons, Belgium, 27,042 D 7 24
Montclair, N.J., 44,043 B 2 129
Monte Carlo, Monaco, 9,948 G 6 26
Monte Cristi, Dominican Republic, 8,252 D 3 48
Montería, Colombia, †167,446 E 2 46
Monterrey, Mexico, 830,336 E 2 42
Montevideo,* Uruguay, 1,154,465 K11 47
Montgomery,* Ala., 133,386 F 6 50
Montluçon, France, 57,638 E 4 26
Montpelier,* Vt., 8,609 B 3 124
Montpellier, France, 152,105 E 6 26
Montréal, Quebec, Canada, 1,214,352 J 6 43
Montreuil, France, 95,420 B 2 26
Monza, Italy, 79,715 B 2 28
Moose Jaw, Saskatchewan, Canada, 31,854 F 5 43
Moradabad, India, 258,251 D 3 34
Moratuwa, Sri Lanka, 77,632 D 7 34
Morelia, Mexico, †209,507 E 4 42
Morioka, Japan, 191,000 F 3 36
Moroni,* Comoro Is., 11,515 P14 39
Moscow,* U.S.S.R., 6,942,000 D 4 30
Most, Czechoslovakia, 56,000 B 1 29
Mostar, Yugoslavia, 53,000 B 3 29
Mosul, Iraq, 315,157 D 2 33
Motherwell and Wishaw, Scotland, 75,022 B 1 23
Moulmein, Burma, †175,000 C 3 35
Mount Vernon, N.Y., 72,778 H 1 133
Mukalla, P.D.R. Yemen, 30,000 E 7 33
Mukden, China, 2,424,000 K 3 37
Mülheim, W. Germany, 191,080 B 3 25
Mulhouse, France, 115,632 G 4 26
Multan, Pakistan, 358,201 C 2 34
Muncie, Ind., 69,082 G 4 83
Munich, W. Germany, 1,326,331 D 4 25
Münster, W. Germany, 204,571 B 3 25
Murcia, Spain, 83,190 F 4 27
Murmansk, U.S.S.R., 309,000 D 3 30
Muroran, Japan, 181,000 F 2 36
Muscat,* Oman, 7,500 G 5 33
Muskegon, Mich., 44,631 C 5 106
Muskogee, Okla., 37,331 R 3 145
Mutankiang, China, 251,000 M 3 37
Muzaffarnagar, India, 114,859 D 3 34
Muzaffarpur, India, 127,045 E 3 34
Mysore, India, 355,636 D 6 34
My Tho, S. Vietnam, 109,967 E 5 35
Nadiad, India, 108,268 C 4 34
Nagano, Japan, 280,000 E 3 36
Nagaoka, Japan, 159,000 E 3 36
Nagapattinam, India, 68,015 E 6 34
Nagasaki, Japan, 422,000 C 4 36
Nagercoil, India, 141,207 D 7 34
Nagoya, Japan, 2,036,022 E 4 36
Nagpur, India, 866,144 D 4 34
Naha, Japan, 284,000 G 4 36
Nairobi,* Kenya, 477,600 O12 39
Nakhon Ratchasima, Thailand, 41,037 D 4 35
Nal'chik, U.S.S.R., 146,000 E 5 30
Namangan, U.S.S.R., 175,000 H 5 30
Nam Dinh, N. Vietnam, 86,132 E 2 35
Namur, Belgium, 32,621 E 7 24
Nanchang, China, 520,000 H 6 37
Nanchung, China, 206,000 G 5 37
Nancy, France, 121,910 G 3 26
Nander, India, 126,400 D 5 34
Nanking, China, 1,455,000 J 5 37
Nanning, China, 206,000 G 7 37
Nantes, France, 253,105 C 4 26
Napier, New Zealand, 36,700 M 6 40
Naples, Italy, 1,119,392 D 4 28
Nara, Japan, 191,000 F 4 36
Narbonne, France, 35,236 E 6 26
Nashua, N.H., 55,820 D 6 124
Nashville,* Tenn., 541,160 H 8 92
Nasik, India, 176,187 C 5 34
Nassau,* Bahamas, †100,000 C 1 48
Natal, Brazil, 250,787 O 5 46
Nazareth, Israel, 26,400 C 2 31
N'Djamena,* Chad, †132,500 K 9 38
Ndola, Zambia, †150,800 M14 39
Neikiang, China, 180,000 F 6 37
Neiva, Colombia, 133,607 F 3 46
Nellore, India, 134,404 E 6 34
Nelson, New Zealand, 27,900 L 6 40
Netanya, Israel, 46,200 B 3 31
Neuchâtel, Switzerland, 36,300 C 2 27
Neuilly, France, 70,787 A 1 26
Neumünster, W. Germany, 84,636 C 1 25
Neuss, W. Germany, 117,599 B 3 25
New Albany, Ind., 38,402 F 8 83
Newark, N.J., 382,288 B 2 129
Newark, Ohio, 41,836 F 5 140
New Bedford, Mass., 101,777 K 6 104
New Britain, Conn., 83,441 E 2 66
New Brunswick, N.J., 41,885 E 3 129
Newburgh, N.Y., 26,219 M 7 133
Newcastle, N.S.W., Australia, 143,025 J 6 40
Newcastle, England, 76,570 E 4 23
New Castle, Pa., 38,559 B 3 150
Newcastle upon Tyne, England, 240,340 F 3 23
New Delhi,* India, 292,857 D 3 34
Newham, England, 252,000 B 5 23
New Haven, Conn., 137,707 D 3 66
New London, Conn., 31,630 G 3 67
New Orleans, La., 593,471 O 4 95
Newport, Ky., 25,998 S 2 93
Newport, R.I., 34,562 J 7 104
Newport, Wales, 112,000 E 5 23
Newport News, Va., 138,177 P 6 163
New Rochelle, N.Y., 75,385 P 7 133
Newton, Mass., 91,263 B 7 104
New Westminster, Br. Columbia, Canada, 42,835 D 6 43
New York, N.Y., 7,895,563 M 9 133
Nha Trang, S. Vietnam, 103,184 F 4 35
Niagara Falls, Ontario, Canada, 67,163 J 7 43
Niagara Falls, N.Y., 85,615 C 4 132
Niamey,* Niger, 42,000 G 9 38
Nice, France, 301,400 G 6 26
Nicosia,* Cyprus, 47,000 B 2 33
Niigata, Japan, 379,000 E 3 36
Nijmegen, Netherlands, 148,790 G 4 24
Nikolayev, U.S.S.R., 331,000 D 5 30
Nîmes, France, 115,561 F 6 26
Ningpo, China, 280,000 K 6 37
Niš, Yugoslavia, 92,000 C 3 29
Nishinomiya, Japan, 357,000 E 4 36
Niterói, Brazil, 291,970 P14 47
Nizamabad, India, 114,868 D 5 34
Nizhniy Tagil, U.S.S.R., 378,000 G 4 30
Nobeoka, Japan, 134,000 C 4 36
Nome, Alaska, 2,488 E 2 53
Norfolk, Va., 307,951 R 7 163
Noril'sk, U.S.S.R., 136,000 J 3 30
Norristown, Pa., 38,169 M 5 151
Norrköping, Sweden, 94,296 C 3 24
Northampton, England, 123,800 F 4 23
North Bay, Ont., Canada, 49,187 J 6 43

Norwalk, Calif., 91,827 C11 60
Norwalk, Conn., 79,113 B 4 66
Norwich, England, 118,800 G 4 23
Norwood, Ohio, 30,420 C 9 140
Nottingham, England, 303,090 F 4 23
Nouakchott,* Mauritania, 14,500 C 8 38
Nouméa,* New Caledonia, 41,853 G 8 41
Nova Lisboa, Angola, 109,000 K14 39
Novara, Italy, 79,188 B 2 28
Novgorod, U.S.S.R., 128,000 D 4 30
Novi Sad, Yugoslavia, 119,000 C 2 29
Novokuznetsk, U.S.S.R., 499,000 J 4 30
Novomoskovsk, U.S.S.R., 134,000 D 4 30
Novorossiysk, U.S.S.R., 133,000 D 5 30
Novosibirsk, U.S.S.R., 1,161,000 H 4 30
Nuevo Laredo, Mexico, †150,922 E 2 42
Nuku'alofa,* Tonga, 15,685 J 8 41
Numazu, Japan, 186,000 E 4 36
Nuneaton, England, 64,650 F 4 23
Nuremberg (Nürnberg), W. Germany, 477,108 D 4 25
Nyíregyháza, Hungary, 65,000 F 3 29
Oakland, Calif., 361,561 J 2 60
Oak Park, Ill., 62,511 B 2 78
Oak Ridge, Tenn., 28,319 N 8 93
Oaxaca, Mexico, †156,587 F 5 42
Oberhausen, W. Ger., 249,045 B 3 25
Obihiro, Japan, 129,000 F 2 36
Odense, Denmark, 103,850 B 3 24
Odessa, Texas, 78,380 B 6 158
Odessa, U.S.S.R., 892,000 D 5 30
Offenbach, W. Germany, 118,754 C 3 25
Ogaki, Japan, 134,000 H 6 36
Ogbomosho, Nigeria, 370,963 G10 38
Ogden, Utah, 69,478 C 2 160
Oita, Japan, 243,000 C 4 36
Okayama, Japan, 322,000 D 4 36
Okazaki, Japan, 200,000 E 4 36
Oklahoma City,* Okla., 368,856 L 4 145
Oldenburg, W. Ger., 131,434 B 2 25
Oldham, England, 108,280 F 4 23
Olomouc, Czechoslovakia, 77,000 D 2 29
Olsztyn, Poland, 80,700 E 2 31
Olympia,* Wash., 23,111 C 3 166
Omaha, Nebr., 346,929 J 3 121
Omdurman, Sudan, 206,000 N 8 38
Omiya, Japan, 248,000 H 2 36
Omsk, U.S.S.R., 821,000 H 4 30
Omuta, Japan, 206,000 C 4 36
Opole, Poland, 78,800 C 3 31
Oporto, Portugal, 324,400 B 2 27
Oradea, Rumania, 132,266 C 2 29
Oran, Algeria, 327,493 F 4 38
Orange, Calif., 77,365 D11 60
Orange, N.J., 32,566 B 2 129
Ordzhonikidze, U.S.S.R., 236,000 E 5 30
örebro, Sweden, 86,977 C 3 24
Orel, U.S.S.R., 232,000 D 4 30
Orenburg, U.S.S.R., 345,000 F 4 30
Orizaba, Mexico, †92,728 H 2 42
Orlando, Fla., 99,006 E 3 68
Orléans, France, 94,382 D 3 26
Orsk, U.S.S.R., 225,000 F 4 30
Oruro, Bolivia, 86,985 G 7 46
Osaka, Japan, 2,980,489 E 4 36
Osh, U.S.S.R., 120,000 H 5 30
Oshkosh, Wis., 53,221 J 7 173
Osijek, Yugoslavia, 78,000 B 2 29
Oslo,* Norway, 483,196 A 1 24
Osnabrück, W. Ger., 141,000 C 2 25
Osorno, Chile, †105,793 F12 47
Ostend, Belgium, 57,749 A 5 24
Ostrava, Czech., 271,905 E 2 29
Otaru, Japan, 205,000 F 2 36
Otsu, Japan, 164,000 F 4 36
Ottawa, Ontario,* Canada, 302,341 J 7 43
Ottumwa, Iowa, 29,610 J 6 84
Ouagadougou,* Upper Volta, 77,500 F 9 38
Oulu, Finland, 85,094 E 2 24
Overland Park, Kans., 79,034 H 3 89
Oviedo, Spain, 91,550 C 1 27
Owensboro, Ky., 50,329 G 5 92
Oxford, England, 109,720 F 5 23
Oxnard, Calif., 71,225 F 9 60
Oyo, Nigeria, 130,290 G10 38
Pabianice, Poland, 60,100 D 3 31
Pachuca, Mexico, †84,543 E 4 42
Padang, Indon., 178,000 B 6 36
Paderborn, W. Ger., 68,735 C 3 25
Padua, Italy, 169,298 C 2 28
Paducah, Ky., 31,627 D 6 92
Pago Pago,* Amer. Samoa, 2,451 J 7 41
Paisley, Scotland, 95,182 D 3 23
Palembang, Indon., 585,000 C 6 36
Palermo, Sicily, Italy, 531,306 D 5 28
Palghat, India, 95,765 D 6 34
Palma, Spain, 136,431 H 3 27
Palmerston North, New Zealand, 49,200 M 6 40
Palmira, Colombia, 164,394 E 3 46
Pamplona, Spain, 59,227 F 1 27
Panamá,* Panama, 418,013 E 3 48
Panihati, India, 148,121 F 1 34
Pankow, E. Ger., 68,785 F 3 25
Paoki, China, 180,000 G 5 37
Paoting, China, 250,000 J 4 37
Paotow, China, 490,000 G 4 37
Papeete,* Tahiti, Society Is., *Fr. Polynesia, 22,278 M 7 41
Paraíba (João Pessoa), Brazil, †189,096 O 5 46
Paramaribo,* Surinam, 135,000 K 2 46
Paraná, Argentina, 107,551 J10 47
Pardubice, Czech., 65,000 C 1 29
Parepare, Indon., 84,000 F 6 36
Paris,* France, 2,580,010 B 2 26
Parkersburg, W. Va., 44,208 D 4 168
Parma, Italy, 118,602 C 2 28
Parma, Ohio, 100,216 H 9 140
Parnaíba, Brazil, 57,031 M 4 46
Parral, Mexico, †61,729 D 2 42
Pasadena, Calif., 112,981 C10 60
Pasadena, Texas, 89,277 J 2 158
Passaic, N.J., 55,124 B 2 129
Pasto, Colombia, 123,153 E 3 46
Pasuruan, Indon., 78,000 K 2 36
Paterson, N.J., 144,824 B 1 129
Patiala, India, 151,903 C 1 34
Patna, India, 474,349 D 2 34
Pátrai, Greece, 95,364 C 4 29
Pau, France, 71,865 C 6 26
Pavia, Italy, 69,581 B 2 28
Pavlodar, U.S.S.R., 187,000 H 4 30
Pawtucket, R.I., 76,984 J 5 104
Paysandú, Uruguay, 47,875 J10 47
Pécs, Hungary, 140,000 E 3 29
Pegu, Burma, 47,378 C 3 35
Pehpei, China, 150,000 G 6 37
Pekalongan, Indon., 125,000 J 2 36
Peking,* China, 4,148,000 J 3 37
Pelotas, Brazil, 150,278 K10 47
Pematangsiantar, Indon., 142,000 B 5 36
Penang, Malaysia, 234,903 C 6 35
Pengpu, China, 330,000 J 5 37
Penki, China, 449,000 K 3 37
Pensacola, Fla., 59,507 B 4 68
Penza, U.S.S.R., 374,000 E 4 30
Peoria, Ill., 126,963 D 3 78
Pereira, Colombia, 224,421 E 3 46
Perm', U.S.S.R., 850,000 F 4 30
Pernambuco (Recife), Brazil, 1,046,454 O 5 46
Perpignan, France, 100,086 E 6 26
Perth,* W. Australia, Australia, †499,969 B 2 40
Perth, Scotland, 41,654 E 2 23
Perth Amboy, N.J., 38,798 E 2 129
Perugia, Italy, 52,534 D 3 28
Pescara, Italy, 81,697 E 3 28
Peshawar, Pakistan, 218,691 C 2 34
Petah Tiqwa, Israel, 58,700 B 3 31
Peterborough, Ontario, Canada, 58,111 J 7 43
Peterborough, England, 66,800 F 4 23
Petersburg, Va., 36,750 N 6 163
Petropavlovsk, U.S.S.R., 173,000 G 4 30
Petropavlovsk-Kamchatskiy, U.S.S.R., 154,000 R 4 30
Petrópolis, Brazil, 116,080 M 8 47
Petrozavodsk, U.S.S.R., 185,000 D 3 30
Pforzheim, W. Ger., 90,780 C 4 25
Phan Thiet, S. Vietnam, 80,122 F 5 35
Philadelphia, Pa., 1,950,098 N 6 151
Phnom Penh,* Cambodia, †500,000 E 5 35
Phoenix,* Ariz., 581,562 C 5 54
Piacenza, Italy, 78,985 B 2 28
Piedras Negras, Mexico, †65,883 E 2 42
Pierre,* S. Dak., 9,699 J 5 154
Pietermaritzburg,* Natal, South Africa, 111,000 N17 39
Pinar del Río, Cuba, 67,600 A 2 48
Pingtung, China, 130,563 K 7 37
Piracicaba, Brazil, 125,490 L 8 46
Piraiévs, Greece, 183,877 C 4 29
Pisa, Italy, 76,846 C 3 28
Piteşti, Rumania, 60,094 D 2 29
Pittsburgh, Pa., 520,117 B 7 150
Pittsfield, Mass., 57,020 A 3 104
Piura, Peru, 111,400 D 5 46
Plainfield, N.J., 46,862 E 2 129
Plauen, E. Germany, 81,739 E 3 25
Pleven, Bulgaria, 79,234 D 3 29
Płock, Poland, 60,300 D 2 31
Ploieşti, Rumania, 156,382 D 2 29
Plovdiv, Bulgaria, 234,547 D 3 29
Plymouth, England, 248,470 E 5 23
Plzeň, Czechoslovakia, 143,945 B 2 29
Podol'sk, U.S.S.R., 169,000 D 4 30
Pointe-à-Pitre, Guadeloupe, 50,000 G 3 48
Pointe-Noire, Congo, 100,000 J12 39
Poitiers, France, 68,082 D 4 26
Poltava, U.S.S.R., 220,000 D 5 30
Pomona, Calif., 87,384 D10 60
Ponce, Puerto Rico, 125,926 G 2 48
Ponta Grossa, Brazil, 92,344 K 8 47
Pontiac, Mich., 85,279 F 6 106
Pontianak, Indon., 185,000 D 5 36
Poole, England, 101,930 E 5 23
Poona, India, 853,226 C 5 34
Popayán, Colombia, 58,500 E 3 46
Pori, Finland, 71,972 D 2 24
Port Arthur, China, 126,000 K 4 37
Port Arthur, Tex., 57,371 K 8 158
Port-au-Prince,* Haiti, 265,000 D 3 48
Port Elizabeth, Cape of Good Hope, S. Africa, 374,100 M18 39
Port Harcourt, Nigeria, 208,237 H11 38
Port Huron, Mich., 35,794 G 6 106
Portland, Maine, 65,116 C 8 98
Portland, Oreg., 380,555 B 2 146
Port Louis,* Mauritius, 138,140 S19 39
Port-Lyautey (Kénitra), Morocco, 125,000 E 5 38
Port Moresby,* Papua New Guinea, 56,206 E 6 41
Porto (Oporto), Portugal, 324,400 B 2 27
Pôrto Alegre, Brazil, 869,795 K10 47
Port of Spain,* Trinidad and Tobago, 86,150 G 5 48
Porto-Novo,* Benin, 80,000 G10 38
Port Said, Egypt, 283,400 N 5 38
Portsmouth, England, 214,800 F 5 23
Portsmouth, Ohio, 27,633 D 8 140
Portsmouth, Va., 110,963 R 7 163
Port Sudan, Sudan, 110,000 O 8 38
Port Talbot, Wales, 50,970 E 5 23
Porz, W. Germany, 78,076 B 3 25
Posadas, Argentina, 70,691 J 9 47
Potosí, Bolivia, 55,233 G 7 46
Potsdam, E. Germany, 110,671 E 2 25
Poughkeepsie, N.Y., 32,029 N 7 133
Poznań, Poland, 446,700 C 2 31
Prague (Praha),* Czechoslovakia, 1,831,070 C 1 29
Prato, Italy, 75,402 C 3 28
Preston, England, 102,100 E 4 23
Pretoria,* Transvaal,* South Africa, 479,700 M17 39
Prince Albert, Saskatchewan, Canada, 28,464 F 5 43
Prince George, Br. Columbia, Canada, 33,101 D 5 43
Priština, Yugoslavia, 43,000 C 3 29
Probolinggo, Indon., 85,000 K 2 36
Prokop'yevsk, U.S.S.R., 275,000 J 4 30
Providence,* R.I., 179,116 J 5 104
Przemyśl, Poland, 51,000 F 4 31
Pskov, U.S.S.R., 127,000 C 4 30
Puebla, Mexico, †521,885 G 2 42
Pueblo, Colo., 97,453 K 6 65
Puerto Cabello, Venezuela, 52,493 G 1 46
Puerto Montt, Chile, †88,750 F12 47
Puerto Plata, Dominican Republic, 32,181 D 3 48
Pula, Yugoslavia, 40,000 A 2 29
Punta Arenas, Chile, †64,958 F14 47
Pusan, South Korea, 1,425,703 C 4 36
P'yŏngyang,* N. Korea, 653,100 B 3 36
Qena, Egypt, 57,417 N 6 38
Québec,* Quebec, Canada, 186,088 J 6 43
Quelimane, Mozambique, †62,717 O16 39
Querétaro, Mexico, †140,379 E 4 42
Quetta, Pakistan, 106,633 B 2 34
Quezaltenango, Guat., 45,195 B 2 48
Quezon City,* Philippines, 545,500 G 3 36
Quilon, India, 124,072 D 7 34
Quincy, Ill., 45,288 B 4 78
Quincy, Mass., 87,966 D 8 104
Qui Nhon, S. Vietnam, 116,821 F 4 35
Quito,* Ecuador, 496,410 E 3 46
Qum, Iran, 134,292 F 3 33
Rabat,* Morocco, 227,445 E 5 38
Rach Gia, S. Vietnam, 66,745 E 5 35
Racine, Wis., 95,162 M 3 173
Radom, Poland, 148,400 E 3 31
Raipur, India, 205,909 E 4 34
Rajahmundry, India, 165,900 E 5 34
Rajkot, India, 300,152 C 4 34
Rákospalota, Hungary, 63,344 E 3 29
Raleigh,* N.C., 123,793 M 3 137
Ramat Gan, Israel, 109,400 B 3 31
Rampur, India, 161,802 D 3 34
Rancagua, Chile, †95,030 N10 47
Ranchi, India, 176,225 F 4 34
Rangoon,* Burma, †1,700,000 C 3 35
Ratlam, India, 118,625 C 4 34
Raurkela, India, 125,427 F 4 34
Ravenna, Italy, 56,815 D 2 28
Rawalpindi, Pakistan, 340,175 C 2 34
Reading, England, 127,530 F 5 23
Reading, Pa., 87,643 L 5 151
Recife, Brazil, 1,046,454 O 5 46
Recklinghausen, W. Ger., 125,535 B 3 25
Redbridge, England, 244,800 C 5 23
Regensburg, W. Ger., 128,083 E 4 25
Reggio di Calabria, Italy, 93,964 E 5 28
Reggio nell'Emilia, Italy, 83,073 C 2 28
Regina,* Saskatchewan, Canada, 139,469 F 5 43
Reigate, England, 57,830 F 5 23
Reims, France, 151,988 E 3 26
Remscheid, W. Ger., 137,374 B 3 25
Rennes, France, 176,024 C 3 26
Reno, Nev., 72,863 B 3 122
Resht, Iran, 143,557 E 2 33
Resistencia, Argentina, 84,036 J 9 47
Reşiţa, Rumania, 58,683 C 2 29
Reutlingen, W. Ger., 77,853 C 4 25
Revere, Mass., 43,159 D 6 104
Reykjavík,* Iceland, 81,476 B 2 22
Reza'iyeh, Iran, 110,749 D 2 33
Rheinhausen, W. Germany, 71,698 B 3 25
Rheydt, W. Ger., 100,633 B 3 25
Rhodes (Ródhos), Greece, 27,393 E 4 29
Rhondda, Wales, 94,300 E 5 23
Ribeirão Prêto, Brazil, 190,897 L 8 46
Richmond, Calif., 79,043 J 1 60
Richmond, Ind., 43,999 H 5 83
Richmond,* Va., 249,430 O 5 163
Richmond upon Thames, England, 176,600 B 5 23
Riga, U.S.S.R., 733,000 C 4 30
Rijeka, Yugoslavia, 108,000 A 2 29
Rimini, Italy, 72,720 D 2 28
Riobamba, Ecuador, 41,625 E 4 46
Rio de Janeiro, Brazil, 4,252,009 P14 47
Rio Grande, Brazil, 98,863 K10 47
Rivera, Uruguay, 42,623 J10 47
Riverside, Calif., 140,089 E10 60
Riyadh,* Saudi Arabia, 225,000 E 5 33
Roanne, France, 53,178 E 4 26
Roanoke, Va., 92,115 H 6 163
Rochdale, England, 86,600 E 4 23
Rochefort, France, 28,223 C 4 26
Rochester, England, 55,810 G 5 23
Rochester, Minn., 53,766 F 6 110
Rochester, N.Y., 296,233 E 4 132
Rockford, Ill., 147,370 D 1 78
Rockhampton, Queensland, Australia, 46,803 J 4 40
Rock Island, Ill., 50,166 C 2 78

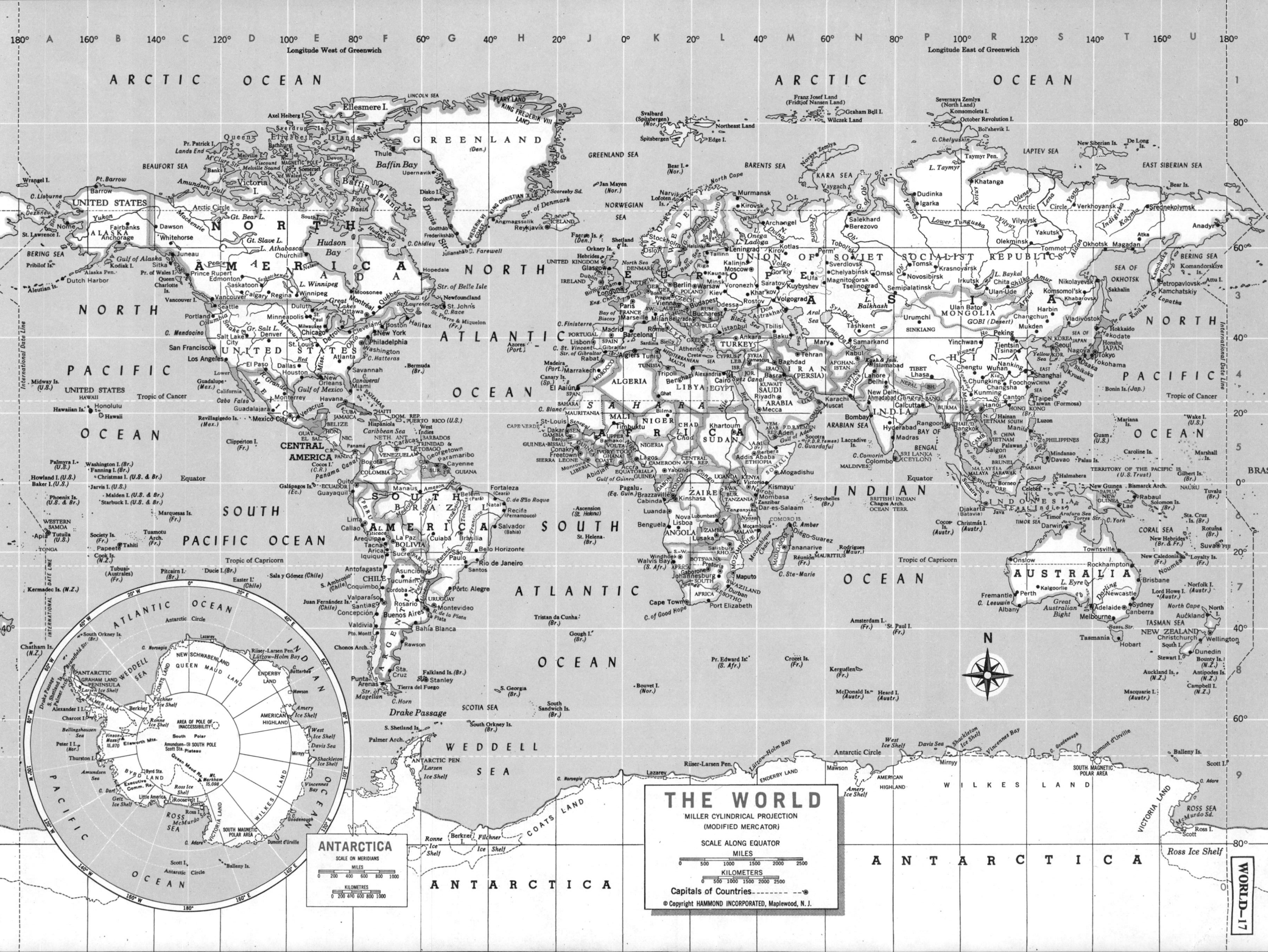
THE WORLD
MILLER CYLINDRICAL PROJECTION
(MODIFIED MERCATOR)
SCALE ALONG EQUATOR
MILES
0 500 1000 1500 2000 2500
KILOMETERS
0 500 1000 1500 2000 2500
Capitals of Countries
© Copyright HAMMOND INCORPORATED, Maplewood, N.J.
ANTARCTICA
SCALE ON MERIDIANS
MILES
0 200 400 600 800 1000
KILOMETRES
0 200 400 600 800 1000
Longitude West of Greenwich
Longitude East of Greenwich
ARCTIC OCEAN
NORTH PACIFIC OCEAN
SOUTH PACIFIC OCEAN
NORTH ATLANTIC OCEAN
SOUTH ATLANTIC OCEAN
INDIAN OCEAN
NORTH AMERICA
SOUTH AMERICA
CENTRAL AMERICA
EUROPE
ASIA
AFRICA
AUSTRALIA
ANTARCTICA
GREENLAND
UNION OF SOVIET SOCIALIST REPUBLICS
UNITED STATES
CANADA
CHINA
INDIA
BRAZIL
Tropic of Cancer
Equator
Tropic of Capricorn
Arctic Circle
Antarctic Circle
International Date Line
WEDDELL SEA
ROSS SEA
WILKES LAND
QUEEN MAUD LAND
VICTORIA LAND
Drake Passage
SCOTIA SEA
TASMAN SEA
CORAL SEA
ARABIAN SEA
BERING SEA
BEAUFORT SEA
GREENLAND SEA
NORWEGIAN SEA
BARENTS SEA
KARA SEA
LAPTEV SEA
EAST SIBERIAN SEA
SEA OF OKHOTSK
Ross Ice Shelf

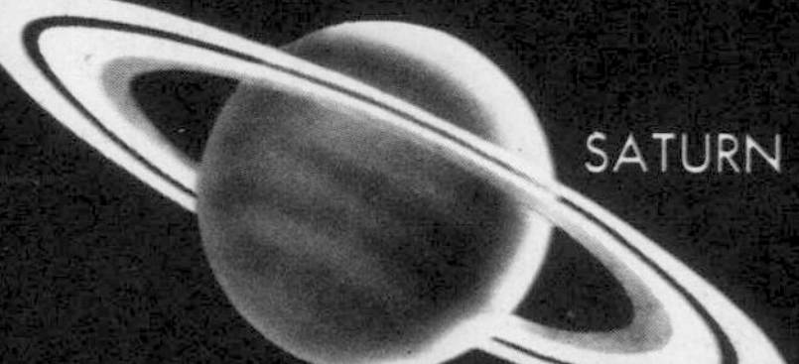

THE SUN The intense light of the sun is the fire produced by the nuclear conversion of hydrogen into helium. The surface temperature is about 11,000 degrees F., but the interior temperature is millions of degrees higher. Periodically, storms erupt from the surface and tongues of flame are hurled millions of miles into space, bombarding the earth's atmosphere with streamers of high energy radiation.

OUR FAMILY

Among the billions of stars in the universe, we believe that there are millions of solar systems similar to our own. To date, however, man has not been able to observe another such group of cold heavenly bodies shining by the reflected light of a mother sun. Ours is not a close family, but extends three and a half billion miles in space. If the sun were a pumpkin, the earth would be a pea over two hundred feet away and the furthest planet, Pluto, another pea two miles beyond.

Just beyond the four inner "dwarf" planets, Mercury, Venus, Earth and Mars, is a girdle of much tinier ones, the asteroids. Beyond these are the four giants, Jupiter, Saturn, Uranus and Neptune, and finally Pluto, another dwarf, which once may have been a moon of Neptune. A total of thirty-one moons and satellites circle the various planets while throughout the solar system fly comets, fiery interplanetary wanderers scattering their embers, the meteors we call shooting stars.

It is a forbidding family. The cold, barren giants are surrounded by deadly gases. The face of Mercury always nearest the sun is an eternally scorched desolation. The extremely high temperatures on the surface of Venus preclude any possibility of life as we know it. The space probe to Mars revealed an inhospitable, cratered landscape that is probably incapable of sustaining any advanced form of life.

OF PLANETS

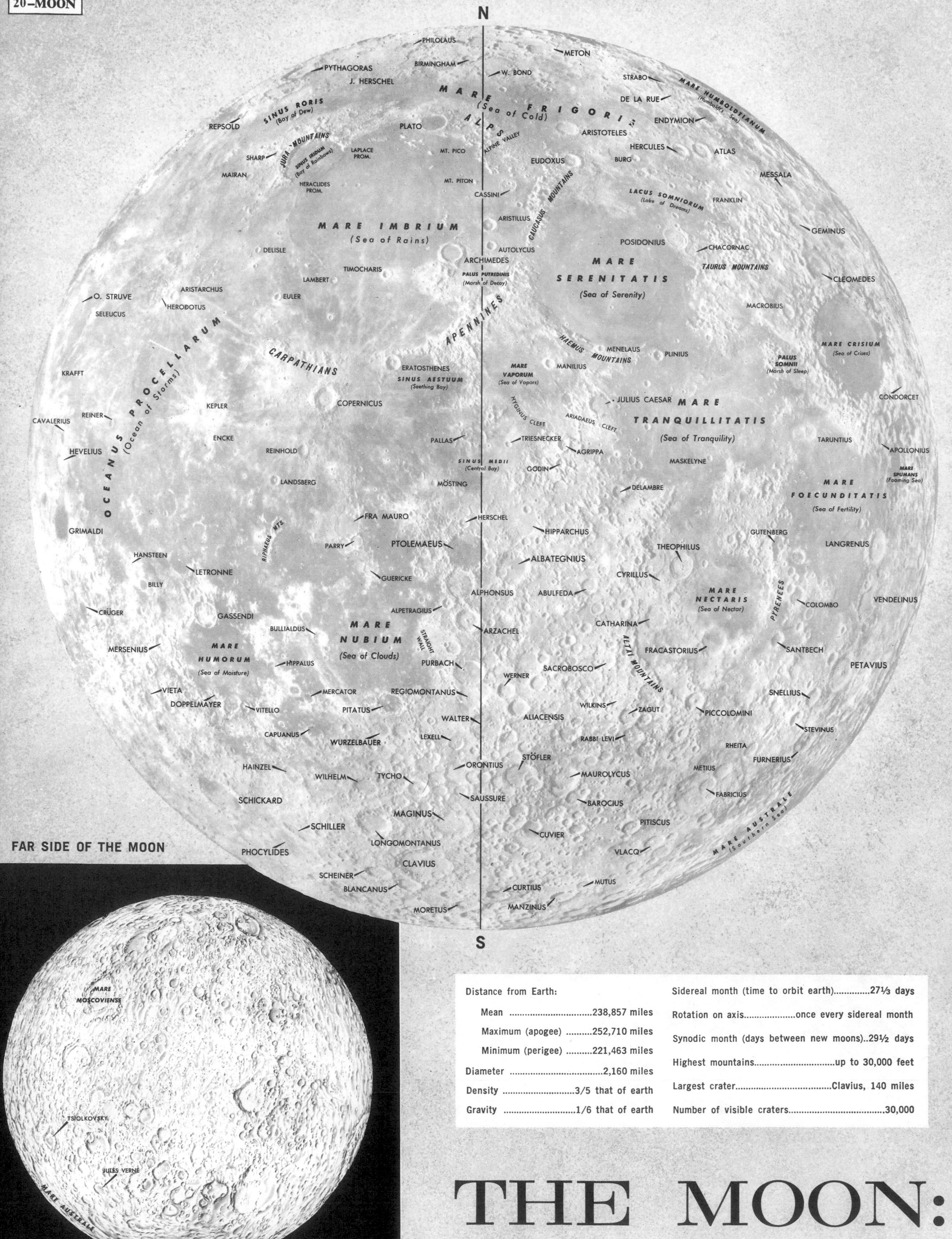

Distance from Earth:	
Mean	238,857 miles
Maximum (apogee)	252,710 miles
Minimum (perigee)	221,463 miles
Diameter	2,160 miles
Density	3/5 that of earth
Gravity	1/6 that of earth

Sidereal month (time to orbit earth)	27⅓ days
Rotation on axis	once every sidereal month
Synodic month (days between new moons)	29½ days
Highest mountains	up to 30,000 feet
Largest crater	Clavius, 140 miles
Number of visible craters	30,000

THE MOON:

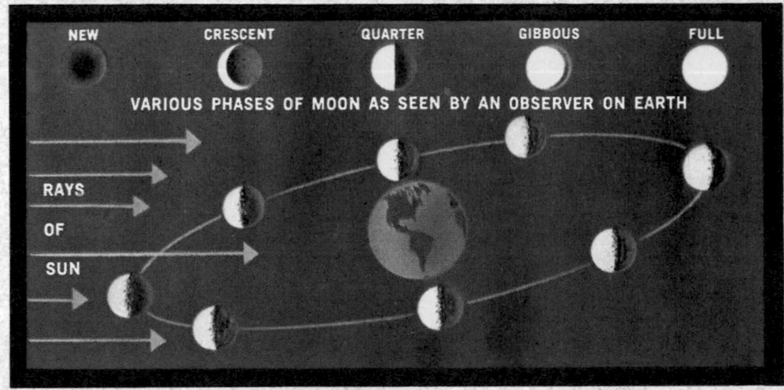

PHASES OF THE MOON

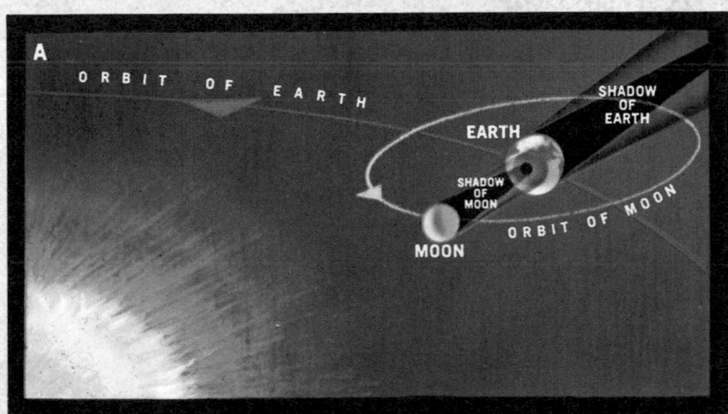

SOLAR ECLIPSE

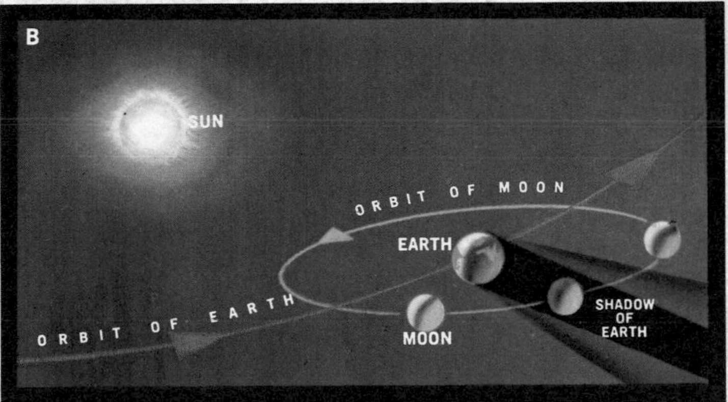

LUNAR ECLIPSE

The moon, which became man's first stepping stone into the silent seas of space, actually is a gigantic stone in the sky . . . an airless, waterless sphere of towering mountain ranges, broad craters, great plains and powdery, gray-brown dust. It rotates around the earth keeping its far side always hidden from our sight. One-quarter the diameter of the earth and having one-sixth its gravity, this uninviting neighbor only 238,000 miles away was formed, we speculate, when a swirling cloud of cosmic gas and particles separated into eddies which contracted to become the sun, the planets and their satellites. Unshielded by protective air, temperatures on its surface range from over 200° F. by day to —200° F. after dark. Yet some day we shall launch space vehicles from there, virtually without gravitational drag and, because it has no atmosphere, clearly observe the furthest heavens on ever-cloudless nights.

In its eccentric but predictable orbit, the moon on occasion crosses directly between the earth and the sun, casting its shadow on the earth's surface. (A) This is the solar eclipse which permits astronomers to acquire certain invaluable data about the area in the sun's vicinity. When the earth passes between sun and moon, hiding it from the sun's light, the eclipse is lunar. (B)

Ancient priests versed in enough primitive astronomy to predict eclipses sometimes used this knowledge to terrorize the people with their power. From the priests of ancient days to today's composers of popular songs, the moon has had an influence on the affairs of man, sometimes profound and far-reaching. The Temple of Diana, Goddess of the Moon, stood for 500 years, one of the Seven Wonders of the World, and there are legends from almost all peoples that deal with the man in the moon. From the belief that the moon affects the mind have come the commonly-rooted words lunar and lunatic. And because its gravitational force pulls the waters of the earth toward it, a major cause of tides, the moon has meant much to the sailors and fishermen of the world.

In days past, a goddess; in days to come, a platform in space — so changes the unchanging face of the moon in the minds of men.

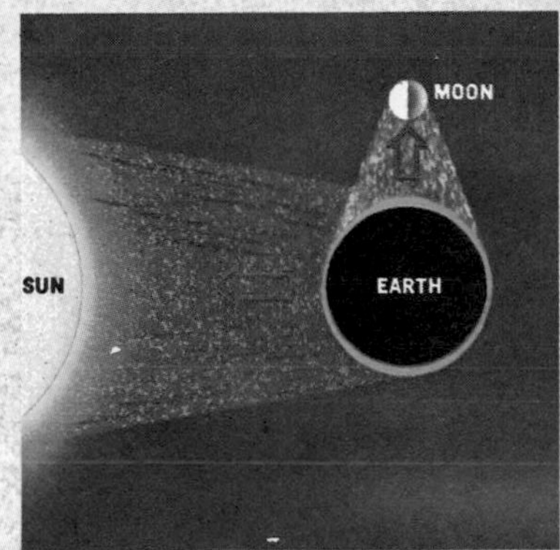

NEAP TIDE is the low monthly tide produced when the sun, earth, and moon form a right angle, and the gravitational pull of the sun partially offsets that of the moon.

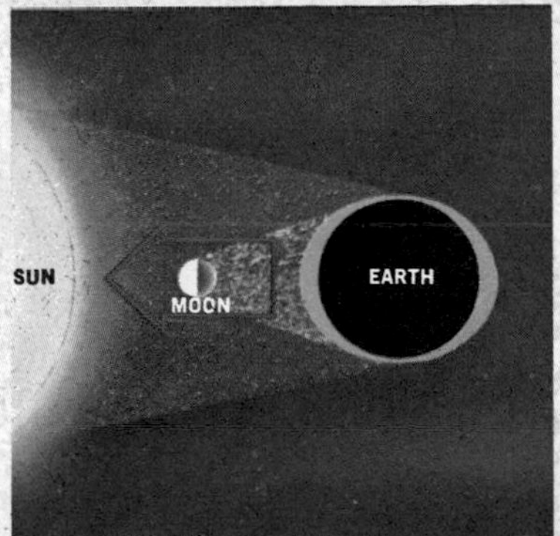

SPRING TIDE is the high monthly tide which results when both sun and moon are in line and their gravitational pull is combined.

Earth's Natural Satellite

EUROPE
LAMBERT AZIMUTHAL EQUAL AREA PROJECTION
SCALE OF MILES
0 100 200 300 400 500
SCALE OF KILOMETRES
0 100 200 300 400 500
Capitals of Countries
International Boundaries
Canals
Copyright by C. S. Hammond & Co., N. Y.
The government of the United States has not recognized the incorporation of Estonia, Latvia and Lithuania into the Soviet Union, nor does it recognize as final the de facto western limit of Polish administration in Germany (the Oder-Neisse line).
Longitude West of Greenwich
Longitude East of Greenwich
NORWEGIAN SEA
BARENTS SEA
NORTH SEA
ATLANTIC OCEAN
BALTIC SEA
MEDITERRANEAN SEA
TYRRHENIAN SEA
IONIAN SEA
BLACK SEA
CASPIAN SEA
Bay of Biscay
English Channel
Arctic Circle
UNION OF SOVIET SOCIALIST REPUBLICS
ICELAND
IRELAND
BRITISH ISLES
UNITED KINGDOM
NORWAY
SWEDEN
FINLAND
DENMARK
POLAND
GERMANY
FRANCE
SPAIN
PORTUGAL
ITALY
YUGOSLAVIA
RUMANIA
BULGARIA
HUNGARY
CZECHOSLOVAKIA
ALBANIA
GREECE
TURKEY
MOROCCO
ALGERIA
TUNISIA
SYRIA
IRAN
CYPRUS

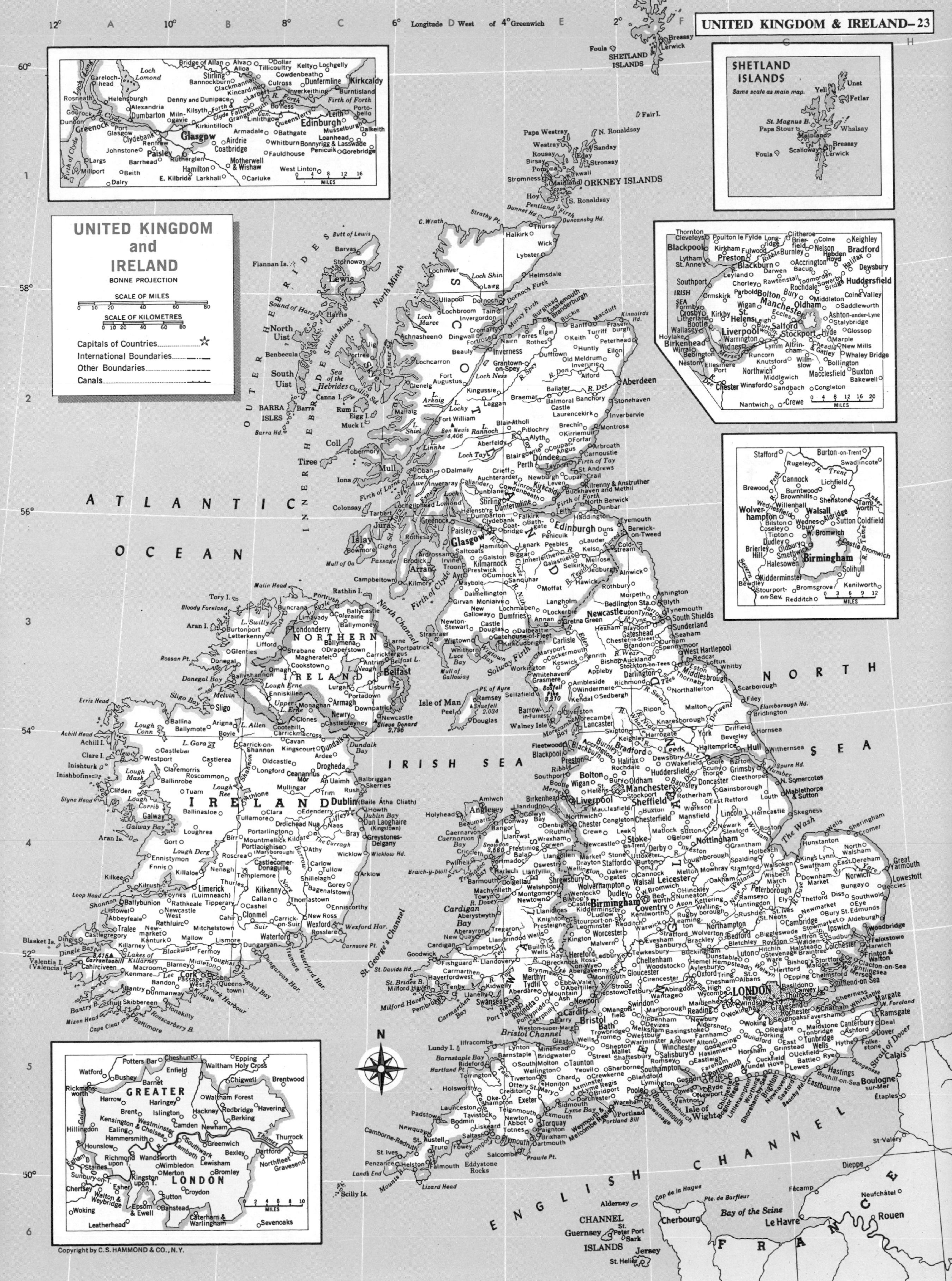
UNITED KINGDOM
and
IRELAND
BONNE PROJECTION
SCALE OF MILES
0 10 20 40 60 80
SCALE OF KILOMETRES
0 10 20 40 60 80
Capitals of Countries
International Boundaries
Other Boundaries
Canals
Longitude West of Greenwich
12° 10° 8° 6° 4° 2°
60° 58° 56° 54° 52° 50°
A B C D E F G H
1 2 3 4 5 6
SHETLAND ISLANDS
Same scale as main map.
Unst
Yell
Fetlar
Whalsay
St. Magnus B.
Papa Stour
Mainland
Bressay
Lerwick
Scalloway
Foula
ORKNEY ISLANDS
ATLANTIC OCEAN
NORTH SEA
IRISH SEA
ENGLISH CHANNEL
OUTER HEBRIDES
INNER HEBRIDES
SCOTLAND
ENGLAND
WALES
NORTHERN IRELAND
IRELAND
FRANCE
CHANNEL ISLANDS
Guernsey
St. Peter Port
Sark
Jersey
St. Helier
Alderney
Isle of Man
Isle of Wight
Edinburgh
Glasgow
Aberdeen
Dundee
Inverness
Belfast
Londonderry
Dublin (Baile Átha Cliath)
Cork
Limerick (Luimneach)
Galway
Waterford
LONDON
Birmingham
Manchester
Liverpool
Leeds
Sheffield
Bristol
Cardiff
Newcastle
Nottingham
Leicester
Coventry
Plymouth
Southampton
Portsmouth
Norwich
Hull
Ben Nevis 4,406
Snowdon 3,560
Scafell Pike 3,210
Slieve Donard 2,796
Carrantuohill 3,415
Bristol Channel
North Channel
St. George's Channel
Calais
Boulogne-sur-Mer
Dieppe
Le Havre
Rouen
Cherbourg
Bay of the Seine
GREATER LONDON
Westminster
Kensington & Chelsea
Camden
Islington
Hackney
Southwark
Lambeth
Greenwich
Croydon
MILES

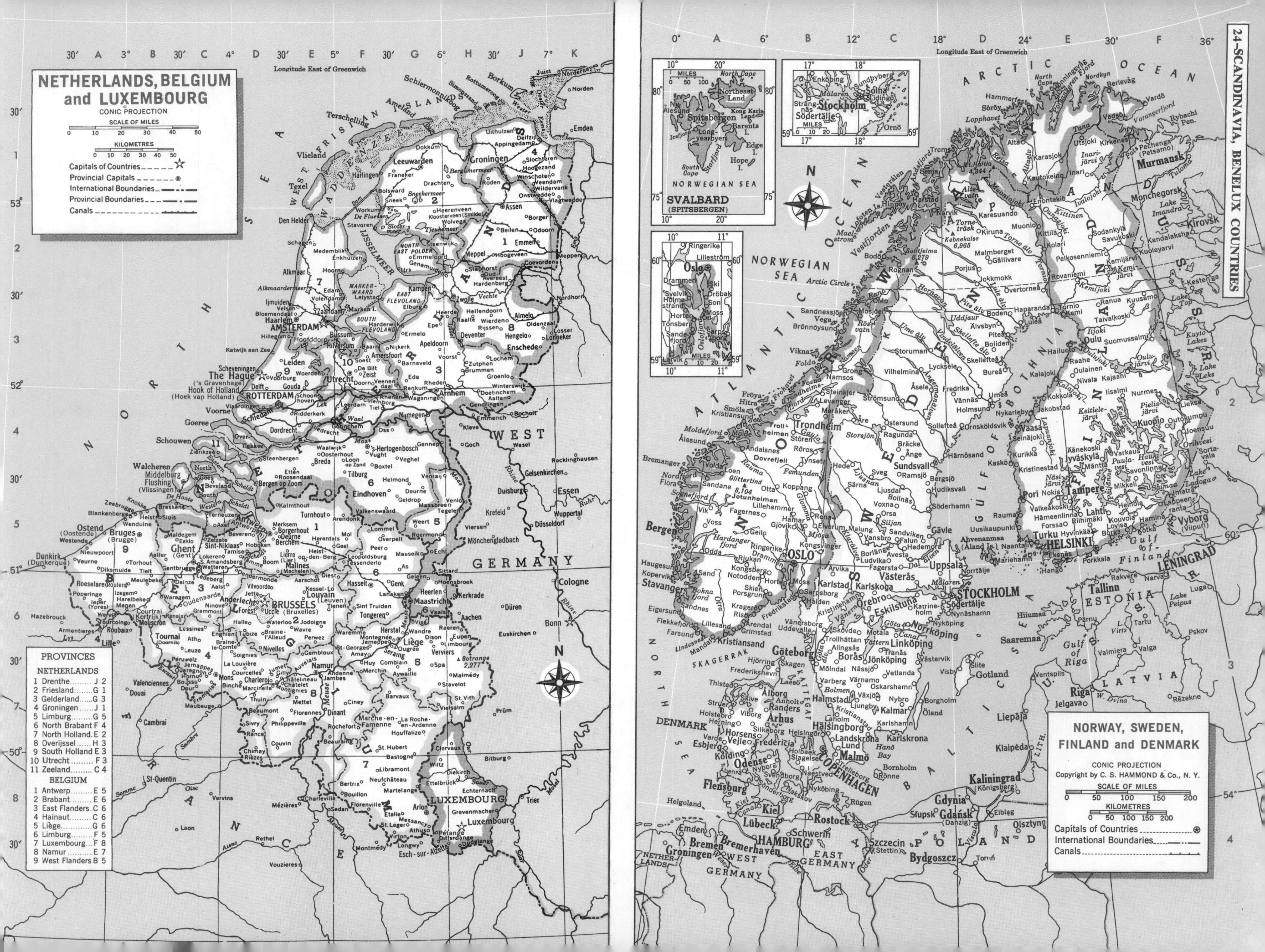
NETHERLANDS, BELGIUM and LUXEMBOURG
CONIC PROJECTION
SCALE OF MILES
KILOMETRES
Capitals of Countries
Provincial Capitals
International Boundaries
Provincial Boundaries
Canals
PROVINCES
NETHERLANDS
1 Drenthe J 2
2 Friesland G 1
3 Gelderland G 3
4 Groningen J 1
5 Limburg G 5
6 North Brabant F 4
7 North Holland E 2
8 Overijssel H 3
9 South Holland E 3
10 Utrecht F 3
11 Zeeland C 4
BELGIUM
1 Antwerp E 5
2 Brabant E 6
3 East Flanders C 6
4 Hainaut C 6
5 Liège G 6
6 Limburg F 5
7 Luxembourg F 8
8 Namur E 7
9 West Flanders B 5
SVALBARD (SPITSBERGEN)
NORWAY, SWEDEN, FINLAND and DENMARK
CONIC PROJECTION
Copyright by C. S. HAMMOND & Co., N. Y.
SCALE OF MILES
KILOMETRES
Capitals of Countries
International Boundaries
Canals

GERMANY
CONIC PROJECTION
SCALE OF MILES
SCALE OF KILOMETERS
Capitals of Countries
State and District Capitals
International Boundaries
State and District Boundaries
Canals
East Germany is divided into districts bearing the same name as their respective capitals.
DENMARK
BALTIC SEA
NORTH SEA
NORTH FRISIAN ISLANDS
EAST FRISIAN ISLANDS
WEST FRISIAN ISLANDS
SCHLESWIG-HOLSTEIN
MECKLENBURG
LOWER SAXONY
BREMEN
HAMBURG
BRANDENBURG
EAST GERMANY
NORTH RHINE-WESTPHALIA
HESSE
THURINGIA
SAXONY
RHINELAND-PALATINATE
SAARLAND
BADEN-WÜRTTEMBERG
BAVARIA
NETHERLANDS
BELGIUM
LUXEMBOURG
FRANCE
SWITZERLAND
AUSTRIA
CZECHOSLOVAKIA
POLAND
BERLIN
WEST
EAST
MILES
Berlin
Hamburg
Bremen
Hannover
Munich
Frankfurt
Stuttgart
Cologne
Düsseldorf
Dresden
Leipzig
Nuremberg

FRANCE
CONIC PROJECTION
SCALE OF MILES
0 20 40 60 80 100
SCALE OF KILOMETRES
0 20 40 60 80 100
Capitals of Countries
Capitals of Departments
International Boundaries
Department Boundaries
Canals
© C.S. HAMMOND & Co., N. Y.
PARIS and ENVIRONS
CORSICA
Same Scale as Main Map
UNITED KINGDOM
ENGLISH CHANNEL
(La Manche)
CHANNEL ISLANDS
NORTH SEA
BAY OF BISCAY
Gulf of Lions
MEDITERRANEAN SEA
BELGIUM
NETHERLANDS
GERMANY
LUXEMBOURG
SWITZERLAND
ITALY
SPAIN
ANDORRA
MONACO
PARIS

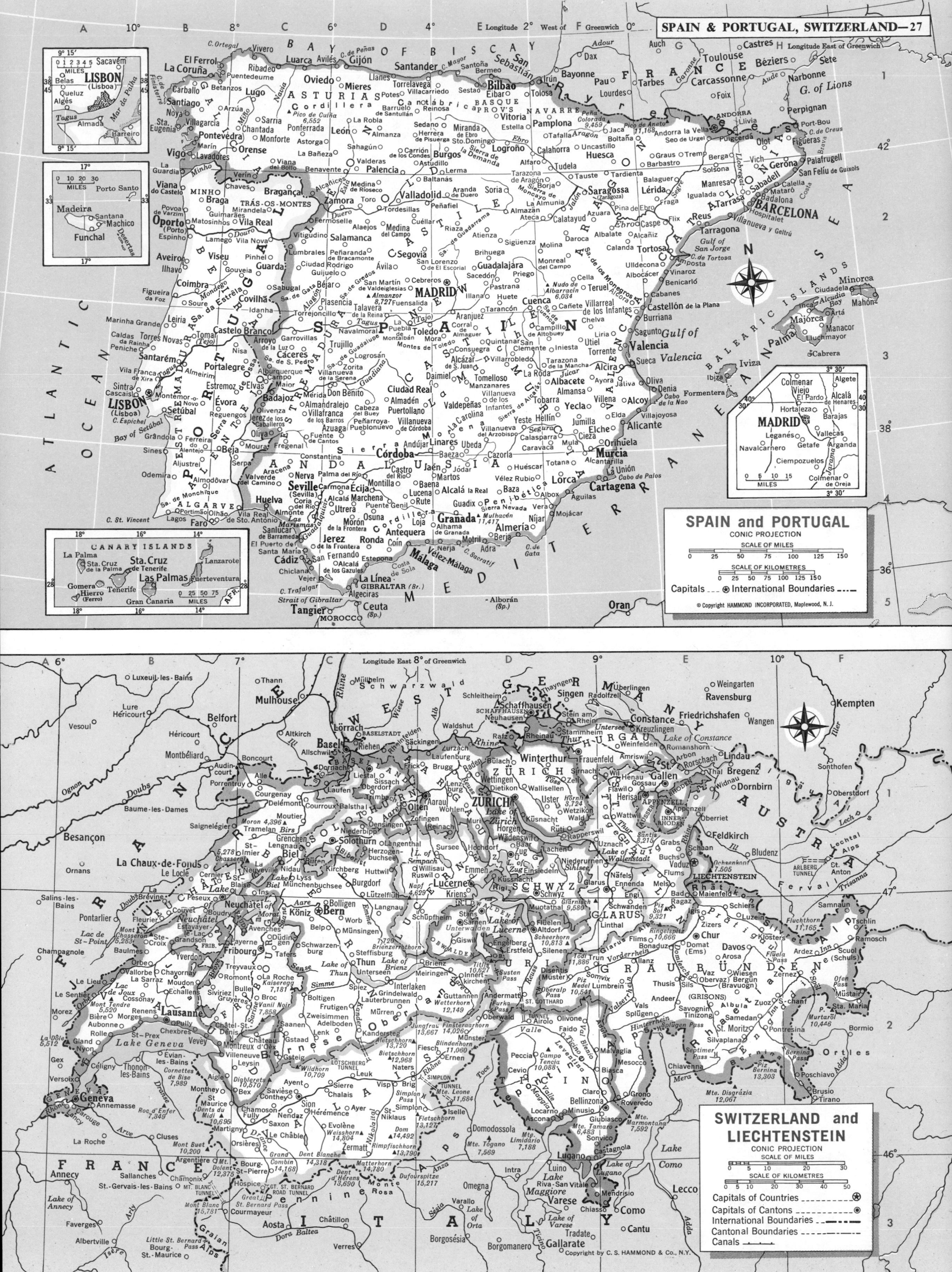
Longitude 2° West of Greenwich 0°
Longitude East of Greenwich
BAY OF BISCAY
ATLANTIC OCEAN
MEDITERRANEAN SEA
SPAIN
PORTUGAL
FRANCE
BALEARIC ISLANDS
LISBON (Lisboa)
MADRID
BARCELONA
Madeira
CANARY ISLANDS
SPAIN and PORTUGAL
CONIC PROJECTION
SCALE OF MILES
0 25 50 75 100 125 150
SCALE OF KILOMETRES
0 25 50 75 100 125 150
Capitals
International Boundaries
© Copyright HAMMOND INCORPORATED, Maplewood, N. J.
Longitude East 8° of Greenwich
GERMANY
AUSTRIA
ITALY
FRANCE
Lake Geneva
Lake of Constance
Lake Maggiore
Lake of Lugano
BERN
ZÜRICH
GENEVA
LIECHTENSTEIN
SWITZERLAND and LIECHTENSTEIN
CONIC PROJECTION
SCALE OF MILES
0 5 10 20 30
SCALE OF KILOMETRES
0 5 10 20 30 40 50
Capitals of Countries
Capitals of Cantons
International Boundaries
Cantonal Boundaries
Canals
Copyright by C. S. HAMMOND & Co., N.Y.

ITALY
CONIC PROJECTION
SCALE OF MILES
0 20 40 60 80 100
SCALE OF KILOMETERS
0 20 40 60 80 100
Capitals of Countries
Regional Capitals
Provincial Capitals
International Boundaries
Regional Boundaries
The regions are subdivided into provinces bearing the same names as their respective capitals, except:
PROVINCE
MASSA-CARRARA
PESARO & URBINO
CAPITAL
Massa
Pesaro
Copyright by C.S. HAMMOND & Co., N.Y.
VATICAN CITY
ROME and ENVIRONS
SWITZERLAND
HUNGARY
AUSTRIA
YUGOSLAVIA
TUNISIA
CORSICA
SARDINIA
SICILY
MALTA
LIGURIAN SEA
TYRRHENIAN SEA
ADRIATIC SEA
IONIAN SEA
MEDITERRANEAN SEA
Gulf of Taranto
Strait of Sicily
Malta Channel
Gulf of Venice
Gulf of Genoa
Gulf of Naples
Gulf of Salerno
Gulf of Gaeta
LIPARI ISLANDS
EGADI ISLANDS
PELAGIE ISLANDS
PONTINE ISLANDS
ROME
MILAN
Turin (Torino)
Genoa (Genova)
Venice (Venezia)
Florence (Firenze)
Naples
Palermo
Bologna
Trieste
Bari
Messina
Catania
Cagliari
Leghorn (Livorno)
SAN MARINO
VATICAN CITY
LIECHTENSTEIN
MONACO
Tunis
Valletta
Longitude East of Greenwich

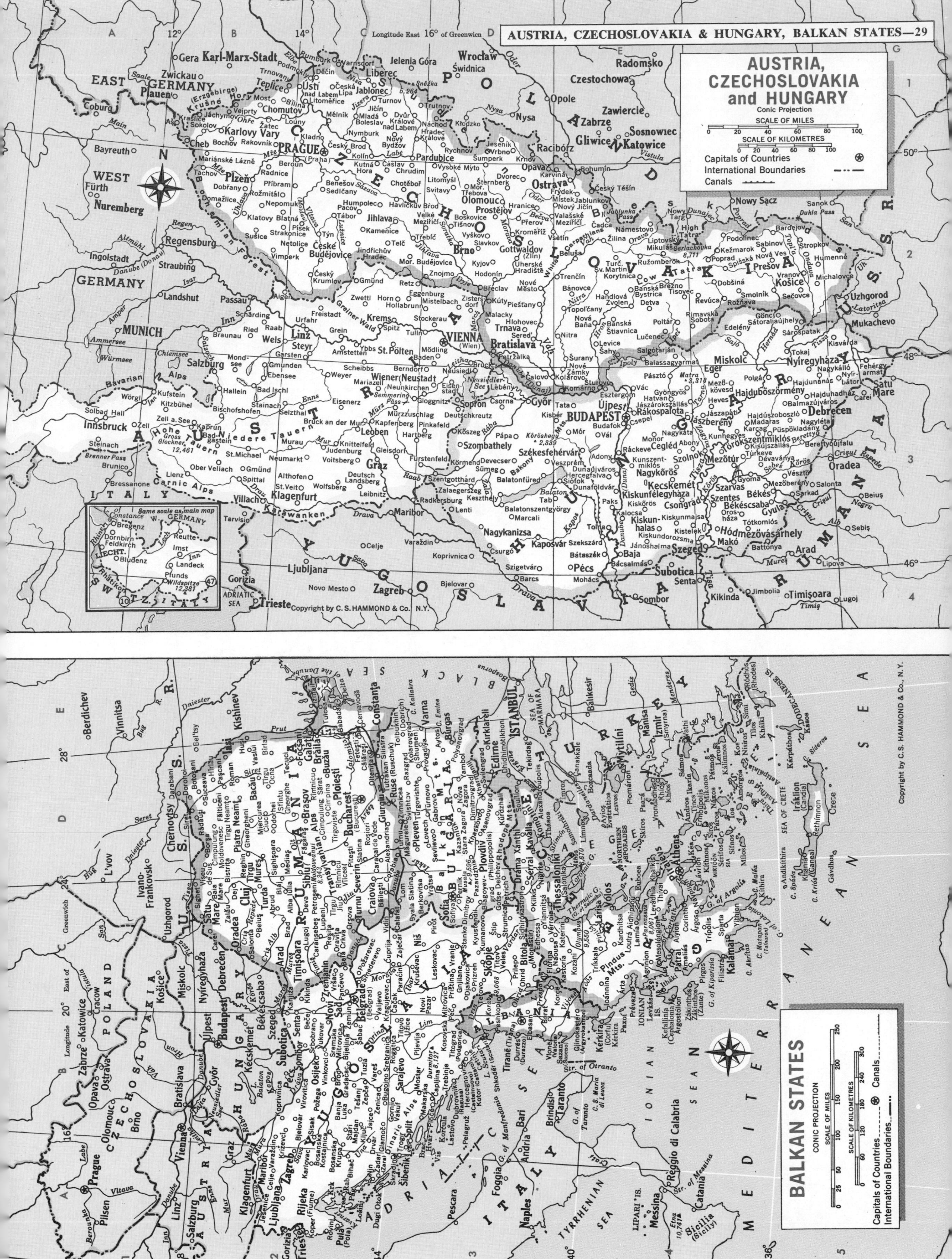
AUSTRIA, CZECHOSLOVAKIA and HUNGARY
Conic Projection
SCALE OF MILES
0 20 40 60 80 100
SCALE OF KILOMETRES
0 20 40 60 80 100
Capitals of Countries
International Boundaries
Canals
Longitude East 16° of Greenwich
Same scale as main map
Copyright by C. S. HAMMOND & Co. N.Y.
EAST GERMANY
WEST GERMANY
GERMANY
POLAND
CZECHOSLOVAKIA
AUSTRIA
HUNGARY
YUGOSLAVIA
RUMANIA
ITALY
U.S.S.R.
PRAGUE
VIENNA
BUDAPEST
Bratislava
Brno
Ostrava
Munich
Nuremberg
Salzburg
Innsbruck
Graz
Linz
Trieste
Zagreb
Ljubljana
Debrecen
Szeged
Miskolc
Košice
BALKAN STATES
CONIC PROJECTION
SCALE OF MILES
0 25 50 100 150 200 250
SCALE OF KILOMETRES
0 60 120 180 240 300
Capitals of Countries
International Boundaries
Canals
Copyright by C.S. HAMMOND & Co., N.Y.
BLACK SEA
ADRIATIC SEA
IONIAN SEA
AEGEAN SEA
MEDITERRANEAN SEA
TYRRHENIAN SEA
SEA OF MARMARA
SEA OF CRETE
BULGARIA
ALBANIA
GREECE
TURKEY
DODECANESE IS.
Bucharest
Sofia
Belgrade
Athens
Tirana
Istanbul
Edirne
Thessaloniki
Sarajevo
Skopje
Constanța
Varna
Plovdiv
Iráklion (Candia)
Sicilia (Sicily)

ADMINISTRATIVE DIVISIONS NOT NAMED ON MAP

Division	Ref.	Division	Ref.
1. Abkhaz A.S.S.R.	E5	13. Khakass Aut. Oblast	J4
2. Adygey Aut. Oblast	D5	14. Komi-Permyak Nat'l Okrug	F4
3. Adzhar A.S.S.R.	E5	15. Mari A.S.S.R.	E4
4. Aginsk Nat'l Okrug	M4	16. Mordvinian A.S.S.R.	E4
5. Chechen-Ingush A.S.S.R.	E5	17. Nagorno-Karabakh Aut. Oblast	E5
6. Chuvash A.S.S.R.	E4	18. Nakhichevan' A.S.S.R.	E6
7. Gorno-Altay Aut. Oblast	J4	19. North Ossetian A.S.S.R.	E5
8. Gorno-Badakhshan Aut. Oblast	H6	20. South Ossetian Aut. Oblast	E5
9. Jewish Aut. Oblast	O5	21. Tatar A.S.S.R.	F4
10. Kabardin-Balkar A.S.S.R.	E5	22. Tuvinian A.S.S.R.	K4
11. Karachay-Cherkess Aut. Oblast	E5	23. Udmurt A.S.S.R.	F4
12. Kara-Kalpak A.S.S.R.	G5	24. Ust'-Ordynskiy Nat'l Okrug	L4

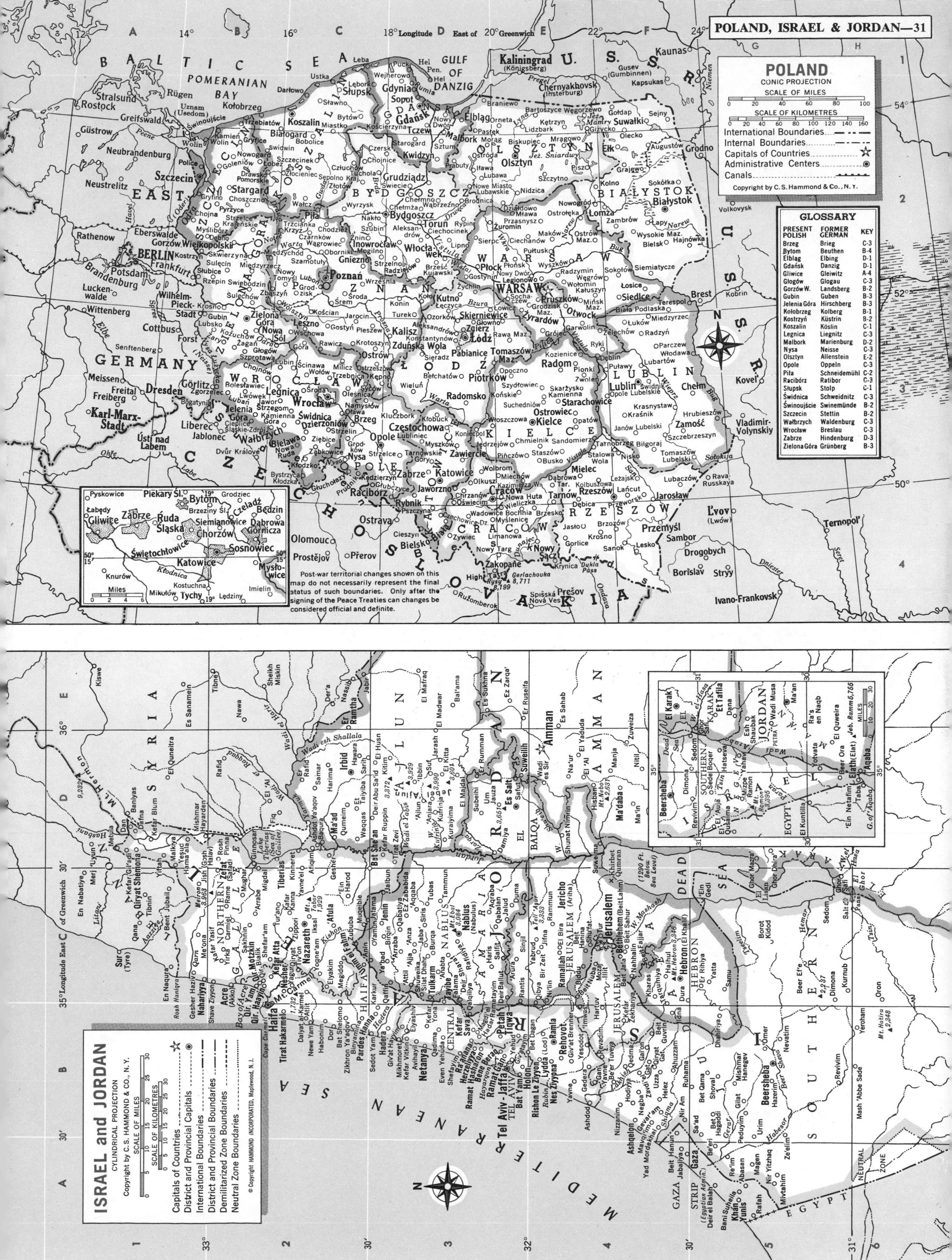
POLAND
CONIC PROJECTION
SCALE OF MILES
0 20 40 60 80 100
SCALE OF KILOMETRES
0 20 40 60 80 100 120 140 160
International Boundaries
Internal Boundaries
Capitals of Countries
Administrative Centers
Canals
Copyright by C. S. Hammond & Co., N. Y.
GLOSSARY
PRESENT POLISH / FORMER GERMAN / KEY
Brzeg Brieg C-3
Bytom Beuthen B-4
Elbląg Elbing D-1
Gdańsk Danzig D-1
Gliwice Gleiwitz A-4
Głogów Glogau C-3
Gorzów W. Landsberg B-2
Gubin Guben B-3
Jelenia Góra Hirschberg B-3
Kołobrzeg Kolberg B-1
Kostrzyń Küstrin B-2
Koszalin Köslin C-1
Legnica Liegnitz C-3
Malbork Marienburg D-2
Nysa Neisse C-3
Olsztyn Allenstein E-2
Opole Oppeln C-3
Piła Schneidemühl C-2
Racibórz Ratibor C-3
Słupsk Stolp C-1
Świdnica Schweidnitz C-3
Świnoujście Swinemünde B-2
Szczecin Stettin B-2
Wałbrzych Waldenburg C-3
Wrocław Breslau C-3
Zabrze Hindenburg D-3
Zielona Góra Grünberg B-3
Post-war territorial changes shown on this map do not necessarily represent the final status of such boundaries. Only after the signing of the Peace Treaties can changes be considered official and definite.
BALTIC SEA
GERMANY
U.S.S.R.
CZECHOSLOVAKIA
Longitude East of Greenwich
ISRAEL and JORDAN
CYLINDRICAL PROJECTION
Copyright by C. S. HAMMOND & CO., N. Y.
SCALE OF MILES
SCALE OF KILOMETRES
Capitals of Countries
District and Provincial Capitals
International Boundaries
District and Provincial Boundaries
Demilitarized Zone Boundaries
Neutral Zone Boundaries
© Copyright HAMMOND INCORPORATED, Maplewood, N. J.
MEDITERRANEAN SEA
SYRIA
JORDAN
EGYPT
DEAD SEA
NEUTRAL ZONE
GAZA STRIP (Egyptian Admin.)

ASIA
LAMBERT AZIMUTHAL EQUAL-AREA PROJECTION
SCALE OF MILES
0 150 300 600 900 1200
SCALE OF KILOMETRES
0 300 600 900 1200
Capitals of Countries
Canals
International Boundaries
Copyright by C. S. Hammond & Co., N.Y.
ATLANTIC OCEAN
ARCTIC OCEAN
North Pole
GREENLAND
Iceland
UNITED STATES ALASKA
BERING SEA
PACIFIC OCEAN
INDIAN OCEAN
ARABIAN SEA
BAY OF BENGAL
SOUTH CHINA SEA
SEA OF OKHOTSK
SEA OF JAPAN
YELLOW SEA
E. CHINA SEA
BLACK SEA
CASPIAN SEA
MEDITERRANEAN SEA
RED SEA
KARA SEA
BARENTS SEA
LAPTEV SEA
NORTH SEA
UNION OF SOVIET SOCIALIST REPUBLICS
RUSSIAN SOVIET FEDERATED SOCIALIST REPUBLICS
SIBERIA
KAZAKH S.S.R.
MONGOLIA
CHINA
MANCHURIA
SINKIANG
TIBET
INNER MONGOLIA
JAPAN
TURKEY
IRAN (PERSIA)
IRAQ
SAUDI ARABIA
AFGHANISTAN
PAKISTAN
INDIA
NEPAL
BHUTAN
BANGLA.
BURMA
THAILAND (SIAM)
CAMBODIA
LAOS
VIETNAM
MALAYSIA
INDONESIA
PHILIPPINES
SRI LANKA (CEYLON)
MALDIVES
AUSTRALIA
AFRICA
Madagascar
Equator
Tropic of Cancer
Tropic of Capricorn
Arctic Circle
MOSCOW
PEKING
TOKYO
SHANGHAI
CALCUTTA
BOMBAY
HONG KONG
Seychelles (Br.)
BRITISH INDIAN OCEAN TERR.
Chagos Archipelago
Diego Garcia
Christmas I. (Australia)
Cocos (Keeling) Is. (Australia)
Amsterdam I. (Fr.)
St. Paul I.
Réunion (Fr.)
MAURITIUS
Rodrigues (To Mauritius)
St. Brandon Group (To Mauritius)
Comoro Is.

NEAR and MIDDLE EAST
CONIC PROJECTION
SCALE OF MILES
0 50 100 200 300 400
SCALE OF KILOMETRES
0 100 200 300 400
Capitals of Countries
International Boundaries
Copyright by C.S. Hammond & Co., N.Y.
Longitude East Greenwich
BLACK SEA
CASPIAN SEA
MEDITERRANEAN SEA
ARABIAN SEA
GULF OF OMAN
TURKEY
SYRIA
LEBANON
ISRAEL
JORDAN
IRAQ
IRAN
AFGHANISTAN
PAKISTAN
INDIA
CHINA
SINKIANG
CYPRUS
KUWAIT
QATAR
BAHRAIN
UNITED ARAB EMIRATES
SAUDI ARABIA
OMAN
YEMEN ARAB REP.
PEOPLES DEM. REP. OF YEMEN
EGYPT
SUDAN
ETHIOPIA
RED SEA
PERSIAN GULF
Rub' al Khali
Ar Rimal
Nubian Desert
Kara-Kum Desert
Kyzyl-Kum Desert
Dasht-i-Kavir
Dasht-i-Lut
Tropic of Cancer

INDIAN SUBCONTINENT
and AFGHANISTAN
CONIC PROJECTION
SCALE OF MILES
0 50 100 200 300
SCALE OF KILOMETRES
0 50 100 200 300
Capitals of Countries
Provincial and State Capitals
International Boundaries
Provincial and State Boundaries
Canals
Longitude 90° East of Greenwich 95°
CALCUTTA
BOMBAY
ARABIAN SEA
BAY OF BENGAL
INDIAN OCEAN
Equator
AFGHANISTAN
BANGLADESH
BHUTAN
SRI LANKA (CEYLON)
MALDIVES
ANDAMAN AND NICOBAR ISLANDS (India)
ANDAMAN SEA
INDONESIA
Tropic of Cancer
KARACHI
DELHI
MADRAS
Rangoon
Kabul
Kathmandu
Colombo

BURMA, THAILAND, INDOCHINA and MALAYA
CONIC PROJECTION
SCALE OF MILES
0 50 100 150 200
SCALE OF KILOMETRES
0 50 100 200 300
International Boundaries
Provincial and State Boundaries
Capitals of Countries
Provincial and State Capitals
Longitude East of Greenwich
BHUTAN
INDIA
BANGLADESH
CHINA
BURMA
KACHIN STATE
SHAN STATE
SAGAING
MANDALAY
KAYAH STATE
KAREN STATE
CHIN STATE
ARAKAN STATE
THAILAND (SIAM)
LAOS
NORTH VIETNAM
SOUTH VIETNAM
CAMBODIA
MALAYA
MALAYSIA
SUMATRA
INDONESIA
ANDAMAN SEA
BAY OF BENGAL
GULF OF TONKIN
GULF OF SIAM
SOUTH CHINA SEA
Gulf of Martaban
Strait of Malacca
Tropic of Cancer
ANDAMAN IS. (India)
NICOBAR IS. (India)
HAINAN
Paracel Is. and Reefs (China)
RANGOON
BANGKOK (Krung Thep)
Hanoi
Vientiane
Phnom Penh
SAIGON
Kuala Lumpur
Singapore
Mandalay
Chiengmai
Haiphong
Da Nang
Hue
Luang Prabang
Isthmus of Kra
Mouths of the Irrawaddy
Mouths of the Mekong
Kunming (Yünnan)
Nanning
Tonle Sap
JOHOR
JOHOR BAHARU
SINGAPORE
MILES 0 10 20
Copyright by C.S. HAMMOND & Co., N.Y.

SOUTHEAST ASIA
LAMBERT AZIMUTHAL EQUAL-AREA PROJECTION
SCALE OF MILES
0 100 200 400 600
SCALE OF KILOMETRES
0 100 200 400 600
Capitals of Countries
Administrative Center
International Boundaries
Territorial Boundaries
Longitude East of Greenwich
Copyright by C. S. HAMMOND & Co., N. Y.
BURMA
THAILAND
LAOS
CAMBODIA
NORTH VIETNAM
SOUTH VIETNAM
CHINA
MALAYA
MALAYSIA
SARAWAK
SABAH (NO. BOR.)
BRUNEI
BORNEO
KALIMANTAN
INDONESIA
PHILIPPINES
WEST IRIAN
PAPUA NEW GUINEA
PORT. TIMOR
AUSTRALIA
BAY OF BENGAL
ANDAMAN SEA
SOUTH CHINA SEA
Gulf of Siam
Gulf of Tonkin
JAVA SEA
SULU SEA
CELEBES SEA
MOLUCCA SEA
BANDA SEA
CERAM SEA
FLORES SEA
Sawu Sea
TIMOR SEA
ARAFURA SEA
PACIFIC OCEAN
INDIAN OCEAN
Equator
Rangoon
Mandalay
Bangkok
Vientiane
Hanoi
Haiphong
Hue
Da Nang
Saigon
Phnom Penh
Kuala Lumpur
SINGAPORE
HONG KONG (Br.)
Macao (Port.)
Manila
Quezon City
Luzon
Mindanao
Davao
Djakarta
Bandung
Semarang
Surabaja
Medan
Palembang
Makasar
Kupang
Dili
Port Moresby
JAVA
EASTERN NEW GUINEA
Same scale as main map
JAPAN and KOREA
CONIC PROJECTION
Copyright by C. S. HAMMOND & CO., N. Y.
SCALE OF MILES
0 50 100 150
KILOMETRES
0 50 100 200 300
Capitals of Countries
International Boundaries
Longitude East of Greenwich
CHINA
MANCHURIA
U. S. S. R.
NORTH KOREA
SOUTH KOREA
JAPAN
HOKKAIDO
HONSHU
SHIKOKU
KYUSHU
SEA OF JAPAN
YELLOW SEA
EAST CHINA SEA
PACIFIC OCEAN
Korea Strait
Tsugaru Strait
KURIL IS. (U.S.S.R.)
RYUKYU IS. (NANSEI SHOTO)
SAKISHIMA ISLANDS
Tropic of Cancer
Okinawa
Naha
P'yŏngyang
Seoul
Inch'ŏn
Pusan
Taegu
Vladivostok
Sapporo
Hakodate
Sendai
Niigata
TOKYO
Yokohama
Nagoya
Kyoto
Osaka
Kobe
Hiroshima
Fukuoka
Nagasaki
Kagoshima

CHINA and MONGOLIA
CONIC PROJECTION
SCALE OF MILES
0 100 200 300 400 500
SCALE OF KILOMETRES
0 100 200 300 400 500
Capitals of Countries.....✩
Provincial Capitals.........◉
Canals
International Boundaries
Provincial Boundaries
Walls
© Copyright HAMMOND INCORPORATED, Maplewood, N.J.
*Wuhan municipality consists of Hankow, Hanyang and Wuchang
Longitude East of Greenwich
PEKING
SHANGHAI
TIENTSIN
Ulan Bator
INNER MONGOLIAN AUTONOMOUS REGION
SINKIANG-UIGHUR AUTONOMOUS REGION
TIBETAN AUTONOMOUS REGION
KWANGSI CHUANG AUTONOMOUS REGION
TSINGHAI
YUNNAN
MANCHURIA
SEA OF JAPAN
SEA OF OKHOTSK
YELLOW SEA
EAST CHINA SEA
SOUTH CHINA SEA
PACIFIC OCEAN
BAY OF BENGAL
Tropic of Cancer
Turfan Depression
Himalayas
Nyenchen Tangha Range
Yablonovyy Range
NORTH KOREA
SOUTH KOREA
Taiwan (Formosa)
PHILIPPINES
HONG KONG (Br.)
NORTH VIETNAM
THAILAND
BANGLADESH
BHUTAN
JAMMU AND KASHMIR
Lake Baykal
Lake Balkhash
RYUKYU ISLANDS (NANSEI SHOTO)
DAITO ISLANDS (Jap.)

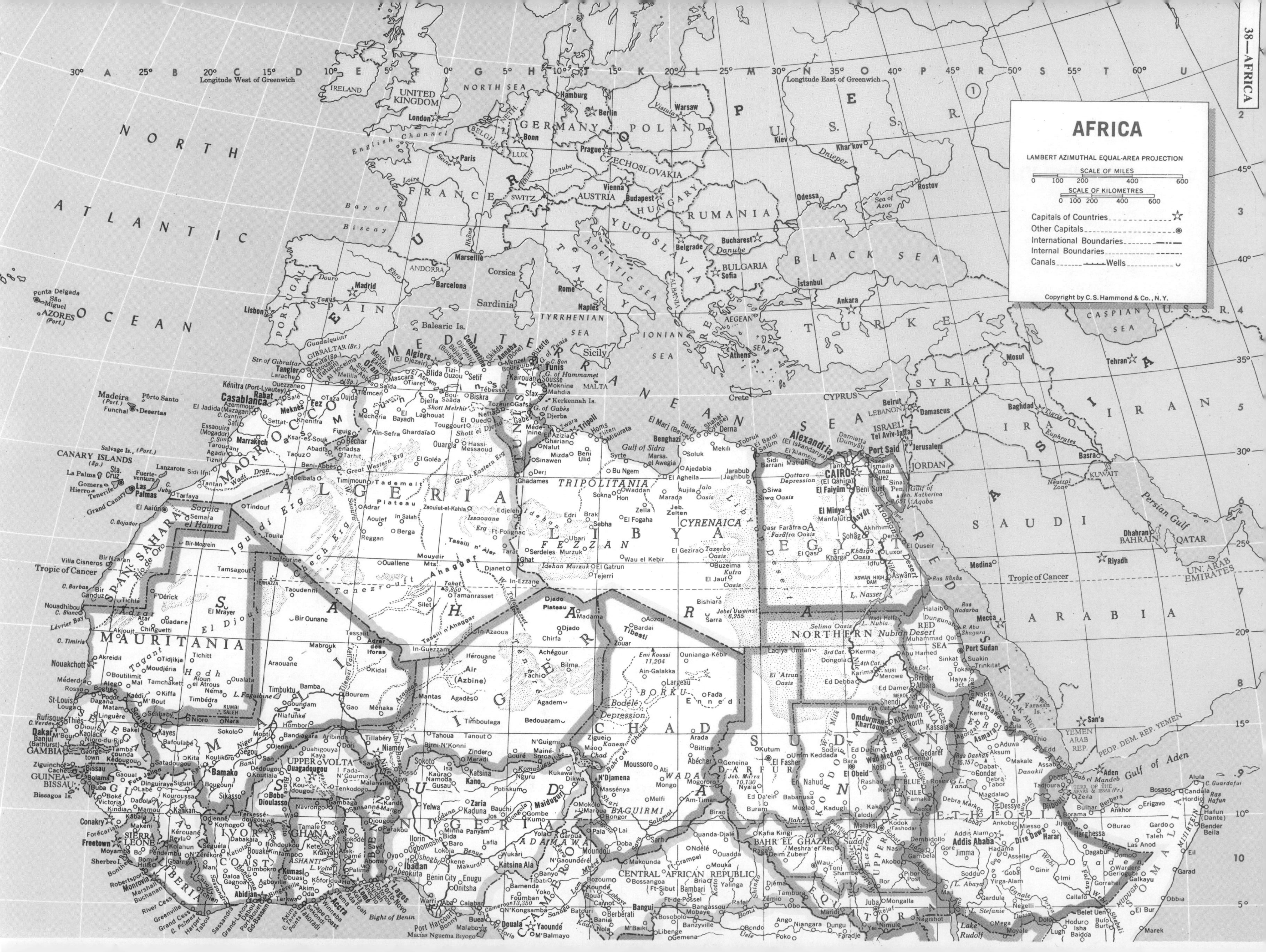
AFRICA
LAMBERT AZIMUTHAL EQUAL-AREA PROJECTION
SCALE OF MILES
0 100 200 400 600
SCALE OF KILOMETRES
0 100 200 400 600
Capitals of Countries
Other Capitals
International Boundaries
Internal Boundaries
Canals
Wells
Copyright by C. S. Hammond & Co., N.Y.

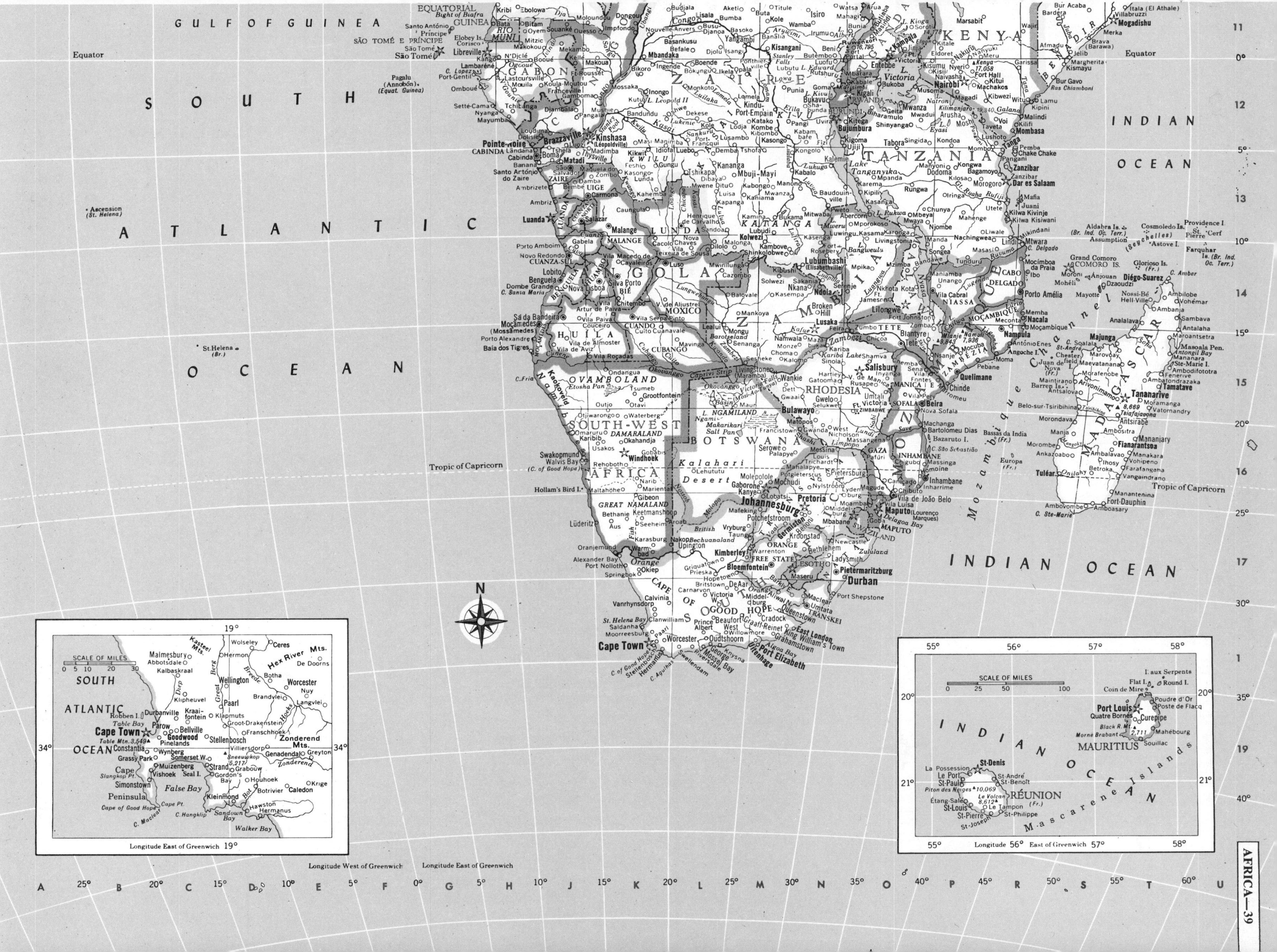

GULF OF GUINEA
SOUTH ATLANTIC OCEAN
INDIAN OCEAN
Equator
Tropic of Capricorn
Mozambique Channel
SOUTH-WEST AFRICA
BOTSWANA
RHODESIA
ANGOLA
ZAIRE
ZAMBIA
TANZANIA
KENYA
GABON
MADAGASCAR
LESOTHO
CAPE OF GOOD HOPE
ORANGE FREE STATE
Kalahari Desert
Luanda
Kinshasa
Brazzaville
Libreville
Nairobi
Mombasa
Dar es Salaam
Zanzibar
Lusaka
Salisbury
Bulawayo
Windhoek
Johannesburg
Pretoria
Kimberley
Bloemfontein
Durban
Pietermaritzburg
Port Elizabeth
East London
Cape Town
Maputo
Beira
Tananarive
Mogadishu
St. Helena (Br.)
Ascension (St. Helena)
Longitude West of Greenwich
Longitude East of Greenwich
SCALE OF MILES
SOUTH ATLANTIC OCEAN
Table Bay
False Bay
Cape Peninsula
Stellenbosch
Paarl
Worcester
Hex River Mts.
Longitude East of Greenwich 19°
INDIAN OCEAN
MAURITIUS
Port Louis
RÉUNION
St-Denis
Mascarene Islands
Longitude 56° East of Greenwich 57°

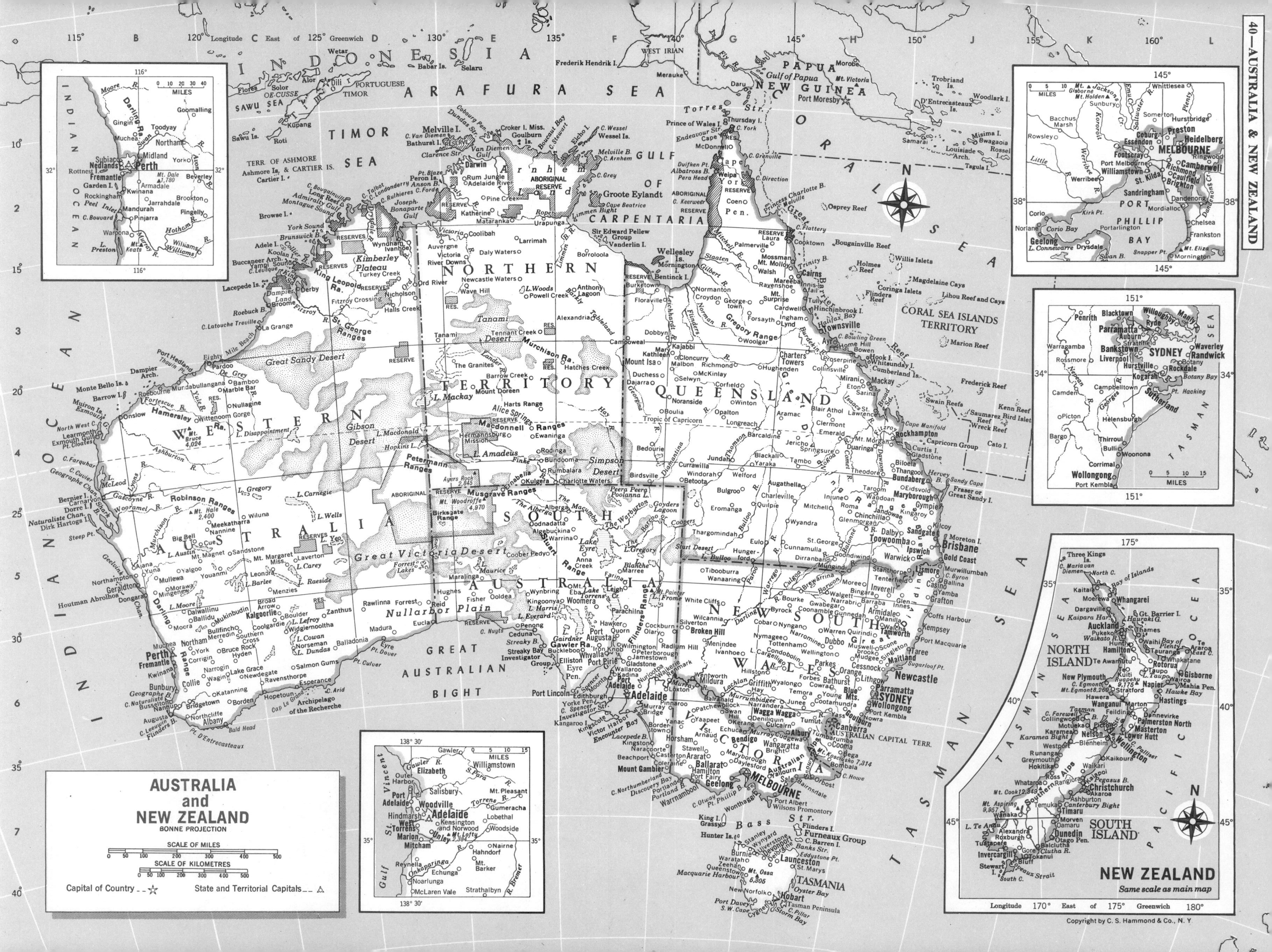
AUSTRALIA
and
NEW ZEALAND
BONNE PROJECTION
SCALE OF MILES
SCALE OF KILOMETRES
Capital of Country
State and Territorial Capitals
NEW ZEALAND
Same scale as main map
NORTH ISLAND
SOUTH ISLAND
TASMANIA
QUEENSLAND
NEW SOUTH WALES
VICTORIA
SOUTH AUSTRALIA
WESTERN AUSTRALIA
NORTHERN TERRITORY
AUSTRALIAN CAPITAL TERR.
CORAL SEA ISLANDS TERRITORY
PAPUA NEW GUINEA
INDONESIA
ARAFURA SEA
TIMOR SEA
CORAL SEA
TASMAN SEA
INDIAN OCEAN
GREAT AUSTRALIAN BIGHT
GULF OF CARPENTARIA
Copyright by C. S. Hammond & Co., N. Y.

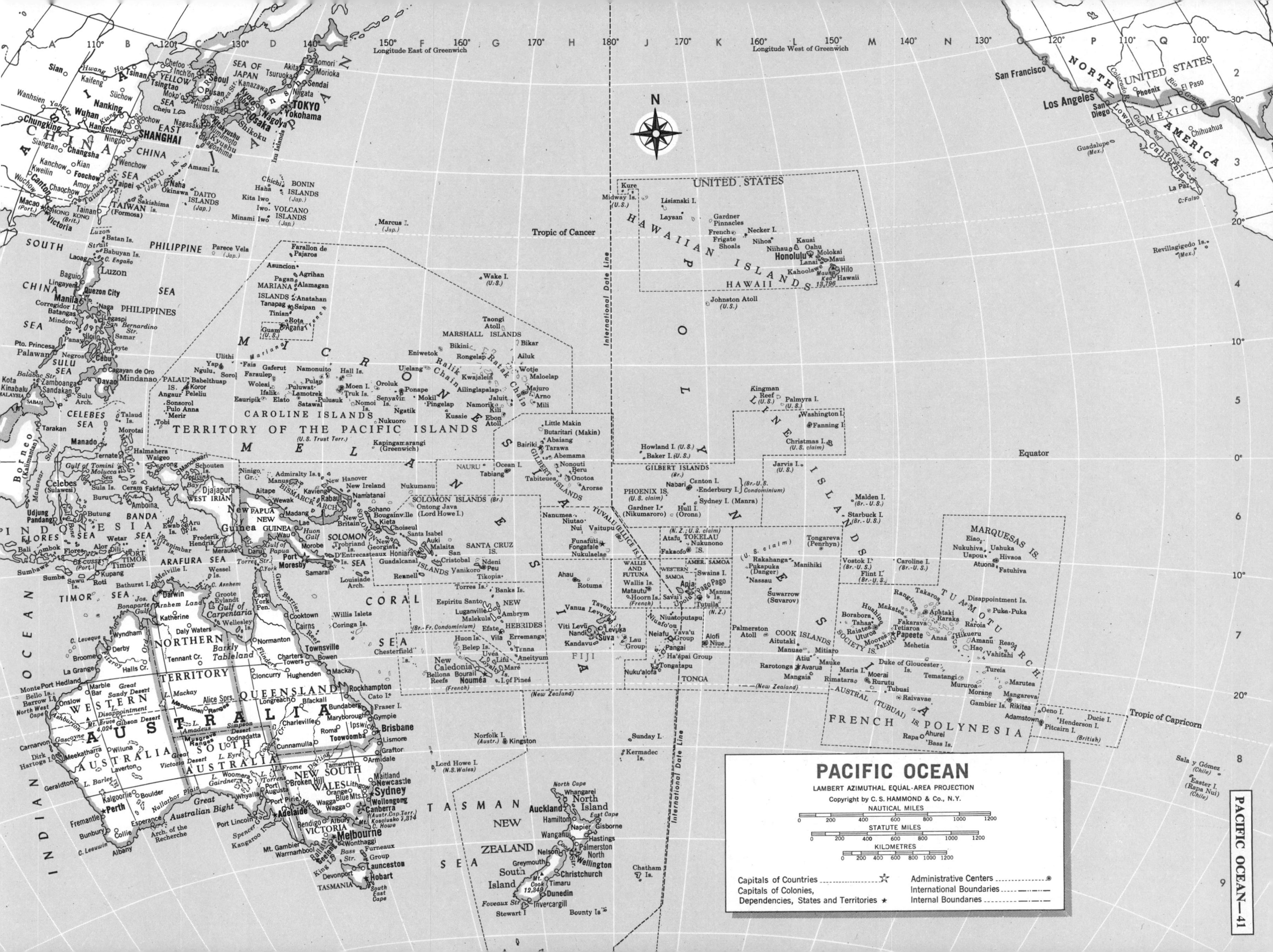
PACIFIC OCEAN
LAMBERT AZIMUTHAL EQUAL-AREA PROJECTION
Copyright by C. S. HAMMOND & Co., N.Y.
NAUTICAL MILES
0 200 400 600 800 1000 1200
STATUTE MILES
0 200 400 600 800 1000 1200
KILOMETRES
0 200 400 600 800 1000 1200
Capitals of Countries
Capitals of Colonies, Dependencies, States and Territories
Administrative Centers
International Boundaries
Internal Boundaries
Longitude East of Greenwich
Longitude West of Greenwich
International Date Line
Equator
Tropic of Cancer
Tropic of Capricorn
NORTH AMERICA
UNITED STATES
MEXICO
ASIA
CHINA
JAPAN
PHILIPPINES
AUSTRALIA
NEW ZEALAND
POLYNESIA
MICRONESIA
MELANESIA
HAWAIIAN ISLANDS
MARQUESAS IS.
FRENCH POLYNESIA
TERRITORY OF THE PACIFIC ISLANDS
CAROLINE ISLANDS
MARSHALL ISLANDS
GILBERT ISLANDS
SOLOMON ISLANDS
NEW HEBRIDES
FIJI
TONGA
TASMAN SEA
CORAL SEA
PHILIPPINE SEA
SOUTH CHINA SEA
INDIAN OCEAN

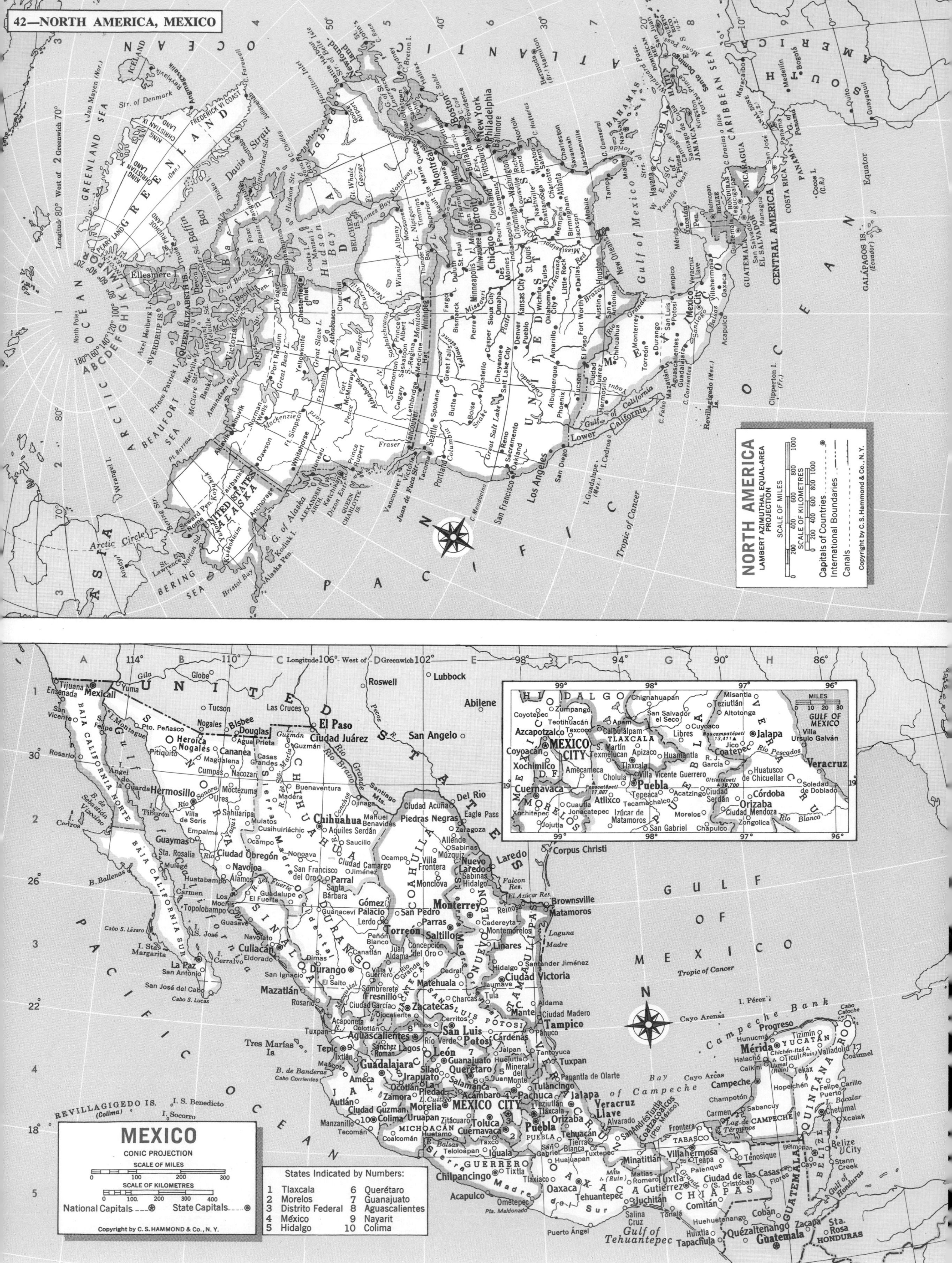
NORTH AMERICA
LAMBERT AZIMUTHAL EQUAL-AREA PROJECTION
SCALE OF MILES
0 200 400 600 800 1000
SCALE OF KILOMETRES
0 200 400 600 800 1000
Capitals of Countries
International Boundaries
Canals
Copyright by C. S. Hammond & Co., N. Y.
MEXICO
CONIC PROJECTION
SCALE OF MILES
0 100 200 300
SCALE OF KILOMETRES
0 100 200 300 400
National Capitals
State Capitals
States Indicated by Numbers:
1 Tlaxcala
2 Morelos
3 Distrito Federal
4 México
5 Hidalgo
6 Querétaro
7 Guanajuato
8 Aguascalientes
9 Nayarit
10 Colima
Copyright by C. S. HAMMOND & Co., N. Y.
ARCTIC OCEAN
ATLANTIC OCEAN
PACIFIC OCEAN
GULF OF MEXICO
CANADA
UNITED STATES
MEXICO
CENTRAL AMERICA
SOUTH AMERICA
GREENLAND
ALASKA
ASIA
MEXICO CITY
Tropic of Cancer
Arctic Circle
Equator

CANADA
CONIC PROJECTION
SCALE OF MILES
0 50 100 200 300
SCALE OF KILOMETRES
0 50 100 200 300 400 500
Capitals of Countries
Provincial Capitals
International Boundaries
Provincial Boundaries
Canals
Copyright by C.S. HAMMOND & Co., N.Y.
QUEEN ELIZABETH ISLANDS
Scale of Miles
0 50 100 200
ARCTIC
OCEAN
BEAUFORT SEA
BAFFIN BAY
DAVIS STRAIT
GREENLAND
HUDSON BAY
ATLANTIC OCEAN
PACIFIC OCEAN
YUKON TERRITORY
DISTRICT OF MACKENZIE
DISTRICT OF FRANKLIN
DISTRICT OF KEEWATIN
NORTHWEST TERRITORIES
BRITISH COLUMBIA
ALBERTA
SASKATCHEWAN
MANITOBA
ONTARIO
QUEBEC
NEWFOUNDLAND
NEW BRUNSWICK
NOVA SCOTIA
PRINCE EDWARD I.
UNITED STATES
ALASKA
Ottawa
Toronto
Montréal
Québec
Winnipeg
Regina
Edmonton
Victoria
Vancouver
Halifax
St. John's

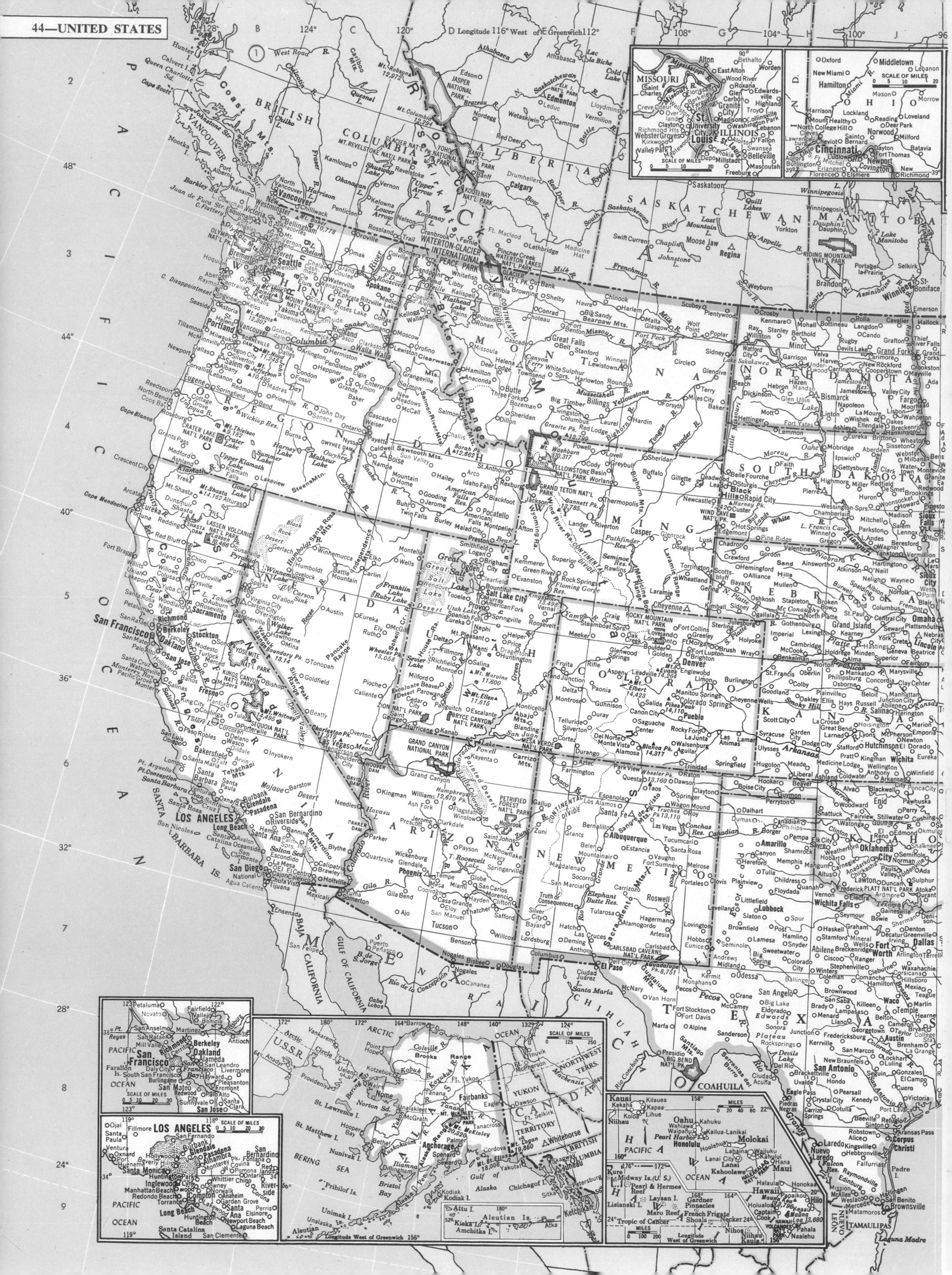
Longitude 116° West of Greenwich
PACIFIC OCEAN
BRITISH COLUMBIA
ALBERTA
SASKATCHEWAN
MANITOBA
WASHINGTON
OREGON
CALIFORNIA
NEVADA
IDAHO
MONTANA
WYOMING
UTAH
COLORADO
ARIZONA
NEW MEXICO
NORTH DAKOTA
SOUTH DAKOTA
NEBRASKA
KANSAS
OKLAHOMA
TEXAS
MEXICO
BAJA CALIFORNIA
GULF OF CALIFORNIA
CHIHUAHUA
COAHUILA
NUEVO LEON
TAMAULIPAS
Vancouver
Victoria
Seattle
Tacoma
Spokane
Portland
Boise
Salt Lake City
Denver
Colorado Springs
Pueblo
Cheyenne
Casper
Billings
Great Falls
Helena
Butte
Edmonton
Calgary
Regina
Saskatoon
Winnipeg
Bismarck
Fargo
Grand Forks
Minot
Rapid City
Pierre
Sioux Falls
Omaha
Lincoln
Wichita
Topeka
Oklahoma City
Tulsa
Amarillo
Lubbock
Dallas
Fort Worth
Austin
San Antonio
Corpus Christi
El Paso
Albuquerque
Santa Fe
Phoenix
Tucson
Las Vegas
Reno
Sacramento
San Francisco
Oakland
San Jose
Fresno
Los Angeles
San Diego
Long Beach
Pasadena
YELLOWSTONE NATIONAL PARK
GRAND CANYON NATIONAL PARK
YOSEMITE NAT'L PARK
Great Salt Lake
SAN FRANCISCO
LOS ANGELES
MISSOURI
ILLINOIS
St. Louis
OHIO
IND.
Cincinnati
ALASKA
YUKON TERRITORY
NORTHWEST TERRS.
CANADA
U.S.S.R.
BERING SEA
ARCTIC OCEAN
Anchorage
Fairbanks
Juneau
Mt. McKinley 20,320
Aleutian Is.
HAWAII
Kauai
Oahu
Honolulu
Molokai
Maui
Hawaii
Hilo
Tropic of Cancer
SCALE OF MILES

UNITED STATES
POLYCONIC PROJECTION
SCALE OF MILES
0 50 100 200 300
SCALE OF KILOMETRES
0 50 100 200 300
Capitals of Countries
State and Provincial Capitals
International Boundaries
State and Provincial Boundaries
Copyright by C. S. Hammond & Co., N. Y.
84° Longitude West 80° of Greenwich 76°
GULF OF MEXICO
ATLANTIC OCEAN
GULF OF ST. LAWRENCE
LAKE SUPERIOR
LAKE MICHIGAN
LAKE HURON
LAKE ONTARIO
LAKE ERIE
NEW YORK
PHILADELPHIA
CHICAGO
DETROIT
BAHAMAS
Copyright by C. S. HAMMOND & CO., N. Y.

CARIBBEAN SEA
ATLANTIC OCEAN
PACIFIC
NETH. ANTILLES
WEST INDIES
BARBADOS
TRINIDAD AND TOBAGO
GRENADA
COSTA RICA
PANAMÁ
CANAL ZONE (U.S.)
COLOMBIA
VENEZUELA
GUYANA
SURINAM
FRENCH GUIANA
ECUADOR
PERU
BOLIVIA
PARAGUAY
AMAPÁ
RORAIMA
AMAZONAS
PARÁ
ACRE
RONDÔNIA
MATO GROSSO
GOIÁS
MARANHÃO
PIAUÍ
CEARÁ
RIO GRANDE DO NORTE
PARAÍBA
PERNAMBUCO
ALAGOAS
SERGIPE
BAHIA
MINAS GERAIS
ESPÍRITO SANTO
SÃO PAULO
DISTRITO FEDERAL
Brasília
Caracas
Bogotá
Quito
Lima
La Paz
Sucre
Georgetown
Paramaribo
Cayenne
Panamá
Port of Spain
Bridgetown
Belém
Manaus
Recife
Salvador (Bahia)
Fortaleza (Ceará)
Belo Horizonte
Amazonas
Equator
Longitude 55° West of 50° Greenwich
GALÁPAGOS ISLANDS (Archipiélago de Colón) (To Ecuador)
Same scale as main map

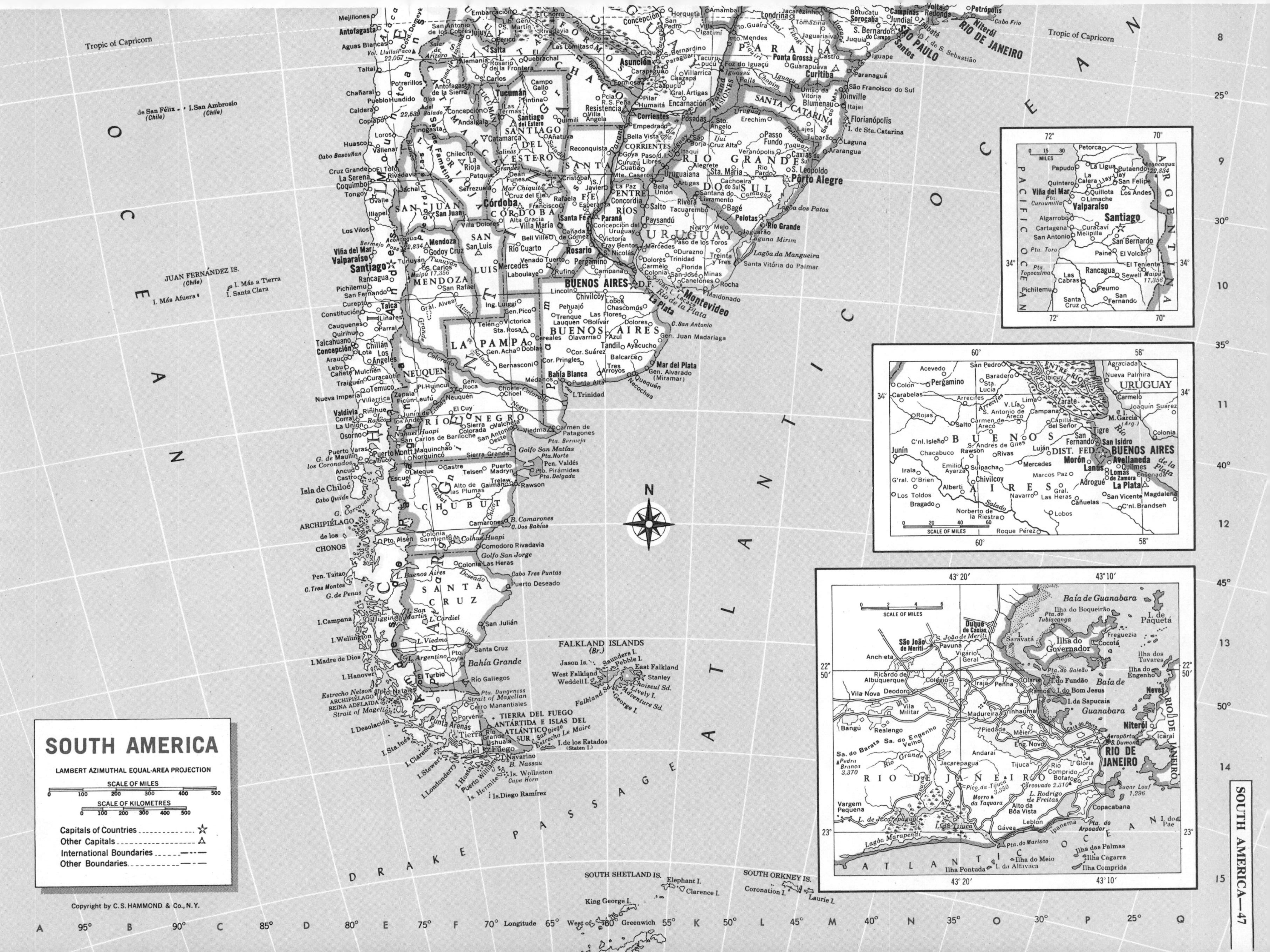
SOUTH AMERICA
LAMBERT AZIMUTHAL EQUAL-AREA PROJECTION
SCALE OF MILES
SCALE OF KILOMETRES
Capitals of Countries
Other Capitals
International Boundaries
Other Boundaries
Copyright by C.S. HAMMOND & Co., N.Y.
ATLANTIC OCEAN
PACIFIC OCEAN
DRAKE PASSAGE
FALKLAND ISLANDS (Br.)
SOUTH SHETLAND IS.
SOUTH ORKNEY IS.
JUAN FERNÁNDEZ IS. (Chile)
Tropic of Capricorn
Longitude West of Greenwich
RIO DE JANEIRO
BUENOS AIRES
Santiago
Montevideo
Asunción
SÃO PAULO
Pôrto Alegre
Valparaíso
Córdoba
Rosario
Mendoza
Tucumán
Concepción
Mar del Plata
Bahía Blanca
TIERRA DEL FUEGO
Cape Horn

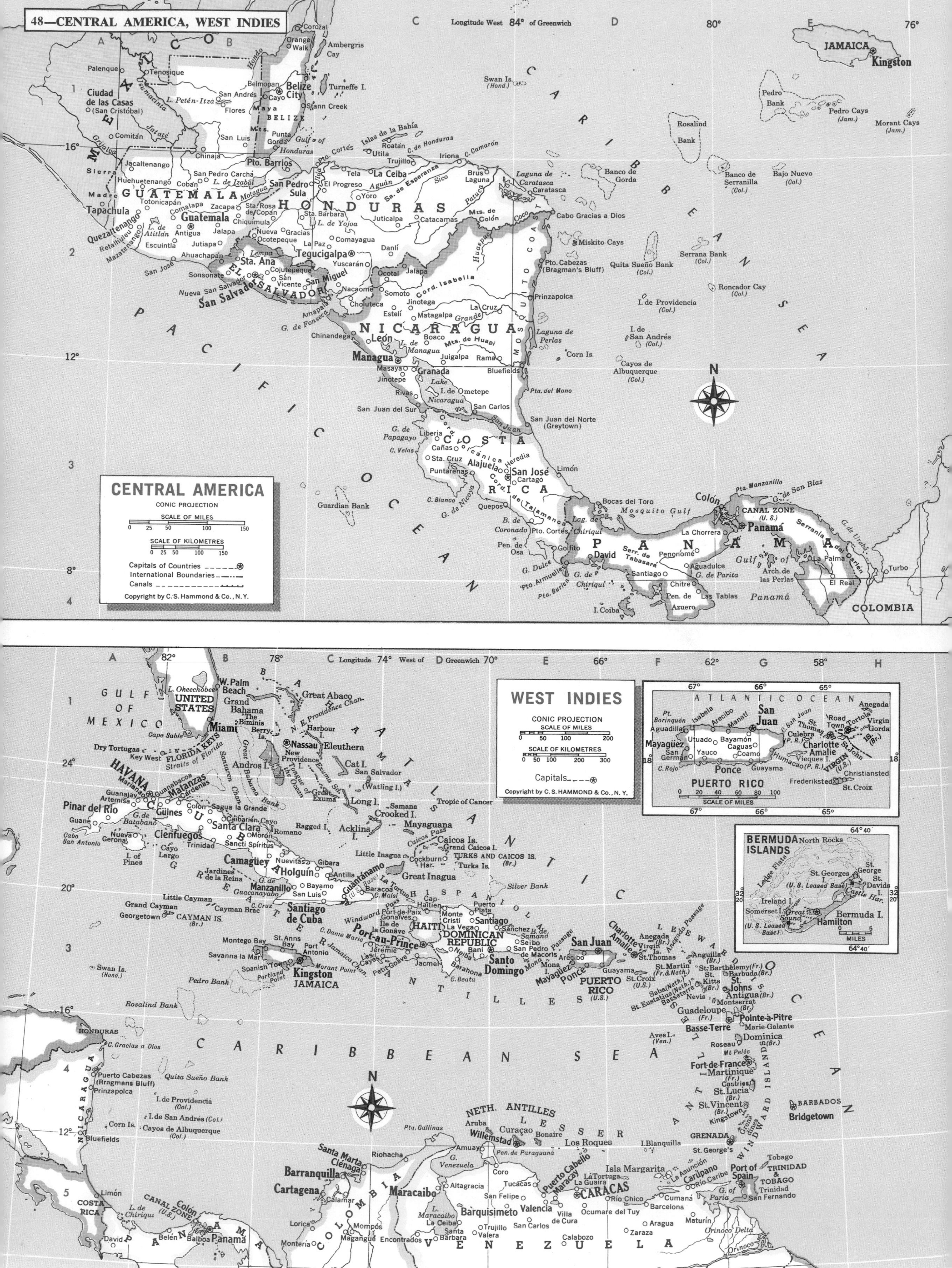

CENTRAL AMERICA
CONIC PROJECTION
SCALE OF MILES
0 25 50 100 150
SCALE OF KILOMETRES
0 25 50 100 150
Capitals of Countries
International Boundaries
Canals
Copyright by C. S. Hammond & Co., N. Y.
Longitude West 84° of Greenwich
MEXICO
GUATEMALA
HONDURAS
EL SALVADOR
NICARAGUA
COSTA RICA
PANAMA
COLOMBIA
BELIZE
JAMAICA
Kingston
CARIBBEAN SEA
PACIFIC OCEAN
Guatemala
Tegucigalpa
San Salvador
Managua
San José
Panamá
Belize City
Belmopan
CANAL ZONE (U. S.)
Colón
Swan Is. (Hond.)
Pedro Bank
Pedro Cays (Jam.)
Morant Cays (Jam.)
Rosalind Bank
Banco de Gorda
Banco de Serranilla (Col.)
Bajo Nuevo (Col.)
Miskito Cays
Serrana Bank (Col.)
Quita Sueño Bank (Col.)
Roncador Cay (Col.)
I. de Providencia (Col.)
I. de San Andrés (Col.)
Corn Is.
Cayos de Albuquerque (Col.)
Cabo Gracias a Dios
Guardian Bank
WEST INDIES
CONIC PROJECTION
SCALE OF MILES
0 50 100 200
SCALE OF KILOMETRES
0 50 100 200 300
Capitals
Copyright by C. S. Hammond & Co., N. Y.
Longitude 74° West of Greenwich 70°
GULF OF MEXICO
UNITED STATES
Miami
FLORIDA KEYS
Straits of Florida
BAHAMA
Nassau
HAVANA
CUBA
CAYMAN IS. (Br.)
Georgetown
HAITI
Port-au-Prince
DOMINICAN REPUBLIC
Santo Domingo
Kingston
JAMAICA
PUERTO RICO (U.S.)
San Juan
TURKS AND CAICOS IS. (Br.)
ATLANTIC OCEAN
Tropic of Cancer
GREATER ANTILLES
LESSER ANTILLES
LEEWARD ISLANDS
WINDWARD ISLANDS
NETH. ANTILLES
Willemstad
BARBADOS
Bridgetown
TRINIDAD & TOBAGO
Port of Spain
GRENADA
St. George's
CARIBBEAN SEA
VENEZUELA
CARACAS
COLOMBIA
Barranquilla
Cartagena
Maracaibo
PUERTO RICO
SCALE OF MILES
0 20 40 60 80 100
ATLANTIC OCEAN
Mayagüez
Ponce
Charlotte Amalie
VIRGIN IS.
BERMUDA ISLANDS
North Rocks
St. George
St. Georges I. (U. S. Leased Base)
Castle Har.
Ireland I.
Somerset I.
Great Sound
Bermuda I.
Hamilton
(U. S. Leased Base)
MILES
0 5
64° 40'

COUNTIES

County	Key
Autauga, 24,460	E 5
Baldwin, 59,382	C 9
Barbour, 22,543	H 7
Bibb, 13,812	D 5
Blount, 26,853	E 2
Bullock, 11,824	G 6
Butler, 22,007	E 7
Calhoun, 103,092	G 3
Chambers, 36,356	H 5
Cherokee, 15,606	G 2
Chilton, 25,180	E 5
Choctaw, 16,589	B 6
Clarke, 26,724	C 7
Clay, 12,636	G 4
Cleburne, 10,996	G 3
Coffee, 34,872	G 8
Colbert, 49,632	C 1
Conecuh, 15,645	E 8
Coosa, 10,662	F 5
Covington, 34,079	F 8
Crenshaw, 13,188	F 7
Cullman, 52,445	E 2
Dale, 52,938	G 8
Dallas, 55,296	D 6
De Kalb, 41,981	G 2
Elmore, 33,535	F 5
Escambia, 34,906	D 8
Etowah, 94,144	F 2
Fayette, 16,252	C 3
Franklin, 23,933	C 2
Geneva, 21,924	G 8
Greene, 10,650	C 5
Hale, 15,888	C 5
Henry, 13,254	H 7
Houston, 56,574	H 8
Jackson, 39,202	F 1
Jefferson, 644,991	E 3
Lamar, 14,335	B 3
Lauderdale, 68,111	C 1
Lawrence, 27,281	D 1
Lee, 61,268	H 5
Limestone, 41,699	E 1
Lowndes, 12,897	E 6
Macon, 24,841	G 6
Madison, 186,540	E 1
Marengo, 23,819	C 6
Marion, 23,788	C 2
Marshall, 54,211	F 2
Mobile, 317,308	B 9
Monroe, 20,883	D 7
Montgomery, 167,790	F 6
Morgan, 77,306	E 2
Perry, 15,388	D 5
Pickens, 20,326	B 4
Pike, 25,038	G 7
Randolph, 18,331	H 4
Russell, 45,394	H 6
Saint Clair, 27,956	F 3
Shelby, 38,037	E 4
Sumter, 16,974	B 5
Talladega, 65,280	F 4
Tallapoosa, 33,840	G 5
Tuscaloosa, 116,029	C 4
Walker, 56,246	D 3
Washington, 16,241	B 8
Wilcox, 16,303	D 7
Winston, 16,654	D 2

CITIES and TOWNS

Zip	Name/Pop.	Key
36310	Abbeville⊙, 2,996	H 7
35440	Abernant, 602	D 4
35005	Adamsville, 2,412	D 3
35540	Addison, 692	D 2
35006	Adger, 1,550	D 4
35441	Akron, 535	C 5
35007	Alabaster, 2,642	E 4
35950	Albertville, 9,963	F 2
† 35115	Aldrich, 476	E 4
35010	Alexander City, 12,358	G 5
36250	Alexandria, 600	G 3
35442	Aliceville, 2,807	B 4
35013	Allgood, 272	F 3
† 35616	Allsboro, 300	B 1
35015	Alton, 500	E 3
35952	Altoona, 781	F 2
36420	Andalusia⊙, 10,092	E 8
35610	Anderson, 400	D 1
36201	Anniston⊙, 31,533	G 3
35016	Arab, 4,399	E 2
35805	Ardmore, 761	E 1
36311	Ariton, 643	G 7
35033	Arkadelphia, 325	E 3
† 35035	Ashby, 500	E 4
36312	Ashford, 1,980	H 8
36251	Ashland⊙, 1,921	G 4
35953	Ashville, 986	F 3
35611	Athens⊙, 14,360	E 1
36502	Atmore, 8,293	C 8
35954	Attalla, 7,510	F 2
36830	Auburn, 22,767	H 5
36003	Autaugaville, 870	E 6
† 36312	Avon, 374	H 8
36505	Axis, 600	B 9
35019	Baileyton, 500	E 2
36004	Baker Hill, 350	H 7
36506	Barlow Bend, 300	C 8
† 36532	Barnwell, 700	C 10
36533	Battles Wharf, 300	C 10
36507	Bay Minette⊙, 6,727	C 9
36509	Bayou La Batre, 2,664	B 10
35543	Bear Creek, 336	C 2
36425	Beatrice, 455	D 7
35544	Beaverton, 265	B 3
† 35653	Belgreen, 500	C 2
36901	Bellamy, 700	B 6
35546	Berry, 679	C 3
35020	Bessemer, 33,428	D 4
* 35201	Birmingham⊙, 300,910	D 3
	Birmingham, ‡739,274	D 3
36902	Bladon Springs, 300	B 7
† 36874	Bleecker, 250	H 5
35031	Blountsville, 1,254	E 2
36201	Blue Mountain, 446	G 3
35226	Bluff Park 12,372	E 4
35957	Boaz, 5,621	F 2
36903	Bolinger, 250	B 7
36007	Bolling, 250	E 7
36511	Bon Secour, 850	C 10
36110	Boylston, 2,943	F 6
36009	Brantley, 1,066	F 7
35034	Brent, 2,093	D 5
36426	Brewton⊙, 6,747	D 8
35740	Bridgeport, 2,908	G 1
35035	Brierfield, 950	E 4
35020	Brighton, 2,277	D 4
35548	Brilliant, 726	C 2
36429	Brooklyn, 350	E 8
35036	Brookside, 990	E 3
35444	Brookwood, 450	D 4
35445	Brownville, 300	C 4
36010	Brundidge, 2,709	G 7
35446	Buhl, 500	C 4
36725	Burkville, 250	E 6
36431	Burnt Corn, 250	D 7
36904	Butler⊙, 2,064	B 6
† 36767	Cahaba, 50	D 6
35040	Calera, 1,655	E 4
36012	Calhoun, 950	F 6
36513	Calvert, 500	B 8
36726	Camden⊙, 1,742	D 7
36850	Camp Hill, 1,554	G 5
36514	Canoe, 560	D 8
† 36726	Canton Bend, 250	D 6
35549	Carbon Hill, 1,929	D 3
36515	Carlton, 275	C 8
35447	Carrollton⊙, 923	B 4
† 36023	Carrville, 895	G 5
† 36548	Carson, 250	C 8
36432	Castleberry, 666	D 8
36013	Cecil, 250	F 6
35959	Cedar Bluff, 956	G 2
36014	Central, 300	F 5
35960	Centre⊙, 2,418	G 2
35042	Centreville⊙, 2,233	D 5
36729	Chance, 350	C 7
36015	Chapman, 400	E 7
36518	Chatom⊙, 1,059	B 8
35043	Chelsea, 615	E 4
35616	Cherokee, 1,484	C 1
36611	Chickasaw, 8,447	B 9
35044	Childersburg, 4,831	F 4
36254	Choccolocco, 300	G 3
36905	Choctaw, 600	B 6
36520	Chrysler, 300	C 8
36521	Chunchula, 400	B 9
36522	Citronelle, 1,935	B 8
35045	Clanton⊙, 5,868	E 5
36015	Clayton⊙, 1,626	G 7
35049	Cleveland, 413	E 3
36017	Clio, 1,065	G 7
35617	Cloverdale, 650	C 1
35449	Coaling, 300	D 4
36523	Coden, 500	B 10
36318	Coffee Springs, 329	G 8
36524	Coffeeville, 441	B 7
35452	Coker, 800	C 4
36010	Collinsville, 1,300	G 2
36319	Columbia, 891	H 8
35051	Columbiana⊙, 2,248	E 4

AREA 51,609 sq. mi.
POPULATION 3,444,165
CAPITAL Montgomery
LARGEST CITY Birmingham
HIGHEST POINT Cheaha Mtn. 2,407 ft.
SETTLED IN 1702
ADMITTED TO UNION December 14, 1819
POPULAR NAME Heart of Dixie; Cotton State
STATE FLOWER Camellia
STATE BIRD Yellowhammer

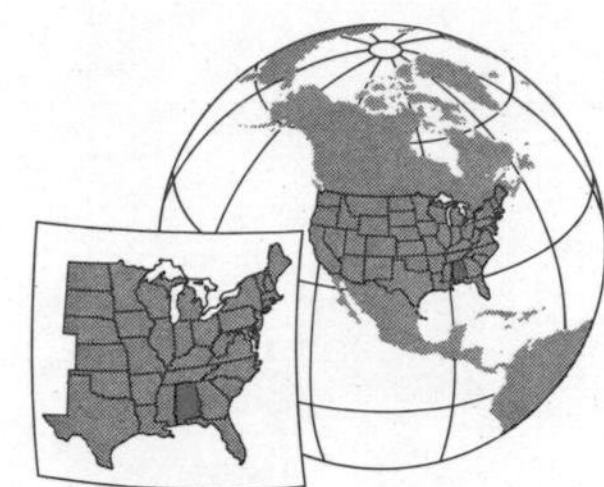

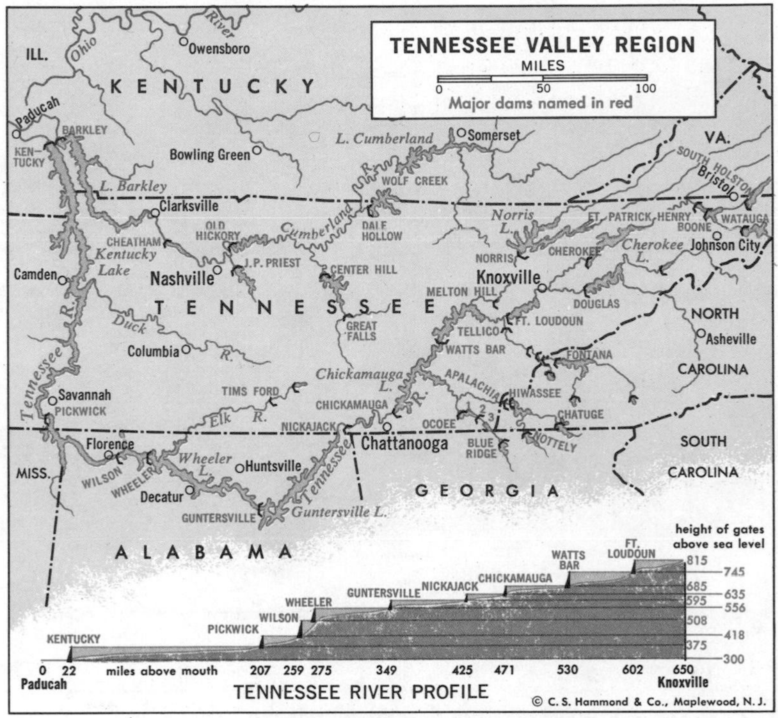

Agriculture, Industry and Resources

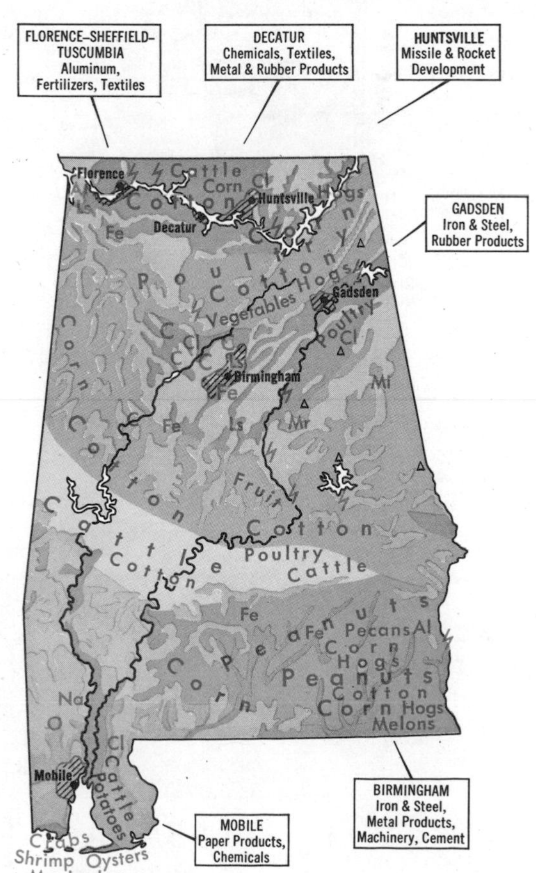

DOMINANT LAND USE

- Specialized Cotton
- Cotton, Livestock
- Cotton, General Farming
- Cotton, Hogs, Peanuts
- Cotton, Forest Products
- Peanuts, General Farming
- Truck and Mixed Farming
- Forests
- Swampland, Limited Agriculture

MAJOR MINERAL OCCURRENCES

Al	Bauxite	Ls	Limestone
At	Asphalt	Mi	Mica
C	Coal	Mr	Marble
Cl	Clay	Na	Salt
Fe	Iron Ore	O	Petroleum

ϟ Water Power

 Major Industrial Areas

▵ Major Textile Manufacturing Centers

Zip	Name/Pop.	Key
36019	Cooper, 250	E 5
36020	Coosada, 600	F 5
35550	Cordova, 2,750	D 3
† 35546	Corona, 300	C 3
35088	Cottage Grove, 300	F 5
35453	Cottondale, 600	D 4
36851	Cottonton, 415	H 6
36320	Cottonwood, 1,149	H 8
35618	Courtland, 547	D 1
36321	Cowarts, 350	H 8
36435	Coy 950	D 7
36525	Creola, 950	B 9
36906	Cromwell, 700	B 6
35962	Crossville, 1,035	G 2
36907	Cuba, 386	B 6
35055	Cullman⊙, 12,601	E 2
36920	Cullomburg, 325	B 7
36852	Cusseta, 250	H 5
36853	Dadeville⊙, 2,847	G 5
36322	Daleville, 5,182	G 8
35619	Danville, 400	D 2
36526	Daphne, 2,382	C 9
36528	Dauphin Island, 950	B 10
36256	Daviston, 247	G 4
36257	De Armanville, 500	G 3
36022	Deatsville, 350	F 5
35601	Decatur⊙, 38,044	D 1
36529	Deer Park, 300	B 8
36732	Demopolis, 7,651	C 6
36436	Dickinson, 350	C 7
36736	Dixons Mills, 285	C 6
35061	Dolomite, 1,237	D 4
35062	Dora, 1,862	D 3
36301	Dothan⊙, 36,733	H 8
35553	Double Springs⊙, 957	D 2
35964	Douglas, 527	F 2
36028	Dozier, 304	F 7
36259	Duke, 250	G 3
35744	Dutton, 423	G 1
† 36507	Dyas, 250	C 9
36260	Eastaboga, 500	F 3
36426	East Brewton, 2,336	E 8
35457	Echola, 300	C 4
36024	Eclectic, 1,184	F 5
† 36317	Edwin, 296	H 7
36323	Elba⊙, 4,634	F 8
36530	Elberta, 395	C 10
35554	Eldridge, 350	C 3
35620	Elkmont, 394	E 1
36025	Elmore, 656	F 5
35458	Elrod, 600	C 4
35459	Emelle, 300	B 5
35063	Empire, 400	D 3
36330	Enterprise, 15,591	G 8
35460	Epes, 293	B 5
36027	Eufaula, 9,102	H 7
35462	Eutaw⊙, 2,805	C 5
36401	Evergreen⊙, 3,924	E 8
36439	Excel, 422	D 8
35746	Fackler, 250	G 1
36854	Fairfax, 2,772	H 5
35064	Fairfield, 14,369	E 3
36532	Fairhope, 5,720	C 10
35208	Fairview, 313	E 2
35622	Falkville, 946	E 2
35555	Fayette⊙, 4,568	C 3
36440	Finchburg, 300	D 7
36855	Five Points, 247	H 4
† 35129	Flat Creek-Wegra, 1,066	D 3
35966	Flat Rock, 750	G 1
36739	Flatwood, 300	C 6
† 35601	Flint City, 404	D 1
36441	Flomaton, 1,584	D 8
36442	Florala, 2,701	F 8
35630	Florence⊙, 34,031	C 1
36535	Foley, 3,368	C 10
35214	Forestdale, 6,091	E 3
36030	Forest Home, 450	E 7
36740	Forkland, 400	C 5
36031	Fort Davis, 500	G 6
36032	Fort Deposit, 1,438	E 7
36856	Fort Mitchell, 2,400	H 6
35967	Fort Payne⊙, 8,435	G 2
35463	Fosters, 400	C 4
36444	Franklin, 500	D 7
36538	Frankville, 350	B 7
† 31833	Fredonia, 300	H 5
36445	Frisco City, 1,286	D 8
36539	Fruitdale, 275	B 8
36446	Fulton, 628	C 7
35068	Fultondale, 5,163	E 3
36741	Furman, 300	E 6
35971	Fyffe, 311	G 2
* 35901	Gadsden⊙, 53,928	G 2
	Gadsden, ‡94,144	G 2
36540	Gainestown, 300	C 8
35464	Gainesville, 255	B 5
35972	Gallant, 475	F 2
36038	Gantt, 380	E 8
35070	Garden City, 745	E 2
35071	Gardendale, 6,502	E 3
36340	Geneva⊙, 4,398	G 8
36033	Georgiana, 2,148	E 7
35974	Geraldine, 1,935	G 2
35559	Glen Allen, 276	C 3
35905	Glencoe, 2,901	G 3
36034	Glenwood, 378	F 7
† 36024	Good Hope, 840	E 2
35072	Goodwater, 2,172	F 4
35466	Gordo, 1,991	C 4
36343	Gordon, 312	H 8
35561	Gorgas, 500	D 3
36035	Goshen, 279	F 7
36450	Gosport, 400	C 7
36036	Grady, 298	F 7
36541	Grand Bay, 950	B 10
35747	Grant, 382	F 1
35073	Graysville, 3,182	D 3
35074	Green Pond, 500	D 4
36744	Greensboro⊙, 3,371	C 5

(continued on following page)

ALABAMA
SCALE
0 5 10 20 30 40 MI.
0 5 10 20 30 40 KM.
State Capitals
County Seats
© C.S. HAMMOND & Co., N.Y.
T E N N E S S E E
G E O R G I A
F L O R I D A
M I S S I S S I P P I
GULF OF MEXICO
88° 87° Longitude West of 30' Greenwich 86° 85°
35° 34° 33° 32° 31°
CHATTANOOGA
CHICKAMAUGA AND CHATTANOOGA NAT'L MIL. PK.
RUSSELL CAVE NAT'L MON.
ATLANTA
KENNESAW MT. NAT. BATTLEFIELD PARK
COLUMBUS
PENSACOLA
BIRMINGHAM
MONTGOMERY
MOBILE
LAUDERDALE
LIMESTONE
MADISON
JACKSON
COLBERT
LAWRENCE
MORGAN
MARSHALL
DE KALB
FRANKLIN
MARION
WINSTON
CULLMAN
ETOWAH
CHEROKEE
BLOUNT
LAMAR
FAYETTE
WALKER
JEFFERSON
ST. CLAIR
CALHOUN
CLEBURNE
PICKENS
TUSCALOOSA
SHELBY
TALLADEGA
CLAY
RANDOLPH
BIBB
COOSA
TALLAPOOSA
CHAMBERS
GREENE
HALE
CHILTON
PERRY
AUTAUGA
ELMORE
LEE
SUMTER
MARENGO
DALLAS
LOWNDES
MACON
RUSSELL
CHOCTAW
WILCOX
MONTGOMERY
BULLOCK
BARBOUR
CLARKE
MONROE
BUTLER
CRENSHAW
PIKE
WASHINGTON
CONECUH
COFFEE
DALE
HENRY
ESCAMBIA
COVINGTON
GENEVA
HOUSTON
BALDWIN
MOBILE
Florence
Sheffield
Tuscumbia
Athens
Huntsville
Decatur
Scottsboro
Guntersville
Ft. Payne
Gadsden
Cullman
Jasper
Anniston
Talladega
Tuscaloosa
Bessemer
Selma
Prattville
Wetumpka
Opelika
Auburn
Tuskegee
Phenix City
Eufaula
Troy
Greenville
Dothan
Enterprise
Andalusia
Brewton
Evergreen
Monroeville
Demopolis
Prichard
Bay Minette
Mobile Bay
Mississippi Sound
Perdido Bay
Pensacola Bay
Choctawhatchee Bay
Lake Martin
Logan Martin Lake
Lake Eufaula
Weiss Res.
L. Seminole
Wheeler Lake
Tennessee R.
Alabama R.
Tombigbee R.
Black Warrior R.
Coosa R.
Tallapoosa R.
Chattahoochee R.
WALTER F. GEORGE DAM
JIM WOODRUFF DAM
MAXWELL A.F.B.
GUNTER A.F.B.
REDSTONE ARSENAL
FT. McCLELLAN
FORT RUCKER
HORSESHOE BEND NAT'L MIL. PK.
2,407 Cheaha Mtn.

Railroad tracks form tangled spider webs leading to voracious steel furnaces. Native coal, iron ore and limestone are delivered to Ensley (Birmingham), Alabama plant.

Topography

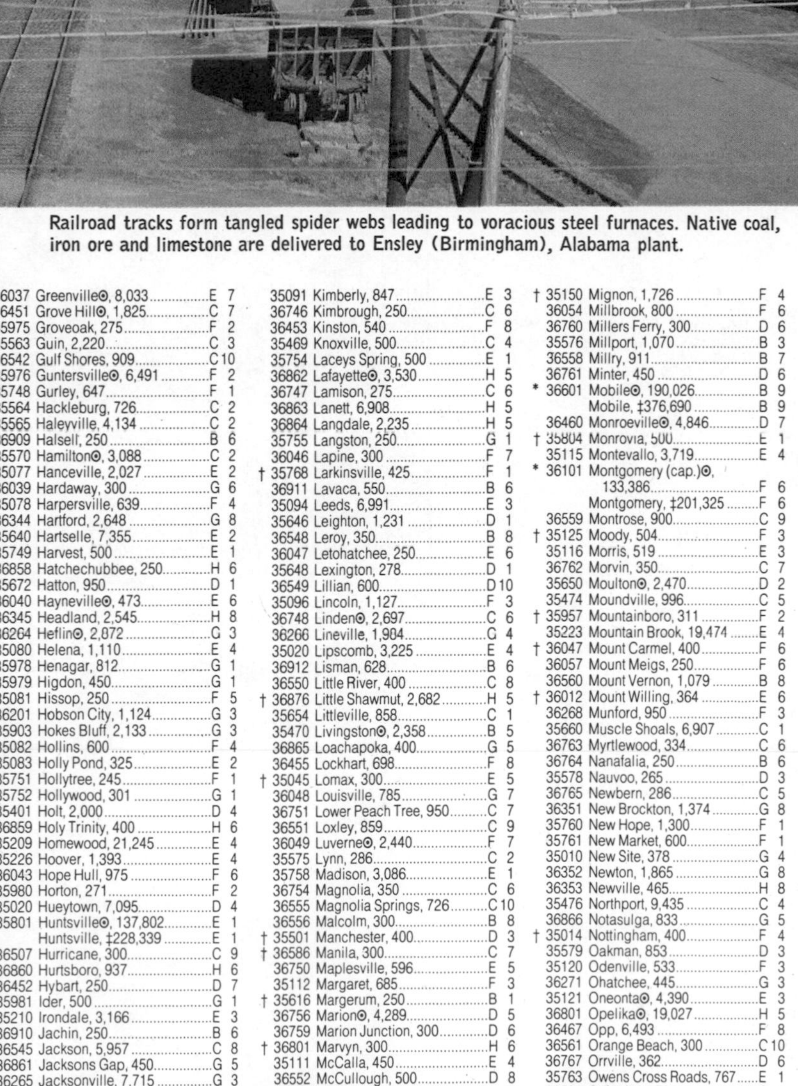

36037 Greenville⊙, 8,033 E 7
36451 Grove Hill⊙, 1,825 C 7
35975 Groveoak, 275 F 2
35563 Guin, 2,220 C 3
36542 Gulf Shores, 909 C 10
35976 Guntersville⊙, 6,491 F 2
35748 Gurley, 647 F 1
35564 Hackleburg, 726 C 2
35565 Haleyville, 4,134 C 2
36909 Halsell, 250 B 6
35570 Hamilton⊙, 3,088 C 2
35077 Hanceville, 2,027 E 2
36039 Hardaway, 300 G 6
35078 Harpersville, 639 F 4
36344 Hartford, 2,648 G 8
35640 Hartselle, 7,355 E 2
35749 Harvest, 500 E 1
36858 Hatchechubbee, 250 H 6
† 35672 Hatton, 950 D 1
36040 Hayneville⊙, 473 E 6
36345 Headland, 2,545 H 8
36264 Heflin⊙, 2,872 G 3
35080 Helena, 1,110 E 4
35978 Henagar, 812 G 1
35979 Higdon, 450 G 1
35081 Hissop, 250 F 5
† 36201 Hobson City, 1,124 G 3
35903 Hokes Bluff, 2,133 G 3
35082 Hollins, 600 F 4
35083 Holly Pond, 325 E 2
35751 Hollytree, 245 F 1
35752 Hollywood, 301 G 1
35401 Holt, 2,000 D 4
36859 Holy Trinity, 400 H 6
35209 Homewood, 21,245 E 4
† 35226 Hoover, 1,393 E 4
36043 Hope Hull, 975 F 6
35980 Horton, 271 F 2
35020 Hueytown, 7,095 D 4
* 35801 Huntsville⊙, 137,802 E 1
Huntsville, ‡228,339 E 1
† 36507 Hurricane, 300 C 9
36860 Hurtsboro, 937 H 6
36452 Hybart, 250 D 7
35981 Ider, 500 G 1
35210 Irondale, 3,166 E 3
36910 Jachin, 250 B 6
36545 Jackson, 5,957 C 8
36861 Jacksons Gap, 450 G 5
36265 Jacksonville, 7,715 G 3
35501 Jasper⊙, 10,798 D 3
36745 Jefferson, 500 C 6
35085 Jemison, 1,423 E 5
† 36268 Jenifer, 300 G 3
35086 Johns, 241 D 4
35087 Joppa, 350 E 2
35089 Kellyton, 500 F 5
35574 Kennedy, 415 B 3
36045 Kent, 500 G 5
35645 Killen, 683 D 1
35091 Kimberly, 847 E 3
36746 Kimbrough, 250 C 6
36453 Kinston, 540 F 8
35469 Knoxville, 500 C 4
35754 Laceys Spring, 500 E 1
36862 Lafayette⊙, 3,530 H 5
36747 Lamison, 275 C 6
36863 Lanett, 6,908 H 5
36864 Langdale, 2,235 H 5
35755 Langston, 250 G 1
36046 Lapine, 300 F 7
† 35768 Larkinsville, 425 F 1
36911 Lavaca, 550 B 6
35094 Leeds, 6,991 E 3
35646 Leighton, 1,231 D 1
36548 Leroy, 350 B 8
36047 Letohatchee, 250 E 6
35648 Lexington, 278 D 1
36549 Lillian, 600 D 10
35096 Lincoln, 1,127 F 3
36748 Linden⊙, 2,697 C 6
36266 Lineville, 1,904 G 4
35020 Lipscomb, 3,225 E 4
36912 Lisman, 628 B 6
36550 Little River, 400 C 8
† 36876 Little Shawmut, 2,682 H 5
35654 Littleville, 858 C 1
35470 Livingston⊙, 2,358 B 5
36865 Loachapoka, 400 G 5
36455 Lockhart, 698 F 8
† 35045 Lomax, 300 E 5
36048 Louisville, 785 G 7
36751 Lower Peach Tree, 950 C 7
36551 Loxley, 859 C 9
36049 Luverne⊙, 2,440 F 7
35575 Lynn, 286 C 2
35758 Madison, 3,086 E 1
36754 Magnolia, 350 C 6
36555 Magnolia Springs, 726 C 10
36556 Malcolm, 300 B 8
† 35501 Manchester, 400 D 3
† 36586 Manila, 300 C 7
36750 Maplesville, 596 E 5
35112 Margaret, 685 F 3
† 35616 Margerum, 250 B 1
36756 Marion⊙, 4,289 D 5
36759 Marion Junction, 300 D 6
† 36801 Marvyn, 300 H 6
35111 McCalla, 450 E 4
36552 McCullough, 500 D 8
36553 McIntosh, 600 B 8
36456 McKenzie, 491 E 7
36753 McWilliams, 525 D 7
36913 Melvin, 300 B 7
35984 Mentone, 407 G 1
35759 Meridianville, 950 F 1
36458 Mexia, 250 D 8
35228 Midfield, 6,399 E 4
36350 Midland City, 1,172 H 8
36053 Midway, 558 H 6
† 35150 Mignon, 1,726 F 4
36054 Millbrook, 800 F 6
36760 Millers Ferry, 300 D 6
35576 Millport, 1,070 B 3
36558 Millry, 911 B 7
36761 Minter, 450 D 6
* 36601 Mobile⊙, 190,026 B 9
Mobile, ‡376,690 B 9
36460 Monroeville⊙, 4,846 D 7
† 35804 Monrovia, 500 E 1
35115 Montevallo, 3,719 E 4
* 36101 Montgomery (cap.)⊙, 133,386 F 6
Montgomery, ‡201,325 F 6
36559 Montrose, 900 C 9
† 35125 Moody, 504 F 3
35116 Morris, 519 E 3
36762 Morvin, 350 C 7
35650 Moulton⊙, 2,470 D 2
35474 Moundville, 996 C 5
† 35957 Mountainboro, 311 F 2
35223 Mountain Brook, 19,474 E 4
† 36047 Mount Carmel, 400 F 6
36057 Mount Meigs, 250 F 6
36560 Mount Vernon, 1,079 B 8
† 36012 Mount Willing, 364 E 6
36268 Munford, 950 F 3
35660 Muscle Shoals, 6,907 C 1
36763 Myrtlewood, 334 C 6
36764 Nanafalia, 250 B 6
35578 Nauvoo, 265 D 3
36765 Newbern, 286 C 5
36351 New Brockton, 1,374 G 8
35760 New Hope, 1,300 F 1
35761 New Market, 600 F 1
35010 New Site, 378 G 4
36352 Newton, 1,865 G 8
36353 Newville, 465 H 8
35476 Northport, 9,435 C 4
36866 Notasulga, 833 G 5
† 35014 Nottingham, 400 F 4
35579 Oakman, 853 D 3
35120 Odenville, 533 F 3
36271 Ohatchee, 445 G 3
35121 Oneonta⊙, 4,390 E 3
36801 Opelika⊙, 19,027 H 5
36467 Opp, 6,493 F 8
36561 Orange Beach, 300 C 10
36767 Orrville, 362 D 6
35763 Owens Cross Roads, 767 E 1
36201 Oxford, 4,361 G 3
36360 Ozark⊙, 13,555 G 8
35477 Panola, 300 B 5
36370 Pansey, 300 H 8
35580 Parrish, 1,742 D 3
35124 Pelham, 931 E 4
35125 Pell City⊙, 5,381 F 3
36916 Pennington, 276 B 6
36562 Perdido, 325 C 8
36530 Perdido Beach, 300 C 10
36471 Peterman, 750 D 7
35478 Peterson, 1,040 D 4
36867 Phenix City⊙, 25,281 H 6
35581 Phil Campbell, 1,230 C 2
36272 Piedmont, 5,063 G 3
36371 Pinckard, 609 G 8
36768 Pine Apple, 347 E 7
36769 Pine Hill, 697 C 7
36065 Pine Level, 300 F 6
35126 Pinson, 2,500 E 3
35765 Pisgah, 519 G 1
36871 Pittsview, 400 H 6
36758 Plantersville, 550 E 5
36564 Point Clear, 850 C 10
36067 Prattville⊙, 13,116 E 6
36610 Prichard, 41,578 B 9
35766 Princeton, 250 F 1
36772 Putnam, 305 B 6
† 36507 Rabun, 300 C 8
35131 Ragland, 1,239 F 3
35901 Rainbow City, 3,107 F 3
35986 Rainsville, 2,099 G 2
35480 Ralph, 500 C 4
36069 Ramer, 750 F 6
36273 Ranburne, 371 H 3
36473 Range, 275 D 8
35582 Red Bay, 2,464 B 2
36474 Red Level, 616 E 8
† 35954 Reece City, 496 G 2
35481 Reform, 1,893 C 4
† 36720 Rehoboth, 300 D 6
† 35160 Renfroe, 400 F 4
36475 Repton, 277 D 8
† 35203 Republic, 500 E 3
36918 Riderwood, 400 B 6
36476 River Falls, 580 E 8
35135 Riverside, 351 F 3
36872 River View, 1,109 H 5
36274 Roanoke, 5,251 H 4
36567 Robertsdale, 2,078 C 9
35136 Rockford⊙, 603 F 5
36274 Rock Mills, 800 H 4
35652 Rogersville, 950 D 1
† 35020 Roosevelt City, 3,663 E 4
35653 Russellville⊙, 7,814 C 2
36071 Rutledge, 353 F 7
35137 Saginaw, 300 E 4
35138 Saint Bernard, 896 E 2
† 35146 Saint Clair Springs, 300 F 3
36568 Saint Elmo, 650 B 10
36569 Saint Stephens, 400 B 7
36874 Salem, 475 H 5
36570 Salitpa, 500 C 7
36477 Samson, 2,257 F 8
36478 Sanford, 256 F 8
35583 Saragossa, 300 D 3
36571 Saraland, 7,840 B 9
36775 Sardis, 300 E 6
36775 Sardis, 368 F 2
36572 Satsuma, 2,035 B 9
35139 Sayre, 700 E 3
35768 Scottsboro⊙, 9,324 F 1
36875 Seale, 400 H 6
35771 Section, 702 G 1
36701 Selma⊙, 27,379 E 6
† 36701 Selmont, 2,270 E 6
36574 Seminole, 275 D 10
36575 Semmes, 800 B 9
36876 Shawmut, 2,181 H 5
35660 Sheffield, 13,115 C 1
35143 Shelby, 500 E 4
36075 Shorter, 500 G 6
36373 Shorterville, 330 H 7
36733 Shortleaf, 253 C 6
36919 Silas, 345 B 7
35144 Siluria, 678 E 4
36576 Silverhill, 552 C 9
† 36268 Silver Run, 250 G 3
35584 Sipsey, 608 D 3
36375 Slocomb, 1,883 G 8
36877 Smiths, 2,500 H 5
35952 Snead, 347 F 2
† 36104 Snowdoun, 250 F 6
36778 Snow Hill, 500 E 7
35901 Southside, 983 F 3
36527 Spanish Fort, 983 C 9
† 35674 Spring Valley, 600 C 1
35146 Springville, 1,153 E 3
35585 Spruce Pine, 600 C 2
36878 Standing Rock, 500 H 4
36578 Stapleton, 975 C 9
35987 Steele, 798 F 3
35147 Sterrett, 450 F 4
35772 Stevenson, 2,390 G 1
† 35150 Stewartville, 250 F 4
36579 Stockton, 1,400 C 9
35586 Sulligent, 1,762 B 3
35148 Sumiton, 2,374 D 3
36580 Summerdale, 550 C 10
36780 Sunny South, 250 C 7
36781 Suttle, 256 D 5
36782 Sweet Water, 265 C 6
35149 Sycamore, 800 F 4
35150 Sylacauga, 12,255 F 4
35988 Sylvania, 476 G 1
35160 Talladega⊙, 17,662 F 4
36078 Tallassee, 4,809 G 5
35671 Tanner, 600 E 1
35217 Tarrant, 6,835 E 3
36582 Theodore, 1,950 B 9
36783 Thomaston, 824 C 6
36784 Thomasville, 3,769 C 7
35171 Thorsby, 944 E 5
35672 Town Creek, 1,203 D 1
35587 Townley, 500 D 3
36921 Toxey, 304 B 7
35172 Trafford, 628 E 3
35673 Trinity, 881 D 1
36081 Troy⊙, 11,482 G 7
35173 Trussville, 2,985 E 3
36479 Tunnel Springs, 300 D 7
35401 Tuscaloosa⊙, 65,773 C 4
Tuscaloosa, ‡116,029 C 4
35674 Tuscumbia⊙, 8,828 C 1
36083 Tuskegee⊙, 11,028 G 6
36088 Tuskegee Institute, 5,800 G 6
36089 Union Springs⊙, 4,324 G 6
36786 Uniontown, 2,133 D 6
36480 Uriah, 1,200 D 8
35775 Valhermoso Springs, 500 E 2
35989 Valley Head, 470 G 1
35176 Vandiver, 700 F 4
36091 Verbena, 350 E 5
35592 Vernon⊙, 2,190 B 3
35216 Vestavia Hills, 8,311 E 4
35593 Vina, 366 B 2
35178 Vincent, 1,419 F 4
35179 Vinemont, 480 E 2
36481 Vredenburgh, 622 D 7
36276 Wadley, 626 G 4
36585 Wagarville, 350 B 8
36586 Walker Springs, 500 C 7
35180 Warrior, 2,621 E 3
35677 Waterloo, 262 B 1
35182 Wattsville, 500 F 3
36879 Waverly, 247 G 5
36277 Weaver, 2,091 G 3
36376 Webb, 354 H 8
36278 Wedowee⊙, 842 H 4
† 35129 Wegra-Flat Creek, 1,066 D 3
35183 Weogufka, 350 F 4
35184 West Blocton, 1,172 D 4
† 36201 West End-Cobb Town, 5,515 G 3
35185 Westover, 1,400 E 4
36092 Wetumpka⊙, 3,786 F 5
36482 Whatley, 500 C 7
† 35618 Wheeler, 300 D 1
† 36040 White Hall, 300 E 6
† 36862 White Plains, 350 G 3
† 35094 Whites Chapel, 334 F 3
36923 Whitfield, 500 B 6
† 36352 Wicksburg, 400 G 8
36587 Wilmer, 720 B 9
35186 Wilsonville, 659 E 4
35187 Wilton, 573 E 4
35594 Winfield, 3,292 C 3
35188 Woodstock, 320 D 4
35776 Woodville, 322 F 1
36924 Yantley, 500 B 6
36789 Yellow Bluff, 350 C 7
36925 York, 3,044 B 6

⊙ County seat.
‡ Population of metropolitan area.
† Zip of nearest p.o.
* Multiple zips

SENATORIAL DISTRICTS

District	Key
Central, 70,996	H 2
Northwestern, 16,763	E 2
South Central, 170,058	G 3
Southeastern, 42,565	L 3

CITIES and TOWNS

Zip	Name/Pop.	Key
99615	Akhiok, 115	H 3
99551	Akiachak, 312	F 2
99552	Akiak, 171	F 2
99553	Akutan, 101	E 4
99554	Alakanuk, 265	E 2
99555	Aleknagik, 128	G 3
99720	Allakaket, 174	H 1
99786	Ambler, 169	G 1
99721	Anaktuvuk Pass, 99	H 1
* 99501	Anchorage⊙, 48,029	B 1
99556	Anchor Point, 102	B 2
† 99760	Anderson, 362	H 2
† 99658	Andreafski (Saint Marys), 384	F 2
99820	Angoon, 400	M 1
99557	Aniak, 205	G 2
99920	Annette, 195	N 2
99558	Anvik, 83	F 2
99722	Arctic Village, 85	K 1
† 99701	Aurora Lodge, 250	J 2
99723	Barrow, 2,104	G 1
† 99747	Barter Island (Kaktovik), 123	K 1
99724	Beaver, 101	J 1
† 99612	Belkofski, 59	F 3
99559	Bethel, 2,416	F 2
† 99726	Bettles, 65	H 1
99726	Bettles Field, 49	H 1
† 99740	Birch Creek, 45	J 1
† 99567	Birchwood, 1,219	C 1
99785	Brevig Mission, 123	E 1
99727	Buckland, 104	F 1
99729	Cantwell, 62	J 2
† 99901	Cape Pole, 123	M 2
99730	Central, 26	J 1
99788	Chalkyitsik, 130	K 1
† 99620	Chaneliak, 100	F 2
99561	Chefornak, 146	F 2
99563	Chevak, 387	E 2
99732	Chicken, 25	K 2
99564	Chignik, 83	G 3
99565	Chignik Lagoon, 70	G 3
† 99564	Chignik Lake, 117	G 3
† 99586	Chistochina, 33	K 2
99566	Chitina, 38	K 2
99567	Chugiak, 489	C 1
99733	Circle, 54	K 1
99568	Clam Gulch, 47	B 1
99569	Clarks Point, 95	G 3
99704	Clear, 504	J 2
99570	Cohoe, 60	B 1
99571	Cold Bay, 256	F 3
99701	College, 3,434	J 1
99572	Cooper Landing, 31	C 1
99573	Copper Center, 206	J 2
99574	Cordova, 1,164	D 1
99921	Craig, 272	M 2
99575	Crooked Creek, 59	G 2
† 99746	Cutoff (Huslia), 159	G 1
99736	Deering, 85	F 1
99737	Delta Junction, 703	J 2
99576	Dillingham, 914	G 3
† 99762	Diomede, 84	E 1
99737	Dot Lake, 42	K 2
† 99685	Dutch Harbor, 30	E 4
99738	Eagle, 36	K 2
99577	Eagle River, 2,437	C 1
† 99901	Edna Bay, 112	M 2
99578	Eek, 186	F 2
99579	Egegik, 148	G 3
† 99569	Ekuk, 51	G 3
99580	Ekwok, 103	G 3
99825	Elfin Cove, 49	M 1
99739	Elim, 174	F 2
99581	Emmonak, 439	E 2
† 99603	English Bay, 58	B 2
† 99674	Eska, 50	B 1
99725	Ester, 264	J 2
99701	Fairbanks⊙, 14,771	J 2
99583	False Pass, 62	F 4
99585	Fortuna Ledge, 175	F 2
99740	Fort Yukon, 448	J 1
99586	Gakona, 88	K 2
99741	Galena, 302	G 2
99742	Gambell, 372	D 2
99587	Girdwood, 144	C 1
99588	Glennallen, 363	D 1
99762	Golovin, 117	F 2
99589	Goodnews Bay, 218	F 3
† 99586	Gulkana, 53	J 2
99826	Gustavus, 64	M 1
99827	Haines, 463	M 1
99743	Healy, 79	H 2
† 99665	Holikachuk, 100	G 2
99602	Holy Cross, 199	G 2
99603	Homer, 1,083	B 2
99829	Hoonah, 748	M 1
99604	Hooper Bay, 490	E 2
99605	Hope, 51	C 1
† 99687	Houston, 69	B 1
99745	Hughes, 85	H 1
99746	Huslia, 159	G 1
99922	Hydaburg, 214	M 2
99923	Hyder, 49	P 2
† 99625	Igiugig, 36	G 3
99606	Iliamna, 58	G 3
99801	Juneau (cap.)⊙, 6,050	N 1
† 99663	Kachemak, 76	B 2
† 99608	Kaguyak, 59	H 3
99830	Kake, 448	M 1
† 99647	Kakhonak, 88	H 3
99747	Kaktovik, 123	K 1
99607	Kalskag, 122	F 2
99748	Kaltag, 206	G 2
99608	Karluk, 98	H 3
99924	Kasaan, 30	N 2
† 99668	Kashegelok, 200	G 2
99609	Kasigluk, 526	F 2
99610	Kasilof, 71	B 1
99611	Kenai, 3,533	B 1
99901	Ketchikan, 6,994	N 2
99749	Kiana, 278	F 1
99612	King Cove, 283	F 4
† 99762	King Island, 100	E 1
99613	King Salmon, 202	G 3
99614	Kipnuk, 325	F 2
99750	Kivalina, 188	E 1
99925	Klawock, 213	M 2
† 99827	Klukwan, 103	M 1
99751	Kobuk, 75	G 1
99615	Kodiak, 3,798	H 3
99576	Koliganek, 142	G 3
99620	Kotlik, 228	F 2
99752	Kotzebue, 1,696	F 1
99753	Koyuk, 122	F 1
99754	Koyukuk, 124	G 1
† 99625	Kvichak, 75	G 3
99621	Kwethluk, 408	F 2
99622	Kwigillingok, 148	F 3
† 99655	Kwinhagak (Quinhagak), 340	F 3
99624	Larsen Bay, 109	H 3
99625	Levelock, 74	G 3
† 99566	Lower Tonsina, 65	J 2
99756	Manley Hot Springs, 34	H 2
99628	Manokotak, 214	G 3
† 99585	Marshall (Fortuna Ledge), 175	F 2
99627	McGrath, 279	H 2
99630	Mekoryuk, 249	E 2
† 99579	Meshik, 75	G 3
99926	Metlakatla, 1,050	N 2
99903	Meyers Chuck, 37	N 2
99758	Minto, 168	J 2
† 99676	Montana, 33	B 1
99631	Moose Pass, 53	C 1
† 99901	Mountain Point, 459	N 2
99632	Mountain Village, 419	E 2
99835	Mount Edgecumbe, 835	M 1
† 99589	Mumtrak (Goodnews Bay), 218	F 3
† 99764	Nabesna, 40	K 2
99633	Naknek, 178	G 3
† 99559	Napaiskak, 259	F 2
99634	Napakiak, 270	F 2
99760	Nenana, 362	J 2
† 99606	Newhalen, 88	H 3
99636	New Stuyahok, 216	G 3
99559	Newtok, 114	F 2
† 99603	Nikolaevsk, 70	B 2
99691	Nikolai, 112	H 2
99638	Nikolski, 57	E 4
99639	Ninilchik, 134	B 1
99761	Noatak, 293	F 1
99762	Nome⊙, 2,488	E 2
99640	Nondalton, 184	G 2
99763	Noorvik, 462	F 1
99705	North Pole, 265	J 2
99764	Northway, 40	K 2
99765	Nulato, 308	G 2
99641	Nunapitchuk, 400	F 2
99643	Old Harbor, 290	H 3
† 99559	Oscarville, 41	F 2
99644	Ouzinkie, 160	H 3
99645	Palmer, 1,140	C 1
99646	Pauloff Harbor, 39	F 4
99737	Paxson, 32	J 2
99647	Pedro Bay, 65	H 3
99832	Pelican, 133	M 1
99648	Perryville, 94	G 3
99833	Petersburg, 2,042	N 2
99649	Pilot Point, 68	G 3
99650	Pilot Station, 290	F 2
† 99658	Pitkas Point, 70	F 2
99651	Platinum, 55	F 3
99766	Point Hope, 386	E 1
† 99587	Portage, 80	C 1
99834	Port Alexander, 36	M 2
† 99827	Port Chilkoot, 220	N 1
† 99603	Port Graham, 107	B 2
† 99579	Port Heiden, 66	G 3
99550	Port Lions, 227	H 3

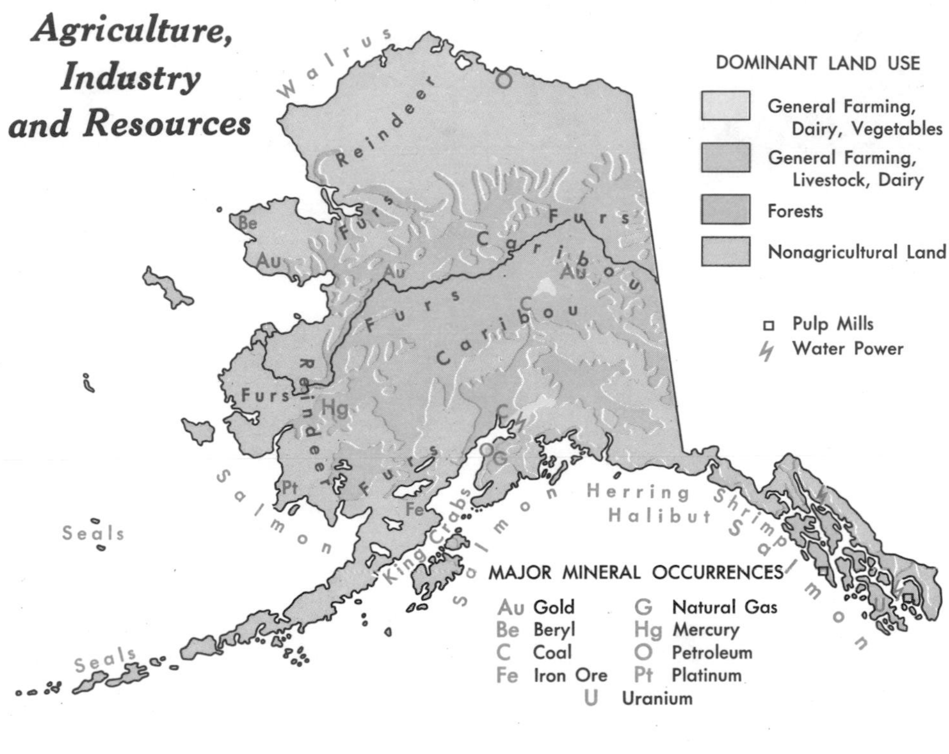

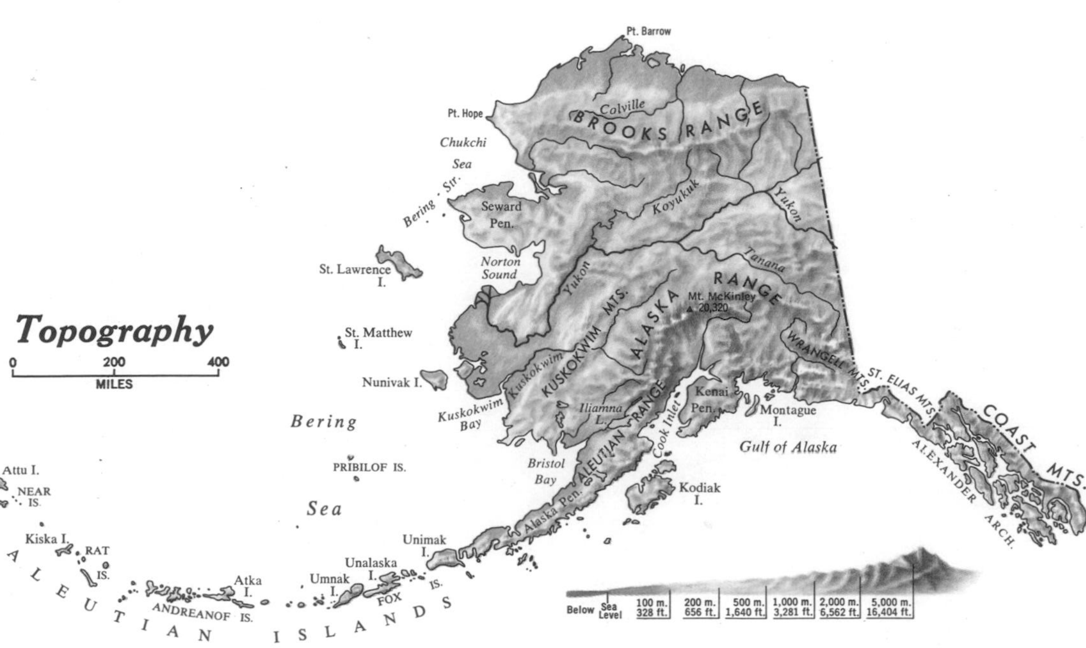

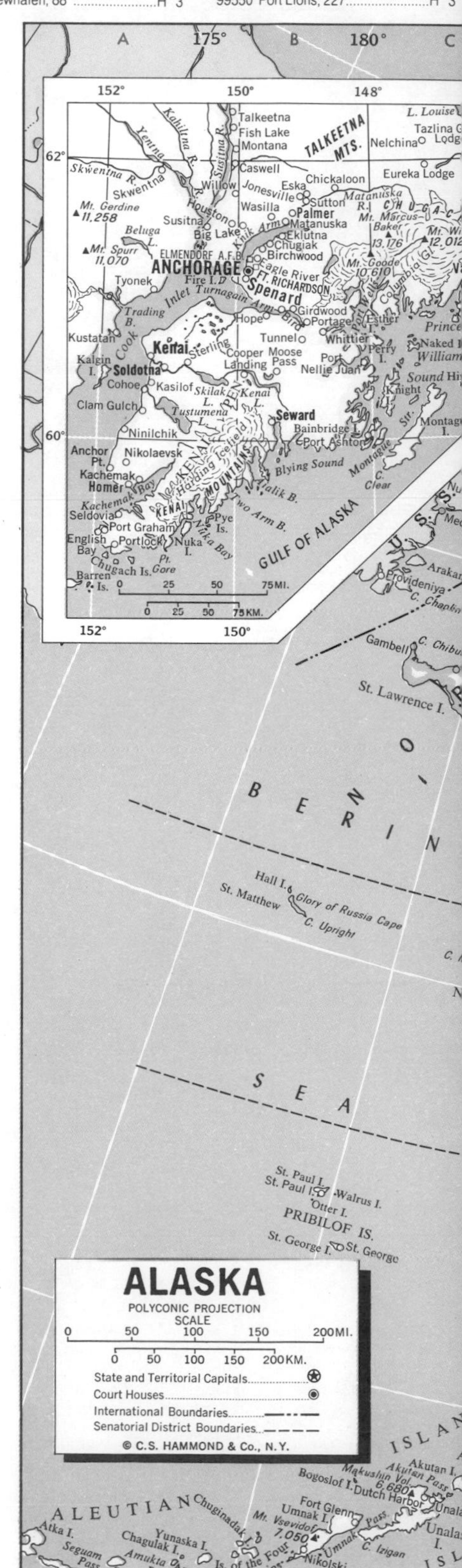

9723 Prudhoe Bay, 49 .... J 1
9655 Quinhagak, 340 .... F 3
9767 Rampart, 36 .... H 1
9656 Red Devil, 81 .... G 2
9768 Ruby, 145 .... G 2
9657 Russian Mission, 146 .... F 2
9660 Saint George, 163 .... E 3
9658 Saint Marys, 384 .... F 2
9659 Saint Michael, 207 .... F 2
9660 Saint Paul Island, 450 .... D 3
9661 Sand Point, 360 .... G 3
9769 Savoonga, 364 .... E 2
9901 Saxman, 135 .... N 2
9662 Scammon Bay, 166 .... E 2
9770 Selawik, 429 .... G 1
9663 Seldovia, 437 .... B 2
9664 Seward, 1,587 .... C 1
9665 Shageluk, 167 .... G 2
9771 Shaktoolik, 151 .... F 2
9666 Sheldon Point, 125 .... E 2
9772 Shishmaref, 267 .... E 1
9773 Shungnak, 165 .... G 1
9835 Sitka, 3,370 .... M 1
9840 Skagway, 675 .... M 1
9668 Sleetmute, 109 .... G 2
9669 Soldotna, 1,202 .... B 1
9670 South Naknek, 154 .... G 3
9503 Spenard, 18,089 .... C 1
9671 Stebbins, 231 .... F 2
9672 Sterling, 30 .... B 1
9774 Stevens Village, 74 .... J 1
9673 Stony River, 74 .... G 2
9729 Summit, 34 .... J 2
9743 Suntrana, 67 .... J 2
9501 Susitna, 50 .... B 1

99674 Sutton, 76 .... C 1
99676 Talkeetna, 182 .... B 1
99776 Tanacross, 84 .... K 2
99777 Tanana, 120 .... H 1
99677 Tatitlek, 111 .... D 1
99778 Teller, 220 .... E 1
99841 Tenakee Springs, 86 .... M 1
99779 Tetlin, 114 .... K 2
† 99801 Thane, 70 .... N 1
† 99901 Thorne Bay, 443 .... M 2
99678 Togiak, 383 .... F 3
99780 Tok, 214 .... K 2
99679 Tuluksak, 195 .... F 2
99680 Tuntutuliak, 158 .... F 2
99681 Tununak, 274 .... E 2
99682 Tyonek, 232 .... B 1
† 99701 Umiat, 45 .... H 1
99684 Unalakleet, 434 .... G 2
99685 Unalaska, 178 .... E 4
99686 Valdez, 1,005 .... D 1
99781 Venetie, 112 .... J 1
99782 Wainwright, 315 .... F 1
99783 Wales, 131 .... E 1
99928 Ward Cove, 105 .... N 2
99687 Wasilla, 300 .... B 1
99784 White Mountain, 87 .... F 2
99501 Whittier, 130 .... C 1
99688 Willow, 38 .... B 1
† 99615 Woody Island, 41 .... H 3
99929 Wrangell, 2,029 .... N 2
99689 Yakutat, 190 .... L 3

⊙ Court House
† Zip of nearest p.o.
* Multiple zips

Arthur A. Twomey — Shostal Associates

Despite its deceptively calm exterior, the Vaughan Lewis Glacier is actually a river of ice, hundreds of feet deep, flowing steadily. Ridges (eskers) are formed by streams under the ice.

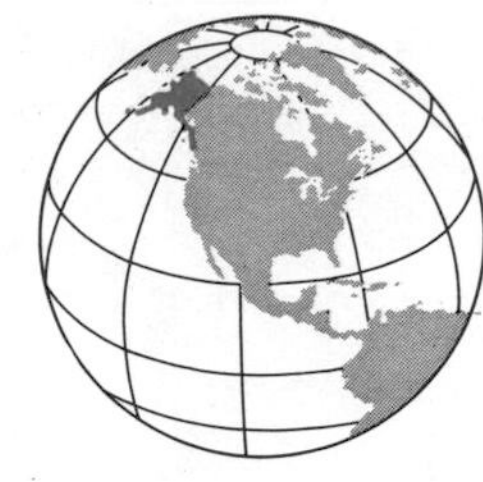

AREA 586,412 sq. mi.
POPULATION 302,173
CAPITAL Juneau
LARGEST CITY Anchorage
HIGHEST POINT Mt. McKinley 20,320 ft.
SETTLED IN 1801
ADMITTED TO UNION January 3, 1959
POPULAR NAME Great Land
STATE FLOWER Forget-me-not
STATE BIRD Willow Ptarmigan

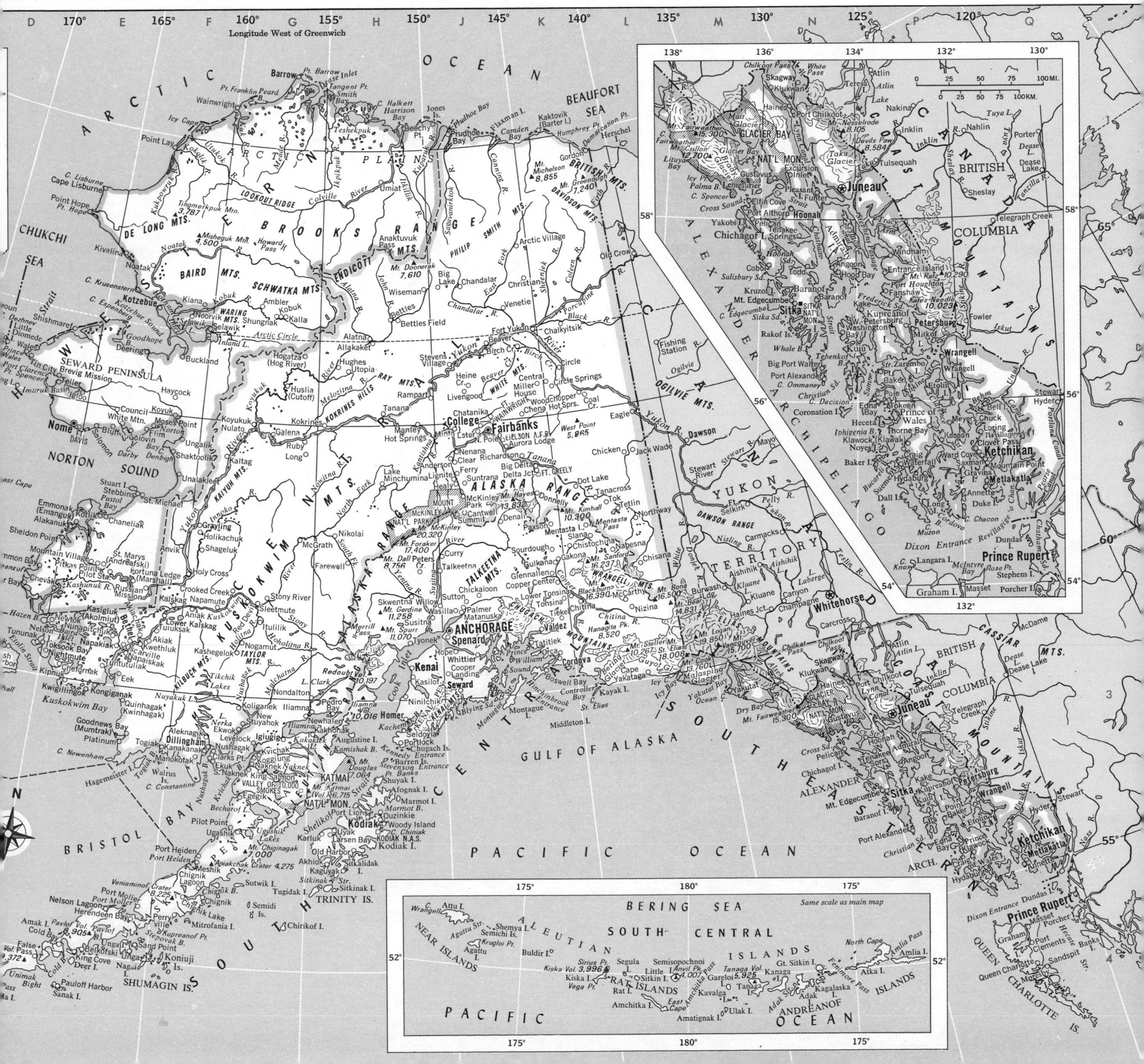

Longitude West of Greenwich

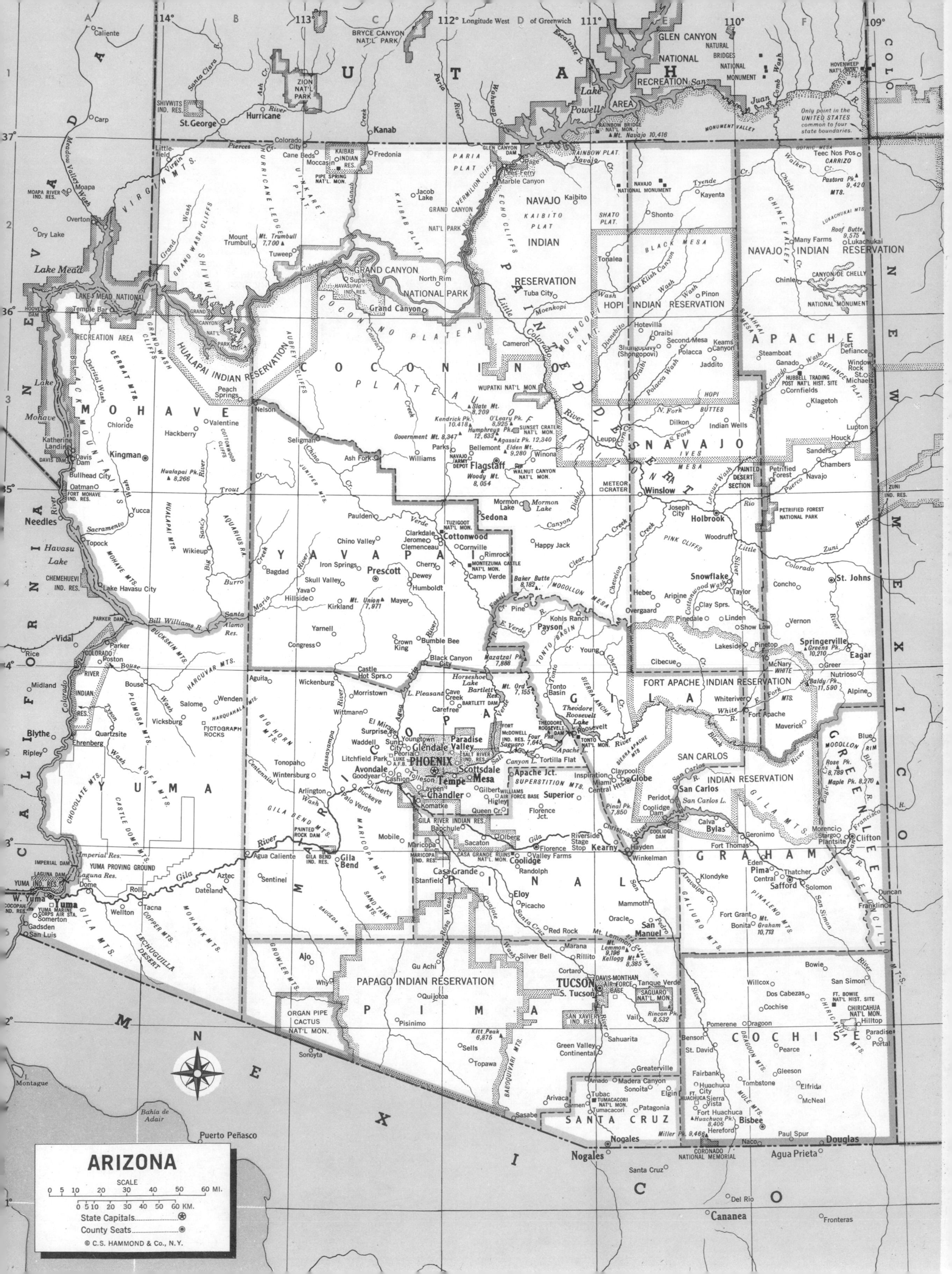
ARIZONA
SCALE
0 5 10 20 30 40 50 60 MI.
0 5 10 20 30 40 50 60 KM.
State Capitals
County Seats
© C.S. HAMMOND & Co., N.Y.
114°
113°
112° Longitude West of Greenwich
111°
110°
109°
37°
36°
35°
34°
33°
32°
31°
A
B
C
D
E
F
U T A H
N E V A D A
C A L I F O R N I A
N E W M E X I C O
C O L O.
M E X I C O
M O H A V E
C O C O N I N O
Y A V A P A I
N A V A J O
A P A C H E
G I L A
M A R I C O P A
Y U M A
P I N A L
P I M A
G R A H A M
G R E E N L E E
C O C H I S E
S A N T A C R U Z
PHOENIX
TUCSON
S. Tucson
Flagstaff
Prescott
Kingman
Yuma
Mesa
Tempe
Scottsdale
Glendale
Chandler
Globe
Holbrook
Winslow
St. Johns
Safford
Clifton
Bisbee
Douglas
Nogales
Florence
Coolidge
Casa Grande
Eloy
Ajo
Sedona
Cottonwood
Payson
Snowflake
Show Low
Springerville
Eagar
Sierra Vista
Needles
Parker
Blythe
Lake Havasu City
Bullhead City
Page
Tuba City
Kayenta
Chinle
Window Rock
Fort Defiance
Ganado
St. George
Hurricane
Kanab
Fredonia
Grand Canyon
North Rim
GRAND CANYON NATIONAL PARK
GLEN CANYON NATIONAL RECREATION AREA
Lake Powell
Lake Mead
LAKE MEAD NATIONAL RECREATION AREA
ZION NAT'L PARK
BRYCE CANYON NAT'L PARK
NATURAL BRIDGES NATIONAL MONUMENT
HOVENWEEP NAT'L MON.
Only point in the UNITED STATES common to four state boundaries.
MONUMENT VALLEY
RAINBOW BRIDGE NAT'L MON.
Mt. Navajo 10,416
NAVAJO NATIONAL MONUMENT
NAVAJO INDIAN RESERVATION
HOPI INDIAN RESERVATION
HUALAPAI INDIAN RESERVATION
HAVASUPAI IND. RES.
KAIBAB INDIAN RES.
PIPE SPRING NAT'L MON.
CANYON DE CHELLY NATIONAL MONUMENT
HUBBELL TRADING POST NAT'L HIST. SITE
PETRIFIED FOREST NATIONAL PARK
PAINTED DESERT SECTION
METEOR CRATER
WUPATKI NAT'L MON.
SUNSET CRATER NAT'L MON.
WALNUT CANYON NAT'L MON.
TUZIGOOT NAT'L MON.
MONTEZUMA CASTLE NAT'L MON.
FORT APACHE INDIAN RESERVATION
SAN CARLOS INDIAN RESERVATION
COLORADO RIVER INDIAN RES.
FORT MOHAVE IND. RES.
CHEMEHUEVI IND. RES.
SALT RIVER IND. RES.
FORT McDOWELL IND. RES.
GILA RIVER INDIAN RES.
MARICOPA IND. RES.
GILA BEND IND. RES.
PAPAGO INDIAN RESERVATION
SAN XAVIER IND. RES.
ORGAN PIPE CACTUS NAT'L MON.
SAGUARO NAT'L MON.
TUMACACORI NAT'L MON.
CHIRICAHUA NAT'L MON.
FT. BOWIE NAT'L HIST. SITE
CORONADO NATIONAL MEMORIAL
CASA GRANDE RUINS NAT'L MON.
YUMA PROVING GROUND
LUKE A.F.B.
WILLIAMS AIR FORCE BASE
DAVIS-MONTHAN AIR FORCE
NAVAJO ARMY DEPOT
PAINTED DESERT
MOGOLLON RIM
COCONINO PLATEAU
KAIBAB PLAT.
KAIBITO PLAT.
BLACK MESA
VERMILION CLIFFS
ECHO CLIFFS
TONTO BASIN
Humphreys Pk. 12,633
Agassiz Pk. 12,340
Mt. Trumbull 7,700
Hualapai Pk. 8,266
Mt. Union 7,971
Baldy Pk. 11,590
Mt. Graham 10,713
Mt. Lemmon 9,196
Miller Pk. 9,466
Mazatzal Pk. 7,888
Kitt Peak 6,875
Rincon Pk. 8,532
Colorado
Gila
Salt
Verde
Little Colorado
Bill Williams R.
San Pedro
Santa Cruz
Puerto Peñasco
Bahía de Adair
Agua Prieta
Cananea
Santa Cruz
Sonoyta
Montague

Topography

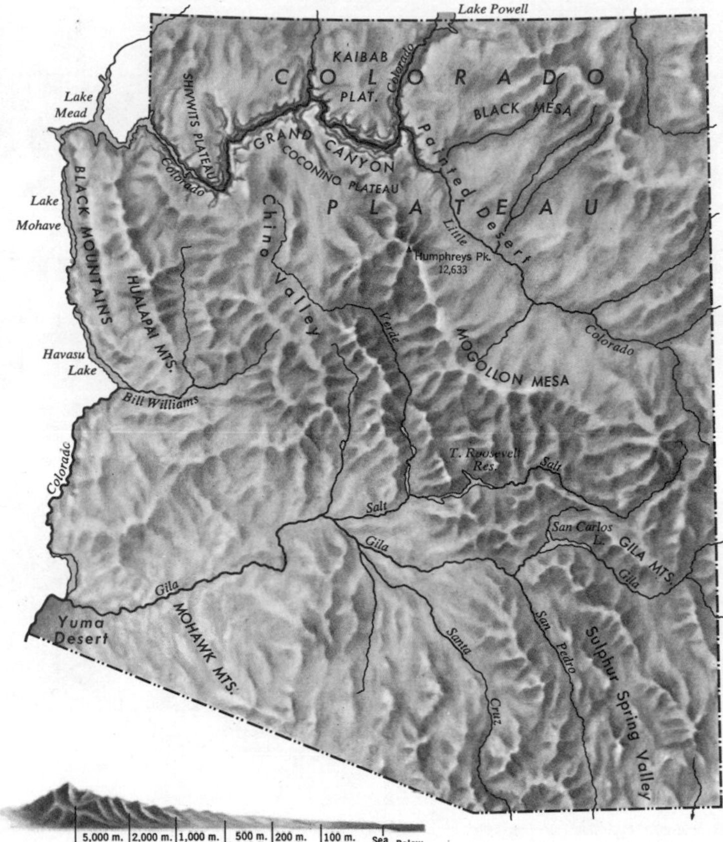

AREA 113,909 sq. mi.
POPULATION 1,772,482
CAPITAL Phoenix
LARGEST CITY Phoenix
HIGHEST POINT Humphreys Pk. 12,633 ft.
SETTLED IN 1580
ADMITTED TO UNION February 14, 1912
POPULAR NAME Grand Canyon State
STATE FLOWER Saguaro Cactus Blossom
STATE BIRD Cactus Wren

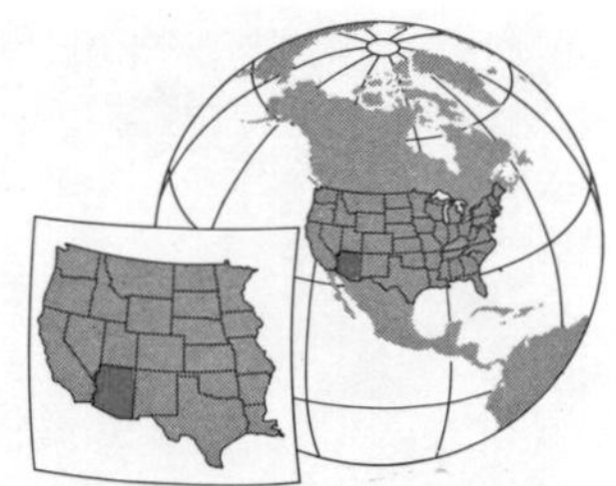

Agriculture, Industry and Resources

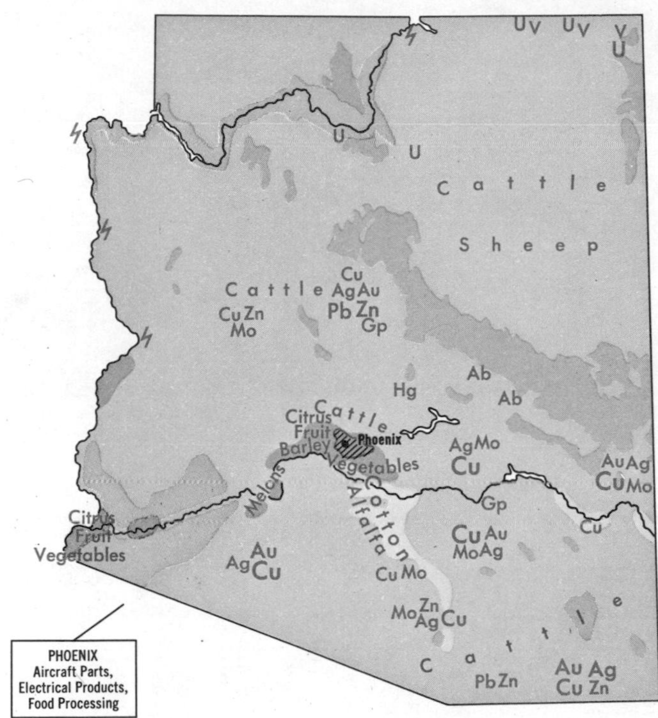

MAJOR MINERAL OCCURRENCES

Ab	Asbestos	Gp	Gypsum	U	Uranium
Ag	Silver	Hg	Mercury	V	Vanadium
Au	Gold	Mo	Molybdenum	Zn	Zinc
Cu	Copper	Pb	Lead		

DOMINANT LAND USE

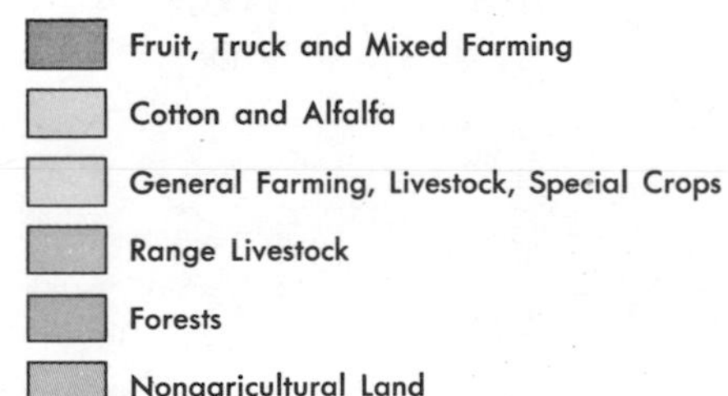

- Fruit, Truck and Mixed Farming
- Cotton and Alfalfa
- General Farming, Livestock, Special Crops
- Range Livestock
- Forests
- Nonagricultural Land

ϟ Water Power

Major Industrial Areas

COUNTIES

Name/Pop.	Key
Apache, 32,298	F 3
Cochise, 61,910	F 7
Coconino, 48,326	C 3
Gila, 29,255	E 5
Graham, 16,578	E 6
Greenlee, 10,330	F 5
Maricopa, 967,522	C 5
Mohave, 25,857	A 3
Navajo, 47,715	E 3
Pima, 351,667	D 6
Pinal, 67,916	D 6
Santa Cruz, 13,966	E 7
Yavapai, 36,733	C 4
Yuma, 60,827	A 5

CITIES and TOWNS

Zip	Name/Pop.	Key
85333	Agua Caliente, 30	B 6
85320	Aguila, 450	B 5
85321	Ajo, 5,881	C 6
85920	Alpine, 450	F 5
85640	Amado, 75	D 7
85220	Apache Junction, 2,390	D 5
85901	Aripine, 25	E 4
85601	Arivaca, 165	D 7
85322	Arlington, 950	C 5
86320	Ash Fork, 800	C 3
85323	Avondale, 6,304	C 5
85333	Aztec, 20	B 6
86321	Bagdad, 2,079	B 4
85221	Bapchule, 300	D 5
86001	Bellemont, 6	D 3
85602	Benson, 2,839	E 7
85603	Bisbee⊙, 8,328	F 7
85324	Black Canyon City, 600	C 4
85922	Blue, 50	F 5
85643	Bonita, 20	E 6
85325	Bouse, 200	A 5
85605	Bowie, 600	F 6
85326	Buckeye, 2,599	C 5
86430	Bullhead City, 2,900	A 3
85327	Bumble Bee, 15	C 4
85530	Bylas, 1,125	E 5
85530	Calva, 10	E 5
86020	Cameron, 600	D 3
86322	Camp Verde, 1,500	D 4
86022	Cane Beds, 30	B 2
85331	Carefree, 350	D 5
85640	Carmen, 200	D 7
85222	Casa Grande, 10,536	D 6
85329	Cashion, 2,705	C 5
85342	Castle Hot Springs, 50	C 5
85331	Cave Creek, 300	D 5
85531	Central, 300	F 6
85501	Central Heights, 2,289	E 5
86502	Chambers, 500	F 3
85224	Chandler, 13,763	D 5
† 86327	Cherry, 20	C 4
86503	Chinle, 500	F 2
86323	Chino Valley, 970	C 4
86431	Chloride, 225	A 3
† 85292	Christmas, 201	E 5
85901	Cibecue, 100	E 4
86324	Clarkdale, 892	C 4
85532	Claypool, 2,245	E 5
† 85934	Clay Springs, 225	E 4
† 86326	Clemenceau, 300	C 4
85533	Clifton⊙, 5,087	F 5
85606	Cochise, 150	F 6
86021	Colorado City, 350	B 2
85924	Concho, 100	F 4
85332	Congress, 350	C 4
† 85640	Continental, 250	D 7
85228	Coolidge, 4,651	D 6
† 85542	Coolidge Dam, 42	E 5
† 86505	Cornfields, 200	F 3
86325	Cornville, 425	D 4
85230	Cortaro, 75	D 6
86326	Cottonwood, 2,815	D 4
86333	Crown King, 100	C 4
85333	Dateland, 100	B 6
† 86430	Davis Dam, 125	A 3
86327	Dewey, 100	C 4
† 86047	Dilkon, 90	E 3
† 85364	Dome, 48	A 6
† 85643	Dos Cabezas, 30	F 6
85607	Douglas, 12,462	F 7
85609	Dragoon, 150	F 6
85534	Duncan, 773	F 6
85925	Eagar, 1,279	F 4
85535	Eden, 89	F 6
85334	Ehrenburg, 93	A 5
† 85617	Elfrida, 700	F 7
† 85637	Elgin, 247	E 7
85335	El Mirage, 3,258	C 5
85231	Eloy, 5,381	D 6
85612	Fairbank, 100	E 7
86001	Flagstaff⊙, 26,117	D 3
85232	Florence⊙, 2,173	D 5
85233	Florence Junction, 35	D 5
85926	Fort Apache, 500	F 5
86504	Fort Defiance, 900	F 3
85643	Fort Grant, 240	E 6
85613	Fort Huachuca, 159	E 7
85536	Fort Thomas, 450	E 5
85534	Franklin, 300	F 6
86022	Fredonia, 798	C 2
85336	Gadsden, 250	A 6
86505	Ganado, 300	F 3
† 85536	Geronimo, 25	F 5
85337	Gila Bend, 1,795	C 6
85234	Gilbert, 1,971	D 5
† 85617	Gleeson, 15	F 7
85301	Glendale, 36,228	C 5
85501	Globe⊙, 7,333	E 5
85338	Goodyear, 2,140	C 5
86023	Grand Canyon, 1,011	C 2
† 85637	Greaterville, 15	E 7
85614	Green Valley, 5,971	D 7
85927	Greer, 60	F 4
† 85634	Gu-Achi, 339	C 6
86401	Hackberry, 250	B 3
86024	Happy Jack, 50	D 4
85235	Hayden, 1,283	E 5
85928	Heber, 750	E 4
85615	Hereford, 10	E 7
85236	Higley, 500	D 5
† 86301	Hillside, 100	B 4
† 85632	Hilltop, 9	F 6
86025	Holbrook⊙, 4,759	E 4
86030	Hotevilla, 600	E 3
86506	Houck, 325	F 3
85616	Huachuca City, 1,233	E 7
86329	Humboldt, 424	C 4
86031	Indian Wells, 150	E 3
85537	Inspiration, 500	D 5
86330	Iron Springs, 175	C 4
86022	Jacob Lake, 16	C 2
† 86025	Jeddito, 20	E 3
86331	Jerome, 290	C 4
86032	Joseph City, 650	E 4
86044	Kaibito, 275	D 2
† 86401	Katherine Landing, 102	A 3
86033	Kayenta, 500	E 2
86034	Keams Canyon, 400	E 3
85237	Kearny, 2,829	E 5
86401	Kingman⊙, 7,312	A 3
86332	Kirkland, 100	C 4
† 86505	Klagetoh, 200	F 3
85643	Klondyke, 86	E 6
85538	Kohls Ranch, 100	D 4
† 85339	Komatke, 300	C 5
86403	Lake Havasu City, 5,700	A 4
85929	Lakeside, 700	E 4
85339	Laveen, 800	C 5
† 86036	Lees Ferry, 10	D 2
86035	Leupp, 150	E 3
† 85326	Liberty, 150	C 5
† 85901	Linden, 50	E 4
85340	Litchfield Park, 1,664	C 5
86432	Littlefield, 40	B 2
86507	Lukachukai, 350	F 2
85341	Lukeville, 50	C 7
86508	Lupton, 250	F 3
† 85637	Madera Canyon, 75	E 7
85618	Mammoth, 1,953	E 6
86503	Many Farms, 250	F 2
85238	Marana, 2,900	D 6
86036	Marble Canyon, 6	D 2
85239	Maricopa, 750	C 5
† 85920	Maverick, 50	F 5
86333	Mayer, 810	C 4
85930	McNary, 950	F 4
85617	McNeal, 100	F 7

(continued on following page)

(continued)

Ray Manley — Shostal Associates

Indigo-blue Lake Mead is surrounded by color-streaked cliffs and ranges, set off by the bright concrete of Arizona's Hoover Dam. One of the world's largest man-made lakes, Lake Mead provides water storage, dependable water supply and water sports.

* 85201 Mesa, 62,853 D 5
85539 Miami, 3,394 E 5
† 85239 Mobile, 100 C 5
86022 Moccasin, 60 C 2
85540 Morenci, 950 F 5
86038 Mormon Lake, 20 D 4
85342 Morristown, 250 C 5
85619 Mount Lemmon, 75 E 6
† 84770 Mount Trumbull, 14 B 2
85620 Naco, 750 E 7
86509 Navajo, 100 F 3
† 86434 Nelson, 39 B 3
85621 Nogales⊙, 8,946 E 7
86022 North Rim, 2 C 2
85932 Nutrioso, 67 F 5
86433 Oatman, 175 A 3
† 85247 Olberg, 65 D 5
85623 Oracle, 1,500 E 6
86039 Oraibi, 600 E 3
85933 Overgaard, 300 E 4
86040 Page, 1,439 D 2
85343 Palo Verde, 500 C 5
85253 Paradise Valley, 7,155 D 5
85344 Parker, 1,948 A 4
86001 Parks, 175 C 3
85624 Patagonia, 630 E 7
86334 Paulden, 4 C 4
† 85607 Paul Spur, 34 F 7
85541 Payson, 1,490 D 4
86434 Peach Springs, 525 B 3
85625 Pearce, 300 F 7
85345 Peoria, 4,792 C 5
85542 Peridot, 950 E 5
86025 Petrified Forest, 80 F 3
* 85001 Phoenix (cap.)⊙, 581,562 C 5
Phoenix, ‡967,522 C 5
85241 Picacho, 1,200 D 6
85543 Pima, 1,184 F 6
85544 Pine, 800 D 4
85934 Pinedale, 86 E 4
85935 Pinetop, 950 F 4
86510 Pinon, 100 E 2
85634 Pisinimo, 187 C 6
† 85540 Plantsite, 1,077 F 5
86042 Polacca, 500 E 3
85627 Pomerene, 365 E 6
85632 Portal, 72 F 7
85371 Poston, 500 A 4
86301 Prescott⊙, 13,030 C 4
85346 Quartzsite, 255 A 5
85242 Queen Creek, 600 D 5
† 85634 Quijotoa, 107 C 6
85243 Randolph, 350 D 6
85245 Red Rock, 100 D 6
85246 Rillito, 400 D 6
86335 Rimrock, 217 D 4
85237 Riverside Stage Stop, 418 D 5
85347 Roll, 700 A 6
85545 Roosevelt, 125 D 5
85247 Sacaton, 300 D 5
85546 Safford⊙, 5,333 F 6
85629 Sahuarita, 200 E 7
85630 Saint David, 1,250 E 7
85936 Saint Johns⊙, 1,320 F 4
86511 Saint Michaels, 250 F 3
85348 Salome, 684 B 5
85550 San Carlos, 2,542 E 5
86512 Sanders, 420 F 3
85349 San Luis, 280 A 6
85631 San Manuel, 4,332 E 6
85632 San Simon, 400 F 6
85633 Sasabe, 50 D 7
* 85251 Scottsdale, 67,823 D 5
86043 Second Mesa, 30 E 3
86336 Sedona, 2,022 D 4
86337 Seligman, 950 B 3
85634 Sells, 1,245 D 7
† 85333 Sentinel, 20 B 6
86044 Shonto, 700 E 2
85901 Show Low, 2,285 F 4
† 86043 Shungopavy (Shongopovi), 570 E 3
85635 Sierra Vista, 6,689 E 7
85270 Silver Bell, 900 D 6
86338 Skull Valley, 250 C 4
85937 Snowflake, 1,833 E 4
85551 Solomon, 700 F 6
85350 Somerton, 2,225 A 6
85637 Sonoita, 50 E 7
85713 South Tucson, 6,220 D 6
85938 Springerville, 1,038 F 4
85272 Stanfield, 150 C 6
† 85540 Stargo, 1,194 F 5
† 86505 Steamboat, 100 F 3
85351 Sun City, 13,670 D 5
86435 Supai, 190 C 2
85273 Superior, 4,975 D 5
85352 Tacna, 950 B 6
† 85701 Tanque Verde, 850 E 6
85939 Taylor, 888 E 4
86514 Teec Nos Pos, 550 F 2
85281 Tempe, 62,907 D 5
86443 Temple Bar, 84 A 2
85552 Thatcher, 2,320 F 6
85353 Tolleson, 3,881 C 5
85638 Tombstone, 1,241 F 7
86044 Tonalea, 125 E 2
85354 Tonopah, 54 B 5
85553 Tonto Basin, 69 D 5
85639 Topawa, 500 D 7
86436 Topock, 325 A 4
85290 Tortilla Flat, 37 D 5
85640 Tubac, 140 E 7
86045 Tuba City, 2,500 D 2
* 85701 Tucson⊙, 262,933 D 6
Tucson, ‡351,667 D 6
85640 Tumacacori, 100 D 7
† 84770 Tuweep, 14 B 2
85641 Vail, 175 E 6
86437 Valentine, 120 B 3
85291 Valley Farms, 240 D 6
85940 Vernon, 75 F 4
† 85348 Vicksburg, 16 B 5
85355 Waddell, 100 C 5
85356 Wellton, 900 A 6
85357 Wenden, 245 B 5
† 85364 West Yuma, 5,552 A 6
85941 Whiteriver, 900 E 5
85321 Why, 65 C 6
85358 Wickenburg, 2,698 C 5
85360 Wikieup, 150 B 4
85643 Willcox, 2,568 F 6
86046 Williams, 2,386 C 3
86515 Window Rock, 600 F 3
85292 Winkelman, 974 E 6
† 86001 Winona, 25 D 3
86047 Winslow, 8,066 E 3
† 85322 Wintersburg, 400 B 5
85361 Wittmann, 600 C 5
85942 Woodruff, 120 E 4
85362 Yarnell, 800 C 4
† 86301 Yava, 40 C 4
85554 Young, 197 D 4
85363 Youngtown, 1,886 C 5
86438 Yucca, 250 A 4
85364 Yuma⊙, 29,007 A 6

⊙ County seat.
‡ Population of metropolitan area.
† Zip of nearest p.o.
* Multiple zips

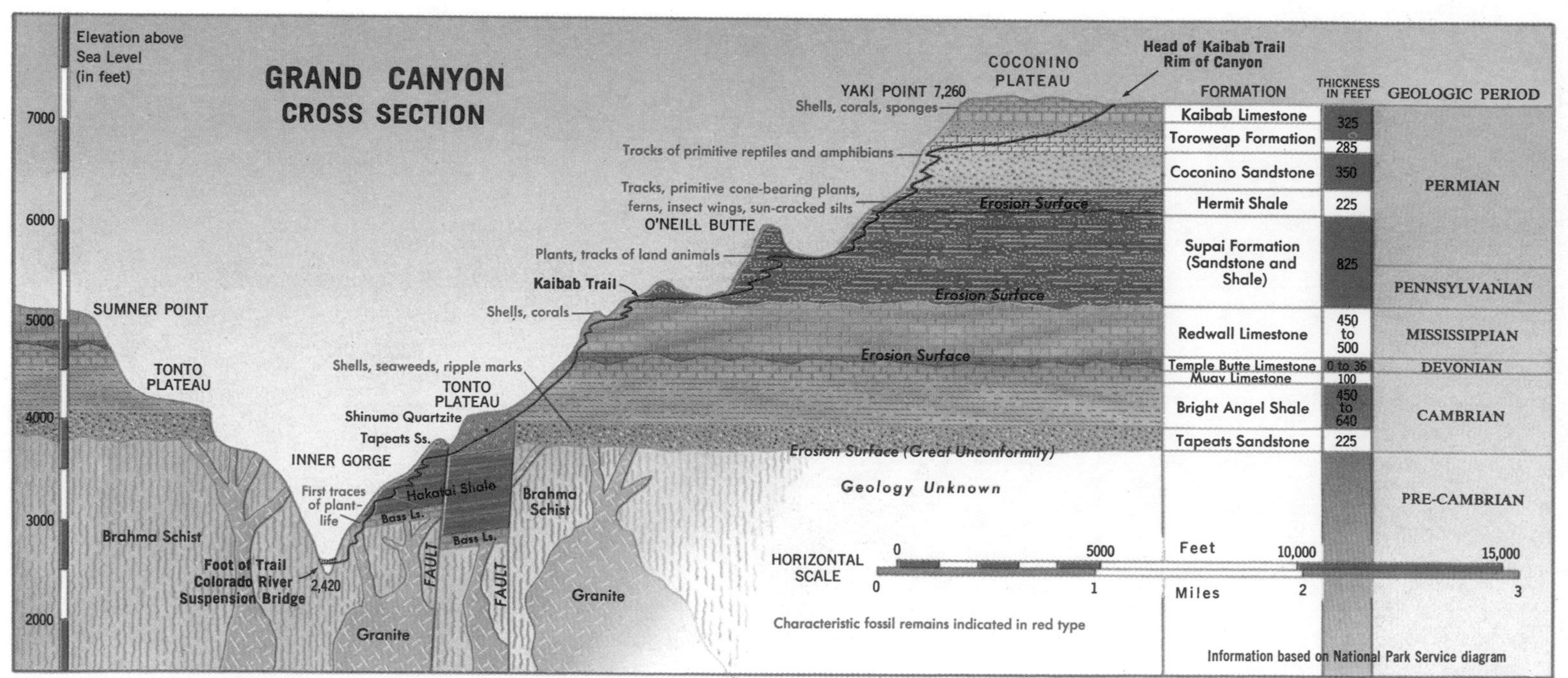

COUNTIES

Arkansas, 23,347 ... H 5
Ashley, 24,976 ... G 7
Baxter, 15,319 ... F 1
Benton, 50,476 ... B 1
Boone, 19,073 ... D 1
Bradley, 12,778 ... F 7
Calhoun, 5,573 ... E 6
Carroll, 12,301 ... C 1
Chicot, 18,164 ... H 7
Clark, 21,537 ... D 5
Clay, 18,771 ... K 1
Cleburne, 10,349 ... F 2
Cleveland, 6,605 ... F 6
Columbia, 25,952 ... D 7
Conway, 16,805 ... E 3
Craighead, 52,068 ... J 2
Crawford, 25,677 ... B 2
Crittenden, 48,106 ... K 3
Cross, 19,783 ... J 3
Dallas, 10,022 ... E 6
Desha, 18,761 ... H 6
Drew, 15,157 ... G 6
Faulkner, 31,572 ... F 3
Franklin, 11,301 ... C 2
Fulton, 7,699 ... G 1
Garland, 54,131 ... D 4
Grant, 9,711 ... F 5
Greene, 24,765 ... J 1
Hempstead, 19,308 ... C 6
Hot Spring, 21,963 ... E 5
Howard, 11,412 ... C 5
Independence, 22,723 ... G 2
Izard, 7,381 ... G 1
Jackson, 20,452 ... H 2
Jefferson, 85,329 ... G 5
Johnson, 13,630 ... C 2
Lafayette, 10,018 ... C 7
Lawrence, 16,320 ... H 1
Lee, 18,884 ... J 4
Lincoln, 12,913 ... G 6
Little River, 11,194 ... B 6
Logan, 16,789 ... C 3
Lonoke, 26,249 ... G 4
Madison, 9,453 ... C 1
Marion, 7,000 ... E 1
Miller, 33,385 ... C 7
Mississippi, 62,060 ... K 2
Monroe, 15,657 ... H 4
Montgomery, 5,821 ... C 4
Nevada, 10,111 ... D 6
Newton, 5,844 ... D 2
Ouachita, 30,896 ... E 6
Perry, 5,634 ... E 4
Phillips, 40,046 ... J 5
Pike, 8,711 ... C 5
Poinsett, 26,822 ... J 2
Polk, 13,297 ... B 5
Pope, 28,607 ... D 3
Prairie, 10,249 ... G 4
Pulaski, 287,189 ... F 4
Randolph, 12,645 ... H 1
Saint Francis, 30,799 ... J 3
Saline, 36,107 ... E 4
Scott, 8,207 ... B 4
Searcy, 7,731 ... E 2
Sebastian, 79,237 ... B 3
Sevier, 11,272 ... B 6
Sharp, 8,233 ... G 1
Stone, 6,838 ... F 2
Union, 45,428 ... E 7
Van Buren, 8,275 ... E 2
Washington, 77,370 ... B 2
White, 39,253 ... G 3
Woodruff, 11,566 ... H 3
Yell, 14,208 ... D 3

AREA 53,104 sq. mi.
POPULATION 1,923,295
CAPITAL Little Rock
LARGEST CITY Little Rock
HIGHEST POINT Magazine Mtn. 2,753 ft.
SETTLED IN 1685
ADMITTED TO UNION June 15, 1836
POPULAR NAME Land of Opportunity; Wonder State
STATE FLOWER Apple Blossom
STATE BIRD Mockingbird

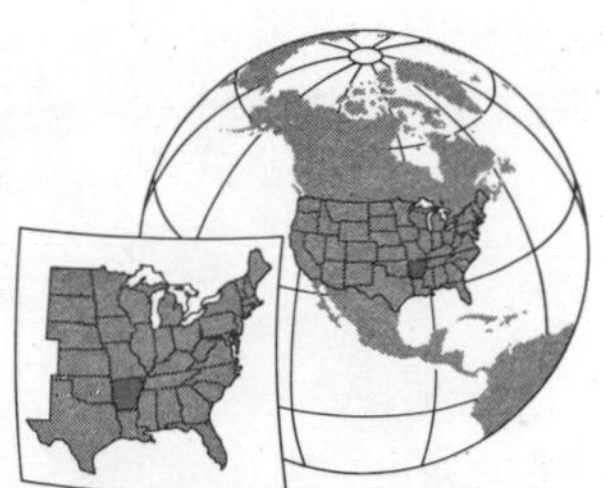

Agriculture, Industry and Resources

DOMINANT LAND USE

- Fruit and Mixed Farming
- Specialized Cotton
- Cotton, General Farming
- Rice, General Farming
- General Farming, Livestock, Truck Farming, Cotton
- Forests
- Swampland, Limited Agriculture

MAJOR MINERAL OCCURRENCES

Al	Bauxite	G	Natural Gas
Ba	Barite	Gp	Gypsum
C	Coal	Mr	Marble
Cl	Clay	O	Petroleum
D	Diamonds	Sp	Soapstone
Zn	Zinc		

Water Power — Major Industrial Areas

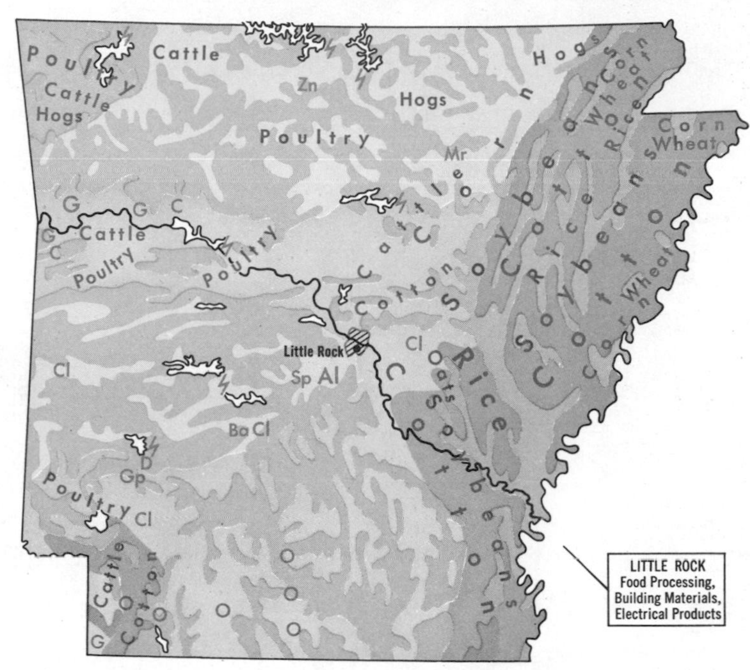

Eric Carle — Shostal Associates

Soybeans, Arkansas' leading cash crop, valued primarily as high protein food and feed, also has a wide range of uses, including plastics and agricultural sprays.

CITIES and TOWNS

Zip Name/Pop. Key

72920 Abbott, 210 ... B 3
72001 Adona, 204 ... E 3
72510 Agnos, 130 ... G 1
72002 Alexander, 297 ... F 4
72410 Alicia, 246 ... H 2
72820 Alix, 250 ... C 3
† 72046 Allport, 307 ... G 4
72921 Alma, 1,613 ... B 3
72003 Almyra, 220 ... H 5
72611 Alpena, 309 ... D 1
72004 Altheimer, 1,037 ... G 5
72821 Altus, 418 ... C 3
72005 Amagon, 136 ... H 2
71921 Amity, 614 ... D 5
71922 Antoine, 182 ... D 5
72822 Appleton, 150 ... E 3
71923 Arkadelphia⊙, 9,841 ... D 5
71630 Arkansas City⊙, 615 ... H 6
† 72055 Arkansas Post, 15 ... H 5
72310 Armorel, 300 ... L 2
71822 Ashdown⊙, 3,522 ... B 6
72513 Ash Flat⊙, 211 ... G 1
72823 Atkins, 2,015 ... E 3
72311 Aubrey, 351 ... J 4
72006 Augusta⊙, 2,777 ... H 3
72007 Austin, 236 ... G 4
72008 Auvergne, 150 ... H 2
72711 Avoca, 173 ... B 1
72010 Bald Knob, 2,094 ... G 3
71631 Banks, 189 ... F 6
72923 Barling, 1,739 ... B 3
72312 Barton, 400 ... J 4
72313 Bassett, 265 ... K 2
72501 Batesville⊙, 7,209 ... G 2
72411 Bay, 751 ... J 2
71720 Bearden, 1,272 ... E 6
72012 Beebe, 2,805 ... G 3
72014 Beedeville, 144 ... H 3
71721 Beirne, 140 ... D 6
72712 Bella Vista, 500 ... B 1
† 72601 Bellefonte, 300 ... D 1
72824 Belleville, 379 ... D 3
71823 Ben Lomond, 155 ... B 6
72015 Benton⊙, 16,499 ... E 4
72712 Bentonville⊙, 5,508 ... B 1
72615 Bergman, 249 ... E 1
72616 Berryville⊙, 2,271 ... C 1
† 72764 Bethel Heights, 284 ... B 1
† 72501 Bethesda, 285 ... G 2
72016 Bigelow, 258 ... E 3
72617 Bigflat, 189 ... F 1
72413 Biggers, 372 ... J 1
† 72386 Birdsong, 150 ... K 3
72017 Biscoe, 340 ... H 4
71929 Bismarck, 200 ... D 5
72414 Black Oak, 272 ... K 2
72415 Black Rock, 498 ... H 1
† 72069 Blackton, 175 ... H 4
71825 Blevins, 265 ... C 6
† 72933 Bloomer, 150 ... B 3
71722 Bluff City, 244 ... D 6
72827 Bluffton, 198 ... C 4
72315 Blytheville⊙, 24,752 ... L 2
† 71858 Bodcaw, 158 ... D 6
72926 Boles, 163 ... B 4
† 72901 Bonanza, 342 ... B 3
72416 Bono, 428 ... J 2
72927 Booneville⊙, 3,239 ... C 3
72020 Bradford, 826 ... G 3
71826 Bradley, 706 ... C 7
72928 Branch, 325 ... C 3
† 72017 Brasfield, 200 ... H 4
72828 Briggsville, 200 ... C 4
72021 Brinkley, 5,275 ... H 4
72417 Brookland, 465 ... J 2
72618 Bruno, 130 ... E 1
72022 Bryant, 1,199 ... F 4
71827 Buckner, 392 ... D 7
72619 Bull Shoals, 430 ... E 1
72321 Burdette, 173 ... L 2
72023 Cabot, 2,903 ... F 4
71935 Caddo Gap, 125 ... C 5
72322 Caldwell, 292 ... J 3
72519 Calico Rock, 723 ... F 1
71724 Calion, 535 ... E 7
71701 Camden⊙, 15,147 ... E 6
† 72201 Cammack Village, 1,165 ... E 4
† 72473 Campbell Station, 218 ... H 2
71829 Canfield, 365 ... C 7
72419 Caraway, 952 ... K 2
72024 Carlisle, 2,048 ... G 4
71725 Carthage, 566 ... E 5
72025 Casa, 208 ... D 3
72421 Cash, 265 ... J 2
72026 Casscoe, 200 ... H 4
† 72951 Caulksville, 208 ... C 3
72521 Cave City, 807 ... G 2
72718 Cave Springs, 469 ... B 1
72930 Cecil, 234 ... C 3
72450 Center Hill, 1,201 ... J 1
71830 Center Point, 144 ... C 5
72027 Center Ridge, 220 ... E 3
72719 Centerton, 312 ... B 1
71901 Central City, 150 ... B 3
† 71832 Chapel Hill, 154 ... B 5
72933 Charleston⊙, 1,497 ... B 3
72522 Charlotte, 158 ... H 2
72323 Chatfield, 150 ... K 3
72542 Cherokee Village, 1,300 ... G 1
† 71953 Cherry Hill, 250 ... B 4
72324 Cherry Valley, 556 ... J 3
71726 Chidester, 232 ... D 6
72029 Clarendon⊙, 2,563 ... H 4
72325 Clarkedale, 250 ... K 3
72830 Clarksville⊙, 4,616 ... D 3
72031 Clinton⊙, 1,029 ... F 2
72832 Coal Hill, 733 ... C 3
72476 College City, 645 ... J 1
71655 College Heights, 2,050 ... G 6
72326 Colt, 301 ... J 3
71831 Columbus, 258 ... C 6
72523 Concord, 163 ... G 2
72032 Conway⊙, 15,510 ... F 3
72422 Corning⊙, 2,705 ... J 1
72626 Cotter, 858 ... E 1
72036 Cotton Plant, 1,657 ... H 3
71937 Cove, 334 ... B 5
72037 Coy, 240 ... G 4
72327 Crawfordsville, 831 ... K 3
71635 Crossett, 6,191 ... G 7
71728 Curtis, 500 ... D 6
72526 Cushman, 427 ... G 2
† 71923 Dalark, 132 ... E 5
72039 Damascus, 255 ... F 3
72833 Danville⊙, 1,362 ... D 3
72834 Dardanelle⊙, 3,297 ... D 3
72424 Datto, 142 ... J 1
72722 Decatur, 847 ... A 1
72723 Delaney, 150 ... C 2
72425 Delaplaine, 145 ... J 1
72835 Delaware, 200 ... D 3
71940 Delight, 439 ... C 5
72426 Dell, 358 ... K 2
72836 Denning, 203 ... C 3
71832 De Queen⊙, 3,863 ... B 5
71638 Dermott, 4,250 ... H 7
72040 Des Arc⊙, 1,714 ... G 4
72041 De Valls Bluff⊙, 622 ... H 4
72042 De Witt⊙, 3,728 ... H 5
72644 Diamond City, 282 ... E 1
72043 Diaz, 283 ... H 2
71833 Dierks, 1,101 ... B 5
71834 Doddridge, 125 ... C 7
71941 Donaldson, 500 ... E 5
72837 Dover, 662 ... D 3
72530 Drasco, 300 ... G 2
† 72943 Driggs, 125 ... C 3
71639 Dumas, 4,600 ... H 6
72935 Dyer, 486 ... B 3
71729 Eagle Mills, 149 ... E 6
72331 Earle, 3,146 ... K 3
71701 East Camden, 589 ... E 6
72044 Edgemont, 125 ... F 2
72332 Edmondson, 412 ... K 3
72333 Elaine, 1,210 ... J 5
71730 El Dorado⊙, 25,283 ... E 7
72727 Elkins, 418 ... C 1
72728 Elm Springs, 260 ... B 1
72045 El Paso, 131 ... F 3
71740 Emerson, 393 ... D 7
71835 Emmet, 433 ... D 6

(continued on following page)

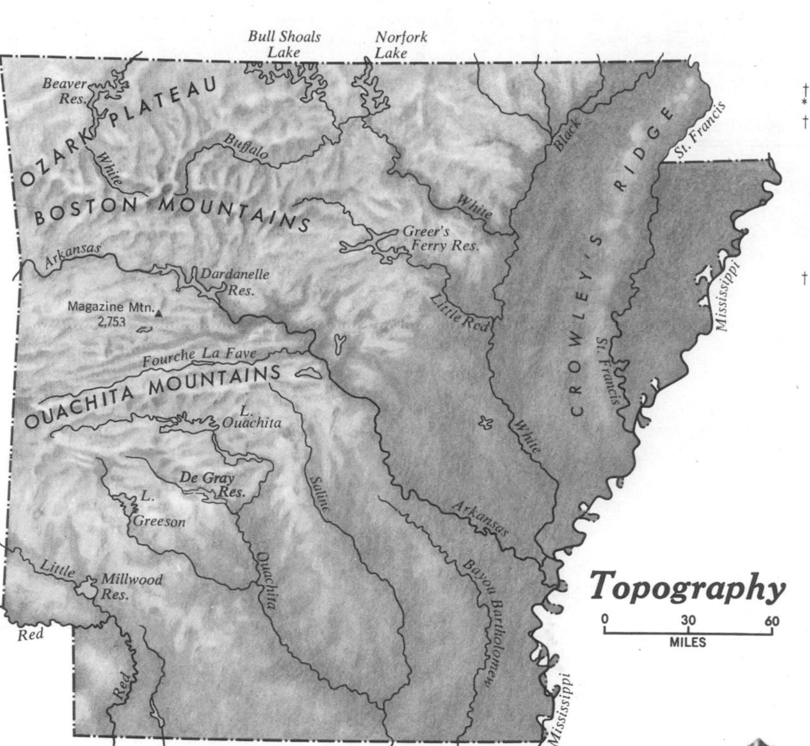

	ZIP	Place	Key
	72046	England, 3,075	G 4
	72047	Enola, 150	F 3
	72048	Ethel, 350	H 5
	72428	Etowah, 150	K 2
	71640	Eudora, 3,687	H 7
	72632	Eureka Springs⊙, 1,670	C 1
	72729	Evansville, 427	B 2
	72532	Evening Shade, 309	G 1
†	72936	Excelsior, 160	B 3
	72397	Fair Oaks, 270	J 3
	72049	Fargo, 206	H 4
	72730	Farmington, 908	B 1
	72701	Fayetteville⊙, 30,729	B 1
†	71747	Felsenthal, 150	F 7
	72429	Fisher, 361	J 2
	72634	Flippen, 626	E 1
	72534	Floral, 165	G 2
	71742	Fordyce⊙, 4,837	F 6
	71836	Foreman, 1,173	B 6
†	72031	Formosa, 224	E 3
	72335	Forrest City⊙, 12,521	J 3
	72901	Fort Smith⊙, 62,802	B 3
		Fort Smith, ‡160,421	B 3
	71837	Fouke, 506	C 7
	71642	Fountain Hill, 266	G 7
	72051	Fox, 200	F 2
	72017	Fredonia (Biscoe), 340	H 4
	71942	Friendship, 150	E 5
	71838	Fulton, 323	C 6
	72732	Garfield, 163	C 1
	71839	Garland, 321	C 7
	72052	Garner, 150	G 3
	72635	Gassville, 434	F 1
	71840	Genoa, 125	C 7
	72734	Gentry, 1,022	A 1
	72054	Georgetown, 137	G 3
	72055	Gillett, 860	H 5
	71841	Gillham, 200	B 5
	72339	Gilmore, 461	K 3
	71943	Glenwood, 1,212	C 5
	72340	Goodwin, 125	J 4
†	72315	Gosnell, 1,386	K 2
	71643	Gould, 1,683	G 6
	71644	Grady, 688	G 5
	71944	Grannis, 177	B 5
	72838	Gravelly, 300	C 4
	72736	Gravette, 1,154	B 1
	72058	Greenbrier, 582	F 3
	72638	Green Forest, 1,354	D 1
	72737	Greenland, 650	B 1
	72430	Greenway, 240	K 1
	72936	Greenwood⊙, 2,032	B 3
†	72067	Greers Ferry, 389	F 2
	72059	Gregory, 311	H 3
	72060	Griffithville, 227	G 3
	72431	Grubbs, 442	H 2
	72540	Guion, 213	G 2
†	71923	Gum Springs, 269	D 5
	71743	Gurdon, 2,075	D 6
	72061	Guy, 179	F 3
	72937	Hackett, 462	B 3
	71645	Halley, 204	H 6
	71646	Hamburg⊙, 3,102	G 7
	71744	Hampton⊙, 1,252	F 6
	72542	Hardy, 692	H 1
	71745	Harrell, 269	F 7
	72432	Harrisburg⊙, 1,931	J 2
	72601	Harrison⊙, 7,239	D 1
	72938	Hartford, 616	B 3
	72840	Hartman, 400	C 3
	72062	Haskell, 239	E 4
	71945	Hatfield, 377	B 5
	72063	Hattieville, 163	E 3
	72842	Havana, 308	D 3
	72341	Haynes, 375	J 4
	72064	Hazen, 1,605	G 4
	72543	Heber Springs⊙, 2,497	G 2
	72843	Hector, 387	E 3
	72342	Helena⊙, 10,415	J 4
	72065	Hensley, 350	F 4
	71647	Hermitage, 399	F 7
	72066	Hickory Plains, 200	G 3
	72347	Hickory Ridge, 410	J 3
	72068	Higginson, 225	G 3
	72739	Hiwasse, 175	B 1
†	72857	Hollis, 275	D 4
	72069	Holly Grove, 840	H 4
†	71923	Hollywood, 175	D 5
	72939	Hon, 250	B 4
	71801	Hope⊙, 8,810	C 6
	71842	Horatio, 748	B 6
	72536	Horseshoe Bend, 321	G 1
	71901	Hot Springs National Park⊙, 35,631	D 4
	72070	Houston, 200	E 3
	72433	Hoxie, 2,265	H 1
†	72315	Huffman, 150	L 2
	72348	Hughes, 1,872	J 4
	72349	Hulbert, 500	K 3
	72072	Humnoke, 398	G 4
	72073	Humphrey, 818	G 5
	72074	Hunter, 131	H 3
	72940	Huntington, 627	B 3
	72740	Huntsville⊙, 1,287	C 1
	71747	Huttig, 822	F 7
	72434	Imboden, 406	H 1
	72075	Jacksonport, 306	H 2
	72076	Jacksonville, 19,832	F 4
	72641	Jasper⊙, 394	D 1
	72079	Jefferson, 250	F 5
	71649	Jennie, 172	H 7
†	72901	Jenny Lind, 250	B 3
†	72327	Jericho, 150	K 3
	72080	Jerusalem, 250	E 3
	71949	Jessieville, 248	D 4
	72741	Johnson, 274	B 1
	72350	Joiner, 839	K 3
	72401	Jonesboro⊙, 27,050	J 2
	72105	Jones Mill, 850	E 5
	72081	Judsonia, 1,667	G 3
	71749	Junction City, 763	E 7
	72351	Keiser, 688	K 2
	72082	Kensett, 1,444	G 3
	72083	Keo, 226	G 4
†	72956	Kibler, 611	B 3
	71652	Kingsland, 304	F 6
	72742	Kingston, 200	C 1
	71950	Kirby, 300	C 5
	72435	Knobel, 375	J 1
	72845	Knoxville, 202	D 3
	72436	Lafe, 160	J 1
	72352	La Grange, 350	J 4
	72437	Lake City⊙, 948	K 2
	71653	Lake Village⊙, 3,310	H 7
	72846	Lamar, 589	D 3
	71929	Lambert, 200	D 5
	71844	Laneburg, 150	D 6
	71952	Langley, 200	C 5
	72941	Lavaca, 532	B 3
	71750	Lawson, 300	F 7
	72438	Leachville, 1,582	K 2
	72644	Lead Hill, 143	D 1
	72084	Leola, 390	E 5
	72354	Lepanto, 1,846	K 2
	72645	Leslie, 563	E 2
	72085	Letona, 191	G 3
	71845	Lewisville⊙, 1,653	C 7
	72355	Lexa, 500	J 4
	72646	Limestone, 200	D 2
	72744	Lincoln, 1,023	B 2
*	72201	Little Rock (cap.)⊛ 132,483	F 4
		Little Rock-North Little Rock ‡323,296	F 4
	71846	Lockesburg, 620	B 6
	72550	Locust Grove, 225	G 2
	72847	London, 539	D 3
	72086	Lonoke⊙, 3,140	G 4
	71751	Louann, 245	E 7
	72745	Lowell, 653	B 1
†	72856	Lurton, 150	D 2
	72358	Luxora, 1,566	K 2
	72440	Lynn, 274	H 2
	72103	Mabelvale, 350	F 4
†	71753	Macedonia, 150	D 7
	72359	Madison, 984	J 4
	72943	Magazine, 677	C 3
	72553	Magness, 139	H 2
†	72104	Magnet, 230	E 5
	71753	Magnolia⊙, 11,303	D 7
	72104	Malvern⊙, 8,739	E 5
	72554	Mammoth Spring, 1,072	G 1
	72442	Manila, 1,961	K 2
	72944	Mansfield, 981	B 3
	72555	Marcella, 136	G 2
†	72114	Marche, 150	F 4
	72360	Marianna⊙, 6,196	J 4
	72364	Marion⊙, 1,634	K 3
	72365	Marked Tree, 3,208	K 2
	72443	Marmaduke, 821	K 1
	72650	Marshall⊙, 1,397	E 2
	72366	Marvell, 1,980	J 4
	72106	Mayflower, 469	F 4
	72444	Maynard, 224	J 1
	72747	Maysville, 200	A 1
†	72006	McClelland, 200	H 3
	72101	McCrory, 1,378	H 3
	72441	McDougal, 328	K 1
	71654	McGehee, 4,683	H 6
	71849	McNab, 201	C 6
	71752	McNeil, 684	D 7
	72102	McRae, 643	G 3
	72556	Melbourne⊙, 1,043	G 1
	71953	Mena⊙, 4,530	B 4
	72107	Menifee, 251	E 3
	72945	Midland, 294	B 3
	71851	Mineral Springs, 761	C 6
†	71639	Mitchellville, 494	H 6
	72447	Monette, 1,076	K 2
	72108	Monroe, 200	H 4
	71655	Monticello⊙, 5,085	G 6
	71658	Montrose, 558	H 7
	72558	Moorefield, 127	G 2
	72109	Morganton, 144	F 3
	72368	Moro, 489	H 4
	72110	Morrilton⊙, 6,814	E 3
	71659	Moscow, 250	G 5
	72946	Mountainburg, 524	B 2
	72653	Mountain Home⊙, 3,936	F 1
	71956	Mountain Pine, 800	D 4
	72560	Mountain View⊙, 1,866	F 2
	71758	Mount Holly, 300	E 7
	71957	Mount Ida⊙, 819	C 4
	72655	Mount Judea, 500	D 2
	72561	Mount Pleasant, 346	G 2
	72111	Mount Vernon, 200	F 3
	72947	Mulberry, 1,340	B 2
	71958	Murfreesboro⊙, 1,350	C 5
	71852	Nashville⊙, 4,016	C 6
	72562	Newark, 849	H 2
	71660	New Edinburg, 304	F 6
	71959	Newhope, 130	C 5
	72112	Newport⊙, 7,725	H 2
	72448	Nimmons, 135	K 1
†	71601	Noble Lake, 350	G 5
	72658	Norfork, 266	F 1
	71960	Norman, 360	C 5
	71759	Norphlet, 755	E 7
†	71635	North Crossett, 2,891	G 7
*	72114	North Little Rock, 60,040	F 4
†	72386	Norvell, 440	K 3
	72660	Oakgrove, 236	C 1
	71961	Oden, 141	C 4
	71853	Ogden, 286	B 6
	72564	Oil Trough, 524	G 2
	72449	O'Kean, 244	J 1
	71962	Okolona, 233	D 5
	72853	Ola, 1,029	D 3
	72662	Omaha, 160	D 1
	72369	Oneida, 300	J 5
†	72110	Oppelo, 147	E 3
	72370	Osceola⊙, 7,204	K 2
	72565	Oxford, 271	G 1
	71855	Ozan, 134	C 6
	72949	Ozark⊙, 2,592	C 3
	72372	Palestine, 755	J 4
	72121	Pangburn, 654	G 3
	72450	Paragould⊙, 10,639	J 1
	72855	Paris⊙, 3,646	C 3
	71661	Parkdale, 459	H 7
	72373	Parkin, 1,731	J 3
	72950	Parks, 358	B 4
	72123	Patterson, 417	H 3
	72453	Peach Orchard, 256	J 1
	71964	Pearcy, 200	D 5
	72751	Pea Ridge, 1,088	B 1
	71965	Pencil Bluff, 200	C 4
	72124	Perla, 227	E 5
	72125	Perry, 218	E 3
	71801	Perrytown, 148	C 6
	72126	Perryville⊙, 815	E 3
	72752	Pettigrew, 300	C 2
	71662	Pickens, 200	H 6
	72454	Piggott⊙, 3,087	K 1
	72669	Pindall, 154	E 1
	71601	Pine Bluff⊙, 57,389	F 5
		Pine Bluff, ‡85,329	F 5
	72857	Plainview, 677	D 4
	72568	Pleasant Plains, 162	G 2
	72127	Plumerville, 724	E 3
	72455	Pocahontas⊙, 4,544	H 1
	72456	Pollard, 253	K 1
	72374	Poplar Grove, 255	J 4
	72457	Portia, 381	H 1
	71663	Portland, 662	H 7
	72858	Pottsville, 411	D 3
	72569	Poughkeepsie, 130	H 1
	72128	Poyen, 265	E 5
	72753	Prairie Grove, 1,582	B 2
	72859	Prairie View, 150	C 3
	72129	Prattsville, 299	F 5
	71857	Prescott⊙, 3,921	D 6
	72672	Pyatt, 137	E 1
	72131	Quitman, 354	F 3
	72951	Ratcliff, 184	C 3
†	72333	Ratio, 200	J 5
	72459	Ravenden, 219	H 1
	71726	Reader, 143	D 6
	71664	Readland, 225	H 7
	72401	Rector, 1,990	K 1
	72132	Redfield, 277	F 5
	71670	Reed, 403	H 6
	72462	Reyno, 356	J 1
	71665	Rison⊙, 1,214	F 6

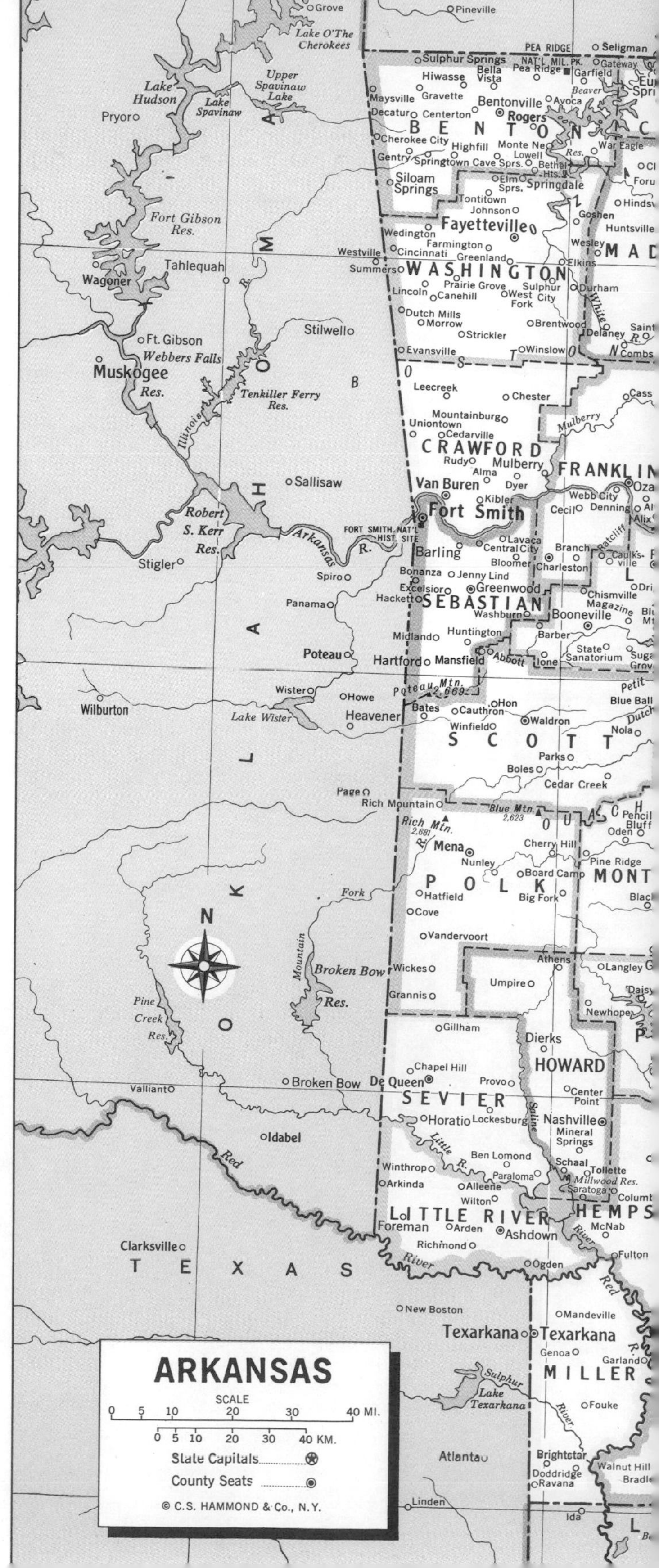

72377 Rivervale, 250 .... K 2
† 72104 Rockport, 158 .... E 5
72134 Roe, 127 .... H 4
72756 Rogers, 11,050 .... B 1
72135 Roland, 350 .... E 4
† 72355 Rondo, 379 .... J 4
72137 Rose Bud, 157 .... F 3
72571 Rosie, 300 .... G 2
72378 Round Pond, 160 .... J 3
72860 Rover, 160 .... D 4
72139 Russell, 231 .... G 3
72801 Russellville⊙, 11,750 .... D 3
72140 Saint Charles, 201 .... H 5
72464 Saint Francis, 297 .... K 1
72675 Saint Joe, 225 .... E 1
72760 Saint Paul, 145 .... C 2
72575 Salado, 175 .... G 2
72576 Salem⊙, 1,277 .... G 1
† 72658 Salesville, 156 .... F 1
71859 Saratoga, 131 .... C 6
† 71851 Schaal, 125 .... C 6
72142 Scott, 200 .... F 4
72862 Scottsville, 241 .... D 3
72863 Scranton, 222 .... C 3
72143 Searcy⊙, 9,040 .... G 3
72465 Sedgwick, 168 .... J 2
† 71670 Selma, 193 .... G 6
72150 Sheridan⊙, 2,480 .... F 5
72152 Sherrill, 208 .... F 5
72116 Sherwood, 2,754 .... F 4
72153 Shirley, 269 .... F 2
72761 Siloam Springs, 6,009 .... B 1
71762 Smackover, 2,058 .... E 7
71763 Sparkman, 663 .... E 6
72764 Springdale, 16,783 .... B 1
72157 Springfield, 160 .... E 3
71860 Stamps, 2,427 .... D 7
71667 Star City⊙, 2,032 .... G 6
72954 State Sanatorium, 700 .... C 3
71764 Stephens, 1,184 .... E 7
72468 Stonewall, 205 .... J 1
72469 Strawberry, 176 .... H 2
71765 Strong, 965 .... F 7
72160 Stuttgart⊙, 10,477 .... H 4
72865 Subiaco, 375 .... C 3
72470 Success, 201 .... J 1
72579 Sulphur Rock, 224 .... H 2
72768 Sulphur Springs, 503 .... B 1
72677 Summit, 321 .... E 1
72164 Sweet Home, 350 .... F 4
72471 Swifton, 703 .... H 2
71861 Taylor, 671 .... D 7
75501 Texarkana⊙, 21,682 .... C 7
Texarkana, ‡101,198 .... C 7
71766 Thornton, 331 .... F 6
71670 Tillar, 293 .... H 6
† 71851 Tollette, 225 .... C 6
† 72041 Tollville, 156 .... G 4
72770 Tontitown, 426 .... B 1
72167 Traskwood, 210 .... E 5
72472 Trumann, 5,938 .... J 2
72168 Tucker, 500 .... G 5
72473 Tuckerman, 1,731 .... H 2
† 71725 Tulip, 150 .... E 5
72015 Tull, 179 .... E 5
72483 Tulot, 170 .... K 2
72169 Tupelo, 246 .... H 3
72384 Turrell, 783 .... K 3
72386 Tyronza, 510 .... K 3
72170 Ulm, 185 .... H 4
72955 Uniontown, 250 .... B 2
71768 Urbana, 500 .... E 7
† 71923 Vaden, 125 .... E 6
72682 Valley Springs, 275 .... D 1
72956 Van Buren⊙, 8,373 .... B 3
72387 Vanndale, 310 .... J 3
72388 Victoria, 198 .... K 2
71769 Village, 200 .... D 7
72173 Vilonia, 423 .... F 3
72583 Viola, 360 .... G 1
72389 Wabash, 275 .... J 5
72175 Wabbaseka, 644 .... G 5
72474 Walcott, 131 .... J 1
72475 Waldenburg, 164 .... J 2
71770 Waldo, 1,658 .... D 7
72958 Waldron⊙, 2,132 .... B 4
72476 Walnut Ridge⊙, 3,800 .... J 1
72176 Ward, 619 .... F 3
71671 Warren⊙, 6,433 .... F 6
† 72936 Washburn, 165 .... B 3
71862 Washington, 290 .... C 6
71863 Waterloo, 150 .... D 6
71674 Watson, 371 .... H 6
72479 Weiner, 915 .... J 2
72177 Weldon, 133 .... H 3
72773 Wesley, 200 .... C 1
71771 Wesson, 160 .... E 7
† 71635 West Crossett, 200 .... F 7
72685 Western Grove, 179 .... D 1
72774 West Fork, 810 .... B 2
72390 West Helena, 11,007 .... J 4
72301 West Memphis, 25,892 .... K 3
72178 West Point, 184 .... G 3
72391 West Ridge, 350 .... K 2
72392 Wheatley, 507 .... H 4
71772 Whelen Springs, 126 .... D 6
† 71635 White, 200 .... G 7
71601 White Hall, 1,300 .... F 5
71973 Wickes, 409 .... B 5
72394 Widener, 292 .... J 3
72482 Williford, 173 .... H 1
71675 Wilmar, 653 .... G 6
71676 Wilmot, 1,132 .... G 7
72395 Wilson, 1,009 .... K 2
71865 Wilton, 427 .... B 6
71677 Winchester, 234 .... G 6
72959 Winslow, 227 .... B 2
71866 Winthrop, 240 .... B 6
72587 Wiseman, 193 .... G 1
72180 Woodson, 600 .... F 4
72181 Wooster, 307 .... F 3
72182 Wright, 175 .... F 5
72183 Wrightsville, 400 .... F 4
72396 Wynne⊙, 6,696 .... J 3
72687 Yellville⊙, 860 .... E 1
71678 Yorktown, 225 .... G 5

⊙ County seat.
‡ Population of metropolitan area.
† Zip of nearest p.o.
* Multiple zips

CALIFORNIA
SCALE
0 10 20 40 60 80 MI.
0 10 20 40 60 80 KM.
State Capitals
County Seats
Canals
© C.S. HAMMOND & Co., N.Y.
Longitude West of Greenwich
SAN FRANCISCO AND VICINITY
0 5 10 15 20 MI.
0 5 10 15 20 KM.
SACRAMENTO AND VICINITY
0 5 10 15 20 MI.
0 5 10 15 20 KM.
LOS ANGELES AND VICINITY
0 5 10 15 20 MI.
0 5 10 15 20 KM.
OREGON
NEVADA
ARIZONA
MEXICO
PACIFIC OCEAN
SANTA BARBARA IS.
Santa Barbara Channel
San Pedro Channel
Gulf of Santa Catalina
SAN FRANCISCO
Sacramento
Oakland
Berkeley
San Jose
Stockton
Fresno
Bakersfield
LOS ANGELES
Long Beach
San Diego
Santa Barbara
Reno
Carson City
Las Vegas
Lake Tahoe
Salton Sea
DEATH VALLEY NATIONAL MONUMENT
LAKE MEAD NATIONAL RECREATION AREA
JOSHUA TREE NAT'L MON.
SEQUOIA NATIONAL PARK
KINGS CANYON NAT'L PARK
YOSEMITE NATIONAL PARK
LASSEN VOLCANIC NAT'L PARK
Mojave Desert
Mt. Whitney 14,494
Lake Mead
Lake Mohave
Tijuana
Mexicali
Ensenada

AREA 158,693 sq. mi.
POPULATION 19,953,134
CAPITAL Sacramento
LARGEST CITY Los Angeles
HIGHEST POINT Mt. Whitney 14,494 ft.
SETTLED IN 1769
ADMITTED TO UNION September 9, 1850
POPULAR NAME Golden State
STATE FLOWER Golden Poppy
STATE BIRD California Valley Quail

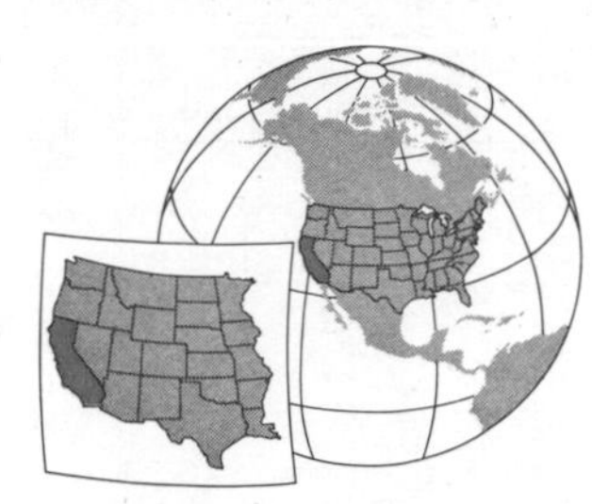

COUNTIES

County	Key
Alameda, 1,073,184	D 6
Alpine, 484	F 5
Amador, 11,821	E 5
Butte, 101,969	D 4
Calaveras, 13,585	E 5
Colusa, 12,430	C 4
Contra Costa, 558,389	D 6
Del Norte, 14,580	B 2
El Dorado, 43,833	E 5
Fresno, 413,053	E 7
Glenn, 17,521	C 4
Humboldt, 99,692	B 3
Imperial, 74,492	K 10
Inyo, 15,571	H 7
Kern, 329,162	G 8
Kings, 64,610	F 8
Lake, 19,548	C 4
Lassen, 14,960	E 3
Los Angeles, 7,032,075	G 9
Madera, 41,519	F 6
Marin, 206,038	C 5
Mariposa, 6,015	E 6
Mendocino, 51,101	B 4
Merced, 104,629	E 6
Modoc, 7,469	E 2
Mono, 4,016	F 5
Monterey, 250,071	D 7
Napa, 79,140	C 5
Nevada, 26,346	E 4
Orange, 1,420,386	H 10
Placer, 77,306	E 4
Plumas, 11,707	E 4
Riverside, 459,074	J 10
Sacramento, 631,498	D 5
San Benito, 18,226	D 7
San Bernardino, 684,072	J 9
San Diego, 1,357,854	J 10
San Francisco (city county), 715,674	J 2
San Joaquin, 290,208	D 6
San Luis Obispo, 105,690	E 8
San Mateo, 556,234	C 6
Santa Barbara, 264,324	E 9
Santa Clara, 1,064,714	D 6
Santa Cruz, 123,790	C 6
Shasta, 77,640	C 3
Sierra, 2,365	E 4
Siskiyou, 33,225	C 2
Solano, 169,941	D 5
Sonoma, 204,885	C 5
Stanislaus, 194,506	D 6
Sutter, 41,935	D 4
Tehama, 29,517	C 3
Trinity, 7,615	B 3
Tulare, 188,322	G 7
Tuolumne, 22,169	F 5
Ventura, 376,430	F 9
Yolo, 91,788	D 5
Yuba, 44,736	D 4

CITIES and TOWNS

Zip	Name/Pop.	Key
92301	Adelanto, 2,115	H 9
96006	Adin, 550	E 2
93601	Ahwahnee, 503	F 6
94501	Alameda, 70,968	J 2
94507	Alamo-Danville, 14,059	K 2
94706	Albany, 14,674	J 2
* 91801	Alhambra, 62,125	C 10
93201	Alpaugh, 800	F 8
92001	Alpine, 1,570	J 11
91001	Altadena, 42,380	C 10
91701	Alta Loma, 6,100	E 10
96101	Alturas⊙, 2,799	E 2
† 95101	Alum Rock, 18,355	L 3
* 92801	Anaheim, 166,701	D 11
	Anaheim-Santa Ana-Garden Grove, ‡1,420,386	D 11
96007	Anderson, 5,492	C 3
95222	Angels Camp, 1,710	E 5
94508	Angwin, 2,690	C 5
94509	Antioch, 28,060	L 1
92307	Apple Valley, 6,702	H 9
95003	Aptos, 8,704	K 4
95912	Arbuckle, 1,037	C 4
95825	Arcade-Arden, 82,498	B 8
91006	Arcadia, 42,868	C 10
95521	Arcata, 8,985	A 3
93202	Armona, 1,392	F 7
93420	Arroyo Grande, 7,454	E 8
90701	Artesia, 14,757	C 11
93203	Arvin, 5,090	G 8
† 94578	Ashland, 14,810	K 2
95413	Asti, 50	C 5
93422	Atascadero, 10,290	E 8
94025	Atherton, 8,085	K 3
95301	Atwater, 11,640	E 6
93602	Auberry, 515	F 6
95603	Auburn⊙, 6,570	C 8
90704	Avalon, 1,520	G 10
93204	Avenal, 3,035	E 8
91702	Azusa, 25,217	D 10
92309	Baker, 600	J 8
* 93301	Bakersfield⊙ 69,515	G 8
	Bakersfield ‡, 329,271	G 8
91706	Baldwin Park, 47,285	D 10
92220	Banning, 12,034	J 10
92311	Barstow, 17,442	H 9
† 95501	Bayview, 2,340	A 3
† 93401	Baywood Park-Los Osos, 3,487	E 8
92223	Beaumont, 5,484	J 10
90201	Bell, 21,836	C 11
90706	Bellflower, 51,454	C 11
94002	Belmont, 23,667	J 3
94920	Belvedere, 2,599	H 2
94510	Benicia, 8,783	K 1
95005	Ben Lomond, 2,793	K 4
* 94701	Berkeley, 116,716	J 2
94511	Bethel Island, 1,398	L 1
* 90210	Beverly Hills, 33,416	B 10
92314	Big Bear City, 850	J 9
92315	Big Bear Lake, 5,268	J 9
95917	Biggs, 1,115	D 4
93513	Big Pine, 839	G 6
93920	Big Sur, 500	D 7
93606	Biola, 950	E 7
93514	Bishop, 3,498	G 6
† 94947	Black Point, 500	J 1
92316	Bloomington, 11,957	E 10
95525	Blue Lake, 1,112	A 3
92225	Blythe, 7,047	L 10
94923	Bodega Bay, 700	B 5
94924	Bolinas, 700	H 1
95415	Boonville, 715	B 5
93516	Boron, 1,999	H 8
92004	Borrego Springs, 860	J 10
95006	Boulder Creek, 1,806	J 4
95707	Bowman, 2,089	C 8
91010	Bradbury, 1,098	D 10
92227	Brawley, 13,746	K 11
92621	Brea, 18,447	D 11
94513	Brentwood, 2,649	L 2
93517	Bridgeport⊙, 525	F 5
94005	Brisbane, 3,003	J 2
95605	Broderick-Bryte, 12,782	B 8
95007	Brookdale, 630	J 4
95605	Bryte-Broderick, 12,782	B 8
93427	Buellton, 1,402	E 9
90620	Buena Park, 63,646	D 11
* 91501	Burbank, 88,871	C 10
94010	Burlingame, 27,320	J 2
96013	Burney, 2,190	D 3
93206	Buttonwillow, 1,193	F 8
94514	Byron, 800	L 2
92230	Cabazon, 598	J 10
92231	Calexico, 10,625	K 11
93501	California City, 1,309	H 8
92233	Calipatria, 1,824	K 10
94515	Calistoga, 1,882	C 5
95418	Calpella, 900	B 4
93745	Calwa, 5,191	F 7
93010	Camarillo, 19,219	F 9
93428	Cambria, 1,716	D 8
95709	Camino, 800	E 5
95008	Campbell, 24,770	K 3
92006	Campo, 850	J 11
95226	Campo Seco, 700	D 9
* 91303	Canoga Park, 109,127	B 10
92672	Capistrano Beach, 4,149	H 10
95010	Capitola, 5,080	K 4
92007	Cardiff-by-the-Sea, 5,724	H 10
92008	Carlsbad, 14,944	H 10
93921	Carmel, 4,525	D 7
93924	Carmel Valley, 3,026	D 7
95608	Carmichael, 37,625	C 8
93013	Carpinteria, 6,982	F 9
90744	Carson, 71,150	C 11
93609	Caruthers, 950	E 7
† 93001	Casitas Springs, 1,113	F 9
95420	Caspar, 578	B 4
91310	Castaic, 800	G 9
94546	Castro Valley, 44,760	K 2
95012	Castroville, 3,235	D 7
92234	Cathedral City, 3,640	J 10
93430	Cayucos, 1,772	E 8
96104	Cedarville, 825	E 2
96019	Central Valley, 2,361	C 3
95307	Ceres, 6,029	D 6
90701	Cerritos, 15,856	C 11
91311	Chatsworth, 24,000	B 10
95044	Chemeketa Park-Redwood Estates, 1,452	K 4
† 94521	Cherryland, 9,969	K 2
96020	Chester, 1,531	D 3
95926	Chico, 19,580	D 4
93555	China Lake, 11,105	H 8
95309	Chinese Camp, 150	E 6
91710	Chino, 20,411	D 10
93610	Chowchilla, 4,349	E 6
* 92010	Chula Vista, 67,901	J 11
95610	Citrus Heights, 21,760	C 8
91711	Claremont, 23,464	D 10
95612	Clarksburg, 554	B 9
94517	Clayton, 1,385	K 2
95422	Clearlake Highlands, 2,836	C 5
95423	Clearlake Oaks, 975	C 4
95425	Cloverdale, 3,251	B 5
93612	Clovis, 13,856	F 7
92236	Coachella, 8,353	J 10
93210	Coalinga, 6,161	E 7
95713	Colfax, 798	E 4
94014	Colma, 537	J 2
92324	Colton, 19,974	E 10
95932	Colusa⊙, 3,842	C 4
† 90001	Commerce, 10,536	C 10
* 90220	Compton, 78,611	C 11
* 94520	Concord, 85,164	K 1
93212	Corcoran, 5,249	F 7
96021	Corning, 3,573	C 4
91720	Corona, 27,519	E 11
92118	Coronado, 20,910	H 11
95076	Corralitos, 600	L 4
94925	Corte Madera, 8,464	J 2
* 92626	Costa Mesa, 72,660	D 11
96022	Cottonwood, 1,288	C 3
95428	Covelo, 900	B 4
91722	Covina, 30,380	D 10
95531	Crescent City⊙, 2,586	A 2
92325	Crestline, 3,509	H 9
94525	Crockett, 2,900	J 1
91730	Cucamonga, 5,796	E 10
90230	Culver City, 31,035	B 10
95014	Cupertino, 18,216	K 3
93615	Cutler, 2,503	F 7
95534	Cutten, 2,228	A 3
90630	Cypress, 31,026	D 11
92327	Daggett, 950	H 9
* 94014	Daly City, 66,922	H 2
92629	Dana Point, 4,745	H 10
94526	Danville-Alamo, 14,059	K 2
95616	Davis, 23,488	B 8
94576	Deer Park, 975	C 5
93215	Delano, 14,559	F 8
95315	Delhi, 2,063	E 6
92014	Del Mar, 3,956	H 11
93940	Del Rey Oaks, 1,823	D 7
92404	Del Rosa, 8,000	E 10
92240	Desert Hot Springs, 2,738	J 9
† 93550	Desert View Highlands, 2,172	G 9
94528	Diablo, 950	K 2
95619	Diamond Springs, 900	D 8
93618	Dinuba, 7,917	F 7
95620	Dixon, 4,432	B 9
96023	Dorris, 840	D 2
93620	Dos Palos, 2,496	E 6
* 90240	Downey, 88,445	C 11
95936	Downieville⊙, 375	E 4
91010	Duarte, 14,981	D 10
94566	Dublin, 13,641	K 2
95937	Dunnigan, 550	C 5
96025	Dunsmuir, 2,214	C 2
95938	Durham, 700	D 4
92241	Eagle Mountain, 2,453	K 10
93219	Earlimart, 3,080	F 8
† 92225	East Blythe, 1,252	L 10
90804	East Los Angeles, 105,033	C 10
93706	Easton, 1,065	F 7
93523	Edwards, 900	G 9
* 92020	El Cajon, 52,273	J 11
92243	El Centro⊙, 19,272	K 11
94530	El Cerrito, 25,190	J 2
95623	El Dorado, 900	C 8
95630	El Dorado Hills, 2,000	C 8
94018	El Granada, 1,473	H 3
95624	Elk Grove, 3,721	B 9
* 91731	El Monte, 69,837	D 10
95318	El Portal, 675	F 6
93030	El Rio, 6,173	F 9
90245	El Segundo, 15,620	B 11
92330	Elsinore, 3,530	F 11
92630	El Toro, 8,654	E 11
94608	Emeryville, 2,681	J 2
95319	Empire, 2,016	D 6
92024	Encinitas, 5,375	H 10
91316	Encino, 40,000	B 10
96001	Enterprise, 11,486	C 3
95320	Escalon, 2,366	E 6
92025	Escondido, 36,792	J 10
95627	Esparto, 1,088	C 5
91739	Etiwanda, 900	E 10
96027	Etna, 667	C 2
95501	Eureka⊙, 24,337	A 3
93221	Exeter, 4,475	F 7
94930	Fairfax, 7,661	H 1
94533	Fairfield⊙, 44,146	K 1
95628	Fair Oaks, 11,256	C 8
92028	Fallbrook, 6,945	H 10
96028	Fall River Mills, 600	D 3
93223	Farmersville, 3,456	F 7
93224	Fellows, 530	F 8
95018	Felton, 2,062	K 4
95536	Ferndale, 1,352	A 3
93015	Fillmore, 6,285	G 9
93622	Firebaugh, 2,517	E 7
95828	Florin, 9,646	B 8
95630	Folsom, 5,810	C 8
92335	Fontana, 20,673	E 10
† 93268	Ford City, 3,503	F 8
† 95703	Foresthill, 900	E 4
94933	Forest Knolls, 900	H 1
95437	Fort Bragg, 4,455	B 4
95538	Fort Dick, 850	A 2
96032	Fort Jones, 515	C 2
95540	Fortuna, 4,203	A 3
94404	Foster City, 9,327	J 2
92708	Fountain Valley, 31,826	D 11
93625	Fowler, 2,239	F 7
93225	Frazier Park, 1,167	F 9
95019	Freedom, 5,563	L 4
* 94536	Fremont, 100,869	K 3
† 93701	Fresno⊙, 165,972	F 7
	Fresno, ‡413,053	F 7
* 92631	Fullerton, 85,987	D 11
95632	Galt, 3,200	C 9
* 90247	Gardena, 41,021	C 11
* 92640	Garden Grove, 122,524	D 11
95634	Georgetown, 700	E 5
96035	Gerber, 800	C 3
95441	Geyserville, 887	B 5
95020	Gilroy, 12,665	D 6
† 92501	Glen Avon Heights, 5,759	E 10
* 91201	Glendale, 132,752	C 10
91740	Glendora, 31,349	D 10
93017	Goleta, 3,500	F 9
93926	Gonzales, 2,575	D 7
93227	Goshen, 1,324	F 7
91344	Granada Hills, 50,000	B 10
92324	Grand Terrace, 5,901	E 10
95945	Grass Valley, 5,149	D 4
95444	Graton, 975	C 5
93308	Greenacres, 2,116	F 8
93927	Greenfield, 2,608	D 7
95947	Greenville, 1,073	E 3
95948	Gridley, 3,534	D 4
93433	Grover City, 5,939	E 8
93434	Guadalupe, 3,145	E 9
95445	Gualala, 585	B 5
95446	Guerneville, 900	B 5
95322	Gustine, 2,793	D 6
94019	Half Moon Bay, 4,023	H 3
95951	Hamilton City, 961	C 4
93230	Hanford⊙, 15,179	F 7
96039	Happy Camp, 925	B 2
90710	Harbor City, 17,500	C 11
90250	Hawthorne, 53,304	C 11
96041	Hayfork, 900	B 3
* 94541	Hayward, 93,058	K 2
95448	Healdsburg, 5,438	B 5
92249	Heber, 875	K 11
92343	Hemet, 12,252	H 10
96113	Herlong, 900	E 3
90254	Hermosa Beach, 17,412	B 11
92345	Hesperia, 4,592	H 9
† 91302	Hidden Hills, 1,529	B 10
92507	Highgrove, 2,158	E 10
92346	Highland, 13,290	H 9
95324	Hilmar, 813	E 6
92347	Hinkley, 900	H 9
95023	Hollister⊙, 7,663	D 7
90028	Hollywood, 85,047	C 10
92250	Holtville, 3,496	K 11
† 91720	Home Gardens, 5,116	E 11
92348	Homeland, 1,187	H 10
95546	Hoopa, 850	B 2
95449	Hopland, 817	B 5
95326	Hughson, 2,144	E 6
* 92646	Huntington Beach, 115,960	C 11
90255	Huntington Park, 33,744	C 11
93234	Huron, 1,525	E 7
92349	Idyllwild, 950	J 10
94947	Ignacio, 4,500	H 1
92251	Imperial, 3,094	K 11
92032	Imperial Beach, 20,244	H 11
93526	Independence⊙, 748	H 7
92201	Indio, 14,459	J 10
* 90301	Inglewood, 89,985	B 11
94937	Inverness, 800	B 5
95640	Ione, 2,369	C 9
93017	Isla Vista, 13,441	E 9
95641	Isleton, 909	L 1
93235	Ivanhoe, 1,595	F 7
95642	Jackson⊙, 1,924	C 9
92034	Jacumba, 700	J 11
95327	Jamestown, 950	E 6
92252	Joshua Tree, 1,211	J 9
95451	Kelseyville, 950	C 5
† 94701	Kensington, 5,823	J 2
93600	Kerman, 2,667	E 7
93238	Kernville, 900	G 8
93239	Kettleman City, 600	E 7
95328	Keyes, 1,875	E 6
93930	King City, 3,717	D 7
95719	Kings Beach, 600	F 4
93631	Kingsburg, 3,843	F 7
95645	Knights Landing, 846	B 8
91011	La Canada, 20,652	C 10
91214	La Crescenta-Montrose, 19,594	C 10
94549	Lafayette, 20,484	K 2
* 92651	Laguna Beach, 14,550	G 10
92653	Laguna Hills, 13,676	D 11
92677	Laguna Niguel, 4,644	H 10
90631	La Habra, 41,350	D 11
94020	La Honda, 650	J 3
92037	La Jolla, 30,000	H 11
92352	Lake Arrowhead, 2,682	H 9
93532	Lake Hughes, 750	G 9
93240	Lake Isabella, 850	G 8
† 92330	Lakeland Village, 1,724	E 11
95453	Lakeport⊙, 3,005	C 4
* 90712	Lakewood, 82,973	C 11
92041	La Mesa, 39,178	H 11
90638	La Mirada, 30,808	D 11
93241	Lamont, 7,007	G 8
93534	Lancaster, 30,948	G 9
* 91744	La Puente, 31,092	D 10
94939	Larkspur, 10,487	H 1
95076	La Selva Beach, 1,171	K 4
95330	Lathrop, 2,137	D 6
93242	Laton, 1,071	F 7
91750	La Verne, 12,965	D 10

(continued on following page)

(continued)

90260 Lawndale, 24,825 .... B 11
95454 Laytonville, 917 .... B 4
95333 Le Grand, 995 .... E 6
92045 Lemon Grove, 19,690 .... J 11
93245 Lemoore, 4,219 .... F 7
90304 Lennox, 16,121 .... B 11
92311 Lenwood, 3,834 .... H 9
92024 Leucadia, 5,900 .... H 10
95648 Lincoln, 3,176 .... B 8
† 95901 Linda, 7,731 .... D 4
93247 Lindsay, 5,206 .... F 7
95953 Live Oak, 2,645 .... D 4
95953 Live Oak, 6,443 .... K 4
94550 Livermore, 37,703 .... L 2
95334 Livingston, 2,588 .... E 6
95237 Lockeford, 890 .... C 9
95240 Lodi, 28,691 .... C 9
95551 Loleta, 800 .... A 3
92354 Loma Linda, 9,797 .... F 10
90717 Lomita, 19,784 .... C 11
93436 Lompoc, 25,284 .... E 9
93545 Lone Pine, 1,241 .... H 7
* 90801 Long Beach, 358,633 .... C 11
95650 Loomis, 1,108 .... C 8
90720 Los Alamitos, 11,346 .... D 11
93440 Los Alamos, 750 .... E 9
94022 Los Altos, 24,956 .... K 3
94022 Los Altos Hills, 6,865 .... J 3
* 90001 Los Angeles⊙, 2,816,061 .... C 10
Los Angeles-Long Beach, ‡7,032,075 .... C 10
93635 Los Banos, 9,188 .... E 6
95030 Los Gatos, 23,735 .... K 4
96055 Los Molinos, 900 .... D 3
† 93401 Los Osos-Baywood Park, 3,487 .... E 8
95457 Lower Lake, 850 .... C 5
96118 Loyalton, 945 .... E 4
95458 Lucerne, 1,300 .... C 4
92356 Lucerne Valley, 850 .... J 9
90262 Lynwood, 43,353 .... C 11
93637 Madera⊙, 16,044 .... E 7
90265 Malibu, 15,000 .... B 10
90266 Manhattan Beach, 35,352 .... B 11
95336 Manteca, 13,845 .... D 6
93252 Maricopa, 740 .... F 8
† 94901 Marinwood, 6,000 .... H 1
95338 Mariposa⊙, 900 .... F 6
96120 Markleeville⊙, 150 .... F 5
94553 Martinez⊙, 16,506 .... K 1
95901 Marysville⊙, 9,353 .... D 4
95955 Maxwell, 850 .... C 4
90270 Maywood, 16,996 .... C 10
96057 McCloud, 1,643 .... C 2
93250 McFarland, 4,177 .... F 8
92254 Mecca, 900 .... K 10
93023 Meiners Oaks, 7,025 .... F 9
95460 Mendocino, 975 .... B 4
93640 Mendota, 2,705 .... E 7
94025 Menlo Park, 26,734 .... J 3
92359 Mentone, 2,900 .... H 9
95340 Merced⊙, 22,670 .... E 6
95461 Middletown, 800 .... C 5
92655 Midway City, 5,900 .... D 11
94030 Millbrae, 20,781 .... J 2
94941 Mill Valley, 12,942 .... H 2
95035 Milpitas, 27,149 .... L 3
91752 Mira Loma, 8,482 .... E 10
92675 Mission Viejo, 11,933 .... D 11
* 95350 Modesto⊙, 61,712 .... D 6
93501 Mojave, 2,573 .... G 8
95245 Mokelumne Hill, 560 .... E 5
91016 Monrovia, 30,015 .... D 10
96064 Montague, 890 .... C 2
93003 Montalvo, 2,400 .... F 9
94037 Montara, 1,459 .... H 3
91763 Montclair, 22,546 .... D 10
90640 Montebello, 42,807 .... C 10
93103 Montecito, 4,900 .... F 9
93940 Monterey, 26,302 .... D 7
91754 Monterey Park, 49,166 .... C 10
95462 Monte Rio, 900 .... B 5
95030 Monte Sereno, 3,089 .... K 4
91020 Montrose-La Crescenta, 19,594 .... C 10
93021 Moorpark, 3,380 .... G 9
94556 Moraga, 14,205 .... K 2
95037 Morgan Hill, 6,485 .... L 4
93442 Morro Bay, 7,109 .... D 8
94038 Moss Beach, 700 .... H 3
95039 Moss Landing, 600 .... C 7
94040 Mountain View, 51,092 .... K 3
96067 Mount Shasta, 2,163 .... C 2
† 95926 Mulberry, 1,795 .... D 4
95247 Murphys, 780 .... E 5
92362 Murrieta, 850 .... H 10
92405 Muscoy, 7,091 .... E 10
94558 Napa⊙, 35,978 .... C 5
92050 National City, 43,184 .... J 11
92363 Needles, 4,051 .... L 9
95959 Nevada City⊙, 2,314 .... D 4
94560 Newark, 27,153 .... K 3
92365 Newberry Springs, 710 .... J 9
95658 Newcastle, 900 .... C 8
91321 Newhall, 9,651 .... G 9
95360 Newman, 2,505 .... D 6
* 92660 Newport Beach, 49,422 .... D 11
92257 Niland, 900 .... K 10
93444 Nipomo, 3,642 .... E 8
91760 Norco, 14,511 .... E 11
93643 North Fork, 575 .... F 6
95660 North Highlands, 31,854 .... B 8
* 91601 North Hollywood, 190,000 .... B 10
90650 Norwalk, 91,827 .... C 11
94947 Novato, 31,006 .... H 1
95361 Oakdale, 6,594 .... E 6
93644 Oakhurst, 800 .... F 6
* 94601 Oakland⊙, 361,561 .... J 2
94561 Oakley, 1,306 .... L 1
93022 Oak View, 4,872 .... F 9
93445 Oceano, 2,564 .... E 8
92054 Oceanside, 40,494 .... H 10
93308 Oildale, 20,879 .... F 8
93023 Ojai, 5,591 .... F 9
* 91761 Ontario, 64,118 .... D 10
95060 Opal Cliffs, 5,425 .... K 4
* 92666 Orange, 77,374 .... D 11

93646 Orange Cove, 3,392 .... F 7
93454 Orcutt, 8,500 .... E 9
95555 Orick, 950 .... A 2
94563 Orinda, 6,790 .... J 2
95963 Orland, 2,884 .... C 4
95556 Orleans, 850 .... B 2
92368 Oro Grande, 700 .... H 9
93647 Orosi, 2,757 .... F 7
95965 Oroville⊙, 7,536 .... D 4
93030 Oxnard, 71,225 .... F 9
Oxnard-Ventura, ‡376,430 .... F 9
94044 Pacifica, 36,020 .... H 2
92109 Pacific Beach, 59,000 .... H 11
93950 Pacific Grove, 13,505 .... C 7
† 95076 Pajaro, 1,407 .... D 7
95968 Palermo, 1,966 .... D 4
93550 Palmdale, 8,511 .... G 9
92260 Palm Desert, 6,171 .... J 10
92262 Palm Springs, 20,936 .... J 10
* 94301 Palo Alto, 55,966 .... K 3
90274 Palos Verdes Estates, 13,641 .... B 11
95969 Paradise, 14,539 .... D 4
90723 Paramount, 34,734 .... C 11
93648 Parlier, 1,993 .... F 7
* 91101 Pasadena, 113,327 .... C 10
† 95060 Pastiempo, 1,115 .... K 4
93446 Paso Robles, 7,168 .... E 8
95363 Patterson, 3,147 .... D 6
93553 Pearblossom, 900 .... H 9
93953 Pebble Beach, 5,000 .... C 7
92370 Perris, 4,228 .... F 11
94060 Pescadero, 625 .... J 4
94952 Petaluma, 24,870 .... H 1
95466 Philo, 700 .... B 4
90660 Pico Rivera, 54,170 .... C 10
94611 Piedmont, 10,917 .... J 2
93650 Pinedale, 1,900 .... F 7
94564 Pinole, 15,850 .... J 1
93040 Piru, 975 .... G 9
93449 Pismo Beach, 4,043 .... E 8
94565 Pittsburg, 20,651 .... L 1
93256 Pixley, 1,584 .... F 8
92670 Placentia, 21,948 .... D 11
95667 Placerville⊙, 5,416 .... C 8
95365 Planada, 2,056 .... E 6
94523 Pleasant Hill, 24,610 .... K 2
94566 Pleasanton, 18,328 .... L 2
95669 Plymouth, 501 .... C 8
95726 Pollock Pines, 850 .... E 5
* 91766 Pomona, 87,384 .... D 10
93257 Poplar, 1,239 .... F 7
93257 Porterville, 12,602 .... G 7
93041 Port Hueneme, 14,295 .... F 9
96122 Portola, 1,625 .... E 4
94025 Portola Valley, 4,999 .... J 3
95469 Potter Valley, 975 .... B 4
92064 Poway, 9,422 .... J 11
96079 Project City, 1,431 .... C 3
93534 Quartz Hill, 4,935 .... G 9
95971 Quincy⊙, 3,343 .... E 4
92065 Ramona, 3,554 .... J 10
95670 Rancho Cordova, 30,451 .... C 8
† 91321 Rancho Santa Clarita, 4,860 .... G 9
92067 Rancho Santa Fe, 975 .... H 10
96080 Red Bluff⊙, 7,676 .... C 3
96001 Redding⊙, 16,659 .... C 3
92373 Redlands, 36,355 .... H 9
* 90277 Redondo Beach, 56,075 .... B 11
* 94061 Redwood City⊙, 55,686 .... J 3
95044 Redwood Estates-Chemeketa Park, 1,452 .... K 4
93654 Reedley, 8,131 .... F 7
91335 Reseda, 60,862 .... B 10
92376 Rialto, 28,370 .... D 10
93261 Richgrove, 1,023 .... F 8
* 94801 Richmond, 79,043 .... J 1
93555 Ridgecrest, 7,629 .... H 8
95562 Rio Dell, 2,817 .... A 3
95673 Rio Linda, 7,524 .... B 8
94571 Rio Vista, 3,135 .... L 1
95366 Ripon, 2,679 .... D 6
95367 Riverbank, 3,949 .... E 6
93656 Riverdale, 1,722 .... E 7
* 92501 Riverside⊙, 140,089 .... E 11
95677 Rocklin, 3,039 .... B 8
94572 Rodeo, 5,356 .... J 1
94928 Rohnert Park, 6,133 .... C 5
95540 Rohnerville, 2,781 .... B 3
90274 Rolling Hills, 2,050 .... B 11
90274 Rolling Hills Estates, 6,027 .... B 11
93560 Rosamond, 2,281 .... G 9
91770 Rosemead, 40,972 .... C 10
95678 Roseville, 17,895 .... B 8
94957 Ross, 2,742 .... H 1
92509 Rubidoux, 13,969 .... E 10
* 95801 Sacramento (cap.)⊙, 254,413 .... B 8
Sacramento, ‡800,592 .... B 8
94574 Saint Helena, 3,173 .... C 5
93901 Salinas⊙, 58,896 .... D 7
Salinas-Monterey, ‡250,071 .... D 7
95563 Salyer, 700 .... B 3
95564 Samoa, 585 .... A 3
95249 San Andreas⊙, 1,564 .... E 5
94960 San Anselmo, 13,031 .... H 1
93450 San Ardo, 750 .... E 7
* 92401 San Bernardino⊙, 104,251 .... E 10
San Bernardino-Riverside-Ontario, ‡1,143,146 .... E 10
94066 San Bruno, 36,254 .... J 2
94070 San Carlos, 25,924 .... J 3
92672 San Clemente, 17,063 .... H 10
* 92101 San Diego⊙, 696,769 .... H 11
San Diego, ‡1,357,854 .... H 11
91773 San Dimas, 15,692 .... D 10
* 91340 San Fernando, 16,571 .... C 10
* 94101 San Francisco⊙, 715,674 .... H 2
San Francisco-Oakland, ‡3,109,519 .... H 2
* 91775 San Gabriel, 29,176 .... C 10
93657 Sanger, 10,088 .... F 7
92383 San Jacinto, 4,385 .... H 10
93660 San Joaquin, 1,506 .... E 7
* 95101 San Jose⊙, 445,779 .... L 3
San Jose, ‡1,064,714 .... L 3

Agriculture, Industry and Resources

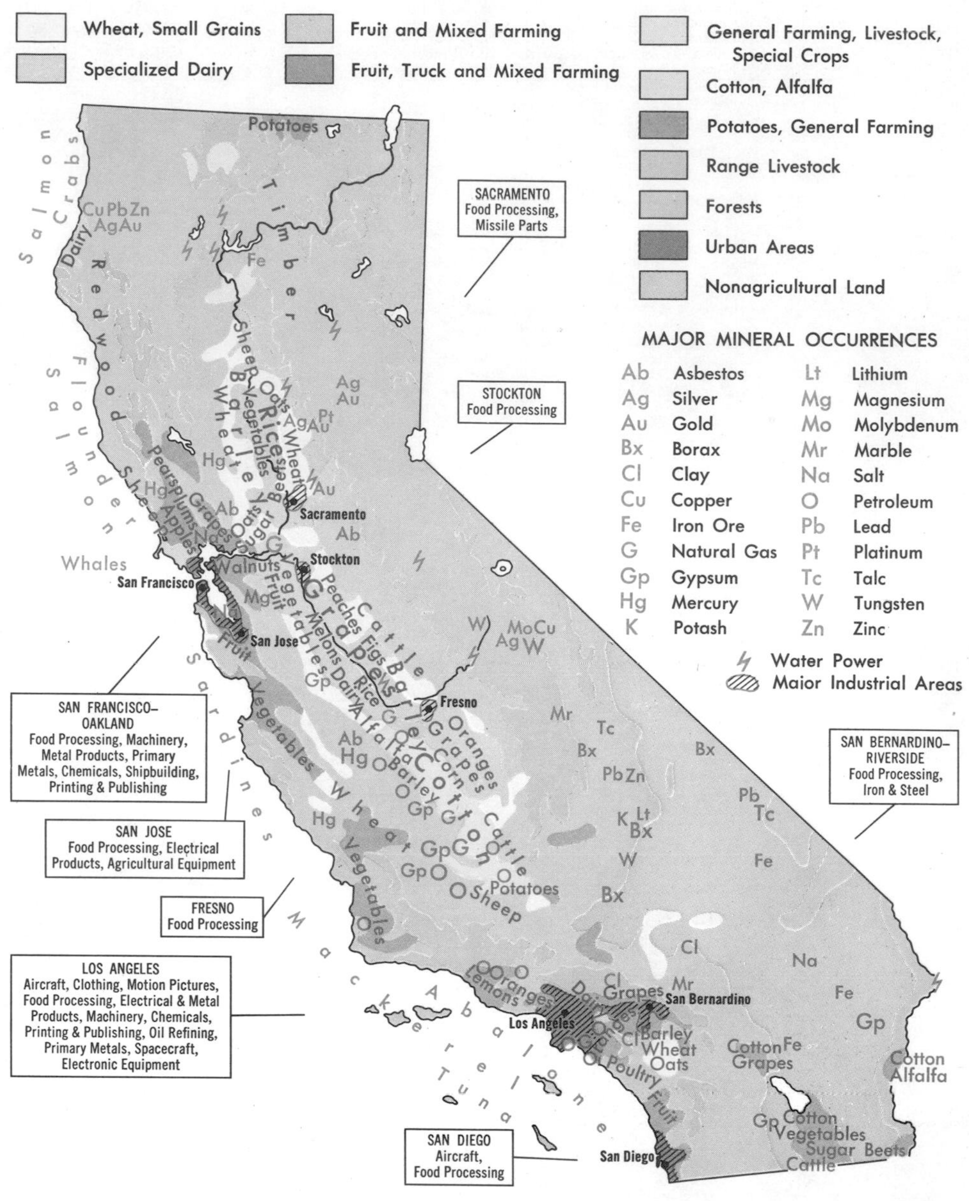

95045 San Juan Bautista, 1,164 .... D 7
92675 San Juan Capistrano, 3,781 .... H 10
* 94577 San Leandro, 68,698 .... J 2
94580 San Lorenzo, 24,633 .... K 2
93401 San Luis Obispo⊙, 28,036 .... E 8
92069 San Marcos, 3,896 .... H 10
91108 San Marino, 14,177 .... D 10
95046 San Martin, 1,392 .... L 4
* 94401 San Mateo, 78,911 .... J 3
93451 San Miguel, 600 .... E 8
94806 San Pablo, 21,461 .... J 1
* 90731 San Pedro, 91,000 .... C 11
* 94901 San Rafael⊙, 38,977 .... J 1
94583 San Ramon, 4,084 .... K 2
* 92701 Santa Ana⊙, 156,601 .... D 11
* 93101 Santa Barbara⊙, 70,215 .... F 9
Santa Barbara, ‡264,324 .... F 9
* 95050 Santa Clara, 87,717 .... K 3
95060 Santa Cruz⊙, 32,076 .... K 4
90670 Santa Fe Springs, 14,750 .... C 11
93453 Santa Margarita, 750 .... E 8
93454 Santa Maria, 32,749 .... E 9
* 90401 Santa Monica, 88,289 .... B 10
93060 Santa Paula, 18,001 .... F 9
* 95401 Santa Rosa⊙, 50,006 .... C 5
93063 Santa Susana, 2,900 .... B 10
† 94901 Santa Venetia, 2,500 .... J 1
92071 Santee, 21,107 .... J 11
95070 Saratoga, 27,110 .... K 4
93003 Saticoy, 2,400 .... F 9
94965 Sausalito, 6,158 .... H 2
95565 Scotia, 950 .... A 3
95060 Scotts Valley, 3,621 .... K 4
90740 Seal Beach, 24 441 .... C 11
93955 Seaside, 35,935 .... D 7
95472 Sebastopol, 3,993 .... C 5
92273 Seeley, 952 .... K 11
93662 Selma, 7,459 .... F 7
91343 Sepulveda, 40,000 .... B 10
93263 Shafter, 5,327 .... F 8
96087 Shasta, 750 .... C 3
93449 Shell Beach, 1,900 .... E 8
91024 Sierra Madre, 12,140 .... D 10
90806 Signal Hill, 5,582 .... C 11

92676 Silverado, 950 .... E 11
93065 Simi Valley, 56,464 .... G 9
92075 Solana Beach, 5,023 .... H 11
93960 Soledad, 6,843 .... D 7
93463 Solvang, 2,004 .... E 9
95476 Sonoma, 4,112 .... C 5
95370 Sonora⊙, 3,100 .... E 6
95073 Soquel, 5,795 .... K 4
93665 South Dos Palos, 850 .... E 7
91733 South El Monte, 13,443 .... C 10
90280 South Gate, 56,909 .... C 11
95705 South Lake Tahoe, 12,921 .... F 5
† 95965 South Oroville, 4,111 .... D 4
91030 South Pasadena, 22,979 .... C 10
† 95801 South Sacramento, 28,574 .... B 8
94080 South San Francisco, 46,646 .... J 2
† 93268 South Taft, 2,214 .... F 8
93265 Springville, 720 .... G 7
94305 Stanford, 8,691 .... J 3
90680 Stanton, 17,947 .... D 11
94970 Stinson Beach, 800 .... H 2
* 95201 Stockton⊙, 107,644 .... D 6
Stockton, ‡290,208 .... D 6
93266 Stratford, 750 .... F 7
93267 Strathmore, 1,221 .... F 7
94585 Suisun City, 2,917 .... K 1
93067 Summerland, 781 .... F 9
92381 Sun City, 5,519 .... F 11
96089 Summit City, 900 .... C 3
91040 Sunland, 22,200 .... C 10
92388 Sunnymead, 6,708 .... F 11
* 94086 Sunnyvale, 95,408 .... K 3
94586 Sunol, 750 .... L 2
90742 Sunset Beach, 1,900 .... C 11
96130 Susanville⊙, 6,608 .... E 3
95982 Sutter, 1,488 .... D 4
95685 Sutter Creek, 1,508 .... C 9
93268 Taft, 4,285 .... F 8
95730 Tahoe City, 1,394 .... E 4
91356 Tarzana, 24,165 .... B 10
93561 Tehachapi, 4,211 .... G 8
91780 Temple City, 29,673 .... D 10
93465 Templeton, 900 .... E 8

93270 Terra Bella, 1,037 .... G 8
92274 Thermal, 975 .... J 10
† 95965 Thermalito, 4,217 .... D 4
95686 Thornton, 850 .... B 9
91360 Thousand Oaks, 36,334 .... G 9
92276 Thousand Palms, 600 .... J 10
94920 Tiburon, 6,209 .... J 2
93272 Tipton, 969 .... F 7
90290 Topanga, 4,800 .... B 10
† 90290 Topanga Beach, 4,500 .... B 10
* 90501 Torrance, 134,584 .... C 11
95376 Tracy, 14,724 .... D 6
93668 Tranquillity, 800 .... E 7
93562 Trona, 975 .... H 8
95734 Truckee, 1,392 .... E 4
91042 Tujunga, 22,000 .... C 10
93274 Tulare, 16,235 .... F 7
96134 Tulelake, 857 .... D 2
95379 Tuolumne, 1,365 .... E 6
95380 Turlock, 13,992 .... E 6
92680 Tustin, 21,178 .... D 11
95383 Twain Harte, 1,484 .... E 6
92277 Twentynine Palms, 5,667 .... K 9
† 95060 Twin Lakes, 3,012 .... K 4
95482 Ukiah⊙, 10,095 .... B 4
94587 Union City, 14,724 .... K 2
90007 University Park, 3,100 .... D 11
91786 Upland, 32,551 .... E 10
95485 Upper Lake, 975 .... C 4
95688 Vacaville, 21,690 .... D 5
91355 Valencia, 4,243 .... G 9
94590 Vallejo, 66,733 .... J 1
Vallejo-Napa, ‡249,081 .... J 1
95252 Valley Springs, 800 .... C 9
* 91401 Van Nuys, 231,600 .... B 10
90291 Venice, 80,500 .... B 11
* 93001 Ventura⊙, 55,797 .... F 9
92392 Victorville, 10,845 .... H 9
92667 Villa Park, 2,723 .... D 11
93277 Visalia⊙, 27,268 .... F 7
92083 Vista, 24,688 .... H 10
91789 Walnut, 5,992 .... D 10
* 94595 Walnut Creek, 39,844 .... K 2
95690 Walnut Grove, 800 .... B 9

93280 Wasco, 8,269 .... F 8
95386 Waterford, 2,243 .... E 6
95076 Watsonville, 14,569 .... D 7
96093 Weaverville⊙, 1,489 .... B 3
96094 Weed, 2,983 .... C 2
* 91790 West Covina, 68,034 .... D 10
† 90025 West Hollywood, 29,448 .... B 10
90025 West Los Angeles, 38,805 .... B 10
92683 Westminster, 59,865 .... D 11
92281 Westmorland, 1,175 .... K 10
94565 West Pittsburg, 5,969 .... K 1
95255 West Point, 950 .... E 5
95691 West Sacramento, 12,002 .... B 8
96137 Westwood, Lassen, 1,862 .... D 3
90024 Westwood, L.A., 45,000 .... B 10
95692 Wheatland, 1,280 .... D 4
* 90601 Whittier, 72,863 .... D 11
95987 Williams, 1,571 .... C 4
95490 Willits, 3,091 .... B 4
95988 Willows⊙, 4,085 .... C 4
90744 Wilmington, 38,000 .... C 11
95492 Windsor, 2,359 .... C 5
92283 Winterhaven, 850 .... L 11
95694 Winters, 2,419 .... D 5
95388 Winton, 3,393 .... E 6
95258 Woodbridge, 1,397 .... B 9
93286 Woodlake, 3,371 .... G 7
95695 Woodland⊙, 20,677 .... B 8
91364 Woodland Hills, 56,420 .... B 10
94062 Woodside, 4,731 .... J 3
92398 Yermo, 1,304 .... J 9
92686 Yorba Linda, 11,856 .... D 11
95389 Yosemite National Park, 857 .... F 6
94599 Yountville, 2,332 .... C 5
96097 Yreka⊙, 5,394 .... C 2
95991 Yuba City⊙, 13,986 .... D 4
92399 Yucaipa, 19,284 .... J 9
92284 Yucca Valley, 3,893 .... J 9

⊙ County seat.
‡ Population of metropolitan area.
† Zip of nearest p.o.
* Multiple zips

AREA 104,247 sq. mi
POPULATION 2,207,259
CAPITAL Denver
LARGEST CITY Denver
HIGHEST POINT Mt. Elbert 14,433 ft.
SETTLED IN 1858
ADMITTED TO UNION August 1, 1876
POPULAR NAME Centennial State
STATE FLOWER Mountain Columbine
STATE BIRD Lark Bunting

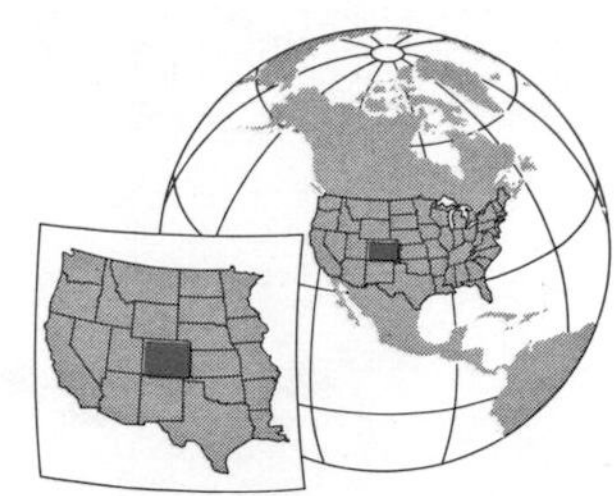

COUNTIES

County		Key
Adams, 185,789		L 3
Alamosa, 11,422		H 7
Arapahoe, 162,142		L 3
Archuleta, 2,733		E 8
Baca, 5,674		O 8
Bent, 6,493		N 7
Boulder, 131,889		J 2
Chaffee, 10,162		G 5
Cheyenne, 2,396		O 5
Clear Creek, 4,819		H 3
Conejos, 7,846		G 8
Costilla, 3,091		J 8
Crowley, 3,086		M 6
Custer, 1,120		J 6
Delta, 15,286		D 5
Denver, 514,678		K 3
Dolores, 1,641		C 7
Douglas, 8,407		K 4
Eagle, 7,498		F 3
Elbert, 3,903		L 4
El Paso, 235,972		K 5
Fremont, 21,942		J 5
Garfield, 14,821		C 3
Gilpin, 1,272		H 3
Grand, 4,107		G 2
Gunnison, 7,578		E 5
Hinsdale, 202		E 7
Huerfano, 6,590		K 7
Jackson, 1,811		G 1
Jefferson, 233,031		J 3
Kiowa, 2,029		O 6
Kit Carson, 7,530		O 4
Lake, 8,282		G 4
La Plata, 19,199		D 8
Larimer, 89,900		H 1
Las Animas, 15,744		L 8
Lincoln, 4,836		M 5
Logan, 18,852		N 1
Mesa, 54,374		B 5
Mineral, 786		F 7
Moffat, 6,525		C 1
Montezuma, 12,952		B 8
Montrose, 18,366		C 6
Morgan, 20,105		M 2
Otero, 23,523		M 7
Ouray, 1,546		D 6
Park, 2,185		H 4
Phillips, 4,131		P 1
Pitkin, 6,185		F 4
Prowers, 13,258		P 7
Pueblo, 118,238		K 6
Rio Blanco, 4,842		C 3
Rio Grande, 10,494		G 7
Routt, 6,592		E 1
Saguache, 3,827		G 6
San Juan, 831		D 7
San Miguel, 1,949		C 6
Sedgwick, 3,405		P 1
Summit, 2,665		G 3
Teller, 3,316		J 5
Washington, 5,550		N 3
Weld, 89,297		L 1
Yuma, 8,544		P 2

CITIES and TOWNS

Zip	Name/Pop.	Key
80101	Agate, 120	M 4
81020	Aguilar, 699	K 8
80720	Akron⊙, 1,775	N 2
81101	Alamosa⊙, 6,985	H 8
80510	Allenspark, 100	J 2
80420	Alma, 73	G 4
81210	Almont, 15	F 5
80721	Amherst, 105	P 1
80801	Anton, 65	N 3
81120	Antonito, 1,113	H 8
80802	Arapahoe, 100	P 5
81021	Arlington, 10	N 6
80804	Arriba, 254	N 4
† 81323	Arriola, 50	B 8
80002	Arvada, 46,814	J 3
81611	Aspen⊙, 2,404	F 4
80722	Atwood, 75	N 1
80610	Ault, 841	K 1
80010	Aurora, 74,974	K 3
81410	Austin, 1,163	D 5
81620	Avon, 50	F 3
81022	Avondale, 750	L 6
80421	Bailey, 200	H 4
† 80624	Barnesville, 20	L 2
81621	Basalt, 419	E 4
81122	Bayfield, 320	D 8
81411	Bedrock, 20	B 6
† 80758	Beecher Island, 5	P 3
80512	Bellvue, 335	J 1
80102	Bennett, 613	L 3
80513	Berthoud, 1,446	J 2
† 80438	Berthoud Pass, 200	H 3
80805	Bethune, 99	P 4
81023	Beulah, 425	K 6
80908	Black Forest, 700	K 4
80422	Black Hawk, 217	J 3
81123	Blanca, 212	H 8
† 81001	Blende, 950	K 6
† 80424	Blue River, 8	G 4
† 81155	Bonanza, 10	G 6
81024	Boncarbo, 50	K 8
80423	Bond, 63	F 3
81025	Boone, 448	L 6
* 80301	Boulder⊙, 66,870	J 2
† 81428	Bowie, 18	D 5
80806	Boyero, 25	N 5
81026	Brandon, 10	P 6
81027	Branson, 70	M 8
80424	Breckenridge⊙, 548	G 4
80611	Briggsdale, 440	L 1
80601	Brighton⊙, 8,309	K 3
81028	Bristol, 250	P 6
† 80901	Broadmoor, 3,871	K 5
† 81212	Brookside, 173	J 6
80020	Broomfield, 7,261	J 3
80723	Brush, 3,377	M 2
† 80742	Buckingham, 6	L 1
81211	Buena Vista, 1,962	G 5
80425	Buffalo Creek, 150	J 4
80807	Burlington⊙, 2,828	P 4
80426	Burns, 100	F 3
80103	Byers, 490	L 3
81320	Cahone, 125	B 7
80808	Calhan, 465	L 4
81029	Campo, 206	O 8
81212	Canon City⊙, 9,206	J 6
81124	Capulin, 600	G 8
81623	Carbondale, 726	E 4
80612	Carr, 47	K 1
80809	Cascade, 950	K 5
80104	Castle Rock⊙, 1,531	K 4
81413	Cedaredge, 581	D 5
81125	Center, 1,470	G 7
80427	Central City⊙, 228	J 3
81126	Chama, 400	J 8
81030	Cheraw, 129	N 6
80810	Cheyenne Wells⊙, 982	P 5
81127	Chimney Rock, 51	E 8
81031	Chivington, 15	O 6
81128	Chromo, 150	F 8
81220	Cimarron, 25	D 6
80428	Clark, 55	F 1
† 80731	Clarkville, 4	P 2
81520	Clifton, 950	C 4
80429	Climax, 975	G 4
81221	Coal Creek, 225	J 6
81222	Coaldale, 104	H 6
80430	Coalmont, 12	F 1
81032	Cokedale, 101	K 8
81624	Collbran, 225	C 4
† 81401	Colona, 54	D 6
81004	Colorado City, 411	K 6
* 80901	Colorado Springs⊙, 135,060	K 5
	Colorado Springs, ‡235,972	K 5
† 80428	Columbine, 12	E 1
80022	Commerce City, 17,407	K 3
80432	Como, 35	H 4
81129	Conejos⊙, 100	G 8
80812	Cope, 125	O 3
80611	Cornish, 2	L 2
81321	Cortez⊙, 6,032	B 8
81223	Cotopaxi, 150	H 6
80434	Cowdrey, 10	G 1
81625	Craig⊙, 4,205	D 2
81415	Crawford, 171	D 5
81130	Creede⊙, 653	E 7
81224	Crested Butte, 372	E 5
81131	Crestone, 34	H 7
80813	Cripple Creek⊙, 425	J 5
80726	Crook, 199	O 1
81033	Crowley, 216	M 6
81055	Cuchara, 43	J 8
80514	Dacono, 360	K 2
† 80728	Dailey, 20	O 1
81630	De Beque, 155	C 4
† 80135	Deckers, 4	J 4
80105	Deer Trail, 374	M 3
81034	Delhi, 10	M 7
81132	Del Norte⊙, 1,569	G 7
81416	Delta⊙, 3,694	D 5
* 80201	Denver (cap.)⊙, 514,678	K 3
	Denver, ‡1,227,529	K 3
81235	Deora, 2	O 7
80435	Dillon, 182	H 3
81610	Dinosaur, 247	B 2
80814	Divide, 50	J 5
81323	Dolores, 820	C 8
81324	Dove Creek⊙, 619	A 7
† 81239	Doyleville, 75	F 6
80515	Drake, 75	J 2
81301	Durango⊙, 10,333	D 8
81036	Eads⊙, 795	O 6
81631	Eagle⊙, 790	F 3
† 81212	East Canon, 1,805	J 6
80615	Eaton, 1,389	K 1
81418	Eckert, 850	C 5
80214	Edgewater, 4,866	J 3
81632	Edwards, 100	F 3
81325	Egnar, 84	B 7
80106	Elbert, 150	L 4
80437	Eldora, 100	H 3
80107	Elizabeth, 493	K 4
81633	Elk Springs, 56	C 2
80438	Empire, 249	H 3
80110	Englewood, 33,695	K 3
80516	Erie, 1,090	K 2
80517	Estes Park, 1,616	J 2
† 81433	Eureka, 25	D 7
80620	Evans, 2,570	K 2
80439	Evergreen, 2,321	J 3
80440	Fairplay⊙, 419	H 4
81037	Farisita, 45	J 7
† 80030	Federal Heights, 1,502	J 3
80520	Firestone, 570	K 2
† 80810	Firstview, 6	O 5
80815	Flagler, 615	N 4
80728	Fleming, 349	O 1
81226	Florence, 2,846	J 6
80816	Florissant, 75	J 5
80521	Fort Collins⊙, 43,337	J 1
81133	Fort Garland, 400	J 8
80621	Fort Lupton, 2,489	K 2
81038	Fort Lyon, 135	N 6
80701	Fort Morgan⊙, 7,594	M 2
80817	Fountain, 3,515	K 5
81039	Fowler, 1,241	L 6
80441	Foxton, 75	J 4
80116	Franktown, 157	K 4
80442	Fraser, 221	H 3
80530	Frederick, 696	K 2
80820	Freshwater (Guffey), 24	H 5
80443	Frisco, 471	G 3
81521	Fruita, 1,822	B 4
† 81501	Fruitvale, 950	C 4
80622	Galeton, 200	K 1
81134	Garcia, 90	J 8
81040	Gardner, 75	J 7
81227	Garfield, 11	G 5
81522	Gateway, 250	B 5
80818	Genoa, 161	N 4
80444	Georgetown⊙, 542	H 3
80623	Gilcrest, 382	K 2
80624	Gill, 250	L 2
81634	Gilman, 400	G 3
81523	Glade Park, 69	B 5
80485	Glendevey, 50	H 1
80532	Glen Haven, 50	H 2
81601	Glenwood Springs⊙, 4,106	E 4
80401	Golden⊙, 9,817	J 3
80625	Goodrich, 85	M 2
80445	Gould, 12	G 2
81041	Granada, 551	P 6
80446	Granby, 554	H 2
81501	Grand Junction⊙, 20,170	B 4
80447	Grand Lake, 189	H 2
81635	Grand Valley, 270	D 4
81228	Granite, 23	G 4
80448	Grant, 50	H 4
80631	Greeley⊙, 38,902	K 2
† 80118	Greenland, 47	K 4
80819	Green Mountain Falls, 359	K 5
81636	Greystone, 2	B 1
80729	Grover, 121	L 1
80820	Guffey, 24	H 5
81042	Gulnare, 100	K 8
81230	Gunnison⊙, 4,613	E 5
81637	Gypsum, 420	F 3
80730	Hale, 12	P 3
81638	Hamilton, 30	D 2
81043	Hartman, 129	P 6
80449	Hartsel, 75	H 4
81044	Hasty, 150	O 6
81045	Haswell, 135	N 6
80731	Haxtun, 899	O 1
81639	Hayden, 763	E 2
80732	Hereford, 50	L 1
81326	Hesperus, 78	C 8
80733	Hillrose, 121	N 2
81232	Hillside, 79	H 6
81046	Hoehne, 400	L 8
81047	Holly, 993	P 6
80734	Holyoke⊙, 1,640	P 1
81136	Hooper, 80	H 7
81419	Hotchkiss, 507	D 5
80451	Hot Sulphur Springs⊙, 220	H 2
81233	Howard, 175	H 6
80641	Hoyt, 175	L 2
80642	Hudson, 518	K 2
80821	Hugo⊙, 759	N 4
80533	Hygiene, 400	J 2
80452	Idaho Springs, 2,003	H 3
80735	Idalia, 100	P 3
81137	Ignacio, 613	D 8
80736	Iliff, 193	N 1
81427	Ironton	D 7
† 80901	Ivywild, 12,000	K 5
80455	Jamestown, 185	J 2
81048	Jansen, 267	K 8
81138	Jaroso, 56	H 8
80456	Jefferson, 45	H 4
80822	Joes, 100	O 3
80534	Johnstown, 1,191	K 2
80737	Julesburg⊙, 1,578	P 1
80823	Karval, 70	N 5
80643	Keenesburg, 427	L 2
80738	Keota, 6	L 1
80644	Kersey, 474	L 2
81049	Kim, 200	N 8
80117	Kiowa⊙, 235	L 4
80824	Kirk, 100	P 3
80825	Kit Carson, 220	O 5
† 80435	Kokomo, 75	G 4
80459	Kremmling, 764	G 2
80826	Kutch, 2	M 5
80026	Lafayette, 3,498	K 3
81139	La Garita, 50	G 7
80739	Laird, 105	P 2
81140	La Jara, 768	H 8
81050	La Junta⊙, 7,938	M 7
81235	Lake City⊙, 91	E 6
80827	Lake George, 29	J 5
80215	Lakewood, 92,787	J 3
81052	Lamar⊙, 7,797	O 6
80535	Laporte, 950	J 1
80118	Larkspur, 350	K 4
80645	La Salle, 1,227	K 2
81054	Las Animas⊙, 3,148	N 6
† 81151	Lasauces, 120	H 8
† 81153	Lavalley, 237	J 8
81055	La Veta, 589	J 8
† 80452	Lawson, 108	H 3
81625	Lay, 8	D 2
81420	Lazear, 60	D 5
80461	Leadville⊙, 4,314	G 4
† 81323	Lebanon, 50	B 8
81327	Lewis, 350	B 8
80828	Limon, 1,814	M 4
† 81212	Lincoln Park, 2,984	J 6
80740	Lindon, 50	N 3
80120	Littleton⊙, 26,466	K 3
80536	Livermore, 20	J 1
† 80701	Log Lane Village, 329	M 2
81524	Loma, 100	B 4
80501	Longmont, 23,209	J 2
† 80135	Longview, 10	J 4
80027	Louisville, 2,409	J 3
80131	Louviers, 306	K 4
80537	Loveland, 16,220	J 2
80646	Lucerne, 150	K 2
81056	Lycan, 4	P 7
80540	Lyons, 958	J 2
81525	Mack, 175	B 4
81421	Maher, 80	D 5
† 80461	Malta, 200	G 4
81141	Manassa, 814	H 8
81328	Mancos, 709	C 8
80829	Manitou Springs, 4,278	J 5
81058	Manzanola, 451	M 6
† 81623	Marble, 1	E 4
81329	Marvel, 100	C 8
80541	Masonville, 200	J 2
† 80649	Masters, 50	L 2
80830	Matheson, 100	M 4
81640	Maybell, 82	C 2
81057	McClave, 165	O 6
80463	McCoy, 14	F 3
80542	Mead, 195	K 2
81641	Meeker⊙, 1,597	D 2
81642	Meredith, 48	F 4
80741	Merino, 260	N 2
81005	Mesa, 295	C 4
81330	Mesa Verde National Park, 70	C 8
81142	Mesita, 50	H 8
80543	Milliken, 702	K 2
80477	Milner, 75	F 2
81645	Minturn, 706	G 3
81059	Model, 19	L 8
81143	Moffat, 98	H 6
81646	Molina, 120	D 4
81144	Monte Vista, 3,909	G 7
80464	Montezuma, 6	H 3

(continued on following page)

Colorado Department of Public Relations

This view of Bear Lake and Longs Peak is typical of the beautiful mountain scenery found in Rocky Mountain National Park, an area which many call "the roof of America."

Topography

0 50 100
MILES

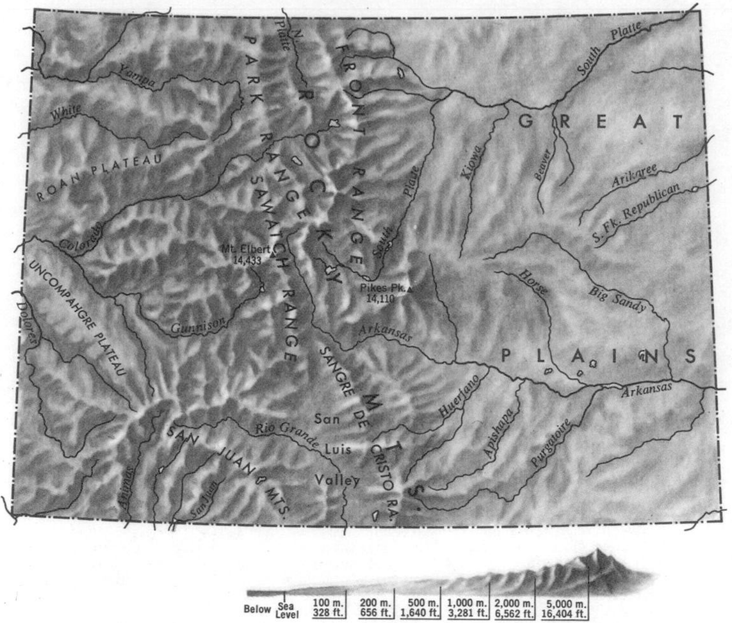

Agriculture, Industry and Resources

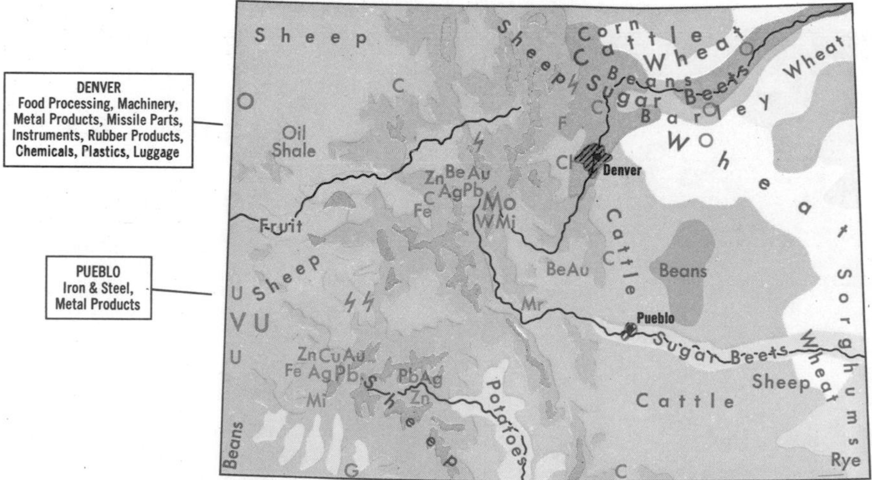

DOMINANT LAND USE

- Specialized Wheat
- Wheat, Range Livestock
- Wheat, Grain Sorghums, Range Livestock
- Dry Beans, General Farming
- Sugar Beets, Dry Beans, Livestock, General Farming
- Fruit, Mixed Farming
- General Farming, Livestock, Special Crops
- Range Livestock
- Forests
- Urban Areas
- Nonagricultural Land

MAJOR MINERAL OCCURRENCES

Ag	Silver	Mi	Mica
Au	Gold	Mo	Molybdenum
Be	Beryl	Mr	Marble
C	Coal	O	Petroleum
Cl	Clay	Pb	Lead
Cu	Copper	U	Uranium
F	Fluorspar	V	Vanadium
Fe	Iron Ore	W	Tungsten
G	Natural Gas	Zn	Zinc

Water Power
Major Industrial Areas

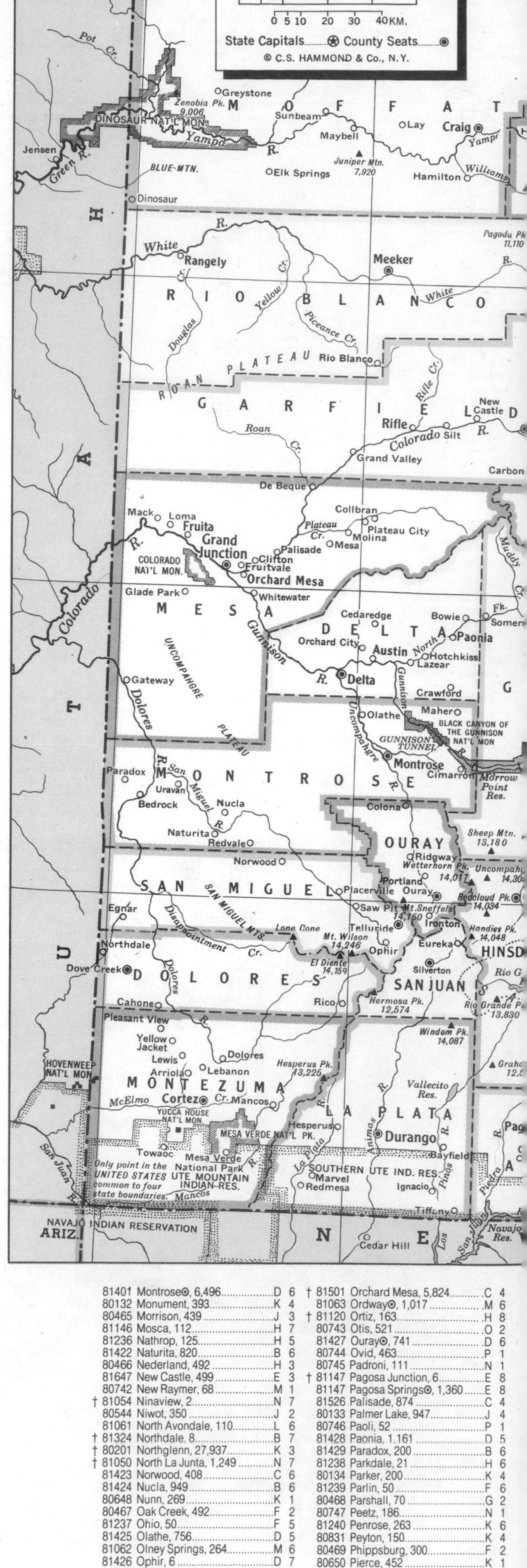

	ZIP	Place	Key			ZIP	Place	Key	
	81401	Montrose⊙, 6,496	D	6	†	81501	Orchard Mesa, 5,824	C	4
	80132	Monument, 393	K	4		81063	Ordway⊙, 1,017	M	6
	80465	Morrison, 439	J	3	†	81120	Ortiz, 163	H	8
	81146	Mosca, 112	H	7		80743	Otis, 521	O	2
	81236	Nathrop, 125	H	5		81427	Ouray⊙, 741	D	6
	81422	Naturita, 820	B	6		80744	Ovid, 463	P	1
	80466	Nederland, 492	H	3		80745	Padroni, 111	N	1
	81647	New Castle, 499	E	3	†	81147	Pagosa Junction, 6	E	8
	80742	New Raymer, 68	M	1		81147	Pagosa Springs⊙, 1,360	E	8
†	81054	Ninaview, 2	N	7		81526	Palisade, 874	C	4
	80544	Niwot, 350	J	2		80133	Palmer Lake, 947	J	4
	81061	North Avondale, 110	L	6		80746	Paoli, 52	P	1
†	81324	Northdale, 8	B	7		81428	Paonia, 1,161	D	5
†	80201	Northglenn, 27,937	K	3		81429	Paradox, 200	B	6
†	81050	North La Junta, 1,249	N	7		81238	Parkdale, 21	H	6
	81423	Norwood, 408	C	6		80134	Parker, 200	K	4
	81424	Nucla, 949	B	6		81239	Parlin, 50	F	6
	80648	Nunn, 269	K	1		80468	Parshall, 70	G	2
	80467	Oak Creek, 492	F	2		80747	Peetz, 186	N	1
	81237	Ohio, 50	F	5		81240	Penrose, 263	K	6
	81425	Olathe, 756	D	5		80831	Peyton, 150	K	4
	81062	Olney Springs, 264	M	6		80469	Phippsburg, 300	F	2
	81426	Ophir, 6	D	7		80650	Pierce, 452	K	1
	80649	Orchard, 85	L	2		80470	Pine, 89	J	4
†	81418	Orchard City (Eckert), 850	C	5		80471	Pinecliffe, 500	J	3

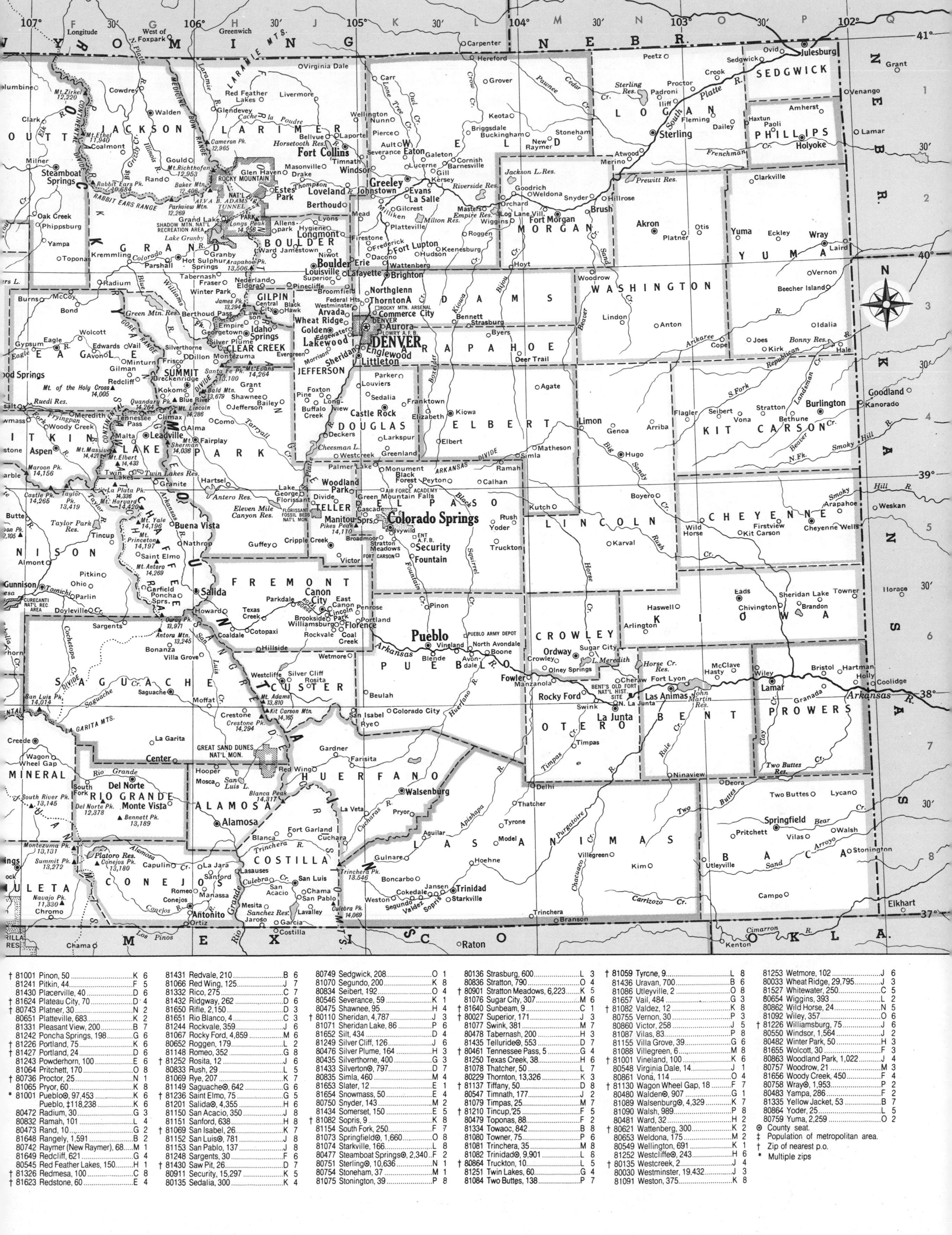

† 81001 Pinon, 50 .... K 6
81241 Pitkin, 44 .... F 5
81430 Placerville, 40 .... D 6
† 81624 Plateau City, 70 .... D 4
† 80743 Platner, 30 .... N 2
80651 Platteville, 683 .... K 2
81331 Pleasant View, 200 .... B 7
81242 Poncha Springs, 198 .... G 6
† 81226 Portland, 75 .... K 6
† 81427 Portland, 24 .... D 6
81243 Powderhorn, 100 .... E 6
81064 Pritchett, 170 .... O 8
† 80736 Proctor, 25 .... N 1
81065 Pryor, 60 .... K 8
* 81001 Pueblo⊙, 97,453 .... K 6
Pueblo, ‡118,238 .... K 6
80472 Radium, 30 .... G 3
80832 Ramah, 101 .... L 4
80473 Rand, 10 .... G 2
81648 Rangely, 1,591 .... B 2
80742 Raymer (New Raymer), 68 .... M 1
81649 Redcliff, 621 .... G 4
80545 Red Feather Lakes, 150 .... H 1
† 81326 Redmesa, 100 .... C 8
† 81623 Redstone, 60 .... E 4

81431 Redvale, 210 .... B 6
81066 Red Wing, 125 .... J 7
81332 Rico, 275 .... C 7
81432 Ridgway, 262 .... D 6
81650 Rifle, 2,150 .... D 3
81651 Rio Blanco, 4 .... C 3
81244 Rockvale, 359 .... J 6
81067 Rocky Ford, 4,859 .... M 6
80652 Roggen, 179 .... L 2
81148 Romeo, 352 .... G 8
† 81252 Rosita, 12 .... J 6
80833 Rush, 29 .... L 5
81069 Rye, 207 .... K 7
81149 Saguache⊙, 642 .... G 6
† 81236 Saint Elmo, 75 .... G 5
81201 Salida⊙, 4,355 .... H 6
81150 San Acacio, 350 .... J 8
81151 Sanford, 638 .... H 8
† 81069 San Isabel, 26 .... K 7
81152 San Luis⊙, 781 .... J 8
81153 San Pablo, 137 .... J 8
81248 Sargents, 30 .... F 6
† 81430 Saw Pit, 26 .... D 7
80911 Security, 15,297 .... K 5
80135 Sedalia, 300 .... K 4

80749 Sedgwick, 208 .... O 1
81070 Segundo, 200 .... K 8
80834 Seibert, 192 .... O 4
80546 Severance, 59 .... K 1
80475 Shawnee, 95 .... H 4
† 80110 Sheridan, 4,787 .... J 3
81071 Sheridan Lake, 86 .... P 6
81652 Silt, 434 .... D 4
81249 Silver Cliff, 126 .... J 6
80476 Silver Plume, 164 .... H 3
80435 Silverthorne, 400 .... G 3
81433 Silverton⊙, 797 .... D 7
80835 Simla, 460 .... M 4
81653 Slater, 12 .... E 1
81654 Snowmass, 50 .... E 4
80750 Snyder, 143 .... M 2
81434 Somerset, 150 .... E 5
† 81082 Sopris, 9 .... K 8
81154 South Fork, 250 .... F 7
81073 Springfield⊙, 1,660 .... O 8
81074 Starkville, 166 .... L 8
80477 Steamboat Springs⊙, 2,340 .... F 2
80751 Sterling⊙, 10,636 .... N 1
80754 Stoneham, 37 .... M 1
81075 Stonington, 39 .... P 8

80136 Strasburg, 600 .... L 3
80836 Stratton, 790 .... O 4
† 80901 Stratton Meadows, 6,223 .... K 5
81076 Sugar City, 307 .... M 6
† 81640 Sunbeam, 9 .... C 1
† 80027 Superior, 171 .... J 3
81077 Swink, 381 .... M 7
80478 Tabernash, 200 .... H 3
81435 Telluride⊙, 553 .... D 7
† 80461 Tennessee Pass, 5 .... G 4
81250 Texas Creek, 38 .... H 6
81078 Thatcher, 50 .... L 7
80229 Thornton, 13,326 .... K 3
† 81137 Tiffany, 50 .... D 8
80547 Timnath, 177 .... J 2
81079 Timpas, 25 .... M 7
† 81210 Tincup, 25 .... F 5
80479 Toponas, 88 .... F 2
81334 Towaoc, 842 .... B 8
81080 Towner, 75 .... P 6
81081 Trinchera, 35 .... M 8
81082 Trinidad⊙, 9,901 .... L 8
† 80864 Truckton, 10 .... L 5
81251 Twin Lakes, 60 .... G 4
81084 Two Buttes, 138 .... P 7

† 81059 Tyrone, 9 .... L 8
81436 Uravan, 700 .... B 6
81086 Utleyville, 2 .... O 8
81657 Vail, 484 .... G 3
† 81082 Valdez, 12 .... K 8
80755 Vernon, 30 .... P 3
80860 Victor, 258 .... J 5
81087 Vilas, 83 .... P 8
81155 Villa Grove, 39 .... G 6
81088 Villegreen, 6 .... M 8
† 81001 Vineland, 100 .... K 6
80548 Virginia Dale, 14 .... J 1
80861 Vona, 114 .... O 4
† 81130 Wagon Wheel Gap, 18 .... F 7
80480 Walden⊙, 907 .... G 1
81089 Walsenburg⊙, 4,329 .... K 7
81090 Walsh, 989 .... P 8
80481 Ward, 32 .... H 2
† 80621 Wattenberg, 300 .... K 2
80653 Weldona, 175 .... M 2
80549 Wellington, 691 .... K 1
81252 Westcliffe⊙, 243 .... H 6
† 80135 Westcreek, 2 .... J 4
80030 Westminster, 19,432 .... J 3
81091 Weston, 375 .... K 8

81253 Wetmore, 102 .... J 6
80033 Wheat Ridge, 29,795 .... J 3
81527 Whitewater, 250 .... C 5
80654 Wiggins, 393 .... L 2
80862 Wild Horse, 24 .... N 5
81092 Wiley, 357 .... O 6
† 81226 Williamsburg, 75 .... J 6
80550 Windsor, 1,564 .... J 2
80482 Winter Park, 50 .... H 3
81655 Wolcott, 30 .... F 3
80863 Woodland Park, 1,022 .... J 4
80757 Woodrow, 21 .... M 3
81656 Woody Creek, 450 .... F 4
80758 Wray⊙, 1,953 .... P 2
80483 Yampa, 286 .... F 2
81335 Yellow Jacket, 53 .... B 7
80864 Yoder, 25 .... L 5
80759 Yuma, 2,259 .... O 2

⊙ County seat.
‡ Population of metropolitan area.
† Zip of nearest p.o.
* Multiple zips

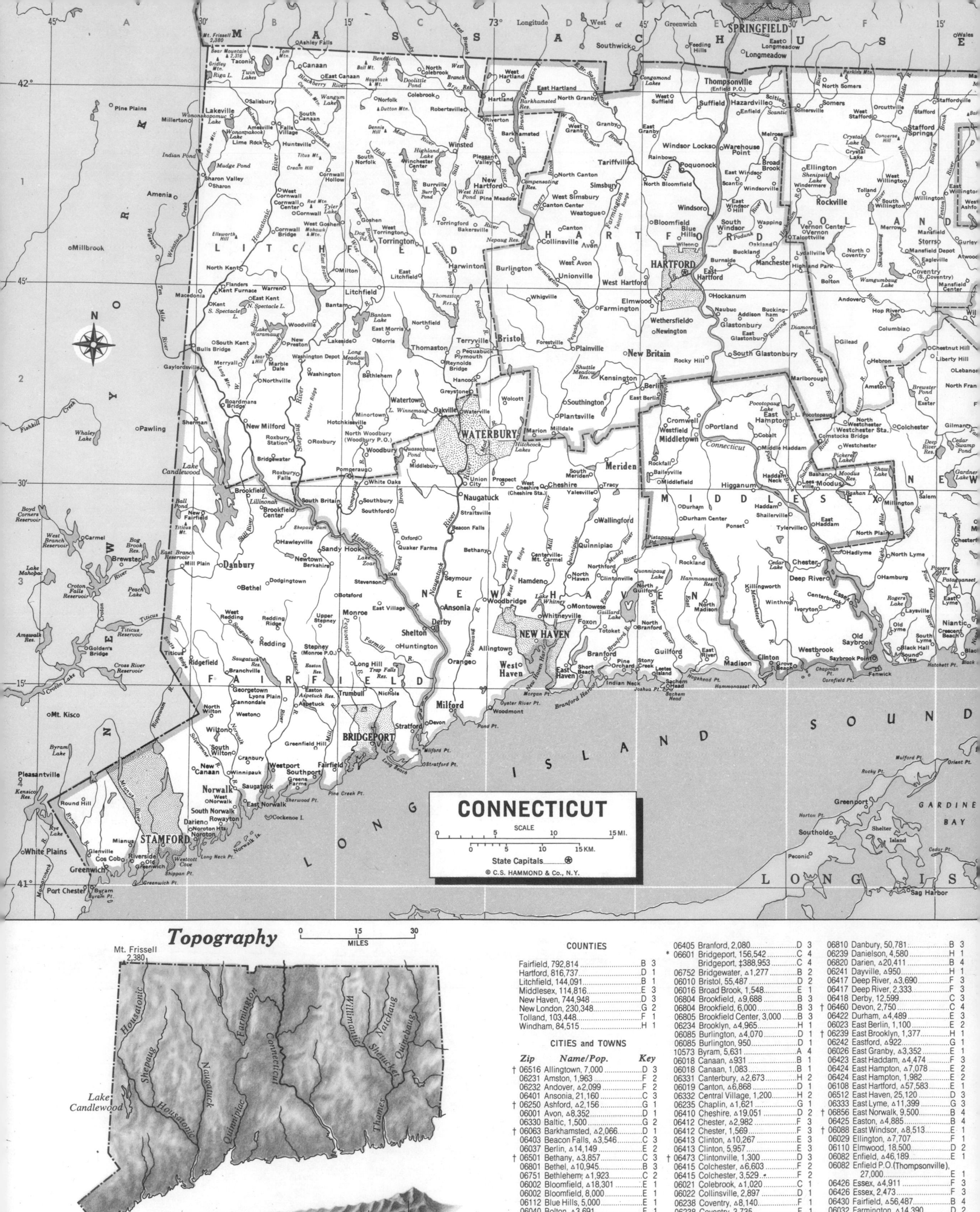

COUNTIES

Name/Pop.	Key
Fairfield, 792,814	B 3
Hartford, 816,737	D 1
Litchfield, 144,091	B 1
Middlesex, 114,816	E 3
New Haven, 744,948	D 3
New London, 230,348	G 2
Tolland, 103,448	F 1
Windham, 84,515	H 1

CITIES and TOWNS

	Zip	Name/Pop.	Key
†	06516	Allingtown, 7,000	D 3
	06231	Amston, 1,963	F 2
	06232	Andover, ▵2,099	F 2
	06401	Ansonia, 21,160	C 3
†	06250	Ashford, ▵2,156	G 1
	06001	Avon, ▵8,352	D 1
	06330	Baltic, 1,500	G 2
†	06063	Barkhamsted, ▵2,066	D 1
	06403	Beacon Falls, ▵3,546	C 3
	06037	Berlin, ▵14,149	E 2
†	06501	Bethany, ▵3,857	C 3
	06801	Bethel, ▵10,945	B 3
	06751	Bethlehem, ▵1,923	C 2
	06002	Bloomfield, ▵18,301	E 1
	06002	Bloomfield, 8,000	E 1
	06112	Blue Hills, 5,000	E 1
	06040	Bolton, ▵3,691	F 1
	06405	Branford, ▵20,444	D 3
	06405	Branford, 2,080	D 3
*	06601	Bridgeport, 156,542	C 4
		Bridgeport, ‡388,953	C 4
	06752	Bridgewater, ▵1,277	B 2
	06010	Bristol, 55,487	D 2
	06016	Broad Brook, 1,548	E 1
	06804	Brookfield, ▵9,688	B 3
	06804	Brookfield, 6,000	B 3
	06805	Brookfield Center, 3,000	B 3
	06234	Brooklyn, ▵4,965	H 1
	06085	Burlington, ▵4,070	D 1
	06085	Burlington, 950	D 1
	10573	Byram, 5,631	A 4
	06018	Canaan, ▵931	B 1
	06018	Canaan, 1,083	B 1
	06331	Canterbury, ▵2,673	H 2
	06019	Canton, ▵6,868	D 1
	06332	Central Village, 1,200	H 2
	06235	Chaplin, ▵1,621	G 1
	06410	Cheshire, ▵19,051	D 2
	06412	Chester, ▵2,982	F 3
	06412	Chester, 1,569	F 3
	06413	Clinton, ▵10,267	E 3
	06413	Clinton, 5,957	E 3
†	06473	Clintonville, 1,300	D 3
	06415	Colchester, ▵6,603	F 2
	06415	Colchester, 3,529	F 2
	06021	Colebrook, ▵1,020	C 1
	06022	Collinsville, 2,897	D 1
	06238	Coventry, ▵8,140	F 1
	06238	Coventry, 3,735	F 1
	06416	Cromwell, ▵7,400	E 2
	06810	Danbury, 50,781	B 3
	06239	Danielson, 4,580	H 1
	06820	Darien, ▵20,411	B 4
	06241	Dayville, ▵950	H 1
	06417	Deep River, ▵3,690	F 3
	06417	Deep River, 2,333	F 3
	06418	Derby, 12,599	C 3
†	06460	Devon, 2,750	C 4
	06422	Durham, ▵4,489	E 3
	06023	East Berlin, 1,100	E 2
†	06239	East Brooklyn, 1,377	H 1
	06242	Eastford, ▵922	G 1
	06026	East Granby, ▵3,352	E 1
	06423	East Haddam, ▵4,474	F 3
	06424	East Hampton, ▵7,078	E 2
	06424	East Hampton, 1,982	E 2
	06108	East Hartford, ▵57,583	E 1
	06512	East Haven, 25,120	D 3
	06333	East Lyme, ▵11,399	G 3
†	06856	East Norwalk, 9,500	B 4
	06425	Easton, ▵4,885	B 4
†	06088	East Windsor, ▵8,513	E 1
	06029	Ellington, ▵7,707	F 1
	06110	Elmwood, 18,500	D 2
	06082	Enfield, ▵46,189	E 1
	06082	Enfield P.O.(Thompsonville), 27,000	E 1
	06426	Essex, ▵4,911	F 3
	06426	Essex, 2,473	F 3
	06430	Fairfield, ▵56,487	B 4
	06032	Farmington, ▵14,390	D 2
†	06010	Forestville, 20,000	D 2

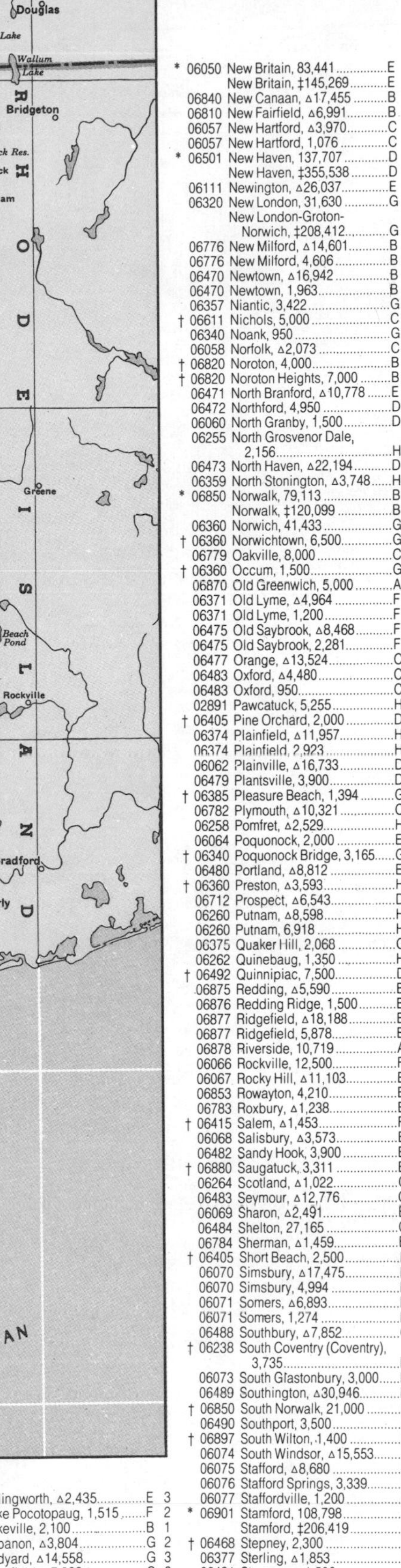

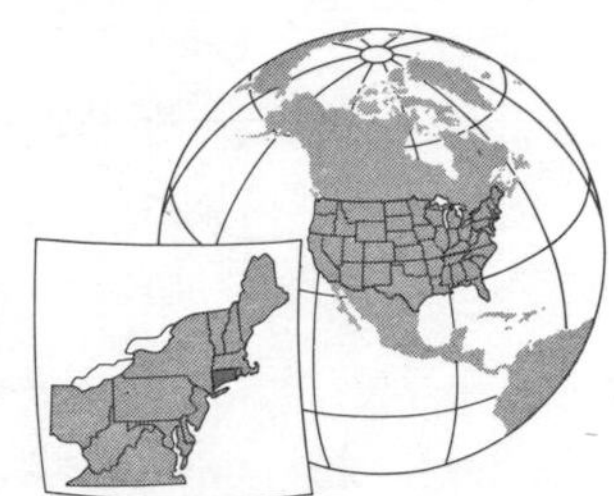

AREA 5,009 sq. mi.
POPULATION 3,032,217
CAPITAL Hartford
LARGEST CITY Hartford
HIGHEST POINT Mt. Frissell (S. Slope) 2,380 ft.
SETTLED IN 1635
ADMITTED TO UNION January 9, 1788
POPULAR NAME Constitution State; Nutmeg State
STATE FLOWER Mountain Laurel
STATE BIRD Robin

Agriculture, Industry and Resources

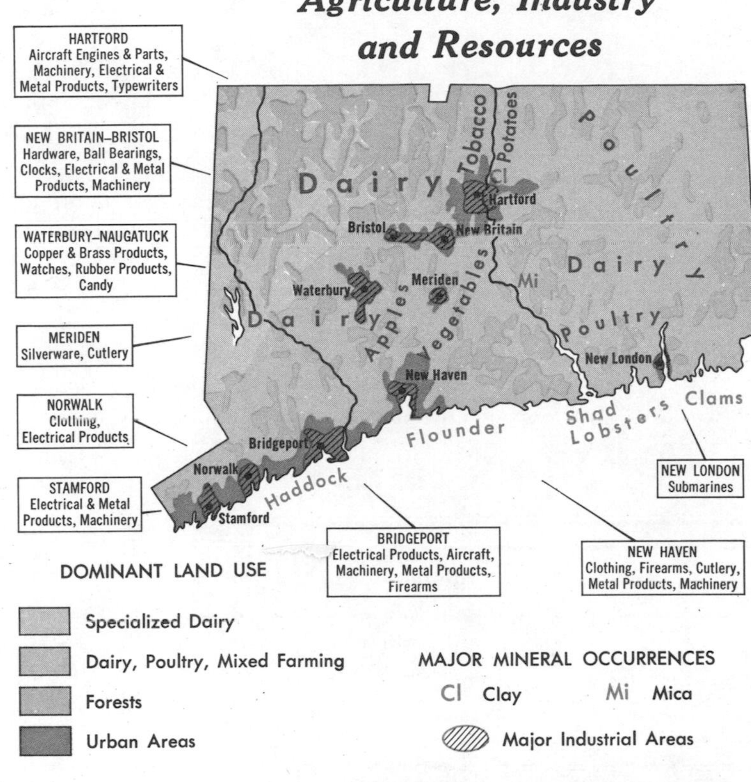

† 06254 Franklin, ∆1,356 G 2
06335 Gales Ferry, 6,200 G 3
06829 Georgetown, 1,101 B 4
06033 Glastonbury, ∆20,651 E 2
06756 Goshen, ∆1,351 C 1
06035 Granby, ∆6,150 D 1
† 06430 Greenfield Hill, 2,500 B 4
06436 Greens Farms, 3,147 B 4
06830 Greenwich, ∆59,755 A 4
06340 Groton, ∆38,523 G 3
06340 Groton, 8,933 G 3
06437 Guilford, ∆12,033 E 3
06437 Guilford, 3,632 E 3
06438 Haddam, ∆4,934 E 3
06438 Haddam, 950 E 3
06514 Hamden, ∆49,357 D 3
06247 Hampton, ∆1,129 G 1
* 06101 Hartford (cap.), 158,017 E 1
Hartford, ‡663,891 E 1
† 06091 Hartland, ∆1,303 D 1
06790 Harwinton, ∆4,318 C 1
06082 Hazardville, 10,000 E 1
06248 Hebron, ∆3,815 F 2
06441 Higganum, 2,600 E 2
† 06108 Hockanum, 6,500 E 2
† 06484 Huntington, 2,000 C 3
† 06405 Indian Neck, 1,500 D 3
06442 Ivoryton, 1,500 F 3
06351 Jewett City, 3,372 H 2
06037 Kensington, 6,000 D 2
06757 Kent, ∆1,990 B 2
† 06241 Killingly, ∆13,573 H 1
† 06413 Killingworth, ∆2,435 E 3
† 06424 Lake Pocotopaug, 1,515 F 2
06039 Lakeville, 2,100 B 1
06249 Lebanon, ∆3,804 G 2
06339 Ledyard, ∆14,558 G 3
06759 Litchfield, ∆7,399 C 2
06759 Litchfield, 1,559 C 2
06443 Madison, ∆9,768 E 3
06443 Madison, 4,310 E 3
06040 Manchester, ∆47,994 E 1
† 06250 Mansfield, ∆19,994 F 1
06444 Marion, 1,800 D 2
† 06424 Marlborough, ∆2,991 F 2
06450 Meriden, 55,959 D 2
Meriden, ‡55,959 D 2
06762 Middlebury, ∆5,542 C 2
06455 Middlefield, ∆4,132 E 2
06457 Middletown, 36,924 E 2
06460 Milford, 50,858 C 4
06467 Milldale, 1,175 D 2
06468 Monroe, ∆12,047 C 3
06468 Monroe P.O. (Stepney), 3,000 B 3
† 06473 Montowese, 2,500 D 3
06353 Montville, 1,688 G 3
06353 Montville, ∆15,662 G 3
06469 Moodus, 1,352 F 2
06354 Moosup, 3,376 H 2
† 06385 Morningside Park, 3,458 G 3
06763 Morris, ∆1,609 C 2
06355 Mystic, 2,568 H 3
06770 Naugatuck, 23,034 C 3

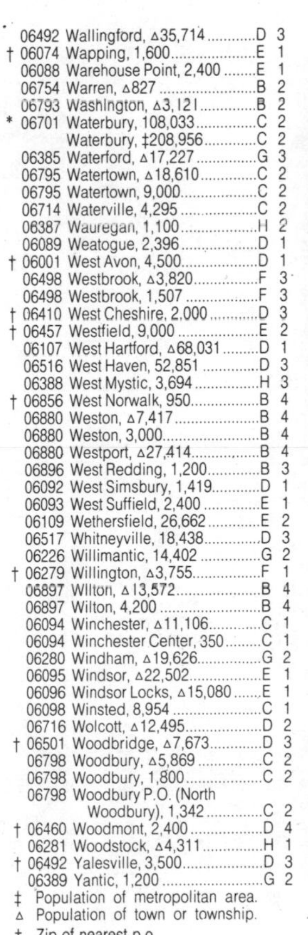

* 06050 New Britain, 83,441 E 2
New Britain, ‡145,269 E 2
06840 New Canaan, ∆17,455 B 4
06810 New Fairfield, ∆6,991 B 3
06057 New Hartford, ∆3,970 C 1
06057 New Hartford, 1,076 C 1
* 06501 New Haven, 137,707 D 3
New Haven, ‡355,538 D 3
06111 Newington, ∆26,037 E 2
06320 New London, 31,630 G 3
New London-Groton-Norwich, ‡208,412 G 3
06776 New Milford, ∆14,601 B 2
06776 New Milford, 4,606 B 2
06470 Newtown, ∆16,942 B 3
06470 Newtown, 1,963 B 3
06357 Niantic, 3,422 G 3
† 06611 Nichols, 5,000 C 4
06340 Noank, 950 G 3
06058 Norfolk, ∆2,073 C 1
† 06820 Noroton, 4,000 B 4
† 06820 Noroton Heights, 7,000 B 4
06471 North Branford, ∆10,778 E 3
06472 Northford, 4,950 D 3
06060 North Granby, 1,500 D 1
06255 North Grosvenor Dale, 2,156 H 1
06473 North Haven, ∆22,194 D 3
06359 North Stonington, ∆3,748 H 3
* 06850 Norwalk, 79,113 B 4
Norwalk, ‡120,099 B 4
06360 Norwich, 41,433 G 2
† 06360 Norwichtown, 6,500 G 2
06779 Oakville, 8,000 C 2
† 06360 Occum, 1,500 G 2
06870 Old Greenwich, 5,000 A 4
06371 Old Lyme, ∆4,964 F 3
06371 Old Lyme, 1,200 F 3
06475 Old Saybrook, ∆8,468 F 3
06475 Old Saybrook, 2,281 F 3
06477 Orange, ∆13,524 C 3
06483 Oxford, ∆4,480 C 3
06483 Oxford, 950 C 3
02891 Pawcatuck, 5,255 H 3
† 06405 Pine Orchard, 2,000 D 3
06374 Plainfield, ∆11,957 H 2
06374 Plainfield, 2,923 H 2
06062 Plainville, ∆16,733 D 2
06479 Plantsville, 3,900 D 2
† 06385 Pleasure Beach, 1,394 G 3
06782 Plymouth, ∆10,321 C 2
06258 Pomfret, ∆2,529 H 1
06064 Poquonock, 2,000 E 1
† 06340 Poquonock Bridge, 3,165 G 3
06480 Portland, ∆8,812 E 2
† 06360 Preston, ∆3,593 H 2
06712 Prospect, ∆6,543 D 2
06260 Putnam, ∆8,598 H 1
06260 Putnam, 6,918 H 1
06375 Quaker Hill, 2,068 G 3
06262 Quinebaug, 1,350 H 1
† 06492 Quinnipiac, 7,500 D 3
06875 Redding, ∆5,590 B 3
06876 Redding Ridge, 1,500 B 3
06877 Ridgefield, ∆18,188 B 3
06877 Ridgefield, 5,878 B 3
06878 Riverside, 10,719 A 4
06066 Rockville, 12,500 F 1
06067 Rocky Hill, ∆11,103 E 2
06853 Rowayton, 4,210 B 4
06783 Roxbury, ∆1,238 B 2
† 06415 Salem, ∆1,453 F 3
06068 Salisbury, ∆3,573 B 1
06482 Sandy Hook, 3,900 B 3
† 06880 Saugatuck, 3,311 B 4
06264 Scotland, ∆1,022 G 2
06483 Seymour, ∆12,776 C 3
06069 Sharon, ∆2,491 B 1
06484 Shelton, 27,165 C 3
06784 Sherman, ∆1,459 B 2
† 06405 Short Beach, 2,500 D 3
06070 Simsbury, ∆17,475 D 1
06070 Simsbury, 4,994 D 1
06071 Somers, ∆6,893 F 1
06071 Somers, 1,274 F 1
06488 Southbury, ∆7,852 C 3
† 06238 South Coventry (Coventry), 3,735 F 1
06073 South Glastonbury, 3,000 E 2
06489 Southington, ∆30,946 D 2
† 06850 South Norwalk, 21,000 B 4
06490 Southport, 3,500 B 4
† 06897 South Wilton, 1,400 B 4
06074 South Windsor, ∆15,553 E 1
06075 Stafford, ∆8,680 F 1
06076 Stafford Springs, 3,339 F 1
06077 Staffordville, 1,200 G 1
* 06901 Stamford, 108,798 A 4
Stamford, ‡206,419 A 4
† 06468 Stepney, 2,300 B 3
06377 Sterling, ∆1,853 H 2
06491 Stevenson, 1,500 C 3
06378 Stonington, ∆15,940 H 3
06378 Stonington, 1,413 H 3
† 06405 Stony Creek, 2,800 E 3
06268 Storrs, 10,691 F 1
06497 Stratford, ∆49,775 C 4
06078 Suffield, ∆8,634 E 1
06380 Taftville, 2,000 G 2
06081 Tariffville, 1,337 D 1
06786 Terryville, 6,900 C 2
† 06360 Thamesville, 1,500 G 2
06787 Thomaston, ∆6,233 C 2
06277 Thompson, ∆7,580 H 1
06277 Thompson, 1,200 H 1
† 06082 Thompsonville, 27,000 E 1
06084 Tolland, ∆7,857 F 1
† 06790 Torringford, 3,500 C 1
06790 Torrington, 31,952 C 1
† 06405 Totoket, 950 D 3
06611 Trumbull, ∆31,394 C 4
06611 Trumbull, 10,000 C 4
06382 Uncasville, 1,750 G 3
† 06076 Union, ∆443 G 1
† 06770 Union City, 5,000 C 2
06085 Unionville, 2,900 D 1
06066 Vernon, ∆27,237 F 1
06384 Voluntown, ∆1,452 H 2

06492 Wallingford, ∆35,714 D 3
† 06074 Wapping, 1,600 E 1
06088 Warehouse Point, 2,400 E 1
06754 Warren, ∆827 B 2
06793 Washington, ∆3,121 B 2
* 06701 Waterbury, 108,033 C 2
Waterbury, ‡208,956 C 2
06385 Waterford, ∆17,227 G 3
06795 Watertown, ∆18,610 C 2
06795 Watertown, 9,000 C 2
06714 Waterville, 4,295 C 2
06387 Wauregan, 1,100 H 2
06089 Weatogue, 2,396 D 1
† 06001 West Avon, 4,500 D 1
06498 Westbrook, ∆3,820 F 3
06498 Westbrook, 1,507 F 3
† 06410 West Cheshire, 2,000 D 3
† 06457 Westfield, 9,000 E 2
06107 West Hartford, ∆68,031 D 1
06516 West Haven, 52,851 D 3
06388 West Mystic, 3,694 H 3
† 06856 West Norwalk, 950 B 4
06880 Weston, ∆7,417 B 4
06880 Weston, 3,000 B 4
06880 Westport, ∆27,414 B 4
06896 West Redding, 1,200 B 3
06092 West Simsbury, 1,419 D 1
06093 West Suffield, 2,400 E 1
06109 Wethersfield, 26,662 E 2
06517 Whitneyville, 18,438 D 3
06226 Willimantic, 14,402 G 2
† 06279 Willington, ∆3,755 F 1
06897 Wilton, ∆13,572 B 4
06897 Wilton, 4,200 B 4
06094 Winchester, ∆11,106 C 1
06094 Winchester Center, 350 C 1
06280 Windham, ∆19,626 G 2
06095 Windsor, ∆22,502 E 1
06096 Windsor Locks, ∆15,080 E 1
06098 Winsted, 8,954 C 1
06716 Wolcott, ∆12,495 D 2
† 06501 Woodbridge, ∆7,673 D 3
06798 Woodbury, ∆5,869 C 2
06798 Woodbury, 1,800 C 2
06798 Woodbury P.O. (North Woodbury), 1,342 C 2
† 06460 Woodmont, 2,400 D 4
06281 Woodstock, ∆4,311 H 1
† 06492 Yalesville, 3,500 D 3
06389 Yantic, 1,200 G 2

‡ Population of metropolitan area.
∆ Population of town or township.
† Zip of nearest p.o.
* Multiple zips

Edmund V. Ballman

Bark whaler "Charles W. Morgan," on view at Mystic, Connecticut, covered more miles and caught more whales than any other ship of her kind.

FLORIDA
SCALE
0 5 10 20 30 40 50MI.
0 5 10 20 30 40 50KM.
State Capitals
County Seats
Canals
© C.S. HAMMOND & Co., N.Y.
Longitude West 83° of Greenwich
ALA.
G E O R G I A
ATLANTIC OCEAN
GULF OF MEXICO
STRAITS OF FLORIDA
FLORIDA KEYS
JACKSON
CALHOUN
GADSDEN
LEON
LIBERTY
WAKULLA
JEFFERSON
MADISON
HAMILTON
TAYLOR
SUWANNEE
COLUMBIA
LAFAYETTE
GULF
FRANKLIN
NASSAU
BAKER
DUVAL
UNION
BRADFORD
CLAY
ST. JOHNS
PUTNAM
ALACHUA
GILCHRIST
DIXIE
LEVY
MARION
FLAGLER
VOLUSIA
CITRUS
SUMTER
LAKE
SEMINOLE
ORANGE
HERNANDO
PASCO
PINELLAS
HILLSBOROUGH
POLK
OSCEOLA
BREVARD
INDIAN RIVER
MANATEE
HARDEE
HIGHLANDS
OKEECHOBEE
ST. LUCIE
SARASOTA
DE SOTO
MARTIN
CHARLOTTE
GLADES
PALM BEACH
LEE
HENDRY
COLLIER
BROWARD
DADE
MONROE
Tallahassee
Jacksonville
Tampa
St. Petersburg
Orlando
Miami
Miami Beach
Key West
Lake Okeechobee
Big Cypress Swamp
EVERGLADES NATIONAL PARK
WESTERN PART OF FLORIDA
Same scale as main map
A L A B A M A
GULF OF MEXICO
ESCAMBIA
SANTA ROSA
OKALOOSA
WALTON
HOLMES
WASHINGTON
BAY
Pensacola
Panama City

COUNTIES

County, Pop.	Key
Alachua, 104,764	D 2
Baker, 9,242	D 1
Bay, 75,283	C 6
Bradford, 14,625	D 2
Brevard, 230,006	F 3
Broward, 620,100	F 5
Calhoun, 7,624	D 6
Charlotte, 27,559	E 5
Citrus, 19,196	D 3
Clay, 32,059	E 2
Collier, 38,040	E 5
Columbia, 25,250	D 1
Dade, 1,287,792	F 6
De Soto, 13,060	E 4
Dixie, 5,480	C 2
Duval, 528,865	E 1
Escambia, 205,334	B 6
Flagler, 4,454	E 2
Franklin, 7,065	B 2
Gadsden, 39,184	B 1
Gilchrist, 3,551	D 2
Glades, 3,669	E 5
Gulf, 10,096	D 7
Hamilton, 7,787	D 1
Hardee, 14,889	E 4
Hendry, 11,859	E 5
Hernando, 17,004	D 3
Highlands, 29,507	E 4
Hillsborough, 490,265	D 4
Holmes, 10,720	C 5
Indian River, 35,992	F 4
Jackson, 34,434	D 5
Jefferson, 8,778	C 1
Lafayette, 2,892	C 2
Lake, 69,305	E 3
Lee, 105,216	E 5
Leon, 103,047	B 1
Levy, 12,756	D 2
Liberty, 3,379	B 1
Madison, 13,481	C 1
Manatee, 97,115	D 4
Marion, 69,030	D 2
Martin, 28,035	F 4
Monroe, 52,586	E 7
Nassau, 20,626	E 1
Okaloosa, 88,187	C 6
Okeechobee, 11,233	F 4
Orange, 344,311	E 3
Osceola, 25,267	E 3
Palm Beach, 348,753	F 5
Pasco, 75,955	D 3
Pinellas, 522,329	D 4
Polk, 227,222	E 4
Putnam, 36,290	E 2
Saint Johns, 30,727	E 2
Saint Lucie, 50,836	F 4
Santa Rosa, 37,741	B 6
Sarasota, 120,413	D 4
Seminole, 83,692	E 3
Sumter, 14,839	D 3
Suwannee, 15,559	C 1
Taylor, 13,641	C 1
Union, 8,112	D 1
Volusia, 169,487	E 2
Wakulla, 6,308	B 1
Walton, 16,087	C 6
Washington, 11,453	C 6

CITIES and TOWNS

	Zip	Name/Pop.	Key
	32615	Alachua, 2,252	D 2
	32420	Alford, 402	D 6
	32421	Altha, 423	A 1
	32702	Altoona, 800	E 3
	33820	Alturas, 468	E 4
	33920	Alva, 900	E 5
	33501	Anna Maria, 1,137	D 4
	32617	Anthony, 500	D 2
	32320	Apalachicola⊙, 3,102	A 2
	33570	Apollo Beach, 1,042	C 3
	32703	Apopka, 4,045.	E 3
	33821	Arcadia⊙, 5,658	E 4
	32618	Archer, 898	D 2
	32422	Argyle, 155	C 6
	33502	Aripeka, 300	D 3
†	32327	Arran, 160	B 1
	32705	Astatula, 388	E 3
	32002	Astor, 300	E 2
	33823	Auburndale, 5,386	E 3
†	32344	Aucilla, 150	C 1
	33825	Avon Park, 6,712	E 4
	33827	Babson Park, 950	E 4
	32530	Bagdad, 850	B 6
	32531	Baker, 500	C 5
	32234	Baldwin, 1,272	E 1
†	33101	Bal Harbour, 2,038	C 4
	32005	Barberville, 300	E 2
†	32533	Barrineau Park, 150	B 6
	32532	Barth, 200	B 6
	33830	Bartow⊙, 12,891	E 4
	32423	Bascom, 200	A 1
	33428	Basinger, 300	F 4
†	33101	Bay Harbour Islands, 4,619	B 4
	33504	Bay Pines, 1,100	B 3
†	33902	Bayshore, 150	E 5
†	36502	Bay Springs, 125	B 6
	33429	Bean City, 155	F 5
	33578	Bee Ridge, 2,100	D 4
	32619	Bell, 227	D 2
	33540	Belleair, 2,962	B 2
†	33540	Belleair Beach, 952	B 2
	33540	Belleair Bluffs, 1,910	B 3
	33430	Belle Glade, 15,949	F 5
†	33430	Belle Glade Camp, 1,892	F 5
†	32801	Belle Isle, 2,705	E 3
	32620	Belleview, 916	D 2
	33152	Biscayne Park, 2,717	B 4
†	32801	Bithlo, 684	E 3
	32424	Blountstown⊙, 2,384	A 1
†	32535	Bluffsprings, 160	B 5
	33921	Boca Grande, 600	D 5
	33432	Boca Raton, 28,506	F 5
	33922	Bokeelia, 750	D 5
	32425	Bonifay⊙, 2,068	C 5
	33923	Bonita Springs, 1,932	E 5
	32007	Bostwick, 500	E 2
	33834	Bowling Green, 1,357	E 4
	33435	Boynton Beach, 18,115	F 5
	33505	Bradenton⊙, 21,040	D 4
	33510	Bradenton Beach, 1,370	D 4
	33835	Bradley, 1,276	D 4
	33511	Brandon, 12,749	D 4
	32008	Branford, 820	D 2
†	33435	Briny Breezes, 481	G 5
	32321	Bristol⊙, 626	B 1
	32621	Bronson⊙, 698	D 2
	32622	Brooker, 340	D 2
	33512	Brooksville⊙, 4,060	D 3
†	33101	Browns Village, 23,442	B 4
	32455	Bruce, 221	C 6
	33439	Bryant, 400	F 5
†	33054	Bunche Park, 5,773	B 4
	32010	Bunnell⊙, 1,687	E 2
	33513	Bushnell⊙, 700	D 3
	32011	Callahan, 772	E 1
	32401	Callaway, 3,240	D 6
	32426	Campbellton, 304	D 5
	33438	Canal Point, 900	F 5
	32624	Candler, 500	E 2
	32533	Cantonment, 3,241	B 6
	32920	Cape Canaveral, 4,258	F 3
	33904	Cape Coral, 10,193	E 5
	33924	Captiva, 150	D 5
	33054	Carol City, 27,361	B 4
	32322	Carrabelle, 1,044	B 2
	32427	Caryville, 724	C 6
	32706	Cassadaga, 250	E 3
	32707	Casselberry, 9,438	E 3
†	32401	Cedar Grove, 689	D 6
	32625	Cedar Key, 714	C 2
	33514	Center Hill, 371	D 3
	32535	Century, 2,679	B 5
†	32302	Chaires, 150	B 1
	33950	Charlotte Harbor, 990	E 5
	32324	Chattahoochee, 7,944	B 1
†	32350	Cherry Lake Farms, 400	C 1
	32626	Chiefland, 1,965	D 2
	32428	Chipley⊙, 3,347	D 6
	33925	Chokoloskee, 230	E 6
	32709	Christmas, 800	E 3
†	32548	Cinco Bayou, 362	B 6
	32627	Citra, 500	D 2
†	32922	City Point, 350	F 3
	32430	Clarksville, 250	D 6
*	33515	Clearwater⊙, 52,074	B 2
	32711	Clermont, 3,661	E 3
†	33950	Cleveland, 150	E 5
	33440	Clewiston, 3,896	E 5
	32922	Cocoa, 16,110	F 3
	32931	Cocoa Beach, 9,952	F 3
†	33060	Coconut Creek, 1,359	F 5
	33521	Coleman, 614	D 3
	32448	Compass Lake, 200	D 6
†	32333	Concord, 300	B 1
	33314	Cooper City, 2,535	F 5
	33926	Copeland, 500	E 6
†	83559	Coral Cove, 1,520	D 4
	33134	Coral Gables, 42,494	B 5
	33836	Cornwell, 700	E 4
	33522	Cortez, 600	D 4
	32533	Cottagehill, 500	B 6
	32431	Cottondale, 765	D 6
	32327	Crawfordville⊙, 750	B 1
	32012	Crescent City, 1,734	E 2
	32536	Crestview⊙, 7,952	C 6
	32628	Cross City⊙, 2,268	C 2
	32463	Crystal Lake, 125	D 6
	32629	Crystal River, 1,696	D 3
	33524	Crystal Springs, 300	D 3
	33157	Cutler Ridge, 17,441	F 6
	32432	Cypress, 266	A 1
	33880	Cypress Gardens, 3,757	E 3
†	33472	Cypress Quarters, 1,310	F 4
	33525	Dade City⊙, 4,241	D 3
	33004	Dania, 9,013	B 4
†	32464	Darlington, 175	C 5
	33837	Davenport, 828	E 3
	33314	Davie, 2,856	B 4
	32013	Day, 200	C 1
*	32014	Daytona Beach, 45,327	F 2
	32016	Daytona Beach Shores, 768	F 2
	32713	De Bary, 3,154	E 3
	33441	Deerfield Beach, 17,130	F 5
	32433	De Funiak Springs⊙, 4,966	C 6
	32720	De Land⊙, 11,641	E 2
	32028	De Leon Springs, 1,134	E 2
	33444	Delray Beach, 19,366	F 5
	32763	Deltona, 4,868	E 3
†	33870	De Soto City, 250	E 4
	32541	Destin, 1,536	C 6
	32030	Doctors Inlet, 800	E 1
	33527	Dover, 2,094	D 4
†	32060	Dowling Park, 200	C 1
	33838	Dundee, 1,660	E 3
	33528	Dunedin, 17,639	B 2
	32630	Dunnellon, 1,146	D 2
	33839	Eagle Lake, 1,373	E 4
	32631	Earleton, 350	D 2
†	33601	East Lake-Orient Park, 5,697	C 2
†	33940	East Naples, 6,152	E 5
	32031	East Palatka, 1,446	E 2
	32328	Eastpoint, 1,188	B 2
	32437	Ebro, 125	C 6
	32032	Edgewater, 3,348	F 3
†	32801	Edgewood, 392	E 3
†	33601	Egypt Lake, 7,556	C 2
	33531	Elfers, 500	D 3
	32033	Elkton, 240	E 2
†	33101	El Portal, 2,068	B 4
	33533	Englewood, 5,182	D 5
	32504	Ensley, 2,400	B 6

(continued on following page)

AREA 58,560 sq. mi.
POPULATION 6,789,443
CAPITAL Tallahassee
LARGEST CITY Jacksonville
HIGHEST POINT 345 ft. (Walton County)
SETTLED IN 1565
ADMITTED TO UNION March 3, 1845
POPULAR NAME Sunshine State; Peninsula State
STATE FLOWER Orange Blossom
STATE BIRD Mockingbird

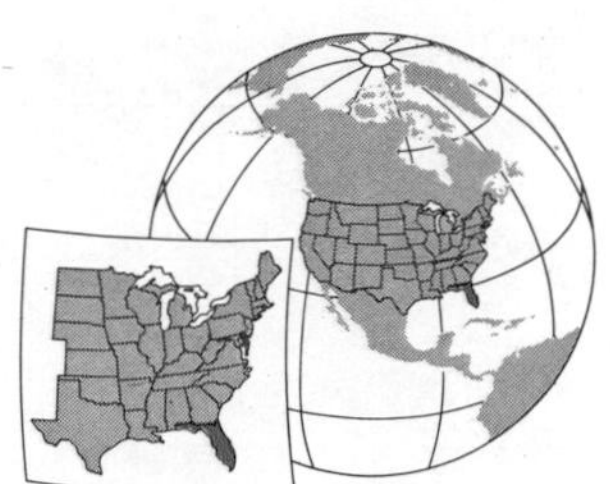

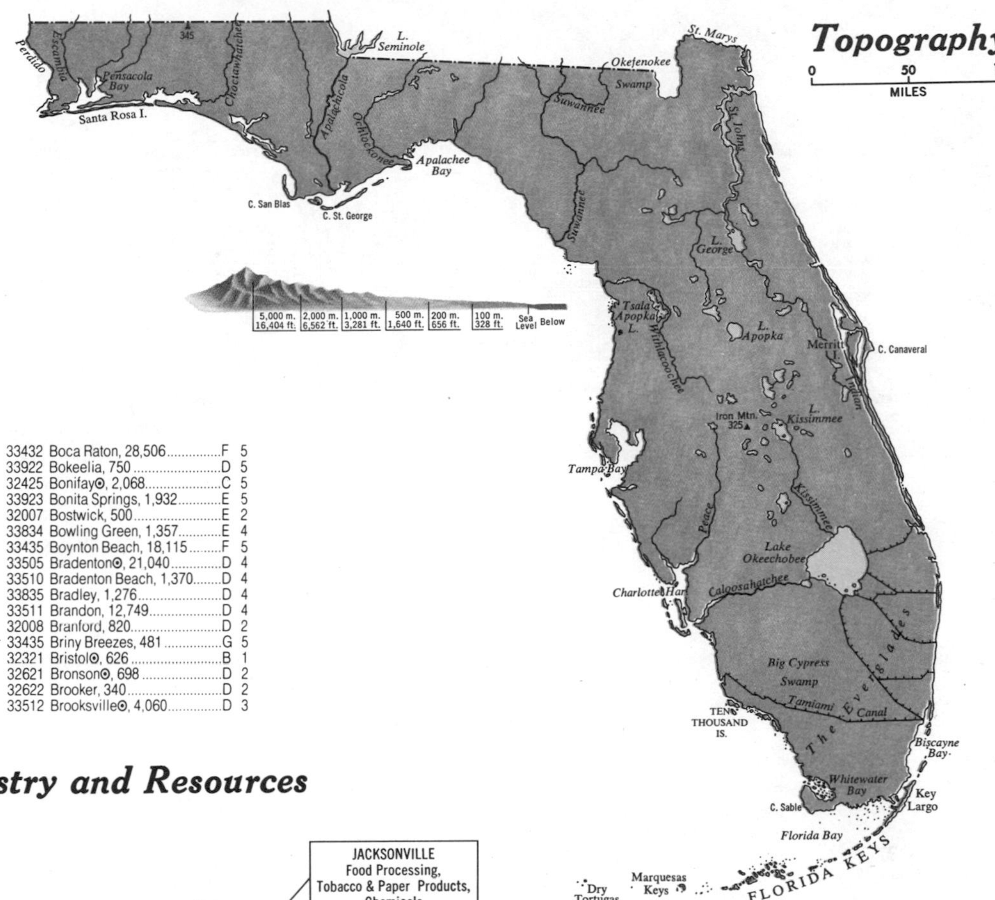

Agriculture, Industry and Resources

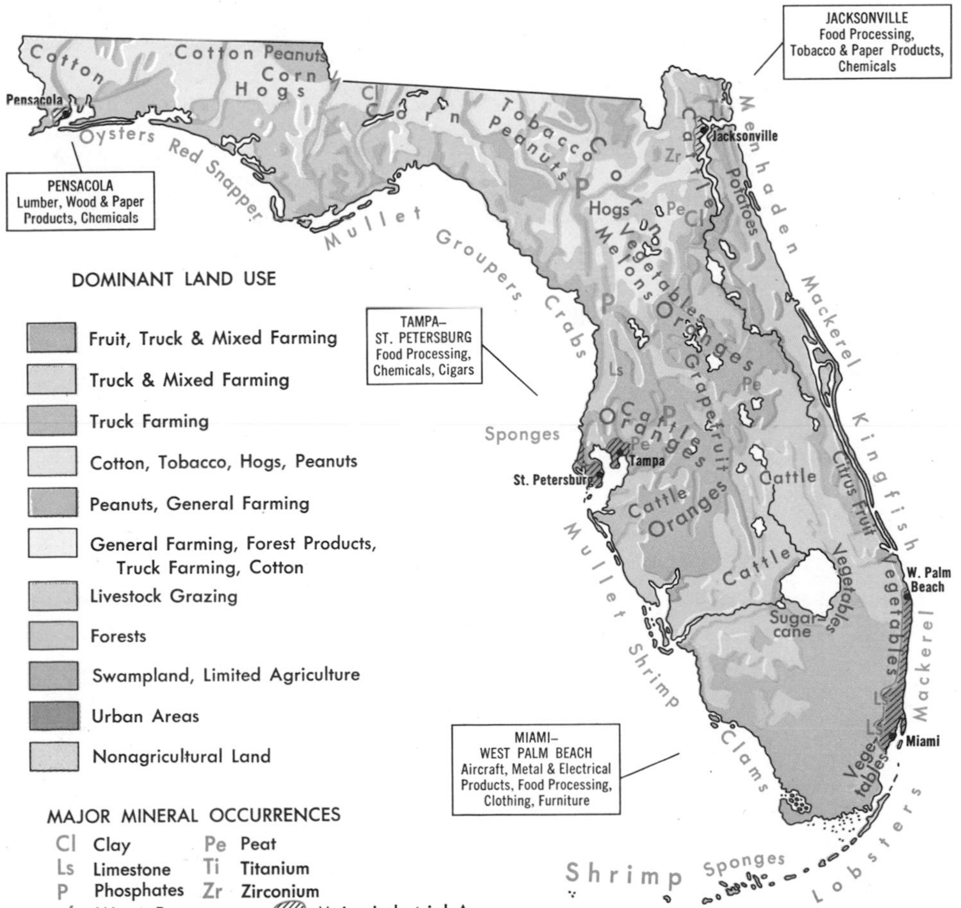

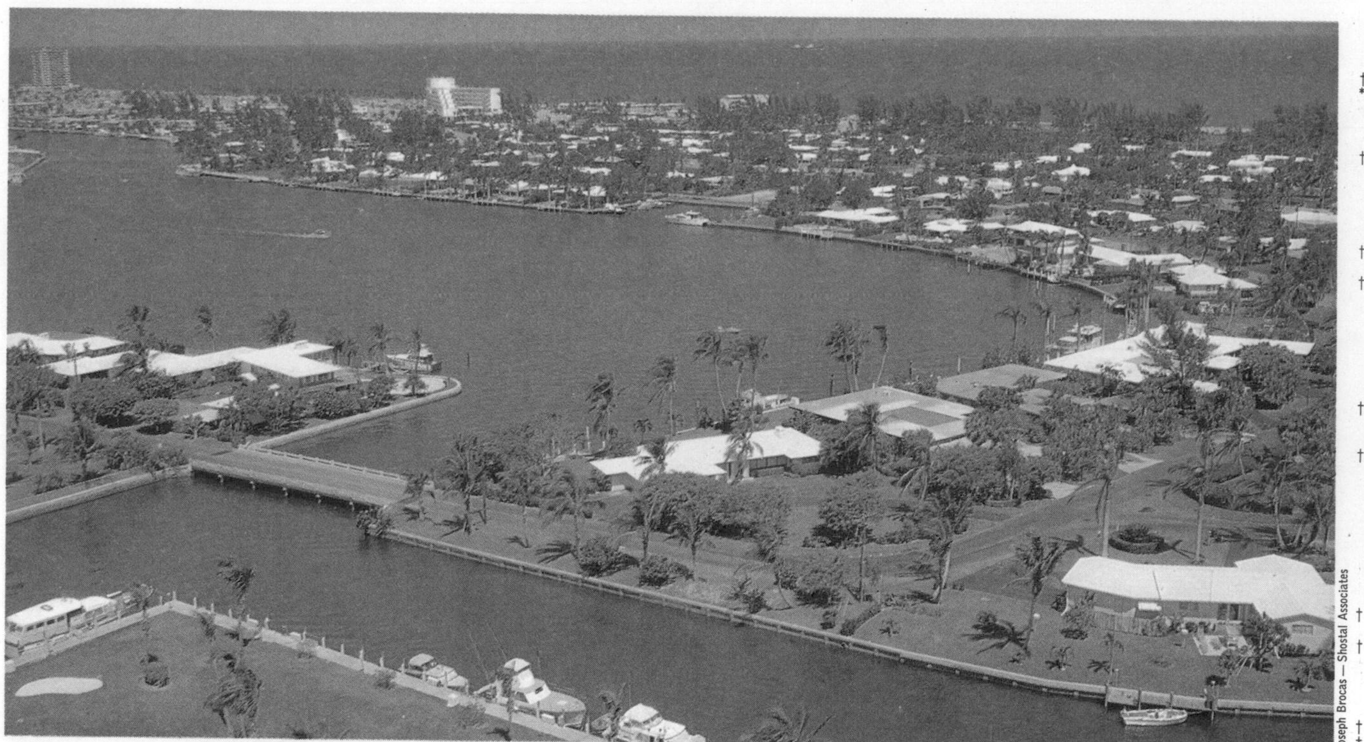
Joseph Brocas — Shostal Associates

Over 150 miles of inland waterways provide a Venetian atmosphere in the modern city of Fort Lauderdale, Florida.

† 32010 Espanola, 300 E 2
33928 Estero, 950 E 5
32425 Esto, 210 C 5
32726 Eustis, 6,722 E 3
33929 Everglades City, 462 E 6
† 32601 Fairbanks, 380 D 2
† 32804 Fairvilla, 950 E 3
33930 Felda, 125 E 5
32948 Fellsmere, 813 F 4
32034 Fernandina Beach⊙, 6,955 E 1
† 33301 Fern Crest Village, 1,009 B 4
32036 Flagler Beach, 1,042 E 2
32635 Florahome, 400 E 2
32636 Floral City, 975 D 3
33030 Florida City, 5,133 F 6
† 32570 Floridatown, 297 B 6
† 32569 Florosa, 200 B 6
† 32347 Foley, 500 C 1
† 33935 Fort Denaud, 300 E 5
† 33472 Fort Drum, 100 F 4
33834 Fort Green, 300 E 4
* 33301 Fort Lauderdale⊙, 139,590 C 4
Fort Lauderdale-Hollywood, ‡620,100 C 4
32637 Fort McCoy, 900 E 2
33841 Fort Meade, 4,374 E 4
* 33901 Fort Myers⊙, 27,351 E 5
33931 Fort Myers Beach, 4,305 E 5
33842 Fort Ogden, 700 E 4
33450 Fort Pierce⊙, 29,721 F 4
32548 Fort Walton Beach, 19,994 C 6
32038 Fort White, 365 D 2
32438 Fountain, 650 D 6
32439 Freeport, 950 C 6
† 32430 Frink, 275 D 6
33843 Frostproof, 2,814 E 4
32731 Fruitland Park, 1,359 D 3
33578 Fruitville, 1,531 D 4
32601 Gainesville⊙, 64,510 D 2
32732 Geneva, 950 E 3
32039 Georgetown, 687 E 2
33534 Gibsonton, 1,900 C 3
32960 Gifford, 5,772 F 4
32040 Glen Saint Mary, 357 D 1
32722 Glenwood, 400 E 2
33160 Golden Beach, 849 C 4
33940 Golden Gate, 1,410 E 5
† 33455 Gomez, 400 F 4
32560 Gonzalez, 750 B 6
33933 Goodland, 500 E 6
† 32502 Goulding, 500 B 6
33170 Goulds, 6,690 F 6
32440 Graceville, 2,560 D 5
32042 Graham, 150 D 2
32638 Grandin, 150 E 2
32442 Grand Ridge, 512 A 1
32949 Grant, 500 F 4
33460 Greenacres City, 1,731 F 5
32043 Green Cove Springs⊙, 3,857 E 2
32330 Greensboro, 716 B 1
32331 Greenville, 1,141 C 1
32443 Greenwood, 515 A 1
32332 Gretna, 883 B 1
33533 Grove City, 1,178 F 5
32736 Groveland, 1,928 E 3
32561 Gulf Breeze, 4,190 B 6
32639 Gulf Hammock, 300 D 2
† 33552 Gulf Harbors, 1,177 D 3
33737 Gulfport, 9,730 B 3
† 33444 Gulf Stream, 408 F 5
† 32601 Hague, 200 D 2
33844 Haines City, 8,956 E 3
33009 Hallandale, 23,849 B 4
32044 Hampton, 386 D 2
33440 Harlem, 2,006 F 5
32563 Harold, 150 B 6
32045 Hastings, 320 E 2
32333 Havana, 2,022 B 1
32640 Hawthorne, 1,126 D 2
32642 Hernando, 524 D 3
* 33010 Hialeah, 102,297 B 4
† 33010 Hialeah Gardens, 492 B 4
33846 Highland City, 900 E 4
† 33515 High Point, 800 B 3
32643 High Springs, 2,787 D 2
32401 Hiland Park, 3,691 C 6
† 33827 Hillcrest Heights, 154 E 4
32046 Hilliard, 1,205 E 1
† 32327 Hilliardville, 150 B 1
† 33060 Hillsboro Beach, 713 F 5
† 32333 Hinson, 250 B 1
33455 Hobe Sound, 2,029 F 4
32645 Holder, 134 D 3
32047 Hollister, 500 E 2
32017 Holly Hill, 8,191 E 2
* 33020 Hollywood, 106,873 B 4
† 33020 Hollywood Ridge Farms, 302 B 4
33509 Holmes Beach, 2,699 D 4
32564 Holt, 850 C 6
33030 Homestead, 13,674 F 6
32646 Homosassa, 850 D 3
32647 Homosassa Springs, 550 D 3
32334 Hosford, 975 B 1
32737 Howey In The Hills, 466 E 3
33568 Hudson, 2,278 D 3
† 33460 Hypoluxo, 336 F 5
33934 Immokalee, 3,764 E 5
32901 Indialantic, 2,685 F 3
32935 Indian Harbour Beach, 5,371 F 3
33535 Indian Rocks Beach, 2,666 B 3
† 33535 Indian Rocks Beach South Shore, 791 B 3
33456 Indiantown, 2,283 F 4
32649 Inglis, 449 D 2
33848 Intercession City, 600 E 3
32048 Interlachen, 478 E 2
32650 Inverness⊙, 2,299 D 3
33036 Islamorada, 1,251 F 7
32654 Island Grove, 200 D 2
* 32201 Jacksonville⊙, 528,865 E 1
Jacksonville, ‡528,865 E 1
32250 Jacksonville Beach, 12,049 E 1
32052 Jasper⊙, 2,221 D 1
32565 Jay, 646 B 5
32053 Jennings, 582 C 1
33457 Jensen Beach, 3,000 F 4
† 32901 June Park, 3,090 F 3
† 33404 Juno Beach, 747 F 5
33458 Jupiter, 3,136 F 5
† 33455 Jupiter Island, 295 F 4
33849 Kathleen, 900 D 3
32739 Kenansville, 450 F 4
33156 Kendall, 35,497 B 5
† 32670 Kendrick, 200 D 2
33709 Kenneth City, 3,862 B 3
33149 Key Biscayne, 4,563 B 5
33051 Key Colony Beach, 371 F 7
33037 Key Largo, 2,866 F 6
32656 Keystone Heights, 800 E 2
33040 Key West⊙, 27,563 E 7
32449 Kinard, 450 D 6
32741 Kissimmee⊙, 7,119 E 3
† 32010 Korona, 200 E 2
33935 La Belle⊙, 1,823 E 5
33537 Lacoochee, 1,380 D 3
32658 La Crosse, 365 D 2
32659 Lady Lake, 382 E 3
33850 Lake Alfred, 2,847 E 3
32054 Lake Butler⊙, 1,598 D 1
† 33601 Lake Carroll, 5,577 C 2
32055 Lake City⊙, 10,575 D 1
32057 Lake Como, 340 E 2
33459 Lake Harbor, 300 F 5
32744 Lake Helen, 1,303 E 3
32745 Lake Jem, 314 E 3
* 33801 Lakeland, 41,550 D 3
† 33601 Lake Magdalene, 9,266 D 3
32746 Lake Mary, 900 E 3
32747 Lake Monroe, 500 E 3
33403 Lake Park, 6,993 F 5
33852 Lake Placid, 656 E 4
† 33471 Lakeport, 375 E 5
33853 Lake Wales, 8,240 E 4
32566 Lakewood, 525 C 5
33460 Lake Worth, 23,714 G 5
32336 Lamont, 500 C 1
33539 Land O'Lakes, 900 D 3
33460 Lantana, 7,126 F 5
33540 Largo, 22,031 B 3
33308 Lauderdale-by-the-Sea, 2,879 C 3
† 33301 Lauderdale Lakes, 10,577 B 4
33313 Lauderhill, 8,465 B 4
32567 Laurel Hill, 418 C 5
33545 Laurel-Nokomis, 3,238 D 4
32058 Lawtey, 636 D 1
32661 Lecanto, 125 D 3
32059 Lee, 240 C 1
32748 Leesburg, 11,869 E 3
33936 Lehigh Acres, 4,394 E 5
33030 Leisure City, 2,900 F 6
† 33601 Leto, 8,458 C 2
33064 Lighthouse Point, 9,071 F 5
† 33865 Limestone, 200 E 4
32060 Live Oak⊙, 6,830 D 1
32337 Lloyd, 225 C 1
32662 Lochloosa, 175 E 2
33548 Longboat Key, 2,850 D 4
33001 Long Key, 150 F 7
32750 Longwood, 3,203 E 3
33857 Lorida, 950 E 4
33858 Loughman, 950 E 3
32663 Lowell, 350 D 2
33470 Loxahatchee, 950 F 5
33549 Lutz, 950 D 3
32444 Lynn Haven, 4,044 C 6
32063 Macclenny⊙, 2,733 D 1
33738 Madeira Beach, 4,158 B 3
32340 Madison⊙, 3,737 C 1
32751 Maitland, 7,157 E 3
32950 Malabar, 634 F 3
32445 Malone, 667 A 1
33550 Mango, 950 D 4
33050 Marathon, 4,397 E 7
33937 Marco, 900 E 6
33063 Margate, 8,867 F 5
32446 Marianna⊙, 6,741 A 1
† 32084 Marineland, 13 E 2
32569 Mary Esther, 3,192 B 6
33512 Masaryktown, 389 D 3
32753 Mascotte, 966 E 3
32066 Mayo⊙, 793 C 1
32568 McDavid, 500 B 5
32664 McIntosh, 287 D 2
† 33101 Medley, 351 B 4
32901 Melbourne, 40,236 F 3
32951 Melbourne Beach, 2,262 F 3
32666 Melrose, 950 D 2
33301 Melrose Park, 6,111 B 4
† 33561 Memphis, 3,207 D 4
32952 Merritt Island, 29,233 F 3
32410 Mexico Beach, 588 D 6
* 33101 Miami⊙, 334,859 B 5
Miami, ‡1,267,792 B 5
33139 Miami Beach, 87,072 C 5
† 33101 Miami Lakes, 3,500 B 4
33153 Miami Shores, 9,425 B 4
33166 Miami Springs, 13,279 B 5
32667 Micanopy, 759 D 2
† 32960 Micco, 400 F 4
32309 Miccosukee, 275 B 1
32068 Middleburg, 950 E 1
32343 Midway, 900 B 1
32537 Milligan, 950 C 6
32570 Milton⊙, 5,360 B 6
32754 Mims, 8,309 F 3
32755 Minneola, 878 E 3
33023 Miramar, 23,973 B 4
32577 Molino, 850 B 6
† 32696 Montbrook, 250 D 2
32344 Monticello⊙, 2,473 C 1
32756 Montverde, 308 E 3
33471 Moore Haven⊙, 974 E 5
32434 Mossy Head, 160 C 6
32757 Mount Dora, 4,543 E 3
32352 Mount Pleasant, 150 B 1
33860 Mulberry, 2,701 E 4
33551 Myakka City, 672 D 4
32506 Myrtle Grove, 16,186 B 6
33940 Naples⊙, 12,042 E 5
† 33940 Naples Park, 1,522 E 5
33030 Naranja, 2,900 F 6
32233 Neptune Beach, 2,868 E 1
32669 Newberry, 1,247 D 2
33552 New Port Richey, 6,098 D 3
32069 New Smyrna Beach, 10,580 F 2
32578 Niceville, 4,024 C 6
33863 Nichols, 300 E 4
33864 Nocatee, 950 E 4
33555 Nokomis-Laurel, 3,238 D 4
32452 Noma, 234 C 5
33141 North Bay Village, 4,831 B 4
33903 North Fort Myers, 8,798 E 5
33161 North Miami, 34,767 B 4
33161 North Miami Beach, 30,723 C 4
† 33940 North Naples, 3,201 E 5
33403 North Palm Beach, 9,035 F 5
33595 North Port Charlotte, 2,244 D 4
† 33708 North Redington Beach, 768 B 3
† 33054 Norwood, 14,973 B 4
32759 Oak Hill, 747 F 3
32760 Oakland, 672 E 3
33307 Oakland Park, 16,261 B 3
32071 O'Brien, 200 D 1
32670 Ocala⊙, 22,583 D 2
† 33457 Ocean Breeze, 714 F 4
33444 Ocean Ridge, 1,074 F 5
33943 Ochopee, 200 E 6
32761 Ocoee, 3,937 E 3
33556 Odessa, 500 D 3
33163 Ojus, 12,000 B 4
32762 Okahumpka, 470 D 3
33472 Okeechobee⊙, 3,715 F 4
32679 Oklawaha, 700 E 2
33557 Oldsmar, 1,538 B 2
32680 Old Town, 500 C 2
32072 Olustee, 400 D 1
33865 Ona, 236 E 4
33558 Oneco, 3,246 D 4
33054 Opa-locka, 11,902 B 4
32763 Orange City, 1,777 E 3
32681 Orange Lake, 900 D 2
32073 Orange Park, 7,619 E 1
32682 Orange Springs, 500 E 2
* 32801 Orlando⊙, 99,006 E 3
Orlando, ‡428,003 E 3
32074 Ormond Beach, 14,063 E 2
33559 Osprey, 1,115 D 4
32764 Osteen, 875 E 3
32683 Otter Creek, 400 D 2
32765 Oviedo, 1,870 E 3
32684 Oxford, 490 D 3
33560 Ozona, 900 D 3
32570 Pace, 1,776 B 6
33476 Pahokee, 5,663 F 5
32077 Palatka⊙, 9,310 E 2
32901 Palm Bay, 6,927 F 3
33480 Palm Beach, 9,086 G 4
† 33404 Palm Beach Shores, 1,214 G 5
33490 Palm City, 900 F 4
33561 Palmetto, 7,422 D 4
33563 Palm Harbor, 1,763 D 3
33619 Palm River-Clair Mel, 8,536 C 3
32935 Palm Shores, 202 F 3
33460 Palm Springs, 4,340 F 5
32346 Panacea, 950 B 1
32401 Panama City⊙, 32,096 C 6
32401 Parker, 4,212 C 6
33564 Parrish, 950 D 4
32538 Paxton, 243 C 5
† 33023 Pembroke Park, 2,949 B 4
33023 Pembroke Pines, 15,520 B 4
32079 Penney Farms, 561 E 2
* 32501 Pensacola⊙, 59,507 B 6
Pensacola, ‡243,075 B 6
33157 Perrine, 10,257 F 6
32347 Perry⊙, 7,701 C 1
33867 Pierce, 500 E 4
32080 Pierson, 654 E 2
33565 Pinellas Park, 22,287 B 3
32350 Pinetta, 300 C 1
† 33042 Pirates Cove, 150 E 7
33946 Placida, 250 D 5
33314 Plantation, 23,523 B 4
33566 Plant City, 15,451 D 3
32768 Plymouth, 950 E 3
33868 Polk City, 151 E 3
32081 Pomona Park, 578 E 2
* 33060 Pompano Beach, 37,724 F 5
32455 Ponce de Leon, 288 C 6
† 32019 Ponce Inlet, 328 F 2
32082 Ponte Vedra Beach, 2,100 E 1
33950 Port Charlotte, 10,769 D 5
† 32439 Portland, 228 C 6
† 33438 Port Mayaca, 400 F 4
32019 Port Orange, 3,781 F 2
33568 Port Richey, 1,259 D 3
32456 Port Saint Joe, 4,401 D 6
33450 Port Saint Lucie, 330 F 4
33492 Port Salerno, 1,161 F 4
33171 Princeton, 1,900 F 6
† 33619 Progress, 1,328 C 3
† 32061 Providence, 150 D 2
33950 Punta Gorda⊙, 3,879 E 5
32351 Quincy⊙, 8,334 B 1
32083 Raiford, 500 D 1
† 32696 Raleigh, 275 D 2
32455 Redbay, 500 C 6
32686 Reddick, 305 D 2
33708 Redington Beach, 1,583 B 3
† 33708 Redington Shores, 1,733 B 3
† 33599 Richland, 928 D 3
† 33158 Richmond Heights, 6,663 F 6
33569 Riverview, 2,225 D 4
33404 Riviera Beach, 21,401 G 5
32955 Rockledge, 10,523 F 3
32957 Roseland, 550 F 4
32447 Round Lake, 275 D 6
33570 Ruskin, 2,414 C 3
33572 Safety Harbor, 3,103 B 2
32084 Saint Augustine⊙, 12,352 E 2
32084 Saint Augustine Beach, 632 E 2
33573 Saint Catherine, 350 D 3
32769 Saint Cloud, 5,041 E 3
33956 Saint James City, 500 D 5
33574 Saint Leo, 1,145 D 3
† 33450 Saint Lucie, 428 F 4
32355 Saint Marks, 366 B 1
* 33701 Saint Petersburg, 216,232 B 3
33736 Saint Petersburg Beach, 8,024 B 3
32356 Salem, 150 C 2
33505 Samoset, 4,070 D 4
† 32069 Samsula, 270 E 2
33576 San Antonio, 473 D 3
32087 Sanderson, 150 D 1
32771 Sanford⊙, 17,393 E 3
33957 Sanibel, 750 D 5
32088 San Mateo, 975 E 2
† 32670 Santos, 150 D 2
* 33577 Sarasota⊙, 40,237 D 4
32935 Satellite Beach, 6,558 F 3
32089 Satsuma, 610 E 2
32775 Scottsmoor, 850 F 3
† 33301 Sea Ranch Lakes, 660 C 3
32958 Sebastian, 825 F 4
33870 Sebring⊙, 7,223 E 4
33584 Seffner, 2,000 D 4
33540 Seminole, 2,410 B 3
32090 Seville, 500 E 2
† 33457 Sewalls Point, 298 F 4
32579 Shalimar, 578 C 6
† 32628 Shamrock, 200 C 2
32959 Sharpes, 427 F 3
32688 Silver Springs, 500 D 2
32460 Sneads, 1,550 B 1
32358 Sopchoppy, 460 B 1
32776 Sorrento, 500 E 3
33493 South Bay, 2,958 F 5
32021 South Daytona, 4,979 F 2
† 36441 South Flomaton, 329 B 5
33143 South Miami, 19,571 B 5
33707 South Pasadena, 2,063 B 3
† 32401 Southport, 1,560 C 6
32690 Sparr, 450 D 2
32401 Springfield, 5,949 D 6
32091 Starke⊙, 4,848 D 2
32359 Steinhatchee, 800 C 2
33494 Stuart⊙, 4,820 F 4
32335 Sumatra, 150 B 1
32691 Summerfield, 450 D 2
33042 Summerland Key, 350 E 7
33586 Sun City, 2,143 D 4
† 33450 Sunland Gardens, 1,900 F 4
33160 Sunny Isles, 950 C 4
† 33577 Sunnyland, 4,900 D 4
32461 Sunnyside, 370 C 6
33313 Sunrise Golf Village, 7,403 B 4
33154 Surfside, 3,614 B 4
32692 Suwannee, 203 C 2
† 33144 Sweetwater, 3,307 B 5
† 33601 Sweetwater Creek, 19,453 B 2
† 32043 Switzerland, 500 E 1
32809 Taft, 1,183 E 3
* 32301 Tallahassee (cap.)⊙, 71,897 B 1
Tallahassee, ‡103,047 B 1
† 33301 Tamarac, 5,078 B 3
* 33601 Tampa⊙, 277,767 C 2
Tampa-Saint Petersburg, ‡1,012,594 C 2
33589 Tarpon Springs, 7,118 C 3
32778 Tavares⊙, 3,261 E 3
33070 Tavernier, 900 F 6
32360 Telogia, 300 B 1
33617 Temple Terrace, 7,347 C 2
33538 Tequesta, 2,642 F 5
33591 Terra Ceia, 450 D 4
33592 Thonotosassa, 900 D 3
33905 Tice, 7,254 E 5
32780 Titusville⊙, 30,515 F 3
33740 Treasure Island, 6,120 B 3
32693 Trenton⊙, 1,074 D 2
33593 Trilby, 930 D 3
32784 Umatilla, 1,600 E 3
32580 Valparaiso, 6,504 C 6
33595 Venice, 6,648 D 4
33960 Venus, 300 E 4
32462 Vernon, 691 C 6
32960 Vero Beach⊙, 11,908 F 4
† 32548 Villa Tasso, 200 C 6
† 33166 Virginia Gardens, 2,524 B 5
32970 Wabasso, 950 F 4
32361 Wacissa, 275 B 1
† 32327 Wakulla, 225 B 1
32694 Waldo, 800 D 2
32568 Walnut Hill, 500 B 5
32507 Warrington, 15,848 B 6
† 32055 Watertown, 3,624 D 1
33873 Wauchula⊙, 3,007 E 4
32463 Wausau, 288 D 6
33877 Waverly, 1,172 E 4
33597 Webster, 739 D 3
32695 Weirsdale, 995 D 3
32093 Welaka, 496 E 2
32094 Wellborn, 600 D 1
32401 Westbay, 350 C 6
† 32901 West Melbourne, 3,050 F 3
† 33101 West Miami, 5,494 B 5
* 33401 West Palm Beach⊙, 57,375 F 5
West Palm Beach, ‡348,753 F 5
32401 West Panama City Beach, 1,052 C 6
32505 West Pensacola, 20,924 B 6
32464 Westville, 475 C 6
† 33101 Westwood Lakes, 12,811 B 5
32465 Wewahitchka⊙, 1,733 D 6
† 32465 White City, 600 F 4
32096 White Springs, 767 D 1
32785 Wildwood, 2,082 D 3
32696 Williston, 1,939 D 2
33305 Wilton Manors, 10,948 B 3
33598 Wimauma, 650 D 4
32786 Windermere, 894 E 3
32971 Winter Beach, 350 F 4
32787 Winter Garden, 5,153 E 3
33880 Winter Haven, 16,136 E 3
32789 Winter Park, 21,895 E 3
32362 Woodville, 900 B 1
32697 Worthington Springs, 214 D 2
32797 Yalaha, 675 E 3
32698 Yankeetown, 490 D 2
32466 Youngstown, 400 D 6
32097 Yulee, 950 E 1
32798 Zellwood, 550 E 3
33599 Zephyrhills, 3,369 D 3
33890 Zolfo Springs, 1,117 E 4

⊙ County seat.
‡ Population of metropolitan area.
† Zip of nearest p.o.
* Multiple zips

A. D'Arazien — Shostal Associates

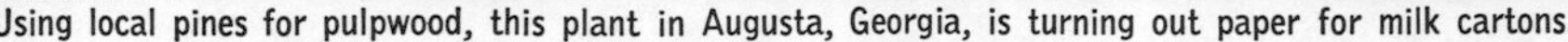
Using local pines for pulpwood, this plant in Augusta, Georgia, is turning out paper for milk cartons.

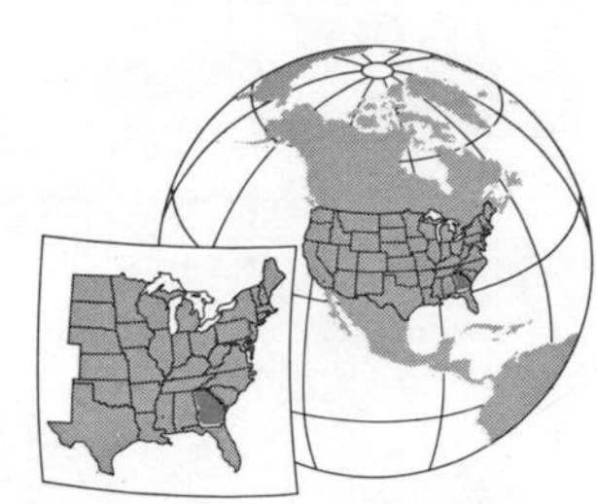

AREA 58,876 sq. mi.
POPULATION 4,589,575
CAPITAL Atlanta
LARGEST CITY Atlanta
HIGHEST POINT Brasstown Bald 4,784 ft.
SETTLED IN 1733
ADMITTED TO UNION January 2, 1788
POPULAR NAME Empire State of the South; Peach State
STATE FLOWER Cherokee Rose
STATE BIRD Brown Thrasher

COUNTIES

Name/Pop.	Key
Appling, 12,726	H 7
Atkinson, 5,879	G 8
Bacon, 8,233	G 7
Baker, 3,875	D 8
Baldwin, 34,240	F 4
Banks, 6,833	E 2
Barrow, 16,859	E 2
Bartow, 32,663	C 2
Ben Hill, 13,171	F 7
Berrien, 11,556	F 8
Bibb, 143,418	E 5
Bleckley, 10,291	F 6
Brantley, 5,940	J 8
Brooks, 13,739	E 9
Bryan, 6,539	K 6
Bulloch, 31,585	J 6
Burke, 18,255	J 4
Butts, 10,560	E 4
Calhoun, 6,606	C 7
Camden, 11,334	J 9
Candler, 6,412	H 6
Carroll, 45,404	B 3
Catoosa, 28,271	B 1
Charlton, 5,680	H 9
Chatham, 187,767	K 6
Chattahoochee, 25,813	C 6
Chattooga, 20,541	B 1
Cherokee, 31,059	D 2
Clarke, 65,177	F 3
Clay, 3,636	B 7
Clayton, 98,043	D 3
Clinch, 6,405	G 9
Cobb, 196,793	C 3
Coffee, 22,828	G 8
Colquitt, 32,200	E 8
Columbia, 22,327	H 3
Cook, 12,129	F 8
Cowela, 32,310	C 4
Crawford, 5,748	E 5
Crisp, 18,087	E 7
Dade, 9,910	A 1
Dawson, 3,639	D 2
Decatur, 22,310	C 9
De Kalb, 415,387	D 3
Dodge, 15,658	F 6
Dooly, 10,404	E 6
Dougherty, 89,639	D 7
Douglas, 28,659	C 3
Early, 12,682	C 8
Echols, 1,924	G 9
Effingham, 13,632	K 6
Elbert, 17,262	G 2
Emanuel, 18,189	H 5
Evans, 7,290	J 6
Fannin, 13,357	D 1
Fayette, 11,364	C 4
Floyd, 73,742	B 2
Forsyth, 16,928	D 2
Franklin, 12,784	F 2
Fulton, 607,592	D 3
Gilmer, 8,956	D 1
Glascock, 2,280	G 4
Glynn, 50,528	J 8
Gordon, 23,570	C 2
Grady, 17,826	D 9
Greene, 10,212	F 3
Gwinnett, 72,349	D 2
Habersham, 20,691	E 1
Hall, 59,405	E 2
Hancock, 9,019	G 4
Haralson, 15,927	B 3
Harris, 11,520	C 5
Hart, 15,814	G 2
Heard, 5,354	B 4
Henry, 23,724	D 4
Houston, 62,924	E 6
Irwin, 8,036	F 7
Jackson, 21,093	E 2
Jasper, 5,760	E 4
Jeff Davis, 9,425	G 7
Jefferson, 17,174	H 4
Jenkins, 8,332	J 5
Johnson, 7,727	G 5
Jones, 12,218	E 5
Lamar, 10,688	D 4
Lanier, 5,031	F 8
Laurens, 32,738	G 6
Lee, 7,044	D 7
Liberty, 17,569	J 7
Lincoln, 5,895	H 3
Long, 3,746	J 7
Lowndes, 55,112	F 9
Lumpkin, 8,728	D 1
Macon, 12,933	D 6
Madison, 13,517	F 2
Marion, 5,099	C 6
McDuffie, 15,276	H 4
McIntosh, 7,371	K 7
Meriwether, 19,461	C 4
Miller, 6,397	C 8
Mitchell, 18,956	D 8
Monroe, 10,991	E 4
Montgomery, 6,099	G 6
Morgan, 9,904	F 3
Murray, 12,986	C 1
Muscogee, 167,377	C 6
Newton, 26,282	E 3
Oconee, 7,915	F 3
Oglethorpe, 7,598	F 3
Paulding, 17,520	C 3
Peach, 15,990	E 5
Pickens, 9,620	D 2
Pierce, 9,281	H 8
Pike, 7,316	D 4
Polk, 29,656	B 3
Pulaski, 8,066	E 6
Putnam, 8,394	F 4
Quitman, 2,180	B 7
Rabun, 8,327	F 1
Randolph, 8,734	C 7
Richmond, 162,347	H 4
Rockdale, 18,152	D 3
Schley, 3,097	D 6
Screven, 12,591	J 5
Seminole, 7,059	C 9
Spalding, 39,514	D 4
Stephens, 20,331	F 1
Stewart, 6,511	C 6
Sumter, 26,931	D 6
Talbot, 6,625	C 5
Taliaferro, 2,423	G 3
Tattnall, 16,557	J 6
Taylor, 7,865	D 5
Telfair, 11,381	G 7
Terrell, 11,416	D 7
Thomas, 34,515	E 9
Tift, 27,288	E 7
Toombs, 19,151	H 6
Towns, 4,565	E 1
Treutlen, 5,647	G 6
Troup, 44,466	B 4
Turner, 8,790	E 7
Twiggs, 8,222	F 5
Union, 6,811	E 1
Upson, 23,505	D 5
Walker, 50,691	B 1
Walton, 23,404	E 3
Ware, 33,525	H 8
Warren, 6,669	G 4
Washington, 17,480	G 4
Wayne, 17,858	J 7
Webster, 2,362	C 6
Wheeler, 4,596	G 6
White, 7,742	E 1
Whitfield, 55,108	B 1
Wilcox, 6,998	F 7
Wilkes, 10,184	G 3
Wilkinson, 9,393	F 5
Worth, 14,770	E 8

CITIES and TOWNS

Zip	Name/Pop.	Key
31001	Abbeville⊙, 781	F 7
30101	Acworth, 3,929	C 2
30103	Adairsville, 1,676	C 2
31620	Adel⊙, 4,972	F 8
31002	Adrian, 705	G 5
30410	Ailey, 487	G 6
30411	Alamo⊙, 833	G 6
31622	Alapaha, 633	F 8
* 31701	Albany⊙, 72,623	D 7
	Albany, ‡89,639	D 7
† 30204	Aldora, 322	D 4
30801	Alexander, 200	J 4
31301	Allenhurst, 230	J 7
31003	Allentown, 295	F 5
31510	Alma⊙, 3,756	G 7
† 30209	Almon, 400	E 3
30201	Alpharetta, 2,455	D 2
30510	Alto, 372	E 2
† 30161	Alto Park, 2,963	B 2
31512	Ambrose, 253	G 7
31709	Americus⊙, 16,091	D 6
31711	Andersonville, 274	D 6
30802	Appling⊙, 212	H 3
31712	Arabi, 305	E 7
30104	Aragon, 850	B 2
† 30549	Arcade, 229	E 2
31520	Arco, 6,009	J 8
31623	Argyle, 206	G 8
31713	Arlington, 1,698	C 8
30105	Armuchee, 600	B 2
31714	Ashburn⊙, 4,209	E 7
† 30521	Ashland, 350	F 2
30601	Athens⊙, 44,342	F 3
* 30301	Atlanta (cap.)⊙, 496,973	D 3
	Atlanta, ‡1,390,164	D 3
31715	Attapulgus, 513	D 9
30203	Auburn, 361	E 2
* 30901	Augusta⊙, 59,864	J 4
	Augusta, ‡253,460	J 4
30001	Austell, 2,632	C 3
† 30557	Avalon, 204	F 1
30803	Avera, 217	G 4
30002	Avondale Estates, 1,735	D 3
31624	Axson, 250	G 8
31716	Baconton, 710	D 8
31717	Bainbridge⊙, 10,887	C 9
30511	Baldwin, 772	E 2
30107	Ball Ground, 617	D 2
30204	Barnesville⊙, 4,935	D 4
† 31601	Barretts, 275	F 8
30413	Bartow, 333	G 5
31720	Barwick, 381	E 9
31513	Baxley⊙, 3,503	H 7
† 31792	Beachton, 200	D 9
30414	Bellville, 234	H 6
† 31601	Bemiss, 325	F 9
31722	Berlin, 422	E 8
30748	Berryton, 200	B 2
30620	Bethlehem, 304	E 3
31904	Bibb City, 812	B 5
30621	Bishop, 235	F 3
31516	Blackshear⊙, 2,624	H 8
30512	Blairsville⊙, 491	E 1
31723	Blakely⊙, 5,267	C 8
† 31308	Blitchton, 256	J 6
31302	Bloomingdale, 1,588	K 6
30513	Blue Ridge⊙, 1,602	D 1
30805	Blythe, 333	H 4
30622	Bogart, 667	E 3
31626	Boston, 1,443	E 9
30623	Bostwick, 289	E 3
30108	Bowdon, 1,753	B 3
30109	Bowdon Junction, 200	B 3
30516	Bowersville, 301	G 2
30624	Bowman, 724	G 2
31801	Box Springs, 600	C 5
30517	Braselton, 386	E 2
30110	Bremen, 3,484	B 3
31701	Bridgeboro, 250	E 8
31725	Brinson, 231	C 9
31726	Bronwood, 500	D 7
31727	Brookfield, 860	F 8
30415	Brooklet, 683	J 6
31519	Broxton, 957	G 7
31520	Brunswick⊙, 19,585	K 8
30113	Buchanan⊙, 800	B 3
31803	Buena Vista⊙, 1,486	C 6
30518	Buford, 4,640	D 2
† 31020	Bullard, 230	F 5
31006	Butler⊙, 1,589	D 5
31007	Byromville, 419	E 6
31008	Byron, 1,368	E 5
31009	Cadwell, 354	G 6
31728	Cairo⊙, 8,061	D 9
30701	Calhoun⊙, 4,748	C 1
31729	Calvary, 500	D 9
30807	Camak, 224	G 4
31730	Camilla⊙, 4,987	D 8
30520	Canon, 709	F 2
30114	Canton⊙, 3,654	C 2
† 30720	Carbondale, 300	B 1
30203	Carl, 234	E 3
30627	Carlton, 294	F 2
30521	Carnesville⊙, 510	F 2
30117	Carrollton⊙, 13,520	C 3
† 30540	Cartecay, 250	D 1
30120	Cartersville⊙, 9,929	C 2
30123	Cassville, 350	C 2
31804	Calaula, 500	C 5
30124	Cave Spring, 1,305	B 2
31627	Cecil, 265	F 8
30125	Cedartown⊙, 9,253	B 2
† 30601	Center, 213	F 2
31093	Centerville, 1,725	E 5
† 31816	Chalybeate Springs, 266	C 5
30341	Chamblee, 9,127	D 3
30705	Chatsworth⊙, 2,706	C 1
31011	Chauncey, 308	F 6
31012	Chester, 409	F 6
30707	Chickamauga, 1,842	B 1
† 30512	Choestoe, 215	E 1
31733	Chula, 300	E 7
30523	Clarkesville⊙, 1,294	F 1
30021	Clarkston, 3,127	D 3
30417	Claxton⊙, 2,669	J 6
30525	Clayton⊙, 1,569	F 1
30128	Clem, 350	B 3
30527	Clermont, 290	E 2
30528	Cleveland⊙, 1,353	E 1
31734	Climax, 275	D 9
31604	Clyattville, 500	F 9
31303	Clyo, 300	K 6
30420	Cobbtown, 321	H 6
31014	Cochran⊙, 5,161	F 6
30710	Cohutta, 300	C 1
30628	Colbert, 532	F 2
30337	College Park, 18,203	C 3
30421	Collins, 574	H 6
31737	Colquitt⊙, 2,026	C 8
* 31901	Columbus⊙, 154,168	C 6
	Columbus, ‡238,584	C 6
30629	Comer, 828	F 2
30529	Commerce, 3,702	E 2
30206	Concord, 312	D 4
30207	Conyers⊙, 4,890	D 3
31738	Coolidge, 717	E 8
30129	Coosa, 600	B 2
31015	Cordele⊙, 10,733	E 7
· 30531	Cornelia, 3,014	E 1
30209	Covington⊙, 10,267	E 3
30630	Crawford, 624	F 3
30631	Crawfordville⊙, 735	G 3
† 30105	Crystal Springs, 500	B 2
31016	Culloden, 272	D 5
30130	Cumming⊙, 2,031	D 2
31805	Cusseta⊙, 1,251	C 6
31740	Cuthbert⊙, 3,972	C 7
30211	Dacula, 782	E 3
30533	Dahlonega⊙, 2,658	D 1
30132	Dallas⊙, 2,133	C 3
30720	Dalton⊙, 18,872	C 1
31741	Damascus, 272	C 8
30633	Danielsville⊙, 378	F 2
31017	Danville, 515	F 5
31305	Darien⊙, 1,826	K 8
31601	Dasher, 452	F 9
31018	Davisboro, 476	G 5
31742	Dawson⊙, 5,383	D 7
30534	Dawsonville⊙, 288	D 2
30808	Dearing, 555	H 4
* 30030	Decatur⊙, 21,943	D 3
† 31501	Deenwood, 3,015	H 8
30535	Demorest, 1,070	F 1
31532	Denton, 244	G 7
31743	De Soto, 321	D 7
31019	Dexter, 438	G 6
† 31520	Dock Junction (Arco), 6,009	J 8
31744	Doerun, 1,157	E 8
31745	Donalsonville⊙, 2,907	C 8
30340	Doraville, 9,039	D 3
31533	Douglas⊙, 10,195	G 7
30134	Douglasville⊙, 5,472	C 3
31020	Dry Branch, 700	F 5
31021	Dublin⊙, 15,143	G 5
31022	Dudley, 423	F 5
30136	Duluth, 1,810	D 2
31630	Du Pont, 252	G 9
30538	Eastanollee, 365	F 1
31021	East Dublin, 1,986	G 5
30539	East Ellijay, 488	C 1
31023	Eastman⊙, 5,416	F 6
† 30263	East Newnan, 1,634	C 4
30344	East Point, 39,315	C 3
31024	Eatonton⊙, 4,125	F 4
31307	Eden, 300	K 6
31746	Edison, 1,210	C 7
† 31093	Elberta, 500	E 5
30635	Elberton⊙, 6,438	G 2
30060	Elizabeth, 950	C 2
31025	Elko, 450	E 6
31308	Ellabell, 400	K 6
31806	Ellaville⊙, 1,391	D 6
31747	Ellenton, 337	E 8
31807	Ellerslie, 615	C 5
30540	Ellijay⊙, 1,326	C 1
30137	Emerson, 813	C 2
31026	Empire, 325	F 6
31749	Enigma, 505	F 8
† 30217	Ephesus, 212	B 4
30541	Epworth, 300	D 1
30724	Eton, 286	C 1
† 31331	Eulonia, 500	K 7
30809	Evans, 1,500	H 3
31536	Everett, 300	J 8
30212	Experiment, 2,256	D 4
30213	Fairburn, 3,143	C 3
30139	Fairmount, 623	C 2
31631	Fargo, 800	G 9
30214	Fayetteville⊙, 2,160	C 4
30140	Felton, 300	B 3
31750	Fitzgerald⊙, 8,015	F 7
† 31313	Flemington, 265	K 7
30215	Flippen, 600	D 3
30216	Flovilla, 289	E 4
30542	Flowery Branch, 779	E 2
31537	Folkston⊙, 2,112	H 9
30050	Forest Park, 19,994	D 3
31029	Forsyth⊙, 3,736	E 4
31751	Fort Gaines⊙, 1,255	C 7
30741	Fort Oglethorpe, 3,869	B 1
31030	Fort Valley⊙, 9,251	E 5
31752	Fowlstown, 400	D 9
30217	Franklin⊙, 749	B 4
30639	Franklin Springs, 501	F 2
37317	Fry, 300	D 1
31753	Funston, 293	E 8
30501	Gainesville⊙, 15,459	E 2
31408	Garden City, 5,741	K 6
30425	Garfield, 214	H 5
31810	Geneva, 250	C 5
31754	Georgetown⊙, 578	B 7
30810	Gibson⊙, 701	G 4
30426	Girard, 241	J 4
30427	Glennville, 2,965	J 7
30428	Glenwood, 670	G 6
30641	Good Hope, 202	E 3
31031	Gordon, 2,553	F 5
30811	Gough, 300	H 4
30812	Gracewood, 1,200	H 4
30220	Grantville, 1,128	C 4
31032	Gray⊙, 2,014	F 4
30221	Grayson, 366	E 3
30642	Greensboro⊙, 2,583	F 3
30222	Greenville⊙, 1,085	C 4
† 31620	Greggs, 250	F 8
30223	Griffin⊙, 22,734	D 4
† 31036	Grovania, 300	E 6
30813	Grovetown, 3,169	H 4
31312	Guyton, 742	K 6
30544	Habersham, 225	F 1
31033	Haddock, 600	F 4
30429	Hagan, 572	J 6
31632	Hahira, 1,326	F 9
31811	Hamilton⊙, 357	C 5
30228	Hampton, 1,551	D 4
30354	Hapeville, 9,567	D 3
31034	Hardwick, 14,047	F 4
30814	Harlem, 1,540	H 4
31035	Harrison, 329	G 5
30643	Hartwell⊙, 4,865	G 2
31036	Hawkinsville⊙, 4,077	E 6
31539	Hazlehurst⊙, 4,065	G 7
30545	Helen, 252	E 1
31037	Helena, 1,230	G 6
30815	Hephzibah, 987	H 4
30546	Hiawassee⊙, 415	E 1
31038	Hillsboro, 250	E 4
30467	Hilltonia, 294	J 5
31313	Hinesville⊙, 4,115	J 7
30141	Hiram, 441	C 3
31542	Hoboken, 424	H 8
30230	Hogansville, 3,075	C 4
30142	Holly Springs, 575	D 2
30523	Hollywood, 300	E 1
† 31537	Homeland, 595	H 9
30547	Homer⊙, 365	F 2
31634	Homerville⊙, 3,025	G 8
31543	Hortense, 400	J 8
30548	Hoschton, 509	E 2
30646	Hull, 222	F 2
30561	Hurst, 216	D 1
31041	Ideal, 543	D 6
30647	Ila, 202	F 2
30231	Indian Springs, 300	E 4
30232	Inman, 475	D 4
31759	Iron City, 351	C 8
31042	Irwinton⊙, 757	F 5
31760	Irwinville, 550	F 7
31406	Isle of Hope, 975	K 7
† 31031	Ivey, 245	F 5
30233	Jackson⊙, 3,778	E 4
31544	Jacksonville, 214	G 7
30143	Jasper⊙, 1,202	D 2

(continued on following page)

GEORGIA
SCALE
0 5 10 20 30 40 MI.
0 5 10 20 30 40 KM.
State Capitals
County Seats
© C.S. HAMMOND & Co., N.Y.
TENNESSEE
NORTH CAROLINA
SOUTH CAROLINA
ALABAMA
FLORIDA
ATLANTIC OCEAN
SEA ISLANDS
Longitude 83° West of Greenwich
ATLANTA
Augusta
Macon
Columbus
Savannah
Chattanooga
Charlotte
Columbia
Tallahassee
Jacksonville
OKEFENOKEE SWAMP
APALACHEE BAY

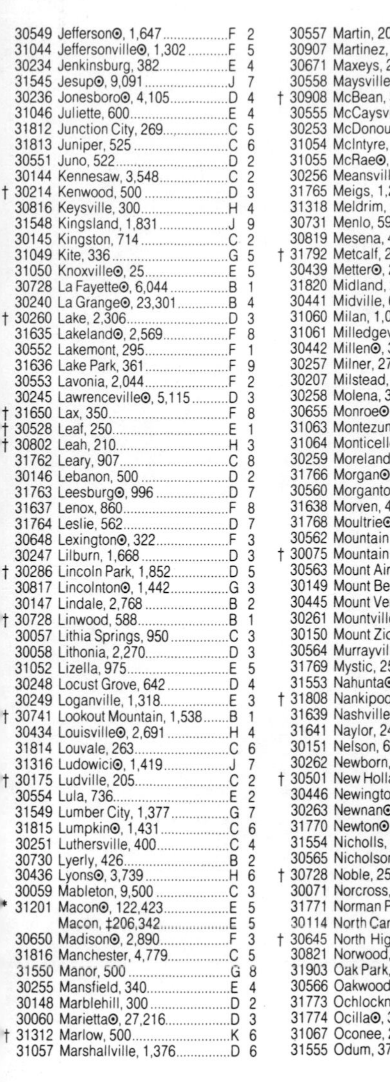

30549 Jefferson⊙, 1,647 ... F 2
31044 Jeffersonville⊙, 1,302 ... F 5
30234 Jenkinsburg, 382 ... E 4
31545 Jesup⊙, 9,091 ... J 7
30236 Jonesboro⊙, 4,105 ... D 4
31046 Juliette, 600 ... E 4
31812 Junction City, 269 ... C 5
31813 Juniper, 525 ... C 6
30551 Juno, 522 ... D 2
30144 Kennesaw, 3,548 ... C 2
† 30214 Kenwood, 500 ... D 3
30816 Keysville, 300 ... H 4
31548 Kingsland, 1,831 ... J 9
30145 Kingston, 714 ... C 2
31049 Kite, 336 ... G 5
31050 Knoxville⊙, 25 ... E 5
30728 La Fayette⊙, 6,044 ... B 1
30240 La Grange⊙, 23,301 ... B 4
† 30260 Lake, 2,306 ... D 3
31635 Lakeland⊙, 2,569 ... F 8
30552 Lakemont, 295 ... F 1
31636 Lake Park, 361 ... F 9
30553 Lavonia, 2,044 ... F 2
30245 Lawrenceville⊙, 5,115 ... D 3
† 31650 Lax, 350 ... F 8
† 30528 Leaf, 250 ... E 1
† 30802 Leah, 210 ... H 3
31762 Leary, 907 ... C 8
30146 Lebanon, 500 ... D 2
31763 Leesburg⊙, 996 ... D 7
31637 Lenox, 860 ... F 8
31764 Leslie, 562 ... D 7
30648 Lexington⊙, 322 ... F 3
30247 Lilburn, 1,668 ... D 3
† 30286 Lincoln Park, 1,852 ... D 5
30817 Lincolnton⊙, 1,442 ... G 3
30147 Lindale, 2,768 ... B 2
† 30728 Linwood, 588 ... B 1
30057 Lithia Springs, 950 ... C 3
30058 Lithonia, 2,270 ... D 3
31052 Lizella, 975 ... E 5
30248 Locust Grove, 642 ... D 4
30249 Loganville, 1,318 ... E 3
† 30741 Lookout Mountain, 1,538 ... B 1
30434 Louisville⊙, 2,691 ... H 4
31814 Louvale, 263 ... C 6
31316 Ludowici⊙, 1,419 ... J 7
† 30175 Ludville, 205 ... C 2
30554 Lula, 736 ... E 2
31549 Lumber City, 1,377 ... G 7
31815 Lumpkin⊙, 1,431 ... C 6
30251 Luthersville, 400 ... C 4
30730 Lyerly, 426 ... B 2
30436 Lyons⊙, 3,739 ... H 6
30059 Mableton, 9,500 ... C 3
* 31201 Macon⊙, 122,423 ... E 5
Macon, ‡206,342 ... E 5
30650 Madison⊙, 2,890 ... F 3
31816 Manchester, 4,779 ... C 5
31550 Manor, 500 ... G 8
30255 Mansfield, 340 ... E 4
30148 Marblehill, 300 ... D 2
30060 Marietta⊙, 27,216 ... D 3
† 31312 Marlow, 500 ... K 6
31057 Marshallville, 1,376 ... D 6

30557 Martin, 201 ... F 2
30907 Martinez, 950 ... H 3
30671 Maxeys, 229 ... F 3
30558 Maysville, 553 ... E 2
† 30908 McBean, 300 ... J 4
30555 McCaysville, 1,619 ... D 1
30253 McDonough⊙, 2,675 ... D 4
31054 McIntyre, 471 ... F 5
31055 McRae⊙, 3,151 ... G 6
30256 Meansville, 313 ... D 4
31765 Meigs, 1,226 ... D 8
31318 Meldrim, 500 ... K 6
30731 Menlo, 593 ... B 2
30819 Mesena, 400 ... G 4
† 31792 Metcalf, 213 ... E 9
30439 Metter⊙, 2,912 ... H 6
31820 Midland, 250 ... C 5
30441 Midville, 665 ... H 5
31060 Milan, 1,084 ... G 6
31061 Milledgeville⊙, 11,601 ... F 4
30442 Millen⊙, 3,713 ... J 5
30257 Milner, 270 ... D 4
30207 Milstead, 1,157 ... D 3
30258 Molena, 389 ... D 4
30655 Monroe⊙, 8,071 ... E 3
31063 Montezuma, 4,125 ... E 6
31064 Monticello⊙, 2,132 ... E 4
30259 Moreland, 363 ... C 4
31766 Morgan⊙, 280 ... C 7
30560 Morganton, 205 ... D 1
31638 Morven, 449 ... E 9
31768 Moultrie⊙, 14,302 ... E 8
30562 Mountain City, 594 ... F 1
† 30075 Mountain Park, 268 ... D 2
30563 Mount Airy, 463 ... F 1
30149 Mount Berry, 1,500 ... B 2
30445 Mount Vernon⊙, 1,579 ... G 6
30261 Mountville, 218 ... C 4
30150 Mount Zion, 264 ... B 3
30564 Murrayville, 550 ... E 2
31769 Mystic, 250 ... F 7
31553 Nahunta⊙, 974 ... H 8
† 31808 Nankipooh, 500 ... C 5
31639 Nashville⊙, 4,323 ... F 8
31641 Naylor, 244 ... F 9
30151 Nelson, 613 ... D 2
30262 Newborn, 294 ... E 3
† 30501 New Holland, 950 ... E 2
30446 Newington, 402 ... J 5
30263 Newnan⊙, 11,205 ... C 4
31770 Newton⊙, 624 ... D 8
31554 Nicholls, 1,150 ... G 7
30565 Nicholson, 397 ... F 2
† 30728 Noble, 250 ... B 1
30071 Norcross, 2,755 ... D 3
31771 Norman Park, 912 ... E 8
30114 North Canton, 950 ... C 2
† 30645 North High Shoals, 165 ... F 3
30821 Norwood, 272 ... G 4
31903 Oak Park, 226 ... H 6
30566 Oakwood, 250 ... E 2
31773 Ochlocknee, 611 ... E 9
31774 Ocilla⊙, 3,185 ... F 7
31067 Oconee, 262 ... G 5
31555 Odum, 379 ... H 7

31556 Offerman, 500 ... H 8
31406 Oglethorpe⊙, 1,286 ... D 6
30449 Oliver, 217 ... J 5
31775 Omega, 831 ... E 8
† 30701 Oostanaula, 300 ... B 1
30267 Oxford, 1,373 ... E 3
30268 Palmetto, 2,045 ... C 3
31777 Parrott, 222 ... D 7
31557 Patterson, 788 ... H 8
31778 Pavo, 775 ... E 9
† 31201 Payne, 236 ... E 5
† 30214 Peachtree City, 793 ... C 4
31642 Pearson⊙, 1,700 ... G 8
31779 Pelham, 4,539 ... D 8
31321 Pembroke⊙, 1,361 ... J 6
30567 Pendergrass, 267 ... E 2
30822 Perkins, 250 ... J 5
31069 Perry⊙, 7,771 ... E 6
† 31794 Phillipsburg, 2,335 ... E 8
† 31629 Pidcock, 210 ... E 9
31071 Pinehurst, 405 ... E 6
30152 Pine Log, 205 ... C 2
31822 Pine Mountain, 862 ... C 5
† 31312 Pineora, 266 ... K 6
† 31728 Pine Park, 330 ... D 9
31071 Pineview, 528 ... F 6
31072 Pitts, 345 ... E 7
31780 Plains, 683 ... D 6
31322 Pooler, 1,517 ... K 6
30450 Portal, 643 ... J 5
30270 Porterdale, 1,773 ... E 3
31407 Port Wentworth, 3,905 ... K 6
31781 Poulan, 766 ... E 8
30073 Powder Springs, 2,559 ... C 3
31824 Preston⊙, 226 ... C 6
30451 Pulaski, 230 ... J 6
31782 Putney, 750 ... D 8
31643 Quitman⊙, 4,818 ... E 9
30568 Rabun Gap, 250 ... F 1
31645 Ray City, 617 ... F 8
30660 Rayle, 300 ... G 3
31783 Rebecca, 266 ... E 7
30272 Red Oak, 3,500 ... C 3
30452 Register, 300 ... J 6
30453 Reidsville⊙, 1,806 ... H 6
31601 Remerton, 523 ... F 9
31075 Rentz, 392 ... G 6
30735 Resaca, 500 ... C 1
31076 Reynolds, 1,253 ... D 5
31077 Rhine, 471 ... F 7
31323 Riceboro, 252 ... K 7
31825 Richland, 1,823 ... C 6
31324 Richmond Hill, 826 ... K 7
31326 Rincon, 1,854 ... K 6
30736 Ringgold⊙, 1,381 ... B 1
30738 Rising Fawn, 400 ... A 1
30274 Riverdale, 2,521 ... D 3
31204 Riverside, 1,159 ... B 2
31078 Roberta, 746 ... D 5
† 30545 Robertstown, 290 ... E 1
31079 Rochelle, 1,380 ... F 7
30153 Rockmart, 3,857 ... B 2
30740 Rocky Face, 500 ... C 1
30455 Rocky Ford, 252 ... J 5
30161 Rome⊙, 30,759 ... B 2

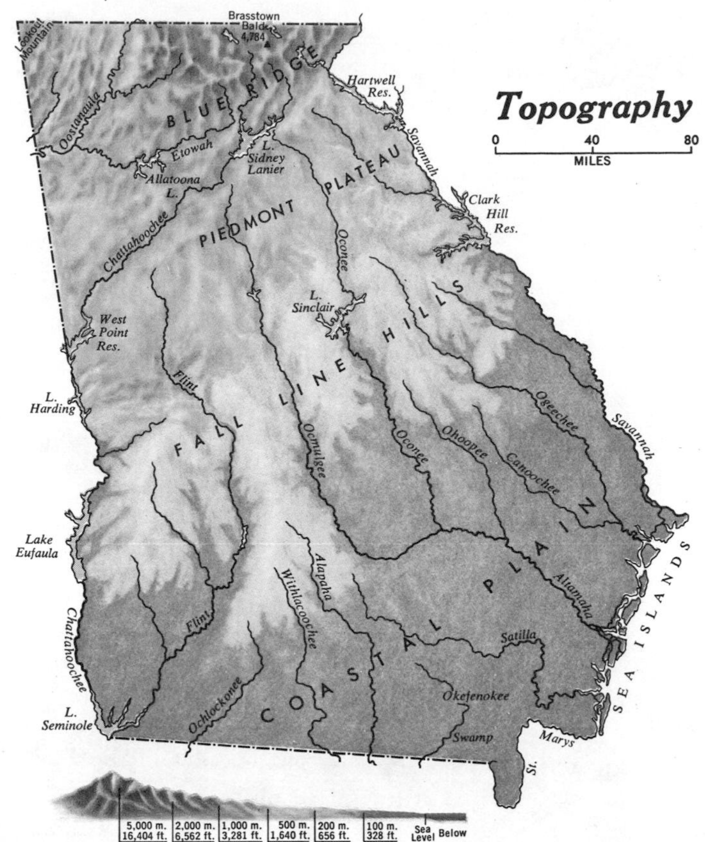

30170 Roopville, 221 ... B 4
30741 Rossville, 3,869 ... B 1
30075 Roswell, 5,430 ... D 2
30662 Royston, 2,428 ... F 2
† 30680 Russell, 378 ... E 3
30663 Rutledge, 628 ... E 3
31646 Saint George, 600 ... H 9
31558 Saint Marys, 3,408 ... J 9
31522 Saint Simons Island, 5,346 ... K 8
31784 Sale City, 323 ... D 8
31082 Sandersville⊙, 5,546 ... G 5
31327 Sapelo Island, 250 ... K 8
30456 Sardis, 643 ... J 5
30275 Sargent, 800 ... C 4
31785 Sasser, 339 ... D 7
30571 Sautee-Nacoochee, 350 ... E 1
* 31401 Savannah⊙, 118,349 ... L 6
Savannah, ‡187,767 ... L 6
31328 Savannah Beach, 1,786 ... L 6
31083 Scotland, 261 ... G 6
31095 Scott, 215 ... G 5
31560 Screven, 936 ... H 7
31561 Sea Island, 600 ... K 8
30276 Senoia, 910 ... C 4
30172 Shannon, 1,563 ... B 2
31786 Shellman, 1,166 ... C 7
31826 Shiloh, 298 ... C 5
† 31781 Shingler, 300 ... E 7
30665 Siloam, 319 ... F 3
30173 Silver Creek, 450 ... B 2
31086 Smarr, 350 ... E 5
31787 Smithville, 713 ... D 7
30080 Smyrna, 19,157 ... D 3
30278 Snellville, 1,990 ... D 3
30279 Social Circle, 1,961 ... E 3
30457 Soperton⊙, 2,596 ... G 6
31647 Sparks, 1,337 ... F 8
31087 Sparta⊙, 2,172 ... F 4
31329 Springfield⊙, 1,001 ... K 6
30705 Spring Place, 241 ... C 1
30823 Stapleton, 390 ... H 4
31648 Statenville⊙, 700 ... G 9
30458 Statesboro⊙, 14,616 ... J 6
30666 Statham, 817 ... E 3
31088 Stevens Pottery, 350 ... F 5
30464 Stillmore, 354 ... H 6
30281 Stockbridge, 1,561 ... D 3
31649 Stockton, 500 ... G 9
30083 Stone Mountain, 1,899 ... D 3
30282 Stonewall, 950 ... C 3
† 30747 Subligna, 300 ... B 1
30572 Suches, 400 ... E 1
30518 Sugar Hill, 1,745 ... E 2
30747 Summerville⊙, 5,043 ... B 2
31789 Sumner, 207 ... E 7
30284 Sunny Side, 209 ... D 4
31563 Surrency, 352 ... H 7
30174 Suwanee, 615 ... D 2
30401 Swainsboro⊙, 7,325 ... H 5
31790 Sycamore, 547 ... E 7
30467 Sylvania⊙, 3,199 ... J 5
31791 Sylvester⊙, 4,226 ... E 7
31827 Talbotton⊙, 1,045 ... C 5
30176 Tallapoosa, 2,896 ... B 3
30573 Tallulah Falls, 255 ... F 1
30177 Tate, 950 ... D 2
30178 Taylorsville, 253 ... C 2
30179 Temple, 864 ... B 3
30751 Tennga, 300 ... C 1
31089 Tennille, 1,753 ... G 5
30286 Thomaston⊙, 10,024 ... D 5
31792 Thomasville⊙, 18,155 ... E 9

30824 Thomson⊙, 6,503 ... H 4
31404 Thunderbolt, 2,750 ... K 6
31794 Tifton⊙, 12,179 ... F 8
30576 Tiger, 312 ... F 1
30668 Tignall, 756 ... G 3
30577 Toccoa⊙, 6,971 ... F 1
31090 Toomsboro, 682 ... F 5
31331 Townsend, 300 ... J 7
30752 Trenton⊙, 1,523 ... A 1
30753 Trion, 1,965 ... B 1
30755 Tunnel Hill, 900 ... C 1
30289 Turin, 242 ... C 4
30471 Twin City, 1,119 ... H 5
31795 Ty Ty, 447 ... E 8
31091 Unadilla, 1,457 ... E 6
30291 Union City, 3,031 ... D 3
30669 Union Point, 1,624 ... F 3
31794 Unionville, 1,646 ... F 8
30473 Uvalda, 663 ... H 6
31601 Valdosta⊙, 32,303 ... F 9
30756 Varnell, 400 ... C 1
30474 Vidalia, 9,507 ... H 6
31092 Vienna⊙, 2,341 ... E 6
30180 Villa Rica, 3,922 ... C 3
30182 Waco, 431 ... B 3
30477 Wadley, 1,989 ... H 5
30183 Waleska, 487 ... D 2
31333 Walthourville, 300 ... J 7
31564 Waresboro, 350 ... H 8
31830 Warm Springs, 523 ... C 5
31093 Warner Robins, 33,491 ... E 5
30828 Warrenton⊙, 2,073 ... G 4
31796 Warwick, 466 ... E 7
30673 Washington⊙, 4,094 ... G 3
30677 Watkinsville⊙, 986 ... E 3
31565 Waverly, 250 ... J 8
31831 Waverly Hall, 671 ... C 5
31501 Waycross⊙, 18,996 ... H 8
30830 Waynesboro⊙, 5,530 ... J 4
31566 Waynesville, 500 ... J 8
31833 West Point, 4,232 ... B 5
31797 Whigham, 381 ... D 9
30184 White, 462 ... C 2
30603 White Hall, 400 ... F 3
30678 White Plains, 236 ... F 4
30185 Whitesburg, 720 ... B 4
30186 Whitestone, 450 ... C 1
† 31833 Whitesville, 250 ... C 5
30581 Wiley, 300 ... F 1
31650 Willacoochee, 1,120 ... G 8
30292 Williamson, 284 ... D 4
31404 Wilmington Island, 3,284 ... L 7
30680 Winder⊙, 6,605 ... E 3
† 30824 Winfield, 444 ... H 3
30187 Winston, 625 ... C 3
30683 Winterville, 551 ... F 3
31569 Woodbine⊙, 1,002 ... J 9
30293 Woodbury, 1,422 ... C 5
31836 Woodland, 689 ... D 5
30188 Woodstock, 870 ... D 2
30670 Woodville, 379 ... F 3
30833 Wrens, 2,204 ... H 4
31096 Wrightsville⊙, 2,106 ... G 5
31097 Yatesville, 423 ... D 5
30582 Young Harris, 544 ... E 1
30295 Zebulon⊙, 776 ... D 4

⊙ County seat.
‡ Population of metropolitan area.
† Zip of nearest p.o.
* Multiple zips

Agriculture, Industry and Resources

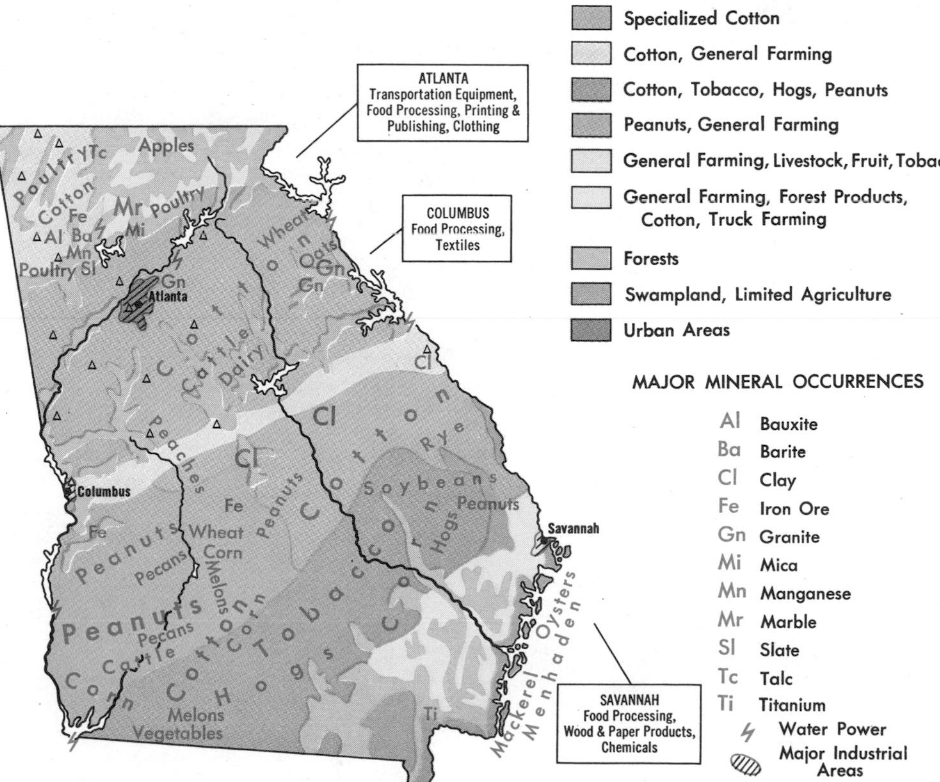

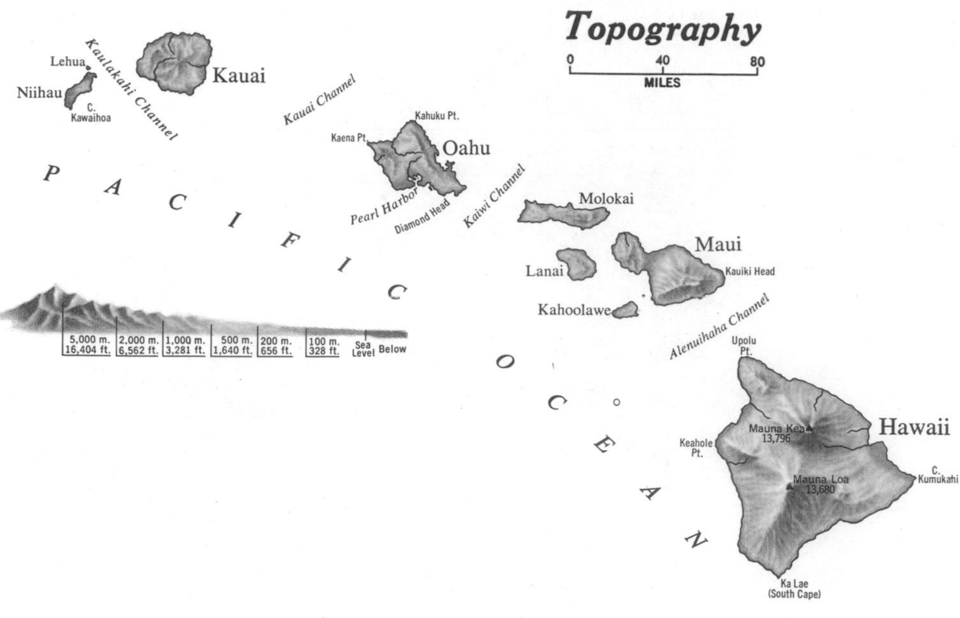

Sharp spikes bristle protectively around their precious fruit crop on Pineapple Hill, west Maui. Second only to sugarcane, pineapples rank high in Hawaii's economy.

Agriculture, Industry and Resources

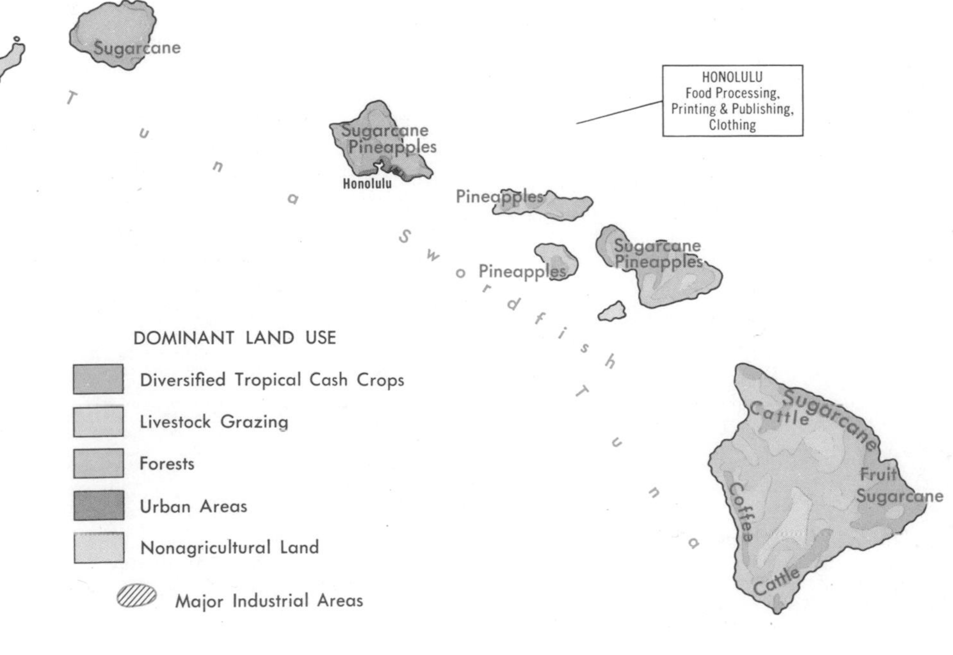

COUNTIES

Name/Pop.	Key
Hawaii, 63,468	K 7
Honolulu, 629,176	D 3
Kalawao, 172	G 1
Kauai, 29,761	A 1
Maui, 45,984	J 1

CITIES and TOWNS

	Zip	Name/Pop.	Key
	96701	Aiea, 12,560	B 3
	96821	Aina Haina, 15,000	F 2
	96703	Anahola, 638	C 1
†	96706	Barbers Point Housing, 1,947	E 2
	96704	Captain Cook, 1,263	G 5
	96705	Eleele, 758	C 2
	96706	Ewa, 2,906	A 4
	96706	Ewa Beach, 7,765	A 4
†	96701	Foster Village, 3,755	B 3
†	96714	Haena, 75	C 1
	96708	Haiku, 464	J 2
	96709	Haina, 333	H 3
	96710	Hakalau, 742	J 4
†	96701	Halawa Heights, 5,809	B 3
	96712	Haleiwa, 2,626	E 1
	96787	Haliimaile, 638	J 2
	96713	Hana, 459	K 2
	96714	Hanalei, 153	C 1
	96715	Hanamaulu, 2,461	C 1
	96716	Hanapepe, 1,388	C 2
	96717	Hauula, 2,048	E 1
	96718	Hawaii National Park, 100	J 6
	96719	Hawi, 797	G 3
	96824	Hickam Housing, 7,352	B 4
	96720	Hilo⊙, 26,353	J 5
	96725	Holualoa, 850	G 5
	96726	Honaunau, 950	G 6
†	96710	Honohina, 125	J 4
	96727	Honokaa, 1,555	H 4
†	96761	Honokahua, 431	H 1
†	96740	Honokohau, 200	G 5
*	96801	Honolulu (cap.)⊙, 324,871	C 4
		Honolulu, ‡630,528	C 4
	96728	Honomu, 737	J 4
†	96706	Honouliuli, 600	A 3
	96729	Hoolehua, 1,090	G 1
†	96740	Huehue, 100	G 5
†	96706	Iroquois Point, 4,572	A 4
†	96801	Iwilei, 1,835	C 4
	96730	Kaaawa, 848	F 1
†	96761	Kaanapali, 250	H 2
†	96801	Kahala, 14,288	D 5
†	96744	Kahaluu, 1,657	E 2
	96731	Kahuku, 917	E 1
	96732	Kahului, 8,280	J 2
	96734	Kailua, 33,783	F 2
†	96740	Kailua, 365	F 5
	96740	Kailua Kona (Kailua), 365	F 5
	96816	Kaimuki, 25,315	D 4

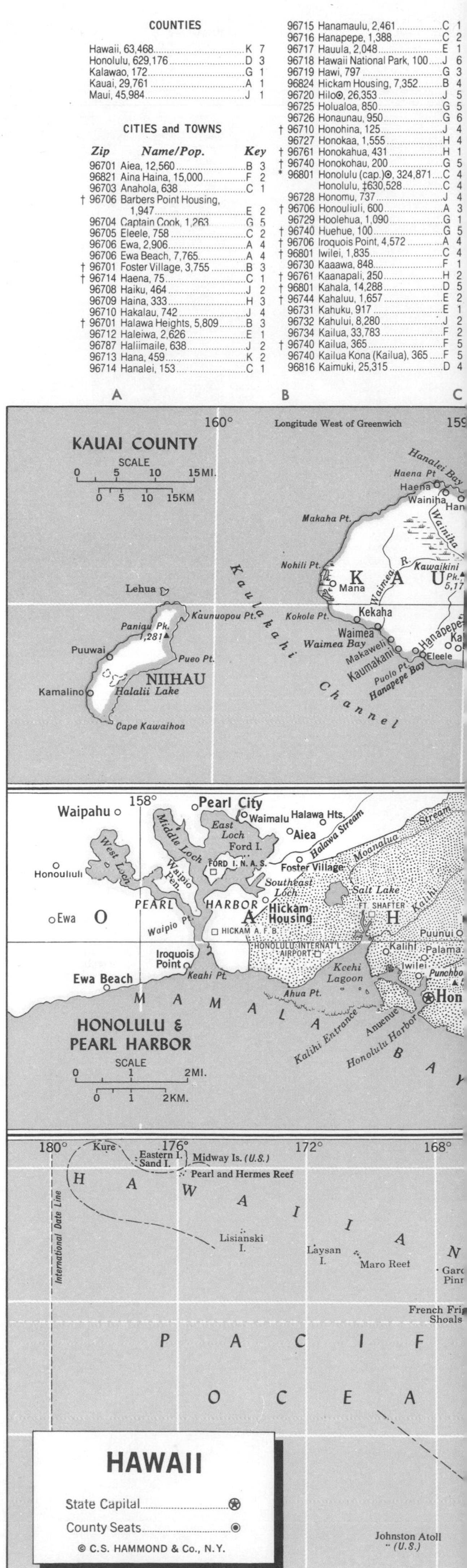

† 96750 Kainaliu, 450 .... G 5
† 96757 Kalae, 150 .... G 1
96741 Kalaheo, 1,514 .... C 2
† 96740 Kalaoa, 300 .... G 5
96742 Kalaupapa⊙, 164 .... G 1
96817 Kalihi, 32,650 .... C 4
† 96748 Kaluaaha, 300 .... H 1
† 96748 Kamalo, 300 .... H 1
96743 Kamuela, 756 .... G 3
96744 Kaneohe, 29,903 .... F 2
96746 Kapaa, 3,794 .... D 1
† 96778 Kapaahu, 850 .... J 6
96755 Kapaau, 237 .... G 3
† 96778 Kapoho, 300 .... K 5
† 96758 Kapulena, 125 .... H 4
96747 Kaumakani, 1,014 .... C 2
96748 Kaunakakai, 1,070 .... G 1
† 96708 Kaupakulua, 100 .... K 2
96743 Kawaihae, 50 .... G 4
† 96712 Kawailoa, 900 .... E 1
96749 Keaau, 951 .... J 5
96750 Kealakekua, 740 .... G 5
96751 Kealia, 600 .... D 1
96751 Kealia, 550 .... G 6
96752 Kekaha, 2,404 .... C 2
† 96704 Keokea, 500 .... G 6
† 96790 Keokea, 750 .... J 2
96753 Kihei, 1,450 .... J 2
96754 Kilauea, 671 .... C 1
† 96713 Koali, 100 .... K 2
† 96755 Kohala (Kapaau), 237 .... G 3
† 96708 Kokomo, 200 .... K 2
96756 Koloa, 1,368 .... C 2
96757 Kualapuu, 441 .... G 1
96758 Kukuihaele, 310 .... H 3
96790 Kula, 800 .... J 2
96759 Kunia, 545 .... E 2
96760 Kurtistown, 900 .... J 5
96761 Lahaina, 3,718 .... H 2
96762 Laie, 3,009 .... E 1
96763 Lanai City, 2,122 .... H 2
96764 Laupahoehoe, 452 .... J 4
96765 Lawai, 950 .... C 2
96766 Lihue⊙, 3,124 .... C 2
† 96779 Lower Paia, 1,105 .... J 1
† 96753 Maalaea, 80 .... J 2
† 96792 Maili, 4,397 .... D 2
† 96792 Makaha, 4,644 .... D 2
† 96706 Makakilo City, 3,499 .... E 2
† 96711 Makapala, 201 .... G 3
96768 Makawao, 1,066 .... K 2
96769 Makaweli, 500 .... B 2
96770 Maunaloa, 872 .... G 1
† 96744 Maunawili, 5,303 .... F 2
† 96786 Mililani, 2,035 .... E 2
† 96704 Milolii, 120 .... G 6
† 96734 Mokapu, 7,860 .... F 2
† 96791 Mokuleia, 880 .... D 1
96771 Mountainview, 419 .... J 5
96772 Naalehu, 1,014 .... H 7
96792 Nanakuli, 6,506 .... D 2
96773 Ninole, 75 .... J 4
† 96761 Olowalu, 750 .... H 2
† 96781 Onomea, 500 .... J 4
96774 Ookala, 486 .... J 4
† 96778 Opihikao, 125 .... K 6
96775 Paauhau, 400 .... H 4
96776 Paauilo, 710 .... H 4
† 96801 Pacific Heights, 5,305 .... C 4
† 96782 Pacific Palisades, 7,846 .... E 2
96777 Pahala, 1,507 .... H 6
96778 Pahoa, 924 .... J 5
96779 Paia, 541 .... J 2
† 96801 Palama, 15,307 .... C 4
† 96704 Papa, 100 .... G 6
96780 Papaaloa, 319 .... J 4
96781 Papaikou, 1,888 .... J 5
† 96781 Paukaa, 450 .... J 5
† 96708 Pauwela, 355 .... K 2
96782 Pearl City, 19,552 .... B 3
96783 Pepeekeo, 1,150 .... J 4
† 96756 Poipu, 466 .... C 2
96766 Puhi, 772 .... C 2
96788 Pukalani, 1,629 .... J 2
† 96748 Pukoo, 300 .... H 1
96784 Puunene, 1,132 .... J 2
† 96801 Puunui, 10,082 .... C 4
† 96769 Puuwai, 200 .... A 2
96786 Schofield Barracks, 13,516 .... E 2
96779 Spreckelsville, 350 .... J 1
† 96790 Ulupalakua, 75 .... J 2
96785 Volcano, 400 .... J 6
96766 Wahiawa, 17,598 .... E 2
† 96788 Waiakoa, 1,050 .... J 2
† 96731 Waialee, 80 .... E 1
96791 Waialua, Oahu, 4,047 .... E 1
96792 Waianae, 3,302 .... D 2
† 96793 Waihee, 346 .... J 2
† 96793 Waikapu, 598 .... J 2
96815 Waikiki, 35,000 .... C 4
† 96748 Wailau, 300 .... H 1
† 96710 Wailea, 315 .... J 4
† 96746 Wailua, 1,379 .... D 2
96793 Wailuku⊙, 7,979 .... J 2
† 96701 Waimalu, 2,982 .... B 3
96795 Waimanalo, 2,081 .... F 2
† 96795 Waimanalo Beach, 3,045 .... F 2
† 96743 Waimea (Kamuela), Hawaii 756 .... G 3
96796 Waimea, Kauai, 1,569 .... B 2
† 96712 Waimea, Oahu, 200 .... E 1
† 96772 Waiohinu, 200 .... G 7
96797 Waipahu, 22,798 .... A 3
† 96786 Waipio Acres, 2,146 .... E 2
† 96786 Whitmore Village, 2,015 .... E 1
† 96801 Woodlawn, 5,569 .... D 4

MIDWAY ISLANDS
Total Population
2,356

⊙ County seat.
‡ Population of metropolitan area.
† Zip of nearest p.o.
* Multiple zips

AREA 6,450 sq. mi.
POPULATION 769,913
CAPITAL Honolulu
LARGEST CITY Honolulu
HIGHEST POINT Mauna Kea 13,796 ft.
SETTLED IN —
ADMITTED TO UNION August 21, 1959
POPULAR NAME Aloha State; Paradise of the Pacific
STATE FLOWER Red Hibiscus
STATE BIRD Nene (Hawaiian Goose)

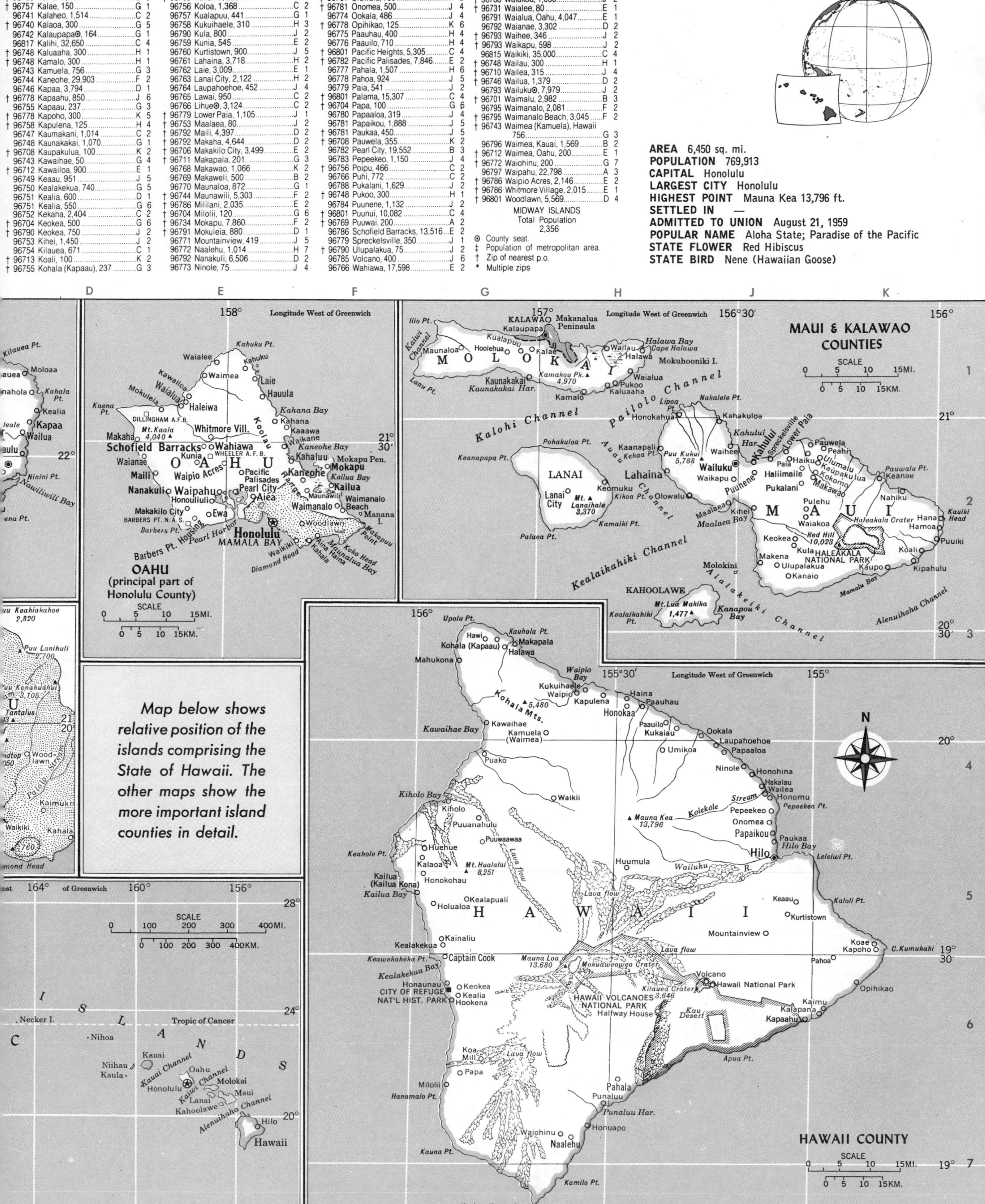

IDAHO
SCALE
0 5 10 20 30 40 50 MI.
0 5 10 20 30 40 50 KM.
State Capitals
County Seats
© C.S. HAMMOND & Co., N.Y.
Topography
0 50 100
MILES
Below Sea Level
100 m. 328 ft.
200 m. 656 ft.
500 m. 1,640 ft.
1,000 m. 3,281 ft.
2,000 m. 6,562 ft.
5,000 m. 16,404 ft.
CLEARWATER MTS.
SALMON RIVER MTS.
SAWTOOTH MTS.
CENTENNIAL MTS.
BITTERROOT RANGE
SNAKE RIVER PLAIN
Borah Pk. 12,662
Hells Canyon
American Falls Res.
Dworshak Res.
L. Pend Oreille
Coeur d'Alene L.
Longitude West of Greenwich
117° 116° 115° 114° 113° 112° 111°
49° 48° 47° 46° 45° 44° 43° 42°
BRITISH COLUMBIA
ALTA.
WASHINGTON
OREGON
NEVADA
UTAH
WYOMING
MONTANA
BOISE
SPOKANE
BUTTE
Missoula
Lewiston
Pocatello
Idaho Falls
Twin Falls
Coeur d'Alene
Nampa
Caldwell
Moscow
Sandpoint
GLACIER NATIONAL PARK
YELLOWSTONE NATIONAL PARK
GRAND TETON NATIONAL PARK
BOUNDARY
BONNER
KOOTENAI
BENEWAH
SHOSHONE
LATAH
CLEARWATER
NEZ PERCE
LEWIS
IDAHO
ADAMS
VALLEY
LEMHI
CUSTER
WASHINGTON
PAYETTE
GEM
BOISE
CANYON
ADA
ELMORE
CAMAS
BLAINE
BUTTE
CLARK
FREMONT
JEFFERSON
MADISON
TETON
BONNEVILLE
BINGHAM
POWER
BANNOCK
CARIBOU
BEAR LAKE
FRANKLIN
ONEIDA
CASSIA
MINIDOKA
JEROME
LINCOLN
GOODING
TWIN FALLS
OWYHEE

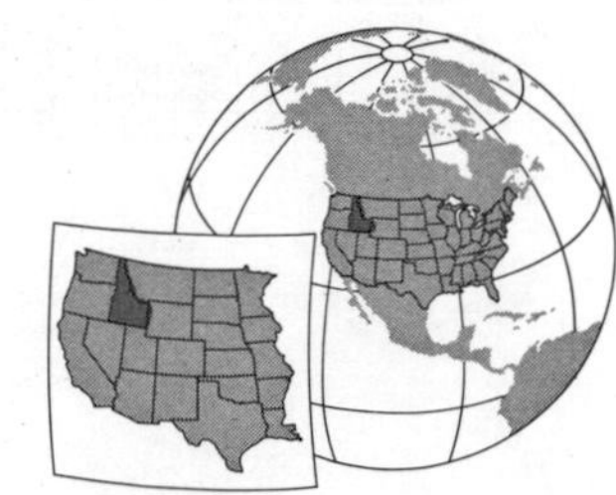

AREA 83,557 sq. mi.
POPULATION 713,008
CAPITAL Boise
LARGEST CITY Boise
HIGHEST POINT Borah Pk. 12,662 ft.
SETTLED IN 1842
ADMITTED TO UNION July 3, 1890
POPULAR NAME Gem State
STATE FLOWER Syringa
STATE BIRD Mountain Bluebird

COUNTIES

Name/Pop.	Key
Ada, 112,230	B 6
Adams, 2,877	B 5
Bannock, 52,200	F 7
Bear Lake, 5,801	G 7
Benewah, 6,230	B 2
Bingham, 29,167	F 6
Blaine, 5,749	D 6
Boise, 1,763	C 6
Bonner, 15,560	B 1
Bonneville, 51,250	G 6
Boundary, 6,371	B 1
Butte, 2,925	E 6
Camas, 728	D 6
Canyon, 61,288	B 6
Caribou, 6,534	G 7
Cassia, 17,017	E 7
Clark, 741	F 5
Clearwater, 10,871	C 3
Custer, 2,967	D 5
Elmore, 17,479	C 6
Franklin, 7,373	G 7
Fremont, 8,710	G 5
Gem, 9,387	B 6
Gooding, 8,645	D 6
Idaho, 12,891	C 4
Jefferson, 11,619	F 6
Jerome, 10,253	D 7
Kootenai, 35,332	B 2
Latah, 24,891	B 3
Lemhi, 5,566	D 4
Lewis, 3,867	B 3
Lincoln, 3,057	D 6
Madison, 13,452	G 6
Minidoka, 15,731	E 7
Nez Perce, 30,376	B 3
Oneida, 2,864	F 7
Owyhee, 6,422	B 7
Payette, 12,401	B 5
Power, 4,864	F 7
Shoshone, 19,718	B 2
Teton, 2,351	G 6
Twin Falls, 41,807	D 7
Valley, 3,609	C 5
Washington, 7,633	B 5

CITIES and TOWNS

Zip	Name/Pop.	Key
83210	Aberdeen, 1,542	F 7
83310	Acequia, 107	E 7
83520	Ahsahka, 500	B 3
83311	Albion, 229	E 7
83312	Almo, 170	E 7
83211	American Falls⊙, 2,769	E 7
83401	Ammon, 1,338	G 6
83212	Arbon, 75	F 7
83213	Arco⊙, 1,244	E 6
83214	Arimo, 252	F 7
83420	Ashton, 1,187	G 5
83801	Athol, 190	B 2
83601	Atlanta, 50	C 6
83215	Atomic City, 24	F 6
83802	Avery, 250	C 2
83461	Baker, 98	E 4
83217	Bancroft, 366	G 7
83264	Banida, 76	G 7
83602	Banks, 49	B 5
83218	Basalt, 349	F 6
83803	Bayview, 300	B 2
83313	Bellevue, 537	D 6
83219	Bennington, 60	G 7
83220	Bern, 135	G 7
83221	Blackfoot⊙, 8,716	F 6
83804	Blanchard, 120	A 1
83314	Bliss, 114	D 7
83223	Bloomington, 186	G 7
* 83701	Boise (cap.)⊙, 74,990	B 6
	Boise, ‡112,230	B 6
83805	Bonners Ferry⊙, 2,796	B 1
83806	Bovill, 343	B 3
† 83651	Bowmont, 100	B 6
83315	Bridge, 140	E 7
83604	Bruneau, 150	C 7
83316	Buhl, 2,975	D 7
83807	Burke, 150	C 2
83318	Burley⊙, 8,279	E 7
† 83213	Butte City, 42	E 6
83808	Calder, 140	B 2
83605	Caldwell⊙, 14,219	B 6
83610	Cambridge, 383	B 5
83320	Carey, 750	E 6
83809	Careywood, 60	B 1
83462	Carmen, 40	E 4
83611	Cascade⊙, 833	C 5
83321	Castleford, 174	C 7
83810	Cataldo, 275	B 2
† 83241	Central, 60	G 7
83226	Challis⊙, 784	D 5
† 83851	Chatcolet, 95	B 2
83421	Chester, 206	G 5
† 83217	Chesterfield, 50	G 7
83201	Chubbuck, 2,924	F 7
83811	Clark Fork, 367	B 1
83812	Clarkia, 147	B 2
83227	Clayton, 36	D 5
83521	Clearwater, 110	C 3
† 83263	Cleveland, 60	G 7
83228	Clifton, 137	F 7
83229	Cobalt, 35	D 4
83814	Coeur d'Alene⊙, 16,228	B 2
83865	Colburn, 200	B 1
83230	Conda, 250	G 7
83821	Coolin, 110	B 1
83322	Corral, 21	D 6
83522	Cottonwood, 867	B 3
83612	Council⊙, 899	B 5
83523	Craigmont, 554	B 3
† 83622	Crouch, 71	B 5
83524	Culdesac, 211	B 3
† 83814	Dalton Gardens, 1,559	B 2
83232	Dayton, 198	F 7
83823	Deary, 411	B 3
83323	Declo, 251	E 7
83824	Desmet, 154	B 2
83324	Dietrich, 84	D 7
83233	Dingle, 300	G 7
83615	Donnelly, 114	B 5
83825	Dover, 300	B 1
83234	Downey, 586	F 7
83422	Driggs⊙, 727	G 6
83423	Dubois⊙, 400	F 5
83616	Eagle, 525	B 6
† 83836	East Hope, 175	B 1
83826	Eastport, 83	B 1
83325	Eden, 343	D 7
83326	Elba, 87	E 7
83525	Elk City, 500	C 4
83827	Elk River, 383	B 3
83235	Ellis, 75	D 5
83828	Emida, 135	B 2
83617	Emmett⊙, 3,945	B 6
83829	Enaville, 90	B 2
83327	Fairfield⊙, 157	D 6
83424	Felt, 90	G 6
83531	Fenn, 45	B 4
83526	Ferdinand, 157	B 3
83830	Fernwood, 360	B 2
83328	Filer, 1,173	D 7
83236	Firth, 362	F 6
83261	Fish Haven, 120	G 7
83203	Fort Hall, 750	F 6
83237	Franklin, 402	G 7
83619	Fruitland, 1,576	B 6
83620	Fruitvale, 90	B 5
83621	Gardena, 44	B 5
83704	Garden City, 2,368	B 6
83622	Garden Valley, 100	C 5
† 83873	Gem, 50	C 2
83832	Genesee, 619	B 3
83238	Geneva, 200	G 7
83239	Georgetown, 421	G 7
83463	Gibbonsville, 85	E 4
83623	Glenns Ferry, 1,386	C 7
83330	Gooding⊙, 2,599	D 7
83241	Grace, 826	G 7
83624	Grand View, 450	B 7
83530	Grangeville⊙, 3,636	B 4
83533	Greencreek, 72	B 3
83626	Greenleaf, 425	B 6
† 83544	Greer, 70	B 3
83332	Hagerman, 436	D 7
83333	Hailey⊙, 1,425	D 6
83425	Hamer, 81	F 6
83627	Hammett, 653	C 7
83334	Hansen, 415	D 7
† 83521	Harpster, 250	C 4
83833	Harrison, 249	B 2
83834	Harvard, 50	B 3
† 83854	Hauser, 349	A 2
† 83835	Hayden, 1,285	B 2
83835	Hayden Lake, 260	B 2
83335	Hazelton, 396	E 7
83535	Headquarters, 350	C 3
† 83443	Heise, 84	G 6
83336	Heyburn, 1,637	E 7
83337	Hill City, 30	D 6
83243	Holbrook, 100	F 7
† 83301	Hollister, 57	D 7
83628	Homedale, 1,411	A 6
83836	Hope, 63	B 1
83629	Horseshoe Bend, 511	B 6
83244	Howe, 428	F 6
† 83854	Huetter, 49	B 2
83631	Idaho City⊙, 164	C 6
83401	Idaho Falls⊙, 35,776	F 6
83632	Indian Valley, 72	B 5
83245	Inkom, 522	F 7
83427	Iona, 890	G 6
83428	Irwin, 228	G 6
83429	Island Park, 136	G 5
83338	Jerome⊙, 4,183	D 7
83535	Juliaetta, 423	B 3
83536	Kamiah, 1,307	B 3
83837	Kellogg, 3,811	B 2
83537	Kendrick, 426	B 3
83340	Ketchum, 1,454	D 6
83538	Keuterville, 26	B 3
† 83423	Kilgore, 50	G 5
83341	Kimberly, 1,557	D 7
83633	King Hill, 150	C 6
83539	Kooskia, 809	C 3
83840	Kootenai, 168	B 1
83634	Kuna, 593	B 6
83841	Laclede, 200	B 1
83635	Lake Fork, 141	B 5
83430	Lamont, 30	G 6
83540	Lapwai, 400	B 3
83246	Lava Hot Springs, 516	F 7
83464	Leadore, 111	E 5
83465	Lemhi, 36	E 5
83249	Leslie, 100	E 6
83636	Letha, 115	B 6
83501	Lewiston⊙, 26,068	A 3
83431	Lewisville, 468	F 6
83432	Lorenzo, 125	G 6
† 83242	Lost River, 58	E 6
83637	Lowman, 45	C 5
83542	Lucile, 105	B 4
† 83241	Lund, 100	G 7
83251	Mackay, 539	E 6
83433	Macks Inn, 150	G 5
83252	Malad City⊙, 1,848	F 7
83342	Malta, 196	E 7
83639	Marsing, 610	B 6
83253	May, 120	E 5
83638	McCall, 1,758	C 5
83250	McCammon, 623	F 7
83640	Meadows, 250	B 5
83641	Melba, 197	B 6
83434	Menan, 545	F 6
83642	Meridian, 2,616	B 6
83643	Mesa, 25	B 5
83644	Middleton, 739	B 6
83645	Midvale, 176	B 5
83343	Minidoka, 131	E 7
83435	Monteview, 110	F 6
83646	Montour, 138	B 6
83254	Montpelier, 2,604	G 7
83255	Moore, 156	E 6
83256	Moreland, 500	F 6
83843	Moscow⊙, 14,146	B 3
83647	Mountain Home⊙, 6,451	C 6
83845	Moyie Springs, 203	B 1
† 83450	Mud Lake, 194	F 6
83846	Mullan, 1,279	C 2
83650	Murphy⊙, 75	B 6
83874	Murray, 100	C 2
83344	Murtaugh, 124	D 7
83345	Naf, 42	E 7
83651	Nampa, 20,768	B 6
83847	Naples, 463	B 1
83436	Newdale, 267	G 6
83654	New Meadows, 605	B 4
83655	New Plymouth, 986	B 6
83543	Nezperce⊙, 555	B 3
83848	Nordman, 168	B 1
83466	North Fork, 150	D 4
83656	Notus, 304	B 6
† 83254	Nounan, 92	G 7
83346	Oakley, 656	D 7
83259	Obsidian, 22	D 6
83657	Ola, 78	B 5
† 99156	Oldtown, 161	A 1
† 83855	Onaway, 166	B 3
83659	Oreana, 115	B 6
83544	Orofino⊙, 3,883	B 3
† 83525	Orogrande, 34	C 4
83849	Osburn, 2,248	B 2
83260	Ovid, 150	G 7
† 83263	Oxford, 75	F 7
83437	Palisades, 95	G 6
83261	Paris⊙, 615	G 7
83438	Parker, 266	G 6
83660	Parma, 1,228	B 6
83347	Paul, 911	E 7
83661	Payette⊙, 4,521	B 5
83545	Peck, 238	B 3
83348	Picabo, 50	D 6
83546	Pierce, 1,218	C 3
83850	Pinehurst, 1,034	B 2
83262	Pingree, 115	F 6
83851	Plummer, 443	B 2
83201	Pocatello⊙, 40,036	F 7
83547	Pollock, 50	B 4
83852	Ponderay, 275	B 1
83853	Porthill, 39	B 1
83854	Post Falls, 2,371	A 2
83855	Potlatch, 871	A 3
83263	Preston⊙, 3,310	G 7
83856	Priest River, 1,493	A 1
83857	Princeton, 124	B 3
83858	Rathdrum, 741	A 2
† 83114	Raymond, 65	G 7
83548	Reubens, 81	B 3
83440	Rexburg⊙, 8,272	G 6
83349	Richfield, 290	D 6
† 89832	Riddle, 44	B 7
83442	Rigby⊙, 2,293	F 6
83549	Riggins, 533	B 4
83443	Ririe, 575	G 6
83444	Roberts, 393	F 6
† 83221	Rockford, 150	F 6
83271	Rockland, 209	F 7
83302	Rogerson, 45	D 7
† 83660	Roswell, 65	A 6
83350	Rupert⊙, 4,563	E 7
83860	Sagle, 100	B 1
83445	Saint Anthony⊙, 2,877	G 6
83272	Saint Charles, 200	G 7
† 83861	Saint Joe, 50	B 2
83861	Saint Maries⊙, 2,571	B 2
83467	Salmon⊙, 2,910	D 4
83252	Samaria, 137	F 7
83862	Samuels, 467	B 1
83863	Sanders, 27	B 2
83864	Sandpoint⊙, 4,144	B 1
83866	Santa, 100	B 2
83274	Shelley, 2,614	F 6
83352	Shoshone⊙, 1,233	D 7
† 83650	Silver City, 1	B 6
† 83423	Small, 35	F 5
83868	Smelterville, 967	B 2
83276	Soda Springs⊙, 2,977	G 7
83550	Southwick, 38	B 3
83446	Spencer, 45	F 5
83869	Spirit Lake, 622	A 2
83277	Springfield, 180	F 6
83447	Squirrel, 43	G 5
83278	Stanley, 47	D 5
83669	Star, 500	B 6
83279	Sterling, 73	F 6
83552	Stites, 263	C 3
83280	Stone, 114	F 7
83448	Sugar City, 617	G 6
83353	Sun Valley, 180	D 6
83281	Swanlake, 145	F 7
83449	Swan Valley, 235	G 6
83670	Sweet, 120	B 6
83468	Tendoy, 150	E 5
83870	Tensed, 151	B 2
83450	Terreton, 42	F 6
83451	Teton, 390	G 6
83452	Tetonia, 176	G 6
83283	Thatcher, 300	G 7
83453	Thornton, 177	G 6
83871	Troy, 541	B 3
83354	Tuttle, 53	D 7
83301	Twin Falls⊙, 21,914	D 7
83454	Ucon, 664	F 6
83455	Victor, 241	G 6
83872	Viola, 300	B 3
† 83234	Virginia, 100	F 7
83873	Wallace⊙, 2,206	C 2
83875	Wardner, 492	B 2
83611	Warm Lake, 200	C 5
83285	Wayan, 50	G 7
83553	Weippe, 713	C 3
83672	Weiser⊙, 4,108	B 5
83355	Wendell, 1,122	D 7
83286	Weston, 230	F 7
83554	White Bird, 185	B 4
83676	Wilder, 564	A 6
83555	Winchester, 274	B 3
83876	Worley, 235	B 2
83677	Yellow Pine, 45	C 4

⊙ County seat.
‡ Population of metropolitan area.
† Zip of nearest p.o.
* Multiple zips

Agriculture, Industry and Resources

MAJOR MINERAL OCCURRENCES

Ag Silver
Au Gold
Co Cobalt
Cu Copper
Fe Iron Ore
Hg Mercury
P Phosphates
Pb Lead
Sb Antimony
Th Thorium
Ti Titanium
V Vanadium
W Tungsten
Zn Zinc
ϟ Water Power

DOMINANT LAND USE

Wheat, General Farming
Wheat, Peas
Specialized Dairy
Potatoes, Beans, Sugar Beets, Livestock, General Farming
General Farming, Dairy, Hay, Sugar Beets
General Farming, Livestock, Special Crops
General Farming, Dairy, Range Livestock
Range Livestock
Forests

Wheat
Timber
Dairy
Cattle
Sheep
Potatoes
Beans
Sugar Beets
Wheat
Barley

The Sun Valley Ski Patrol adds a touch of color to the slopes of Baldy Mountain. Here, in one of the country's most popular resorts, visitors acquire tropical tans while swimming in heated pools, skiing, skijoring, dogsledding or just sunbathing in the glacial air.

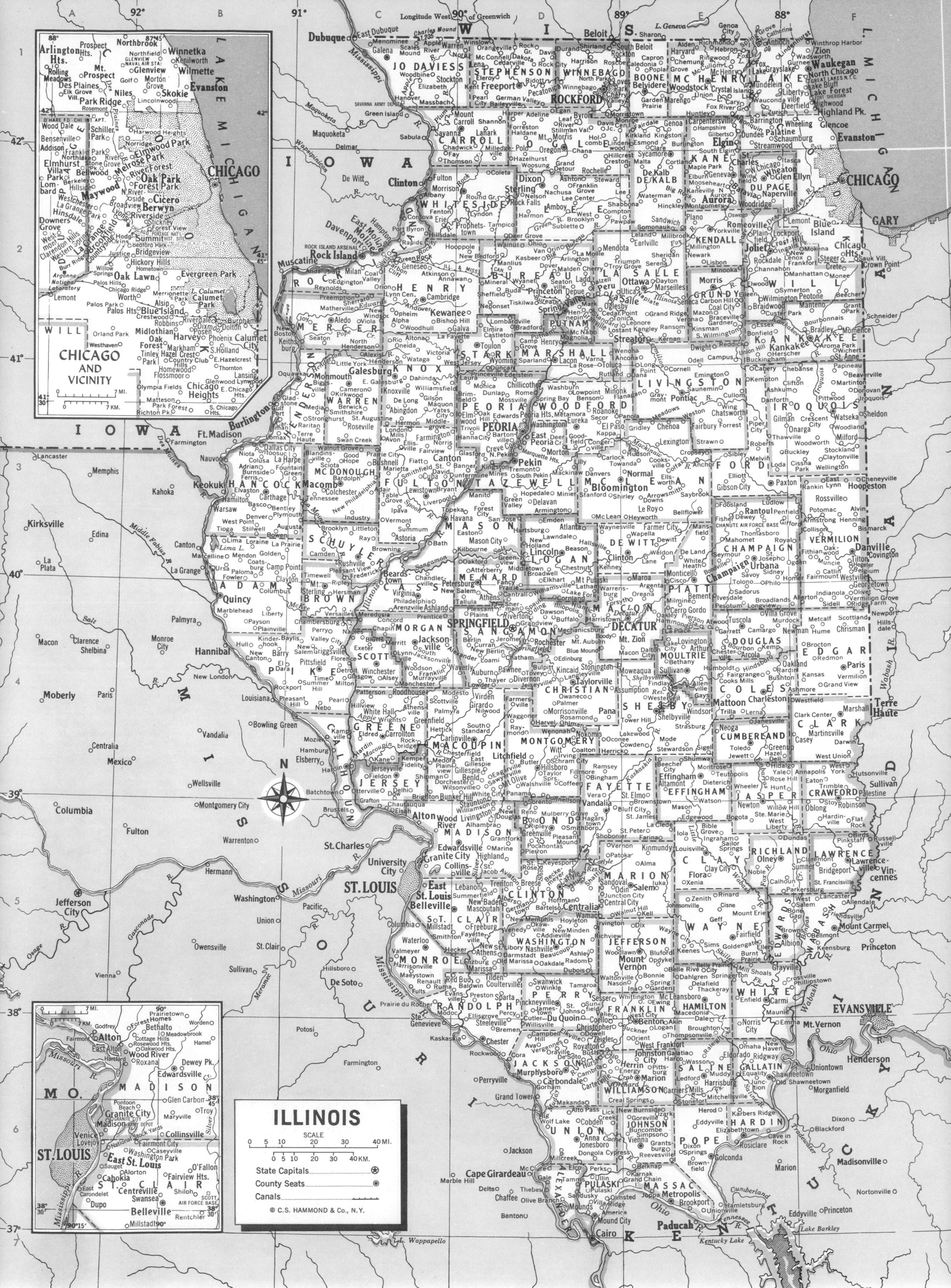

ILLINOIS
SCALE
0 5 10 20 30 40 MI.
0 10 20 30 40 KM.
State Capitals
County Seats
Canals
© C.S. HAMMOND & Co., N.Y.
CHICAGO AND VICINITY
Longitude West of Greenwich
WISCONSIN
IOWA
MISSOURI
KENTUCKY
INDIANA
LAKE MICHIGAN
L. MICHIGAN
MO.
MADISON
ST. LOUIS
ST. CLAIR
CHICAGO
SPRINGFIELD
PEORIA
ROCKFORD
ST. LOUIS
JO DAVIESS
STEPHENSON
WINNEBAGO
BOONE
MC HENRY
LAKE
CARROLL
OGLE
DE KALB
KANE
DU PAGE
COOK
WHITESIDE
LEE
KENDALL
WILL
ROCK ISLAND
HENRY
BUREAU
LA SALLE
GRUNDY
KANKAKEE
MERCER
PUTNAM
STARK
MARSHALL
LIVINGSTON
IROQUOIS
HENDERSON
WARREN
KNOX
PEORIA
WOODFORD
FORD
HANCOCK
MC DONOUGH
FULTON
TAZEWELL
MC LEAN
VERMILION
ADAMS
SCHUYLER
BROWN
MASON
LOGAN
DE WITT
CHAMPAIGN
CASS
MENARD
PIATT
MORGAN
SANGAMON
MACON
DOUGLAS
EDGAR
PIKE
SCOTT
MOULTRIE
CHRISTIAN
COLES
GREENE
CALHOUN
MACOUPIN
MONTGOMERY
SHELBY
CUMBERLAND
CLARK
JERSEY
FAYETTE
EFFINGHAM
JASPER
CRAWFORD
MADISON
BOND
CLAY
RICHLAND
LAWRENCE
MARION
CLINTON
ST. CLAIR
WASHINGTON
JEFFERSON
WAYNE
EDWARDS
WABASH
MONROE
RANDOLPH
PERRY
FRANKLIN
HAMILTON
WHITE
JACKSON
WILLIAMSON
SALINE
GALLATIN
UNION
JOHNSON
POPE
HARDIN
ALEXANDER
PULASKI
MASSAC

COUNTIES

Adams, 70,861 B 4
Alexander, 12,015 D 6
Bond, 14,012 D 5
Boone, 25,440 E 1
Brown, 5,586 C 4
Bureau, 38,541 D 2
Calhoun, 5,675 C 4
Carroll, 19,276 D 1
Cass, 14,219 C 4
Champaign, 163,281 E 3
Christian, 35,948 D 4
Clark, 16,216 F 4
Clay, 14,735 E 5
Clinton, 28,315 D 5
Coles, 47,815 E 4
Cook, 5,492,369 F 2
Crawford, 19,824 F 4
Cumberland, 9,772 E 4
De Kalb, 71,654 E 2
De Witt, 16,975 E 3
Douglas, 18,997 E 4
Du Page, 491,882 E 2
Edgar, 21,591 F 4
Edwards, 7,090 E 5
Effingham, 24,608 E 4
Fayette, 20,752 D 4
Ford, 16,382 E 3
Franklin, 38,329 E 5
Fulton, 41,890 C 3
Gallatin, 7,418 E 6
Greene, 17,014 C 4
Grundy, 26,535 E 2
Hamilton, 8,665 E 5
Hancock, 23,645 B 3
Hardin, 4,914 E 6
Henderson, 8,451 C 3
Henry, 53,217 C 2
Iroquois, 33,532 F 3
Jackson, 55,008 D 6
Jasper, 10,741 E 4
Jefferson, 31,446 E 5
Jersey, 18,492 C 4
Jo Daviess, 21,766 C 1
Johnson, 7,550 E 6
Kane, 251,005 E 2
Kankakee, 97,250 F 2
Kendall, 26,374 E 2
Knox, 61,280 C 3
Lake, 382,638 E 1
La Salle, 111,409 E 2
Lawrence, 17,522 F 5
Lee, 37,947 D 2
Livingston, 40,690 E 3
Logan, 33,538 D 3
Macon, 125,010 E 4
Macoupin, 44,557 D 4
Madison, 250,934 D 5
Marion, 38,986 E 5
Marshall, 13,302 D 2
Mason, 16,161 D 3
Massac, 13,889 E 6
McDonough, 36,653 C 3
McHenry, 111,555 E 1
McLean, 104,389 E 3
Menard, 9,685 D 3
Mercer, 17,294 C 2
Monroe, 18,831 C 5
Montgomery, 30,260 D 4
Morgan, 36,174 C 4
Moultrie, 13,263 E 4
Ogle, 42,867 D 1
Peoria, 195,318 D 3
Perry, 19,757 D 5
Piatt, 15,509 E 4
Pike, 19,185 C 4
Pope, 3,857 E 6
Pulaski, 8,741 D 6
Putnam, 5,007 D 2
Randolph, 31,379 D 5
Richland, 16,829 E 5
Rock Island, 166,734 C 2
Saint Clair, 285,176 D 5
Saline, 25,721 E 6
Sangamon, 161,335 D 4
Schuyler, 8,135 C 3
Scott, 6,096 C 4
Shelby, 22,589 E 4
Stark, 7,510 D 2
Stephenson, 48,861 D 1
Tazewell, 118,649 D 3
Union, 16,071 D 6
Vermilion, 97,047 F 3
Wabash, 12,841 F 5
Warren, 21,595 C 3
Washington, 13,780 D 5
Wayne, 17,004 E 5
White, 17,312 E 5
Whiteside, 62,877 D 2
Will, 249,498 F 2
Williamson, 49,021 E 6
Winnebago, 246,623 D 1
Woodford, 28,012 D 3

CITIES and TOWNS

Zip *Name/Pop.* *Key*

61410 Abingdon, 3,936 C 3
60101 Addison, 24,482 A 2
61230 Albany, 942 C 2
62215 Albers, 656 D 5
62806 Albion⊙, 1,791 E 5
61231 Aledo⊙, 3,325 C 2
61412 Alexis, 946 C 2
60102 Algonquin, 3,515 E 1
62001 Alhambra, 594 D 5
† 62207 Alorton, 3,573 B 6
61413 Alpha, 771 C 2
† 60601 Alsip, 11,141 B 2
62411 Altamont, 1,929 E 4
62002 Alton, 39,700 A 6
61310 Amboy, 2,184 D 2
61232 Andalusia, 950 C 2
62906 Anna, 4,766 D 6
61234 Annawan, 787 C 2
60002 Antioch, 3,189 E 1
61910 Arcola, 2,276 E 4
62501 Argenta, 1,034 E 4
* 60004 Arlington Heights, 64,884 A 1
60910 Aroma Park, 896 F 2
61911 Arthur, 2,214 E 4
60911 Ashkum, 590 E 3
62612 Ashland, 1,128 C 4
62808 Ashley, 655 D 5
61006 Ashton, 1,112 D 2
62510 Assumption, 1,487 E 4
61501 Astoria, 1,281 C 3
62613 Athens, 1,158 D 4
61235 Atkinson, 1,053 C 2
61723 Atlanta, 1,640 D 3
61913 Atwood, 1,264 E 4
62615 Auburn, 2,594 D 4
62311 Augusta, 824 C 3
* 60504 Aurora, 74,182 E 2
62907 Ava, 728 D 6
62216 Aviston, 828 D 5
61415 Avon, 1,013 C 3
61007 Baileyville, 600 D 1
60010 Barrington, 7,701 E 1
62312 Barry, 1,444 B 4
61607 Bartonville, 7,221 D 3
60510 Batavia, 8,994 E 2
62618 Beardstown, 6,222 C 3
62219 Beckemeyer, 1,069 D 5
† 60601 Bedford Park, 583 B 2
60401 Beecher, 1,770 F 2
† 61883 Belgium, 578 F 3
* 62220 Belleville⊙, 41,699 B 6
60104 Bellwood, 22,096 A 2
61008 Belvidere⊙, 14,061 E 1
61813 Bement, 1,638 E 4
62009 Benld, 1,736 D 4
60106 Bensenville, 12,833 A 1
62812 Benton⊙, 6,833 E 6
60162 Berkeley, 6,152 A 2
60402 Berwyn, 52,502 B 2
62010 Bethalto, 7,074 B 6
61914 Bethany, 1,235 E 4
61420 Blandinsville, 922 C 3
61701 Bloomington⊙, 39,992 D 3
Bloomington-Normal, ‡104,389 D 3
60406 Blue Island, 22,958 B 2
62513 Blue Mound, 1,181 D 4
62621 Bluffs, 866 C 4
60914 Bourbonnais, 5,909 F 2
60407 Braceville, 668 E 2
61421 Bradford, 885 D 2
60915 Bradley, 9,881 F 2
60408 Braidwood, 2,323 E 2
62230 Breese, 2,885 D 5
62417 Bridgeport, 2,262 F 5
60455 Bridgeview, 12,522 B 2
62012 Brighton, 1,889 C 4
61517 Brimfield, 729 D 3
60153 Broadview, 9,307 A 2
60513 Brookfield, 20,284 A 2
† 62059 Brooklyn (Lovejoy), 1,702 A 6
62910 Brookport, 1,046 E 6
62418 Brownstown, 689 E 5
60918 Buckley, 680 F 3
61314 Buda, 675 D 2
62014 Bunker Hill, 1,465 D 4
† 60601 Burnham, 3,634 B 2
† 60558 Burr Ridge, 1,637 A 2
61422 Bushnell, 3,703 C 3
61010 Byron, 1,749 D 1
62206 Cahokia, 20,649 B 6
62914 Cairo⊙, 6,277 D 6
60409 Calumet City, 32,956 B 2
† 60601 Calumet Park, 10,069 B 2
62915 Cambria, 798 D 6
61238 Cambridge⊙, 2,095 C 2
62320 Camp Point, 1,143 B 3
61520 Canton, 14,217 C 3
61012 Capron, 654 E 1
61239 Carbon Cliff, 1,369 C 2
62901 Carbondale, 22,816 D 6
62626 Carlinville⊙, 5,675 D 4
62231 Carlyle⊙, 3,139 D 5
62821 Carmi⊙, 6,033 E 5
60110 Carpentersville, 24,059 E 1
62917 Carriers Mills, 2,013 E 6
62016 Carrollton⊙, 2,866 C 4
62918 Carterville, 3,061 D 6
62321 Carthage⊙, 3,350 B 3
60013 Cary, 4,358 E 1
62420 Casey, 2,994 F 4
62232 Caseyville, 3,411 B 6
61817 Catlin, 2,093 F 3
61013 Cedarville, 578 D 1
† 62801 Central City, 1,377 D 5
62801 Centralia, 15,217 D 5
62206 Centreville, 11,378 B 6
61818 Cerro Gordo, 1,368 E 4
61014 Chadwick, 605 D 1
61820 Champaign, 56,532 E 3
Champaign-Urbana, ‡163,281 E 3
62627 Chandlerville, 762 C 3
60410 Channahon, 1,505 E 2
62628 Chapin, 552 C 4
61920 Charleston⊙, 16,421 E 4
62629 Chatham, 2,788 D 4
60921 Chatsworth, 1,255 E 3
60922 Chebanse, 1,185 F 3
61726 Chenoa, 1,860 E 3
61016 Cherry Valley, 952 D 1
62233 Chester⊙, 5,310 D 6
* 60601 Chicago⊙, 3,366,957 B 2
Chicago, ‡6,978,947 B 2
60411 Chicago Heights, 40,900 B 3
60415 Chicago Ridge, 9,187 A 2
61523 Chillicothe, 6,052 D 3
61924 Chrisman, 1,285 F 4
62822 Christopher, 2,910 D 6
60650 Cicero, 67,058 B 2
62823 Cisne, 615 E 5
60924 Cissna Park, 773 F 3
60514 Clarendon Hills, 6,750 A 2
62824 Clay City, 1,049 E 5
62324 Clayton, 727 B 3
60927 Clifton, 1,339 F 3
61727 Clinton⊙, 7,570 E 3
60416 Coal City, 3,040 E 2
61240 Coal Valley, 3,088 C 2
62920 Cobden, 1,114 D 6
62017 Coffeen, 641 D 4
62326 Colchester, 1,747 C 3
61728 Colfax, 935 E 3
62234 Collinsville, 17,773 B 6
62236 Columbia, 4,188 C 5
61242 Cordova, 589 C 2
62018 Cottage Hills, 1,261 B 6
62237 Coulterville, 1,186 D 5
60477 Country Club Hills, 6,920 B 3
† 60525 Countryside, 2,888 A 2
62922 Creal Springs, 830 E 6
60928 Crescent City, 597 F 3
60435 Crest Hill, 7,460 E 2
60113 Creston, 595 D 2
60445 Crestwood, 5,543 B 2
60417 Crete, 4,656 F 2
61611 Creve Coeur, 6,440 D 3
62827 Crossville, 860 F 5
60014 Crystal Lake, 14,541 E 1
61427 Cuba, 1,581 C 3
60929 Cullom, 572 E 3
62330 Dallas City, 1,284 B 3
61320 Dalzell, 579 D 2
61732 Danvers, 854 D 3
61832 Danville⊙, 42,570 F 3
* 62521 Decatur⊙, 90,397 E 4
Decatur, ‡125,010 E 4

(continued on following page)

AREA 56,400 sq. mi.
POPULATION 11,113,976
CAPITAL Springfield
LARGEST CITY Chicago
HIGHEST POINT Charles Mound 1,235 ft.
SETTLED IN 1720
ADMITTED TO UNION December 3, 1818
POPULAR NAME Prairie State
STATE FLOWER Violet
STATE BIRD Cardinal

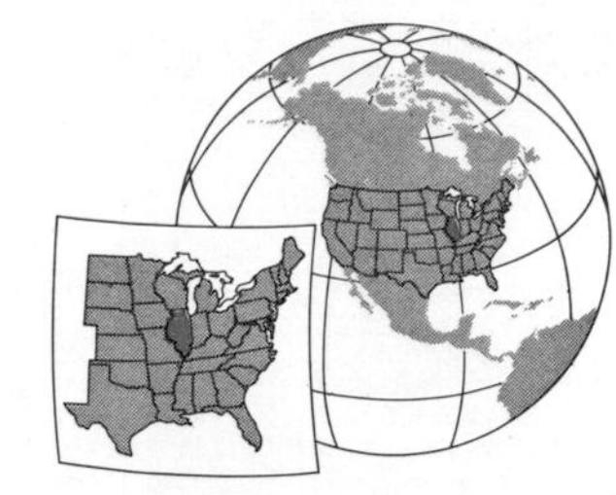

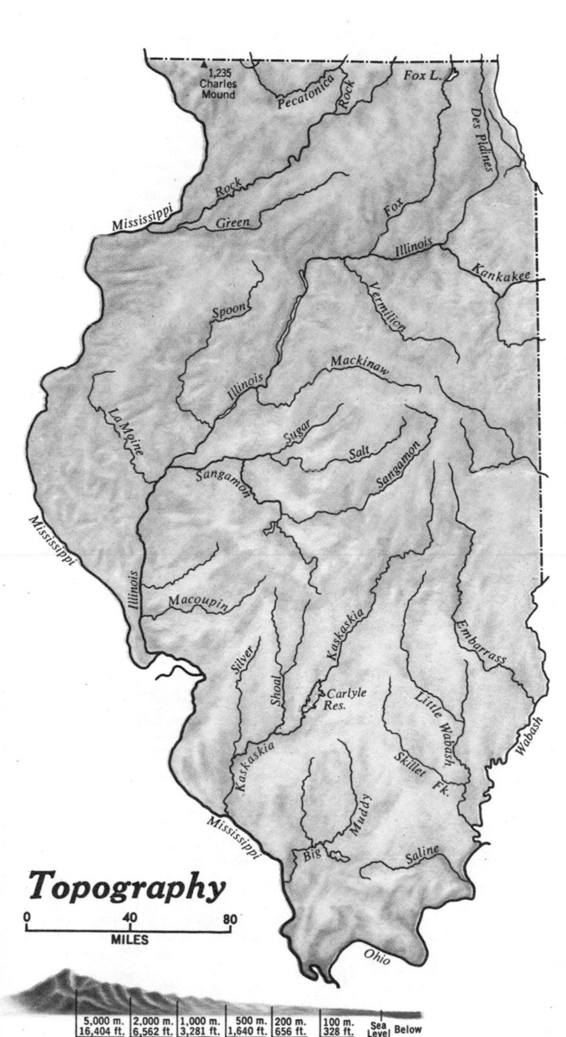

Topography

0 40 80
MILES

5,000 m. 16,404 ft. | 2,000 m. 6,562 ft. | 1,000 m. 3,281 ft. | 500 m. 1,640 ft. | 200 m. 656 ft. | 100 m. 328 ft. | Sea Level | Below

Agriculture, Industry and Resources

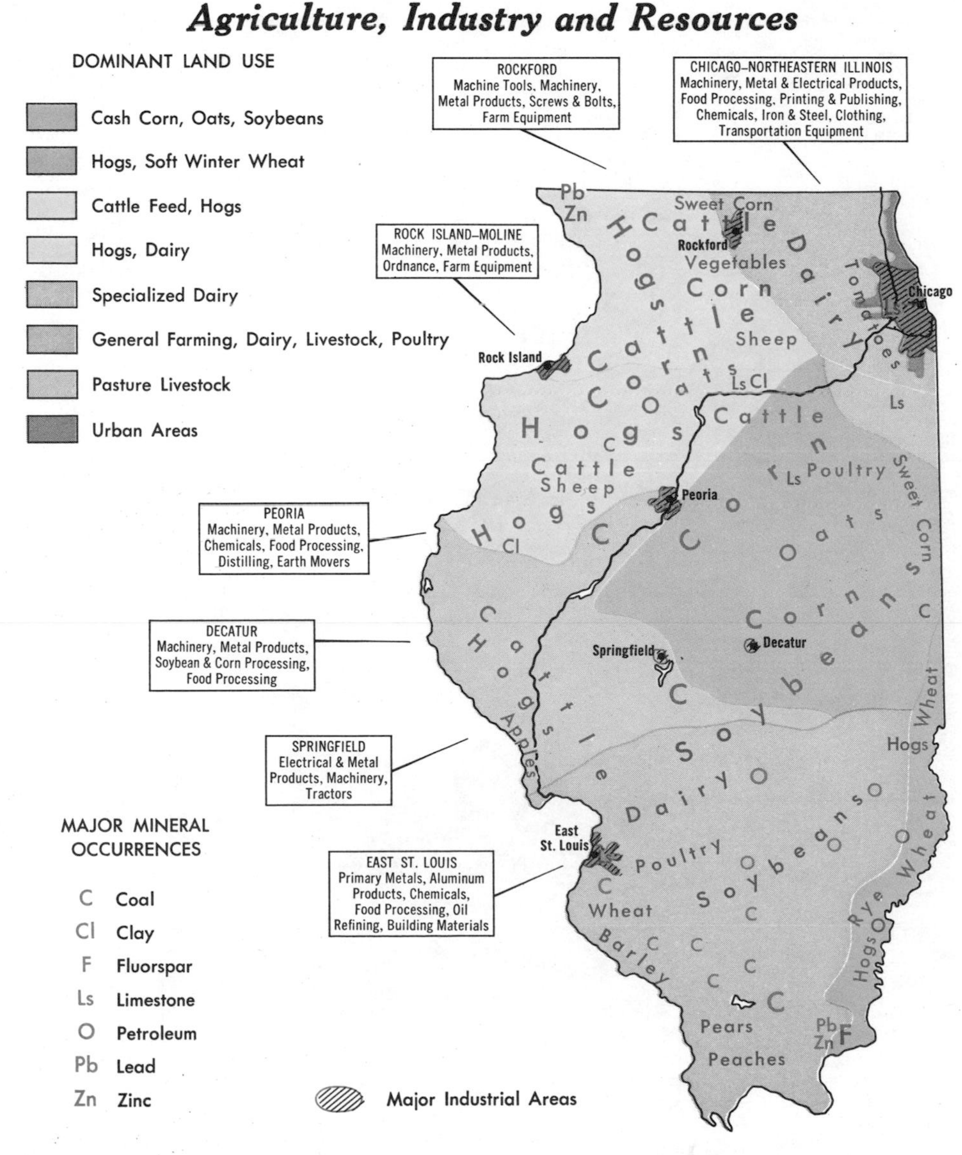

(continued)

61733 Deer Creek, 647 D 3
60015 Deerfield, 18,949 F 1
60115 De Kalb, 32,949 E 2
61734 Delavan, 1,844 D 3
61322 Depue, 1,919 D 2
62924 De Soto, 966 D 6
* 60016 Des Plaines, 57,239 A 1
† 62025 Dewey Park, 2,029 B 6
62530 Divernon, 1,010 D 4
† 60469 Dixmoor, 4,735 B 2
61021 Dixon⊙, 18,147 D 2
60419 Dolton, 25,937 B 2
62926 Dongola, 825 D 6
60515 Downers Grove, 32,751 A 2
61736 Downs, 651 E 3
60118 Dundee (East and West Dundee), 6,215 E 1
61525 Dunlap, 656 D 3
62239 Dupo, 2,842 A 6
62832 Du Quoin, 6,691 D 5
61024 Durand, 972 D 1
60420 Dwight, 3,841 E 2
60518 Earlville, 1,410 E 2
62024 East Alton, 7,309 B 6
† 60411 East Chicago Heights, 5,000 B 3
61025 East Dubuque, 2,408 C 1
† 60118 East Dundee (Dundee), 2,920 E 1
61430 East Galesburg, 706 C 3
† 60429 East Hazelcrest, 1,885 B 2
61244 East Moline, 20,832 C 2
61611 East Peoria, 18,455 D 3
* 62201 East Saint Louis, 69,996 B 6
62531 Edinburg, 1,153 D 4
62025 Edwardsville⊙, 11,070 B 6
62401 Effingham⊙, 9,458 E 4
60119 Elburn, 1,122 E 2
62930 Eldorado, 3,876 E 6
60120 Elgin, 55,691 E 1
61028 Elizabeth, 707 C 1
62931 Elizabethtown⊙, 436 E 6
60007 Elk Grove Village, 24,516 A 1
62932 Elkville, 850 D 6
60126 Elmhurst, 50,547 A 2
61529 Elmwood, 2,014 D 3
60635 Elmwood Park, 26,160 B 2
61738 El Paso, 2,291 D 3
60421 Elwood, 794 E 2
62635 Emden, 552 D 3
62933 Energy, 812 E 6
62835 Enfield, 764 E 5
62934 Equality, 732 E 6
61250 Erie, 1,566 C 2
61530 Eureka⊙, 3,028 D 3
* 60201 Evanston, 79,808 B 1
62242 Evansville, 838 D 5
60642 Evergreen Park, 25,487 B 2
61739 Fairbury, 3,359 E 3
62837 Fairfield⊙, 5,897 E 5
† 62002 Fairmont, 1,521 A 6
† 62201 Fairmont City, 2,769 B 6
61841 Fairmount, 785 F 3
61432 Fairview 601 C 3
62232 Fairview Heights, 8,625 B 6
62838 Farina, 634 E 5
61842 Farmer City, 2,217 E 3
61531 Farmington, 2,959 C 3
62534 Findlay, 809 E 4
61843 Fisher, 1,525 E 3
61844 Fithian, 562 F 3
61740 Flanagan, 878 E 3
62839 Flora, 5,283 E 5
60422 Flossmoor, 7,846 B 3
† 62018 Forest Homes, 1,998 B 6
60130 Forest Park, 15,472 B 2
† 60402 Forest View, 927 B 2
61741 Forrest, 1,219 E 3
61030 Forreston, 1,227 D 1
60020 Fox Lake, 4,511 E 1
60021 Fox River Grove, 2,245 E 1
60423 Frankfort, 2,325 F 2
62638 Franklin, 565 C 4
61031 Franklin Grove, 968 D 2
60131 Franklin Park, 20,497 A 2
62243 Freeburg, 2,495 D 5
61032 Freeport⊙, 27,736 D 1
61252 Fulton, 3,630 C 2
62935 Galatia, 792 E 6
61036 Galena⊙, 3,930 C 1
61401 Galesburg⊙, 36,290 C 3
61434 Galva, 3,061 D 2
60424 Gardner, 1,212 E 2
61254 Geneseo, 5,840 C 2
60134 Geneva⊙, 9,115 E 2
60135 Genoa, 3,003 E 1
61846 Georgetown, 3,984 F 4
62245 Germantown, 1,108 D 5
60936 Gibson City, 3,454 E 3
61847 Gifford, 814 E 3
62033 Gillespie, 3,457 D 4
60938 Gilman, 1,786 E 3
62640 Girard, 1,881 D 4
61533 Glasford, 1,066 D 3
62034 Glen Carbon, 1,897 B 6
60022 Glencoe, 10,542 F 1
60137 Glen Ellyn, 21,909 F 2
60025 Glenview, 24,880 B 1
60425 Glenwood, 7,416 B 3
62035 Godfrey, 1,225 A 6
62938 Golconda⊙, 922 E 6
62339 Golden, 571 B 3
62939 Goreville, 1,109 E 6
62037 Grafton, 1,018 C 5
61325 Grand Ridge, 698 E 2
62942 Grand Tower, 664 D 6
† 62701 Grandview, 2,242 D 4
62040 Granite City, 40,440 B 6
60940 Grant Park, 801 F 2
61326 Granville, 1,232 D 2
60030 Grayslake, 4,907 E 1
62844 Grayville, 2,035 E 5
62044 Greenfield, 1,179 C 4
† 61241 Green Rock, 2,744 C 2
62428 Greenup, 1,618 E 4
61534 Green Valley, 617 D 3
62642 Greenview, 740 D 3
62246 Greenville⊙, 4,631 D 5
61744 Gridley, 1,007 E 3
62340 Griggsville, 1,245 C 4
60031 Gurnee, 2,738 E 1
62341 Hamilton, 2,764 B 3
60140 Hampshire, 1,611 E 1
61256 Hampton, 1,612 C 2
61536 Hanna City, 1,282 D 3
61041 Hanover, 1,243 C 1
62047 Hardin⊙, 1,035 C 4
62946 Harrisburg⊙, 9,535 E 6
62048 Hartford, 2,243 B 6
60033 Harvard, 5,177 E 1
60426 Harvey, 34,636 B 2
60656 Harwood Heights, 9,060 B 1
62644 Havana⊙, 4,376 D 3
60429 Hazel Crest, 10,329 B 2
60034 Hebron, 781 E 1
† 61832 Hegeler, 1,595 F 3
61327 Hennepin⊙, 535 D 2
61537 Henry, 2,610 D 2
62948 Herrin, 9,623 E 6
60941 Herscher, 988 E 2
61745 Heyworth, 1,441 E 3
60457 Hickory Hills, 13,176 B 2
62249 Highland, 5,981 D 5
60035 Highland Park, 32,263 F 1
60040 Highwood, 4,973 F 1
61244 Hillcrest, 630 D 2
62049 Hillsboro⊙, 4,267 D 4
60162 Hillside, 8,888 A 2
60520 Hinckley, 1,053 E 2
60521 Hinsdale, 15,918 A 2
60525 Hodgkins, 2,270 A 2
61849 Homer, 1,354 F 3
60456 Hometown, 6,729 B 2
60430 Homewood, 18,871 B 3
60942 Hoopeston, 6,461 F 3
61747 Hopedale, 923 D 3
61748 Hudson, 802 E 3
62343 Hull, 585 B 4
60142 Huntley, 1,432 E 1
62949 Hurst, 934 D 6
62539 Illiopolis, 1,122 D 4
61440 Industry, 558 C 3
† 60431 Ingalls Park, 5,615 F 2
61441 Ipava, 608 C 3
62051 Irving, 599 D 4
60042 Island Lake, 1,973 E 1
60143 Itasca, 4,638 F 2
62650 Jacksonville⊙, 20,553 C 4
† 62701 Jerome, 1,673 D 4
62052 Jerseyville⊙, 7,446 C 4
62951 Johnston City, 3,928 E 6
* 60431 Joliet⊙, 80,378 E 2
62952 Jonesboro⊙, 1,676 D 6
† 60453 Justice, 9,473 A 2
60901 Kankakee⊙, 30,944 F 2
61933 Kansas, 779 F 4
62956 Karnak, 641 E 6
† 63673 Kaskaskia, 79 C 6
61442 Keithsburg, 836 B 2
60043 Kenilworth, 2,980 B 1
61443 Kewanee, 15,762 C 2
62540 Kincaid, 1,424 D 4
62854 Kinmundy, 759 E 5
60146 Kirkland, 1,138 E 1
61447 Kirkwood, 817 C 3
61448 Knoxville, 2,930 C 3
61540 Lacon⊙, 2,147 D 2
61329 Ladd, 1,328 D 2
60525 La Grange, 16,773 A 2
60525 La Grange Park, 15,626 A 2
61450 La Harpe, 1,240 C 3
60044 Lake Bluff, 4,979 F 1
† 60002 Lake Catherine, 1,219 E 1
60045 Lake Forest, 15,642 F 1
60047 Lake Zurich, 4,082 E 1
61330 La Moille, 669 D 2
61046 Lanark, 1,495 D 1
60438 Lansing, 25,805 B 3
61301 La Salle, 10,736 E 2
62439 Lawrenceville⊙, 5,863 F 5
61047 Leaf River, 633 D 1
62254 Lebanon, 3,564 D 5
60531 Leland, 743 E 2
60439 Lemont, 5,080 A 2
61048 Lena, 1,691 D 1
61752 Le Roy, 2,435 E 3
61542 Lewistown⊙, 2,706 C 3
61753 Lexington, 1,615 E 3
60048 Libertyville, 11,684 F 1
62656 Lincoln⊙, 17,582 D 3
† 60601 Lincolnwood, 12,929 B 1
60046 Lindenhurst, 3,141 F 1
62056 Litchfield, 7,190 D 4
62058 Livingston, 916 D 5
60441 Lockport, 9,985 F 2
61454 Lomax, 565 B 3
60148 Lombard, 35,977 A 2
61544 London Mills, 600 C 3
62858 Louisville⊙, 1,020 E 5
62059 Lovejoy, 1,702 A 6
61111 Loves Park, 12,390 E 1
61937 Lovington, 1,303 E 4
61261 Lyndon, 673 D 2
† 60411 Lynwood, 1,042 B 3
60534 Lyons, 11,124 B 2
61755 Mackinaw, 1,293 D 3
61455 Macomb⊙, 19,643 C 3
62544 Macon, 1,249 E 4
62060 Madison, 7,042 B 6
61853 Mahomet, 1,296 E 3
60150 Malta, 961 E 2
60442 Manhattan, 1,530 F 2
61546 Manito, 1,334 D 3
61854 Mansfield, 870 E 3
60950 Manteno, 2,864 F 2
60151 Maple Park, 660 E 2
60152 Marengo, 4,235 E 1
62061 Marine, 882 D 5
62059 Marion⊙, 11,724 E 6
62257 Marissa, 2,004 D 5
60426 Markham, 15,987 B 2
61756 Maroa, 1,467 E 3
† 61554 Marquette Heights, 2,758 D 3
61341 Marseilles, 4,320 E 2
62441 Marshall⊙, 3,468 F 4
62442 Martinsville, 1,374 F 4
62062 Maryville, 809 B 6
62258 Mascoutah, 5,045 D 5
62664 Mason City, 2,611 D 3
61263 Matherville, 699 C 2
60443 Matteson, 4,741 B 3
61938 Mattoon, 19,681 E 4
60153 Maywood, 30,036 A 2
60444 Mazon, 727 E 2
62957 McClure, 800 D 6
† 60050 McCullom Lake, 873 E 1
60050 McHenry, 6,772 E 1
61754 McLean, 820 D 3
62859 McLeansboro⊙, 2,630 E 5
† 62010 Meadowbrook, 1,295 B 6
* 60160 Melrose Park, 22,706 A 2
62351 Mendon, 883 B 3
61342 Mendota, 6,902 D 2
62665 Meredosia, 1,178 C 4
† 60601 Merrionette Park, 2,303 B 2
61548 Metamora, 2,176 D 3
62960 Metropolis⊙, 6,940 E 6
62666 Middletown, 626 D 3
60445 Midlothian, 15,939 B 2
61264 Milan, 4,873 C 2
60953 Milford, 1,656 F 3
61051 Milledgeville, 1,130 D 1
62260 Millstadt, 2,168 B 6
61759 Minier, 986 D 3
61760 Minonk, 2,267 D 3
60447 Minooka, 768 E 2
60448 Mokena, 1,643 F 2
61265 Moline, 46,237 C 2
60954 Momence, 2,836 F 2
60449 Monee, 940 F 2
61462 Monmouth⊙, 11,022 C 3
60538 Montgomery, 3,278 E 2
61856 Monticello⊙, 4,130 E 3
60539 Mooseheart, 850 E 2
60450 Morris⊙, 8,194 E 2
61270 Morrison⊙, 4,387 C 2
62546 Morrisonville, 1,178 D 4
† 61101 Morristown, 669 D 1
61550 Morton, 10,419 D 3
60053 Morton Grove, 26,369 B 1
62963 Mound City⊙, 1,177 D 6
62964 Mounds, 1,718 D 6
62863 Mount Carmel⊙, 8,096 F 5
61053 Mount Carroll⊙, 2,143 D 1
61054 Mount Morris, 3,173 D 1
62069 Mount Olive, 2,288 D 4
60056 Mount Prospect, 34,995 A 1
62548 Mount Pulaski, 1,677 D 3
62353 Mount Sterling⊙, 2,182 C 4
62864 Mount Vernon⊙, 15,980 E 5
62549 Mount Zion, 2,343 E 4
62550 Moweaqua, 1,687 E 4
62262 Mulberry Grove, 697 D 5
60060 Mundelein, 16,128 E 1
62966 Murphysboro⊙, 10,013 C 6
62668 Murrayville, 595 C 4
60540 Naperville, 23,885 E 2
† 61350 Naplate, 686 E 2
62263 Nashville⊙, 3,027 D 5
62354 Nauvoo, 1,047 B 3
62447 Neoga, 1,270 E 4
60541 Newark, 590 E 2
62264 New Athens, 2,000 D 5
62265 New Baden, 1,953 D 5
62670 New Berlin, 754 D 4
61272 New Boston, 706 B 2
62867 New Haven, 606 E 6
60451 New Lenox, 2,855 F 2
61942 Newman, 1,018 F 4
62448 Newton⊙, 3,024 E 5
61465 New Windsor, 723 C 2
62551 Niantic, 705 D 4
60648 Niles, 31,432 A 1
62868 Noble, 719 E 5
62075 Nokomis, 2,532 D 4
61761 Normal, 26,396 E 3
† 60601 Norridge, 16,880 B 1
62869 Norris City, 1,319 F 6
60542 North Aurora, 4,833 E 2
60062 Northbrook, 27,297 A 1
60064 North Chicago, 47,275 F 1
60093 Northfield, 5,010 B 1
60164 Northlake, 14,212 A 2
† 61101 North Park, 15,679 D 1
† 61554 North Pekin, 1,886 D 3
60546 North Riverside, 8,097 B 2
† 61373 North Utica (Utica), 974 E 2
60452 Oak Forest, 17,870 B 2
61943 Oakland, 1,012 F 4
* 60453 Oak Lawn, 60,305 B 2
60303 Oak Park, 62,511 B 2
61858 Oakwood, 1,367 F 3
† 62095 Oakwood Heights, 3,229 B 6
62449 Oblong, 1,860 F 5
60460 Odell, 1,076 E 2
62870 Odin, 1,263 D 5
62269 O'Fallon, 7,268 B 6
61348 Oglesby, 4,175 D 2
62271 Okawville, 992 D 5
62969 Olive Branch, 600 D 6
62450 Olney⊙, 8,974 E 5
60461 Olympia Fields, 3,478 B 3
60955 Onarga, 1,436 F 3
61467 Oneida, 728 C 2
61469 Oquawka⊙, 1,352 C 3
62554 Oreana, 1,092 E 4
61061 Oregon⊙, 3,539 D 1
61273 Orion, 1,801 C 2
60462 Orland Park, 6,391 A 2
60543 Oswego, 1,862 E 2
61350 Ottawa⊙, 18,716 E 2
60067 Palatine, 25,904 E 1
62451 Palestine, 1,640 F 4
62674 Palmyra, 776 C 4
60463 Palos Heights, 9,915 A 2
60465 Palos Hills, 6,629 A 2
60464 Palos Park, 3,297 A 2
62557 Pana, 6,326 D 4
61944 Paris⊙, 9,971 F 4
60466 Park Forest, 30,638 B 3
60068 Park Ridge, 42,466 A 1
62875 Patoka, 562 D 5
62558 Pawnee, 1,936 D 4
61353 Pawpaw, 846 E 2
60957 Paxton⊙, 4,373 E 3
62360 Payson, 589 B 4
61063 Pecatonica, 1,781 D 1
61554 Pekin⊙, 31,375 D 3
* 61601 Peoria⊙, 126,963 D 3
Peoria, ‡341,979 D 3
61614 Peoria Heights, 7,943 D 3
60468 Peotone, 2,345 F 2
62272 Percy, 967 D 5
61354 Peru, 11,772 D 2
62675 Petersburg⊙, 2,632 D 4
61864 Philo, 1,022 E 3
† 60426 Phoenix, 3,596 B 2
62274 Pinckneyville⊙, 3,377 D 5
60959 Piper City, 817 E 3
62363 Pittsfield⊙, 4,244 C 4
60544 Plainfield, 2,928 E 2
60545 Plano, 4,664 E 2
62366 Pleasant Hill, 1,064 C 4
62677 Pleasant Plains, 644 D 4
62367 Plymouth, 740 C 3
62275 Pocahontas, 764 D 5
61074 Polo, 2,542 D 1
61764 Pontiac⊙, 9,031 E 3
61065 Poplar Grove, 607 E 1
61275 Port Byron, 1,222 C 2
60469 Posen, 5,498 B 2
61865 Potomac, 909 F 3
61470 Prairie City, 630 C 3
62277 Prairie du Rocher, 658 C 5
61356 Princeton⊙, 6,959 D 2
61559 Princeville, 1,455 D 3
61277 Prophetstown, 1,915 D 2
60070 Prospect Heights, 13,333 A 1
62301 Quincy⊙, 45,288 B 4
62080 Ramsey, 830 D 4
60960 Rankin, 727 F 3
61866 Rantoul, 25,562 E 3
61278 Rapids City, 656 C 2
62560 Raymond, 890 D 4
62278 Red Bud, 2,559 D 5
61279 Reynolds, 610 C 2
60071 Richmond, 1,153 E 1
60471 Richton Park, 2,558 B 3
61870 Ridge Farm, 1,015 F 4
62979 Ridgway, 1,160 E 6
60627 Riverdale, 15,806 B 2
60305 River Forest, 13,402 B 2
60171 River Grove, 11,465 A 2
60546 Riverside, 10,432 B 2
62561 Riverton, 2,090 D 4
61561 Roanoke, 2,040 D 3
60472 Robbins, 9,641 B 2
62454 Robinson⊙, 7,178 F 5
61068 Rochelle, 8,594 D 2
62563 Rochester, 1,667 D 4
60436 Rockdale, 2,085 E 2
61071 Rock Falls, 10,287 D 2
* 61101 Rockford⊙, 147,370 D 1
Rockford, ‡272,063 D 1
61201 Rock Island⊙, 50,166 C 2
Rock Island-Moline-Davenport, ‡362,638 C 2
61072 Rockton, 2,099 E 1
60008 Rolling Meadows, 19,178 A 1
61562 Rome, 1,919 D 3
† 60441 Romeoville, 12,674 E 2
62082 Roodhouse, 2,357 C 4
61073 Roscoe, 949 D 1
60018 Rosemont, 4,360 A 1
61473 Roseville, 1,111 C 3
† 62024 Rosewood Heights, 3,391 B 6
62982 Rosiclare, 1,421 F 6
60963 Rossville, 1,420 F 3
62084 Roxana, 1,882 B 6
62983 Royalton, 1,166 D 6
62681 Rushville⊙, 3,300 C 3
60964 Saint Anne, 1,271 F 2
60174 Saint Charles, 12,928 E 2
61563 Saint David, 773 C 3
62458 Saint Elmo, 1,676 E 4
62460 Saint Francisville, 997 F 5
62281 Saint Jacob, 659 D 5
61873 Saint Joseph, 1,554 E 3
62881 Salem⊙, 6,187 E 5
62882 Sandoval, 1,332 D 5
60548 Sandwich, 5,056 E 2
62682 San Jose, 681 D 3
60411 Sauk Village, 7,479 F 2
61074 Savanna, 4,942 C 1
61874 Savoy, 592 E 3
61770 Saybrook, 814 E 3
60172 Schaumburg, 18,730 E 1
60176 Schiller Park, 12,712 A 1
† 62049 Schram City, 657 D 4
61360 Seneca, 1,781 E 2
62884 Sesser, 2,125 D 5
61875 Seymour, 850 E 3
60550 Shabbona, 730 E 2
61078 Shannon, 848 D 1
62984 Shawneetown⊙, 1,742 E 6
61361 Sheffield, 1,038 D 2
62565 Shelbyville⊙, 4,597 E 4
60966 Sheldon, 1,455 F 3
60551 Sheridan, 724 E 2
61281 Sherrard, 808 C 2
† 62220 Shiloh, 945 B 6
61876 Sidell, 645 F 4
61877 Sidney, 915 E 3
61282 Silvis, 5,907 C 2
60076 Skokie, 68,627 B 1
62285 Smithton, 847 C 5
60552 Somonauk, 1,112 E 2
62086 Sorento, 625 D 5
61080 South Beloit, 3,804 E 1
60411 South Chicago Heights, 4,923 B 3
60177 South Elgin, 4,289 E 2
60473 South Holland, 23,931 B 2
62650 South Jacksonville, 2,950 C 4
61564 South Pekin, 955 D 3
60474 South Wilmington, 725 E 2
61565 Sparland, 585 D 2
62286 Sparta, 4,307 D 5
* 62701 Springfield (cap.)⊙, 91,753 D 4
Springfield, ‡161,335 D 4
61362 Spring Valley, 5,605 D 2
61774 Stanford, 657 D 3
62088 Staunton, 4,396 D 5
62288 Steeleville, 1,957 D 6
60475 Steger, 8,104 F 2
61081 Sterling, 16,113 D 2
62463 Stewardson, 729 E 4
60402 Stickney, 6,601 B 2
61084 Stillman Valley, 871 D 1
61085 Stockton, 1,930 C 1
60165 Stone Park, 4,451 A 2
62567 Stonington, 1,096 D 4
60103 Streamwood, 18,176 E 1
61364 Streator, 15,600 E 2
61480 Stronghurst, 836 C 3
61951 Sullivan⊙, 4,112 E 4
60501 Summit, 11,569 B 2
62466 Sumner, 1,201 F 5
62221 Swansea, 5,432 B 6
60178 Sycamore⊙, 7,843 E 2
62688 Tallula, 643 D 4
62888 Tamaroa, 799 D 5
62988 Tamms, 645 D 6
61283 Tampico, 838 D 2
62089 Taylor Springs, 620 D 4
62568 Taylorville⊙, 10,644 D 4
62467 Teutopolis, 1,249 E 4
62689 Thayer, 616 D 4
61878 Thomasboro, 806 E 3
61285 Thomson, 617 C 2
60476 Thornton, 3,714 B 3
62292 Tilden, 909 D 5
† 61832 Tilton, 2,544 F 3
60477 Tinley Park, 12,382 B 2
61368 Tiskilwa, 973 D 2
62468 Toledo⊙, 1,068 E 4
61880 Tolono, 2,027 E 3
61369 Toluca, 1,319 D 2
61370 Tonica, 821 E 2
61483 Toulon⊙, 1,207 D 2
61776 Towanda, 578 E 3
62571 Tower Hill, 683 E 4
61568 Tremont, 1,942 D 3
62293 Trenton, 2,328 D 5
62294 Troy, 2,144 B 6
61953 Tuscola⊙, 3,917 E 4
60180 Union, 579 E 1
61801 Urbana⊙, 32,800 E 3
61373 Utica, 974 E 2
62891 Valier, 628 D 5
62295 Valmeyer, 733 C 5
62471 Vandalia⊙, 5,160 D 5
62090 Venice, 4,680 A 6
61484 Vermont, 947 C 3
61485 Victoria, 782 C 2
62995 Vienna⊙, 1,325 E 6
61956 Villa Grove, 2,605 E 4
60181 Villa Park, 25,891 A 2
61486 Viola, 946 C 2
62690 Virden, 3,504 D 4
62691 Virginia⊙, 1,814 C 4
60083 Wadsworth, 756 F 1
61376 Walnut, 1,295 D 2
† 62801 Wamac, 1,347 D 5
61777 Wapella, 572 E 3
61087 Warren, 1,523 C 1
62573 Warrensburg, 738 D 4
62379 Warsaw, 1,758 B 3
61570 Washburn, 1,173 D 3
61571 Washington, 6,790 D 3
62204 Washington Park, 9,524 B 6
61488 Wataga, 570 C 2
62298 Waterloo⊙, 4,546 C 5
60556 Waterman, 990 E 2
60970 Watseka⊙, 5,294 F 3
60084 Wauconda, 5,460 E 1
60085 Waukegan⊙, 65,269 F 1
62692 Waverly, 1,442 D 4
62895 Wayne City, 985 E 5
61882 Weldon, 553 E 3
61377 Wenona, 1,080 E 2
60153 Westchester, 20,033 A 2
60185 West Chicago, 10,111 E 2
† 62812 West City, 637 E 5
† 60118 West Dundee (Dundee), 3,295 E 1
60558 Western Springs, 12,147 A 2
62474 Westfield, 678 F 4
62896 West Frankfort, 8,836 E 6
60559 Westmont, 8,482 A 2
62476 West Salem, 979 F 5
61883 Westville, 3,655 F 3
60187 Wheaton⊙, 31,138 E 2
60090 Wheeling, 14,746 F 1
62092 White Hall, 2,979 C 4
61489 Williamsfield, 552 C 3
62693 Williamsville, 923 D 4
62997 Willisville, 659 D 6
60480 Willow Springs, 3,318 A 2
60091 Wilmette, 32,134 B 1
60481 Wilmington, 4,335 E 2
62093 Wilsonville, 691 D 4
62694 Winchester⊙, 1,788 C 4
61957 Windsor, 1,126 E 4
† 61465 Windsor (New Windsor), 723 C 2
60190 Winfield, 4,285 E 2
61088 Winnebago, 1,285 D 1
60093 Winnetka, 14,131 B 1
60096 Winthrop Harbor, 4,794 F 1
62094 Witt, 1,040 D 4
60191 Wood Dale, 8,831 A 1
61490 Woodhull, 898 C 2
60515 Woodridge, 11,028 E 2
62095 Wood River, 13,186 B 6
60098 Woodstock⊙, 10,226 E 1
62097 Worden, 1,091 B 6
60482 Worth, 11,999 A 2
61379 Wyanet, 1,005 D 2
61491 Wyoming, 1,563 D 2
61572 Yates City, 840 C 3
60560 Yorkville⊙, 2,049 E 2
62999 Zeigler, 1,940 D 6
60099 Zion, 17,268 F 1

⊙ County seat.
‡ Population of metropolitan area.
† Zip of nearest p.o.
* Multiple zips

Fred Boler.—Shostal Associates

Sailboats lie anchored in Lake Michigan while many of their owners turn the wheels of industry behind Chicago's steel and glass facade.

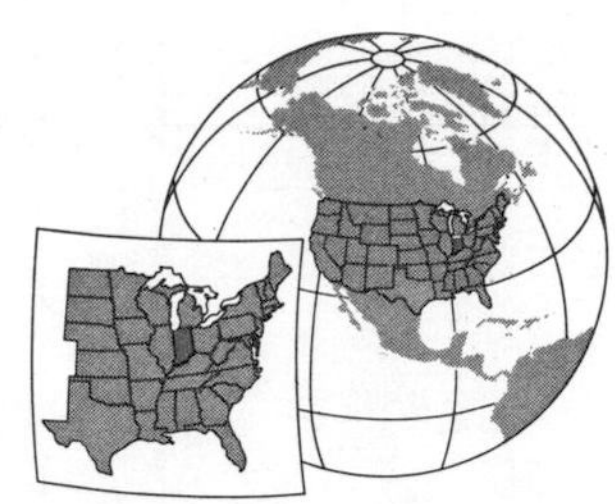

AREA 36,291 sq. mi.
POPULATION 5,193,669
CAPITAL Indianapolis
LARGEST CITY Indianapolis
HIGHEST POINT 1,257 ft. (Wayne County)
SETTLED IN 1730
ADMITTED TO UNION December 11, 1816
POPULAR NAME Hoosier State
STATE FLOWER Peony
STATE BIRD Cardinal

COUNTIES

County	Key
Adams, 26,871	H 3
Allen, 280,455	G 2
Bartholomew, 57,022	F 6
Benton, 11,262	C 3
Blackford, 15,888	G 4
Boone, 30,870	E 4
Brown, 9,057	E 6
Carroll, 17,734	D 3
Cass, 40,456	E 3
Clark, 75,876	F 8
Clay, 23,933	C 6
Clinton, 30,547	E 4
Crawford, 8,033	E 8
Daviess, 26,602	C 7
Dearborn, 29,430	H 6
Decatur, 22,738	G 6
De Kalb, 30,837	H 2
Delaware, 129,219	G 4
Dubois, 30,934	D 8
Elkhart, 126,529	F 1
Fayette, 26,216	G 5
Floyd, 55,622	F 8
Fountain, 18,257	C 4
Franklin, 16,943	G 6
Fulton, 16,984	E 2
Gibson, 30,444	B 8
Grant, 83,955	F 3
Greene, 26,894	D 6
Hamilton, 54,532	E 4
Hancock, 35,096	F 5
Harrison, 20,423	E 8
Hendricks, 53,974	D 5
Henry, 52,603	G 5
Howard, 83,198	E 4
Huntington, 34,970	G 3
Jackson, 33,187	E 7
Jasper, 20,429	C 2
Jay, 23,575	G 4
Jefferson, 27,006	G 7
Jennings, 19,454	F 7
Johnson, 61,138	E 6
Knox, 41,546	C 7
Kosciusko, 48,127	F 2
Lagrange, 20,890	G 1
Lake, 546,253	C 2
LaPorte, 105,342	D 1
Lawrence, 38,038	E 7
Madison, 138,451	F 4
Marion, 792,299	E 5
Marshall, 34,986	E 2
Martin, 10,969	D 7
Miami, 39,246	E 3
Monroe, 84,849	D 6
Montgomery, 33,930	D 4
Morgan, 44,176	E 6
Newton, 11,606	C 3
Noble, 31,382	G 2
Ohio, 4,289	H 7
Orange, 16,968	E 7
Owen, 12,163	D 6
Parke, 14,600	C 5
Perry, 19,075	D 8
Pike, 12,281	C 8
Porter, 87,114	C 2
Posey, 21,740	B 8
Pulaski, 12,534	D 2
Putnam, 26,932	D 5
Randolph, 28,915	G 4
Ripley, 21,138	G 6
Rush, 20,352	G 5
Saint Joseph, 245,045	E 1
Scott, 17,144	F 7
Shelby, 37,797	F 5
Spencer, 17,134	C 9
Starke, 19,280	D 2
Steuben, 20,159	G 1
Sullivan, 19,889	C 6
Switzerland, 6,306	G 7
Tippecanoe, 109,378	D 4
Tipton, 16,650	E 4
Union, 6,582	H 5
Vanderburgh, 168,772	B 8
Vermillion, 16,793	C 5
Vigo, 114,528	C 6
Wabash, 35,553	F 3
Warren, 8,705	C 4
Warrick, 27,972	C 8
Washington, 19,278	E 7
Wayne, 79,109	G 5
Wells, 23,821	G 3
White, 20,995	D 3
Whitley, 23,395	F 2

CITIES and TOWNS

Zip	Name/Pop.	Key
47240	Adams, 300	F 6
† 46947	Adamsboro, 325	E 3
46102	Advance, 561	D 5
46910	Akron, 1,019	E 2
47320	Albany, 2,293	G 4
46701	Albion⊙, 1,498	G 2
† 47283	Alert, 210	F 6
46001	Alexandria, 5,097	F 4
† 46738	Altona, 209	G 2
47917	Ambia, 300	C 4
46911	Amboy, 473	F 3
† 46131	Amity, 400	E 6
46103	Amo, 422	D 5
* 46011	Anderson⊙, 70,787	F 4
	Anderson, ‡138,451	F 4
† 47024	Andersonville, 250	G 5
46702	Andrews, 1,207	F 3
46703	Angola⊙, 5,117	G 1
46030	Arcadia, 1,338	E 4
46704	Arcola, 325	G 2
† 46624	Ardmore, 800	E 1
46501	Argos, 1,393	E 2
46104	Arlington, 550	F 5
46705	Ashley, 721	G 1
46031	Atlanta, 620	E 4
47918	Attica, 4,262	C 4
46502	Atwood, 300	F 2
46706	Auburn⊙, 7,337	G 2
47001	Aurora, 4,293	H 6
47102	Austin, 4,902	F 7
46710	Avilla, 881	G 2
47420	Avoca, 400	D 7
46105	Bainbridge, 703	D 5
46106	Bargersville, 873	E 5
47006	Batesville, 3,799	G 6
47920	Battle Ground, 818	D 3
47421	Bedford⊙, 13,087	E 7
46107	Beech Grove, 13,468	E 5
† 46526	Benton, 221	F 2
46711	Berne, 2,988	H 3
46301	Beverly Shores, 946	C 1
47512	Bicknell, 3,717	C 7
46713	Bippus, 220	F 3
47513	Birdseye, 404	D 8
† 46401	Blackoak, 9,624	C 1
47831	Blanford, 700	B 5
47170	Blocher, 350	F 7
47424	Bloomfield⊙, 2,565	D 6
47832	Bloomingdale, 391	C 5
47401	Bloomington⊙, 42,890	D 6
† 47360	Blountsville, 220	G 4
† 46176	Blue Ridge, 236	F 5
46714	Bluffton⊙, 8,297	G 3
46110	Boggstown, 200	F 5
46302	Boone Grove, 225	C 2
47601	Boonville⊙, 5,736	C 8
47106	Borden, 337	F 8
47324	Boston, 210	H 5
47921	Boswell, 998	C 3
46504	Bourbon, 1,606	E 2
47833	Bowling Green, 200	D 6
47107	Bradford, 400	E 8
47834	Brazil⊙, 8,163	C 5
46506	Bremen, 3,487	E 2
47836	Bridgeton, 350	C 5
† 45030	Bright, 450	H 6
46720	Brimfield, 258	G 2
46913	Bringhurst, 250	E 3
46507	Bristol, 1,100	F 1
† 47354	Bronson (Losantville), 212	G 4
47922	Brook, 919	C 3
46111	Brooklyn, 911	E 5
47923	Brookston, 1,232	D 3
47012	Brookville⊙, 2,864	G 6
46112	Brownsburg, 5,186	E 5
47220	Brownstown⊙, 2,376	F 7
47325	Brownsville, 285	H 5
47516	Bruceville, 627	C 7
47326	Bryant, 320	G 3
47924	Buck Creek, 260	D 4
47517	Buckskin, 275	C 8
47925	Buffalo, 350	D 3
46914	Bunker Hill, 956	E 3
46508	Burket, 210	F 2
46915	Burlington, 685	E 4
47926	Burnettsville, 510	D 3
47222	Burney, 344	F 6
† 46401	Burns Harbor, 1,284	C 1
46916	Burrows, 259	E 3
46721	Butler, 2,394	H 2
47223	Butlerville, 275	F 6
† 46371	Byron, 200	C 5
† 47362	Cadiz, 207	G 5
47327	Cambridge City, 2,481	G 5
46917	Camden, 577	D 3
47108	Campbellsburg, 678	E 7
47520	Cannelton⊙, 2,280	D 9
47837	Carbon, 344	C 5
47838	Carlisle, 714	C 7
46032	Carmel, 6,568	E 5
46114	Cartersburg, 400	E 5
46115	Carthage, 946	F 5
† 47460	Cataract, 200	D 6
47928	Cayuga, 1,090	C 5
47016	Cedar Grove, 248	H 6
46303	Cedar Lake, 7,589	C 2
47521	Celestine, 300	D 8
† 47842	Centenary, 225	B 5
46918	Center, 310	E 4
47840	Centerpoint, 275	C 6
46116	Centerton, 250	E 5
47330	Centerville, 2,380	H 5
47929	Chalmers, 544	D 3
47610	Chandler, 2,032	C 8
47111	Charlestown, 5,890	F 8
46117	Charlottesville, 500	F 5
† 47138	Chelsea, 200	F 7
46017	Chesterfield, 3,001	F 4
46304	Chesterton, 6,177	D 1
47611	Chrisney, 550	C 8
46723	Churubusco, 1,528	G 2
46034	Cicero, 1,378	E 4
47225	Clarksburg, 347	G 6
47930	Clarks Hill, 741	D 4
47130	Clarksville, 13,806	F 8
47841	Clay City, 900	C 6
46510	Claypool, 468	F 2
46118	Clayton, 736	D 5
47426	Clear Creek, 250	E 6
† 46737	Clear Lake, 271	H 1
47226	Clifford, 275	F 6
47842	Clinton, 5,340	C 5
46120	Cloverdale, 870	D 5
47427	Coal City, 300	D 6
47845	Coalmont, 400	C 6
46121	Coatesville, 453	D 5
47931	Colburn, 300	D 3
46035	Colfax, 633	D 4
47978	Collegeville, 1,700	C 3
46725	Columbia City⊙, 4,911	G 2
47201	Columbus⊙, 27,141	E 6
47331	Connersville⊙, 17,604	G 5
46919	Converse, 1,163	F 3
47228	Cortland, 200	F 7
46730	Corunna, 359	G 2
47112	Corydon⊙, 2,719	E 8
47932	Covington⊙, 2,641	C 4
† 47302	Cowan, 428	G 4
47522	Crane, 339	D 7
47933	Crawfordsville⊙, 13,842	D 4
46732	Cromwell, 475	F 2
47229	Crothersville, 1,663	F 7
46307	Crown Point⊙, 10,931	C 2
46511	Culver, 1,783	E 2
46229	Cumberland, 479	E 5
47612	Cynthiana, 793	B 8
47523	Dale, 1,113	D 8
47334	Daleville, 1,730	F 4
47847	Dana, 720	C 5
46122	Danville⊙, 3,771	D 5
47940	Darlington, 802	D 4
47941	Dayton, 840	D 4
46733	Decatur⊙, 8,445	H 3
47524	Decker, 268	B 7
† 46917	Deer Creek, 250	E 3
46923	Delphi⊙, 2,582	D 3
46310	Demotte, 1,697	C 2
46926	Denver, 566	E 3
47230	Deputy, 255	F 7
47302	Desoto, 385	G 4
47018	Dillsboro, 840	G 6
46513	Donaldson, 250	E 2
† 47118	Doolittle Mills, 200	D 8
47335	Dublin, 1,021	G 5
47525	Dubois, 500	D 8
47848	Dugger, 1,150	C 6
† 46304	Dune Acres, 301	C 1
47336	Dunkirk, 3,465	G 4
† 46514	Dunlap, 1,900	F 1
47337	Dunreith, 200	F 5
47231	Dupont, 357	G 7
46311	Dyer, 4,906	C 1
† 46074	Eagletown, 365	E 4
47942	Earl Park, 478	C 3
46312	East Chicago, 46,982	C 1
47019	East Enterprise, 250	H 7
46405	East Gary, 9,858	C 1
† 47370	East Germantown (Pershing), 447	G 5
47338	Eaton, 1,594	G 4
47116	Eckerty, 200	D 8
47339	Economy, 285	G 5
† 46011	Edgewood, 2,326	F 4
46124	Edinburg, 4,906	E 6
47528	Edwardsport, 482	C 7
† 47150	Edwardsville, 700	F 8
47613	Elberfeld, 834	C 8
47232	Elizabethtown, 519	F 6
46514	Elkhart, 43,152	F 1
47429	Ellettsville, 1,627	D 6
47529	Elnora, 873	C 7
† 47018	Elrod, 200	G 6
† 47901	Elston, 500	D 4
46036	Elwood, 11,196	F 4
46125	Eminence, 200	D 5
47118	English⊙, 664	E 8
46524	Etna Green, 516	E 2
† 47928	Eugene, 300	B 5
* 47701	Evansville⊙, 138,764	C 9
	Evansville, ‡232,775	C 9
46126	Fairland, 950	F 5
46928	Fairmount, 3,427	F 4
† 47842	Fairview Park, 1,067	C 5
47850	Farmersburg, 962	C 6
47340	Farmland, 1,262	G 4
47532	Ferdinand, 1,432	D 8
46128	Fillmore, 600	D 5
46129	Finly, 350	F 5
46038	Fishers, 628	E 5
47234	Flat Rock, 289	F 6
46929	Flora, 1,877	E 3
47119	Floyds Knobs, 350	F 8
47851	Fontanet, 200	C 5
46039	Forest, 400	E 4
47533	Fort Branch, 2,535	B 8
46040	Fortville, 2,460	F 5
* 46801	Fort Wayne⊙, 177,671	G 2
	Fort Wayne, ‡280,455	G 2
47341	Fountain City, 852	H 5
46130	Fountaintown, 225	F 5
47944	Fowler⊙, 2,643	C 3
46930	Fowlerton, 337	F 4
47946	Francesville, 1,015	D 3
47534	Francisco, 621	B 8
46041	Frankfort⊙, 14,956	E 4
46131	Franklin⊙, 11,477	E 6
46044	Frankton, 1,796	F 4
47120	Fredericksburg, 207	E 8
47431	Freedom, 262	D 6
47535	Freelandville, 710	C 7
47235	Freetown, 550	E 7
46737	Fremont, 1,043	H 1
47432	French Lick, 2,059	D 7
46931	Fulton, 372	E 3
† 47119	Galena, 250	F 8
46932	Galveston, 1,284	E 3
46738	Garrett, 4,715	G 2
* 46401	Gary, 175,415	C 1
	Gary-Hammond-East Chicago, ‡633,367	C 1
46933	Gas City, 5,742	F 4
47342	Gaston, 928	G 4
46740	Geneva, 1,100	H 3
47537	Gentryville, 281	C 8
47122	Georgetown, 1,273	F 8
47343	Glenwood, 452	G 5
† 47567	Glezen, 300	C 8
46045	Goldsmith, 235	E 4
47948	Goodland, 1,176	C 3
46526	Goshen⊙, 17,171	F 1
47433	Gosport, 692	D 6
46741	Grabill, 570	H 2
47615	Grandview, 696	C 9
46530	Granger, 200	E 1
46135	Greencastle⊙, 8,852	D 5
† 47025	Greendale, 3,783	H 6
46140	Greenfield⊙, 9,986	F 5
47344	Greensboro, 225	G 5
47240	Greensburg⊙, 8,620	G 6
47345	Greens Fork, 444	H 5
46936	Greentown, 1,870	E 4
47124	Greenville, 611	F 8
46142	Greenwood, 11,408	E 5
46319	Griffith, 18,168	C 1
46144	Gwynneville, 240	F 5
47346	Hagerstown, 2,059	G 5
46742	Hamilton, 537	H 1
46532	Hamlet, 761	D 2
* 46320	Hammond, 107,790	B 1
46340	Hanna, 500	D 2
47243	Hanover, 3,018	F 7
47125	Hardinsburg, 263	E 8
46743	Harlan, 840	H 2
47853	Harmony, 750	C 5
47434	Harrodsburg, 400	D 6
47348	Hartford City⊙, 8,207	G 4
47244	Hartsville, 434	F 6
47617	Hatfield, 800	C 9
47539	Haubstadt, 1,171	B 8
† 47546	Haysville, 585	D 8
47540	Hazleton, 416	B 8
46341	Hebron, 1,624	C 2
47436	Heltonville, 400	E 7
46937	Hemlock, 200	F 4
47126	Henryville, 1,500	F 7
46322	Highland, 24,947	B 1
46046	Hillisburg, 225	E 4
47949	Hillsboro, 505	C 4
47854	Hillsdale, 500	C 5
46745	Hoagland, 530	H 3
46342	Hobart, 21,485	C 1
46047	Hobbs, 400	F 4
47541	Holland, 662	C 8
47023	Holton, 610	G 6
46146	Homer, 245	F 5
47246	Hope, 1,603	F 6
† 46069	Hortonville, 240	E 4
46746	Howe, 800	G 1
46747	Hudson, 464	G 1
46552	Hudson Lake, 1,134	D 1
46748	Huntertown, 775	G 2
47542	Huntingburg, 4,794	D 8
46750	Huntington⊙, 16,217	G 3
† 46064	Huntsville, 450	G 4
47437	Huron, 580	D 7
47855	Hymera, 907	C 6
47950	Idaville, 600	D 3
* 46201	Indianapolis (cap.)⊙ 744,624	E 5
	Indianapolis, ‡1,109,882	E 5
46048	Ingalls, 888	F 5
47545	Ireland, 527	C 8
46147	Jamestown, 938	D 5
47438	Jasonville, 2,335	C 6
47546	Jasper⊙, 8,641	D 8
47130	Jeffersonville⊙, 20,008	F 8
† 47565	Johnson, 250	B 8
† 46074	Jolietville, 265	E 4
46938	Jonesboro, 2,466	F 4
47247	Jonesville, 202	F 6
46049	Kempton, 469	E 4
46755	Kendallville, 6,838	G 2
47351	Kennard, 518	G 5
47951	Kentland⊙, 1,864	C 3
46939	Kewanna, 614	E 2
46759	Keystone, 200	G 3
46760	Kimmell, 350	F 2
47952	Kingman, 530	C 5
46345	Kingsbury, 314	D 1
46346	Kingsford Heights, 1,200	D 2
46050	Kirklin, 736	E 4
46148	Knightstown, 2,456	F 5
47857	Knightsville, 788	C 5
46534	Knox⊙, 3,519	D 2
46901	Kokomo⊙, 44,042	E 4
† 46574	Koontz Lake, 900	D 2
46347	Kouts, 1,388	C 2
46348	La Crosse, 696	D 2
47954	Ladoga, 1,099	D 5
* 47901	Lafayette⊙, 44,955	D 4
	Lafayette-West Lafayette, ‡109,378	D 4
46940	La Fontaine, 793	F 3
46761	Lagrange⊙, 2,053	F 1
46941	Lagro, 552	F 3
† 46703	Lake James, 400	H 1
46943	Laketon, 500	F 3
46349	Lake Village, 600	C 2
46536	Lakeville, 712	E 1
† 46567	Lake Wawasee, 600	F 2
47136	Lanesville, 586	E 8
46763	Laotto, 312	G 2
46537	Lapaz, 604	E 2
46051	Lapel, 1,725	F 4
46350	LaPorte⊙, 22,140	D 1
46764	Larwill, 324	F 2
47024	Laurel, 753	G 6
46226	Lawrence, 16,646	E 5
47025	Lawrenceburg⊙, 4,636	H 6
47137	Leavenworth, 330	E 8
46052	Lebanon⊙, 9,766	D 4
46538	Leesburg, 561	F 2
46945	Leiters Ford, 250	E 2
46765	Leo, 500	G 2
46355	Leroy, 350	C 2
† 47240	Letts, 247	F 6
47352	Lewisville, 530	G 5
47138	Lexington, 400	F 7
47353	Liberty⊙, 1,831	H 5
46766	Liberty Center, 300	G 3
46946	Liberty Mills, 200	F 2
46767	Ligonier, 3,034	F 2
47955	Linden, 713	D 4
46769	Linn Grove, 300	H 3
47441	Linton, 5,450	C 6
† 46755	Lisbon, 200	G 2
46149	Lizton, 397	D 5
46947	Logansport⊙, 19,255	E 3
† 46360	Long Beach, 2,740	D 1
47553	Loogootee, 2,953	D 7
47354	Losantville, 212	G 4
46356	Lowell, 3,839	C 2
† 46601	Lydick, 1,341	E 1
† 47874	Lyford, 400	C 5
47355	Lynn, 1,360	H 4
47619	Lynnville, 556	C 8
47443	Lyons, 702	C 7
46951	Macy, 273	E 3
47250	Madison⊙, 13,081	G 7
† 47001	Manchester, 250	H 6
46150	Manilla, 300	F 5
† 47872	Mansfield, 200	C 5
47140	Marengo, 767	E 8
47556	Mariah Hill, 275	D 8
† 46176	Marietta, 280	F 6
46952	Marion⊙, 39,607	F 3
46770	Markle, 963	G 3
46056	Markleville, 457	F 5
47859	Marshall, 365	C 5
46151	Martinsville⊙, 9,723	D 6
46957	Matthews, 728	F 4
46154	Maxwell, 245	F 5
46055	McCordsville, 500	F 5
47860	Mecca, 800	C 5
47957	Medaryville, 732	D 2
47260	Medora, 788	E 7
47958	Mellott, 325	C 4
47143	Memphis, 324	F 8
46539	Mentone, 830	E 2
47861	Merom, 305	B 6
46410	Merrillville, 15,918	C 2
47030	Metamora, 400	G 6
† 46703	Metz, 200	H 1
46958	Mexico, 850	E 3
46959	Miami, 420	E 3
46360	Michigan City, 39,369	C 1

(continued on following page)

D'Arazien — Shostal Associates

Ore being unloaded in the storage yard at steel plant docks in Gary, Indiana. Aided by the state's outstanding natural supply of limestone, mills in the Lake Michigan area produce more than 15 million tons of steel yearly.

(continued)

46057 Michigantown, 457 E 4
46540 Middlebury, 1,055 F 1
47356 Middletown, 2,046 F 4
47445 Midland, 220 C 6
47031 Milan, 1,260 G 6
46542 Milford, 1,264 F 2
46543 Millersburg, 618 F 1
47261 Millhousen, 252 G 6
47145 Milltown, 829 E 8
† 47362 Millville, 275 G 5
46156 Milroy, 750 G 6
47357 Milton, 694 G 5
46544 Mishawaka, 35,517 E 1
47446 Mitchell, 4,092 E 7
47358 Modoc, 275 G 4
46771 Mongo, 225 G 1
47959 Monon, 1,548 D 3
46772 Monroe, 622 H 3
47557 Monroe City, 603 C 7
46773 Monroeville, 1,353 H 3
46157 Monrovia, 750 E 5
46960 Monterey, 268 D 2
47862 Montezuma, 1,192 C 5
47558 Montgomery, 411 C 7
47960 Monticello⊙, 4,869 D 3
47962 Montmorenci, 350 D 4
47359 Montpelier, 2,093 G 3
47360 Mooreland, 495 G 5
47032 Moores Hill, 616 G 6
46158 Mooresville, 5,800 E 5
46160 Morgantown, 1,134 E 6
47963 Morocco, 1,285 C 3
47033 Morris, 435 G 6
46161 Morristown, 838 F 5
47361 Mount Summit, 395 G 4
47620 Mount Vernon⊙, 6,770 B 9
46058 Mulberry, 1,075 D 4
* 47302 Muncie⊙, 69,080 G 4
Muncie, ‡129,219 G 4
46321 Munster, 16,514 B 1
47147 Nabb, 204 F 7
47034 Napoleon, 282 G 6
46550 Nappanee, 4,159 F 2
47448 Nashville⊙, 527 E 6
† 47421 Needmore, 200 E 7
47150 New Albany⊙, 38,402 F 8
47449 Newberry, 295 C 7
47630 Newburgh, 2,302 C 9
46552 New Carlisle, 1,434 E 1
47362 New Castle⊙, 21,215 G 5
† 46342 New Chicago, 2,231 C 1
47863 New Goshen, 500 B 5
47631 New Harmony, 971 B 8
46774 New Haven, 5,728 H 2
47366 New Lisbon, 350 G 5
† 46979 New London, 200 E 4
47965 New Market, 640 D 5
46163 New Palestine, 863 F 5
46553 New Paris, 1,080 F 2
† 47165 New Pekin, 912 F 7
47263 New Point, 381 G 6
47966 Newport⊙, 708 C 5
† 47106 New Providence (Borden), 337 F 8
47967 New Richmond, 381 D 4
47968 New Ross, 318 D 5
† 46173 New Salem, 270 G 5
47161 New Salisbury, 350 E 8
47969 Newtown, 286 C 4
47035 New Trenton, 200 H 6
47162 New Washington, 1,100 F 7
46184 New Whiteland, 4,200 E 5
46060 Noblesville⊙, 7,548 F 4
46366 North Judson, 1,738 D 2
46554 North Liberty, 1,259 E 1
46962 North Manchester, 5,791 F 3
46165 North Salem, 601 D 5
47805 North Terre Haute, 1,400 C 5
47265 North Vernon, 4,582 F 6
46555 North Webster, 456 F 2
† 47960 Norway, 250 D 3
46556 Notre Dame, 8,400 E 1
† 47331 Nulltown, 250 G 5
46965 Oakford, 300 E 4
47560 Oakland City, 3,289 C 8
47561 Oaktown, 726 C 7
47367 Oakville, 250 G 4
47562 Odon, 1,433 C 7
† 46401 Ogden Dunes, 1,361 C 1
47036 Oldenburg, 758 G 6
47451 Oolitic, 1,155 E 7
† 47343 Orange, 200 G 5
46063 Orestes, 519 F 4
46776 Orland, 457 G 1
47452 Orleans, 1,834 D 7
46561 Osceola, 1,572 E 1
47037 Osgood, 1,346 G 6
46777 Ossian, 1,538 G 3
46367 Otis, 300 D 1
47163 Otisco, 375 F 7
47970 Otterbein, 899 C 4
47564 Otwell, 850 C 8
47453 Owensburg, 700 D 7
47565 Owensville, 1,056 B 8
47971 Oxford, 1,098 C 3
† 46508 Palestine, 200 F 2
47164 Palmyra, 483 E 8
47454 Paoli⊙, 3,281 E 7
46166 Paragon, 538 D 6
47368 Parker, 1,179 G 4
47566 Patoka, 529 B 8
47455 Patricksburg, 265 D 6
47038 Patriot, 216 H 7
47865 Paxton, 250 C 6
47165 Pekin, 950 E 7
46064 Pendleton, 2,243 F 5
47369 Pennville, 798 G 4
† 46011 Perkinsville, 300 F 4
47974 Perrysville, 510 C 4
47370 Pershing, 447 G 5
† 46975 Pershing, 425 E 2
46970 Peru⊙, 14,139 E 3
47567 Petersburg⊙, 2,697 C 7
46778 Petroleum, 200 G 3
46562 Pierceton, 1,175 F 2
47866 Pimento, 200 C 6
† 46350 Pine Lake, 1,954 D 1
47975 Pine Village, 291 C 4
46167 Pittsboro, 867 D 5
46168 Plainfield, 8,211 E 5
47568 Plainville, 538 C 7
46779 Pleasant Lake, 650 H 1
46563 Plymouth⊙, 7,661 E 2
47868 Poland, 300 C 6
46781 Poneto, 286 G 3
46368 Portage, 19,127 C 1
46304 Porter, 3,058 C 1
47371 Portland⊙, 7,115 H 4
47633 Poseyville, 1,035 B 8
† 46360 Pottawattamie Park, 374 C 1
47869 Prairie Creek, 225 C 6
47870 Prairieton, 400 B 6
† 46164 Princes Lakes, 597 E 6
47570 Princeton⊙, 7,431 B 8
46170 Putnamville, 200 D 5
47456 Quincy, 250 D 6
47573 Ragsdale, 200 C 7
46737 Ray, 200 H 1
† 47274 Reddington, 245 F 6
47373 Redkey, 1,667 G 4
46171 Reelsville, 210 D 5
47977 Remington, 1,127 C 3
47978 Rensselaer⊙, 4,688 C 3
47980 Reynolds, 641 D 3
47634 Richland, 650 C 9
47374 Richmond⊙, 43,999 H 5
47380 Ridgeville, 924 G 4
47871 Riley, 257 C 6
47040 Rising Sun⊙, 2,305 H 7
46172 Roachdale, 1,004 D 5
46974 Roann, 509 F 3
46783 Roanoke, 858 G 3
46975 Rochester⊙, 4,631 E 2
46977 Rockfield, 300 D 3
47635 Rockport⊙, 2,565 C 9
47872 Rockville⊙, 2,820 C 5
46371 Rolling Prairie, 2,500 D 1
47574 Rome, 1,354 D 9
46784 Rome City, 1,385 G 1
47981 Romney, 420 D 4
47874 Rosedale, 817 C 5
† 46601 Roseland, 895 E 1
46372 Roselawn, 200 C 2
46065 Rossville, 830 D 4
46978 Royal Center, 987 E 3
† 47302 Royerton, 411 G 4
46173 Rushville⊙, 6,686 G 5
46175 Russellville, 390 D 5
46975 Russiaville, 844 E 4
47575 Saint Anthony, 460 D 8
47875 Saint Bernice, 900 C 5
46785 Saint Joe, 564 H 2
46373 Saint John, 1,757 C 2
† 45030 Saint Leon, 435 H 6
47876 Saint Mary-of-the-Woods, 1,200 B 6
† 46556 Saint Marys, 1,600 E 1
47577 Saint Meinrad, 1,100 D 8
47272 Saint Paul, 785 F 6
† 47012 Saint Peter, 200 H 6
† 47620 Saint Philip, 400 B 9
† 47638 Saint Wendel, 250 B 8
47167 Salem⊙, 5,041 E 7
47578 Sandborn, 528 C 7
† 47401 Sanders, 200 E 6
46374 San Pierre, 300 D 2
47579 Santa Claus, 125 D 8
47382 Saratoga, 406 H 4
† 47283 Sardinia, 225 F 6
46375 Schererville, 3,663 C 2
46376 Schneider, 426 C 2
47273 Scipio, 250 F 6
47170 Scottsburg⊙, 4,791 F 7
47878 Seelyville, 1,195 C 6
47172 Sellersburg, 3,177 F 8
47383 Selma, 890 G 4
47274 Seymour, 13,352 F 7
46068 Sharpsville, 672 E 4
47879 Shelburn, 1,281 C 6
46377 Shelby, 400 C 2
46176 Shelbyville⊙, 15,094 F 6
47880 Shepardsville, 325 B 5
46069 Sheridan, 2,137 E 4
† 47338 Shideler, 275 G 4
46565 Shipshewana, 448 F 1
47384 Shirley, 958 F 5

Topography

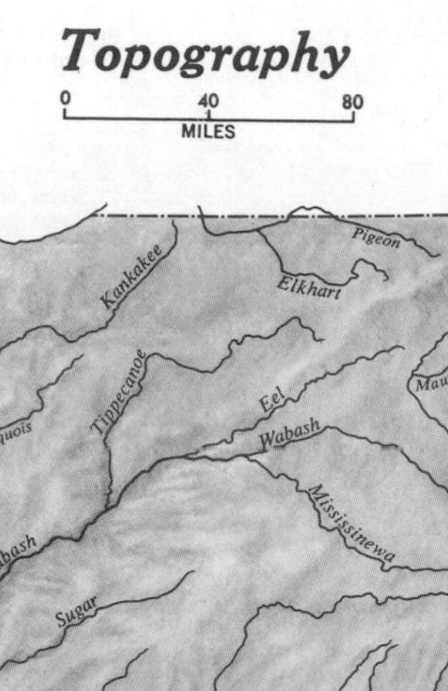

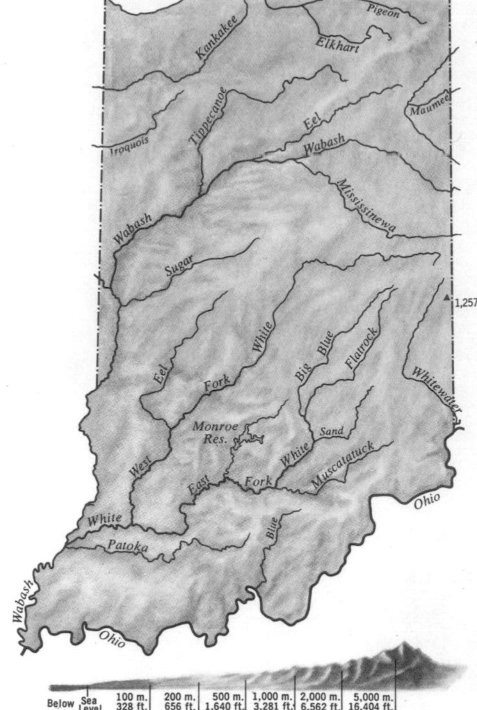

Agriculture, Industry and Resources

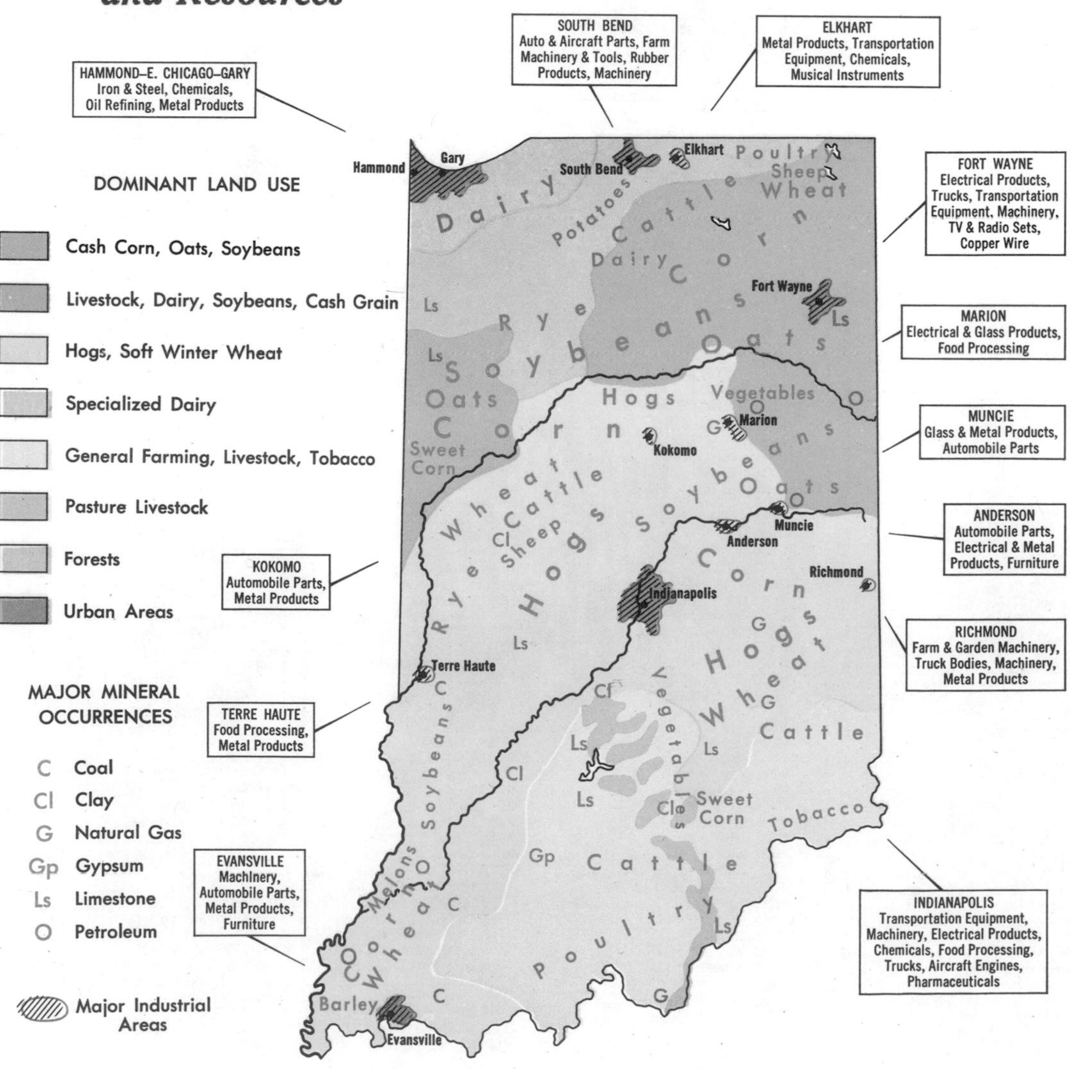

† 46797 Shirley City (Woodburn), 688 H 2
47581 Shoals⊙, 1,039 D 7
46982 Silver Lake, 588 F 2
46983 Sims, 250 F 3
† 46142 Smith Valley, 1,679 E 5
47458 Smithville, 350 D 6
46984 Somerset, 296 F 3
47583 Somerville, 313 C 8
* 46601 South Bend⊙, 125,580 E 1
South Bend, ‡280,031 E 1
46786 South Milford, 437 G 1
† 46201 Southport, 2,505 E 5
46787 South Whitley, 1,362 F 2
† 47355 Spartanburg, 201 H 4
47172 Speed, 800 F 8
46224 Speedway, 15,056 E 5
47460 Spencer⊙, 2,423 D 6
46788 Spencerville, 320 G 2
47385 Spiceland, 957 F 5
† 47374 Spring Grove, 437 H 5
† 46140 Spring Lake, 263 F 5
47386 Springport, 236 G 4
47462 Springville, 205 D 7
47584 Spurgeon, 285 C 8
47463 Stanford, 200 D 6
46985 Star City, 500 D 3
47881 Staunton, 582 C 6
47585 Stendal, 225 C 8
47636 Stewartsville, 275 B 8
46180 Stilesville, 352 D 5
46351 Stillwell, 225 D 1
47464 Stinesville, 291 D 6
47983 Stockwell, 500 D 4
47387 Straughn, 329 G 5
46789 Stroh, 600 G 1
47882 Sullivan⊙, 4,683 C 6
47388 Sulphur Springs, 387 G 4
46379 Sumava Resorts, 265 C 2
46070 Summitville, 1,104 F 4
47041 Sunman, 707 G 6
46986 Swayzee, 1,073 F 4
46987 Sweetser, 1,076 F 3
47465 Switz City, 301 C 6
46567 Syracuse, 1,546 F 2
47280 Taylorsville, 1,275 F 6
47586 Tell City, 7,933 D 9
47637 Tennyson, 335 C 8
* 47801 Terre Haute⊙, 70,286 C 6
Terre Haute, ‡175,143 C 6
46381 Thayer, 350 C 2
46071 Thorntown, 1,399 D 4
46570 Tippecanoe, 285 E 2
46072 Tipton⊙, 5,176 E 4
46571 Topeka, 677 F 1
† 46360 Town of Pines, 1,007 D 1
46181 Trafalgar, 457 E 6
† 46360 Trail Creek, 2,697 D 1
† 46725 Tri Lakes, 1,193 G 2
47588 Troy, 575 D 9
46988 Twelve Mile, 225 E 3
47177 Underwood, 550 F 7
47390 Union City, 3,995 H 4
46791 Uniondale, 349 G 3
46382 Union Mills, 350 D 2
47468 Unionville, 250 E 6
47884 Universal, 462 C 5
46989 Upland, 3,202 F 4
46990 Urbana, 400 F 3
† 47130 Utica, 300 F 8
47281 Vallonia, 600 E 7
46383 Valparaiso⊙, 20,020 C 2
46991 Van Buren, 1,057 F 3
47987 Veedersburg, 1,837 C 4
47282 Vernon⊙, 440 F 7
47042 Versailles⊙, 1,020 G 6
47043 Vevay⊙, 1,463 G 7
47591 Vincennes⊙, 19,867 C 7
46992 Wabash⊙, 13,379 F 3
47638 Wadesville, 300 B 8
46573 Wakarusa, 1,160 F 1
46182 Waldron, 800 F 6
† 47201 Walesboro, 214 F 6
46574 Walkerton, 2,006 E 2
† 46802 Wallen, 945 G 2
46994 Walton, 1,054 E 3
46390 Wanatah, 773 D 2
46792 Warren, 1,229 G 3
46580 Warsaw⊙, 7,506 F 2
47501 Washington⊙, 11,358 C 7
46793 Waterloo, 1,876 G 2
47989 Waveland, 557 D 5
† 46151 Waverly, 225 E 5
46794 Wawaka, 293 F 2
47990 Waynetown, 993 C 4
47392 Webster, 300 H 5
47469 West Baden Springs, 930 D 7
† 47353 West College Corner, 709 H 5
46074 Westfield, 1,837 E 4
† 45030 West Harrison, 395 H 6
47906 West Lafayette, 19,157 D 4
47991 West Lebanon, 899 C 4
46995 West Middleton, 450 E 4
47596 Westphalia, 300 C 7
47992 Westpoint, 300 C 4
47283 Westport, 1,170 F 6
47885 West Terre Haute, 2,704 B 6
46391 Westville, 2,614 D 1
46392 Wheatfield, 713 C 2
47597 Wheatland, 562 C 7
46393 Wheeler, 550 C 1
46184 Whiteland, 1,492 E 5
46075 Whitestown, 569 E 5
46394 Whiting, 7,247 C 1
46186 Wilkinson, 480 F 5
47470 Williams, 350 D 7
47993 Williamsport⊙, 1,661 C 4
46996 Winamac⊙, 2,341 D 2
47394 Winchester⊙, 5,493 G 4
46076 Windfall, 946 F 4
47994 Wingate, 437 C 4
46590 Winona Lake, 2,811 F 2
47598 Winslow, 1,030 C 8
47995 Wolcott, 894 C 3
46795 Wolcottville, 915 G 1
46796 Wolflake, 333 F 2
46797 Woodburn, 688 H 2
† 46624 Woodland, 400 E 1
47471 Worthington, 1,691 C 6
47179 Wyandotte, 26 E 8
46595 Wyatt, 305 E 1
† 47630 Yankeetown, 250 C 9
46798 Yoder, 250 G 3
47396 Yorktown, 1,673 G 4
46998 Young America, 250 E 3
† 47808 Youngstown, 350 C 6
46799 Zanesville, 350 G 3
46077 Zionsville, 1,857 E 5

⊙ County seat.
‡ Population of metropolitan area.
† Zip of nearest p.o.
* Multiple zips

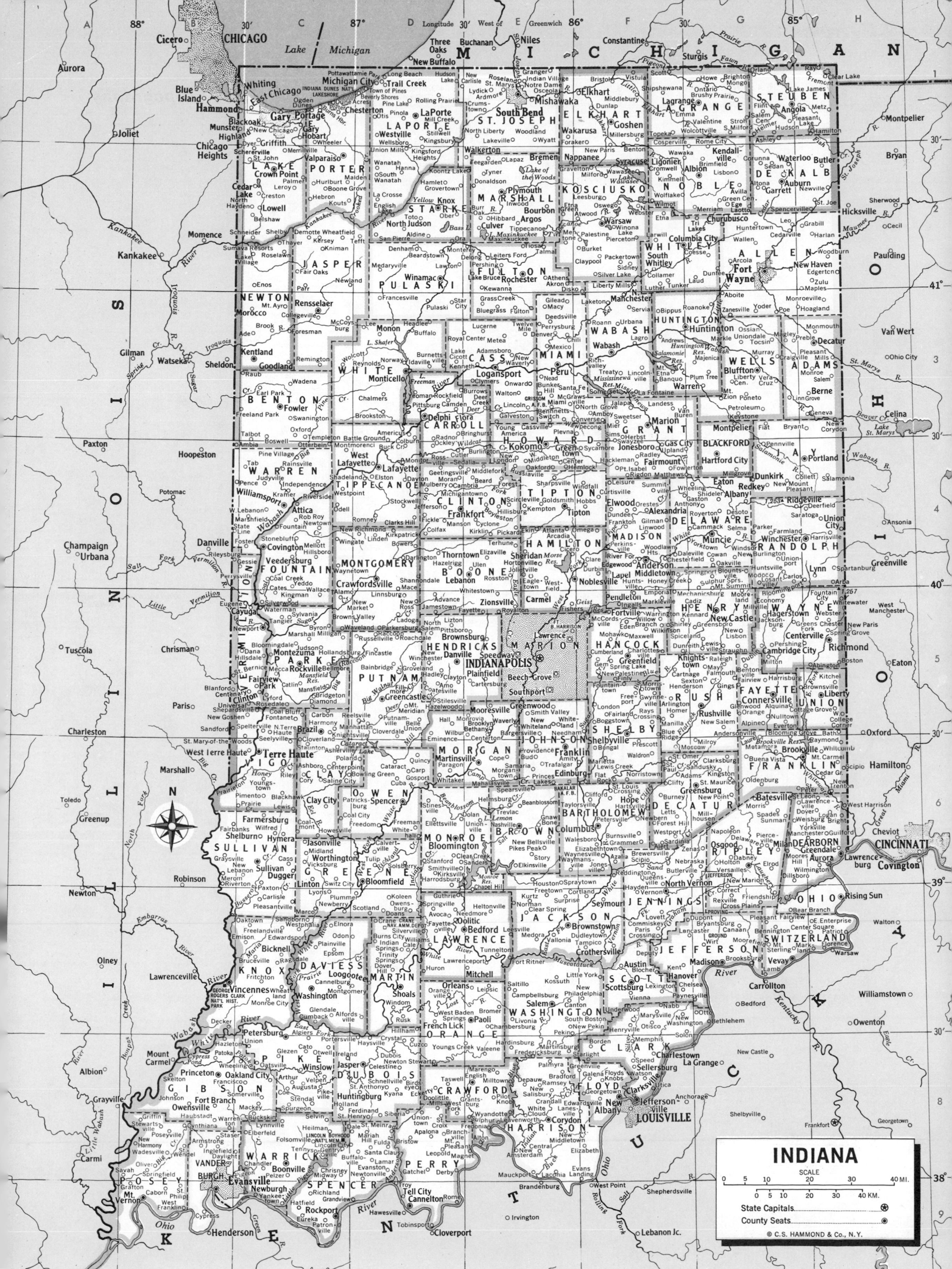

INDIANA
SCALE
0 5 10 20 30 40 MI.
0 5 10 20 30 40 KM.
State Capitals
County Seats
© C.S. HAMMOND & Co., N.Y.
Longitude 30' West of Greenwich 86°
88° 30' 87° 30' 85°
41° 30' 40° 30' 39° 30' 38° 30'
A B C D E F G H
1 2 3 4 5 6 7 8 9
MICHIGAN
ILLINOIS
OHIO
KENTUCKY
Lake Michigan
CHICAGO
INDIANAPOLIS
LOUISVILLE
CINCINNATI
LAKE
PORTER
LAPORTE
ST. JOSEPH
ELKHART
LAGRANGE
STEUBEN
NOBLE
DE KALB
KOSCIUSKO
MARSHALL
STARKE
JASPER
NEWTON
PULASKI
FULTON
WHITLEY
ALLEN
BENTON
WHITE
CASS
MIAMI
WABASH
HUNTINGTON
WELLS
ADAMS
CARROLL
HOWARD
GRANT
BLACKFORD
JAY
WARREN
TIPPECANOE
CLINTON
TIPTON
MADISON
DELAWARE
RANDOLPH
FOUNTAIN
MONTGOMERY
BOONE
HAMILTON
HENRY
WAYNE
VERMILLION
PARKE
PUTNAM
HENDRICKS
MARION
HANCOCK
RUSH
FAYETTE
UNION
VIGO
CLAY
MORGAN
JOHNSON
SHELBY
DECATUR
FRANKLIN
OWEN
MONROE
BROWN
BARTHOLOMEW
SULLIVAN
GREENE
JACKSON
JENNINGS
RIPLEY
DEARBORN
OHIO
SWITZERLAND
KNOX
DAVIESS
MARTIN
LAWRENCE
SCOTT
JEFFERSON
WASHINGTON
ORANGE
CLARK
PIKE
DUBOIS
CRAWFORD
FLOYD
HARRISON
GIBSON
POSEY
VANDERBURGH
WARRICK
SPENCER
PERRY
Gary
Hammond
East Chicago
Michigan City
South Bend
Mishawaka
Elkhart
Goshen
Fort Wayne
Logansport
Peru
Kokomo
Marion
Lafayette
Muncie
Anderson
Richmond
Terre Haute
Bloomington
Columbus
Evansville
New Albany
Jeffersonville
Vincennes
Crown Point
Valparaiso
Plymouth
Warsaw
Huntington
Wabash
Frankfort
Noblesville
Greenfield
New Castle
Connersville
Franklin
Martinsville
Shelbyville
Madison
Bedford
Jasper
Princeton
Mt. Vernon
Rockport
Cannelton
Tell City
Kankakee River
Wabash River
White River
Ohio River
Tippecanoe River
Whitewater River

COUNTIES

County, Pop.	Key
Adair, 9,487	E 6
Adams, 6,322	D 6
Allamakee, 14,968	L 2
Appanoose, 15,007	H 7
Audubon, 9,595	D 5
Benton, 22,885	J 4
Black Hawk, 132,916	J 4
Boone, 25,470	F 5
Bremer, 22,737	J 3
Buchanan, 21,746	K 4
Buena Vista, 20,693	C 3
Butler, 16,953	H 3
Calhoun, 14,287	D 4
Carroll, 22,912	D 4
Cass, 17,007	D 6
Cedar, 17,655	L 5
Cerro Gordo, 49,335	G 2
Cherokee, 17,269	B 3
Chickasaw, 14,969	J 2
Clarke, 7,581	F 6
Clay, 18,464	C 2
Clayton, 20,606	L 3
Clinton, 56,749	M 5
Crawford, 18,780	C 4
Dallas, 26,085	E 5
Davis, 8,207	J 7
Decatur, 9,737	F 7
Delaware, 18,770	L 4
Des Moines, 46,982	L 7
Dickinson, 12,565	C 2
Dubuque, 90,609	M 4
Emmet, 14,009	D 2
Fayette, 26,898	K 3
Floyd, 19,860	H 2
Franklin, 13,255	G 3
Fremont, 9,282	B 7
Greene, 12,716	E 5
Grundy, 14,119	H 4
Guthrie, 12,243	D 5
Hamilton, 18,383	F 4
Hancock, 13,227	F 2
Hardin, 22,248	G 4
Harrison, 16,240	B 5
Henry, 18,114	K 6
Howard, 11,442	J 2
Humboldt, 12,519	E 3
Ida, 9,190	C 4
Iowa, 15,419	J 5
Jackson, 20,839	M 4
Jasper, 35,425	G 5
Jefferson, 15,774	K 6
Johnson, 72,127	K 5
Jones, 19,868	L 4
Keokuk, 13,943	J 6
Kossuth, 22,937	E 2
Lee, 42,996	L 7
Linn, 163,213	K 4
Louisa, 10,682	L 6
Lucas, 10,163	G 6
Lyon, 13,340	A 2
Madison, 11,558	E 6
Mahaska, 22,177	H 6
Marion, 26,352	G 6
Marshall, 41,076	G 4
Mills, 11,606	B 6
Mitchell, 13,108	H 2
Monona, 12,069	B 4
Monroe, 9,357	H 7
Montgomery, 12,781	C 6
Muscatine, 37,181	L 5
O'Brien, 17,522	B 2
Osceola, 8,555	B 2
Page, 18,507	C 7
Palo Alto, 13,289	D 2
Plymouth, 24,312	A 3
Pocahontas, 12,729	D 3
Polk, 286,101	F 5
Pottawattamie, 86,991	B 6
Poweshiek, 18,803	H 5
Ringgold, 6,373	E 7
Sac, 15,573	C 4
Scott, 142,687	M 5
Shelby, 15,528	C 5
Sioux, 27,996	A 2
Story, 62,783	G 4
Tama, 20,147	H 4
Taylor, 8,790	D 7
Union, 13,557	E 7
Van Buren, 8,643	K 7
Wapello, 42,149	J 6
Warren, 27,432	F 6
Washington, 18,967	K 6
Wayne, 8,405	G 7
Webster, 48,391	E 4
Winnebago, 12,990	F 2
Winneshiek, 21,758	K 2
Woodbury, 103,052	B 4
Worth, 8,968	G 2
Wright, 17,294	F 3

CITIES and TOWNS

Zip	Name/Pop.	Key
50601	Ackley, 1,794	G 3
50002	Adair, 750	D 6
50003	Adel⊙, 2,419	E 5
50830	Afton, 823	E 6
52530	Agency, 610	J 7
52201	Ainsworth, 455	K 6
51001	Akron, 1,324	A 3
50510	Albert City, 683	C 3
52531	Albia⊙, 4,151	H 6
50005	Albion, 772	H 4
52202	Alburnett, 418	K 4
50006	Alden, 876	G 4
50420	Alexander, 249	G 3
50511	Algona⊙, 6,032	E 2
50008	Allerton, 643	G 7
50602	Allison⊙, 1,071	H 3
51002	Alta, 1,717	C 3
50603	Alta Vista, 283	J 2
51003	Alton, 1,018	A 3
50009	Altoona, 2,854	G 5
52203	Amana, 610	K 5
50010	Ames, 39,505	F 4
52205	Anamosa⊙, 4,389	L 4
52030	Andrew, 335	M 4
50020	Anita, 1,101	D 6
50021	Ankeny, 9,151	F 5
51004	Anthon, 711	B 4
50604	Aplington, 936	H 3
51430	Arcadia, 414	C 4
50606	Arlington, 481	K 3
50514	Armstrong, 1,061	D 2
51331	Arnolds Park, 970	C 2
51431	Arthur, 273	C 4
† 52001	Asbury, 410	M 4
51232	Ashton, 483	B 2
52720	Atalissa, 244	L 5
52206	Atkins, 581	K 4
50022	Atlantic⊙, 7,306	D 6
51433	Auburn, 329	D 4
50025	Audubon⊙, 2,907	D 5
51005	Aurelia, 1,065	C 3
50607	Aurora, 229	K 3
51521	Avoca, 1,535	C 6
50515	Ayrshire, 243	D 2
50516	Badger, 465	E 3
50026	Bagley, 365	E 5
50517	Bancroft, 1,103	E 2
50027	Barnes City, 238	H 6
52533	Batavia, 525	J 7
51006	Battle Creek, 837	B 4
50028	Baxter, 788	G 5
50029	Bayard, 628	D 5
52534	Beacon, 338	H 6
50609	Beaman, 222	H 4
50833	Bedford⊙, 1,733	D 7
52208	Belle Plaine, 2,810	J 5
52031	Bellevue, 2,336	M 4

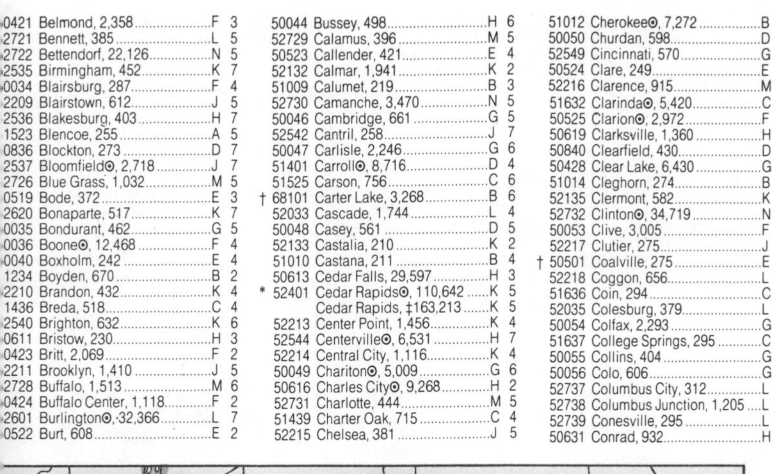

- 0421 Belmond, 2,358 ..... F 3
- 2721 Bennett, 385 ..... L 5
- 2722 Bettendorf, 22,126 ..... N 5
- 2535 Birmingham, 452 ..... K 7
- 0034 Blairsburg, 287 ..... F 4
- 2209 Blairstown, 612 ..... J 5
- 2536 Blakesburg, 403 ..... H 7
- 1523 Blencoe, 255 ..... A 5
- 0836 Blockton, 273 ..... D 7
- 2537 Bloomfield⊙, 2,718 ..... J 7
- 2726 Blue Grass, 1,032 ..... M 5
- 0519 Bode, 372 ..... E 3
- 2620 Bonaparte, 517 ..... K 7
- 0035 Bondurant, 462 ..... G 5
- 0036 Boone⊙, 12,468 ..... F 4
- 0040 Boxholm, 242 ..... E 4
- 1234 Boyden, 670 ..... B 2
- 2210 Brandon, 432 ..... K 4
- 1436 Breda, 518 ..... C 4
- 2540 Brighton, 632 ..... K 6
- 0611 Bristow, 230 ..... H 3
- 0423 Britt, 2,069 ..... F 2
- 2211 Brooklyn, 1,410 ..... J 5
- 2728 Buffalo, 1,513 ..... M 6
- 0424 Buffalo Center, 1,118 ..... F 2
- 2601 Burlington⊙, 32,366 ..... L 7
- 0522 Burt, 608 ..... E 2
- 50044 Bussey, 498 ..... H 6
- 52729 Calamus, 396 ..... M 5
- 50523 Callender, 421 ..... E 4
- 52132 Calmar, 1,941 ..... K 2
- 51009 Calumet, 219 ..... B 3
- 52730 Camanche, 3,470 ..... N 5
- 50046 Cambridge, 661 ..... G 5
- 52542 Cantril, 258 ..... J 7
- 50047 Carlisle, 2,246 ..... G 6
- 51401 Carroll⊙, 8,716 ..... D 4
- 51525 Carson, 756 ..... C 6
- † 68101 Carter Lake, 3,268 ..... B 6
- 52033 Cascade, 1,744 ..... L 4
- 50048 Casey, 561 ..... D 5
- 52133 Castalia, 210 ..... K 2
- 51010 Castana, 211 ..... B 4
- 50613 Cedar Falls, 29,597 ..... H 3
- * 52401 Cedar Rapids⊙, 110,642 ..... K 5
- Cedar Rapids, ‡163,213 ..... K 5
- 52213 Center Point, 1,456 ..... K 4
- 52544 Centerville⊙, 6,531 ..... H 7
- 52214 Central City, 1,116 ..... K 4
- 50049 Chariton⊙, 5,009 ..... G 6
- 50616 Charles City⊙, 9,268 ..... H 2
- 52731 Charlotte, 444 ..... M 5
- 51439 Charter Oak, 715 ..... C 4
- 52215 Chelsea, 381 ..... J 5
- 51012 Cherokee⊙, 7,272 ..... B 3
- 50050 Churdan, 598 ..... D 4
- 52549 Cincinnati, 570 ..... G 7
- 50524 Clare, 249 ..... E 3
- 52216 Clarence, 915 ..... M 5
- 51632 Clarinda⊙, 5,420 ..... C 7
- 50525 Clarion⊙, 2,972 ..... F 3
- 50619 Clarksville, 1,360 ..... H 3
- 50840 Clearfield, 430 ..... D 7
- 50428 Clear Lake, 6,430 ..... G 2
- 51014 Cleghorn, 274 ..... B 3
- 52135 Clermont, 582 ..... K 3
- 52732 Clinton⊙, 34,719 ..... N 5
- 50053 Clive, 3,005 ..... F 5
- 52217 Clutier, 275 ..... J 4
- † 50501 Coalville, 275 ..... E 4
- 52218 Coggon, 656 ..... L 4
- 51636 Coin, 294 ..... C 7
- 52035 Colesburg, 379 ..... L 3
- 50054 Colfax, 2,293 ..... G 5
- 51637 College Springs, 295 ..... C 7
- 50055 Collins, 404 ..... G 5
- 50056 Colo, 606 ..... G 4
- 52737 Columbus City, 312 ..... L 6
- 52738 Columbus Junction, 1,205 ..... L 6
- 52739 Conesville, 295 ..... L 6
- 50631 Conrad, 932 ..... H 4

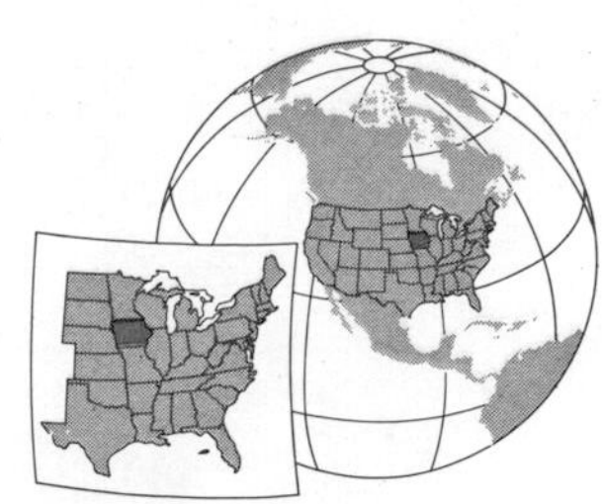

AREA 56,290 sq. mi.
POPULATION 2,825,041
CAPITAL Des Moines
LARGEST CITY Des Moines
HIGHEST POINT Ocheyedan Mound 1,675 ft.
SETTLED IN 1788
ADMITTED TO UNION December 28, 1846
POPULAR NAME Hawkeye State
STATE FLOWER Wild Rose
STATE BIRD Eastern Goldfinch

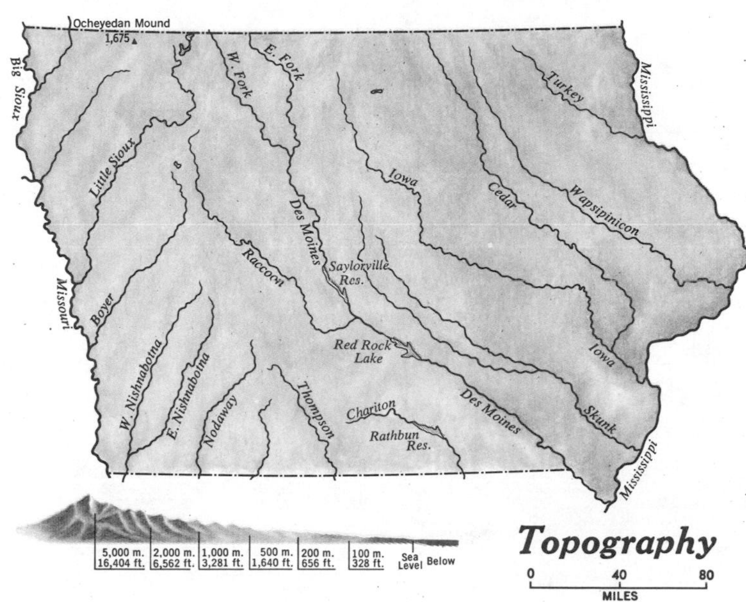

- 50058 Coon Rapids, 1,381 ..... D 5
- 52240 Coralville, 6,130 ..... K 5
- 50841 Corning⊙, 2,095 ..... D 7
- 51016 Correctionville, 870 ..... B 4
- 50430 Corwith, 407 ..... F 3
- 50060 Corydon⊙, 1,745 ..... G 7
- 50431 Coulter, 262 ..... G 3
- 51501 Council Bluffs⊙, 60,348 ..... B 6
- 52621 Crawfordsville, 288 ..... K 6
- 51526 Crescent, 284 ..... B 6
- 52136 Cresco⊙, 3,927 ..... J 2
- 50801 Creston⊙, 8,234 ..... E 6
- 50432 Crystal Lake, 276 ..... F 2
- 50843 Cumberland, 385 ..... D 6
- 50529 Dakota City⊙, 746 ..... E 3
- 50062 Dallas, 438 ..... G 6
- 50063 Dallas Center, 1,128 ..... E 5
- 51019 Danbury, 527 ..... B 4
- 52623 Danville, 948 ..... L 7
- * 52801 Davenport⊙, 98,469 ..... M 5
- Davenport-Rock Island-Moline, ‡362,638 ..... M 5
- 50065 Davis City, 301 ..... F 7
- 50066 Dawson, 232 ..... E 5
- 50530 Dayton, 909 ..... E 4
- 52101 Decorah⊙, 7,458 ..... K 2
- 51440 Dedham, 325 ..... D 5
- 52222 Deep River, 323 ..... J 5
- 51527 Defiance, 392 ..... C 5
- 52223 Delhi, 527 ..... L 4
- 52037 Delmar, 599 ..... M 4
- 51441 Deloit, 279 ..... C 4
- 52550 Delta, 475 ..... J 6
- 51442 Denison⊙, 5,882 ..... C 4
- 52624 Denmark, 375 ..... L 7
- 50622 Denver, 1,169 ..... J 3
- * 50301 Des Moines (cap.)⊙, 200,587 ..... G 5
- Des Moines, ‡286,101 ..... G 5
- 50069 De Soto, 369 ..... E 5
- 52742 De Witt, 3,647 ..... N 5
- 50070 Dexter, 652 ..... E 5
- 50845 Diagonal, 327 ..... E 7
- 51333 Dickens, 240 ..... C 2
- 50624 Dike, 794 ..... H 4
- 52745 Dixon, 276 ..... M 5
- 52746 Donahue, 216 ..... M 5
- 52625 Donnellson, 798 ..... K 7
- 51235 Doon, 437 ..... A 2
- 52551 Douds, 247 ..... J 7
- 51528 Dow City, 571 ..... B 5
- 50071 Dows, 777 ..... F 3
- 52001 Dubuque⊙, 62,309 ..... M 3
- Dubuque, ‡90,609 ..... M 3
- 50625 Dumont, 724 ..... H 3
- 50532 Duncombe, 418 ..... E 4
- 50626 Dunkerton, 563 ..... J 3
- 51529 Dunlap, 1,292 ..... B 5
- 52747 Durant, 1,472 ..... M 5
- 52040 Dyersville, 3,437 ..... L 3
- 52224 Dysart, 1,251 ..... J 4
- 50533 Eagle Grove, 4,489 ..... F 3
- 50072 Earlham, 974 ..... E 6
- 51530 Earling, 573 ..... C 5
- 52041 Earlville, 751 ..... L 4
- 50535 Early, 727 ..... C 4
- 52553 Eddyville, 945 ..... H 6
- 52042 Edgewood, 786 ..... K 3
- 52554 Eldon, 1,319 ..... J 7
- 50627 Eldora⊙, 3,223 ..... G 4
- 52748 Eldridge, 1,535 ..... M 5
- 52141 Elgin, 613 ..... K 3
- 52043 Elkader⊙, 1,592 ..... L 3
- 50073 Elkhart, 269 ..... F 5
- 51531 Elk Horn, 667 ..... C 5
- † 50700 Elk Run Heights, 1,175 ..... J 4
- 51532 Elliott, 423 ..... C 6
- 50075 Ellsworth, 443 ..... F 4
- 50628 Elma, 601 ..... J 2
- 52227 Ely, 275 ..... K 5
- 51533 Emerson, 484 ..... C 6
- 50536 Emmetsburg⊙, 4,150 ..... D 2
- 52045 Epworth, 1,132 ..... M 4
- 51638 Essex, 770 ..... C 7
- 51334 Estherville⊙, 8,108 ..... D 2
- 50707 Evansdale, 5,038 ..... J 4
- 51338 Everly, 699 ..... C 2
- 50076 Exira, 966 ..... D 5
- 52555 Exline, 224 ..... H 7
- 50629 Fairbank, 810 ..... K 3
- 52228 Fairfax, 635 ..... K 5
- 52556 Fairfield⊙, 8,715 ..... J 6
- 52046 Farley, 1,096 ..... L 4
- 52047 Farmersburg, 232 ..... L 3
- 52626 Farmington, 800 ..... K 7
- 50538 Farnhamville, 393 ..... D 4
- 51639 Farragut, 521 ..... C 7
- 52142 Fayette, 1,947 ..... K 3
- 50539 Fenton, 403 ..... E 2
- 50434 Fertile, 394 ..... G 2
- 50435 Floyd, 380 ..... H 2
- 50540 Fonda, 980 ..... D 3
- 50846 Fontanelle, 752 ..... E 6
- 50436 Forest City⊙, 3,841 ..... F 2
- 52144 Fort Atkinson, 339 ..... J 2
- 50501 Fort Dodge⊙, 31,263 ..... E 3
- 52627 Fort Madison⊙, 13,996 ..... L 7
- 51340 Fostoria, 219 ..... C 2
- 50630 Fredericksburg, 912 ..... J 3
- 52561 Fremont, 480 ..... H 6
- 51020 Galva, 319 ..... C 3
- 50103 Garden Grove, 285 ..... F 7
- 52049 Garnavillo, 634 ..... L 3
- 50438 Garner⊙, 2,217 ..... F 2
- 52229 Garrison, 383 ..... J 4
- 50632 Garwin, 563 ..... H 4
- 51237 George, 1,194 ..... B 2
- 50105 Gilbert, 521 ..... F 4
- 50634 Gilbertville, 655 ..... J 4
- 50106 Gilman, 513 ..... H 5
- 50541 Gilmore City, 766 ..... D 3
- 50635 Gladbrook, 961 ..... H 4
- 51534 Glenwood⊙, 4,195 ..... B 6
- 51443 Glidden, 964 ..... D 4
- 50542 Goldfield, 722 ..... F 3
- 50439 Goodell, 218 ..... F 3
- 52750 Gooselake, 218 ..... N 5
- 50543 Gowrie, 1,225 ..... E 4
- 51342 Graettinger, 907 ..... D 2
- 50440 Grafton, 254 ..... G 2
- 50107 Grand Junction, 967 ..... E 4
- 52751 Grand Mound, 627 ..... M 5
- 50108 Grand River, 211 ..... F 7
- 52752 Grandview, 357 ..... L 6
- 50109 Granger, 661 ..... F 5
- 51022 Granville, 383 ..... B 3
- 50848 Gravity, 286 ..... D 7
- 52050 Greeley, 323 ..... L 3
- 50636 Greene, 1,363 ..... H 3
- 50849 Greenfield⊙, 2,212 ..... D 6
- 50111 Grimes, 834 ..... F 5
- 50112 Grinnell, 8,402 ..... H 5
- 51535 Griswold, 1,181 ..... C 6
- 50638 Grundy Center⊙, 2,712 ..... H 4
- 50115 Guthrie Center⊙, 1,834 ..... D 5
- 52052 Guttenberg, 2,177 ..... L 3
- 51444 Halbur, 235 ..... D 4
- 51640 Hamburg, 1,640 ..... B 7
- 50441 Hampton⊙, 4,376 ..... G 3
- 51536 Hancock, 228 ..... C 6
- 50544 Harcourt, 305 ..... E 4
- 51537 Harlan⊙, 5,049 ..... C 5
- 52146 Harpers Ferry, 227 ..... L 2
- 50118 Hartford, 582 ..... G 6
- 51346 Hartley, 1,694 ..... C 2
- 50119 Harvey, 217 ..... H 6
- 51540 Hastings, 229 ..... C 6
- 50546 Havelock, 220 ..... D 3
- 51023 Hawarden, 2,789 ..... A 2
- 52147 Hawkeye, 529 ..... J 3
- 50641 Hazleton, 626 ..... K 3
- 52563 Hedrick, 790 ..... J 6
- 51541 Henderson, 211 ..... B 6
- 52233 Hiawatha, 2,416 ..... K 4
- 52235 Hills, 507 ..... K 5
- 52630 Hillsboro, 252 ..... K 7
- 51024 Hinton, 488 ..... A 3
- 50642 Holland, 258 ..... H 4
- 51025 Holstein, 1,445 ..... B 4
- 52053 Holy Cross, 290 ..... L 3
- 52237 Hopkinton, 800 ..... L 4
- 51026 Hornick, 250 ..... A 4
- 51238 Hospers, 646 ..... B 2
- 50122 Hubbard, 846 ..... G 4
- 50643 Hudson, 1,535 ..... H 4
- 51239 Hull, 1,523 ..... A 2
- 50548 Humboldt, 4,665 ..... E 3
- 50123 Humeston, 673 ..... G 7
- 50124 Huxley, 937 ..... F 5
- 51445 Ida Grove⊙, 2,261 ..... B 4
- 50644 Independence⊙, 5,910 ..... K 4
- 50125 Indianola⊙, 8,852 ..... F 6
- 51240 Inwood, 644 ..... A 2
- 50645 Ionia, 270 ..... J 2
- 52240 Iowa City⊙, 46,850 ..... L 5
- 50126 Iowa Falls, 6,454 ..... G 3
- 51027 Ireton, 582 ..... A 3
- 51446 Irwin, 446 ..... C 5
- 50128 Jamaica, 271 ..... E 5
- 50647 Janesville, 741 ..... J 3
- 50129 Jefferson⊙, 4,735 ..... E 4
- 50648 Jesup, 1,662 ..... J 4
- 50130 Jewell, 1,152 ..... F 4
- 50131 Johnston, 222 ..... F 5
- 52247 Kalona, 1,488 ..... K 6
- 50132 Kamrar, 243 ..... F 4
- 50447 Kanawha, 705 ..... F 3
- 50133 Kellerton, 299 ..... E 7

(continued on following page)

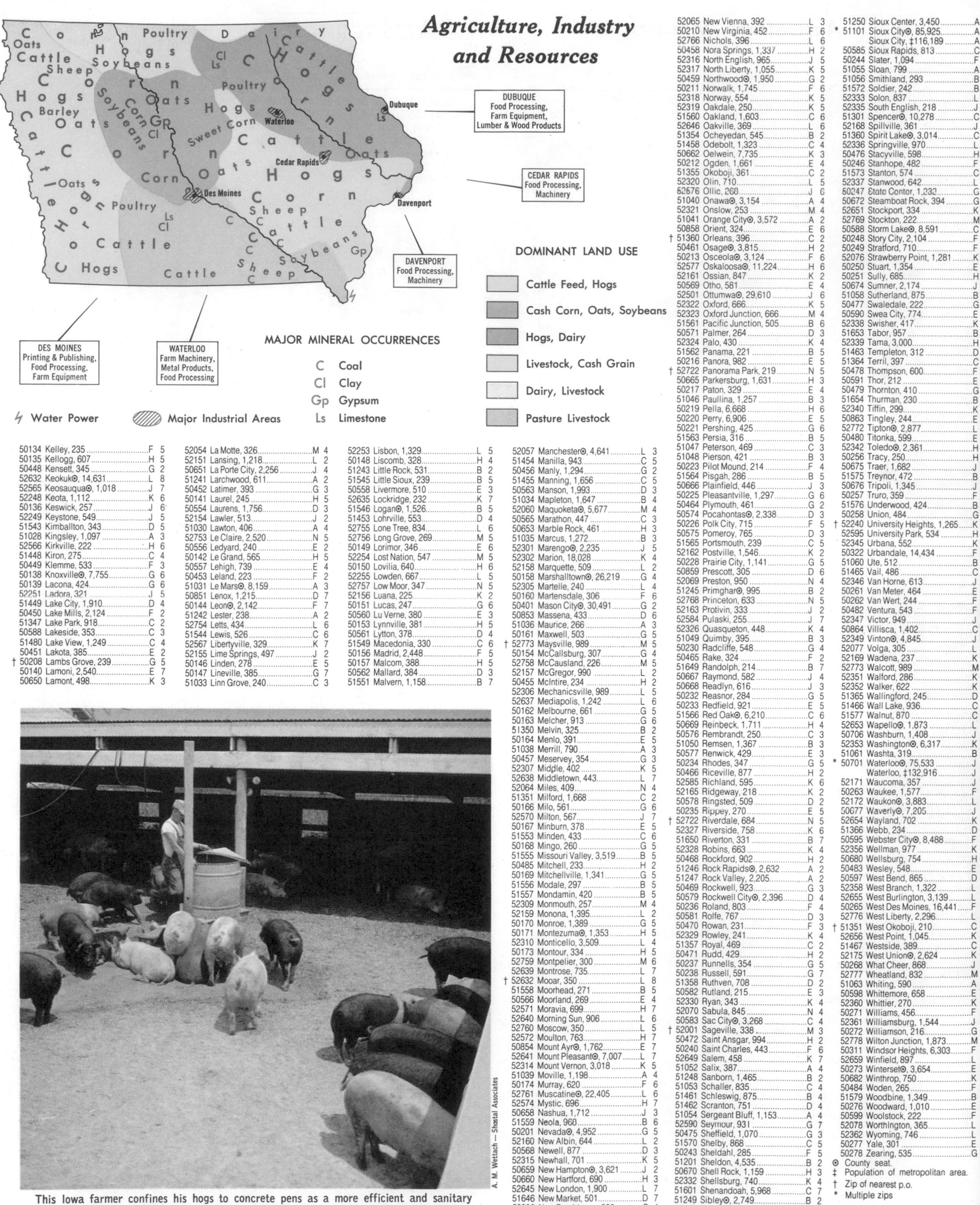

This Iowa farmer confines his hogs to concrete pens as a more efficient and sanitary method of raising healthy animals for market. Iowa's record-breaking hog production is due largely to the availability of corn for fodder.

50134 Kelley, 235 .... F 5
50135 Kellogg, 607 .... H 5
50448 Kensett, 345 .... G 2
52632 Keokuk⊙, 14,631 .... L 8
52565 Keosauqua⊙, 1,018 .... J 7
52248 Keota, 1,112 .... K 6
50136 Keswick, 257 .... J 6
52249 Keystone, 549 .... J 5
51543 Kimballton, 343 .... D 5
51028 Kingsley, 1,097 .... A 3
52566 Kirkville, 222 .... H 6
51448 Kiron, 275 .... C 4
50449 Klemme, 533 .... F 3
50138 Knoxville⊙, 7,755 .... G 6
50139 Lacona, 424 .... G 6
52251 Ladora, 321 .... J 5
51449 Lake City, 1,910 .... D 4
50450 Lake Mills, 2,124 .... F 2
51347 Lake Park, 918 .... C 2
50588 Lakeside, 353 .... C 3
51480 Lake View, 1,249 .... C 4
50451 Lakota, 385 .... E 2
† 50208 Lambs Grove, 239 .... G 5
50140 Lamoni, 2,540 .... E 7
50650 Lamont, 498 .... K 3
52054 La Motte, 326 .... M 4
52151 Lansing, 1,218 .... L 2
50651 La Porte City, 2,256 .... J 4
51241 Larchwood, 611 .... A 2
50452 Latimer, 393 .... G 3
50141 Laurel, 245 .... H 5
50554 Laurens, 1,756 .... D 3
52154 Lawler, 513 .... J 2
51030 Lawton, 406 .... A 4
52753 Le Claire, 2,520 .... N 5
50556 Ledyard, 240 .... E 2
50142 Le Grand, 565 .... H 5
50557 Lehigh, 739 .... E 4
50453 Leland, 223 .... F 2
51031 Le Mars⊙, 8,159 .... A 3
50851 Lenox, 1,215 .... D 7
50144 Leon⊙, 2,142 .... F 7
51242 Lester, 238 .... A 2
52754 Letts, 434 .... L 6
51544 Lewis, 526 .... C 6
52567 Libertyville, 329 .... K 7
52155 Lime Springs, 497 .... J 2
50146 Linden, 278 .... E 5
50147 Lineville, 385 .... G 7
51033 Linn Grove, 240 .... C 3
52253 Lisbon, 1,329 .... L 5
50148 Liscomb, 328 .... H 4
51243 Little Rock, 531 .... B 2
51545 Little Sioux, 239 .... B 5
50558 Livermore, 510 .... E 3
52635 Lockridge, 232 .... K 7
51546 Logan⊙, 1,526 .... B 5
51453 Lohrville, 553 .... D 4
52755 Lone Tree, 834 .... L 6
52756 Long Grove, 269 .... M 5
50149 Lorimor, 346 .... E 6
52254 Lost Nation, 547 .... M 5
50150 Lovilia, 640 .... H 6
52255 Lowden, 667 .... L 5
52757 Low Moor, 347 .... N 5
52156 Luana, 225 .... K 2
50151 Lucas, 247 .... G 6
50560 Lu Verne, 380 .... E 3
50153 Lynnville, 381 .... H 5
50561 Lytton, 378 .... D 4
51549 Macedonia, 330 .... C 6
50156 Madrid, 2,448 .... F 5
50157 Malcom, 388 .... H 5
50562 Mallard, 384 .... D 3
51551 Malvern, 1,158 .... B 7
52057 Manchester⊙, 4,641 .... L 3
51454 Manilla, 943 .... C 5
50456 Manly, 1,294 .... G 2
51455 Manning, 1,656 .... C 5
50563 Manson, 1,993 .... D 3
51034 Mapleton, 1,647 .... B 4
52060 Maquoketa⊙, 5,677 .... M 4
50565 Marathon, 447 .... C 3
50653 Marble Rock, 461 .... H 3
51035 Marcus, 1,272 .... B 3
52301 Marengo⊙, 2,235 .... J 5
52302 Marion, 18,028 .... K 4
52158 Marquette, 509 .... L 2
50158 Marshalltown⊙, 26,219 .... G 4
52305 Martelle, 240 .... L 4
50160 Martensdale, 306 .... F 6
50401 Mason City⊙, 30,491 .... G 2
50853 Massena, 433 .... D 6
51036 Maurice, 266 .... A 3
50161 Maxwell, 503 .... G 5
† 52773 Maysville, 989 .... M 5
50154 McCallsburg, 307 .... G 4
52758 McCausland, 226 .... M 5
52157 McGregor, 990 .... L 2
50455 McIntire, 234 .... H 2
52306 Mechanicsville, 989 .... L 5
52637 Mediapolis, 1,242 .... L 6
50162 Melbourne, 661 .... G 5
50163 Melcher, 913 .... G 6
51350 Melvin, 325 .... B 2
50164 Menlo, 391 .... E 5
51038 Merrill, 790 .... A 3
50457 Meservey, 354 .... G 3
52307 Middle, 402 .... K 5
52638 Middletown, 443 .... L 7
52064 Miles, 409 .... N 4
51351 Milford, 1,668 .... C 2
50166 Milo, 561 .... G 6
52570 Milton, 567 .... J 7
50167 Minburn, 378 .... E 5
51553 Minden, 433 .... C 6
50168 Mingo, 260 .... G 5
51555 Missouri Valley, 3,519 .... B 5
50485 Mitchell, 233 .... H 2
50169 Mitchellville, 1,341 .... G 5
51556 Modale, 297 .... B 5
51557 Mondamin, 420 .... B 5
52309 Monmouth, 257 .... M 4
52159 Monona, 1,395 .... L 2
50170 Monroe, 1,389 .... G 5
50171 Montezuma⊙, 1,353 .... H 5
52310 Monticello, 3,509 .... L 4
50173 Montour, 334 .... H 5
52759 Montpelier, 300 .... M 6
52639 Montrose, 735 .... L 7
† 52632 Mooar, 350 .... L 8
51558 Moorhead, 271 .... B 5
50566 Moorland, 269 .... E 4
52571 Moravia, 699 .... H 7
52640 Morning Sun, 906 .... L 6
52760 Moscow, 350 .... L 5
52572 Moulton, 763 .... H 7
50854 Mount Ayr⊙, 1,762 .... E 7
52641 Mount Pleasant⊙, 7,007 .... L 7
52314 Mount Vernon, 3,018 .... K 5
51039 Moville, 1,198 .... A 4
50174 Murray, 620 .... F 6
52761 Muscatine⊙, 22,405 .... L 6
52574 Mystic, 696 .... H 7
50658 Nashua, 1,712 .... J 3
51559 Neola, 968 .... B 6
50201 Nevada⊙, 4,952 .... G 5
52160 New Albin, 644 .... L 2
50568 Newell, 877 .... D 3
52315 Newhall, 701 .... K 5
50659 New Hampton⊙, 3,621 .... J 2
50660 New Hartford, 690 .... H 3
52645 New London, 1,900 .... L 7
51646 New Market, 501 .... D 7
50206 New Providence, 208 .... G 4
50207 New Sharon, 944 .... H 6
50208 Newton⊙, 15,619 .... H 5
52065 New Vienna, 392 .... L 3
50210 New Virginia, 452 .... F 6
52766 Nichols, 396 .... L 6
50458 Nora Springs, 1,337 .... H 2
52316 North English, 965 .... J 5
52317 North Liberty, 1,055 .... K 5
50459 Northwood⊙, 1,950 .... G 2
50211 Norwalk, 1,745 .... F 6
52318 Norway, 554 .... K 5
52319 Oakdale, 250 .... K 5
51560 Oakland, 1,603 .... C 6
52646 Oakville, 369 .... L 6
51354 Ocheyedan, 545 .... B 2
51458 Odebolt, 1,323 .... C 4
50662 Oelwein, 7,735 .... K 3
50212 Ogden, 1,661 .... E 4
51355 Okoboji, 361 .... C 2
52320 Olin, 710 .... L 5
52576 Ollie, 268 .... J 6
51040 Onawa⊙, 3,154 .... A 4
52321 Onslow, 253 .... M 4
51041 Orange City⊙, 3,572 .... A 2
50858 Orient, 324 .... E 6
† 51360 Orleans, 396 .... C 2
50461 Osage⊙, 3,815 .... H 2
50213 Osceola⊙, 3,124 .... F 6
52577 Oskaloosa⊙, 11,224 .... H 6
52161 Ossian, 847 .... K 2
50569 Otho, 581 .... E 4
52501 Ottumwa⊙, 29,610 .... J 6
52322 Oxford, 666 .... K 5
52323 Oxford Junction, 666 .... M 4
51561 Pacific Junction, 505 .... B 6
50571 Palmer, 264 .... D 3
52324 Palo, 430 .... K 4
51562 Panama, 221 .... B 5
50216 Panora, 982 .... E 5
† 52722 Panorama Park, 219 .... N 5
50665 Parkersburg, 1,631 .... H 3
50217 Paton, 329 .... E 4
51046 Paullina, 1,257 .... B 3
50219 Pella, 6,668 .... H 6
50220 Perry, 6,906 .... E 5
50221 Pershing, 425 .... G 6
51563 Persia, 316 .... B 5
51047 Peterson, 469 .... C 3
51048 Pierson, 421 .... B 3
50223 Pilot Mound, 214 .... F 4
51564 Pisgah, 286 .... B 5
50666 Plainfield, 446 .... J 3
50225 Pleasantville, 1,297 .... G 6
50464 Plymouth, 461 .... G 2
50574 Pocahontas⊙, 2,338 .... D 3
50226 Polk City, 715 .... F 5
50575 Pomeroy, 765 .... D 3
51565 Portsmouth, 239 .... C 5
52162 Postville, 1,546 .... K 2
50228 Prairie City, 1,141 .... G 5
50859 Prescott, 305 .... D 6
52069 Preston, 950 .... N 4
51245 Primghar⊙, 995 .... B 2
52768 Princeton, 633 .... N 5
52163 Protivin, 333 .... J 2
52584 Pulaski, 255 .... J 7
52326 Quasqueton, 448 .... K 4
51049 Quimby, 395 .... B 3
50230 Radcliffe, 548 .... G 4
50465 Rake, 324 .... F 2
51649 Randolph, 214 .... B 7
50667 Raymond, 582 .... J 4
50668 Readlyn, 616 .... J 3
50232 Reasnor, 284 .... G 5
50233 Redfield, 921 .... E 5
51566 Red Oak⊙, 6,210 .... C 6
50669 Reinbeck, 1,711 .... H 4
50576 Rembrandt, 250 .... C 3
51050 Remsen, 1,367 .... B 3
50577 Renwick, 429 .... E 3
50234 Rhodes, 347 .... G 5
50466 Riceville, 877 .... H 2
52585 Richland, 595 .... K 6
52165 Ridgeway, 218 .... K 2
50578 Ringsted, 509 .... D 2
50235 Rippey, 270 .... E 5
† 52722 Riverdale, 684 .... N 5
52327 Riverside, 758 .... K 6
51650 Riverton, 331 .... B 7
52328 Robins, 663 .... K 4
50468 Rockford, 902 .... H 2
51246 Rock Rapids⊙, 2,632 .... A 2
51247 Rock Valley, 2,205 .... A 2
50469 Rockwell, 923 .... G 3
50579 Rockwell City⊙, 2,396 .... D 4
50236 Roland, 803 .... F 4
50581 Rolfe, 767 .... D 3
50470 Rowan, 231 .... F 3
52329 Rowley, 241 .... K 4
51357 Royal, 469 .... C 2
50471 Rudd, 429 .... H 2
50237 Runnells, 354 .... G 5
50238 Russell, 591 .... G 7
51358 Ruthven, 708 .... D 2
50582 Rutland, 215 .... E 3
52330 Ryan, 343 .... K 4
52070 Sabula, 845 .... N 4
50583 Sac City⊙, 3,268 .... C 4
† 52001 Sageville, 338 .... M 3
50472 Saint Ansgar, 994 .... H 2
50240 Saint Charles, 443 .... F 6
52649 Salem, 458 .... K 7
51052 Salix, 387 .... A 4
51248 Sanborn, 1,465 .... B 2
51053 Schaller, 835 .... C 4
51461 Schleswig, 875 .... B 4
51462 Scranton, 751 .... D 4
51054 Sergeant Bluff, 1,153 .... A 4
52590 Seymour, 931 .... G 7
50475 Sheffield, 1,070 .... G 3
51570 Shelby, 868 .... C 5
50243 Sheldahl, 285 .... F 5
51201 Sheldon, 4,535 .... B 2
50670 Shell Rock, 1,159 .... H 3
52332 Shellsburg, 740 .... K 4
51601 Shenandoah, 5,968 .... C 7
51249 Sibley⊙, 2,749 .... B 2
51652 Sidney⊙, 1,061 .... B 7
52591 Sigourney⊙, 2,319 .... J 6
51571 Silver City, 272 .... B 6
51250 Sioux Center, 3,450 .... A 2
* 51101 Sioux City⊙, 85,925 .... A 3
Sioux City, ‡116,189 .... A 3
50585 Sioux Rapids, 813 .... C 3
50244 Slater, 1,094 .... F 5
51055 Sloan, 799 .... A 4
51056 Smithland, 293 .... B 4
51572 Soldier, 242 .... B 5
52333 Solon, 837 .... L 5
52335 South English, 218 .... J 6
51301 Spencer⊙, 10,278 .... C 2
52168 Spillville, 361 .... J 2
51360 Spirit Lake⊙, 3,014 .... C 2
52336 Springville, 970 .... L 4
50476 Stacyville, 598 .... H 2
50246 Stanhope, 482 .... F 4
51573 Stanton, 574 .... C 7
52337 Stanwood, 642 .... L 5
50247 State Center, 1,232 .... G 5
50672 Steamboat Rock, 394 .... G 4
52651 Stockport, 334 .... K 7
52769 Stockton, 222 .... M 5
50588 Storm Lake⊙, 8,591 .... C 3
50248 Story City, 2,104 .... F 4
50249 Stratford, 710 .... F 4
52076 Strawberry Point, 1,281 .... K 3
50250 Stuart, 1,354 .... E 6
50251 Sully, 685 .... H 5
50674 Sumner, 2,174 .... J 3
51058 Sutherland, 875 .... B 3
50477 Swaledale, 222 .... G 3
50590 Swea City, 774 .... E 2
52338 Swisher, 417 .... K 5
51653 Tabor, 957 .... B 7
52339 Tama, 3,000 .... H 5
51463 Templeton, 312 .... D 5
51364 Terril, 397 .... C 2
50478 Thompson, 600 .... F 2
50591 Thor, 212 .... E 3
50479 Thornton, 410 .... G 3
51654 Thurman, 230 .... B 7
52340 Tiffin, 299 .... K 5
50863 Tingley, 244 .... E 7
52772 Tipton⊙, 2,877 .... L 5
50480 Titonka, 599 .... E 2
52342 Toledo⊙, 2,361 .... H 4
50256 Tracy, 250 .... H 6
50675 Traer, 1,682 .... J 4
51575 Treynor, 472 .... B 6
50676 Tripoli, 1,345 .... J 3
50257 Truro, 359 .... F 6
51576 Underwood, 424 .... B 6
50258 Union, 484 .... G 4
† 52240 University Heights, 1,265 .... K 5
52595 University Park, 534 .... H 6
52345 Urbana, 552 .... K 4
50322 Urbandale, 14,434 .... F 5
51060 Ute, 512 .... B 4
51465 Vail, 486 .... C 4
52346 Van Horne, 613 .... J 4
50261 Van Meter, 464 .... E 5
50262 Van Wert, 244 .... F 7
50482 Ventura, 543 .... F 2
52347 Victor, 949 .... J 5
50864 Villisca, 1,402 .... C 7
52349 Vinton⊙, 4,845 .... J 4
52077 Volga, 305 .... L 3
52169 Wadena, 237 .... K 3
52773 Walcott, 989 .... M 5
52351 Walford, 286 .... K 5
52352 Walker, 622 .... K 4
51365 Wallingford, 245 .... D 2
51466 Wall Lake, 936 .... C 4
51577 Walnut, 870 .... C 6
52653 Wapello⊙, 1,873 .... L 6
50706 Washburn, 1,408 .... J 4
52353 Washington⊙, 6,317 .... K 6
51061 Washta, 319 .... B 3
* 50701 Waterloo⊙, 75,533 .... J 4
Waterloo, ‡132,916 .... J 4
52171 Waucoma, 357 .... J 2
50263 Waukee, 1,577 .... F 5
52172 Waukon⊙, 3,883 .... L 2
50677 Waverly⊙, 7,205 .... J 3
52654 Wayland, 702 .... K 6
51366 Webb, 234 .... D 3
50595 Webster City⊙, 8,488 .... F 4
52356 Wellman, 977 .... K 6
50680 Wellsburg, 754 .... H 4
50483 Wesley, 548 .... E 2
50597 West Bend, 865 .... D 3
52358 West Branch, 1,322 .... L 5
52655 West Burlington, 3,139 .... L 7
50265 West Des Moines, 16,441 .... F 5
52776 West Liberty, 2,296 .... L 5
† 51351 West Okoboji, 210 .... C 2
52656 West Point, 1,045 .... K 7
51467 Westside, 389 .... C 4
52175 West Union⊙, 2,624 .... K 3
50268 What Cheer, 868 .... J 6
52777 Wheatland, 832 .... M 5
51063 Whiting, 590 .... A 4
50598 Whittemore, 658 .... E 2
52360 Whittier, 270 .... K 4
50271 Williams, 456 .... F 3
52361 Williamsburg, 1,544 .... J 5
50272 Williamson, 216 .... G 6
52778 Wilton Junction, 1,873 .... M 5
50311 Windsor Heights, 6,303 .... F 5
52659 Winfield, 897 .... L 6
50273 Winterset⊙, 3,654 .... E 6
50682 Winthrop, 750 .... K 4
50484 Woden, 265 .... F 2
51579 Woodbine, 1,349 .... B 5
50276 Woodward, 1,010 .... E 5
50599 Woolstock, 222 .... F 3
52078 Worthington, 365 .... L 4
52362 Wyoming, 746 .... L 4
50277 Yale, 301 .... E 5
50278 Zearing, 535 .... G 4

⊙ County seat.
‡ Population of metropolitan area.
† Zip of nearest p.o.
* Multiple zips

Agriculture, Industry and Resources

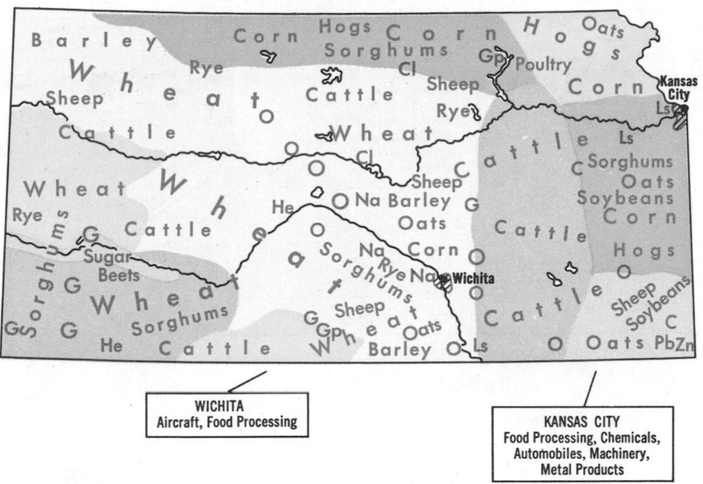

AREA 82,264 sq. mi.
POPULATION 2,249,071
CAPITAL Topeka
LARGEST CITY Wichita
HIGHEST POINT Mt. Sunflower 4,039 ft.
SETTLED IN 1831
ADMITTED TO UNION January 29, 1861
POPULAR NAME Sunflower State
STATE FLOWER Sunflower
STATE BIRD Western Meadowlark

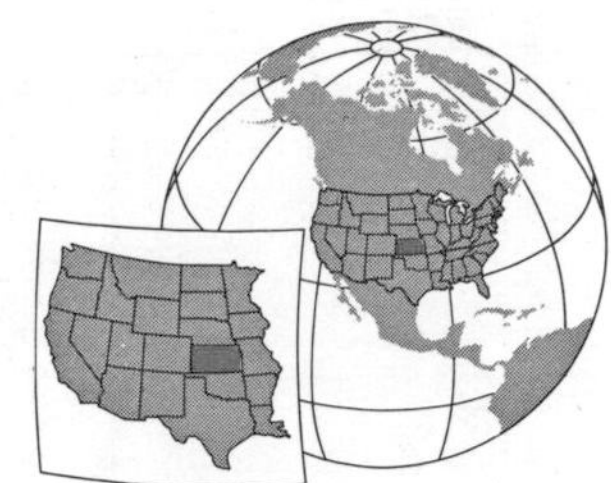

DOMINANT LAND USE

- Specialized Wheat
- Wheat, General Farming
- Wheat, Range Livestock
- Wheat, Grain Sorghums, Range Livestock
- Cattle Feed, Hogs
- Livestock, Cash Grain
- Livestock, Cash Grain, Dairy
- General Farming, Livestock, Cash Grain
- General Farming, Livestock, Special Crops
- Range Livestock

MAJOR MINERAL OCCURRENCES

C	Coal	Ls	Limestone
Cl	Clay	Na	Salt
G	Natural Gas	O	Petroleum
Gp	Gypsum	Pb	Lead
He	Helium	Zn	Zinc

Major Industrial Areas

Robert Leahey — Shostal Associates

Loaded with wheat for storage, a truck pulls onto a weighing platform at the Salina grain elevators. Wheat is grown here on such a scale that Kansas is known as the Breadbasket of the World.

COUNTIES

County, Pop.	Key
Allen, 15,043	G 4
Anderson, 8,501	G 3
Atchison, 19,165	G 2
Barber, 7,016	D 4
Barton, 30,663	D 3
Bourbon, 15,215	H 4
Brown, 11,685	G 2
Butler, 38,658	F 4
Chase, 3,408	F 3
Chautauqua, 4,642	F 4
Cherokee, 21,549	H 4
Cheyenne, 4,256	A 2
Clark, 2,896	C 4
Clay, 9,890	E 2
Cloud, 13,466	E 2
Coffey, 7,397	G 3
Comanche, 2,702	C 4
Cowley, 35,012	F 4
Crawford, 37,850	H 4
Decatur, 4,988	B 2
Dickinson, 19,993	E 3
Doniphan, 9,107	G 2
Douglas, 57,932	G 3
Edwards, 4,581	C 4
Elk, 3,858	F 4
Ellis, 24,730	C 3
Ellsworth, 6,146	D 3
Finney, 18,947	B 3
Ford, 22,587	C 4
Franklin, 19,548	G 3
Geary, 28,111	F 3
Gove, 3,940	B 3
Graham, 4,751	C 2
Grant, 5,961	A 4
Gray, 4,516	B 4
Greeley, 1,819	A 3
Greenwood, 9,141	F 4
Hamilton, 2,747	A 3
Harper, 7,871	D 4
Harvey, 27,236	E 3
Haskell, 3,672	B 4
Hodgeman, 2,662	C 3
Jackson, 10,342	G 2
Jefferson, 11,945	G 2
Jewell, 6,099	D 2
Johnson, 217,662	H 3
Kearny, 3,047	A 3
Kingman, 8,886	D 4
Kiowa, 4,088	C 4
Labette, 25,775	G 4
Lane, 2,707	B 3
Leavenworth, 53,340	G 2
Lincoln, 4,582	D 2
Linn, 7,770	H 3
Logan, 3,814	A 3
Lyon, 32,071	F 3
Marion, 13,935	E 3
Marshall, 13,139	F 2
McPherson, 24,778	E 3
Meade, 4,912	B 4
Miami, 19,254	H 3
Mitchell, 8,010	D 2
Montgomery, 39,949	G 4
Morris, 6,432	F 3
Morton, 3,576	A 4
Nemaha, 11,825	F 2
Neosho, 18,812	G 4
Ness, 4,791	C 3
Norton, 7,279	C 2
Osage, 13,352	G 3
Osborne, 6,416	D 2
Ottawa, 6,183	E 2
Pawnee, 8,484	C 3
Phillips, 7,888	C 2
Pottawatomie, 11,755	F 2
Pratt, 10,056	D 4
Rawlins, 4,393	A 2
Reno, 60,765	D 4
Republic, 8,498	E 2
Rice, 12,320	D 3
Riley, 56,788	F 2
Rooks, 7,628	C 2
Rush, 5,117	C 3
Russell, 9,428	D 3
Saline, 46,592	E 3
Scott, 5,606	B 3
Sedgwick, 350,694	E 4
Seward, 15,744	B 4
Shawnee, 155,322	G 2
Sheridan, 3,859	B 2
Sherman, 7,792	A 2
Smith, 6,757	D 2
Stafford, 5,943	D 3
Stanton, 2,287	A 4
Stevens, 4,198	A 4
Sumner, 23,553	E 4
Thomas, 7,501	A 2
Trego, 4,436	C 3
Wabaunsee, 6,397	F 3
Wallace, 2,215	A 3
Washington, 9,249	E 2
Wichita, 3,274	A 3
Wilson, 11,317	G 4
Woodson, 4,789	G 4
Wyandotte, 186,845	H 2

CITIES and TOWNS

	Zip	Name/Pop.	Key
	67510	Abbyville, 143	D 4
	67410	Abilene⊙, 6,661	E 3
	67414	Ada, 120	E 2
	66830	Admire, 144	F 3
	66930	Agenda, 107	E 2
	67621	Agra, 294	C 2
	67511	Albert, 235	C 3
	67512	Alden, 238	D 3
	67513	Alexander, 129	C 3
	66833	Allen, 175	F 3
	66401	Alma⊙, 905	F 2
	67622	Almena, 489	C 2
	67330	Altamont, 845	G 4
	66834	Alta Vista, 402	F 3
	67623	Alton, 214	D 2
	66710	Altoona, 475	G 4
	66835	Americus, 441	F 3
	67001	Andale, 500	E 4
	67002	Andover, 1,880	E 4
	67003	Anthony⊙, 2,653	D 4
	66711	Arcadia, 388	H 4
	67004	Argonia, 591	E 4
	67005	Arkansas City, 13,216	E 4
	67514	Arlington, 503	D 4
	66712	Arma, 1,348	H 4
	67831	Ashland⊙, 1,244	C 4
	67416	Assaria, 303	E 3
	66002	Atchison⊙, 12,565	G 2
	66932	Athol, 108	D 2
	67008	Atlanta, 216	F 4
	67009	Attica, 639	D 4
	67730	Atwood⊙, 1,658	B 2
	66402	Auburn, 261	G 3
	67010	Augusta, 5,977	F 4
	67417	Aurora, 120	E 2
	66403	Axtell, 456	F 2
	66404	Baileyville, 110	F 2
	66006	Baldwin City, 2,520	G 3
	67418	Barnard, 190	D 2
	66933	Barnes, 209	F 2
	67332	Bartlett, 138	G 4
	66007	Basehor, 724	G 2
	66713	Baxter Springs, 4,489	H 4
	67516	Bazine, 386	C 3
	66406	Beattie, 288	F 2
	67012	Beaumont, 135	F 4
	67013	Belle Plaine, 1,553	E 4
	66935	Belleville⊙, 3,063	E 2
	67420	Beloit⊙, 4,121	D 2
	67519	Belpre, 191	C 4
	66407	Belvue, 161	F 2
	67422	Bennington, 561	E 2
	67016	Bentley, 260	E 4
	67017	Benton, 517	E 4
	66408	Bern, 191	F 2
	67423	Beverly, 193	E 2
	67731	Bird City, 671	A 2
	67520	Bison, 285	C 3
	66010	Blue Mound, 308	H 3
	66411	Blue Rapids, 1,148	F 2
	67018	Bluff City, 109	E 4
	67625	Bogue, 257	C 2
	66012	Bonner Springs, 3,662	H 2
	67732	Brewster, 320	A 2
	66716	Bronson, 397	H 4
	67425	Brookville, 238	E 3
	67834	Bucklin, 771	C 4
	66013	Bucyrus, 196	H 3
	66717	Buffalo, 321	G 4
	67522	Buhler, 1,019	E 3
	67626	Bunker Hill, 181	D 3
	67019	Burden, 503	F 4
	67523	Burdett, 285	C 3
	66838	Burdick, 120	F 3
	66413	Burlingame, 999	G 3
	66839	Burlington⊙, 2,099	G 3
	66840	Burns, 268	F 3
	66936	Burr Oak, 426	D 2
	67020	Burrton, 808	E 3
	67427	Bushton, 397	D 3
	67022	Caldwell, 1,540	E 4
	67023	Cambridge, 110	F 4
	67333	Caney, 2,192	G 4
	67428	Canton, 893	E 3
	66414	Carbondale, 1,041	G 3
	66842	Cassoday, 123	F 3
	67627	Catharine, 126	C 3
	67430	Cawker City, 726	D 2
	67024	Cedar Vale, 665	F 4
	66415	Centralia, 511	F 2
	66720	Chanute, 10,341	G 4
	67431	Chapman, 1,132	E 3
	67524	Chase, 800	D 3
	67334	Chautauqua, 137	F 4
	67025	Cheney, 1,160	E 4
	66724	Cherokee, 790	H 4
	67335	Cherryvale, 2,609	G 4
	67336	Chetopa, 1,596	G 4
†	66762	Chicopee, 300	H 4
	87835	Cimarron⊙, 1,373	B 4
	66416	Circleville, 178	G 2
	67525	Claflin, 887	D 3
	67432	Clay Center⊙, 4,963	E 2
	67629	Clayton, 127	B 2
	67026	Clearwater, 1,435	E 4
	66937	Clifton, 718	E 2
	66938	Clyde, 946	E 2
	67028	Coats, 152	D 4
	67337	Coffeyville, 15,116	G 4
	67701	Colby⊙, 4,658	A 2
	67029	Coldwater⊙, 1,016	C 4
	67631	Collyer, 182	B 2
	66015	Colony, 382	G 3
	66725	Columbus⊙, 3,356	H 4
	67030	Colwich, 879	E 4
	66901	Concordia⊙, 7,221	E 2
	67031	Conway Springs, 1,153	E 4
	67836	Coolidge, 102	A 3
	67837	Copeland, 267	B 4
	66417	Corning, 162	F 2
	66845	Cottonwood Falls⊙, 987	F 3
	66846	Council Grove⊙, 2,403	F 3
	66939	Courtland, 403	E 2
	66728	Crestline, 102	H 4
	66940	Cuba, 290	E 2
†	67124	Cullison, 117	D 4
	67435	Culver, 148	E 3
	66016	Cummings, 826	G 2
	67035	Cunningham, 483	D 4
	67632	Damar, 245	C 2
	67340	Dearing, 338	G 4
	67838	Deerfield, 474	A 4
	66418	Delia, 168	G 2
	67436	Delphos, 599	E 2
	66419	Denison, 248	G 2
	67341	Dennis, 120	G 4
	66017	Denton, 162	G 2
	67037	Derby, 7,947	E 4
	66018	De Soto, 1,839	H 3
	67038	Dexter, 286	F 4
	67839	Dighton⊙, 1,540	B 3
	67801	Dodge City⊙, 14,127	B 4
	67634	Dorrance, 234	D 3
	67039	Douglass, 1,126	F 4
	66420	Dover, 122	G 3
	67437	Downs, 1,268	D 2
	67635	Dresden, 103	B 2
	66848	Dunlap, 102	F 3
	67438	Durham, 143	E 3
	66849	Dwight, 322	F 3
	66731	Earlton, 102	G 4
†	67201	Eastborough, 1,141	E 4
	66020	Easton, 435	G 2
	66021	Edgerton, 513	H 3
	67342	Edna, 418	G 4
	66022	Edwardsville, 619	H 2
	66023	Effingham, 605	G 2
	67041	Elbing, 128	E 3
	67042	El Dorado⊙, 12,308	F 4
	67361	Elgin, 115	F 4
	67344	Elk City, 432	G 4
	67345	Elk Falls, 124	F 4
	67950	Elkhart⊙, 2,089	A 4
	67526	Ellinwood, 2,416	D 3
	67637	Ellis, 2,137	C 3

(continued on following page)

(continued)

67439 Ellsworth⊙, 2,080 .... D 3
66850 Elmdale, 102 .... F 3
† 66603 Elmont, 112 .... G 2
66732 Elsmore, 116 .... G 4
66024 Elwood, 1,283 .... H 2
66422 Emmett, 156 .... F 2
66801 Emporia⊙, 23,327 .... F 3
67840 Englewood, 158 .... C 4
67841 Ensign, 237 .... B 4
67441 Enterprise, 868 .... E 3
66733 Erie⊙, 1,414 .... G 4
66941 Esbon, 206 .... D 2
66423 Eskridge, 589 .... F 3
66025 Eudora, 2,071 .... G 3
67045 Eureka⊙, 3,576 .... F 4
66424 Everest, 304 .... G 2
66425 Fairview, 283 .... G 2
67047 Fall River, 191 .... G 4
67442 Falun, 105 .... E 3
66851 Florence, 716 .... E 3
66026 Fontana, 160 .... H 3
67842 Ford, 246 .... C 4
66942 Formoso, 180 .... D 2
67843 Fort Dodge, 450 .... C 4
66027 Fort Leavenworth, 8,060 .... H 2
66701 Fort Scott⊙, 8,967 .... H 4
67844 Fowler, 588 .... B 4
66427 Frankfort, 960 .... F 2
66735 Franklin, 620 .... H 4
66736 Fredonia⊙, 3,080 .... G 4
66762 Frontenac, 2,223 .... H 4
66738 Fulton, 213 .... H 4
66739 Galena, 3,712 .... H 4
66740 Galesburg, 146 .... G 4
67443 Galva, 522 .... E 3
67846 Garden City⊙, 14,708 .... B 4
67050 Garden Plain, 678 .... E 4
66030 Gardner, 1,839 .... H 3
67529 Garfield, 261 .... C 3
66741 Garland, 125 .... H 4
66032 Garnett⊙, 3,169 .... G 3
66742 Gas, 438 .... G 4
67638 Gaylord, 211 .... D 2
67444 Geneseo, 453 .... D 3
67051 Geuda Springs, 223 .... E 4
66743 Girard⊙, 2,591 .... H 4
67639 Glade, 180 .... C 2
67445 Glasco, 767 .... E 2
67446 Glen Elder, 422 .... D 2
67052 Goddard, 955 .... E 4
67053 Goessel, 386 .... E 3
66428 Goff, 207 .... G 2
67735 Goodland⊙, 5,510 .... A 2
67640 Gorham, 379 .... D 3
67736 Gove⊙, 172 .... B 3
67737 Grainfield, 374 .... B 2
† 66441 Grandview Plaza, 734 .... F 2
66429 Grantville, 190 .... G 2
67530 Great Bend⊙, 16,133 .... D 3
66033 Greeley, 368 .... G 3
67447 Green, 163 .... E 2
66943 Greenleaf, 448 .... E 2
67054 Greensburg⊙, 1,907 .... C 4
67346 Grenola, 290 .... F 4
66852 Gridley, 328 .... G 3
67738 Grinnell, 449 .... B 2
67448 Gypsum, 391 .... E 3
66944 Haddam, 289 .... E 2
66744 Hallowell, 135 .... H 4
67056 Halstead, 1,716 .... E 4
66853 Hamilton, 349 .... F 4
66945 Hanover, 793 .... F 2
67849 Hanston, 282 .... C 3
67057 Hardtner, 300 .... D 4
67058 Harper, 1,665 .... D 4
66854 Hartford, 478 .... F 3
66431 Harveyville, 279 .... F 3
67347 Havana, 144 .... G 4
67543 Haven, 1,146 .... E 4
66432 Havensville, 163 .... F 2
67059 Haviland, 705 .... C 4
67601 Hays⊙, 15,396 .... C 3
67060 Haysville, 6,483 .... E 4
67061 Hazelton, 176 .... D 4
67850 Healy, 251 .... B 3
66746 Hepler, 152 .... H 4
67449 Herington, 3,165 .... E 3
67739 Herndon, 268 .... B 2
67062 Hesston, 1,926 .... E 3
66434 Hiawatha⊙, 3,365 .... G 2
66035 Highland, 899 .... G 2
67642 Hill City⊙, 2,071 .... C 2
67063 Hillsboro, 2,730 .... E 3
66036 Hillsdale, 250 .... H 3
67544 Hoisington, 3,710 .... D 3
67851 Holcomb, 272 .... B 3
66436 Holton⊙, 3,063 .... G 2
67450 Holyrood, 593 .... D 3
66438 Home, 120 .... F 2
67451 Hope, 438 .... E 3
† 67879 Horace, 137 .... A 3
66439 Horton, 2,177 .... G 2
67349 Howard⊙, 918 .... F 4
67740 Hoxie⊙, 1,419 .... B 2
66440 Hoyt, 420 .... G 2
67545 Hudson, 181 .... D 3
67951 Hugoton⊙, 2,739 .... A 4
66748 Humboldt, 2,249 .... G 4
67452 Hunter, 150 .... D 2
66038 Huron, 106 .... G 2
67501 Hutchinson⊙, 36,885 .... D 3
67301 Independence⊙, 10,347 .... G 4
67853 Ingalls, 235 .... B 4
67546 Inman, 836 .... E 3
66749 Iola⊙, 6,493 .... G 4
67065 Isabel, 147 .... D 4
67066 Iuka, 210 .... D 4
66948 Jamestown, 470 .... E 2
67643 Jennings, 224 .... B 2
67854 Jetmore⊙, 936 .... B 3
66949 Jewell, 569 .... D 2
67855 Johnson⊙, 1,038 .... A 4
66441 Junction City⊙, 19,018 .... F 2
67454 Kanopolis, 626 .... D 3
67741 Kanorado, 278 .... A 2
* 66101 Kansas City⊙, 168,213 .... H 2
Kansas City, ‡1,253,916 .... H 2
67067 Kechi, 229 .... E 4
67857 Kendall, 160 .... A 4
66951 Kensington, 653 .... C 2
66039 Kincaid, 189 .... G 3
67068 Kingman⊙, 3,622 .... D 4
67547 Kinsley⊙, 2,212 .... C 4
67070 Kiowa, 1,414 .... D 4
67644 Kirwin, 293 .... C 2
67859 Kismet, 294 .... B 4
67350 Labette, 105 .... G 4
67548 La Crosse⊙, 1,583 .... C 3
66040 La Cygne, 989 .... H 3
66750 Lafontaine, 140 .... G 4
66751 La Harpe, 509 .... G 4
67860 Lakin⊙, 1,570 .... A 4
66041 Lancaster, 279 .... G 2
66042 Lane, 254 .... G 3
66043 Lansing, 3,797 .... H 2
67550 Larned⊙, 4,567 .... C 3
67072 Latham, 156 .... F 4
66044 Lawrence⊙, 45,698 .... G 3
66048 Leavenworth⊙, 25,147 .... H 2
66206 Leawood, 10,349 .... H 3
66952 Lebanon, 517 .... D 2
66856 Lebo, 589 .... G 3
66050 Lecompton, 434 .... G 2
67073 Lehigh, 168 .... E 3
67645 Lenora, 439 .... C 2
67074 Leon, 510 .... F 4

KANSAS

SCALE

0 5 10 20 30 40 50 MI.

0 5 10 20 30 40 50 KM.

State Capitals ⊛

County Seats ⊙

Zip	Place, population	Key
66449	Leonardville, 412	F 2
67861	Leoti⊙, 1,916	A 3
66857	Le Roy, 551	G 3
67743	Levant, 425	A 2
67552	Lewis, 525	C 4
67901	Liberal⊙, 13,471	B 4
67351	Liberty, 185	G 4
67553	Liebenthal, 169	C 3
67455	Lincoln⊙, 1,582	D 2
66858	Lincolnville, 218	F 3
67456	Lindsborg, 2,764	E 3
66953	Linn, 388	E 2
66052	Linwood, 323	G 2
67457	Little River, 493	E 3
67646	Logan, 760	C 2
67647	Long Island, 195	C 2
67352	Longton, 304	F 4
67459	Lorraine, 153	D 3
66859	Lost Springs, 103	E 3
66053	Louisburg, 1,033	H 3
66450	Louisville, 204	F 2
67648	Lucas, 524	D 2
67649	Luray, 303	D 2
66451	Lyndon⊙, 958	G 3
67554	Lyons⊙, 4,355	D 3
67557	Macksville, 484	D 4
66860	Madison, 1,061	F 3
66955	Mahaska, 122	E 2
67101	Maize, 785	E 4
66502	Manhattan⊙, 27,575	F 2
66956	Mankato⊙, 1,287	D 2
67862	Manter, 219	A 4
66507	Maple Hill, 327	F 2
66754	Mapleton, 112	H 3
67863	Marienthal, 120	A 3
66861	Marion⊙, 2,052	F 3
67464	Marquette, 578	E 3
66508	Marysville⊙, 3,588	F 2
66509	Mayetta, 246	G 2
67103	Mayfield, 110	E 4
67556	McCracken, 333	C 3
66753	McCune, 487	G 4
67745	McDonald, 269	A 2
66501	McFarland, 209	F 2
66054	McLouth, 623	G 2
67460	McPherson⊙, 10,851	E 3
67864	Meade⊙, 1,899	B 4
67104	Medicine Lodge⊙, 2,545	D 4
67558	Medora, 110	E 3
66510	Melvern, 455	G 3
66512	Meriden, 472	G 2
66203	Merriam, 10,851	H 3

Topography

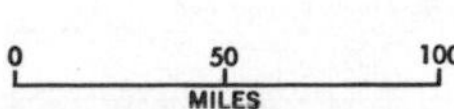

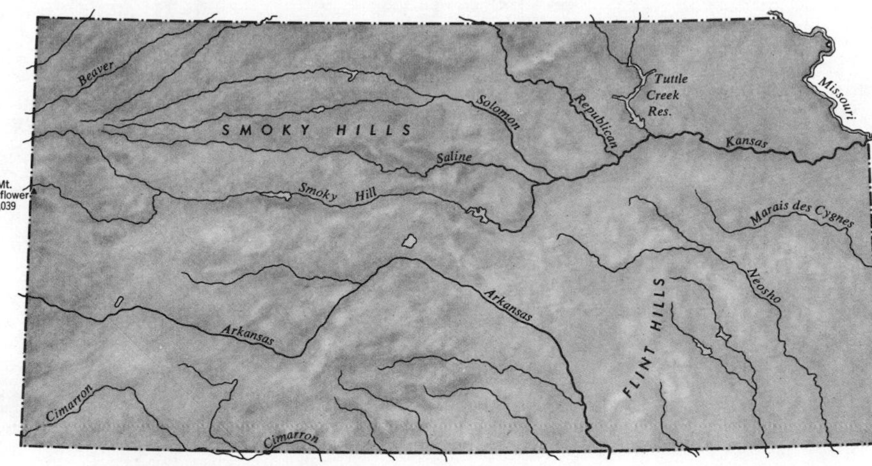

5,000 m. 16,404 ft. | 2,000 m. 6,562 ft. | 1,000 m. 3,281 ft. | 500 m. 1,640 ft. | 200 m. 656 ft. | 100 m. 328 ft. | Sea Level | Below

Zip	Place, population	Key
67105	Milan, 162	E 4
66514	Milford, 296	F 2
67466	Miltonvale, 718	E 2
67467	Minneapolis⊙, 1,971	E 2
67865	Minneola, 630	C 4
66222	Mission, 8,376	H 2
67353	Moline, 555	F 4
67867	Montezuma, 606	B 4
66755	Moran, 550	G 4
67468	Morganville, 257	E 2
67650	Morland, 300	B 2
66515	Morrill, 308	G 2
66958	Morrowville, 201	E 2
67952	Moscow, 228	A 4
66056	Mound City⊙, 714	H 3
67107	Moundridge, 1,271	E 3
67354	Mound Valley, 467	G 4
67108	Mount Hope, 665	E 4
66758	Mulberry, 622	H 4
67109	Mullinville, 376	C 4
67110	Mulvane, 3,185	E 4
66959	Munden, 123	E 2
† 67601	Munjor, 200	C 3
66058	Muscotah, 206	G 2
66960	Narka, 130	E 2
67112	Nashville, 107	D 4
67651	Natoma, 603	D 2
66757	Neodesha, 3,295	G 4
66758	Neosho Falls, 184	G 3
66864	Neosho Rapids, 234	F 3
67560	Ness City⊙, 1,756	C 3
66516	Netawaka, 192	G 2
67470	New Cambria, 160	E 3
67114	Newton⊙, 15,439	E 3
67561	Nickerson, 1,187	D 3
67653	Norcatur, 284	B 2
67117	North Newton, 963	E 3
67654	Norton⊙, 3,627	C 2
66060	Nortonville, 727	G 2
67118	Norwich, 414	E 4
67748	Oakley⊙, 2,327	B 2
67749	Oberlin⊙, 2,291	B 2
67562	Odin, 117	D 3
67563	Offerle, 212	C 4
67656	Ogallah, 110	C 3
66517	Ogden, 1,491	F 2
66518	Oketo, 133	F 2
66061	Olathe⊙, 17,917	H 3
67564	Olmitz, 161	D 3
66865	Olpe, 453	F 3
66520	Olsburg, 151	F 2
66521	Onaga, 761	F 2
66522	Oneida, 112	G 2
66760	Opolis, 160	H 4
66523	Osage City, 2,600	G 3
66064	Osawatomie, 4,294	H 3
67473	Osborne⊙, 1,980	D 2
66066	Oskaloosa⊙, 955	G 2
67356	Oswego⊙, 2,200	G 4
67565	Otis, 387	C 3
66067	Ottawa⊙, 11,036	G 3
66524	Overbrook, 748	G 3
66204	Overland Park, 76,623	H 3
67119	Oxford, 1,113	E 4
66070	Ozawkie, 137	G 2
67657	Palco, 398	C 2
66962	Palmer, 166	E 2
66071	Paola⊙, 4,622	H 3
67658	Paradise, 145	D 2
67751	Park, 178	B 2
67219	Park City, 2,529	E 4
66072	Parker, 255	H 3
67357	Parsons, 13,015	G 4
67566	Partridge, 302	D 4
66619	Pauline, 800	G 3
67567	Pawnee Rock, 442	D 3
66526	Paxico, 216	F 2
66866	Peabody, 1,368	E 3
67120	Peck, 150	E 4
66073	Perry, 664	G 2
67360	Peru, 289	F 4
67660	Pfeifer, 175	C 3
67661	Phillipsburg⊙, 3,241	C 2
67122	Piedmont, 116	F 4
67868	Pierceville, 175	B 4
66761	Piqua, 107	G 4
66762	Pittsburg, 20,171	H 4
67869	Plains, 857	B 4
67663	Plainville, 2,627	C 2
66075	Pleasanton, 1,216	H 3
67568	Plevna, 124	D 4
66076	Pomona, 541	G 3
67474	Portis, 178	D 2
67123	Potwin, 497	F 4
66527	Powhattan, 111	G 2
67664	Prairie View, 201	C 2
66208	Prairie Village, 28,138	H 2
67124	Pratt⊙, 6,736	D 4
66767	Prescott, 222	H 3
67569	Preston, 239	D 4
67570	Pretty Prairie, 561	D 4
66078	Princeton, 159	G 3
67127	Protection, 673	C 4
66528	Quenemo, 429	G 3
67752	Quinter, 930	B 2
67475	Ramona, 121	E 3
66963	Randall, 195	D 2
66554	Randolph, 106	F 2
67572	Ransom, 416	C 3
66079	Rantoul, 163	G 3
67573	Raymond, 133	D 3
66868	Reading, 247	F 3
66769	Redfield, 138	H 4
66964	Republic, 243	E 2
66529	Reserve, 117	G 2
67753	Rexford, 231	B 2
66080	Richmond, 464	G 3
66531	Riley, 668	F 2
66770	Riverton, 500	H 4
66532	Robinson, 278	G 2
† 66205	Roeland Park, 9,974	H 2
67954	Rolla, 400	A 4
67132	Rosalia, 130	F 4
67133	Rose Hill, 387	E 4
66533	Rossville, 934	G 2
67476	Roxbury, 110	E 3
67574	Rozel, 236	C 3
67575	Rush Center, 237	C 3
67665	Russell⊙, 5,371	D 3
66534	Sabetha, 2,376	G 2
67756	Saint Francis⊙, 1,725	A 2
66535	Saint George, 241	F 2
67576	Saint John⊙, 1,477	D 3
66536	Saint Marys, 1,434	G 2
66771	Saint Paul, 804	G 4
67401	Salina⊙, 37,714	E 3
67870	Satanta, 1,161	B 4
66772	Savonburg, 109	G 4
67134	Sawyer, 164	D 4
66773	Scammon, 457	H 4
66966	Scandia, 567	E 2
67667	Schoenchen, 182	C 3
67871	Scott City⊙, 4,001	B 3
66537	Scranton, 575	G 3
67361	Sedan⊙, 1,555	F 4
67135	Sedgwick, 1,083	E 4
67757	Selden, 271	B 2
66538	Seneca⊙, 2,182	F 2
66081	Severance, 128	G 2
67137	Severy, 384	F 4
67872	Shallow Water, 106	B 3
67138	Sharon, 265	D 4
67758	Sharon Springs⊙, 1,012	A 3
66203	Shawnee, 20,482	H 2
67874	Shields, 110	B 3
66539	Silver Lake, 811	G 2
67478	Simpson, 131	E 2
66967	Smith Center⊙, 2,389	D 2
67479	Smolan, 175	E 3
66540	Soldier, 173	G 2
67480	Solomon, 973	E 3
67140	South Haven, 413	E 4
† 67501	South Hutchinson, 1,879	D 3
67876	Spearville, 738	C 4
66083	Spring Hill, 1,186	H 3
67578	Stafford, 1,414	D 4
66084	Stanley, 450	H 3
66775	Stark, 124	G 4
67579	Sterling, 2,312	D 3
66085	Stilwell, 350	H 3
67669	Stockton⊙, 1,818	C 2
66869	Strong City, 545	F 3
67877	Sublette⊙, 1,208	B 4
66541	Summerfield, 254	F 2
67143	Sun City, 119	D 4
66019	Sunflower, 1,744	H 3
67363	Sycamore, 125	G 4
67581	Sylvia, 390	D 4
67878	Syracuse⊙, 1,720	A 3
67482	Talmage, 125	E 2
67483	Tampa, 154	E 3
66542	Tecumseh, 270	G 2
67484	Tescott, 393	E 2
66776	Thayer, 430	G 4
67582	Timken, 123	C 3
67485	Tipton, 315	D 2
66086	Tonganoxie, 1,717	G 2
* 66601	Topeka (cap.)⊙, 125,011	G 2
	Topeka, ‡155,322	G 2
66777	Toronto, 431	G 4
67144	Towanda, 1,190	E 4
66778	Treece, 225	H 4
67879	Tribune⊙, 1,013	A 3
66087	Troy⊙, 1,047	G 2
67583	Turon, 430	D 4
67364	Tyro, 206	G 4
67146	Udall, 668	E 4
67880	Ulysses⊙, 3,779	A 4
66779	Uniontown, 286	G 4
67584	Utica, 297	B 3
67147	Valley Center, 2,551	E 4
66088	Valley Falls, 1,169	G 2
66544	Vermillion, 191	F 2
67671	Victoria, 1,246	C 3
67149	Viola, 193	E 4
66870	Virgil, 179	F 4
67672	WaKeeney⊙, 2,334	C 2
67487	Wakefield, 583	E 2
67673	Waldo, 123	D 2
67761	Wallace, 112	A 3
66780	Walnut, 330	G 4
67151	Walton, 211	E 3
66547	Wamego, 2,507	F 2
66968	Washington⊙, 1,584	F 2
66548	Waterville, 632	F 2
66090	Wathena, 1,150	H 2
66871	Waverly, 510	G 3
66781	Weir, 740	H 4
66091	Welda, 149	G 3
67152	Wellington⊙, 8,072	E 4
66092	Wellsville, 1,183	G 3
67762	Weskan, 350	A 3
66782	West Mineral, 232	H 4
66549	Westmoreland⊙, 485	F 2
66093	Westphalia, 185	G 3
67869	West Plains (Plains), 857	B 4
66550	Wetmore, 392	G 2
66551	Wheaton, 106	F 2
66872	White City, 458	F 3
66094	White Cloud, 210	G 2
67154	Whitewater, 520	E 4
66552	Whiting, 256	G 2
* 67201	Wichita⊙, 276,554	E 4
	Wichita, ‡389,352	E 4
† 66601	Willard, 124	G 2
66095	Williamsburg, 286	G 3
66873	Wilsey, 169	F 3
67490	Wilson, 870	D 3
66097	Winchester, 492	G 2
67491	Windom, 183	E 3
67156	Winfield⊙, 11,405	F 4
67764	Winona, 293	A 2
67492	Woodbine, 170	E 3
67675	Woodston, 211	C 2
67882	Wright, 173	C 4
66783	Yates Center⊙, 1,967	G 4
67585	Yoder, 155	E 4
67159	Zenda, 142	D 4
67676	Zurich, 189	C 2

⊙ County seat.
‡ Population of metropolitan area.
† Zip of nearest p.o.
* Multiple zips

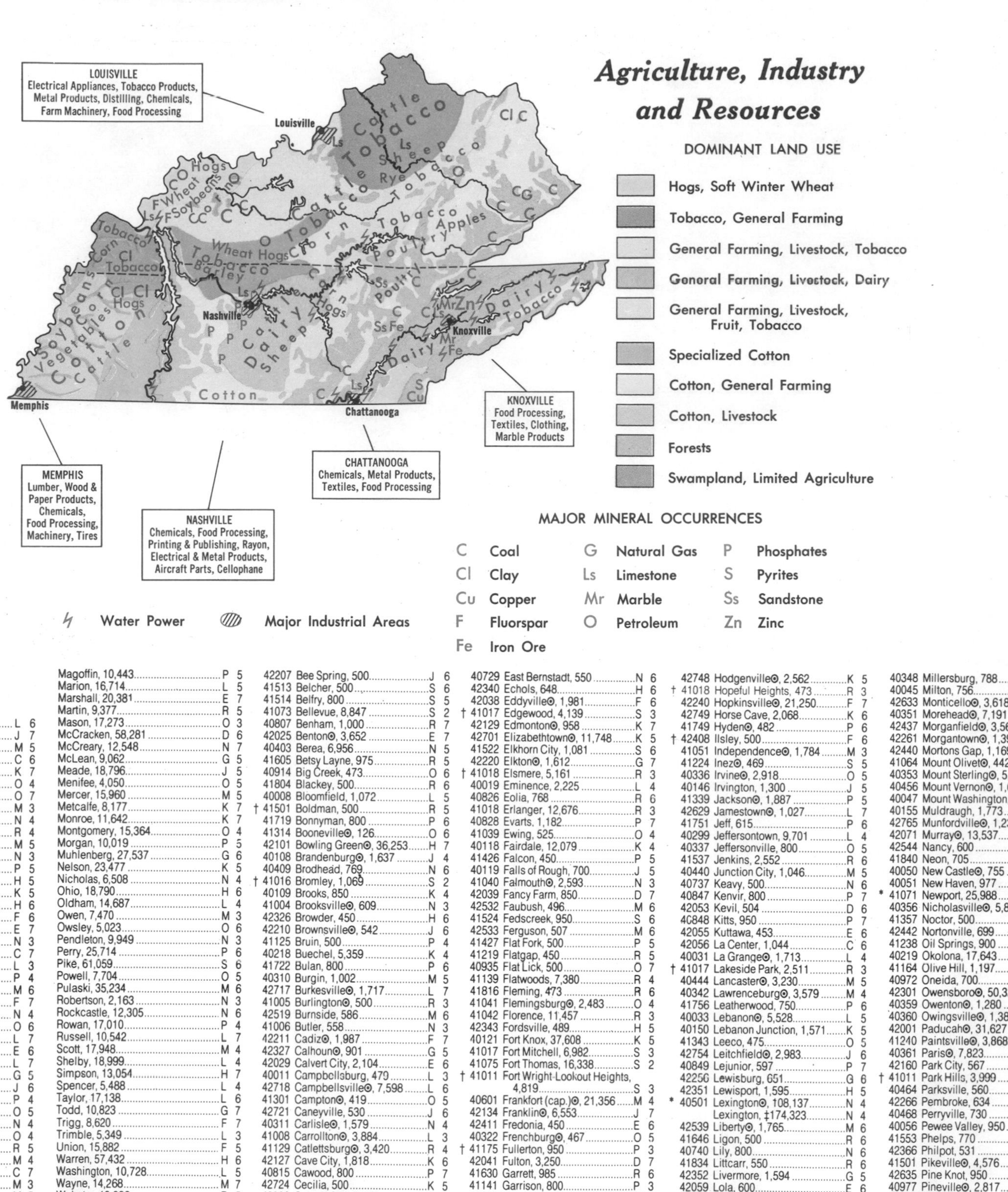

KENTUCKY

COUNTIES

Adair, 13,037 L 6
Allen, 12,598 J 7
Anderson, 9,358 M 5
Ballard, 8,276 C 6
Barren, 28,677 K 7
Bath, 9,235 O 4
Bell, 31,087 O 7
Boone, 32,812 M 3
Bourbon, 18,476 N 4
Boyd, 52,376 R 4
Boyle, 21,090 M 5
Bracken, 7,227 N 3
Breathitt, 14,221 P 5
Breckinridge, 14,789 H 5
Bullitt, 26,090 K 5
Butler, 9,723 H 6
Caldwell, 13,179 F 6
Calloway, 27,692 E 7
Campbell, 88,501 N 3
Carlisle, 5,354 C 7
Carroll, 8,523 L 3
Carter, 19,850 P 4
Casey, 12,930 M 6
Christian, 56,224 F 7
Clark, 24,090 N 4
Clay, 18,481 O 6
Clinton, 8,174 L 7
Crittenden, 8,493 E 6
Cumberland, 6,850 L 7
Daviess, 79,486 G 5
Edmonson, 8,751 J 6
Elliott, 5,933 P 4
Estill, 12,752 O 5
Fayette, 174,323 N 4
Fleming, 11,366 O 4
Floyd, 35,889 R 5
Franklin, 34,481 M 4
Fulton, 10,183 C 7
Gallatin, 4,134 M 3
Garrard, 9,457 M 5
Grant, 9,999 M 3
Graves, 30,939 D 7
Grayson, 16,445 J 5
Green, 10,350 K 6
Greenup, 33,192 R 3
Hancock, 7,080 H 5
Hardin, 78,421 K 5
Harlan, 37,370 P 7
Harrison, 14,158 N 4
Hart, 13,980 K 6
Henderson, 36,031 F 5
Henry, 10,910 L 4
Hickman, 6,264 C 7
Hopkins, 38,167 F 6
Jackson, 10,005 N 6
Jefferson, 695,055 K 4
Jessamine, 17,430 M 5
Johnson, 17,539 R 5
Kenton, 129,440 M 3
Knott, 14,698 R 6
Knox, 23,689 O 7
Larue, 10,672 K 5
Laurel, 27,386 N 6
Lawrence, 10,726 R 4
Lee, 6,587 O 5
Leslie, 11,623 P 6
Letcher, 23,165 R 6
Lewis, 12,355 P 3
Lincoln, 16,663 M 6
Livingston, 7,596 E 6
Logan, 21,793 H 7
Lyon, 5,562 E 6
Madison, 42,730 N 5
Magoffin, 10,443 P 5
Marion, 16,714 L 5
Marshall, 20,381 E 7
Martin, 9,377 R 5
Mason, 17,273 O 3
McCracken, 58,281 D 6
McCreary, 12,548 N 7
McLean, 9,062 G 5
Meade, 18,796 J 5
Menifee, 4,050 O 5
Mercer, 15,960 M 5
Metcalfe, 8,177 K 7
Monroe, 11,642 K 7
Montgomery, 15,364 O 4
Morgan, 10,019 P 5
Muhlenberg, 27,537 G 6
Nelson, 23,477 K 5
Nicholas, 6,508 N 4
Ohio, 18,790 H 6
Oldham, 14,687 L 4
Owen, 7,470 M 3
Owsley, 5,023 O 6
Pendleton, 9,949 N 3
Perry, 25,714 P 6
Pike, 61,059 S 6
Powell, 7,704 O 5
Pulaski, 35,234 M 6
Robertson, 2,163 N 3
Rockcastle, 12,305 N 6
Rowan, 17,010 P 4
Russell, 10,542 L 7
Scott, 17,948 M 4
Shelby, 18,999 L 4
Simpson, 13,054 H 7
Spencer, 5,488 L 4
Taylor, 17,138 L 6
Todd, 10,823 G 7
Trigg, 8,620 F 7
Trimble, 5,349 L 3
Union, 15,882 F 5
Warren, 57,432 H 6
Washington, 10,728 L 5
Wayne, 14,268 M 7
Webster, 13,282 F 5
Whitley, 24,145 N 7
Wolfe, 5,669 O 5
Woodford, 14,434 M 4

CITIES and TOWNS

Zip *Name/Pop.* *Key*

42202 Adairville, 973 H 7
41510 Aflex, 475 S 5
42602 Albany⊙, 1,891 L 7
41001 Alexandria⊙, 3,844 N 3
41601 Allen, 724 R 5
40223 Anchorage, 1,477 K 4
40402 Annville, 500 O 6
40902 Arjay, 975 O 7
42021 Arlington, 549 D 7
41101 Ashland, 29,245 R 4
Ashland-Huntington, ‡253,743 R 4
42206 Auburn, 1,160 H 7
† 40201 Audubon Park, 1,862 K 4
41002 Augusta, 1,434 N 3
41602 Auxier, 900 R 5
41603 Banner, 550 R 5
40906 Barbourville⊙, 3,549 O 7
40004 Bardstown⊙, 5,816 L 5
42023 Bardwell⊙, 1,049 D 7
42024 Barlow, 746 D 6
41311 Beattyville⊙, 923 O 5
41203 Beauty, 800 S 5
42320 Beaver Dam, 2,622 H 6
40006 Bedford⊙, 780 L 3
40359 Beechwood, 1,788 K 4
42207 Bee Spring, 500 J 6
41513 Belcher, 500 S 6
41514 Belfry, 800 S 5
41073 Bellevue, 8,847 S 2
40807 Benham, 1,000 R 7
42025 Benton⊙, 3,652 E 7
40403 Berea, 6,956 N 5
41605 Betsy Layne, 975 R 5
40914 Big Creek, 473 O 6
41804 Blackey, 500 R 6
40008 Bloomfield, 1,072 L 5
† 41501 Boldman, 500 R 5
41719 Bonnyman, 800 P 6
41314 Booneville⊙, 126 O 6
42101 Bowling Green⊙, 36,253 H 7
40108 Brandenburg⊙, 1,637 J 4
40409 Brodhead, 769 N 6
† 41016 Bromley, 1,069 S 2
40109 Brooks, 850 K 4
41004 Brooksville⊙, 609 N 3
42326 Browder, 450 H 6
42210 Brownsville⊙, 542 J 6
41125 Bruin, 500 P 4
40218 Buechel, 5,359 K 4
41722 Bulan, 800 P 6
40310 Burgin, 1,002 M 5
42717 Burkesville⊙, 1,717 L 7
41005 Burlington⊙, 500 R 3
42519 Burnside, 586 M 6
41006 Butler, 558 N 3
42211 Cadiz⊙, 1,987 F 7
42327 Calhoun⊙, 901 G 5
42029 Calvert City, 2,104 E 6
40011 Campbellsburg, 479 L 3
42718 Campbellsville⊙, 7,598 L 6
41301 Campton⊙, 419 O 5
42721 Caneyville, 530 J 6
40311 Carlisle⊙, 1,579 N 4
41008 Carrollton⊙, 3,884 L 3
41129 Catlettsburg⊙, 3,420 R 4
42127 Cave City, 1,818 K 6
40815 Cawood, 800 P 7
42724 Cecilia, 500 K 5
42330 Central City, 3,455 G 6
41727 Chavies, 500 P 6
42726 Clarkson, 660 J 6
42404 Clay, 1,426 F 6
40312 Clay City, 983 O 5
40313 Clearfield, 550 P 4
42031 Clinton⊙, 1,618 D 7
40414 Clover Bottom, 600 N 5
40111 Cloverport, 1,388 H 5
41076 Cold Spring, 5,348 T 3
42728 Columbia⊙, 3,234 L 6
41729 Combs, 900 P 6
42609 Cooper, 500 M 7
40701 Corbin, 7,317 N 7
42406 Corydon, 880 F 5
* 41011 Covington, 52,535 S 2
40419 Crab Orchard, 861 M 6
† 41016 Crescent Springs, 1,662 R 2
† 41076 Crestview, 657 S 2
† 41017 Crestview Hills, 1,114 R 3
42217 Crofton, 631 G 6
42034 Crutchfield, 500 D 7
40823 Cumberland, 3,317 R 6
42035 Cunningham, 700 D 7
41031 Cynthiana⊙, 6,356 N 4
41733 Daisy, 500 P 6
40422 Danville⊙, 11,542 M 5
42408 Dawson Springs, 2,830 F 6
41074 Dayton, 8,691 T 2
42409 Dixon⊙, 572 F 5
41520 Dorton, 750 R 6
42337 Drakesboro, 907 H 6
41035 Dry Ridge, 1,100 M 3
42410 Earlington, 2,321 F 6
40729 East Bernstadt, 550 N 6
42340 Echols, 648 H 6
42038 Eddyville⊙, 1,981 F 6
† 41017 Edgewood, 4,139 S 3
42129 Edmonton⊙, 958 K 7
42701 Elizabethtown⊙, 11,748 K 5
41522 Elkhorn City, 1,081 S 6
42220 Elkton⊙, 1,612 G 7
† 41018 Elsmere, 5,161 R 3
40019 Eminence, 2,225 L 4
40826 Eolia, 768 R 6
41018 Erlanger, 12,676 R 3
40828 Evarts, 1,182 P 7
41039 Ewing, 525 O 4
40118 Fairdale, 12,079 K 4
41426 Falcon, 450 P 5
40119 Falls of Rough, 700 J 5
41040 Falmouth⊙, 2,593 N 3
42039 Fancy Farm, 850 D 7
42532 Faubush, 496 M 6
41524 Fedscreek, 950 S 6
42533 Ferguson, 507 M 6
41427 Flat Fork, 500 P 5
41219 Flatgap, 450 R 5
40935 Flat Lick, 500 O 7
41139 Flatwoods, 7,380 R 4
41816 Fleming, 473 R 6
41041 Flemingsburg⊙, 2,483 O 4
41042 Florence, 11,457 R 3
42343 Fordsville, 489 H 5
40121 Fort Knox, 37,608 K 5
41017 Fort Mitchell, 6,982 S 3
41075 Fort Thomas, 16,338 S 2
† 41011 Fort Wright-Lookout Heights, 4,819 S 3
40601 Frankfort (cap.)⊙, 21,356 M 4
42134 Franklin⊙, 6,553 J 7
42411 Fredonia, 450 E 6
40322 Frenchburg⊙, 467 O 5
† 41175 Fullerton, 950 P 3
42041 Fulton, 3,250 D 7
41630 Garrett, 985 R 6
41141 Garrison, 800 P 3
40324 Georgetown⊙, 8,629 M 4
40943 Girdler, 500 O 7
42141 Glasgow⊙, 11,301 J 7
41046 Glencoe, 500 M 3
42232 Gracey, 450 F 7
42344 Graham, 500 G 6
41142 Grahn, 450 P 4
40734 Gray, 800 O 7
40434 Gray Hawk, 500 N 6
41143 Grayson⊙, 2,184 R 4
42743 Greensburg⊙, 1,990 K 6
41144 Greenup⊙, 1,284 R 3
42345 Greenville⊙, 3,875 G 6
41329 Guage, 450 P 5
42234 Guthrie, 1,200 G 7
41820 Hall, 500 R 6
40947 Hammond, 500 O 7
42048 Hardin, 522 E 7
40143 Hardinsburg⊙, 1,547 H 5
41531 Hardy, 950 S 5
40831 Harlan⊙, 3,318 P 7
40330 Harrodsburg⊙, 6,741 M 5
42347 Hartford⊙, 1,868 H 6
41514 Hatfield, 700 S 5
42348 Hawesville⊙, 1,262 H 5
41701 Hazard⊙, 5,459 P 6
41048 Hebron, 550 R 2
42420 Henderson⊙, 22,976 F 5
42050 Hickman⊙, 3,048 C 7
41076 Highland Heights, 4,400 T 3
40951 Hima, 600 O 6
† 41203 Himlerville (Beauty), 800 S 5
41822 Hindman⊙, 808 R 6
41146 Hitchins, 500 R 4
42748 Hodgenville⊙, 2,562 K 5
† 41018 Hopeful Heights, 473 R 3
42240 Hopkinsville⊙, 21,250 F 7
42749 Horse Cave, 2,068 K 6
41749 Hyden⊙, 482 P 6
† 42408 Ilsley, 500 F 6
41051 Independence⊙, 1,784 M 3
41224 Inez⊙, 469 S 5
40336 Irvine⊙, 2,918 O 5
40146 Irvington, 1,300 J 5
41339 Jackson⊙, 1,887 P 5
42629 Jamestown⊙, 1,027 L 7
41751 Jeff, 615 P 6
40299 Jeffersontown, 9,701 L 4
40337 Jeffersonville, 800 O 5
41537 Jenkins, 2,552 R 6
40440 Junction City, 1,046 M 5
40737 Keavy, 500 N 6
40847 Kenvir, 800 P 7
42053 Kevil, 504 D 6
40848 Kitts, 950 P 7
42055 Kuttawa, 453 E 6
42056 La Center, 1,044 C 6
40031 La Grange⊙, 1,713 L 4
† 41017 Lakeside Park, 2,511 R 3
40444 Lancaster⊙, 3,230 M 5
40342 Lawrenceburg⊙, 3,579 M 4
41756 Leatherwood, 750 P 6
40033 Lebanon⊙, 5,528 L 5
40150 Lebanon Junction, 1,571 K 5
41343 Leeco, 475 O 5
42754 Leitchfield⊙, 2,983 J 6
40849 Lejunior, 597 P 7
42256 Lewisburg, 651 G 6
42351 Lewisport, 1,595 H 5
* 40501 Lexington⊙, 108,137 N 4
Lexington, ‡174,323 N 4
42539 Liberty⊙, 1,765 M 6
41646 Ligon, 500 R 6
40740 Lily, 800 N 6
41834 Littcarr, 550 R 6
42352 Livermore, 1,594 G 5
42059 Lola, 600 E 6
40741 London⊙, 4,337 N 6
42001 Lone Oak, 3,759 D 6
41542 Lookout, 600 S 6
40037 Loretto, 985 L 5
41348 Lost Creek, 500 P 6
41701 Lothair, 800 P 6
41230 Louisa⊙, 1,781 R 4
* 40201 Louisville⊙, 361,472 K 4
Louisville, ‡826,553 K 4
41231 Lovely, 500 S 5
41232 Lowmansville, 500 R 5
40854 Loyall, 1,212 P 7
41016 Ludlow, 5,815 S 2
40855 Lynch, 800 R 7
† 40201 Lynnview, 1,165 K 4
42431 Madisonville⊙, 15,332 F 6
41547 Majestic, 600 S 5
40962 Manchester⊙, 1,664 O 6
42064 Marion⊙, 3,008 E 6
42631 Marshes Siding, 950 M 7
41649 Martin, 786 R 5
42066 Mayfield⊙, 10,724 D 7
41056 Maysville⊙, 7,411 O 3
41543 McAndrews, 975 S 5
40447 McKee⊙, 255 O 6
40448 McKinney, 475 M 6
41835 McRoberts, 1,037 R 6
41546 McVeigh, 700 S 5
41059 Melbourne, 500 T 3
41501 Meta, 600 S 5
40965 Middlesboro, 11,844 O 7
40243 Middletown, 2,500 L 4
40347 Midway, 1,278 M 4
41501 Millard, 600 S 6
40348 Millersburg, 788 N 4
40045 Milton, 756 L 3
42633 Monticello⊙, 3,618 M 7
40351 Morehead⊙, 7,191 P 4
42437 Morganfield⊙, 3,563 E 5
42261 Morgantown⊙, 1,394 H 6
42440 Mortons Gap, 1,169 F 6
41064 Mount Olivet⊙, 442 N 3
40353 Mount Sterling⊙, 5,083 N 4
40456 Mount Vernon⊙, 1,639 N 6
40047 Mount Washington, 2,020 K 4
40155 Muldraugh, 1,773 J 5
42765 Munfordville⊙, 1,233 J 6
42071 Murray⊙, 13,537 E 7
42544 Nancy, 600 M 6
41840 Neon, 705 R 6
40050 New Castle⊙, 755 L 4
40051 New Haven, 977 K 5
* 41071 Newport, 25,988 S 2
40356 Nicholasville⊙, 5,829 N 5
41357 Noctor, 500 P 5
42442 Nortonville, 699 G 6
41238 Oil Springs, 900 P 5
40219 Okolona, 17,643 K 4
41164 Olive Hill, 1,197 P 4
40972 Oneida, 700 O 6
42301 Owensboro⊙, 50,329 G 5
40359 Owenton⊙, 1,280 M 3
40360 Owingsville⊙, 1,381 O 4
42001 Paducah⊙, 31,627 D 6
41240 Paintsville⊙, 3,868 R 5
40361 Paris⊙, 7,823 N 4
42160 Park City, 567 J 6
† 41011 Park Hills, 3,999 S 2
40464 Parksville, 560 M 5
42266 Pembroke, 634 G 7
40468 Perryville, 730 M 5
40056 Pewee Valley, 950 L 4
41553 Phelps, 770 S 6
42366 Philpot, 531 H 5
41501 Pikeville⊙, 4,576 S 6
42635 Pine Knot, 950 M 7
40977 Pineville⊙, 2,817 O 7
40755 Pittsburg, 938 N 6
40258 Pleasure Ridge Park, 28,566 J 4
40057 Pleasureville, 747 L 4
42367 Powderly, 631 G 6
41845 Premium, 489 R 6
41653 Prestonsburg⊙, 3,422 R 5
42445 Princeton⊙, 6,292 F 6
40059 Prospect, 500 K 4
42450 Providence, 4,270 F 6
41169 Raceland, 1,857 R 3
40160 Radcliff, 7,881 K 5
40472 Ravenna, 784 O 5
42638 Revelo, 500 N 7
40475 Richmond⊙, 16,861 N 5
42452 Robards, 701 F 5
41169 Russell, 1,982 R 3
42642 Russell Springs, 1,641 L 6
42276 Russellville⊙, 6,456 H 7
40207 Saint Matthews, 13,152 K 4
42078 Salem, 650 E 6
40371 Salt Lick, 441 O 4
40372 Salvisa, 500 M 5
41465 Salyersville⊙, 1,196 P 5
41171 Sandy Hook⊙, 192 P 4
40982 Scalf, 500 O 7
42553 Science Hill, 470 M 6
42164 Scottsville⊙, 3,584 J 7
42455 Sebree, 1,092 F 5
† 41385 Sewell, 500 P 5
40983 Sextons Creek, 975 O 6
41562 Shelbiana, 800 R 6
40065 Shelbyville⊙, 4,182 L 4
40165 Shepherdsville⊙, 2,769 K 4

216 Shively, 19,223 ..... K 4
984 Sibert, 500 ..... O 6
085 Silver Grove, 1,365 ..... T 3
067 Simpsonville, 628 ..... L 4
763 Slemp, 500 ..... P 6
764 Smilax, 856 ..... P 6
081 Smithland⊙, 514 ..... E 6
171 Smiths Grove, 756 ..... J 6
546 Smith Town, 500 ..... M 7
173 Soldier, 600 ..... P 4
501 Somerset⊙, 10,436 ..... M 6
071 Southgate, 3,212 ..... S 2
174 South Portsmouth, 950 ..... P 3
175 South Shore, 676 ..... R 3
561 South Williamson, 850 ..... S 5
458 Spottsville, 914 ..... G 5
069 Springfield⊙, 2,961 ..... L 5
256 Staffordsville, 700 ..... R 5
484 Stanford⊙, 2,474 ..... M 5
380 Stanton⊙, 2,037 ..... O 5
647 Stearns, 900 ..... N 7
170 Stephensport, 500 ..... H 5
567 Stone, 850 ..... S 5
459 Sturgis, 2,210 ..... F 5
558 Tateville, 680 ..... M 7
011 Taylor Mill, 3,253 ..... S 3
071 Taylorsville⊙, 897 ..... L 4
259 Thealka, 550 ..... R 5
189 Tollesboro, 500 ..... O 3
167 Tompkinsville⊙, 2,207 ..... K 7
286 Trenton, 496 ..... G 7
486 Tyner, 590 ..... O 6
091 Union, 500 ..... M 3
461 Uniontown, 1,255 ..... F 5
784 Upton, 552 ..... K 6
272 Valley Station, 24,471 ..... K 4
179 Vanceburg⊙, 1,773 ..... P 3
265 Van Lear, 1,033 ..... R 5
872 Verda, 950 ..... P 7
092 Verona, 500 ..... M 3
383 Versailles⊙, 5,679 ..... M 4
017 Villa Hills, 1,647 ..... R 2
175 Vine Grove, 2,987 ..... K 5
572 Virgie, 600 ..... R 6
094 Walton, 1,801 ..... M 3
095 Warsaw⊙, 1,232 ..... M 3
667 Weeksbury, 950 ..... R 6
472 West Liberty⊙, 1,387 ..... P 5
177 West Point, 1,741 ..... J 4
564 West Somerset, 850 ..... M 6
268 West Van Lear, 975 ..... R 5
101 Westwood, 2,900 ..... R 4
669 Wheelwright, 793 ..... R 6
464 White Plains, 729 ..... G 6
858 Whitesburg⊙, 1,137 ..... R 6
378 Whitesville, 752 ..... H 5
653 Whitley City⊙, 1,060 ..... N 7
087 Wickliffe⊙, 1,211 ..... C 7
071 Wilders, 823 ..... S 3
769 Williamsburg⊙, 3,687 ..... N 7
097 Williamstown⊙, 2,063 ..... M 3
390 Wilmore, 3,466 ..... M 5
391 Winchester⊙, 13,402 ..... N 4
088 Wingo, 593 ..... D 7
011 Winston Park, 578 ..... S 3
394 Wolverine, 500 ..... P 5
771 Woodbine, 700 ..... N 7
001 Woodlawn, 1,639 ..... D 6
071 Woodlawn, 525 ..... S 2
776 Wooton, 750 ..... P 6
183 Worthington, 1,364 ..... R 3
501 Zebulon, 800 ..... R 5

TENNESSEE

COUNTIES

derson, 60,300 ..... N 8
dford, 25,039 ..... J 9
Benton, 12,126 ..... E 8
Bledsoe, 7,643 ..... L 9
Blount, 63,744 ..... O 9
Bradley, 50,686 ..... M 10
Campbell, 26,045 ..... N 8
Cannon, 8,467 ..... J 9
Carroll, 25,741 ..... E 9
Carter, 42,575 ..... S 8
Cheatham, 13,199 ..... G 8
Chester, 9,927 ..... D 10
Claiborne, 19,420 ..... O 8
Clay, 6,624 ..... K 7
Cocke, 25,283 ..... P 9
Coffee, 32,572 ..... J 9
Crockett, 14,402 ..... C 9
Cumberland, 20,733 ..... L 9
Davidson, 447,877 ..... H 8
Decatur, 9,457 ..... E 9
De Kalb, 11,151 ..... K 9
Dickson, 21,977 ..... G 8
Dyer, 30,427 ..... C 8
Fayette, 22,692 ..... C 10
Fentress, 12,593 ..... M 8
Franklin, 27,244 ..... J 10
Gibson, 47,871 ..... D 9
Giles, 22,138 ..... G 10
Grainger, 13,948 ..... O 8
Greene, 47,630 ..... R 8
Grundy, 10,631 ..... K 10
Hamblen, 38,696 ..... P 8
Hamilton, 254,236 ..... L 10
Hancock, 6,719 ..... P 7
Hardeman, 22,435 ..... C 10
Hardin, 18,212 ..... E 10
Hawkins, 33,726 ..... P 8
Haywood, 19,596 ..... C 9
Henderson, 17,291 ..... E 9
Henry, 23,749 ..... E 8
Hickman, 12,096 ..... G 9
Houston, 5,845 ..... F 8
Humphreys, 13,560 ..... F 8
Jackson, 8,141 ..... K 8
Jefferson, 24,940 ..... P 8
Johnson, 11,569 ..... T 7
Knox, 276,293 ..... O 9
Lake, 7,896 ..... B 8
Lauderdale, 20,271 ..... B 9
Lawrence, 29,097 ..... G 10
Lewis, 6,761 ..... F 9
Lincoln, 24,318 ..... H 10
Loudon, 24,266 ..... N 9
Macon, 12,315 ..... J 7
Madison, 65,727 ..... D 9
Marion, 20,577 ..... K 10
Marshall, 17,319 ..... H 10
Maury, 43,376 ..... G 9
McMinn, 35,462 ..... M 10
McNairy, 18,369 ..... D 10
Meigs, 5,219 ..... M 9
Monroe, 23,475 ..... N 10
Montgomery, 62,721 ..... G 8
Moore, 3,568 ..... J 10
Morgan, 13,619 ..... M 8
Obion, 29,936 ..... C 8
Overton, 14,866 ..... L 8
Perry, 5,238 ..... F 9
Pickett, 3,774 ..... M 7
Polk, 11,669 ..... N 10
Putnam, 35,487 ..... K 8
Rhea, 17,202 ..... M 9
Roane, 38,881 ..... M 9
Robertson, 29,102 ..... H 7
Rutherford, 59,428 ..... J 9
Scott, 14,762 ..... M 8
Sequatchie, 6,331 ..... L 10
Sevier, 28,241 ..... O 9
Shelby, 722,014 ..... B 10
Smith, 12,509 ..... J 8
Stewart, 7,319 ..... F 7

KENTUCKY

AREA 40,395 sq. mi.
POPULATION 3,219,311
CAPITAL Frankfort
LARGEST CITY Louisville
HIGHEST POINT Black Mtn. 4,145 ft.
SETTLED IN 1774
ADMITTED TO UNION June 1, 1792
POPULAR NAME Blue Grass State
STATE FLOWER Goldenrod
STATE BIRD Cardinal

TENNESSEE

AREA 42,244 sq. mi.
POPULATION 3,924,164
CAPITAL Nashville
LARGEST CITY Memphis
HIGHEST POINT Clingmans Dome 6,643 ft.
SETTLED IN 1757
ADMITTED TO UNION June 1, 1796
POPULAR NAME Volunteer State
STATE FLOWER Iris
STATE BIRD Mockingbird

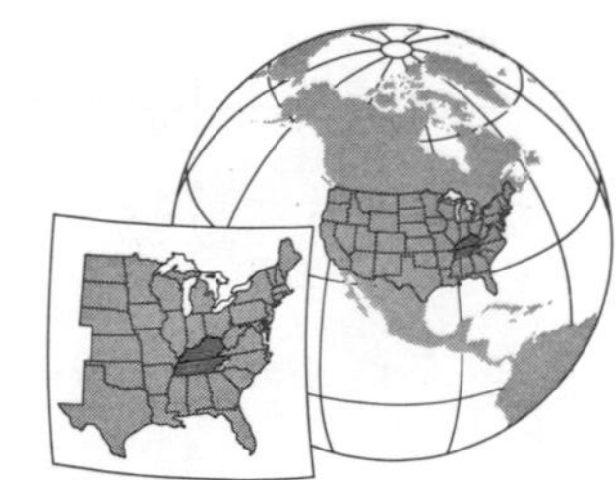

Sullivan, 127,329 ..... S 7
Sumner, 56,106 ..... J 8
Tipton, 28,001 ..... B 9
Trousdale, 5,155 ..... J 8
Unicoi, 15,254 ..... S 8
Union, 9,072 ..... O 8
Van Buren, 3,758 ..... L 9
Warren, 26,972 ..... K 9
Washington, 73,924 ..... R 8
Wayne, 12,365 ..... F 10
Weakley, 28,827 ..... D 8
White, 17,088 ..... L 9
Williamson, 34,330 ..... H 9
Wilson, 36,999 ..... J 8

CITIES and TOWNS

Zip *Name/Pop.* *Key*

37010 Adams, 458 ..... G 7
38310 Adamsville, 1,344 ..... E 10
37616 Afton, 550 ..... R 8
38001 Alamo⊙, 2,499 ..... C 9
37701 Alcoa, 7,739 ..... N 9
37012 Alexandria, 680 ..... J 8
38501 Algood, 1,808 ..... K 8
38504 Allardt, 610 ..... M 8
38541 Allons, 600 ..... L 8
37301 Altamont⊙, 546 ..... K 10
38449 Ardmore, 601 ..... H 10
38002 Arlington, 1,349 ..... B 10
38506 Armathwaite, 625 ..... M 8
37707 Arthur, 500 ..... O 7
37015 Ashland City⊙, 2,027 ..... G 8
37303 Athens⊙, 11,790 ..... M 10
38004 Atoka, 446 ..... B 10
38220 Atwood, 937 ..... D 9
37304 Bakewell, 600 ..... L 10
† 37650 Banner Hill, 2,517 ..... R 8
38005 Bartlett, 1,150 ..... B 10
38311 Bath Springs, 725 ..... E 10
38544 Baxter, 1,229 ..... K 8
37708 Bean Station, 500 ..... P 8
37018 Beechgrove, 600 ..... J 9
37305 Beersheba Springs, 560 ..... K 10
37205 Belle Meade ..... H 8
38006 Bells, 1,474 ..... C 9
38314 Bemis, 1,883 ..... D 9
37307 Benton⊙, 749 ..... M 10
† 37201 Berry Hill ..... H 8
† 37027 Berry's Chapel, 1,345 ..... H 9
38315 Bethel Springs, 781 ..... D 10
38221 Big Sandy, 539 ..... E 8
37308 Birchwood, 900 ..... M 10
37709 Blaine, 650 ..... O 8
37660 Bloomingdale, 3,120 ..... R 7
38545 Bloomington Springs, 800 ..... K 8
37617 Blountville⊙, 900 ..... S 7
37618 Bluff City, 947 ..... S 8
38008 Bolivar⊙, 6,674 ..... C 10
38316 Bradford, 968 ..... D 8
37658 Braemar-Hampton, 1,100 ..... S 8
37027 Brentwood, 1,091 ..... H 8
37710 Briceville, 850 ..... N 8
38011 Brighton, 952 ..... B 10
37620 Bristol, 20,064 ..... S 7
38012 Brownsville⊙, 7,011 ..... C 9
38317 Bruceton, 1,450 ..... E 8
38014 Brunswick, 500 ..... B 10
38318 Buena Vista, 500 ..... E 9
37711 Bulls Gap, 774 ..... P 8
37640 Butler, 500 ..... T 8
38549 Byrdstown⊙, 582 ..... L 7
37309 Calhoun, 624 ..... M 10
38320 Camden⊙, 3,052 ..... E 8
38129 Capleville, 450 ..... B 10
37030 Carthage⊙, 2,491 ..... K 8
37714 Caryville, 648 ..... N 8
38551 Celina⊙, 1,370 ..... K 7
37033 Centerville⊙, 2,592 ..... G 9
37034 Chapel Hill, 752 ..... H 9
37310 Charleston, 792 ..... M 10
37036 Charlotte⊙, 610 ..... G 8
* 37401 Chattanooga⊙, 119,082 ..... K 10
Chattanooga, ‡304,927 ..... K 10
37642 Church Hill, 2,822 ..... R 7
37715 Clairfield, 650 ..... O 7
38553 Clarkrange, 675 ..... L 8
37040 Clarksville⊙, 31,719 ..... G 7
37311 Cleveland⊙, 20,651 ..... M 10
38425 Clifton, 737 ..... F 10
37716 Clinton⊙, 4,794 ..... N 8
37719 Coalfield, 712 ..... N 8
37313 Coalmont, 518 ..... K 10
37314 Cokercreek, 500 ..... N 10
37315 Collegedale, 3,031 ..... M 10
38017 Collierville, 3,625 ..... B 10
38450 Collinwood, 922 ..... F 10
37663 Colonial Heights, 3,027 ..... R 8
38401 Columbia⊙, 21,471 ..... G 9
37720 Concord, 500 ..... N 9
38501 Cookeville⊙, 14,270 ..... L 8
37317 Copperhill, 563 ..... N 10
38018 Cordova, 600 ..... B 10
37047 Cornersville, 655 ..... H 10
37721 Corryton, 500 ..... O 8
38326 Counce, 975 ..... E 10
38019 Covington⊙, 5,801 ..... B 9
37318 Cowan, 1,772 ..... K 10
37723 Crab Orchard, 900 ..... M 9
38555 Crossville⊙, 5,381 ..... L 9
37051 Cumberland Furnace, 800 ..... G 8
38452 Cypress Inn, 500 ..... F 10
37725 Dandridge⊙, 1,270 ..... O 8
37321 Dayton⊙, 4,361 ..... L 9
37322 Decatur⊙, 698 ..... M 9
38329 Decaturville⊙, 958 ..... E 9
37324 Decherd, 2,148 ..... J 10
37055 Dickson, 5,665 ..... G 8
37214 Donelson ..... H 8
37058 Dover⊙, 1,179 ..... F 8
38559 Doyle, 1,205 ..... K 9
38225 Dresden⊙, 1,939 ..... D 8
38023 Drummonds, 700 ..... A 10
37326 Ducktown, 562 ..... N 10
37327 Dunlap⊙, 1,672 ..... L 10
38330 Dyer, 2,501 ..... D 8
38024 Dyersburg⊙, 14,523 ..... C 8
† 37801 Eagleton, 5,345 ..... O 9
† 37311 East Cleveland, 1,870 ..... M 10
37412 East Ridge, 21,799 ..... L 11
37732 Elgin, 500 ..... M 8
37643 Elizabethton⊙, 12,269 ..... S 8
37734 Elk Valley, 750 ..... N 7
38029 Ellendale, 1,500 ..... B 10
† 37601 Embreeville Junction, 1,293 ..... R 8
37735 Emory Gap, 500 ..... M 9
37329 Englewood, 1,878 ..... M 10
37061 Erin⊙, 1,157 ..... F 8
37650 Erwin⊙, 4,715 ..... S 8
37330 Estill Springs, 919 ..... J 10
38456 Ethridge, 600 ..... G 10
37331 Etowah, 3,736 ..... M 10
37332 Evensville, 475 ..... M 9
37062 Fairview, 1,630 ..... G 9
37656 Fall Branch, 825 ..... R 8
37334 Fayetteville⊙, 7,030 ..... H 10
38030 Finley, 950 ..... B 8
37335 Flintville, 500 ..... H 10
38031 Forest Hill, 850 ..... B 10
† 37201 Forest Hills ..... H 8
38032 Fort Pillow, 700 ..... B 9
37064 Franklin⊙, 9,404 ..... H 9
38034 Friendship, 441 ..... C 9
37737 Friendsville, 575 ..... N 9
38337 Gadsden, 523 ..... D 9
38562 Gainesboro⊙, 1,101 ..... K 8
37066 Gallatin⊙, 13,093 ..... H 8
38037 Gates, 523 ..... C 9
37738 Gatlinburg, 2,329 ..... O 9
38038 Germantown, 3,474 ..... B 10
37071 Gladeville, 500 ..... J 8
38229 Gleason, 1,314 ..... D 8
37072 Goodlettsville ..... H 8
38563 Gordonsville, 601 ..... K 8
37337 Grandview, 1,250 ..... M 9
37338 Graysville, 951 ..... L 10
37073 Green Brier, 2,279 ..... H 8
37743 Greeneville⊙, 13,722 ..... R 8
38230 Greenfield, 2,050 ..... D 8
38565 Grimsley, 500 ..... L 2
37339 Gruetli, 910 ..... K 10
† 37766 Habersham, 800 ..... N 8
38040 Halls, 2,323 ..... C 9
38461 Hampshire, 500 ..... G 9
37658 Hampton-Braemar, 1,100 ..... S 8
37748 Harriman, 8,734 ..... M 9
37341 Harrison, 500 ..... L 10
37752 Harrogate, 950 ..... O 8
37074 Hartsville⊙, 2,243 ..... J 8
37755 Helenwood, 675 ..... M 8
38340 Henderson⊙, 3,581 ..... D 10
38041 Henning, 605 ..... B 9
37343 Hixson, 6,188 ..... L 10
38462 Hohenwald⊙, 3,385 ..... F 9
38342 Hollow Rock, 722 ..... E 8
38343 Humboldt, 10,066 ..... D 9
38344 Huntingdon⊙, 3,661 ..... E 8
37345 Huntland, 849 ..... J 10
37756 Huntsville⊙, 337 ..... N 8
37079 Indian Mound, 600 ..... F 7
† 37201 Inglewood ..... H 8
38463 Iron City, 504 ..... F 10
37757 Jacksboro⊙, 689 ..... N 8
38301 Jackson⊙, 39,996 ..... D 9
38556 Jamestown⊙, 1,899 ..... M 8
37347 Jasper⊙, 1,811 ..... K 10
37760 Jefferson City, 5,124 ..... P 8
37762 Jellico, 2,235 ..... N 7
37601 Johnson City, 33,770 ..... S 8
37659 Jonesboro⊙, 1,510 ..... R 8
37921 Karns, 1,105 ..... N 9
38233 Kenton, 1,439 ..... C 8
† 34347 Kimball, 807 ..... K 10
* 37660 Kingsport, 31,938 ..... R 7
37763 Kingston⊙, 4,142 ..... N 9
* 37901 Knoxville⊙, 174,587 ..... O 9
Knoxville, ‡400,337 ..... O 9
37349 Laager, 675 ..... K 10
37083 Lafayette⊙, 2,583 ..... J 7
37766 La Follette, 6,902 ..... N 8
37769 Lake City, 1,923 ..... N 8
37416 Lake Hills-Murray Hills, 7,806 ..... L 10
† 37138 Lakewood, 2,500 ..... H 8
37086 La Vergne, 2,825 ..... H 9
38464 Lawrenceburg⊙, 8,889 ..... G 10
37087 Lebanon⊙, 12,492 ..... J 8
37771 Lenoir City, 5,324 ..... N 9
37091 Lewisburg⊙, 7,207 ..... H 10
38351 Lexington⊙, 4,955 ..... E 9
37681 Limestone, 500 ..... R 8
37096 Linden⊙, 1,062 ..... F 9
38570 Livingston⊙, 3,050 ..... L 8
37097 Lobelville, 773 ..... F 9
† 37662 Long Island, 1,352 ..... S 7
37350 Lookout Mountain, 1,741 ..... L 11
38469 Loretto, 1,375 ..... G 10
37774 Loudon⊙, 3,728 ..... N 9
37777 Louisville, 500 ..... N 9
37351 Lupton City, 750 ..... L 10
37779 Luttrell, 819 ..... O 8
38471 Lutts, 850 ..... F 10

(continued on following page)

Jack Zehrt — Shostal Associates

Sleek racehorses enjoy a patch of shade on a Calumet Farm pasture in Lexington, Kentucky. More than half the country's winning racehorses are from Inner Bluegrass area farms.

Eugene Belt — Shostal Associates

Using field glasses to bridge the gap, a naturalist observes the wildlife in Cades Cove, Tennessee. Mist-shrouded Great Smoky Mountains are in the distance.

(continued)

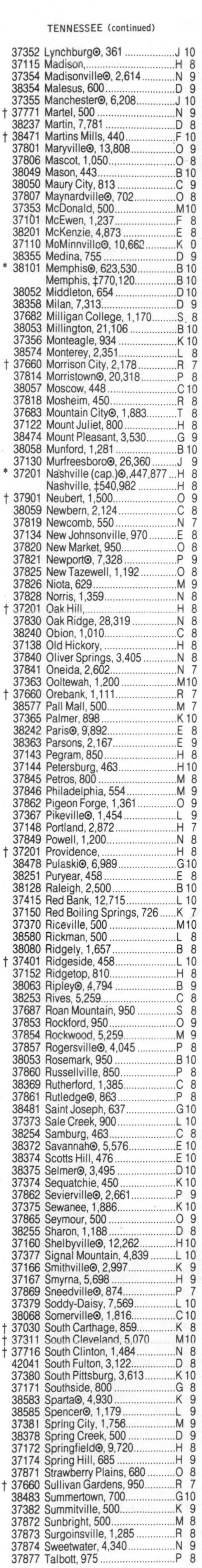

TENNESSEE (continued)

37352 Lynchburg⊙, 361 ....J 10
37115 Madison,..............................H 8
37354 Madisonville⊙, 2,614..........N 9
38354 Malesus, 600........................D 9
37355 Manchester⊙, 6,208.............J 10
† 37771 Martel, 500 ....N 9
38237 Martin, 7,781 ....D 8
† 38471 Martins Mills, 440.................F 10
37801 Maryville⊙, 13,808...............O 9
37806 Mascot, 1,050.......................O 8
38049 Mason, 443...........................B 10
38050 Maury City, 813 ....C 9
37807 Maynardville⊙, 702..............O 8
37353 McDonald, 500.....................M10
37101 McEwen, 1,237.....................F 8
38201 McKenzie, 4,873 ....E 8
37110 McMinnville⊙, 10,662..........K 0
38355 Medina, 755 ....D 9
* 38101 Memphis⊙, 623,530.............B 10
Memphis, ‡770,120.............B 10
38052 Middleton, 654 ....D 10
38358 Milan, 7,313.........................D 9
37682 Milligan College, 1,170.........S 8
38053 Millington, 21,106 ....B 10
37356 Monteagle, 934 ....K 10
38574 Monterey, 2,351....................L 8
† 37660 Morrison City, 2,178 ....R 7
37814 Morristown⊙, 20,318............P 8
38057 Moscow, 448 ....C 10
37818 Mosheim, 450........................R 8
37683 Mountain City⊙, 1,883..........T 8
37122 Mount Juliet, 800...................H 8
38474 Mount Pleasant, 3,530..........G 9
38058 Munford, 1,281 ....B 10
37130 Murfreesboro⊙, 26,360 ....J 9
* 37201 Nashville (cap.)⊙, 447,877 ...H 8
Nashville, ‡540,982 ....H 8
† 37901 Neubert, 1,500.......................O 9
38059 Newbern, 2,124 ....C 8
37819 Newcomb, 550 ....N 7
37134 New Johnsonville, 970 ....E 8
37820 New Market, 950....................O 8
37821 Newport⊙, 7,328 ....P 9
37825 New Tazewell, 1,192 ....O 8
37826 Niota, 629..............................M 9
37828 Norris, 1,359..........................N 8
† 37201 Oak Hill,.................................H 8
37830 Oak Ridge, 28,319 ....N 8
38240 Obion, 1,010..........................C 8
37138 Old Hickory, ...H 8
37840 Oliver Springs, 3,405 ....N 8
37841 Oneida, 2,602........................N 7
37363 Ooltewah, 1,200 ....M10
† 37660 Orebank, 1,111.......................R 7
38577 Pall Mall, 500.........................M 7
37365 Palmer, 898 ....K 10
38242 Paris⊙, 9,892........................E 8
38363 Parsons, 2,167.......................E 9
37143 Pegram, 850..........................H 8
37144 Petersburg, 463.....................H 10
37845 Petros, 800 ....M 8
37846 Philadelphia, 554 ....M 9
37862 Pigeon Forge, 1,361 ....O 9
37367 Pikeville⊙, 1,454 ....L 9
37148 Portland, 2,872......................H 7
37849 Powell, 1,200.........................N 8
† 37201 Providence, ...H 8
38478 Pulaski⊙, 6,989 ....G 10
38251 Puryear, 458 ....E 8
38128 Raleigh, 2,500........................B 10
37415 Red Bank, 12,715...................L 10
37150 Red Boiling Springs, 726 ......K 7
37370 Riceville, 500 ....M10
38580 Rickman, 500 ....L 8
38080 Ridgely, 1,657 ....B 8
† 37401 Ridgeside, 458........................L 10
37152 Ridgetop, 810.........................H 8
38063 Ripley⊙, 4,794 ....B 9
38253 Rives, 5,259...........................C 8
37687 Roan Mountain, 950 ....S 8
37853 Rockford, 950.........................O 9
37854 Rockwood, 5,259....................M 9
37857 Rogersville⊙, 4,045 ....P 8
38053 Rosemark, 950 ....B 10
37860 Russellville, 850.....................P 8
38369 Rutherford, 1,385....................C 8
37861 Rutledge⊙, 863 ....P 8
38481 Saint Joseph, 637...................G 10
37373 Sale Creek, 900 ....L 10
38254 Samburg, 463.........................C 8
38372 Savannah⊙, 5,576..................E 10
38374 Scotts Hill, 476 ....E 10
38375 Selmer⊙, 3,495 ....D 10
37374 Sequatchie, 450 ....K 10
37862 Sevierville⊙, 2,661..................P 9
37375 Sewanee, 1,886.......................K 10
37865 Seymour, 500 ....O 9
38255 Sharon, 1,188 ....D 8
37160 Shelbyville⊙, 12,262...............H 10
37377 Signal Mountain, 4,839 ....L 10
37166 Smithville⊙, 2,997...................K 9
37167 Smyrna, 5,698 ....H 9
37869 Sneedville⊙, 874.....................P 7
37379 Soddy-Daisy, 7,569.................L 10
38068 Somerville⊙, 1,816..................C 10
† 37030 South Carthage, 859...............K 8
† 37311 South Cleveland, 5,070 ....M10
† 37716 South Clinton, 1,484................N 8
42041 South Fulton, 3,122..................D 8
37380 South Pittsburg, 3,613.............K 10
37171 Southside, 800 ....G 8
38583 Sparta⊙, 4,930 ....K 9
38585 Spencer⊙, 1,179 ....L 9
37381 Spring City, 1,756.....................M 9
38378 Spring Creek, 500 ....D 9
37172 Springfield⊙, 9,720...................H 8
37174 Spring Hill, 685 ....H 9
37871 Strawberry Plains, 680 ....O 8
† 37660 Sullivan Gardens, 950...............R 7
38483 Summertown, 700.....................G 10
37382 Summitville, 500.......................K 9
37872 Sunbright, 500..........................M 8
37873 Surgoinsville, 1,285 ....R 8
37874 Sweetwater, 4,340....................N 9
37877 Talbott, 975 ....P 8

37879 Tazewell⊙, 1,860 ....O 8
37385 Tellico Plains, 773..................N 10
37880 Ten Mile, 700..........................M 9
37178 Tennessee Ridge, 664 ....F 8
† 37401 Tiftona, 1,750..........................L 11
38079 Tiptonville⊙, 2,229..................B 8
37387 Tracy City, 1,388 ....K 10
37883 Treadway, 712.........................P 8
38382 Trenton⊙, 4,226......................D 9
38258 Trezevant, 877 ....D 8
38259 Trimble, 675 ....C 8
38260 Troy, 826..................................C 8
37388 Tullahoma, 15,311...................J 10
37743 Tusculum, 1,157 ....R 8
37692 Unicoi, 500...............................S 8
38261 Union City⊙, 11,925...............C 8
37393 Victoria, 800 ....K 10
37885 Vonore, 524 ....N 9
37887 Wartburg⊙, 541.......................M 9
37183 Wartrace, 616...........................J 9
37184 Watertown, 1,061.....................J 8
37185 Waverly⊙, 3,794......................F 8
38485 Waynesboro⊙, 1,983..............F 10
38074 Western State Hospital,
2,900..C 10
37186 Westmoreland, 1,423 ....J 7
37187 White Bluff, 516 ....G 8
38116 Whitehaven, 19,000.................A 10
37188 White House, 650 ....H 8
37890 White Pine, 1,532 ....P 8
37891 Whitesburg, 500.......................P 8
37396 Whiteside, 523 ....K 10
38075 Whiteville, 992..........................C 10
37397 Whitwell, 1,669.........................K 10
37398 Winchester⊙, 5,211.................J 10
37892 Winfield, 950 ....M 7
37190 Woodbury⊙, 1,725 ....J 9
37191 Woodlawn, 500.........................G 7

⊙ County seat.
‡ Population of metropolitan area.
† Zip of nearest p.o.
* Multiple zips

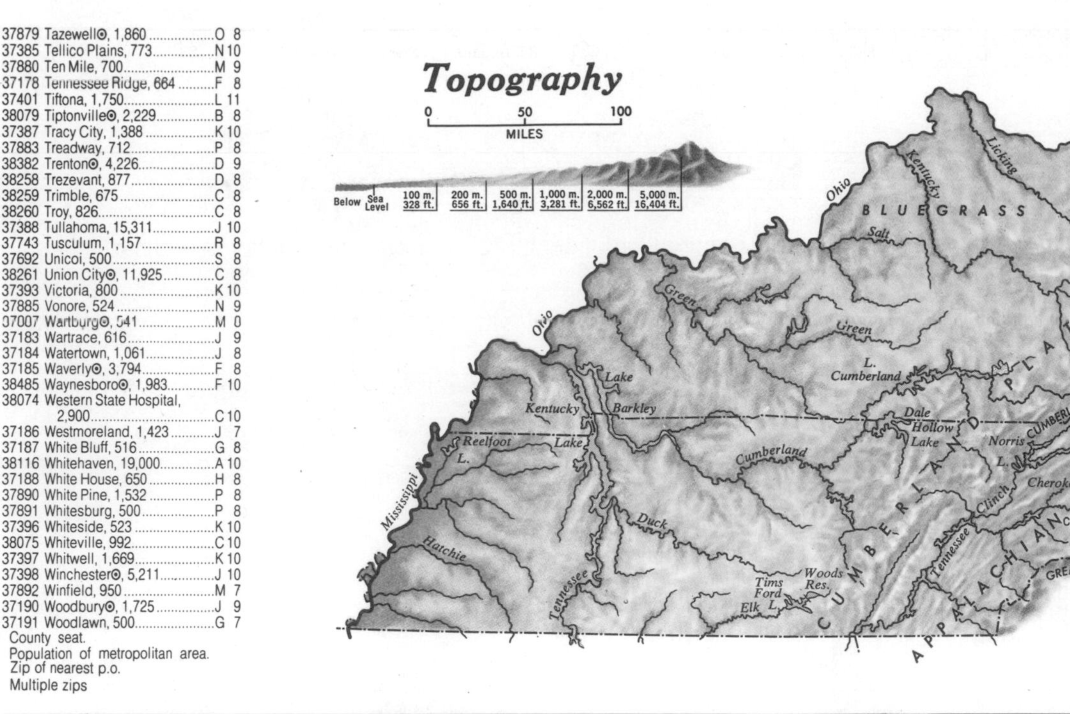

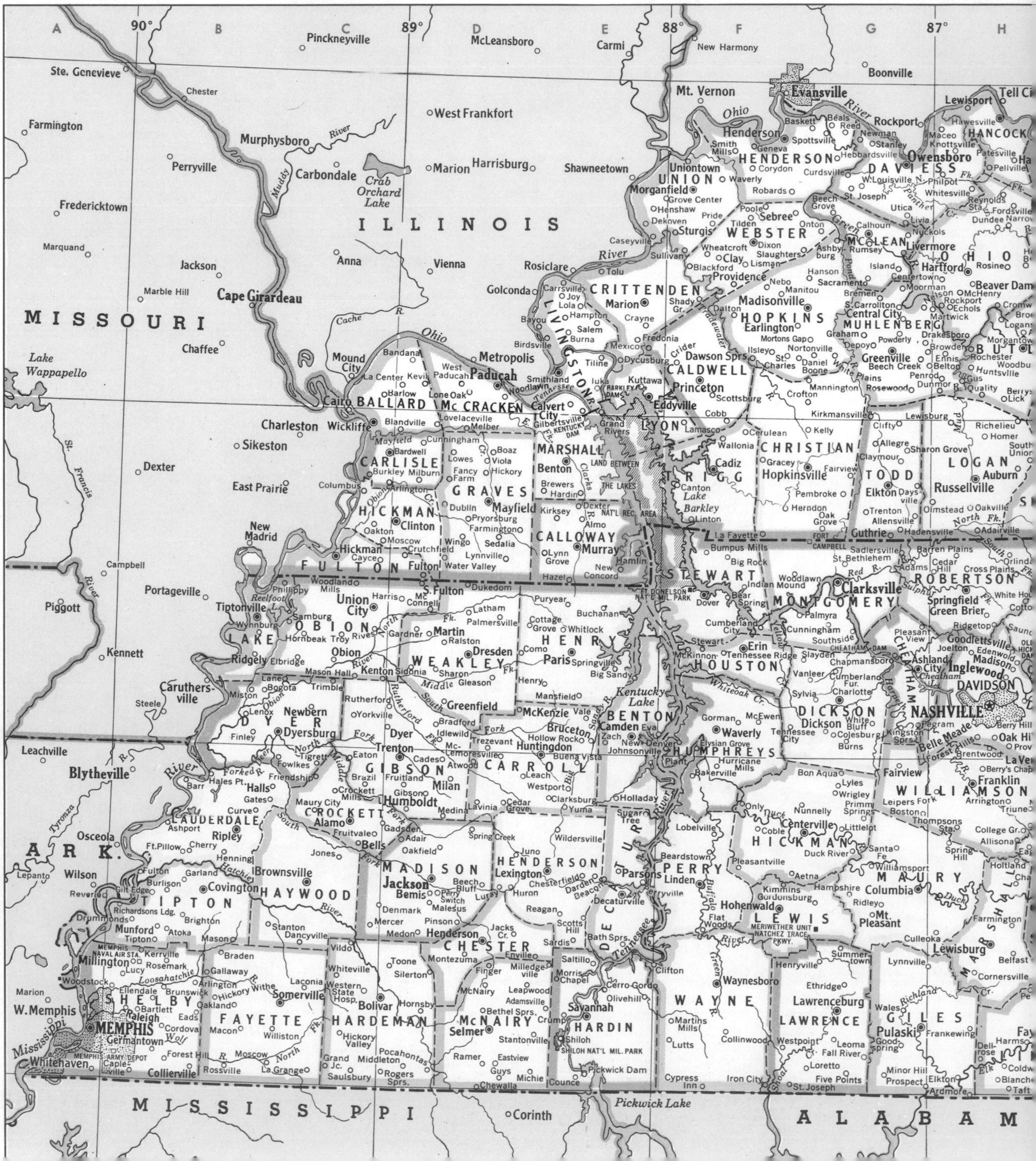

KENTUCKY
and
TENNESSEE
SCALE
0 5 10 20 30 40 MI.
0 5 10 20 30 40 KM.
State Capitals
County Seats
© C.S. HAMMOND & Co., N.Y.
OHIO
INDIANA
WEST VIRGINIA
VIRGINIA
NORTH CAROLINA
SOUTH CAROLINA
GEORGIA
CINCINNATI
LOUISVILLE
Lexington
Frankfort
KNOXVILLE
CHATTANOOGA
DAYTON
INDIANAPOLIS

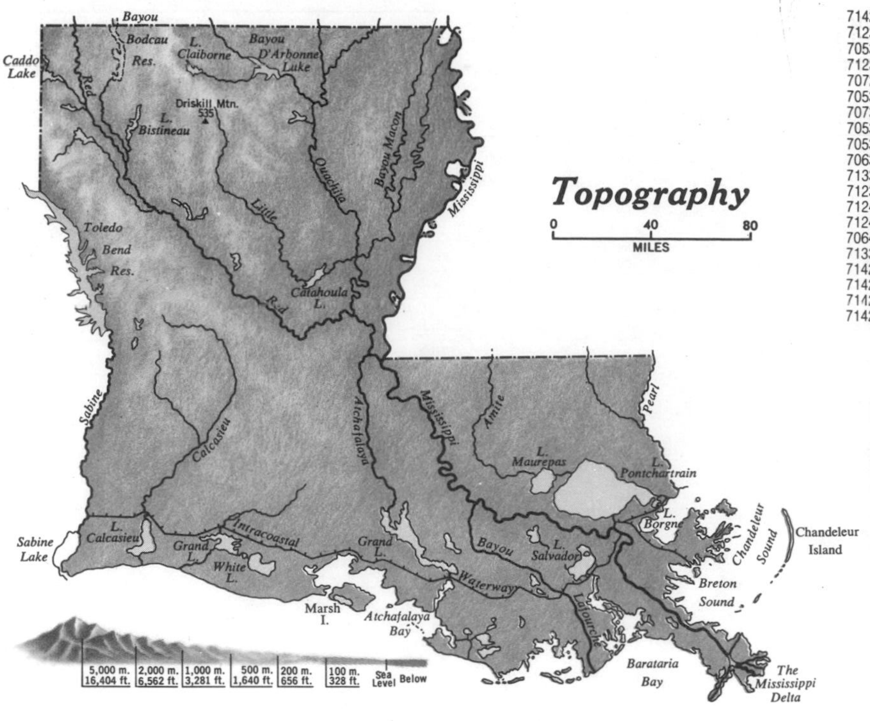

PARISHES

Acadia, 52,109 .... F 6
Allen, 20,794 .... E 5
Ascension, 37,086 .... J 6
Assumption, 19,654 .... H 7
Avoyelles, 37,751 .... G 4
Beauregard, 22,888 .... D 5
Bienville, 16,024 .... D 2
Bossier, 64,519 .... C 1
Caddo, 230,184 .... C 1
Calcasieu, 145,415 .... D 6
Caldwell, 9,354 .... F 2
Cameron, 8,194 .... D 7
Catahoula, 11,769 .... G 3
Claiborne, 17,024 .... D 1
Concordia, 22,578 .... G 4
De Soto, 22,764 .... C 2
East Baton Rouge, 285,167 .... K 1
East Carroll, 12,884 .... H 1
East Feliciana, 17,657 .... H 5
Evangeline, 31,932 .... F 5
Franklin, 23,946 .... G 2
Grant, 13,671 .... E 3
Iberia, 57,397 .... G 7
Iberville, 30,746 .... H 6
Jackson, 15,963 .... E 2
Jefferson, 337,568 .... K 7
Jefferson Davis, 29,554 .... E 6
Lafayette, 109,716 .... F 6
Lafourche, 68,941 .... K 7
La Salle, 13,295 .... F 3
Lincoln, 33,800 .... E 1
Livingston, 36,511 .... L 2
Madison, 15,065 .... H 2
Morehouse, 32,463 .... G 1
Natchitoches, 35,219 .... D 3
Orleans, 593,471 .... L 6
Ouachita, 115,387 .... F 2
Plaquemines, 25,225 .... L 8
Pointe Coupee, 22,022 .... G 5
Rapides, 118,078 .... E 4
Red River, 9,226 .... D 2
Richland, 21,774 .... G 2
Sabine, 18,638 .... C 3
Saint Bernard, 51,185 .... L 7
Saint Charles, 29,550 .... K 7
Saint Helena, 9,937 .... J 5
Saint James, 19,733 .... L 3
Saint John the Baptist, 23,813 .... M 3
Saint Landry, 80,364 .... F 5
Saint Martin, 32,453 .... G 6
Saint Mary, 60,752 .... H 7
Saint Tammany, 63,585 .... L 6
Tangipahoa, 65,875 .... K 5
Tensas, 9,732 .... H 2
Terrebonne, 76,049 .... J 8
Union, 18,447 .... F 1
Vermilion, 43,071 .... F 7
Vernon, 53,794 .... D 4
Washington, 41,987 .... K 5
Webster, 39,939 .... D 1
West Baton Rouge, 16,864 .... H 6
West Carroll, 13,028 .... H 1
West Feliciana, 11,376 .... H 5
Winn, 16,369 .... E 3

CITIES and TOWNS

Zip Name/Pop. Key

70510 Abbeville⊙, 10,996 .... F 7
70420 Abita Springs, 839 .... L 6
71316 Acme, 212 .... G 4
† 70774 Acy, 570 .... L 3
70710 Addis, 724 .... J 2
† 70544 Adeline, 200 .... G 7
70711 Albany, 700 .... M 1
† 71016 Alberta, 300 .... D 2
71301 Alexandria⊙, 41,557 .... E 4
70340 Amelia, 2,292 .... H 7
70422 Amite⊙, 3,593 .... K 5
71403 Anacoco, 575 .... D 4
† 71301 Anandale, 1,779 .... F 4
70426 Angie, 317 .... L 5
70712 Angola, 550 .... G 5
70032 Arabi, 12,000 .... K 7
† 70736 Arbroth, 250 .... H 5
71001 Arcadia⊙, 2,970 .... E 1
71218 Archibald, 300 .... G 2
† 71343 Archie, 280 .... G 3
† 70456 Arcola, 200 .... K 5
70512 Arnaudville, 1,673 .... G 6
71002 Ashland, 211 .... D 2
71003 Athens, 387 .... E 1
71404 Atlanta, 342 .... E 3
70513 Avery Island, 591 .... G 7
70713 Bains, 400 .... H 5
70714 Baker, 8,281 .... K 1
70514 Baldwin, 2,117 .... H 7
71405 Ball, 500 .... F 4
† 70401 Baptist, 150 .... M 1
70036 Barataria, 950 .... K 7
70515 Basile, 1,779 .... E 5
71219 Baskin, 177 .... G 2
71220 Bastrop⊙, 14,713 .... G 1
* 70801 Baton Rouge (cap.)⊙, 165,963 .... K 2
Baton Rouge, ‡285,167 .... K 2
† 70754 Bayou Barbary, 200 .... M 2
† 70360 Bayou Cane, 9,077 .... J 7
70716 Bayou Goula, 850 .... J 3
70380 Bayou Vista, 5,121 .... H 7
† 71220 Beekman, 300 .... G 1
70675 Bel, 150 .... D 6
71004 Belcher, 400 .... C 1
70630 Bell City, 350 .... D 6
† 70341 Belle Alliance, 350 .... K 3
70037 Belle Chasse, 950 .... O 4
† 71330 Belledeau, 450 .... F 4
70341 Belle Rose, 900 .... K 3
† 71468 Bellwood, 150 .... D 3
71406 Belmont, 150 .... C 3
71005 Benson, 200 .... C 3
71407 Bentley, 300 .... E 3
71006 Benton⊙, 1,493 .... C 1
71222 Bernice, 1,794 .... E 1
† 70040 Bertrandville, 175 .... L 7
70342 Berwick, 4,168 .... H 7
71007 Bethany, 250 .... B 2
71008 Bienville, 287 .... D 2
71009 Blanchard, 806 .... C 1
70427 Bogalusa, 18,412 .... L 5
† 71064 Bolinger, 250 .... C 1
71223 Bonita, 533 .... G 1
70038 Boothville, 300 .... M 8
71320 Bordelonville, 450 .... G 4
71224 Bosco, 480 .... F 2
71010 Bossier City, 41,595 .... C 1
† 70353 Boudreaux, 275 .... J 8
70343 Bourg, 900 .... J 7
70039 Boutte, 950 .... N 4
71409 Boyce, 1,240 .... E 4
70040 Braithwaite, 550 .... P 4
70517 Breaux Bridge, 4,942 .... G 6
70718 Brittany, 290 .... L 3
70518 Broussard, 1,707 .... F 6
70719 Brusly, 1,282 .... J 2
71322 Bunkie, 5,395 .... F 5
70041 Buras-Triumph, 4,113 .... L 8
70738 Burnside, 500 .... L 3
70431 Bush, 275 .... L 5
70519 Cade, 800 .... G 6
71433 Calcasieu, 400 .... E 4
71225 Calhoun, 653 .... F 2
71410 Calvin, 286 .... E 3
70631 Cameron⊙, 975 .... D 7
71411 Campti, 1,078 .... D 3
† 70584 Cankton, 260 .... F 6
70520 Carencro, 2,302 .... G 6
70042 Carlisle, 975 .... L 7
70721 Carville, 950 .... K 3
71016 Castor, 178 .... D 2
70521 Cecelia, 550 .... G 6
71323 Center Point, 850 .... F 4
70522 Centerville, 500 .... H 7
† 70723 Central, 546 .... L 3
† 70395 Chacahoula, 150 .... J 7
70043 Chalmette⊙, 15,000 .... P 4
70523 Charenton, 950 .... H 7
71324 Chase, 150 .... G 2
70524 Chataignier, 725 .... F 5
71226 Chatham, 827 .... F 2
70344 Chauvin, 900 .... J 8
71325 Cheneyville, 1,082 .... F 4
71227 Choudrant, 555 .... F 1
70525 Church Point, 3,865 .... F 6
71414 Clarence, 448 .... E 3
71415 Clarks, 889 .... F 2
71228 Clay, 400 .... E 2
71326 Clayton, 1,103 .... H 3
70722 Clinton⊙, 1,884 .... J 5
71416 Cloutierville, 250 .... E 3
71417 Colfax⊙, 1,892 .... E 3
71229 Collinston, 397 .... G 1
71418 Columbia⊙, 1,000 .... F 2
70723 Convent⊙, 650 .... L 3
71419 Converse, 375 .... C 3
† 70785 Corbin, 189 .... L 1
71327 Cottonport, 1,846 .... F 5
71018 Cotton Valley, 1,261 .... D 1
† 71018 Couchwood, 150 .... D 1
71019 Coushatta⊙, 1,492 .... D 2
70433 Covington⊙, 7,170 .... K 5
† 70656 Cravens, 475 .... E 5
70632 Creole, 175 .... D 7
† 70764 Crescent, 300 .... J 2
71020 Creston, 150 .... E 3
70526 Crowley⊙, 16,104 .... F 6
71230 Crowville, 400 .... G 2
71021 Cullen, 1,956 .... D 1
70345 Cut Off, 750 .... K 7
† 70040 Dalcour, 275 .... P 4
70725 Darrow, 500 .... K 3
70046 Davant, 650 .... L 7
70528 Delcambre, 1,975 .... G 7
71232 Delhi, 2,887 .... H 2
71233 Delta, 153 .... J 2
70726 Denham Springs, 6,752 .... L 1
70633 De Quincy, 3,448 .... D 6
70634 De Ridder⊙, 8,030 .... D 5
70030 Des Allemands, 2,318 .... N 4
70047 Destrehan, 800 .... N 4
71328 Deville, 500 .... F 4
70048 Diamond, 370 .... L 7
71022 Dixie, 330 .... C 1
† 71055 Dixie Inn, 456 .... D 1
71422 Dodson, 457 .... E 2
70346 Donaldsonville⊙, 7,367 .... K 3
70352 Donner, 500 .... J 7
71234 Downsville, 250 .... F 1
71023 Doyline, 716 .... D 1
70637 Dry Creek, 480 .... D 5
71423 Dry Prong, 352 .... E 3
71235 Dubach, 1,096 .... E 1
71024 Dubberly, 212 .... D 1
70353 Dulac, 225 .... J 8
71236 Dunn, 225 .... G 2
70728 Duplessis, 700 .... K 2
70529 Duson, 1,199 .... F 6
† 71247 East Hodge, 200 .... E 2
70530 Easton, 365 .... F 5
71025 East Point, 200 .... D 2
71330 Echo, 450 .... F 4
70049 Edgard⊙, 300 .... M 3
† 71019 Edgefield, 201 .... D 2
† 70668 Edgerly, 250 .... C 6
71331 Effie, 950 .... F 4
70638 Elizabeth, 504 .... E 5
71424 Elmer, 445 .... E 4
† 71051 Elm Grove, 350 .... C 2
† 70775 Elm Park, 200 .... H 5
70532 Elton, 1,598 .... E 6
70050 Empire, 700 .... L 8
71425 Enterprise, 300 .... G 3
71237 Epps, 448 .... G 1
70533 Erath, 2,024 .... F 7
71238 Eros, 164 .... F 2
70729 Erwinville, 790 .... H 5
70534 Estherwood, 661 .... F 6
70730 Ethel, 350 .... H 5
70535 Eunice, 11,390 .... F 6
70537 Evangeline, 400 .... F 6
70639 Evans, 400 .... D 5
71333 Evergreen, 307 .... F 5
71239 Extension, 950 .... G 3
71240 Fairbanks, 150 .... F 1
71241 Farmerville⊙, 3,416 .... F 1
70640 Fenton, 404 .... E 6
71334 Ferriday, 5,239 .... G 3
71426 Fisher, 300 .... D 4
71427 Flatwoods, 450 .... E 4
71428 Flora, 200 .... D 3
71429 Florien, 639 .... D 4
70436 Fluker, 400 .... K 5
70437 Folsom, 249 .... K 5
70732 Fordoche, 488 .... G 5
71242 Forest, 221 .... H 1
71430 Forest Hill, 370 .... E 4
† 71449 Fort Jesup, 950 .... C 3
71243 Fort Necessity, 150 .... G 2
70538 Franklin⊙, 9,325 .... G 7
70438 Franklinton⊙, 3,562 .... K 5
70733 French Settlement, 800 .... L 2
71027 Frierson, 700 .... C 2
† 70753 Frost, 500 .... L 2
† 71039 Fryeburg, 150 .... D 2
70354 Galliano, 950 .... K 8
† 70769 Galvez, 200 .... L 2
70540 Garden City, 515 .... H 7
70051 Garyville, 2,474 .... M 3
70734 Geismar, 300 .... K 3
71432 Georgetown, 300 .... G 3
71028 Gibsland, 1,380 .... E 1
70356 Gibson, 950 .... J 7
71336 Gilbert, 746 .... G 2
71029 Gilliam, 211 .... C 1
71244 Girard, 250 .... G 2
† 70538 Glencoe, 200 .... G 7
71433 Glenmora, 1,651 .... E 5
71030 Gloster, 975 .... C 2
70736 Glynn, 400 .... H 5
70357 Golden Meadow, 2,681 .... K 8
71031 Goldonna, 337 .... D 2
70737 Gonzales, 4,512 .... L 2
70079 Good Hope, 950 .... N 3
71337 Good Pine, 535 .... F 3
71245 Grambling, 4,407 .... E 1
70052 Gramercy, 2,567 .... M 3
71032 Grand Cane, 284 .... C 2
70643 Grand Chenier, 710 .... E 7
70541 Grand Coteau, 1,301 .... G 6
70358 Grand Isle, 2,236 .... L 8
† 70601 Grand Lake, 400 .... D 6

LOUISIANA

SCALE
0 5 10 20 30 40 MI.
0 5 10 20 30 40 KM.

State Capitals .... ⊛
Parish Seats .... ⊙
Canals ....

70644 Grant, 225 .... E 5
70359 Gray, 750 .... J 7
71435 Grayson, 516 .... F 2
70441 Greensburg⊙, 652 .... J 5
70739 Greenwell Springs, 225 .... K 1
71033 Greenwood, 212 .... B 2
70053 Gretna⊙, 24,875 .... O 4
70740 Grosse Tete, 710 .... G 6
70542 Gueydan, 1,984 .... E 6
70730 Gurley, 150 .... H 5
70645 Hackberry, 750 .... D 7
70057 Hahnville⊙, 2,483 .... N 4
71246 Haile, 300 .... F 1
71034 Hall Summit, 190 .... D 2
70401 Hammond, 12,487 .... N 1
70083 Happy Jack, 800 .... L 7
70123 Harahan, 13,037 .... N 4
71340 Harrisonburg⊙, 626 .... G 3
70058 Harvey, 6,347 .... O 4
71037 Haughton, 885 .... C 1

70646 Hayes, 800 .... E 6
71038 Haynesville, 3,055 .... D 1
† 70462 Head of Island, 420 .... L 2
71436 Hebert, 150 .... G 2
71039 Heflin, 314 .... D 2
71341 Hessmer, 454 .... F 4
70743 Hester, 280 .... L 3
71437 Hicks, 369 .... E 4
71247 Hodge, 818 .... E 2
70744 Holden, 750 .... M 1
71248 Holly Ridge, 200 .... G 2
† 70663 Hollywood, 2,328 .... D 6
† 70083 Homeplace, 600 .... L 8
71040 Homer⊙, 4,483 .... D 1
71439 Hornbeck, 525 .... D 4
71043 Hosston, 428 .... C 1
70360 Houma⊙, 30,922 .... J 7
† 70356 Humphreys, 900 .... J 7
70746 Iberville, 221 .... K 2
71044 Ida, 370 .... C 1

70443 Independence, 1,770 .... M 1
70747 Innis, 300 .... G 5
70543 Iota, 1,271 .... E 6
70647 Iowa, 1,944 .... D 6
† 70427 Isabel, 365 .... K 5
70748 Jackson, 4,697 .... H 5
71045 Jamestown, 153 .... D 2
70544 Jeanerette, 6,322 .... G 7
70121 Jefferson Heights, 16,489 .... O 4
71342 Jena⊙, 2,389 .... F 3
70546 Jennings⊙, 11,783 .... E 6
71249 Jigger, 400 .... G 2
† 70631 Johnsons Bayou, 300 .... C 7
71250 Jones, 200 .... G 1
71251 Jonesboro⊙, 5,072 .... E 2
71343 Jonesville, 2,761 .... G 3
71440 Joyce, 700 .... E 3
71749 Junction City, 733 .... E 1
70548 Kaplan, 5,540 .... F 6
71046 Keatchie, 328 .... C 2

(continued on following page)

AREA 48,523 sq. mi.
POPULATION 3,643,180
CAPITAL Baton Rouge
LARGEST CITY New Orleans
HIGHEST POINT Driskill Mtn. 535 ft.
SETTLED IN 1699
ADMITTED TO UNION April 30, 1812
POPULAR NAME Pelican State
STATE FLOWER Magnolia
STATE BIRD Eastern Brown Pelican

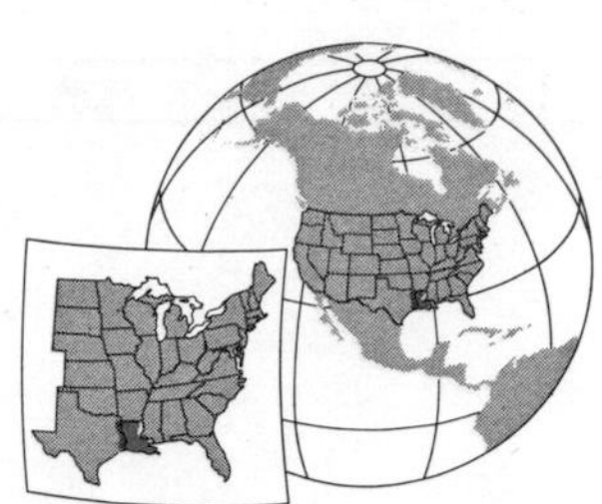

NEW ORLEANS, BATON ROUGE AND VICINITY

Agriculture, Industry and Resources

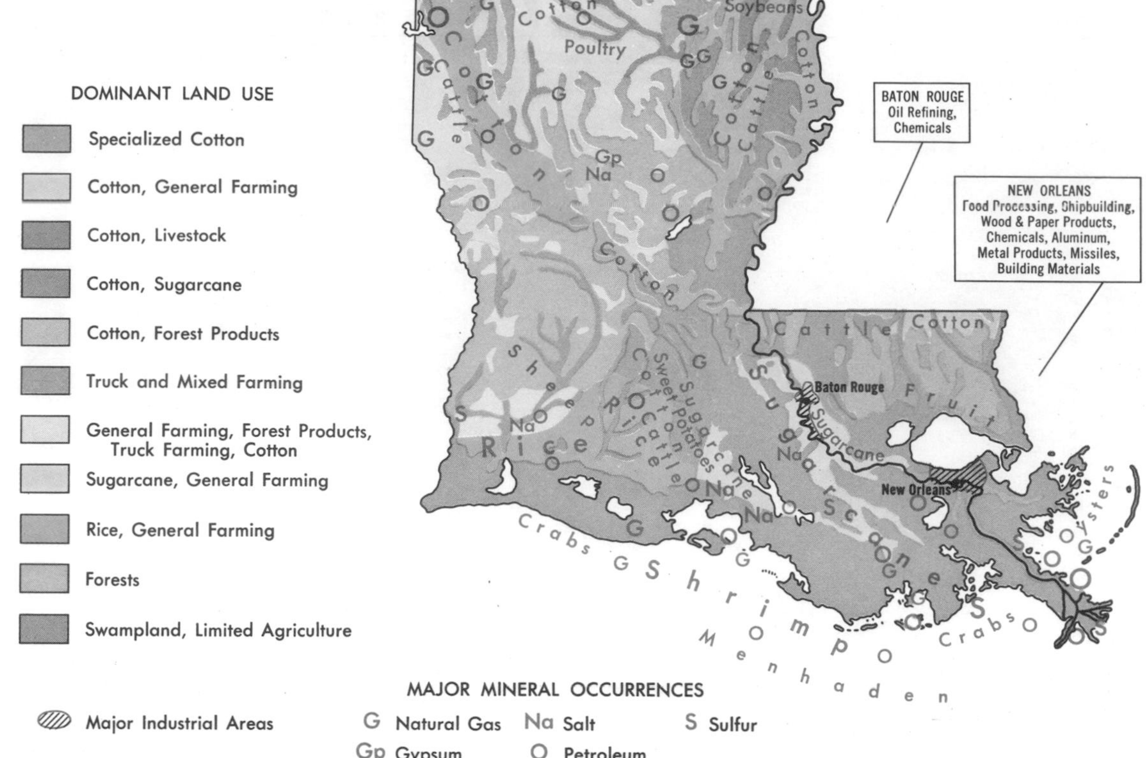

	Zip	Place	Key
	71047	Keithville, 500	C 2
	71441	Kelly, 250	F 3
	70062	Kenner, 29,858	N 4
	70444	Kentwood, 2,736	J 5
	71253	Kilbourne, 370	H 1
†	70462	Killian, 275	M 2
	70066	Killona, 600	M 3
	70648	Kinder, 2,307	E 6
	70370	Klotzville, 248	K 3
	70371	Kraemer, 510	M 4
	70750	Krotz Springs, 1,435	G 5
	70372	Labadieville, 700	K 4
	70650	Lacassine, 494	E 6
	70445	Lacombe, 750	L 6
	70501	Lafayette⊙, 68,908	F 6
		Lafayette, ‡109,716	F 6
	70067	Lafitte, 1,223	K 7
†	70301	Lafourche, 200	J 7
	70549	Lake Arthur, 3,551	E 6
	70601	Lake Charles⊙, 77,998	D 6
		Lake Charles, ‡145,415	D 6
	70752	Lakeland, 400	H 5
	71254	Lake Providence⊙, 6,183	H 1
	70068	Laplace, 5,953	N 3
	70373	Larose, 4,267	K 7
	71344	Larto, 500	G 4
	70550	Lawtell, 600	F 5
	71345	Lebeau, 270	F 5
	71346	Lecompte, 1,518	F 4
	71446	Leesville⊙, 8,928	D 4
	71447	Lena, 250	E 4
	70551	Leonville, 512	G 6
	70753	Lettsworth, 200	G 5
†	70525	Lewisburg, 265	F 6
	71348	Libuse, 500	F 4
	71256	Lillie, 160	E 1
	71048	Lisbon, 151	E 1
†	71343	Lismore, 380	G 3
†	70062	Little Farms, 15,713	N 4
	70754	Livingston⊙, 1,398	L 1
	70755	Livonia, 611	G 5
	70374	Lockport, 1,995	K 7
	71049	Logansport, 1,330	C 3
†	71367	Lonepine, 850	F 5
	71448	Longleaf, 250	E 4
	71050	Longstreet, 182	B 2
	70652	Longville, 250	D 5
	70446	Loranger, 200	N 1
	70552	Loreauville, 728	G 6
	70756	Lottie, 350	G 5
	70069	Lucy, 825	M 3
	70070	Luling, 3,255	N 4
	70071	Lutcher, 3,911	L 3
	70447	Madisonville, 801	K 6
	70554	Mamou, 3,275	F 5
	70448	Mandeville, 2,282	L 6
	71259	Mangham, 544	G 2
	71052	Mansfield⊙, 6,432	C 2
	71350	Mansura, 1,699	G 4
	71449	Many⊙, 3,112	C 3
	70663	Maplewood, 1,900	D 6
	70757	Maringouin, 1,365	G 6
	71260	Marion, 796	F 1
	71351	Marksville⊙, 4,519	G 4
	70072	Marrero, 29,015	O 4
	70375	Mathews, 600	J 7
	70449	Maurepas, 200	M 2
	70555	Maurice, 476	F 6
†	71433	McNary, 220	E 5
	71451	Melder, 200	E 4
	71353	Melville, 2,076	G 5
	70556	Mermentau, 756	E 6
	71261	Mer Rouge, 819	G 1
	70653	Merryville, 1,286	D 5
*	70001	Metairie, 135,816	O 4
	70557	Midland, 500	F 6
	70558	Milton, 500	F 6
	71055	Minden⊙, 13,996	D 1
	70376	Modeste, 230	K 3
	71201	Monroe⊙, 56,374	F 1
		Monroe, ‡115,387	F 1
	70377	Montegut, 950	J 8
	71354	Monterey, 800	G 4
	71454	Montgomery, 923	E 3
	70422	Montpelier, 211	M 1
†	70068	Montz, 200	M 3
	71060	Mooringsport, 830	B 1
	71455	Mora, 378	E 4
	71355	Moreauville, 807	G 4
	70380	Morgan City, 16,586	H 7
	70759	Morganza, 836	G 5
	71356	Morrow, 350	F 5
	70559	Morse, 759	F 6
	70076	Mount Airy, 700	M 3
	70077	Nairn, 500	L 8
	70390	Napoleonville⊙, 1,008	K 4
	70451	Natalbany, 900	N 1
	71456	Natchez, 600	D 3
	71457	Natchitoches⊙, 15,974	D 3
†	71342	Nebo, 200	F 3
	71460	Negreet, 200	C 4
	71357	Newellton, 1,403	H 2
†	71354	New Era, 200	G 4
	70560	New Iberia⊙, 30,147	G 6
	71461	Newllano, 1,800	D 4
*	70101	New Orleans⊙, 593,471	O 4
		New Orleans, ‡1,045,809	O 4
	70760	New Roads⊙, 3,945	G 5
	70078	New Sarpy, 1,643	N 4
	71462	Noble, 209	C 3
	70079	Norco, 4,773	N 3
†	71247	North Hodge, 640	E 2
	70761	Norwood, 348	H 5
	71463	Oakdale, 7,301	E 5
	71263	Oak Grove⊙, 1,980	H 1
	71264	Oak Ridge, 276	G 1
	70655	Oberlin⊙, 1,857	E 5
†	71369	Odenburg, 175	G 5
	71061	Oil City, 907	C 1
†	70560	Olivier, 300	G 7
	71465	Olla, 1,387	F 3
	70570	Opelousas⊙, 20,121	G 5
	70762	Oscar, 700	H 5
	71358	Palmetto, 312	G 5
	70391	Paincourtville, 600	K 3
	70080	Paradis, 750	M 4
	70582	Parks, 491	G 6
†	70544	Patoutville, 230	G 7
	70392	Patterson, 4,409	H 7
	70763	Paulina, 500	L 3
	70452	Pearl River, 1,361	L 6
†	70548	Pecan Island, 480	F 7
	70575	Perry, 225	F 7
†	70042	Phoenix, 525	L 7
	70453	Pine Grove, 500	J 5
	70576	Pine Prairie, 515	E 5
	71360	Pineville, 8,951	F 4
	71266	Pioneer, 188	H 1
	70656	Pitkin, 700	E 5
	71064	Plain Dealing, 2,116	C 1
	70764	Plaquemine⊙, 7,739	J 2
	70393	Plattenville, 400	K 4
	71362	Plaucheville, 224	G 5
	71065	Pleasant Hill, 826	C 3
	70082	Pointe a la Hache⊙, 750	L 7
	71467	Pollock, 341	F 3
	70454	Ponchatoula, 4,545	N 2
	70767	Port Allen⊙, 5,728	J 2
	70577	Port Barre, 2,133	G 5
†	70791	Port Hudson, 200	J 1
	70083	Port Sulphur, 3,022	L 8
†	70726	Port Vincent, 387	L 2
	71066	Powhatan, 277	D 3
	70769	Prairieville, 500	K 2
	71067	Princeton, 350	C 1
	71468	Provencal, 530	D 3
	71268	Quitman, 169	E 2
	70394	Raceland, 4,880	J 7
	70578	Rayne, 9,510	F 6
	71269	Rayville⊙, 3,962	G 2
	70580	Reddell, 800	F 5
	70658	Reeves, 214	D 5
†	70085	Reggio, 400	L 7
†	70763	Remy, 850	L 3
	70084	Reserve, 6,381	M 3
	71334	Ridgecrest, 1,076	G 3
	71068	Ringgold, 1,731	D 2
†	70427	Rio, 250	L 5
	70581	Roanoke, 640	E 6
	71469	Robeline, 274	D 3
	70455	Robert, 600	N 1
	71069	Rodessa, 273	B 1
	70772	Rosedale, 621	G 6
	70456	Roseland, 1,273	J 5
	70659	Rosepine, 587	D 5
	71365	Ruby, 350	F 4
	71270	Ruston⊙, 17,365	E 1
	70774	Saint Amant, 900	L 2
	70457	Saint Benedict, 200	K 5
	70085	Saint Bernard, 750	L 7
	70775	Saint Francisville⊙ 1,603	H 5
	70776	Saint Gabriel, 975	K 2
	70086	Saint James, 600	L 3
	71366	Saint Joseph⊙, 1,864	H 3
	71367	Saint Landry, 950	F 5
	70582	Saint Martinville⊙, 7,153	G 6
	71471	Saint Maurice, 650	E 3
	70087	Saint Rose, 2,106	N 4
	71070	Saline, 307	E 2
	71301	Samtown, 4,210	F 4
	71071	Sarepta, 882	D 1
	70395	Schriever, 700	J 7
	70807	Scotlandville, 22,557	J 1
	70583	Scott, 1,334	F 6
†	70560	Segura, 200	G 6
†	70764	Seymourville, 2,506	J 2
	71072	Shongaloo, 173	D 1
*	71101	Shreveport⊙, 182,064	C 1
		Shreveport, ‡294,703	C 1
	71073	Sibley, 869	D 1
	71368	Sicily Island, 630	G 3
	71472	Sieper, 200	E 4
	71473	Sikes, 237	F 2
	71369	Simmesport, 2,027	G 5
	71474	Simpson, 491	D 4
	71275	Simsboro, 412	E 1
	70660	Singer, 400	D 5
	71475	Slagle, 200	D 4
	70777	Slaughter, 580	H 5
	70458	Slidell, 16,101	L 6
†	70346	Smoke Bend, 300	K 3
	71276	Sondheimer, 325	H 1
	70778	Sorrento, 1,182	L 3
†	71052	South Mansfield, 439	C 3
	71277	Spearsville, 197	E 1
	70462	Springfield, 423	M 2
	71075	Springhill, 6,496	D 1
†	71465	Standard, 190	F 3
	70661	Starks, 750	C 6
	71279	Start, 200	G 2
	71280	Sterlington, 1,118	F 1
	71078	Stonewall, 500	C 2
	70663	Sulphur, 13,551	D 6
	71079	Summerfield, 170	E 1
	70463	Sun, 288	L 5
	70584	Sunset, 1,675	F 6
	70780	Sunshine, 900	K 2
	70396	Supreme, 617	K 4
	71281	Swartz, 650	G 1
†	70601	Sweet Lake, 300	D 7
	70464	Talisheek, 292	L 5
	71282	Tallulah⊙, 9,643	H 2
	70465	Tangipahoa, 469	J 5
	71080	Taylor, 500	D 1
†	71290	Tendal, 200	H 2
†	70053	Terry Town, 13,832	O 4
	70397	Theriot, 950	J 8
	70301	Thibodaux⊙, 14,925	J 7
	70466	Tickfaw, 370	M 1
	71477	Tioga, 457	F 4
	71286	Transylvania, 400	H 1
	71081	Trees, 247	B 1
†	70041	Triumph-Buras, 4,113	L 8
	71371	Trout, 500	F 3
	71479	Tullos, 600	F 3
	70782	Tunica, 475	G 5
	70585	Turkey Creek, 280	F 5
	70723	Union, 665	L 3
	71480	Urania, 950	F 3
	70090	Vacherie, 2,145	L 3
†	70757	Valverda, 200	G 5
	70467	Varnado, 320	L 5
	70091	Venice, 900	M 8
	71372	Vick, 500	F 4
	71373	Vidalia⊙, 5,538	G 3
	71270	Vienna, 250	E 1
	70586	Ville Platte⊙, 9,692	F 5
	70668	Vinton, 3,454	C 6
	70092	Violet, 975	P 4
	71082	Vivian, 4,046	B 1
	70784	Wakefield, 200	H 5
	70785	Walker, 1,363	L 1
†	70049	Wallace, 200	M 3
	71374	Walters, 500	G 3
	71289	Warden, 350	H 1
†	71301	Wardville, 1,087	F 4
	70589	Washington, 1,473	G 5
	71375	Waterproof, 1,438	H 3
	70786	Watson, 700	L 1
	71290	Waverly, 350	H 2
†	70569	Weeks, 400	G 7
	70093	Welcome, 450	L 3
	70591	Welsh, 3,203	E 6
	70669	Westlake, 4,082	D 6
	71291	West Monroe, 14,868	F 1
†	70082	West Pointe a la Hache, 250	L 7
	70094	Westwego, 11,402	O 4
	70787	Weyanoke, 500	H 5
	70788	White Castle, 2,206	J 3
†	70462	Whitehall, 380	M 2
	71376	Whiteville, 450	F 5
	71377	Wildsville, 650	G 3
	70789	Wilson, 606	H 5
	71483	Winnfield⊙, 7,142	E 3
	71295	Winnsboro⊙, 5,349	G 2
	71378	Wisner, 1,339	G 3
	71485	Woodworth, 409	E 4
	70592	Youngsville, 1,002	G 6
	70791	Zachary, 4,964	K 1
	71486	Zwolle, 2,169	C 3

⊙ Parish seat.
‡ Population of metropolitan area.
† Zip of nearest p.o.
* Multiple zips

Pushed by powerful tugboats, barges make their way from the Mississippi down the shallow Gulf Intracoastal Waterway to deliver their cargoes to New Orleans, Morgan City and Lake Charles, Louisiana.

AREA 33,215 sq. mi.
POPULATION 993,663
CAPITAL Augusta
LARGEST CITY Portland
HIGHEST POINT Katahdin 5,268 ft.
SETTLED IN 1624
ADMITTED TO UNION March 15, 1820
POPULAR NAME Pine Tree State
STATE FLOWER Pine Cone & Tassel
STATE BIRD Chickadee

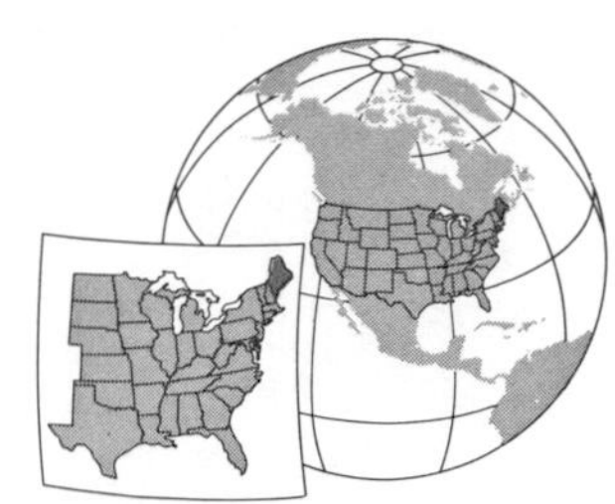

COUNTIES

Name/Pop.	Key
Androscoggin, 91,279	C 7
Aroostook, 92,463	F 2
Cumberland, 192,528	C 8
Franklin, 22,444	B 5
Hancock, 34,590	G 6
Kennebec, 95,247	D 7
Knox, 29,013	E 7
Lincoln, 20,537	D 7
Oxford, 43,457	B 7
Penobscot, 125,393	F 5
Piscataquis, 16,285	E 4
Sagadahoc, 23,452	D 7
Somerset, 40,597	C 4
Waldo, 23,328	E 6
Washington, 29,859	H 6
York, 111,576	B 9

CITIES and TOWNS

Zip	Name/Pop.	Key
04406	Abbot Village, ▵453	D 5
04001	Acton, ▵697	B 8
04606	Addison, ▵773	H 6
04910	Albion, ▵1,056	E 6
04610	Alexander, ▵169	H 5
04002	Alfred⊙, ▵1,211	B 9
04774	Allagash, ▵456	F 1
04938	Allens Mills, 150	C 6
04535	Alna, ▵315	D 7
04468	Alton, ▵340	F 5
04408	Amherst, ▵148	G 6
04216	Andover, ▵791	B 6
04216	Andover, 350	B 6
04911	Anson, ▵2,168	D 6
04911	Anson, 950	D 6
04862	Appleton, ▵628	E 7
04732	Ashland, ▵1,761	G 2
04732	Ashland, 750	G 2
04912	Athens, ▵592	D 6
04912	Athens, 200	D 6
04426	Atkinson, ▵213	E 5
04210	Auburn⊙, 24,151	C 7
04330	Augusta (cap.)⊙, 21,945	D 7
04408	Aurora, ▵72	G 6
04003	Bailey Island, 400	D 8
04409	Bancroft, ▵53	H 4
04401	Bangor⊙, 33,168	F 6
04609	Bar Harbor, ▵3,716	G 7
04609	Bar Harbor, 2,392	G 7
04610	Baring, 150	J 5
04004	Bar Mills, 800	C 8
04653	Bass Harbor, 413	G 7
04530	Bath⊙, 9,679	D 8
04915	Bayside, 238	F 7
04611	Beals, ▵663	H 7
04622	Beddington, ▵32	H 6
04915	Belfast⊙, 5,957	F 7
04917	Belgrade, ▵1,302	D 7
04917	Belgrade, 300	D 7
04918	Belgrade Lakes, 700	D 6
04915	Belmont, ▵349	E 7
04733	Benedicta, ▵177	G 4
04919	Benton, ▵1,729	D 6
03901	Berwick, ▵3,136	B 9
03901	Berwick, 1,765	B 9
04285	Berry Mills, 245	C 6
04217	Bethel, ▵2,220	B 7
04217	Bethel, 750	B 7
04005	Biddeford, 19,983	B 9
04006	Biddeford Pool, 500	C 9
04920	Bingham, ▵1,254	D 5
04920	Bingham, 1,184	D 5
04613	Birch Harbor, 210	H 7
04734	Blaine, ▵903	H 2
04734	Blaine-Mars Hill, 1,854	H 2
04406	Blanchard, ▵56	D 5
04614	Blue Hill, ▵1,367	F 7
04615	Blue Hill Falls, 850	F 7
04040	Bolsters Mills, 150	B 7
04537	Boothbay, ▵1,814	D 8
04537	Boothbay, 700	D 8
04538	Boothbay Harbor, 2,320	D 8
04008	Bowdoinham, ▵1,294	D 7
04481	Bowerbank, ▵29	E 5
04410	Bradford, ▵569	F 5
04410	Bradford, 150	F 5
04411	Bradley, ▵1,010	F 6
04412	Brewer, 9,300	F 6
04735	Bridgewater, ▵895	H 3
04009	Bridgton, ▵2,967	B 7
04009	Bridgton, 1,779	B 7
† 04990	Brighton, ▵58	D 5
04539	Bristol, ▵1,721	D 8
04539	Bristol, 160	D 8
04616	Brooklin, ▵598	F 7
04921	Brooks, ▵751	E 6
04617	Brooksville, ▵673	F 7
04413	Brookton, 225	H 4
04010	Brownfield, ▵478	B 8
04010	Brownfield, 200	B 8
04414	Brownville, ▵1,490	E 5
04414	Brownville, 1,641	E 5
04415	Brownville Junction, 950	E 5
04011	Brunswick, ▵16,195	C 8
04011	Brunswick, 10,867	C 8
04219	Bryant Pond, 350	B 7
04220	Buckfield, ▵929	C 7
04618	Bucks Harbor, 161	J 6
04416	Bucksport, ▵3,756	F 6
04416	Bucksport, 2,456	F 6
04417	Burlington, ▵266	G 5
04922	Burnham, ▵802	E 6
† 04093	Buxton, ▵3,135	C 8
† 04275	Byron, ▵132	B 6
04619	Calais, 4,044	J 5
04923	Cambridge, ▵281	E 5
04843	Camden, ▵4,115	F 7
04843	Camden, 3,492	F 7
04924	Canaan, ▵904	D 6
04221	Canton, ▵742	C 7
03902	Cape Neddick, 850	B 9
04014	Cape Porpoise, 500	C 9
04925	Caratunk, ▵96	C 5
04418	Cardville, 223	F 5
04736	Caribou, 10,419	G 2
04419	Carmel, ▵1,301	E 6
04420	Carroll, ▵132	G 5
† 04224	Carthage, ▵354	C 6
† 04465	Cary, ▵184	H 4
04015	Casco, ▵1,256	B 7
04015	Casco, 250	B 7
04421	Castine, ▵1,080	F 7
† 04623	Centerville, ▵19	H 6
† 04757	Chapman, ▵328	G 2
04422	Charleston, ▵909	F 5
† 04666	Charlotte, ▵199	J 5
04017	Chebeague Island, 400	C 8
† 04345	Chelsea, ▵2,095	D 7
04622	Cherryfield, ▵771	H 6
† 04458	Chester, ▵255	F 5
† 04938	Chesterville, ▵643	C 6
04926	China, ▵1,850	E 7
04926	China, 336	E 7
04222	Chisholm, 1,530	C 7
† 04428	Clifton, ▵233	G 6
04927	Clinton, ▵1,971	D 6
04927	Clinton, 1,124	D 6
† 04623	Columbia, ▵162	H 6
04623	Columbia Falls, ▵367	H 6
† 04638	Cooper, ▵88	H 6
04341	Coopers Mills, 200	E 7
04624	Corea, 300	H 7
04928	Corinna, ▵1,700	E 6
04020	Cornish, ▵839	B 8
† 04976	Cornville, ▵623	D 6
04423	Costigan, 200	F 5
04625	Cranberry Isles, ▵186	G 7
† 04610	Crawford, ▵74	H 5
† 04015	Crescent Lake, 175	C 7
04738	Crouseville, 300	G 2
† 04747	Crystal, ▵281	G 4
04021	Cumberland Center, ▵4,096	C 8
04021	Cumberland Center, 950	C 8
04011	Cundys Harbor, 150	D 8
† 04563	Cushing, ▵522	E 7
04626	Cutler, ▵588	J 6
04626	Cutler, 153	J 6
04543	Damariscotta, ▵1,264	E 7
04543	Damariscotta-Newcastle, 1,188	E 7
04424	Danforth, ▵794	H 4
04424	Danforth, 650	H 4
† 04622	Deblois, ▵20	H 6
† 04429	Dedham, ▵522	F 6
04627	Deer Isle, ▵1,211	F 7
04627	Deer Isle, 600	F 7
04022	Denmark, ▵397	B 8
04628	Dennysville, ▵278	J 6
04425	Derby, 300	E 5
04929	Detroit, ▵663	E 6
04930	Dexter, ▵3,725	E 5
04936	Dexter, 2,732	E 5
04224	Dixfield, ▵2,188	C 6
04224	Dixfield, 1,535	C 6
04932	Dixmont, ▵559	E 6
04426	Dover-Foxcroft, ▵4,178	E 5
04426	Dover-Foxcroft⊙, 3,102	E 5
04342	Dresden, ▵787	D 7
04225	Dryden, 675	C 6
† 04039	Dry Mills, 700	C 8
† 04747	Dyer Brook, ▵165	G 3
04739	Eagle Lake, ▵908	F 1
04739	Eagle Lake, 675	F 1
04226	East Andover, 194	B 6
04024	East Baldwin, 175	B 8
04629	East Blue Hill, 150	G 7
04544	East Boothbay, 400	D 8
04427	East Corinth, 525	F 5
04227	East Dixfield, 288	C 6
04428	East Eddington, 200	F 6
04026	East Hiram, 198	B 8
04429	East Holden, 450	F 6
04027	East Lebanon, 950	B 9
† 04049	East Limington, 200	B 8
04228	East Livermore, 290	C 7
04630	East Machias, ▵1,057	J 6
04630	East Machias, 750	J 6
† 04950	East Madison, 400	D 6
04430	East Millinocket, ▵2,567	F 4
04430	East Millinocket, 2,564	F 4
04740	Easton, ▵1,305	H 2
† 04270	East Otisfield, 200	B 7
04229	East Peru, 350	C 7
04230	East Poland, 700	C 7
04631	Eastport, 1,989	K 6
04231	East Stoneham, 150	B 7
04632	East Sullivan, 300	G 6
† 04862	East Union, 220	E 7
04935	East Vassalboro, 300	D 7
04030	East Waterboro, 365	B 8
04234	East Wilton, 650	C 6
† 04428	Eddington, ▵1,358	F 6
† 04428	Eddington, 250	F 6
04545	Edgecomb, ▵549	D 8
† 04628	Edmunds, 229	J 6
03903	Eliot, ▵3,497	B 9
04605	Ellsworth⊙, 4,603	F 6
04433	Enfield, ▵1,148	F 5
04433	Enfield, 150	F 5
04434	Etna, ▵526	E 6
04936	Eustis, ▵595	B 5
04435	Exeter, ▵663	E 6
† 04938	Fairbanks, 300	C 6
04937	Fairfield, ▵5,684	D 6
04937	Fairfield, 3,694	D 6
† 04937	Fairfield Center, 975	D 6
04105	Falmouth, ▵6,291	C 8
04105	Falmouth, 1,621	C 8
† 04105	Falmouth Foreside (Falmouth), 1,621	C 8
† 04345	Farmingdale, ▵2,423	D 7
† 04345	Farmingdale, 1,832	D 7
04938	Farmington, ▵5,657	C 6
04938	Farmington⊙, 3,096	C 6
04940	Farmington Falls, 500	C 6
04344	Fayette, ▵447	C 7
04546	Five Islands, 161	D 8
04742	Fort Fairfield, ▵4,859	H 2
04742	Fort Fairfield, 2,322	H 2
04743	Fort Kent, ▵4,575	F 1
04743	Fort Kent, 2,876	F 1
04744	Fort Kent Mills, 300	F 1
04438	Frankfort, ▵620	F 6
04634	Franklin, ▵708	G 6
04634	Franklin, 350	G 6
04941	Freedom, ▵373	E 7
04032	Freeport, ▵4,781	C 8
04032	Freeport, 1,822	C 8
04745	Frenchville, ▵1,375	G 1
04745	Frenchville, 800	G 1
04547	Friendship, ▵834	E 7
04547	Friendship, 700	E 7
04037	Fryeburg, ▵2,208	A 7
04037	Fryeburg, 1,075	A 7
04345	Gardiner, 6,685	D 7
04939	Garland, ▵596	E 5
04939	Garland, 300	E 5
04548	Georgetown, ▵464	D 8
04548	Georgetown, 190	D 8
† 04217	Gilead, ▵153	B 7
† 04401	Glenburn, ▵1,196	F 6
04846	Glen Cove, 300	E 7
† 04005	Goodwins Mills, 340	B 8
† 04046	Goose Rocks Beach, 200	C 9
04038	Gorham, ▵7,839	C 8
04038	Gorham, 3,337	C 8
04636	Gouldsboro, ▵1,310	H 7
04636	Gouldsboro, 296	H 7
04746	Grand Isle, ▵797	G 1
04746	Grand Isle, 400	G 1
04637	Grand Lake Stream, ▵186	H 5
04039	Gray, ▵2,939	C 8
04039	Gray, 525	C 8
04236	Greene, ▵1,772	C 7
04441	Greenville, ▵1,894	D 5
04441	Greenville, 1,714	D 5
04442	Greenville Junction, 150	D 5
04443	Guilford, ▵1,694	E 5
04443	Guilford, 1,216	E 5
04347	Hallowell, 2,814	D 7
† 04785	Hamlin, ▵357	H 1
04444	Hampden, ▵4,693	F 6
04444	Hampden, 2,207	F 6
04445	Hampden Highlands, 950	F 6
04640	Hancock, ▵1,070	G 6
04237	Hanover, ▵275	B 7
04942	Harmony, ▵650	D 6
04942	Harmony, 350	D 6
† 04011	Harpswell, ▵2,552	D 8
04643	Harrington, ▵553	H 6
04040	Harrison, ▵1,045	B 7
† 04221	Hartford, ▵312	C 7
04943	Hartland, ▵1,414	D 6
04943	Hartland, 975	D 6
04446	Haynesville, ▵157	G 4
04238	Hebron, ▵532	C 7
† 04401	Hermon, ▵2,376	F 6
† 04082	Highland Lake, 600	C 8
04944	Hinckley, 317	D 6
04041	Hiram, ▵686	B 8
04041	Hiram, 175	B 8
04730	Hodgdon, ▵933	H 3
† 04429	Holden, ▵1,789	H 3
† 04429	Holden, 900	H 3
04042	Hollis Center, ▵1,560	B 8
04847	Hope, ▵500	E 7
04847	Hope, 175	E 7
04730	Houlton, ▵8,111	H 3
04730	Houlton⊙, 6,760	H 3
04448	Howland, ▵1,468	F 5
04448	Howland, 1,418	F 5
04449	Hudson, ▵482	F 5
04644	Hulls Cove, 200	G 7
04747	Island Falls, ▵913	G 3
04645	Isle au Haut, ▵45	F 7
04848	Islesboro, ▵421	F 7
04848	Islesboro, 200	F 7
04945	Jackman, ▵848	C 4
04945	Jackman, 700	C 4
04647	Jacksonville, 200	J 6
04239	Jay, ▵3,954	C 7
04239	Jay, 850	C 7
04348	Jefferson, ▵1,242	D 7
04648	Jonesboro, ▵448	J 6
04649	Jonesport, ▵1,326	H 6
04649	Jonesport, 1,073	H 6
04748	Keegan, 450	G 1
04450	Kenduskeag, ▵733	E 6
04043	Kennebunk, ▵5,646	B 9
04043	Kennebunk, 2,764	B 9
04046	Kennebunkport, ▵2,160	C 9
04046	Kennebunkport, 1,097	C 9
04349	Kents Hill, 250	D 7
04047	Kezar Falls, 680	B 8
04947	Kingfield, ▵877	C 6
04451	Kingman, 250	G 4
† 04990	Kingsbury, ▵7	D 5
03904	Kittery, ▵11,028	B 9
03904	Kittery, 7,363	B 9
03905	Kittery Point, 1,172	B 9
† 04986	Knox, ▵443	E 6
04453	La Grange, ▵393	F 5
04453	La Grange, 250	F 5
† 04463	Lake View, ▵16	F 5
† 04605	Lamoine, ▵615	G 7
04455	Lee, ▵599	G 5
† 04263	Leeds, ▵1,031	C 7
04456	Levant, ▵862	F 6
04240	Lewiston, 41,779	C 7
	Lewiston-Auburn, ‡72,474	C 7
04949	Liberty, ▵515	E 7
04949	Liberty, 200	E 7
04749	Lille, 300	G 1
04048	Limerick, ▵963	B 8
04750	Limestone, ▵8,745	H 2
04750	Limestone, 1,572	H 2
04049	Limington, ▵1,066	B 8
04049	Limington, 250	B 8
04457	Lincoln, ▵4,759	G 5
04457	Lincoln, 3,482	G 5
04458	Lincoln Center, 325	G 5
04849	Lincolnville, ▵955	E 7
04849	Lincolnville, 800	E 7
04755	Linneus, ▵608	H 3
04250	Lisbon, ▵6,544	C 7
* 04250	Lisbon-Lisbon Center, 1,475	C 7
04252	Lisbon Falls, 3,257	D 7
04350	Litchfield, ▵1,222	D 7
04650	Little Deer Isle, 275	F 7
† 04760	Littleton, ▵958	H 3
04253	Livermore, ▵1,610	C 7
04253	Livermore, 280	C 7
04254	Livermore Falls, ▵3,450	C 7
04254	Livermore Falls, 2,378	C 7
04255	Locke Mills, 300	B 7
04051	Lovell, ▵607	B 7
04051	Lovell, 180	B 7
† 04433	Lowell, ▵154	F 5
04652	Lubec, ▵1,949	K 6
04652	Lubec, 900	K 6
† 04730	Ludlow, ▵259	G 3
04654	Machias, ▵2,441	J 6
04654	Machias⊙, 1,368	J 6
04655	Machiasport, ▵887	H 6
04655	Machiasport, 374	H 6
† 04451	Macwahoc, ▵126	G 4
04756	Madawaska, ▵5,585	G 1
04756	Madawaska, 4,452	G 1
04950	Madison, ▵4,278	D 6
04950	Madison, 2,920	D 6
† 04966	Madrid, ▵107	B 6
04351	Manchester, ▵1,331	D 7
04757	Mapleton, ▵1,598	G 2
04758	Mars Hill, ▵1,875	H 2
04758	Mars Hill-Blaine, 1,854	H 2
04759	Masardis, ▵317	G 3
04459	Mattawamkeag, ▵988	G 5
04256	Mechanic Falls, ▵2,193	C 7
04256	Mechanic Falls, 1,872	C 7
04657	Meddybemps, ▵76	J 5
† 04453	Medford, ▵146	F 5
04460	Medway, ▵1,491	G 4
04957	Mercer, ▵313	D 6
04257	Mexico, ▵4,309	B 6
04257	Mexico, 3,325	B 6
04658	Milbridge, ▵1,154	H 6
04461	Milford, ▵1,828	F 6
04461	Milford, 1,519	F 6
04462	Millinocket, ▵7,742	F 4
04462	Millinocket, 7,558	F 4
04463	Milo, ▵2,572	F 5
04463	Milo, 1,514	F 5
04258	Minot, ▵919	C 7
04258	Minot, 250	C 7
04852	Monhegan, ▵44	E 8
04259	Monmouth, ▵2,062	D 7

(continued on following page)

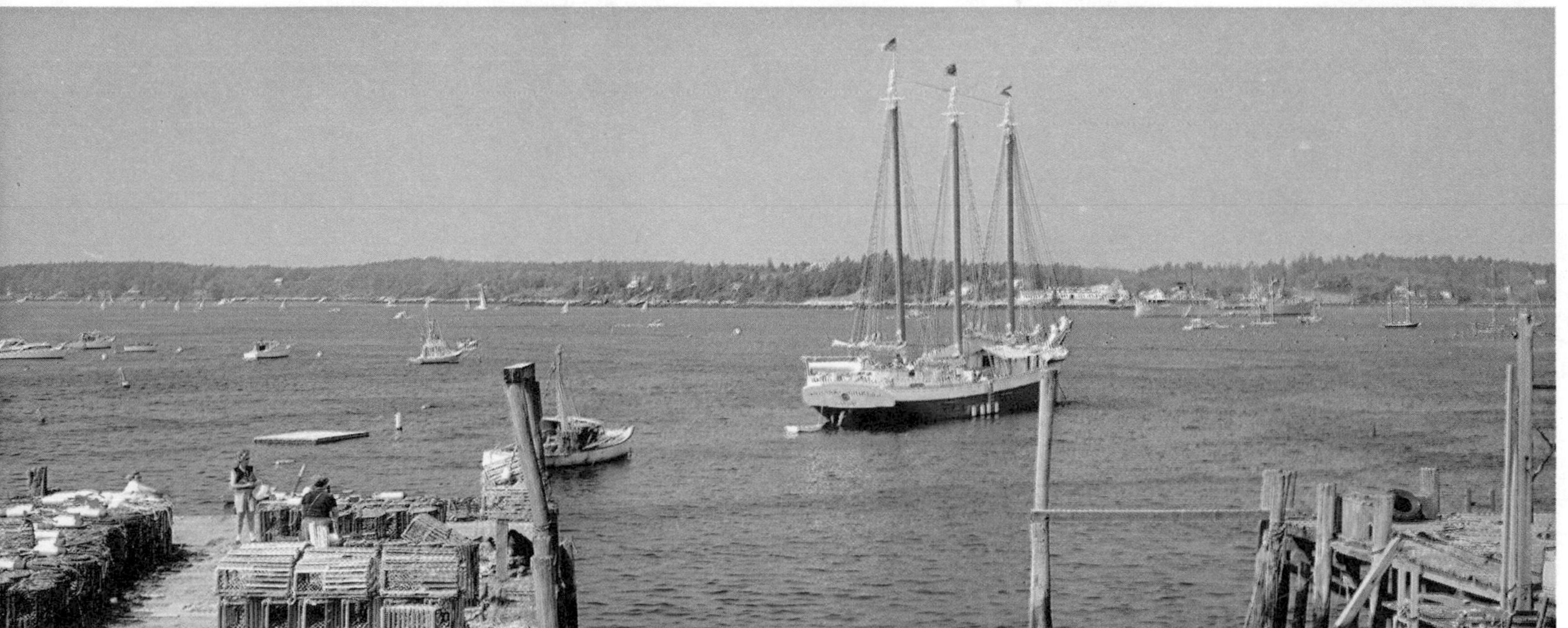

Boothbay Harbor offers facilities for a variety of sailing craft — yachts, rented party boats and commercial fishermen, all seen here at anchor. This active port rates high among Maine's popular coastal resort towns.

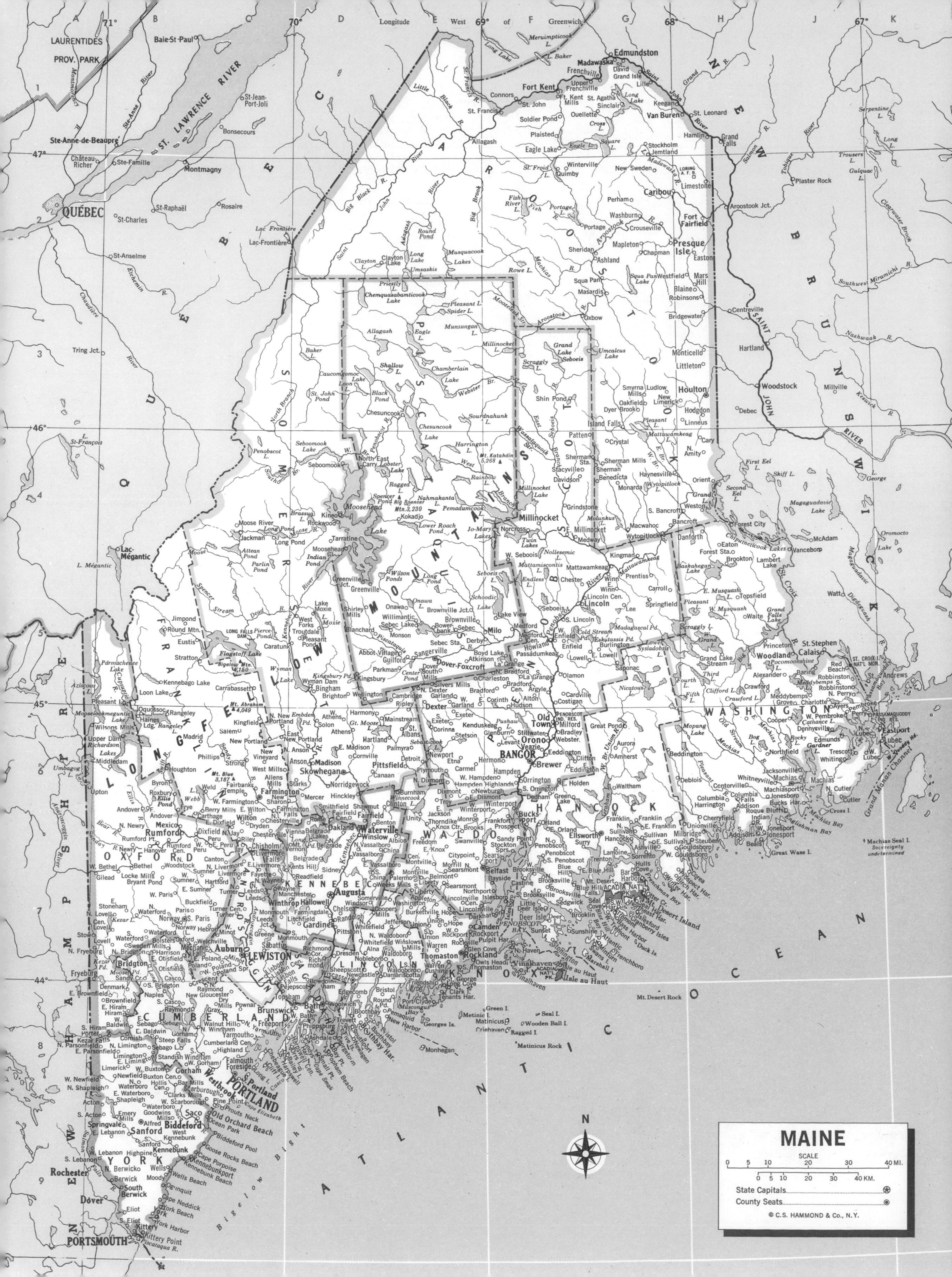

MAINE
SCALE
0 5 10 20 30 40 MI.
0 5 10 20 30 40 KM.
State Capitals
County Seats
© C.S. HAMMOND & Co., N.Y.
Longitude West of Greenwich
71° 70° 69° 68° 67°
47° 46° 45° 44°
A B C D E F G H J K
1 2 3 4 5 6 7 8 9
QUÉBEC
NEW BRUNSWICK
NEW HAMPSHIRE
ATLANTIC OCEAN
ST. LAWRENCE RIVER
LAURENTIDES PROV. PARK
AROOSTOOK
PISCATAQUIS
PENOBSCOT
SOMERSET
FRANKLIN
OXFORD
WASHINGTON
HANCOCK
WALDO
KENNEBEC
ANDROSCOGGIN
CUMBERLAND
YORK
LINCOLN
KNOX
SAGADAHOC
LONGFELLOW MOUNTAINS
Moosehead Lake
Mt. Katahdin 5,268
Mt. Abraham 4,049
Mt. Blue 3,187
Bigelow Mtn. 4,150
ACADIA NAT'L PK.
Mt. Desert Island
Augusta
Bangor
Portland
Lewiston
Auburn
Presque Isle
Houlton
Caribou
Millinocket
Waterville
Brunswick
Bath
Rockland
Belfast
Ellsworth
Machias
Eastport
Calais
Biddeford
Saco
Sanford
Kittery
Portsmouth
Edmundston
Fort Kent
Van Buren
Madawaska
Dover-Foxcroft
Skowhegan
Farmington
Rumford
Old Town
Orono
Brewer
Bigelow Bight
Grand Manan Channel
Machias Seal I. Sovereignty undetermined
Mt. Desert Rock
Matinicus Rock

04259 Monmouth, 500...D 7
04951 Monroe, ∆478...E 6
04464 Monson, ∆669...E 5
04760 Monticello, ∆1,072...H 3
04941 Montville, ∆430...E 7
04054 Moody, 500...B 9
04945 Moose River, ∆255...C 4
04952 Morrill, ∆410...E 7
04660 Mount Desert, ∆1,659...G 7
04352 Mount Vernon, ∆680...D 7
04055 Naples, ∆956...B 8
04445 Newburgh, ∆835...F 6
04553 Newcastle, ∆1,076...D 7
04553 Newcastle-Damariscotta, 1,188...E 7
04056 Newfield, ∆458...B 8
04056 Newfield, 165...B 8
04260 New Gloucester, ∆2,811...C 8
04260 New Gloucester, 400...C 8
04554 New Harbor, 580...E 8
04761 New Limerick, ∆427...G 3
04953 Newport, ∆2,260...E 6
04953 Newport, 1,588...E 6
04954 New Portland, ∆559...C 6
04954 New Portland, 201...C 6
04261 Newry, ∆208...B 6
04955 New Sharon, ∆725...C 6
04762 New Sweden, ∆639...G 2
04762 New Sweden, 400...G 2
04956 New Vineyard, ∆444...C 6
04555 Nobleboro, ∆850...D 7
04957 Norridgewock, ∆1,964...D 6
04957 Norridgewock, 1,067...D 6
04958 North Anson 950...D 6
04959 North Belgrade, 300...D 7
03906 North Berwick, ∆2,224...B 9
03906 North Berwick, 1,449...B 9
04057 North Bridgton, 200...B 7
04626 North Cutler, 153...J 6
04662 Northeast Harbor, 700...G 7
04654 Northfield, ∆57...H 6
04058 North Fryeburg, 250...B 7
04853 North Haven, ∆399...F 7
04853 North Haven, 300...F 7
04262 North Jay, 800...C 6
04049 North Limington, 400...B 8
04254 North Livermore, 280...C 7
04663 North Lubec, 250...J 6
04961 North New Portland, 300...C 6
04849 Northport, ∆744...E 7
04664 North Sullivan, 280...G 6
04266 North Turner, 300...C 7
04962 North Vassalboro, 950...D 7
04572 North Waldoboro, 250...E 7
04061 North Waterboro, 200...B 8
04267 North Waterford, 217...B 7
04284 North Wayne, 175...C 7
04353 North Whitefield, 300...D 7
04062 North Windham, 600...C 8

† 04219 North Woodstock, 400...B 7
† 04096 North Yarmouth, ∆1,383...C 8
† 04096 North Yarmouth, 500...C 8
04268 Norway, ∆3,595...B 7
04268 Norway, 2,430...B 7
04763 Oakfield, ∆836...G 3
04963 Oakland, ∆5,273...D 6
04963 Oakland, 2,261...D 6
03907 Ogunquit, 800...B 9
04064 Old Orchard Beach, ∆5,404...C 9
04064 Old Orchard Beach, 5,273...C 9
04468 Old Town, 9,057...F 6
04964 Oquossoc, 210...B 6
04471 Orient, ∆83...H 4
04472 Orland, ∆1,307...F 6
04472 Orland, 500...F 6
04473 Orono, ∆9,989...F 6
04473 Orono, 9,146...F 6
04474 Orrington, ∆2,702...F 6
04474 Orrington, 250...F 6
04066 Orrs Island, 500...D 8
† 04270 Otisfield, ∆589...B 7
04665 Otter Creek, 350...G 7
04854 Owls Head, ∆1,281...F 7
04764 Oxbow, ∆92...G 3
04270 Oxford, ∆1,892...B 7
04270 Oxford, 550...B 7
04354 Palermo, ∆645...E 7
04965 Palmyra, ∆1,104...E 6
04271 Paris, ∆3,739...B 7
† 04443 Parkman, ∆457...D 5
04475 Passadumkeag, ∆326...F 5
04765 Patten, ∆1,266...F 4
04765 Patten, 1,068...F 4
04067 Pejepscott, 200...D 8
04558 Pemaquid, 160...E 8
04666 Pembroke, ∆700...J 6
04666 Pembroke, 300...J 6
04476 Penobscot, ∆786...F 7
04766 Perham, ∆436...G 2
04667 Perry, ∆878...J 6
04272 Peru, ∆1,345...C 6
04966 Phillips, ∆979...C 6
04562 Phippsburg, ∆1,229...D 8
04562 Phippsburg, 280...D 8
† 04064 Pine Point, 650...C 8
04967 Pittsfield, ∆4,274...E 6
04967 Pittsfield, 3,398...E 6
† 04345 Pittston, ∆1,617...D 7
04969 Plymouth, ∆542...E 6
04273 Poland, ∆2,015...C 7
04273 Poland, 300...C 7
04768 Portage, ∆477...G 2
04855 Port Clyde, 300...E 8
04068 Porter, ∆1,115...B 8
04068 Porter, 225...B 8
* 04101 Portland⊙, 65,116...C 8
Portland, ‡141,625...C 8
04069 Pownal, ∆800...C 8

04477 Prentiss, ∆159...G 5
04769 Presque Isle, 11,452...H 2
04668 Princeton, ∆956...H 5
† 04981 Prospect, ∆358...F 6
04669 Prospect Harbor, 350...H 7
† 04345 Randolph, ∆1,741...D 7
† 04345 Randolph, 1,548...D 7
04970 Rangeley, ∆941...B 6
04970 Rangeley, 600...B 6
04071 Raymond, ∆1,328...B 8
04071 Raymond, 550...B 8
04355 Readfield, ∆1,258...D 7
04355 Readfield, 300...D 7
04670 Red Beach, 210...J 5
04357 Richmond, ∆2,168...D 7
04357 Richmond, 1,449...D 7
† 04357 Richmond Corner, 200...D 7
† 04930 Ripley, ∆297...E 5
04671 Robbinston, ∆396...J 5
04671 Robbinston, 200...J 5
† 04734 Robinsons, 487...H 3
04841 Rockland⊙, 8,505...E 7
04856 Rockport, ∆2,067...F 7
04856 Rockport, 875...F 7
† 04841 Rockville, 250...E 7
04478 Rockwood, 250...D 4
† 04957 Rome, ∆362...D 6
† 04654 Roque Bluffs, ∆153...H 6
04564 Round Pond, 375...E 8
04275 Roxbury, ∆271...B 6
04276 Rumford, ∆9,363...B 6
04276 Rumford, 6,198...B 6
04278 Rumford Center, 325...B 7
04280 Sabattus, 950...C 7
04072 Saco, 11,678...C 8
04772 Saint Agatha, ∆868...G 1
04971 Saint Albans, ∆1,041...E 6
04773 Saint David, 915...G 1
04774 Saint Francis, ∆811...E 1
04857 Saint George, ∆1,639...E 7
04857 Saint George, 250...E 7
† 04743 Saint John, ∆377...F 1
† 04983 Salem, 300...C 6
04972 Sandy Point, 300...F 7
04073 Sanford, ∆10,457...B 9
04073 Sanford, 15,812...B 9
04479 Sangerville, ∆1,107...E 5
04074 Scarborough, ∆7,845...C 8
04074 Scarborough, 500...C 8
04675 Seal Harbor, 336...G 7
04973 Searsmont, ∆624...E 7
04973 Searsmont, 400...E 7
04974 Searsport, ∆1,951...F 7
04974 Searsport, 1,110...F 7
04075 Sebago Lake, 500...B 8
04481 Sebec, ∆325...E 5
04484 Seboeis, ∆63...F 5
04676 Sedgwick, ∆578...F 7
04076 Shapleigh, ∆559...B 8

04975 Shawmut, 250...D 6
04775 Sheridan, 250...F 2
† 04777 Sherman, ∆949...G 4
† 04777 Sherman, 165...G 4
04776 Sherman Mills, 600...G 4
04777 Sherman Station, 300...F 4
04485 Shirley Mills, ∆174...D 5
04485 Shirley Mills, 180...D 5
† 04330 Sidney, ∆1,319...D 7
04779 Sinclair, 260...G 1
04976 Skowhegan, ∆7,601...D 6
04976 Skowhegan⊙, 6,571...D 6
04978 Smithfield, ∆527...D 6
04780 Smyrna Mills, ∆318...G 3
04780 Smyrna Mills, 250...G 3
04781 Soldier Pond, 500...F 1
04979 Solon, ∆712...D 6
† 04341 Somerville, ∆215...D 7
04677 Sorrento, ∆199...G 7
03908 South Berwick, ∆3,488...B 9
03908 South Berwick, 1,863...B 9
04568 South Bristol, ∆664...D 8
04077 South Casco, 200...B 8
04358 South China, 225...D 7
† 03903 South Eliot, 1,635...B 9
04079 South Harpswell, 650...C 8
04080 South Hiram, 175...B 8
† 04862 South Hope, 200...E 7
† 03901 South Lebanon, 200...A 9
† 04259 South Monmouth, 168...D 7
† 04474 South Orrington, 400...F 6
04281 South Paris⊙, 2,315...C 7
† 04569 Southport, ∆473...D 8
04569 Southport, 175...D 8
04106 South Portland, 23,267...C 8
† 04073 South Sanford, 850...B 9
04858 South Thomaston, ∆831...E 7
† 04864 South Union, 180...E 7
† 04572 South Waldoboro, 300...E 7
04081 South Waterford, 320...B 7
04679 Southwest Harbor, ∆1,657...G 7
04082 South Windham, 1,453...C 8
04487 Springfield, ∆336...G 5
04083 Springvale, 2,914...B 9
04782 Stacyville, ∆547...F 4
04084 Standish, ∆3,122...B 8
04084 Standish, 700...B 8
04980 Starks, ∆323...D 6
04085 Steep Falls, 500...B 8
04488 Stetson, ∆395...E 6
04680 Steuben, ∆697...H 6
04680 Steuben, 200...H 6
04489 Stillwater, 600...F 6
04783 Stockholm, ∆388...G 1
04981 Stockton Springs, ∆1,142...F 7
04981 Stockton Springs, 500...F 7
04681 Stonington, ∆1,291...F 7
† 04058 Stow, ∆109...A 7
04982 Stratton, 450...B 5

04983 Strong, ∆1,132...C 6
04682 Sullivan, ∆824...G 6
† 04292 Sumner, ∆525...C 7
04683 Sunset, 170...F 7
† 04627 Sunshine, 175...G 7
04684 Surry, ∆623...F 7
04685 Swans Island, ∆323...G 7
† 04915 Swanville, ∆487...E 6
† 04040 Sweden, ∆110...B 7
04984 Temple, ∆367...C 6
04860 Tenants Harbor, 600...E 8
04861 Thomaston, ∆2,646...E 7
04861 Thomaston, 2,160...E 7
04986 Thorndike, ∆439...E 6
04490 Topsfield, 180...H 5
04086 Topsham, ∆5,022...D 8
04086 Topsham, 2,700...D 8
† 04653 Tremont, ∆1,003...G 7
† 04653 Tremont, 175...G 7
† 04605 Trenton, ∆392...G 7
† 04652 Trescott, 200...J 6
04571 Trevett, 275...D 8
04987 Troy, ∆543...E 6
04282 Turner, ∆2,246...C 7
04282 Turner, 400...C 7
04862 Union, ∆1,189...E 7
04862 Union, 300...E 7
04988 Unity, ∆1,280...E 6
04784 Upper Frenchville, 375...G 1
04261 Upton, ∆54...B 6
04785 Van Buren, ∆3,971...G 1
04785 Van Buren, 3,429...G 1
04491 Vanceboro, ∆263...J 4
04989 Vassalboro, ∆2,618...D 7
04401 Veazie, ∆1,556...F 6
04401 Veazie, 1,174...F 6
04360 Vienna, ∆205...D 6
04863 Vinalhaven, ∆1,135...F 7
04492 Waite, ∆70...H 5
† 04915 Waldo, ∆431...E 7
04572 Waldoboro, ∆3,146...E 7
04572 Waldoboro, 824...E 7
† 04021 Walnut Hill, 400...C 8
† 04605 Waltham, ∆167...G 6
04864 Warren, ∆1,864...E 7
04864 Warren, 770...E 7
04786 Washburn, ∆1,914...G 2
04786 Washburn, 1,098...G 2
04574 Washington, ∆723...E 7
04087 Waterboro, ∆1,208...B 8
04087 Waterboro, 400...B 8
04088 Waterford, ∆760...B 7
04901 Waterville, 18,192...D 6
04284 Wayne, ∆577...D 7
04284 Wayne, 175...D 7
04361 Weeks Mills, 235...E 7
04285 Weld, ∆360...C 6
04990 Wellington, ∆232...D 5
04090 Wells, ∆4,448...B 9

04090 Wells, 950...B 9
04090 Wells Beach, 600...B 9
04686 Wesley, ∆110...H 6
† 04530 West Bath, ∆836...D 8
04286 West Bethel, 155...B 7
04092 Westbrook, 14,444...C 8
† 04617 West Brooksville, 156...F 7
04093 West Buxton, 185...B 8
04493 West Enfield, 500...F 5
04992 West Farmington, 700...C 6
04787 Westfield, ∆517...G 2
† 04634 West Franklin, 350...G 6
† 04345 West Gardiner, ∆1,435...D 7
† 04445 West Hampden, 800...E 6
04649 West Jonesport, 400...H 6
† 04652 West Lubec, 275...J 6
04288 West Minot, 200...C 7
04095 West Newfield, 225...B 8
04494 Weston, ∆162...H 4
04289 West Paris, ∆1,171...B 7
04290 West Peru, 650...C 7
04291 West Poland, 300...C 7
04865 West Rockport, 350...E 7
04074 West Scarborough, 850...C 8
04690 West Tremont, 200...G 7
04362 Whitefield, ∆1,131...D 7
04362 Whitefield, 550...D 7
04691 Whiting, ∆269...J 6
04692 Whitneyville, ∆155...H 6
† 04443 Willimantic, ∆126...E 5
04294 Wilton, ∆3,802...C 6
04294 Wilton, 2,225...C 6
04363 Windsor, ∆1,097...D 7
04495 Winn, ∆516...G 5
04495 Winn, 250...G 5
04901 Winslow, ∆7,299...D 6
04901 Winslow, 5,389...D 6
04693 Winter Harbor, ∆1,028...G 7
04496 Winterport, ∆1,963...F 6
04496 Winterport, 900...F 6
04788 Winterville, ∆164...F 2
04364 Winthrop, ∆4,335...C 7
04364 Winthrop, 2,571...C 7
04578 Wiscasset⊙, ∆2,244...D 7
04694 Woodland, 1,534...H 5
04579 Woolwich, ∆1,710...D 8
† 04920 Wyman Dam, 300...D 5
04497 Wytopitlock, 200...G 4
04096 Yarmouth, ∆4,854...C 8
04096 Yarmouth, 2,421...C 8
03909 York, ∆5,690...B 9
03909 York, 2,912...B 9
03910 York Beach, 900...B 9
03911 York Harbor, 950...B 9

⊙ County seat.
‡ Population of metropolitan area.
∆ Population of town or township.
† Zip of nearest p.o.
* Multiple zips

Agriculture, Industry and Resources

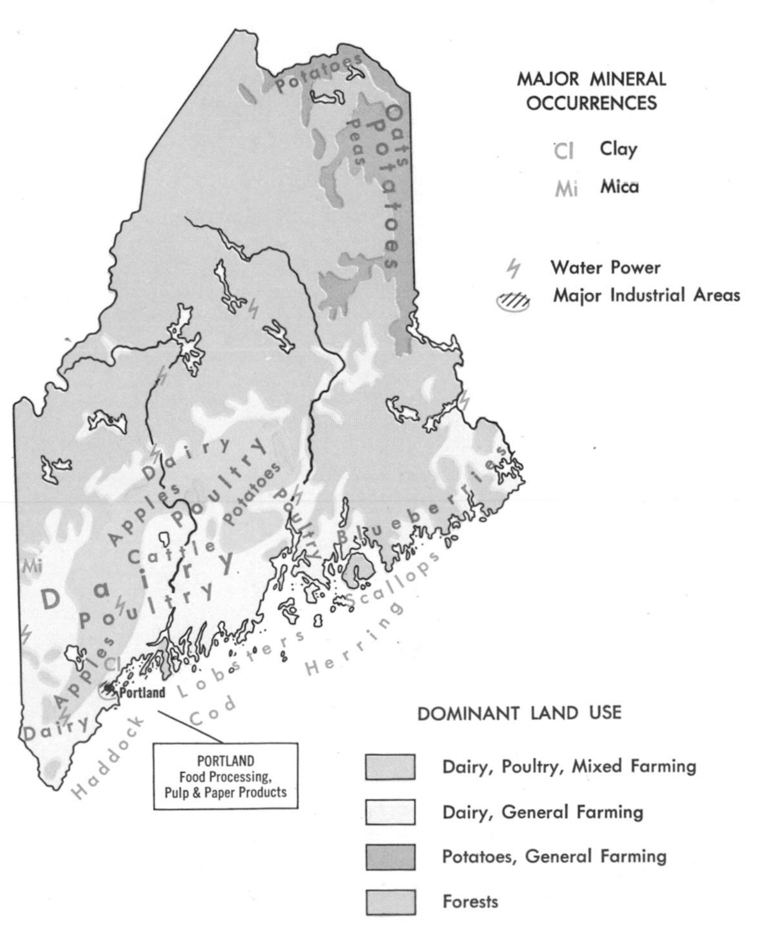

Topography

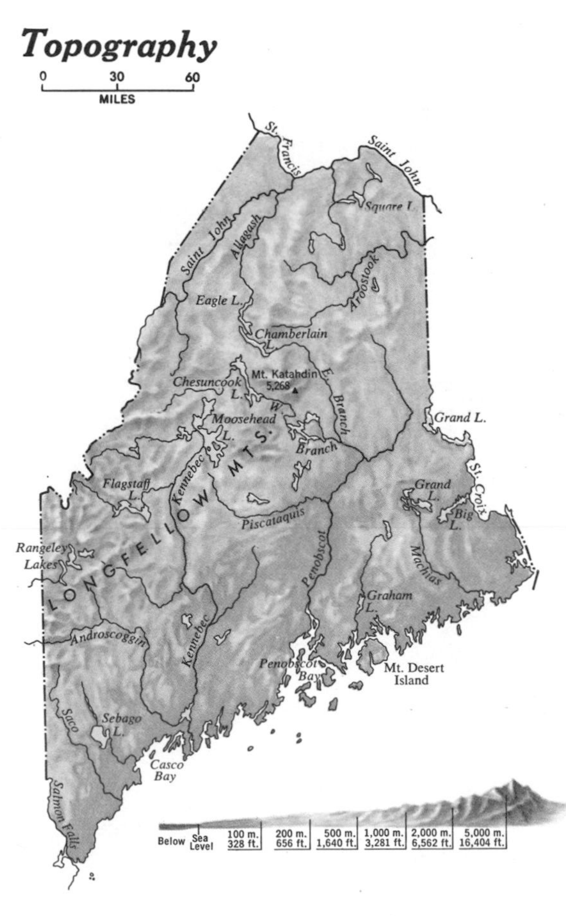

MARYLAND

COUNTIES

Allegany, 84,044 C 2
Anne Arundel, 297,539 M 4
Baltimore, 621,077 M 3
Baltimore (city county), 905,759 M 3
Calvert, 20,682 M 6
Caroline, 19,781 P 5
Carroll, 69,006 K 2
Cecil, 53,291 P 2
Charles, 47,678 K 6
Dorchester, 29,405 O 7
Frederick, 84,927 J 3
Garrett, 21,476 A 2
Harford, 115,378 N 2
Howard, 61,911 L 4
Kent, 16,146 O 3
Montgomery, 522,809 J 4
Prince Georges, 660,567 L 5
Queen Annes, 18,422 P 4
Saint Marys, 47,388 M 7
Somerset, 18,924 R 8
Talbot, 23,692 O 5
Washington, 103,829 G 2
Wicomico, 54,236 R 7
Worcester, 24,442 S 8

CITIES and TOWNS

Zip Name/Pop. Key
21001 Aberdeen, 12,375 O 2
21009 Abingdon, 3,000 N 3
21520 Accident, 237 A 2
20607 Accokeek, 450 L 6
21710 Adamstown, 265 H 3
21810 Allen, 200 R 7
† 21043 Allview, 2,314 L 4
* 21401 Annapolis (cap.)⊙, 29,592 M 5
20701 Annapolis Junction, 775 M 4
† 21782 Antietam, 150 H 3
20608 Aquasco, 950 L 6
† 20785 Ardmore, 500 G 4
† 20015 Aspen Hill, 16,799 K 4
* 21201 Baltimore, 905,759 M 3
Baltimore, ‡2,070,670 M 3
21607 Barclay, 187 P 4
20703 Barnesville, 162 J 4
20610 Barstow, 500 M 6
21521 Barton, 723 B 2
† 21901 Bayview, 250 P 2
21014 Bel Air⊙, 6,307 N 2
20611 Bel Alton, 675 L 7
† 21662 Bellevue, 300 O 6
20705 Beltsville, 8,912 G 3
20612 Benedict, 700 M 6
21811 Berlin, 1,942 T 7
† 20740 Berwyn Heights, 3,934 G 4
20014 Bethesda, 71,621 E 4
21609 Bethlehem, 200 P 6
21610 Betterton, 327 O 3
21611 Bishops Head, 250 O 7
21813 Bishopville, 300 T 7
21814 Bivalve, 450 P 7
20710 Bladensburg, 7,488 G 4
21523 Bloomington, 235 B 3
21713 Boonsboro, 1,410 H 2
† 21532 Borden Shaft, 208 B 2
21020 Boring, 283 L 2
† 20027 Boulevard Heights, 500 F 5
† 20678 Bowens, 250 M 6
20715 Bowie, 35,028 L 4
20720 Boyds, 300 J 4
21612 Bozman, 500 N 5
20613 Brandywine, 525 L 6
20722 Brentwood, 3,426 F 4
21715 Brownsville, 185 H 3
21716 Brunswick, 3,566 H 3
21717 Buckeystown, 400 J 3
21718 Burkittsville, 221 H 3
20730 Burtonsville, 3,000 L 4
20618 Bushwood, 675 L 7
21023 Butler, 150 M 2
20731 Cabin John, 2,500 E 4
20619 California, 350 M 7
† 20705 Calverton, 6,453 L 4
21613 Cambridge⊙, 11,595 O 6
20031 Camp Springs, 22,776 G 6
20027 Capitol Heights, 2,852 G 5
21024 Cardiff, 510 N 2
† 20780 Carrollton, 13,395 G 4
21025 Carrollton, 174 L 2
† 21034 Castleton, 675 N 2
† 21788 Catoctin Furnace, 516 J 2
21228 Catonsville, 54,812 M 3
21720 Cavetown, 325 H 2
21912 Cecilton, 581 P 3
† 20767 Cedar Grove, 300 K 4
† 20027 Cedar Heights, 6,049 G 5
21617 Centreville⊙, 1,853 O 4
21816 Chance, 500 P 8
20621 Chaptico, 300 M 7
21914 Charlestown, 721 P 2
20622 Charlotte Hall, 200 M 7
21027 Chase, 900 N 3
20623 Cheltenham, 950 L 6
† 21921 Cherry Hill, 214 P 2
20732 Chesapeake Beach, 934 N 6
21915 Chesapeake City, 1,031 P 2
21619 Chester, 950 N 5
21620 Chestertown⊙, 3,476 O 4
20785 Cheverly, 6,696 G 4
20015 Chevy Chase, 16,424 E 4
21721 Chewsville, 350 H 2
20783 Chillum, 35,656 F 4
21623 Church Hill, 247 O 4
21028 Churchville, 500 N 2
21624 Claiborne, 150 N 5
20734 Clarksburg, 400 J 4
21029 Clarksville, 500 L 4
21722 Clear Spring, 499 G 2
20624 Clements, 800 L 7
20735 Clinton, 1,900 G 6
21030 Cockeysville, 2,900 M 3
20740 College Park, 26,156 G 4
† 20722 Colmar Manor, 1,715 F 4
21917 Colora, 500 O 2
20626 Coltons Point, 310 M 8
21043 Columbia, 8,815 L 5
20627 Compton, 500 M 7
21918 Conowingo, 150 O 2
21723 Cooksville, 497 K 3
† 20027 Coral Hills, 7,105 G 5
21625 Cordova, 365 O 5
21524 Corriganville, 850 C 2
† 20722 Cottage City, 993 F 4
† 20611 Cox Station (Bel Alton), 675 L 7
† 21788 Creagerstown, 240 J 2
21525 Crellin, 500 A 3
21502 Cresaptown, 1,731 C 2
21817 Crisfield, 3,078 P 9
21627 Crocheron, 150 O 8
21113 Crofton, 4,478 M 4
21032 Crownsville, 1,900 M 4
21628 Crumpton, 375 P 4
21502 Cumberland⊙, 29,724 D 2
20750 Damascus, 2,638 K 3
20628 Dameron, 500 N 8
21820 Dames Quarter, 300 P 8
† 25425 Dargan, 245 H 3
21034 Darlington, 800 N 2
20760 Darnestown, 950 J 4
21035 Davidsonville, 250 M 5
20751 Deale, 1,059 M 5
21821 Deal Island, 800 P 8
21550 Deer Park, 310 A 3
† 19940 Delmar, 1,191 R 7
21629 Denton⊙, 1,561 P 5
20855 Derwood, 450 K 4
20753 Dickerson, 500 J 4
20028 District Heights, 8,424 G 5
† 21710 Doubs, 273 J 3
† 21795 Downsville, 255 G 2
20630 Drayden, 450 N 8
† 21154 Dublin, 366 N 2
21222 Dundalk, 85,377 N 3
† 20608 Eagle Harbor, 200 M 6
† 21146 Earleigh Heights, 1,500 M 4
21631 East New Market, 251 P 6
21601 Easton⊙, 6,809 O 5
21528 Eckhart Mines, 900 C 2
21040 Edgewood, 8,551 N 3
† 20781 Edmonston, 1,441 F 4
† 21784 Eldersburg, 1,739 L 3
21920 Elk Mills, 500 P 2
† 21901 Elk Neck, 700 P 2
21227 Elkridge, 4,900 M 4
21921 Elkton⊙, 5,362 P 2
21529 Ellerslie, 950 C 2
21043 Ellicott City⊙, 9,506 L 3
21727 Emmitsburg, 1,532 J 2
21221 Essex, 38,193 N 3
21824 Ewell, 350 O 9
† 21620 Fairlee, 300 O 4
† 20027 Fairmont Heights, 1,972 G 5
21047 Fallston, 617 N 2
21632 Federalsburg, 1,917 P 6
21061 Ferndale, 9,929 M 4
21048 Finksburg, 950 L 3
21634 Fishing Creek, 595 N 7
21530 Flintstone, 395 D 2
† 20907 Forest Glen, 1,900 F 4
† 20001 Forest Heights, 3,600 F 5
21050 Forest Hill, 450 N 2
† 20028 Forestville, 16,152 G 5
† 20013 Fort Foote, 700 F 6
† 20735 Fort Washington, 1,650 L 6
† 21740 Fountain Head, 2,029 H 2
† 21760 Foxville, 400 J 2
21701 Frederick⊙, 23,641 J 3
21053 Freeland, 500 M 2
21531 Friendsville, 566 A 2
† 21157 Frizzellburg, 300 K 2
21532 Frostburg, 7,327 C 2
21826 Fruitland, 2,315 R 7
21734 Funkstown, 1,051 H 2
20760 Gaithersburg, 8,344 K 4
21635 Galena, 361 P 3
21054 Gambrills, 460 M 4
20766 Garrett Park, 1,258 E 3
21055 Garrison, 950 L 3
20767 Germantown, 260 J 4
21829 Girdletree, 850 S 8
20801 Glenarden, 4,502 G 4
21057 Glen Arm, 350 N 3
21061 Glen Burnie, 38,608 M 4
20768 Glen Echo, 297 E 4
† 20013 Glen Echo Heights, 2,025 E 4
21737 Glenelg, 400 L 3
21071 Glyndon-Reisterstown, 14,037 L 3
21636 Goldsboro, 231 P 4
† 20715 Good Luck, 10,584 G 4
† 21788 Graceham, 300 J 2
† 21163 Granite, 950 L 3
21536 Grantsville, 517 B 2
21638 Grasonville, 1,182 O 5
20770 Greenbelt, 18,199 G 4
21122 Green Haven, 1,841 M 4
21072 Greenmount, 325 L 2
21639 Greensboro, 1,173 P 5
21740 Hagerstown⊙, 35,862 G 2
† 21740 Halfway, 6,106 G 2
† 20850 Halpine, 5,912 K 4
21074 Hampstead, 961 L 2
21750 Hancock, 1,832 F 2
21201 Hanover, 500 M 4
† 21787 Harney, 250 K 2
21078 Havre de Grace, 9,791 O 2
21830 Hebron, 705 R 7
21080 Henryton, 400 L 3
† 21111 Hereford, 680 M 2
21753 Highfield, 500 J 2
† 20901 Hillandale, 19,520 F 4
† 20001 Hillcrest Heights, 24,037 F 5
21641 Hillsboro, 177 P 5
20636 Hollywood, 500 M 7
21642 Hoopersville, 300 O 7
20637 Hughesville, 500 L 6
20639 Huntingtown, 450 M 6
21643 Hurlock, 1,056 P 6
† 21864 Hursley Station (Stockton), 500 S 8
20734 Hyattstown, 150 J 3
* 20780 Hyattsville, 14,998 F 4
20640 Indian Head, 1,350 K 6
21644 Ingleside, 180 P 4

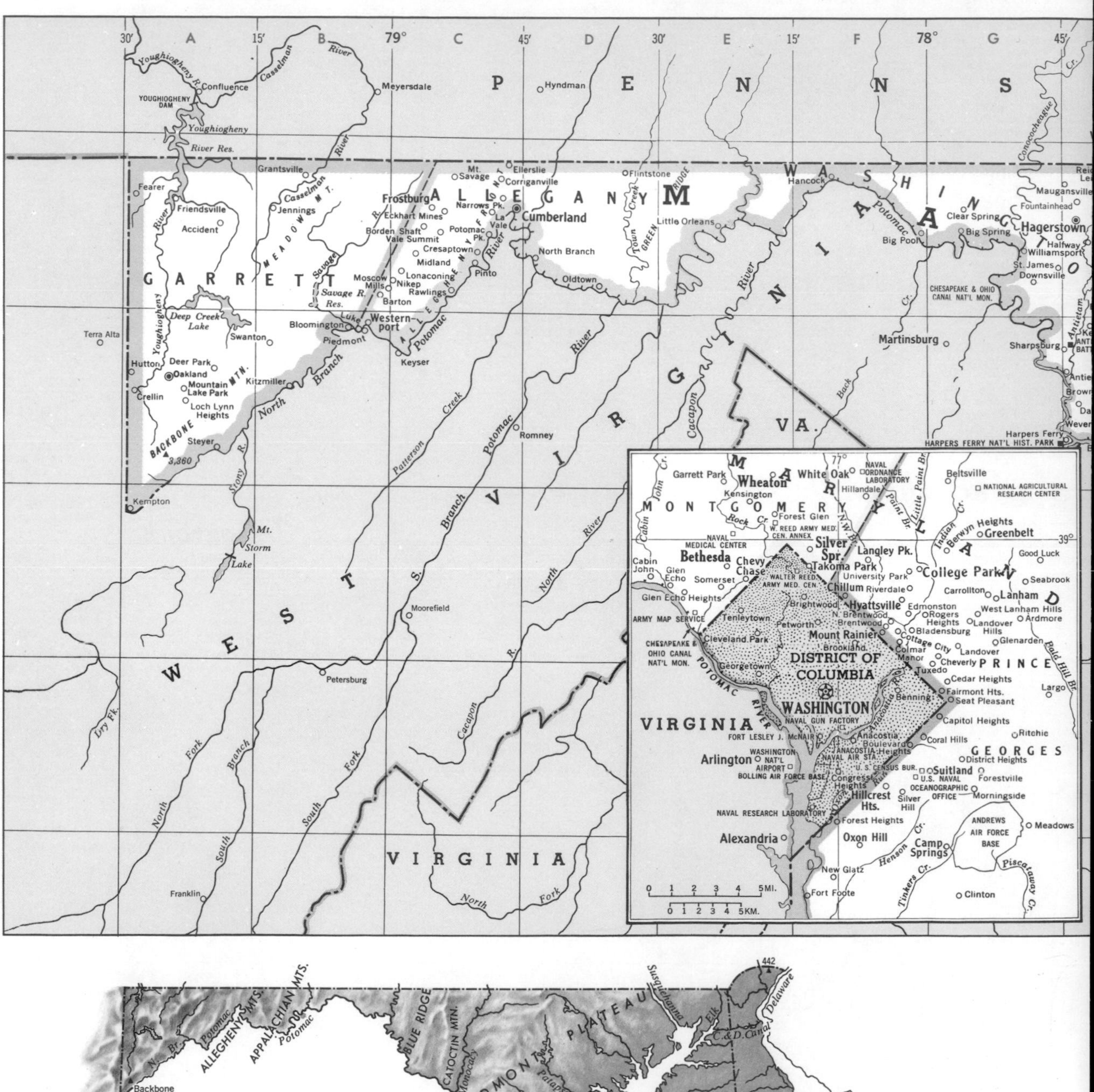

Topography

0 30 60 MILES

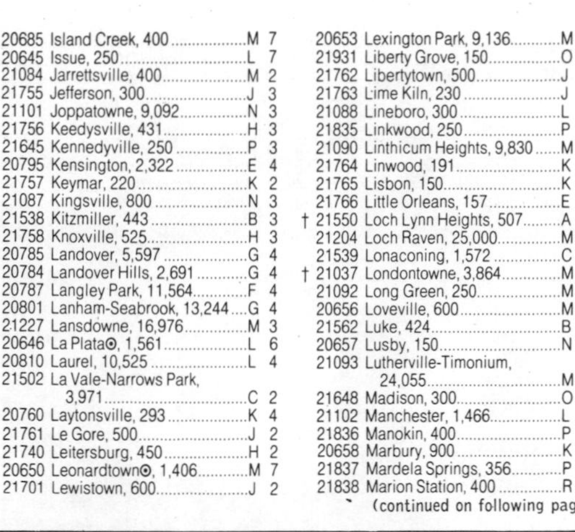

† 20685	Island Creek, 400	M	7
20645	Issue, 250	L	7
21084	Jarrettsville, 400	M	2
21755	Jefferson, 300	J	3
† 21101	Joppatowne, 9,092	N	3
21756	Keedysville, 431	H	3
21645	Kennedyville, 250	P	3
20795	Kensington, 2,322	E	4
21757	Keymar, 220	K	2
21087	Kingsville, 800	N	3
21538	Kitzmiller, 443	B	3
21758	Knoxville, 525	H	3
20785	Landover, 5,597	G	4
20784	Landover Hills, 2,691	G	4
20787	Langley Park, 11,564	F	4
20801	Lanham-Seabrook, 13,244	G	4
21227	Lansdowne, 16,976	M	3
20646	La Plata⊙, 1,561	L	6
20810	Laurel, 10,525	L	4
21502	La Vale-Narrows Park, 3,971	C	2
20760	Laytonsville, 293	K	4
21761	Le Gore, 500	J	2
† 21740	Leitersburg, 450	H	2
20650	Leonardtown⊙, 1,406	M	7
21701	Lewistown, 600	J	2
20653	Lexington Park, 9,136	M	7
21931	Liberty Grove, 150	O	2
21762	Libertytown, 500	J	3
21763	Lime Kiln, 230	J	3
21088	Lineboro, 300	L	2
21835	Linkwood, 250	P	6
21090	Linthicum Heights, 9,830	M	4
21764	Linwood, 191	K	2
21765	Lisbon, 150	K	3
21766	Little Orleans, 157	E	2
† 21550	Loch Lynn Heights, 507	A	3
21204	Loch Raven, 25,000	M	3
21539	Lonaconing, 1,572	C	2
† 21037	Londontowne, 3,864	M	4
21092	Long Green, 250	M	3
20656	Loveville, 600	M	7
21562	Luke, 424	B	3
20657	Lusby, 150	N	7
21093	Lutherville-Timonium, 24,055	M	3
21648	Madison, 300	O	6
21102	Manchester, 1,466	L	2
21836	Manokin, 400	P	8
20658	Marbury, 900	K	6
21837	Mardela Springs, 356	P	7
21838	Marion Station, 400	R	8

(continued on following page)

MARYLAND

AREA 10,577 sq. mi.
POPULATION 3,922,399
CAPITAL Annapolis
LARGEST CITY Baltimore
HIGHEST POINT Backbone Mtn. 3,360 ft.
SETTLED IN 1634
ADMITTED TO UNION April 28, 1788
POPULAR NAME Old Line State; Free State
STATE FLOWER Black-eyed Susan
STATE BIRD Baltimore Oriole

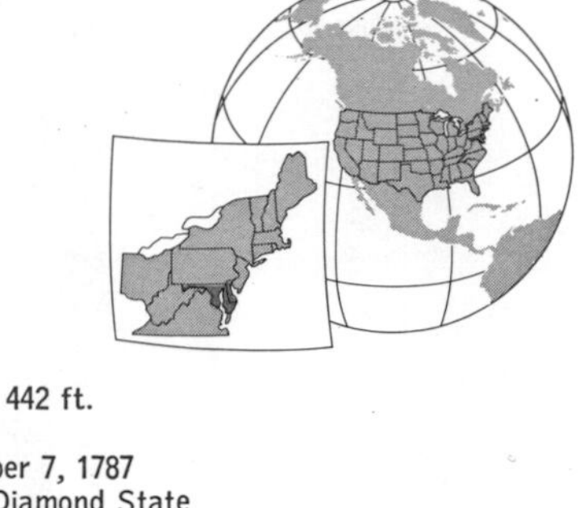

DELAWARE

AREA 2,057 sq. mi.
POPULATION 548,104
CAPITAL Dover
LARGEST CITY Wilmington
HIGHEST POINT Ebright Road 442 ft.
SETTLED IN 1631
ADMITTED TO UNION December 7, 1787
POPULAR NAME First State; Diamond State
STATE FLOWER Peach Blossom
STATE BIRD Blue Hen Chicken

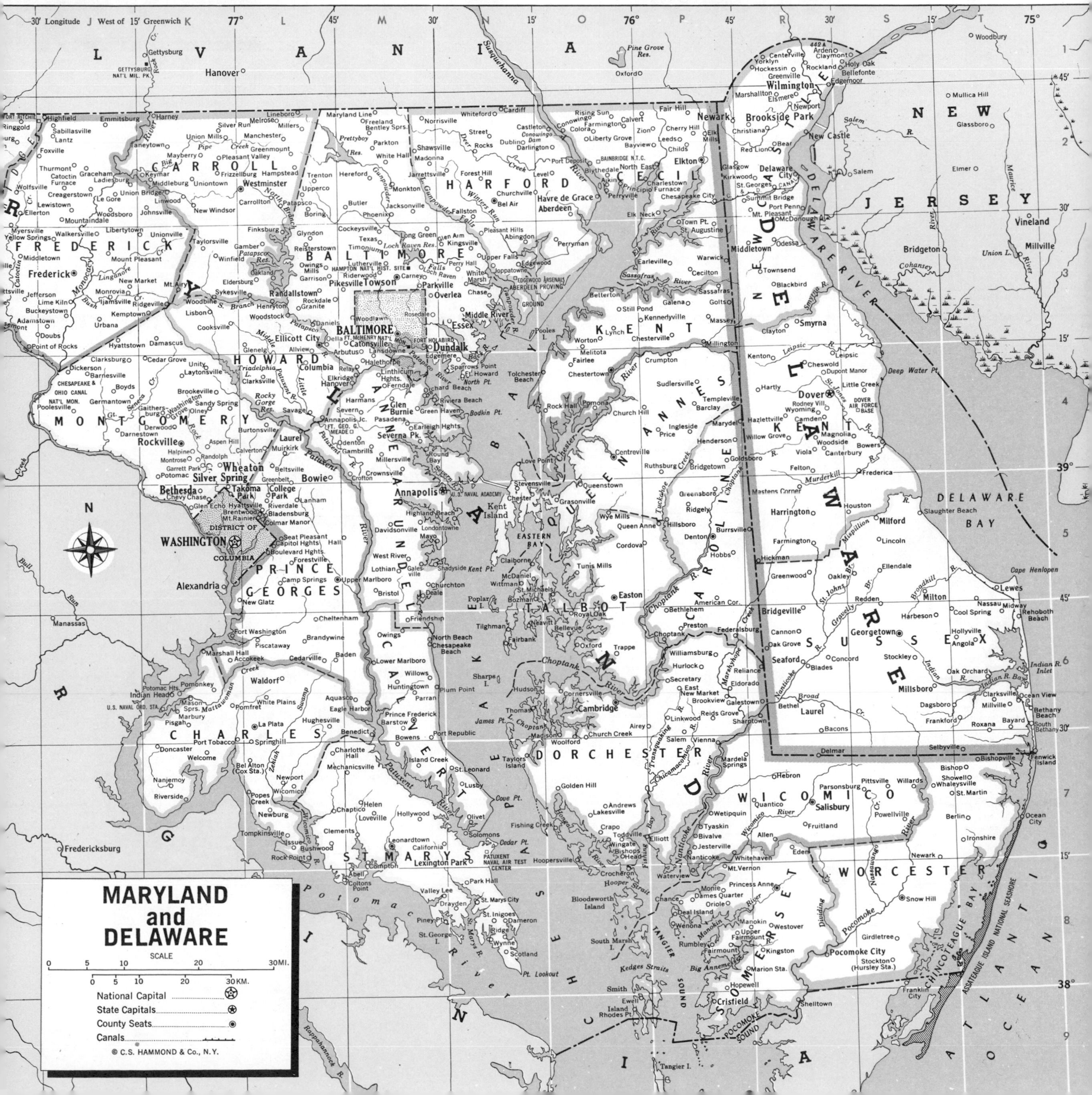

MARYLAND and DELAWARE

SCALE
0 5 10 20 30 MI.
0 5 10 20 30 KM.

National Capital
State Capitals
County Seats
Canals

MARYLAND (continued)

† 20616 Marshall Hall, 325 .... K 6
21649 Marydel, 176 .... P 4
21105 Maryland Line, 250 .... M 2
21650 Massey, 220 .... P 3
21767 Maugansville, 1,069 .... H 2
21106 Mayo, 2,154 .... M 5
21647 McDaniel, 325 .... N 5
† 20870 Meadows, 200 .... G 5
20659 Mechanicsville, 784 .... M 7
21708 Middleburg, 200 .... K 2
21220 Middle River, 19,935 .... N 3
21769 Middletown, 1,262 .... J 3
21542 Midland, 665 .... C 2
21108 Millersville, 380 .... M 4
21651 Millington, 474 .... P 3
21111 Monkton, 307 .... M 2
21770 Monrovia, 300 .... J 3
† 20850 Montrose, 6,140 .... K 4
† 20028 Morningside, 1,665 .... G 5
† 21521 Moscow Mills, 275 .... B 2
† 21701 Mountaindale, 400 .... J 2
21550 Mountain Lake Park, 1,263 .... A 3
21771 Mount Airy, 1,825 .... K 3
† 21701 Mount Pleasant, 400 .... J 3
20822 Mount Rainier, 8,180 .... F 4
21545 Mount Savage, 1,413 .... C 2
† 21853 Mount Vernon, 900 .... P 8
† 20705 Muirkirk, 950 .... L 4
21773 Myersville, 450 .... H 3
20662 Nanjemoy, 238 .... K 7
21840 Nanticoke, 400 .... P 7
† 21502 Narrows Park-La Vale, 3,971 .... C 2
21652 Neavitt, 241 .... N 6
21841 Newark, 800 .... S 7
20664 Newburg, 550 .... L 7
† 20013 New Glatz, 950 .... F 6
21774 New Market, 339 .... J 3
21776 New Windsor, 788 .... K 2
21546 Nikep, 400 .... C 2
20831 North Beach, 761 .... N 6
† 20722 North Brentwood, 758 .... F 4
21901 North East, 1,818 .... P 2
21550 Oakland⊙, 1,786 .... A 3
21550 Oakland, 1,256 .... L 3
21842 Ocean City, 1,493 .... T 7
21113 Odenton, 5,989 .... M 4
† 21043 Oella, 600 .... L 3
21555 Oldtown, 400 .... D 2
20832 Olney, 2,138 .... K 4
† 21122 Orchard Beach, 200 .... M 4
21206 Overlea, 13,086 .... N 3
20836 Owings, 700 .... M 6
21117 Owings Mills, 7,360 .... L 3
21654 Oxford, 750 .... O 6
20021 Oxon Hill, 11,974 .... F 6
20667 Park Hall, 600 .... N 8
21120 Parkton, 290 .... M 2
21234 Parkville, 33,897 .... M 3
† 20639 Parran, 200 .... M 6
21849 Parsonsburg, 200 .... R 7
21122 Pasadena, 2,380 .... M 4
21127 Patapsco, 160 .... L 2
21128 Perry Hall, 5,446 .... N 3
21130 Perryman, 665 .... O 3
21903 Perryville, 2,091 .... O 2
21131 Phoenix, 165 .... M 2
21208 Pikesville, 25,395 .... M 3
20674 Piney Point, 950 .... M 8
21556 Pinto, 165 .... C 2
20640 Pisgah, 650 .... K 6
21850 Pittsville, 477 .... S 7
† 21087 Pleasant Hills, 1,754 .... N 3
21851 Pocomoke City, 3,573 .... R 8
21777 Point of Rocks, 400 .... J 3
20675 Pomfret, 600 .... L 6
20837 Poolesville, 349 .... J 4
21904 Port Deposit, 906 .... O 2
20677 Port Tobacco, 590 .... K 6
20854 Potomac (Potomac Valley), 5,094 .... K 4
20640 Potomac Heights, 1,983 .... K 6
† 21502 Potomac Park, 2,253 .... C 2
21852 Powellville, 450 .... S 7
21655 Preston, 509 .... P 6
20678 Prince Frederick⊙, 950 .... M 6
21853 Princess Anne⊙, 975 .... P 8
21856 Quantico, 200 .... R 7
21657 Queen Anne, 292 .... O 5
21658 Queenstown, 387 .... O 5
21133 Randallstown, 33,683 .... L 3
† 20853 Randolph, 13,233 .... K 4
21557 Rawlings, 600 .... C 2
21136 Reisterstown-Glyndon, 14,037 .... L 3
21139 Riderwood, 8,000 .... M 3
20680 Ridge, 550 .... N 8
21660 Ridgely, 822 .... P 5
21911 Rising Sun, 956 .... O 2
† 20013 Ritchie, 950 .... G 5
20840 Riverdale, 5,724 .... F 4
21122 Riviera Beach, 7,464 .... N 4
21661 Rock Hall, 1,125 .... O 4
20682 Rock Point, 300 .... L 7
* 20850 Rockville⊙, 41,564 .... K 4
† 20780 Rogers Heights, 3,000 .... G 4
21779 Rohrersville, 500 .... H 3
21237 Rosedale, 19,417 .... M 3
21662 Royal Oak, 600 .... O 6
21780 Sabillasville, 200 .... J 2
20684 Saint Inigoes, 750 .... N 8
21781 Saint James, 400 .... G 2
20685 Saint Leonard, 244 .... N 7
20686 Saint Marys City, 1,900 .... N 8
21663 Saint Michaels, 1,456 .... N 5
21801 Salisbury⊙, 15,252 .... R 7
20860 Sandy Spring, 500 .... K 4
20863 Savage, 2,116 .... L 4
20687 Scotland, 660 .... N 8
20801 Seabrook-Lanham, 13,244 .... G 4
20027 Seat Pleasant, 7,217 .... G 5
21664 Secretary, 352 .... P 6
21146 Severna Park, 16,358 .... M 4
20867 Shady Side, 1,562 .... N 5
21782 Sharpsburg, 833 .... G 3
21861 Sharptown, 660 .... R 6

Antietam Battlefield, near Sharpsburg, Maryland, the scene of the country's bloodiest one-day battle on September 17, 1862. A national battlefield site today, it is surrounded by farms, some of whose cattle graze among the cannons and monuments.

J. C. Maycock — Shostal Associates

In Lewes, Delaware, settled by the Dutch in 1631, the Thompson Country Store sign establishes its origin as c.1800. The home of generations of Delaware River ship pilots, this seafaring town survives a history of shipwreck, bombardment and plundering.

Dorothy Bacheller

21862 Showell, 250 .... T 7
20023 Silver Hill-Suitland, 30,355 .... F 5
* 20901 Silver Spring, 77,496 .... F 4
21783 Smithsburg, 671 .... H 2
21863 Snow Hill⊙, 2,201 .... S 8
20688 Solomons, 250 .... N 7
† 20015 Somerset, 1,303 .... E 4
21666 Stevensville, 500 .... N 5
21667 Still Pond, 250 .... O 3
21864 Stockton, 500 .... S 8
21154 Street, 200 .... N 2
21668 Sudlersville, 417 .... P 4
20023 Suitland-Silver Hill, 30,355 .... F 5
21561 Swanton, 223 .... A 3
21784 Sykesville, 1,399 .... K 3
20012 Takoma Park, 18,455 .... F 4
21787 Taneytown, 1,731 .... K 2
21669 Taylors Island, 375 .... N 7
21788 Thurmont, 2,359 .... J 2
21671 Tilghman, 950 .... N 6
21093 Timonium-Lutherville, 24,055 .... M 3
21672 Toddville, 300 .... O 7
21204 Towson⊙, 77,809 .... M 3
21673 Trappe, 426 .... O 6
20781 Tuxedo, 500 .... G 5
21791 Union Bridge, 904 .... K 2
21157 Uniontown, 250 .... K 2
21792 Unionville, 250 .... K 3
† 20740 University Park, 2,926 .... F 4
21155 Upperco, 500 .... L 2
21867 Upper Fairmount, 300 .... P 8
21156 Upper Falls, 900 .... N 3
20870 Upper Marlboro⊙, 646 .... M 5
20692 Valley Lee, 600 .... M 8
21869 Vienna, 358 .... P 7
20601 Waldorf, 7,368 .... L 6
21793 Walkersville, 1,269 .... J 3
21912 Warwick, 550 .... P 3
20880 Washington Grove, 688 .... K 4
20693 Welcome, 438 .... K 7
21870 Wenona, 323 .... P 8
21562 Westernport, 3,106 .... B 3
† 20784 West Lanham Hills, 950 .... G 4
21157 Westminster⊙, 7,207 .... L 2
21871 Westover, 450 .... R 8
20881 West River, 796 .... M 5
20902 Wheaton, 66,247 .... E 3
21160 Whiteford, 500 .... N 2
21161 White Hall, 350 .... M 2
21162 White Marsh, 500 .... N 3
† 20901 White Oak, 19,769 .... F 3
20695 White Plains, 1,600 .... L 6
21874 Willards, 494 .... S 7
21674 Williamsburg, 300 .... P 6
21795 Williamsport, 2,270 .... G 2
21675 Wingate, 200 .... O 7
21676 Wittman, 500 .... N 5
21797 Woodbine, 872 .... K 3
† 21201 Woodlawn, 28,811 .... M 3
21798 Woodsboro, 439 .... J 2
21163 Woodstock, 700 .... L 3
21677 Woolford, 295 .... O 7
21678 Worton, 315 .... O 3
21679 Wye Mills, 300 .... O 5
† 21701 Yellow Springs, 940 .... H 3

DELAWARE

COUNTIES

Kent, 81,892 .... R 4
New Castle, 385,856 .... R 2
Sussex, 80,356 .... S 6

CITIES and TOWNS

Zip *Name/Pop.* *Key*

† 19801 Arden, 3,340 .... R 1
19701 Bear, 200 .... R 2
19809 Bellefonte, 1,442 .... S 1
19930 Bethany Beach, 189 .... T 6
19931 Bethel, 219 .... R 6
† 19973 Blades, 632 .... R 6
19993 Bridgeville, 1,317 .... R 6
19711 Brookside Park, 7,856 .... R 2
19934 Camden, 1,241 .... R 4
† 19801 Centerville, 1,260 .... R 1
19936 Cheswold, 286 .... R 4
19702 Christiana, 550 .... R 2
19937 Clarksville, 350 .... T 6
19703 Claymont, 6,584 .... S 1
19938 Clayton, 1,015 .... R 3
19930 Dagsboro, 375 .... S 6
19706 Delaware City, 2,024 .... R 2
19940 Delmar, 943 .... R 7
19901 Dover (cap.)⊙, 17,488 .... R 4
† 19901 Dupont Manor, 1,256 .... R 4
† 19801 Edgemoor, 2,100 .... S 1
19941 Ellendale, 399 .... S 5
† 19801 Elsmere, 8,415 .... R 2
19943 Felton, 495 .... R 4
19945 Frankford, 635 .... S 6
19946 Frederica, 878 .... S 4
19947 Georgetown⊙, 1,844 .... S 6
19807 Greenville, 230 .... R 1
19950 Greenwood, 654 .... R 5
19951 Harbeson, 312 .... S 6
19952 Harrington, 2,407 .... R 5
19953 Hartly, 180 .... R 4
19707 Hockessin, 950 .... R 1
† 19801 Holly Oak, 1,140 .... S 1
19954 Houston, 317 .... S 5
19955 Kenton, 205 .... R 4
19708 Kirkwood, 450 .... R 2
19956 Laurel, 2,408 .... R 6
19958 Lewes, 2,563 .... T 5
19960 Lincoln, 757 .... S 5
19961 Little Creek, 215 .... S 4
19962 Magnolia, 319 .... R 4
19808 Marshallton, 1,240 .... R 2
19709 Middletown, 2,644 .... R 3
19963 Milford, 5,314 .... S 5
19966 Millsboro, 1,073 .... S 6
19967 Millville, 224 .... T 6
19968 Milton, 1,490 .... S 5
19711 Newark, 20,757 .... P 2
19720 New Castle, 4,814 .... R 2
19804 Newport, 1,366 .... R 2
19970 Ocean View, 411 .... T 6
19730 Odessa, 547 .... R 3
19731 Port Penn, 325 .... R 2
19971 Rehoboth Beach, 1,614 .... T 6
19901 Rodney Village, 2,127 .... R 4
19733 Saint Georges, 450 .... R 2
19973 Seaford, 5,537 .... R 6
19975 Selbyville, 1,099 .... S 7
19977 Smyrna, 4,243 .... R 3
19734 Townsend, 505 .... R 3
19979 Viola, 154 .... R 4
* 19801 Wilmington⊙, 80,386 .... R 2
Wilmington, ‡498,977 .... R 2
19980 Woodside, 223 .... R 4
19934 Wyoming, 1,062 .... R 4
19736 Yorklyn, 300 .... R 1

DISTRICT OF COLUMBIA

CITIES and TOWNS

Zip *Name/Pop.* *Key*

20007 Georgetown, ... E 5
* 20001 Washington, D.C. (cap.), U.S. 756,510 .... F 5
Washington, ‡2,861,123 .... F 5

⊙ County seat.
‡ Population of metropolitan area.
† Zip of nearest p.o.
* Multiple zips

Agriculture, Industry and Resources

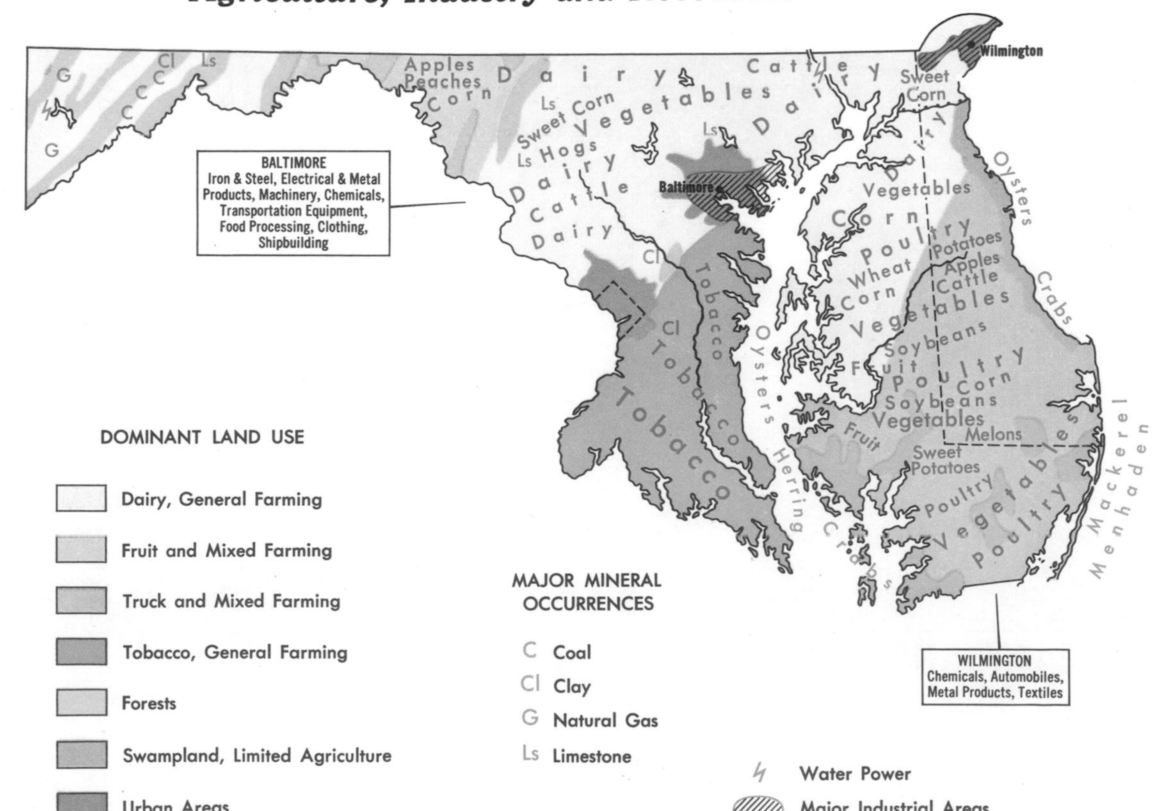

MASSACHUSETTS

AREA 8,257 sq. mi.
POPULATION 5,689,170
CAPITAL Boston
LARGEST CITY Boston
HIGHEST POINT Mt. Greylock 3,491 ft.
SETTLED IN 1620
ADMITTED TO UNION February 6, 1788
POPULAR NAME Bay State; Old Colony
STATE FLOWER Mayflower
STATE BIRD Chickadee

RHODE ISLAND

AREA 1,214 sq. mi.
POPULATION 949,723
CAPITAL Providence
LARGEST CITY Providence
HIGHEST POINT Jerimoth Hill 812 ft.
SETTLED IN 1636
ADMITTED TO UNION May 29, 1790
POPULAR NAME Little Rhody
STATE FLOWER Violet
STATE BIRD Rhode Island Red

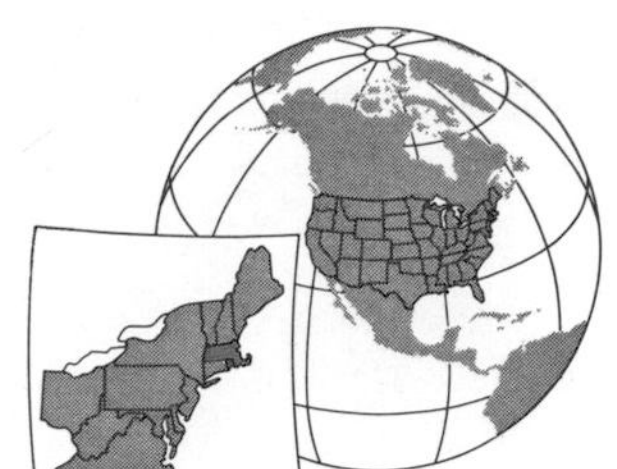

Agriculture, Industry and Resources

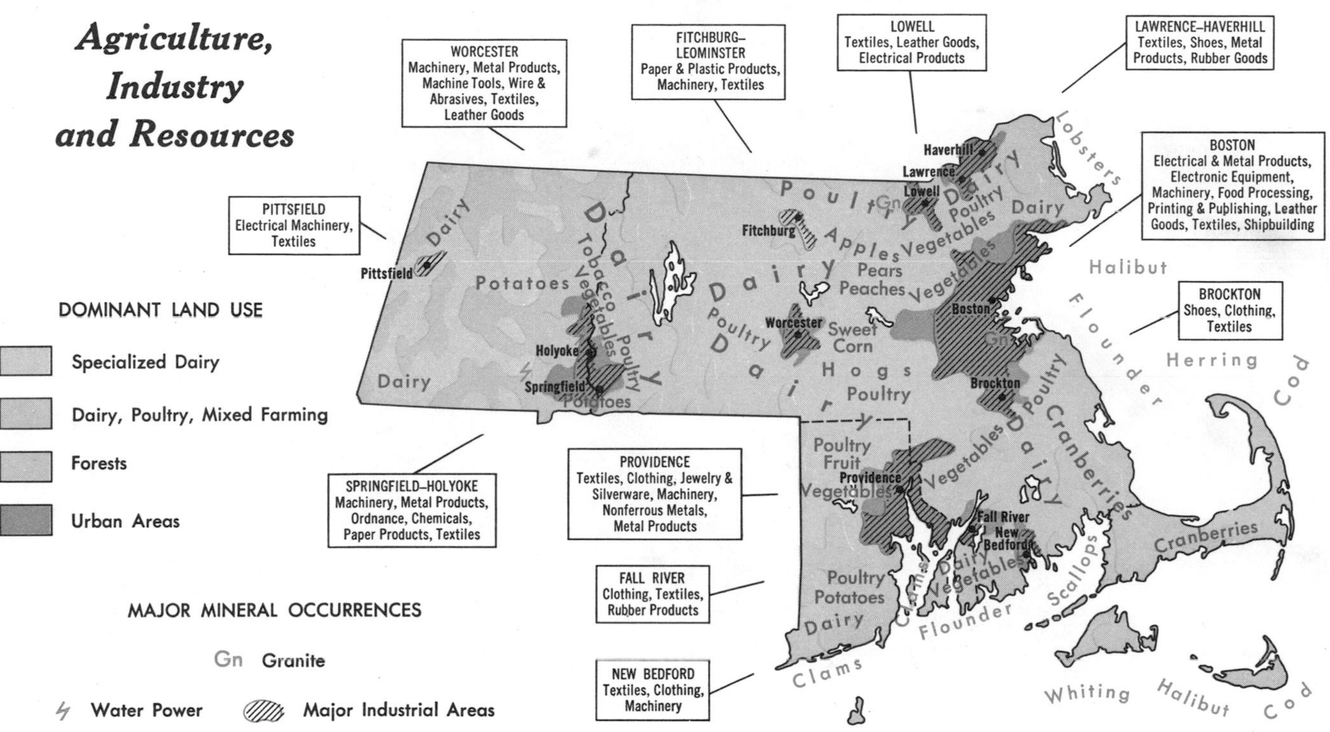

MASSACHUSETTS

COUNTIES

Name/Pop.	Key
Barnstable, 96,656	N 6
Berkshire, 149,402	B 3
Bristol, 444,301	K 5
Dukes, 6,117	M 7
Essex, 637,887	L 2
Franklin, 59,210	D 2
Hampden, 459,050	D 4
Hampshire, 123,981	D 3
Middlesex, 1,397,268	J 3
Nantucket, 3,774	O 7
Norfolk, 605,051	K 4
Plymouth, 333,314	L 5
Suffolk, 735,190	K 3
Worcester, 637,969	G 3

CITIES and TOWNS

	Zip	*Name/Pop.*	*Key*
	02351	Abington, ∆12,334	L 4
	02351	Abington, 5,900	L 4
	01720	Acton, ∆14,770	J 3
	01220	Adams, ∆11,772	B 2
	01220	Adams, 11,256	B 2
	01001	Agawam, ∆21,717	D 4
	01261	Alford, ∆302	A 4
	01913	Amesbury, ∆11,388	L 1
	01913	Amesbury, 10,088	L 1
	01002	Amherst, ∆26,331	E 3
	01002	Amherst, 17,926	E 3
	01810	Andover, ∆23,695	K 2
	02174	Arlington, ∆53,524	C 6
	01430	Ashburnham, ∆3,484	G 2
	01431	Ashby, ∆2,274	G 2
	01330	Ashfield, ∆1,274	C 2
	01721	Ashland, ∆8,882	J 3
	01331	Athol, ∆11,185	F 2
	01331	Athol, 9,723	F 2
	02703	Attleboro, 32,907	J 5
	02763	Attleboro Falls, 5,000	J 5
	01501	Auburn, ∆15,347	G 4
	02166	Auburndale, 7,235	B 7
	02322	Avon, ∆5,295	K 4
	01432	Ayer, ∆7,393	H 2
	02630	Barnstable⊙, ∆19,842	N 6
	01005	Barre, ∆3,825	F 3
	01223	Becket, ∆929	B 3
	01730	Bedford, ∆13,513	B 6
	01007	Belchertown, ∆5,936	E 3
	02019	Bellingham, ∆13,967	J 4
	02019	Bellingham, 4,228	J 4
	02178	Belmont, ∆28,285	C 6
	02780	Berkley, ∆2,027	K 5
	01503	Berlin, ∆2,099	H 3
	01337	Bernardston, ∆1,659	D 2
	01915	Beverly, 38,348	E 5
	01821	Billerica, ∆31,648	J 2
	01504	Blackstone, ∆6,566	H 4
	01008	Blandford, ∆863	C 4
	01740	Bolton, ∆1,905	H 3
*	02101	Boston (cap.)⊙, 641,071	D 7
		Boston, ‡2,753,700	D 7
	02532	Bourne, ∆12,636	M 6
†	01720	Boxborough, ∆1,451	H 3
	01921	Boxford, ∆4,032	L 2
	01505	Boylston, ∆2,774	H 3
	02184	Braintree, ∆35,050	D 8
	02631	Brewster, ∆1,790	O 5
	02324	Bridgewater, ∆11,829	K 5
	02324	Bridgewater, 4,032	K 5
	01010	Brimfield, ∆1,907	F 4
*	02401	Brockton, 89,040	K 4
		Brockton, ‡189,820	K 4
	01506	Brookfield, ∆2,063	F 4
	02147	Brookline, ∆58,886	C 7
	01338	Buckland, ∆1,892	C 2
	01803	Burlington, ∆21,980	C 5
†	02138	Cambridge⊙, 100,361	C 7
	02021	Canton, ∆17,100	C 8
	01741	Carlisle, ∆2,871	J 2
	02330	Carver, ∆2,420	M 5
	01339	Charlemont, ∆897	C 2
	01507	Charlton, ∆4,654	F 4
	02633	Chatham, ∆4,554	P 6
	01824	Chelmsford, ∆31,432	J 2
	02150	Chelsea, 30,625	D 6
	01225	Cheshire, ∆3,006	B 2
	01011	Chester, ∆1,025	C 3
	01012	Chesterfield, ∆704	C 3
*	01013	Chicopee, 66,676	D 4
	02535	Chilmark, ∆340	M 7.
	01510	Clinton, ∆13,383	H 3
	01778	Cochituate, 6,000	A 7
	02025	Cohasset, ∆6,954	F 7
	02025	Cohasset, 3,900	F 7
†	01826	Collinsville, 4,000	J 2
	01340	Colrain, ∆1,420	D 2
	01742	Concord, ∆16,148	B 6
	01742	Concord, 5,900	B 6
	01341	Conway, ∆998	D 2
	01026	Cummington, ∆562	C 3
	01226	Dalton, ∆7,505	B 3
	01923	Danvers, ∆26,151	D 5
	02714	Dartmouth, ∆18,800	K 6
	02026	Dedham⊙, ∆26,938	C 7
	01342	Deerfield, ∆3,850	D 2
	02638	Dennis, ∆6,454	O 5
	02715	Dighton, ∆4,667	K 5
†	02122	Dorchester, 153,061	D 7
†	01516	Douglas, ∆2,947	H 4
	02030	Dover, ∆4,529	B 7
	01826	Dracut, ∆18,214	J 2
	01570	Dudley, ∆8,087	G 4
	01827	Dunstable, ∆1,292	J 2
	02332	Duxbury, ∆7,636	M 4
	02332	Duxbury, 2,477	M 4
†	02184	East Braintree, 12,000	D 8
	02333	East Bridgewater, ∆8,347	L 4
	01515	East Brookfield, ∆1,800	G 4
	02642	Eastham, ∆2,043	O 5
	01027	Easthampton, ∆13,012	D 3
	01028	East Longmeadow, ∆13,029	E 4
†	02186	East Milton, 9,500	D 7
	02334	Easton, ∆12,157	K 4
	01437	East Pepperell, 4,200	H 2
†	01906	East Saugus, 4,200	D 6
	02032	East Walpole, 4,500	C 8
†	02189	East Weymouth, 20,000	E 8
	02539	Edgartown, ∆1,481	M 7
	02539	Edgartown⊙, 1,006	M 7
	01344	Erving, ∆1,260	E 2
	02112	Essex, ∆2,670	L 2
	02149	Everett, 42,485	D 6
	02719	Fairhaven, ∆16,332	L 6
*	02720	Fall River, 96,898	K 6
		Fall River, ‡149,976	K 6
*	02540	Falmouth, ∆15,942	M 6
*	02540	Falmouth, 5,806	M 6
	01030	Feeding Hills, 9,500	D 4
	01420	Fitchburg, 43,343	G 2
		Fitchburg-Leominster, ‡97,164	G 2
†	01247	Florida, ∆672	B 2
	02035	Foxboro, ∆14,218	J 4
	02035	Foxboro, 4,090	J 4
	01701	Framingham, 64,048	A 7
	01701	Framingham Center, 16,000	J 3
	02038	Franklin, ∆17,830	J 4
	02038	Franklin, 8,863	J 4
	01440	Gardner, 19,748	G 2
†	02535	Gay Head, ∆118	L 7
	01830	Georgetown, ∆5,290	L 2
†	01376	Gill, ∆1,100	D 2
	01930	Gloucester, 27,941	M 2
	01032	Goshen, ∆483	C 3
	01519	Grafton, ∆11,659	H 4
	01033	Granby, ∆5,473	E 3
	01034	Granville, ∆1,008	C 4
	01230	Great Barrington, ∆7,537	A 4
	01301	Greenfield, ∆18,116	D 2
	01301	Greenfield⊙, 14,642	D 2
	01880	Greenwood, 7,500	D 6
	01450	Groton, ∆5,109	H 2
	01830	Groveland, ∆5,382	L 1
	01035	Hadley, ∆3,750	D 3
	02338	Halifax, ∆3,537	L 5
	01936	Hamilton, ∆6,373	L 2
	01036	Hampden, ∆4,572	E 4
	01237	Hancock, ∆675	A 2
	02339	Hanover, ∆10,107	L 4
	02341	Hanson, ∆7,148	L 4
	01037	Hardwick, ∆2,379	F 3
	01451	Harvard, ∆13,426	H 2
	02645	Harwich, ∆5,892	O 6
	02645	Harwich, 3,842	O 6
	01038	Hatfield, ∆2,825	D 3
	01830	Haverhill, 46,120	K 1
	01346	Heath, ∆383	C 2
	02043	Hingham, ∆18,845	E 8
	01235	Hinsdale, ∆1,588	B 3
	02343	Holbrook, ∆11,775	D 8
	01520	Holden, ∆12,564	G 3
†	01550	Holland, ∆931	F 4
	01746	Holliston, ∆12,069	A 8
	01746	Holliston, 3,900	A 8
	01040	Holyoke, 50,112	D 4
	01747	Hopedale, ∆4,292	H 4
	01748	Hopkinton, ∆5,981	J 4
	01452	Hubbardston, ∆1,437	F 3
	01749	Hudson, ∆16,084	H 3
	01749	Hudson, 14,283	H 3
	02045	Hull, ∆9,961	E 7
	01050	Huntington, ∆1,593	C 4
	02601	Hyannis, 6,847	N 6
	02136	Hyde Park, 25,000	C 7
	01938	Ipswich, ∆10,750	L 2
	01938	Ipswich, 5,022	I ?
	02090	Islington, 3,800	C 8
	02130	Jamaica Plain, 50,000	C 7
	02360	Kingston, ∆5,999	M 5
	02360	Kingston, 3,772	M 5
	02346	Lakeville, ∆4,376	L 5
	01523	Lancaster, ∆6,095	H 3
	01237	Lanesboro, ∆2,972	A 2
*	01840	Lawrence, 66,915	K 2
		Lawrence-Haverhill, ‡232,395	K 2
	01238	Lee, ∆6,426	B 3
	01524	Leicester, ∆9,140	G 4
	01240	Lenox, ∆5,804	A 3
	01240	Lenox, 2,208	A 3
	01453	Leominster, 32,939	G 2
	01054	Leverett, ∆1,005	E 3
	02173	Lexington, ∆31,886	B 6
†	01301	Leyden, ∆376	D 2
	01773	Lincoln, ∆7,567	B 6
	01460	Littleton, ∆6,380	H 2
	01106	Longmeadow, ∆15,630	D 4
*	01850	Lowell, 94,239	J 2
		Lowell, ‡212,860	J 2
	01056	Ludlow, ∆17,580	E 4
	02745	Lunds Corner, 7,020	L 6
	01462	Lunenburg, ∆7,419	H 2
*	01901	Lynn, 90,294	D 6
	01940	Lynnfield, ∆10,826	D 5
†	01940	Lynnfield Center (Lynnfield P.O.), 6,500	C 5
	02148	Malden, 56,127	D 6
	01944	Manchester, ∆5,151	F 5
	02048	Mansfield, ∆9,939	J 4
	02048	Mansfield, 4,778	J 4
	01945	Marblehead, ∆21,295	E 7
	02738	Marion, ∆3,466	L 6
	01752	Marlborough, 27,936	H 3
	02050	Marshfield, ∆15,223	M 4
	02649	Mashpee, ∆1,288	M 6
	02126	Mattapan, 18,500	C 7
	02739	Mattapoisett, ∆4,500	L 6
	01754	Maynard, ∆9,710	J 3
	02052	Medfield, ∆9,821	B 8
	02052	Medfield, 3,900	B 8
	02155	Medford, 64,397	C 6
	02053	Medway, ∆7,938	J 4
	02053	Medway, 3,716	J 4
	02176	Melrose, 33,180	D 6
	01756	Mendon, ∆2,524	H 4
	01860	Merrimac, ∆4,245	L 1
	01844	Methuen, 35,456	K 2
	02346	Middleboro, ∆13,607	L 5
	02346	Middleboro, 6,259	L 5
	01243	Middlefield, ∆288	B 3
	01949	Middleton, ∆4,044	K 2
	01757	Milford, ∆19,352	H 4
	01757	Milford, 13,740	H 4
	01527	Millbury, ∆11,987	H 4
	02054	Millis, ∆5,686	A 8
	01529	Millville, ∆1,764	H 4
	02186	Milton, ∆27,190	D 7
	01057	Monson, ∆7,355	E 4
	01351	Montaque, ∆8,451	E 2
	01245	Monterey, ∆600	B 4
†	12517	Mount Washington, ∆52	A 4
	01908	Nahant, ∆4,119	E 6
	02554	Nantucket, ∆3,774	O 7
	02554	Nantucket⊙, 2,461	O 7
	01760	Natick, ∆31,057	A 7
	02192	Needham, ∆29,748	B 7
	02194	Needham Heights, 10,000	B 7
†	02122	Neponset, 25,000	D 7
*	02740	New Bedford, 101,777	K 6
		New Bedford, ‡152,642	K 6
	01531	New Braintree, ∆631	F 3
	01950	Newbury, ∆3,804	L 1
	01950	Newburyport, 15,807	L 1
†	01230	New Marlboro, ∆1,031	B 4
	01355	New Salem, ∆474	E 2
†	02158	Newton, 91,066	C 7
†	02159	Newton Center, 20,790	C 7
†	02161	Newton Highlands, 6,900	C 7
†	02160	Newtonville, 14,000	C 7
	02790	Noquochoke P.O. (Westport), ∆950	K 6
	02056	Norfolk, ∆4,656	J 4
	02351	North Abington, 6,200	L 4
	01247	North Adams, 19,195	B 2
	01060	Northampton⊙, 29,664	D 3
	01845	North Andover, ∆16,284	K 2
*	02760	North Attleboro, ∆18,665	J 5
	01862	North Billerica, 4,900	J 2
	01532	Northboro, ∆9,218	H 3
	01532	Northboro, 3,900	H 3
	01536	Northbridge, ∆11,795	H 4
	01535	North Brookfield, ∆3,967	F 3
	01863	North Chelmsford, 3,700	J 2
	02747	North Dartmouth, 6,000	K 6
	02356	North Easton, 6,000	K 4
	01360	Northfield, ∆2,631	E 2
	01536	North Grafton, 5,500	H 4
	01864	North Reading, ∆11,264	C 5
	02060	North Scituate, 5,507	F 8
†	02191	North Weymouth, 13,000	D 8
	01067	North Wilbraham, 5,700	E 4
	02766	Norton, ∆9,487	K 5
	02061	Norwell, ∆7,796	F 8
	02062	Norwood, ∆30,815	B 8
	02557	Oak Bluffs, ∆1,385	M 7
	01068	Oakham, ∆730	F 3
†	01566	Old Sturbridge Village, 500	F 4
	01364	Orange, ∆6,104	E 2
	01364	Orange, 3,847	E 2
	02653	Orleans, ∆3,055	O 5
	01253	Otis, ∆820	B 4
	01540	Oxford, ∆10,345	G 4
	01540	Oxford, 6,109	G 4
	01069	Palmer, ∆11,680	E 4
	01069	Palmer, 3,649	E 4
	01612	Paxton, ∆3,731	G 3
	01960	Peabody, 48,080	E 5
†	01002	Pelham, ∆937	E 3
	02359	Pembroke, ∆11,193	L 4
	01463	Pepperell, ∆5,887	H 2
	01366	Petersham, ∆1,014	F 3
†	01331	Phillipston, ∆872	F 2
	01866	Pinehurst, 5,681	B 5
	01201	Pittsfield⊙, 57,020	A 3
		Pittsfield, ‡79,727	A 3
	01070	Plainfield, ∆287	C 2
	02762	Plainville, ∆4,953	J 4
*	02360	Plymouth, ∆18,606	M 5
*	02360	Plymouth⊙, 6,940	M 5
	02367	Plympton, ∆1,224	L 5
†	02726	Pottersville, 3,722	K 6
	01541	Princeton, ∆1,681	G 3
	02657	Provincetown, ∆2,911	O 4
†	02169	Quincy, 87,966	D 7
	02368	Randolph, ∆27,035	D 8
	02767	Raynham, ∆6,705	K 5
	01867	Reading, ∆22,539	C 5
	02137	Readville, 10,000	C 8
	02769	Rehoboth, ∆6,512	K 5
	02151	Revere, 43,159	D 6
	01254	Richmond, ∆1,461	A 3
	02770	Rochester, ∆1,770	L 6
	02370	Rockland, ∆15,674	L 4
	01966	Rockport, ∆5,636	M 2
	01966	Rockport, 4,166	M 2
	01367	Rowe, ∆277	C 2
	01969	Rowley, ∆3,040	L 2
†	02119	Roxbury, 200,000	C 7
	01368	Royalston, ∆809	F 2
	01071	Russell, ∆1,382	C 4
	01543	Rutland, ∆3,198	G 3
	01970	Salem⊙, 40,556	E 5
	01950	Salisbury, ∆4,179	L 1
	01255	Sandisfield, ∆547	B 4
	02563	Sandwich, ∆5,239	N 5
	01906	Saugus, ∆25,110	D 6
	01256	Savoy, ∆322	B 2
	01701	Saxonville, 15,000	A 7
	02066	Scituate, ∆16,973	F 8
	02066	Scituate, 3,738	F 8
	02771	Seekonk, ∆11,116	J 5
	02067	Sharon, ∆12,367	K 4
	01810	Shawsheen Village, 5,200	K 2
	01257	Sheffield, ∆2,374	A 4
	01770	Sherborn, ∆3,309	A 8
	01464	Shirley, ∆4,909	H 2
	01545	Shrewsbury, ∆19,196	H 3
	01072	Shutesbury, ∆489	E 3
	02726	Somerset, ∆18,088	K 5
†	02143	Somerville, 88,779	C 6
	01073	Southampton, ∆3,069	C 4
	01772	Southborough, ∆5,798	H 3
†	02185	South Braintree, 6,000	D 8

(continued on following page)

Massachusetts and Rhode Island

(continued)

MASSACHUSETTS (continued)

01550 Southbridge, ▵17,057 .... G 4
01550 Southbridge, 14,261 .... G 4
02748 South Dartmouth, 9,209 .... L 6
02375 South Easton, 4,400 .... K 4
01075 South Hadley, ▵17,033 .... D 4
01075 South Hadley Falls, 6,500 .... D 4
† 02190 South Weymouth, 17,500 .... E 8
01077 Southwick, ▵6,330 .... C 4
02664 South Yarmouth, 5,380 .... O 6
01562 Spencer, ▵8,779 .... F 3
01562 Spencer, 5,895 .... F 3
* 01101 Springfield⊙, 163,905 .... D 4
Springfield-Chicopee-Holyoke, ‡529,921 .... D 4
01564 Sterling, ▵4,247 .... G 3
01262 Stockbridge, ▵2,312 .... A 3
01262 Stockbridge, 1,147 .... A 3
02180 Stoneham, ▵20,725 .... C 6
02072 Stoughton, ▵23,459 .... K 4
01775 Stow, ▵3,984 .... H 3
01566 Sturbridge, ▵4,878 .... F 4
01776 Sudbury, ▵13,506 .... A 6
01375 Sunderland, ▵2,236 .... D 3
† 01527 Sutton, ▵4,590 .... G 4
01907 Swampscott, ▵13,578 .... E 6
02777 Swansea, ▵12,640 .... K 5
02780 Taunton⊙, 43,756 .... K 5
01468 Templeton, ▵5,863 .... F 2
01876 Tewksbury, ▵22,755 .... K 2
† 01034 Tolland, ▵172 .... B 4
01983 Topsfield, ▵5,225 .... L 2
01469 Townsend, ▵4,281 .... H 2
02666 Truro, ▵1,234 .... O 5
01376 Turners Falls, 5,168 .... D 2
01879 Tyngsboro, ▵4,204 .... J 2
01264 Tyringham, ▵234 .... A 4
01568 Upton, ▵3,484 .... H 4
01569 Uxbridge, ▵8,253 .... H 4
02568 Vineyard Haven, 1,599 .... M 7
† 02168 Waban, 6,871 .... B 7
01880 Wakefield, ▵25,402 .... C 5
01081 Wales, ▵852 .... F 4
02081 Walpole, ▵18,149 .... B 8
02154 Waltham, 61,582 .... B 6
01082 Ware, ▵8,187 .... E 3
01082 Ware, 6,509 .... E 3
02571 Wareham, ▵11,492 .... L 5
01083 Warren, ▵3,633 .... F 4
01378 Warwick, ▵492 .... E 2
† 01223 Washington, ▵406 .... B 3
02172 Watertown, ▵39,307 .... C 6
02179 Waverley, 15,000 .... B 6
01778 Wayland, ▵13,461 .... A 7
01570 Webster, ▵14,917 .... G 4
01570 Webster, 12,432 .... G 4
02181 Wellesley, ▵28,051 .... B 7
02181 Wellesley Hills, 15,000 .... B 7
02667 Wellfleet, ▵1,743 .... O 5
01379 Wendell, ▵405 .... E 2
01984 Wenham, ▵3,849 .... L 2
01581 Westboro, ▵12,594 .... H 3
01581 Westboro, 4,474 .... H 3
01583 West Boylston, ▵6,369 .... G 3
02379 West Bridgewater, ▵7,152 .... K 4
01585 West Brookfield, ▵2,653 .... F 4
01085 Westfield, 31,433 .... D 4
01886 Westford, ▵10,368 .... J 2
† 01027 Westhampton, ▵793 .... C 3
01473 Westminster, ▵4,273 .... G 2
01985 West Newbury, ▵2,254 .... L 1
† 02165 West Newton, 13,500 .... B 7
02193 Weston, ▵10,870 .... B 6
02790 Westport, ▵9,791 .... K 6
02790 Westport P.O. (North Westport), 4,000 .... K 6
01089 West Springfield, ▵28,461 .... D 4
01266 West Stockbridge, ▵1,354 .... A 3
02575 West Tisbury, ▵453 .... M 7
02090 Westwood, ▵12,750 .... B 8
02673 West Yarmouth, 3,699 .... N 6
† 02188 Weymouth, 54,610 .... D 8
01093 Whately, ▵1,145 .... D 3
01588 Whitinsville, 5,210 .... H 4
02382 Whitman, ▵13,059 .... L 4
01095 Wilbraham, ▵11,984 .... E 4
01095 Wilbraham, 3,540 .... E 4
01096 Williamsburg, ▵2,342 .... C 3
01267 Williamstown, ▵8,454 .... B 2
01267 Williamstown, 4,285 .... B 2
01887 Wilmington, ▵17,102 .... C 5
01887 Wilmington, 3,900 .... C 5
01475 Winchendon, ▵6,635 .... F 2
01475 Winchendon, 3,997 .... F 2
01890 Winchester, ▵22,269 .... C 6
01270 Windsor, ▵468 .... B 2
02152 Winthrop, ▵20,335 .... D 6
01801 Woburn, 37,406 .... C 6
02543 Woods Hole, 750 .... M 6
* 01601 Worcester⊙, 176,572 .... H 3
Worcester, ‡339,730 .... H 3
01098 Worthington, ▵712 .... C 3
02093 Wrentham, ▵7,315 .... J 4
† 02675 Yarmouth, ▵12,033 .... O 6

RHODE ISLAND

COUNTIES

Bristol, 45,937 .... J 6
Kent, 142,382 .... H 6
Newport, 94,559 .... K 6
Providence, 580,261 .... H 5
Washington, 83,586 .... H 7

CITIES and TOWNS

Zip	Name/Pop.	Key
02816	Anthony, 7,000	H 6
† 02887	Apponaug, 6,533	J 6
02806	Barrington, ▵17,554	J 6
02806	Barrington, 13,000	J 6
02809	Bristol, ▵17,860	J 6
02809	Bristol⊙, 14,000	J 6
02911	Centerdale, 8,000	H 5
02863	Central Falls, 18,716	J 5
02813	Charlestown, ▵2,863	H 7
02816	Coventry, ▵22,947	H 6
02816	Coventry, 7,000	H 6
02910	Cranston, 73,037	J 5
02818	East Greenwich⊙, ▵9,577	H 6
02914	East Providence, 48,151	J 5
02822	Exeter, ▵3,245	H 6
02825	Foster, ▵2,626	H 5
02828	Greenville, 3,500	H 5
02833	Hopkinton, ▵5,392	H 7
02835	Jamestown, ▵2,911	J 6

⊙ County seat or courthouse.
‡ Population of metropolitan area.
▵ Population of town or township.
† Zip of nearest p.o.
• Multiple zips

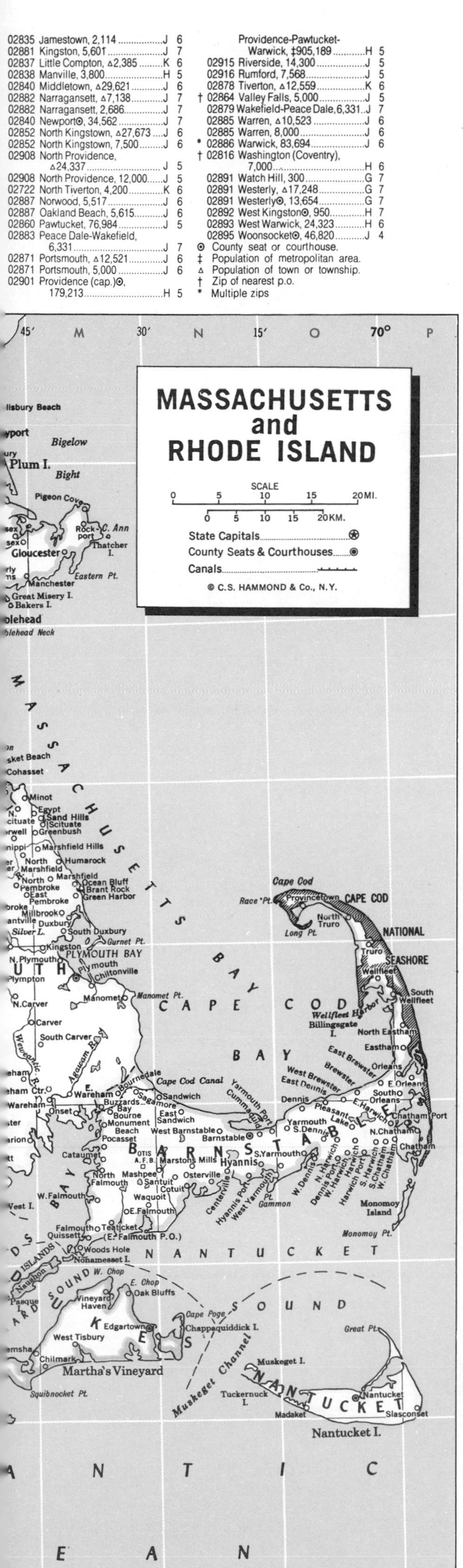

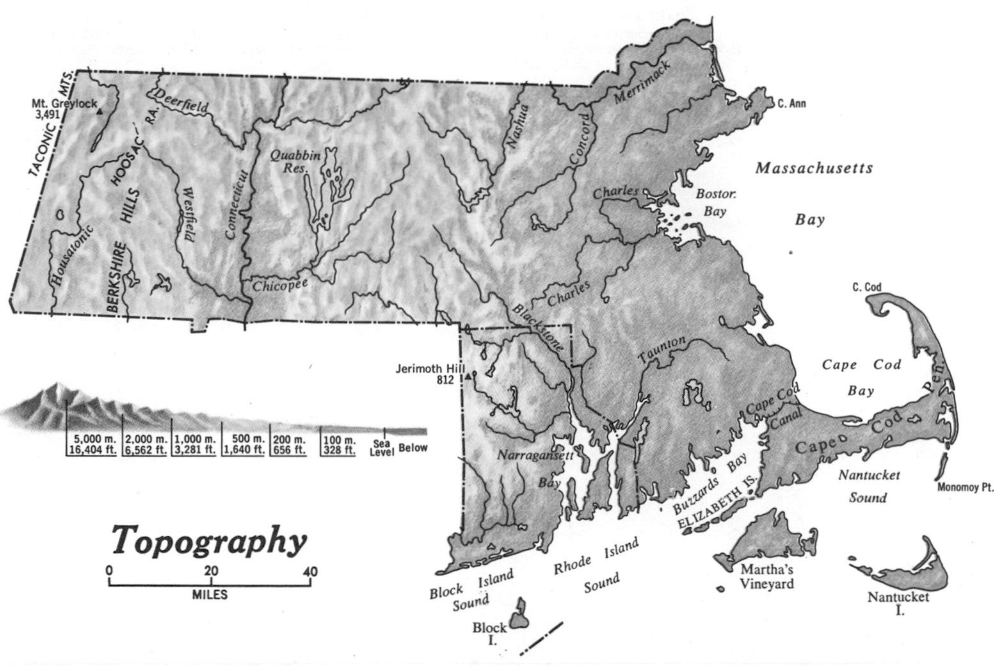

Marking the site of the first battle of the Revolutionary War on April 19, 1775, the Minuteman Statue faces the line of advancing Redcoats at Lexington, Massachusetts.

Typical Newport turn-of-the-century grandeur in a French chalet-style mansion, with mansard roof and wrought iron gates.

MICHIGAN
SCALE
0 5 10 20 30 40 50 MI.
0 5 10 20 30 40 50 KM.
State Capitals
County Seats
Canals
© C.S. HAMMOND & Co., N.Y.
Longitude 86° West of
88° 87° 85° 83°
47° 46° 45° 44° 43° 42°
A B C D E F G
1 2 3 4 5 6 7
Same scale as main map.
KEWEENAW
ISLE ROYALE (NATIONAL PARK)
L. SUPERIOR
Same scale as main map
LAKE SUPERIOR
HOUGHTON
ONTONAGON
GOGEBIC
IRON
BARAGA
MARQUETTE
DICKINSON
MENOMINEE
DELTA
ALGER
SCHOOLCRAFT
LUCE
MACKINAC
CHIPPEWA
EMMET
CHEBOYGAN
PRESQUE ISLE
CHARLEVOIX
ANTRIM
OTSEGO
MONTMORENCY
ALPENA
LEELANAU
BENZIE
GRAND TRAVERSE
KALKASKA
CRAWFORD
OSCODA
ALCONA
MANISTEE
WEXFORD
MISSAUKEE
ROSCOMMON
OGEMAW
IOSCO
MASON
LAKE
OSCEOLA
CLARE
GLADWIN
ARENAC
OCEANA
NEWAYGO
MECOSTA
ISABELLA
MIDLAND
BAY
HURON
TUSCOLA
SANILAC
MUSKEGON
MONTCALM
GRATIOT
SAGINAW
OTTAWA
KENT
IONIA
CLINTON
SHIAWASSEE
GENESEE
LAPEER
ST. CLAIR
ALLEGAN
BARRY
EATON
INGHAM
LIVINGSTON
OAKLAND
MACOMB
VAN BUREN
KALAMAZOO
CALHOUN
JACKSON
WASHTENAW
WAYNE
CASS
ST. JOSEPH
BRANCH
HILLSDALE
LENAWEE
MONROE
LAKE MICHIGAN
LAKE HURON
LAKE ST. CLAIR
LAKE ERIE
Green Bay
Saginaw Bay
Whitefish Bay
North Channel
Straits of Mackinac
WISCONSIN
INDIANA
OHIO
ONTARIO
ILL.
CAN.
Lansing
Detroit
Grand Rapids
Flint
Saginaw
Bay City
Midland
Kalamazoo
Battle Creek
Jackson
Ann Arbor
Pontiac
Muskegon
Marquette
Sault Ste. Marie
Escanaba
Traverse City
Alpena
Port Huron
Monroe
Toledo
Windsor
Milwaukee
South Bend
Green Bay
Sheboygan
Racine
Kenosha
Manitowoc
Two Rivers
Menominee
Marinette
Ludington
Manistee
Cadillac
Mt. Pleasant
Holland
Benton Harbor
St. Joseph
Niles
Coldwater
Hillsdale
Adrian
Ypsilanti
Owosso
Alma
Big Rapids
Petoskey
Cheboygan
Rogers City
Gaylord
Grayling
Houghton
Hancock
Ironwood
Iron Mountain
Ishpeming
Negaunee
Munising
Manistique
St. Ignace
Newberry
PICTURED ROCKS NAT'L LAKESHORE
SLEEPING BEAR NAT'L LAKESHORE
L'ANSE INDIAN RES.
K. I. SAWYER A.F.B.
KINCHELOE A.F.B.
WURTSMITH AIR FORCE BASE
SELFRIDGE AIR FORCE BASE
POINT PELEE NAT'L PARK
PERRY'S VICTORY & INT'L PEACE MEM. NAT'L MON.
Bloomfield Hills
Troy
Birmingham
Sterling Hts.
Royal Oak
Warren
Berkley
Oak Park
Ferndale
Hamtramck
Highland Park
Grosse Pte. Woods
Grosse Pte. Shores
Grosse Pte. Farms
Grosse Pointe
Grosse Pte. Park
Dearborn
Inkster
Melvindale
Allen Park
Taylor
River Rouge
Ecorse
Lincoln Park
Wyandotte
Riverview
Trenton
Grosse Ile
ONT.
0 5 10 MI.
0 5 10 KM.

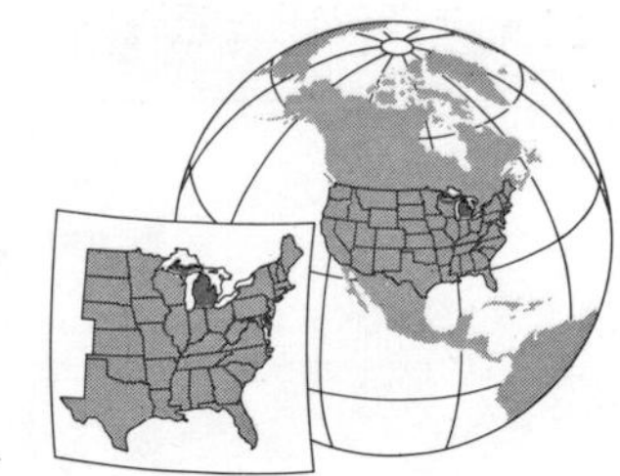

AREA 58,216 sq. mi.
POPULATION 8,875,083
CAPITAL Lansing
LARGEST CITY Detroit
HIGHEST POINT Mt. Curwood 1,980 ft.
SETTLED IN 1650
ADMITTED TO UNION January 26, 1837
POPULAR NAME Wolverine State
STATE FLOWER Apple Blossom
STATE BIRD Robin

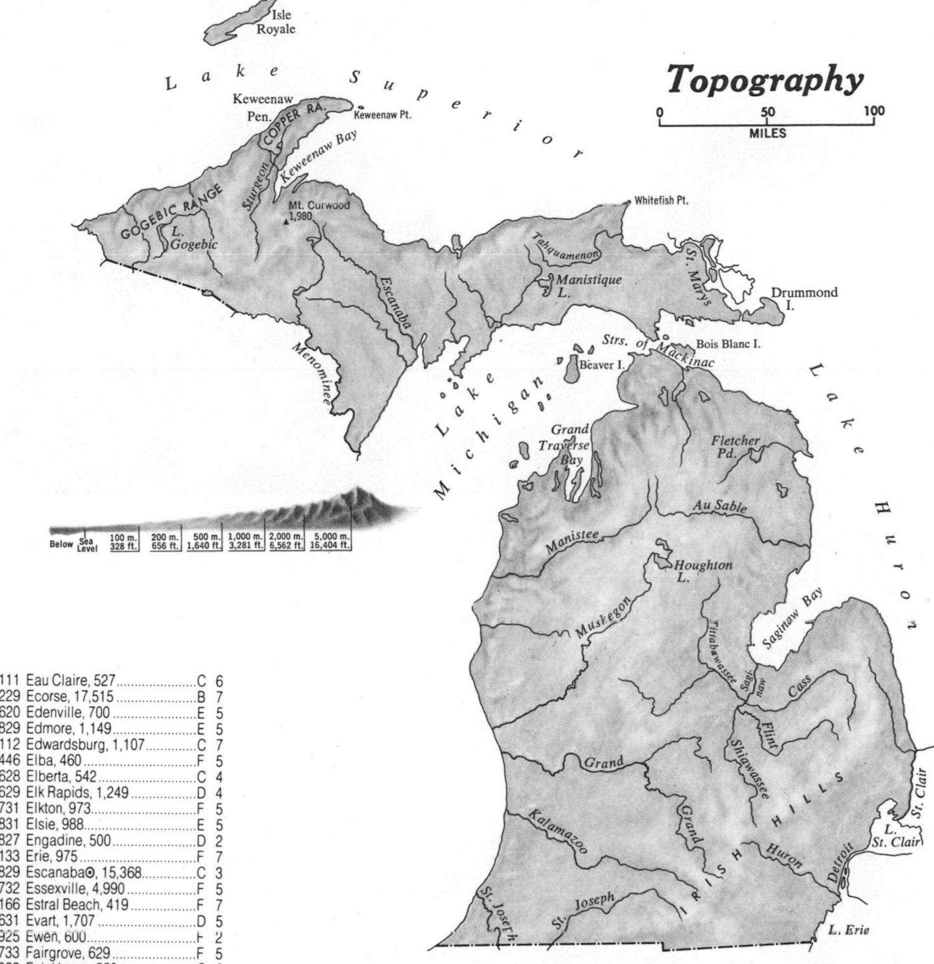

COUNTIES

Name/Pop.	Key
Alcona, 7,113	F 4
Alger, 8,568	C 2
Allegan, 66,575	D 6
Alpena, 30,708	F 4
Antrim, 12,612	D 3
Arenac, 11,149	F 4
Baraga, 7,789	A 2
Barry, 38,166	D 6
Bay, 117,339	E 5
Benzie, 8,593	C 4
Berrien, 163,875	C 7
Branch, 37,906	D 7
Calhoun, 141,963	D 6
Cass, 43,312	C 7
Charlevoix, 16,541	D 3
Cheboygan, 16,573	E 3
Chippewa, 32,412	E 2
Clare, 16,695	E 5
Clinton, 48,492	E 6
Crawford, 6,482	E 4
Delta, 35,924	C 2
Dickinson, 23,753	B 2
Eaton, 68,892	E 6
Emmet, 18,331	E 3
Genesee, 444,341	F 5
Gladwin, 13,471	E 4
Gogebic, 20,676	F 2
Grand Traverse, 39,175	D 4
Gratiot, 39,246	E 5
Hillsdale, 37,171	E 7
Houghton, 34,652	G 1
Huron, 34,083	F 5
Ingham, 261,039	E 6
Ionia, 45,848	D 6
Iosco, 24,905	F 4
Iron, 13,813	G 2
Isabella, 44,594	E 5
Jackson, 143,274	E 6
Kalamazoo, 201,550	D 6
Kalkaska, 5,272	D 4
Kent, 411,044	D 5
Keweenaw, 2,264	A 1
Lake, 5,661	D 5
Lapeer, 52,317	F 5
Leelanau, 10,872	D 4
Lenawee, 81,609	E 7
Livingston, 58,967	F 6
Luce, 6,789	D 2
Mackinac, 9,660	D 2
Macomb, 625,309	G 6
Manistee, 20,094	C 4
Marquette, 64,686	B 2
Mason, 22,612	C 4
Mecosta, 27,992	D 5
Menominee, 24,587	B 3
Midland, 63,769	E 5
Missaukee, 7,126	D 4
Monroe, 118,479	F 7
Montcalm, 39,660	D 5
Montmorency, 5,247	E 3
Muskegon, 157,246	C 5
Newaygo, 27,992	D 5
Oakland, 907,871	F 6
Oceana, 17,984	C 5
Ogemaw, 11,903	E 4
Ontonagon, 10,548	F 1
Osceola, 14,838	D 5
Oscoda, 4,726	E 4
Otsego, 10,422	E 3
Ottawa, 128,181	C 6
Presque Isle, 12,836	F 3
Roscommon, 9,892	E 4
Saginaw, 219,743	E 5
Saint Clair, 120,175	G 6
Saint Joseph, 47,392	D 7
Sanilac, 34,889	G 5
Schoolcraft, 8,226	C 2
Shiawassee, 63,075	E 6
Tuscola, 48,603	F 5
Van Buren, 56,173	C 6
Washtenaw, 234,103	F 6
Wayne, 2,666,751	F 6
Wexford, 19,717	D 4

CITIES and TOWNS

Zip	Name/Pop.	Key
49220	Addison, 595	E 7
49221	Adrian⊙, 20,382	F 7
48701	Akron, 525	F 5
48764	Alabaster, 46	F 4
49224	Albion, 12,112	E 6
48001	Algonac, 3,684	G 6
49010	Allegan⊙, 4,516	D 6
48101	Allen Park, 40,747	B 7
48801	Alma, 9,790	E 5
48003	Almont, 1,634	F 6
49707	Alpena⊙, 13,805	F 3
49903	Amasa, 450	G 2
48004	Anchorville, 440	G 6
* 48103	Ann Arbor⊙, 99,797	F 6
	Ann Arbor, ‡234,103	F 6
† 49659	Antrim, 475	D 4
48410	Argyle, 800	G 5
48005	Armada, 1,352	G 6
48806	Ashley, 521	E 5
49011	Athens, 996	D 6
49709	Atlanta⊙, 475	E 3
49905	Atlantic Mine, 785	G 1
48611	Auburn, 1,919	F 5
48057	Auburn Heights, 7,500	F 6
48703	Au Gres, 564	F 4
49012	Augusta, 1,025	D 6
† 48750	Au Sable-Oscoda, 3,475	F 4
† 48640	Averill, 800	E 5
48413	Bad Axe⊙, 2,999	G 5
49304	Baldwin⊙, 612	D 5
48414	Bancroft, 724	E 6
49013	Bangor, 2,050	C 6
49908	Baraga, 1,116	G 1
49807	Bark River, 550	B 3
49101	Baroda, 439	C 7
48808	Bath, 600	E 6
* 49014	Battle Creek, 38,931	D 6
48706	Bay City⊙, 49,449	F 5
	Bay City, ‡117,339	F 5
48720	Bay Port, 600	F 5
49770	Bay View, 500	E 3
48612	Beaverton, 954	E 5
49020	Bedford, 450	D 6
† 49423	Beechwood, 2,714	C 6
48809	Belding, 5,121	D 5
49615	Bellaire⊙, 897	D 4
48111	Belleville, 2,406	F 6
49021	Bellevue, 1,297	E 6
49022	Benton Harbor, 16,481	C 6
† 49022	Benton Heights, 8,067	C 6
49910	Bergland, 635	F 1
48072	Berkley, 22,618	B 6
49103	Berrien Springs, 1,951	C 7
49911	Bessemer⊙, 2,805	F 2
49617	Beulah⊙, 461	C 4
49307	Big Rapids⊙, 11,995	D 5
48415	Birch Run, 932	F 5
* 48008	Birmingham, 26,170	B 6
49228	Blissfield, 2,753	F 7
48013	Bloomfield Hills, 3,672	B 6
49026	Bloomingdale, 496	C 6
49712	Boyne City, 2,969	E 3
48615	Breckenridge, 1,257	E 5
48722	Bridgeport, 1,900	F 5
49106	Bridgman, 1,621	C 7
48116	Brighton, 2,457	F 6
49715	Brimley, 490	E 2
49229	Britton, 697	F 6
49028	Bronson, 2,390	D 7
49230	Brooklyn, 1,112	E 6
48416	Brown City, 1,142	G 5
49716	Brutus, 431	E 3
49107	Buchanan, 4,645	C 7
49314	Burnips, 725	D 6
49030	Burr Oak, 873	D 7
48418	Byron, 655	E 6
49315	Byron Center, 900	D 6
49601	Cadillac⊙, 9,990	D 4
49316	Caledonia, 716	D 6
49913	Calumet, 1,007	A 1
48014	Capac, 1,279	G 5
48117	Carleton, 1,503	F 6
48723	Caro⊙, 3,701	F 5
48724	Carrollton, 7,300	E 5
48811	Carson City, 1,217	E 5
48419	Carsonville, 621	G 5
48725	Caseville, 607	F 5
49915	Caspian, 1,165	G 2
48726	Cass City, 1,974	F 5
49031	Cassopolis⊙, 2,108	C 7
49422	Castle Park, 500	C 6
49319	Cedar Springs, 1,807	D 5
49719	Cedarville, 800	E 2
49233	Cement City, 531	F 6
48015	Center Line, 10,379	B 6
49622	Central Lake, 741	D 3
49032	Centreville⊙, 1,044	D 7
49814	Champion, 550	B 2
49815	Channing, 550	B 2
49720	Charlevoix⊙, 3,519	D 3
48813	Charlotte⊙, 8,244	E 6
49623	Chase, 534	D 5
49721	Cheboygan⊙, 5,553	E 3
48118	Chelsea, 3,858	E 6
48616	Chesaning, 2,876	E 5
48617	Clare, 2,639	E 5
49234	Clarklake, 500	E 6
48016	Clarkston, 1,034	F 6
48017	Clawson, 17,617	B 6
49235	Clayton, 505	E 7
48727	Clifford, 472	F 5
49034	Climax, 594	D 6
49236	Clinton, 1,677	F 6
48420	Clio, 2,357	F 5
49036	Coldwater⊙, 9,099	D 7
48618	Coleman, 1,295	E 5
49038	Coloma, 1,814	C 6
49040	Colon, 1,172	D 7
48421	Columbiaville, 935	F 5
49041	Comstock, 5,003	D 6
49237	Concord, 983	E 6
49042	Constantine, 1,733	D 7
49722	Conway, 560	F 3
49404	Coopersville, 2,129	C 5
49818	Cornell, 640	B 3
48817	Corunna⊙, 2,829	E 6
49043	Covert, 650	C 6
48422	Croswell, 1,954	G 5
48818	Crystal, 649	E 5
49920	Crystal Falls⊙, 2,000	A 2
† 49501	Cutlerville, 6,267	D 6
48819	Dansville, 486	E 6
48423	Davison, 5,259	F 5
* 48120	Dearborn, 104,199	B 7
48127	Dearborn Heights, 80,069	B 7
49045	Decatur, 1,764	C 6
48427	Deckerville, 817	G 5
49238	Deerfield, 834	F 7
49725	De Tour Village, 494	E 3
* 48201	Detroit⊙, 1,511,482	B 7
	Detroit, ‡4,199,931	B 7
† 48161	Detroit Beach, 2,053	F 7
48820	De Witt, 1,829	E 6
48130	Dexter, 1,729	F 6
48821	Dimondale, 970	E 6
49922	Dollar Bay, 950	G 1
49323	Dorr, 550	D 6
49406	Douglas, 813	C 6
49047	Dowagiac, 6,583	D 6
48020	Drayton Plains, 16,462	F 6
49726	Drummond Island, 700	F 3
48428	Dryden, 654	F 6
48131	Dundee, 2,472	F 7
48429	Durand, 3,678	E 6
49924	Eagle River⊙, 36	A 1
48021	East Detroit, 45,920	B 6
† 49506	East Grand Rapids, 12,565	D 6
49727	East Jordan, 2,041	D 3
† 49801	East Kingsford, 1,155	A 3
49626	Eastlake, 512	C 4
48823	East Lansing, 47,540	E 6
48730	East Tawas, 2,372	F 4
† 49001	Eastwood, 9,682	D 6
48827	Eaton Rapids, 4,494	E 6
49111	Eau Claire, 527	C 6
48229	Ecorse, 17,515	B 7
48620	Edenville, 700	E 5
48829	Edmore, 1,149	E 5
49112	Edwardsburg, 1,107	C 7
† 48446	Elba, 460	F 5
49628	Elberta, 542	C 4
49629	Elk Rapids, 1,249	D 4
48731	Elkton, 973	F 5
48831	Elsie, 988	E 5
49827	Engadine, 500	D 2
48133	Erie, 975	F 7
49829	Escanaba⊙, 15,368	C 3
48732	Essexville, 4,990	F 5
† 48166	Estral Beach, 419	F 7
49631	Evart, 1,707	D 5
49925	Ewen, 600	F 2
48733	Fairgrove, 629	F 5
48023	Fair Haven, 550	G 6
49022	Fair Plain, 3,680	C 6
48621	Fairview, 600	F 4
48024	Farmington, 13,337	F 6
48622	Farwell, 777	E 5
49408	Fennville, 811	C 6
48430	Fenton, 8,284	F 6
48220	Ferndale, 30,850	B 6
49409	Ferrysburg, 2,196	C 5
48134	Flat Rock, 5,643	F 6
* 48501	Flint⊙, 193,317	F 6
	Flint, ‡496,658	F 6
48433	Flushing, 7,190	F 5
48835	Fowler, 1,020	E 5
48836	Fowlerville, 1,978	F 6
48734	Frankenmuth, 2,834	F 5
49635	Frankfort, 1,660	C 4
48025	Franklin, 3,344	B 6
48026	Fraser, 11,868	B 6
48623	Freeland, 1,303	E 5
49325	Freeport, 501	D 6
49412	Fremont, 3,465	D 5
49415	Fruitport, 1,409	C 5
49052	Fulton, 500	D 6
49927	Gaastra, 479	G 2
49053	Galesburg, 1,355	D 6
49113	Galien, 691	C 7
49735	Gaylord⊙, 3,012	E 3
48437	Genesee, 950	F 5
49836	Germfask, 750	C 2
48173	Gibraltar, 3,325	F 6
49837	Gladstone, 5,237	C 3
48624	Gladwin⊙, 2,071	E 5
49055	Gobles, 801	D 6
49737	Good Hart, 500	D 3
48438	Goodrich, 774	F 6
48439	Grand Blanc, 5,132	F 6
49417	Grand Haven⊙, 11,884	C 5
48837	Grand Ledge, 6,032	E 6
49839	Grand Marais, 650	D 2
* 49501	Grand Rapids⊙, 197,649	D 5
	Grand Rapids, ‡539,225	D 5
49418	Grandville, 10,764	D 6
49327	Grant, 772	D 5
49240	Grass Lake, 1,061	E 6
49738	Grayling⊙, 2,143	E 4
48738	Greenbush, 650	F 4
48838	Greenville, 7,493	D 5
48138	Grosse Ile, 7,799	B 7
48236	Grosse Pointe, 6,637	B 7
† 48236	Grosse Pointe Farms, 11,701	B 6
† 48236	Grosse Pointe Park, 15,585	B 7
† 48236	Grosse Pointe Shores, 3,042	B 6
† 48236	Grosse Pointe Woods, 21,878	B 6
49840	Gulliver, 962	D 2
49841	Gwinn, 1,054	B 2
48739	Hale, 500	F 4
48139	Hamburg, 500	F 6
49419	Hamilton, 950	C 6
48212	Hamtramck, 27,245	B 6
49930	Hancock, 4,820	G 1
49241	Hanover, 513	E 6
48441	Harbor Beach, 2,134	G 5
49740	Harbor Springs, 1,662	D 3
48236	Harper Woods, 20,186	B 6
48625	Harrison⊙, 1,460	E 4
48740	Harrisville⊙, 541	F 4
48028	Harsens Island, 750	G 6
49420	Hart⊙, 2,139	C 5
49057	Hartford, 2,508	C 6
48840	Haslett, 3,492	E 6
49058	Hastings⊙, 6,501	D 6
48030	Hazel Park, 23,784	B 6
48626	Hemlock, 900	E 5
48841	Henderson, 600	E 5
49847	Hermansville, 950	B 3
49744	Herron, 950	F 3
49421	Hesperia, 877	D 5
49745	Hessel, 500	E 2
48203	Highland Park, 35,444	B 6
49242	Hillsdale⊙, 7,728	E 7
49423	Holland, 26,337	C 6
48442	Holly, 4,355	F 6
48842	Holt, 6,980	E 6
49425	Holton, 500	C 5
49245	Homer, 1,617	E 6
49328	Hopkins, 566	D 6
49931	Houghton⊙, 6,067	G 1
48629	Houghton Lake, 500	E 4
48630	Houghton Lake Heights, 1,252	E 4
49329	Howard City, 1,060	D 5
48843	Howell⊙, 5,224	E 6
49934	Hubbell, 1,251	A 1
49247	Hudson, 2,618	E 7
49426	Hudsonville, 3,523	D 6
48140	Ida, 970	F 7
49642	Idlewild, 800	D 5
48444	Imlay City, 1,980	F 5
49749	Indian River, 950	E 3
48141	Inkster, 38,595	B 7
49643	Interlochen, 800	D 4
48846	Ionia⊙, 6,361	D 6
49801	Iron Mountain⊙, 8,702	B 3
49935	Iron River, 2,684	G 2
49938	Ironwood, 8,711	F 2
49849	Ishpeming, 8,245	B 2
48847	Ithaca⊙, 2,749	E 5
* 49201	Jackson⊙, 45,484	E 6
	Jackson, ‡143,274	E 6
49428	Jenison, 11,266	D 6
49061	Jones, 420	D 7
49250	Jonesville, 2,081	E 6
* 49001	Kalamazoo⊙, 85,555	D 6
	Kalamazoo, ‡201,550	D 6
49646	Kalkaska⊙, 1,475	D 4
48631	Kawkawlin, 450	F 5
48030	Keego Harbor, 3,092	F 6
49330	Kent City, 686	D 5
49508	Kentwood, 20,310	D 6
48445	Kinde, 618	G 5
49801	Kingsford, 5,276	A 3
49649	Kingsley, 632	D 4
48741	Kingston, 464	F 5
48848	Laingsburg, 1,159	E 6
48632	Lake, 600	E 5
49651	Lake City⊙, 704	D 4
48143	Lakeland, 720	F 6
49945	Lake Linden, 1,214	A 1
† 49039	Lake Michigan Beach, 1,201	C 6
48849	Lake Odessa, 1,924	D 6
48850	Lakeview, 1,198	D 5
† 49440	Lakewood Club, 590	C 5
48144	Lambertville, 5,721	F 7
49946	L'Anse⊙, 2,538	G 1
* 48901	Lansing (cap.), 131,546	E 6
	Lansing, ‡378,423	E 6
48446	Lapeer⊙, 6,270	F 5
49913	Laurium, 2,868	A 1
49064	Lawrence, 790	C 6
49065	Lawton, 1,358	D 6
49654	Leland⊙, 776	D 3
49251	Leslie, 1,894	E 6
49755	Levering, 967	E 3
49756	Lewiston, 750	E 4
48450	Lexington, 834	G 5
48146	Lincoln Park, 52,984	B 7
48451	Linden, 1,546	F 6
48634	Linwood, 950	F 5
49252	Litchfield, 1,167	E 6
49833	Little Lake, 950	B 2
* 48150	Livonia, 110,109	F 6
48743	Long Lake, 900	F 4
49331	Lowell, 3,068	D 6
49431	Ludington⊙, 9,021	C 5
48157	Luna Pier, 1,418	F 7
48851	Lyons, 758	E 6
49757	Mackinac Island, 517	E 3
49701	Mackinaw City, 810	E 3
48071	Madison Heights, 38,599	F 6
49659	Mancelona, 1,255	E 4
48158	Manchester, 1,650	E 6
49660	Manistee⊙, 7,723	C 4
49854	Manistique⊙, 4,324	C 3
49663	Manton, 1,107	D 4
48853	Maple Rapids, 683	E 5
49067	Marcellus, 1,139	D 6
49947	Marenisco, 865	F 2
48039	Marine City, 4,567	G 6
49665	Marion, 891	D 4
48453	Marlette, 1,706	G 5
49435	Marne, 950	D 5
49855	Marquette⊙, 21,967	B 2
49068	Marshall⊙, 7,253	E 6
49070	Martin, 502	D 6
48040	Marysville, 5,610	G 6
48854	Mason⊙, 5,468	E 6
49948	Mass, 850	G 1
49071	Mattawan, 1,569	D 6
48159	Maybee, 485	F 6
48744	Mayville, 872	F 5
49657	McBain, 520	D 4
48122	Melvindale, 13,862	B 7
48041	Memphis, 1,121	G 6
49072	Mendon, 949	D 7
49858	Menominee⊙, 10,748	B 3

(continued on following page)

A. D'Arazien — Shostal Associates

Turning out more than one car a minute keeps these inspectors on their toes during the final step on an assembly line in Detroit, Michigan.

	Zip	Place, population	Key
	48637	Merrill, 961	E 5
	48455	Metamora, 468	F 6
	49758	Metz, 495	F 3
	49254	Michigan Center, 4,900	E 6
	48856	Middleton, 500	E 5
	49333	Middleville, 1,865	D 6
	48640	Midland⊙, 35,176	E 5
	48160	Milan, 4,533	F 6
	48042	Milford, 4,699	F 6
	48746	Millington, 1,099	F 5
	48647	Mio⊙, 975	E 4
	49950	Mohawk, 800	A 1
	49335	Moline, 750	D 6
	48161	Monroe⊙, 23,894	F 7
	49437	Montague, 2,396	C 5
	48457	Montrose, 1,789	F 5
	49256	Morenci, 2,132	E 7
	49336	Morley, 481	D 5
	48857	Morrice, 734	E 6
	48043	Mount Clemens⊙, 20,476	G 6
	48458	Mount Morris, 3,778	F 5
	48858	Mount Pleasant⊙, 20,504	E 5
	48860	Muir, 617	D 5
	48861	Mulliken, 454	E 6
	48747	Munger, 432	F 5
	49862	Munising⊙, 3,677	C 2
*	49440	Muskegon⊙, 44,631	C 5
		Muskegon-Muskegon Heights, ‡157,426	C 5
	49444	Muskegon Heights, 17,304	C 5
	49261	Napoleon, 650	E 6
	49073	Nashville, 1,558	D 6
	49865	National Mine, 565	B 2
	49866	Negaunee, 5,248	B 2
	49337	Newaygo, 1,381	D 5
	48047	New Baltimore, 4,132	G 6
	49868	Newberry⊙, 2,334	D 2
	48164	New Boston, 800	F 6
	49117	New Buffalo, 2,784	C 7
	49446	New Era, 466	C 5
	48048	New Haven, 1,855	G 6
	48460	New Lothrop, 596	F 5
	49119	New Troy, 430	C 7
	49120	Niles, 12,988	C 7
	49262	North Adams, 574	E 7
	48461	North Branch, 932	F 5
	49445	North Muskegon, 4,243	C 5
	49670	Northport, 594	D 3
	48167	Northville, 5,400	F 6
†	49444	Norton Shores, 22,271	C 5
	49870	Norway, 3,033	B 3
	48050	Novi, 9,668	F 6
	48237	Oak Park, 36,762	B 6
	49763	Ocqueoc, 500	F 3
	48864	Okemos, 7,770	E 6
	49076	Olivet, 1,629	E 6
	49765	Onaway, 1,262	E 3
	49675	Onekama, 638	C 4
	49265	Onsted, 555	E 6
	49953	Ontonagon⊙, 2,432	F 1
	48033	Orchard Lake, 1,487	F 6
	48462	Ortonville, 983	F 6
	48750	Oscoda-Au Sable, 3,475	F 4
	48463	Otisville, 724	F 5
	49078	Otsego, 3,957	D 6
†	49735	Otsego Lake, 500	E 4
	48464	Otter Lake, 551	F 5
	48866	Ovid, 1,650	E 5
	48867	Owosso, 17,179	E 5
	48051	Oxford, 2,536	F 6
	49955	Painesdale, 600	G 1
	49871	Palmer, 950	B 2
	49268	Palmyra, 600	E 7
	49004	Parchment, 2,027	D 6
	49269	Parma, 880	E 6
	49079	Paw Paw⊙, 3,160	D 6
†	49038	Paw Paw Lake, 3,726	C 6
	48052	Pearl Beach, 1,744	G 6
	48466	Peck, 580	G 5
	49769	Pellston, 469	E 3
	49449	Pentwater, 993	C 5
	48871	Perrinton, 489	E 5
	48872	Perry, 1,531	E 6
	49270	Petersburg, 1,227	F 7
	49770	Petoskey⊙, 6,342	E 3
	48873	Pewamo, 498	E 5
	49774	Pickford, 800	E 2
	48755	Pigeon, 1,174	F 5
	48169	Pinckney, 921	F 6
	48650	Pinconning, 1,320	F 5
	49271	Pittsford, 610	E 7
	49080	Plainwell, 3,195	D 6
	48069	Pleasant Ridge, 3,989	B 6
	48170	Plymouth, 11,758	F 6
*	48053	Pontiac⊙, 85,279	F 6
	49081	Portage, 33,590	D 6
	48467	Port Austin, 883	F 4
	48060	Port Huron⊙, 35,794	G 6
	48875	Portland, 3,817	E 6
	48469	Port Sanilac, 493	G 5
	48876	Potterville, 1,280	E 6
	49874	Powers, 560	B 3
	48651	Prudenville, 500	E 4
	49082	Quincy, 1,540	E 7
	49876	Quinnesec, 770	A 3
	49959	Ramsay, 1,068	F 2
	49676	Rapid City, 450	D 4
	49878	Rapid River, 950	C 3
	49451	Ravenna, 1,048	D 5
	49274	Reading, 1,125	E 7
	49677	Reed City⊙, 2,286	D 5
	48757	Reese, 1,050	F 5
	49340	Remus, 425	D 5
	49879	Republic, 900	B 2
	49083	Richland, 728	D 6
	48062	Richmond, 3,234	G 6
	48758	Richville, 650	F 5
	48218	River Rouge, 15,947	B 7
	49084	Riverside, 650	C 6
	48192	Riverview, 11,342	B 7
	48063	Rochester, 7,054	F 6
	49341	Rockford, 2,428	D 5
	49960	Rockland, 450	G 1
	48173	Rockwood, 3,119	F 6
	49779	Rogers City⊙, 4,275	F 3
	48065	Romeo, 4,012	F 6
	48174	Romulus, 3,900	F 6
	49444	Roosevelt Park, 4,176	C 5
	48653	Roscommon⊙, 810	E 4
	48878	Rosebush, 439	E 5
	48654	Rose City, 530	E 4
	48066	Roseville, 60,529	G 6
*	48067	Royal Oak, 85,499	B 6
	49780	Rudyard, 950	E 2
*	48601	Saginaw⊙, 91,849	F 5
		Saginaw, ‡219,743	F 5
	48655	Saint Charles, 2,046	E 5
	48079	Saint Clair, 4,770	G 6
*	48080	Saint Clair Shores, 88,093	G 6
	48656	Saint Helen, 700	E 4
	49781	Saint Ignace⊙, 2,892	E 3
	48879	Saint Johns⊙, 6,672	E 6
	49085	Saint Joseph⊙, 11,042	C 6
	48880	Saint Louis, 4,101	E 5
	48176	Saline, 4,811	F 6
	48471	Sandusky⊙, 2,071	G 5
	48657	Sanford, 818	E 5
	48881	Saranac, 1,223	D 6
	49453	Saugatuck, 1,022	C 6
	49783	Sault Sainte Marie⊙, 15,136	E 2
	49125	Sawyer, 650	C 7
	49087	Schoolcraft, 1,277	D 6
	49454	Scottville, 1,202	C 5
	48759	Sebewaing, 2,053	F 5
	49455	Shelby, 1,703	C 5
	48883	Shepherd, 1,416	E 5
	48884	Sheridan, 653	D 5
†	49085	Shoreham, 666	C 6
†	49126	Shorewood Hills, 1,620	C 7
	49047	Sister Lakes, 700	C 6
	48075	Southfield, 69,285	F 6
	48192	Southgate, 33,909	F 6
	49090	South Haven, 6,471	C 6
	48178	South Lyon, 2,675	F 6
†	48161	South Monroe, 3,012	F 7
	49963	South Range, 898	G 1
	48179	South Rockwood, 1,477	F 7
	49886	Spalding, 600	B 3
†	48060	Sparlingville, 1,845	G 6
	49345	Sparta, 3,094	D 5
	49283	Spring Arbor, 1,832	E 6
	49015	Springfield, 3,994	D 6
	49456	Spring Lake, 3,034	C 5
	49284	Springport, 723	E 6
	49964	Stambaugh, 1,458	G 2
	48658	Standish⊙, 1,184	F 5
	48888	Stanton⊙, 1,089	D 5
	49887	Stephenson, 800	B 3
	48659	Sterling, 507	E 4
*	48077	Sterling Heights, 61,365	B 6
	49127	Stevensville, 1,107	C 6
	49285	Stockbridge, 1,190	E 6
	49681	Stronach, 500	C 4
	49790	Strongs, 450	E 2
	49091	Sturgis, 9,295	D 7
	48890	Sunfield, 497	D 6
	49682	Suttons Bay, 522	D 3
	48473	Swartz Creek, 4,928	F 6
†	48053	Sylvan Lake, 2,219	F 6
	48763	Tawas City⊙, 1,666	F 4
	48180	Taylor, 70,020	B 7
	49286	Tecumseh, 7,120	E 7
	49092	Tekonsha, 739	E 6
	48182	Temperance, 2,900	F 7
	49128	Three Oaks, 1,750	C 7
	49093	Three Rivers, 7,355	D 7
	49792	Tower, 425	E 3
	49684	Traverse City⊙, 18,048	D 4
	48183	Trenton, 24,127	B 7
	48084	Troy, 39,419	B 6
	49347	Trufant, 600	D 5
	48475	Ubly, 899	G 5
	49094	Union City, 1,740	D 6
	49129	Union Pier, 900	C 7
	48767	Unionville, 647	F 5
	48087	Utica, 3,504	F 6
	49095	Vandalia, 427	D 7
	49795	Vanderbilt, 522	E 3
	48768	Vassar, 2,802	F 5
	49096	Vermontville, 857	E 6
	48476	Vernon, 818	F 6
	48891	Vestaburg, 680	E 5
	49097	Vicksburg, 2,139	D 6
	49892	Vulcan, 975	B 3
	49968	Wakefield, 2,757	F 2
	49288	Waldron, 564	E 7
	49504	Walker, 11,492	D 6
	48088	Walled Lake, 3,759	F 6
	49796	Walloon Lake, 550	E 3
*	48089	Warren, 179,260	B 6
	49969	Watersmeet, 700	G 2
	49098	Watervliet, 2,059	C 6
	49348	Wayland, 2,054	D 6
	48184	Wayne, 21,054	F 6
	48892	Webberville, 1,251	E 6
	48893	Weidman, 450	D 5
	49894	Wells, 1,085	B 3
	48661	West Branch⊙, 1,912	E 4
	48185	Westland, 86,749	F 6
	48894	Westphalia, 806	E 6
	49349	White Cloud⊙, 1,044	D 5
	49461	Whitehall, 3,017	C 5
	49099	White Pigeon, 1,455	D 7
	49971	White Pine, 1,218	F 1
	48189	Whitmore Lake, 2,763	F 6
	48190	Whittaker, 500	F 6
	48770	Whittemore, 460	F 4
	48895	Williamston, 2,600	E 6
	48191	Willis, 500	F 6
	49896	Wilson, 500	B 3
	48896	Winn, 600	E 5
	48096	Wixom, 2,010	F 6
	49442	Wolf Lake, 2,258	D 5
	48183	Woodhaven, 3,330	F 6
	48897	Woodland, 473	D 6
	48192	Wyandotte, 41,061	B 7
	49509	Wyoming, 56,560	D 6
	48097	Yale, 1,505	G 5
	48197	Ypsilanti, 29,538	F 6
	49464	Zeeland, 4,734	D 6
†	48601	Zilwaukee, 2,072	F 5

⊙ County seat.
‡ Population of metropolitan area.
† Zip of nearest p.o.
* Multiple zips

Agriculture, Industry and Resources

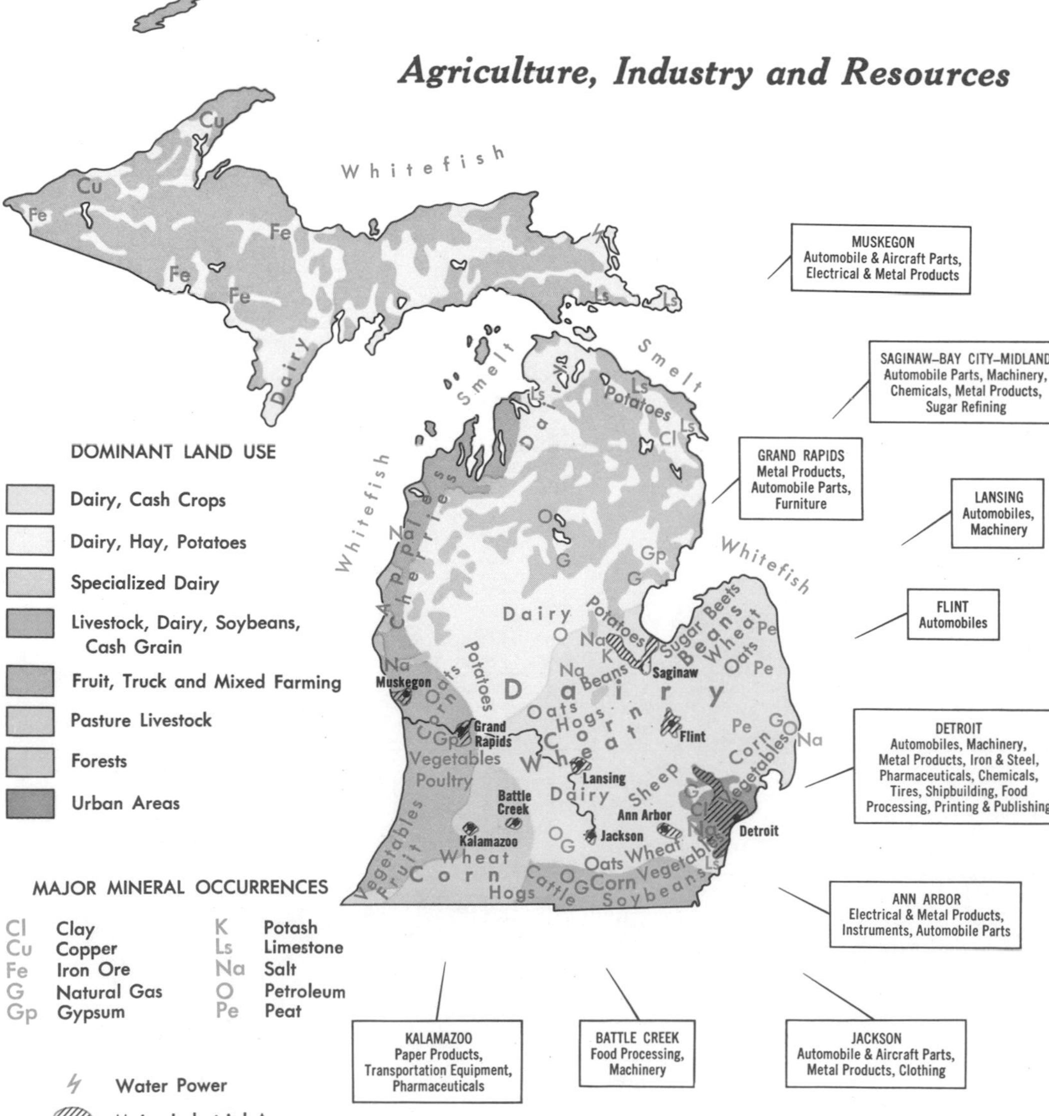

AREA 84,068 sq. mi.
POPULATION 3,805,069
CAPITAL St. Paul
LARGEST CITY Minneapolis
HIGHEST POINT Eagle Mtn. 2,301 ft.
SETTLED IN 1805
ADMITTED TO UNION May 11, 1858
POPULAR NAME North Star State; Gopher State
STATE FLOWER Lady-slipper
STATE BIRD Loon

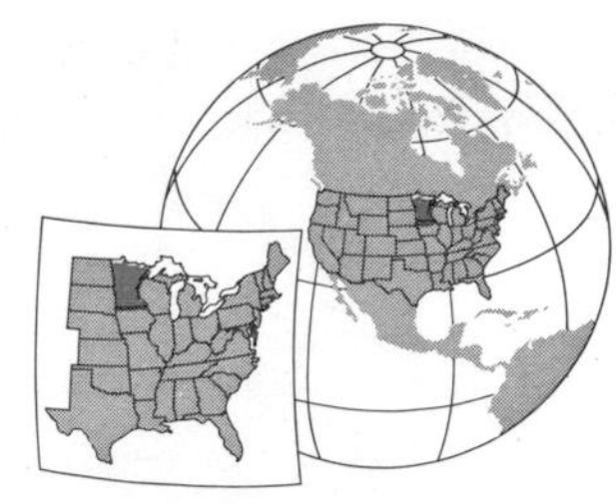

COUNTIES

Aitkin, 11,403 E 4
Anoka, 154,556 E 5
Becker, 24,372 C 4
Beltrami, 26,373 C 2
Benton, 20,841 D 5
Big Stone, 7,941 B 5
Blue Earth, 52,322 D 6
Brown, 28,887 D 6
Carlton, 28,072 F 4
Carver, 28,310 E 6
Cass, 17,323 D 4
Chippewa, 15,109 C 5
Chisago, 17,492 F 5
Clay, 46,585 B 4
Clearwater, 8,013 C 3
Cook, 3,423 H 3
Cottonwood, 14,887 C 6
Crow Wing, 34,826 D 4
Dakota, 139,808 E 6
Dodge, 13,037 F 7
Douglas, 22,892 C 5
Faribault, 20,896 D 7
Fillmore, 21,916 F 7
Freeborn, 38,064 E 7
Goodhue, 34,763 F 6
Grant, 7,462 B 5
Hennepin, 960,080 E 5
Houston, 17,556 G 7
Hubbard, 10,583 D 3
Isanti, 16,560 E 5
Itasca, 35,530 E 3
Jackson, 14,352 C 7
Kanabec, 9,775 E 5
Kandiyohi, 30,548 C 5
Kittson, 6,853 B 2
Koochiching, 17,731 E 2
Lac qui Parle, 11,164 B 6
Lake, 13,351 G 3
Lake of the Woods, 3,987 D 2
Le Sueur, 21,332 E 6
Lincoln, 8,143 B 6
Lyon, 24,273 C 6
Mahnomen, 5,638 C 3
Marshall, 13,060 B 2
Martin, 24,316 D 7
McLeod, 27,662 D 6
Meeker, 18,810 D 5
Mille Lacs, 15,703 E 5
Morrison, 26,949 D 4
Mower, 43,783 F 7
Murray, 12,508 C 6
Nicollet, 24,518 D 6
Nobles, 23,208 C 7
Norman, 10,008 B 3
Olmsted, 84,104 F 7
Otter Tail, 46,097 C 4
Pennington, 13,266 B 2
Pine, 16,821 F 4
Pipestone, 12,791 B 6
Polk, 34,435 B 3
Pope, 11,107 C 5
Ramsey, 476,255 E 5
Red Lake, 5,388 B 3
Redwood, 20,024 C 6
Renville, 21,139 C 6
Rice, 41,582 E 6
Rock, 11,346 B 7
Roseau, 11,569 C 2
Saint Louis, 220,693 F 3
Scott, 32,423 E 6
Sherburne, 18,344 E 5
Sibley, 15,845 D 6
Stearns, 95,400 D 5
Steele, 26,931 E 7
Stevens, 11,218 B 5
Swift, 13,177 C 5
Todd, 22,114 D 4
Traverse, 6,254 B 5
Wabasha, 17,224 F 6
Wadena, 12,412 D 4
Waseca, 16,663 E 6
Washington, 82,948 F 5
Watonwan, 13,298 D 7
Wilkin, 9,389 B 4
Winona, 44,409 G 6
Wright, 38,933 D 5
Yellow Medicine, 14,418 B 6

CITIES and TOWNS

Zip *Name/Pop.* *Key*

56510 Ada⊙, 2,076 B 3
55909 Adams, 771 F 7
56110 Adrian, 1,350 C 7
55001 Afton, 248 F 6
56430 Ah-Gwah-Ching, 500 D 3
56431 Aitkin⊙, 1,553 E 4
56433 Akeley, 468 D 3
56307 Albany, 1,599 D 5
56207 Alberta, 140 B 5
56007 Albert Lea⊙, 19,418 E 7
55301 Albertville, 451 E 5
56009 Alden, 713 E 7
56308 Alexandria⊙, 6,973 C 5
55002 Almelund, 150 F 5
56111 Alpha, 179 D 7
55910 Altura, 334 G 6
56710 Alvarado, 302 B 2
56010 Amboy, 571 D 7
55703 Angora, 287 F 3
55302 Annandale, 1,234 D 5
55303 Anoka⊙, 13,489 E 5
56208 Appleton, 1,789 C 5
55378 Apple Valley, 8,502 G 6
56113 Arco, 121 B 6
56713 Argyle, 739 B 2
55307 Arlington, 1,823 D 6
55801 Arnold, 750 F 4
56309 Ashby, 415 C 4
55704 Askov, 287 F 4
56209 Atwater, 956 D 5
56511 Audubon, 297 C 4
55705 Aurora, 2,531 F 3
55912 Austin⊙, 25,074 E 7
56114 Avoca, 203 C 7
56310 Avon, 725 D 5
55706 Babbitt, 3,076 G 3
56435 Backus, 257 D 4
56714 Badger, 327 B 2
56621 Bagley⊙, 1,314 C 3
56115 Balaton, 649 C 6
56622 Ball Club, 150 E 3
56514 Barnesville, 1,782 B 4
55707 Barnum, 382 F 4
56311 Barrett, 342 B 5
56515 Battle Lake, 772 C 4
56623 Baudette⊙, 1,547 D 2
† 56401 Baxter, 1,556 D 4
† 56444 Bay Lake, 250 E 4
55003 Bayport, 2,987 F 5
56211 Beardsley, 366 B 5
† 55723 Bear River, 250 E 3
55601 Beaver Bay, 362 G 3
56116 Beaver Creek, 235 B 7
55308 Becker, 365 E 5
56516 Bejou, 157 B 3
56312 Belgrade, 713 C 5
† 55027 Bellechester, 199 F 6
56011 Belle Plaine, 2,328 E 6
56212 Bellingham, 263 B 5
56517 Beltrami, 171 B 3
56214 Belview, 429 C 6
56601 Bemidji⊙, 11,490 D 3
56626 Bena, 169 D 3
56215 Benson⊙, 3,484 C 5
56437 Bertha, 512 C 4
56117 Bigelow, 262 C 7
56627 Big Falls, 534 E 2
56628 Bigfork, 399 E 3
55309 Big Lake, 1,015 E 5
56118 Bingham Lake, 214 C 7
55310 Bird Island, 1,309 D 6
55708 Biwabik, 1,483 F 3
56630 Blackduck, 595 D 3
† 55303 Blaine, 20,640 G 5
† 56011 Blakeley, 125 E 6
56216 Blomkest, 172 D 6
55917 Blooming Prairie, 1,804 E 7
55420 Bloomington, 81,970 G 6
56013 Blue Earth⊙, 3,965 D 7
56518 Bluffton, 195 C 4
56519 Borup, 128 B 3
55709 Bovey, 858 E 3
56314 Bowlus, 268 D 5
56218 Boyd, 311 C 6
55006 Braham, 744 E 5
56401 Brainerd⊙, 11,667 D 4
† 55056 Branch, 880 F 5
56315 Brandon, 414 C 5
56520 Breckenridge⊙, 4,200 B 4
† 56472 Breezy Point Village, 233 D 4
56119 Brewster, 563 C 7
56014 Bricelyn, 470 E 7
55710 Britt, 175 F 3
55429 Brooklyn Center, 35,173 G 5
† 55401 Brooklyn Park, 26,230 G 5
56715 Brooks, 163 B 3
55711 Brookston, 137 F 4
56316 Brooten, 615 C 5
56438 Browerville, 665 D 4
55918 Brownsdale, 625 F 7
56219 Browns Valley, 906 B 5
55919 Brownsville, 417 G 7
55312 Brownton, 688 D 6
55712 Bruno, 130 F 4
† 55051 Brunswick, 144 E 5
56317 Buckman, 158 D 5
55313 Buffalo⊙, 3,275 E 5
55314 Buffalo Lake, 758 D 6
55713 Buhl, 1,303 F 3
55378 Burnsville, 19,940 E 6
56318 Burtrum, 135 D 5
56120 Butterfield, 619 D 7
† 56723 Bygland, 475 B 3
55920 Byron, 1,419 F 6
55921 Caledonia⊙, 2,619 G 7
56521 Callaway, 233 C 3
55716 Calumet, 460 E 3
55008 Cambridge⊙, 3,467 E 5
56522 Campbell, 339 B 4
56220 Canby, 2,081 B 6
55009 Cannon Falls, 2,072 F 6
55922 Canton, 391 F 7
55717 Canyon, 125 F 3
56319 Carlos, 260 C 5
55718 Carlton⊙, 884 F 4
55315 Carver, 669 E 6
56633 Cass Lake, 1,317 D 3
55010 Castle Rock, 150 E 6
55012 Center City⊙, 324 F 5
† 55038 Centerville, 534 E 5
56121 Ceylon, 487 D 7
55316 Champlin, 2,275 G 5
56122 Chandler, 319 C 7
55317 Chanhassen, 4,879 F 6
55318 Chaska⊙, 4,352 F 6
55923 Chatfield, 1,885 F 7
55013 Chisago City, 1,068 E 5
55719 Chisholm, 5,913 E 3
56221 Chokio, 455 B 5
55014 Circle Pines, 3,918 G 5
56222 Clara City, 1,491 C 6
55924 Claremont, 520 E 6
56440 Clarissa, 599 C 4
56223 Clarkfield, 1,084 C 6
56016 Clarks Grove, 480 E 7
56634 Clearbrook, 599 C 3
55319 Clear Lake, 280 E 5
55320 Clearwater, 282 D 5
56224 Clements, 252 D 6
56017 Cleveland, 492 E 6
56523 Climax, 255 B 3
56225 Clinton, 608 B 5
56524 Clitherall, 131 C 4
56226 Clontarf, 147 C 5
55720 Cloquet, 8,699 F 4
55015 Cloverton, 150 F 4
55721 Cohasset, 536 E 3
55321 Cokato, 1,735 D 5
56320 Cold Spring, 2,006 D 5
55722 Coleraine, 1,086 E 3
56321 Collegeville, 1,600 D 5
55322 Cologne, 518 E 6
55421 Columbia Heights, 23,997 G 5
56019 Comfrey, 525 D 6
56525 Comstock, 135 B 4
56020 Conger, 167 E 7
55723 Cook, 687 F 3
55433 Coon Rapids, 30,505 G 5
† 55340 Corcoran, 1,656 F 5
56228 Cosmos, 570 D 6
55016 Cottage Grove, 13,419 F 6
55724 Cotton, 350 F 3
56229 Cottonwood, 794 C 6
56021 Courtland, 360 D 6
55725 Crane Lake, 350 F 2
55726 Cromwell, 181 F 4
56716 Crookston⊙, 8,312 B 3
56441 Crosby, 2,241 D 4
56442 Crosslake, 358 E 4
† 55005 Crown, 200 E 5
† 55401 Crystal, 30,925 G 5
55323 Crystal Bay, 6,787 F 5
56123 Currie, 368 C 6
56323 Cyrus, 289 C 5
55925 Dakota, 369 G 7
56324 Dalton, 221 C 4
56230 Danube, 497 C 6
56231 Danvers, 136 C 5
56022 Darfur, 179 D 6
55324 Darwin, 224 D 5
55325 Dassel, 1,058 D 5
56232 Dawson, 1,699 B 6
55327 Dayton, 517 E 5
55391 Deephaven, 3,853 G 5
56527 Deer Creek, 287 C 4
56636 Deer River, 815 E 3
56444 Deerwood, 448 E 4
56233 De Graff, 195 C 5
55328 Delano, 1,851 E 5
56023 Delavan, 281 D 7
56234 Delhi, 154 C 6
† 55110 Dellwood, 514 F 5
55018 Dennison, 162 E 6
56528 Dent, 156 C 4
56501 Detroit Lakes⊙, 5,797 C 4
55926 Dexter, 252 F 7
56529 Dilworth, 2,321 B 4
55927 Dodge Center, 1,603 F 6
56235 Donnelly, 252 B 5
55929 Dover, 321 F 7
55930 Dresbach, 250 G 7
* 55801 Duluth⊙, 100,578 F 4
Duluth-Superior, ‡265,350 F 4
56236 Dumont, 204 B 5
55019 Dundas, 460 E 6
56126 Dundee, 138 C 7
56127 Dunnell, 237 D 7
56446 Eagle Bend, 557 D 4
† 55005 East Bethel, 2,586 E 5
56024 Eagle Lake, 839 E 6
† 56031 East Chain, 171 D 7
56721 East Grand Forks, 7,607 B 3
† 56401 East Gull Lake, 440 D 4
56025 Easton, 352 E 7
56237 Echo, 356 C 6
55343 Eden Prairie, 6,938 G 6
55329 Eden Valley, 776 D 5
56128 Edgerton, 1,119 B 7
55424 Edina, 44,046 G 6
56639 Effie, 165 E 3
55931 Eitzen, 208 G 7
† 55910 Elba, 158 F 6
56531 Elbow Lake⊙, 1,484 B 5
55932 Elgin, 580 F 6
56533 Elizabeth, 188 B 4
55330 Elk River⊙, 2,252 E 5
55933 Elkton, 134 F 7
56026 Ellendale, 569 E 7
56129 Ellsworth, 588 C 7
56027 Elmore, 910 D 7
56325 Elrosa, 203 C 5
55731 Ely, 4,904 G 3
56028 Elysian, 445 E 6
55732 Embarrass, 195 F 3
56447 Emily, 386 E 4
56029 Emmons, 412 E 7
56534 Erhard, 748 B 4
56640 Ericsburg, 300 E 2
56535 Erskine, 571 B 3
55733 Esko, 500 F 4
56722 Euclid, 130 B 3
56238 Evan, 126 D 6
56326 Evansville, 553 C 4
55734 Eveleth, 4,721 F 3
55331 Excelsior, 2,563 E 6
55934 Eyota, 639 F 7
55332 Fairfax, 1,432 D 6
55383 Fairhaven, 129 D 5
56031 Fairmont⊙, 10,751 D 7
55113 Falcon Heights, 5,507 G 5
55021 Faribault⊙, 16,595 E 6
55024 Farmington, 3,104 E 6
56641 Federal Dam, 147 D 3
56536 Felton, 232 B 3
56537 Fergus Falls⊙, 12,443 B 4
56540 Fertile, 955 B 3
56448 Fifty Lakes, 143 D 4
55603 Finland, 300 G 3
55735 Finlayson, 192 F 4
56723 Fisher, 383 B 3
56328 Flensburg, 259 D 5
55736 Floodwood, 650 E 4
† 55792 Florenton, 635 F 3
56329 Foley⊙, 1,271 D 5
† 56308 Forada, 158 C 5
55738 Forbes, 225 F 3
55025 Forest Lake, 3,207 F 5
56330 Foreston, 273 E 5
56542 Fosston, 1,684 C 3
55935 Fountain, 347 F 7
56543 Foxhome, 185 B 4
55333 Franklin, 557 D 6
56544 Frazee, 1,015 C 4
56032 Freeborn, 296 E 7
56331 Freeport, 593 D 5
† 55801 French River, 200 G 4
55421 Fridley, 29,233 G 5
55026 Frontenac, 223 F 6
56033 Frost, 290 D 7
56131 Fulda, 1,226 C 7
56034 Garden City, 270 D 6
56332 Garfield, 198 C 5
56450 Garrison, 125 E 4
56132 Garvin, 201 C 6
56545 Gary, 265 B 3
55334 Gaylord⊙, 1,720 D 6
56035 Geneva, 358 E 7
56717 Gentilly, 163 B 3
56546 Georgetown, 141 B 3
55740 Gheen, 145 F 3
56239 Ghent, 301 C 6
55335 Gibbon, 877 D 6
55741 Gilbert, 2,287 F 3
† 56431 Glen, 125 E 4
55336 Glencoe⊙, 4,217 D 6
56036 Glenville, 740 E 7
56334 Glenwood⊙, 2,584 C 5
56547 Glyndon, 674 B 4
55427 Golden Valley, 24,246 G 5
56644 Gonvick, 344 C 3
55027 Goodhue, 539 F 6
55742 Goodland, 175 E 3
56725 Goodridge, 144 C 2
56037 Good Thunder, 489 D 6
55027 Goodview, 1,829 G 6
56240 Graceville, 735 B 5
56039 Granada, 381 D 7
55604 Grand Marais⊙, 1,301 G 2
55936 Grand Meadow, 869 F 7
55744 Grand Rapids⊙, 7,247 E 3
55029 Grandy, 155 E 5
56241 Granite Falls⊙, 3,225 C 6
55030 Grasston, 132 E 5
56726 Greenbush, 787 B 2
† 55373 Greenfield, 977 F 5
55338 Green Isle, 363 E 6
56242 Green Valley, 129 C 6
56335 Greenwald, 244 D 5
56336 Grey Eagle, 325 D 5
56243 Grove City, 502 D 5
56727 Grygla, 211 C 2
56452 Hackensack, 220 D 4
56133 Hadley, 119 C 7
56728 Hallock⊙, 1,477 A 2
56548 Halstad, 598 B 3
55339 Hamburg, 377 D 6
55340 Hamel, 2,396 F 5
55938 Hammond, 179 F 6
55031 Hampton, 369 E 6
56244 Hancock, 806 C 5
56245 Hanley Falls, 265 C 6
55341 Hanover, 365 E 5
56041 Hanska, 442 D 6
56364 Harding, 119 E 4
56134 Hardwick, 274 B 7
55939 Harmony, 1,130 F 7
55032 Harris, 559 F 5
56042 Hartland, 331 E 7
† 55374 Hassan, 778 E 5
55033 Hastings⊙, 12,195 F 6
56549 Hawley, 1,371 B 4
55940 Hayfield, 939 F 7
56043 Hayward, 261 E 7
55342 Hector, 1,178 D 6
56044 Henderson, 730 E 6
56136 Hendricks, 712 B 6
56550 Hendrum, 311 B 3
56551 Henning, 850 C 4
56248 Herman, 619 B 5
56137 Heron Lake, 777 C 7
56453 Hewitt, 198 C 4
55746 Hibbing, 16,104 F 3
55748 Hill City, 357 E 4
56138 Hills, 571 B 7
55037 Hinckley, 885 E 4
56552 Hitterdal, 178 B 4
56339 Hoffman, 627 C 5
55941 Hokah, 697 G 7
56340 Holdingford, 551 D 5
56139 Holland, 263 B 6
56045 Hollandale, 287 E 7
56249 Holloway, 146 C 5
55749 Holyoke, 190 F 4
55942 Homer, 150 G 6
56045 Hope, 125 E 7
55343 Hopkins, 13,428 G 5
55943 Houston, 1,090 G 7
55606 Hovland, 150 G 2
55349 Howard Lake, 1,162 D 5
55750 Hoyt Lakes, 3,634 F 3
55038 Hugo, 751 E 5
56047 Huntley, 139 D 7
55350 Hutchinson, 8,031 D 6
56140 Ihlen, 132 B 7
† 55359 Independence, 1,993 F 5
56649 International Falls⊙, 6,439 E 2
55075 Inver Grove Heights, 12,148 E 6
56141 Iona, 260 C 7
55751 Iron, 150 F 3
56455 Ironton, 562 D 4
55040 Isanti, 679 E 5
56342 Isle, 551 E 4
56142 Ivanhoe⊙, 738 B 6
56143 Jackson⊙, 3,550 C 7
55752 Jacobson, 225 E 4
56048 Janesville, 1,557 E 6
56144 Jasper, 754 B 7
56145 Jeffers, 436 C 6
56456 Jenkins, 148 D 4
55352 Jordan, 1,836 E 6
† 56669 Kabetogama, 150 F 2
56251 Kandiyohi, 295 D 5
56732 Karlstad, 727 B 2
56050 Kasota, 732 D 6
55944 Kasson, 1,883 F 6
55753 Keewatin, 1,382 E 3
56650 Kelliher, 289 D 3
55945 Kellogg, 403 G 6
55754 Kelly Lake, 950 F 3
55755 Kelsey, 151 F 3
56733 Kennedy, 424 B 2
56343 Kensington, 308 C 5
56553 Kent, 139 B 4
55946 Kenyon, 1,575 E 6
56252 Kerkhoven, 641 C 5
55757 Kettle River, 173 E 4
56051 Kiester, 681 E 7
56052 Kilkenny, 182 E 6
55353 Kimball, 567 D 5
55758 Kinney, 325 F 3
55609 Knife River, 350 G 4
55947 La Crescent, 3,142 G 7
56054 Lafayette, 498 D 6
56149 Lake Benton, 759 B 6
56734 Lake Bronson, 325 B 2
55041 Lake City, 3,594 F 6
56055 Lake Crystal, 1,807 D 6
55042 Lake Elmo, 4,032 F 6
56150 Lakefield, 1,820 C 7
† 55398 Lake Fremont (Zimmerman), 495 E 5
56458 Lake George, 200 D 3
55043 Lakeland, 962 F 6
56253 Lake Lillian, 316 C 6
56554 Lake Park, 658 B 4
† 55043 Lake Saint Croix Beach, 1,111 F 6
† 56401 Lake Shore, 410 D 4
55044 Lakeville, 7,556 E 6
56151 Lake Wilson, 378 B 7
56152 Lamberton, 962 C 6
56735 Lancaster, 382 B 2
55949 Lanesboro, 850 G 7
55950 Lansing, 300 F 7
56461 Laporte, 154 D 3
† 55744 La Prairie, 413 E 3
56056 La Salle, 132 D 6

(continued on following page)

Superior National Forest in Minnesota contains the nation's largest wilderness park with primitive virgin timberlands, protected wildlife and 5,000 restocked lakes.

MINNESOTA
SCALE
0 5 10 20 30 40 50 MI.
0 5 10 20 30 40 50 KM.
State Capitals
County Seats
© C.S. HAMMOND & Co., N.Y.
NORTHEASTERN PART OF MINNESOTA
Same scale as main map
CANADA
MANITOBA
ONTARIO
NORTH DAKOTA
SOUTH DAKOTA
IOWA
WISCONSIN
LAKE SUPERIOR
Lake of the Woods
KITTSON
ROSEAU
LAKE OF THE WOODS
MARSHALL
KOOCHICHING
PENNINGTON
BELTRAMI
RED LAKE
POLK
NORMAN
MAHNOMEN
CLEARWATER
ITASCA
SAINT LOUIS
LAKE
COOK
CLAY
BECKER
HUBBARD
CASS
AITKIN
CARLTON
WILKIN
OTTER TAIL
WADENA
CROW WING
PINE
GRANT
DOUGLAS
TODD
MORRISON
MILLE LACS
KANABEC
TRAVERSE
STEVENS
POPE
STEARNS
BENTON
SHERBURNE
ISANTI
CHISAGO
BIG STONE
SWIFT
KANDIYOHI
MEEKER
WRIGHT
ANOKA
CHIPPEWA
LAC QUI PARLE
YELLOW MEDICINE
RENVILLE
MCLEOD
CARVER
HENNEPIN
RAMSEY
WASHINGTON
SCOTT
DAKOTA
SIBLEY
LINCOLN
LYON
REDWOOD
NICOLLET
LE SUEUR
RICE
GOODHUE
WABASHA
BROWN
PIPESTONE
MURRAY
COTTONWOOD
WATONWAN
BLUE EARTH
WASECA
STEELE
DODGE
OLMSTED
WINONA
ROCK
NOBLES
JACKSON
MARTIN
FARIBAULT
FREEBORN
MOWER
FILLMORE
HOUSTON
ST. PAUL
MINNEAPOLIS
DULUTH
Superior
Rochester
St. Cloud
Mankato
Moorhead
Fargo
Grand Forks
Sioux Falls
La Crosse

56344 Lastrup, 161 D 4
† 55101 Lauderdale, 2,419 G 5
56057 Le Center⊙, 1,890 E 6
56651 Lengby, 140 C 3
† 55734 Leonidas, 157 F 3
56153 Leota, 285 C 7
55951 Le Roy, 870 F 7
55354 Lester Prairie, 1,162 D 6
56058 Le Sueur, 3,745 E 6
55952 Lewiston, 1,000 G 7
56060 Lewisville, 291 D 7
† 55014 Lexington, 1,926 G 5
† 55050 Lilydale, 664 G 5
55045 Lindstrom, 1,260 F 5
† 55038 Lino Lakes, 3,692 G 5
56155 Lismore, 323 B 7
55355 Litchfield⊙, 5,262 D 5
56345 Little Falls⊙, 7,467 D 5
56653 Littlefork, 824 E 2
55611 Little Marais, 175 G 3
† 56334 Long Beach, 219 C 5
55356 Long Lake, 1,506 F 5
56347 Long Prairie⊙, 2,416 D 5
56655 Longville, 171 D 4
55046 Lonsdale, 622 E 6
55357 Loretto, 340 F 5
56349 Lowry, 257 C 5
56255 Lucan, 254 C 6
55612 Lutsen, 620 F 2
56156 Luverne⊙, 4,703 B 7
55953 Lyle, 522 F 7
56157 Lynd, 267 C 6
55954 Mabel, 888 G 7
56062 Madelia, 2,316 D 6
56256 Madison⊙, 2,242 B 5
56063 Madison Lake, 587 E 6
56158 Magnolia, 233 B 7
56557 Mahnomen⊙, 1,313 C 3
55115 Mahtomedi, 2,640 F 5
55762 Mahtowa, 167 F 4
56001 Mankato⊙, 30,895 E 6
55955 Mantorville⊙, 479 F 6
† 55369 Maple Grove, 6,275 F 5
55358 Maple Lake, 1,124 D 5
55359 Maple Plain, 1,169 F 5
56065 Mapleton, 1,307 E 7
† 55912 Mapleview, 328 E 7
55109 Maplewood, 25,222 G 5
55764 Marble, 682 E 3
56657 Marcell, 350 E 3
56257 Marietta, 264 B 5
55047 Marine on Saint Croix, 513 F 5
56258 Marshall⊙, 9,886 C 6
55360 Mayer, 325 E 6
56260 Maynard, 455 C 6
55956 Mazeppa, 498 F 6
55760 McGregor, 331 E 4
56556 McIntosh, 753 C 3
55761 McKinley, 317 F 3
55765 Meadowlands, 128 F 3
55049 Medford, 690 E 6
55427 Medicine Lake, 930 G 5
† 55340 Medina (Hamel), 2,396 F 5
† 56352 Meire Grove, 171 C 5
56352 Melrose, 2,273 D 5
56464 Menahga, 835 C 4
55050 Mendota, 327 G 5
† 55050 Mendota Heights, 6,165 G 6
56736 Mentor, 236 B 3
56465 Merrifield, 300 D 4
56737 Middle River, 369 B 2
† 55033 Miesville, 192 F 6
56353 Milaca⊙, 1,940 E 5
56262 Milan, 427 C 5
55957 Millville, 139 F 6
56263 Milroy, 247 C 6
56354 Miltona, 172 C 4
* 55401 Minneapolis⊙, 434,400 G 5
Minneapolis-Saint Paul, ‡1,813,647 G 5
56264 Minneota, 1,320 C 6
55959 Minnesota City, 301 G 6
56068 Minnesota Lake, 738 E 7
55343 Minnetonka, 35,776 G 5
† 55364 Minnetrista, 2,878 F 5
56265 Montevideo⊙, 5,661 C 6
56069 Montgomery, 2,281 E 6
55362 Monticello, 1,636 E 5
55363 Montrose, 379 E 5
56560 Moorhead⊙, 29,687 B 4
Moorhead-Fargo, ‡120,238 B 4
55767 Moose Lake, 1,400 F 4
56266 Mora⊙, 2,582 E 5
56266 Morgan, 972 D 6
56267 Morris⊙, 5,366 C 5
55052 Morristown, 659 E 6
56270 Morton, 591 C 6
56466 Motley, 351 D 4
55364 Mound, 7,572 E 6
† 55112 Mounds View, 9,988 G 5
55768 Mountain Iron, 1,698 F 3
56159 Mountain Lake, 1,986 D 7
56271 Murdock, 358 C 5
55769 Nashwauk, 1,341 E 3
56272 Nassau, 126 B 5
56566 Naytahwaush, 350 C 3
56355 Nelson, 175 C 5
55053 Nerstrand, 221 E 6
55772 Nett Lake, 470 E 2
56467 Nevis, 308 D 4
55366 New Auburn, 274 D 6
55112 New Brighton, 19,507 G 5
56738 Newfolden, 390 B 2
55367 New Germany, 303 E 6
56273 New London, 736 C 5
55054 New Market, 215 E 6
56356 New Munich, 307 D 5
55055 Newport, 2,922 F 6
56071 New Prague, 2,680 E 6
56072 New Richland, 1,113 E 7
† 55031 New Trier, 153 F 6
56073 New Ulm⊙, 13,051 D 6
56567 New York Mills, 791 C 4
† 56431 Nichols, 125 E 4
56074 Nicollet, 618 D 6
56568 Nielsville, 156 B 3
56468 Nisswa, 1,011 D 4
55770 Nopeming, 268 F 4
56274 Norcross, 137 B 5
55056 North Branch, 1,106 F 5
† 56442 North Crosslake, 362 D 4
55057 Northfield, 10,235 E 6
56001 North Mankato, 7,347 D 6
56661 Northome, 351 D 3
56275 North Redwood, 155 D 6
56075 Northrop, 188 D 7
55109 North Saint Paul, 11,950 E 5
55368 Norwood, 1,058 E 6
56276 Odessa, 194 B 5
56160 Odin, 166 D 7
56569 Ogema, 236 C 3
56358 Ogilvie, 384 E 5
56161 Okabena, 237 C 7
56742 Oklee, 536 C 3
56277 Olivia⊙, 2,553 C 6
56359 Onamia, 670 E 4
† 55044 Orchard Lake, 200 E 6
56162 Ormsby, 199 D 7
† 55323 Orono (Crystal Bay), 6,787 F 5
55960 Oronoco, 564 F 6
55771 Orr, 315 F 2
56278 Ortonville⊙, 2,665 B 5
56570 Osage, 175 C 4
56360 Osakis, 1,306 C 5
56744 Oslo, 417 A 2
55369 Osseo, 2,908 G 5
55961 Ostrander, 216 F 7
† 56058 Ottawa, 125 E 6
56571 Ottertail, 180 C 4
56662 Outing, 425 E 4
55060 Owatonna⊙, 15,341 E 6
56469 Palisade, 149 E 4
† 55801 Palmers, 150 G 4
† 55705 Palo, 158 F 3
56361 Parkers Prairie, 882 C 4
56470 Park Rapids⊙, 2,772 D 4
56362 Paynesville, 1,920 D 5
56363 Pease, 187 E 5
† 56472 Pelican Lakes (Breezy Point Village), 233 D 4
56572 Pelican Rapids, 1,835 B 4
56078 Pemberton, 128 E 7
55775 Pengilly, 625 E 3
56279 Pennock, 255 C 5
56472 Pequot Lakes, 499 D 4
56573 Perham, 1,933 C 4
56574 Perley, 149 B 3
55962 Peterson, 269 G 7
† 55948 Pickwick, 150 G 7
56364 Pierz, 893 D 5
56473 Pillager, 374 D 4
55063 Pine City⊙, 2,143 F 5
55963 Pine Island, 1,640 F 6
56474 Pine River, 803 D 4
56164 Pipestone⊙, 5,328 B 7
55964 Plainview, 2,093 F 6
55370 Plato, 303 D 6
56748 Plummer, 285 B 3
† 55401 Plymouth, 17,593 G 5
56666 Ponemah, 531 D 2
56280 Porter, 207 B 6
55965 Preston⊙, 1,413 F 7
55371 Princeton, 2,531 E 5
56281 Prinsburg, 448 C 6
55372 Prior Lake, 1,114 E 6
55810 Proctor, 3,123 F 4
† 55752 Rabey, 125 E 4
55967 Racine, 197 F 7
56475 Randall, 536 D 4
55065 Randolph, 350 E 6
56668 Ranier, 255 E 2
56669 Ray, 200 E 2
56282 Raymond, 589 C 5
56165 Reading, 150 C 7
55968 Reads Landing, 150 F 6
56670 Redby, 475 D 3
56671 Redlake, 300 C 3
56750 Red Lake Falls⊙, 1,740 B 3
55066 Red Wing⊙, 10,441 F 6
56283 Redwood Falls⊙, 4,774 C 6
56672 Remer, 403 E 3
56284 Renville, 1,252 C 6
56166 Revere, 166 C 6
56367 Rice, 366 D 5
55423 Richfield, 47,231 G 6
56368 Richmond, 866 D 5
55422 Robbinsdale, 16,845 G 5
55901 Rochester⊙, 53,766 F 6
55067 Rock Creek, 805 F 5
55373 Rockford, 730 F 5
56369 Rockville, 302 D 5
55374 Rogers, 544 E 5
55969 Rollingstone, 450 G 6
56371 Roscoe, 195 D 5
56751 Roseau⊙, 2,552 C 2
55970 Rose Creek, 390 F 7
† 56216 Roseland, 123 C 6
55068 Rosemount, 1,337 E 6
55113 Roseville, 34,518 G 5
56579 Rothsay, 448 B 4
56167 Round Lake, 506 C 7
56373 Royalton, 534 D 5
55069 Rush City, 1,130 F 5
55971 Rushford, 1,318 G 7
56168 Rushmore, 394 C 7
56169 Russell, 398 C 6
56170 Ruthton, 405 B 6
55778 Rutledge, 123 F 4
56580 Sabin, 333 B 4
56285 Sacred Heart, 707 C 6
55779 Saginaw, 407 F 4
55414 Saint Anthony Falls, 9,239 G 5
55375 Saint Bonifacius, 685 F 5
55972 Saint Charles, 1,942 F 7
56080 Saint Clair, 488 E 6
56301 Saint Cloud⊙, 39,691 D 5
55070 Saint Francis, 897 E 5
56554 Saint Hilaire, 337 B 2
56081 Saint James⊙, 4,027 D 7
56374 Saint Joseph, 1,786 D 5
55426 Saint Louis Park, 48,883 G 5
56376 Saint Martin, 188 D 5
55376 Saint Michael, 1,021 E 5
* 55101 Saint Paul (cap.)⊙, 309,980 G 6
55071 Saint Paul Park, 5,587 G 6
56082 Saint Peter⊙, 8,339 E 6
56375 Saint Stephen, 331 D 5
56755 Saint Vincent, 177 A 2
56083 Sanborn, 505 C 6
55072 Sandstone, 1,641 F 4
56377 Sartell, 1,323 D 5
56378 Sauk Centre, 3,750 C 5
56379 Sauk Rapids, 5,051 D 5
55378 Savage, 3,611 G 6
55780 Sawyer, 200 F 4
55073 Scandia, 200 F 5
† 55720 Scanlon, 1,132 F 4
55613 Schroeder, 550 G 3
56287 Seaforth, 132 C 6
56084 Searles, 160 D 6
56477 Sebeka, 668 C 4
55074 Shafer, 149 F 5
55379 Shakopee⊙, 6,876 F 6
56581 Shelly, 260 B 3
56171 Sherburn, 1,190 D 7
56676 Shevlin, 185 C 3
† 55021 Shieldsville, 150 E 6
† 55331 Shorewood, 4,223 F 5
55614 Silver Bay, 3,504 G 3
55380 Silver Creek, 125 D 5
55381 Silver Lake, 694 D 6
† 56001 Skyline, 400 D 6
56172 Slayton⊙, 2,351 C 7
56085 Sleepy Eye, 3,461 D 6
† 56345 Sobieski, 189 D 5
55782 Soudan, 900 F 3
55382 South Haven, 238 D 5
56679 South International Falls, 2,116 E 2
55075 South Saint Paul, 25,016 G 6
56288 Spicer, 586 C 5
56087 Springfield, 2,530 C 6
55974 Spring Grove, 1,290 G 7
55432 Spring Lake Park, 6,417 E 5
55384 Spring Park, 1,087 E 5
55975 Spring Valley, 2,572 F 7
55079 Stacy, 278 E 5
55080 Stanchfield, 155 E 5
56479 Staples, 2,657 D 4
56381 Starbuck, 1,138 C 5
56173 Steen, 191 B 7
56757 Stephen, 904 A 2
55385 Stewart, 666 D 6
55976 Stewartville, 2,802 F 7
55082 Stillwater⊙, 10,191 F 5
55988 Stockton, 346 G 6
56174 Storden, 364 C 6
56758 Strandquist, 138 B 2
55783 Sturgeon Lake, 167 F 4
56289 Sunburg, 144 C 5
† 55075 Sunfish Lake, 269 E 6
56290 Svea, 125 C 6
56382 Swanville, 300 D 5
55785 Swatara, 250 E 4
55786 Taconite, 352 E 3
56291 Taunton, 195 B 6
55084 Taylors Falls, 587 F 5
56683 Tenstrike, 138 D 3
56701 Thief River Falls⊙, 8,618 B 2
† 56319 Thomson, 159 F 4
56583 Tintah, 167 B 5
55615 Tofte, 400 H 3
55789 Toivola, 185 F 3
† 55331 Tonka Bay, 1,397 F 5
55790 Tower, 699 F 3
56175 Tracy, 2,516 C 6
56176 Trimont, 835 D 7
56088 Truman, 1,137 D 7
55791 Twig, 165 F 4
56089 Twin Lakes, 230 E 7
56584 Twin Valley, 868 B 3
55616 Two Harbors⊙, 4,437 G 3
56178 Tyler, 1,069 B 6
56585 Ulen, 486 B 3
56586 Underwood, 278 C 4
56384 Upsala, 312 D 5
† 56361 Urbank, 125 C 4
55979 Utica, 240 G 7
† 55101 Vadnais Heights, 3,391 G 5
56587 Vergas, 281 C 4
55085 Vermillion, 359 F 6
56481 Verndale, 570 C 4
† 55752 Verndon, 135 E 4
56090 Vernon Center, 347 D 7
55086 Veseli, 150 E 6
56292 Vesta, 330 C 6
55386 Victoria, 850 F 6
56385 Villard, 221 C 5
56588 Vining, 121 C 4
55792 Virginia, 12,450 F 3
55981 Wabasha⊙, 2,371 G 6
56293 Wabasso, 738 C 6
55387 Waconia, 2,445 E 6
56482 Wadena⊙, 4,640 C 4
56386 Wahkon, 208 E 4
56387 Waite Park, 2,824 D 5
56091 Waldorf, 285 E 7
56484 Walker⊙, 2,073 D 3
56180 Walnut Grove, 756 C 6
56092 Walters, 152 E 7
55982 Waltham, 189 F 7
55983 Wanamingo, 574 F 6
56294 Wanda, 124 C 6
55743 Warba, 148 E 3
56762 Warren⊙, 1,999 B 2
56763 Warroad, 1,086 C 2
55087 Warsaw, 200 E 6
56093 Waseca⊙, 6,789 E 6
55388 Watertown, 1,390 E 6
56096 Waterville, 1,539 E 6
55389 Watkins, 785 D 5
56295 Watson, 228 C 5
56589 Waubun, 345 C 3
55390 Waverly, 546 E 5
55391 Wayzata, 3,700 G 5
55088 Webster, 175 E 6
56181 Welcome, 694 D 7
56097 Wells, 2,791 E 7
56590 Wendell, 247 B 4
56183 Westbrook, 990 C 6
55985 West Concord, 718 F 6
55118 West Saint Paul, 18,799 G 5
56296 Wheaton⊙, 2,029 B 5
56485 Whipholt, 142 D 3
55110 White Bear Lake, 23,313 G 5
56591 White Earth, 150 C 3
56184 Wilder, 132 C 7
55090 Willernie, 697 G 5
56686 Williams, 220 D 2
56201 Willmar⊙, 12,869 C 5
55795 Willow River, 331 F 4
56185 Wilmont, 390 C 7
56687 Wilton, 119 C 3
56101 Windom⊙, 3,952 C 7
56592 Winger, 228 B 3
56098 Winnebago, 1,791 D 7
55987 Winona⊙, 26,438 G 6
55395 Winsted, 1,266 D 6
55396 Winthrop, 1,391 D 6
55796 Winton, 193 G 3
56594 Wolverton, 171 B 4
† 55798 Woodbury, 6,184 F 6
56297 Wood Lake, 418 C 6
56186 Woodstock, 217 B 7
56187 Worthington⊙, 9,825 C 7
55797 Wrenshall, 147 F 4
55798 Wright, 132 E 4
55990 Wykoff, 450 F 7
55092 Wyoming, 695 F 5
55397 Young America, 611 E 6
55799 Zim, 608 F 3
55398 Zimmerman, 495 E 5
55991 Zumbro Falls, 203 F 6
55992 Zumbrota, 1,929 F 6

⊙ County seat.
‡ Population of metropolitan area.
† Zip of nearest p.o.
* Multiple zips

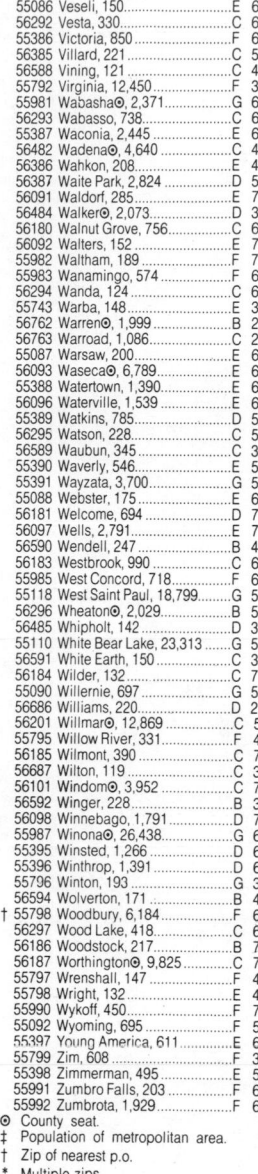

Agriculture, Industry and Resources

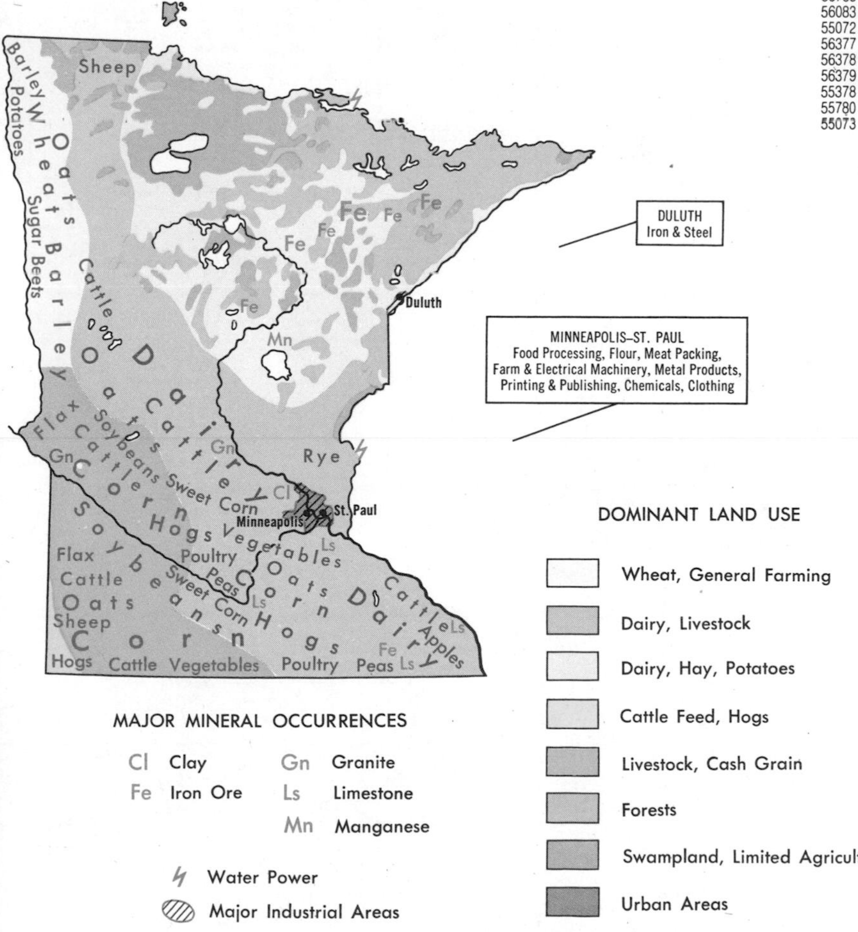

Topography

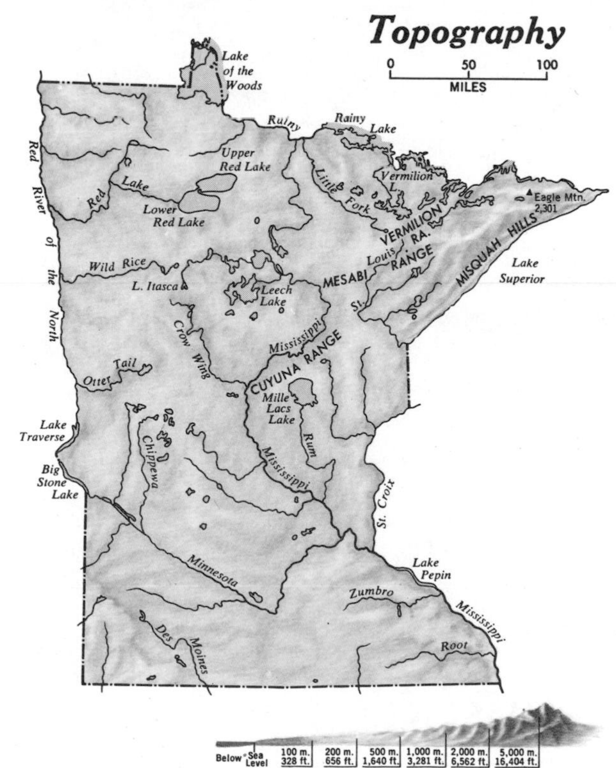

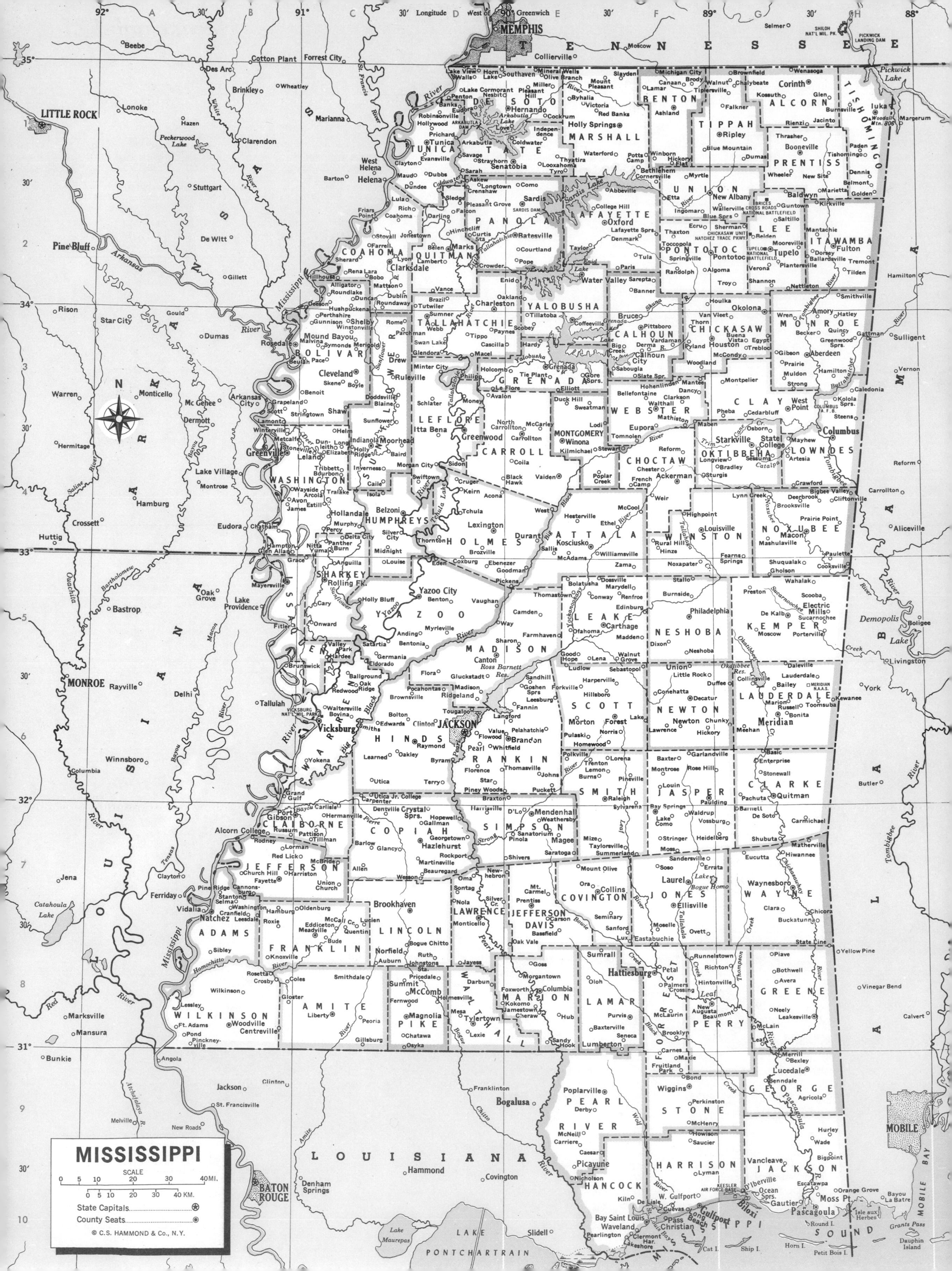

MISSISSIPPI
SCALE
0 5 10 20 30 40 MI.
0 5 10 20 30 40 KM.
State Capitals
County Seats
© C.S. HAMMOND & Co., N.Y.
Longitude West of Greenwich
TENNESSEE
ARKANSAS
LOUISIANA
ALABAMA
MEMPHIS
LITTLE ROCK
BATON ROUGE
MOBILE
JACKSON
MONROE
LAKE PONTCHARTRAIN
MISSISSIPPI SOUND
Mississippi River
DE SOTO
MARSHALL
BENTON
TIPPAH
ALCORN
TISHOMINGO
TUNICA
TATE
PRENTISS
UNION
PANOLA
LAFAYETTE
PONTOTOC
LEE
ITAWAMBA
COAHOMA
QUITMAN
YALOBUSHA
CALHOUN
CHICKASAW
MONROE
BOLIVAR
TALLAHATCHIE
SUNFLOWER
GRENADA
WEBSTER
CLAY
LEFLORE
CARROLL
MONTGOMERY
CHOCTAW
OKTIBBEHA
LOWNDES
WASHINGTON
HUMPHREYS
HOLMES
ATTALA
WINSTON
NOXUBEE
SHARKEY
YAZOO
ISSAQUENA
MADISON
LEAKE
NESHOBA
KEMPER
WARREN
HINDS
RANKIN
SCOTT
NEWTON
LAUDERDALE
SMITH
JASPER
CLARKE
CLAIBORNE
COPIAH
SIMPSON
JEFFERSON
COVINGTON
JONES
WAYNE
ADAMS
FRANKLIN
LINCOLN
LAWRENCE
JEFFERSON DAVIS
WILKINSON
AMITE
PIKE
WALTHALL
MARION
LAMAR
FORREST
PERRY
GREENE
PEARL RIVER
STONE
GEORGE
HANCOCK
HARRISON
JACKSON

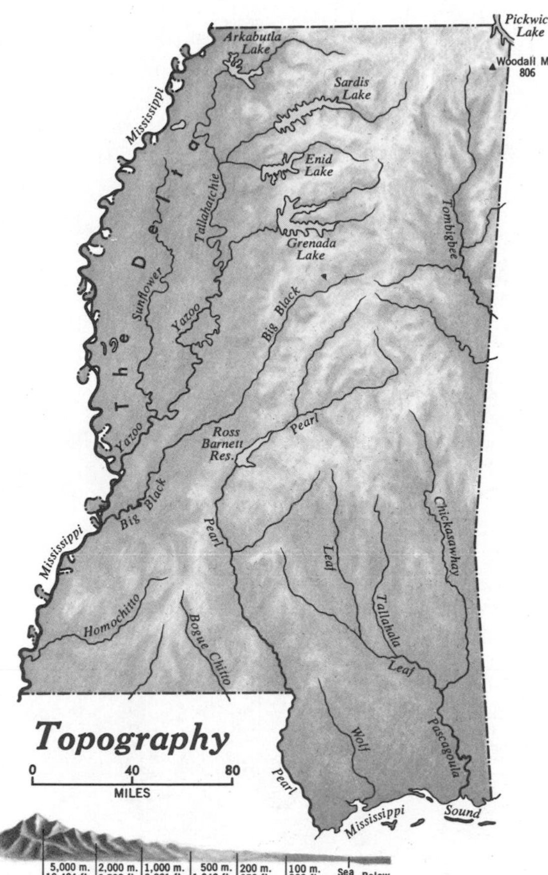

AREA 47,716 sq. mi.
POPULATION 2,216,912
CAPITAL Jackson
LARGEST CITY Jackson
HIGHEST POINT Woodall Mtn. 806 ft.
SETTLED IN 1716
ADMITTED TO UNION December 10, 1817
POPULAR NAME Magnolia State
STATE FLOWER Magnolia
STATE BIRD Mockingbird

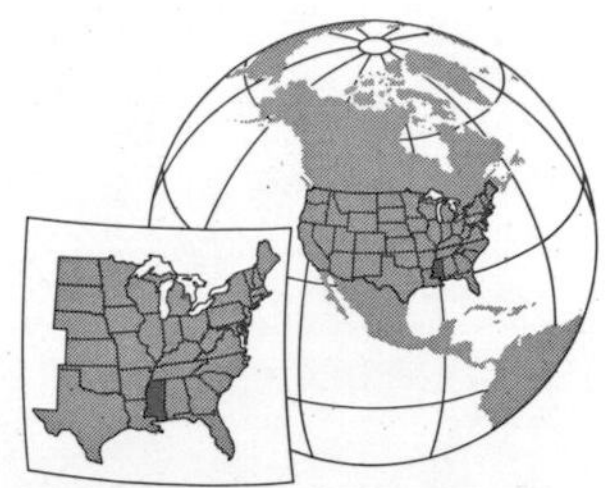

Gracious antebellum houses of brick and stucco, shaded by moss-draped oaks, add a sense of permanence to the older section of Biloxi, Mississippi.

COUNTIES

County, Pop.	Key
Adams, 37,293	B 8
Alcorn, 27,179	G 1
Amite, 13,763	C 8
Attala, 19,570	E 4
Benton, 7,505	F 1
Bolivar, 49,409	C 3
Calhoun, 14,623	F 3
Carroll, 9,397	E 4
Chickasaw, 16,805	G 3
Choctaw, 8,440	F 4
Claiborne, 10,086	C 7
Clarke, 15,049	G 6
Clay, 18,840	G 3
Coahoma, 40,447	C 2
Copiah, 24,749	D 7
Covington, 14,002	E 7
De Soto, 35,885	E 1
Forrest, 57,849	F 8
Franklin, 8,011	C 8
George, 12,459	G 9
Greene, 8,545	G 8
Grenada, 19,854	E 3
Hancock, 17,387	E 10
Harrison, 134,582	F 10
Hinds, 214,973	D 6
Holmes, 23,120	D 4
Humphreys, 14,601	C 4
Issaquena, 2,737	B 5
Itawamba, 16,847	H 2
Jackson, 87,975	G 9
Jasper, 15,994	F 6
Jefferson, 9,295	B 7
Jefferson Davis, 12,936	E 7
Jones, 56,357	F 7
Kemper, 10,233	G 5
Lafayette, 24,181	E 2
Lamar, 15,209	E 8
Lauderdale, 67,087	G 6
Lawrence, 11,137	D 7
Leake, 17,085	E 5
Lee, 46,148	G 2
Leflore, 42,111	D 3
Lincoln, 26,198	D 8
Lowndes, 49,700	H 4
Madison, 29,737	D 5
Marion, 22,871	E 8
Marshall, 24,027	E 1
Monroe, 34,043	H 3
Montgomery, 12,918	E 4
Neshoba, 20,802	F 5
Newton, 18,983	F 6
Noxubee, 14,288	G 4
Oktibbeha, 28,752	G 4
Panola, 26,829	E 2
Pearl River, 27,802	E 9
Perry, 9,065	G 8
Pike, 31,756	D 8
Pontotoc, 17,363	F 2
Prentiss, 20,133	G 1
Quitman, 15,888	D 2
Rankin, 43,933	E 6
Scott, 21,369	E 6
Sharkey, 8,937	C 5
Simpson, 19,947	E 7
Smith, 13,561	E 6
Stone, 8,101	F 9
Sunflower, 37,047	C 3
Tallahatchie, 19,338	D 3
Tate, 18,544	E 1
Tippah, 15,852	G 1
Tishomingo, 14,940	H 1
Tunica, 11,854	D 1
Union, 19,096	F 2
Walthall, 12,500	D 8
Warren, 44,981	C 6
Washington, 70,581	C 4
Wayne, 16,650	G 7
Webster, 10,047	F 3
Wilkinson, 11,099	B 8
Winston, 18,406	F 4
Yalobusha, 11,915	E 2
Yazoo, 27,304	D 5

CITIES and TOWNS

	Zip	Name/Pop.	Key
	38601	Abbeville, 600	F 2
	39730	Aberdeen⊙, 6,157	H 3
	39735	Ackerman⊙, 1,502	F 4
†	39095	Acona, 200	D 4
†	39452	Agricola, 200	G 9
	39096	Alcorn College, 2,380	B 7
	38820	Algoma, 150	G 2
	38720	Alligator, 280	C 2
	38821	Amory, 7,236	H 3
	38721	Anguilla, 612	C 5
	38722	Arcola, 517	C 4
	38602	Arkabutla, 195	D 1
	39736	Artesia, 444	G 4
	38603	Ashland⊙, 348	F 1
	38604	Askew, 200	D 1
†	39664	Auburn, 500	C 8
	38912	Avalon, 275	D 3
†	39456	Avera, 150	G 8
	38723	Avon, 400	B 4
	39320	Bailey, 320	G 6
	38724	Baird, 212	C 4
	38824	Baldwyn, 2,366	G 2
†	38801	Ballardsville, 105	H 2
†	38664	Banks, 100	D 1
	38913	Banner, 200	F 2
	39421	Bassfield, 354	E 8
	38606	Batesville⊙, 3,796	E 2
†	39343	Baxter, 225	F 6
†	39455	Baxterville, 100	E 8
	39520	Bay Saint Louis⊙, 6,752	F 10
	39422	Bay Springs⊙, 1,801	F 7
	39423	Beaumont, 1,061	G 8
†	39191	Beauregard, 199	D 7
	38825	Becker, 450	G 3
	38826	Belden, 241	G 2
	38609	Belen, 500	D 2
	39737	Bellefontaine, 360	F 3
	38827	Belmont, 968	H 1
	39038	Belzoni⊙, 3,146	C 4
†	39450	Benndale, 500	G 9
	38725	Benoit, 473	C 3
	39039	Benton, 500	D 5
	39040	Bentonia, 544	D 5
†	38659	Bethlehem, 210	F 1
	38726	Beulah, 443	B 3
	39453	Bexley, 130	G 9
	39738	Bigbee Valley, 370	H 4
	38914	Big Creek, 148	F 3
†	39567	Bigpoint, 100	H 9
*	39530	Biloxi, 48,486	G 10
		Biloxi-Gulfport, ‡134,582	G 10
	38918	Black Hawk, 100	E 4
	38610	Blue Mountain, 677	G 1
	38828	Blue Springs, 125	G 2
	38728	Bobo, 200	C 2
	39629	Bogue Chitto, 658	D 8
	39041	Bolton, 787	D 6
	39550	Bond, 350	F 9
	39321	Bonita, 300	G 6
	38829	Booneville⊙, 5,895	G 1
†	39456	Bothwell, 100	G 8
	38729	Bourbon, 350	C 4
	38730	Boyle, 861	C 3
	39042	Brandon⊙, 2,685	E 6
	39044	Braxton, 180	D 6
	38956	Brazil, 229	D 2
	39601	Brookhaven⊙, 10,700	C 7
	39425	Brooklyn, 750	F 8
	39739	Brooksville, 978	G 4
†	38683	Brownfield, 300	G 1
†	39041	Brownsville, 200	D 6
†	39095	Brozville, 150	D 4
	38915	Bruce, 2,033	F 3
†	39180	Brunswick, 90	C 5
	39322	Buckatunna, 500	G 7
	39630	Bude, 1,146	C 8
†	39153	Burns, 100	E 6
	38833	Burnsville, 435	H 1
	38611	Byhalia, 702	E 1
†	39205	Byram, 250	D 6
†	38754	Caile, 350	C 4
	39740	Caledonia, 245	H 3
	38916	Calhoun City, 1,847	F 3
	39045	Camden, 248	E 5
	38612	Canaan, 200	F 1
†	39120	Cannonsburg, 240	B 7
	39046	Canton⊙, 10,503	D 5
	39049	Carlisle, 350	C 7
†	39360	Carmichael, 150	G 7
	39426	Carriere, 900	E 9
	38917	Carrollton⊙, 295	E 4
	39427	Carson, 285	E 7
	39051	Carthage⊙, 3,031	E 5
	39054	Cary, 517	C 5
	38920	Cascilla, 150	D 3
	39741	Cedarbluff, 180	G 3
	39631	Centreville, 1,819	B 8
	38684	Chalybeate, 350	G 1
	38921	Charleston⊙, 2,821	D 2
	39632	Chatawa, 300	D 8
†	39483	Cheraw, 100	E 8
	39323	Chunky, 280	G 6
	39324	Clara, 400	G 7
	38614	Clarksdale⊙, 21,673	D 2
†	39752	Clarkson, 100	F 3
	39551	Clermont Harbor, 200	F 10
	38732	Cleveland⊙, 13,327	C 3
	39742	Cliftonville, 280	H 4
	39056	Clinton, 7,246	D 6
	38617	Coahoma, 350	C 2
	38922	Coffeeville⊙, 1,024	E 3
	38618	Coldwater, 1,450	E 1
	39639	Coles, 195	C 8
†	38655	College Hill, 175	E 2
	39428	Collins⊙, 1,934	E 7
	39325	Collinsville, 700	G 6
	39429	Columbia⊙, 7,587	E 8
	39701	Columbus⊙, 25,795	H 3
	38619	Como, 1,003	E 1
†	39051	Conway, 125	E 5
	38834	Corinth⊙, 11,581	G 1
†	38659	Cornersville, 235	F 1
	38620	Courtland, 316	E 2
†	39095	Coxburg, 300	D 5
†	39120	Cranfield, 100	B 7
	39743	Crawford, 391	G 4
	38621	Crenshaw, 1,271	D 2
	39633	Crosby, 491	B 8
	38622	Crowder, 815	D 2
	38924	Cruger, 415	D 4
	39059	Crystal Springs, 4,180	D 7
†	39571	Cuevas, 200	F 10
†	38606	Curtis Station, 200	D 2
†	39751	Dancy, 116	F 3
†	39643	Darbun, 100	D 8
	38623	Darling, 250	D 2
	39327	Decatur⊙, 1,311	F 6
	39328	De Kalb⊙, 1,072	G 5
†	39571	De Lisle, 450	F 10
	39061	Delta City, 300	C 4
	38838	Dennis, 175	H 1
†	39470	Derby, 189	E 9
	38839	Derma, 660	F 3
	39360	De Soto, 150	G 7
	39532	D'Iberville, 7,288	G 10
†	39350	Dixon, 125	F 5
	39062	D'Lo, 485	E 7
	38736	Doddsville, 276	C 3
	38840	Dorsey, 100	H 2
	38737	Drew, 2,574	C 3
	38739	Dublin, 385	C 2
	38925	Duck Hill, 809	E 3
†	39337	Duffee, 100	G 6
	38625	Dumas, 200	G 1
	38740	Duncan, 599	C 2
†	38756	Dunleith, 140	C 4
	39063	Durant, 2,752	E 4
	39436	Eastabuchie, 200	F 8
	39064	Ebenezer, 150	D 5
	38841	Ecru, 417	F 2
	39634	Eddiceton, 175	C 8
	39065	Eden, 152	D 5
†	39051	Edinburg, 200	F 5
	39066	Edwards, 1,236	C 6
	38842	Egypt, 100	G 3
	39329	Electric Mills, 200	G 5
	38742	Elizabeth, 540	C 4
	38926	Elliott, 200	E 3
	39437	Ellisville⊙, 4,643	F 7
	39330	Enterprise, 458	G 6
	39552	Escatawpa, 1,579	G 10
†	38748	Estill, 100	C 4
	39067	Ethel, 560	F 4
	38627	Etta, 100	F 2
†	38632	Eudora, 200	D 1
	39744	Eupora, 1,792	F 3
	38628	Falcon, 230	D 2
	38629	Falkner, 500	G 1
†	39042	Fannin, 250	E 6
	38630	Farrell, 400	C 2
	39069	Fayette⊙, 1,725	B 7
	39635	Fernwood, 600	D 8
	39070	Fitler, 800	B 5
	39071	Flora, 987	D 5
	39073	Florence, 404	D 6
†	39201	Flowood, 352	D 6
	39074	Forest⊙, 4,085	F 6
	39076	Forkville, 180	E 6
	39636	Fort Adams, 129	B 8
	39483	Foxworth, 950	E 8
	39745	French Camp, 174	F 4
	38631	Friars Point, 1,177	C 2
	38843	Fulton⊙, 2,899	H 2
†	39345	Garlandville, 150	F 6
	38844	Gattman, 175	H 3
	39553	Gautier, 2,087	G 10
	39078	Georgetown, 339	D 7
†	39083	Glancy, 120	C 7
	38846	Glen, 250	H 1
	38744	Glen Allan, 400	B 4
	38928	Glendora, 201	D 3
	39638	Gloster, 1,401	B 8
†	39110	Gluckstadt, 150	D 5
	38847	Golden, 115	H 2
†	39094	Good Hope, 125	E 5
	39079	Goodman, 1,194	E 5
	38929	Gore Springs, 120	E 3
†	39042	Goshen Springs, 100	E 6
†	39429	Goss, 100	E 8
	38745	Grace, 325	C 5
†	38725	Grapeland, 200	B 3
	38701	Greenville⊙, 39,648	B 4
	38930	Greenwood⊙, 22,400	D 4
	38848	Greenwood Springs, 170	H 3
	38901	Grenada⊙, 9,944	E 3
	39501	Gulfport⊙, 40,791	F 10
	38746	Gunnison, 545	C 3
	38849	Guntown, 304	G 2
	39746	Hamilton, 350	H 3
†	38744	Hampton, 200	B 4
†	39177	Hardee, 100	C 5
	39080	Harperville, 260	E 6
	39081	Harriston, 500	C 7
	39082	Harrisville, 500	D 7
†	38821	Hatley, 500	H 3
	39401	Hattiesburg⊙, 38,277	F 8
	39083	Hazlehurst⊙, 4,577	D 7
	39439	Heidelberg, 1,112	F 7
	39086	Hermanville, 500	C 7
	38632	Hernando⊙, 2,499	E 1
†	39192	Hesterville, 100	E 4
	39332	Hickory, 570	F 6
	38633	Hickory Flat, 354	F 1
	39087	Hillsboro, 350	E 6
†	38646	Hinchcliff, 125	D 2
†	39462	Hintonville, 100	F 8
†	39108	Hinze, 140	F 4
	39333	Hiwannee, 250	G 7
†	39751	Hohenlinden, 96	F 3
	38748	Hollandale, 3,260	C 4
	39088	Holly Bluff, 250	C 5
	38749	Holly Ridge, 375	C 4
	38635	Holly Springs⊙, 5,728	E 1
†	38676	Hollywood, 125	D 1
†	39648	Holmesville, 200	D 8
†	39059	Hopewell, 300	D 7
	38637	Horn Lake, 850	D 1
	38850	Houlka, 646	G 2
	38851	Houston⊙, 2,720	G 3
	39555	Hurley, 500	H 9
†	38774	Hushpuckena, 100	C 2
	38638	Independence, 150	E 1
	38751	Indianola⊙, 8,947	C 4
†	38652	Ingomar, 150	F 2
	38753	Inverness, 1,119	C 4
	38754	Isola, 458	C 4
	38941	Itta Bena, 2,489	D 4
	38852	Iuka⊙, 2,389	H 1
†	38865	Jacinto, 150	H 1
*	39201	Jackson (cap.)⊙, 153,968	D 6
		Jackson, ‡258,906	D 6
†	38748	James, 100	B 4
	39641	Jayess, 150	D 8
†	39042	Johns, 90	E 6
	38639	Jonestown, 1,110	D 2
	39334	Kewanee, 100	H 6
	39747	Kilmichael, 543	E 4
	39556	Kiln, 750	F 10
†	38856	Kirkville, 200	H 2
†	39661	Knoxville, 100	B 8
	39643	Kokomo, 150	E 8
†	39740	Kolola Springs, 150	H 3
	39090	Kosciusko⊙, 7,266	E 4
	38834	Kossuth, 227	G 1
	39092	Lake, 441	F 6
†	39422	Lake Como, 150	F 7
	38641	Lake Cormorant, 300	D 1
	39558	Lakeshore, 550	F 10
†	38680	Lake View, 125	D 1
	38642	Lamar, 135	F 1
	38643	Lambert, 1,511	D 2
	38755	Lamont, 450	B 3
†	39042	Langford, 100	E 6
	39335	Lauderdale, 600	G 5
	39440	Laurel⊙, 24,145	F 7
	39336	Lawrence, 200	F 6
	39450	Leaf, 350	G 8
	39451	Leakesville⊙, 1,090	G 8
	39093	Learned, 116	C 6
	38942	Le Flore, 99	D 3
	38756	Leland, 6,000	C 4
†	39074	Lemon, 90	E 6
	39094	Lena, 233	E 5
	39644	Lessley, 100	B 8
†	39667	Lexie, 270	D 8
	39095	Lexington⊙, 2,756	D 4
	39645	Liberty⊙, 612	C 8
	39337	Little Rock, 130	F 5
†	38828	Long, 110	C 4
	39560	Long Beach, 6,170	F 10
†	38665	Longtown, 150	D 1
	39749	Longview, 800	G 4
†	38668	Looxahoma, 200	E 1
†	39153	Lorena, 90	F 6
	39096	Lorman, 500	B 7
	39338	Louin, 382	F 6
	39097	Louise, 444	C 5
	39339	Louisville⊙, 6,626	G 4
	39452	Lucedale⊙, 2,083	G 9
	39098	Ludlow, 300	E 5
	38644	Lula, 445	C 2
	39455	Lumberton, 2,084	E 8
†	39501	Lyman, 500	F 10
	38645	Lyon, 383	D 2
	39750	Maben, 862	F 3
	39341	Macon⊙, 2,612	G 4
	39109	Madden, 450	F 5
	39110	Madison, 853	D 6
	39111	Magee, 2,973	E 7
	39652	Magnolia⊙, 1,913	D 8

(continued on following page)

(continued)

† 38769 Malvina, 100 .... C 3
38855 Mantachie, 200 .... H 2
39751 Mantee, 142 .... F 3
38856 Marietta, 250 .... H 2
39342 Marion, 550 .... G 6
38646 Marks⊙, 2,609 .... D 2
† 39083 Martinsville, 250 .... D 7
† 39051 Marydell, 125 .... F 5
† 39341 Mashulaville, 227 .... G 4
† 39360 Matherville, 150 .... G 7
39752 Mathiston, 570 .... F 3
38758 Mattson, 200 .... C 2
† 39425 Maxie, 100 .... F 9
39113 Mayersville⊙, 500 .... B 5
39753 Mayhew, 200 .... G 4
39107 McAdams, 240 .... E 4
39647 McCall Creek, 250 .... C 7
38943 McCarley, 250 .... E 3
39648 McComb, 11,969 .... D 8
38854 McCondy, 150 .... G 3
39108 McCool, 225 .... F 4
39561 McHenry, 550 .... F 9
39456 McLain, 632 .... G 8
† 39401 McLaurin, 100 .... F 8
39457 McNeill, 800 .... E 9
39653 Meadville⊙, 594 .... C 8
† 39301 Meehan, 100 .... G 6
39114 Mendenhall⊙, 2,402 .... E 7
39301 Meridian⊙, 45,083 .... G 6
38759 Merigold, 772 .... C 3
† 39452 Merrill, 100 .... G 9
38760 Metcalfe, 600 .... B 4
38647 Michigan City, 350 .... F 1
39115 Midnight, 450 .... C 4
38648 Mineral Wells, 250 .... E 1
38944 Minter City, 300 .... D 3
39116 Mize, 372 .... E 7
38945 Money, 350 .... D 3
39654 Monticello⊙, 1,790 .... D 7
39754 Montpelier, 200 .... G 3
39343 Montrose, 160 .... F 6
38857 Mooreville, 200 .... G 2
38761 Moorhead, 2,284 .... C 4
38946 Morgan City, 300 .... D 4
39484 Morgantown, 305 .... E 8
39117 Morton, 2,672 .... E 6
39459 Moselle, 525 .... F 8
39460 Moss, 150 .... F 7
39563 Moss Point, 19,321 .... G 10
38762 Mound Bayou, 2,134 .... C 3
39119 Mount Olive, 923 .... E 7
38649 Mount Pleasant, 250 .... E 1
† 38748 Murphy, 100 .... C 4
38650 Myrtle, 308 .... F 1
39120 Natchez⊙, 19,704 .... B 7
39461 Neely, 200 .... G 8
38651 Nesbit, 300 .... D 1
39344 Neshoba, 250 .... F 5
38858 Nettleton, 1,591 .... G 2
38652 New Albany⊙, 6,426 .... G 2
39462 New Augusta⊙, 511 .... F 8
39140 Newhebron, 456 .... D 7
39345 Newton, 3,556 .... F 6
39463 Nicholson, 400 .... E 10
38763 Nitta Yuma, 150 .... C 4
† 39665 Nola, 120 .... D 7
† 39629 Norfield, 225 .... C 8
38947 North Carrollton, 611 .... E 3
39346 Noxapater, 554 .... F 5
38948 Oakland, 493 .... E 2
† 39154 Oakley, 420 .... D 6
† 39180 Oak Ridge, 350 .... C 6
39656 Oak Vale, 166 .... E 8
39564 Ocean Springs, 9,580 .... G 10
39141 Ofahoma, 850 .... E 5
38860 Okolona⊙, 3,002 .... G 2
38654 Olive Branch, 1,513 .... E 1
† 39482 Oloh, 100 .... E 8
39142 Oma, 100 .... D 7
† 39428 Ora, 140 .... E 7
† 39501 Orange Grove, 200 .... H 10
39657 Osyka, 628 .... D 8
39464 Ovett, 250 .... F 8
38655 Oxford⊙, 13,846 .... F 2
38764 Pace, 629 .... C 3
39347 Pachuta, 271 .... G 6
38861 Paden, 97 .... H 1
† 39401 Palmers Crossing, 250 .... F 8
38765 Panther Burn, 400 .... C 4
38738 Parchman, 200 .... D 3
38949 Paris, 253 .... F 2
39567 Pascagoula⊙, 27,264 .... G 10
39571 Pass Christian, 2,979 .... F 10
39144 Pattison, 540 .... C 7
39348 Paulding⊙, 769 .... F 6
39349 Paulette, 230 .... H 4
† 38920 Paynes, 100 .... D 3
39208 Pearl, 9,623 .... D 6
39572 Pearlington, 500 .... E 10
39145 Pelahatchie, 1,306 .... E 6
† 38664 Penton, 175 .... D 1
† 39645 Peoria, 100 .... C 8
39573 Perkinston, 950 .... F 9
39465 Petal, 6,986 .... F 8
39755 Pheba, 280 .... G 3
39350 Philadelphia⊙, 6,274 .... F 5
38950 Philipp, 975 .... D 3
† 39476 Piave, 250 .... G 8
39466 Picayune, 10,467 .... E 9
39146 Pickens, 1,012 .... E 5
† 39120 Pine Ridge, 175 .... B 7
39148 Piney Woods, 300 .... D 6
39149 Pinola, 102 .... E 7
38951 Pittsboro⊙, 188 .... F 3
38862 Plantersville, 910 .... G 2
38657 Pleasant Grove, 150 .... D 2
† 38651 Pleasant Hill, 400 .... E 1
39118 Polkville, 500 .... E 6
38863 Pontotoc⊙, 3,453 .... G 2
38568 Pope, 210 .... E 2
† 39747 Poplar Creek, 100 .... E 4
39470 Poplarville⊙, 2,312 .... E 9
39352 Porterville, 150 .... G 5
39150 Port Gibson⊙, 2,589 .... B 7
38659 Potts Camp, 459 .... F 1
39353 Prairie Point, 150 .... H 4
39474 Prentiss⊙, 1,789 .... E 7
39354 Preston, 120 .... G 5
† 39666 Pricedale, 400 .... D 8
38660 Prichard, 150 .... D 1
39151 Puckett, 333 .... E 6
39152 Pulaski, 108 .... E 6
39475 Purvis⊙, 1,860 .... F 8
† 38851 Pyland, 120 .... F 3
39660 Quentin, 150 .... C 8
39355 Quitman⊙, 2,702 .... G 6

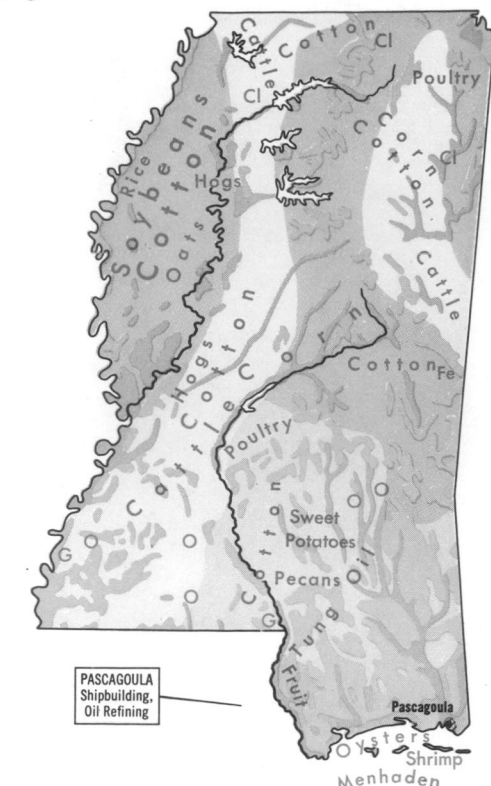

Agriculture, Industry and Resources

DOMINANT LAND USE

Specialized Cotton
Cotton, Livestock
Cotton, General Farming
Cotton, Forest Products
Truck and Mixed Farming
Forests
Swampland, Limited Agriculture

MAJOR MINERAL OCCURRENCES

Cl Clay
Fe Iron Ore
G Natural Gas
O Petroleum

Major Industrial Areas

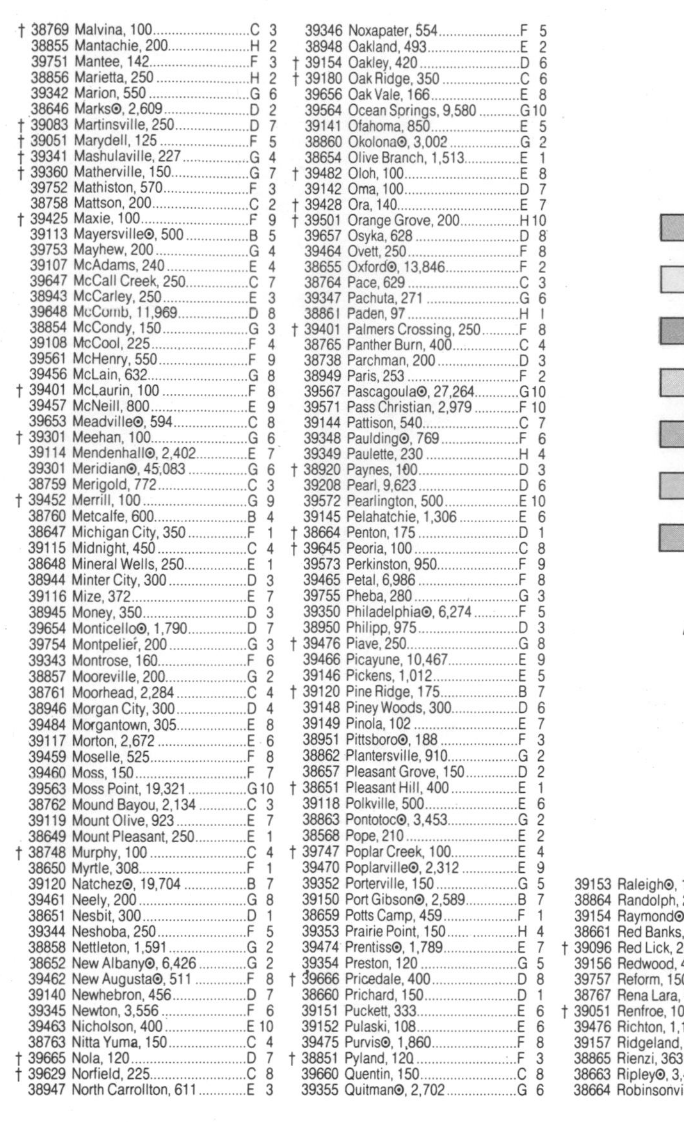

39153 Raleigh⊙, 1,018 .... F 6
38864 Randolph, 205 .... F 2
39154 Raymond⊙, 1,620 .... D 6
38661 Red Banks, 350 .... F 1
† 39096 Red Lick, 250 .... B 7
39156 Redwood, 400 .... C 6
39757 Reform, 150 .... F 4
38767 Rena Lara, 400 .... C 2
† 39051 Renfroe, 100 .... F 5
39476 Richton, 1,110 .... G 8
39157 Ridgeland, 1,650 .... D 6
38865 Rienzi, 363 .... G 1
38663 Ripley⊙, 3,482 .... G 1
38664 Robinsonville, 285 .... D 1
† 39083 Rockport, 100 .... D 7
† 39096 Rodney, 200 .... B 7
39159 Rolling Fork⊙, 2,034 .... C 5
38768 Rome, 171 .... C 3
38769 Rosedale⊙, 2,599 .... B 3
39356 Rose Hill, 300 .... F 6
† 38614 Roundaway, 175 .... C 2
† 38740 Roundlake, 105 .... C 2
39661 Roxie, 662 .... B 8
38771 Ruleville, 2,351 .... D 3
† 39401 Runnelstown, 200 .... F 8
† 39108 Rural Hill, 125 .... F 4
39357 Russell, 300 .... G 6
39662 Ruth, 150 .... D 8
† 38955 Sabougla, 100 .... F 3
39160 Sallis, 213 .... E 4
38866 Saltillo, 836 .... G 2
39112 Sanatorium, 400 .... E 7
39477 Sandersville, 694 .... F 7
39161 Sandhill, 392 .... E 5
39478 Sandy Hook, 108 .... E 8
39479 Sanford, 150 .... F 8
38665 Sarah, 300 .... D 1
38666 Sardis⊙, 2,391 .... E 2
38867 Sarepta, 650 .... F 2
39574 Saucier, 100 .... F 9
38667 Savage, 100 .... D 1
38952 Schlater, 398 .... D 3
38953 Scobey, 100 .... E 3
39358 Scooba, 626 .... G 5
38772 Scott, 500 .... B 3
39359 Sebastopol, 268 .... F 5
39479 Seminary, 269 .... E 7
38668 Senatobia⊙, 4,247 .... E 1
39758 Sessums, 100 .... G 4
38868 Shannon, 575 .... G 2
38773 Shaw, 2,513 .... C 3
38774 Shelby, 2,645 .... C 3
38669 Sherard, 160 .... C 2
38869 Sherman, 468 .... G 2
39164 Shivers, 100 .... E 7
39360 Shubuta, 602 .... G 7
39361 Shuqualak, 591 .... G 5
39165 Sibley, 250 .... B 8
38954 Sidon, 348 .... D 4
39166 Silver City, 370 .... C 4
39663 Silver Creek, 257 .... D 7
38775 Skene, 300 .... C 3
38955 Slate Spring, 105 .... F 3
† 38642 Slayden, 310 .... F 1
38670 Sledge, 516 .... D 2
39664 Smithdale, 200 .... C 8
38870 Smithville, 552 .... H 2
39665 Sontag, 200 .... D 7
39480 Soso, 230 .... F 7
38671 Southaven, 8,931 .... E 1
† 38863 Springville, 100 .... F 2
† 39350 Stallo, 100 .... F 5
39167 Star, 575 .... D 6
39759 Starkville⊙, 11,369 .... G 4
39762 State College, 4,595 .... G 4
39362 State Line, 598 .... G 8
39766 Steens, 125 .... H 3
39767 Stewart, 150 .... F 4
38776 Stoneville, 700 .... C 4
39363 Stonewall, 1,161 .... G 6
38672 Stovall, 260 .... C 2
† 38665 Strayhorn, 800 .... D 1
39481 Stringer, 340 .... F 7
38777 Stringtown, 300 .... C 3
39769 Sturgis, 321 .... G 4
† 39168 Summerland, 150 .... F 7
39666 Summit, 1,640 .... D 8
38957 Sumner⊙, 533 .... D 3
39482 Sumrall, 955 .... E 8
38778 Sunflower, 983 .... C 3
38958 Swan Lake, 250 .... D 3
38959 Swiftown, 400 .... D 4
39153 Sylvarena, 115 .... F 6
† 38769 Symonds, 200 .... C 3
38673 Taylor, 92 .... E 2
39168 Taylorsville, 1,299 .... F 7
39169 Tchula, 1,729 .... D 4
39170 Terry, 546 .... D 6
38871 Thaxton, 250 .... F 2
39171 Thomastown, 350 .... E 5
38872 Thorn, 125 .... F 3
39172 Thornton, 120 .... D 4
† 38829 Thrasher, 800 .... G 1
† 38668 Thyatira, 100 .... E 1
38960 Tie Plant, 950 .... E 3
† 38843 Tilden, 250 .... H 2
38961 Tillatoba, 102 .... E 3
38674 Tiplersville, 120 .... G 1
38962 Tippo, 200 .... D 3
38873 Tishomingo, 410 .... H 1
38874 Toccopola, 175 .... F 2
39770 Tomnolen, 225 .... F 4
39364 Toomsuba, 500 .... G 6
39174 Tougaloo, 1,720 .... D 6
38757 Tralake, 200 .... C 4
38875 Trebloc, 750 .... G 3
38876 Tremont, 250 .... H 2
38779 Tribbett, 200 .... C 4
† 38863 Troy, 150 .... G 2
38675 Tula, 100 .... F 2
38676 Tunica⊙, 1,685 .... D 1
38801 Tupelo⊙, 20,471 .... G 2
38963 Tutwiler, 1,103 .... D 2
39667 Tylertown⊙, 1,736 .... D 8
39365 Union, 1,856 .... F 5
39668 Union Church, 194 .... C 7
39175 Utica, 1,019 .... C 6
39175 Utica Junior College, 700 .... C 6
39176 Vaiden⊙, 716 .... E 4
39177 Valley Park, 350 .... C 5
39178 Value, 327 .... D 6
38964 Vance, 500 .... D 2
† 39564 Vancleave, 505 .... G 9
† 38851 Van Vleet, 300 .... G 3
38878 Vardaman, 777 .... F 3
38879 Verona, 1,877 .... G 2
39180 Vicksburg⊙, 25,478 .... C 6
38679 Victoria, 400 .... E 1
39366 Vossburg, 250 .... F 7
39575 Wade, 800 .... G 9
† 39422 Waldrup, 125 .... F 7
38680 Walls, 850 .... D 1
38683 Walnut, 458 .... G 1
39189 Walnut Grove, 398 .... F 5
† 39180 Waltersville, 150 .... C 6
39771 Walthall⊙, 161 .... F 3
39190 Washington, 250 .... B 7
38685 Waterford, 375 .... E 1
38965 Water Valley⊙, 3,285 .... E 2
39576 Waveland, 3,108 .... F 10
39367 Waynesboro⊙, 4,368 .... G 7
38780 Wayside, 250 .... C 4
38966 Webb, 751 .... D 3
39772 Weir, 573 .... F 4
38886 Wenasoga, 125 .... G 1
39191 Wesson, 1,253 .... D 7
39192 West, 305 .... E 4
† 39501 West-Gulfport, 6,996 .... F 10
39773 West Point⊙, 8,714 .... G 3
38880 Wheeler, 600 .... G 1
39193 Whitfield, 6,200 .... E 6
39577 Wiggins⊙, 2,995 .... F 9
† 39090 Williamsville, 250 .... F 4
† 38659 Winborn, 122 .... F 1
38967 Winona⊙, 5,521 .... E 4
38781 Winstonville, 536 .... C 3
38782 Winterville, 500 .... B 4
39776 Woodland, 130 .... F 3
39669 Woodville⊙, 1,734 .... B 8
† 39730 Wren, 150 .... G 3
39194 Yazoo City⊙, 10,796 .... D 5
† 39090 Zama, 125 .... F 5

⊙ County seat.
‡ Population of metropolitan area.
† Zip of nearest p.o.
* Multiple zips

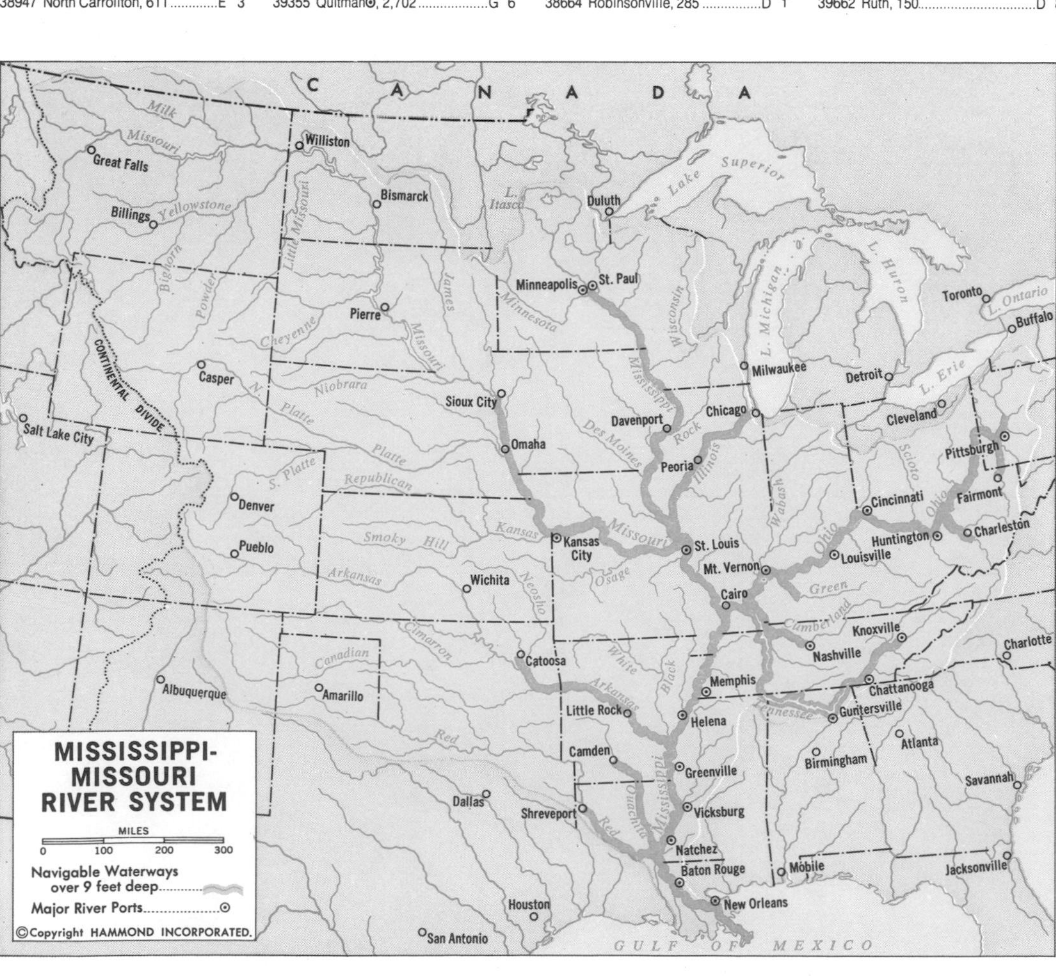

AREA 69,686 sq. mi.
POPULATION 4,677,399
CAPITAL Jefferson City
LARGEST CITY St. Louis
HIGHEST POINT Taum Sauk Mtn. 1,772 ft.
SETTLED IN 1764
ADMITTED TO UNION August 10, 1821
POPULAR NAME Show Me State
STATE FLOWER Hawthorn
STATE BIRD Bluebird

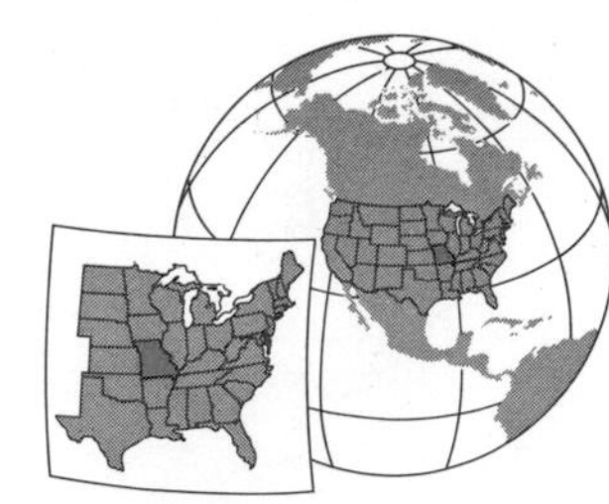

COUNTIES

Adair, 22,472 G 2
Andrew, 11,913 C 3
Atchison, 9,240 B 2
Audrain, 25,362 J 4
Barry, 19,597 E 9
Barton, 10,431 D 7
Bates, 15,468 D 6
Benton, 9,695 F 6
Bollinger, 8,820 M 8
Boone, 80,911 H 4
Buchanan, 86,915 C 3
Butler, 33,529 M 9
Caldwell, 8,351 E 3
Callaway, 25,850 J 5
Camden, 13,315 G 6
Cape Girardeau, 49,350 N 8
Carroll, 12,565 F 4
Carter, 3,878 L 9
Cass, 39,448 D 5
Cedar, 9,424 E 7
Chariton, 11,084 F 3
Christian, 15,124 F 9
Clark, 8,260 J 2
Clay, 123,322 D 4
Clinton, 12,462 D 3
Cole, 46,228 H 6
Cooper, 14,732 G 5
Crawford, 14,828 K 7
Dade, 6,850 E 8
Dallas, 10,054 F 7
Daviess, 8,420 E 3
De Kalb, 7,305 D 3
Dent, 11,457 J 7
Douglas, 9,268 G 9
Dunklin, 33,742 M10
Franklin, 55,116 K 6
Gasconade, 11,878 J 6
Gentry, 8,060 D 2
Greene, 152,929 F 8
Grundy, 11,819 E 2
Harrison, 10,257 E 2
Henry, 18,451 E 6
Hickory, 4,481 F 7
Holt, 6,654 B 2
Howard, 10,561 G 4
Howell, 23,521 J 9
Iron, 9,529 L 7
Jackson, 654,558 D 5
Jasper, 79,852 D 8
Jefferson, 105,248 L 6
Johnson, 34,172 E 5
Knox, 5,692 H 2
Laclede, 19,944 G 7
Lafayette, 26,626 E 4
Lawrence, 24,585 E 8
Lewis, 10,993 J 2
Lincoln, 18,041 L 4
Linn, 15,125 F 3
Livingston, 15,368 E 3
Macon, 15,432 G 3
Madison, 8,641 M 8
Maries, 6,851 J 6
Marion, 28,121 J 3
McDonald, 12,357 D 9
Mercer, 4,910 E 2
Miller, 15,026 H 6
Mississippi, 16,647 O 9
Moniteau, 10,742 G 5
Monroe, 9,542 H 3
Montgomery, 11,000 K 5
Morgan, 10,068 G 6
New Madrid, 23,420 N 9
Newton, 32,901 D 9
Nodaway, 22,467 C 2
Oregon, 9,180 K 9
Osage, 10,994 J 6
Ozark, 6,226 H 9
Pemiscot, 26,373 N10
Perry, 14,393 N 7
Pettis, 34,137 F 5
Phelps, 29,481 J 7
Pike, 16,928 K 4
Platte, 32,081 C 4
Polk, 15,415 F 7
Pulaski, 53,781 H 7
Putnam, 5,916 F 2
Ralls, 7,764 J 3
Randolph, 22,434 G 3
Ray, 17,599 E 4
Reynolds, 6,106 L 8
Ripley, 9,803 L 9
Saint Charles, 92,954 L 5
Saint Clair, 7,667 E 6
Sainte Genevieve, 12,867 M 7
Saint Francois, 36,818 M 7
Saint Louis, 951,353 M 5
Saint Louis (city county), 622,236 M 5
Saline, 24,633 F 4
Schuyler, 4,665 G 2
Scotland, 5,499 H 2
Scott, 33,250 N 8
Shannon, 7,196 K 8
Shelby, 7,906 H 3
Stoddard, 25,771 N 9
Stone, 9,921 F 9
Sullivan, 7,572 F 2
Taney, 13,023 F 9
Texas, 18,320 J 8
Vernon, 19,065 D 7
Warren, 9,699 K 5
Washington, 15,086 L 7
Wayne, 8,546 L 8
Webster, 15,562 G 8
Worth, 3,359 D 2
Wright, 13,667 H 8

CITIES and TOWNS

Zip *Name/Pop.* *Key*

64720 Adrian, 1,259 D 6
63730 Advance, 903 N 8
63123 Affton, 24,067 P 3
64836 Airport Drive, 300 C 8
64830 Alba, 365 D 8
64402 Albany⊙, 1,804 D 2
63430 Alexandria, 453 K 2
63001 Allenton, 800 N 3
64001 Alma, 380 E 4
64620 Altamont, 225 D 3
63732 Altenburg, 277 O 7
65606 Alton⊙, 715 K 9
64421 Amazonia, 326 C 3
64722 Amoret, 219 C 6
64831 Anderson, 1,065 D 9
63620 Annapolis, 330 L 8
63820 Anniston, 515 O 9
64724 Appleton City, 1,058 D 6
63821 Arbyrd, 575 M10
63621 Arcadia, 627 L 7
64725 Archie, 525 D 5
65001 Argyle, 262 J 6
65230 Armstrong, 354 G 4
63010 Arnold, 11,994 P 4
65604 Ash Grove, 934 E 8
65010 Ashland, 769 H 5
63530 Atlanta, 377 H 3
63332 Augusta, 259 M 3
65605 Aurora, 5,359 E 9
65231 Auxvasse, 808 J 4
65608 Ava⊙, 2,504 G 9
64010 Avondale, 748 P 5
63011 Ballwin, 10,656 O 3
63531 Baring, 206 H 2
64423 Barnard, 206 C 2
64011 Bates City, 229 E 5
† 65619 Battlefield, 291 F 8
63622 Belgrade, 349 L 7
63735 Bell City, 424 N 8
65013 Belle, 1,133 J 6
† 63101 Bellefontaine Neighbors, 13,987 R 2
63623 Belleview, 225 L 7
63333 Bellflower, 360 K 4
64012 Belton, 9,783 C 5
63736 Benton⊙, 640 O 8
63014 Berger, 226 K 5
63134 Berkeley, 19,743 P 2
63822 Bernie, 1,641 M 9
63823 Bertrand, 604 O 9
64424 Bethany⊙, 2,914 E 2
63532 Bevier, 806 G 3
65610 Billings, 760 F 8
65438 Birch Tree, 573 K 9
† 64068 Birmingham, 266 P 5
63624 Bismarck, 1,387 L 7
65321 Blackburn, 294 F 4
† 63031 Black Jack, 3,500 P 2
65322 Blackwater, 249 G 5
65014 Bland, 621 J 6
63824 Blodgett, 220 O 8
63825 Bloomfield⊙, 1,584 M 9
63627 Bloomsdale, 411 M 6
64015 Blue Springs, 6,779 R 6
† 64101 Blue Summit, 1,283 R 5
64426 Blythedale, 213 E 2
64622 Bogard, 294 E 4
65612 Bois D'Arc, 250 F 8
64427 Bolckow, 225 C 2
65613 Bolivar⊙, 4,769 F 7
63628 Bonne Terre, 3,622 L 7
65016 Bonnots Mill, 210 J 5
65233 Boonville⊙, 7,514 G 5
64723 Bosworth, 386 F 4
65441 Bourbon, 955 K 6
63334 Bowling Green⊙, 2,936 K 4
63826 Braggadocio, 285 N10
63827 Bragg City, 210 N10
65616 Branson, 2,175 F 9
63533 Brashear, 316 H 2
64624 Braymer, 919 E 3
64625 Breckenridge, 598 E 3
† 63101 Breckenridge Hills, 7,011 O 2
63144 Brentwood, 11,248 P 3
63044 Bridgeton, 19,992 O 2
64728 Bronaugh, 203 C 7
64628 Brookfield, 5,491 F 3
64630 Browning, 412 F 2
65236 Brunswick, 1,870 F 4
64631 Bucklin, 654 G 3
64016 Buckner, 1,695 R 5
65622 Buffalo⊙, 1,915 F 7
65237 Bunceton, 437 G 5
63629 Bunker, 447 K 8
64428 Burlington Junction, 634 B 2
64730 Butler⊙, 3,984 D 6
65689 Cabool, 1,848 H 8
63630 Cadet, 300 L 6
64632 Cainsville, 454 E 2
65239 Cairo, 248 H 4
65323 Calhoun, 360 E 6
65018 California⊙, 3,105 H 5
63534 Callao, 373 G 3
64017 Camden, 286 D 4
65020 Camdenton⊙, 1,636 G 6
64429 Cameron, 3,960 D 3
63933 Campbell, 1,979 M 9
63828 Canalou, 358 N 9
63435 Canton, 2,680 J 2
63701 Cape Girardeau, 31,282 O 8
63829 Cardwell, 859 M10
64834 Carl Junction, 1,661 C 8
64633 Carrollton⊙, 4,847 E 4
64835 Carterville, 1,716 D 8
64836 Carthage⊙, 11,035 D 8
63830 Caruthersville⊙, 7,350 N10
65625 Cassville⊙, 1,910 E 9
63015 Catawissa, 250 N 4
65022 Cedar City, 454 H 5
63016 Cedar Hill, 500 L 6
63436 Center, 588 J 3
65023 Centertown, 277 H 5
64019 Centerview, 234 E 5
63633 Centerville⊙, 209 L 8
65240 Centralia, 3,618 H 4
63740 Chaffee, 2,793 N 8
65024 Chamois, 615 J 5
63834 Charleston⊙, 5,131 O 9
63017 Chesterfield, 13,000 O 3
64733 Chilhowee, 297 E 5
64601 Chillicothe⊙, 9,519 E 3
64635 Chula, 244 F 3
63437 Clarence, 1,050 H 3
65243 Clark, 271 H 4
65025 Clarksburg, 343 G 5
64430 Clarksdale, 248 D 3
63336 Clarksville, 668 K 4
63837 Clarkton, 1,177 M10
64119 Claycomo, 1,841 P 5
63105 Clayton⊙, 16,222 P 3
64431 Clearmont, 226 C 1
64734 Cleveland, 256 C 5
65631 Clever, 430 F 8
64735 Clinton⊙, 7,504 E 6
65325 Cole Camp, 1,038 F 6
65201 Columbia⊙, 58,804 H 5
63742 Commerce, 234 O 8
64434 Conception Junction, 237 C 2
64020 Concordia, 1,854 E 5
65632 Conway, 547 G 7
63839 Cooter, 414 N10
64021 Corder, 476 E 4
63338 Cottleville, 275 N 2
† 64501 Country Club Village, 221 C 3
64637 Cowgill, 232 E 3
64437 Craig, 369 B 2
65633 Crane, 1,003 E 9
64739 Creighton, 294 D 6
63018 Crescent, 425 N 3
† 63101 Crestwood, 15,398 O 3
63141 Creve Coeur, 8,967 O 3
65452 Crocker, 814 H 7
65634 Cross Timbers, 204 F 6
63019 Crystal City, 3,898 M 6
65453 Cuba, 2,070 K 6
63339 Curryville, 337 K 4
64439 Dearborn, 543 C 3
64740 Deepwater, 565 E 6
64440 De Kalb, 287 C 3
63744 Delta, 462 N 8
63636 Des Arc, 222 L 8
63601 Desloge, 2,818 M 7
63020 De Soto, 5,984 M 6
63131 Des Peres, 5,333 O 3
63841 Dexter, 6,024 N 9
64840 Diamond, 554 D 9
65459 Dixon, 1,387 H 6
63637 Doe Run, 900 M 7
63935 Doniphan⊙, 1,850 L 9
† 65550 Doolittle, 509 J 7
63844 Dorena, 500 O 9
63536 Downing, 406 H 2
64742 Drexel, 723 C 6
63936 Dudley, 248 M 9
64841 Duenweg, 656 D 8
† 64801 Duquesne, 738 D 8
64442 Eagleville, 388 D 2
64743 East Lynne, 255 D 5
63845 East Prairie, 3,275 O 9
65462 Edgar Springs, 450 J 7
64444 Edgerton, 477 C 4
63537 Edina⊙, 1,574 H 2
65026 Eldon, 3,520 G 6
64744 El Dorado Springs, 3,300 E 7
63638 Ellington, 1,094 L 8
63011 Ellisville, 4,681 N 3
63937 Ellsinore, 342 L 9
63343 Elsberry, 1,398 L 4
63639 Elvins, 1,603 L 7
65466 Eminence⊙, 520 K 8
65327 Emma, 224 F 5
63344 Eolia, 321 L 4
63846 Essex, 493 N 9
† 63601 Esther, 1,040 M 7
63025 Eureka, 2,384 N 3
65646 Everton, 264 E 8
63440 Ewing, 330 J 2
64024 Excelsior Springs, 9,411 R 4
65647 Exeter, 434 D 9
64446 Fairfax, 835 B 2
65648 Fair Grove, 431 F 8
65649 Fair Play, 328 E 7
64842 Fairview, 263 D 9
63345 Farber, 470 J 4
63640 Farmington⊙, 6,590 M 7
65248 Fayette⊙, 3,520 G 4
63026 Fenton, 2,275 P 3
63135 Ferguson, 28,915 P 2
63028 Festus, 7,530 M 6
64449 Fillmore, 251 C 2
63940 Fisk, 503 M 9
63601 Flat River, 4,550 M 7
* 63031 Florissant, 65,908 P 2
63347 Foley, 224 L 4
65652 Fordland, 399 G 8
64451 Forest City, 365 B 3
63348 Foristell, 273 M 2
65653 Forsyth⊙, 803 F 9
63441 Frankford, 472 K 4
65250 Franklin, 252 G 4
63645 Fredericktown⊙, 3,799 M 7
65035 Freeburg, 577 J 6
64746 Freeman, 417 C 5
63748 Frohna, 225 N 7
† 63101 Frontenac, 3,920 O 3
65251 Fulton⊙, 12,148 J 5
65655 Gainesville⊙, 627 G 9
65656 Galena⊙, 391 F 9
64640 Gallatin⊙, 1,833 E 3
64641 Galt, 261 F 2
64747 Garden City, 633 D 5
65036 Gasconade, 235 J 5
63037 Gerald, 762 K 6
63848 Gideon, 1,112 N10
65330 Gilliam, 248 F 4
64642 Gilman City, 376 D 2
64118 Gladstone, 23,128 P 5
65254 Glasgow, 1,336 G 4
† 64068 Glenaire, 505 R 5
63038 Glencoe, 2,500 N 3
63122 Glendale, 6,891 P 3
64748 Golden City, 810 D 8
63843 Goodman, 565 C 9
63543 Gorin, 220 H 2
64454 Gower, 758 C 3
64455 Graham, 213 C 2
64029 Grain Valley, 709 S 6
64844 Granby, 1,678 D 9
63943 Grandin, 243 L 9
64030 Grandview, 17,456 P 6
63650 Graniteville, 375 L 7
64456 Grant City⊙, 1,095 D 2
65037 Gravois Mills, 994 G 6
63850 Grayridge, 300 N 9
63039 Gray Summit, 950 M 3
63544 Green Castle, 235 G 2
63545 Green City, 629 F 2
65661 Greenfield⊙, 1,172 E 8
65332 Green Ridge, 403 F 5
63546 Greentop, 351 H 2
63944 Greenville⊙, 328 M 8
64034 Greenwood, 925 R 6
63040 Grover, 550 O 3
64643 Hale, 461 F 3
65255 Hallsville, 790 H 4
64644 Hamilton, 1,645 E 3
63401 Hannibal, 18,609 K 3
64035 Hardin, 683 E 4
64701 Harrisonville⊙, 4,928 D 5
65667 Hartville⊙, 524 G 8
63349 Hawk Point, 354 K 5
63851 Hayti, 3,841 N10
* 63042 Hazelwood, 14,082 P 2
63047 Hematite, 300 L 6
64460 Hemple, 350 D 3
64036 Henrietta, 466 E 4
63048 Herculaneum, 1,885 M 6
65041 Hermann⊙, 2,658 K 5
65668 Hermitage⊙, 284 F 7
65257 Higbee, 641 H 4
64037 Higginsville, 4,318 E 4
63049 High Ridge, 350 O 4
63050 Hillsboro⊙, 432 L 6
63852 Holcomb, 593 N10
64040 Holden, 2,089 E 5
63853 Holland, 329 N10
65672 Hollister, 906 F 9
64048 Holt, 319 D 4
64461 Hopkins, 656 C 1
† 63070 Horine, 850 M 6
63855 Hornersville, 693 M10
63051 House Springs, 500 O 4
65483 Houston⊙, 2,178 J 8
65333 Houstonia, 312 F 5
65674 Humansville, 825 E 7
64752 Hume, 350 C 6
63443 Hunnewell, 304 J 3
65259 Huntsville⊙, 1,442 H 4
63547 Hurdland, 225 H 2
65486 Iberia, 741 H 6
63754 Illmo, 1,232 O 8
63052 Imperial, 900 P 4
* 64050 Independence⊙, 111,662 R 5
63648 Irondale, 319 L 7
63650 Ironton⊙, 1,452 L 7
63755 Jackson⊙, 5,896 N 8
64648 Jamesport, 614 E 3
65046 Jamestown, 243 G 5
64755 Jasper, 796 D 8
65101 Jefferson City (cap.)⊙, 32,407 H 5
63136 Jennings, 19,379 P 2
63351 Jonesburg, 479 K 5
64801 Joplin, 39,256 C 8
† 63385 Josephville, 250 N 2
63445 Kahoka⊙, 2,207 J 2
* 64101 Kansas City, 507,087 P 5
Kansas City, ‡1,253,916 P 5
64060 Kearney, 984 D 4
63758 Kelso, 401 O 8
63857 Kennett⊙, 9,852 M10
65261 Keytesville⊙, 730 G 4
64649 Kidder, 231 D 3
63053 Kimmswick, 268 M 6
64463 King City, 1,023 D 2
64650 Kingston⊙, 291 E 3
64061 Kingsville, 284 D 5
63140 Kinloch, 5,629 P 2
63501 Kirksville⊙, 15,560 H 2
63122 Kirkwood, 31,890 O 3
65336 Knob Noster, 2,264 E 5
63446 Knox City, 284 H 2
63054 Koch, 600 P 4
65692 Koshkonong, 216 J 9
† 63090 Krakow, 300 K 6
63055 Labadie, 350 N 3
63447 La Belle, 848 J 2
64651 Laclede, 430 F 3
63352 Laddonia, 745 J 4
† 64758 Ladue, 10,491 P 3
63448 La Grange, 1,237 K 2
64063 Lake Lotawana, 1,786 R 6
65049 Lake Ozark, 507 G 6
† 64015 Lake Tapawingo, 867 R 6
† 64034 Lake Winnebago, 432 R 6
64759 Lamar⊙, 3,760 D 8
65337 La Monte, 814 F 5
64847 Lanagan, 374 C 9
63548 Lancaster⊙, 821 H 1
63549 La Plata, 1,377 H 2
64652 Laredo, 383 E 2
64465 Lathrop, 1,268 D 3
64062 Lawson, 1,034 D 4
† 63640 Leadington, 299 M 7
63653 Leadwood, 1,397 L 7
65535 Leasburg, 218 K 6
65536 Lebanon⊙, 8,616 G 7
64063 Lee's Summit, 16,230 R 6
64761 Leeton, 425 E 5
63125 Lemay, 40,115 P 3
63654 Lesterville, 275 L 8
64066 Levasy, 283 S 5
63452 Lewistown, 615 J 2
64067 Lexington⊙, 5,388 E 4
64762 Liberal, 644 D 7
64068 Liberty⊙, 13,679 R 5
65542 Licking, 1,002 J 8
63862 Lilbourn, 1,152 N 9
65338 Lincoln, 574 F 6
65051 Linn⊙, 1,289 J 5
65052 Linn Creek, 268 G 6
64653 Linneus⊙, 400 F 3
65682 Lockwood, 887 E 8
65054 Loose Creek, 370 J 5
63353 Louisiana, 4,533 K 4
64763 Lowry City, 520 E 6
63762 Lutesville, 626 M 8
63552 Macon⊙, 5,301 H 3
65263 Madison, 540 H 4
64466 Maitland, 319 B 2
63863 Malden, 5,374 M 9
65339 Malta Bend, 342 F 4
65704 Mansfield, 1,056 G 8
63143 Maplewood, 12,785 P 3
63764 Marble Hill⊙, 589 N 8
64658 Marceline, 2,622 F 3
65705 Marionville, 1,496 E 8
63655 Marquand, 400 M 8
65340 Marshall⊙, 11,847 F 4
65706 Marshfield⊙, 2,961 G 8
63866 Marston, 666 N 9
63357 Marthasville, 415 L 5
65264 Martinsburg, 318 J 4
64468 Maryville⊙, 9,970 C 2
63857 Matthews, 538 N 9
64469 Maysville⊙, 1,045 D 3
64071 Mayview, 330 E 4
64657 McFall, 203 D 2
64659 Meadville, 409 F 3
63555 Memphis⊙, 2,081 H 2
64660 Mendon, 289 F 3
64661 Mercer, 364 F 2
65058 Meta, 387 H 6
65265 Mexico⊙, 11,807 J 4
65344 Miami, 205 F 4
63359 Middletown, 235 J 4
63556 Milan⊙, 1,794 F 2
65707 Miller, 676 E 8
63952 Mill Spring, 207 L 8
64769 Mindenmines, 279 D 8
63659 Mine La Motte, 200 M 7
† 63801 Miner, 640 N 9
63660 Mineral Point, 369 L 7
64072 Missouri City, 375 R 5
65270 Moberly, 12,988 G 4

(continued on following page)

The Gateway Arch soars in silhouette against the St. Louis skyline. A Saarinen design, the monument is the centerpiece of the Jefferson National Expansion Memorial. Internal passenger trains carry sightseers up either leg to the long observation room.

Agriculture, Industry and Resources

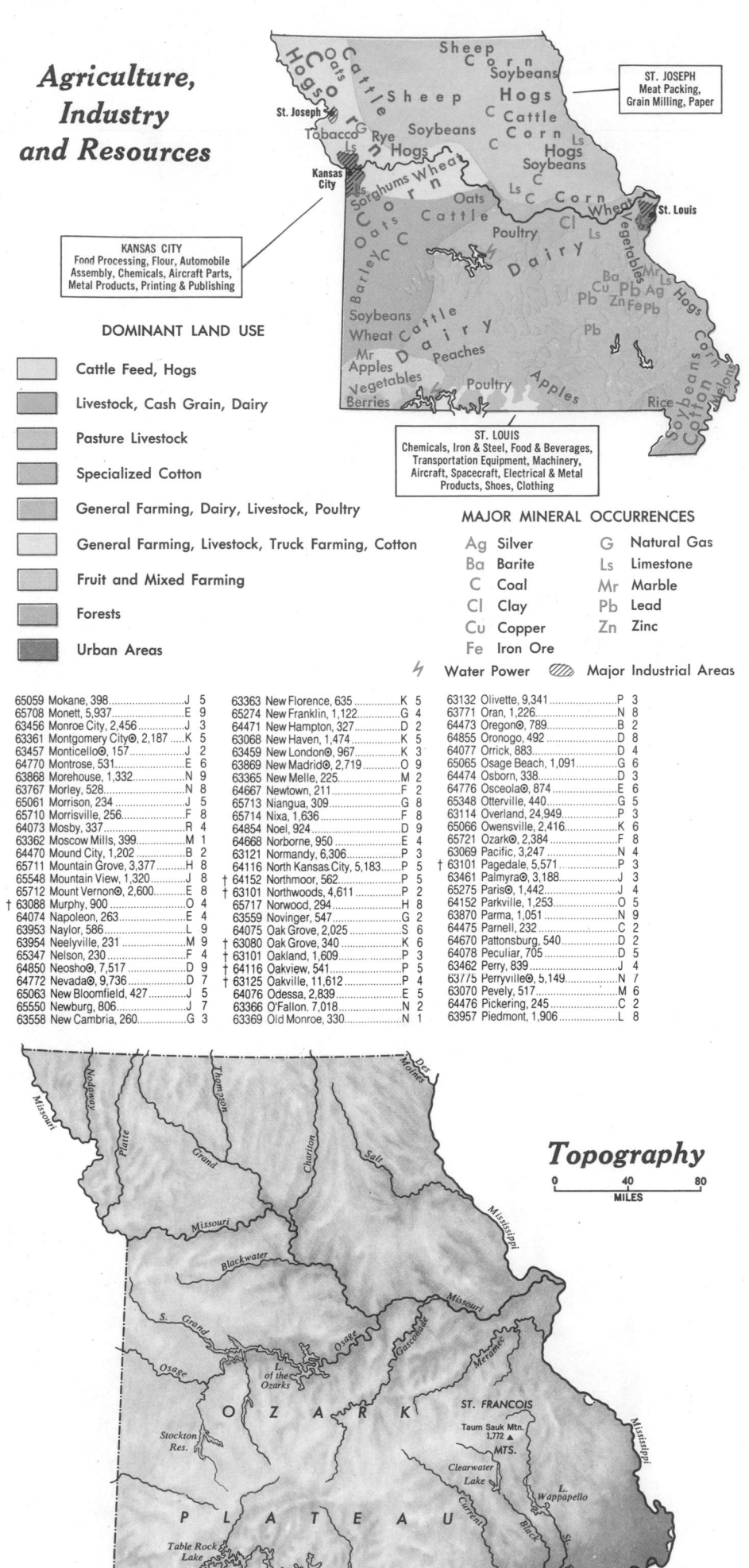

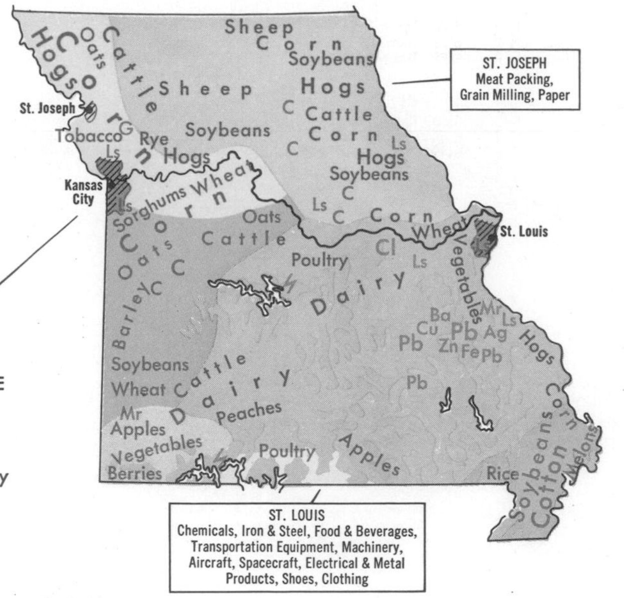

ST. JOSEPH
Meat Packing, Grain Milling, Paper

KANSAS CITY
Food Processing, Flour, Automobile Assembly, Chemicals, Aircraft Parts, Metal Products, Printing & Publishing

ST. LOUIS
Chemicals, Iron & Steel, Food & Beverages, Transportation Equipment, Machinery, Aircraft, Spacecraft, Electrical & Metal Products, Shoes, Clothing

DOMINANT LAND USE

- Cattle Feed, Hogs
- Livestock, Cash Grain, Dairy
- Pasture Livestock
- Specialized Cotton
- General Farming, Dairy, Livestock, Poultry
- General Farming, Livestock, Truck Farming, Cotton
- Fruit and Mixed Farming
- Forests
- Urban Areas

MAJOR MINERAL OCCURRENCES

Ag	Silver	G	Natural Gas
Ba	Barite	Ls	Limestone
C	Coal	Mr	Marble
Cl	Clay	Pb	Lead
Cu	Copper	Zn	Zinc
Fe	Iron Ore		

Water Power — Major Industrial Areas

65059 Mokane, 398 .... J 5
65708 Monett, 5,937 .... E 9
63456 Monroe City, 2,456 .... J 3
63361 Montgomery City⊙, 2,187 .... K 5
63457 Monticello⊙, 157 .... J 2
64770 Montrose, 531 .... E 6
63868 Morehouse, 1,332 .... N 9
63767 Morley, 528 .... N 8
65061 Morrison, 234 .... J 5
65710 Morrisville, 256 .... F 8
64073 Mosby, 337 .... R 4
63362 Moscow Mills, 399 .... M 1
64470 Mound City, 1,202 .... B 2
65711 Mountain Grove, 3,377 .... H 8
65548 Mountain View, 1,320 .... J 8
65712 Mount Vernon⊙, 2,600 .... E 8
† 63088 Murphy, 900 .... O 4
64074 Napoleon, 263 .... E 4
63953 Naylor, 586 .... L 9
63954 Neelyville, 231 .... M 9
65347 Nelson, 230 .... F 4
64850 Neosho⊙, 7,517 .... D 9
64772 Nevada⊙, 9,736 .... D 7
65063 New Bloomfield, 427 .... J 5
65550 Newburg, 806 .... J 7
63558 New Cambria, 260 .... G 3
63363 New Florence, 635 .... K 5
65274 New Franklin, 1,122 .... G 4
64471 New Hampton, 327 .... D 2
63068 New Haven, 1,474 .... K 5
63459 New London⊙, 967 .... K 3
63869 New Madrid⊙, 2,719 .... O 9
63365 New Melle, 225 .... M 2
64667 Newtown, 211 .... F 2
65713 Niangua, 309 .... G 8
65714 Nixa, 1,636 .... F 8
64854 Noel, 924 .... D 9
64668 Norborne, 950 .... E 4
63121 Normandy, 6,306 .... P 3
64116 North Kansas City, 5,183 .... P 5
† 64152 Northmoor, 562 .... P 5
† 63101 Northwoods, 4,611 .... P 2
65717 Norwood, 294 .... H 8
63559 Novinger, 547 .... G 2
64075 Oak Grove, 2,025 .... S 6
† 63080 Oak Grove, 340 .... K 6
† 63101 Oakland, 1,609 .... P 3
† 64116 Oakview, 541 .... P 5
† 63125 Oakville, 11,612 .... P 4
64076 Odessa, 2,839 .... E 5
63366 O'Fallon. 7,018 .... N 2
63369 Old Monroe, 330 .... N 1
63132 Olivette, 9,341 .... P 3
63771 Oran, 1,226 .... N 8
64473 Oregon⊙, 789 .... B 2
64855 Oronogo, 492 .... D 8
64077 Orrick, 883 .... D 4
65065 Osage Beach, 1,091 .... G 6
64474 Osborn, 338 .... D 3
64776 Osceola⊙, 874 .... E 6
65348 Otterville, 440 .... G 5
63114 Overland, 24,949 .... P 3
65066 Owensville, 2,416 .... K 6
65721 Ozark⊙, 2,384 .... F 8
63069 Pacific, 3,247 .... N 4
† 63101 Pagedale, 5,571 .... P 3
63461 Palmyra⊙, 3,188 .... J 3
65275 Paris⊙, 1,442 .... J 4
64152 Parkville, 1,253 .... O 5
63870 Parma, 1,051 .... N 9
64475 Parnell, 232 .... C 2
64670 Pattonsburg, 540 .... D 2
64078 Peculiar, 705 .... D 5
63462 Perry, 839 .... J 4
63775 Perryville⊙, 5,149 .... N 7
63070 Pevely, 517 .... M 6
64476 Pickering, 245 .... C 2
63957 Piedmont, 1,906 .... L 8

Topography

0 40 80 MILES

5,000 m. 16,404 ft. | 2,000 m. 6,562 ft. | 1,000 m. 3,281 ft. | 500 m. 1,640 ft. | 200 m. 656 ft. | 100 m. 328 ft. | Sea Level | Below

65723 Pierce City, 1,097 .... E 8
65276 Pilot Grove, 701 .... G 5
63663 Pilot Knob, 582 .... L 7
63120 Pine Lawn, 5,773 .... P 3
64856 Pineville⊙, 444 .... D 9
64079 Platte City⊙, 2,022 .... C 4
† 64152 Platte Woods, 484 .... O 5
64477 Plattsburg⊙, 1,832 .... D 3
64080 Pleasant Hill, 3,396 .... D 5
65725 Pleasant Hope, 265 .... F 8
† 64836 Pleasant Valley, 1,535 .... R 5
63779 Pocahontas, 604 .... N 8
64671 Polo, 438 .... D 3
65789 Pomona, 250 .... J 9
63901 Poplar Bluff⊙, 16,653 .... L 9
63373 Portage Des Sioux, 509 .... P 2
63873 Portageville, 3,117 .... N 10
65067 Portland, 250 .... J 5
63664 Potosi⊙, 2,761 .... L 7
65068 Prairie Home, 231 .... G 5
64673 Princeton⊙, 1,328 .... E 2
64857 Purcell, 325 .... D 8
64674 Purdin, 236 .... F 3
65734 Purdy, 588 .... E 9
63960 Puxico, 759 .... M 9
63561 Queen City, 588 .... H 2
63961 Qulin, 496 .... M 9
64858 Racine, 274 .... C 9
64479 Ravenwood, 336 .... C 2
65555 Raymondville, 284 .... J 8
64083 Raymore, 587 .... D 5
64133 Raytown, 33,632 .... P 6
65737 Reeds Spring, 286 .... F 9
65738 Republic, 2,411 .... E 8
64779 Rich Hill, 1,661 .... D 6
65556 Richland, 1,783 .... H 7
64085 Richmond⊙, 4,948 .... D 4
63117 Richmond Heights, 13,802 .... P 3
64481 Ridgeway, 469 .... D 2
63874 Risco, 412 .... N 9
† 63601 Rivermines, 402 .... L 7
64168 Riverside, 2,123 .... O 5
† 63101 Riverview, 3,741 .... R 2
65279 Rocheport, 307 .... H 5
† 63101 Rock Hill, 7,275 .... P 3
64482 Rock Port⊙, 1,575 .... B 2

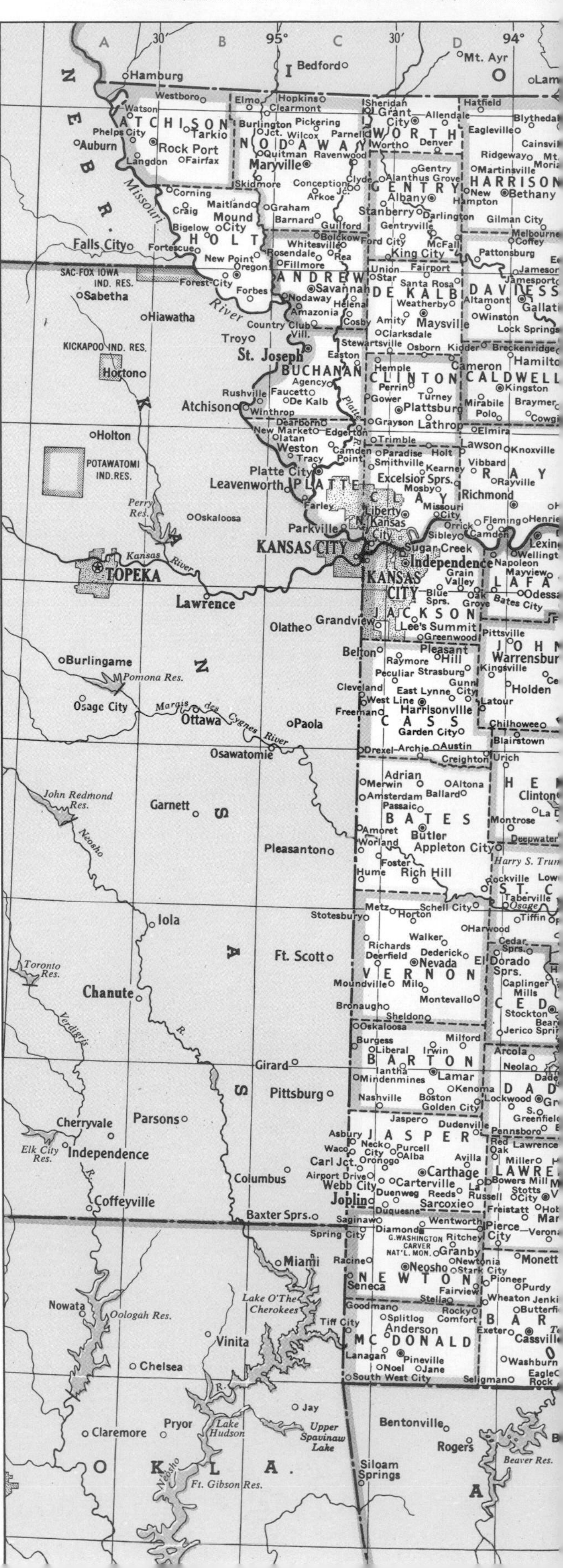

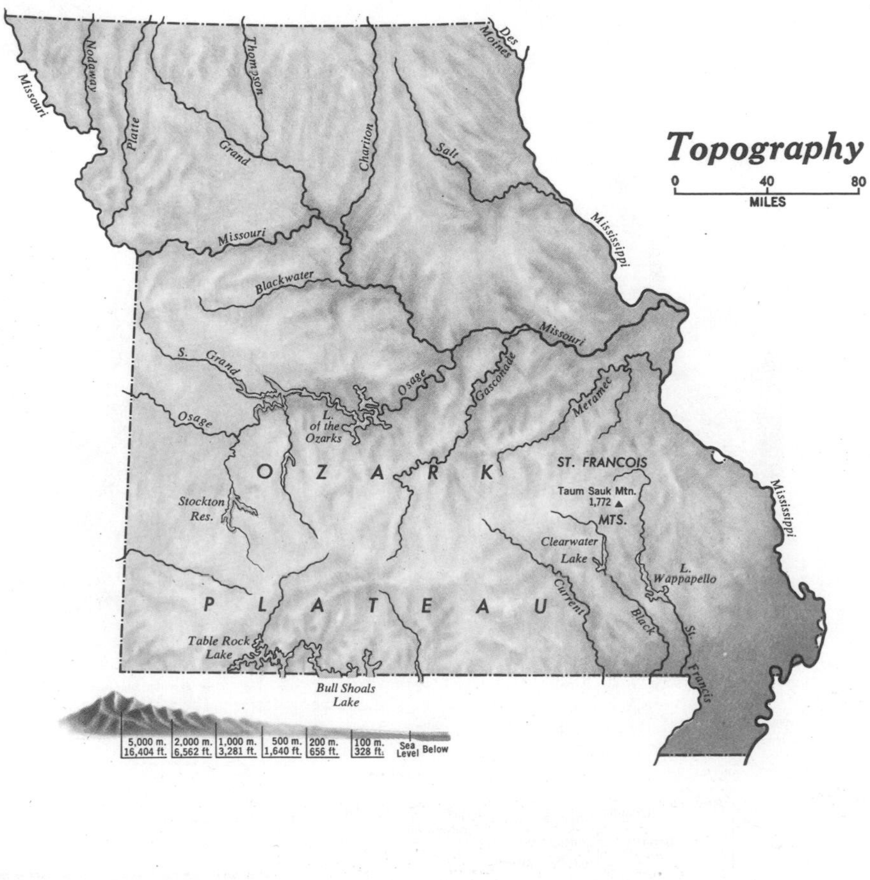

64780 Rockville, 203 .... D 6
65742 Rogersville, 574 .... G 8
65401 Rolla⊙, 13,245 .... J 7
63091 Rosebud, 305 .... K 6
64483 Rosendale, 245 .... C 2
64484 Rushville, 300 .... B 3
65074 Russellville, 557 .... H 6
63074 Saint Ann, 18,215 .... O 2
63301 Saint Charles⊙, 31,834 .... O 2
63077 Saint Clair, 2,978 .... L 6
63670 Sainte Genevieve⊙, 4,468 .... M 6
65075 Saint Elizabeth, 287 .... H 6
63101 Saint George, 1,806 .... P 3
65559 Saint James, 2,787 .... J 6
63114 Saint John, 8,960 .... P 2
64501 Saint Joseph⊙, 72,691 .... C 3
Saint Joseph, ‡86,915 .... C 3
63101 Saint Louis⊙, 622,236 .... P 3
Saint Louis, ‡2,363,017 .... P 3
63673 Saint Marys, 645 .... M 7
63376 Saint Peters, 486 .... N 2
65560 Salem⊙, 4,363 .... J 7
65281 Salisbury, 1,960 .... G 4
64862 Sarcoxie, 1,175 .... D 8
64485 Savannah⊙, 3,324 .... C 3
64783 Schell City, 367 .... D 6
63780 Scott City, 2,464 .... O 8
65301 Sedalia⊙, 22,847 .... F 5
65745 Seligman, 424 .... D 9
63876 Senath, 1,484 .... M 10
64865 Seneca, 1,577 .... C 9
65746 Seymour, 1,208 .... G 8
63468 Shelbina, 2,060 .... H 3
63469 Shelbyville⊙, 601 .... H 3
64784 Sheldon, 498 .... D 7
64486 Sheridan, 251 .... C 1
† 63101 Shrewsbury, 5,896 .... P 3
64088 Sibley, 279 .... S 5
63801 Sikeston, 14,699 .... N 9
63377 Silex, 306 .... K 4
64487 Skidmore, 440 .... B 2
65349 Slater, 2,576 .... G 4
65350 Smithton, 402 .... F 5
64089 Smithville, 1,785 .... D 4
64863 South West City, 453 .... D 9
† 63101 Spanish Lake, 15,647 .... P 2
65753 Sparta, 380 .... F 9
64679 Spickard, 408 .... F 2
* 65801 Springfield⊙, 120,096 .... F 8
Springfield, ‡152,929 .... F 8
64489 Stanberry, 1,479 .... C 2
63079 Stanton, 350 .... K 6
63877 Steele, 2,107 .... N 10
65565 Steelville⊙, 1,392 .... K 7
64490 Stewartsville, 634 .... C 3
65785 Stockton⊙, 1,063 .... E 7
65567 Stoutland, 205 .... G 7
65078 Stover, 849 .... G 6
65757 Strafford, 491 .... F 8
65284 Sturgeon, 787 .... H 4
64054 Sugar Creek, 4,755 .... R 5
63080 Sullivan, 5,100 .... K 6
65571 Summersville, 435 .... J 8
† 63101 Sunset Hills, 3,728 .... P 3
65351 Sweet Springs, 1,716 .... F 5
64491 Tarkio, 2,517 .... B 2
† 64063 Tarsney Lakes, 401 .... R 6
65791 Thayer, 1,609 .... J 9
† 63025 Times Beach, 1,265 .... O 3
65081 Tipton, 1,914 .... G 5
64091 Tracy, 252 .... C 4
64683 Trenton⊙, 6,063 .... E 2
64492 Trimble, 206 .... D 4
63379 Troy⊙, 2,538 .... L 5
63380 Truesdail, 262 .... K 5
65082 Tuscumbia⊙, 256 .... H 6
63084 Union⊙, 5,183 .... L 6
64494 Union Star, 417 .... C 2
63565 Unionville⊙, 2,075 .... G 2
64063 Unity, 242 .... R 6
63130 University City, 46,309 .... P 3
65767 Urbana, 369 .... F 7
64788 Urich, 433 .... E 6
64686 Utica, 275 .... E 3
63088 Valley Park, 3,662 .... O 3
63965 Van Buren⊙, 714 .... L 8
63382 Vandalia, 3,160 .... J 4
63784 Vanduser, 306 .... N 9
65769 Verona, 515 .... E 9
65084 Versailles⊙, 2,244 .... G 6
65566 Viburnum, 520 .... K 7
65580 Vichy, 250 .... J 6
† 63020 Victoria, 250 .... M 6
65581 Vida, 300 .... J 7
65582 Vienna⊙, 505 .... H 6
64790 Walker, 227 .... D 7
65770 Walnut Grove, 442 .... F 8
63966 Wappapello, 254 .... M 9
63879 Wardell, 275 .... N 10
† 65101 Wardsville, 460 .... H 5
64093 Warrensburg⊙, 13,125 .... E 5
63383 Warrenton⊙, 2,057 .... K 5
65355 Warsaw⊙, 1,423 .... F 6
65772 Washburn, 250 .... E 9
63090 Washington, 8,499 .... K 5
64096 Waverly, 827 .... E 4
63472 Wayland, 467 .... J 2
65583 Waynesville⊙, 3,375 .... H 7
† 64152 Weatherby Lake, 832 .... O 5
65774 Weaubleau, 343 .... F 7
64870 Webb City, 6,811 .... C 8
63119 Webster Groves, 26,995 .... P 3
64097 Wellington, 720 .... E 4
63112 Wellston, 7,050 .... P 3
63384 Wellsville, 1,565 .... K 4
63385 Wentzville, 3,223 .... M 2
63386 Westalton, 435 .... R 2
64498 Westboro, 234 .... B 1
64098 Weston, 1,267 .... C 4
65085 Westphalia, 332 .... J 6
65775 West Plains⊙, 6,893 .... J 9
65779 Wheatland, 317 .... F 7
64874 Wheaton, 360 .... E 9
64688 Wheeling, 268 .... F 3
65781 Willard, 1,018 .... F 8
63977 Williamsville, 398 .... L 9
65793 Willow Springs, 2,045 .... H 9
65360 Windsor, 2,734 .... E 5
63389 Winfield, 620 .... L 5
65588 Winona, 973 .... K 8
† 63101 Woodson Terrace, 5,936 .... P 2
63390 Wright City, 943 .... K 5
63474 Wyaconda, 356 .... J 2
63882 Wyatt, 562 .... O 9

⊙ County seat.
‡ Population of metropolitan area.
† Zip of nearest p.o.
* Multiple zips

COUNTIES

County	Key
Beaverhead, 8,187	C 5
Big Horn, 10,057	J 5
Blaine, 6,727	G 2
Broadwater, 2,526	E 4
Carbon, 7,080	G 5
Carter, 1,956	M 5
Cascade, 81,804	E 3
Chouteau, 6,473	F 3
Custer, 12,174	L 4
Daniels, 3,083	L 2
Dawson, 11,269	M 3
Deer Lodge, 15,652	C 5
Fallon, 4,050	M 4
Fergus, 12,611	G 3
Flathead, 39,460	B 2
Gallatin, 32,505	E 5
Garfield, 1,796	J 3
Glacier, 10,783	C 2
Golden Valley, 931	G 4
Granite, 2,737	C 4
Hill, 17,358	F 2
Jefferson, 5,238	D 4
Judith Basin, 2,667	F 4
Lake, 14,445	B 3
Lewis and Clark, 33,281	D 3
Liberty, 2,359	E 2
Lincoln, 18,063	A 2
Madison, 5,014	D 5
McCone, 2,875	L 3
Meagher, 2,122	F 4
Mineral, 2,958	B 3
Missoula, 58,263	C 3
Musselshell, 3,734	H 4
Park, 11,197	F 5
Petroleum, 675	H 3
Phillips, 5,386	J 2
Pondera, 6,611	D 2
Powder River, 2,862	L 5
Powell, 6,660	D 4
Prairie, 1,752	L 4
Ravalli, 14,409	B 4
Richland, 9,837	M 3
Roosevelt, 10,365	L 2
Rosebud, 6,032	K 4
Sanders, 7,093	A 3
Sheridan, 5,779	M 2
Silver Bow, 41,981	D 5
Stillwater, 4,632	G 5
Sweet Grass, 2,980	G 5
Teton, 6,116	D 3
Toole, 5,839	E 2
Treasure, 1,069	J 4
Valley, 11,471	K 2
Wheatland, 2,529	G 4
Wibaux, 1,465	M 4
Yellowstone, 87,367	H 4
Yellowstone Nat'l Park, 64	F 6

CITIES and TOWNS

	Zip	Name/Pop.	Key
	59001	Absarokee, 700	G 5
	59820	Alberton, 363	B 3
	59710	Alder, 100	D 5
†	59634	Alhambra, 50	E 4
†	59741	Amsterdam, 200	E 5
	59711	Anaconda⊙, 9,771	C 4
	59211	Antelope, 95	M 2
	59821	Arlee, 220	B 3
†	59412	Armington, 62	F 3
	59003	Ashland, 200	K 5
	59410	Augusta, 400	D 3
	59713	Avon, 250	D 4
	59411	Babb, 50	C 2
	59212	Bainville, 217	M 2
	59313	Baker⊙, 2,584	M 4
	59006	Ballantine, 350	J 5
†	59725	Bannack, 20	C 5
	59613	Basin, 230	D 4
	59007	Bearcreek, 31	G 5
†	59441	Becket, 35	G 4
	59008	Belfry, 250	H 5
	59714	Belgrade, 1,307	E 5
†	59046	Belmont, 75	G 4
	59412	Belt, 656	E 3
†	59462	Benchland, 100	F 3
	59314	Biddle, 83	L 5
	59910	Big Arm, 150	B 3
	59911	Bigfork, 500	C 2
	59010	Bighorn, 40	J 4
	59520	Big Sandy, 827	G 2
	59011	Big Timber⊙, 1,592	G 5
*	59101	Billings⊙, 61,581	H 5
		Billings, ‡87,367	H 5
	59414	Black Eagle, 1,500	E 3
	59415	Blackfoot, 100	D 2
	59823	Bonner, 250	C 4
	59632	Boulder⊙, 1,342	E 4
	59521	Box Elder, 200	F 2
	59715	Bozeman⊙, 18,670	E 5
	59416	Brady, 230	E 2
	59014	Bridger, 717	H 5
	59317	Broadus⊙, 799	L 5
	59015	Broadview, 123	H 4
	59213	Brockton, 401	M 2
	59214	Brockway, 80	L 3
	59417	Browning, 1,700	C 2
	59016	Busby, 600	J 5
	59701	Butte⊙, 23,368	D 5
†	59857	Camas Prairie, 160	B 3
†	59601	Canyon Ferry, 100	E 4
	59721	Cardwell, 36	E 5
	59420	Carter, 100	E 3
†	59347	Cartersville, 140	K 4
	59421	Cascade, 714	E 3
†	59701	Centerville, 2,284	D 4
	59824	Charlo, 150	B 3
	59522	Chester⊙, 936	E 2
	59523	Chinook⊙, 1,813	G 2
	59422	Choteau⊙, 1,586	D 3
	59423	Christina, 44	G 3
	59215	Circle⊙, 964	L 3
	59634	Clancy, 550	E 4
	59825	Clinton, 250	C 4
	59018	Clyde Park, 244	F 5
	59424	Coffee Creek, 79	F 3
	59323	Colstrip, 160	K 5
	59912	Columbia Falls, 2,652	B 2
	59019	Columbus⊙, 1,173	G 5
	59826	Condon, 250	C 3
	59827	Conner, 150	B 5
	59425	Conrad⊙, 2,770	D 2
	59020	Cooke City, 45	G 5
	59913	Coram, 450	C 2
	59828	Corvallis, 467	C 4
†	59648	Craig, 100	D 3
	59217	Crane, 152	M 3
	59022	Crow Agency, 975	J 5
	59218	Culbertson, 821	M 2
	59024	Custer, 193	J 4
	59427	Cut Bank⊙, 4,004	D 2
	59219	Dagmar, 55	M 2
	59829	Darby, 538	B 4
	59914	Dayton, 60	B 3
†	59028	Dean, 32	G 5
	59830	De Borgia, 95	A 3
	59722	Deer Lodge⊙, 4,306	D 4
	59724	Dell, 50	D 6
†	59053	Delpine, 33	F 4
	59430	Denton, 398	G 3
	59431	Devon, 33	E 2
	59725	Dillon⊙, 4,548	D 5
	59727	Divide, 105	D 5
	59831	Dixon, 300	B 3
	59524	Dodson, 196	H 2
	59832	Drummond, 494	D 4
	59432	Dupuyer, 105	D 2
	59433	Dutton, 415	E 3
	59434	East Glacier Park, 340	C 2
	59635	East Helena, 1,651	E 4
	59026	Edgar, 150	H 5
	59324	Ekalaka⊙, 663	M 5
†	59701	Elk Park, 53	D 4
	59728	Elliston, 300	D 4
	59915	Elmo, 150	B 3
	59729	Ennis, 501	E 5
	59325	Epsie, 60	L 5
	59916	Essex, 35	C 2
	59917	Eureka, 1,195	B 2
	59436	Fairfield, 638	D 3
	59221	Fairview, 956	M 3
	59326	Fallon, 200	L 4
	59028	Fishtail, 52	G 5
	59222	Flaxville, 185	L 2
†	59701	Floral Park, 5,113	D 5
	59833	Florence, 500	B 4
	59440	Floweree, 306	E 3
	59441	Forestgrove, 90	H 3
	59327	Forsyth⊙, 1,873	K 4
†	59526	Fort Belknap, 185	H 2
	59442	Fort Benton⊙, 1,863	F 3
	59918	Fortine, 250	A 2
	59223	Fort Peck, 975	K 2
	59443	Fort Shaw, 450	E 3
†	59075	Fort Smith, 300	J 5
	59224	Four Buttes, 50	L 2
	59225	Frazer, 300	K 2
	59834	Frenchtown, 300	B 3
	59226	Froid, 330	M 2
	59029	Fromberg, 364	H 5
	59444	Galata, 48	E 2
†	59722	Galen, 210	D 4
	59730	Gallatin Gateway, 200	E 5
	59030	Gardiner, 479	F 5
	59445	Garneill, 55	G 4
	59731	Garrison, 350	D 4
	59446	Geraldine, 370	F 3
	59447	Geyser, 567	F 3
	59525	Gildford, 285	F 2

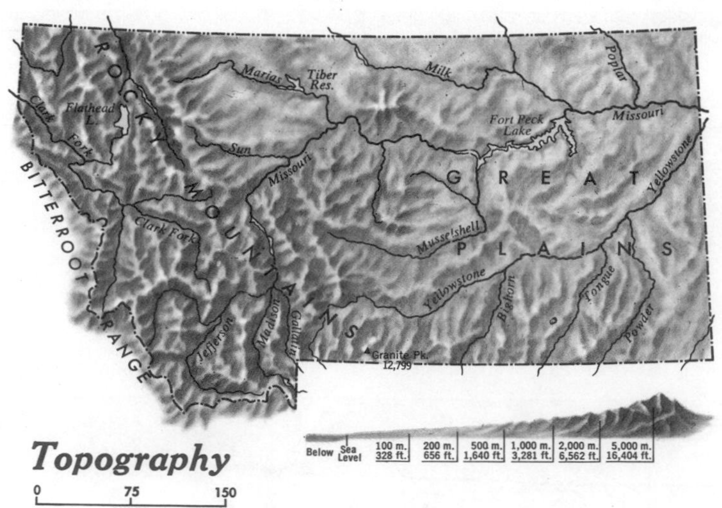

Topography

0 75 150
MILES

MONTANA

SCALE

0 5 10 20 40 60 MI.

0 5 10 20 40 60 KM.

State Capitals ⊛

County Seats ⊙

Surrounded by the wide open spaces, a Montana ranch basks in the reflected glory of the Rocky Mountains while it awaits cattle returning from the range. Ranches accommodate so many head of cattle that the state's residents are outnumbered six to one.

Ray Manley—Shostal Associates

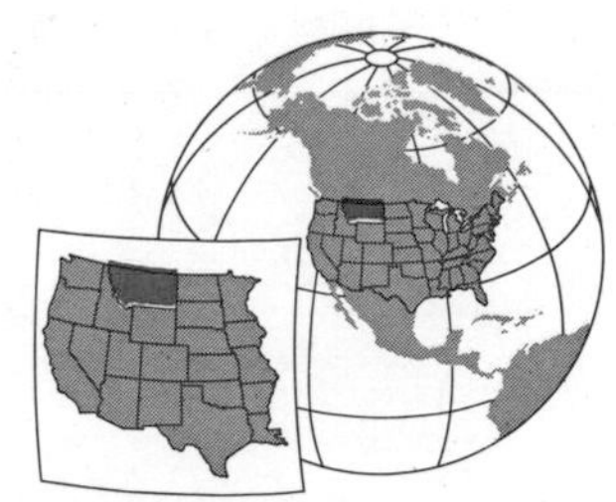

AREA 147,138 sq. mi.
POPULATION 694,409
CAPITAL Helena
LARGEST CITY Billings
HIGHEST POINT Granite Pk. 12,799 ft.
SETTLED IN 1809
ADMITTED TO UNION November 8, 1889
POPULAR NAME Treasure State
STATE FLOWER Bitterroot
STATE BIRD Western Meadowlark

Agriculture, Industry and Resources

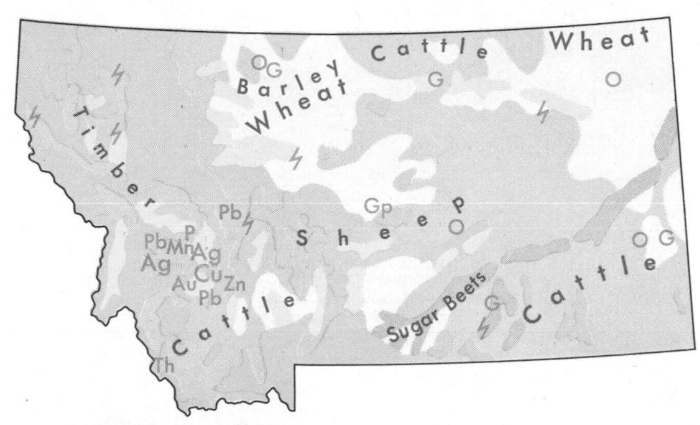

DOMINANT LAND USE

- Specialized Wheat
- Wheat, Range Livestock
- General Farming, Dairy, Range Livestock
- General Farming, Livestock, Special Crops
- Range Livestock
- Sugar Beets, Beans, Livestock, General Farming
- Forests

MAJOR MINERAL OCCURRENCES

Ag	Silver	O	Petroleum
Au	Gold	P	Phosphates
Cu	Copper	Pb	Lead
G	Natural Gas	Th	Thorium
Gp	Gypsum	Zn	Zinc
Mn	Manganese		

ϟ Water Power

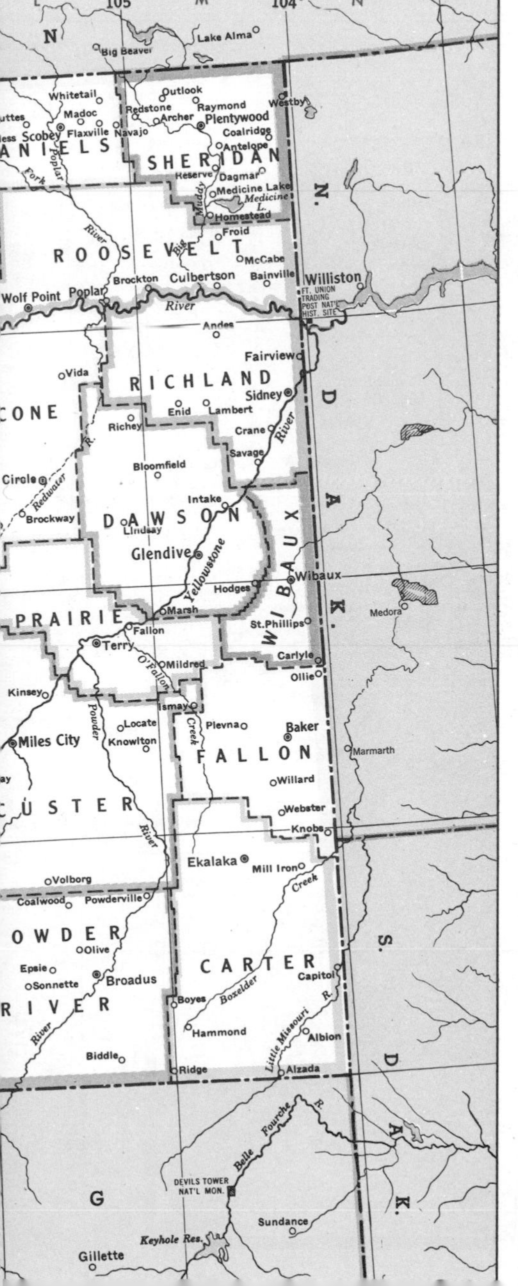

59230 Glasgow⊙, 4,700 K 2
† 59725 Glen, 100 D 5
59330 Glendive⊙, 6,305 M 3
59240 Glentana, 40 K 2
59733 Goldcreek, 76 D 4
59835 Grantsdale, 250 B 4
59032 Grassrange, 181 H 3
59401 Great Falls⊙, 60,091 E 3
Great Falls, ‡81,804 E 3
59836 Greenough, 100 C 4
59837 Hall, 95 C 4
59840 Hamilton⊙, 2,499 B 4
59034 Hardin⊙, 2,733 J 5
59526 Harlem, 1,094 H 2
59036 Harlowton⊙, 1,375 F 4
59735 Harrison, 275 E 5
59333 Hathaway, 45 K 4
59842 Haugan, 40 A 3
59501 Havre⊙, 10,558 G 2
59527 Hays, 950 H 2
59448 Heart Butte, 450 C 2
59601 Helena (cap.)⊙, 22,730 E 4
59843 Helmville, 76 C 4
59844 Heron, 185 A 2
59450 Highwood, 360 F 3
59451 Hilger, 40 G 3
59528 Hingham, 262 F 2
59241 Hinsdale, 500 K 2
59452 Hobson, 192 G 4
† 59353 Hodges, 50 M 4
59529 Hogeland, 68 H 2
59242 Homestead, 75 M 2
59845 Hot Springs, 664 B 3
59919 Hungry Horse, 700 C 2
59037 Huntley, 225 H 5
59846 Huson, 40 B 3
59038 Hysham⊙, 373 J 4
59039 Ingomar, 55 J 4
59335 Intake, 60 M 3
59530 Inverness, 150 F 2
59336 Ismay, 40 M 4
59736 Jackson, 196 C 5
59737 Jeffers, 70 E 5
59638 Jefferson City, 99 E 4
† 59721 Jefferson Island, 31 E 5
59041 Joliet, 412 G 5
59531 Joplin, 350 F 2
59337 Jordan⊙, 529 J 3
59453 Judith Gap, 160 G 4
59901 Kalispell⊙, 10,526 B 2
59454 Kevin, 250 D 2
59920 Kila, 44 B 2
† 59072 Klein, 200 H 4
59532 Kremlin, 347 F 2
59922 Lakeside, 663 B 2
59243 Lambert, 141 M 3
59043 Lame Deer, 460 K 5
59533 Landusky, 50 H 3
59244 Larslan, 140 K 2
59044 Laurel, 4,454 H 5
59738 Laurin, 60 D 5
59046 Lavina, 169 H 4
59457 Lewistown⊙, 6,437 G 3
59923 Libby⊙, 3,286 A 2
59739 Lima, 351 D 6
59639 Lincoln, 473 D 4
59339 Lindsay, 40 L 3
59047 Livingston⊙, 6,883 F 5
59535 Lloyd, 70 G 2
59340 Locate, 49 L 4
† 59101 Lockwood, 950 H 5
59050 Lodge Grass, 806 J 5
† 59524 Lodgepole, 39 H 2
59763 Logan, 53 E 5
59847 Lolo, 300 B 4
59460 Loma, 172 F 3
59461 Lothair, 35 E 2
59538 Malta⊙, 2,195 J 2
59741 Manhattan, 816 E 5
59925 Marion, 120 B 2
59053 Martinsdale, 203 F 4
59640 Marysville, 42 D 4
59742 Maudlow, 75 E 4
53850 Maxville, 44 C 4
59740 McAllister, 62 E 5
59247 Medicine Lake, 393 M 2
59743 Melrose, 350 D 5
59054 Melstone, 227 H 4
59055 Melville, 150 F 4
59301 Miles City⊙, 9,023 L 4
59851 Milltown, 500 C 4
59801 Missoula⊙, 29,497 C 4
59462 Moccasin, 100 F 3
59463 Monarch, 80 F 3
59464 Moore, 219 G 4
59059 Musselshell, 32 H 4
59248 Nashua, 513 K 2
59465 Neihart, 109 F 4
59745 Norris, 37 E 5
† 59501 North Havre, 1,073 G 2
59853 Noxon, 250 A 3
† 59936 Nyack, 31 C 2
59061 Nye, 65 G 5
59466 Oilmont, 75 E 2
59927 Olney, 250 B 2
59250 Opheim, 306 K 2
59251 Oswego, 75 L 2
59252 Outlook, 153 M 2
59854 Ovando, 102 C 3
59855 Pablo, 350 B 3
59856 Paradise, 500 B 3
59063 Park City, 400 H 5
59253 Peerless, 100 L 2
59467 Pendroy, 35 D 2
59858 Philipsburg⊙, 1,128 C 4
59859 Plains, 1,046 B 3
59254 Plentywood⊙, 2,381 M 2
59344 Plevna, 189 M 4
59860 Polson⊙, 2,464 B 3
59064 Pompeys Pillar, 69 J 5
59747 Pony, 111 E 5
59255 Poplar, 1,389 L 2
59862 Potomac, 58 C 4
59468 Power, 91 E 3
59929 Proctor, 108 B 3
59066 Pryor, 150 H 5
59641 Radersburg, 65 E 4
59748 Ramsay, 140 D 4
59067 Rapelje, 295 G 5
59863 Ravalli, 150 B 3
59256 Raymond, 34 M 2
59469 Raynesford, 100 F 3
59068 Red Lodge⊙, 1,844 G 5
59257 Redstone, 77 M 2
59069 Reedpoint, 125 G 5
59258 Reserve, 90 M 2
59930 Rexford, 243 A 2
59259 Richey, 389 L 3
59260 Richland, 37 K 2
59642 Ringling, 51 F 4
59070 Roberts, 291 G 5
† 59521 Rocky Boy, 150 G 2
59931 Rollins, 200 B 3
59864 Ronan, 1,347 C 3
59347 Rosebud, 120 K 4
59072 Roundup⊙, 2,116 H 4
59471 Roy, 175 H 3
59540 Rudyard, 550 F 2
59074 Ryegate⊙, 261 G 4
59261 Saco, 356 J 2
59865 Saint Ignatius, 925 C 3
59866 Saint Regis, 500 A 3
59075 Saint Xavier, 110 J 5
59867 Saltese, 95 A 3
59472 Sand Coulee, 500 E 3
59076 Sanders, 50 J 4
59473 Santa Rita, 125 D 2
59262 Savage, 300 M 3
59263 Scobey⊙, 1,486 L 2
59868 Seeley Lake, 400 C 3
59078 Shawmut, 60 G 4
† 59347 Sheffield, 40 K 4
59474 Shelby⊙, 3,111 E 2
59079 Shepherd, 100 H 5
59749 Sheridan, 636 D 5
59270 Sidney⊙, 4,543 M 3
59080 Silesia, 90 H 5
† 59701 Silver Bow Park, 5,524 D 4
59751 Silver Star, 100 D 5
59477 Simms, 299 E 3
59541 Simpson, 70 F 2
59932 Somers, 950 B 2
59348 Sonnette, 42 L 5
† 59442 Square Butte, 48 F 3
59479 Stanford⊙, 505 F 3
† 59846 Stark, 51 B 3
59870 Stevensville, 829 C 4
59480 Stockett, 500 E 3
59933 Stryker, 60 B 2
59481 Suffolk, 45 G 3
59482 Sunburst, 604 E 2
59483 Sun River, 190 E 3
59872 Superior⊙, 993 B 3
59911 Swan Lake, 200 C 3
59484 Sweetgrass, 120 E 2
59349 Terry⊙, 870 L 4
59873 Thompson Falls⊙, 1,356 A 3
59752 Three Forks, 1,188 E 5
† 59347 Thurlow, 40 K 4
59643 Toston, 75 E 4
59644 Townsend⊙, 1,371 E 4
59934 Trego, 50 B 2
59753 Trident, 50 E 5
59874 Trout Creek, 200 A 3
59935 Troy, 1,046 A 2
59542 Turner, 175 H 2
59754 Twin Bridges, 613 D 5
59085 Twodot, 118 F 4
59485 Ulm, 450 E 3
59452 Utica, 40 F 4
59486 Valier, 651 D 2
† 59237 Vananda, 50 K 4
59487 Vaughn, 345 E 3
59875 Victor, 500 B 4
59274 Vida, 52 L 3
59755 Virginia City⊙, 149 E 5
59701 Walkerville, 1,097 D 4
59756 Warmsprings, 1,600 D 4
59757 Waterloo, 102 D 5
† 59214 Watkins, 40 K 3
59275 Westby, 287 M 2
59936 West Glacier, 348 C 2
59758 West Yellowstone, 756 E 6
59937 Whitefish, 3,349 B 2
59759 Whitehall, 1,035 D 5
† 59784 Whitepine, 50 A 3
59645 White Sulphur Springs⊙, 1,200 E 4
59276 Whitetail, 125 L 2
59544 Whitewater, 100 J 2
59353 Wibaux⊙, 644 M 3
59760 Willow Creek, 325 E 5
59086 Wilsall, 200 F 5
59488 Windham, 60 F 3
59489 Winifred, 190 G 3
59087 Winnett⊙, 271 H 4
59647 Winston, 115 E 4
59761 Wisdom, 155 C 5
59762 Wise River, 125 C 5
59648 Wolf Creek, 200 D 3
59201 Wolf Point⊙, 3,095 L 2
† 59875 Woodside, 80 B 4
59088 Worden, 350 H 5
59089 Wyola, 110 J 5
† 59935 Yaak, 75 A 2
59547 Zurich, 89 G 2

⊙ County seat.
‡ Population of metropolitan area.
† Zip of nearest p.o.
* Multiple zips

COUNTIES

County, Pop.	Key
Adams, 30,553	F 4
Antelope, 9,047	F 2
Arthur, 606	C 3
Banner, 1,034	A 3
Blaine, 847	E 3
Boone, 8,190	F 3
Box Butte, 10,094	A 2
Boyd, 3,752	F 2
Brown, 4,021	E 2
Buffalo, 31,222	E 4
Burt, 9,247	H 3
Butler, 9,461	G 3
Cass, 18,076	H 4
Cedar, 12,192	G 2
Chase, 4,129	C 4
Cherry, 6,846	C 2
Cheyenne, 10,778	A 3
Clay, 8,266	F 4
Colfax, 9,498	G 3
Cuming, 12,034	H 3
Custer, 14,092	E 3
Dakota, 13,137	H 2
Dawes, 9,693	A 2
Dawson, 19,467	E 4
Deuel, 2,717	B 3
Dixon, 7,453	H 2
Dodge, 34,782	H 3
Douglas, 389,455	H 3
Dundy, 2,926	C 4
Fillmore, 8,137	G 4
Franklin, 4,566	F 4
Frontier, 3,982	D 4
Furnas, 6,897	E 4
Gage, 25,719	H 4
Garden, 2,929	B 3
Garfield, 2,411	F 3
Gosper, 2,178	E 4
Grant, 1,019	C 3
Greeley, 4,000	F 3
Hall, 42,851	F 4
Hamilton, 8,867	F 4
Harlan, 4,357	E 4
Hayes, 1,530	C 4
Hitchcock, 4,051	C 4
Holt, 12,933	F 2
Hooker, 939	C 3
Howard, 6,807	F 3
Jefferson, 10,436	G 4
Johnson, 5,743	H 4
Kearney, 6,707	F 4
Keith, 8,487	C 3
Keya Paha, 1,340	E 2
Kimball, 6,009	A 3
Knox, 11,723	G 2
Lancaster, 167,972	H 4
Lincoln, 29,538	D 4
Logan, 991	D 3
Loup, 854	E 3
Madison, 27,402	G 3
McPherson, 623	C 3
Merrick, 8,751	F 3
Morrill, 5,813	A 3
Nance, 5,142	F 3
Nemaha, 8,976	J 4
Nuckolls, 7,404	F 4
Otoe, 15,576	H 4
Pawnee, 4,473	H 4
Perkins, 3,423	C 4
Phelps, 9,553	E 4
Pierce, 8,493	G 2
Platte, 26,508	G 3
Polk, 6,468	G 3
Red Willow, 12,191	D 4
Richardson, 12,277	J 4
Rock, 2,231	E 2
Saline, 12,809	G 4
Sarpy, 63,696	H 3
Saunders, 17,018	H 3
Scotts Bluff, 36,432	A 3
Seward, 14,460	G 4
Sheridan, 7,285	B 2
Sherman, 4,725	F 3
Sioux, 2,034	A 2
Stanton, 5,758	G 3
Thayer, 7,779	G 4
Thomas, 954	D 3
Thurston, 6,942	H 2
Valley, 5,783	E 3
Washington, 13,310	H 3
Wayne, 10,400	G 2
Webster, 6,477	F 4
Wheeler, 1,054	F 3
York, 13,685	G 4

CITIES and TOWNS

Zip	Name/Pop.	Key
68301	Adams, 463	H 4
69210	Ainsworth⊙, 2,073	D 2
68620	Albion⊙, 2,074	F 3
68810	Alda, 456	F 4
68710	Allen, 309	H 2
69301	Alliance⊙, 6,862	A 2
68920	Alma⊙, 1,299	E 4
68814	Ansley, 631	E 3
68922	Arapahoe, 1,147	E 4
68815	Arcadia, 418	F 3
68002	Arlington, 910	H 3
69120	Arnold, 752	D 3
69121	Arthur⊙, 175	C 3
68003	Ashland, 2,176	H 3
68713	Atkinson, 1,406	E 2
68305	Auburn⊙, 3,650	J 4
68818	Aurora⊙, 3,180	F 4
68924	Axtell, 500	E 4
68004	Bancroft, 545	H 2
68622	Bartlett⊙, 193	F 3
69020	Bartley, 283	D 4
68714	Bassett⊙, 983	E 2
68715	Battle Creek, 1,158	G 3
69334	Bayard, 1,338	A 3
68310	Beatrice⊙, 12,389	H 4
68926	Beaver City⊙, 802	E 4
68313	Beaver Crossing, 400	G 4
68716	Beemer, 699	H 3
68005	Bellevue, 19,449	J 3
68624	Bellwood, 361	G 3
69021	Benkelman⊙, 1,349	C 4
68317	Bennet, 489	H 4
68007	Bennington, 683	H 3
68927	Bertrand, 662	E 4
69122	Big Springs, 472	B 3
68928	Bladen, 293	F 4
68008	Blair⊙, 6,106	H 3
68718	Bloomfield, 1,287	G 2
68930	Blue Hill, 1,201	F 4
68318	Blue Springs, 494	H 4
68010	Boys Town, 989	H 3
68319	Bradshaw, 347	G 4
69123	Brady, 311	D 3
68626	Brainard, 309	G 3
68821	Brewster⊙, 54	D 3
69336	Bridgeport⊙, 1,490	A 3
68822	Broken Bow⊙, 3,734	E 3
68321	Brownville, 174	J 4
69127	Brule, 423	C 3
68322	Bruning, 315	G 4
68823	Burwell⊙, 1,341	E 3
68722	Butte⊙, 575	F 2
68824	Cairo, 686	F 3
68825	Callaway, 523	D 3
69022	Cambridge, 1,145	D 4
68932	Campbell, 447	F 4
68015	Cedar Bluffs, 616	H 3
68627	Cedar Rapids, 449	F 3
68724	Center⊙, 111	G 2
68826	Central City⊙, 2,803	F 3
68017	Ceresco, 474	H 3
69337	Chadron⊙, 5,853	B 2
68725	Chambers, 321	F 2
68827	Chapman, 371	F 3
69129	Chappell⊙, 1,204	B 3
68327	Chester, 459	G 4
68628	Clarks, 480	G 3
68629	Clarkson, 805	G 3
68933	Clay Center⊙, 952	F 4
68726	Clearwater, 398	F 2
68727	Coleridge, 608	G 2
68601	Columbus⊙, 15,471	G 3
68329	Cook, 328	H 4
68331	Cortland, 326	H 4
69130	Cozad, 4,219	E 4
68019	Craig, 295	H 3
69339	Crawford, 1,291	A 2
68729	Creighton, 1,461	G 2
68333	Crete, 4,444	G 4
68730	Crofton, 677	G 2
69024	Culbertson, 801	C 4
69025	Curtis, 1,166	D 4
68731	Dakota City⊙, 1,057	H 2
69131	Dalton, 354	B 3
68831	Dannebrog, 384	F 3
68335	Davenport, 427	G 4
68632	David City⊙, 2,380	G 3
68020	Decatur, 679	H 2
68340	Deshler, 937	G 4
68341	De Witt, 651	G 4
68342	Diller, 287	H 4
69133	Dix, 342	A 3
68633	Dodge, 704	H 3
68832	Doniphan, 542	F 4
68343	Dorchester, 492	G 4
68634	Duncan, 298	G 3
68347	Eagle, 441	H 4
68935	Edgar, 707	F 4
68636	Elgin, 917	F 3
68022	Elkhorn, 1,184	H 3
68836	Elm Creek, 798	E 4
68349	Elmwood, 548	H 4
68937	Elwood⊙, 601	E 4
68733	Emerson, 850	H 2
69028	Eustis, 400	D 4
68735	Ewing, 552	F 2
68351	Exeter, 759	G 4
68352	Fairbury⊙, 5,265	G 4
68938	Fairfield, 487	G 4
68354	Fairmont, 761	G 4
68355	Falls City⊙, 5,444	J 4
68358	Firth, 328	H 4
68023	Fort Calhoun, 642	J 3
68939	Franklin⊙, 1,193	E 4
68025	Fremont⊙, 22,962	H 3
68359	Friend, 1,126	G 4
68638	Fullerton⊙, 1,444	F 3
68361	Geneva⊙, 2,275	G 4
68640	Genoa, 1,174	G 3
69341	Gering⊙, 5,639	A 3
68840	Gibbon, 1,388	F 4
68841	Giltner, 408	F 4
68941	Glenvil, 332	F 4
69343	Gordon, 2,106	B 2
69138	Gothenburg, 3,154	D 4
68801	Grand Island⊙, 31,269	F 4
69140	Grant⊙, 1,099	C 4
68842	Greeley⊙, 580	F 3
68366	Greenwood, 506	H 3
68028	Gretna, 1,557	H 3
68942	Guide Rock, 318	F 4
68843	Hampton, 387	G 4
69345	Harrisburg⊙, 80	A 3
69346	Harrison⊙, 377	A 2
68739	Hartington⊙, 1,581	G 2
68944	Harvard, 1,230	F 4
68901	Hastings⊙, 23,580	F 4
69032	Hayes Center⊙, 237	C 4
69347	Hay Springs, 682	B 2
68370	Hebron⊙, 1,667	G 4
69348	Hemingford, 734	A 2
68371	Henderson, 901	G 4
68029	Herman, 323	H 3
69143	Hershey, 526	D 3
68372	Hickman, 415	H 4
68947	Hildreth, 352	E 4
68948	Holbrook, 307	D 4
68949	Holdrege⊙, 5,635	E 4
68030	Homer, 457	H 2
68031	Hooper, 895	H 3
68641	Howells, 682	H 3
68376	Humboldt, 1,194	J 4

Miles of pens hold thousands of head of cattle in the Union Stockyards, Omaha. Next stop — the meat packers' plant.

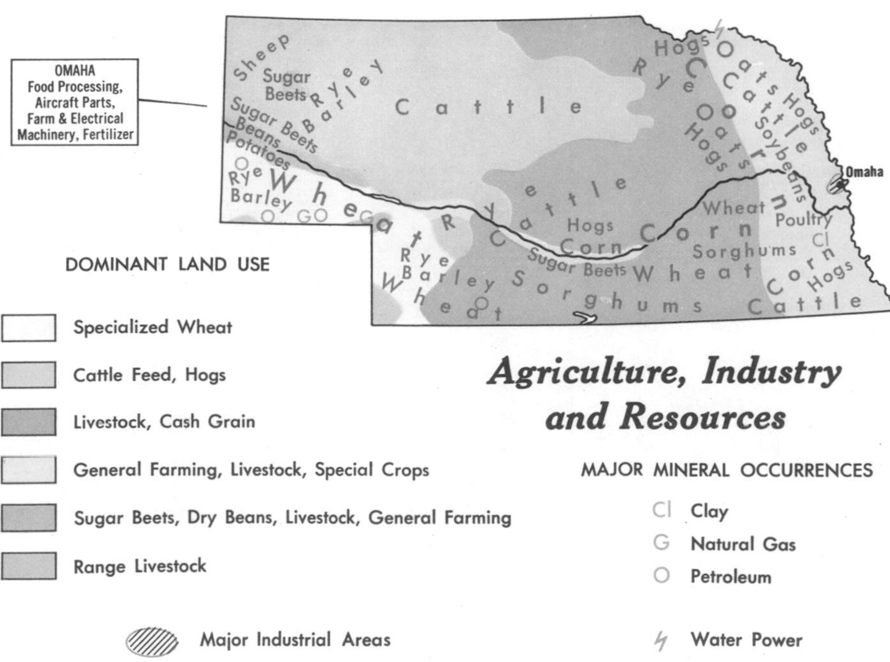

Agriculture, Industry and Resources

MAJOR MINERAL OCCURRENCES

- Cl Clay
- G Natural Gas
- O Petroleum
- Water Power

Zip	Place	Key
68642	Humphrey, 862	G 3
69350	Hyannis⊙, 345	C 3
69033	Imperial⊙, 1,589	C 4
69034	Indianola, 672	D 4
68378	Johnson, 350	J 4
68955	Juniata, 480	F 4
68847	Kearney⊙, 19,181	E 4
68956	Kenesaw, 728	F 4
68034	Kennard, 336	H 3
69145	Kimball⊙, 3,680	A 3
68745	Laurel, 1,009	G 2
68046	La Vista, 4,807	J 3
68957	Lawrence, 343	F 4
68643	Leigh, 501	G 3
69147	Lewellen, 376	B 3
68850	Lexington⊙, 5,618	E 4
68501	Lincoln (cap.)⊙, 149,518	H 4
	Lincoln, ‡167,972	H 4
68644	Lindsay, 291	G 3
69149	Lodgepole, 407	B 3
69217	Long Pine, 363	E 2
68958	Loomis, 323	E 4
68037	Louisville, 1,036	H 3
68853	Loup City⊙, 1,456	E 3
69352	Lyman, 561	A 3
68746	Lynch, 375	F 2
68038	Lyons, 1,177	H 3
68039	Macy, 550	H 2
68748	Madison⊙, 1,595	G 3
69038	Maywood, 309	D 4
69001	McCook⊙, 8,285	D 4
68401	McCool Junction, 289	G 4
68041	Mead, 488	H 3
68752	Meadow Grove, 372	G 2
68856	Merna, 322	E 3
68405	Milford, 1,846	H 4
68137	Millard, 7,460	H 3
68406	Milligan, 319	G 4
69356	Minatare, 939	A 3
68959	Minden⊙, 2,669	F 4
69357	Mitchell, 1,842	A 3
69358	Morrill, 937	A 3
69152	Muilen⊙, 667	C 2
68409	Murray, 286	J 4
68410	Nebraska City⊙, 7,441	J 4
68413	Nehawka, 298	H 4
68756	Neligh⊙, 1,764	G 2
68961	Nelson⊙, 746	F 4
68757	Newcastle, 347	H 2
68758	Newman Grove, 863	G 3
68760	Niobrara, 602	G 2
68701	Norfolk, 16,607	G 2
68649	North Bend, 1,350	H 3
68859	North Loup, 441	F 3
69101	North Platte⊙, 19,447	D 3
68761	Oakdale, 322	F 2
68045	Oakland, 1,355	H 3
68415	Odell, 349	H 4
69153	Ogallala⊙, 4,976	C 3
* 68101	Omaha⊙, 347,328	J 3
	Omaha, ‡540,142	J 3
68763	O'Neill⊙, 3,753	F 2
68764	Orchard, 467	F 2
68862	Ord⊙, 2,439	F 3
68966	Orleans, 592	E 4
68651	Osceola⊙, 923	G 3
69154	Oshkosh⊙, 1,067	B 3
68765	Osmond, 883	G 2
68863	Overton, 506	E 4
68967	Oxford, 1,116	E 4
69040	Palisade, 372	C 4
68864	Palmer, 391	F 3
68418	Palmyra, 386	H 4
68046	Papillion⊙, 5,606	J 3
† 68801	Parkview, 1,089	F 4
68420	Pawnee City⊙, 1,267	H 4
69155	Paxton, 503	C 3
68047	Pender⊙, 1,229	H 2
68421	Peru, 1,380	J 4
68652	Petersburg, 370	G 3
68865	Phillips, 341	F 4
68767	Pierce⊙, 1,360	G 2
68768	Pilger, 470	G 2
68769	Plainview, 1,494	G 2
68653	Platte Center, 384	G 3
68048	Plattsmouth⊙, 6,371	J 3
68424	Plymouth, 424	G 4
68654	Polk, 413	G 3
68770	Ponca⊙, 984	H 2
69156	Potter, 356	A 3
68050	Prague, 291	H 3
68127	Ralston, 4,265	J 3
68771	Randolph, 1,130	G 2
68869	Ravenna, 1,356	F 4
68970	Red Cloud⊙, 2,195	F 4
68658	Rising City, 344	G 3
68431	Rulo, 299	J 4
69360	Rushville⊙, 1,137	B 2
68660	Saint Edward, 853	G 3
68873	Saint Paul⊙, 2,026	F 3
68874	Sargent, 789	E 3
68661	Schuyler⊙, 3,597	G 3
68875	Scotia, 354	F 3
69361	Scottsbluff, 14,507	A 3
68057	Scribner, 1,031	H 3
68434	Seward⊙, 5,294	H 4
68662	Shelby, 647	G 3
68876	Shelton, 1,028	F 4
68436	Shickley, 385	G 4
69162	Sidney⊙, 6,403	B 3
68663	Silver Creek, 483	G 3
68664	Snyder, 383	H 3
68776	South Sioux City, 7,920	H 2
68665	Spalding, 676	F 3
68777	Spencer, 606	F 2
68059	Springfield, 795	H 3
68778	Springview⊙, 260	E 2
68779	Stanton⊙, 1,363	G 3
69163	Stapleton⊙, 311	D 3
68443	Sterling, 476	H 4
69042	Stockville⊙, 61	D 4
69043	Stratton, 481	C 4
68666	Stromsburg, 1,215	G 3
68780	Stuart, 561	E 2
68978	Superior, 2,779	F 4
69165	Sutherland, 840	C 3
68979	Sutton, 1,361	G 4
68446	Syracuse, 1,562	H 4
68447	Table Rock, 429	H 4
68448	Talmage, 285	H 4
68879	Taylor⊙, 240	E 3
68450	Tecumseh⊙, 2,058	H 4
68061	Tekamah⊙, 1,848	H 3
† 69341	Terrytown, 747	A 3
69166	Thedford⊙, 303	D 3
68781	Tilden, 947	G 2
69044	Trenton⊙, 770	D 4
69167	Tryon⊙, 138	C 3
68669	Ulysses, 312	G 3
68456	Utica, 602	G 4
69201	Valentine⊙, 2,662	D 2
68064	Valley, 1,595	H 3
68065	Valparaiso, 415	H 3
68783	Verdigre, 570	F 2
68066	Wahoo⊙, 3,835	H 3
68784	Wakefield, 1,160	H 2
68067	Walthill, 897	H 2
69045	Wauneta, 738	C 4
68786	Wausa, 720	G 2
68462	Waverly, 1,152	H 4
68787	Wayne⊙, 5,379	G 2
68463	Weeping Water, 1,143	J 4
68464	Western, 344	G 4
68070	Weston, 285	H 3
68788	West Point⊙, 3,385	H 3
68465	Wilber⊙, 1,483	G 4
68071	Winnebago, 675	H 2
68790	Winside, 453	G 2
68791	Wisner, 1,315	H 3
68882	Wolbach, 366	F 3
68883	Wood River, 1,061	F 4
68466	Wymore, 1,790	H 4
68467	York⊙, 6,778	G 4
68073	Yutan, 507	H 3

⊙ County seat.
‡ Population of metropolitan area.
† Zip of nearest p.o.
* Multiple zips

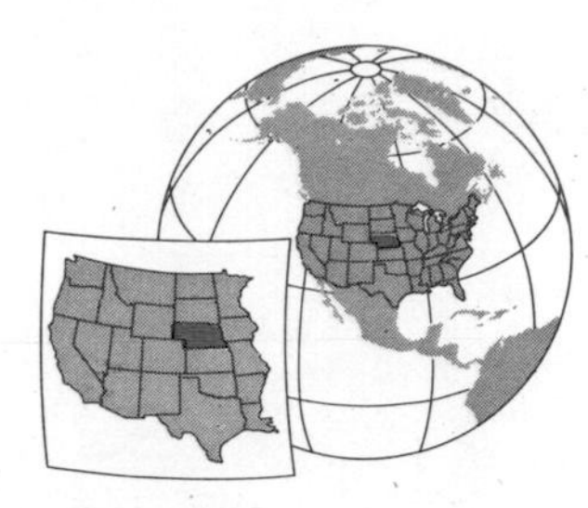

AREA 77,227 sq. mi.
POPULATION 1,483,791
CAPITAL Lincoln
LARGEST CITY Omaha
HIGHEST POINT 5,426 ft. (Kimball Co.)
SETTLED IN 1847
ADMITTED TO UNION March 1, 1867
POPULAR NAME Cornhusker State
STATE FLOWER Goldenrod
STATE BIRD Western Meadowlark

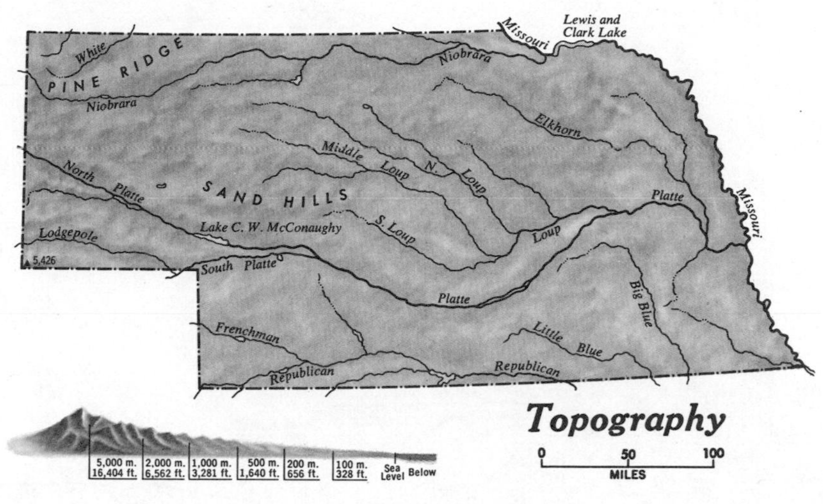

Topography

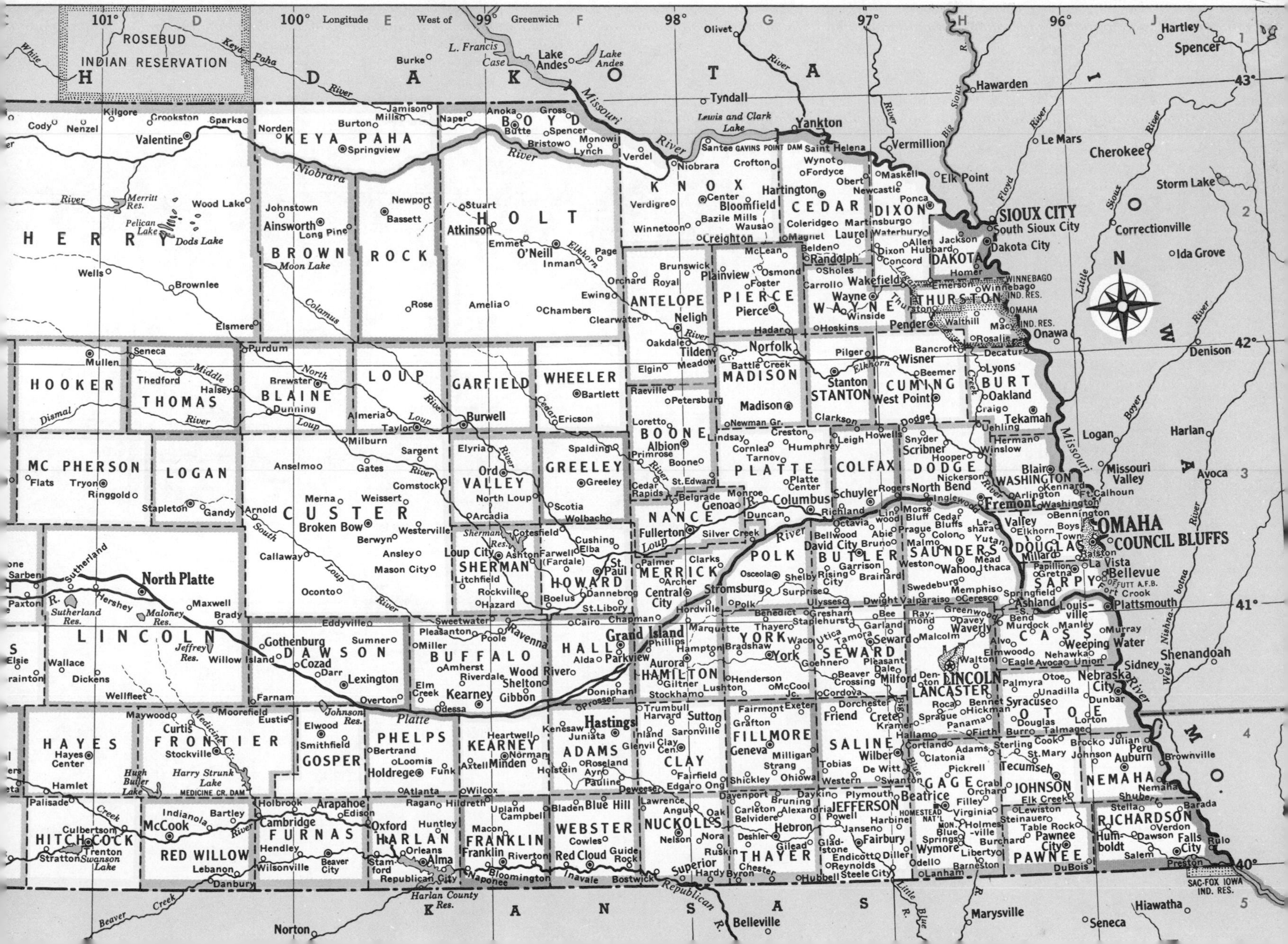

5,000 m. 16,404 ft. | 2,000 m. 6,562 ft. | 1,000 m. 3,281 ft. | 500 m. 1,640 ft. | 200 m. 656 ft. | 100 m. 328 ft. | Sea Level | Below

0 50 100 MILES

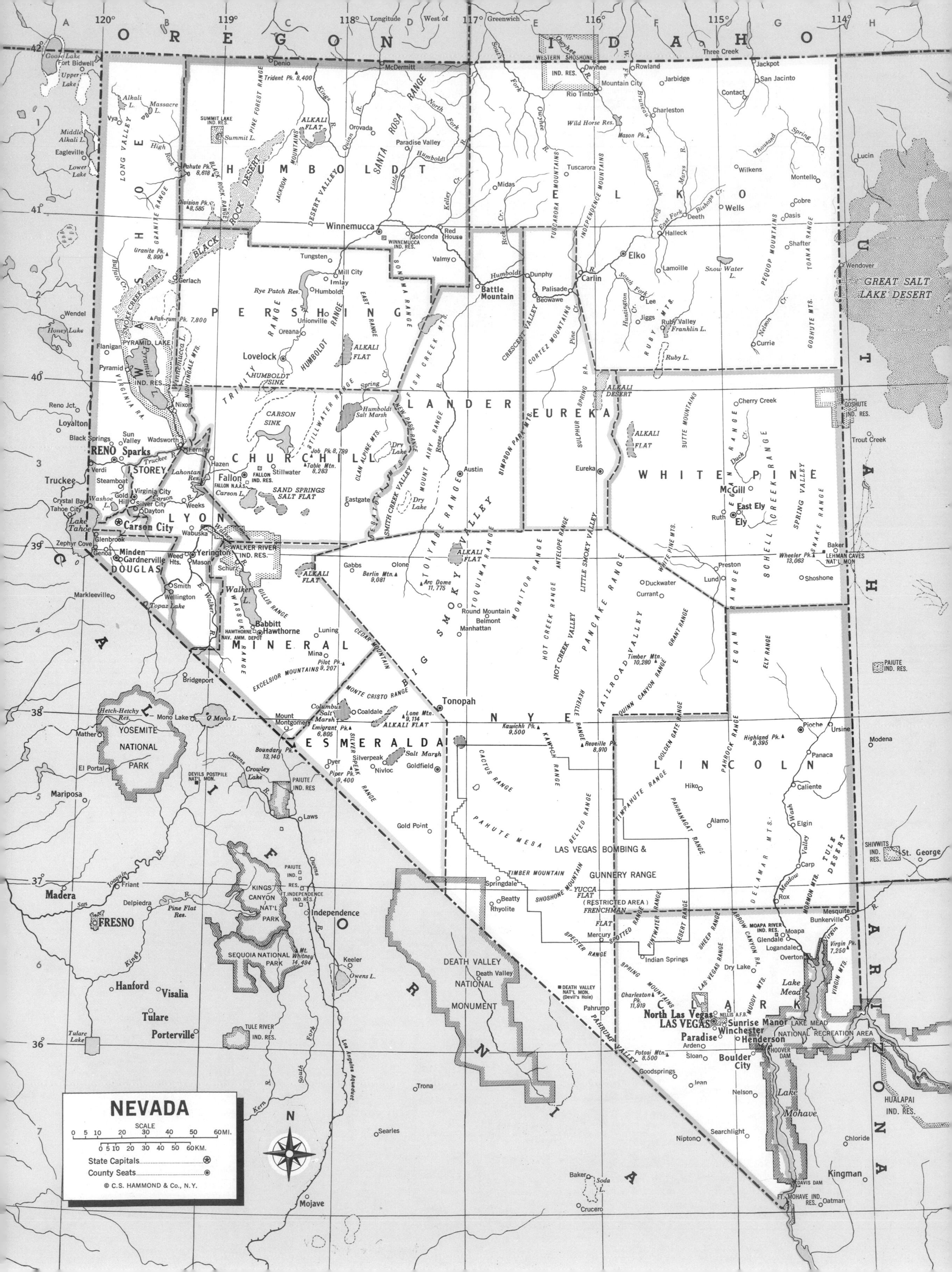

NEVADA
SCALE
0 5 10 20 30 40 50 60 MI.
0 5 10 20 30 40 50 60 KM.
State Capitals
County Seats
© C.S. HAMMOND & Co., N.Y.
N
Longitude West of Greenwich
120° 119° 118° 117° 116° 115° 114°
42° 41° 40° 39° 38° 37° 36°
A B C D E F G H
1 2 3 4 5 6 7
OREGON
IDAHO
UTAH
ARIZONA
CALIFORNIA
HUMBOLDT
PERSHING
WASHOE
CHURCHILL
LANDER
EUREKA
ELKO
WHITE PINE
STOREY
LYON
DOUGLAS
MINERAL
ESMERALDA
NYE
LINCOLN
CLARK
Carson City
RENO
Sparks
Winnemucca
Elko
Ely
East Ely
McGill
Ruth
Tonopah
Goldfield
Hawthorne
Babbitt
Fallon
Lovelock
Battle Mountain
Austin
Eureka
Pioche
Yerington
Minden
Gardnerville
LAS VEGAS
North Las Vegas
Sunrise Manor
Winchester
Paradise
Henderson
Boulder City
Carlin
Wells
Denio
McDermitt
Jackpot
San Jacinto
Jarbidge
Contact
Rowland
Mountain City
Owyhee
Rio Tinto
Charleston
Tuscarora
Midas
Golconda
Red House
Valmy
Tungsten
Mill City
Imlay
Humboldt
Unionville
Oreana
Gerlach
Vya
Orovada
Paradise Valley
Dunphy
Palisade
Beowawe
Halleck
Deeth
Lamoille
Lee
Jiggs
Ruby Valley
Currie
Wilkens
Montello
Cobre
Oasis
Shafter
Wendover
Lucin
Cherry Creek
Trout Creek
Baker
Preston
Lund
Shoshone
Duckwater
Currant
Round Mountain
Belmont
Manhattan
Gabbs
Ione
Luning
Mina
Schurz
Mason
Weed Hts.
Smith
Wellington
Wabuska
Weeks
Hazen
Stillwater
Eastgate
Wadsworth
Nixon
Fernley
Sun Valley
Verdi
Steamboat
Virginia City
Gold Hill
Silver City
Dayton
Glenbrook
Genoa
Zephyr Cove
Crystal Bay
Tahoe City
Truckee
Black Springs
Reno Jct.
Loyalton
Flanigan
Pyramid
Wendel
Eagleville
Fort Bidwell
Markleeville
Topaz Lake
Bridgeport
Mono Lake
Mount Montgomery
Coaldale
Dyer
Silverpeak
Nivloc
Gold Point
Laws
Beatty
Rhyolite
Springdale
Mercury
Indian Springs
Pahrump
Arden
Sloan
Goodsprings
Jean
Nelson
Searchlight
Nipton
Hiko
Alamo
Caliente
Panaca
Ursine
Modena
Elgin
Carp
Rox
Mesquite
Bunkerville
Moapa
Glendale
Logandale
Overton
Dry Lake
St. George
Kingman
Chloride
Oatman
Independence
Keeler
Death Valley
Trona
Searles
Baker
Crucero
Mojave
Fresno
Madera
Friant
Delpiedra
Mariposa
El Portal
Mather
Hanford
Visalia
Tulare
Porterville
YOSEMITE NATIONAL PARK
KINGS CANYON NAT'L PARK
SEQUOIA NATIONAL PARK
DEATH VALLEY NATIONAL MONUMENT
DEVILS POSTPILE NAT'L MON.
DEATH VALLEY NAT'L MON. (Devil's Hole)
LEHMAN CAVES NAT'L MON.
LAKE MEAD NATIONAL RECREATION AREA
LAS VEGAS BOMBING & GUNNERY RANGE
YUCCA FLAT (RESTRICTED AREA)
FRENCHMAN FLAT
HAWTHORNE NAV. AMM. DEPOT
FALLON N.A.A.S.
NELLIS A.F.B.
HOOVER DAM
DAVIS DAM
WESTERN SHOSHONE IND. RES.
SUMMIT LAKE IND. RES.
WINNEMUCCA IND. RES.
FALLON IND. RES.
WALKER RIVER IND. RES.
GOSHUTE IND. RES.
PAIUTE IND. RES.
SHIVWITS IND. RES.
MOAPA RIVER IND. RES.
HUALAPAI IND. RES.
FT. MOHAVE IND. RES.
TULE RIVER IND. RES.
INDEPENDENCE IND. RES.
IND. RES.
GREAT SALT LAKE DESERT
BLACK ROCK DESERT
SMOKE CREEK DESERT
ALKALI DESERT
TULE DESERT
ALKALI FLAT
SAND SPRINGS SALT FLAT
CARSON SINK
HUMBOLDT SINK
Humboldt Salt Marsh
Columbus Salt Marsh
Salt Marsh
PYRAMID LAKE
Pyramid L.
Winnemucca L.
Lake Tahoe
Walker L.
Rye Patch Res.
Lahontan Res.
Carson L.
Wild Horse Res.
Snow Water L.
Franklin L.
Ruby L.
Lake Mead
Lake Mohave
Owens L.
Crowley Lake
Mono L.
Honey Lake
Goose Lake
Upper Lake
Middle Alkali L.
Lower Lake
Summit L.
Washoe L.
Tulare Lake
Pine Flat Res.
Hetch-Hetchy Res.
Soda L.
Dry Lake
Humboldt R.
Truckee R.
Carson R.
Walker R.
E. Walker R.
Reese R.
Quinn R.
Kings R.
Little Humboldt R.
Owyhee R.
South Fork
North Fork
Bruneau R.
Marys R.
Thousand Spring Cr.
Virgin R.
Meadow Valley Wash
Owens R.
Kern R.
Los Angeles Aqueduct
PAHRUMP VALLEY
LONG VALLEY
DESERT VALLEY
SMITH CREEK VALLEY
BIG SMOKY VALLEY
CRESCENT VALLEY
HOT CREEK VALLEY
LITTLE SMOKY VALLEY
RAILROAD VALLEY
SPRING VALLEY
GRANITE RANGE
PINE FOREST RANGE
BLACK ROCK RANGE
JACKSON MOUNTAINS
SANTA ROSA RANGE
SONOMA RANGE
EAST RANGE
HUMBOLDT RANGE
TRINITY RANGE
STILLWATER RANGE
CLAN ALPINE MTS.
DESATOYA MTS.
NEW PASS RANGE
FISH CREEK MTS.
SHOSHONE MTS.
TOIYABE RANGE
TOQUIMA RANGE
MONITOR RANGE
ANTELOPE RANGE
HOT CREEK RANGE
PANCAKE RANGE
SIMPSON PARK MTS.
CORTEZ MOUNTAINS
SULPHUR SPRING RA.
TUSCARORA MOUNTAINS
INDEPENDENCE MOUNTAINS
RUBY MTS.
PEQUOP MOUNTAINS
TOANA RANGE
GOSHUTE MTS.
BUTTE MOUNTAINS
EGAN RANGE
SCHELL CREEK RANGE
SNAKE RANGE
WHITE PINE MTS.
GRANT RANGE
QUINN CANYON RANGE
REVEILLE RANGE
KAWICH RANGE
CACTUS RANGE
PAHUTE MESA
BELTED RANGE
TIMBER MOUNTAIN
SHOSHONE MOUNTAIN
GOLDEN GATE RANGE
TIMPAHUTE RANGE
PAHRANAGAT RANGE
PAHROCK RANGE
ELY RANGE
DELAMAR MTS.
MORMON MTS.
VIRGIN MTS.
SPOTTED RANGE
PINTWATER RANGE
DESERT RANGE
SHEEP RANGE
ARROW CANYON RA.
LAS VEGAS RANGE
MUDDY MTS.
SPRING MOUNTAINS
SPECTER RANGE
SILVER PEAK RANGE
MONTE CRISTO RANGE
EXCELSIOR MOUNTAINS
CEDAR MOUNTAIN
WASSUK RANGE
GILLIS RANGE
MOUNT AIRY RANGE
VIRGINIA RA.
NIGHTINGALE MTS.
Trident Pk. 8,400
Pahute Pk. 8,618
Division Pk. 8,585
Granite Pk. 8,990
Pah-rum Pk. 7,800
Job Pk. 8,799
Table Mtn. 8,283
Berlin Mtn. 9,081
Arc Dome 11,775
Mason Pk.
Wheeler Pk. 13,063
Pilot Pk. 9,207
Lone Mtn. 9,114
Emigrant Pk. 6,805
Boundary Pk. 13,140
Piper Pk. 9,400
Kawichi Pk. 9,500
Reveille Pk. 8,910
Timber Mtn. 10,280
Highland Pk. 9,395
Charleston Pk. 11,919
Potosi Mtn. 8,500
Virgin Pk. 7,250
Mt. Whitney 14,494
Three Creek

COUNTIES

County	Key
Carson City (city), 15,468	B 3
Churchill, 10,513	C 3
Clark, 273,288	F 6
Douglas, 6,882	B 4
Elko, 13,958	F 1
Esmeralda, 629	D 5
Eureka, 948	E 3
Humboldt, 6,375	C 1
Lander, 2,666	D 3
Lincoln, 2,557	F 5
Lyon, 8,221	B 3
Mineral, 7,051	C 4
Nye, 5,599	E 4
Pershing, 2,670	C 2
Storey, 695	B 3
Washoe, 121,068	B 2
White Pine, 10,150	F 3

CITIES and TOWNS

	Zip	Name/Pop.	Key
	89001	Alamo, 300	F 5
	89310	Austin⊙, 300	E 3
	89416	Babbitt, 1,579	C 4
	89311	Baker, 75	G 3
	89820	Battle Mountain, 1,856	E 2
	89003	Beatty, 570	E 6
	89045	Belmont, 25	E 4
	89821	Beowawe, 104	E 2
	89508	Black Springs, 2,500	B 3
	89005	Boulder City, 5,223	G 7
	89007	Bunkerville, 150	G 6
	89008	Caliente, 916	G 5
	89822	Carlin, 1,313	E 2
	89009	Carp, 32	G 5
	89701	Carson City (cap.), 15,468	B 3
	89801	Charleston, 14	F 1
	89312	Cherry Creek, 75	G 3
	89049	Coaldale, 31	D 4
	89830	Cobre, 14	G 1
	89825	Contact, 9	G 1
	89402	Crystal Bay, 950	A 3
	89314	Currant, 30	F 4
	89313	Currie, 15	G 2
	89403	Dayton, 350	B 3
	89823	Deeth, 27	F 1
	89404	Denio, 28	C 1
	89040	Dry Lake, 5	G 6
	89314	Duckwater, 85	F 4
	89821	Dunphy, 25	E 2
	89010	Dyer, 60	C 5
	89315	East Ely, 1,992	G 3
	89406	Eastgate, 17	D 3
	89112	East Las Vegas, 6,501	F 6
	89009	Elgin, 8	G 5
	89801	Elko⊙, 7,621	F 2
	89301	Ely⊙, 4,176	G 3
	89316	Eureka⊙, 300	E 3
	89406	Fallon⊙, 2,959	C 3
	89408	Fernley, 750	B 3
	89409	Gabbs, 874	D 4
	89410	Gardnerville, 800	B 4
	89411	Genoa, 170	B 4
	89412	Gerlach, 150	B 2
	89413	Glenbrook, 800	B 3
	89025	Glendale, 20	G 6
	89414	Golconda, 150	D 2
	89013	Goldfield⊙, 213	D 5
	89440	Gold Hill, 50	B 3
	89013	Gold Point, 10	D 5
	89019	Goodsprings, 120	F 7
	89824	Halleck, 50	F 2
	89415	Hawthorne⊙, 3,539	C 4
	89417	Hazen, 60	C 3
	89015	Henderson, 16,395	G 6
	89017	Hiko, 150	F 5
†	89418	Humboldt, 12	C 2
	89418	Imlay, 150	C 2
	89018	Indian Springs, 500	F 6
†	89310	Ione, 15	D 4
	89825	Jackpot, 400	G 1
	89826	Jarbidge, 25	F 1
	89019	Jean, 100	F 7
	89827	Jiggs, 6	F 2
	89828	Lamoille, 51	F 2
*	89101	Las Vegas⊙, 125,787	F 6
		Las Vegas, ‡273,288	F 6
	89829	Lee, 180	F 2
	89021	Logandale, 410	G 6
	89419	Lovelock⊙, 1,571	C 2
	89317	Lund, 300	F 4
	89420	Luning, 55	C 4
	89022	Manhattan, 28	E 4
†	89447	Mason, 200	B 4
	89421	McDermitt, 300	D 1
	89318	McGill, 2,164	G 3
	89023	Mercury, 2,200	E 6
	89024	Mesquite, 500	G 6
†	89414	Midas, 6	E 1
†	89418	Mill City, 4	D 2
	89422	Mina, 375	C 4
	89423	Minden⊙, 520	B 4
	89025	Moapa, 250	G 6
	89830	Montello, 150	G 1
	89831	Mountain City, 80	F 1
†	89422	Mount Montgomery, 10	C 5
†	89046	Nelson, 67	G 7
	89424	Nixon, 300	B 3
	89030	North Las Vegas, 36,216	F 6
†	89830	Oasis, 5	G 1
†	89419	Oreana, 18	C 2
	89425	Orovada, 250	D 1
	89040	Overton, 900	G 6
	89832	Owyhee, 100	F 1
	89041	Pahrump, 400	E 6
†	89822	Palisade, 5	E 2
	89042	Panaca, 500	G 5
†	89101	Paradise, 24,477	F 6
	89426	Paradise Valley, 110	D 1
	89043	Pioche⊙, 525	G 5
†	89301	Preston, 44	G 4
†	89414	Red House, 4	D 2
*	89501	Reno⊙, 72,863	B 3
		Reno, ‡121,068	B 3
†	89003	Rhyolite, 8	E 6
†	89831	Rio Tinto, 5	E 1
	89045	Round Mountain, 100	E 4
†	89831	Rowland, 10	F 1
†	89009	Rox, 12	G 6
	89833	Ruby Valley, 225	F 2
	89319	Ruth, 750	F 3
†	89825	San Jacinto, 8	G 1
	89427	Schurz, 350	C 4
	89046	Searchlight, 279	F 7
†	89835	Shafter, 7	G 2
†	89301	Shoshone, 15	G 4
	89428	Silver City, 100	B 3
	89047	Silverpeak, 80	D 5
†	89114	Sloan, 25	F 7
	89430	Smith, 300	B 4
	89431	Sparks, 24,187	B 3
	89436	Steamboat, 560	B 3
†	89406	Stillwater, 30	C 3
†	89101	Sunrise Manor, 10,886	F 6
†	89431	Sun Valley, 2,414	B 3
	89049	Tonopah⊙, 1,716	D 4
	89834	Tuscarora, 15	E 1
†	89418	Unionville, 18	C 2
†	89043	Ursine, 40	G 5
	89438	Valmy, 50	D 2
	89439	Verdi, 100	B 3
	89440	Virginia City⊙, 300	B 3
†	96104	Vya, 12	B 1
†	89447	Wabuska, 50	B 3
	89442	Wadsworth, 375	B 3
	89443	Weed Heights, 750	B 4
†	89447	Weeks, 15	B 3
	89444	Wellington, 100	B 4
	89835	Wells, 1,081	G 1
†	89835	Wilkins, 6	G 1
†	89101	Winchester, 13,981	F 6
	89445	Winnemucca⊙, 3,587	D 2
	89447	Yerington⊙, 2,010	B 4
	89448	Zephyr Cove, 400	A 3

⊙ County seat.
‡ Population of metropolitan area.
† Zip of nearest p.o.
* Multiple zips

AREA 110,540 sq. mi.
POPULATION 488,738
CAPITAL Carson City
LARGEST CITY Las Vegas
HIGHEST POINT Boundary Pk. 13,140 ft.
SETTLED IN 1850
ADMITTED TO UNION October 31, 1864
POPULAR NAME Silver State
STATE FLOWER Sagebrush
STATE BIRD Mountain Bluebird

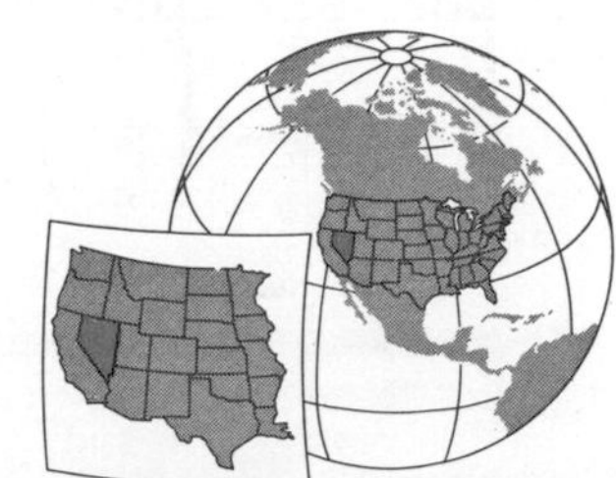

Bill McKinney — Shostal Associates

An incandescent oasis in the Nevada desert, Reno beckons travelers to its varied diversions — from games of chance and nightclub entertainment to annual rodeos and skiing in the Sierra Nevada.

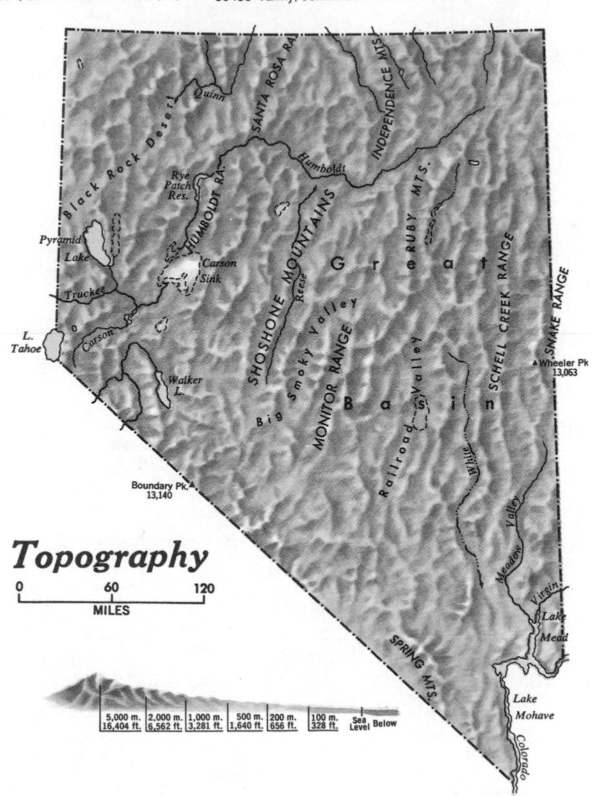

Topography

0 60 120 MILES

Agriculture, Industry and Resources

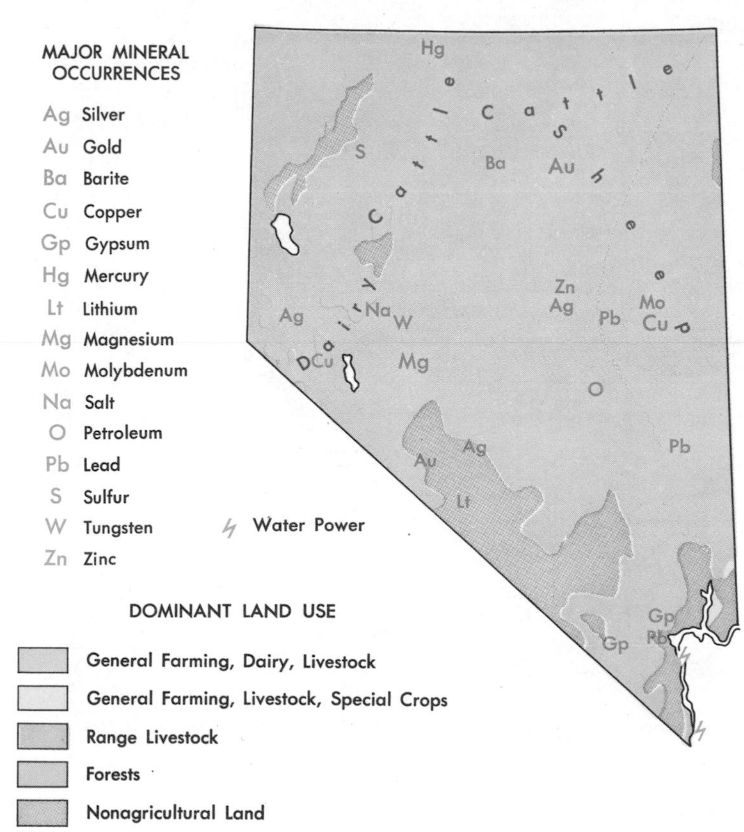

MAJOR MINERAL OCCURRENCES

Ag Silver
Au Gold
Ba Barite
Cu Copper
Gp Gypsum
Hg Mercury
Lt Lithium
Mg Magnesium
Mo Molybdenum
Na Salt
O Petroleum
Pb Lead
S Sulfur
W Tungsten
Zn Zinc
Water Power

DOMINANT LAND USE

General Farming, Dairy, Livestock
General Farming, Livestock, Special Crops
Range Livestock
Forests
Nonagricultural Land

NEW HAMPSHIRE
and VERMONT
SCALE
0 5 10 15 20 25 MI.
0 5 10 15 20 25 KM.
State Capitals
County Seats
© C.S. HAMMOND & Co., N.Y.
CANADA
QUÉBEC
NEW YORK
MAINE
MASSACHUSETTS
VERMONT
NEW HAMPSHIRE
GRAND ISLE
FRANKLIN
ORLEANS
ESSEX
LAMOILLE
CALEDONIA
CHITTENDEN
WASHINGTON
ADDISON
ORANGE
RUTLAND
WINDSOR
BENNINGTON
WINDHAM
COOS
GRAFTON
CARROLL
BELKNAP
SULLIVAN
MERRIMACK
STRAFFORD
CHESHIRE
HILLSBORO
ROCKINGHAM
ATLANTIC OCEAN
LAKE CHAMPLAIN
Montpelier
Concord
Burlington
Rutland
Manchester
Nashua
Portsmouth
Longitude West of Greenwich
73°
72°
71°
45°
44°
43°

NEW HAMPSHIRE

COUNTIES

Belknap, 32,367 D 4
Carroll, 18,548 E 4
Cheshire, 52,364 C 6
Coos, 34,291 E 2
Grafton, 54,914 D 4
Hillsboro, 223,941 D 6
Merrimack, 80,925 D 5
Rockingham, 138,951 E 5
Strafford, 70,431 E 5
Sullivan, 30,949 C 5

CITIES and TOWNS

Zip *Name/Pop.* *Key*
03601 Acworth, ▵459 C 5
† 03864 Albany, ▵259 E 4
† 03222 Alexandria, ▵466 D 4
† 03275 Allenstown, ▵2,732 E 5
03602 Alstead, ▵1,185 C 5
03602 Alstead, 450 C 5
03809 Alton, ▵1,647 E 5
03809 Alton, 450 E 5
03031 Amherst, ▵4,605 D 6
03810 Amherst, 600 D 6
03216 Andover, ▵1,138 D 5
03216 Andover, 500 D 5
03440 Antrim, ▵2,122 D 5
03440 Antrim, 750 D 5
03217 Ashland, ▵1,599 D 4
03217 Ashland, 1,391 D 4
03441 Ashuelot, 750 C 6
03811 Atkinson, ▵2,291 E 6
03032 Auburn, ▵2,035 E 5
03218 Barnstead, ▵1,119 E 5
03218 Barnstead, 400 E 5
† 03825 Barrington, ▵1,865 F 5
03812 Bartlett, ▵1,098 E 3
03812 Bartlett, 600 E 3
03740 Bath, ▵607 D 3
03102 Bedford, ▵5,859 D 6
03220 Belmont, ▵2,493 E 5
03220 Belmont, 900 E 5
03442 Bennington, ▵639 D 5
† 03785 Benton, ▵194 D 3
03570 Berlin, 15,256 E 3
03574 Bethlehem, ▵1,142 D 3
03574 Bethlehem, 500 D 3
03301 Boscawen, ▵3,162 D 5
† 03301 Bow Mills, 600 D 5
03221 Bradford, ▵679 D 5
† 03833 Brentwood, ▵1,468 E 6
03575 Bretton Woods, 6 E 3
† 03222 Bridgewater, ▵398 D 4
03222 Bristol, ▵1,670 D 4
03222 Bristol, 1,080 D 4
† 03872 Brookfield, ▵198 E 4
03033 Brookline, ▵1,167 D 6
03223 Campton, ▵1,171 D 4
03741 Canaan, ▵1,923 C 4
03741 Canaan, 500 C 4
03034 Candia, ▵1,997 E 5
† 03079 Canobie Lake, 500 E 6
03224 Canterbury, ▵895 D 5
† 03595 Carroll, ▵310 D 3
03813 Center Conway, 450 E 4
03226 Center Harbor, ▵540 E 4
03814 Center Ossipee, 550 E 4
03603 Charlestown, ▵3,274 C 5
03603 Charlestown, 1,285 C 5
† 04037 Chatham, ▵134 E 3
03036 Chester, ▵1,382 E 6
03443 Chesterfield, ▵1,817 C 6
03443 Chesterfield, 450 C 5
† 03258 Chichester, ▵1,083 E 5
03743 Claremont, 14,221 C 5
† 05902 Clarksville, ▵166 E 1
03576 Colebrook, ▵2,094 E 2
03576 Colebrook, 1,070 E 2
03301 Concord (cap.)⊙, 30,022 D 5
03229 Contoocook, 975 D 5
03818 Conway, ▵4,865 E 4
03818 Conway, 1,489 E 4
† 03753 Croydon, ▵396 C 5
† 03598 Dalton, ▵425 D 3
03230 Danbury, ▵489 D 4
03819 Danville, ▵924 E 6
03037 Deerfield, ▵1,178 E 5
† 03244 Deering, ▵578 D 5
03038 Derry, ▵11,712 E 6
03038 Derry, 6,090 E 6

NEW HAMPSHIRE
AREA 9,304 sq. mi.
POPULATION 737,681
CAPITAL Concord
LARGEST CITY Manchester
HIGHEST POINT Mt. Washington 6,288 ft.
SETTLED IN 1623
ADMITTED TO UNION June 21, 1788
POPULAR NAME Granite State
STATE FLOWER Purple Lilac
STATE BIRD Purple Finch

† 03266 Dorchester, ▵141 D 4
03820 Dover⊙, 20,850 F 5
03444 Dublin, ▵837 C 6
† 03588 Dummer, ▵225 E 2
† 03301 Dunbarton, ▵825 D 5
03824 Durham, ▵8,869 F 5
03824 Durham, 7,221 F 5
03231 East Andover, 450 D 5
03041 East Derry, 600 E 6
03827 East Kingston, ▵838 F 6
† 03580 Easton, ▵92 D 3
03446 East Swanzey, 500 C 6
† 03894 East Wolfeboro, 400 E 4
03832 Eaton, ▵221 E 4
† 03264 Ellsworth, ▵13 D 4
03748 Enfield, ▵2,345 C 4
03748 Enfield, 1,408 C 4
03042 Epping, ▵2,356 E 5
03042 Epping, 1,097 E 5
03234 Epsom, ▵1,469 E 5
03579 Errol, ▵199 E 2
03750 Etna, 550 C 4
03833 Exeter, ▵8,892 F 6
03833 Exeter⊙, 6,439 F 6
03835 Farmington, ▵3,588 E 5
03835 Farmington, 2,884 E 5
03447 Fitzwilliam, ▵1,362 C 6
03447 Fitzwilliam, 750 C 6
03043 Francestown, ▵525 D 6
03580 Franconia, ▵655 D 3
03235 Franklin, 7,292 D 5
03836 Freedom, ▵387 E 4

VERMONT
AREA 9,609 sq. mi.
POPULATION 444,732
CAPITAL Montpelier
LARGEST CITY Burlington
HIGHEST POINT Mt. Mansfield 4,393 ft.
SETTLED IN 1764
ADMITTED TO UNION March 4, 1791
POPULAR NAME Green Mountain State
STATE FLOWER Red Clover
STATE BIRD Hermit Thrush

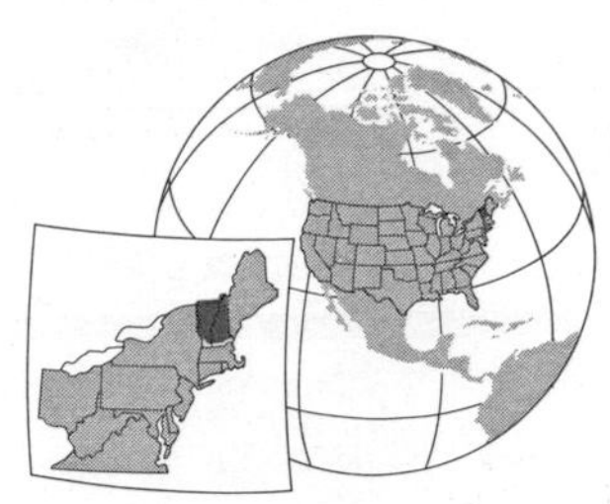

Topography

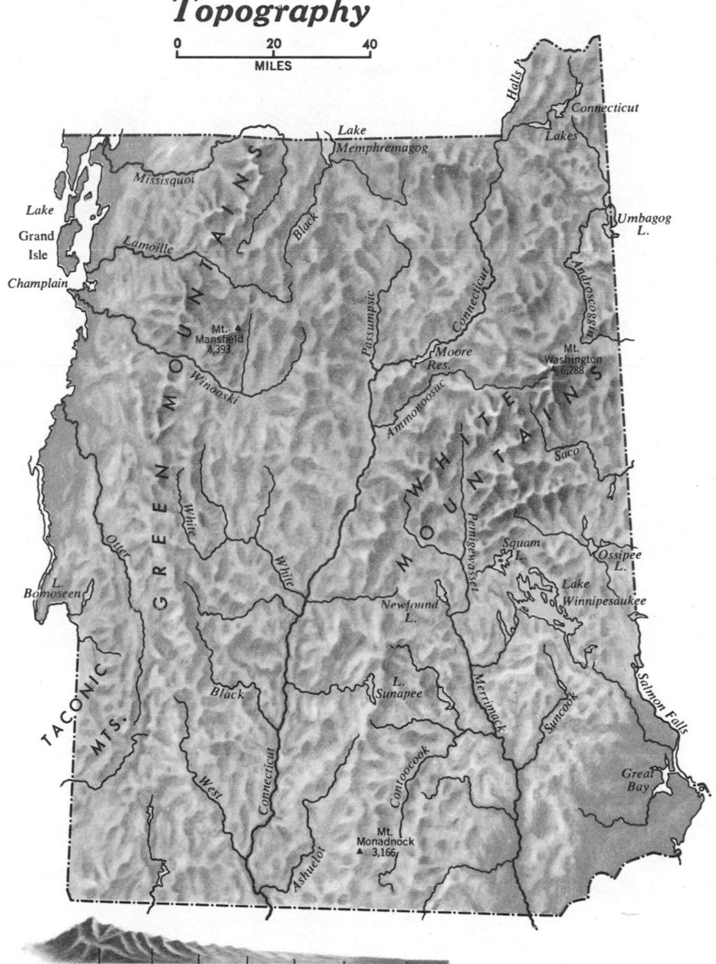

Agriculture, Industry and Resources

Dairy
Maple Syrup
Potatoes
Apples
Vegetables
Poultry
Ab Tc Gn Mr Sl Mi Be Th

Manchester

MANCHESTER
Leather Goods, Textiles, Electrical Products

DOMINANT LAND USE

Specialized Dairy
Dairy, General Farming
Dairy, Poultry, Mixed Farming
Forests

Water Power
Major Industrial Areas

MAJOR MINERAL OCCURRENCES

Ab Asbestos
Be Beryl
Gn Granite
Mi Mica
Mr Marble
Sl Slate
Tc Talc
Th Thorium

03044 Fremont, ▵993 E 6
† 03246 Gilford, ▵3,219 E 4
03237 Gilmanton, ▵1,010 E 5
03448 Gilsum, ▵570 C 5
03045 Goffstown, ▵9,284 D 5
03045 Goffstown, 2,272 D 5
03581 Gorham, ▵2,998 E 3
03581 Gorham, 2,020 E 3
03752 Goshen, ▵395 C 5
03239 Gossville, 800 E 5
03240 Grafton, ▵370 D 4
03753 Grantham, ▵366 C 5
03045 Grasmere, 513 D 5
03047 Greenfield, ▵1,058 D 6
03840 Greenland, ▵1,784 F 5
03048 Greenville, ▵1,587 D 6
03048 Greenville, 1,332 D 6
† 03241 Groton, ▵120 D 4
03582 Groveton, 1,597 D 2
03841 Hampstead, ▵2,401 E 6
03841 Hampstead, 500 E 6
03842 Hampton, ▵8,011 F 6
03842 Hampton, 5,407 F 6
03842 Hampton Beach, 975 F 6
03844 Hampton Falls, ▵1,254 F 6
03449 Hancock, ▵909 C 6
03755 Hanover, ▵8,494 C 4
03755 Hanover, 6,147 C 4
03450 Harrisville, ▵584 C 6
03765 Haverhill, ▵3,090 C 3
03765 Haverhill, 400 C 3
03241 Hebron, ▵234 D 4
03242 Henniker, ▵2,348 D 5
03242 Henniker, 950 D 5
03243 Hill, ▵450 D 4
03244 Hillsboro, ▵2,775 D 5
03244 Hillsboro, 1,784 D 5
03451 Hinsdale, ▵3,276 C 6
03451 Hinsdale, 1,059 C 6
03245 Holderness, ▵1,048 D 4
03049 Hollis, ▵2,616 D 6
03049 Hollis, 500 D 6
03106 Hooksett. ▵5,564 E 5
03106 Hooksett. 1,303 E 5
03301 Hopkinton, ▵3,007 D 5
03301 Hopkinton, 500 D 5
03051 Hudson, ▵10,638 E 6
03051 Hudson, 4,900 E 6
03845 Intervale, 500 E 3
03846 Jackson, ▵404 E 3
03452 Jaffrey, ▵3,353 C 6
03452 Jaffrey, 1,922 C 6
03583 Jefferson, ▵714 D 3
03431 Keene⊙, 20,467 C 6
03848 Kingston, ▵2,882 E 6
03246 Laconia⊙, 14,888 E 4
03584 Lancaster, ▵3,166 D 3
03584 Lancaster⊙, 2,120 D 3
† 03585 Landaff, ▵292 D 3
† 03602 Langdon, ▵337 C 5
03766 Lebanon, 9,725 C 4
† 03857 Lee, ▵1,481 F 5
03606 Lempster, ▵360 C 5
03251 Lincoln, ▵1,341 D 3
03251 Lincoln, 900 D 3
03585 Lisbon, ▵1,480 D 3
03585 Lisbon, 1,247 D 3
† 03051 Litchfield, ▵1,420 E 6
03561 Littleton, ▵5,290 D 3
03561 Littleton, 4,180 D 3
03252 Lochmere, 500 D 5
03053 Londonderry, ▵5,346 E 6
03301 Loudon, ▵1,707 E 5
† 03585 Lyman, ▵213 D 3
03768 Lyme, ▵1,112 C 4
03768 Lyme, 400 C 4
† 03082 Lyndeboro, ▵789 D 6
† 03820 Madbury, ▵704 F 5
03849 Madison, ▵572 E 4
* 03101 Manchester, 87,754 E 6
Manchester, ‡108,461 E 6
03455 Marlborough, ▵1,671 C 6
03455 Marlborough, 1,231 C 6
03456 Marlow, ▵390 C 5
03253 Meredith, ▵2,904 D 4
03253 Meredith, 1,017 D 4
03770 Meriden, 495 C 4
03054 Merrimack, ▵8,595 D 6
03054 Merrimack, 850 D 6
† 03887 Middleton, ▵430 E 5
03588 Milan, ▵713 E 2
03055 Milford, ▵6,622 D 6
03055 Milford, 4,997 D 6
03851 Milton, ▵1,859 F 5
03851 Milton, 750 F 5
03771 Monroe, ▵385 C 3
03057 Mont Vernon, ▵906 D 6
03254 Moultonboro, ▵1,310 E 4
03060 Nashua⊙, 55,820 D 6
† 03457 Nelson, ▵304 C 5
03070 New Boston, ▵1,390 D 6
03070 New Boston, 450 D 6
03255 Newbury, ▵509 C 5
03854 New Castle, ▵975 F 5
03855 New Durham, ▵583 E 5
03856 Newfields, ▵843 F 5
03256 New Hampton, ▵946 D 4
† 03801 Newington, ▵798 F 5
03071 New Ipswich, ▵1,803 D 6
03257 New London, ▵2,236 D 5
03257 New London, 1,347 D 5
03857 Newmarket, ▵3,361 F 5
03857 Newmarket, 2,645 F 5
03773 Newport, ▵5,899 C 5
03773 Newport⊙, 3,296 C 5
03858 Newton, ▵1,920 E 6
03858 Newton, 483 E 6
03859 Newton Junction, 500 E 6
03258 North Chichester, 450 E 5
03860 North Conway, 1,723 E 3
† 03276 Northfield, ▵2,193 D 5
† 03276 Northfield-Tilton, 2,420 D 5
03862 North Hampton, ▵3,259 F 6
03862 North Hampton, 750 F 6
03774 North Haverhill, 750 D 3
† 03773 North Newport, 500 C 5
03073 North Salem, 950 E 6
03590 North Stratford, 650 D 2
† 03582 Northumberland, ▵2,493 D 2
† 03608 North Walpole, 950 C 5
† 03281 North Weare, 600 D 5
03261 Northwood, ▵1,526 E 5

(continued on following page)

NEW HAMPSHIRE (continued)

03262 North Woodstock, 650 ..... D 3
03290 Nottingham, ∆952 ..... E 5
† 03741 Orange, ∆103 ..... D 4
03777 Orford, ∆793 ..... C 4
03864 Ossipee⊙, ∆1,647 ..... E 4
03076 Pelham, ∆5,408 ..... E 6
† 03275 Pembroke, ∆4,261 ..... E 5
03458 Peterborough, ∆3,807 ..... D 6
03458 Peterborough, 2,078 ..... D 6
03779 Piermont, ∆462 ..... C 4
03592 Pittsburg, ∆726 ..... E 1
03263 Pittsfield, ∆2,517 ..... E 5
03263 Pittsfield, 1,662 ..... E 5
03781 Plainfield, ∆1,323 ..... C 4
03865 Plaistow, ∆4,712 ..... E 6
03865 Plaistow, 950 ..... E 6
03264 Plymouth, ∆4,225 ..... D 4
03264 Plymouth, 3,109 ..... D 4
03801 Portsmouth, 25,717 ..... F 5
03593 Randolph, ∆169 ..... E 3
03077 Raymond, ∆3,003 ..... E 5
† 03470 Richmond, ∆287 ..... C 6
03461 Rindge, ∆2,175 ..... C 6
03867 Rochester, 17,938 ..... E 5
† 03431 Roxbury, ∆161 ..... C 6
03266 Rumney, ∆870 ..... D 4
03870 Rye, ∆4,083 ..... F 5
03870 Rye, 750 ..... F 5
03871 Rye Beach, 750 ..... F 6
† 03870 Rye North Beach, 700 ..... F 5
03079 Salem, ∆20,142 ..... E 6
03079 Salem, 950 ..... E 6
† 03079 Salem Depot, 975 ..... E 6
03268 Salisbury, ∆589 ..... D 5
† 03820 Salmon Falls, 950 ..... F 5
03269 Sanbornton, ∆1,022 ..... D 5
03872 Sanbornville, 550 ..... F 4
03873 Sandown, ∆741 ..... E 6
03270 Sandwich, ∆666 ..... E 4
03874 Seabrook, ∆3,053 ..... F 6
03874 Seabrook, 950 ..... F 6
† 03458 Sharon, ∆136 ..... D 6
† 03581 Shelburne, ∆199 ..... E 3
03878 Somersworth, 9,026 ..... F 5
† 03037 South Deerfield, 500 ..... E 5
† 01913 South Hampton, ∆558 ..... F 6
03083 South Merrimack, 650 ..... D 6
† 03874 South Seabrook, 500 ..... F 6
03462 Spofford, 631 ..... C 6
† 03284 Springfield, ∆310 ..... C 4
† 03582 Stark, ∆343 ..... E 2
† 03576 Stewartstown, ∆1,008 ..... E 2
03464 Stoddard, ∆242 ..... C 5
03884 Strafford, ∆965 ..... E 5
† 03590 Stratford, ∆980 ..... D 2
03885 Stratham, ∆1,512 ..... F 5
03585 Sugar Hill, ∆336 ..... D 3
† 03445 Sullivan, ∆376 ..... C 5
03782 Sunapee, ∆1,384 ..... C 5
03782 Sunapee, 750 ..... C 5
03275 Suncook, 4,280 ..... D 5
03431 Surry, ∆507 ..... C 5
† 03260 Sutton, ∆642 ..... D 5
† 03431 Swanzey, ∆4,254 ..... C 6
† 03431 Swanzey, 950 ..... C 6
03886 Tamworth, ∆1,054 ..... E 4
03084 Temple, ∆441 ..... D 6
† 03285 Thornton, ∆594 ..... D 4
03276 Tilton, ∆2,579 ..... D 5
03276 Tilton-Northfield, 2,420 ..... D 5
03465 Troy, ∆1,713 ..... C 6
† 03816 Tuftonboro, ∆910 ..... E 4
† 03743 Unity, ∆709 ..... C 5
03888 Wakefield, ∆1,420 ..... F 4
03608 Walpole, ∆2,966 ..... C 5
03608 Walpole, 900 ..... C 5
03278 Warner, ∆1,441 ..... D 5
03278 Warner, 600 ..... D 5
03279 Warren, ∆539 ..... D 4
03280 Washington, ∆248 ..... C 5
03223 Waterville Valley, ∆109 ..... D 4
03281 Weare, ∆1,851 ..... D 5
03281 Weare P.O. (North Weare), 600 ..... D 5
† 03301 Webster, ∆680 ..... D 5
03282 Wentworth, ∆376 ..... D 4
† 03579 Wentworths Location, ∆37 ..... E 2
† 03038 West Derry (Derry), 6,090 ..... E 6
03784 West Lebanon, 4,200 ..... C 4
03467 Westmoreland, ∆998 ..... C 6
03597 West Stewartstown, 600 ..... E 2
03469 West Swanzey, 950 ..... C 6
03892 Westville, 500 ..... E 6
03598 Whitefield, ∆1,538 ..... D 3
03598 Whitefield, 1,093 ..... D 3
† 03287 Wilmot, ∆516 ..... D 5
03086 Wilton, ∆2,276 ..... D 6
03086 Wilton, 1,161 ..... D 6
03470 Winchester, ∆2,869 ..... C 6
03470 Winchester, 938 ..... C 6
03087 Windham, ∆3,008 ..... E 6
03289 Winnisquam, 500 ..... E 5
03894 Wolfeboro, ∆3,036 ..... E 4
03894 Wolfeboro, 1,718 ..... E 4
03896 Wolfeboro Falls, 650 ..... E 4
03293 Woodstock, ∆897 ..... D 4
03785 Woodsville⊙, 1,336 ..... C 3

VERMONT

COUNTIES

Addison, 24,266 ..... A 3
Bennington, 29,282 ..... A 6
Caledonia, 22,789 ..... C 2
Chittenden, 99,131 ..... A 3
Essex, 5,416 ..... D 2
Franklin, 31,282 ..... B 2
Grand Isle, 3,574 ..... A 2
Lamoille, 13,309 ..... B 2
Orange, 17,676 ..... C 3
Orleans, 20,153 ..... C 2
Rutland, 52,637 ..... A 4
Washington, 47,659 ..... B 3
Windham, 33,074 ..... B 5
Windsor, 44,082 ..... B 4

CITIES and TOWNS

Zip Name/Pop. Key

† 05491 Addison, ∆717 ..... A 3
05820 Albany, ∆528 ..... C 2
05440 Alburg, ∆1,271 ..... A 2
05440 Alburg, 520 ..... A 2
† 05143 Andover, ∆239 ..... B 5
05250 Arlington, ∆1,934 ..... A 5
05250 Arlington, 1,212 ..... A 5
05030 Ascutney, 500 ..... C 5
05901 Averill, ∆8 ..... D 2
05441 Bakersfield, ∆635 ..... B 2
05031 Barnard, ∆569 ..... B 4
05821 Barnet, ∆1,342 ..... C 3
05641 Barre, 10,209 ..... C 3
05641 Barre, ∆6,509 ..... C 3
05822 Barton, ∆2,874 ..... C 2
05822 Barton, 1,051 ..... C 2
05902 Beecher Falls, 640 ..... D 2
05101 Bellows Falls, 3,505 ..... C 5
05442 Belvidere, ∆189 ..... B 2
05201 Bennington, ∆14,586 ..... A 6
05201 Bennington⊙, 7,950 ..... A 6
05731 Benson, ∆583 ..... A 4
† 05476 Berkshire, ∆931 ..... B 2
05032 Bethel, ∆1,347 ..... B 4
† 03590 Bloomfield, ∆196 ..... D 2
† 05466 Bolton, ∆427 ..... B 3
05732 Bomoseen, 500 ..... A 4
05033 Bradford, ∆1,627 ..... C 3
05033 Bradford, 709 ..... C 3
05646 Braintree, ∆751 ..... B 4
05733 Brandon, ∆3,697 ..... A 4
05733 Brandon, 1,720 ..... A 4
05301 Brattleboro, ∆12,239 ..... B 6
05301 Brattleboro, 9,055 ..... B 6
05034 Bridgewater, ∆783 ..... B 4
05734 Bridport, ∆809 ..... A 4
05443 Bristol, ∆2,744 ..... A 3
05443 Bristol, 1,737 ..... A 3
05036 Brookfield, ∆606 ..... B 3
† 05345 Brookline, ∆180 ..... B 5
† 05860 Brownington, ∆522 ..... C 2
† 05871 Burke, ∆1,053 ..... D 2
05401 Burlington⊙, 38,633 ..... A 3
05647 Cabot, ∆663 ..... C 3
05648 Calais, ∆749 ..... B 3
05444 Cambridge, ∆1,528 ..... B 2
05903 Canaan, ∆949 ..... D 2
05735 Castleton, ∆2,837 ..... A 4
05735 Castleton, 450 ..... A 4
05142 Cavendish, ∆1,264 ..... B 5
05736 Center Rutland, 500 ..... A 4
05445 Charlotte, ∆1,802 ..... A 3
05038 Chelsea⊙, ∆983 ..... C 4
05038 Chelsea, 525 ..... C 4
05143 Chester, ∆2,371 ..... B 5
05143 Chester, 950 ..... B 5
05144 Chester Depot, 500 ..... B 5
05737 Chittenden, ∆646 ..... B 4
05737 Chittenden, 525 ..... B 4
† 05759 Clarendon, ∆1,537 ..... A 4
05446 Colchester, ∆8,776 ..... A 2
05824 Concord, ∆896 ..... D 3
05039 Corinth, ∆683 ..... C 3
† 05753 Cornwall, ∆900 ..... A 4
05825 Coventry, ∆492 ..... C 2
05826 Craftsbury, ∆632 ..... C 2
05739 Danby, ∆910 ..... A 5
05828 Danville, ∆1,405 ..... C 3
05828 Danville, 450 ..... C 3
05829 Derby, ∆3,252 ..... C 2
05829 Derby (Derby Center), 547 ..... C 2
05830 Derby Line, 834 ..... C 2
05251 Dorset, ∆1,293 ..... A 5
05251 Dorset, 450 ..... A 5
† 05676 Duxbury, ∆621 ..... B 3
05252 East Arlington, 500 ..... A 5
05649 East Barre, 950 ..... C 3
05448 East Fairfield, 700 ..... B 2
05837 East Haven, ∆197 ..... D 2
05740 East Middlebury, 500 ..... A 4
05651 East Montpelier, ∆1,597 ..... B 3
05651 East Montpelier, 550 ..... B 3
05652 Eden, ∆513 ..... B 2
05450 Enosburg Falls, 1,266 ..... B 2
05451 Essex, ∆10,951 ..... A 2
05451 Essex, 850 ..... A 2
05452 Essex Junction, 6,511 ..... A 3
05454 Fairfax, ∆1,366 ..... B 2
05455 Fairfield, ∆1,285 ..... B 2
05743 Fair Haven, ∆2,777 ..... A 4
05743 Fair Haven, 2,287 ..... A 4
05045 Fairlee, ∆604 ..... C 4
05045 Fairlee, 425 ..... C 4
05456 Ferrisburg, ∆1,875 ..... A 3
† 05444 Fletcher, ∆456 ..... B 2
05745 Forest Dale, 500 ..... A 4
05457 Franklin, ∆821 ..... B 2
† 05478 Georgia, ∆1.711 ..... A 2
05904 Gilman, 700 ..... D 3
05839 Glover, ∆649 ..... C 2
05146 Grafton, ∆465 ..... B 5
05840 Granby, ∆52 ..... D 2
05458 Grand Isle, ∆809 ..... A 2
05654 Graniteville, 1,120 ..... C 3
05747 Granville, ∆255 ..... B 4
05841 Greensboro, ∆593 ..... C 2
05046 Groton, ∆666 ..... C 3
05046 Groton, 438 ..... C 3
05905 Guildhall⊙, ∆169 ..... D 2
† 05301 Guilford, ∆1,108 ..... B 6
† 05358 Halifax, ∆295 ..... B 6
05748 Hancock, ∆283 ..... B 4
05843 Hardwick, ∆2,466 ..... C 2
05843 Hardwick, 1,503 ..... C 2
05047 Hartford, ∆6,477 ..... C 4
05047 Hartford, 650 ..... C 4
05047 Hartland, ∆1,806 ..... C 4
† 05459 Highgate, ∆1,936 ..... B 2
05459 Highgate Center, 927 ..... B 2
05461 Hinesburg, ∆1,775 ..... A 3
† 05830 Holland, ∆383 ..... D 2
05749 Hubbardton, ∆228 ..... A 4
05462 Huntington, ∆748 ..... B 3
05655 Hyde Park, ∆1,347 ..... B 2
05655 Hyde Park⊙, 418 ..... B 2
05750 Hydeville, 450 ..... A 4
† 05777 Ira, ∆284 ..... A 4
05845 Irasburg, ∆775 ..... C 2
05846 Island Pond, 1,123 ..... D 2
05463 Isle La Motte, ∆262 ..... A 2
05343 Jamaica, ∆590 ..... B 5
† 05859 Jay, ∆182 ..... C 2
05465 Jericho, ∆2,343 ..... B 3
05465 Jericho, 450 ..... A 2
05656 Johnson, ∆1,927 ..... B 2
05656 Johnson, 1,296 ..... B 2
† 05752 Leicester, ∆583 ..... A 4
† 03576 Lemington, ∆120 ..... D 2
† 05443 Lincoln, ∆599 ..... B 3
05148 Londonderry, ∆1,037 ..... B 5
05847 Lowell, ∆515 ..... C 2
05149 Ludlow, ∆2,463 ..... B 5
05149 Ludlow, 1,508 ..... B 5
05906 Lunenburg, ∆1,061 ..... D 3
05849 Lyndon, ∆3,705 ..... C 2
05851 Lyndonville, 1,415 ..... D 2
† 05905 Maidstone, ∆94 ..... D 2
05254 Manchester, ∆2,919 ..... A 5
05254 Manchester⊙, 435 ..... A 5
05255 Manchester Center, 900 ..... A 5
05256 Manchester Depot, 1,560 ..... B 5
05344 Marlboro, ∆592 ..... B 6
05658 Marshfield, ∆1,033 ..... C 3
† 05701 Mendon, ∆743 ..... B 4
05753 Middlebury, ∆6,532 ..... A 3
05753 Middlebury⊙, 4,500 ..... A 3
† 05602 Middlesex, ∆857 ..... B 3
05757 Middletown Springs, ∆426 ..... A 5
05468 Milton, ∆4,495 ..... A 2
05468 Milton, 1,164 ..... A 2
05469 Monkton, ∆765 ..... A 3
05470 Montgomery, ∆651 ..... B 2
05602 Montpelier (cap.)⊙, 8,609 ..... B 3
05660 Moretown, ∆904 ..... B 3
05853 Morgan, ∆286 ..... D 2
† 05661 Morristown, ∆4,052 ..... B 2
05661 Morrisville, 2,116 ..... B 2
05758 Mount Holly, ∆687 ..... B 5
† 05739 Mount Tabor, ∆184 ..... B 5
† 05871 Newark, ∆144 ..... D 2
05051 Newbury, ∆1,440 ..... C 3
05051 Newbury, 450 ..... C 3
05345 Newfane, ∆900 ..... B 6
05345 Newfane⊙, 183 ..... B 6
05472 New Haven, ∆1,039 ..... A 3
05855 Newport, ∆1,125 ..... C 2
05855 Newport⊙, 4,664 ..... C 2
05257 North Bennington, 984 ..... A 6
05759 North Clarendon, 750 ..... B 4
05663 Northfield, ∆4,870 ..... B 3
05663 Northfield, 2,139 ..... B 3
05664 Northfield Falls, 700 ..... B 3
05474 North Hero⊙, ∆364 ..... A 2
05260 North Pownal, 600 ..... A 6
05150 North Springfield, 1,100 ..... B 5
05859 North Troy, 774 ..... C 2
05907 Norton, ∆207 ..... D 2
05055 Norwich, ∆1,966 ..... C 4
05055 Norwich, 500 ..... C 4
† 05649 Orange, ∆540 ..... C 3
05860 Orleans, 1,138 ..... C 2
05760 Orwell, ∆851 ..... A 4
† 05491 Panton, ∆416 ..... A 3
05761 Pawlet, ∆1,184 ..... A 5
05862 Peacham, ∆446 ..... C 3
05152 Peru, ∆243 ..... B 5
05762 Pittsfield, ∆249 ..... B 4
05763 Pittsford, ∆2,306 ..... A 4
05763 Pittsford, 682 ..... A 4
05667 Plainfield, ∆1,399 ..... C 3
05667 Plainfield, 949 ..... C 3
05056 Plymouth, ∆283 ..... B 4
† 05067 Pomfret, ∆620 ..... B 4
05764 Poultney, ∆3,217 ..... A 4
05764 Poultney, 1,914 ..... A 4
05261 Pownal, ∆2,441 ..... A 6
05261 Pownal, 700 ..... A 6
05765 Proctor, ∆2,095 ..... A 4
05765 Proctor, 1,950 ..... A 4
05153 Proctorsville, 512 ..... B 5
05346 Putney, ∆1,727 ..... B 6
05346 Putney, 1,115 ..... B 6
05059 Quechee, 420 ..... C 4
05060 Randolph, ∆3,882 ..... B 4
05060 Randolph, 2,115 ..... B 4
05062 Reading, ∆564 ..... B 5
05350 Readsboro, ∆638 ..... B 6
05350 Readsboro, 469 ..... B 6
05476 Richford, ∆2,116 ..... B 2
05476 Richford, 1,527 ..... B 2
05477 Richmond, ∆2,249 ..... A 3
05477 Richmond, 935 ..... A 3
05766 Ripton, ∆187 ..... A 4
05767 Rochester, ∆884 ..... B 4
† 05101 Rockingham, ∆5,501 ..... C 5
05669 Roxbury, ∆354 ..... B 3
05063 Royalton, ∆1,399 ..... B 4
05768 Rupert, ∆582 ..... A 5
05701 Rutland, ∆2,248 ..... B 4
05701 Rutland⊙, 19,293 ..... B 4
05042 Ryegate, ∆830 ..... C 3
05478 Saint Albans, ∆3,270 ..... A 2
05478 Saint Albans⊙, 8,082 ..... A 2
† 05401 Saint George, ∆477 ..... A 2
05819 Saint Johnsbury, ∆8,409 ..... D 3
05819 Saint Johnsbury⊙, 7,000 ..... D 3
05769 Salisbury, ∆649 ..... A 4
† 05250 Sandgate, ∆127 ..... A 5
05154 Saxtons River, 581 ..... B 5
† 05363 Searsburg, ∆84 ..... A 6
05262 Shaftsbury, ∆2,411 ..... A 6
05065 Sharon, ∆541 ..... C 4
05866 Sheffield, ∆307 ..... C 2
05482 Shelburne, ∆3,728 ..... A 3
05482 Shelburne, 2,591 ..... A 3
05483 Sheldon, ∆1,481 ..... B 2
05770 Shoreham, ∆790 ..... A 4
† 05738 Shrewsbury, ∆570 ..... B 4
05670 South Barre, 865 ..... B 3
05401 South Burlington, ∆10,032 ..... A 3
05486 South Hero, ∆868 ..... A 2
05155 South Londonderry, 600 ..... B 5
05068 South Royalton, 625 ..... C 4
05156 Springfield, ∆10,063 ..... B 5
05156 Springfield, 5,632 ..... B 5
† 01247 Stamford, ∆752 ..... A 6
05487 Starksboro, ∆668 ..... A 3
05772 Stockbridge, ∆389 ..... B 4
05672 Stowe, ∆2,388 ..... B 3
05672 Stowe, 435 ..... B 3
05072 Strafford, ∆536 ..... C 4
† 05360 Stratton, ∆104 ..... B 5
† 05733 Sudbury, ∆253 ..... A 4
† 05250 Sunderland, ∆601 ..... A 5
05867 Sutton, ∆438 ..... C 2
05488 Swanton, ∆4,622 ..... A 2
05488 Swanton, 2,630 ..... A 2
05074 Thetford, ∆1,422 ..... C 4
† 05773 Tinmouth, ∆268 ..... A 5
05076 Topsham, ∆686 ..... C 3
05353 Townshend, ∆668 ..... B 5
05868 Troy, ∆1,457 ..... C 2
05077 Tunbridge, ∆791 ..... C 4
05489 Underhill, ∆1,198 ..... B 2
05491 Vergennes, 2,242 ..... A 3
05354 Vernon, ∆1,024 ..... B 6
05079 Vershire, ∆299 ..... C 4
05673 Waitsfield, ∆837 ..... B 3
† 05873 Walden, ∆442 ..... C 3
05773 Wallingford, ∆1,676 ..... B 5
05773 Wallingford, 815 ..... B 5
† 05491 Waltham, ∆265 ..... A 3
05355 Wardsboro, ∆391 ..... B 5
05674 Warren, ∆588 ..... B 3
05675 Washington, ∆667 ..... C 3
05676 Waterbury, ∆4,614 ..... B 3
05676 Waterbury, 2,840 ..... B 3
05677 Waterbury Center, 900 ..... B 3
05492 Waterville, ∆397 ..... B 2
05678 Websterville, 700 ..... B 3
05774 Wells, ∆560 ..... A 5
05081 Wells River, 419 ..... C 3
05301 West Brattleboro, 2,200 ..... B 6
05083 West Fairlee, ∆337 ..... C 4
05874 Westfield, ∆375 ..... C 2
05494 Westford, ∆991 ..... A 2
† 05743 West Haven, ∆240 ..... A 4
05158 Westminster, ∆1,875 ..... C 5
† 05860 Westmore, ∆195 ..... C 2
05161 Weston, ∆507 ..... B 5
05161 Weston, 450 ..... B 5
05777 West Rutland, ∆2,381 ..... A 4
05777 West Rutland, 1,875 ..... A 4
† 05753 Weybridge, ∆618 ..... A 3
† 05851 Wheelock, ∆238 ..... C 2
05001 White River Junction, 2,379 ..... C 4
05778 Whiting, ∆359 ..... A 4
05361 Whitingham, ∆1,011 ..... B 6
05088 Wilder, 1,328 ..... C 4
05679 Williamstown, ∆1,822 ..... B 3
05679 Williamstown, 650 ..... B 3
05495 Williston, ∆3,187 ..... A 3
05363 Wilmington, ∆1,184 ..... B 6
05363 Wilmington, 544 ..... B 6
† 05359 Windham, ∆174 ..... B 5
05089 Windsor, ∆4,158 ..... C 5
05089 Windsor, 3,400 ..... C 5
05404 Winooski, 7,309 ..... A 3
05680 Wolcott, ∆676 ..... C 2
† 05681 Woodbury, ∆399 ..... C 3
† 05201 Woodford, ∆286 ..... A 6
05091 Woodstock, ∆2,608 ..... B 4
05091 Woodstock⊙, 1,154 ..... B 4
05682 Worcester, ∆505 ..... B 3

⊙ County seat.
∆ Population of town or township.
‡ Population of metropolitan area.
† Zip of nearest p.o.
* Multiple zips

Edmund V. Ballman

Designed to protect wooden structures from the ravages of weather, a few early covered bridges are still standing in New Hampshire. This barn-red relic is in Jackson.

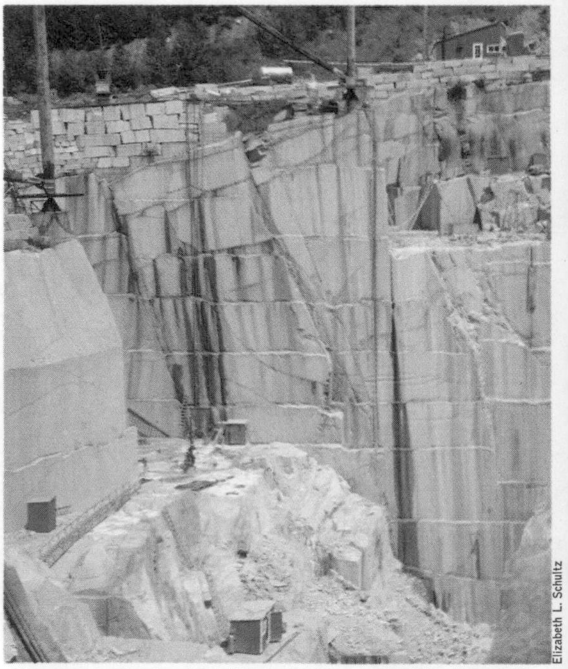
Elizabeth L. Schultz

Located in the heart of Vermont, Barre rightfully boasts of its granite quarries which provide a sculptured panorama set off by surrounding green hills.

AREA 7,836 sq. mi.
POPULATION 7,168,164
CAPITAL Trenton
LARGEST CITY Newark
HIGHEST POINT High Point 1,803 ft.
SETTLED IN 1617
ADMITTED TO UNION December 18, 1787
POPULAR NAME Garden State
STATE FLOWER Violet
STATE BIRD Eastern Goldfinch

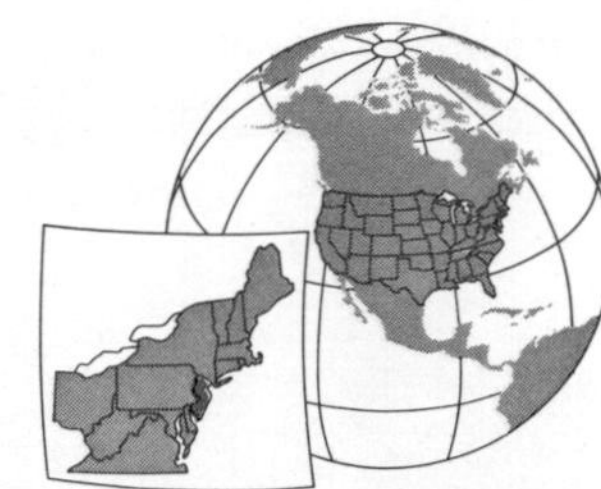

COUNTIES

County	Key
Atlantic, 175,043	D 5
Bergen, 898,012	E 2
Burlington, 323,132	D 4
Camden, 456,291	D 4
Cape May, 59,554	D 5
Cumberland, 121,374	C 5
Essex, 929,986	E 2
Gloucester, 172,681	C 4
Hudson, 609,266	E 2
Hunterdon, 69,718	D 2
Mercer, 303,968	D 3
Middlesex, 583,813	E 3
Monmouth, 459,379	E 3
Morris, 383,454	D 2
Ocean, 208,470	E 4
Passaic, 460,782	E 1
Salem, 60,346	C 4
Somerset, 198,372	D 2
Sussex, 77,528	D 1
Union, 543,116	E 2
Warren, 73,879	C 2

CITIES and TOWNS

Zip	Name/Pop.	Key
08201	Absecon, 6,094	D 5
07820	Allamuchy, 600	D 2
07401	Allendale, 6,240	B 1
07711	Allenhurst, 1,012	F 3
08501	Allentown, 1,603	D 3
08720	Allenwood, 2,200	E 3
08001	Alloway, 850	C 4
08865	Alpha, 2,829	C 2
07620	Alpine, 1,344	C 1
07821	Andover, 813	D 2
08801	Annandale, 675	D 2
07712	Asbury Park, 16,533	F 3
08033	Ashland, 2,500	B 3
08004	Atco, 2,980	D 4
08401	Atlantic City, 47,859	E 5
	Atlantic City, ‡175,043	E 5
07716	Atlantic Highlands, 5,102	F 3
08106	Audubon, 10,802	B 3
08106	Audubon Park, 1,492	B 3
08202	Avalon, 1,283	D 5
07001	Avenel, 10,250	E 2
07717	Avon by the Sea, 2,163	F 3
08005	Barnegat, 900	E 4
08006	Barnegat Light, 554	E 4
08007	Barrington, 8,409	B 3
07920	Basking Ridge, 2,500	D 2
08742	Bay Head, 1,083	E 3
07002	Bayonne, 72,743	B 2
08721	Bayville, 6,000	E 4
08008	Beach Haven, 1,488	E 4
08722	Beachwood, 4,390	E 4
07921	Bedminster, 1,250	D 2
07718	Belford, 7,000	E 3
08502	Belle Mead, 1,950	D 3
07109	Belleville, 34,643	B 2
08030	Bellmawr, 15,618	B 3
07719	Belmar, 5,782	E 3
07823	Belvidere⊙, 2,641	C 2
07621	Bergenfield, 33,131	C 1
07922	Berkeley Heights, ▵13,078	E 2
08009	Berlin, 4,997	D 4
07924	Bernardsville, 6,652	D 2
08010	Beverly, 3,105	D 3
08012	Blackwood, 9,500	C 4
07825	Blairstown, 1,900	C 2
07003	Bloomfield, 52,029	B 2
07403	Bloomingdale, 7,797	E 1
08804	Bloomsbury, 879	C 2
07603	Bogota, 8,125	B 2
07005	Boonton, 9,261	E 2
08505	Bordentown, 4,490	D 3
08805	Bound Brook, 10,450	D 2
07720	Bradley Beach, 4,163	F 3
07826	Branchville, 911	D 1
08723	Breton Woods, 1,900	E 3
08723	Brick Town, ▵35,057	E 3
08014	Bridgeport, 950	C 4
08302	Bridgeton⊙, 20,435	C 5
08730	Brielle, 3,594	E 3
08203	Brigantine, 6,741	E 5
08030	Brooklawn, 2,870	B 3
07926	Brookside, 1,300	D 2
08015	Browns Mills, 7,144	D 4
07828	Budd Lake, 3,168	D 2
08310	Buena, 3,283	D 4
08016	Burlington, 11,991	D 3
07405	Butler, 7,051	E 2
07006	Caldwell, 8,719	B 2
07830	Califon, 970	D 2
* 08101	Camden⊙, 102,551	B 3
† 08701	Candlewood, 5,629	E 3
08204	Cape May, 4,392	D 6
08210	Cape May Court House⊙, 2,062	D 5
07072	Carlstadt, 7,947	B 2
08069	Carneys Point, 3,900	C 4
07008	Carteret, 23,137	E 2
08018	Cedar Brook, 600	D 4
07009	Cedar Grove, ▵15,582	B 2
07927	Cedar Knolls, 3,900	E 2
08311	Cedarville, 900	C 5
† 08723	Cedarwood Park, 1,400	E 3
07928	Chatham, 9,566	E 2
08019	Chatsworth, 700	D 4
08879	Cheesequake, 2,900	E 3
08034	Cherry Hill, ▵64,395	B 3
† 08089	Chesilhurst, 801	D 4
07930	Chester, 1,299	D 2
† 08505	Chesterfield, ▵3,190	D 3
07066	Clark, ▵18,829	A 3
08020	Clarksboro, 1,500	C 4
08510	Clarksburg, 800	E 3
08312	Clayton, 5,193	C 4
08021	Clementon, 4,492	D 4
07010	Cliffside Park, 14,387	C 2
07721	Cliffwood, 7,056	E 3
* 07011	Clifton, 82,437	B 2
08809	Clinton, 1,742	D 2
07624	Closter, 8,604	C 1
08108	Collingswood, 17,422	B 3
08213	Cologne, 800	D 4
07067	Colonia, 12,000	E 2
07722	Colts Neck, 950	E 3
08022	Columbus, 800	D 3
07961	Convent Station, 6,587	E 2
08512	Cranbury, 1,253	E 3
07016	Cranford, ▵27,391	E 2
07626	Cresskill, 7,164	C 1
08515	Crosswicks, 700	D 3
07723	Deal, 2,401	F 3
08023	Deepwater, 800	C 4
08110	Delair, 2,800	B 3
08075	Delanco, ▵4,157	D 3
08075	Delran, 675	B 3
07627	Demarest, 6,262	C 1
08214	Dennisville, 990	D 5
07834	Denville, ▵14,045	E 2
08096	Deptford, ▵24,232	B 4
08317	Dorothy, 850	D 5
07801	Dover, 15,039	D 2
07628	Dumont, 17,534	C 1
08812	Dunellen, 7,072	D 2
08816	East Brunswick, ▵34,166	E 3
07936	East Hanover, ▵7,734	E 2
07734	East Keansburg, 5,000	F 3
08873	East Millstone, 950	D 3
† 07100	East Newark, 1,922	B 2
* 07017	East Orange, 75,471	B 2
07407	East Paterson, 22,749	B 2
07073	East Rutherford, 8,536	B 2
07724	Eatontown, 14,619	E 3
07020	Edgewater, 4,849	C 2
† 08010	Edgewater Park, ▵7,412	D 3
08817	Edison, ▵67,120	E 2
08215	Egg Harbor City, 4,304	D 4
07740	Elberon, 2,900	F 3
* 07201	Elizabeth⊙, 112,654	B 2
08318	Elmer, 1,592	C 4
07630	Emerson, 8,428	B 1
* 07631	Englewood, 24,985	C 2
07632	Englewood Cliffs, 5,938	C 2
† 08330	English Creek, 950	D 5
07726	Englishtown, 1,048	E 3
07849	Espanong (Lake Hopatcong), 1,941	D 2
07021	Essex Fells, 2,541	B 2
07006	Fairfield, 6,731	A 2
07701	Fair Haven, 6,142	E 3
07410	Fair Lawn, 37,975	B 1
08320	Fairton, 600	C 5
07022	Fairview, 10,698	C 2
07023	Fanwood, 8,920	E 2
07931	Far Hills, 780	D 2
07727	Farmingdale, 1,148	E 3
† 08505	Fieldsboro, 615	D 3
08821	Flagtown, 800	D 2
07836	Flanders, 3,875	D 2
08822	Flemington⊙, 3,917	D 2
08518	Florence-Roebling, 7,551	D 3
07932	Florham Park, 8,094	E 2
† 08037	Folsom, 1,767	D 4
08863	Fords, 14,000	E 2
08731	Forked River, 1,422	E 4
07024	Fort Lee, 30,631	C 2
07416	Franklin, ▵30,389	D 3
07416	Franklin, 4,236	D 1
07417	Franklin Lakes, 7,550	B 1
08322	Franklinville, 2,500	C 4
07728	Freehold⊙, 10,545	E 3
08825	Frenchtown, 1,459	C 2
07026	Garfield, 30,722	B 2
07027	Garwood, 5,260	E 2
08026	Gibbsboro, 2,634	B 4
08027	Gibbstown, 3,400	C 4
† 08753	Gilford Park, 4,007	E 4
07933	Gillette, 2,950	E 2
08028	Glassboro, 12,938	C 4
08029	Glendora, 10,280	B 4
08826	Glen Gardner, 874	D 2
07028	Glen Ridge, 8,518	B 2
07452	Glen Rock, 13,011	B 1
08030	Gloucester City, 14,707	B 3
08219	Green Creek, 975	D 5
07435	Green Pond, 800	E 1
07935	Green Village, 800	D 2
08323	Greenwich, ▵963	C 5
08032	Grenloch, 950	C 4
07950	Greystone Park, 5,500	D 2
08620	Groveville, 2,800	D 3
07093	Guttenberg, 5,754	C 2
* 07601	Hackensack⊙, 35,911	B 2
07840	Hackettstown, 9,472	D 2
08033	Haddonfield, 13,118	B 3
08035	Haddon Heights, 9,365	B 3
08036	Hainesport, ▵2,990	D 4
07508	Haledon, 6,767	B 1
07419	Hamburg, 1,820	D 1
08690	Hamilton Square, 11,300	D 3
08037	Hammonton, 11,464	D 4
08827	Hampton, 1,386	D 2
07640	Harrington Park, 4,841	C 1
07029	Harrison, 11,811	B 2
08039	Harrisonville, 950	C 4
† 08057	Hartford, 650	D 4
07604	Hasbrouck Heights, 13,651	B 2
07641	Haworth, 3,760	C 1
07507	Hawthorne, 19,173	B 2
07730	Hazlet, 15,000	E 3
08828	Helmetta, 955	E 3
07421	Hewitt, 950	E 1
08829	High Bridge, 2,606	D 2
08904	Highland Park, 14,385	D 2
07732	Highlands, 3,916	F 3
08520	Hightstown, 5,431	D 3
07502	Hillcrest, 1,975	C 2
07642	Hillsdale, 11,768	B 1
07205	Hillside, ▵21,636	B 2
† 08083	Hi-Nella, 1,195	B 4
07030	Hoboken, 45,380	C 2
07423	Ho-ho-kus, 4,348	B 1
07733	Holmdel, 5,500	E 3
07843	Hopatcong, 9,052	D 2
07844	Hope, 950	D 2
08525	Hopewell, 2,271	D 3
07727	Howell, ▵21,756	E 3
† 08865	Huntington, 1,900	C 2
† 07712	Interlaken, 1,182	E 3
07845	Ironia, 1,500	D 2
07111	Irvington, 59,743	B 2
08830	Iselin, 19,000	E 2

(continued on following page)

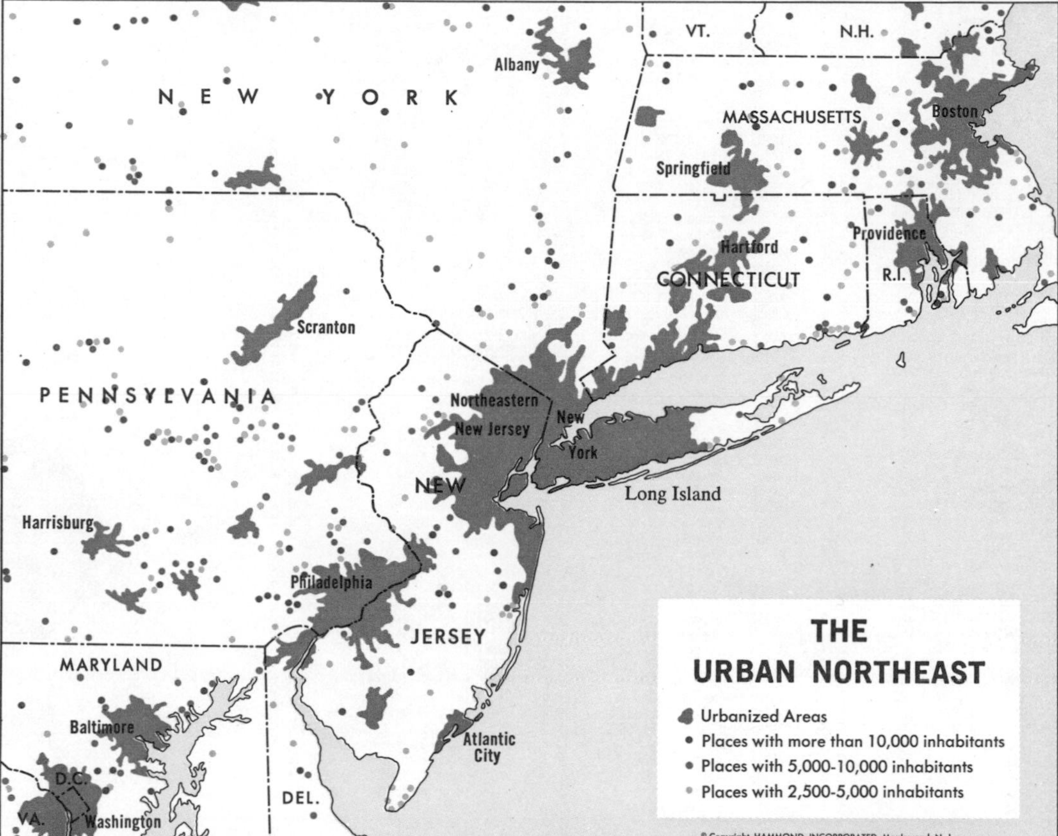

Agriculture, Industry and Resources

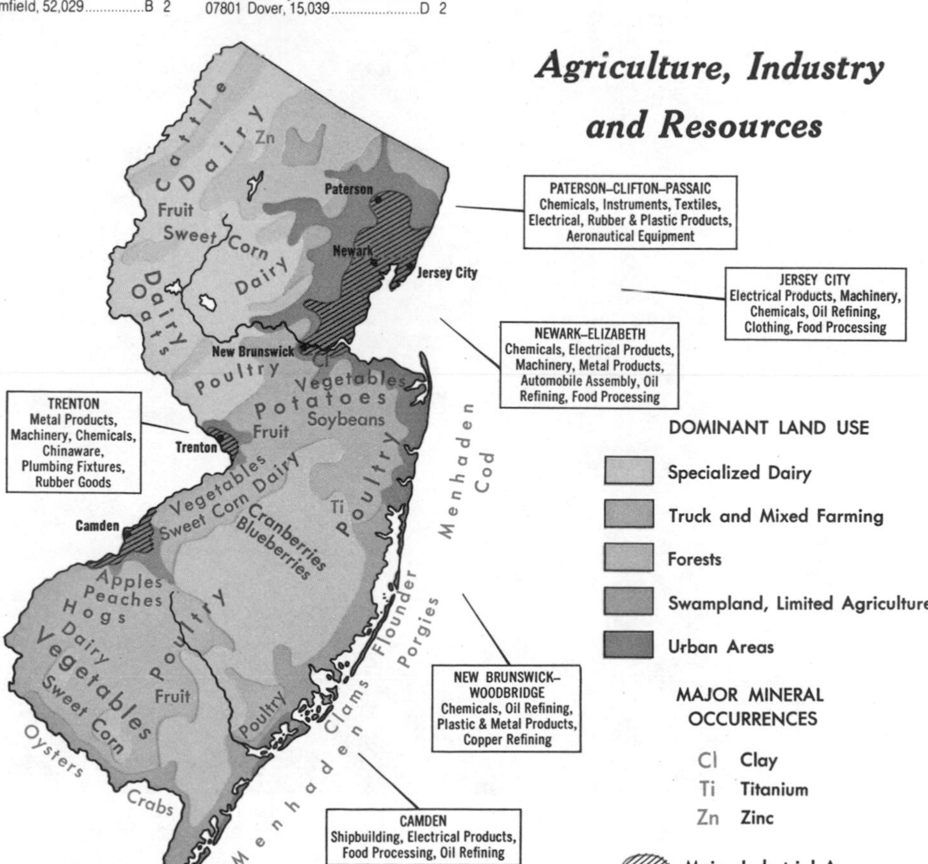

(continued)

Zip	Place	Key
08732	Island Heights, 1,397	E 4
08527	Jackson, ▵18,276	E 3
08831	Jamesburg, 4,584	E 3
* 07301	Jersey City⊙, 260,545	B 2
	Jersey City, ‡609,266	B 2
07734	Keansburg, 9,720	E 3
07032	Kearny, 37,585	B 2
08832	Keasbey, 1,200	E 2
08824	Kendall Park, 7,412	D 3
07033	Kenilworth, 9,165	E 2
07735	Keyport, 7,205	E 3
08528	Kingston, 1,200	D 3
07405	Kinnelon, 7,600	E 2
08043	Kirkwood, 800	D 4
07848	Lafayette, 900	D 1
07034	Lake Hiawatha, 11,389	E 2
07849	Lake Hopatcong, 1,941	D 2
08733	Lakehurst, 2,641	E 3
† 07871	Lake Mohawk, 6,262	D 1
08701	Lakewood, 17,874	E 3
08530	Lambertville, 4,359	D 3
07850	Landing, 2,370	D 2
08734	Lanoka Harbor, 1,066	E 4
08021	Laurel Springs, 2,566	B 4
08879	Laurence Harbor, 6,715	E 3
08735	Lavallette, 1,509	E 4
08045	Lawnside, 2,757	B 3
08648	Lawrenceville, 1,464	D 3
08833	Lebanon, 885	D 2
07852	Ledgewood, 2,800	D 2
08327	Leesburg, 800	D 5
07737	Leonardo, 4,000	E 3
07605	Leonia, 8,847	C 2
07938	Liberty Corner, 1,900	D 2
07035	Lincoln Park, 9,034	A 1
07738	Lincroft, 4,900	E 3
07036	Linden, 41,409	A 3
08021	Lindenwold, 12,199	B 4
08221	Linwood, 6,159	D 5
07424	Little Falls, ▵11,727	B 2
07643	Little Ferry, 9,042	B 2
07739	Little Silver, 6,010	F 3
07039	Livingston, ▵30,127	E 2
07644	Lodi, 25,213	B 2
08008	Long Branch, 31,774	F 3
08403	Longport, 1,225	D 5
07853	Long Valley, 1,645	D 2
08048	Lumberton, 600	D 4
07071	Lyndhurst, ▵22,729	B 2
07939	Lyons, 3,900	D 2
07940	Madison, 16,710	E 2
08049	Magnolia, 5,893	B 3
07430	Mahwah, ▵10,539	E 1
08328	Malaga, 950	C 4
08050	Manahawkin, 1,278	E 4
08736	Manasquan, 4,971	E 3
08051	Mantua, 5,530	C 4
08835	Manville, 13,029	D 2
08052	Maple Shade, ▵16,464	B 3
07040	Maplewood, ▵24,932	E 2
† 07866	Marcella, 540	E 2
08402	Margate City, 10,576	E 5
07746	Marlboro, 2,380	E 3
08053	Marlton, 10,180	D 4
08223	Marmora, 650	D 5
08836	Martinsville, 3,500	D 2
08054	Masonville, 900	D 4
07747	Matawan, 9,136	E 3
08330	Mays Landing⊙, 1,272	D 5
07607	Maywood, 11,087	B 2
07428	McAfee, 800	D 1
† 08232	McKee City, 950	D 5
08055	Medford, 1,448	D 4
08055	Medford Lakes, 4,792	D 4
07945	Mendham, 3,729	D 2
08817	Menlo Park, 10,000	E 2
08619	Mercerville, 5,456	D 3
08109	Merchantville, 4,425	B 3
08840	Metuchen, 16,031	E 2
08056	Mickleton, 950	C 4
08846	Middlesex, 15,038	E 2
07748	Middletown, ▵54,623	E 3
07432	Midland Park, 8,159	B 1
08848	Milford, 1,230	C 2
07041	Millburn, ▵21,307	E 2
07946	Millington, 975	D 2
08849	Millstone, 630	D 2
08850	Milltown, 6,470	E 3
08332	Millville, 21,366	C 5
07438	Milton, 2,220	D 1
† 07801	Mine Hill, ▵3,557	D 2
08342	Mizpah, 900	D 5
07750	Monmouth Beach, 2,042	F 3
08852	Monmouth Junction, 1,900	D 3
07434	Monroe, ▵9,138	E 3
† 12771	Montague, 750	D 1
* 07042	Montclair, 44,043	B 2
07645	Montvale, 7,327	B 1
07045	Montville, 4,900	E 2
07074	Moonachie, 2,937	B 2
08057	Moorestown, 14,179	B 3
07950	Morris Plains, 5,540	D 2
07960	Morristown⊙, 17,662	D 2
07046	Mountain Lakes, 4,739	E 2
07092	Mountainside, 7,520	E 2
† 07470	Mountain View, 9,000	B 2
07856	Mount Arlington, 3,590	D 2
08059	Mount Ephraim, 5,625	B 3
07970	Mount Freedom, 1,621	D 2
08060	Mount Holly⊙, ▵12,713	D 4
† 07885	Mount Hope, 1,510	D 2
08061	Mount Royal, 850	C 4
08062	Mullica Hill, 800	C 4
† 08087	Mystic Islands, 900	E 4
08063	National Park, 3,730	B 3
07752	Navesink, 2,400	E 3
07753	Neptune, ▵27,863	E 3
07753	Neptune City, 5,502	E 3
† 08853	Neshanic, 752	D 3
07857	Netcong, 2,858	D 2
* 07101	Newark⊙, 382,417	B 2
	Newark, ‡2,056,556	B 2
* 08901	New Brunswick⊙, 41,885	E 3
08533	New Egypt, 1,769	E 3
08344	Newfield, 1,487	D 4
07435	Newfoundland, 900	D 1
08224	New Gretna, 700	E 4
07646	New Milford, 20,201	B 1
08345	Newport, 700	C 5
07974	New Providence, 13,796	E 2
07724	New Shrewsbury, 5,925	E 3
07860	Newton⊙, 7,297	D 1
08346	Newtonville, 750	D 4
07976	New Vernon, 1,900	D 2
08817	Nixon, 12,000	E 2
08347	Norma, 1,200	C 4
07032	North Arlington, 18,096	B 2
07047	North Bergen, ▵47,751	B 2
08876	North Branch, 610	D 2
08902	North Brunswick, ▵16,691	E 3
† 07006	North Caldwell, 6,425	B 2
08204	North Cape May, 3,812	C 6
08225	Northfield, 8,875	D 5
07508	North Haledon, 7,614	B 1
07060	North Plainfield, 21,796	E 2
07647	Northvale, 5,177	F 1
08260	North Wildwood, 3,914	D 6
07648	Norwood, 4,398	C 1
07110	Nutley, 32,099	B 2
07755	Oakhurst, 5,558	E 3
07436	Oakland, 14,420	B 1
08107	Oaklyn, 4,626	B 3
07438	Oak Ridge, 750	E 1
08226	Ocean City, 10,575	D 5
08740	Ocean Gate, 1,081	E 4
07756	Ocean Grove, 7,000	F 3
07757	Oceanport, 7,503	F 3
08230	Ocean View, 950	D 5
08231	Oceanville, 600	D 5
07439	Ogdensburg, 2,222	D 1
08857	Old Bridge, 25,176	E 3
07675	Old Tappan, 3,917	C 1
08858	Oldwick, 600	D 2
07649	Oradell, 8,903	B 1
* 07050	Orange, 32,566	B 2
08723	Osbornsville, 3,900	E 3
07863	Oxford, 1,411	C 2
07470	Packanack Lake, 4,000	B 1
† 08226	Palermo, 600	D 5
07650	Palisades Park, 13,351	C 2
08065	Palmyra, 6,969	B 3
07652	Paramus, 29,495	B 1
† 08087	Parkertown, 600	E 4
07656	Park Ridge, 8,709	B 1
07054	Parsippany, ▵55,112	E 2
* 07055	Passaic, 55,124	E 2
* 07501	Paterson⊙, 144,824	B 2
	Paterson-Clifton-Passaic, ‡1,358,794	B 2
08066	Paulsboro, 8,084	C 4
07977	Peapack-Gladstone, 1,924	D 2
08067	Pedricktown, 1,500	C 4
08068	Pemberton, 1,344	D 4
08534	Pennington, 2,151	D 3
08110	Pennsauken, ▵36,394	B 3
08069	Penns Grove, 5,727	C 4
08070	Pennsville, 11,014	C 4
07440	Pequannock, 4,900	B 1
* 08861	Perth Amboy, 38,798	E 2
08865	Phillipsburg, 17,849	C 2
08741	Pine Beach, 1,395	E 4
07058	Pine Brook, 3,500	E 2
08021	Pine Hill, 5,132	D 4
08854	Piscataway, ▵36,418	D 2
08071	Pitman, 10,257	C 4
* 07060	Plainfield, 46,862	E 2
08536	Plainsboro, 1,200	D 3
08232	Pleasantville, 13,778	D 5
08742	Point Pleasant, 15,968	E 3
08742	Point Pleasant Beach, 4,882	E 3
08240	Pomona, 900	D 5
07442	Pompton Lakes, 11,397	A 1
07444	Pompton Plains, 9,500	B 1
07758	Port Monmouth, 4,556	E 3
† 07850	Port Morris, 950	D 2
07865	Port Murray, 800	D 2
08349	Port Norris, 1,955	C 5
07064	Port Reading, 4,900	E 2
08241	Port Republic, 586	D 4
08540	Princeton, 12,311	D 3
08550	Princeton Junction, 950	D 3
† 07885	Prospect Park, 5,176	B 1
08072	Quinton, 575	C 4
* 07065	Rahway, 29,114	E 2
† 07945	Ralston, 650	D 2
† 08057	Ramblewood, 5,556	D 4
07446	Ramsey, 12,571	B 1
08869	Raritan, 6,691	D 2
07701	Red Bank, 12,847	E 3
08350	Richland, 950	D 5
07657	Ridgefield, 11,308	B 2
07660	Ridgefield Park, 14,453	B 2
* 07450	Ridgewood, 27,547	B 1
08551	Ringoes, 682	D 3
07456	Ringwood, 10,393	E 1
08242	Rio Grande, 1,203	D 5
07457	Riverdale, 2,729	A 1
07661	River Edge, 12,850	B 1
08075	Riverside, ▵8,616	B 3
08077	Riverton, 3,412	B 3
08691	Robbinsville, 650	D 3
07662	Rochelle Park, ▵6,380	B 2
07866	Rockaway, ▵18,955	D 2
07866	Rockaway, 6,383	D 2
08553	Rocky Hill, 917	D 3
08554	Roebling-Florence, 7,551	D 3
08555	Roosevelt, 814	E 3
07068	Roseland, 4,453	A 2
07203	Roselle, 22,585	B 2
07204	Roselle Park, 14,277	A 2
08352	Rosenhayn, 950	C 5
† 07876	Roxbury, ▵15,754	D 2
07760	Rumson, 7,421	F 3
08078	Runnemede, 10,475	B 3
* 07070	Rutherford, 20,802	B 2
07662	Saddle Brook, ▵15,098	B 1
07458	Saddle River, 2,437	B 1
08079	Salem⊙, 7,648	C 4
08872	Sayreville, 32,508	E 3
07076	Scotch Plains, ▵22,279	E 2
07760	Sea Bright, 1,339	F 3
08302	Seabrook, 1,569	C 5
08750	Sea Girt, 2,207	E 3
08243	Sea Isle City, 1,712	D 5
08751	Seaside Heights, 1,248	E 4
08752	Seaside Park, 1,432	E 4
07094	Secaucus, 13,228	B 2
07077	Sewaren, 3,200	E 2
08080	Sewell, 2,210	C 4
08353	Shiloh, 573	C 5
08008	Ship Bottom, 1,079	E 4
07078	Short Hills, 14,000	E 2
07701	Shrewsbury, 3,315	E 3
08081	Sicklerville, 1,700	D 4
† 07424	Singac, 3,942	B 2
08558	Skillman, 1,955	D 3
† 07728	Smithburg, 750	E 3
08083	Somerdale, 6,510	B 4
08244	Somers Point, 7,919	D 5
08876	Somerville⊙, 13,652	D 2
08879	South Amboy, 9,338	E 3
† 07719	South Belmar, 1,490	E 3
08880	South Bound Brook, 4,525	E 2
† 08852	South Brunswick, ▵14,058	E 3
07079	South Orange, 16,971	A 2
07080	South Plainfield, 21,142	E 2
08882	South River, 15,428	E 3
08246	South Seaville, 600	D 5
08753	South Toms River, 3,981	E 4
07871	Sparta, 3,000	D 1
08884	Spotswood, 7,891	E 3
07081	Springfield, ▵15,740	E 2
07762	Spring Lake, 3,896	F 3
07762	Spring Lake Heights, 4,602	E 3
07874	Stanhope, 3,040	D 2
08885	Stanton, 700	D 2
08886	Stewartsville, 950	C 2
07980	Stirling, 1,450	E 2
07460	Stockholm, 1,477	D 1
08559	Stockton, 619	D 3
08247	Stone Harbor, 1,089	D 5
08084	Stratford, 9,801	B 4
† 07747	Strathmore, 7,674	E 3
07876	Succasunna, 5,000	D 2
07901	Summit, 23,620	E 2
08008	Surf City, 1,129	E 4
07461	Sussex, 2,038	D 1
08085	Swedesboro, 2,287	C 4
07878	Tabor, 1,500	E 2
07666	Teaneck, ▵42,355	B 2
07670	Tenafly, 14,827	C 1
07608	Teterboro, 14	B 2
08086	Thorofare, 4,200	B 4
08887	Three Bridges, 750	D 2
08560	Titusville, 900	D 3
08753	Toms River⊙, 7,303	E 4
07511	Totowa, 11,580	B 1
07082	Towaco, 2,500	E 2
* 08601	Trenton (cap.)⊙, 104,638	D 3
	Trenton, ‡303,968	D 3
08087	Tuckerton, 1,926	E 4
07083	Union, ▵53,077	A 2
07735	Union Beach, 6,472	E 3
07087	Union City, 58,537	C 2
† 07421	Upper Greenwood Lake 1,505	E 1
† 07458	Upper Saddle River, 7,949	B 1
† 07724	Vail Homes, 1,164	E 3
07088	Vauxhall, 9,245	A 2
08406	Ventnor City, 10,385	E 5
07462	Vernon, 800	E 1
07044	Verona, 15,067	B 2
08251	Villas, 3,155	D 5
08088	Vincentown, 900	D 4
08360	Vineland, 47,399	C 5
	Vineland-Millville-Bridgeton, ‡121,374	C 5
07463	Waldwick, 12,313	B 1
07719	Wall, ▵16,498	E 3
07055	Wallington, 10,284	B 2
† 07712	Wanamassa, 4,600	E 3
07465	Wanaque, 8,636	B 1
08758	Waretown, 1,800	E 4
07882	Washington, 5,943	D 2
07060	Watchung, 4,750	E 2
08089	Waterford Works, 950	D 4
07470	Wayne, ▵49,141	A 1
07087	Weehawken, ▵13,383	C 2
08090	Wenonah, 2,364	C 4
07006	West Caldwell, 11,887	A 2
† 08204	West Cape May, 1,005	D 6
08092	West Creek, 630	E 4
* 07090	Westfield, 33,720	E 2
07764	West Long Branch, 6,845	F 3
07480	West Milford, 950	E 1
07093	West New York, 40,627	C 2
07052	West Orange, 43,715	A 2
07424	West Paterson, 11,692	B 2
08628	West Trenton, 5,900	D 3
08093	Westville, 5,170	B 3
07675	Westwood, 11,105	B 1
07885	Wharton, 5,535	D 2
07981	Whippany, 7,500	E 2
08888	Whitehouse, 800	D 2
08889	White House Station, 1,019	D 2
08252	Whitesboro, 700	D 5
† 08701	Whitesville, 600	E 3
08759	Whiting, 750	E 4
07765	Wickatunk, 950	E 3
08260	Wildwood, 4,110	D 6
08260	Wildwood Crest, 3,483	D 6
08094	Williamstown, 4,075	D 4
08046	Willingboro, ▵43,414	D 3
† 07036	Winfield, ▵2,184	B 2
08270	Woodbine, 2,625	D 5
07095	Woodbridge, ▵98,944	E 2
08096	Woodbury⊙, 12,408	B 4
08097	Woodbury Heights, 3,621	B 4
07675	Woodcliff Lake, 5,506	B 1
08107	Wood-Lynne, 3,101	B 3
† 07885	Woodport, 2,100	D 2
07075	Wood-Ridge, 8,311	B 2
08098	Woodstown, 3,137	C 4
08562	Wrightstown, 2,719	D 3
07481	Wyckoff, ▵16,039	B 1
08620	Yardville, 9,500	D 3

⊙ County seat.
‡ Population of metropolitan area.
▵ Population of town or township.
† Zip of nearest p.o
* Multiple zips

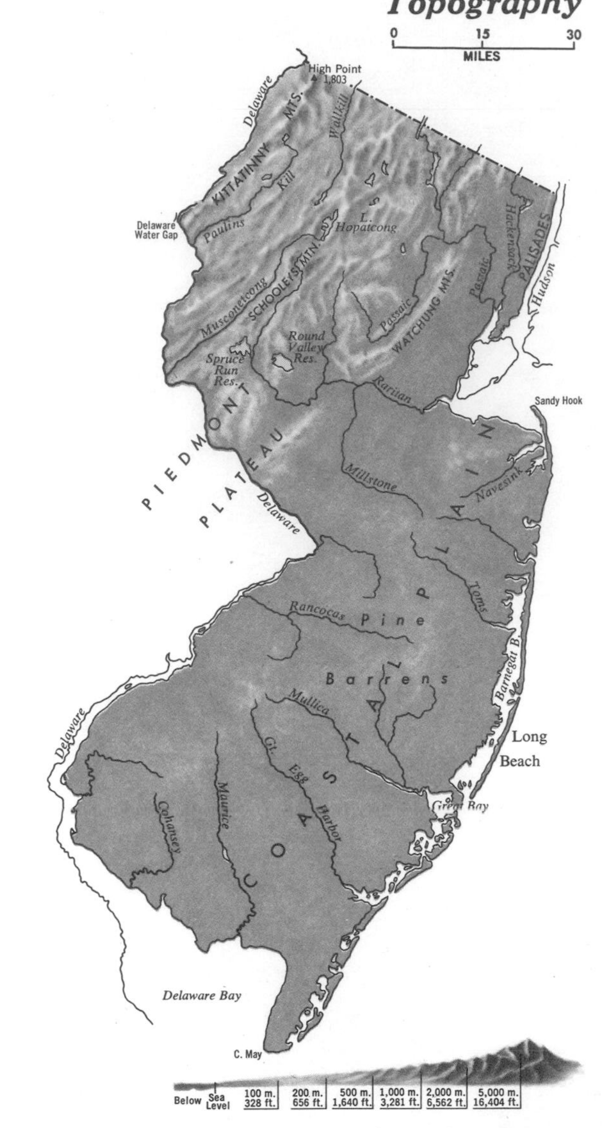

New Jersey towns become suburbs of Manhattan, thanks to connecting links like the Holland and Lincoln Tunnels and the George Washington Bridge. Scene above is the Fort Lee approach to the Bridge.

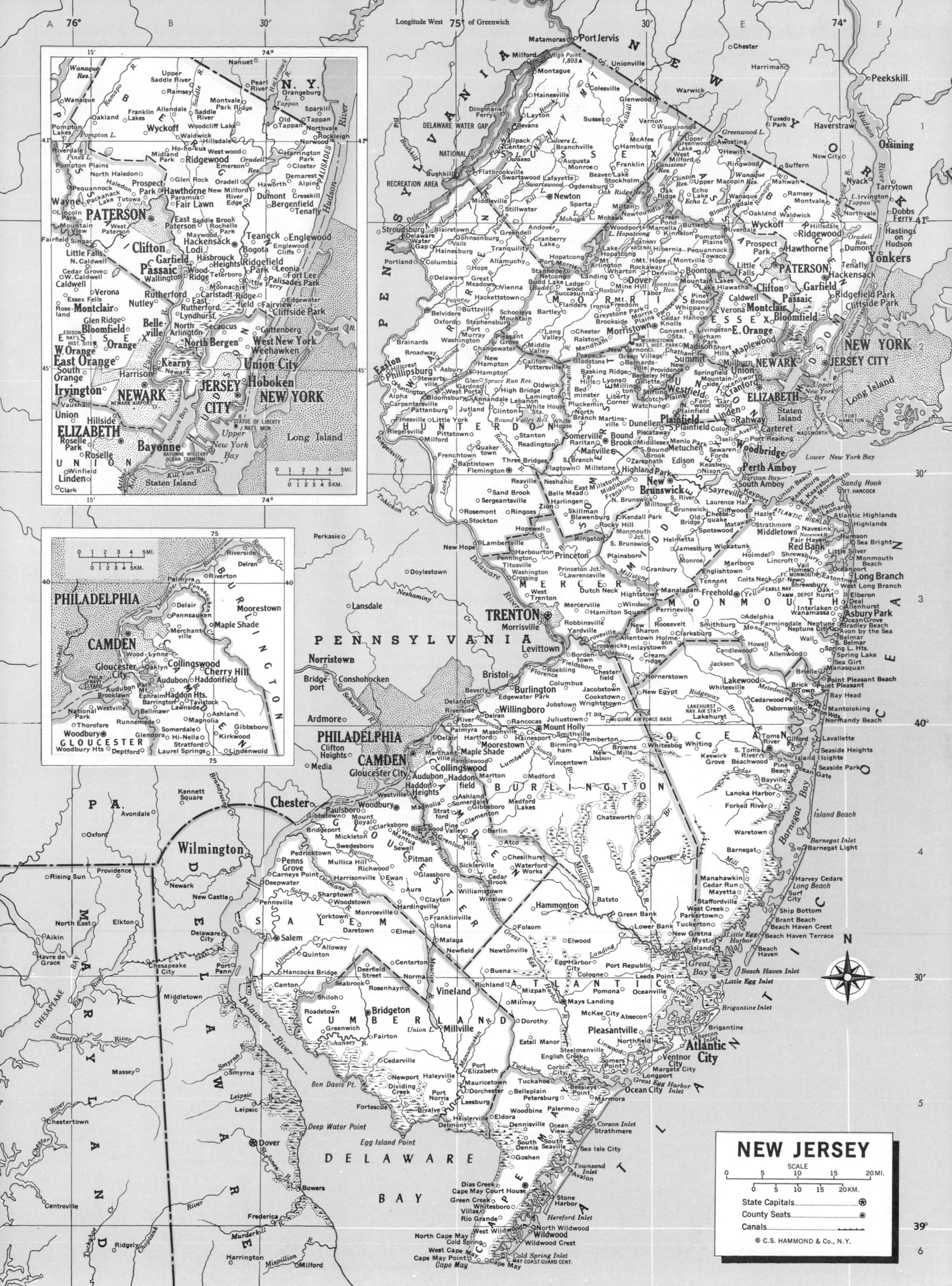

NEW JERSEY
SCALE
0 5 10 15 20 MI.
0 5 10 15 20 KM.
State Capitals
County Seats
Canals
© C.S. HAMMOND & Co., N.Y.
Longitude West 75° of Greenwich
76°
30′
74°
41°
40°
39°
A
B
C
D
E
F
1
2
3
4
5
6
PENNSYLVANIA
NEW YORK
DELAWARE
MARYLAND
ATLANTIC OCEAN
DELAWARE BAY
Lower New York Bay
Long Island
SUSSEX
PASSAIC
BERGEN
WARREN
MORRIS
ESSEX
HUDSON
UNION
HUNTERDON
SOMERSET
MIDDLESEX
MERCER
MONMOUTH
BURLINGTON
OCEAN
CAMDEN
GLOUCESTER
SALEM
CUMBERLAND
ATLANTIC
CAPE MAY
TRENTON
NEWARK
JERSEY CITY
NEW YORK
PATERSON
ELIZABETH
Perth Amboy
New Brunswick
Atlantic City
Camden
Philadelphia
Wilmington
Chester
Port Jervis
High Point 1,803
DELAWARE WATER GAP
NATIONAL RECREATION AREA
Newton
Morristown
Flemington
Somerville
Freehold
Toms River
Mount Holly
Woodbury
Salem
Bridgeton
Mays Landing
Cape May Court House
Cape May
Wildwood
Ocean City
Vineland
Millville
Asbury Park
Long Branch
Red Bank
Sandy Hook
Barnegat Bay
Barnegat Inlet
Little Egg Inlet
Brigantine Inlet
Hereford Inlet
Cold Spring Inlet
Lakehurst Nav. Air Sta.
McGuire Air Force Base
Ft. Dix
Staten Island
Upper New York Bay
Statue of Liberty Nat'l Mon.
Newark Airport
PHILADELPHIA
BURLINGTON
CAMDEN
GLOUCESTER
0 1 2 3 4 5MI.
0 1 2 3 4 5KM.

COUNTIES

County	Key
Bernalillo, 315,774	C 4
Catron, 2,198	A 4
Chaves, 43,335	E 5
Colfax, 12,170	E 2
Curry, 39,517	F 4
De Baca, 2,547	E 4
Dona Ana, 69,773	C 6
Eddy, 41,119	E 6
Grant, 22,030	A 5
Guadalupe, 4,969	E 4
Harding, 1,348	F 3
Hidalgo, 4,734	A 7
Lea, 49,554	F 6
Lincoln, 7,560	D 5
Los Alamos, 15,198	C 3
Luna, 11,706	B 6
McKinley, 43,208	A 3
Mora, 4,673	E 3
Otero, 41,097	D 6
Quay, 10,903	F 3
Rio Arriba, 25,170	B 2
Roosevelt, 16,479	F 4
Sandoval, 17,492	C 3
San Juan, 52,517	A 2
San Miguel, 21,951	D 3
Santa Fe, 53,756	C 3
Sierra, 7,189	B 5
Socorro, 9,763	C 5
Taos, 17,516	D 2
Torrance, 5,290	D 4
Union, 4,925	F 2
Valencia, 40,539	A 4

CITIES and TOWNS

	Zip	Name/Pop.	Key
	87510	Abiquiu, 310	C 2
†	87049	Acoma, 150	B 4
†	87049	Acomita, 975	B 3
	87114	Alameda, 5,000	C 3
	88310	Alamogordo⊙, 23,035	C 6
*	87101	Albuquerque⊙, 243,751	C 3
		Alburquerque, ‡315,774	C 3
	87511	Alcalde, 975	C 2
	87001	Algodones, 195	C 3
	88312	Alto, 104	D 5
	87512	Amalia, 200	D 2
	88020	Animas, 75	A 7
	88021	Anthony, 1,728	C 6
	87711	Anton Chico, 600	D 3
†	88351	Arabela, 65	D 5
	87820	Aragon, 85	A 5
	87930	Arrey, 367	B 6
	87513	Arroyo Hondo, 400	D 2
	87514	Arroyo Seco, 500	D 2
	88210	Artesia, 10,315	E 6
	87410	Aztec⊙, 3,354	B 2
	88023	Bayard, 2,908	A 6
	87002	Belen, 4,823	C 4
	88314	Bent, 157	D 5
	88024	Berino, 300	C 6
	87004	Bernalillo⊙, 2,016	C 3
	87815	Bingham, 60	C 5
	87412	Blanco, 150	B 2
	87413	Bloomfield, 1,574	A 2
	87005	Bluewater, 300	A 3
	87006	Bosque, 300	C 4
	87712	Buena Vista, 178	D 3
	87515	Canjilon, 300	C 2
	87516	Canones, 200	C 2
	88316	Capitan, 439	D 5
	88414	Capulin, 100	F 2
	88220	Carlsbad⊙, 21,297	E 6
	88301	Carrizozo⊙, 1,123	D 5
	87007	Casa Blanca, 560	B 4
	88113	Causey, 150	F 5
	87518	Cebolla, 150	C 2
	87008	Cedar Crest, 600	C 3
†	87410	Cedar Hill, 145	B 2
	88026	Central, 1,864	A 6
	87010	Cerrillos, 118	D 3
	87519	Cerro, 400	D 2
	87713	Chacon, 200	D 2
	87520	Chama, 899	C 2
	88027	Chamberino, 400	C 6
	87521	Chamisal, 637	D 2
†	87059	Chilili, 80	C 4
	87522	Chimayo, 900	D 3
	87714	Cimarron, 927	E 2
	88415	Clayton⊙, 2,931	F 2
	87715	Cleveland, 500	D 2
	88028	Cliff, 350	A 6
	88317	Cloudcroft, 525	D 6
	88101	Clovis⊙, 28,495	F 4
†	87041	Cochiti, 300	C 3
	88029	Columbus, 241	B 7
	88416	Conchas Dam, 192	E 3
	87523	Cordova, 600	D 2
	88318	Corona, 262	D 4
	87048	Corrales, 975	C 3
	87524	Costilla, 400	D 2
	87012	Coyote, 125	C 2
	87313	Crownpoint, 876	A 3
†	86504	Crystal, 200	A 2
	87013	Cuba, 750	B 2
	87014	Cubero, 300	B 3
	88417	Cuervo, 150	E 3
	87522	Cundiyo, 98	D 3
	87821	Datil, 150	B 4
	88030	Deming⊙, 8,343	B 6
	87933	Derry, 350	B 6
	88418	Des Moines, 204	F 2
	88230	Dexter, 746	E 5
†	87711	Dilia, 125	D 3
	87527	Dixon, 640	D 2
	88032	Dona Ana, 800	C 6
	88115	Dora, 196	F 5
	87528	Dulce, 450	B 2
	88319	Duran, 100	D 4
	87718	Eagle Nest, 300	D 2
	87015	Edgewood, 75	C 3
	87935	Elephant Butte, 75	B 5
	88116	Elida, 233	F 5
†	87731	El Porvenir, 90	D 3
	87529	El Prado, 200	D 2
	87530	El Rito, 475	C 2
	87531	Embudo, 400	C 2
	88321	Encino, 250	D 4
	87532	Espanola, 4,528	C 3
	87016	Estancia⊙, 721	D 4
	88231	Eunice, 2,641	F 6
	88033	Fairacres, 500	C 6
	87720	Farley, 81	E 2
	87401	Farmington, 21,979	A 2
	88034	Faywood, 75	B 6
†	88041	Fierro, 200	A 6

NEW MEXICO

SCALE 0 5 10 20 30 40 50 60 MI.
0 5 10 20 30 40 50 60 KM.

State Capitals ⊛
County Seats ⊙

87415 Flora Vista, 500 .... A 2
88118 Floyd, 248 .... F 4
88322 Flying H, 61 .... E 5
88419 Folsom, 75 .... F 2
88036 Fort Bayard, 390 .... A 6
88323 Fort Stanton, 389 .... D 5
88119 Fort Sumner⊙, 1,615 .... E 4
87316 Fort Wingate, 800 .... A 3
87416 Fruitland, 600 .... A 2
† 87540 Galisteo, 125 .... D 3
87017 Gallina, 500 .... C 2
87301 Gallup⊙, 14,596 .... A 3
87317 Gamerco, 800 .... A 3
87936 Garfield, 600 .... B 6
88421 Garita, 154 .... E 3
88038 Gila, 300 .... A 6
88324 Glencoe, 140 .... D 5
88039 Glenwood, 175 .... A 5
87535 Glorieta, 300 .... D 3
88120 Grady, 104 .... F 4
87020 Grants, 8,768 .... B 3
87722 Guadalupita, 305 .... D 2
88232 Hagerman, 953 .... E 5
88041 Hanover, 350 .... A 6
87937 Hatch, 867 .... B 6
87537 Hernandez, 500 .... C 2
88325 High Rolls Mountain Park, 650 .... D 5
88042 Hillsboro, 125 .... B 6
88240 Hobbs, 26,025 .... F 6
87723 Holman, 510 .... D 2
88336 Hondo, 250 .... D 5
88250 Hope, 90 .... E 6
87901 Hot Springs (Truth or Consequences), 4,656 .... B 5
88121 House, 119 .... F 4
88251 Humble City, 65 .... F 6
88043 Hurley, 1,796 .... A 6
87538 Ilfeld, 68 .... D 3
87022 Isleta, 1,080 .... C 4
88252 Jal, 2,602 .... F 6
87023 Jarales, 525 .... C 4
87024 Jemez Pueblo, 1,197 .... C 3
87025 Jemez Springs, 356 .... C 3
87417 Kirtland, 800 .... A 2
† 87712 La Cueva, 200 .... D 3
87026 Laguna, 900 .... B 3
87027 La Jara, 210 .... B 2
87028 Lajoya, 97 .... C 4
88253 Lake Arthur, 306 .... E 5
88337 La Luz, 800 .... C 6
87539 La Madera, 200 .... C 2
88044 La Mesa, 900 .... C 6
87540 Lamy, 66 .... D 3
87418 La Plata, 150 .... A 2
88001 Las Cruces⊙, 37,857 .... C 6
87541 Las Tablas, 65 .... C 2
87701 Las Vegas (city)⊙, 7,528 .... D 3
† 88021 La Union, 200 .... C 7
87725 Ledoux, 400 .... D 3
87823 Lemitar, 400 .... B 4
88338 Lincoln, 100 .... D 5
87543 Llano, 270 .... D 2
88255 Loco Hills, 350 .... F 6
88426 Logan, 386 .... F 3
88045 Lordsburg⊙, 3,429 .... A 6
87544 Los Alamos⊙, 11,310 .... C 3
87031 Los Lunas⊙, 973 .... C 4
† 87101 Los Ranchos de Albuquerque, 1,900 .... C 3
88256 Loving, 1,192 .... E 6
88260 Lovington⊙, 8,915 .... F 6
87547 Lumberton, 190 .... C 2
87824 Luna, 175 .... A 5
87825 Magdalena, 652 .... B 4
88263 Malaga, 250 .... E 6
87318 Manuelito, 200 .... A 3
† 87016 Manzano, 110 .... C 4
87728 Maxwell, 393 .... E 2
88339 Mayhill, 200 .... D 6

88262 McDonald, 170 .... F 5
† 79901 Meadow Vista, 1,402 .... C 7
88124 Melrose, 636 .... F 4
87319 Mentmore, 315 .... A 3
88340 Mescalero, 950 .... D 5
88046 Mesilla, 1,713 .... C 6
88047 Mesilla Park, 1,500 .... C 6
88048 Mesquite, 950 .... C 6
87320 Mexican Springs, 150 .... A 3
87729 Miami, 200 .... E 2
87020 Milan, 2,185 .... B 3
88049 Mimbres, 155 .... B 6
87731 Montezuma, 110 .... D 3
87939 Monticello, 125 .... B 5
88265 Monument, 250 .... F 6
87732 Mora⊙, 1,400 .... D 3
87035 Moriarty, 758 .... D 4
87733 Mosquero⊙, 244 .... F 3
87036 Mountainair, 1,022 .... C 4
† 87501 Nambe, 100 .... D 3
88430 Nara Visa, 400 .... F 3
87328 Navajo, 920 .... A 3
† 87325 Newcomb, 300 .... A 2
88431 Newkirk, 75 .... E 3
87038 New Laguna, 450 .... B 4
88341 Nogal, 80 .... D 5
87734 Ocate, 288 .... E 2
88266 Oil Center, 300 .... F 6
87549 Ojo Caliente, 500 .... D 2
87735 Ojo Feliz, 146 .... E 2
87550 Ojo Sarco, 184 .... D 2
88052 Organ, 500 .... C 6
88342 Orogrande, 80 .... D 6
† 88220 Otis, 200 .... E 6
87040 Paguate, 775 .... B 3
87551 Park View, 788 .... C 2
87552 Pecos, 598 .... D 3
87041 Penablanca, 320 .... C 3
87553 Penasco, 1,169 .... D 2
87042 Peralta, 400 .... C 4
87554 Petaca, 84 .... C 2
88343 Picacho, 120 .... D 5
87827 Pie Town, 99 .... A 4
88053 Pinos Altos, 200 .... A 6
87043 Placitas, 88 .... C 3
87044 Ponderosa, 400 .... C 3
88130 Portales⊙, 10,554 .... F 4
87045 Prewitt, 300 .... B 3
88432 Puerto de Luna, 180 .... E 4
88433 Quay, 75 .... F 4
87829 Quemado, 520 .... A 4
87556 Questa, 1,095 .... D 2
88054 Radium Springs, 150 .... B 6
87736 Rainsville, 300 .... D 2
87321 Ramah, 574 .... A 3
87557 Ranches of Taos, 2,900 .... D 2
87740 Raton⊙, 6,962 .... E 2
87558 Red River, 125 .... D 2
87046 Regina, 65 .... B 2
87322 Rehoboth, 300 .... A 3
87830 Reserve⊙, 800 .... A 5
87560 Ribera, 400 .... D 3
87940 Rincon, 300 .... C 6
87742 Rociada, 164 .... D 3
87561 Rodarte, 650 .... D 2
88056 Rodeo, 100 .... A 7
88201 Roswell⊙, 33,908 .... E 5
87562 Rowe, 150 .... D 3
87743 Roy, 476 .... E 3
88345 Ruidoso, 2,216 .... D 5
88346 Ruidoso Downs, 702 .... D 5
87563 Rutheron, 90 .... C 2
87941 Salem, 400 .... B 6
87831 San Acacia, 150 .... B 4
87832 San Antonio, 359 .... B 5
87564 San Cristobal, 275 .... D 2
87047 Sandia Park, 200 .... C 3
† 87001 San Felipe, 1,187 .... C 3
87049 San Fidel, 150 .... B 3
† 87501 San Ildefonso, 140 .... C 3

88434 San Jon, 308 .... F 3
87565 San Jose, 115 .... D 3
87566 San Juan Pueblo, 900 .... C 2
88057 San Lorenzo, 264 .... B 6
87050 San Mateo, 200 .... B 3
88058 San Miguel, 400 .... C 6
88348 San Patricio, 250 .... D 5
87051 San Rafael, 300 .... A 3
87567 Santa Cruz, 754 .... D 2
87501 Santa Fe (cap.)⊙, 41,167 .... C 3
88059 Santa Rita, 600 .... B 6
88435 Santa Rosa⊙, 2,485 .... E 4
87052 Santo Domingo Pueblo, 1,662 .... C 3
87053 San Ysidro, 280 .... C 3
87745 Sapello, 144 .... D 3
87055 Seboyeta, 125 .... B 3
87568 Sena, 150 .... D 3
87569 Serafina, 280 .... D 3
87420 Shiprock, 800 .... A 2
88061 Silver City⊙, 7,751 .... A 6
87801 Socorro⊙, 4,687 .... C 4
† 87565 Soham, 104 .... D 3
87746 Solano, 70 .... E 3
87747 Springer, 1,574 .... E 2
87056 Stanley, 60 .... D 3
87057 Tajique, 150 .... C 4
87571 Taos⊙, 2,475 .... D 2
† 87571 Taos Pueblo, 1,030 .... D 2
88267 Tatum, 982 .... F 5
87574 Tesuque, 800 .... C 3
88135 Texico, 772 .... F 4
87323 Thoreau, 550 .... A 3
87575 Tierra Amarilla⊙, 850 .... C 2
87059 Tijeras, 500 .... C 3
88351 Tinnie, 95 .... D 5
87324 Toadlena, 200 .... A 2
87325 Tohatchi, 500 .... A 3
87060 Tome, 500 .... C 4
87061 Torreon, 100 .... C 4
87576 Trampas, 76 .... D 2
88439 Trementina, 80 .... E 3
87577 Tres Piedras, 200 .... D 2
87578 Truchas, 275 .... D 2
87748 Trujillo, 148 .... E 3
87901 Truth or Consequences⊙, 4,656 .... B 5
88401 Tucumcari⊙, 7,189 .... F 3
88352 Tularosa, 2,851 .... C 5
88065 Tyrone, 100 .... A 6
88001 University Park, 4,165 .... C 6
87749 Ute Park, 75 .... D 2
87579 Vadito, 335 .... D 2
88072 Vado, 350 .... C 6
87580 Valdez, 190 .... D 2
† 87031 Valencia, 500 .... C 4
87581 Vallecitos, 450 .... C 2
88073 Vanadium, 300 .... A 6
88353 Vaughn, 867 .... D 4
87582 Velarde, 365 .... C 2
† 81091 Vermejo Park, 85 .... D 2
87583 Villanueva, 300 .... D 3
† 88055 Virden, 151 .... A 6
87752 Wagon Mound, 630 .... E 2
87421 Waterflow, 475 .... A 2
87753 Watrous, 250 .... D 3
87544 White Rock, 3,861 .... C 3
88002 White Sands Missile Range, 4,167 .... C 6
88268 Whites City, 300 .... E 6
87063 Willard, 209 .... D 4
87942 Williamsburg, 367 .... B 5
88136 Yeso, 200 .... E 4
87064 Youngsville, 130 .... C 2
† 87053 Zia Pueblo, 600 .... C 3
87327 Zuni, 3,958 .... A 3

⊙ County seat.
‡ Population of metropolitan area.
† Zip of nearest p.o.
* Multiple zips

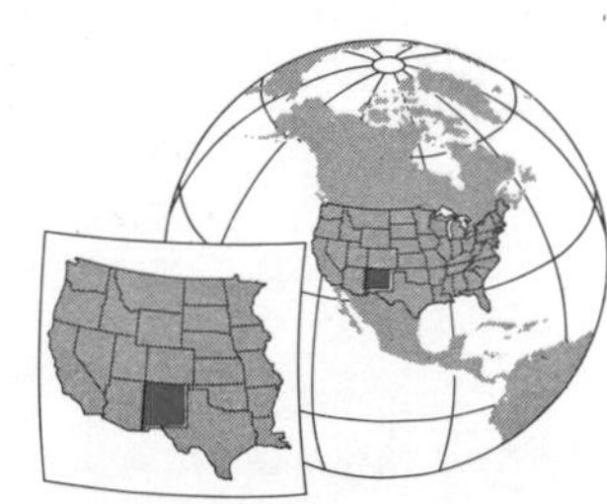

AREA 121,666 sq. mi.
POPULATION 1,016,000
CAPITAL Santa Fe
LARGEST CITY Albuquerque
HIGHEST POINT Wheeler Pk. 13,161 ft.
SETTLED IN 1605
ADMITTED TO UNION January 6, 1912
POPULAR NAME Land of Enchantment
STATE FLOWER Yucca
STATE BIRD Road Runner

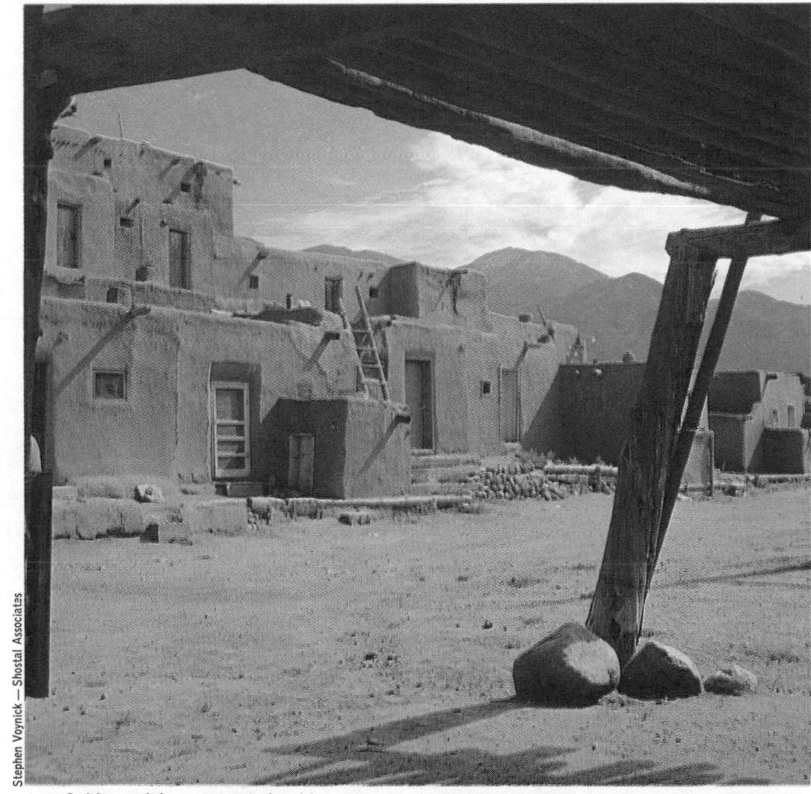
Stephen Voynick — Shostal Associates

Golden adobe against the blue Sangre de Cristo Mountains. Clear, pure colors, magnificent surroundings and congenial atmosphere combine to draw artists and writers to Taos, New Mexico.

Topography

0 50 100 MILES

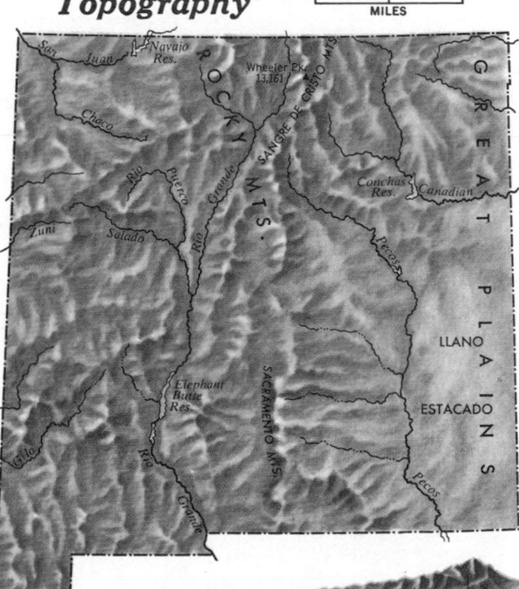

Agriculture, Industry and Resources

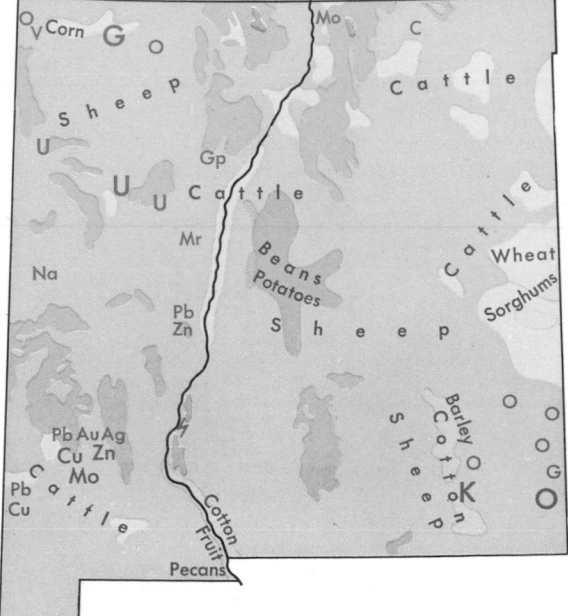

DOMINANT LAND USE

- Wheat, Grain Sorghums, Range Livestock
- General Farming, Livestock, Special Crops
- General Farming, Livestock, Cash Grain
- Dry Beans, General Farming
- Cotton, Forest Products
- Range Livestock
- Forests
- Nonagricultural Land

MAJOR MINERAL OCCURRENCES

Ag	Silver	Gp	Gypsum	U	Uranium
Au	Gold	K	Potash	V	Vanadium
C	Coal	Mo	Molybdenum	Zn	Zinc
Cu	Copper	Mr	Marble	O	Petroleum
G	Natural Gas	Na	Salt	Pb	Lead

ϟ Water Power

Corn
Sheep
Cattle
Wheat
Sorghums
Beans
Potatoes
Barley
Cotton
Fruit
Pecans

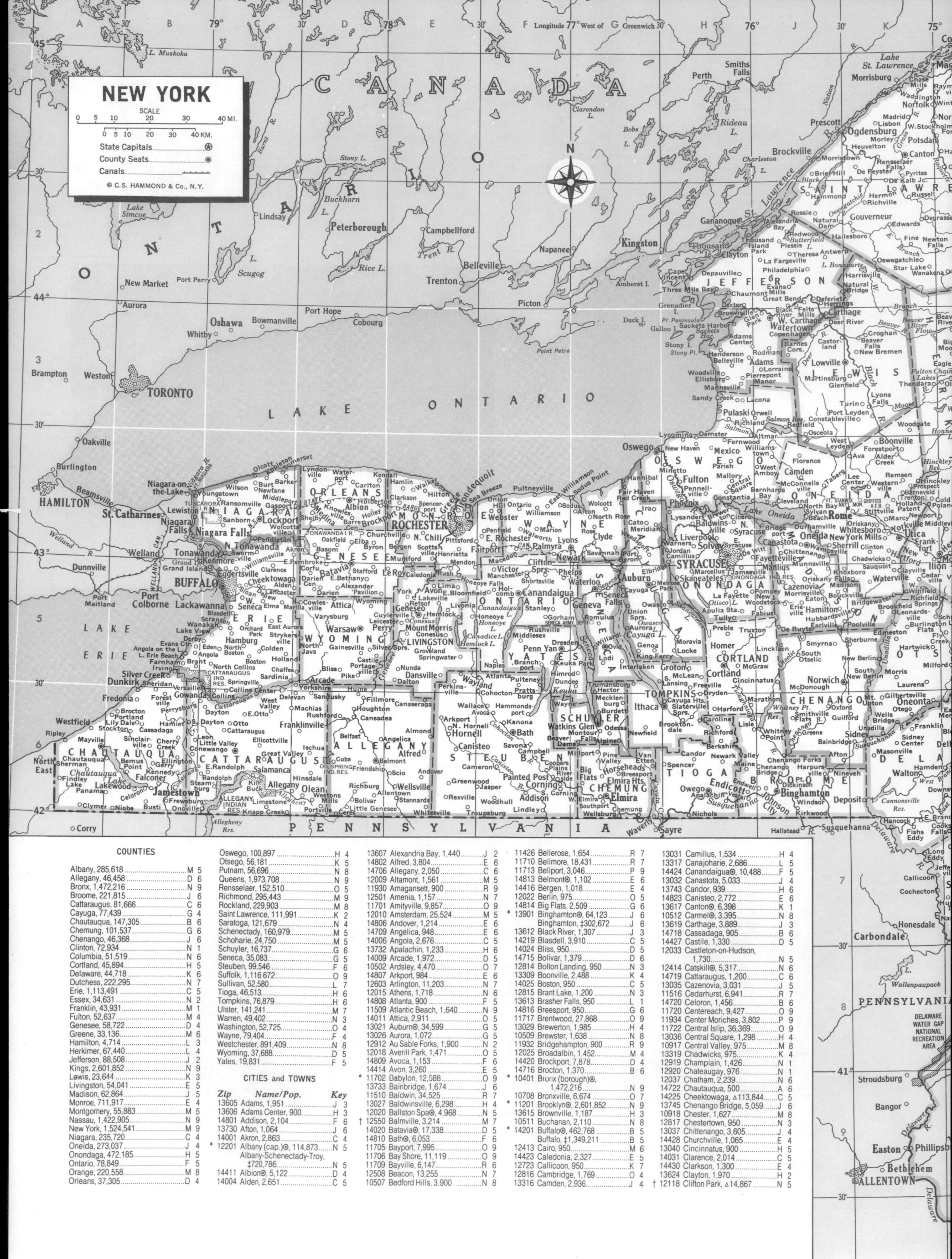

COUNTIES

Albany, 285,618 ..... M 5
Allegany, 46,458 ..... D 6
Bronx, 1,472,216 ..... N 9
Broome, 221,815 ..... J 6
Cattaraugus, 81,666 ..... C 6
Cayuga, 77,439 ..... G 4
Chautauqua, 147,305 ..... B 6
Chemung, 101,537 ..... G 6
Chenango, 46,368 ..... J 6
Clinton, 72,934 ..... N 1
Columbia, 51,519 ..... N 6
Cortland, 45,894 ..... H 5
Delaware, 44,718 ..... K 6
Dutchess, 222,295 ..... N 7
Erie, 1,113,491 ..... C 5
Essex, 34,631 ..... N 2
Franklin, 43,931 ..... M 1
Fulton, 52,637 ..... M 4
Genesee, 58,722 ..... D 4
Greene, 33,136 ..... M 6
Hamilton, 4,714 ..... L 3
Herkimer, 67,440 ..... L 4
Jefferson, 88,508 ..... J 2
Kings, 2,601,852 ..... N 9
Lewis, 23,644 ..... K 3
Livingston, 54,041 ..... E 5
Madison, 62,864 ..... J 5
Monroe, 711,917 ..... E 4
Montgomery, 55,883 ..... M 5
Nassau, 1,422,905 ..... N 9
New York, 1,524,541 ..... M 9
Niagara, 235,720 ..... C 4
Oneida, 273,037 ..... J 4
Onondaga, 472,185 ..... H 5
Ontario, 78,849 ..... F 5
Orange, 220,558 ..... M 8
Orleans, 37,305 ..... D 4
Oswego, 100,897 ..... H 4
Otsego, 56,181 ..... K 5
Putnam, 56,696 ..... N 8
Queens, 1,973,708 ..... N 9
Rensselaer, 152,510 ..... O 5
Richmond, 295,443 ..... M 9
Rockland, 229,903 ..... M 8
Saint Lawrence, 111,991 ..... K 2
Saratoga, 121,679 ..... N 4
Schenectady, 160,979 ..... M 5
Schoharie, 24,750 ..... M 5
Schuyler, 16,737 ..... G 6
Seneca, 35,083 ..... G 5
Steuben, 99,546 ..... F 6
Suffolk, 1,116 672 ..... O 9
Sullivan, 52,580 ..... L 7
Tioga, 46,513 ..... H 6
Tompkins, 76,879 ..... H 6
Ulster, 141,241 ..... M 7
Warren, 49,402 ..... N 3
Washington, 52,725 ..... O 4
Wayne, 79,404 ..... F 4
Westchester, 891,409 ..... N 8
Wyoming, 37,688 ..... D 5
Yates, 19,831 ..... F 5

CITIES and TOWNS

	Zip	Name/Pop.	Key
	13605	Adams, 1,951	J 3
	13606	Adams Center, 900	H 3
	14801	Addison, 2,104	F 6
	13730	Afton, 1,064	J 6
	14001	Akron, 2,863	C 4
*	12201	Albany (cap.)⊙, 114,873	N 5
		Albany-Schenectady-Troy, ‡720,786	N 5
	14411	Albion⊙, 5,122	D 4
	14004	Alden, 2,651	C 5
	13607	Alexandria Bay, 1,440	J 2
	14802	Alfred, 3,804	E 6
	14706	Allegany, 2,050	C 6
	12009	Altamont, 1,561	M 5
	11930	Amagansett, 900	R 9
	12501	Amenia, 1,157	N 7
	11701	Amityville, 9,857	O 9
	12010	Amsterdam, 25,524	M 5
	14806	Andover, 1,214	E 6
	14709	Angelica, 948	E 6
	14006	Angola, 2,676	C 5
	13732	Apalachin, 1,233	H 6
	14009	Arcade, 1,972	D 5
	10502	Ardsley, 4,470	O 7
	14807	Arkport, 984	E 6
	12603	Arlington, 11,203	N 7
	12015	Athens, 1,718	N 6
	14808	Atlanta, 900	F 5
	11509	Atlantic Beach, 1,640	N 9
	14011	Attica, 2,911	D 5
	13021	Auburn⊙, 34,599	G 5
	13026	Aurora, 1,072	G 5
	12912	Au Sable Forks, 1,900	N 2
	12018	Averill Park, 1,471	O 5
	14809	Avoca, 1,153	F 6
	14414	Avon, 3,260	E 5
*	11702	Babylon, 12,588	O 9
	13733	Bainbridge, 1,674	J 6
	11510	Baldwin, 34,525	R 7
	13027	Baldwinsville, 6,298	H 4
	12020	Ballston Spa⊙, 4,968	N 5
†	12550	Balmville, 3,214	M 7
	14020	Batavia⊙, 17,338	D 5
	14810	Bath⊙, 6,053	F 6
	11705	Bayport, 7,995	O 9
	11706	Bay Shore, 11,119	O 9
	11709	Bayville, 6,147	R 6
	12508	Beacon, 13,255	N 7
	10507	Bedford Hills, 3.900	N 8
	11426	Bellerose, 1,654	R 7
	11710	Bellmore, 18,431	R 7
	11713	Bellport, 3,046	P 9
	14813	Belmont⊙, 1,102	E 6
	14416	Bergen, 1,018	E 4
	12022	Berlin, 975	O 5
	14814	Big Flats, 2,509	G 6
*	13901	Binghamton⊙, 64,123	J 6
		Binghamton, ‡302,672	J 6
	13612	Black River, 1,307	J 3
	14219	Blasdell, 3,910	C 5
	14024	Bliss, 950	D 5
	14715	Bolivar, 1,379	D 6
	12814	Bolton Landing, 950	N 3
	13309	Boonville, 2,488	K 4
	14025	Boston, 950	C 5
	12815	Brant Lake, 1,200	N 3
	13613	Brasher Falls, 950	L 1
	14816	Breesport, 950	G 6
	11717	Brentwood, 27,868	O 9
	13029	Brewerton, 1,985	H 4
	10509	Brewster, 1,638	N 8
	11932	Bridgehampton, 900	R 9
	12025	Broadalbin, 1,452	M 4
	14420	Brockport, 7,878	D 4
	14716	Brocton, 1,370	B 6
*	10401	Bronx (borough)⊙, 1,472,216	N 9
	10708	Bronxville, 6,674	O 7
*	11201	Brooklyn⊙, 2,601,852	N 9
	13615	Brownville, 1,187	H 3
	10511	Buchanan, 2,110	N 8
*	14201	Buffalo⊙, 462,768	B 5
		Buffalo, ‡1,349,211	B 5
	12413	Cairo, 950	M 6
	14423	Caledonia, 2,327	E 5
	12723	Callicoon, 950	K 7
	12816	Cambridge, 1,769	O 4
	13316	Camden, 2,936	J 4
	13031	Camillus, 1,534	H 4
	13317	Canajoharie, 2,686	L 5
	14424	Canandaigua⊙, 10,488	F 5
	13032	Canastota, 5,033	J 4
	13743	Candor, 939	H 6
	14823	Canisteo, 2,772	E 6
	13617	Canton⊙, 6,398	K 1
	10512	Carmel⊙, 3,395	N 8
	13619	Carthage, 3,889	J 3
	14718	Cassadaga, 905	B 6
	14427	Castile, 1,330	D 5
	12033	Castleton-on-Hudson, 1,730	N 5
	12414	Catskill⊙, 5,317	N 6
	14719	Cattaraugus, 1,200	C 6
	13035	Cazenovia, 3,031	J 5
	11516	Cedarhurst, 6,941	R 7
	14720	Celoron, 1,456	B 6
	11720	Centereach, 9,427	O 9
	11934	Center Moriches, 3,802	P 9
	11722	Central Islip, 36,369	O 9
	13036	Central Square, 1,298	H 4
	10917	Central Valley, 975	M 8
	13319	Chadwicks, 975	K 4
	12919	Champlain, 1,426	N 1
	12920	Chateaugay, 976	N 1
	12037	Chatham, 2,239	N 6
	14722	Chautauqua, 500	A 6
	14225	Cheektowaga, ▵113,844	C 5
	13745	Chenango Bridge, 5,059	J 6
	10918	Chester, 1,627	M 8
	12817	Chestertown, 950	N 3
	13037	Chittenango, 3,605	J 4
	14428	Churchville, 1,065	E 4
	13040	Cincinnatus, 900	H 5
	14031	Clarence, 2,014	C 5
	14430	Clarkson, 1,300	E 4
	13624	Clayton, 1,970	H 2
†	12118	Clifton Park, ▵14,867	N 5

AREA 49,576 sq. mi.
POPULATION 18,241,266
CAPITAL Albany
LARGEST CITY New York
HIGHEST POINT Mt. Marcy 5,344 ft.
SETTLED IN 1614
ADMITTED TO UNION July 26, 1788
POPULAR NAME Empire State
STATE FLOWER Rose
STATE BIRD Bluebird

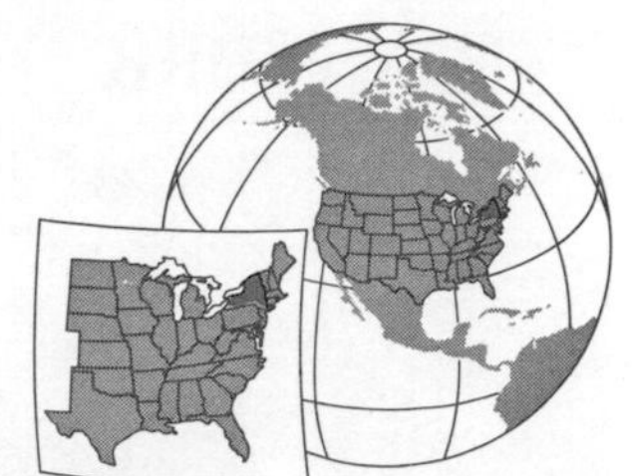

Topography

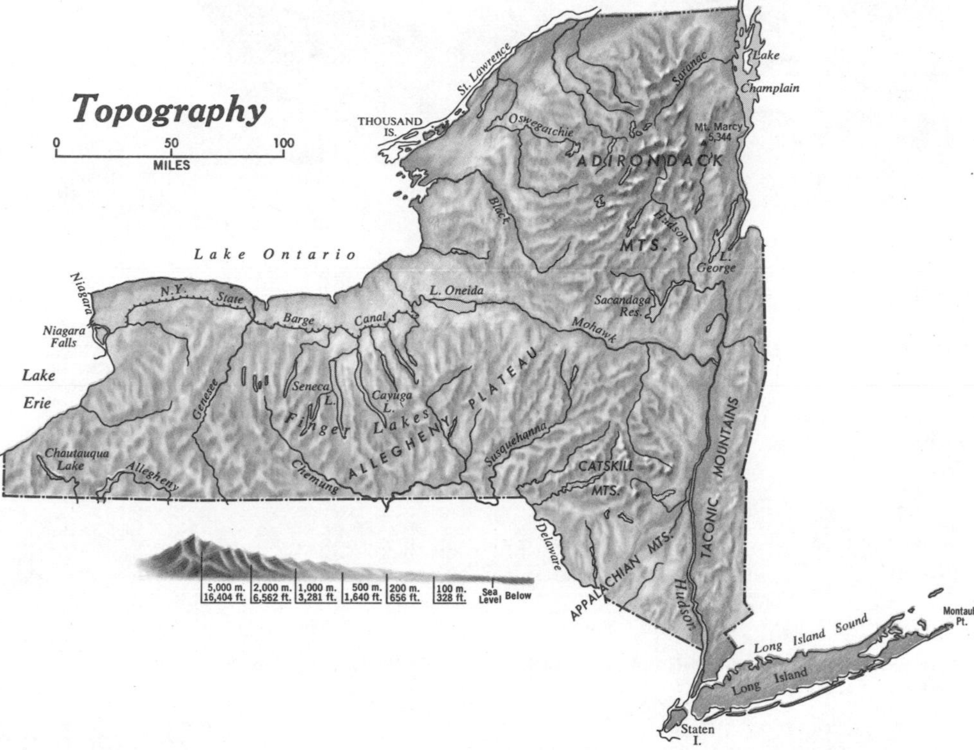

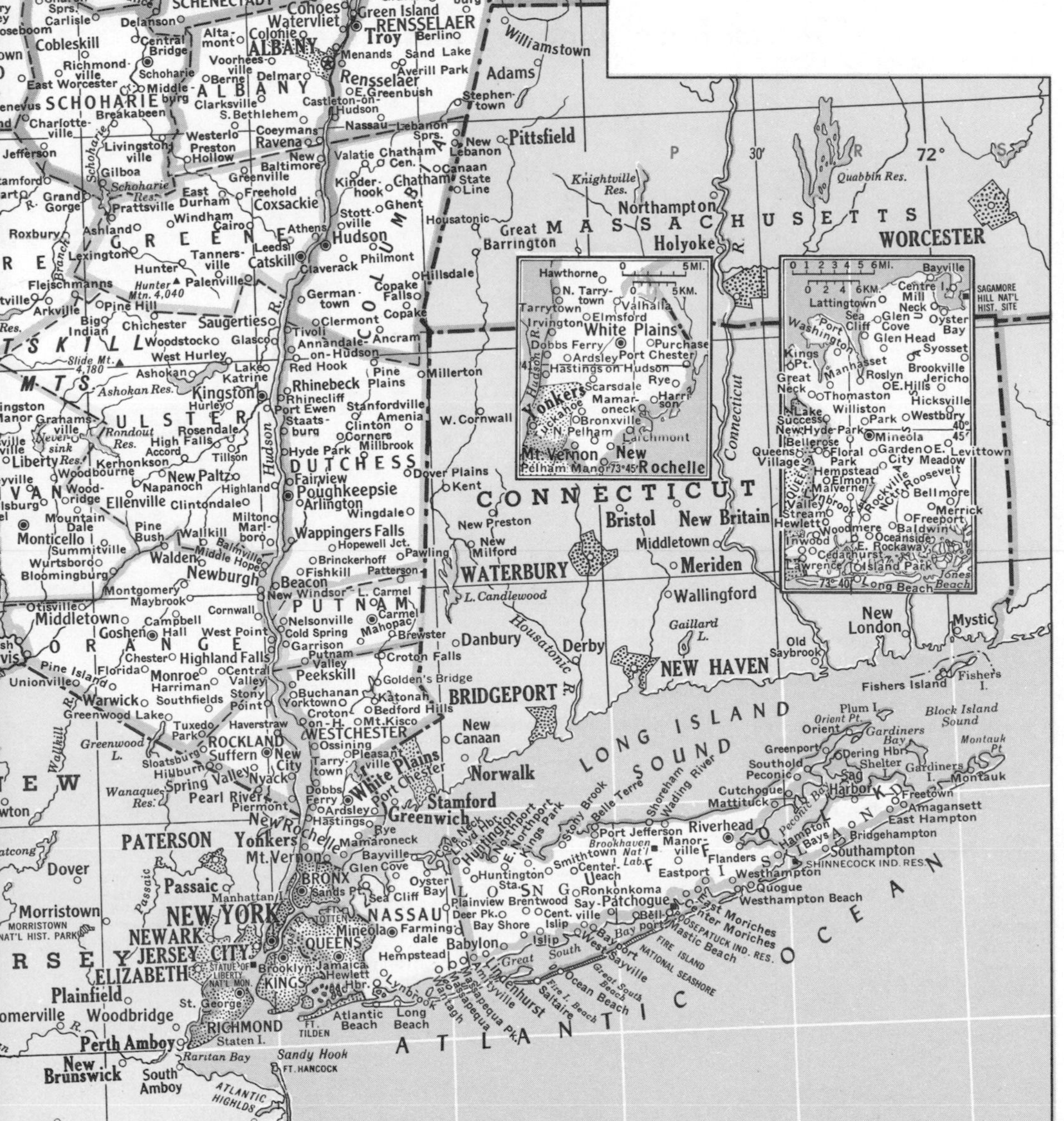

14432 Clifton Springs, 2,058 .... F 4
13323 Clinton, 2,271 .... K 4
14433 Clyde, 2,828 .... G 4
12043 Cobleskill, 4,368 .... L 5
12045 Coeymans, 975 .... N 6
12047 Cohoes, 18,613 .... N 5
14033 Colden, 950 .... C 5
10516 Cold Spring, 2,083 .... N 8
† 12201 Colonie, 8,701 .... N 5
13326 Cooperstown⊙, 2,403 .... L 5
12022 Corinth, 3,267 .... N 4
14830 Corning, 15,792 .... F 6
12518 Cornwall, 2,032 .... M 8
13045 Cortland⊙, 19,621 .... H 5
12051 Coxsackie, 2,399 .... N 6
10519 Croton Falls, 950 .... N 8
10520 Croton-on-Hudson, 7,523 .... N 8
14727 Cuba, 1,735 .... D 6
12929 Dannemora, 3,735 .... N 1
14437 Dansville, 5,436 .... E 5
11729 Deer Park, 31,120 .... O 9
14042 Delevan, 994 .... D 6
13753 Delhi⊙, 3,017 .... L 6
12054 Delmar, 7,500 .... N 5
14043 Depew, 22,158 .... C 5
13754 Deposit, 2,061 .... K 6
14047 Derby, 4,900 .... B 5
13214 DeWitt, 10,032 .... H 4
13634 Dexter, 1,061 .... H 2
10522 Dobbs Ferry, 10,353 .... O 6
13329 Dolgeville, 2,872 .... L 4
12522 Dover Plains, 975 .... O 7
13053 Dryden, 1,490 .... H 6
14837 Dundee, 1,539 .... F 5
14048 Dunkirk, 16,855 .... B 5
13054 Durhamville, 975 .... J 4
13332 Earlville, 1,050 .... J 5
14052 East Aurora, 7,033 .... C 5
12061 East Greenbush, 985 .... N 5
11937 East Hampton, 1.753 .... R 9
11554 East Meadow, 46,252 .... R 7
11940 East Moriches, 1,702 .... P 9
11731 East Northport, 12,392 .... O 9
11941 Eastport, 1,308 .... P 9
14445 East Rochester, 8,347 .... F 4
11518 East Rockaway, 10,323 .... R 7
13057 East Syracuse, 4,333 .... H 4
14057 Eden, 2,962 .... C 5
† 14226 Eggertsville, 55,000 .... C 5
13060 Elbridge, 1,040 .... G 5
12932 Elizabethtown⊙, 607 .... N 2
12428 Ellenville, 4,482 .... M 7
14731 Ellicottville, 955 .... C 6
14059 Elma, 2,784 .... C 5
* 14901 Elmira⊙, 39,945 .... G 6
14903 Elmira Heights, 4,906 .... G 6
11003 Elmont, 29,363 .... R 7
10523 Elmsford, 3,911 .... P 6
13760 Endicott, 16,556 .... H 6
13760 Endwell, 15,999 .... H 6
14450 Fairport, 6,474 .... F 4
† 12601 Fairview, 8,517 .... N 7
14733 Falconer, 2,983 .... B 6
11735 Farmingdale, 9,297 .... N 9
13066 Fayetteville, 4,996 .... J 4
12524 Fishkill, 913 .... N 7
* 11001 Floral Park, 18,422 .... R 7
10921 Florida, 1,674 .... M 8
13337 Fly Creek, 910 .... K 5
12068 Fonda⊙, 1,120 .... M 5
14062 Forestville, 908 .... B 6
12937 Fort Covington, 983 .... M 1
12828 Fort Edward, 3,733 .... O 4
13339 Fort Plain, 2,809 .... L 5
13340 Frankfort, 3,305 .... K 4
14737 Franklinville, 1,948 .... D 6
14063 Fredonia, 10,326 .... B 6
11520 Freeport, 40,374 .... R 7
14738 Frewsburg, 1,772 .... B 6
14739 Friendship, 1,285 .... D 6
13069 Fulton, 14,003 .... H 4
11530 Garden City, 25,373 .... R 7
10524 Garrison, 975 .... N 8
14067 Gasport, 950 .... C 4
14454 Geneseo⊙, 5,714 .... E 5
14456 Geneva, 16,793 .... G 5
14740 Gerry, 950 .... B 6
12432 Glasco, 1,169 .... M 6
11542 Glen Cove, 25,770 .... R 6
11545 Glen Head, 4,000 .... R 7
12801 Glens Falls, 17,222 .... N 4
12078 Gloversville, 19,677 .... M 4
10526 Golden's Bridge, 1,101 .... N 8
10924 Goshen⊙, 4,342 .... M 8
13642 Gouverneur, 4,574 .... K 2
14070 Gowanda, 3,110 .... B 6
12434 Grand Gorge, 950 .... L 6
14072 Grand Island, 900 .... B 5
12832 Granville, 2,784 .... O 4
* 11020 Great Neck, 10,724 .... R 7
14616 Greece, ∆75,136 .... E 4
13778 Greene, 1,874 .... J 6
12183 Green Island, 3,297 .... N 5
11944 Greenport, 2,481 .... P 8
12834 Greenwich, 2,092 .... O 4
10925 Greenwood Lake, 2,262 .... M 8
13073 Groton, 2,112 .... H 5
13780 Guilford, 995 .... J 6
12086 Hagaman, 1,410 .... M 5
14075 Hamburg, 10,215 .... C 5
13346 Hamilton, 3,636 .... J 5
14840 Hammondsport, 1,066 .... F 6
11946 Hampton Bays, 1,862 .... R 9
13783 Hancock, 1,688 .... K 7
10926 Harriman, 955 .... M 8
10528 Harrison, 9,250 .... P 7
10706 Hastings on Hudson, 9,479 .... O 7
10927 Haverstraw, 8,198 .... M 8
10532 Hawthorne, 5,000 .... O 6
* 11550 Hempstead, 39,411 .... R 7
13650 Henderson, 900 .... H 3
13350 Herkimer⊙, 8,960 .... L 4

(continued on following page)

(continued)

Lower Manhattan's skyline in an unusual view from a pier at the Brooklyn Port Authority Marine Terminal.

Eric Carle — Shostal Associates

11557 Hewlett, 6,796 .... R 7
* 11801 Hicksville, 48,075 .... R 7
12440 High Falls, 950 .... M 7
12528 Highland, 2,184 .... M 7
10928 Highland Falls, 4,638 .... M 8
10931 Hillburn, 1,058 .... M 8
14468 Hilton, 2,440 .... E 4
14080 Holland, 950 .... C 5
14470 Holley, 1,868 .... D 4
13077 Homer, 4,143 .... H 5
14472 Honeoye Falls, 2,248 .... F 5
12090 Hoosick Falls, 3,897 .... O 5
12533 Hopewell Junction, 2,055 .... N 7
14843 Hornell, 12,144 .... E 6
14845 Horseheads, 7,989 .... G 6
14744 Houghton, 1,620 .... D 6
12534 Hudson⊙, 8,940 .... N 6
12839 Hudson Falls⊙, 7,917 .... O 4
11743 Huntington, 12,130 .... O 9
11746 Huntington Station, 28,817 .... O 9
12443 Hurley, 4,081 .... M 7
12538 Hyde Park, 2,805 .... N 6
13357 Ilion, 9,808 .... K 5
12842 Indian Lake, 950 .... M 3
11696 Inwood, 8,433 .... R 7
14617 Irondequoit, ∆63,675 .... E 4
10533 Irvington, 5,878 .... O 6
11558 Island Park, 5,396 .... R 8
11751 Islip, 7,962 .... O 9
14850 Ithaca⊙, 26,226 .... G 6
* 11401 Jamaica⊙, 765,078 .... N 9
14701 Jamestown, 39,795 .... B 6
13078 Jamesville, 900 .... H 5
11753 Jericho, 14,010 .... S 7
13790 Johnson City, 18,025 .... J 6
12095 Johnstown⊙, 10,045 .... M 4
13080 Jordan, 1,493 .... H 4
10536 Katonah, 4,189 .... N 8
12944 Keeseville, 2,122 .... O 2
14271 Kenmore, 20,980 .... C 5
14747 Kennedy, 950 .... B 6
12446 Kerhonkson, 1,243 .... M 7
14478 Keuka Park, 990 .... F 5
12106 Kinderhook, 1,233 .... N 6
* 11201 Kings (Brooklyn) (borough), 2,601,852 .... N 9
11754 Kings Park, 5,555 .... O 9
11024 Kings Point, 5,525 .... R 7
12401 Kingston⊙, 25,544 .... M 7
14218 Lackawanna, 28,657 .... B 5
10512 Lake Carmel, 4,796 .... N 8
12845 Lake George⊙, 1,046 .... N 4
12449 Lake Katrine, 1,092 .... M 7
12846 Lake Luzerne, 900 .... N 4
12946 Lake Placid, 2,731 .... N 2
12108 Lake Pleasant⊙, 364 .... M 4
11040 Lake Success, 3,254 .... R 7
14085 Lake View, 6,000 .... B 5
14750 Lakewood, 3,864 .... B 6
14086 Lancaster, 13,365 .... C 5
10538 Larchmont, 7,203 .... P 7
11559 Lawrence, 6,566 .... R 7
14482 Le Roy, 5,118 .... E 5
11756 Levittown, 65,440 .... S 7
14092 Lewiston, 3,292 .... B 4
12754 Liberty, 4,293 .... L 7
14485 Lima, 1,686 .... E 5
11757 Lindenhurst, 28,338 .... O 9
13365 Little Falls, 7,629 .... L 4
14755 Little Valley⊙, 1,340 .... C 6
13088 Liverpool, 3,307 .... H 4
12758 Livingston Manor, 1,522 .... L 7
14487 Livonia, 1,278 .... E 5
14094 Lockport⊙, 25,399 .... C 4
11561 Long Beach, 33,127 .... R 8
13367 Lowville, 3,671 .... J 3
11563 Lynbrook, 23,776 .... R 7
12952 Lyon Mountain, 1,200 .... N 1
14489 Lyons⊙, 4,496 .... F 4
14502 Macedon, 1,168 .... F 4
13660 Madrid, 950 .... K 1
10541 Mahopac, 5,265 .... N 8
13103 Mallory, 900 .... H 4
12953 Malone⊙, 8,048 .... M 1
11565 Malverne, 10,036 .... R 7
10543 Mamaroneck, 18,909 .... P 7
14504 Manchester, 1,305 .... F 5
11030 Manhasset, 8,541 .... R 7
* 10001 Manhattan (borough), 1,524,541 .... M 9
13104 Manlius, 4,295 .... J 5
13803 Marathon, 1,053 .... J 6
13108 Marcellus, 1,456 .... H 5
13403 Marcy, 2,417 .... K 4

14505 Marion, 925 .... F 4
12542 Marlboro, 1,580 .... M 7
11758 Massapequa, 26,951 .... O 9
11762 Massapequa Park, 22,112 .... O 9
13662 Massena, 14,042 .... L 1
11950 Mastic Beach, 4,870 .... P 9
11952 Mattituck, 1,995 .... P 9
12543 Maybrook, 1,536 .... M 8
12117 Mayfield, 981 .... M 4
14757 Mayville⊙, 1,567 .... A 6
13101 McGraw, 1,319 .... H 5
12118 Mechanicville, 6,247 .... N 5
14103 Medina, 6,415 .... D 4
† 13021 Melrose Park, 2,189 .... G 5
† 12201 Menands, 3,449 .... N 5
11566 Merrick, 25,904 .... S 7
13114 Mexico, 1,555 .... H 4
12122 Middleburg, 1,410 .... M 5
12550 Middle Hope, 2,327 .... M 7
14105 Middleport, 2,132 .... C 4
10940 Middletown, 22,607 .... L 8
12545 Millbrook, 1,735 .... N 7
12546 Millerton, 1,042 .... O 7
11765 Mill Neck, 982 .... R 6
12547 Milton, 1,900 .... M 7
12547 Milton, 1,861 .... N 4
11501 Mineola⊙, 21,845 .... R 7
13115 Minetto, 950 .... H 4
12956 Mineville-Witherbee, 1,967 .... O 2
13407 Mohawk, 3,301 .... L 4
10950 Monroe, 4,439 .... M 8
12549 Montgomery, 1,533 .... M 7
12701 Monticello⊙, 5,991 .... L 7
14865 Montour Falls, 1,534 .... G 6
13118 Moravia, 1,642 .... H 5
12960 Moriah, 953 .... N 2
12962 Morrisonville, 1,276 .... N 1
13408 Morrisville, 2,296 .... J 5
12763 Mountain Dale, 950 .... L 7
10549 Mount Kisco, 8,172 .... N 8
14510 Mount Morris, 3,417 .... E 5
* 10550 Mount Vernon, 72,778 .... O 7
12458 Napanoch, 975 .... M 7
14512 Naples, 1,324 .... F 5
12123 Nassau, 1,466 .... N 5
14513 Newark, 11,644 .... G 4
13811 Newark Valley, 1,286 .... H 6
13411 New Berlin, 1,369 .... K 5
12550 Newburgh, 26,219 .... M 7
10956 New City⊙, 27,344 .... N 8
14108 Newfane, 2,588 .... C 4
13413 New Hartford, 2,433 .... K 4
11040 New Hyde Park, 10,116 .... R 7
12561 New Paltz, 6,058 .... M 7
13416 Newport, 908 .... K 4
* 10801 New Rochelle, 75,385 .... P 7
12550 New Windsor, 8,803 .... N 8
* 10001 New York (5 boroughs)⊙, 7,867,760 .... M 9
New York, ‡11,517,483 .... M 9
13417 New York Mills, 3,805 .... K 4
* 14301 Niagara Falls, 85,615 .... C 4
12309 Niskayuna, 6,186 .... N 5
13667 Norfolk, 1,379 .... K 1
14110 North Boston, 1,635 .... C 5
14514 North Chili, 3,163 .... E 4
14111 North Collins, 1,675 .... C 5
15853 North Creek, 950 .... M 3
14113 North Java, 950 .... D 5
11768 Northport, 7,440 .... O 9
13212 North Syracuse, 8,687 .... H 4
10591 North Tarrytown, 8,334 .... O 6
14120 North Tonawanda, 36,012 .... C 4
12134 Northville, 1,192 .... M 4
13815 Norwich⊙, 8,843 .... J 5
13668 Norwood, 2,098 .... L 1
14517 Nunda, 1,254 .... E 5
10960 Nyack, 6,659 .... N 8
14125 Oakfield, 1,964 .... D 4
11572 Oceanside, 35,028 .... R 7
13669 Ogdensburg, 14,554 .... K 1
14126 Olcott, 1,592 .... C 4
13420 Old Forge, 950 .... L 3
14760 Olean, 19,169 .... D 6
13421 Oneida, 11,658 .... J 4
13820 Oneonta, 16,030 .... K 6
14127 Orchard Park, 3,732 .... C 5
13424 Oriskany, 1,627 .... K 4
13425 Oriskany Falls, 927 .... J 5
10562 Ossining, 21,659 .... N 8
13126 Oswego⊙, 23,844 .... G 4
13825 Otego, 956 .... K 6
10963 Otisville, 933 .... L 8
14521 Ovid⊙, 779 .... G 5
13827 Owego⊙, 5,152 .... H 6

13830 Oxford, 1,944 .... J 6
11771 Oyster Bay, 14,330 .... S 6
14870 Painted Post, 2,496 .... F 6
14522 Palmyra, 3,776 .... F 4
12768 Parksville, 950 .... L 7
11772 Patchogue, 11,582 .... P 9
12563 Patterson, 975 .... N 7
12137 Pattersonville, 950 .... M 5
12564 Pawling, 1,914 .... N 7
10965 Pearl River, 17,146 .... M 8
10566 Peekskill, 18,881 .... N 8
† 10803 Pelham Manor, 6,673 .... O 7
14526 Penfield, 8,904 .... F 4
14527 Penn Yan⊙, 5,168 .... F 5
14530 Perry, 4,538 .... D 5
12972 Peru, 1,261 .... N 1
14532 Phelps, 1,989 .... F 5
12565 Philmont, 1,674 .... N 6
13135 Phoenix, 2,617 .... H 4
10968 Piermont, 2,386 .... M 8
12566 Pine Bush, 1,183 .... M 7
10969 Pine Island, 925 .... L 8
12567 Pine Plains, 950 .... N 7
14534 Pittsford, 1,755 .... E 4
11803 Plainview, 32,195 .... O 9

12901 Plattsburgh⊙, 18,715 .... O 1
10570 Pleasantville, 7,110 .... N 8
13140 Port Byron, 1,330 .... G 4
10573 Port Chester, 25,803 .... P 7
12466 Port Ewen, 2,882 .... N 7
12974 Port Henry, 1,532 .... O 2
11777 Port Jefferson, 5,515 .... P 9
12771 Port Jervis, 8,852 .... L 8
14770 Portville, 1,304 .... D 6
11050 Port Washington, 15,923 .... R 6
13676 Potsdam, 9,985 .... K 1
* 12601 Poughkeepsie⊙, 32,029 .... N 7
13142 Pulaski, 2,480 .... H 3
10577 Purchase, 2,900 .... P 7
10579 Putnam Valley, ∆975 .... N 8
* 11101 Queens (borough), 1,973,708 .... N 9
11429 Queens Village, 72,000 .... R 7
14772 Randolph, 1,498 .... C 6
14131 Ransomville, 1,034 .... C 4
12143 Ravena, 2,797 .... N 6
12571 Red Hook, 1,680 .... N 7
12144 Rensselaer, 10,136 .... N 5
12572 Rhinebeck, 2,336 .... N 7
13439 Richfield Springs, 1,540 .... K 5
14775 Ripley, 1,173 .... A 6
11901 Riverhead⊙, 7,585 .... P 9
† 14830 Riverside, 911 .... F 6
* 14601 Rochester⊙, 296,233 .... E 4
Rochester, ‡882,667 .... E 4
* 11570 Rockville Centre, 27,444 .... R 7
13440 Rome, 50,148 .... J 4
11779 Ronkonkoma, 7,284 .... O 9
11575 Roosevelt, 15,008 .... R 7
12776 Roscoe, 1,300 .... L 7
12472 Rosendale, 1,220 .... M 7
11576 Roslyn, 2,546 .... R 7
12979 Rouses Point, 2,250 .... O 1
10580 Rye, 15,869 .... P 7
13685 Sackets Harbor, 1,202 .... H 3
11963 Sag Harbor, 2,363 .... R 8
10301 Saint George⊙, 13,000 .... M 9
13452 Saint Johnsville, 2,089 .... L 5
14779 Salamanca, 7,877 .... C 6
12865 Salem, 1,025 .... O 4
† 11050 Sands Point, 2,916 .... N 9
12983 Saranac Lake, 6,086 .... M 2
12866 Saratoga Springs, 18,845 .... N 4
12477 Saugerties, 4,190 .... M 6
13456 Sauquoit, 1,900 .... K 5
14879 Savona, 933 .... F 6
11782 Sayville, 11,680 .... O 9
10583 Scarsdale, 19,229 .... P 7
* 12301 Schenectady⊙, 77,859 .... M 5
12157 Schoharie⊙, 1,125 .... M 5
12870 Schroon Lake, 950 .... N 3
12871 Schuylerville, 1,402 .... N 4
12302 Scotia, 8,224 .... N 5

14546 Scottsville, 1,967 .... E 4
† 14075 Scranton, 925 .... C 5
† 14617 Sea Breeze, 1,200 .... F 4
11579 Sea Cliff, 5,890 .... R 6
13148 Seneca Falls, 7,794 .... G 5
13460 Sherburne, 1,613 .... K 5
13461 Sherrill, 2,986 .... J 4
14548 Shortsville, 1,516 .... F 5
13838 Sidney, 4,789 .... K 6
14136 Silver Creek, 3,182 .... B 5
13152 Skaneateles, 3,055 .... H 5
† 14201 Sloan, 5,216 .... C 5
10974 Sloatsburg, 3,134 .... M 8
11787 Smithtown, 15,000 .... O 9
14551 Sodus, 1,813 .... G 4
14555 Sodus Point, 1,172 .... G 4
13209 Solvay, 8,280 .... H 4
11968 Southampton, 4,904 .... R 9
14830 South Corning, 1,414 .... F 6
12779 South Fallsburg, 1,590 .... L 7
† 12801 South Glens Falls, 4,013 .... N 4
11971 Southold, 2,030 .... P 8
† 14901 Southport, 8,685 .... G 6
14559 Spencerport, 2,929 .... E 4
10977 Spring Valley, 18,112 .... M 8
14141 Springville, 4,350 .... C 5
12167 Stamford, 1,286 .... L 6
* 10301 Staten Island (borough), 295,443 .... M 9
12170 Stillwater, 1,428 .... N 5
11790 Stony Brook, 6,391 .... O 9
10980 Stony Point, 8,270 .... M 8
12172 Stottville, 1,106 .... N 6
10901 Suffern, 8,273 .... M 8
11791 Syosset, 9,970 .... S 7
* 13201 Syracuse⊙, 197,208 .... H 4
Syracuse, ‡635,946 .... H 4
10591 Tarrytown, 11,115 .... O 6
13691 Theresa, 985 .... J 2
† 11020 Thomaston, 2,486 .... R 7
12883 Ticonderoga, 3,268 .... N 3
12486 Tillson, 1,256 .... M 7
14150 Tonawanda, 21,898 .... B 4
* 12180 Troy⊙, 62,918 .... N 5
14886 Trumansburg, 1,618 .... G 5
10707 Tuckahoe, 6,236 .... O 7
12986 Tupper Lake, 4,854 .... M 2
13849 Unadilla, 1,489 .... K 6
13160 Union Springs, 1,183 .... G 5
* 13501 Utica⊙, 91,611 .... K 4
Utica-Rome, ‡337,477 .... K 4
12184 Valatie, 1,288 .... N 6
10595 Valhalla, 6,000 .... P 6
* 11580 Valley Stream, 40,413 .... N 9
13850 Vestal, 8,303 .... H 6
14564 Victor, 2,187 .... F 5
12186 Voorheesville, 2,826 .... M 5
13694 Waddington, 955 .... K 1

11792 Wading River, 975 .... P 9
12586 Walden, 5,277 .... M 7
12589 Wallkill, 1,849 .... M 7
13856 Walton, 3,744 .... K 6
13163 Wampsville⊙, 586 .... J 4
† 14075 Wanakah, 1,600 .... C 5
11793 Wantagh, 21,873 .... N 9
12590 Wappingers Falls, 5,607 .... N 7
12885 Warrensburg, 2,743 .... N 3
14569 Warsaw⊙, 3,619 .... D 5
10990 Warwick, 3,604 .... M 8
12188 Waterford, 2,879 .... N 5
13165 Waterloo⊙, 5,418 .... G 5
13601 Watertown⊙, 30,787 .... J 3
13480 Waterville, 1,808 .... K 5
12189 Watervliet, 12,404 .... N 5
14891 Watkins Glen⊙, 2,716 .... G 6
14892 Waverley, 5,261 .... G 7
14572 Wayland, 2,022 .... E 5
14580 Webster, 5,037 .... F 4
13166 Weedsport, 1,900 .... G 4
14895 Wellsville, 5,815 .... E 6
11590 Westbury, 15,362 .... R 7
† 13619 West Carthage, 2,047 .... J 3
† 14901 West Elmira, 5,901 .... G 6
14787 Westfield, 3,651 .... A 6
† 12801 West Glens Falls, 3,363 .... N 4
11977 Westhampton, 1,156 .... P 9
11978 Westhampton Beach, 1,926 .... P 9
10996 West Point, 8,100 .... M 8
11796 West Sayville, 7,386 .... O 9
14224 West Seneca, ∆48,404 .... C 5
13491 West Winfield, 1,018 .... K 5
12887 Whitehall, 3,764 .... O 3
* 10601 White Plains⊙, 50,220 .... P 6
13492 Whitesboro, 4,805 .... K 4
13862 Whitney Point, 1,058 .... J 6
14589 Williamson, 1,991 .... F 4
14221 Williamsville, 6,835 .... C 5
11596 Williston Park, 9,154 .... R 7
12996 Willsboro, 950 .... N 2
14172 Wilson, 1,284 .... C 4
13865 Windsor, 1,098 .... J 6
12998 Witherbee-Mineville, 1,967 .... N 2
14590 Wolcott, 1,617 .... G 4
12788 Woodbourne, 1,155 .... M 7
11598 Woodmere, 19,831 .... R 7
12789 Woodridge, 1,071 .... L 7
12498 Woodstock, 1,073 .... M 6
* 10701 Yonkers, 204,370 .... O 7
† 10598 Yorktown, 9,008 .... N 8
13495 Yorkville, 3,425 .... K 4
14174 Youngstown, 2,169 .... C 4

⊙ County seat.
‡ Population of metropolitan area.
∆ Population of town or township.
† Zip of nearest p.o.
* Multiple zips

Agriculture, Industry and Resources

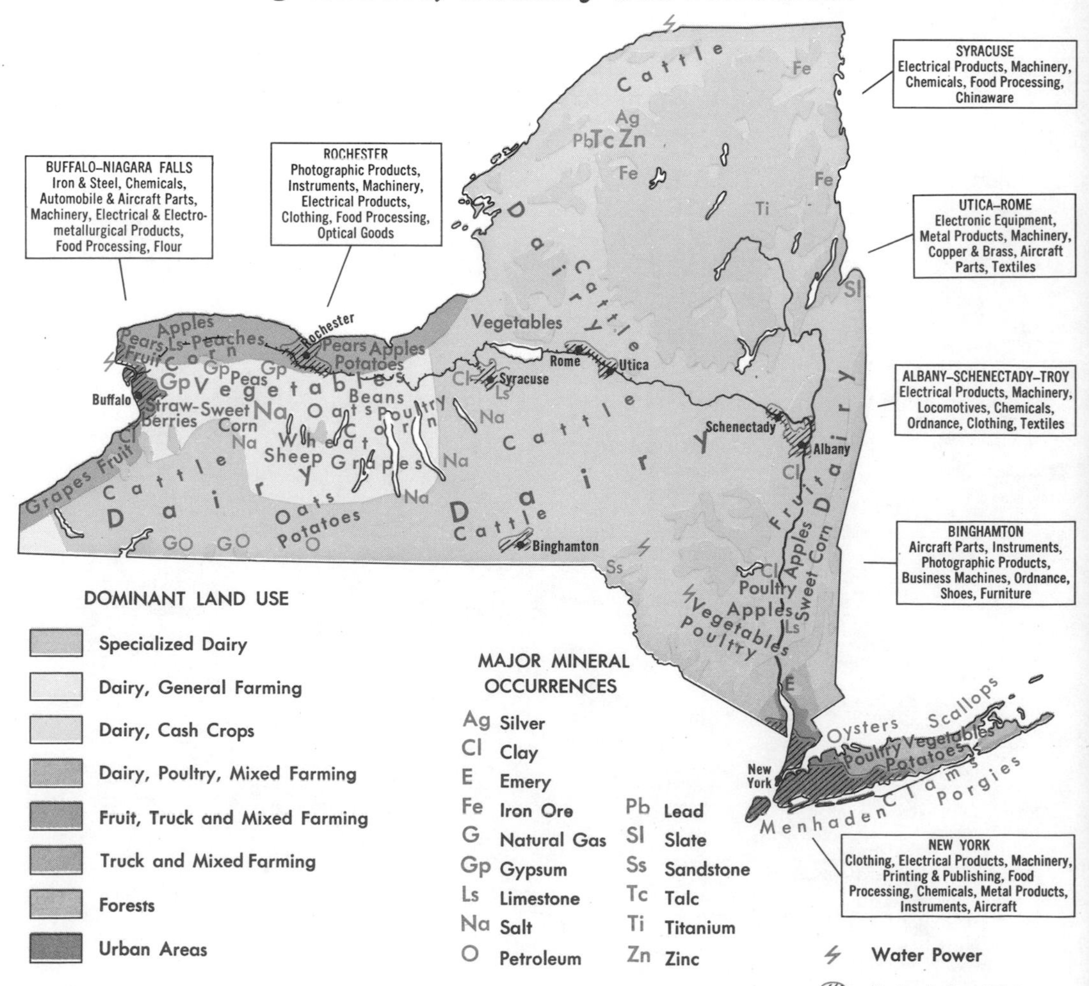

COUNTIES

Alamance, 96,362 L 3
Alexander, 19,466 G 3
Alleghany, 8,134 G 1
Anson, 23,488 J 4
Ashe, 19,571 F 2
Avery, 12,655 F 2
Beaufort, 35,980 R 4
Bertie, 20,528 P 2
Bladen, 26,477 M 5
Brunswick, 24,223 N 6
Buncombe, 145,056 D 3
Burke, 60,364 F 3
Cabarrus, 74,629 H 4
Caldwell, 56,699 F 3
Camden, 5,453 S 2
Carteret, 31,603 R 5
Caswell, 19,055 L 2
Catawba, 90,873 G 3
Chatham, 29,554 L 3
Cherokee, 16,330 A 4
Chowan, 10,764 R 2
Clay, 5,180 B 4
Cleveland, 72,556 F 4
Columbus, 46,937 M 6
Craven, 62,554 P 4
Cumberland, 212,042 M 4
Currituck, 6,976 S 2
Dare, 6,995 T 3
Davidson, 95,627 J 3
Davie, 18,855 H 3
Duplin, 38,015 O 5
Durham, 132,681 M 3
Edgecombe, 52,341 O 3
Forsyth, 214,348 J 2
Franklin, 26,820 N 2
Gaston, 148,415 G 4
Gates, 8,524 R 2
Graham, 6,562 B 4
Granville, 32,762 M 2
Greene, 14,967 O 3
Guilford, 288,590 K 3
Halifax, 53,884 O 2
Harnett, 49,667 M 4
Haywood, 41,710 C 3
Henderson, 42,804 D 4
Hertford, 23,529 P 2
Hoke, 16,436 L 4
Hyde, 5,571 S 3
Iredell, 72,197 H 3
Jackson, 21,593 C 4
Johnston, 61,737 N 4
Jones, 9,779 P 4
Lee 30,467 L 4
Lenoir, 55,204 O 4
Lincoln, 32,682 G 3
Macon, 15,788 B 4
Madison, 16,003 D 3
Martin, 24,730 P 3
McDowell, 30,648 E 3
Mecklenburg, 354,656 H 4
Mitchell, 13,447 E 2
Montgomery, 19,267 K 4
Moore, 39,048 L 4
Nash, 59,122 O 2
New Hanover, 82,996 O 6
Northampton, 24,009 P 2
Onslow, 103,126 P 5
Orange, 57,707 L 2
Pamlico, 9,467 R 4
Pasquotank, 26,824 S 2
Pender, 18,149 O 5
Perquimans, 8,351 S 2
Person, 25,914 M 2
Pitt, 73,900 P 3
Polk, 11,735 E 4
Randolph, 76,358 K 3
Richmond, 39,889 K 4
Robeson, 84,842 L 5
Rockingham, 72,402 K 2
Rowan, 90,035 H 3
Rutherford, 47,337 E 4
Sampson, 44,954 N 4
Scotland, 26,929 L 5
Stanly, 42,822 J 4
Stokes, 23,782 J 2
Surry, 51,415 H 2
Swain, 7,861 B 3
Transylvania, 19,713 D 4
Tyrrell, 3,806 S 3
Union, 54,714 H 4
Vance, 32,691 N 2
Wake, 228,453 M 3
Warren, 15,810 N 2
Washington, 14,038 R 3
Watauga, 23,404 F 2
Wayne, 85,408 N 4
Wilkes, 49,524 G 2
Wilson, 57,486 O 3
Yadkin, 24,599 H 2
Yancey, 12,629 E 3

CITIES and TOWNS

Zip *Name/Pop.* *Key*

28321 Abbottsburg, 425 M 5
28315 Aberdeen, 1,592 L 4
27006 Advance, 206 J 3
27910 Ahoskie, 5,105 P 2
27201 Alamance, 450 K 2
† 28713 Alarka, 900 C 4
28001 Albemarle⊙, 11,126 J 4
† 27589 Alert, 200 N 2
28701 Alexander, 200 D 3
28509 Alliance, 577 R 4
† 28364 Alma, 200 L 5
28702 Almond, 200 B 4
27202 Altamahaw, 900 L 2
28901 Andrews, 1,384 B 4
27501 Angier, 1,431 M 4
28007 Ansonville, 694 J 4
27502 Apex, 2,192 M 3
28510 Arapahoe, 212 R 4
27263 Archdale, 6,103 K 3
27589 Arcola, 300 N 2
28704 Arden, 850 D 4
† 28642 Arlington, 711 H 2
28420 Ash, 250 N 6
27203 Asheboro⊙, 10,797 K 3
* 28801 Asheville⊙, 57,681 D 3
Asheville, ‡145,056 D 3
28603 Ashford, 225 F 3
† 27983 Askewville, 247 R 2
28421 Atkinson, 325 N 5
28511 Atlantic, 950 S 5
28512 Atlantic Beach, 300 R 5
27805 Aulander, 947 P 2
27806 Aurora, 620 R 4
28318 Autryville, 213 M 4
27915 Avon, 400 U 4
† 28076 Avondale-Henrietta, 1,307 F 4
28513 Ayden, 3,450 P 4
28009 Badin, 1,626 J 4
27503 Bahama, 280 M 2
27807 Bailey, 724 N 3
28705 Bakersville⊙, 409 E 2
28706 Balfour, 2,014 E 4
† 27203 Balfours, 4,836 K 3
28707 Balsam, 300 C 4
† 27030 Bannertown, 1,138 H 1
27917 Barco, 325 T 2
† 28739 Barker Heights, 2,933 D 4
28710 Bat Cave, 400 E 4
27808 Bath, 231 R 4
27809 Battleboro, 688 O 2
28515 Bayboro⊙, 665 R 4
27207 Bear Creek, 500 L 3
28516 Beaufort⊙, 3,368 R 5
27810 Belhaven, 2,259 R 3
28012 Belmont, 4,814 H 4
27919 Belvidere, 275 S 2
† 28621 Benham, 400 G 2
27208 Bennett, 200 K 3
27504 Benson, 2,267 N 4
† 27565 Berea, 200 M 2
28016 Bessemer City, 5,217 G 4
† 28779 Beta, 500 C 4
27812 Bethel, 1,514 P 3
28518 Beulaville, 1,156 O 5
† 28803 Biltmore Forest, 1,298 E 3
27209 Biscoe, 1,244 K 4
27813 Black Creek, 449 O 3
28711 Black Mountain, 3,204 E 3
28320 Bladenboro, 783 M 5
27212 Blanch, 210 L 2
28605 Blowing Rock, 801 F 2
† 28438 Boardman, 233 M 6
28092 Boger City, 2,203 G 4
† 28570 Bogue, 600 R 5
28461 Boiling Spring Lakes, 245 N 7
28017 Boiling Springs, 2,284 F 4
28423 Bolton, 534 N 6
27213 Bonlee, 275 L 3
28606 Boomer, 212 G 2
28607 Boone⊙, 8,754 F 2
27011 Boonville, 687 H 2
28322 Bowdens, 250 N 4
28712 Brevard⊙, 5,243 D 4
28519 Bridgeton, 520 R 4
27505 Broadway, 694 L 4
28601 Brookford, 590 G 3
27214 Browns Summit, 500 K 2
28424 Brunswick, 206 M 6
28713 Bryson City⊙, 1,290 C 4
† 28377 Buies, 275 L 5
27506 Buies Creek, 2,024 M 4
27507 Bullock, 550 M 2
27508 Bunn, 284 N 3
28323 Bunnlevel, 200 M 4
28425 Burgaw⊙, 1,744 N 5
27215 Burlington, 35,930 K 2
28714 Burnsville⊙, 1,348 E 3
27509 Butner, 3,538 M 2
28324 Butters, 225 M 5
27920 Buxton, 700 U 4
27228 Bynum, 400 L 3
28325 Calypso, 462 N 4
27921 Camden⊙, 300 S 2
28326 Cameron, 204 L 4
28715 Candler, 950 D 3
27229 Candor, 561 K 4
28716 Canton, 5,158 D 3
28019 Caroleen, 975 F 4
28428 Carolina Beach, 1,663 O 6
27510 Carrboro, 3,472 L 3
28327 Carthage⊙, 1,034 K 4
27511 Cary, 7,430 M 3
28020 Casar, 350 F 3
28717 Cashiers, 230 C 4
27816 Castalia, 265 O 2
28429 Castle Hayne, 900 O 6
28609 Catawba, 565 G 3
† 28754 Catharine Lake, 500 O 5
27230 Cedar Falls, 500 K 3
28520 Cedar Island, 250 S 5
28718 Cedar Mountain, 250 D 4
28431 Chadbourn, 2,213 M 6
27514 Chapel Hill, 25,537 M 3
* 28201 Charlotte⊙, 241,178 H 4
Charlotte, ‡409,370 H 4
28719 Cherokee, 975 C 4
28021 Cherryville, 5,258 G 4
28023 China Grove, 1,788 H 3
28521 Chinquapin, 350 O 5
27817 Chocowinity, 566 P 4
28610 Claremont, 788 G 3
28432 Clarendon, 300 M 6
28433 Clarkton, 662 M 6
27520 Clayton, 3,103 N 3
27012 Clemmons, 4,900 J 2
27013 Cleveland, 614 H 3
28024 Cliffside, 950 F 4
27233 Climax, 475 K 3
28328 Clinton⊙, 7,157 N 5
28721 Clyde, 900 D 3
27521 Coats, 1,051 M 4
27922 Cofield, 422 R 2
27923 Coinjock, 650 S 2
27924 Colerain, 373 R 2
27234 Coleridge, 600 K 3
28611 Collettsville, 275 F 3
27925 Columbia⊙, 902 S 3
28722 Columbus⊙, 731 E 4
28522 Comfort, 340 O 5
27818 Como, 211 P 1
28025 Concord⊙, 18,464 H 4
28612 Connellys Springs, 500 F 3
28613 Conover, 3,355 G 3
27820 Conway, 694 P 2
27014 Cooleemee, 1,115 H 3
28031 Cornelius, 1,296 H 4
28523 Cove City, 485 P 4
28032 Cramerton, 2,142 G 4
27522 Creedmoor, 1,405 M 2
27928 Creswell, 633 S 3
28033 Crouse, 850 G 4
† 28716 Cruso, 800 D 4
28723 Cullowhee, 6,300 C 4
28331 Cumberland, 800 M 5
28435 Currie, 294 N 6
27929 Currituck⊙, 500 T 2
27015 Cycle, 210 H 2
28034 Dallas, 4,059 G 4
† 27043 Dalton, 400 J 2
27016 Danbury⊙, 152 J 2
28036 Davidson, 2,931 H 4
28524 Davis, 600 R 5
28436 Delco, 450 N 6
27239 Denton, 1,017 J 3
28725 Dillsboro, 215 C 4
27017 Dobson⊙, 933 H 2
† 28685 Dockery, 300 G 2
28526 Dover, 585 P 4
28619 Drexel, 1,431 F 3
28332 Dublin, 283 M 5
28334 Dunn, 8,302 M 4
* 27701 Durham⊙, 95,438 M 2
Durham, ‡190,388 M 2
† 28761 Dysartsville, 950 F 3
27242 Eagle Springs, 500 K 4
28038 Earl, 300 F 4
27018 East Bend, 485 H 2
28726 East Flat Rock, 2,627 E 4
28352 East Laurinburg, 487 L 5
† 28752 East Marion, 3,015 F 3
28039 East Spencer, 2,217 J 3
27288 Eden, 15,871 K 1
27932 Edenton⊙, 4,766 R 2
27243 Efland, 600 L 2
27909 Elizabeth City⊙, 14,069 S 2
28337 Elizabethtown⊙, 1,418 M 5
28621 Elkin, 2,899 H 2
28622 Elk Park, 503 F 2
28040 Ellenboro, 465 F 4
28338 Ellerbe, 913 K 4
27822 Elm City, 1,201 O 3
27244 Elon College, 2,150 L 2
27823 Enfield, 3,272 O 2
27824 Engelhard, 500 T 3
28728 Enka, 500 D 3
28527 Ernul, 350 P 4
28339 Erwin, 2,852 M 4
27247 Ether, 375 K 4
28729 Etowah, 700 D 4
27830 Eureka, 263 O 3
28438 Evergreen, 250 M 6
28439 Fair Bluff, 1,039 M 6
27826 Fairfield, 954 S 3
28340 Fairmont, 2,827 L 6
28730 Fairview, 800 D 3
28341 Faison, 598 N 4
28041 Faith, 506 J 3
28342 Falcon, 357 M 4
† 27028 Farmington, 300 H 3
27828 Farmville, 4,424 O 3
* 28301 Fayetteville⊙, 53,510 M 4
Fayetteville, ‡212,042 M 4
28731 Flat Rock, 650 E 4
28732 Fletcher, 950 E 4
28043 Forest City, 7,179 E 4
† 27028 Fork, 250 J 3
27829 Fountain, 434 O 3
27524 Four Oaks, 1,057 M 4
28734 Franklin⊙, 2,336 C 4
27525 Franklinton, 1,459 N 2
27248 Franklinville, 794 K 3
28440 Freeland, 500 N 6
27830 Fremont, 1,596 N 3
27936 Frisco, 325 T 4
27526 Fuquay-Varina, 3,576 M 3
28441 Garland, 656 N 5
27529 Garner, 4,923 M 3
27831 Garysburg, 231 O 2

(continued on following page)

AREA 52,586 sq. mi.
POPULATION 5,082,059
CAPITAL Raleigh
LARGEST CITY Charlotte
HIGHEST POINT Mt. Mitchell 6,684 ft.
SETTLED IN 1650
ADMITTED TO UNION November 21, 1789
POPULAR NAME Tarheel State
STATE FLOWER Flowering Dogwood
STATE BIRD Cardinal

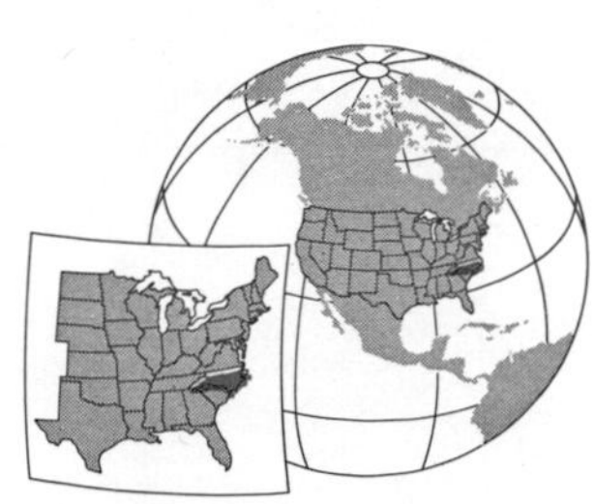

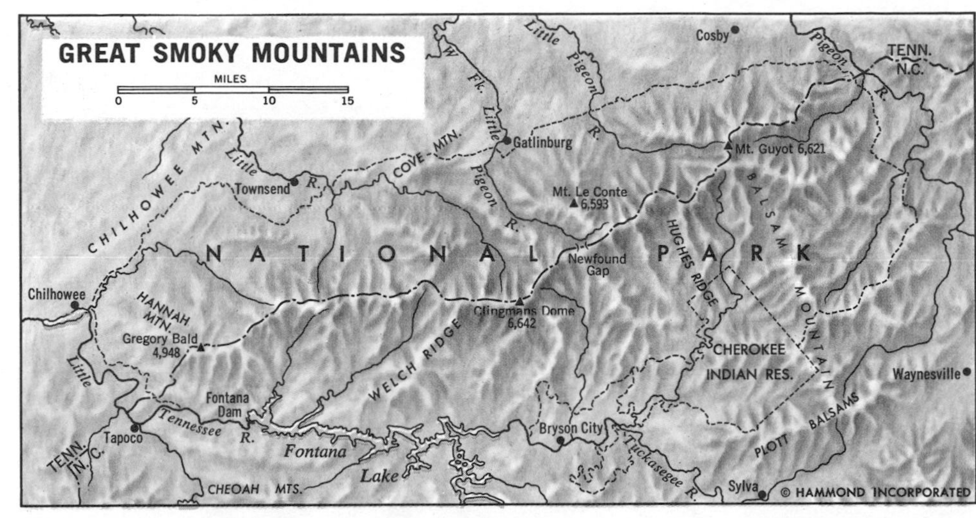

Agriculture, Industry and Resources

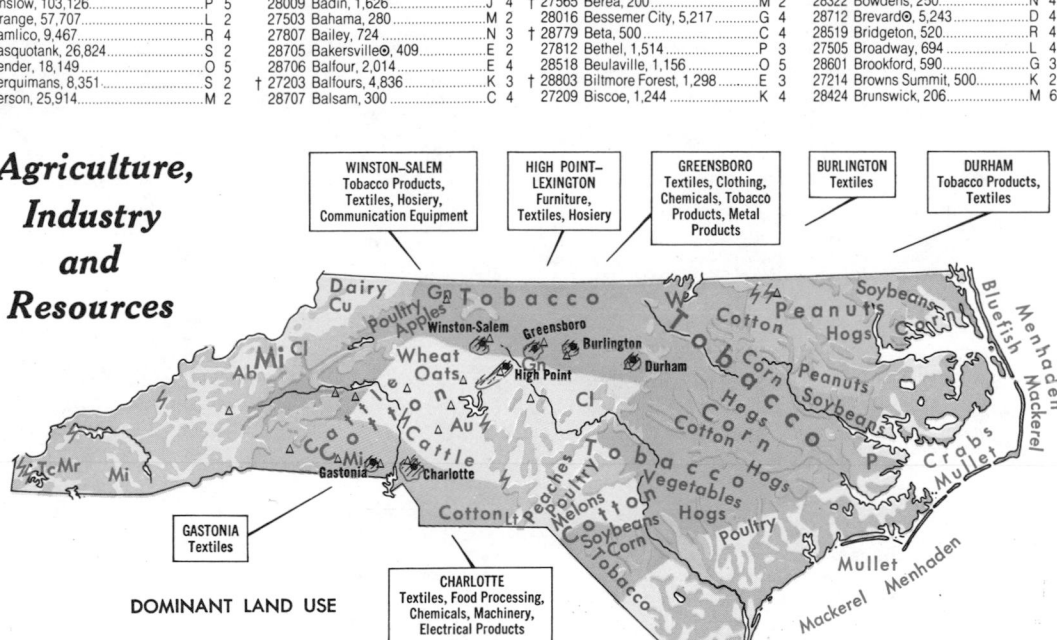

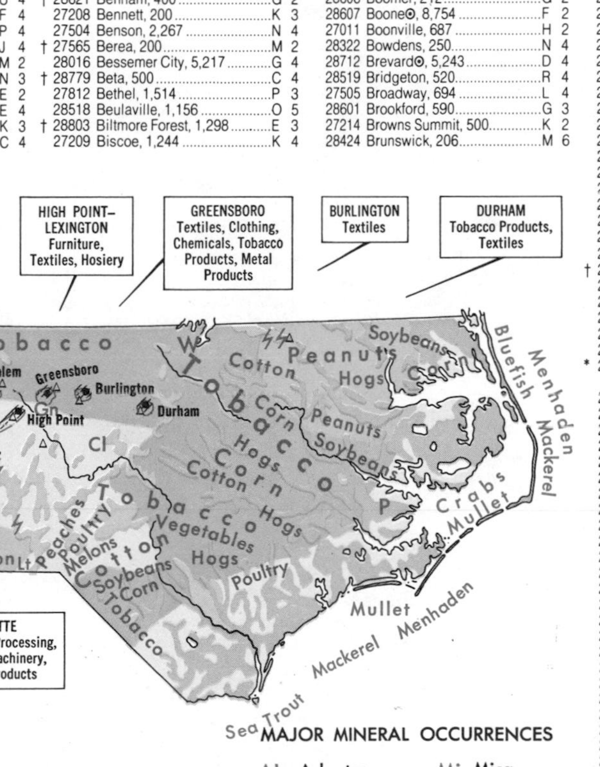

DOMINANT LAND USE

- Specialized Cotton
- Cotton, General Farming
- Cotton and Tobacco
- Tobacco, General Farming
- Peanuts, General Farming
- General Farming, Livestock, Fruit, Tobacco
- General Farming, Truck Farming, Tobacco, Livestock
- Forests
- Swampland, Limited Agriculture
- Nonagricultural Land

MAJOR MINERAL OCCURRENCES

Ab Asbestos
Au Gold
Cl Clay
Cu Copper
Gn Granite
Lt Lithium
Mi Mica
Mr Marble
P Phosphates
Tc Talc
W Tungsten

Water Power
Major Industrial Areas
Major Textile Manufacturing Centers

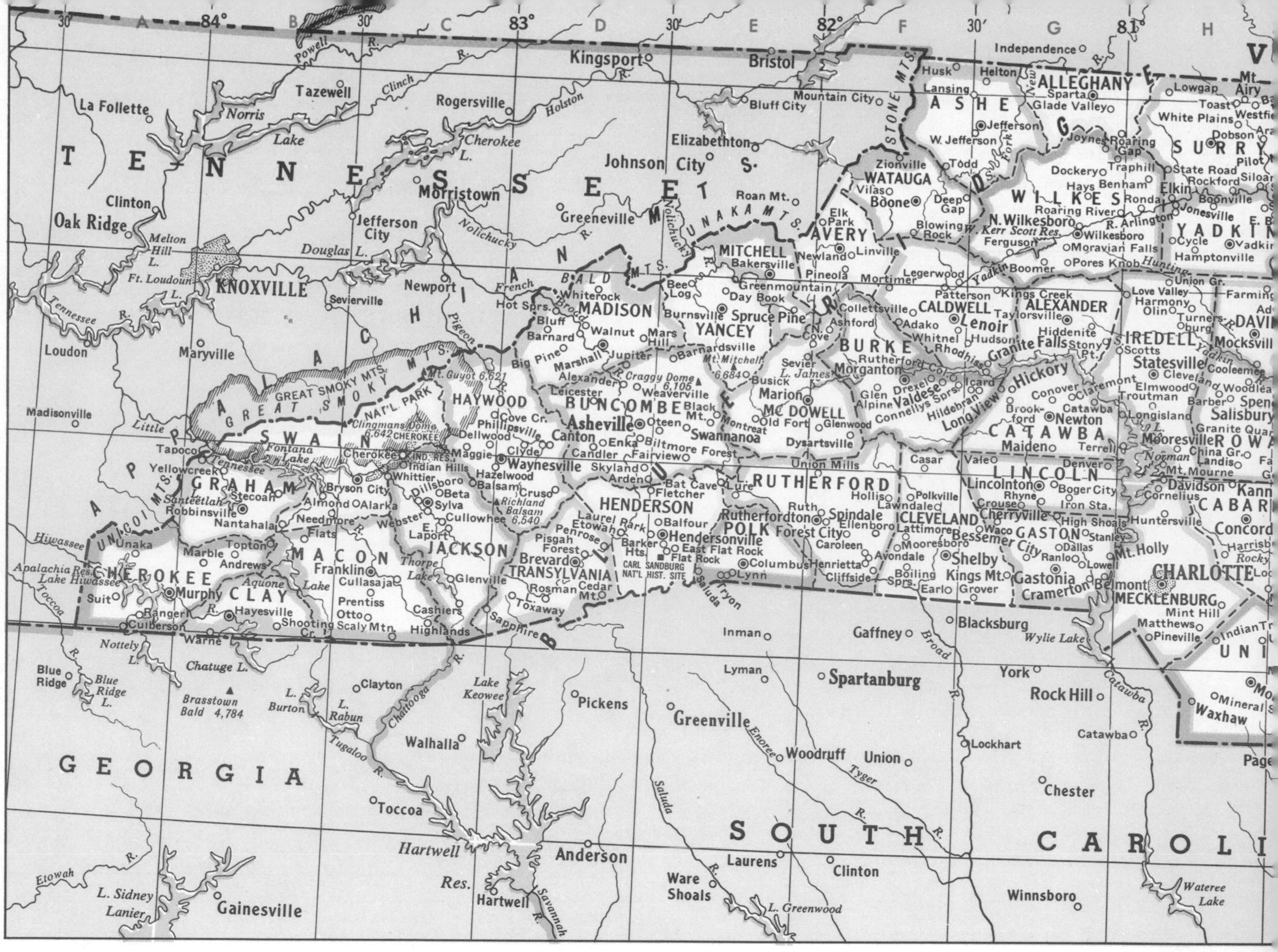

27832 Gaston, 1,105 O 1
28052 Gastonia⊙, 47,142 G 4
27937 Gates, 225 R 2
27938 Gatesville⊙, 338 R 2
28343 Gibson, 502 K 5
27249 Gibsonville, 2,019 K 2
28628 Glen Alpine, 797 F 3
27251 Glendon, 250 L 4
27215 Glen Raven, 2,848 L 2
28736 Glenville, 400 C 4
28737 Glenwood, 400 F 3
28071 Gold Hill, 350 J 3
27530 Goldsboro⊙, 26,810 O 4
27252 Goldston, 364 L 3
27253 Graham⊙, 8,172 L 2
27939 Grandy, 425 T 2
28630 Granite Falls, 2,388 G 3
28072 Granite Quarry, 1,344 H 3
28529 Grantsboro, 900 R 4
28740 Greenmountain, 500 E 3
* 27401 Greensboro⊙, 144,076 K 2
Greensboro-Winston-Salem-High Point, ‡603,895 K 2
27834 Greenville⊙, 29,063 P 3
28530 Grifton, 1,860 P 4
27837 Grimesland, 394 P 3
28073 Grover, 555 G 4
27256 Gulf, 300 L 3
27839 Halifax⊙, 335 O 2
28442 Hallsboro, 300 M 6
27840 Hamilton, 579 P 3
28345 Hamlet, 4,627 K 5
28443 Hampstead, 400 O 6
27020 Hamptonville, 250 H 2
27941 Harbinger, 460 T 2
28531 Harkers Island, 1,633 R 5
28634 Harmony, 377 H 3
28444 Harrells, 249 N 5
28075 Harrisburg, 800 H 4
27943 Hatteras, 500 T 4
28532 Havelock, 5,283 P 5
27258 Haw River, 1,542 L 2
28904 Hayesville⊙, 428 B 4
† 28318 Hayne, 300 M 5
28635 Hays, 750 G 2
† 27559 Haywood, 500 L 3
28738 Hazelwood, 2,057 C 4
27536 Henderson⊙, 13,896 N 2
28739 Hendersonville⊙, 6,443 E 4
28076 Henrietta-Avondale, 1,307 F 4
27944 Hertford⊙, 2,023 S 2
28601 Hickory, 20,569 G 3
28636 Hiddenite, 800 G 3
28741 Highlands, 583 C 4
* 27260 High Point, 63,204 J 3
28077 High Shoals, 900 G 4
28637 Hildebran, 481 F 3
27278 Hillsborough⊙, 1,444 L 2
27843 Hobgood, 530 P 2
28537 Hobucken, 500 S 4
28347 Hoffman, 434 K 4
27844 Hollister, 750 O 2
28445 Holly Ridge, 415 P 6
27540 Holly Springs, 697 M 3
28538 Hookerton, 441 O 4
28348 Hope Mills, 1,721 M 5
28743 Hot Springs, 653 D 3
28539 Hubert, 980 P 5
28638 Hudson, 2,820 G 3
28078 Huntersville, 1,538 H 4
28666 Icard, 1,100 G 3
28079 Indian Trail, 405 H 4
27589 Inez, 250 N 2
28080 Iron Station, 250 G 4
27845 Jackson⊙, 762 P 2
27281 Jackson Springs, 225 K 4
28540 Jacksonville⊙, 16,021 O 5
28550 James City, 2,577 R 4
27282 Jamestown, 1,297 K 3
27846 Jamesville, 533 R 3
27947 Jarvisburg, 350 T 2
28640 Jefferson⊙, 943 G 2
† 28352 Johns, 250 K 5
28642 Jonesville, 1,659 H 2
27283 Julian, 300 K 3
28787 Jupiter, 208 D 3
28081 Kannapolis, 36,293 H 4
27847 Kelford, 295 P 2
28349 Kenansville⊙, 762 O 5
27542 Kenly, 1,370 N 3
27284 Kernersville, 4,815 J 2
27948 Kill Devil Hills, 357 T 3
27021 King, 1,033 J 2
28086 Kings Mountain, 8,465 G 4
28501 Kinston⊙, 22,309 O 4
27544 Kittrell, 427 M 2
27949 Kitty Hawk, 600 T 2

27545 Knightdale, 815 N 3
27950 Knotts Island, 450 T 2
28449 Kure Beach, 394 O 7
28551 La Grange, 2,558 O 4
28746 Lake Lure, 456 E 4
28747 Lake Toxaway, 750 D 4
28350 Lakeview, 449 L 4
28450 Lake Waccamaw, 924 M 6
28088 Landis, 2,297 H 3
28643 Lansing, 283 F 1
28089 Lattimore, 257 F 4
28351 Laurel Hill, 1,215 K 5
† 28739 Laurel Park, 581 D 4
28352 Laurinburg⊙, 8,859 K 5
28090 Lawndale, 544 F 4
27291 Leasburg, 400 L 2
28748 Leicester, 265 D 3
28451 Leland, 500 N 6
28645 Lenoir⊙, 14,705 G 3
27849 Lewiston, 327 P 2
27292 Lexington⊙. 17,205 J 3
27298 Liberty, 2,167 K 3
28091 Lilesville, 641 K 5
27546 Lillington⊙, 1,155 M 4
28092 Lincolnton⊙, 5,293 G 4
28356 Linden, 205 M 4
28646 Linville, 400 F 2
27299 Linwood, 300 J 3
27850 Littleton, 903 O 2
28461 Long Beach, 493 N 7
27548 Longhurst, 1,485 L 2
28648 Longisland, 350 H 3
28601 Long View, 3,360 F 3
28452 Longwood, 650 N 6
† 28345 Longwood Park, 1,284 K 5
27549 Louisburg⊙, 2,941 N 2
28098 Lowell, 3,307 G 4
27024 Lowgap, 660 H 1
28552 Lowland, 538 S 4
27851 Lucama, 610 N 3

28358 Lumberton⊙, 16,961 L 5
28750 Lynn, 550 E 4
27852 Macclesfield, 536 O 3
27951 Mackeys, 250 R 3
27025 Madison, 2,018 J 2
28751 Maggie, 400 C 3
28453 Magnolia, 614 O 5
28650 Maiden, 2,416 G 3
27552 Mamers, 500 L 4
† 28387 Manly, 225 L 4
27953 Manns Harbor, 365 T 3
27954 Manteo⊙, 547 T 3
† 27855 Mapleton, 250 P 2
28905 Marble, 950 B 4
28752 Marion⊙, 3,335 E 3
28753 Marshall⊙, 982 D 3
28553 Marshallberg, 700 S 5
28754 Mars Hill, 1,623 D 3
28103 Marshville, 1,405 J 4
28105 Matthews, 783 H 4
28554 Maury, 421 O 4
28364 Maxton, 1,885 L 5
27027 Mayodan, 2,875 K 2
28555 Maysville, 912 P 5
28361 McCain, 950 L 4
27302 Mebane, 2,433 L 2
† 28516 Merrimon, 500 R 5
27555 Micro, 300 N 3
27557 Middlesex, 729 N 3
28107 Midland, 950 J 4
† 28377 Midstate Mill, 925 L 5
28544 Midway Park, 4,900 O 5
27305 Milton, 235 L 1
27854 Milwaukee, 376 P 2
28212 Mint Hill, 1,200 H 4
28109 Misenheimer, 1,450 J 4
27028 Mocksville⊙, 2,529 H 3
27559 Moncure, 800 L 3
28110 Monroe⊙, 11,282 J 5
28757 Montreat, 450 E 3

28114 Mooresboro, 275 F 4
28115 Mooresville, 8,808 H 3
28654 Moravian Falls, 375 G 2
28557 Morehead City, 5,233 R 5
28655 Morganton⊙, 13,625 F 3
28119 Morven, 562 J 5
27030 Mount Airy, 7,325 H 1
27306 Mount Gilead, 1,286 K 4
28120 Mount Holly, 5,107 H 4
28123 Mount Mourne, 950 H 3
28365 Mount Olive, 4,914 O 4
28124 Mount Pleasant, 1,174 J 4
27345 Mount Vernon Springs, 225 L 3
27958 Moyock, 350 S 1
27855 Murfreesboro, 3,508 R 2
28906 Murphy⊙, 2,082 B 4
27959 Nags Head, 414 T 3
27856 Nashville⊙, 1,670 O 3
27561 Neuse, 500 M 3
28560 New Bern⊙, 14,660 P 4
28657 Newland⊙, 524 F 2
28127 New London, 285 J 4
28570 Newport, 1,735 R 5
28658 Newton⊙, 7,857 G 3
28366 Newton Grove, 546 N 4
27563 Norlina, 969 N 2
† 28752 North Cove, 257 F 3
† 28532 North Harlowe, 975 R 5
28659 North Wilkesboro, 3,357 G 2
27564 Northside, 400 M 2
28128 Norwood, 1,896 J 4
28129 Oakboro, 568 J 4
27857 Oak City, 559 P 3
27310 Oak Ridge, 950 K 2
27960 Ocracoke, 500 T 4
28762 Old Fort, 676 E 3
27961 Old Trap, 400 T 2
28368 Olivia, 400 L 4
28571 Oriental, 445 R 4
28805 Oteen, 2,863 E 3

27565 Oxford⊙, 7,178 M 2
27860 Pantego, 218 R 3
28371 Parkton, 550 M 5
27861 Parmele, 373 P 3
28661 Patterson, 344 F 3
28133 Peachland, 556 J 5
† 28091 Pee Dee, 210 K 5
27311 Pelham, 350 L 1
28372 Pembroke, 1,982 L 5
28766 Penrose, 600 D 4
† 28716 Phillipsville, 1,239 D 3
27863 Pikeville, 580 N 4
27041 Pilot Mountain, 1,309 H 2
28373 Pinebluff, 570 K 4
27042 Pine Hall, 550 K 2
28374 Pinehurst, 1,056 K 4
27568 Pine Level, 983 N 4
28662 Pineola, 875 F 2
27864 Pinetops, 1,379 O 3
27865 Pinetown, 278 R 3
28134 Pineville, 1,948 H 4
28572 Pink Hill, 522 O 4
27043 Pinnacle, 725 J 2
28768 Pisgah Forest, 850 D 4
27312 Pittsboro⊙, 1,447 L 3
27866 Pleasant Hill, 250 O 1
27962 Plymouth⊙, 4,774 R 3
28135 Polkton, 845 J 4
28136 Polkville, 450 F 4
28573 Pollocksville, 456 P 5
27965 Poplar Branch, 400 T 2
27966 Powells Point, 375 T 2
27967 Powellsville, 247 R 2
27569 Princeton, 1,044 N 4
† 27886 Princeville, 654 P 3
28376 Raeford⊙, 3,180 L 5
* 27601 Raleigh (cap.)⊙, 121,577 M 3
Raleigh, ‡228,453 M 3
27316 Ramseur, 1,328 K 3
27317 Randleman, 2,312 K 3

† 28906 Ranger, 500 A 4
28052 Ranlo, 2,092 G 4
27868 Red Oak, 359 N 2
28377 Red Springs, 3,383 L 5
27320 Reidsville, 13,636 K 2
28378 Rex, 975 M 5
28667 Rhodhiss, 784 F 3
† 28092 Rhyne, 2,273 G 4
28137 Richfield, 306 J 4
28574 Richlands, 935 O 5
27869 Rich Square, 1,254 P 2
27570 Ridgeway, 500 N 2
28456 Riegelwood, 459 N 6
27870 Roanoke Rapids, 13,508 O 2
28668 Roaring Gap, 450 H 2
28669 Roaring River, 500 G 2
27325 Robbins, 1,059 K 4
28771 Robbinsville⊙, 777 B 4
† 28379 Roberdel, 350 K 5
27871 Robersonville, 1,910 P 3
28379 Rockingham⊙, 5,852 K 5
28138 Rockwell, 999 J 3
27801 Rocky Mount, 34,284 O 3
28457 Rocky Point, 975 O 6
27571 Rolesville, 529 N 3
28670 Ronda, 465 H 2
27970 Roper, 649 R 3
28382 Roseboro, 1,235 N 5
28458 Rose Hill, 1,448 N 5
28772 Rosman, 407 D 4
27572 Rougemont, 400 L 2
28383 Rowland, 1,358 L 5
27573 Roxboro⊙, 5,370 M 2
27872 Roxobel, 347 P 2
† 27587 Royal Cotton Mills, 600 M 2
27326 Ruffin, 600 K 2
27045 Rural Hall, 2,338 J 2
† 28139 Ruth, 360 E 4
28671 Rutherford College, 950 F 3
28139 Rutherfordton⊙. 3,245 E 4

Topography

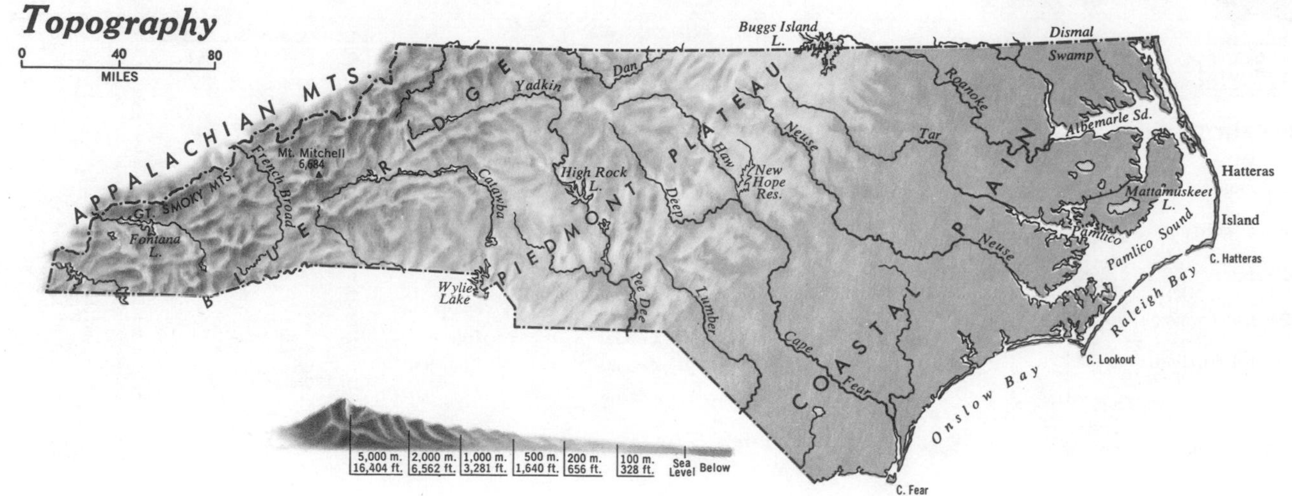

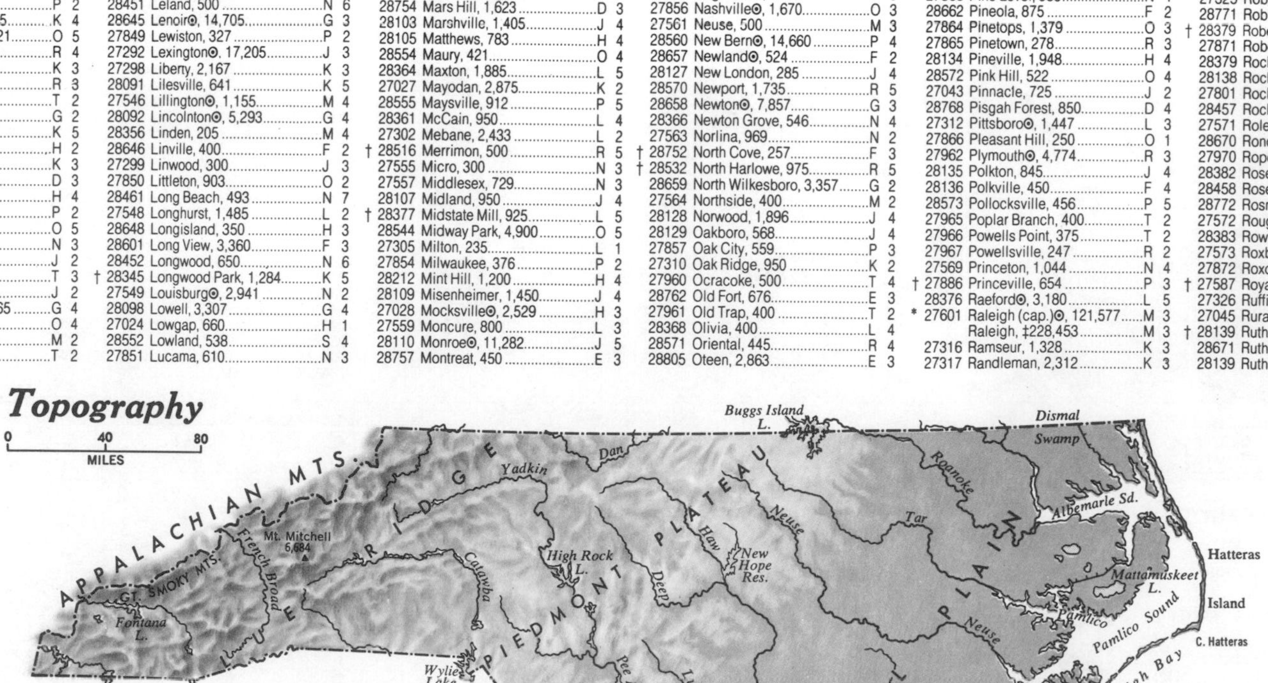

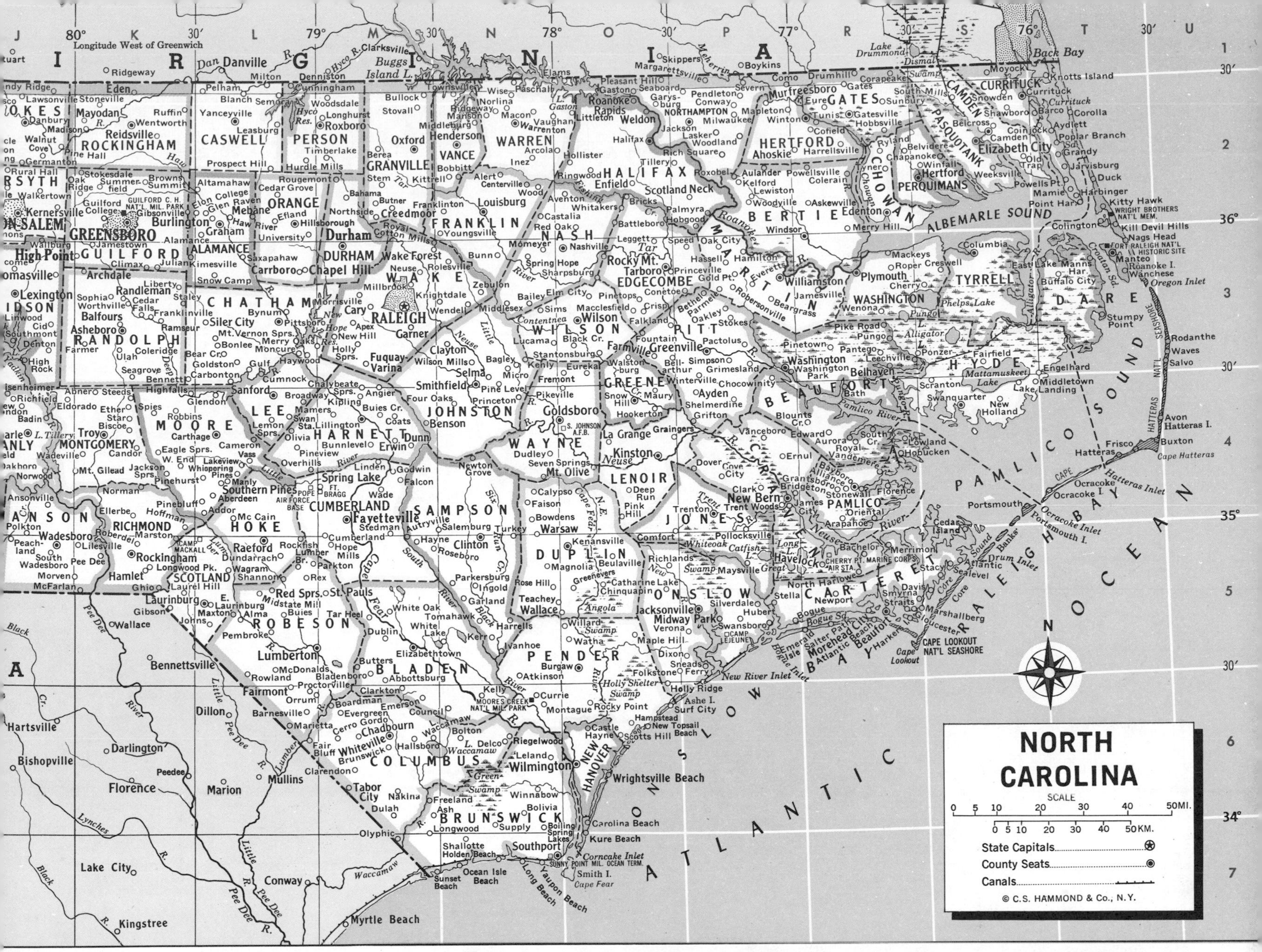

NORTH CAROLINA

SCALE
0 5 10 20 30 40 50 MI.
0 5 10 20 30 40 50 KM.

State Capitals ⊛
County Seats ⊙
Canals

	Zip	Place	Key
	28384	Saint Pauls, 2,011	M 5
	28385	Salemburg, 669	N 4
	28144	Salisbury⊙, 22,515	H 3
	28575	Salter Path, 500	R 5
	28773	Saluda, 546	E 4
	27046	Sandy Ridge, 500	J 1
	27330	Sanford⊙, 11,716	L 4
	27340	Saxapahaw, 950	L 3
	28775	Scaly Mountain, 250	C 4
	27874	Scotland Neck, 2,869	P 2
	27875	Scranton, 220	S 4
	27876	Seaboard, 611	O 1
	27341	Seagrove, 354	K 3
	28577	Sealevel, 600	S 5
	27576	Selma, 4,356	N 3
	27343	Semora, 250	L 2
	27877	Severn, 356	P 2
†	28752	Sevier, 302	E 3
	28459	Shallotte, 597	N 7
	27878	Sharpsburg, 789	O 3
	27973	Shawboro, 300	S 2
	28150	Shelby⊙, 16,328	G 4
†	27043	Shoals, 350	J 2
†	28904	Shooting Creek, 250	B 4
	27344	Siler City, 4,680	L 3
†	28539	Silverdale, 250	P 5
	27880	Sims, 205	N 3
	27879	Simpson, 300	P 3
	28776	Skyland, 2,177	D 4
	27577	Smithfield⊙, 6,677	N 3
	28579	Smyrna, 225	R 5
	28460	Sneads Ferry, 700	P 5
	28580	Snow Hill⊙, 1,359	O 4
	27350	Sophia, 700	K 3
	28387	Southern Pines, 5,937	L 4
	27976	South Mills, 950	S 2
	27351	Southmont, 950	J 3
	28461	Southport⊙, 2,220	N 7
	28675	Sparta⊙, 1,304	G 1
	28159	Spencer, 3,075	H 3
	28160	Spindale, 3,848	F 4
	27882	Spring Hope, 1,334	N 3
	28390	Spring Lake, 3,968	M 4
	28777	Spruce Pine, 2,333	E 3
	28581	Stacy, 410	S 5
	27355	Staley, 239	K 3
	28163	Stanfield, 458	J 4
	28164	Stanley, 2,336	G 4
†	27045	Stanleyville, 2,362	J 2
	27883	Stantonsburg, 869	O 3
	27356	Star, 892	K 4
	28676	State Road, 800	H 2
	28677	Statesville⊙, 19,996	H 3
†	28771	Stecoah, 250	B 4
	28391	Stedman, 505	M 4
†	27341	Steeds, 300	K 4
	28582	Stella, 300	P 5
	27581	Stem, 242	M 2
	27357	Stokesdale, 800	K 2
	27048	Stoneville, 1,030	K 2
	28583	Stonewall, 335	R 4
	28678	Stony Point, 1,001	G 3
	27582	Stovall, 405	M 2
	27358	Summerfield, 900	K 2
	27979	Sunbury, 350	R 2
	28462	Supply, 300	N 6
	28778	Swannanoa, 1,966	E 3
	27885	Swanquarter⊙, 175	S 4
	28584	Swansboro, 1,207	P 5
	28779	Sylva⊙, 1,561	C 4
	28463	Tabor City, 2,400	M 6
	27886	Tarboro⊙, 9,425	O 3
	28681	Taylorsville⊙, 1,231	G 3
	28464	Teachey, 219	N 5
	28682	Terrell, 319	G 3
	27360	Thomasville, 15,230	J 3
	27887	Tillery, 300	O 2
	27040	Toast, 2,636	H 2
	28781	Topton, 240	B 4
	27584	Townsville, 250	N 1
	28685	Traphill, 350	H 2
	28585	Trenton⊙, 539	P 4
†	28560	Trent Woods, 719	P 4
	28166	Troutman, 797	H 3
	27371	Troy⊙, 2,429	K 4
	28782	Tryon, 1,951	E 4
	28393	Turkey, 329	N 4
	27980	Tyner, 252	R 2
†	27203	Ulah, 500	K 3
	28908	Unaka, 300	A 4
	28167	Union Mills, 500	F 3
	28690	Valdese, 3,182	F 3
	28586	Vanceboro, 758	P 4
	28587	Vandemere, 379	R 4
	28394	Vass, 885	L 4
	28540	Verona, 300	O 5
	28692	Vilas, 250	F 2
	28169	Waco, 245	G 4
	28395	Wade, 315	M 4
	28170	Wadesboro⊙, 3,977	J 5
	28396	Wagram, 718	L 5
	27587	Wake Forest, 3,148	M 3
	27051	Walkertown, 1,652	J 2
	28466	Wallace, 2,905	N 5
	27373	Wallburg, 225	J 3
	27052	Walnut Cove, 1,213	J 2
	27981	Wanchese, 975	T 3
	28909	Warne, 350	B 5
	27589	Warrenton⊙, 1,035	N 2
	28398	Warsaw, 2,701	N 4
	27889	Washington⊙, 8,961	R 3
†	27889	Washington Park, 517	R 3
	28173	Waxhaw, 1,248	H 5
	28786	Waynesville⊙, 6,488	D 4
	28787	Weaverville, 1,280	D 3
	27909	Weeksville, 300	S 2
	27374	Welcome, 975	J 3
	27890	Weldon, 2,304	O 2
	27591	Wendell, 1,929	N 3
	27375	Wentworth⊙, 150	K 2
	27376	West End, 950	K 4
	27053	Westfield, 500	H 2
	28694	West Jefferson, 889	F 2
	28327	Whispering Pines, 362	L 4
	27891	Whitakers, 926	O 2
	28337	White Lake, 232	M 5
	27031	White Plains, 350	H 2
	28472	Whiteville⊙, 4,195	M 6
	28645	Whitnel, 975	F 3
	28789	Whittier, 325	C 4
	28697	Wilkesboro⊙, 1,974	G 2
	28478	Willard, 300	O 5
	27892	Williamston⊙, 6,570	R 3
	28401	Wilmington⊙, 46,169	N 6
		Wilmington, ‡107,219	N 6
	27893	Wilson⊙, 29,347	O 3
	27593	Wilson Mills, 283	M 3
	27983	Windsor⊙, 2,199	P 2
	27985	Winfall, 581	S 2
	28174	Wingate, 2,569	J 5
*	27101	Winston-Salem⊙, 132,913	J 2
	28590	Winterville, 1,437	P 3
	27986	Winton⊙, 917	P 2
	27594	Wise, 500	N 2
	27897	Woodland, 744	P 2
	27054	Woodleaf, 750	H 3
†	27849	Woodville, 253	P 2
	28480	Wrightsville Beach, 1,701	O 6
	27055	Yadkinville⊙, 2,232	H 2
	27379	Yanceyville⊙, 1,274	L 2
†	28461	Yaupon Beach, 334	N 7
†	28771	Yellowcreek, 204	A 4
	27596	Youngsville, 555	N 2
	27597	Zebulon, 1,839	N 3
	28698	Zionville, 350	F 2

⊙ County seat.
‡ Population of metropolitan area.
† Zip of nearest p.o.
* Multiple zips

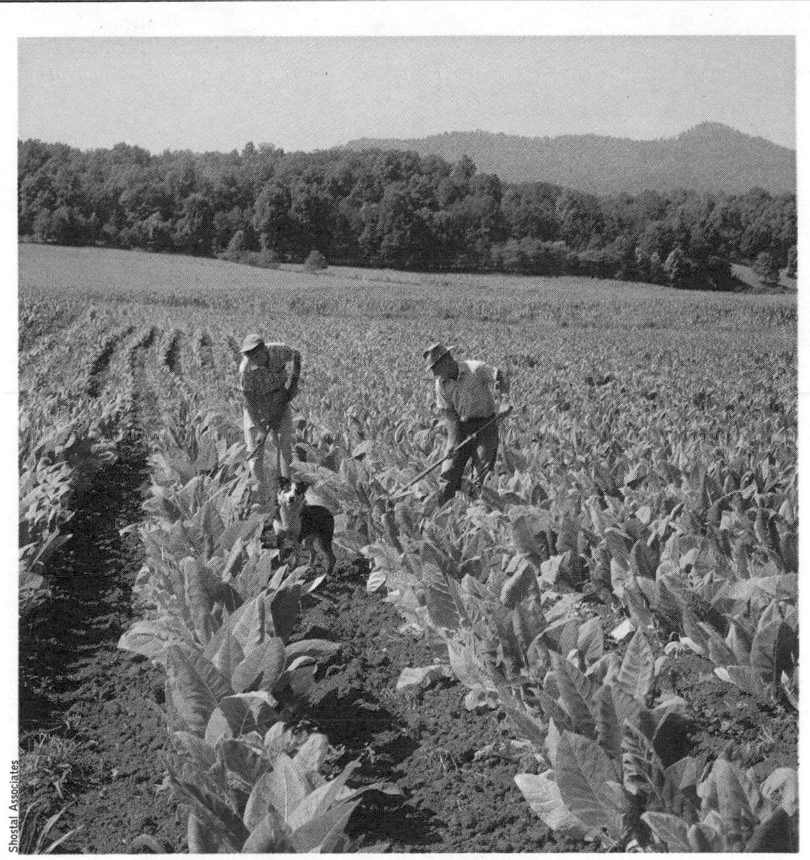
Shostal Associates

Weeding "green gold" — tobacco is North Carolina's money crop.

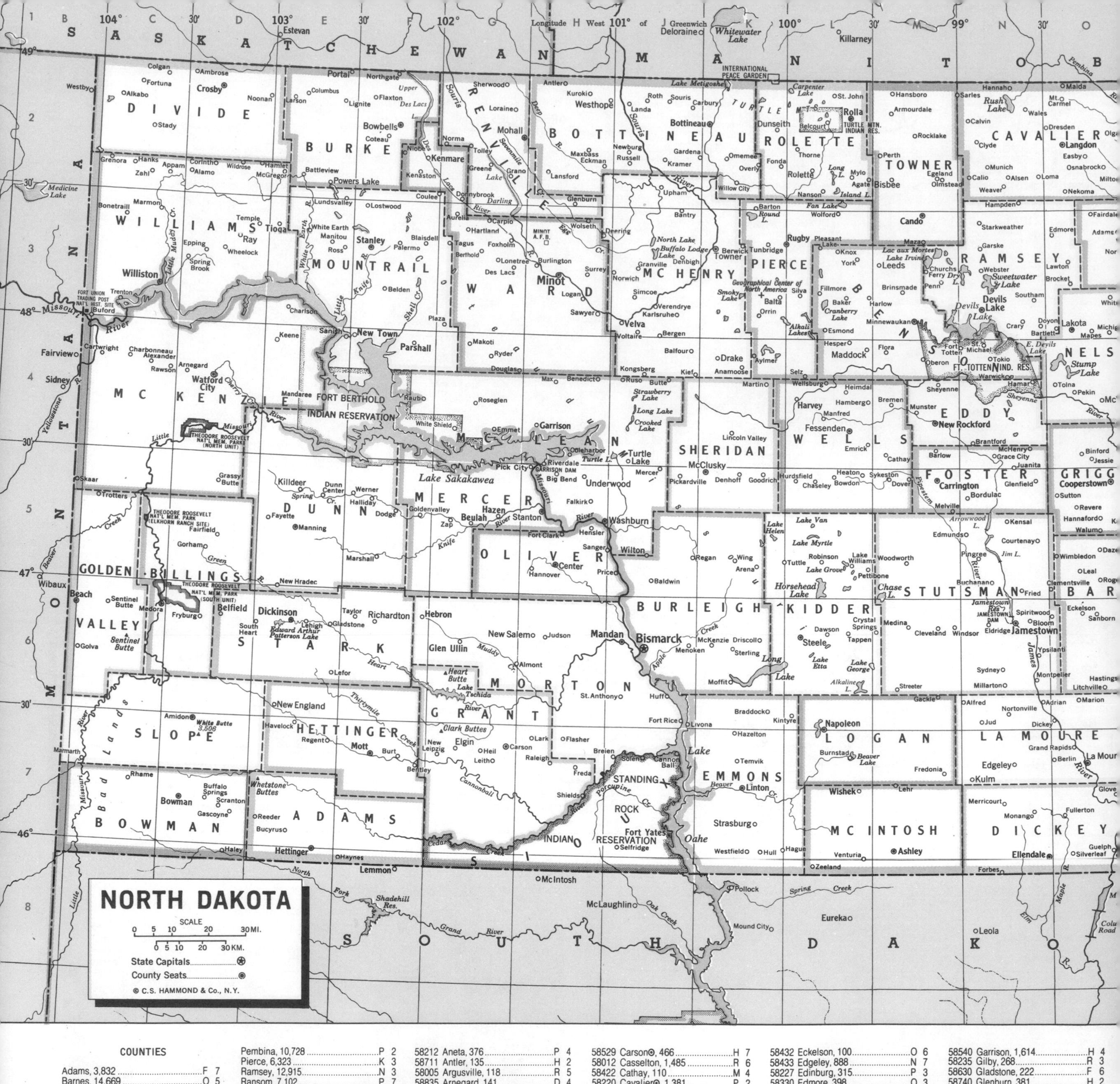

COUNTIES

County	Key
Adams, 3,832	F 7
Barnes, 14,669	O 5
Benson, 8,245	M 3
Billings, 1,198	D 5
Bottineau, 9,496	J 2
Bowman, 3,901	C 7
Burke, 4,739	E 2
Burleigh, 40,714	J 6
Cass, 73,653	R 5
Cavalier, 8,213	N 2
Dickey, 6,976	N 7
Divide, 4,564	C 2
Dunn, 4,895	E 5
Eddy, 4,103	N 4
Emmons, 7,200	K 7
Foster, 4,832	N 5
Golden Valley, 2,611	C 5
Grand Forks, 61,102	P 3
Grant, 5,009	G 6
Griggs, 4,184	O 5
Hettinger, 5,075	E 7
Kidder, 4,362	L 6
La Moure, 7,117	N 7
Logan, 4,245	L 7
McHenry, 8,977	J 3
McIntosh, 5,545	L 7
McKenzie, 6,127	D 4
McLean, 11,251	G 4
Mercer, 6,175	G 5
Morton, 20,310	H 6
Mountrail, 8,437	E 3
Nelson, 5,776	O 4
Oliver, 2,322	H 5
Pembina, 10,728	P 2
Pierce, 6,323	K 3
Ramsey, 12,915	N 3
Ransom, 7,102	P 7
Renville, 3,828	G 2
Richland, 18,089	R 7
Rolette, 11,549	L 2
Sargent, 5,937	P 7
Sheridan, 3,232	K 4
Sioux, 3,632	H 7
Slope, 1,484	C 7
Stark, 19,613	E 6
Steele, 3,749	P 4
Stutsman, 23,550	M 5
Towner, 4,645	M 2
Traill, 9,571	R 5
Walsh, 16,251	P 3
Ward, 58,560	G 3
Wells, 7,847	L 4
Williams, 19,301	C 3

CITIES and TOWNS

	Zip	Name/Pop.	Key
	58001	Abercrombie, 262	S 7
	58210	Adams, 284	O 3
	58830	Alamo, 124	D 2
	58831	Alexander, 208	C 4
	58003	Alice, 83	P 6
	58520	Almont, 109	H 6
	58311	Alsen, 201	N 2
	58833	Ambrose, 109	D 2
	58620	Amidon⊙, 54	D 7
	58710	Anamoose, 401	K 4
	58212	Aneta, 376	P 4
	58711	Antler, 135	H 2
	58005	Argusville, 118	R 5
	58835	Arnegard, 141	D 4
	58006	Arthur, 412	R 5
	58214	Arvilla, 115	P 4
	58413	Ashley⊙, 1,236	M 7
	58712	Balfour, 93	J 4
	58313	Balta, 133	K 3
	58008	Barney, 81	S 7
	58216	Bathgate, 133	P 2
	58621	Beach⊙, 1,408	C 6
	58316	Belcourt, 950	L 2
	58622	Belfield, 1,130	D 6
	58718	Berthold, 398	G 3
	58523	Beulah, 1,344	G 5
	58416	Binford, 242	O 4
	58317	Bisbee, 305	M 2
	58501	Bismarck (cap.)⊙, 34,703	J 6
	58318	Bottineau⊙, 2,760	J 2
	58721	Bowbells⊙, 584	F 2
	58418	Bowdon, 229	L 5
	58623	Bowman⊙, 1,762	D 7
	58524	Braddock, 106	K 6
	58321	Brocket, 95	O 3
	58420	Buchanan, 100	N 5
	58011	Buffalo, 241	R 6
	58722	Burlington, 247	H 3
	58723	Butte, 193	J 4
	58218	Buxton, 235	R 4
	58324	Cando⊙, 1,512	M 3
	58528	Cannon Ball, 550	J 7
†	58241	Canton (Hensel), 81	P 2
	58725	Carpio, 215	G 3
	58421	Carrington⊙, 2,491	M 5
	58529	Carson⊙, 466	H 7
	58012	Casselton, 1,485	R 6
	58422	Cathay, 110	M 4
	58220	Cavalier⊙, 1,381	P 2
	58013	Cayuga, 116	R 7
	58530	Center⊙, 619	H 5
	58014	Chaffee, 99	R 6
	58015	Christine, 108	S 6
	58325	Church's Ferry, 139	M 3
	58424	Cleveland, 128	M 6
	58016	Clifford, 84	R 5
	58017	Cogswell, 203	P 7
	58727	Columbus, 465	E 2
	58425	Cooperstown⊙, 1,485	O 5
	58426	Courtenay, 125	N 5
	58327	Crary, 150	N 3
	58730	Crosby⊙, 1,545	D 2
	58222	Crystal, 272	P 2
	58021	Davenport, 147	R 6
	58428	Dawson, 131	L 6
	58429	Dazey, 128	O 5
	58430	Denhoff, 85	K 5
	58733	Des Lacs, 197	G 3
	58301	Devils Lake⊙, 7,078	N 3
	58431	Dickey, 118	N 6
	58601	Dickinson⊙, 12,405	E 6
	58625	Dodge, 121	F 5
	58734	Donnybrook, 163	G 2
	58735	Douglas, 144	G 4
	58736	Drake, 636	K 4
	58225	Drayton, 1,095	R 2
	58532	Driscoll, 128	K 6
	58626	Dunn Center, 107	E 5
	58329	Dunseith, 811	K 2
	58024	Dwight, 93	S 7
	58432	Eckelson, 100	O 6
	58433	Edgeley, 888	N 7
	58227	Edinburg, 315	P 3
	58330	Edmore, 398	O 3
	58331	Egeland, 96	M 2
	58533	Elgin, 839	G 7
	58436	Ellendale⊙, 1,517	N 7
	58228	Emerado, 515	R 4
	58027	Enderlin, 1,343	P 6
	58843	Epping, 140	D 3
	58029	Erie, 100	R 5
	58332	Esmond, 416	L 3
	58229	Fairdale, 102	O 3
	58030	Fairmount, 412	S 7
	58102	Fargo⊙, 53,365	S 6
		Fargo-Moorhead, ‡120,238	S 6
	58438	Fessenden⊙, 815	L 4
	58031	Fingal, 166	P 6
	58230	Finley⊙, 809	P 4
	58535	Flasher, 467	H 7
	58737	Flaxton, 286	F 2
	58439	Forbes, 88	N 8
	58231	Fordville, 361	P 3
	58233	Forest River, 169	P 3
	58032	Forman⊙, 596	P 7
	58033	Fort Ransom, 121	P 6
	58335	Fort Totten, 550	M 4
	58844	Fortuna, 216	C 2
	58538	Fort Yates⊙, 1,153	J 7
	58440	Fredonia, 100	M 7
	58441	Fullerton, 110	O 7
	58442	Gackle, 470	M 6
	58035	Galesburg, 134	R 5
	58739	Gardena, 84	J 2
	58036	Gardner, 96	R 5
	58540	Garrison, 1,614	H 4
	58235	Gilby, 268	R 3
	58630	Gladstone, 222	F 6
	58740	Glenburn, 381	H 2
	58443	Glenfield, 127	N 5
	58631	Glen Ullin, 1,070	G 6
	58541	Goldenvalley, 235	F 5
	58632	Golva, 104	C 6
	58444	Goodrich, 300	K 5
	58445	Grace City, 87	N 4
	58237	Grafton⊙, 5,946	R 3
	58201	Grand Forks⊙, 39,008	R 4
	58038	Grandin, 187	R 5
	58741	Granville, 282	J 3
	58039	Great Bend, 86	S 7
	58845	Grenora, 401	C 2
	58040	Gwinner, 623	P 7
	58542	Hague, 146	L 7
	58636	Halliday, 413	F 5
	58238	Hamilton, 110	R 2
	58338	Hampden, 114	N 2
	58041	Hankinson, 1,125	S 7
	58448	Hannaford, 244	O 5
	58239	Hannah, 145	N 2
	58340	Harlow, 85	M 3
	58341	Harvey, 2,361	L 4
	58042	Harwood, 200	S 6
	58240	Hatton, 808	R 4
	58043	Havana, 156	P 8
	58544	Hazelton, 374	K 7
	58545	Hazen, 1,240	G 5
	58638	Hebron, 1,103	G 6
	58342	Heimdal, 101	L 4
	58547	Hensler, 100	H 5
	58639	Hettinger⊙, 1,655	E 8

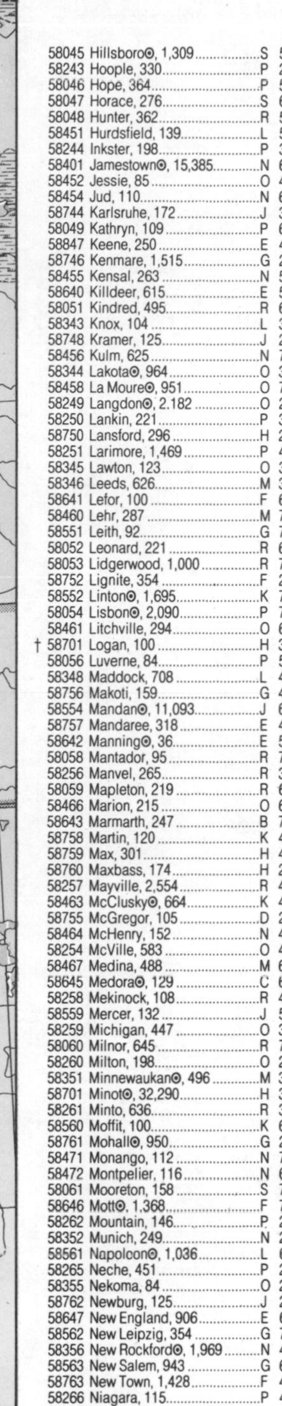

58045 Hillsboro⊙, 1,309 .... S 5
58243 Hoople, 330 .... P 2
58046 Hope, 364 .... P 5
58047 Horace, 276 .... S 6
58048 Hunter, 362 .... R 5
58451 Hurdsfield, 139 .... L 5
58244 Inkster, 198 .... P 3
58401 Jamestown⊙, 15,385 .... N 6
58452 Jessie, 85 .... O 4
58454 Jud, 110 .... N 6
58744 Karlsruhe, 172 .... J 3
58049 Kathryn, 109 .... P 6
58847 Keene, 250 .... E 4
58746 Kenmare, 1,515 .... G 2
58455 Kensal, 263 .... N 5
58640 Killdeer, 615 .... E 5
58051 Kindred, 495 .... R 6
58343 Knox, 104 .... L 3
58748 Kramer, 125 .... J 2
58456 Kulm, 625 .... N 7
58344 Lakota⊙, 964 .... O 3
58458 La Moure⊙, 951 .... O 7
58249 Langdon⊙, 2.182 .... O 2
58250 Lankin, 221 .... P 3
58750 Lansford, 296 .... H 2
58251 Larimore, 1,469 .... P 4
58345 Lawton, 123 .... O 3
58346 Leeds, 626 .... M 3
58641 Lefor, 100 .... F 6
58460 Lehr, 287 .... M 7
58551 Leith, 92 .... G 7
58052 Leonard, 221 .... R 6
58053 Lidgerwood, 1,000 .... R 7
58752 Lignite, 354 .... F 2
58552 Linton⊙, 1,695 .... K 7
58054 Lisbon⊙, 2,090 .... P 7
58461 Litchville, 294 .... O 6
† 58701 Logan, 100 .... H 3
58056 Luverne, 84 .... P 5
58348 Maddock, 708 .... L 4
58756 Makoti, 159 .... G 4
58554 Mandan⊙, 11,093 .... J 6
58757 Mandaree, 318 .... E 4
58642 Manning⊙, 36 .... E 5
58058 Mantador, 95 .... R 7
58256 Manvel, 265 .... R 3
58059 Mapleton, 219 .... R 6
58466 Marion, 215 .... O 6
58643 Marmarth, 247 .... B 7
58758 Martin, 120 .... K 4
58759 Max, 301 .... H 4
58760 Maxbass, 174 .... H 2
58257 Mayville, 2,554 .... R 4
58463 McClusky⊙, 664 .... K 4
58755 McGregor, 105 .... D 2
58464 McHenry, 152 .... N 4
58254 McVille, 583 .... O 4
58467 Medina, 488 .... M 6
58645 Medora⊙, 129 .... C 6
58258 Mekinock, 108 .... R 4
58559 Mercer, 132 .... J 5
58259 Michigan, 447 .... O 3
58060 Milnor, 645 .... R 7
58260 Milton, 198 .... O 2
58351 Minnewaukan⊙, 496 .... M 3
58701 Minot⊙, 32,290 .... H 3
58261 Minto, 636 .... R 3
58560 Moffit, 100 .... K 6
58761 Mohall⊙, 950 .... G 2
58471 Monango, 112 .... N 7
58472 Montpelier, 116 .... N 6
58061 Mooreton, 158 .... S 7
58646 Mott⊙, 1,368 .... F 7
58262 Mountain, 146 .... P 2
58352 Munich, 249 .... N 2
58561 Napoleon⊙, 1,036 .... L 6
58265 Neche, 451 .... P 2
58355 Nekoma, 84 .... O 2
58762 Newburg, 125 .... J 2
58647 New England, 906 .... E 6
58562 New Leipzig, 354 .... G 7
58356 New Rockford⊙, 1,969 .... N 4
58563 New Salem, 943 .... G 6
58763 New Town, 1,428 .... F 4
58266 Niagara, 115 .... P 4
58062 Nome, 103 .... P 6

AREA 70,665 sq. mi.
POPULATION 617,761
CAPITAL Bismarck
LARGEST CITY Fargo
HIGHEST POINT White Butte 3,506 ft.
SETTLED IN 1780
ADMITTED TO UNION November 2, 1889
POPULAR NAME Flickertail State; Sioux State
STATE FLOWER Prairie Rose
STATE BIRD Meadowlark

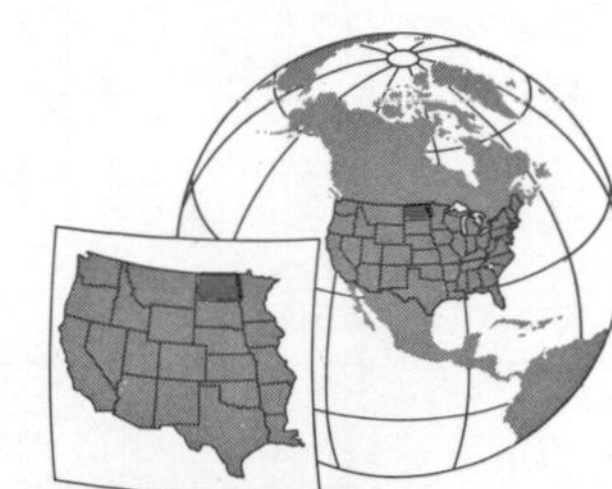

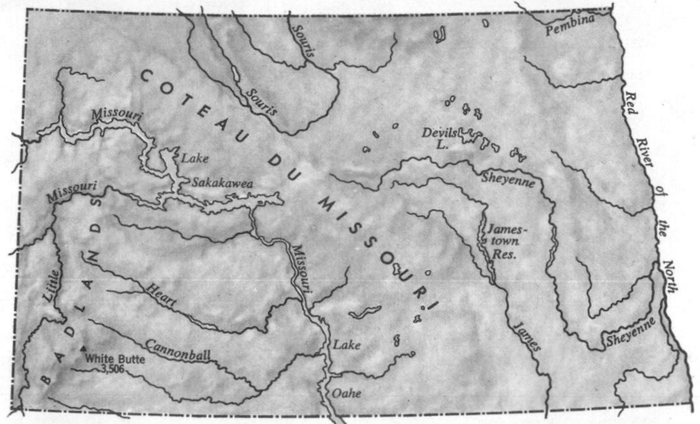

Topography

0 50 100 MILES

58765 Noonan, 403 .... D 2
58267 Northwood, 1,189 .... P 4
58473 Nortonville, 90 .... N 6
58474 Oakes, 1,742 .... O 7
† 58237 Oakwood, 91 .... R 3
58357 Oberon, 151 .... M 4
58063 Oriska, 128 .... P 6
58269 Osnabrock, 255 .... O 2
58064 Page, 367 .... P 5
58769 Palermo, 146 .... F 3
58270 Park River, 1,680 .... P 3
58770 Parshall, 1,246 .... F 4
58361 Pekin, 120 .... O 4
58271 Pembina, 741 .... R 2
58272 Petersburg, 266 .... P 3
58475 Pettibone, 173 .... L 5
† 58545 Pick City, 119 .... G 5
58273 Pisek, 154 .... P 3
58771 Plaza, 291 .... G 3
58772 Portal, 251 .... E 2
58274 Portland, 534 .... R 5
58773 Powers Lake, 523 .... E 2
58849 Ray, 776 .... D 3
58649 Reeder, 306 .... E 7
58650 Regent, 344 .... E 7
58275 Reynolds, 236 .... R 4
58651 Rhame, 206 .... C 7
58652 Richardton, 799 .... F 6
58565 Riverdale, 600 .... H 4
58478 Robinson, 125 .... L 5
58365 Rocklake, 270 .... M 2
58479 Rogers, 96 .... O 5
58366 Rolette, 579 .... L 2
58367 Rolla⊙, 1,458 .... L 2
58776 Ross, 125 .... E 3
58368 Rugby⊙, 2,889 .... L 3
58067 Rutland, 225 .... P 7
58779 Ryder, 211 .... G 4
58369 Saint John, 367 .... L 2
58276 Saint Thomas, 508 .... R 2
58480 Sanborn, 255 .... O 6
58780 Sanish, 25 .... E 4
58372 Sarles, 148 .... N 2
58781 Sawyer, 373 .... H 3
58653 Scranton, 360 .... D 7
58568 Selfridge, 346 .... J 7
58373 Selz, 110 .... L 4
58654 Sentinel Butte, 125 .... C 6
58277 Sharon, 201 .... P 4
58068 Sheldon, 192 .... P 6
58782 Sherwood, 369 .... G 2
58374 Sheyenne, 362 .... M 4
58569 Shields, 125 .... H 7
58570 Solen, 180 .... J 7
58783 Souris, 151 .... J 2
58655 South Heart, 132 .... D 6
58481 Spiritwood, 100 .... N 6
58784 Stanley⊙, 1,581 .... F 3
58571 Stanton⊙, 517 .... H 5
58377 Starkweather, 193 .... N 3
58482 Steele⊙, 696 .... L 6
58573 Strasburg, 642 .... K 7
58483 Streeter, 324 .... M 6
58785 Surrey, 361 .... H 3
58484 Sutton, 87 .... O 5
58486 Sykeston, 232 .... M 5
58487 Tappen, 294 .... L 6
58656 Taylor, 162 .... F 6
58278 Thompson, 291 .... R 4
58852 Tioga, 1,667 .... E 3
58379 Tokio, 130 .... N 4
58787 Tolley, 163 .... G 2
58380 Tolna, 247 .... O 4
58071 Tower City, 289 .... P 6
58788 Towner⊙, 870 .... K 3
58853 Trenton, 150 .... C 3
58575 Turtle Lake, 712 .... J 4
58488 Tuttle, 216 .... L 5
58576 Underwood, 781 .... H 5
58789 Upham, 272 .... J 2
58072 Valley City⊙, 7,843 .... P 6
58790 Velva, 1,241 .... J 3
58490 Verona, 140 .... O 7
58075 Wahpeton⊙, 7,076 .... S 7
58077 Walcott, 175 .... R 6
58281 Wales, 116 .... N 2
58282 Walhalla, 1,471 .... P 2
58577 Washburn⊙, 804 .... J 5
58854 Watford City⊙, 1,768 .... D 4
58078 West Fargo, 5,161 .... S 6
† 58078 West Fargo Industrial Park, 104 .... S 6
58793 Westhope, 705 .... H 2
58794 White Earth, 128 .... E 3
58795 Wildrose, 235 .... D 2
58801 Williston⊙, 11,280 .... C 3
58384 Willow City, 403 .... K 2
58579 Wilton, 695 .... J 5
58492 Wimbledon, 337 .... O 5
58494 Wing, 223 .... K 5
58495 Wishek, 1,275 .... L 7
58496 Woodworth, 139 .... M 5
58081 Wyndmere, 516 .... R 7
58386 York, 102 .... L 3
58497 Ypsilanti, 139 .... N 6
58580 Zap, 271 .... G 5
58581 Zeeland, 313 .... L 8

⊙ County seat.
‡ Population of metropolitan area.
† Zip of nearest p.o.
* Multiple zips

North Dakota's wealth springs from her soil. The state has the largest farms and leads in production of barley, wheat and flaxseed.

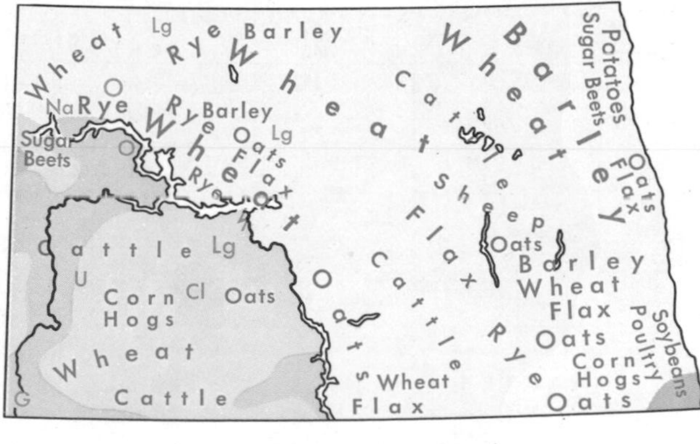

Agriculture, Industry and Resources

DOMINANT LAND USE

- Specialized Wheat
- Wheat, General Farming
- Wheat, Range Livestock
- Livestock, Cash Grain
- Sugar Beets, Dry Beans, Livestock, General Farming
- Range Livestock
- Water Power

MAJOR MINERAL OCCURRENCES

- Cl Clay
- G Natural Gas
- Lg Lignite
- Na Salt
- O Petroleum
- U Uranium

OHIO
SCALE
0 5 10 20 30 40 MI.
0 5 10 20 30 40 KM.
State Capitals
County Seats
© C.S. HAMMOND & Co., N.Y.
83° Longitude E West of 30′ Greenwich F
MICHIGAN
ONTARIO
LAKE ERIE
INDIANA
KENTUCKY
WEST VIRGINIA
PENNSYLVANIA
POINT PELEE NAT'L PARK
PERRY'S VICTORY AND INTERNATIONAL PEACE MEMORIAL NAT'L. MON.
MOUND CITY GROUP NAT'L. MON.
CLINTON CO. A.F.B.
CLEVELAND
CINCINNATI
Columbus
Toledo
Dayton
Akron
Youngstown
Canton
WILLIAMS
FULTON
LUCAS
OTTAWA
DEFIANCE
HENRY
WOOD
SANDUSKY
ERIE
LORAIN
CUYAHOGA
LAKE
GEAUGA
ASHTABULA
TRUMBULL
PORTAGE
SUMMIT
MEDINA
HURON
SENECA
HANCOCK
PUTNAM
PAULDING
VAN WERT
ALLEN
WYANDOT
CRAWFORD
RICHLAND
ASHLAND
WAYNE
STARK
MAHONING
COLUMBIANA
MERCER
AUGLAIZE
HARDIN
MARION
MORROW
KNOX
HOLMES
TUSCARAWAS
CARROLL
JEFFERSON
SHELBY
LOGAN
UNION
DELAWARE
LICKING
COSHOCTON
HARRISON
DARKE
MIAMI
CHAMPAIGN
FRANKLIN
MUSKINGUM
GUERNSEY
BELMONT
PREBLE
MONTGOMERY
CLARK
MADISON
FAIRFIELD
PERRY
NOBLE
MONROE
GREENE
PICKAWAY
HOCKING
MORGAN
WASHINGTON
BUTLER
WARREN
CLINTON
FAYETTE
ROSS
VINTON
ATHENS
HAMILTON
CLERMONT
HIGHLAND
PIKE
JACKSON
MEIGS
BROWN
ADAMS
SCIOTO
GALLIA
LAWRENCE
Ohio River

COUNTIES

Adams, 18,957 .... D 8
Allen, 111,144 .... B 4
Ashland, 43,303 .... F 4
Ashtabula, 98,237 .... J 2
Athens, 54,889 .... F 7
Auglaize, 38,602 .... B 4
Belmont, 80,917 .... J 5
Brown, 26,635 .... C 8
Butler, 226,207 .... A 7
Carroll, 21,579 .... H 4
Champaign, 30,491 .... C 5
Clark, 157,115 .... C 6
Clermont, 95,725 .... B 7
Clinton, 31,464 .... C 7
Columbiana, 108,310 .... J 4
Coshocton, 33,486 .... G 5
Crawford, 50,364 .... E 4
Cuyahoga, 1,721,300 .... G 3
Darke, 49,141 .... A 5
Defiance, 36,949 .... A 3
Delaware, 42,908 .... D 5
Erie, 75,909 .... E 3
Fairfield, 73,301 .... E 6
Fayette, 25,461 .... D 6
Franklin, 833,249 .... E 5
Fulton, 33,071 .... B 2
Gallia, 25,239 .... F 8
Geauga, 62,977 .... H 3
Greene, 125,057 .... C 6
Guernsey, 37,665 .... H 5
Hamilton, 924,018 .... A 7
Hancock, 61,217 .... C 3
Hardin, 30,813 .... C 4
Harrison, 17,013 .... H 5
Henry, 27,058 .... B 3
Highland, 28,996 .... C 7
Hocking, 20,322 .... F 6
Holmes, 23,024 .... G 4
Huron, 49,587 .... E 3
Jackson, 27,174 .... E 7
Jefferson, 96,193 .... J 5
Knox, 41,795 .... F 5
Lake, 197,200 .... H 2
Lawrence, 56,868 .... E 8
Licking, 107,799 .... F 5
Logan, 35,072 .... C 5
Lorain, 256,843 .... F 3
Lucas, 484,370 .... C 2
Madison, 28,318 .... D 6
Mahoning, 303,424 .... J 4
Marion, 64,724 .... D 4
Medina, 82,717 .... G 3
Meigs, 19,799 .... F 7
Mercer, 35,265 .... A 4
Miami, 84,342 .... B 5
Monroe, 15,739 .... H 6
Montgomery, 606,148 .... B 6
Morgan, 12,375 .... G 6
Morrow, 21,348 .... E 4
Muskingum, 77,826 .... G 5
Noble, 10,428 .... G 6
Ottawa, 37,099 .... D 2
Paulding, 19,329 .... A 3
Perry, 27,434 .... F 6
Pickaway, 40,071 .... D 6
Pike, 19,114 .... D 7
Portage, 125,868 .... H 3
Preble, 34,719 .... A 6
Putnam, 31,134 .... B 3
Richland, 129,997 .... E 4
Ross, 61,211 .... D 7
Sandusky, 60,983 .... D 3
Scioto, 76,951 .... D 8
Seneca, 60,696 .... D 3
Shelby, 37,748 .... B 5
Stark, 372,210 .... H 4
Summit, 553,371 .... G 3
Trumbull, 232,579 .... J 3
Tuscarawas, 77,211 .... H 5
Union, 23,786 .... D 5
Van Wert, 29,194 .... A 4
Vinton, 9,420 .... E 7
Warren, 84,925 .... B 7
Washington, 57,160 .... H 7
Wayne, 87,123 .... G 4
Williams, 33,669 .... A 2
Wood, 09,722 .... C 3
Wyandot, 21,826 .... D 4

CITIES and TOWNS

Zip *Name/Pop.* *Key*

45101 Aberdeen, 1,165 .... C 8
45810 Ada, 5,309 .... C 4
45001 Addyston, 1,336 .... B 9
43901 Adena, 1,134 .... J 5
* 44301 Akron⊙, 275,425 .... G 3
Akron, ‡679,239 .... G 3
45710 Albany, 899 .... F 7
43001 Alexandria, 588 .... E 5
45812 Alger, 1,071 .... C 4
44601 Alliance, 26,547 .... H 4
43102 Amanda, 788 .... E 6
† 45201 Amberley, 5,574 .... C 9
45102 Amelia, 820 .... D 10
44001 Amherst, 9,902 .... F 3
43903 Amsterdam, 882 .... J 5
44003 Andover, 1,179 .... J 2
45302 Anna, 792 .... B 5
45303 Ansonia, 1,044 .... A 5
45813 Antwerp, 1,735 .... A 3
44606 Apple Creek, 784 .... G 4
44804 Arcadia, 689 .... D 3
45304 Arcanum, 1,993 .... A 6
43502 Archbold, 3,047 .... B 2
45814 Arlington, 1,066 .... C 4
† 45201 Arlington Heights, 1,476 .... C 9
44805 Ashland⊙, 19,872 .... F 4
43003 Ashley, 1,034 .... E 5
44004 Ashtabula, 24,313 .... J 2
43103 Ashville, 1,772 .... E 6
45701 Athens⊙, 23,310 .... F 7
44807 Attica, 1,005 .... E 3
44201 Atwater, 975 .... H 3
44202 Aurora, 6,549 .... H 3
44010 Austinburg, 900 .... J 2
44515 Austintown, 29,393 .... J 3
44011 Avon, 7,214 .... F 3
44012 Avon Lake, 12,261 .... F 2
† 43512 Ayersville, 950 .... B 3
45612 Bainbridge, 1,057 .... D 7
† 43420 Ballville, 1,652 .... D 3
43804 Baltic, 571 .... G 5
43105 Baltimore, 2,418 .... E 6
44203 Barberton, 33,052 .... G 4
43713 Barnesville, 4,292 .... H 6
43905 Barton, 975 .... J 5
45103 Batavia⊙, 1,894 .... B 7
† 44870 Bay View, 798 .... E 3
44140 Bay Village, 18,163 .... G 9
44608 Beach City, 1,133 .... G 4
† 44101 Beachwood, 9,631 .... J 9
45808 Beaverdam, 525 .... C 4
44146 Bedford, 17,552 .... H 9
† 44146 Bedford Heights, 13,063 .... J 9
43906 Bellaire, 9,655 .... J 5
45305 Bellbrook, 1,268 .... C 6
43310 Belle Center, 985 .... C 4
43311 Bellefontaine⊙, 11,255 .... C 5
44811 Bellevue, 8,604 .... E 3
44813 Bellville, 1,685 .... E 4
43718 Belmont, 666 .... J 5
44609 Beloit, 921 .... J 4
45714 Belpre, 7,189 .... G 7
44017 Berea, 22,396 .... G 10
43908 Bergholz, 914 .... J 4
44814 Berlin Heights, 828 .... F 3
45106 Bethel, 2,214 .... B 8
43719 Bethesda, 1,157 .... H 5
44815 Bettsville, 833 .... D 3
45715 Beverly, 1,396 .... G 6
43209 Bexley, 14,888 .... E 6
45107 Blanchester, 3,080 .... B 7
44817 Bloomdale, 727 .... D 3
43106 Bloomingburg, 895 .... D 6
44818 Bloomville, 884 .... D 3
† 45201 Blue Ash, 8,324 .... C 9
45817 Bluffton, 2,935 .... C 4
44512 Boardman, 30,852 .... J 3
44612 Bolivar, 1,084 .... G 4
† 44264 Boston Heights, 846 .... J 10
45306 Botkins, 1,057 .... B 5
43402 Bowling Green⊙, 21,760 .... C 3
45308 Bradford, 2,163 .... B 5
43406 Bradner, 1,140 .... C 3
† 44101 Bratenahl, 1,613 .... H 9
44141 Brecksville, 9,137 .... H 10
43107 Bremen, 1,413 .... F 6
44613 Brewster, 2,020 .... G 4
† 44215 Briarwood Beach, 508 .... G 3
43912 Bridgeport, 3,001 .... J 5
† 45201 Bridgetown, 13,352 .... B 9
43913 Brilliant, 2,178 .... J 5
44240 Brimfield, 950 .... H 3
44402 Bristolville, 900 .... J 3
† 44141 Broadview Heights, 11,463 .... H 10
44403 Brookfield, 1,200 .... J 3
44144 Brooklyn, 13,142 .... H 9
† 44131 Brooklyn Heights, 1,527 .... H 9
44142 Brook Park, 30,774 .... G 9
† 43912 Brookside, 939 .... J 5
45309 Brookville, 4,403 .... B 6
44212 Brunswick, 15,852 .... G 3
43506 Bryan⊙, 7,008 .... A 3
45716 Buchtel, 592 .... F 7
43008 Buckeye Lake, 2,961 .... F 6
44820 Bucyrus⊙, 13,111 .... E 4
43722 Buffalo, 710 .... G 6
† 45680 Burlington, 900 .... F 9
44021 Burton, 1,214 .... H 3
44822 Butler, 1,052 .... F 4
43723 Byesville, 2,097 .... G 6
43907 Cadiz⊙, 3,060 .... J 5
45820 Cairo, 587 .... B 4
43920 Calcutta, 2,900 .... J 4
43724 Caldwell⊙, 2,082 .... G 6
43314 Caledonia, 792 .... D 4
43725 Cambridge⊙, 13,656 .... G 5
45311 Camden, 1,507 .... A 6
44405 Campbell, 12,577 .... J 3
45111 Camp Dennison, 550 .... D 9
44614 Canal Fulton, 2,367 .... H 4
43110 Canal Winchester, 2,412 .... E 6
44406 Canfield, 4,997 .... J 3
* 44701 Canton⊙, 110,053 .... H 4
Canton, ‡372,210 .... H 4
43315 Cardington, 1,730 .... E 5
43316 Carey, 3,523 .... D 4
45005 Carlisle, 3,821 .... B 6
43112 Carroll, 614 .... E 6
44615 Carrollton⊙, 2,817 .... J 4
44824 Castalia, 1,045 .... E 3
45314 Cedarville, 2,342 .... C 6
45822 Celina⊙, 7,779 .... A 4
43011 Centerburg, 1,038 .... E 5
45459 Centerville, 10,333 .... B 6
44022 Chagrin Falls, 4,848 .... J 9
44024 Chardon⊙, 3,991 .... H 2
45719 Chauncey, 1,117 .... F 7
† 45202 Cherry Grove, 850 .... C 10
45619 Chesapeake, 1,364 .... E 9
44026 Chesterland, 11,500 .... H 2
† 45211 Cheviot, 11,135 .... B 9
45601 Chillicothe⊙, 24,842 .... E 7
45389 Christiansburg, 724 .... C 5
* 45201 Cincinnati⊙, 452,524 .... B 9
Cincinnati, ‡1,384,851 .... B 9
43113 Circleville⊙, 11,687 .... D 6
45113 Clarksville, 574 .... C 7
45315 Clayton, 773 .... B 6
* 44101 Cleveland⊙, 750,903 .... H 9
Cleveland, ‡2,074,194 .... H 9
44118 Cleveland Heights, 60,767 .... H 9
45002 Cleves, 2,044 .... B 9
44216 Clinton, 1,335 .... G 4
43410 Clyde, 5,503 .... E 3
† 45638 Coal Grove, 2,759 .... E 9
45621 Coalton, 550 .... E 7
45828 Coldwater, 3,533 .... A 5
† 44034 Colebrook, 700 .... J 2
44028 Columbia Station, 518 .... G 10
44408 Columbiana, 4,959 .... J 4
* 43201 Columbus (cap.)⊙, 539,677 .... E 6
Columbus, ‡916,228 .... E 6
45830 Columbus Grove, 2,290 .... B 4

(continued on following page)

AREA 41,222 sq. mi.
POPULATION 10,652,017
CAPITAL Columbus
LARGEST CITY Cleveland
HIGHEST POINT Campbell Hill 1,550 ft.
SETTLED IN 1788
ADMITTED TO UNION March 1, 1803
POPULAR NAME Buckeye State
STATE FLOWER Scarlet Carnation
STATE BIRD Cardinal

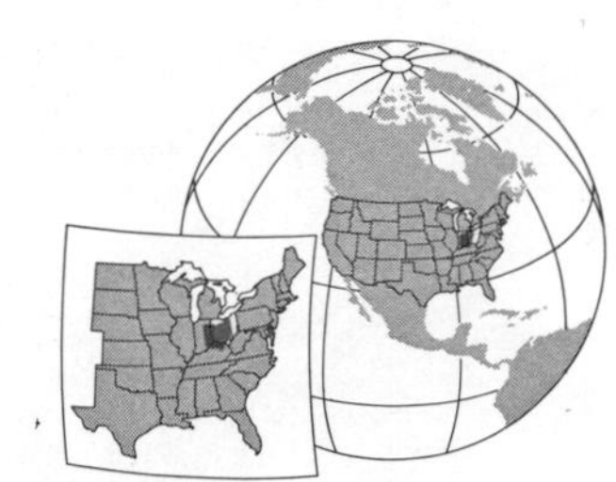

Topography

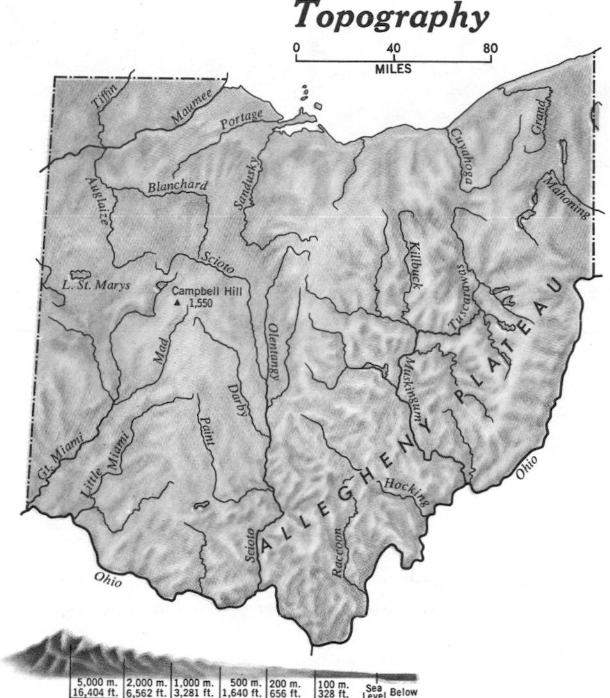

Agriculture, Industry and Resources

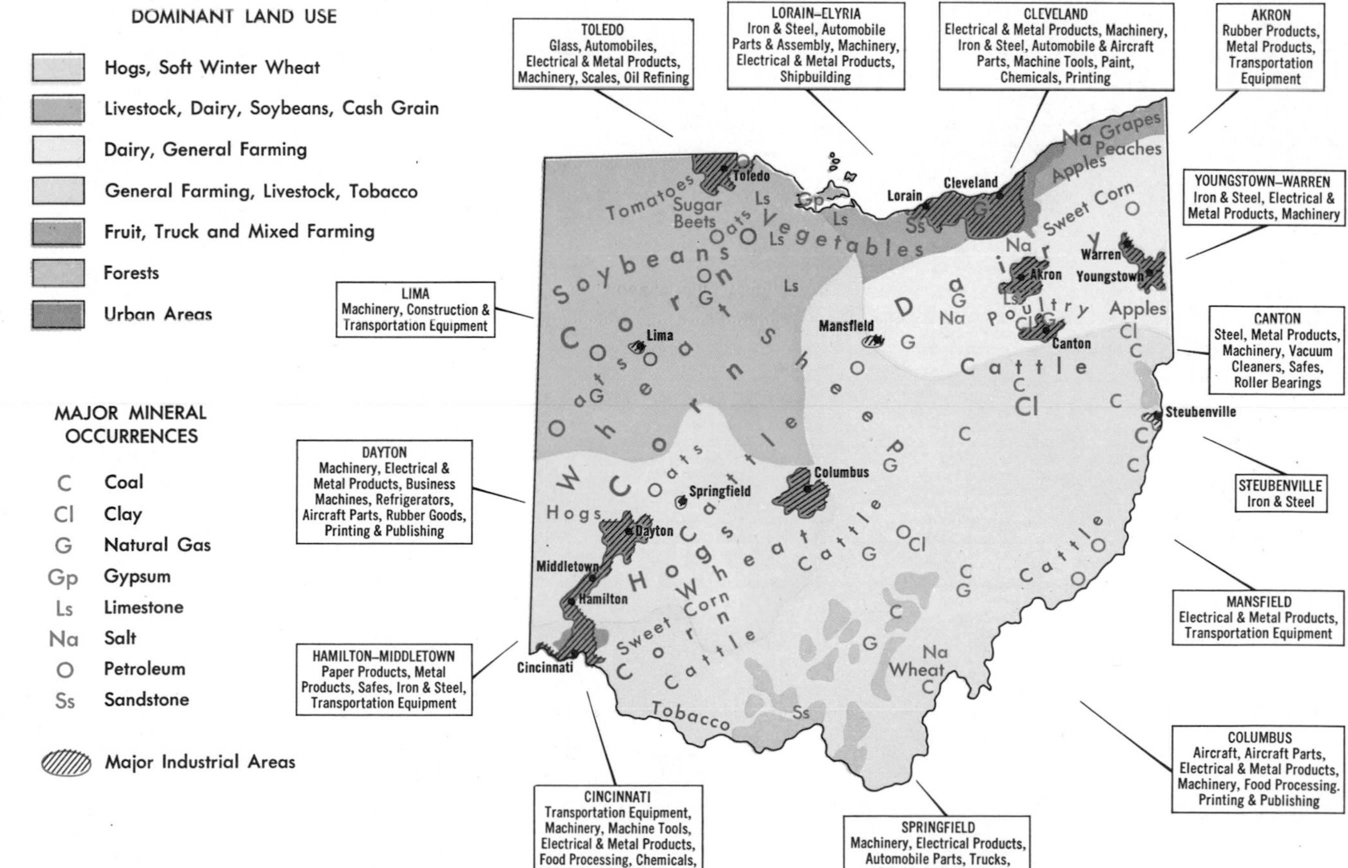

(continued)

Lou Moore — Shostal Associates

Reminiscent of children's book illustrations, the tugboat "Washington" guides ore-carrier "Peter Robertson" through Cleveland's Industrial Flats, past a Milwaukee fuel tanker.

44030	Conneaut, 14,552	J 2
45831	Continental, 1,185	B 3
45832	Convoy, 991	A 4
45723	Coolville, 672	G 7
43730	Corning, 838	F 6
44410	Cortland, 2,525	J 3
43812	Coshocton⊙, 13,747	G 5
† 45201	Covedale, 6,639	B 10
45318	Covington, 2,575	B 5
† 44429	Craig Beach, 1,451	H 3
44827	Crestline, 5,947	E 4
44217	Creston, 1,632	G 3
45806	Cridersville, 1,103	B 4
43731	Crooksville, 2,828	F 6
† 45341	Crystal Lakes, 5,851	C 6
* 44221	Cuyahoga Falls, 49,678	G 3
† 44101	Cuyahoga Heights, 866	H 9
43413	Cygnet, 629	C 3
44618	Dalton, 1,177	G 4
43014	Danville, 1,025	F 5
43123	Darbydale, 743	D 6
* 45401	Dayton⊙, 243,601	B 6
	Dayton, ‡850,266	B 6
44411	Deerfield, 800	H 3
45236	Deer Park, 7,415	C 9
43512	Defiance⊙, 16,281	B 3
43318	Degraff, 1,117	C 5
43015	Delaware⊙, 15,008	E 5
45833	Delphos, 7,608	B 4
43515	Delta, 2,544	B 2
44621	Dennison, 3,506	H 5
† 45202	Dent, 800	B 9
43516	Deshler, 1,938	C 3
45750	Devola, 1,989	H 7
43917	Dillonvale, 1,095	J 5
44622	Dover, 11,516	G 4
44230	Doylestown, 2,373	G 4
43821	Dresden, 1,516	G 5
43017	Dublin, 681	D 5
43734	Duncan Falls, 900	G 6
45836	Dunkirk, 1,036	C 4
44730	East Canton, 1,631	H 4
44112	East Cleveland, 39,600	H 9
44094	Eastlake, 19,690	J 8
43920	East Liverpool, 20,020	J 4
44413	East Palestine, 5,604	J 4
44626	East Sparta, 959	H 4
45320	Eaton⊙, 6,020	A 6
† 44035	Eaton Estates, 2,076	G 3
43517	Edgerton, 2,126	A 3
44004	Edgewood, 3,437	J 2
43320	Edison, 569	E 4
43518	Edon, 803	A 2
45807	Elida, 1,211	B 4
43416	Elmore, 1,316	D 3
45216	Elmwood Place, 3,525	B 9
* 44035	Elyria⊙, 53,427	F 3
45322	Englewood, 7,885	B 6
45323	Enon, 1,929	C 6
44117	Euclid, 71,552	J 9
† 45201	Evendale, 1,967	C 9
45042	Excello, 900	B 7
45324	Fairborn, 32,267	B 6
† 45201	Fairfax, 2,705	C 9
45014	Fairfield, 14,680	A 7
44313	Fairlawn, 6,102	G 3
44077	Fairport Harbor, 3,665	H 2
44126	Fairview Park, 21,681	G 9
45325	Farmersville, 865	A 6
43521	Fayette, 1,175	B 2
45120	Felicity, 786	B 8
45840	Findlay⊙, 35,800	C 3
45326	Fletcher, 539	B 5
43977	Flushing, 1,207	J 5
43843	Forest, 1,535	C 4
45405	Forest Park, 15,139	B 9
† 45202	Forestville, 950	C 10
45844	Fort Jennings, 533	B 4
45845	Fort Loramie, 744	B 5
† 45401	Fort McKinley, 11,536	B 6
45846	Fort Recovery, 1,348	A 5
† 45801	Fort Shawnee, 3,436	B 4
44830	Fostoria, 16,037	D 3
45628	Frankfort, 949	D 7
45005	Franklin, 10,075	B 6
45629	Franklin Furnace, 975	E 8
43822	Frazeysburg, 941	F 5
44627	Fredericksburg, 601	G 4
43019	Fredericktown, 1,935	F 5
43420	Fremont⊙, 18,490	D 3
45630	Friendship, 600	D 8
43230	Gahanna, 12,400	E 5
44833	Galion, 13,123	E 4
45631	Gallipolis⊙, 7,490	F 8
43022	Gambier, 1,571	F 5
44125	Garfield Heights, 41,417	J 9
44231	Garrettsville, 1,718	H 3
44040	Gates Mills, 2,378	J 9
44041	Geneva, 6,449	J 2
44043	Geneva-on-the-Lake, 877	H 2
43430	Genoa, 2,139	D 2
45121	Georgetown⊙, 2,949	C 8
45327	Germantown, 4,088	B 6
45328	Gettysburg, 526	A 5
43431	Gibsonburg, 2,585	D 3
44420	Girard, 14,119	J 3
45848	Glandorf, 732	B 3
45246	Glendale, 2,690	C 9
† 44139	Glenwillow, 526	J 10
45732	Glouster, 2,121	F 6
44629	Gnadenhutten, 1,466	G 5
† 45201	Golf Manor, 5,170	C 9
45122	Goshen, 1,174	B 7
44044	Grafton, 1,771	F 3
43522	Grand Rapids, 976	C 3
44045	Grand River, 613	H 2
† 43201	Grandview Heights, 8,460	D 6
43023	Granville, 3,963	E 5
45330	Gratis, 621	A 6
43322	Green Camp, 537	D 4
45123	Greenfield, 4,780	D 7
45218	Greenhills, 6,092	B 9
44232	Greensburg, 950	G 4
44836	Green Springs, 1,279	E 3
44630	Greentown, 1,150	H 4
45331	Greenville⊙, 12,380	A 5
44837	Greenwich, 1,473	E 3
45239	Groesbeck, 5,000	B 9
43123	Grove City, 13,911	D 6
43125	Groveport, 2,490	E 6
45849	Grover Hill, 536	B 3
45634	Hamden, 953	F 7
45130	Hamersville, 567	C 8
* 45011	Hamilton⊙, 67,865	A 7
	Hamilton-Middletown, ‡226,207	A 7
43524	Hamler, 681	B 3
43931	Hannibal, 550	J 6
† 43055	Hanover, 626	F 5
43126	Harrisburg, 556	D 6
45030	Harrison, 4,408	A 9
45850	Harrod, 533	C 4
† 44085	Hartsgrove, 775	J 2
44632	Hartville, 1,752	H 4
43525	Haskins, 549	C 3
43127	Haydenville, 1,650	F 7
43055	Heath, 6,768	F 5
43025	Hebron, 1,699	E 6
43526	Hicksville, 3,461	A 3
† 44143	Highland Heights, 5,926	J 9
43026	Hilliard, 8,369	D 5
45133	Hillsboro⊙, 5,584	C 7
44234	Hiram, 1,484	H 3
43527	Holgate, 1,541	B 3
43528	Holland, 1,108	C 2
45033	Hooven, 550	A 9
43976	Hopedale, 916	J 5
44425	Hubbard, 8,583	J 3
45424	Huber Heights, 18,943	B 6
44236	Hudson, 3,933	H 3
† 44022	Hunting Valley, 797	J 9
44839	Huron, 6,896	E 3
44131	Independence, 7,034	H 9
† 45201	Indian Hill, 5,651	C 9
43932	Irondale, 602	J 4
45638	Ironton⊙, 15,030	E 8
45640	Jackson⊙, 6,843	E 7
45334	Jackson Center, 1,119	B 5
45740	Jacksonville, 545	F 7
45335	Jamestown, 1,790	C 6
44047	Jefferson⊙, 2,472	J 2
† 43162	Jefferson (West Jefferson), 3,664	D 6
43128	Jeffersonville, 1,031	C 6
44840	Jeromesville, 559	F 4
43986	Jewett, 901	H 5
43031	Johnstown, 3,208	E 5
43748	Junction City, 732	F 6
45853	Kalida, 900	B 4
44240	Kent, 28,183	H 3
43326	Kenton⊙, 8,315	C 4
45429	Kettering, 69,599	B 6
44637	Killbuck, 893	G 5
45034	Kings Mills, 800	B 7
45644	Kingston, 1,157	E 7
44048	Kingsville, 1,129	J 2
44428	Kinsman, 900	J 3
43033	Kirkersville, 578	E 6
44094	Kirtland, 5,530	H 2
43951	Lafferty, 900	H 5
44050	Lagrange, 1,074	F 3
44250	Lakemore, 2,708	H 3
43440	Lakeside, 850	E 2
43331	Lakeview, 1,026	C 4
44107	Lakewood, 70,173	G 9
43130	Lancaster⊙, 32,911	E 6
43934	Lansing, 950	J 5
43332	La Rue, 867	D 4
43135	Laurelville, 624	E 7
† 45501	Lawrenceville, 687	C 6
44430	Leavittsburg, 4,979	J 3
45036	Lebanon⊙, 7,934	B 7
45135	Leesburg, 984	D 7
44431	Leetonia, 2,342	J 4
45856	Leipsic, 2,072	C 3
44251	Leroy, 715	G 3
45338	Lewisburg, 1,553	A 6
44904	Lexington, 2,972	E 4
43532	Liberty Center, 1,007	B 3
* 45801	Lima⊙, 53,734	B 4
	Lima, ‡171,472	B 4
† 45201	Lincoln Heights, 6,099	C 9
43442	Lindsey, 652	D 3
44432	Lisbon⊙, 3,521	J 4
44253	Litchfield, 650	F 3
43136	Lithopolis, 705	E 6
45742	Little Hocking, 520	G 7
45215	Lockland, 5,288	C 9
44254	Lodi, 2,399	F 3
43138	Logan⊙, 6,269	F 6
43140	London⊙, 6,481	C 6
* 44052	Lorain, 78,185	F 3
	Lorain-Elyria, ‡256,843	F 3
44842	Loudonville, 2,865	F 4
44641	Louisville, 6,298	H 4
45140	Loveland, 7,144	D 9
45744	Lowell, 852	H 6
44436	Lowellville, 1,836	J 3
44843	Lucas, 771	F 4
45648	Lucasville, 900	E 8
43443	Luckey, 996	D 3
45142	Lynchburg, 1,186	C 7
44124	Lyndhurst, 19,749	J 9
43533	Lyons, 630	B 2
44056	Macedonia, 6,375	J 10
† 45202	Mack, 5,000	B 9
45243	Madeira, 6,713	C 9
44057	Madison, 1,678	H 2
44643	Magnolia, 1,064	H 4
43758	Malta, 1,017	G 6
44644	Malvern, 1,256	H 4
45144	Manchester, 2,195	C 8
* 44901	Mansfield⊙, 55,047	F 4
	Mansfield, ‡129,997	F 4
44255	Mantua, 1,199	H 3
44137	Maple Heights, 34,093	H 9
† 43440	Marblehead, 726	E 2
45860	Maria Stein, 950	A 5
45227	Mariemont, 4,540	C 9
45750	Marietta⊙, 16,861	G 7
43302	Marion⊙, 38,646	D 4
44645	Marshallville, 693	G 4
43935	Martins Ferry, 10,757	J 5
43040	Marysville⊙, 5,744	D 5
45040	Mason, 5,677	B 7
44646	Massillon, 32,539	H 4
44438	Masury, 2,060	J 3
45069	Maud, 550	B 7
43537	Maumee, 15,937	C 2
† 44121	Mayfield, 3,548	J 9
† 44101	Mayfield Heights, 22,139	J 9
45651	McArthur⊙, 1,543	F 7
43534	McClure, 699	C 3
45858	McComb, 1,329	C 3
43756	McConnelsville⊙, 2,107	G 6
44437	McDonald, 3,177	J 3
45859	McGuffey, 704	C 4
43044	Mechanicsburg, 1,686	D 5
44256	Medina⊙, 10,913	G 3
45862	Mendon, 672	A 4
44060	Mentor, 36,912	H 2
44060	Mentor-on-the-Lake, 6,517	G 2
43540	Metamora, 594	C 2
45342	Miamisburg, 14,797	B 6
45041	Miamitown, 800	A 9
44652	Middlebranch, 600	H 4
† 44017	Middleburg Heights, 12,367	G 10
44062	Middlefield, 1,726	H 3
45863	Middle Point, 543	B 4
45760	Middleport, 2,784	F 7
45042	Middletown, 48,767	A 6
44653	Midvale, 636	H 5
44846	Milan, 1,405	E 3
45150	Milford, 4,828	D 9
43045	Milford Center, 753	D 5
43447	Millbury, 771	D 2
44654	Millersburg⊙, 2,979	F 4
43046	Millersport, 777	E 6
45013	Millville, 697	A 7
44656	Mineral City, 860	H 4
44440	Mineral Ridge, 1,500	J 3
44657	Minerva, 4,359	H 4
† 43201	Minerva Park, 1,402	E 5
43938	Mingo Junction, 5,278	J 5
45865	Minster, 2,405	B 5
44260	Mogadore, 3,858	H 3
45050	Monroe, 3,492	B 7
44847	Monroeville, 1,455	E 3
45242	Montgomery, 5,683	C 9
43543	Montpelier, 4,184	A 2
45439	Moraine, 4,898	B 6
† 44022	Moreland Hills, 3,000	J 9
45152	Morrow, 1,486	B 7
43338	Mount Gilead⊙, 2,971	E 4
45231	Mount Healthy, 7,446	B 9
45154	Mount Orab, 1,306	C 7
43939	Mount Pleasant, 635	J 5
43143	Mount Sterling, 1,536	D 6
43050	Mount Vernon⊙, 13,373	E 5
43340	Mount Victory, 633	D 4
44262	Munroe Falls, 3,794	H 3
43144	Murray City, 562	F 6
43545	Napoleon⊙, 7,791	B 3
44662	Navarre, 1,607	H 4
43940	Neffs, 900	J 5
44441	Negley, 600	J 4
45764	Nelsonville, 4,812	F 7
44849	Nevada, 917	D 4
43054	New Albany, 513	E 5
43055	Newark⊙, 41,836	F 5
45662	New Boston, 3,325	E 8
45869	New Bremen, 2,185	B 5
† 44101	Newburgh Heights, 3,396	H 9
† 45201	New Burlington, 900	B 9
45344	New Carlisle, 6,112	C 6
43832	Newcomerstown, 4,155	G 5
43762	New Concord, 2,318	G 6
43145	New Holland, 796	D 6
45871	New Knoxville, 852	B 5
45345	New Lebanon, 4,248	B 6
43764	New Lexington⊙, 4,921	F 6
44851	New London, 2,336	F 3
45346	New Madison, 959	A 6
45767	New Matamoras, 940	J 6
45011	New Miami, 3,273	A 7
44442	New Middletown, 1,664	J 4
45347	New Paris, 1,692	A 6
44663	New Philadelphia⊙, 15,184	G 5
45768	Newport, 975	H 7
45157	New Richmond, 2,650	B 8
43766	New Straitsville, 947	F 6
44444	Newton Falls, 5,378	J 3
45244	Newtown, 2,047	C 10
45159	New Vienna, 849	C 7
44854	New Washington, 1,251	E 4
44445	New Waterford, 735	J 4
44446	Niles, 21,581	J 3
45872	North Baltimore, 3,143	C 3
45052	North Bend, 638	B 9
44450	North Bloomfield, 650	J 3
44720	North Canton, 15,228	H 4
45239	North College Hill, 12,363	B 9
44855	North Fairfield, 540	E 3
44067	Northfield, 1,089	J 10
44707	North Industry, 2,000	H 4
44068	North Kingsville, 2,458	J 2
43060	North Lewisburg, 840	C 5
44452	North Lima, 800	J 4
44070	North Olmsted, 34,861	G 9
† 44081	North Perry, 851	H 2
† 44101	North Randall, 1,212	H 9
44035	North Ridgeville, 13,152	F 3
44133	North Royalton, 12,807	H 10
† 43601	Northwood, 4,222	D 2
† 43701	North Zanesville, 3,399	G 6
44203	Norton, 12,308	G 3
44857	Norwalk⊙, 13,386	E 3
45212	Norwood, 30,420	C 9
43449	Oak Harbor, 2,807	D 2
45656	Oak Hill, 1,642	E 8
45873	Oakwood, 10,095	B 6
45873	Oakwood, 3,127	B 3
45873	Oakwood, 804	B 3
44074	Oberlin, 8,761	F 3
43207	Obetz, 2,248	E 6
45874	Ohio City, 816	A 4
44138	Olmsted Falls, 2,504	G 9
44862	Ontario, 4,345	E 4
† 44101	Orange, 2,112	J 9
43616	Oregon, 16,563	D 2
44667	Orrville, 7,408	G 4
44076	Orwell, 965	J 2
45875	Ottawa⊙, 3,622	B 3
† 43601	Ottawa Hills, 4,270	C 2
45876	Ottoville, 914	B 4
45160	Owensville, 707	B 7
45056	Oxford, 15,868	A 6
44077	Painesville⊙, 16,536	H 2
45877	Pandora, 857	C 4
44080	Parkman, 750	H 3
44129	Parma, 100,216	H 9
† 44129	Parma Heights, 27,192	G 9
43062	Pataskala, 1,831	E 5
45879	Paulding⊙, 2,983	A 3
45880	Payne, 1,351	A 3
45660	Peebles, 1,629	D 8
43450	Pemberville, 1,301	C 3
44264	Peninsula, 692	G 3
44124	Pepper Pike, 5,933	J 9
44081	Perry, 917	H 2
43551	Perrysburg, 7,693	C 2
44864	Perrysville, 752	F 4
45354	Phillipsburg, 831	B 6
43771	Philo, 846	G 6
43147	Pickerington, 696	E 6
45661	Piketon, 1,347	E 7
43554	Pioneer, 968	A 2
45356	Piqua, 20,741	B 5
43064	Plain City, 2,254	D 5
45359	Pleasant Hill, 1,025	B 5
43148	Pleasantville, 754	F 6
44865	Plymouth, 1,993	E 4
† 45042	Poasttown, 650	B 6
44514	Poland, 3,097	J 3
45760	Pomeroy⊙, 2,672	G 7
43452	Port Clinton⊙, 7,202	E 2
45770	Portland, 550	G 7
45662	Portsmouth⊙, 27,633	D 8
43837	Port Washington, 550	G 5
43942	Powhatan Point, 2,167	J 6
45669	Proctorville, 881	F 9
43342	Prospect, 1,031	D 5
43456	Put-in-Bay, 135	E 2
43773	Quaker City, 510	H 6
43343	Quincy, 686	C 5
45771	Racine, 583	G 8
43066	Radnor, 950	D 5
44265	Randolph, 900	H 3
44266	Ravenna⊙, 11,780	H 3
43943	Rayland, 617	J 5
45215	Reading, 14,303	C 9
† 45202	Remington, 600	C 9
45773	Reno, 576	H 7
† 43412	Reno Beach, 1,049	D 2
44867	Republic, 705	D 3
43068	Reynoldsburg, 13,921	E 6
44286	Richfield, 3,228	G 3
43944	Richmond, 777	J 5
† 44045	Richmond (Grand River), 613	H 2
45673	Richmond Dale, 950	E 7
44143	Richmond Heights, 9,220	H 9
43344	Richwood, 2,072	D 5
45674	Rio Grande, 814	F 8
45167	Ripley, 2,745	C 8
43457	Risingsun, 730	C 3
44270	Rittman, 6,308	G 4
† 43085	Riverlea, 558	D 5
44670	Robertsville, 600	H 4
44084	Rock Creek, 731	J 2
45882	Rockford, 1,207	A 4
44116	Rocky River, 22,958	G 9
44085	Rome, 648	J 2
44272	Rootstown, 900	H 3
† 45662	Rosemount, 1,786	D 8
43777	Roseville, 1,767	F 6
45061	Ross (Venice), 1,661	B 9
43460	Rossford, 5,302	C 2
45236	Rossmoyne, 2,900	C 9
† 43943	Rush Run, 560	J 5
43347	Rushsylvania, 526	C 5
43348	Russells Point, 1,104	C 5
45775	Rutland, 663	F 7
45169	Sabina, 2,160	C 7
† 44067	Sagamore Hills, 4,100	J 10
45217	Saint Bernard, 6,080	B 9
43950	Saint Clairsville⊙, 4,754	J 5
45883	Saint Henry, 1,276	A 5
45885	Saint Marys, 7,699	B 4
43072	Saint Paris, 1,646	C 5
44460	Salem, 14,186	J 4
43945	Salineville, 1,686	J 4
44870	Sandusky⊙, 32,674	E 3
44671	Sandyville, 543	H 4
45171	Sardinia, 824	C 7
43946	Sardis, 700	J 6
43988	Scio, 1,002	H 5
† 45662	Sciotodale, 950	E 8
45679	Seaman, 866	C 8
44672	Sebring, 4,954	H 4
† 44101	Seven Hills, 12,700	H 9
45062	Seven Mile, 699	A 7
44273	Seville, 1,402	G 3
43947	Shadyside, 5,070	J 6
44120	Shaker Heights, 36,306	H 9
45241	Sharonville, 10,985	C 9
43782	Shawnee, 914	F 6
† 44052	Sheffield, 1,730	F 3
44054	Sheffield Lake, 8,734	F 3
44875	Shelby, 9,847	E 4
43556	Sherwood, 784	A 3
44878	Shiloh, 817	E 4
44676	Shreve, 1,635	F 4
45365	Sidney⊙, 16,332	B 5
† 44221	Silver Lake, 3,637	G 3
† 45201	Silverton, 6,588	C 9
43948	Smithfield, 1,245	J 5
44677	Smithville, 1,278	G 4
44139	Solon, 11,519	J 9
43783	Somerset, 1,417	F 6
† 44001	South Amherst, 2,913	F 3
† 43103	South Bloomfield, 610	D 6
45368	South Charleston, 1,500	C 6
44121	South Euclid, 29,579	H 9
45065	South Lebanon, 3,014	B 7
45680	South Point, 2,243	E 9
† 44022	South Russell, 2,673	H 3
45369	South Vienna, 545	C 6
45682	South Webster, 825	E 8
43701	South Zanesville, 1,436	F 6
44275	Spencer, 758	F 3
45887	Spencerville, 2,241	B 4
45066	Springboro, 2,799	B 6
45246	Springdale, 8,127	B 9
* 45501	Springfield⊙, 81,926	C 6
	Springfield, ‡157,115	C 6
45370	Spring Valley, 667	C 6
44276	Sterling, 550	G 4
43952	Steubenville⊙, 30,771	J 5
	Steubenville-Weirton, ‡165,627	J 5
43154	Stoutsville, 573	E 6
44224	Stow, 19,847	H 3
44680	Strasburg, 1,874	G 4
44240	Streetsboro, 7,966	H 3
44136	Strongsville, 15,182	G 10
44471	Struthers, 15,343	J 3
43557	Stryker, 1,296	B 3
† 44260	Suffield, 650	H 3
44681	Sugarcreek, 1,771	G 5
43074	Sunbury, 2,512	E 5
43558	Swanton, 2,927	C 2
44882	Sycamore, 1,096	D 4
43560	Sylvania, 12,031	C 2
45779	Syracuse, 684	G 7
44278	Tallmadge, 15,274	H 3
† 43771	Taylorsville (Philo), 846	G 6
45174	Terrace Park, 2,266	D 9
45780	The Plains, 1,568	F 7
43076	Thornville, 679	F 6
44883	Tiffin⊙, 21,596	D 3
43963	Tiltonsville, 2,123	J 5
† 44094	Timberlake, 964	J 8
45371	Tipp City, 5,090	B 6
† 45245	Tobasco, 950	C 10
* 43601	Toledo⊙, 383,818	D 2
	Toledo, ‡692,571	D 2
43964	Toronto, 7,705	J 5
45067	Trenton, 5,278	B 7
45782	Trimble, 542	F 7
45373	Troy⊙, 17,186	B 5
44682	Tuscarawas, 830	H 5
44087	Twinsburg, 6,432	J 10
44683	Uhrichsville, 5,731	H 5
45322	Union, 3,654	B 6
† 47390	Union City, 1,808	A 5
44685	Uniontown, 875	H 4
44118	University Heights, 17,055	H 9
43221	Upper Arlington, 38,630	D 6
43351	Upper Sandusky⊙, 5,645	D 4
43078	Urbana⊙, 11,237	C 5
† 43123	Urbancrest, 754	D 6
43080	Utica, 1,977	F 5
† 43201	Valley View, 909	D 6
† 44101	Valley View, 1,422	H 9
45377	Vandalia, 10,796	B 6
45890	Vanlue, 539	C 4
45891	Van Wert⊙, 11,320	A 4
44870	Venice, 1,661	B 9
44089	Vermilion, 9,872	F 3
45378	Verona, 593	A 6
45380	Versailles, 2,441	A 5
44473	Vienna, 1,200	J 3
† 44473	Vienna (South Vienna), 545	C 6
44281	Wadsworth, 13,142	G 3
† 44094	Waite Hill, 514	H 2
44889	Wakeman, 514	F 3
43465	Walbridge, 3,208	C 2
44687	Walnut Creek, 550	G 4
† 44146	Walton Hills, 2,508	J 10
45895	Wapakoneta⊙, 7,324	B 4
* 44481	Warren⊙, 63,494	J 3
† 44100	Warrensville Heights, 18,925	H 9
43844	Warsaw, 725	G 5
43160	Washington Court House⊙, 12,495	D 6
44490	Washingtonville, 747	J 4
45786	Waterford, 600	G 6
43566	Waterville, 2,940	C 3
43567	Wauseon⊙, 4,932	B 2
45690	Waverly⊙, 4,858	D 7
43466	Wayne, 921	C 3
44688	Waynesburg, 1,337	H 4
45896	Waynesfield, 704	C 4
45068	Waynesville, 1,638	B 6
44090	Wellington, 4,137	F 3
45692	Wellston, 5,410	F 7
43968	Wellsville, 5,891	J 4
45381	West Alexandria, 1,553	A 6
45449	West Carrollton, 10,748	B 6
43081	Westerville, 12,530	D 5
44491	West Farmington, 650	J 3
43162	West Jefferson, 3,664	D 6
43845	West Lafayette, 1,719	G 5
44145	Westlake, 15,689	G 9
43357	West Liberty, 1,580	C 5
43358	West Mansfield, 753	C 5
45383	West Milton, 3,696	B 6
43569	Weston, 1,269	C 3
† 45662	West Portsmouth, 3,396	D 8
44287	West Salem, 1,058	F 4
45693	West Union⊙, 1,951	C 8
43570	West Unity, 1,589	B 2
† 44138	Westview, 2,523	G 10
45694	Wheelersburg, 3,709	E 8
43213	Whitehall, 25,263	E 6
43571	Whitehouse, 1,542	C 2
44092	Wickliffe, 21,354	J 9
44890	Willard, 5,510	E 3
45176	Williamsburg, 2,054	B 7
44093	Williamsfield, 950	J 2
43164	Williamsport, 857	D 6
44094	Willoughby, 18,634	J 8
† 44094	Willoughby Hills, 5,247	J 9
44094	Willowick, 21,237	J 8
45898	Willshire, 623	A 4
45177	Wilmington⊙, 10,051	C 7
45697	Winchester, 760	C 8
44288	Windham, 3,360	H 3
43952	Wintersville, 4,921	J 5
45245	Withamsville, 975	C 10
† 45201	Woodlawn, 3,251	C 9
† 44101	Woodmere, 976	J 9
43793	Woodsfield⊙, 3,239	H 6
43469	Woodville, 1,834	D 3
44691	Wooster⊙, 18,703	G 4
43085	Worthington, 15,326	E 5
45215	Wyoming, 9,089	C 9
45385	Xenia⊙, 25,373	C 6
45387	Yellow Springs, 4,624	C 6
43971	Yorkville, 1,656	J 5
* 44501	Youngstown⊙, 139,788	J 3
	Youngstown-Warren, ‡536,003	J 3
43701	Zanesville⊙, 33,045	G 6

⊙ County seat.
‡ Population of metropolitan area.
† Zip of nearest p.o.
* Multiple zips

COUNTIES

County, Pop.	Key
Adair, 15,141	S 3
Alfalfa, 7,224	K 1
Atoka, 10,972	O 6
Beaver, 6,282	E 1
Beckham, 15,754	G 4
Blaine, 11,794	K 3
Bryan, 25,552	O 7
Caddo, 28,931	K 4
Canadian, 32,245	K 3
Carter, 37,349	M 6
Cherokee, 23,174	R 3
Choctaw, 15,141	P 6
Cimarron, 4,145	A 1
Cleveland, 81,839	M 4
Coal, 5,525	O 5
Comanche, 108,144	K 5
Cotton, 6,832	K 6
Craig, 14,722	R 1
Creek, 45,532	O 3
Custer, 22,665	H 3
Delaware, 17,767	S 2
Dewey, 5,656	H 2
Ellis, 5,129	G 2
Garfield, 55,365	L 2
Garvin, 24,874	M 5
Grady, 29,354	L 5
Grant, 7,117	L 1
Greer, 7,979	G 5
Harmon, 5,136	G 5
Harper, 5,151	G 1
Haskell, 9,578	R 4
Hughes, 13,228	O 4
Jackson, 30,902	H 5
Jefferson, 7,125	L 6
Johnston, 7,870	N 6
Kay, 48,791	M 1
Kingfisher, 12,857	L 3
Kiowa, 12,532	J 5
Latimer, 8,601	R 5
Le Flore, 32,137	S 5
Lincoln, 19,482	N 3
Logan, 19,645	M 3
Love, 5,637	M 7
Major, 7,529	K 2
Marshall, 7,682	N 6
Mayes, 23,302	R 2
McClain, 14,157	M 5
McCurtain, 28,642	S 6
McIntosh, 12,472	P 4
Murray, 10,669	M 6
Muskogee, 59,542	R 3
Noble, 10,043	M 2
Nowata, 9,773	P 1
Okfuskee, 10,683	O 3
Oklahoma, 526,805	M 3
Okmulgee, 35,358	P 3
Osage, 29,750	O 1
Ottawa, 29,800	S 1
Pawnee, 11,338	N 2
Payne, 50,654	N 2
Pittsburg, 37,521	P 5
Pontotoc, 27,867	N 5
Pottawatomie, 43,134	N 4
Pushmataha, 9,385	R 6
Roger Mills, 4,452	G 3
Rogers, 28,425	P 2
Seminole, 25,144	N 4
Sequoyah, 23,370	S 3
Stephens, 35,902	L 6
Texas, 16,352	C 1
Tillman, 12,901	J 6
Tulsa, 401,663	P 2
Wagoner, 22,163	P 3
Washington, 42,277	P 1
Washita, 12,141	J 4
Woods, 11,920	J 1
Woodward, 15,537	H 2

CITIES and TOWNS

Zip	Name/Pop.	Key
74720	Achille, 382	O 7
74820	Ada⊙, 14,859	N 5
74330	Adair, 459	R 2
73901	Adams, 175	D 1
74520	Adamson, 150	P 5
73520	Addington, 123	L 6
74331	Afton, 1,022	S 1
74824	Agra, 335	N 3
† 74955	Akins, 250	S 3
74721	Albany, 100	O 7
73001	Albert, 110	K 4
74521	Albion, 186	R 5
74522	Alderson, 215	P 5
73002	Alex, 492	L 5
† 73015	Alfalfa, 70	J 4
73716	Aline, 260	K 1
74825	Allen, 974	O 5
73521	Altus⊙, 23,302	H 5
73717	Alva⊙, 7,440	J 1
73004	Amber, 300	L 4
73718	Ames, 227	K 2
† 73723	Amorita, 63	K 1
73719	Anadarko⊙, 6,682	K 4
74523	Antlers⊙, 2,685	P 6
73006	Apache, 1,421	K 5
† 74633	Apperson, 40	N 1
73620	Arapaho⊙, 531	H 3
73007	Arcadia, 500	M 3
73401	Ardmore⊙, 20,881	M 6
74901	Arkoma, 2,098	T 4
73832	Arnett⊙, 711	G 2
74826	Asher, 437	N 5
74524	Ashland, 73	O 5
74525	Atoka⊙, 3,346	O 6
74827	Atwood, 200	O 5
74001	Avant, 439	O 2
73833	Avard, 59	J 1
74526	Bache, 100	P 5
74420	Bacone, 786	R 3
73930	Baker, 63	D 1
73931	Balko, 100	E 1
74002	Barnsdall, 1,579	O 1
† 74965	Baron, 100	S 3
74003	Bartlesville⊙, 29,683	O 1
74722	Battiest, 150	S 6
74828	Bearden, 260	O 4
73932	Beaver⊙, 1,853	F 1
74421	Beggs, 1,107	P 3
† 74523	Belzoni, 50	R 6
74929	Bengal, 75	R 5
74723	Bennington, 288	P 7
74527	Bentley, 125	O 6
† 73662	Berlin, 50	G 4
74331	Bernice, 189	S 1
73622	Bessie, 210	H 4
73008	Bethany, 21,785	L 3
74724	Bethel, 297	S 6
† 74801	Bethel Acres, 1,083	M 4
74332	Big Cabin, 198	R 1
74630	Billings, 618	M 1
73009	Binger, 730	K 4
73720	Bison, 80	L 2
74008	Bixby, 3,973	P 3
74058	Blackburn, 88	N 2
† 74962	Blackgum, 258	S 3
74631	Blackwell, 8,645	M 1
73526	Blair, 1,114	H 5
73010	Blanchard, 1,580	L 4
74528	Blanco, 200	P 5
74529	Blocker, 151	P 4
74725	Blue, 150	O 7
74333	Bluejacket, 234	R 1
† 74525	Boggy Depot, 100	O 6
73933	Boise City⊙, 1,993	B 1
74726	Bokchito, 607	O 6
74930	Bokoshe, 588	S 4
74829	Boley, 514	O 4
74727	Boswell, 755	P 6
74830	Bowlegs, 540	N 4
74009	Bowring, 100	O 1
74422	Boynton, 522	P 3
73011	Bradley, 247	L 5
74423	Braggs, 325	R 3
74632	Braman, 295	M 1
73012	Bray, 90	L 5
73721	Breckinridge, 70	L 2
74424	Briartown, 100	R 4
73013	Bridgeport, 142	K 3
74010	Bristow, 4,653	O 3
74012	Broken Arrow, 11,787	P 2
74728	Broken Bow, 2,980	S 7
74530	Bromide, 231	N 6
† 74873	Brooksville, 80	M 4
† 74437	Bryant, 86	P 4
73834	Buffalo⊙, 1,579	G 1
74931	Bunch, 90	S 3
74633	Burbank, 188	N 1
73722	Burlington, 165	K 1
73430	Burneyville, 106	M 7
73624	Burns Flat, 988	H 4
73625	Butler, 315	H 3
74831	Byars, 247	N 5
† 74820	Byng, 50	N 5
73723	Byron, 72	K 1
73527	Cache, 1,106	J 5
74729	Caddo, 886	O 6
74730	Calera, 1,063	O 7
73014	Calumet, 386	K 3
74531	Calvin, 359	O 5
73835	Camargo, 236	H 2
74932	Cameron, 311	T 4
74425	Canadian, 304	P 4
74533	Caney, 200	O 6
73724	Canton, 844	J 2
73626	Canute, 420	H 4
73725	Capron, 80	J 1
74335	Cardin, 950	S 1
73726	Carmen, 519	J 1
73015	Carnegie, 1,723	J 4
74832	Carney, 396	N 3
73727	Carrier, 125	K 2
73627	Carter, 311	H 4
† 74633	Carter Nine, 50	N 1
74934	Cartersville, 119	S 4
73016	Cashion, 329	L 3
74833	Castle, 212	O 4
74015	Catoosa, 970	P 2
73017	Cement, 892	K 5
† 74820	Center, 100	N 5
74534	Centrahoma, 155	O 5
74336	Centralia, 43	R 1
74834	Chandler⊙, 2,529	N 3
73528	Chattanooga, 302	J 6
74426	Checotah, 3,074	R 4
74016	Chelsea, 1,622	P 1
73728	Cherokee⊙, 2,119	K 1
73838	Chester, 135	J 2
73628	Cheyenne⊙, 892	G 3
73018	Chickasha⊙, 14,194	L 4
74635	Chilocco, 712	M 1
73020	Choctaw, 4,750	M 3
74337	Chouteau, 1,046	R 2
† 74965	Christie, 70	S 3
74017	Claremore⊙, 9,084	R 2
74535	Clarita, 90	O 6
74536	Clayton, 718	R 5
74835	Clearview, 350	O 4
† 73437	Clemscot, 150	L 6
† 74331	Cleora, 87	S 1
73729	Cleo Springs, 344	K 2
74020	Cleveland, 2,573	O 2
73601	Clinton, 8,513	H 3
73632	Cloud Chief, 40	J 4
74537	Cloudy, 175	R 6
74538	Coalgate⊙, 1,859	O 5
† 73059	Cogar, 40	K 4
74733	Colbert, 814	O 7
74338	Colcord, 438	S 2
† 73010	Cole, 75	L 4
73432	Coleman, 125	O 6
74021	Collinsville, 3,009	P 2
73021	Colony, 250	J 4
73529	Comanche, 1,862	L 6
74339	Commerce, 2,593	R 1
73022	Concho, 500	L 3
74836	Connerville, 150	N 6
73023	Cooperton, 55	J 5
74022	Copan, 558	P 1
73632	Cordell⊙, 3,261	H 4
† 74751	Corinne, 100	R 6
73024	Corn, 409	J 4
† 73456	Cornish, 90	L 6
74428	Council Hill, 135	P 3
73025	Countyline, 500	L 6
73730	Covington, 605	L 2
74429	Coweta, 2,457	P 3
† 74934	Cowlington, 751	S 4
73082	Cox City, 285	L 5
73027	Coyle, 303	M 3
73028	Crescent, 1,568	L 3
74837	Cromwell, 287	N 4
74430	Crowder, 339	P 4
73433	Cumberland, 150	N 6
74023	Cushing, 7,529	N 3
73639	Custer, 486	J 3
73029	Cyril, 1,302	K 5
73731	Dacoma, 226	J 1
74540	Daisy, 250	P 5
74838	Dale, 155	M 4
† 74523	Darwin, 50	P 6
74026	Davenport, 831	N 3
73530	Davidson, 515	J 6
73030	Davis, 2,223	M 5
74636	Deer Creek, 203	L 1
74027	Delaware, 534	P 1
73115	Del City, 27,133	L 4
73640	Delhi, 41	G 4
74028	Depew, 739	O 3
73531	Devol, 129	J 6
74431	Dewar, 933	P 4
74029	Dewey, 3,958	P 1
† 74868	Dewright, 100	N 4
73031	Dibble, 184	L 4
† 73401	Dickson, 798	M 6
73641	Dill City, 578	H 4
74340	Disney, 303	S 2
73032	Dougherty, 211	M 6
73733	Douglas, 79	L 2
73734	Dover, 566	L 3
74541	Dow, 300	P 5
73735	Drummond, 326	L 2
74030	Drumright, 2,931	O 3
73532	Duke, 486	G 5
73533	Duncan⊙, 19,718	L 5
74701	Durant⊙, 11,118	O 6
73642	Durham, 43	G 3
74839	Dustin, 502	O 4
73643	Eagle City, 56	J 3
74734	Eagletown, 850	S 6
73033	Eakly, 228	K 4
74840	Earlsboro, 248	N 4
† 73532	East Duke, 250	H 5
73034	Edmond, 16,633	M 3
73537	Eldorado, 737	G 6
73538	Elgin, 840	K 5
73644	Elk City, 7,323	G 4
73539	Elmer, 138	H 6
73035	Elmore City, 653	M 5
73036	El Reno⊙, 14,510	K 3
73701	Enid⊙, 44,008	L 2
† 74561	Enterprise, 130	R 4
73645	Erick, 1,285	G 4
74342	Eucha, 66	S 2
74432	Eufaula⊙, 2,355	P 4
74637	Fairfax, 1,889	N 1
74343	Fairland, 814	S 1
73736	Fairmont, 154	L 2
73737	Fairview⊙, 2,894	J 2
74935	Fanshawe, 199	S 5
73840	Fargo, 262	G 2
74542	Farris, 100	P 6
73540	Faxon, 121	J 6
73646	Fay, 75	J 3
† 74561	Featherston, 75	P 4
73937	Felt, 105	A 1
73434	Fillmore, 250	N 6
74543	Finley, 400	R 6
74842	Fittstown, 325	N 5
74843	Fitzhugh, 212	N 5
73541	Fletcher, 950	K 5
74638	Foraker, 52	Q 1
† 73101	Forest Park, 835	M 3
73938	Forgan, 496	E 1
73038	Fort Cobb, 722	K 4
74434	Fort Gibson, 1,418	R 3
73841	Fort Supply, 550	G 1
74735	Fort Towson, 430	R 7
73647	Foss, 150	H 4
73039	Foster, 50	M 5
73435	Fox, 400	M 6
74031	Foyil, 164	R 2
74844	Francis, 283	N 5
73542	Frederick⊙, 6,132	H 6
73842	Freedom, 292	H 1
73843	Gage, 536	G 2
74936	Gans, 238	S 4
73738	Garber, 1,011	M 2
74736	Garvin, 117	S 7
73844	Gate, 151	F 1
73040	Geary, 1,380	K 3
73436	Gene Autry, 120	N 6
73543	Geronimo, 587	K 6
74544	Gerty, 139	O 5
74032	Glencoe, 421	M 2
74033	Glenpool, 770	P 3
74728	Glover, 244	S 6
74737	Golden, 275	S 6
† 73093	Goldsby, 298	M 4
73739	Goltry, 282	K 1
† 74740	Goodwater, 100	S 7
73939	Goodwell, 1,467	C 1
74435	Gore, 478	R 3
73041	Gotebo, 376	J 4

(continued on following page)

AREA 69,919 sq. mi.
POPULATION 2,559,253
CAPITAL Oklahoma City
LARGEST CITY Oklahoma City
HIGHEST POINT Black Mesa 4,973 ft.
SETTLED IN 1889
ADMITTED TO UNION November 16, 1907
POPULAR NAME Sooner State
STATE FLOWER Mistletoe
STATE BIRD Scissor-tailed Flycatcher

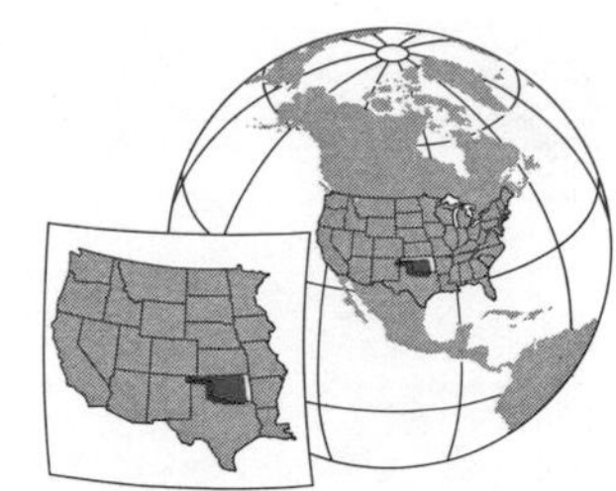

Agriculture, Industry and Resources

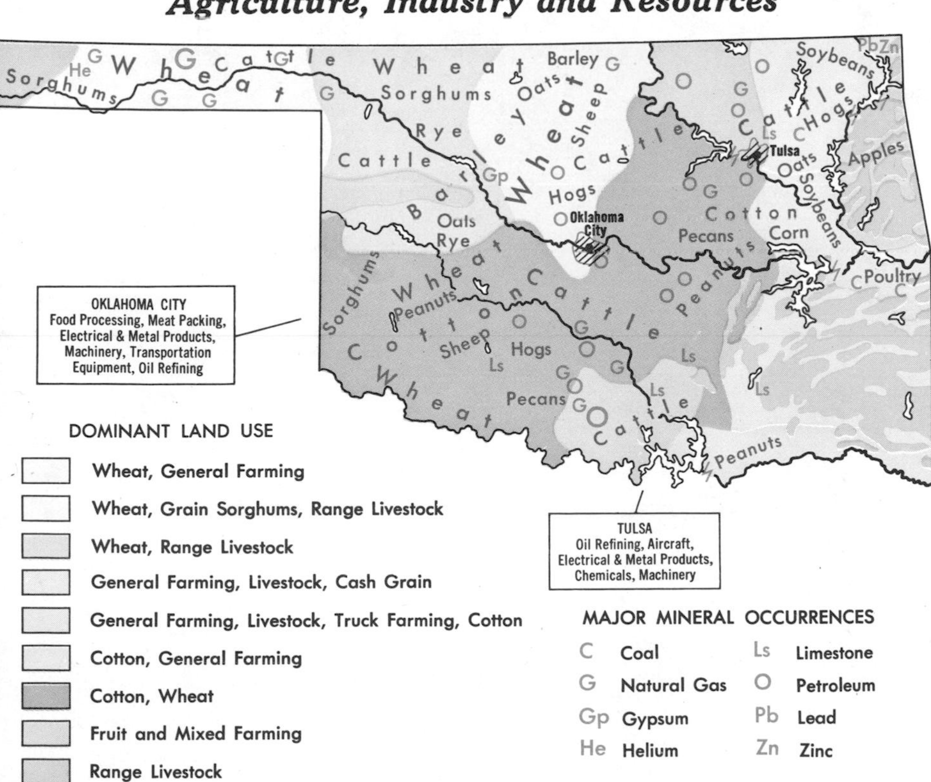

D. Elliott Stribling—Shostal Associates

Aesthetic drawbacks are outweighed by substantial revenues from oil wells obstructing the view of Oklahoma's capitol building.

(continued)

73544 Gould, 368 ... G 5
74545 Gowen, 350 ... R 5
73042 Gracemont, 424 ... K 4
73437 Graham, 250 ... M 6
74639 Grainola, 66 ... N 1
73546 Grandfield, 1,524 ... J 6
73547 Granite, 1,808 ... H 5
74738 Grant, 273 ... R 7
† 74437 Grayson (Wildcat), 142 ... P 3
73043 Greenfield, 143 ... K 3
74344 Grove, 2,000 ... S 1
73044 Guthrie⊙, 9,575 ... M 3
73942 Guymon⊙, 7,674 ... D 1
74546 Haileyville, 928 ... P 5
74034 Hallett, 125 ... N 2
73650 Hammon, 677 ... H 3
74845 Hanna, 181 ... P 4
† 74955 Hanson, 250 ... S 4
74846 Harden City, 150 ... N 5
73944 Hardesty, 223 ... D 1
73045 Harrah, 1,931 ... M 4
74739 Harris, 200 ... S 7
74547 Hartshorne, 2,121 ... R 5
74436 Haskell, 2,063 ... P 3
73548 Hastings, 184 ... K 6
74740 Haworth, 293 ... S 7
74548 Haywood, 175 ... P 5
73549 Headrick, 139 ... H 5
73438 Healdton, 2,324 ... M 6
74937 Heavener, 2,566 ... S 5
73741 Helena, 769 ... K 1
74741 Hendrix, 117 ... O 7
73046 Hennepin, 306 ... M 5
73742 Hennessey, 2,181 ... L 2
74437 Henryetta, 6,430 ... O 4
† 73539 Hess, 65 ... H 6
† 73086 Hickory, 62 ... N 5
73743 Hillsdale, 77 ... K 1
73047 Hinton, 889 ... K 4
73744 Hitchcock, 160 ... K 3
74438 Hitchita, 160 ... P 3
73651 Hobart⊙, 4,638 ... J 5
74345 Hockerville, 125 ... S 1
74939 Hodgen, 150 ... S 5
74439 Hoffman, 262 ... P 4
74848 Holdenville⊙, 5,181 ... O 4
73550 Hollis⊙, 3,150 ... G 5
73551 Hollister, 105 ... J 6
73745 Homestead, 75 ... K 2
74035 Hominy, 2,274 ... O 2
74549 Honobia, 250 ... R 5
73945 Hooker, 1,615 ... D 1
73746 Hopeton, 75 ... J 1
74940 Howe, 403 ... S 5
74440 Hoyt, 110 ... R 4
74743 Hugo⊙, 6,585 ... R 6
† 67333 Hulah, 50 ... O 1
74441 Hulbert, 505 ... R 3
† 73521 Humphreys, 44 ... H 5
74640 Hunter, 274 ... L 1
73048 Hydro, 805 ... J 3
74745 Idabel⊙, 5,946 ... S 7
73552 Indiahoma, 434 ... J 5
74442 Indianola, 205 ... P 4
74036 Inola, 948 ... P 2
73747 Isabella, 89 ... K 2
74346 Jay⊙, 1,594 ... S 2
73748 Jefferson, 128 ... L 1
74037 Jenks, 1,997 ... P 2
74038 Jennings, 338 ... N 2
73749 Jet, 317 ... K 1
73049 Jones, 1,666 ... M 3
74551 Jumbo, 40 ... P 6
74347 Kansas, 317 ... S 2
74641 Kaw, 283 ... N 1
† 74401 Keefeton, 70 ... R 3
74039 Kellyville, 685 ... O 3
74747 Kemp, 153 ... O 7
† 74741 Kemp City (Hendrix), 117 ... O 7
74040 Kendrick, 126 ... N 3
74748 Kenefic, 153 ... O 6
74348 Kenwood, 125 ... S 2
74941 Keota, 685 ... S 4
74349 Ketchum, 238 ... R 1
73947 Keyes, 569 ... B 1
† 74574 Kiamichi, 100 ... R 5
74041 Kiefer, 803 ... O 3
74642 Kildare, 79 ... M 1
73750 Kingfisher⊙, 4,042 ... L 3
73439 Kingston, 710 ... N 7
74552 Kinta, 247 ... R 4
74553 Kiowa, 754 ... P 5

73847 Knowles, 52 ... F 1
74849 Konawa, 1,719 ... N 5
† 74557 Kosoma, 50 ... P 6
74554 Krebs, 1,515 ... P 5
73753 Kremlin, 200 ... L 1
73754 Lahoma, 299 ... K 2
74850 Lamar, 153 ... O 4
74643 Lamont, 478 ... L 1
74555 Lane, 218 ... O 6
74350 Langley, 481 ... R 2
73050 Langston, 486 ... M 3
73848 Laverne, 1,373 ... G 1
73501 Lawton⊙, 74,470 ... K 5
Lawton, ‡108,144 ... K 5
74351 Leach, 75 ... S 2
73440 Lebanon, 240 ... N 7
73654 Leedey, 465 ... H 3
74942 Leflore, 175 ... S 5
74556 Lehigh, 296 ... O 6
74042 Lenapah, 325 ... P 1
73441 Leon, 112 ... M 7
74043 Leonard, 115 ... P 3
74943 Lequire, 100 ... R 4
73051 Lexington, 1,516 ... M 4
† 74858 Lima (New Lima), 238 ... D 4
73052 Lindsay, 3,705 ... L 5
† 74637 Little Chief, 40 ... N 1
† 73446 Little City, 80 ... N 6
73442 Loco, 193 ... L 6
74352 Locust Grove, 1,090 ... R 2
73443 Lone Grove, 1,240 ... M 6
73655 Lone Wolf, 584 ... H 5
73755 Longdale, 331 ... K 2
73053 Lookeba, 165 ... K 4
73756 Loyal, 107 ... K 3

73757 Lucien, 150 ... M 2
† 74825 Lula, 40 ... O 5
73054 Luther, 836 ... M 3
† 74578 Lutie, 250 ... R 5
74852 Macomb, 41 ... M 4
73446 Madill⊙, 2,875 ... N 6
73758 Manchester, 165 ... L 1
73554 Mangum⊙, 4,066 ... G 5
73555 Manitou, 308 ... J 5
74044 Mannford, 892 ... O 2
73447 Mannsville, 364 ... N 6
74045 Maramec, 128 ... N 2
74945 Marble City, 299 ... S 3
73448 Marietta⊙, 2,013 ... M 7
74644 Marland, 236 ... M 1
73055 Marlow, 3,995 ... K 5
73056 Marshall, 420 ... L 2
73556 Martha, 268 ... H 5
74853 Mason, 75 ... O 3
74854 Maud, 1,143 ... N 4
73851 May, 91 ... G 1
73057 Maysville, 1,380 ... M 5
74353 Mazie, 300 ... R 2
74501 McAlester⊙, 18,802 ... P 5
74944 McCurtain, 575 ... R 4
74851 McLoud, 2,159 ... M 4
73449 Mead, 210 ... O 7
73759 Medford⊙, 1,304 ... L 1
73557 Medicine Park, 562 ... J 5
74855 Meeker, 683 ... N 4
† 74074 Mehan, 60 ... M 2
73760 Meno, 119 ... K 2
73058 Meridian, 104 ... M 3
74354 Miami⊙, 13,880 ... S 1
† 74882 Micawber, 41 ... N 3

73110 Midwest City, 48,114 ... M 4
73450 Milburn, 275 ... O 6
74046 Milfay, 150 ... N 3
74856 Mill Creek, 234 ... N 6
74750 Millerton, 350 ... S 7
73451 Milo, 85 ... M 6
† 74944 Milton, 90 ... S 4
73059 Minco, 1,129 ... L 4
74946 Moffett, 312 ... S 4
74947 Monroe, 300 ... S 4
74444 Moodys, 200 ... S 2
† 71821 Moon, 50 ... S 7
73060 Moore, 18,761 ... M 4
73852 Mooreland, 1,196 ... H 2
74445 Morris, 1,119 ... P 3
73061 Morrison, 421 ... M 2
74047 Mounds, 766 ... O 3
73559 Mountain Park, 458 ... J 5
73062 Mountain View, 1,110 ... J 4
74557 Moyers, 125 ... P 6
74948 Muldrow, 1,680 ... S 4
73063 Mulhall, 250 ... M 2
74949 Muse, 75 ... S 5
74401 Muskogee⊙, 37,331 ... R 3
73064 Mustang, 2,637 ... L 4
73853 Mutual, 94 ... H 2
74646 Nardin, 135 ... M 1
73761 Nash, 294 ... K 1
74558 Nashoba, 100 ... R 6
† 74056 Nelagoney, 62 ... O 1
74857 Newalla, 350 ... M 4
74049 New Alluwe, 116 ... R 1
73065 Newcastle, 1,271 ... L 4
† 73632 New Cordell (Cordell)⊙, 3,261 ... H 4

74647 Newkirk⊙, 2,173 ... N 1
74858 New Lima, 238 ... O 4
† 74060 New Prue (Prue), 202 ... O 2
† 73466 New Woodville (Woodville), 118 ... N 7
† 73101 Nichols Hills, 4,478 ... L 3
73066 Nicoma Park, 2,560 ... M 4
73067 Ninnekah, 300 ... L 5
73068 Noble, 2,241 ... M 4
73069 Norman⊙, 52,117 ... M 4
† 73701 North Enid, 730 ... L 2
74358 North Miami, 503 ... R 1
74048 Nowata⊙, 3,679 ... P 1
74050 Oakhurst, 500 ... P 2
73452 Oakland, 317 ... N 6
74359 Oaks, 219 ... S 2
73658 Oakwood, 129 ... J 3
74051 Ochelata, 330 ... P 1
74958 Octavia, 40 ... S 5
74052 Oilton, 1,087 ... N 2
73762 Okarche, 826 ... L 3
74446 Okay, 419 ... R 3
73763 Okeene, 1,421 ... K 2
74859 Okemah⊙, 2,913 ... O 4
† 74003 Okesa, 165 ... O 1
* 73101 Oklahoma City (cap.)⊙, 366,481 ... L 4
Oklahoma City, ‡640,889 ... L 4
74447 Okmulgee⊙, 15,180 ... O 3
74450 Oktaha, 193 ... R 3
74751 Oleta, 50 ... R 6
† 74030 Olive, 100 ... O 2
† 74538 Olney, 42 ... O 6
73560 Olustee, 819 ... H 5
74053 Oologah, 458 ... P 2

73948 Optima, 103 ... D 1
73073 Orlando, 202 ... M 2
74054 Osage, 170 ... O 2
73561 Oscar, 61 ... L 7
73453 Overbrook, 120 ... M 6
74055 Owasso, 3,491 ... P 2
74860 Paden, 442 ... N 3
74951 Panama, 1,121 ... S 4
74559 Panola, 100 ... R 5
73074 Paoli, 480 ... M 5
74451 Park Hill, 125 ... R 3
† 74824 Parkland, 55 ... N 3
73075 Pauls Valley⊙, 5,769 ... M 5
74056 Pawhuska⊙, 4,238 ... O 1
74058 Pawnee⊙, 2,443 ... N 2
74861 Pearson, 60 ... N 4
74648 Peckham, 65 ... M 1
74452 Peggs, 82 ... R 2
† 74301 Pensacola, 56 ... H 2
† 66713 Peoria, 179 ... S 1
74059 Perkins, 1,029 ... M 3
73076 Pernell, 117 ... M 5
73077 Perry⊙, 5,341 ... M 2
74862 Pharoah, 100 ... O 4
† 74538 Phillips, 106 ... O 6
74360 Picher, 2,363 ... S 1
74752 Pickens, 350 ... S 6
73078 Piedmont, 269 ... L 3
74560 Pittsburg, 282 ... P 5
74753 Platter, 275 ... O 7
74952 Plunkettville, 125 ... S 6
73079 Pocasset, 200 ... L 4
74902 Pocola, 1,840 ... T 4
74601 Ponca City, 25,940 ... M 1
73766 Pondcreek, 903 ... L 1

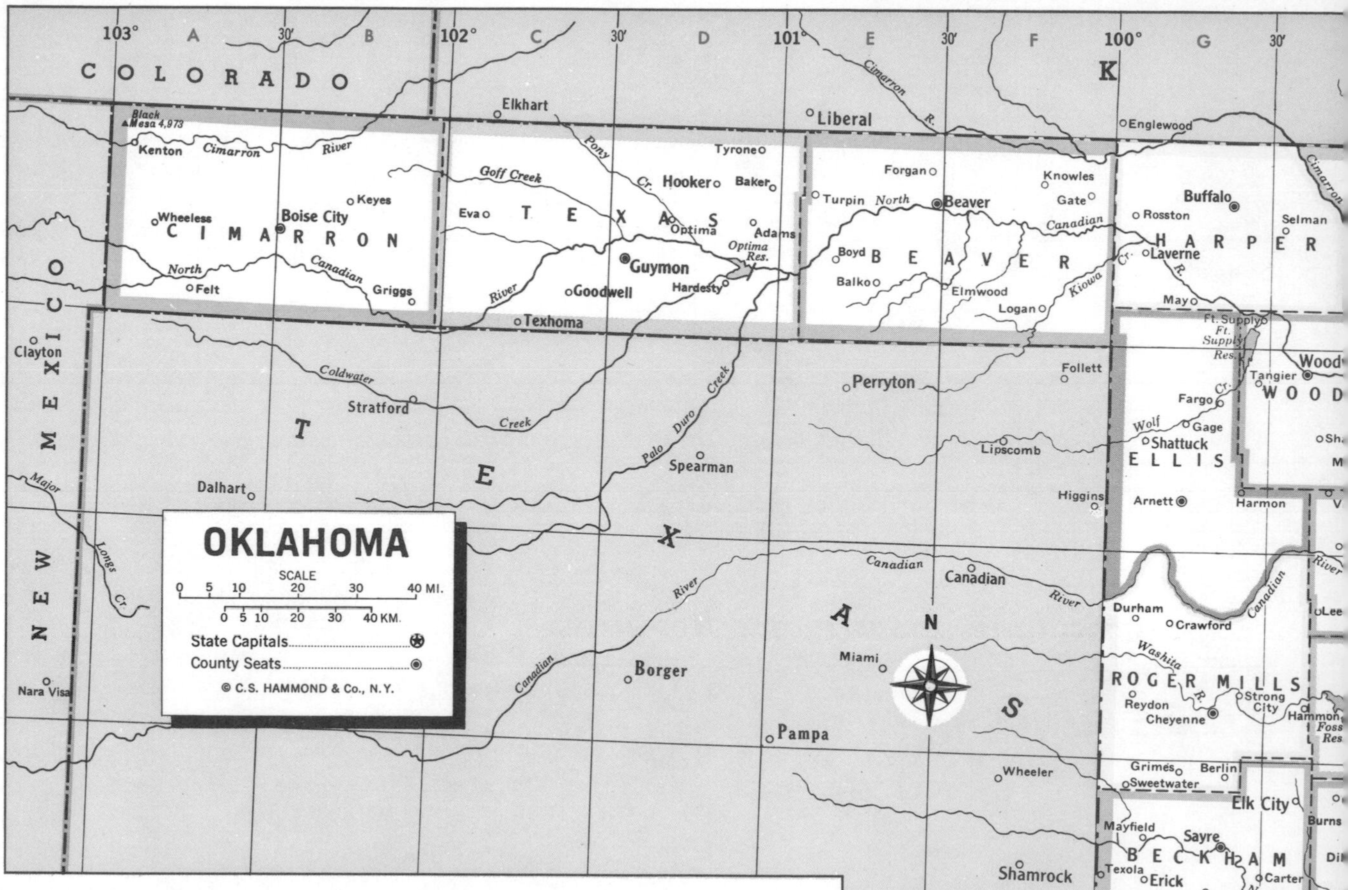

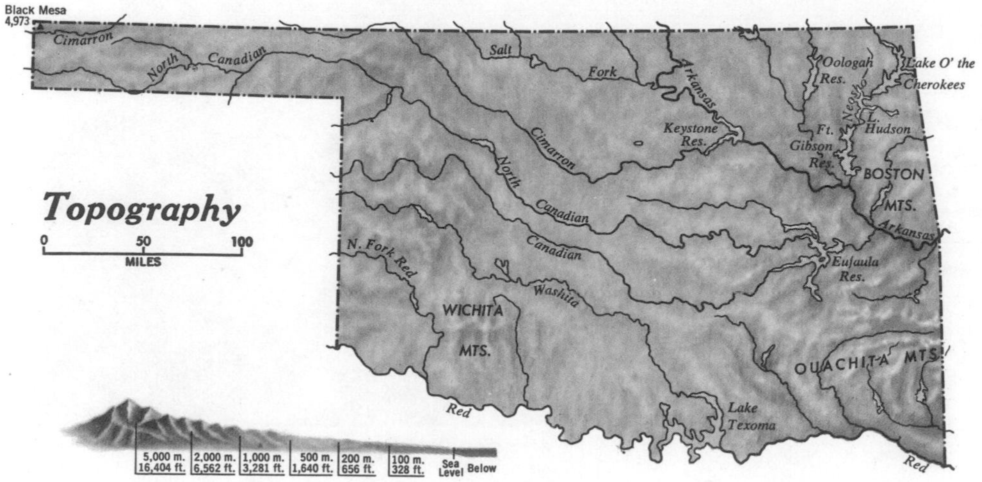

OKLAHOMA

SCALE 0 5 10 20 30 40 MI.
0 5 10 20 30 40 KM.
State Capitals ⊛
County Seats ⊙
© C.S. HAMMOND & Co., N.Y.

Topography

0 50 100 MILES

74863 Pontotoc, 150 .... N 6
73454 Pooleville, 75 .... M 6
74454 Porter, 624 .... R 3
74455 Porum, 658 .... R 4
74953 Poteau⊙, 5,500 .... S 4
74864 Prague, 1,802 .... N 4
74456 Preston, 300 .... P 3
74457 Proctor, 175 .... S 3
74060 Prue, 202 .... O 2
74361 Pryor⊙, 7,057 .... R 2
73080 Purcell⊙, 4,076 .... M 4
73659 Putnam, 84 .... J 3
74363 Quapaw, 967 .... S 1
† 74085 Quay, 41 .... N 2
† 73852 Quinlan, 81 .... J 2
74561 Quinton, 1,262 .... R 4
74650 Ralston, 443 .... N 2
74061 Ramona, 600 .... P 1
73562 Randlett, 384 .... K 6
73081 Ratliff City, 250 .... M 6
74562 Rattan, 350 .... R 6
73455 Ravia, 373 .... N 6
† 73460 Reagan, 175 .... N 6
74458 Redbird, 230 .... P 3
74563 Red Oak, 609 .... R 5
74651 Redrock, 233 .... M 2
73563 Reed, 64 .... G 5
74459 Rentiesville, 96 .... R 4
73660 Reydon, 215 .... G 3
73456 Ringling, 1,206 .... L 6
73768 Ringwood, 241 .... K 2
74062 Ripley, 307 .... N 2
† 74701 Roberta, 45 .... O 7
74933 Rock Island, 97 .... T 4
73661 Rocky, 260 .... J 4
74865 Roff, 632 .... N 5
74954 Roland, 827 .... S 4
73564 Roosevelt, 353 .... J 5
74364 Rose, 120 .... R 2
74831 Rosedale, 98 .... M 5
73855 Rosston, 56 .... G 1
73457 Rubottom, 110 .... M 7
74755 Rufe, 54 .... R 6
73082 Rush Springs, 1,381 .... L 5
73565 Ryan, 1,011 .... L 6
† 74017 Sageeyah, 49 .... P 2
74866 Saint Louis, 207 .... N 4
74365 Salina, 1,024 .... R 2
74955 Sallisaw⊙, 4,888 .... S 4
74063 Sand Springs, 11,519 .... O 2
74066 Sapulpa⊙, 15,159 .... O 3
74564 Sardis, 58 .... R 5
74867 Sasakwa, 321 .... N 5
74565 Savanna, 948 .... P 5
74756 Sawyer, 210 .... R 7
73662 Sayre⊙, 2,712 .... G 4
74460 Schulter, 200 .... P 3
74566 Scipio, 100 .... P 4
73663 Seiling, 1,033 .... J 2
73856 Selman, 93 .... H 1
74868 Seminole, 7,878 .... N 4
73664 Sentinel, 984 .... H 4
74956 Shady Point, 350 .... S 4
74068 Shamrock, 204 .... N 3
73857 Sharon, 155 .... H 2
73858 Shattuck, 1,546 .... G 2
74801 Shawnee⊙, 25,075 .... N 4
74757 Sherwood, 60 .... S 6
74652 Shidler, 717 .... N 1
† 72955 Short, 200 .... S 3
74069 Skedee, 117 .... N 2
74070 Skiatook, 2,930 .... O 2
74071 Slick, 171 .... O 3
74957 Smithville, 144 .... S 6
74567 Snow, 150 .... R 6
73566 Snyder, 1,671 .... J 5
74759 Soper, 322 .... P 6
73770 Southard, 130 .... K 2
74072 South Coffeyville, 646 .... P 1
74869 Sparks, 183 .... N 3
74366 Spavinaw, 470 .... R 2
73084 Spencer, 3,603 .... M 3
74760 Spencerville, 275 .... R 6
74073 Sperry, 1,123 .... P 2
74959 Spiro, 2,057 .... S 4
73458 Springer, 256 .... M 6
73567 Sterling, 675 .... K 5
74461 Stidham, 53 .... P 4
74462 Stigler⊙, 2,347 .... R 4
74074 Stillwater⊙, 31,126 .... N 2
74960 Stilwell⊙, 2,134 .... S 3
† 74436 Stonebluff, 50 .... P 3
74871 Stonewall, 653 .... O 5
74367 Strang, 164 .... R 2
74872 Stratford, 1,278 .... M 5
74569 Stringtown, 397 .... P 6
74079 Stroud, 2,502 .... N 3
74570 Stuart, 294 .... O 5
† 73565 Sugden, 54 .... L 6
73086 Sulphur⊙, 5,158 .... N 5
74966 Summerfield, 210 .... S 5
74761 Swink, 88 .... R 6
74463 Taft, 525 .... R 3
74464 Tahlequah⊙, 9,254 .... R 3
74080 Talala, 163 .... P 1
74571 Talihina, 1,227 .... S 5
73667 Taloga⊙, 363 .... J 2
† 74462 Tamaha, 83 .... S 4
73087 Tatums, 502 .... M 6
74873 Tecumseh, 4,451 .... N 4
73568 Temple, 1,354 .... K 6
74081 Terlton, 111 .... O 2
73569 Terral, 636 .... L 7
73949 Texhoma, 921 .... C 1
73668 Texola, 144 .... G 4
73459 Thackerville, 257 .... M 7
73120 The Village, 13,695 .... L 3
73669 Thomas, 1,336 .... J 3
† 74017 Tiawah, 119 .... P 2
73570 Tipton, 1,206 .... H 6
73460 Tishomingo⊙, 2,663 .... N 6
74762 Tom, 600 .... S 7
74653 Tonkawa, 3,337 .... M 1
† 74852 Tribbey, 60 .... M 4
† 74856 Troy, 92 .... N 6
74875 Tryon, 301 .... N 3
74466 Tullahassee, 183 .... P 3
* 74101 Tulsa⊙, 331,638 .... O 2
Tulsa, ‡476,945 .... O 2
74572 Tupelo, 485 .... O 5
73950 Turpin, 295 .... E 1
74573 Tushka, 400 .... O 6
74574 Tuskahoma, 200 .... R 5
73088 Tussy, 150 .... L 6
73089 Tuttle, 1,640 .... L 4
73951 Tyrone, 588 .... D 1
74601 Uncas, 53 .... M 1
73090 Union, 306 .... L 4
74763 Utica, 177 .... O 7
† 73101 Valley Brook, 2,869 .... M 4
74764 Valliant, 840 .... R 6
74876 Vanoss, 130 .... N 5
73091 Velma, 611 .... L 6
74082 Vera, 215 .... P 2
73092 Verden, 439 .... K 4
† 74017 Verdigris, 307 .... P 2
74877 Vernon, 84 .... P 4
74962 Vian, 1,131 .... S 4
73859 Vici, 694 .... H 2
74301 Vinita⊙, 5,847 .... R 1
73571 Vinson, 51 .... G 5
74765 Wade, 50 .... O 7
74467 Wagoner⊙, 4,959 .... R 3
74468 Wainwright, 135 .... R 3
73771 Wakita, 426 .... L 1
73572 Walters⊙, 2,611 .... K 6
74878 Wanette, 303 .... M 5
74083 Wann, 135 .... P 1
73461 Wapanucka, 425 .... N 6
74576 Wardville, 100 .... P 5
74469 Warner, 1,217 .... R 4
73123 Warr Acres, 9,887 .... L 3
74879 Warwick, 146 .... M 3
73093 Washington, 322 .... M 4
73094 Washita, 160 .... K 4
73772 Watonga⊙, 3,696 .... K 3
74963 Watson, 48 .... S 6
74964 Watts, 326 .... S 2
73773 Waukomis, 241 .... K 2
73573 Waurika⊙, 1,833 .... L 6
73095 Wayne, 618 .... M 5
73860 Waynoka, 1,444 .... J 1
73096 Weatherford, 7,959 .... J 4
† 74560 Weathers, 100 .... P 5
74654 Webb City, 186 .... N 1
74470 Webbers Falls, 485 .... R 3
74369 Welch, 651 .... R 1
74880 Weleetka, 1,199 .... O 4
74471 Welling, 50 .... S 3
74881 Wellston, 789 .... M 3
74882 Welty, 89 .... O 3
† 72761 West Siloam Springs, 210 .... S 2
74965 Westville, 934 .... S 2
74883 Wetumka, 1,687 .... O 4
74884 Wewoka⊙, 5,284 .... O 4
74472 Whitefield, 250 .... R 4
† 74301 Whiteoak, 200 .... R 1
74577 Whitesboro, 300 .... S 5
74578 Wilburton⊙, 2,280 .... R 5
† 74437 Wildcat, 142 .... P 3
73462 Willis, 250 .... N 7
73673 Willow, 188 .... G 4
73463 Wilson, 1,569 .... M 6
73464 Wirt, 350 .... L 6
74966 Wister, 927 .... S 5
73466 Woodville, 118 .... N 7
73801 Woodward⊙, 8,710 .... H 2
74766 Wright City, 1,068 .... R 6
74370 Wyandotte, 297 .... S 1
73098 Wynnewood, 2,374 .... M 5
74084 Wynona, 547 .... O 1
74085 Yale, 1,239 .... N 2
† 74574 Yanush, 350 .... R 5
74885 Yeager, 107 .... O 4
74767 Yuba, 63 .... O 7
73099 Yukon, 8,411 .... L 3

⊙ County seat.
‡ Population of metropolitan area.
† Zip of nearest p.o.
* Multiple zips

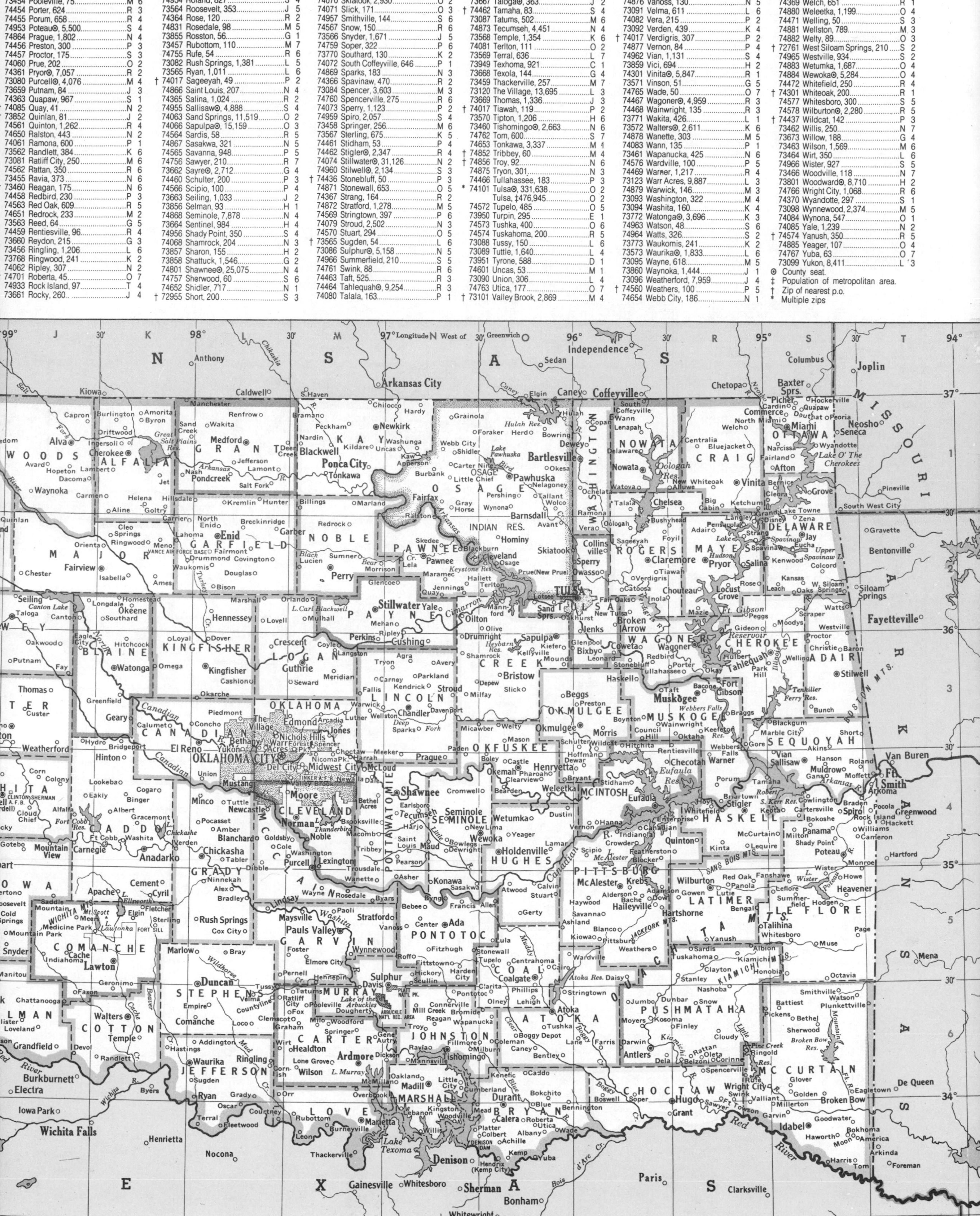

COUNTIES

County, Pop.	Key
Baker, 14,919	K 3
Benton, 53,776	D 3
Clackamas, 166,088	E 2
Clatsop, 28,473	D 1
Columbia, 28,790	D 2
Coos, 56,515	C 4
Crook, 9,985	G 3
Curry, 13,006	C 5
Deschutes, 30,442	F 4
Douglas, 71,743	D 4
Gilliam, 2,342	G 2
Grant, 6,996	J 3
Harney, 7,215	H 4
Hood River, 13,187	F 2
Jackson, 94,533	E 5
Jefferson, 8,548	F 3
Josephine, 35,746	D 5
Klamath, 50,021	F 5
Lake, 6,343	G 5
Lane, 213,358	E 4
Lincoln, 25,755	D 3
Linn, 71,914	E 3
Malheur, 23,169	K 4
Marion, 151,309	E 3
Morrow, 4,465	H 2
Multnomah, 556,667	E 2
Polk, 35,349	D 3
Sherman, 2,139	G 2
Tillamook, 17,930	D 2
Umatilla, 44,923	J 2
Union, 19,377	J 2
Wailowa, 6,247	K 2
Wasco, 20,133	F 2
Washington, 157,920	D 2
Wheeler, 1,849	G 3
Yamhill, 40,213	D 2

CITIES and TOWNS

	Zip	Name/Pop.	Key
	97810	Adams, 219	J 2
	97620	Adel, 200	H 5
	97901	Adrian, 200	K 4
	97320	Agate Beach, 975	C 3
	97406	Agness, 120	C 5
†	97361	Airlie, 45	D 3
	97321	Albany⊙, 18,181	D 3
†	97601	Algoma, 77	F 5
	97811	Alicel, 30	J 2
	97407	Allegany, 200	D 4
	97006	Aloha, 6,000	A 2
	97408	Alpine, 80	D 3
	97324	Alsea, 600	D 3
†	97601	Altamont, 15,746	F 5
	97409	Alvadore, 350	D 3
	97101	Amity, 708	D 2
	97001	Antelope, 51	G 3
	97530	Applegate, 125	D 5
	97458	Arago, 200	C 4
	97812	Arlington, 375	G 2
†	97473	Ash, 80	D 4
	97520	Ashland, 12,342	E 5
	97103	Astoria⊙, 10,244	D 1
	97813	Athena, 872	J 2
	97325	Aumsville, 590	E 3
	97002	Aurora, 306	B 2
|	97817	Austin, 170	J 3
	97410	Azalea, 40	D 5
	97814	Baker⊙, 9,354	K 3
†	97378	Ballston, 120	D 2
†	97458	Bancroft, 25	D 5
	97411	Bandon, 1,832	C 4
	97106	Banks, 430	A 1
	97003	Barlow, 105	B 2
†	97009	Barton, 100	B 2
†	97136	Bar View, 75	C 2
	97817	Bates, 430	J 3
	97107	Bay City, 898	D 2
	97621	Beatty, 50	F 5
	97108	Beaver, 450	D 2
	97004	Beavercreek, 708	B 2
	97005	Beaverton, 18,577	A 2
†	97456	Bellfountain, 50	D 3
	97701	Bend⊙, 13,710	F 3
†	97058	Biggs, 50	G 2
	97016	Birkenfeld, 45	D 1
	97412	Blachly, 425	D 3
†	97108	Blaine, 150	D 2
	97326	Blodgett, 150	D 3
	97413	Blue River, 350	E 3
	97622	Bly, 500	F 5
	97818	Boardman, 192	H 2
	97623	Bonanza, 230	F 5
	97008	Bonneville, 130	F 2
	97009	Boring, 150	E 2
†	97021	Boyd, 26	F 2
†	97342	Breitenbush, 50	F 3
	97010	Bridal Veil, 155	E 2
†	97458	Bridge, 250	D 4
	97819	Bridgeport, 45	K 3
†	97136	Brighton, 52	C 2
	97001	Brightwood, 420	E 2
†	97032	Broadacres, 80	A 3
	97414	Broadbent, 265	C 4
	97903	Brogan, 140	K 3
	97415	Brookings, 2,720	C 5
	97305	Brooks, 490	A 3
†	97840	Brownlee, 50	L 3
†	97524	Brownsboro, 150	E 5
	97327	Brownsville, 1,034	E 3
†	97351	Buena Vista, 90	D 3
†	97420	Bunker Hill, 1,549	C 4
	97720	Burns⊙, 3,293	H 4
	97522	Butte Falls, 358	E 5
†	97002	Butteville, 385	A 2
	97109	Buxton, 163	D 2
	97416	Camas Valley, 665	D 4
	97730	Camp Sherman, 87	F 3
†	97493	Canary, 50	D 4
	97013	Canby, 3,813	B 2
	97110	Cannon Beach, 779	D 2
	97820	Canyon City⊙, 600	J 3
	97417	Canyonville, 940	D 5
	97111	Carlton, 1,126	D 2
†	97415	Carpenterville, 30	C 5
†	97015	Carver, 500	B 2
	97014	Cascade Locks, 574	E 2
	97329	Cascadia, 150	E 3
	97523	Cave Junction, 415	D 5
	97821	Cayuse, 300	J 2
	97822	Cecil, 75	H 2
	97225	Cedar Hills, 2,900	A 2
†	97005	Cedar Mill, 1,500	A 2
†	97058	Celilo, 50	G 2
	97501	Central Point, 4,004	D 5
	97420	Charleston, 500	C 4
	97306	Chemawa, 900	A 3
	97731	Chemult, 580	F 4
†	97058	Chenoweth, 2,329	F 2
	97119	Cherry Grove, 200	D 2
†	97055	Cherryville, 280	E 2
	97419	Cheshire, 750	D 3
	97624	Chiloquin, 826	F 5
	97015	Clackamas, 6,000	B 2
	97016	Clatskanie, 1,286	D 1
	97112	Cloverdale, 151	D 2
	97401	Coburg, 665	E 3
	97017	Colton, 305	B 3

PORTLAND, SALEM AND VICINITY

	ZIP	Place	Key
	97018	Columbia City, 537	E 2
	97823	Condon⊙, 973	G 2
	97420	Coos Bay, 13,466	C 4
	97423	Coquille⊙, 4,437	C 4
	97113	Cornelius, 1,903	A 2
	97330	Corvallis⊙, 35,153	D 3
	97424	Cottage Grove, 6,004	D 4
	97824	Cove, 363	K 2
†	97148	Cove Orchard, 50	D 2
	97335	Crabtree, 350	E 3
	97732	Crane, 63	J 4
†	97601	Crater Lake, 30	E 5
	97336	Crawfordsville, 350	E 3
	97733	Crescent, 850	F 4
	97425	Crescent Lake, 70	F 4
	97426	Creswell, 1,199	D 4
†	97401	Crow, 200	D 4
	97427	Culp Creek, 194	E 4
	97734	Culver, 407	F 3
	97428	Curtin, 300	D 4
†	97439	Cushman, 175	D 4
	97625	Dairy, 74	F 5
	97880	Dale, 25	J 3
	97338	Dallas⊙, 6,361	D 3
†	97910	Danner, 40	K 5
	97429	Days Creek, 602	D 5
	97114	Dayton, 949	A 3
	97825	Dayville, 197	H 3
	97054	Deer Island, 120	E 2
	97341	Depoe Bay, 450	C 3
	97342	Detroit, 328	E 3
	97431	Dexter, 450	E 4
	97731	Diamond Lake, 56	E 4
	97432	Dillard, 602	D 4
†	97116	Dilley, 250	A 2
	97433	Disston, 123	E 4
	97020	Donald, 231	A 3
†	97458	Dora, 30	D 4
	97434	Dorena, 550	E 4
	97435	Drain, 1,204	D 4
	97484	Drew, 60	E 5
	97021	Dufur, 493	F 2
	97115	Dundee, 588	A 2
†	97493	Dunes (Westlake), 976	C 4
†	97233	Durham, 410	A 2
	97905	Durkee, 140	K 3
	97022	Eagle Creek, 250	E 2
	97524	Eagle Point, 1,241	E 5
	97420	Eastside, 1,331	C 4
	97826	Echo, 479	H 2
	97343	Eddyville, 50	D 3
	97827	Elgin, 1,375	K 2
†	97391	Elk City, 30	D 3
	97436	Elkton, 176	D 4
	97437	Elmira, 950	D 3
†	97138	Elsie, 30	D 2
	97828	Enterprise⊙, 1,680	K 2
	97023	Estacada, 1,164	E 2
*	97401	Eugene⊙, 76,346	D 3
		Eugene, ‡213,358	D 3
	97024	Fairview, 1,045	B 2
†	97601	Falcon Heights, 1,389	F 5
	97438	Fall Creek, 58	E 4
	97344	Falls City, 745	D 3
	97710	Fields, 150	J 5
†	97828	Flora, 25	K 2
	97439	Florence, 2,246	C 4
	97116	Forest Grove, 8,275	A 2
	97626	Fort Klamath, 150	E 5
	97735	Fort Rock, 75	G 4
	97830	Fossil⊙, 511	G 2
	97345	Foster, 850	E 3
	97301	Four Corners, 6,199	A 3
	97831	Fox, 75	H 3
	97736	Frenchglen, 45	H 5

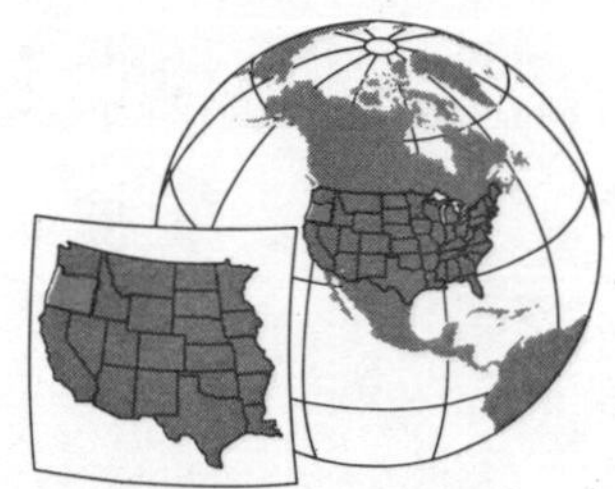

AREA 96,981 sq. mi.
POPULATION 2,091,385
CAPITAL Salem
LARGEST CITY Portland
HIGHEST POINT Mt. Hood 11,235 ft.
SETTLED IN 1810
ADMITTED TO UNION February 14, 1859
POPULAR NAME Beaver State
STATE FLOWER Oregon Grape
STATE BIRD Western Meadowlark

Topography

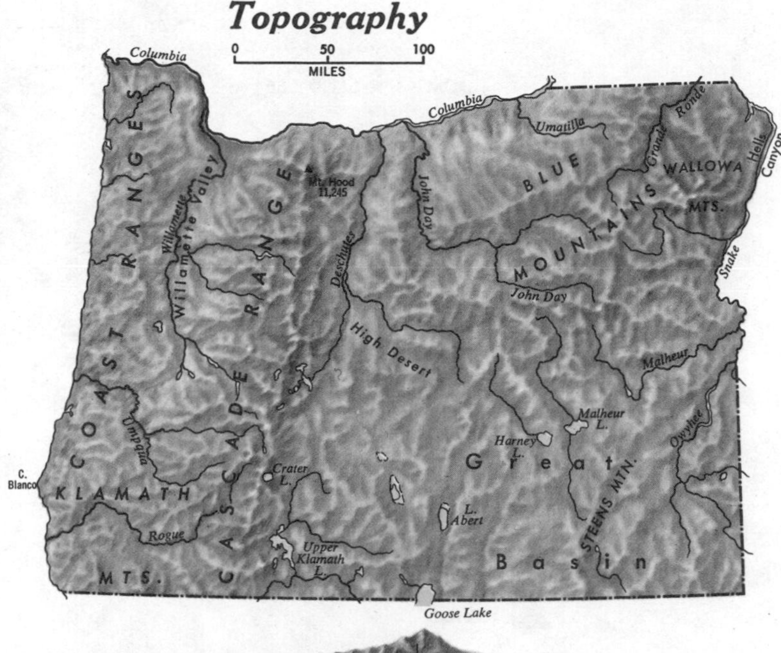

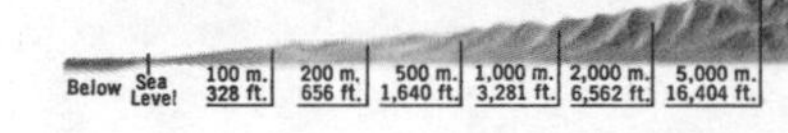

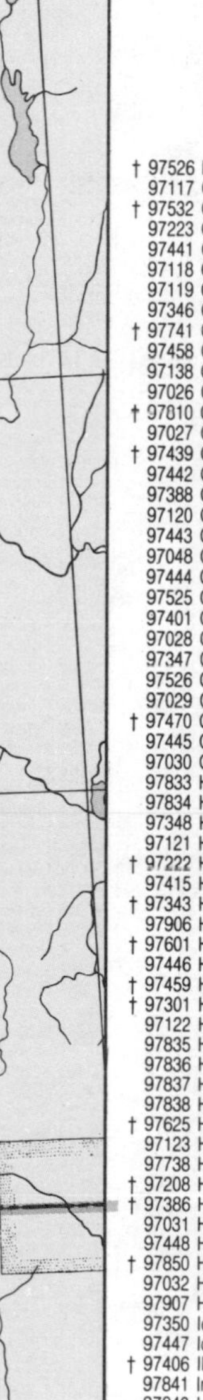

	ZIP	Place	Key
†	97526	Fruitdale, 2,655	D 5
	97117	Gales Creek, 500	D 2
†	97532	Galice, 30	D 5
	97223	Garden Home, 2,900	A 2
	97441	Gardiner, 500	C 4
	97118	Garibaldi, 1,083	D 2
	97119	Gaston, 429	D 2
	97346	Gates, 250	E 3
†	97741	Gateway, 95	F 3
	97458	Gaylord, 125	C 5
	97138	Gearhart, 829	C 1
	97026	Gervais, 746	A 3
†	97810	Gibbon, 100	J 2
	97027	Gladstone, 6,237	B 2
†	97439	Glenada, 75	C 4
	97442	Glendale, 709	D 5
	97388	Gleneden Beach, 400	C 3
	97120	Glenwood, 500	D 2
	97443	Glide, 470	D 4
	97048	Goble, 108	E 1
	97444	Gold Beach⊙, 1,554	C 5
	97525	Gold Hill, 603	D 5
	97401	Goshen, 98	D 4
	97028	Government Camp, 175	F 2
	97347	Grand Ronde, 289	D 2
	97526	Grants Pass⊙, 12,455	D 5
	97029	Grass Valley, 153	G 2
†	97470	Green, 1,612	D 4
	97445	Greenleaf, 47	D 3
	97030	Gresham, 9,875	B 2
	97833	Haines, 212	J 3
	97834	Halfway, 317	K 3
	97348	Halsey, 467	D 3
	97121	Hammond, 500	C 1
†	97222	Happy Valley, 1,392	B 2
	97415	Harbor, 750	C 5
†	97343	Harlan, 35	D 3
	97906	Harper, 102	K 4
†	97601	Harriman, 50	E 5
	97446	Harrisburg, 1,311	D 3
†	97459	Hauser, 400	C 4
†	97301	Hayesville, 5,518	A 3
	97122	Hebo, 350	D 2
	97835	Helix, 152	J 2
	97836	Heppner⊙, 1,429	H 2
	97837	Hereford, 50	K 3
	97838	Hermiston, 4,893	H 2
†	97625	Hildebrand, 50	F 5
	97123	Hillsboro⊙, 14,675	A 2
	97738	Hines, 1,407	H 4
†	97208	Holbrook, 494	A 1
†	97386	Holley, 250	E 3
	97031	Hood River⊙, 3,991	F 2
	97448	Horton, 188	D 3
†	97850	Hot Lake, 60	K 2
	97032	Hubbard, 975	A 3
	97907	Huntington, 507	K 3
	97350	Idanha, 382	E 3
	97447	Idleyld Park, 150	D 4
†	97406	Illahe, 30	C 5
	97841	Imbler, 139	J 2
	97842	Imnaha, 37	L 2
	97351	Independence, 2,594	D 3
	97843	Ione, 355	H 2
	97908	Ironside, 36	K 3
	97844	Irrigon, 261	H 2
	97851	Island City, 202	K 2
	97530	Jacksonville, 1,611	D 5
	97909	Jamieson, 103	K 3
	97401	Jasper, 231	E 3
	97352	Jefferson, 936	D 3
	97267	Jennings Lodge, 3,500	B 2
	97845	John Day, 1,566	J 3
	97910	Jordan Valley, 196	K 5
	97846	Joseph, 839	K 2
	97448	Junction City, 2,373	D 3
	97911	Juntura, 56	K 4
†	97761	Kah-Nee-Ta, 50	F 3
	97303	Keizer, 11,405	A 3
	97627	Keno, 500	F 5
	97033	Kent, 58	G 2
	97531	Kerby, 650	D 5
†	97367	Kernville, 50	D 3
	97848	Kimberly, 30	H 3
†	97123	King City, 1,427	A 2
	97353	Kings Valley, 100	D 3
	97849	Kinzua, 400	H 3
	97601	Klamath Falls⊙, 15,775	F 5
†	97103	Knappa, 950	D 1
	97354	Lacomb, 450	E 3
	97127	Lafayette, 786	A 2
	97850	La Grande⊙, 9,645	J 2
†	97524	Lakecreek, 160	E 5
	97034	Lake Oswego, 14,573	B 2
	97449	Lakeside, 350	C 4
	97630	Lakeview⊙, 2,705	G 5
	97450	Langlois, 150	C 5
	97739	La Pine, 1,500	F 4
†	97060	Latourell Falls, 40	E 2
	97740	Lawen, 95	J 4
	97401	Leaburg, 630	E 3
	97355	Lebanon, 6,636	E 3
†	97478	Leland, 70	D 5
	97839	Lexington, 230	H 2
†	97042	Liberal, 60	B 3
†	97341	Lincoln Beach, 275	C 3
	97367	Lincoln City, 4,198	C 3
†	97405	Logan, 450	B 2
	97357	Logsden, 55	D 3
	97856	Long Creek, 196	H 3
	97857	Lostine, 196	K 2
	97452	Lowell, 567	E 4
	97358	Lyons, 645	E 3
	97741	Madras⊙, 1,689	F 3
	97632	Malin, 486	F 5
	97136	Manhattan Beach, 70	D 2
	97130	Manzanita, 261	C 2
	97453	Mapleton, 950	C 3
	97454	Marcola, 900	E 3
	97359	Marion, 450	D 3
	97362	Marquam, 40	B 3
†	97016	Marshland, 30	D 1
	97037	Maupin, 428	F 2
†	97016	Mayger, 35	D 1
†	97850	May Park, 1,466	J 2
†	97201	Maywood Park, 1,230	B 2
†	97338	McCoy, 40	D 2
	97401	McKenzie Bridge, 100	E 3
	97128	McMinnville⊙, 10,125	D 2
	97858	McNary, 330	H 2
	97859	Meacham, 130	J 2
	97501	Medford⊙, 28,454	E 5
	97860	Medical Springs, 45	K 2
	97384	Mehama, 250	E 3
†	97470	Melrose, 30	D 4
	97532	Merlin, 500	D 5
	97033	Merrill, 722	F 5
	97742	Metolius, 270	F 3
†	97223	Metzger, 2,900	A 2
	97634	Midland, 205	F 5
	97861	Mikkalo, 40	G 2
	97360	Mill City, 1,451	E 3
	97455	Milo, 600	E 5
	97862	Milton-Freewater, 4,105	J 2
	97222	Milwaukie, 16,379	B 2
	97016	Mist, 40	D 1
	97750	Mitchell, 196	G 3
†	97624	Modoc Point, 65	F 5
†	97477	Mohawk, 50	E 3
	97038	Molalla, 2,005	B 3
	97072	Monitor, 82	B 3
	97361	Monmouth, 5,237	D 3
	97456	Monroe, 443	D 3
	97864	Monument, 161	H 3
	97039	Moro⊙, 290	G 2
	97040	Mosier, 217	F 2
†	97106	Mountaindale, 50	A 1
	97362	Mount Angel, 1,973	B 3
	97041	Mount Hood, 215	F 2
	97865	Mount Vernon, 423	H 3
	97042	Mulino, 600	B 2
	97533	Murphy, 300	D 5
	97457	Myrtle Creek, 2,733	D 4
	97458	Myrtle Point, 2,511	C 4
	97131	Nehalem, 241	D 2
	97364	Neotsu, 259	C 2
	97149	Neskowin, 500	D 2
	97143	Netarts, 975	C 2
	97132	Newberg, 6,507	A 2
†	97870	New Bridge, 50	K 3
†	97013	New Era, 50	B 2
	97635	New Pine Creek, 260	G 5
	97365	Newport⊙, 5,188	C 3
	97459	North Bend, 8,553	C 4
	97133	North Plains, 800	A 2
	97043	North Portland, 950	B 1
	97867	North Powder, 304	K 2
	97460	Norway, 115	C 4
	97913	Nyssa, 2,620	K 4
	97268	Oak Grove, 6,300	B 2
	97462	Oakland, 1,010	D 4
	97463	Oakridge, 3,422	E 4
	97534	O'Brien, 315	D 5
	97134	Oceanside, 165	C 2
	97044	Odell, 450	F 2
	97812	Olex, 40	G 2

(continued on following page)

OREGON

SCALE
0 5 10 20 30 40 50 60 MI.
0 5 10 20 30 40 50 60 KM.
State Capitals ⊛
County Seats ⊙

(continued)

Agriculture, Industry and Resources

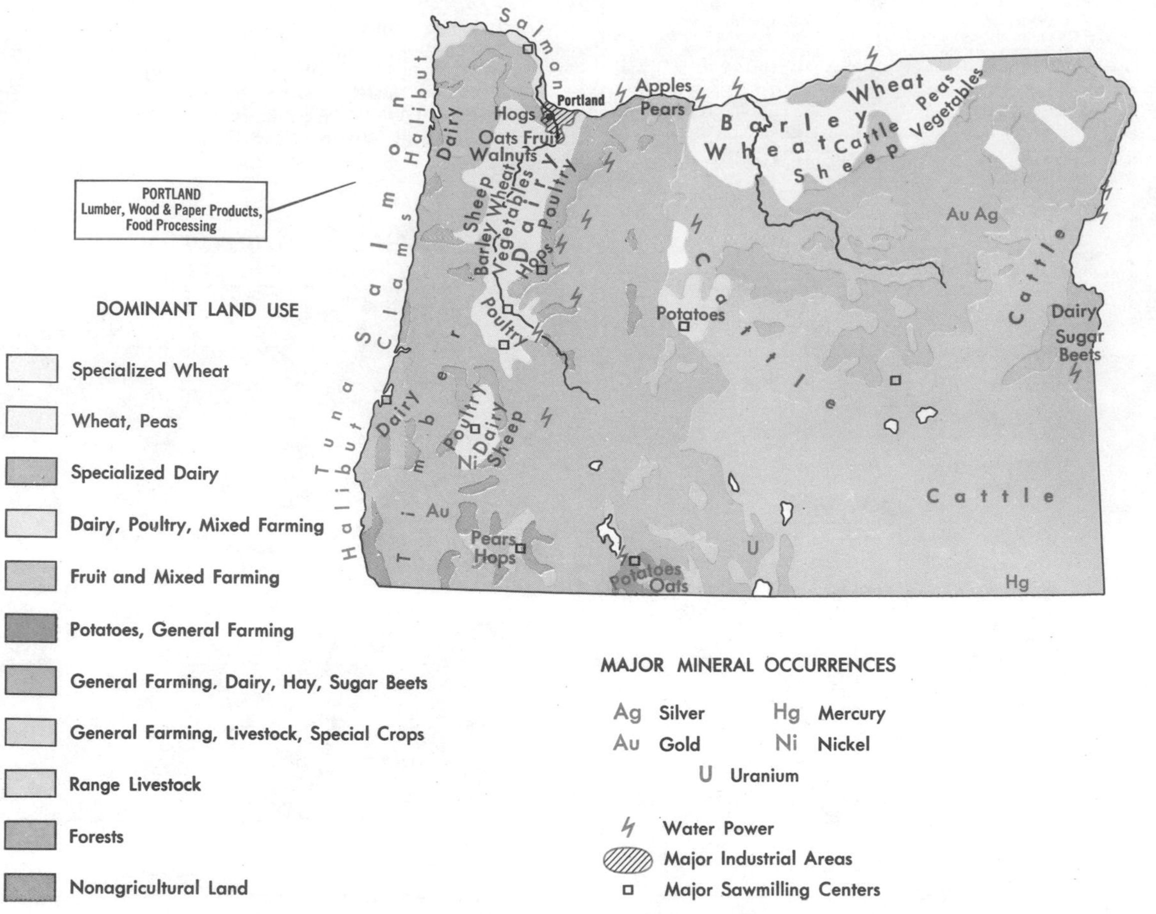

Oregon's magnificently rugged coastline — sandy beaches interspersed with rock fragments ("stacks") torn from the cliffs.

Oregon State Highway Department

	Zip	Place	Key
†	97103	Olney, 75	D 1
	97914	Ontario, 6,523	K 3
	97464	Ophir, 250	C 5
	97045	Oregon City⊙, 9,176	B 2
†	97123	Orenco, 200	A 2
	97368	Otis, 200	D 2
	97369	Otter Rock, 150	C 3
	97840	Oxbow, 75	L 2
	97135	Pacific City, 500	C 2
	97636	Paisley, 260	G 5
	97047	Parkdale, 300	F 2
†	97045	Park Place, 1,200	B 2
	97751	Paulina, 50	G 3
†	97361	Pedee, 45	D 3
	97801	Pendleton⊙, 13,197	J 2
†	97850	Perry, 100	J 2
	97101	Perrydale, 200	D 2
	97370	Philomath, 1,688	D 3
	97535	Phoenix, 1,287	E 5
	97868	Pilot Rock, 1,612	J 2
	97444	Pistol River, 75	C 5
†	97478	Placer, 50	D 5
	97637	Plush, 50	H 5
*	97201	Portland⊙, 382,619	B 2
		Portland, ‡1,009,129	B 2
	97465	Port Orford, 1,037	C 5
	97753	Powell Butte, 550	G 3
	97466	Powers, 842	D 5
	97869	Prairie City, 867	J 3
†	97301	Pratum, 40	A 3
†	97048	Prescott, 105	D 1
	97721	Princeton, 68	J 4
	97754	Prineville⊙, 4,101	G 3
†	97233	Progress, 100	A 2
	97536	Prospect, 200	E 5
†	97411	Prosper, 110	C 4
†	97413	Rainbow, 100	E 3
	97048	Rainier, 1,731	E 1
†	97045	Redland, 700	B 2
	97756	Redmond, 3,721	F 3
	97467	Reedsport, 4,039	C 4
†	97005	Reedville, 1,200	A 2
	97468	Remote, 96	D 5
	97870	Richland, 133	K 3
	97371	Rickreall, 250	D 3
	97469	Riddle, 1,042	D 5
	97871	Rieth, 300	J 2
	97758	Riley, 85	H 4
	97423	Riverton, 150	C 4
	97136	Rockaway, 665	C 2
	97537	Rogue River, 841	D 5
†	97910	Rome, 33	K 5
	97470	Roseburg⊙, 14,461	D 4
	97372	Rose Lodge, 300	D 3
†	97058	Rowena, 50	F 2
†	97106	Roy, 150	A 2
	97050	Rufus, 317	G 2
	97472	Saginaw, 150	E 4
	97373	Saint Benedict, 300	B 3
	97051	Saint Helens⊙, 6,212	E 2
†	97026	Saint Louis, 125	A 3
	97137	Saint Paul, 347	A 3
*	97301	Salem (cap.)⊙, 68,296	A 3
†	97525	Sams Valley, 450	E 5
	97055	Sandy, 1,544	E 2
	97056	Scappoose, 1,859	E 2
†	97123	Scholls, 50	A 2
	97374	Scio, 447	E 3
†	97109	Scofield, 259	D 2
	97473	Scottsburg, 200	D 4
	97375	Scotts Mills, 208	B 3
	97376	Seal Rock, 430	C 3
	97138	Seaside, 4,402	D 2
	97538	Selma, 200	D 5
	97873	Seneca, 400	J 3
	97057	Shaniko, 58	G 3
†	97325	Shaw, 210	A 3
†	97910	Sheaville, 53	K 4
	97377	Shedd, 850	D 3
	97378	Sheridan, 1,881	D 2
	97140	Sherwood, 1,396	A 2
	97380	Siletz, 596	D 3
	97638	Silver Lake, 200	F 4
	97381	Silverton, 4,301	B 3
	97759	Sisters, 516	F 3
	97476	Sixes, 250	C 5
†	97355	Sodaville, 125	E 3
†	97223	Somerset West, 562	A 2
	97366	Southbeach, 300	C 3
†	97501	South Medford, 3,497	E 5
	97639	Sprague River, 200	F 5
	97874	Spray, 161	H 3
†	97132	Springbrook, 75	A 2
	97477	Springfield, 27,047	E 3
	97875	Stanfield, 891	H 2
	97383	Stayton, 3,170	E 3
	97385	Sublimity, 634	E 3
•	97876	Summerville, 76	K 2
†	97420	Sumner, 200	C 4
	97877	Sumpter, 120	J 3
	97478	Sunny Valley, 159	D 5
	97479	Sutherlin, 3,070	D 4
†	97103	Svensen, 950	D 1
	97386	Sweet Home, 3,799	E 3
	97480	Swisshome, 450	D 3
†	97201	Sylvan, 1,440	B 2
	97540	Talent, 1,389	E 5
	97389	Tangent, 350	D 3
	97878	Telocaset, 50	K 2
	97481	Tenmile, 100	D 4
	97760	Terrebonne, 521	F 3
	97058	The Dalles⊙, 10,423	F 2
	97390	Tidewater, 50	D 3
†	97453	Tiernan, 75	C 3
	97223	Tigard, 5,302	A 2
	97141	Tillamook⊙, 3,968	D 2
	97484	Tiller, 300	E 5
	97144	Timber, 150	D 2
	97391	Toledo, 2,818	D 3
	97145	Tolovana Park, 180	C 2
	97541	Trail, 160	E 5
†	97431	Trent, 125	E 4
	97060	Troutdale, 575	E 2
†	97885	Troy, 30	K 2
	97062	Tualatin, 750	A 2
†	97701	Tumalo, 300	F 3
	97392	Turner, 846	E 3
†	97136	Twin Rocks, 185	C 2
	97063	Tygh Valley, 238	F 2
	97880	Ukiah, 375	J 2
	97881	Umapine, 100	J 2
	97882	Umatilla, 679	H 2
	97486	Umpqua, 357	D 4
	97883	Union, 1,531	K 2
†	97536	Union Creek, 35	E 5
	97884	Unity, 312	J 3
	97918	Vale⊙, 1,448	K 4
	97393	Valsetz, 500	D 3
	97487	Veneta, 1,377	D 3
†	97116	Verboort, 280	A 2
	97064	Vernonia, 1,643	D 2
	97488	Vida, 75	E 3
	97394	Waldport, 700	C 3
†	97426	Walker, 50	D 4
	97885	Wallowa, 811	K 2
	97489	Walterville, 150	E 3
	97490	Walton, 300	D 3
	97063	Wamic, 146	F 2
	97761	Warm Springs, 550	F 3
	97053	Warren, 900	E 2
	97146	Warrenton, 1,825	C 1
	97065	Wasco, 412	G 2
	97395	Waterloo, 186	E 3
	97491	Wedderburn, 400	C 5
†	97067	Welches, 100	E 2
	97067	Wemme, 400	E 2
	97492	Westfir, 800	E 4
	97493	Westlake, 976	C 4
	97068	West Linn, 7,091	B 2
	97886	Weston, 660	J 2
	97016	Westport, 650	D 1
†	97071	West Woodburn, 185	A 3
	97147	Wheeler, 262	D 2
	97501	White City, 450	E 5
†	97128	Whiteson, 100	D 2
	97494	Wilbur, 476	D 4
	97543	Wilderville, 200	D 5
	97396	Willamina, 1,193	D 2
	97544	Williams, 750	D 5
†	97741	Willowdale, 115	G 3
	97070	Wilsonville, 900	A 2
	97495	Winchester, 900	D 4
	97467	Winchester Bay, 245	C 4
	97496	Winston, 2,468	D 4
	97497	Wolf Creek, 500	D 5
†	97526	Wonder, 50	D 5
	97071	Woodburn, 7,495	A 3
†	97060	Wood Village, 1,533	B 2
†	97601	Worden, 32	F 5
	97498	Yachats, 441	C 3
	97148	Yamhill, 516	D 2
†	97365	Yaquina, 175	C 3
	97499	Yoncalla, 675	D 4
	97073	Zigzag, 170	F 2

⊙ County seat.
‡ Population of metropolitan area.
† Zip of nearest p.o.
* Multiple zips

Agriculture, Industry and Resources

AREA 45,333 sq. mi.
POPULATION 11,793,909
CAPITAL Harrisburg
LARGEST CITY Philadelphia
HIGHEST POINT Mt. Davis 3,213 ft.
SETTLED IN 1682
ADMITTED TO UNION December 12, 1787
POPULAR NAME Keystone State
STATE FLOWER Mountain Laurel
STATE BIRD Ruffed Grouse

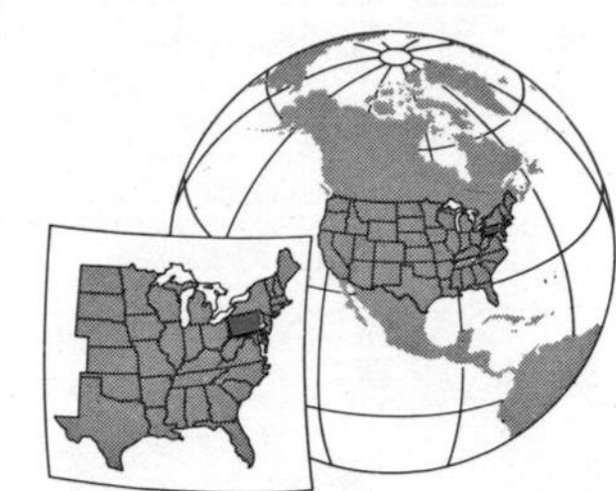

DOMINANT LAND USE

- Specialized Dairy
- Dairy, General Farming
- Fruit and Mixed Farming
- Fruit, Truck and Mixed Farming
- General Farming, Livestock, Tobacco
- General Farming, Livestock, Fruit, Tobacco
- Forests
- Urban Areas

MAJOR MINERAL OCCURRENCES

C	Coal	G	Natural Gas	Sl	Slate
Cl	Clay	Ls	Limestone	Ss	Sandstone
Co	Cobalt	O	Petroleum	Zn	Zinc
Fe	Iron Ore				

Water Power
Major Industrial Areas

ERIE
Machinery, Electrical & Metal Products, Paper

SCRANTON–WILKES-BARRE–HAZLETON
Clothing, Textiles, Metal Products

ALLENTOWN–BETHLEHEM–EASTON
Iron & Steel, Clothing, Cement, Electrical & Metal Products, Textiles, Trucks, Chemicals, Paper Products

READING
Clothing, Textiles, Hosiery, Machinery, Electrical & Metal Products, Automobile Parts

PHILADELPHIA
Machinery, Textiles, Clothing, Electrical & Metal Products, Chemicals, Oil Refining, Food Processing, Printing & Publishing, Iron & Steel, Rugs & Carpets, Leather Goods, Cigars, Instruments

LANCASTER
Machinery, Textiles, Food Processing, Clothing, Electrical & Metal Products, Watches, Farm Equipment, Floor Coverings

YORK
Machinery, Metal Products, Paper Products, Air Conditioning Equipment, Clothing & Textiles

HARRISBURG
Food Processing, Iron & Steel, Clothing, Metal Products

JOHNSTOWN
Iron & Steel

PITTSBURGH
Iron & Steel, Machinery, Electrical & Metal Products, Chemicals, Paint, Glass, Barges, Food Processing

COUNTIES

Adams, 56,937 H 6
Allegheny, 1,605,016 B 5
Armstrong, 75,590 D 4
Beaver, 208,418 B 4
Bedford, 42,353 E 6
Berks, 296,382 K 5
Blair, 135,356 F 4
Bradford, 57,962 J 2
Bucks, 415,056 M 5
Butler, 127,941 C 4
Cambria, 186,785 E 4
Cameron, 7,096 F 3
Carbon, 50,573 L 4
Centre, 99,267 G 4
Chester, 278,311 L 6
Clarion, 38,414 D 3
Clearfield, 74,619 F 3
Clinton, 37,721 G 3
Columbia, 55,114 K 3
Crawford, 81,342 B 2
Cumberland, 158,177 H 5
Dauphin, 223,834 J 5
Delaware, 600,035 M 6
Elk, 37,770 E 3
Erie, 263,654 B 2
Fayette, 154,667 C 6
Forest, 4,926 D 2
Franklin, 100,833 G 6
Fulton, 10,776 F 6
Greene, 36,090 B 6
Huntingdon, 39,108 F 5
Indiana, 79,451 D 4
Jefferson, 43,695 D 3
Juniata, 16,712 H 4
Lackawanna, 234,107 L 3
Lancaster, 319,693 K 5
Lawrence, 107,374 B 4
Lebanon, 99,665 K 5
Lehigh, 255,304 L 4
Luzerne, 342,301 L 3
Lycoming, 113,296 H 3
McKean, 51,915 E 2
Mercer, 127,175 B 3
Mifflin, 45,268 G 4
Monroe, 45,422 M 3
Montgomery, 623,799 M 5
Montour, 16,508 J 3
Northampton, 214,368 M 4
Northumberland, 99,190 J 4
Perry, 28,615 H 5
Philadelphia (city county), 1,948,609 M 6
Pike, 11,818 M 3
Potter, 16,395 G 2
Schuylkill, 160,089 K 4
Snyder, 29,269 H 4
Somerset, 76,037 D 6
Sullivan, 5,961 J 3
Susquehanna, 34,344 L 2
Tioga, 39,691 H 2
Union, 28,603 H 4
Venango, 62,353 C 3
Warren, 47,682 D 2
Washington, 210,876 B 5
Wayne, 29,581 M 2
Westmoreland, 376,935 D 5
Wyoming, 19,082 K 2
York, 272,603 J 6

CITIES and TOWNS

Zip *Name/Pop.* *Key*

19001 Abington, 8,594 M 5
19501 Adamstown, 1,202 K 5
17501 Akron, 3,149 K 5
16401 Albion, 1,768 B 2
18011 Alburtis, 1,142 L 5
19018 Aldan, 5,001 M 7
15001 Aliquippa, 22,277 B 4
* 18101 Allentown⊙, 109,527 L 4
Allentown-Bethlehem-Easton, ‡543,551 L 4
15101 Allison Park, 7,500 C 4
* 16601 Altoona, 62,900 F 4
Altoona, ‡135,356 F 4
19002 Ambler, 7,800 M 5
15003 Ambridge, 11,324 B 4
19020 Andalusia, 8,169 N 5
17003 Annville, 4,704 J 5
15613 Apollo, 2,308 C 4
18403 Archbald, 6,118 M 2
19003 Ardmore, 5,801 M 6
15068 Arnold, 8,174 C 4
17921 Ashland, 4,737 K 4
18706 Ashley, 4,095 L 3
15215 Aspinwall, 3,541 C 6
18810 Athens, 4,173 K 2
17851 Atlas, 1,527 K 4
15202 Avalon, 7,065 B 6
15312 Avella, 1,109 B 5
17721 Avis, 1,749 H 3
18641 Avoca, 3,543 L 3
19311 Avondale, 1,025 L 6
15618 Avonmore, 1,267 C 4
15005 Baden, 5,536 B 4
17502 Bainbridge, 950 J 5
19004 Bala-Cynwyd, 6,483 M 6
† 15201 Baldwin, 26,729 B 7
19503 Bally, 1,197 L 5
18013 Bangor, 5,425 M 4
15714 Barnesboro, 2,708 E 4
18014 Bath, 1,829 M 4
15009 Beaver⊙, 6,100 B 4
15921 Beaverdale, 1,579 E 5
15010 Beaver Falls, 14,375 B 4
18216 Beaver Meadows, 1,274 L 4
15522 Bedford⊙, 3,302 F 5
16823 Bellefonte⊙, 6,828 G 4
15012 Belle Vernon, 1,496 C 5
17004 Belleville, 1,817 G 4
15202 Bellevue, 11,586 B 6
16617 Bellwood, 2,395 F 4
† 15201 Ben Avon, 2,713 B 6
15314 Bentleyville, 2,714 B 5
17814 Benton, 1,027 K 3
15530 Berlin, 1,766 E 6
18603 Berwick, 12,274 K 3
19312 Berwyn, 14,000 L 5
16112 Bessemer, 1,427 B 4
19507 Bethel, 950 K 5
15102 Bethel Park, 34,791 B 7
* 18015 Bethlehem, 72,686 M 4
17307 Biglerville, 977 H 6
19508 Birdsboro, 3,196 L 5
15716 Black Lick, 1,074 D 4
15717 Blairsville, 4,411 D 5
18447 Blakely, 6,391 L 2
15238 Blawnox, 1,907 C 6
15224 Bloomfield (New Bloomfield)⊙, 1,032 H 5
17815 Bloomsburg⊙, 11,652 J 3
16912 Blossburg, 1,753 H 2
17214 Blue Ridge Summit, 950 G 6
16827 Boalsburg, 950 G 4
15315 Bobtown, 1,055 B 6
17007 Boiling Springs, 1,521 H 5
19061 Boothwyn, 8,900 L 7
15135 Boston, 2,500 C 7
15531 Boswell, 1,529 E 5
19512 Boyertown, 4,428 L 5
15104 Brackenridge, 4,796 C 4
15104 Braddock, 8,682 C 7
16701 Bradford, 12,672 E 2
15227 Brentwood, 13,732 B 7
19405 Bridgeport, 5,630 M 5
15017 Bridgeville, 6,717 B 5
15009 Bridgewater, 966 B 4
19007 Bristol (borough), 12,085 N 5
19007 Bristol (urban township), 67,498 N 5
15824 Brockway, 2,529 E 3
19015 Brookhaven, 7,370 M 7
15825 Brookville⊙, 4,314 D 3
19008 Broomall, 20,000 M 6
15236 Broughton, 3,276 B 7
17417 Brownsville, 4,856 C 5
19009 Bryn Athyn, 970 M 5
19010 Bryn Mawr, 5,737 M 5
15021 Burgettstown, 2,118 A 5
17009 Burnham, 2,607 H 4
16001 Butler⊙, 18,691 C 4
16212 Cadogan, ▵563 C 4
15419 California, 6,635 C 5
16403 Cambridge Springs, 1,998 C 2
17011 Camp Hill, 9,931 H 5
18325 Canadensis, 950 M 3
15317 Canonsburg, 11,439 B 5
17724 Canton, 2,037 J 2
18407 Carbondale, 12,808 L 2
17013 Carlisle⊙, 18,079 H 5
15106 Carnegie, 10,864 B 7
15722 Carrolltown, 1,507 E 4
15234 Castle Shannon, 11,899 B 7
18032 Catasauqua, 5,702 M 4
17820 Catawissa, 1,701 K 4
15321 Cecil, 1,900 B 5
16404 Centerville, 4,175 B 6
15920 Central City, 1,547 E 5
17927 Centralia, 1,165 K 4
16828 Centre Hall, 1,202 G 4
18914 Chalfont, 2,366 M 5
17201 Chambersburg⊙, 17,315 G 6
15022 Charleroi, 6,723 C 5
† 19380 Chatwood, 7,168 L 6
19012 Cheltenham, ▵40,238 M 5
* 19013 Chester, 56,331 L 7
19017 Chester Heights, 1,277 L 7
15024 Cheswick, 2,580 C 6
16025 Chicora, 1,166 C 4
17509 Christiana, 1,132 K 6
† 15201 Churchill, 4,690 C 7
15025 Clairton, 15,051 C 7
16214 Clarion⊙, 6,095 D 3
18411 Clarks Summit, 5,376 L 3
16625 Claysburg, 1,516 F 5
15323 Claysville, 951 B 5
16830 Clearfield⊙, 8,176 F 3
19018 Clifton Heights, 8,348 M 7
15728 Clymer, 2,054 E 4
18218 Coaldale, 3,023 L 4
19320 Coatesville, 12,331 L 5
16314 Cochranton, 1,229 B 2
19426 Collegeville, 3,191 M 5
19023 Collingdale, 10,605 N 7
18915 Colmar, 950 M 5
17512 Columbia, 11,237 K 5
16405 Columbus, 950 C 2
15927 Colver, 1,175 E 4
† 19023 Colwyn, 3,169 N 7
15424 Confluence, 954 D 6
16406 Conneautville, 1,032 A 2
15425 Connellsville, 11,643 C 5
19428 Conshohocken, 10,195 M 5
15027 Conway, 2,822 B 4
18219 Conyngham, 1,850 K 3
18036 Coopersburg, 2,326 M 5
18037 Coplay, 3,642 L 4
15108 Coraopolis, 8,435 B 4
17016 Cornwall, 2,111 K 5
16407 Corry, 7,435 C 2
16915 Coudersport⊙, 2,831 G 2
15624 Crabtree, 1,021 D 5
15205 Crafton, 8,233 B 7
16630 Cresson, 2,446 E 5
17929 Cressona, 1,814 K 4
19022 Crum Lynne, 3,700 M 7
15031 Cuddy, 2,500 B 5
16833 Curwensville, 3,189 E 4
† 15901 Dale, 2,274 E 5
18612 Dallas, 2,913 K 3
17313 Dallastown, 3,560 J 6
18414 Dalton, 1,282 L 2
17821 Danville⊙, 6,176 J 4
19023 Darby, 13,729 M 7
17018 Dauphin, 990 J 5
15626 Delmont, 1,934 D 5
17517 Denver, 2,248 K 5
15627 Derry, 3,338 D 5
18519 Dickson City, 7,698 L 3
17019 Dillsburg, 1,441 H 5
15734 Dixonville, 950 D 4
15033 Donora, 8,825 C 5
15216 Dormont, 12,856 B 7
19518 Douglassville, 975 L 5
17315 Dover, 1,168 J 6
19335 Downingtown, 7,437 L 5
18901 Doylestown⊙, 8,270 M 5
15034 Dravosburg, 2,916 C 7
19026 Drexel Hill, 50,000 M 6
18221 Drifton, 1,295 L 3
15801 DuBois, 10,112 E 3
† 17701 Duboistown, 1,468 H 3
15431 Dunbar, 1,499 C 6
17020 Duncannon, 1,739 H 5
16635 Duncansville, 2,210 F 5
18512 Dunmore, 17,300 L 3
15110 Duquesne, 11,410 C 7
18642 Duryea, 5,264 L 3
17316 East Berlin, 1,086 J 6
† 18603 East Berwick, 2,090 K 3
16028 East Brady, 1,218 C 3
15909 East Conemaugh, 2,710 E 5
† 17701 East Faxon, 4,175 J 3
18041 East Greenville, 2,003 L 5
† 19050 East Lansdowne, 3,186 M 7
18042 Easton⊙, 30,256 M 4
17520 East Petersburg, 3,407 K 5
18301 East Stroudsburg, 7,894 M 4
† 15301 East Washington, 2,198 B 5
15931 Ebensburg⊙, 4,318 E 5
† 15005 Economy, 7,176 B 4
19020 Eddington, 20,517 N 5
19013 Eddystone, 2,706 M 7
† 15201 Edgewood, 5,101 B 7
† 15143 Edgeworth, 2,200 B 4
16412 Edinboro, 4,871 B 2
16731 Eldred, 1,092 F 2
15037 Elizabeth, 2,206 C 5
17022 Elizabethtown, 8,072 J 5
17023 Elizabethville, 1,629 J 4
16920 Elkland, 1,942 H 1
15331 Ellsworth, 1,268 B 5
16117 Ellwood City, 10,857 B 4
15038 Elrama, 950 C 5
17824 Elysburg, 1,337 K 4
18049 Emmaus, 11,511 M 4
15834 Emporium⊙, 3,074 F 2
15202 Emsworth, 3,332 B 6
17025 Enola, 4,900 J 5
17522 Ephrata, 9,662 K 5
* 16501 Erie⊙, 129,231 B 1
Erie, ‡263,654 B 1
17815 Espy, 1,652 K 4
19029 Essington, 3,100 M 7
15223 Etna, 5,819 B 6
16033 Evans City, 2,144 B 4
15537 Everett, 2,243 F 5
15631 Everson, 1,143 C 5
15632 Export, 1,402 C 5
15436 Fairchance, 1,906 C 6
19030 Fairless Hills, 16,000 N 5
16415 Fairview, 1,707 B 1
15840 Falls Creek, 1,255 E 3
16121 Farrell, 11,022 A 3
15438 Fayette City, 968 C 5
17222 Fayetteville, 2,449 G 6
18921 Ferndale, 2,482 E 5
19522 Fleetwood, 3,064 L 5
17745 Flemington, 1,519 G 3
† 17552 Florin, 975 J 5
19032 Folcroft, 9,610 M 7
19033 Folsom, 7,815 M 7
16226 Ford City, 4,749 D 4
18421 Forest City, 2,322 L 2
15221 Forest Hills, 9,561 C 7
18704 Forty Fort, 6,114 L 3
† 18015 Fountain Hill, 5,384 L 4
15238 Fox Chapel, 4,684 C 6
17931 Frackville, 5,445 K 4
16323 Franklin⊙, 8,629 C 3
17026 Fredericksburg, 1,073 B 2
17026 Fredericksburg, 950 J 5
15333 Fredericktown, 1,067 C 6
15042 Freedom, 2,643 B 4
18224 Freeland, 4,784 L 3
18017 Freemansburg, 1,681 M 4
16229 Freeport, 2,375 C 4
† 16117 Frisco, 950 B 4
16922 Galeton, 1,552 G 2
16641 Gallitzin, 2,496 E 4
17527 Gap, 1,022 L 6
† 17701 Garden View, 2,662 H 3
15904 Geistown, 3,633 E 5
17325 Gettysburg⊙, 7,275 H 6
17934 Gilberton, 1,293 K 4
16417 Girard, 2,613 B 2
17935 Girardville, 2,450 K 4
15045 Glassport, 7,450 C 7
18617 Glen Lyon, 3,408 K 3
19036 Glenolden, 8,697 M 7
19037 Glen Riddle, 950 L 7
17327 Glen Rock, 1,600 J 6
15116 Glenshaw, 19,500 C 6
19038 Glenside, 17,353 M 5
15634 Grapeville, 1,000 C 5
17225 Greencastle, 3,293 G 6
15601 Greensburg⊙, 15,870 D 5
† 15201 Greentree, 6,441 B 7
16125 Greenville, 8,704 B 3
16127 Grove City, 8,312 B 3
18822 Hallstead, 1,447 L 2
19526 Hamburg, 3,909 L 4
17331 Hanover, 15,623 J 6
† 15201 Harmarville, 1,900 C 6
16037 Harmony, 1,207 B 4
* 17101 Harrisburg (cap.)⊙, 68,061 H 5
Harrisburg, ‡410,626 H 5
18618 Harveys Lake, 1,693 K 3
16646 Hastings, 1,791 E 4
19040 Hatboro, 8,880 M 5
19440 Hatfield, 2,385 M 5
19041 Haverford, ▵55,132 M 6
19083 Havertown, 42,500 M 6
16840 Hawk Run, 1,020 F 4
18428 Hawley, 1,331 M 3
18201 Hazleton, 30,426 L 4
15106 Heidelberg, 2,034 B 7
17406 Hellam, 1,825 J 6
18055 Hellertown, 6,613 M 4
15637 Herminie, 975 C 5
17033 Hershey, 7,407 J 5
† 17044 Highland Park, 1,704 H 4
17034 High Spire, 2,947 J 5
16132 Hillsville, 950 A 4
16648 Hollidaysburg⊙, 6,262 F 5
17748 Homer City, 2,465 D 4
15120 Homestead, 6,309 B 7
18431 Honesdale⊙, 5,224 M 2
19344 Honey Brook, 1,115 L 5
15936 Hooversville, 962 E 5
15445 Hopwood, 2,190 C 6

(continued on following page)

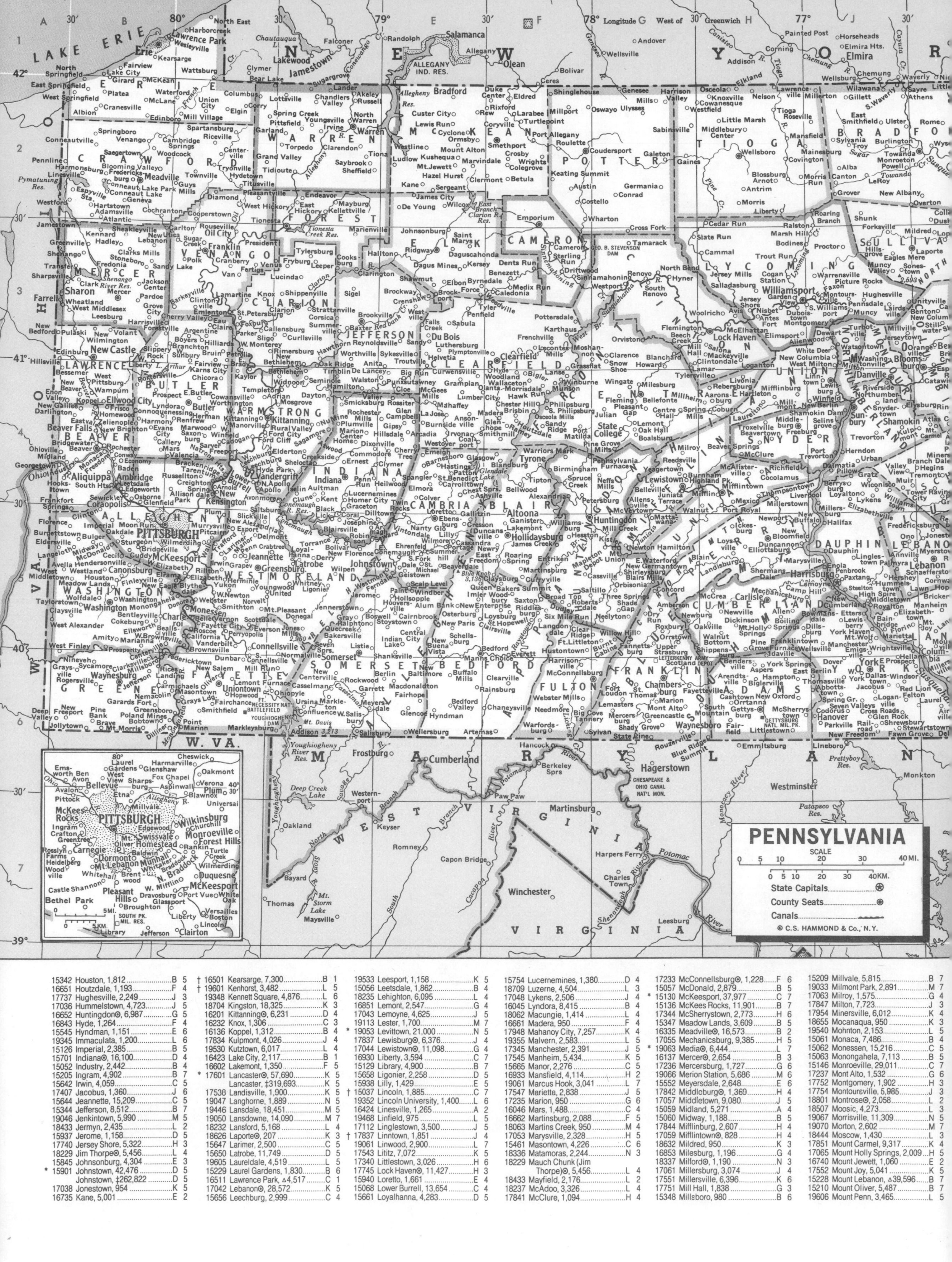

15342 Houston, 1,812 B 5
16651 Houtzdale, 1,193 F 4
17737 Hughesville, 2,249 J 3
17036 Hummelstown, 4,723 J 5
16652 Huntingdon⊙, 6,987 G 5
16843 Hyde, 1,264 F 4
15545 Hyndman, 1,151 E 6
19345 Immaculata, 1,200 L 6
15126 Imperial, 2,385 B 5
15701 Indiana⊙, 16,100 D 4
15052 Industry, 2,442 B 4
15205 Ingram, 4,902 B 7
15642 Irwin, 4,059 C 5
17407 Jacobus, 1,360 J 6
15644 Jeannette, 15,209 C 5
15344 Jefferson, 8,512 B 7
19046 Jenkintown, 5,990 M 5
18433 Jermyn, 2,435 L 2
15937 Jerome, 1,158 D 5
17740 Jersey Shore, 5,322 H 3
18229 Jim Thorpe⊙, 5,456 L 4
15845 Johnsonburg, 4,304 E 3
* 15901 Johnstown, 42,476 D 5
Johnstown, ‡262,822 D 5
17038 Jonestown, 954 K 5
16735 Kane, 5,001 E 2
† 16501 Kearsarge, 7,300 B 1
† 19601 Kenhorst, 3,482 L 5
19348 Kennett Square, 4,876 L 6
18704 Kingston, 18,325 K 3
16201 Kittanning⊙, 6,231 D 4
16232 Knox, 1,306 C 3
16136 Koppel, 1,312 B 4
17834 Kulpmont, 4,026 J 4
19530 Kutztown, 6,017 L 4
16423 Lake City, 2,117 B 1
16602 Lakemont, 1,350 F 5
* 17601 Lancaster⊙, 57,690 K 5
Lancaster, ‡319,693 K 5
17538 Landisville, 1,900 K 5
19047 Langhorne, 1,889 N 5
19446 Lansdale, 18,451 M 5
19050 Lansdowne, 14,090 M 7
18232 Lansford, 5,168 L 4
18626 Laporte⊙, 207 K 3
15647 Larimer, 2,500 C 5
15650 Latrobe, 11,749 D 5
19605 Laureldale, 4,519 L 5
15229 Laurel Gardens, 1,830 B 6
16511 Lawrence Park, Δ4,517 C 1
17042 Lebanon⊙, 28,572 K 5
15656 Leechburg, 2,999 C 4
19533 Leesport, 1,158 K 5
15056 Leetsdale, 1,862 B 4
18235 Lehighton, 6,095 L 4
16851 Lemont, 2,547 G 4
17043 Lemoyne, 4,625 J 5
19113 Lester, 1,700 M 7
* 19053 Levittown, 21,000 N 5
17837 Lewisburg⊙, 6,376 J 4
17044 Lewistown⊙, 11,098 G 4
16930 Liberty, 3,594 C 7
15129 Library, 4,900 B 7
15658 Ligonier, 2,258 D 5
15938 Lilly, 1,429 E 5
† 15037 Lincoln, 1,885 C 7
19352 Lincoln University, 1,400 L 6
16424 Linesville, 1,265 A 2
19468 Linfield, 975 L 5
17112 Linglestown, 3,500 J 5
† 17837 Linntown, 1,851 J 4
19061 Linwood, 2,900 L 7
17543 Lititz, 7,072 K 5
17340 Littlestown, 3,026 H 6
17745 Lock Haven⊙, 11,427 H 3
15940 Loretto, 1,661 E 4
15068 Lower Burrell, 13,654 C 4
15661 Loyalhanna, 4,283 D 5
15754 Lucernemines, 1,380 D 4
18709 Luzerne, 4,504 L 3
17048 Lykens, 2,506 J 4
16045 Lyndora, 8,415 B 4
18062 Macungie, 1,414 L 4
16661 Madera, 950 F 4
17948 Mahanoy City, 7,257 K 4
19355 Malvern, 2,583 L 5
17345 Manchester, 2,391 J 5
17545 Manheim, 5,434 K 5
15665 Manor, 2,276 C 5
16933 Mansfield, 4,114 H 2
19061 Marcus Hook, 3,041 L 7
17547 Marietta, 2,838 J 5
17235 Marion, 950 G 6
16046 Mars, 1,488 C 4
16662 Martinsburg, 2,088 F 5
18063 Martins Creek, 950 M 4
17053 Marysville, 2,328 H 5
15461 Masontown, 4,226 C 6
18336 Matamoras, 2,244 N 3
18229 Mauch Chunk (Jim Thorpe)⊙, 5,456 L 4
18433 Mayfield, 2,176 L 2
18237 McAdoo, 3,326 L 4
17841 McClure, 1,094 H 4
17233 McConnellsburg⊙, 1,228 F 6
15057 McDonald, 2,879 B 5
* 15130 McKeesport, 37,977 C 7
15136 McKees Rocks, 11,901 B 7
17344 McSherrystown, 2,773 H 6
15347 Meadow Lands, 3,609 B 5
16335 Meadville⊙, 16,573 B 2
17055 Mechanicsburg, 9,385 H 5
* 19063 Media⊙, 6,444 L 7
16137 Mercer⊙, 2,654 B 3
17236 Mercersburg, 1,727 G 6
19066 Merion Station, 5,686 M 6
15552 Meyersdale, 2,648 E 6
17842 Middleburg⊙, 1,369 H 4
17057 Middletown, 9,080 J 5
15059 Midland, 5,271 A 4
15060 Midway, 1,188 B 5
17844 Mifflinburg, 2,607 H 4
17059 Mifflintown⊙, 828 H 4
18632 Mildred, 950 K 3
16853 Milesburg, 1,196 G 4
18337 Milford⊙, 1,190 N 3
17061 Millersburg, 3,074 J 4
17551 Millersville, 6,396 K 6
17751 Mill Hall, 1,838 G 3
15348 Millsboro, 980 B 6
15209 Millvale, 5,815 B 7
19033 Milmont Park, 2,891 M 7
17063 Milroy, 1,575 G 4
17847 Milton, 7,723 J 3
17954 Minersville, 6,012 K 4
18655 Mocanaqua, 950 K 3
19540 Mohnton, 2,153 L 5
15061 Monaca, 7,486 B 4
15062 Monessen, 15,216 C 5
15063 Monongahela, 7,113 B 5
15146 Monroeville, 29,011 C 7
17237 Mont Alto, 1,532 G 6
17752 Montgomery, 1,902 H 3
17754 Montoursville, 5,985 J 3
18801 Montrose⊙, 2,058 L 2
18507 Moosic, 4,273 L 3
19067 Morrisville, 11,309 N 5
19070 Morton, 2,602 M 7
18444 Moscow, 1,430 L 3
17851 Mount Carmel, 9,317 K 4
17065 Mount Holly Springs, 2,009 H 5
16740 Mount Jewett, 1,060 E 2
17552 Mount Joy, 5,041 K 5
15228 Mount Lebanon, Δ39,596 B 7
15210 Mount Oliver, 5,487 B 7
19606 Mount Penn, 3,465 L 5

5666 Mount Pleasant, 5,895 ... D 5
8344 Mount Pocono, 1,019 ... M 3
7066 Mount Union, 3,662 ... G 5
7554 Mountville, 1,454 ... K 5
7347 Mount Wolf, 1,811 ... J 5
7756 Muncy, 2,872 ... J 3
5120 Munhall, 16,674 ... C 7
5668 Murrysville, 3,900 ... C 5
7067 Myerstown, 3,645 ... K 5
8634 Nanticoke, 14,632 ... K 3
5943 Nanty Glo, 4,298 ... E 5
9072 Narberth, 5,151 ... M 6
5065 Natrona Heights, 15,000 ... C 4
8064 Nazareth, 5,815 ... M 4
5351 Nemacolin, 1,273 ... B 6
8635 Nescopeck, 1,897 ... K 3
8240 Nesquehoning, 3,338 ... L 4
6141 New Beaver, 1,426 ... B 4
6140 New Bedford, 950 ... A 3
6242 New Bethlehem, 1,406 ... D 3
7068 New Bloomfield⊙, 1,032 ... H 5
5066 New Brighton, 7,637 ... B 4
8901 New Britain, 2,428 ... M 5
6101 New Castle⊙, 38,559 ... B 3
7070 New Cumberland, 9,803 ... J 5
5067 New Eagle, 2,497 ... B 5
17349 New Freedom, 1,495 ... J 6
17557 New Holland, 3,971 ... K 5
18938 New Hope, 978 ... N 5
15068 New Kensington, 20,312 ... C 4
18834 New Milford, 1,143 ... L 2
17350 New Oxford, 1,495 ... H 6
17959 New Philadelphia, 1,528 ... K 4
17074 Newport, 1,747 ... H 5
15468 New Salem, 1,337 ... C 6
15626 New Salem (Delmont), 1,934 ... D 5
18940 Newtown, 2,216 ... N 5
19073 Newtown Square, 16,000 ... L 6
17241 Newville, 1,631 ... H 5
16142 New Wilmington, 2,721 ... B 3
17759 Nisbet, 950 ... H 3
* 19401 Norristown⊙, 38,169 ... M 5
18067 Northampton, 8,389 ... M 4
15673 North Apollo, 1,618 ... D 4
15104 North Braddock, 10,838 ... C 7
† 18032 North Catasauqua, 2,941 ... L 4
16428 North East, 3,846 ... C 1
17857 Northumberland, 4,102 ... J 4
19454 North Wales, 3,911 ... M 5
16365 North Warren, 1,360 ... D 2
15674 Norvelt, 2,588 ... C 5

19074 Norwood, 7,229 ... M 7
18636 Noxen, 950 ... K 3
18241 Nuremberg, 950 ... K 4
15071 Oakdale, 1,614 ... B 5
† 19047 Oakford, 3,800 ... N 5
15139 Oakmont, 7,550 ... C 6
† 15059 Ohioville, 3,918 ... B 4
16301 Oil City, 15,033 ... C 3
18518 Old Forge, 9,522 ... L 3
15472 Oliver, 3,091 ... C 6
18447 Olyphant, 5,422 ... L 3
17961 Orwigsburg, 2,661 ... K 4
16666 Osceola Mills, 1,671 ... F 4
19363 Oxford, 3,658 ... K 6
† 15963 Paint, 1,233 ... E 5
18071 Palmerton, 5,620 ... L 4
17078 Palmyra, 7,615 ... J 5
19301 Paoli, 5,835 ... M 5
17562 Paradise, 975 ... K 5
19365 Parkesburg, 2,701 ... L 6
† 19013 Parkside, 2,343 ... M 7
† 17331 Parkville, 5,120 ... J 6
16668 Patton, 2,762 ... E 4
17111 Paxtang, 2,160 ... J 5
18072 Pen Argyl, 3,668 ... M 4
17103 Penbrook, 3,379 ... J 5
18073 Pennsburg, 2,260 ... M 5
† 19003 Penn Wynne, 6,038 ... M 6
18944 Perkasie, 5,451 ... M 5
15473 Perryopolis, 2,043 ... C 5
* 19101 Philadelphia⊙, 1,948,609 ... N 6
Philadelphia, ‡4,817,914 ... N 6
16866 Philipsburg, 3,700 ... F 4
19460 Phoenixville, 14,823 ... L 5
17963 Pine Grove, 2,197 ... K 4
16868 Pine Grove Mills, 950 ... G 4
15140 Pitcairn, 4,741 ... C 5
* 15201 Pittsburgh⊙, 520,117 ... B 7
Pittsburgh, ‡2,401,245 ... B 7
* 18640 Pittston, 11,113 ... L 3
18705 Plains, 6,606 ... L 3
16823 Pleasant Gap, 1,773 ... G 4
15236 Pleasant Hills, 10,409 ... B 7
16341 Pleasantville, 1,005 ... C 2
15239 Plum, 21,932 ... C 5
18651 Plymouth, 9,536 ... K 3
† 16830 Plymptonville, 1,040 ... E 3
15474 Point Marion, 1,750 ... C 6
16342 Polk, 3,673 ... C 3
15946 Portage, 4,151 ... E 5
16743 Port Allegany, 2,703 ... F 2
17965 Port Carbon, 2,717 ... K 4
15133 Port Vue, 5,862 ... C 7
19464 Pottstown, 25,355 ... L 5
17901 Pottsville⊙, 19,715 ... K 4
19018 Primos, 3,900 ... M 7
16052 Prospect, 973 ... B 4
19076 Prospect Park, 7,250 ... M 7
15767 Punxsutawney, 7,792 ... E 4
18951 Quakertown, 7,276 ... M 5
17566 Quarryville, 1,571 ... K 6
† 15104 Rankin, 3,817 ... C 7
* 19601 Reading⊙, 87,643 ... L 5
Reading, ‡415,056 ... L 5
17567 Reamstown, 1,050 ... K 5
18076 Red Hill, 1,201 ... L 5
17356 Red Lion, 5,645 ... J 6
17084 Reedsville, 950 ... G 4
17764 Renovo, 2,620 ... G 3
15851 Reynoldsville, 2,771 ... D 3
17087 Richland, 1,444 ... K 5
15853 Ridgway⊙, 6,022 ... E 3
19078 Ridley Park, 9,025 ... M 7
18077 Riegelsville, 1,050 ... M 4
15678 Rillton, 975 ... C 5
16248 Rimersburg, 1,146 ... D 3
17868 Riverside, 1,905 ... J 4
16673 Roaring Spring, 2,811 ... F 5
19551 Robesonia, 1,685 ... K 5
15949 Robinson, 975 ... D 5
15074 Rochester, 4,819 ... B 4
19111 Rockledge, 2,564 ... M 5
15557 Rockwood, 1,051 ... D 6
15477 Roscoe, 1,176 ... C 5
19010 Rosemont, 4,900 ... M 5
18013 Roseto, 1,538 ... M 4
17250 Rouzerville, 1,419 ... G 6
† 17067 Royalton, 1,040 ... J 5
19468 Royersford, 4,235 ... L 5
16249 Rural Valley, 962 ... D 4

16345 Russell, 950 ... D 2
15076 Russellton, 1,597 ... C 4
19070 Rutledge, 1,167 ... M 7
16433 Saegertown, 1,348 ... B 2
17970 Saint Clair, 4,576 ... K 4
15857 Saint Marys, 7,470 ... E 3
15951 Saint Michael, 1,248 ... E 5
15681 Saltsburg, 1,037 ... C 4
† 15801 Sandy, 2,000 ... E 3
16056 Saxonburg, 1,191 ... C 4
18840 Sayre, 7,473 ... K 2
15963 Scalp Level, 1,353 ... E 5
17088 Schaefferstown, 1,027 ... K 5
18078 Schnecksville, 1,550 ... L 4
17972 Schuylkill Haven, 6,125 ... K 4
18354 Sciota, 950 ... M 4
15683 Scottdale, 5,818 ... C 5
* 18501 Scranton⊙, 103,564 ... L 3
Scranton, ‡234,107 ... L 3
19018 Secane, 5,700 ... M 7
17870 Selinsgrove, 5,116 ... J 4
18960 Sellersville, 2,829 ... M 5
15143 Sewickley, 5,660 ... B 4
17872 Shamokin, 11,719 ... J 4
17876 Shamokin Dam, 1,562 ... J 4
16146 Sharon, 22,653 ... B 3
19079 Sharon Hill, 7,464 ... N 7
15215 Sharpsburg, 5,499 ... B 6
16150 Sharpsville, 6,126 ... A 3
16347 Sheffield, 1,564 ... D 2
17976 Shenandoah, 8,287 ... K 4
18655 Shickshinny, 1,685 ... K 3
19607 Shillington, 6,249 ... K 5
16748 Shinglehouse, 1,320 ... F 2
17257 Shippensburg, 6,536 ... H 5
19555 Shoemakersville, 1,427 ... K 4
17361 Shrewsburv, 1,716 ... J 6
18407 Simpson, 1,900 ... L 2
19608 Sinking Spring, 2,862 ... K 5
19474 Skippack, 975 ... M 5
18080 Slatington, 4,687 ... L 4
15684 Slickville, 1,066 ... C 5
16057 Slippery Rock, 4,949 ... B 3
16749 Smethport⊙, 1,883 ... F 2
15478 Smithfield, 969 ... C 6
15501 Somerset⊙, 6,269 ... D 6
18964 Souderton, 6,366 ... M 5
15425 South Connellsville, 2,385 ... C 6
15956 South Fork, 1,661 ... E 5
† 14892 South Waverly, 1,307 ... J 2
17701 South Williamsport, 7,153 ... J 3
15775 Spangler, 3,109 ... E 4
19475 Spring City, 3,578 ... L 5
15144 Springdale, 5,202 ... C 4
19064 Springfield, ▵2,446 ... M 7
17362 Spring Grove, 1,669 ... J 6
16801 State College, 33,778 ... G 4
17113 Steelton, 8,556 ... J 5
17363 Stewartstown, 1,157 ... K 6
16153 Stoneboro, 1,129 ... B 3
19464 Stowe, 3,596 ... L 5
17579 Strasburg, 1,897 ... K 6
18360 Stroudsburg⊙, 5,451 ... M 4
† 16323 Sugarcreek, 5,944 ... C 3
18706 Sugar Notch, 1,333 ... L 3
18250 Summit Hill, 3,811 ... L 4
17801 Sunbury⊙, 13,025 ... J 4
18847 Susquehanna, 2,319 ... L 2
19081 Swarthmore, 6,156 ... M 7
15218 Swissvale, 13,821 ... C 7
15865 Sykesville, 1,311 ... E 3
18252 Tamaqua, 9,246 ... L 4
15084 Tarentum, 7,379 ... C 4
18517 Taylor, 6,977 ... L 3
18969 Telford, 3,409 ... M 5
19560 Temple, 1,667 ... L 5
16259 Templeton, 950 ... C 4
17581 Terre Hill, 1,129 ... L 5
18512 Throop, 4,307 ... L 3
16353 Tionesta⊙, 711 ... C 2
16354 Titusville, 7,331 ... C 2
19562 Topton, 1,744 ... L 5
19374 Toughkenamon, 1,233 ... L 6
18848 Towanda⊙, 4,224 ... J 2
17980 Tower City, 1,774 ... J 4
15085 Trafford, 4,383 ... C 5
† 19013 Trainer, 2,336 ... L 7
17981 Tremont, 1,833 ... K 4
18254 Tresckow, 1,146 ... K 4
17881 Trevorton, 2,196 ... J 4

16947 Troy, 1,315 ... J 2
19007 Tullytown, 2,194 ... N 5
18657 Tunkhannock⊙, 2,251 ... L 2
15145 Turtle Creek, 8,308 ... C 7
15960 Twin Rocks, 975 ... E 4
16686 Tyrone, 7,072 ... F 4
16438 Union City, 3,631 ... C 2
15401 Uniontown⊙, 16,282 ... C 6
15689 United, 975 ... D 5
15235 Universal, 1,900 ... C 7
† 19013 Upland, 3,930 ... L 7
* 19082 Upper Darby, ▵95,910 ... M 6
19481 Valley Forge, 400 ... L 5
17983 Valley View, 1,585 ... J 4
15690 Vandergrift, 7,873 ... D 4
15147 Verona, 3,737 ... C 6
15132 Versailles, 2,754 ... C 7
19085 Villanova, 5,250 ... M 6
† 15148 Wall, 1,265 ... C 5
19086 Wallingford, 3,500 ... L 7
18088 Walnutport, 1,942 ... L 4
16157 Wampum, 1,189 ... B 4
16365 Warren⊙, 12,998 ... D 2
15301 Washington⊙, 19,827 ... B 5
16441 Waterford, 1,468 ... B 2
17777 Watsontown, 2,514 ... J 3
18472 Waymart, 1,122 ... M 2
19087 Wayne, 12,500 ... M 6
17268 Waynesboro, 10,011 ... G 6
15370 Waynesburg⊙, 5,152 ... B 6
18255 Weatherly, 2,554 ... L 4
16901 Wellsboro⊙, 4,003 ... H 2
19565 Wernersville, 1,761 ... K 5
16510 Wesleyville, 3,920 ... C 1
15417 West Brownsville, 1,426 ... C 5
19380 West Chester⊙, 19,301 ... L 6
16950 Westfield, 1,273 ... H 2
19390 West Grove, 1,870 ... L 6
18201 West Hazleton, 6,059 ... K 4
† 16201 West Kittanning, 956 ... C 4
19609 West Lawn, 1,973 ... K 5
† 15656 West Leechburg, 1,422 ... C 4
16159 West Middlesex, 1,293 ... B 3
15122 West Mifflin, 28,070 ... C 7
† 15901 Westmont, 6,673 ... D 5
15089 West Newton, 3,648 ... C 5
15229 West View, 8,312 ... B 6
† 17401 West York, 5,314 ... J 6
16161 Wheatland, 1,421 ... B 3
15120 Whitaker, 1,697 ... C 7
18052 Whitehall, 16,551 ... B 7
18661 White Haven, 2,134 ... L 3
15131 White Oak, 9,304 ... C 7
17097 Wiconisco, 1,236 ... J 4
15870 Wilcox, 950 ... E 2
* 18701 Wilkes-Barre⊙, 58,856 ... L 3
Wilkes-Barre-Hazleton, ‡342,301 ... L 3
15221 Wilkinsburg, 26,780 ... C 7
16693 Williamsburg, 1,704 ... F 5
17701 Williamsport⊙, 37,918 ... H 3
17098 Williamstown, 1,919 ... J 4
19090 Willow Grove, 16,494 ... M 5
15148 Wilmerding, 3,218 ... C 7
15025 Wilson, 8,482 ... M 4
15963 Windber, 6,332 ... E 5
18091 Windgap, 2,270 ... M 4
17366 Windsor, 1,298 ... J 6
† 18434 Winton, 4,948 ... M 3
† 15301 Wolfdale, 1,202 ... B 5
19567 Womelsdorf, 1,551 ... K 5
19094 Woodlyn, 6,500 ... M 7
17368 Wrightsville, 2,668 ... J 5
19096 Wynnewood, 9,200 ... M 6
18644 Wyoming, 4,195 ... L 3
19610 Wyomissing, 7,136 ... K 5
19067 Yardley, 2,616 ... N 5
19050 Yeadon, 12,136 ... N 7
17099 Yeagertown, 1,363 ... G 4
* 17401 York⊙, 50,335 ... J 6
York, ‡329,540 ... J 6
16371 Youngsville, 2,158 ... D 2
15697 Youngwood, 3,057 ... D 5
16063 Zelienople, 3,602 ... B 4

⊙ County seat.
‡ Population of metropolitan area.
▵ Population of town of township.
† Zip of nearest p.o.
* Multiple zips

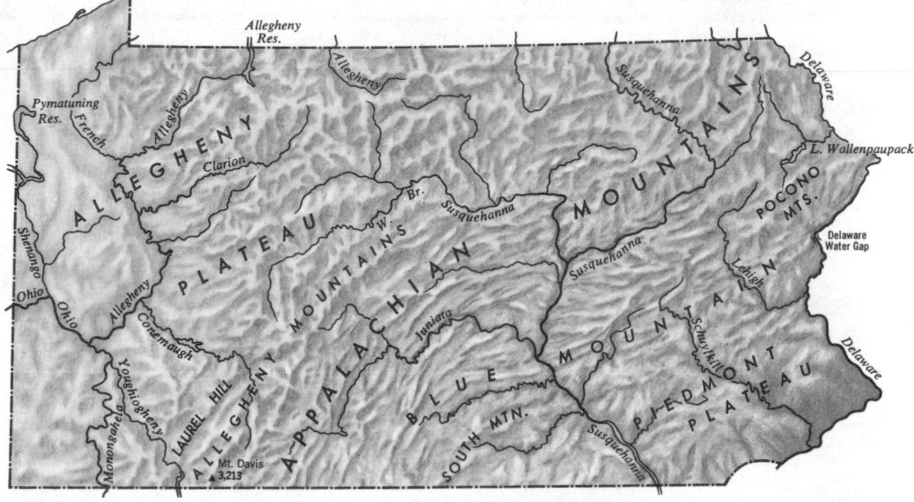

Topography

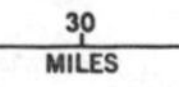

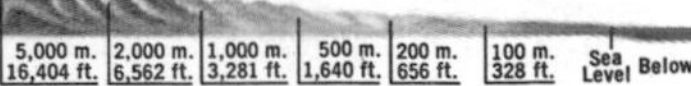

COUNTIES

County, Pop.	Key
Abbeville, 21,112	B 3
Aiken, 91,023	D 4
Allendale, 9,692	E 6
Anderson, 105,474	B 2
Bamberg, 15,950	E 5
Barnwell, 17,176	E 5
Beaufort, 51,136	F 7
Berkeley, 56,199	G 5
Calhoun, 10,780	F 4
Charleston, 247,650	H 6
Cherokee, 36,791	D 1
Chester, 29,811	E 2
Chesterfield, 33,667	G 2
Clarendon, 25,604	G 4
Colleton, 27,622	F 6
Darlington, 53,442	H 3
Dillon, 28,838	J 3
Dorchester, 32,276	G 5
Edgefield, 15,692	D 4
Fairfield, 19,999	E 3
Florence, 89,636	H 3
Georgetown, 33,500	J 5
Greenville, 240,546	C 2
Greenwood, 49,686	C 3
Hampton, 15,878	E 6
Horry, 69,992	J 4
Jasper, 11,885	E 6
Kershaw, 34,727	F 3
Lancaster, 43,328	F 2
Laurens, 49,713	D 2
Lee, 18,323	G 3
Lexington, 89,012	E 4
Marion, 30,270	J 3
Marlboro, 27,151	H 2
McCormick, 7,955	C 4
Newberry, 29,273	D 3
Oconee, 40,728	A 2
Orangeburg, 69,789	F 5
Pickens, 58,956	B 2
Richland, 233,868	F 3
Saluda, 14,528	D 3
Spartanburg, 173,724	D 2
Sumter, 79,425	G 4
Union, 29,230	D 2
Williamsburg, 34,243	H 4
York, 85,216	E 2

CITIES and TOWNS

	Zip	Name/Pop.	Key
	29620	Abbeville⊙, 5,515	C 3
	29426	Adams Run, 500	G 6
	29801	Aiken⊙, 13,436	D 4
	29001	Alcolu, 600	G 4
	29810	Allendale⊙, 3,620	E 5
	29621	Anderson⊙, 27,556	B 2
	29510	Andrews, 2,879	H 5
†	29020	Antioch, 500	F 3
	29320	Arcadia, 1,887	C 2
†	29201	Arcadia Lakes, 741	F 3
†	29201	Ardincaple, 726	E 3
	29640	Ariail, 1,150	B 2
†	29301	Arkwright, 2,059	C 2
	29511	Aynor, 536	J 3
	29706	Baldwin-Aragon Mills, 1,042	E 2
	29002	Ballentine, 550	E 3
	29003	Bamberg⊙, 3,406	E 5
	29812	Barnwell⊙, 4,439	E 5
	29006	Batesburg, 4,036	D 4
	29816	Bath, 1,576	D 5
	29902	Beaufort⊙, 9,434	F 7
	29842	Beech Island, 400	D 5
	29627	Belton, 5,257	C 2
	29512	Bennettsville⊙, 7,468	H 2
	29601	Berea, 7,186	C 2
	29009	Bethune, 506	G 3
	29010	Bishopville⊙, 3,404	G 3
	29702	Blacksburg, 1,977	D 1
	29817	Blackville, 2,395	E 5
	29910	Bluffton, 529	F 7
	29016	Blythewood, 600	E 3
	29431	Bonneau, 365	H 5
	29703	Bowling Green, 542	E 1
	29018	Bowman, 1,095	F 5
†	29201	Boyden Arbor, 416	F 3
	29019	Boykin, 350	F 3
	29432	Branchville, 1,011	F 5
	29911	Brunson, 559	E 6
	29321	Buffalo, 1,461	D 2
†	29834	Burnettown, 434	D 5
	29902	Burton, 900	F 7
	29628	Calhoun Falls, 2,234	B 3
	29020	Camden⊙, 8,532	F 3
	29030	Cameron, 476	F 4
	29322	Campobello, 530	C 1
†	29902	Capehart, 4,490	F 7
	29031	Carlisle, 670	D 2
	29629	Cateechee, 450	B 2
	29033	Cayce, 9,967	E 4
	29630	Central, 1,550	B 2
†	29372	Central Pacolet, 483	D 2
	29036	Chapin, 342	E 3
*	29401	Charleston⊙, 66,945	G 6
		Charleston, ‡303,849	G 6
	29520	Cheraw, 5,627	H 2
	29323	Chesnee, 1,069	D 1
	29706	Chester⊙, 7,045	E 2
	29709	Chesterfield⊙, 1,667	G 2
	29611	City View, 2,497	C 2
†	29501	Claussen, 500	H 3
	29822	Clearwater, 1,500	D 4
	29631	Clemson, 5,578	B 2
	29324	Clifton, 950	D 2
	29325	Clinton, 8,138	D 3
	29525	Clio, 936	H 2
	29710	Clover, 3,506	E 1
*	29201	Columbia (cap.)⊙, 113,542	F 4
		Columbia, ‡322,880	F 4
	29636	Conestee, 600	C 2
	29329	Converse, 900	D 2
	29526	Conway⊙, 8,151	J 4
	29912	Coosawhatchie, 500	F 6
	29434	Cordesville, 900	H 5
	29435	Cottageville, 497	G 6
	29530	Coward, 466	H 4
	29330	Cowpens, 2,109	D 1
	29331	Cross Anchor, 350	D 2
	29332	Cross Hill, 579	D 3
†	29640	Dacusville, 350	B 2
	29914	Dale, 500	F 6
	29040	Dalzell, 625	G 3
	29532	Darlington⊙, 6,990	H 3
	29042	Denmark, 3,571	E 5
	29536	Dillon⊙, 5,991	J 3
	29638	Donalds, 392	C 3
†	29532	Doneraile, 1,417	H 3
	29437	Dorchester, 400	G 5
	29540	Dovesville, 500	H 3
	29639	Due West, 1,380	C 3
	29334	Duncan, 1,266	C 2
	29640	Easley, 11,175	B 2
†	29340	East Gaffney, 3,750	D 1
	29044	Eastover, 817	F 4
	29824	Edgefield⊙, 2,750	C 4
	29712	Edgemoor, 500	E 2
	29438	Edisto Island, 900	G 6
	29081	Ehrhardt, 478	E 5
	29045	Elgin, 374	F 3
	29046	Elliott, 500	G 3
	29047	Elloree, 940	F 4
	29335	Enoree, 850	D 2
	29918	Estill, 1,954	E 6
†	29706	Eureka (Hemlock), 1,524	E 2
	29048	Eutawville, 386	G 5
	29827	Fairfax, 1,937	E 6
	29643	Fair Play, 500	A 2
	29501	Florence⊙, 25,997	H 3
	29542	Floyd Dale, 500	J
	29439	Folly Beach, 1,157	H
	29206	Forest Acres, 6,808	F
†	29928	Forest Beach, 500	F
	29714	Fort Lawn, 510	F
	29715	Fort Mill, 4,505	F
	29050	Fort Motte, 950	F
	29644	Fountain Inn, 3,391	C
	29052	Gadsden, 500	F
	29340	Gaffney⊙, 13,253	D
†	29601	Gantt, 11,386	C
	29440	Georgetown⊙, 10,449	J
	29923	Gifford, 500	E
	29346	Glendale, 850	D
	29347	Glenn Springs, 350	D
	29828	Gloverville, 1,682	D
	29445	Goose Creek, 3,656	H
	29348	Gramling, 500	C
	29829	Graniteville, 1,127	D
	29645	Gray Court, 859	C
	29055	Great Falls, 2,727	F
	29056	Greeleyville, 542	H
	29446	Green Pond, 500	F
	29545	Green Sea, 500	J
*	29601	Greenville⊙, 61,208	C
		Greenville, ‡299,502	C
	29646	Greenwood⊙, 21,069	C
	29651	Greer, 10,642	C
	29546	Gresham, 350	J
†	29569	Gurley, 425	J
	29924	Hampton⊙, 2,845	E
	29410	Hanahan, 8,376	H

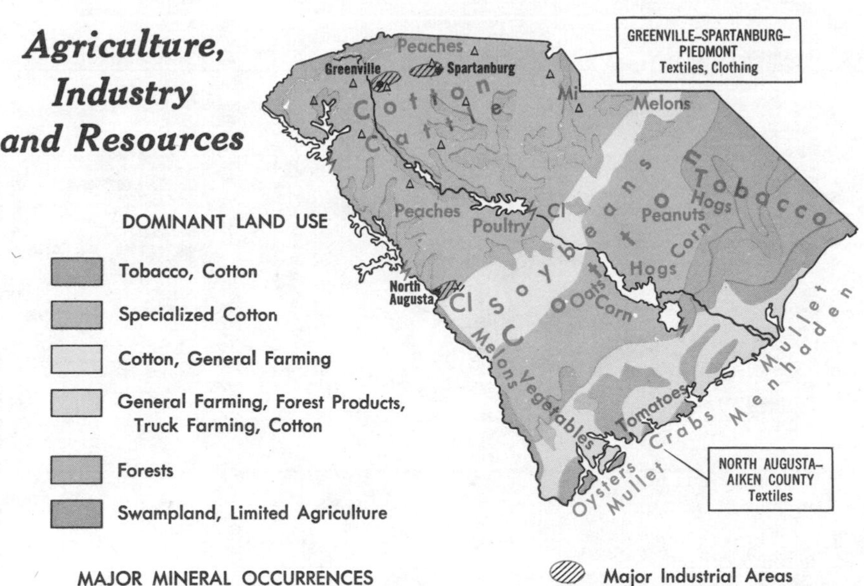

MAJOR MINERAL OCCURRENCES

Cl Clay

Mi Mica

Major Industrial Areas

Water Power

Major Textile Centers

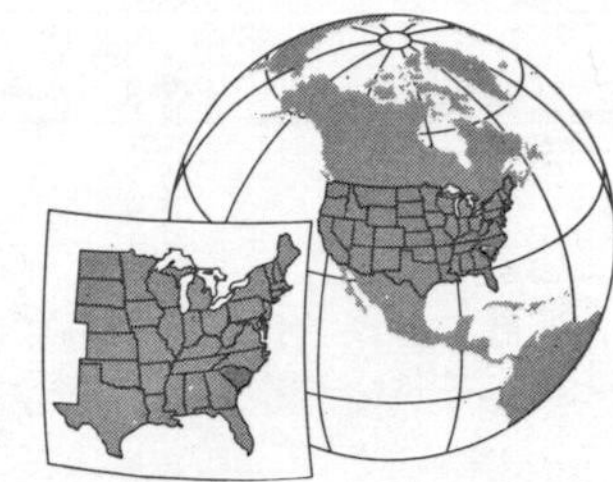

AREA 31,055 sq. mi.
POPULATION 2,590,516
CAPITAL Columbia
LARGEST CITY Columbia
HIGHEST POINT Sassafras Mtn. 3,560 ft.
SETTLED IN 1670
ADMITTED TO UNION May 23, 1788
POPULAR NAME Palmetto State
STATE FLOWER Yellow Jessamine
STATE BIRD Carolina Wren

29927 Hardeeville, 853 .... E 7
29448 Harleyville, 704 .... G 5
29550 Hartsville, 8,017 .... G 3
29058 Heath Springs, 955 .... F 2
29554 Hemingway, 1,026 .... J 4
29706 Hemlock, 1,524 .... E 2
29717 Hickory Grove, 377 .... E 2
29813 Hilda, 331 .... E 5
29928 Hilton Head Island, 450 .... F 7
29059 Holly Hill, 1,178 .... G 5
29449 Hollywood, 339 .... G 6
29654 Honea Path, 3,707 .... C 3
29062 Horatio, 500 .... F 3
29450 Huger, 500 .... H 5
29349 Inman, 1,661 .... C 1
29063 Irmo, 517 .... E 3
29720 Irwin, 1,424 .... F 2
29451 Isle of Palms, 2,657 .... H 6
29655 Iva, 1,114 .... B 3
29831 Jackson, 1,928 .... D 5
29452 Jacksonboro, 550 .... G 6
29483 Jedburg, 900 .... G 5
29718 Jefferson, 709 .... G 2
29351 Joanna, 1,631 .... D 3
29455 Johns Island, 675 .... G 6
29555 Johnsonville, 1,267 .... J 4
29832 Johnston, 2,552 .... D 4
29353 Jonesville, 1,447 .... D 2
29067 Kershaw, 1,818 .... G 2
29556 Kingstree⊙, 3,381 .... H 4
29814 Kline, 305 .... E 5
29456 Ladson, 600 .... G 6

29656 La France, 875 .... B 2
29560 Lake City, 6,247 .... H 4
29563 Lake View, 949 .... J 3
29069 Lamar, 1,250 .... G 3
29720 Lancaster⊙, 9,186 .... F 2
† 29720 Lancaster Mills, 2,558 .... F 2
29724 Lando, 775 .... E 2
29356 Landrum, 1,859 .... C 1
29564 Lane, 517 .... H 5
29834 Langley, 975 .... D 4
29565 Latta, 1,764 .... J 3
29360 Laurens⊙, 10,298 .... C 3
29070 Leesville, 1,907 .... E 4
29734 Lesslie, 500 .... E 2
29072 Lexington⊙, 969 .... E 4
29657 Liberty, 2,860 .... B 2
† 29483 Lincolnville, 504 .... G 6
29566 Little River, 500 .... K 4
29931 Lobeco, 350 .... F 6
29569 Loris, 1,741 .... K 3
29078 Lugoff, 500 .... F 3
29079 Lydia, 400 .... G 3
29325 Lydia Mills, 925 .... D 3
29365 Lyman, 1,159 .... C 2
29080 Lynchburg, 546 .... G 3
29660 Madison, 350 .... A 2
29102 Manning⊙, 4,025 .... G 4
29661 Marietta-Slater, 1,764 .... C 1
29571 Marion⊙, 7,435 .... J 3
29662 Mauldin, 3,797 .... C 2
29104 Mayesville, 757 .... G 4
29368 Mayo, 800 .... D 1
29101 McBee, 592 .... G 3
29570 McColl, 2,524 .... H 2
29835 McCormick⊙, 1,864 .... C 4
† 29379 Monarch Mills, 1,726 .... D 2
29461 Moncks Corner⊙, 2,314 .... G 5
29105 Monetta, 850 .... D 4
29839 Montmorenci, 700 .... D 4
29664 Mountain Rest, 500 .... A 2
29464 Mount Pleasant, 6,155 .... H 6
29574 Mullins, 6,006 .... J 3
29576 Murrells Inlet, 850 .... K 4
29577 Myrtle Beach, 8,536 .... K 4
29408 Naval Base, 13,565 .... G 6
29107 Neeses, 388 .... E 4
29580 Nesmith, 350 .... H 4
29108 Newberry⊙, 9,218 .... D 3
29809 New Ellenton, 2,546 .... D 5
29665 Newry, 874 .... B 2
† 29536 New Town, 950 .... J 3
29581 Nichols, 549 .... J 3
29666 Ninety Six, 2,166 .... C 3
29667 Norris, 757 .... B 2
29112 North, 1,076 .... E 4
29841 North Augusta, 12,883 .... C 5
29406 North Charleston, 19,854 .... G 6
† 29550 North Hartsville, 1,485 .... G 3
29582 North Myrtle Beach, 1,957 .... K 4
29113 Norway, 579 .... E 5
29114 Olanta, 640 .... H 4
29843 Olar, 423 .... E 5
29115 Orangeburg⊙, 13,252 .... F 4
29372 Pacolet, 1,418 .... D 2
29373 Pacolet Mills, 1,504 .... D 2
29728 Pageland, 2,122 .... G 2
29583 Pamplico, 1,068 .... H 4
29584 Patrick, 421 .... G 2
29374 Pauline, 750 .... D 2
29585 Pawleys Island, 650 .... J 5
29670 Pendleton, 2,615 .... B 2
29671 Pickens⊙, 2,954 .... B 2
29673 Piedmont, 2,242 .... C 2
† 29169 Pineridge, 633 .... E 4
29468 Pineville, 900 .... H 5
29125 Pinewood, 687 .... G 4
29469 Pinopolis, 788 .... G 5
29935 Port Royal, 2,865 .... F 7
29127 Prosperity, 762 .... D 3
† 29501 Quinby, 788 .... H 3
29589 Rains, 600 .... J 3
29470 Ravenel, 931 .... G 6
29375 Reidville, 460 .... C 2
29128 Rembert, 350 .... G 3
29936 Ridgeland⊙, 1,165 .... E 7

29129 Ridge Spring, 644 .... D 4
29472 Ridgeville, 563 .... G 5
29130 Ridgeway, 437 .... F 3
29131 Rimini, 400 .... G 4
29473 Ritter, 350 .... F 6
29730 Rock Hill, 33,846 .... E 2
29740 Rodman, 500 .... E 2
29133 Rowesville, 392 .... F 5
29741 Ruby, 306 .... G 2
29475 Ruffin, 400 .... F 6
29407 Saint Andrews, 9,202 .... G 6
29134 Saint Charles, 350 .... G 3
29477 Saint George⊙, 1,806 .... F 5
29135 Saint Matthews⊙, 2,403 .... F 4
† 29148 Saint Paul, 725 .... G 4
29479 Saint Stephen, 1,506 .... H 5
29137 Salley, 450 .... E 4
29138 Saluda⊙, 2,442 .... D 4
† 29301 Saxon, 4,807 .... D 2
29591 Scranton, 732 .... H 4
29940 Seabrook, 500 .... F 6
29592 Sellers, 561 .... H 3
29678 Seneca, 6,027 .... A 2
† 29150 Shannontown, 7,491 .... G 4
29941 Sheldon, 950 .... F 6
29480 Shulerville, 375 .... H 5
29681 Simpsonville, 3,308 .... C 2
29682 Six Mile, 361 .... B 2
29683 Slater-Marietta, 1,764 .... C 1
29593 Society Hill, 806 .... H 2
† 29512 South Bennettsville, 1,726 .... H 2
† 29169 South Congaree, 1,434 .... E 4
* 29301 Spartanburg⊙, 44,546 .... C 1
29169 Springdale, 2,638 .... E 4
† 29720 Springdale, 3,193 .... F 2
29146 Springfield, 724 .... E 4
† 29067 Spring Mills, 975 .... F 2
29377 Startex, 1,203 .... C 2
29482 Sullivans Island, 1,426 .... H 6
29148 Summerton, 1,305 .... G 4
29483 Summerville, 3,839 .... G 5
29150 Sumter⊙, 24,435 .... G 4
29685 Sunset, 450 .... B 2
29577 Surfside Beach, 1,329 .... K 4
29160 Swansea, 691 .... E 4
29686 Tamassee, 420 .... A 2
29687 Taylors, 6,831 .... C 2
29688 Tigerville, 975 .... C 1
29161 Timmonsville, 2,246 .... H 3
29690 Travelers Rest, 2,241 .... C 2
29847 Trenton, 362 .... D 4
29162 Turbeville, 442 .... G 4
29379 Union⊙, 10,775 .... D 2
† 29678 Utica, 1,299 .... B 2
29944 Varnville, 1,555 .... E 6
29850 Vaucluse, 575 .... D 7
29607 Wade-Hampton, 17,152 .... C 2
29164 Wagener, 723 .... E 4
29691 Walhalla⊙, 3,662 .... A 2
29488 Walterboro⊙, 6,257 .... F 6
29692 Ware Shoals, 2,480 .... C 3
29851 Warrenville, 1,059 .... D 4
† 29360 Watts Mills, 1,181 .... D 2
29385 Wellford, 1,298 .... C 2
29169 West Columbia, 7,838 .... E 4
29693 Westminster, 2,521 .... A 2
29669 West Pelzer, 861 .... B 2
29696 West Union, 388 .... B 2
29178 Whitmire, 2,226 .... D 3
29303 Whitney, 2,891 .... D 1
29697 Williamston, 3,991 .... B 2
29853 Williston, 2,594 .... E 5
29856 Windsor, 590 .... E 5
† 29501 Windy Hill, 1,671 .... H 3
29180 Winnsboro⊙, 3,411 .... E 3
† 29180 Winnsboro Mills, 2,312 .... E 3
29388 Woodruff, 4,576 .... D 2
29945 Yemassee, 745 .... F 6
29494 Yonges Island, 350 .... G 6
29745 York⊙, 5,081 .... E 1
† 29574 Zion, 400 .... J 3

⊙ County seat.
‡ Population of metropolitan area.
† Zip of nearest p.o.
* Multiple zips

Colorful materials being Sanforized in a South Carolina textile mill. Textiles are by far the most important of the state's industries.

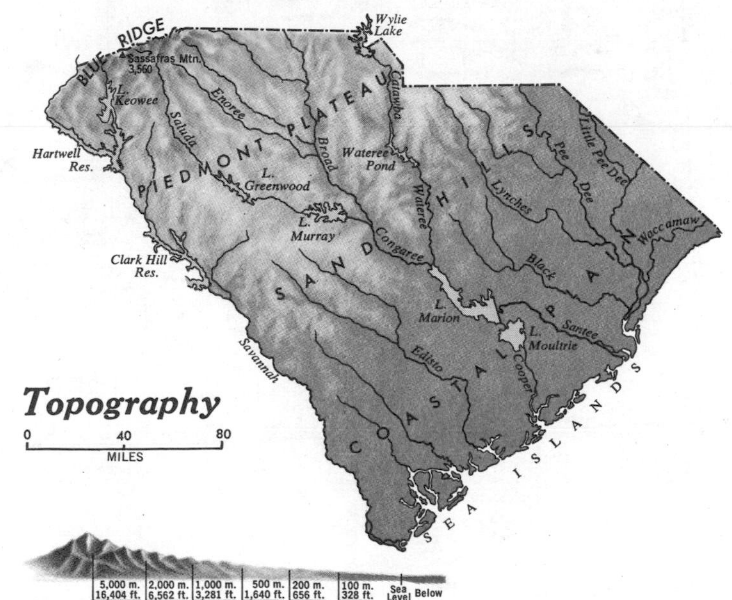

COUNTIES

County, Pop.	Key
Aurora, 4,183	M 6
Beadle, 20,877	N 5
Bennett, 3,088	F 7
Bon Homme, 8,577	O 7
Brookings, 22,158	R 5
Brown, 36,920	N 2
Brule, 5,870	L 6
Buffalo, 1,739	L 5
Butte, 7,825	B 4
Campbell, 2,866	J 2
Charles Mix, 9,994	M 7
Clark, 5,515	O 4
Clay, 12,923	P 8
Codington, 19,140	P 4
Corson, 4,994	G 2
Custer, 4,698	B 6
Davison, 17,319	N 6
Day, 8,713	O 3
Deuel, 5,686	R 4
Dewey, 5,170	G 3
Douglas, 4,569	N 7
Edmunds, 5,548	L 3
Fall River, 7,505	B 7
Faulk, 3,893	L 3
Grant, 9,005	R 3
Gregory, 6,710	L 7
Haakon, 2,802	F 5
Hamlin, 5,172	P 4
Hand, 5,883	L 4
Hanson, 3,781	O 6
Harding, 1,855	B 2
Hughes, 11,632	J 5
Hutchinson, 10,379	O 7
Hyde, 2,515	K 4
Jackson, 1,531	F 6
Jerauld, 3,310	M 5
Jones, 1,882	H 6
Kingsbury, 7,657	O 5
Lake, 11,456	P 5
Lawrence, 17,453	B 5
Lincoln, 11,761	R 7
Lyman, 4,060	J 6
Marshall, 5,965	O 2
McCook, 7,246	P 6
McPherson, 5,022	L 2
Meade, 16,618	D 5
Mellette, 2,420	H 6
Miner, 4,454	O 5
Minnehaha, 95,209	R 6
Moody, 7,622	R 5
Pennington, 59,349	C 6
Perkins, 4,769	D 3
Potter, 4,449	J 3
Roberts, 11,678	P 2
Sanborn, 3,697	N 5
Shannon, 8,198	D 7
Spink, 10,595	N 4
Stanley, 2,457	H 5
Sully, 2,362	J 4
Todd, 6,606	H 7
Tripp, 8,171	K 7
Turner, 9,872	P 7
Union, 9,643	R 8
Walworth, 7,842	J 3
Washabaugh, 1,389	F 6
Yankton, 19,039	P 7
Ziebach, 2,221	F 4

CITIES and TOWNS

	Zip	Name/Pop.	Key
	57401	Aberdeen⊙, 26,476	M 3
	57310	Academy, 17	M 7
	57520	Agar, 156	J 4
	57420	Akaska, 46	J 3
	57210	Albee, 26	S 3
	57001	Alcester, 627	R 7
	57311	Alexandria⊙, 598	O 6
	57714	Allen, 150	F 7
	57312	Alpena, 307	N 5
	57211	Altamont, 54	R 4
	57421	Amherst, 75	O 2
	57422	Andover, 138	O 3
	57715	Ardmore, 14	B 7
	57212	Arlington, 954	P 5
	57313	Armour⊙, 925	N 7
	57423	Artas, 73	K 2
	57314	Artesian, 277	O 6
	57424	Ashton, 137	N 3
	57213	Astoria, 153	S 4
	57425	Athol, 50	M 3
	57002	Aurora, 237	R 5
	57315	Avon, 610	N 8
	57214	Badger, 122	P 5
	57003	Baltic, 364	R 6
	57316	Bancroft, 48	O 4
	57426	Barnard, 72	N 2
	57716	Batesland, 135	E 7
	57427	Bath, 150	N 3
	57717	Belle Fourche⊙, 4,236	B 4
	57521	Belvidere, 96	G 6
	57215	Bemis, 28	R 4
	57004	Beresford, 1,655	R 7
	57216	Big Stone City, 631	S 3
†	57310	Bijou Hills, 12	L 6
	57620	Bison⊙, 406	E 2
	57718	Black Hawk, 550	C 5
	57522	Blunt, 445	J 4
	57317	Bonesteel, 354	M 7
	57318	Bonilla, 33	N 4
	57428	Bowdle, 667	K 3
	57719	Box Elder, 607	D 5
	57217	Bradley, 157	O 3
	57005	Brandon, 1,431	R 6
	57218	Brandt, 132	R 4
	57429	Brentford, 94	N 3
	57319	Bridgewater, 633	P 6
	57219	Bristol, 470	O 3
	57430	Britton⊙, 1,465	O 2
†	57350	Broadland, 45	N 4
	57006	Brookings⊙, 13,717	R 5
	57220	Bruce, 217	R 5
	57221	Bryant, 502	P 4
	57720	Buffalo⊙, 393	B 2
	57722	Buffalo Gap, 155	C 6
	57621	Bullhead, 449	G 2
	57010	Burbank, 96	R 8
	57523	Burke⊙, 892	L
	57011	Bushnell, 65	R
	57222	Butler, 38	O
	57724	Camp Crook, 150	B
	57012	Canistota, 636	P
	57524	Canning, 40	K
	57321	Canova, 204	O
	57013	Canton⊙, 2,665	R
	57725	Caputa, 43	D
†	57533	Carlock, 13	L
	57322	Carpenter, 50	O
	57526	Carter, 17	J
	57323	Carthage, 362	O
	57223	Castlewood, 523	R
	57324	Cavour, 134	N
†	57058	Center, 18	P
	57014	Centerville, 910	R
	57727	Central City, 188	B
	57325	Chamberlain⊙, 2,626	L
	57015	Chancellor, 220	R
	57431	Chelsea, 45	M
	57622	Cherry Creek, 275	F
	57016	Chester, 260	R
	57224	Claire City, 100	P
	57432	Claremont, 214	N
	57225	Clark⊙, 1,356	O

SOUTH DAKOTA

SCALE

0 5 10 20 40 60 MI.

0 5 10 20 40 60 KM.

State Capitals ⊛

County Seats ⊙

† 57332 Clayton, 13 .... O 7
57581 Clearfield, 20 .... K 7
57226 Clear Lake⊙, 1,157 .... R 4
57017 Colman, 456 .... R 6
57528 Colome, 375 .... K 7
57018 Colton, 601 .... P 6
57433 Columbia, 240 .... N 2
57434 Conde, 279 .... N 3
57227 Corona, 133 .... R 3
57328 Corsica, 615 .... N 7
57019 Corson, 101 .... R 6
57728 Cottonwood, 16 .... F 6
57228 Crandall, 17 .... O 3
57435 Cresbard, 224 .... M 3
57229 Crocker, 40 .... O 3
57020 Crooks, 200 .... R 6
57730 Custer⊙, 1,597 .... B 6
57529 Dallas, 233 .... K 7
57329 Dante, 88 .... N 7
57021 Davis, 101 .... P 7
57732 Deadwood⊙, 2,409 .... B 5
57022 Dell Rapids, 1,991 .... R 6
57330 Delmont, 260 .... N 7
57230 Dempster, 75 .... R 4
57231 De Smet⊙, 1,336 .... O 5
57331 Dimock, 167 .... O 7
57530 Dixon, 15 .... L 7
57436 Doland, 430 .... N 4
57023 Dolton, 60 .... P 7
57531 Draper, 200 .... J 6
57623 Dupree⊙, 523 .... F 3
57625 Eagle Butte, 530 .... G 4
57232 Eden, 132 .... P 2
57735 Edgemont. 1,174 .... B 7
57024 Egan, 281 .... R 6
57025 Elk Point⊙, 1,372 .... R 8
57026 Elkton, 541 .... S 5
57736 Elm Springs, 16 .... D 5
57332 Emery, 452 .... O 6
57737 Enning, 35 .... E 4
† 57321 Epiphany, 64 .... O 6
57233 Erwin, 106 .... P 5
57333 Esmond, 19 .... O 5
57234 Estelline, 276 .... R 4
57334 Ethan, 309 .... N 6
57437 Eureka, 1,547 .... K 2
57738 Fairburn, 50 .... C 6
57335 Fairfax, 199 .... M 7
57027 Fairview, 72 .... R 7
57626 Faith, 576 .... E 4
57336 Farmer, 58 .... O 6
57740 Farmingdale, 30 .... D 6
57438 Faulkton⊙, 955 .... L 3
57337 Fedora, 75 .... O 5
57439 Ferney, 72 .... N 3
57628 Firesteel, 17 .... G 3
57028 Flandreau⊙, 2,027 .... R 5
57235 Florence, 175 .... P 3
57338 Forestburg, 150 .... N 5
57741 Fort Meade, 900 .... C 5
57532 Fort Pierre⊙, 1,448 .... H 5
57339 Fort Thompson, 750 .... L 5
57440 Frankfort, 192 .... N 4
† 57042 Franklin, 14 .... P 6
57441 Frederick, 359 .... N 2
57029 Freeman, 1,357 .... O 7
57742 Fruitdale, 74 .... B 4
57340 Fulton, 101 .... O 6
57341 Gannvalley⊙, 80 .... L 5
57236 Garden City, 126 .... O 4
57030 Garretson, 847 .... S 6
57237 Gary, 366 .... S 4
57031 Gayville, 269 .... P 8
57342 Geddes, 308 .... M 7
57442 Gettysburg⊙, 1,915 .... K 3
57630 Glencross, 75 .... H 3
57631 Glenham, 178 .... J 2
57238 Goodwin, 114 .... R 4

(continued on following page)

AREA 77,047 sq. mi.
POPULATION 666,257
CAPITAL Pierre
LARGEST CITY Sioux Falls
HIGHEST POINT Harney Pk. 7,242 ft.
SETTLED IN 1856
ADMITTED TO UNION November 2, 1889
POPULAR NAME Coyote State; Sunshine State
STATE FLOWER Pasqueflower
STATE BIRD Ring-necked Pheasant

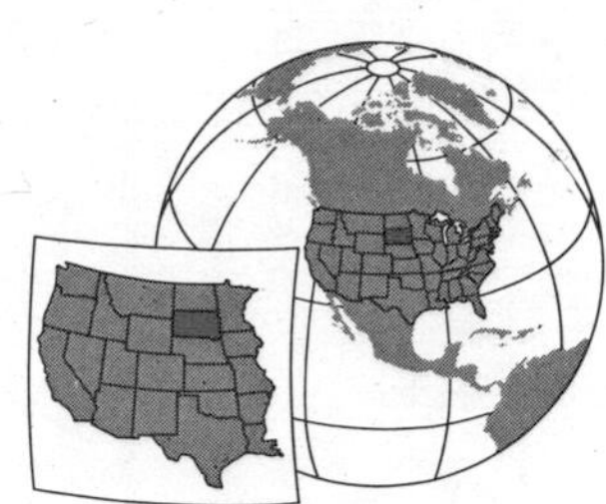

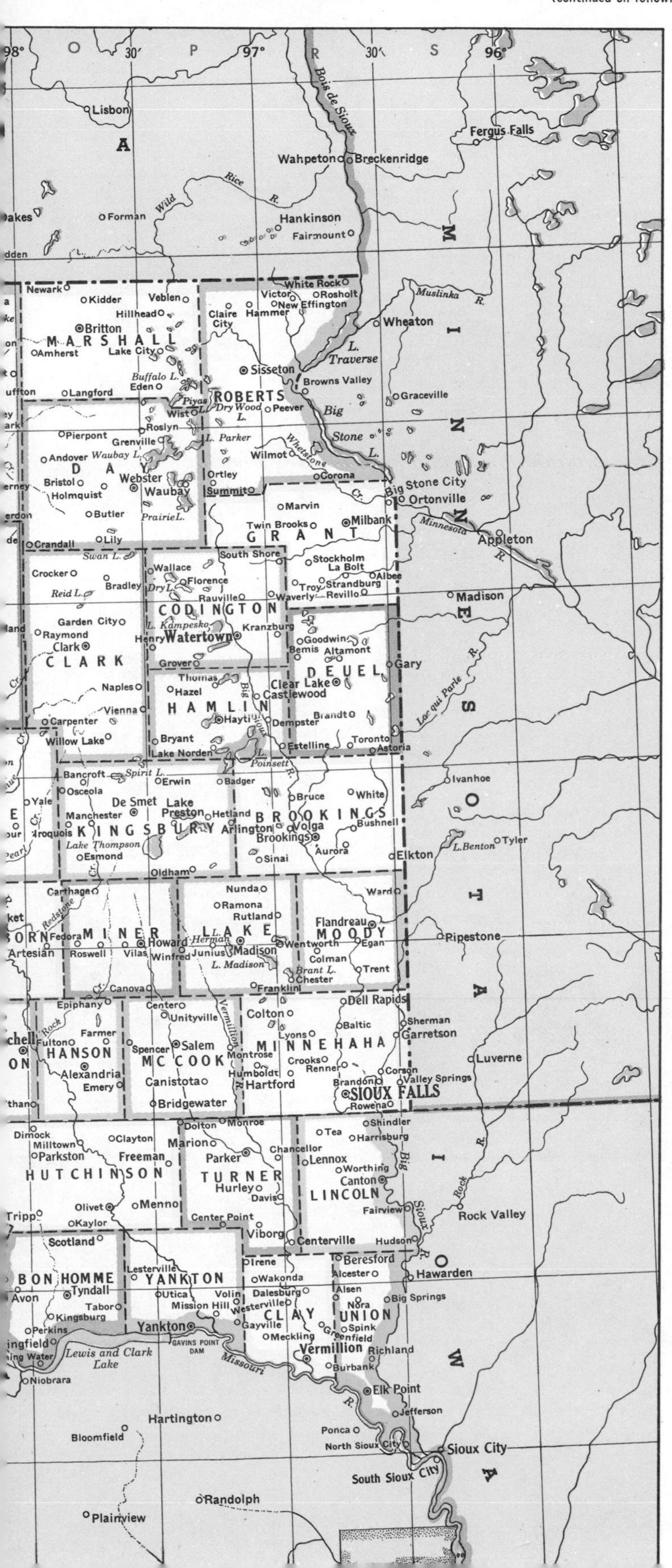

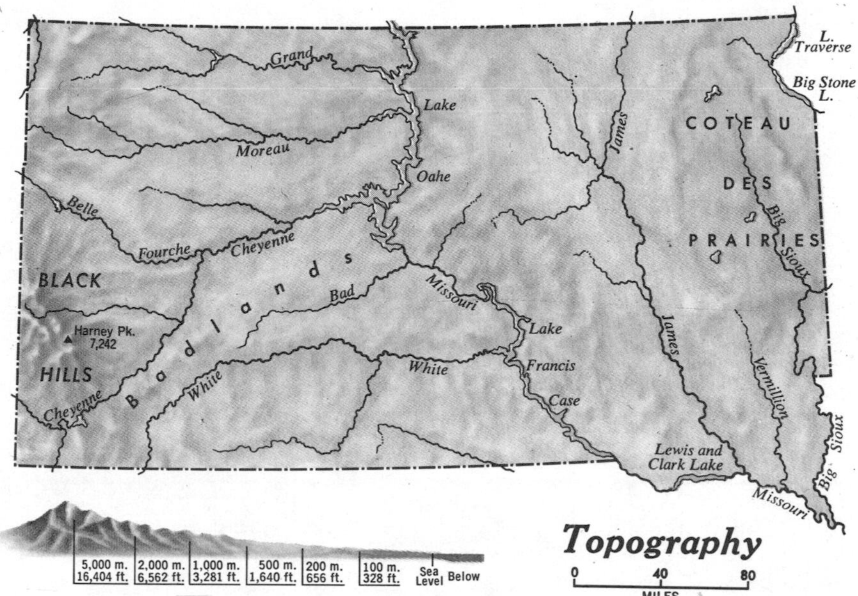

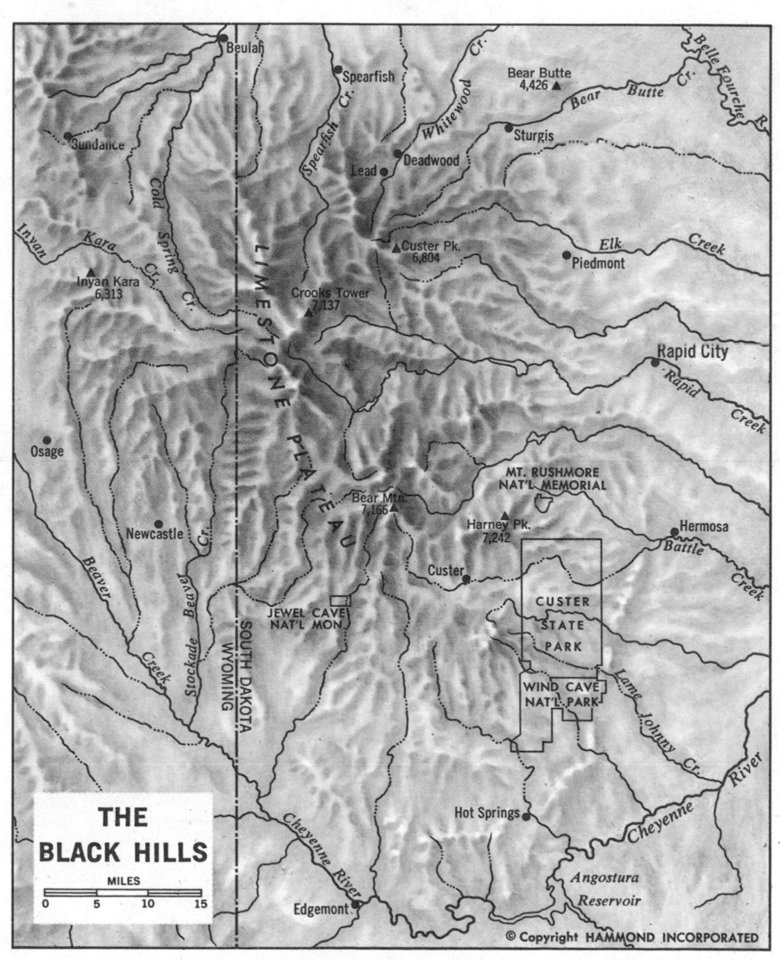

† 57010 Greenfield, 12 ... R 8
† 57380 Greenwood, 90 ... N 8
57533 Gregory, 1,756 ... L 7
57239 Grenville, 154 ... O 3
57445 Groton, 1,021 ... N 3
† 57201 Grover, 12 ... P 4
57534 Hamill, 57 ... K 6
57240 Hammer, 30 ... R 2
57535 Harrington, 54 ... G 7
57032 Harrisburg, 338 ... R 7
57344 Harrison, 68 ... M 7
57536 Harrold, 184 ... K 4
57033 Hartford, 800 ... P 6
57537 Hayes, 28 ... H 5
57241 Hayti⊙, 393 ... P 4
57242 Hazel, 101 ... P 4
57446 Hecla, 407 ... N 2
57243 Henry, 182 ... P 4
57744 Hermosa, 150 ... C 6
57632 Herreid, 672 ... K 2
57538 Herrick, 126 ... L 7
57244 Hetland, 81 ... P 5
† 69501 Hidden Timber, 30 ... J 7
57345 Highmore⊙, 1,173 ... L 4
57745 Hill City, 389 ... B 6
† 57270 Hillhead, 26 ... O 2
† 57437 Hillsview, 19 ... L 2
† 57701 Hisega, 36 ... C 5
57348 Hitchcock, 150 ... M 4
57540 Holabird, 32 ... K 4
† 57274 Holmquist, 13 ... O 3
57448 Hosmer, 437 ... L 2
57747 Hot Springs⊙, 4,434 ... C 7
57449 Houghton, 90 ... N 2
57450 Hoven, 671 ... K 3
57349 Howard⊙, 1,175 ... P 5
57034 Hudson, 366 ... R 7
57035 Humboldt, 411 ... P 6
57036 Hurley, 399 ... P 7
57350 Huron⊙, 14,299 ... N 5
57541 Ideal, 135 ... K 6
† 57774 Igloo, 20 ... B 7
57750 Interior, 81 ... F 6
57451 Ipswich⊙, 1,187 ... L 3
57037 Irene, 461 ... P 7
57353 Iroquois, 375 ... O 5
57633 Isabel, 394 ... G 3
57452 Java, 305 ... K 3
57038 Jefferson, 474 ... S 8
† 57042 Junius, 50 ... P 6
57543 Kadoka⊙, 815 ... F 6
57354 Kaylor, 110 ... O 7
57634 Keldron, 35 ... F 2
57642 Kenel, 245 ... H 2
57544 Kennebec⊙, 372 ... K 6
57751 Keystone, 475 ... C 6
57453 Kidder, 140 ... O 2
57355 Kimball, 825 ... M 6
57245 Kranzburg, 143 ... R 4
57752 Kyle, 500 ... E 7
57246 La Bolt, 90 ... R 3
57356 Lake Andes⊙, 948 ... M 7
57247 Lake City, 44 ... O 2
57248 Lake Norden, 393 ... P 4
57249 Lake Preston, 812 ... P 5
57358 Lane, 94 ... N 5
57454 Langford, 328 ... O 2
57636 Lantry, 52 ... G 3
57637 La Plant, 165 ... H 3
57754 Lead, 5,420 ... B 5
57455 Lebanon, 182 ... K 3
57638 Lemmon, 1,997 ... E 2
57039 Lennox, 1,487 ... R 7
57456 Leola⊙, 787 ... M 2
57040 Lesterville, 181 ... O 7
57359 Letcher, 201 ... N 6
57250 Lily, 62 ... O 3
57639 Little Eagle, 975 ... H 2
57640 Lodgepole, 25 ... D 2
57457 Longlake, 128 ... L 2
57547 Longvalley, 16 ... F 7
57360 Loomis, 150 ... N 6
57548 Lower Brule, 500 ... K 5
57458 Lowry, 35 ... K 3
57549 Lucas, 13 ... L 7
† 57569 Lyman, 15 ... K 6
57041 Lyons, 89 ... R 6
57042 Madison⊙, 6,315 ... P 6
57643 Mahto, 23 ... H 2
† 57353 Manchester, 25 ... O 5
57756 Manderson, 350 ... D 7
57460 Mansfield, 150 ... N 3
57043 Marion, 844 ... P 7
57551 Martin⊙, 1,248 ... F 7
57361 Marty, 225 ... N 8
57251 Marvin, 65 ... R 3
57627 Maurine, 12 ... E 3
57641 McIntosh⊙, 563 ... G 2
57642 McLaughlin, 863 ... H 2
57044 Meckling, 100 ... R 8
57461 Mellette, 199 ... N 3
57045 Menno, 796 ... P 7
57552 Midland, 270 ... G 5
57252 Milbank⊙, 3,727 ... R 3
57362 Miller⊙, 2,148 ... L 4
† 57366 Milltown, 28 ... O 7
57462 Mina, 18 ... M 3
57463 Miranda, 60 ... M 4
57555 Mission, 739 ... H 7
57046 Mission Hill, 161 ... P 8
57301 Mitchell⊙, 13,425 ... N 6
57601 Mobridge, 4,545 ... J 2
57047 Monroe, 134 ... P 7
57048 Montrose, 377 ... P 6
57645 Morristown, 144 ... F 2
57558 Mosher, 19 ... J 7
57646 Mound City⊙, 164 ... K 2
57363 Mount Vernon, 398 ... N 6
57559 Murdo⊙, 865 ... H 6
† 57778 Mystic, 16 ... B 5
57254 Naples, 38 ... O 4
57759 Nemo, 100 ... B 5
† 57453 Newark, 25 ... O 2
57255 New Effington, 258 ... R 2
57760 Newell, 664 ... C 4
57364 New Holland, 131 ... M 7
57761 New Underwood, 416 ... D 5
† 57584 New Witten, 102 ... K 7

Agriculture, Industry and Resources

DOMINANT LAND USE

- Specialized Wheat
- Wheat, General Farming
- Wheat, Range Livestock
- Cattle Feed, Hogs
- Livestock, Cash Grain
- General Farming, Livestock, Special Crops
- Range Livestock
- Forests

ϟ Water Power

MAJOR MINERAL OCCURRENCES

Ag	Silver	Mi	Mica
Au	Gold	O	Petroleum
Be	Beryl	U	Uranium
Gn	Granite	V	Vanadium

57762 Nisland, 157 ... C 4
57560 Norris, 42 ... G 7
† 57625 North Eagle Butte, 1,351 ... G 3
57049 North Sioux City, 860 ... R 8
57465 Northville, 119 ... M 3
57050 Nunda, 85 ... P 5
57365 Oacoma, 215 ... L 6
57763 Oelrichs, 94 ... C 7
57764 Oglala, 250 ... D 7
57562 Okaton, 65 ... H 6
† 57501 Okobojo, 15 ... J 4
57563 Okreek, 300 ... J 7
57051 Oldham, 244 ... P 5
57052 Olivet⊙, 103 ... O 7
57466 Onaka, 69 ... L 3
57564 Onida⊙, 785 ... K 4
57766 Oral, 45 ... C 7
57467 Orient, 131 ... L 4
57256 Ortley, 111 ... P 3
† 57353 Osceola, 32 ... O 5
57053 Parker⊙, 1,005 ... P 7
57366 Parkston, 1,611 ... O 7
57566 Parmelee, 475 ... G 7
† 57529 Paxton, 18 ... L 7
† 57729 Pedro, 15 ... E 5
57257 Peever, 202 ... R 2
57567 Philip⊙, 983 ... F 5
57367 Pickstown, 300 ... M 7
57769 Piedmont, 650 ... C 5
57468 Pierpont, 241 ... O 3
57501 Pierre (cap.)⊙, 9,699 ... J 5
57770 Pine Ridge, 2,768 ... E 7
57368 Plankinton⊙, 613 ... N 6
57369 Platte, 1,351 ... M 7
57648 Pollock, 341 ... J 2
57772 Porcupine, 200 ... E 7
† 57750 Potato Creek, 40 ... F 6
57649 Prairie City, 55 ... D 2
57568 Presho, 922 ... J 6
57773 Pringle, 86 ... B 6
57774 Provo, 45 ... B 7
57370 Pukwana, 208 ... L 6
57402 Putney, 24 ... N 2
57775 Quinn, 105 ... E 5
57054 Ramona, 227 ... P 5
57701 Rapid City⊙, 43,836 ... C 5
57357 Ravinia, 109 ... N 7
57258 Raymond, 114 ... O 4
57469 Redfield⊙, 2,943 ... N 4
57776 Redig, 13 ... C 3
57777 Redowl, 14 ... D 4
57371 Ree Heights, 183 ... L 4
57569 Reliance, 204 ... K 6
57055 Renner, 260 ... R 6
57259 Revillo, 142 ... R 3
† 57025 Richland, 70 ... R 8
57652 Ridgeview, 65 ... H 3
57778 Rochford, 20 ... B 5
57701 Rockerville, 48 ... C 6
57470 Rockham, 60 ... M 4
† 57772 Rockyford, 50 ... E 7
57471 Roscoe, 398 ... L 3
57570 Rosebud, 650 ... H 7
57260 Rosholt, 456 ... R 2
57261 Roslyn, 250 ... P 2
57372 Roswell, 32 ... O 6
57056 Rowena, 76 ... R 6
57057 Rutland, 100 ... P 5
57571 Saint Charles, 33 ... L 7
57572 Saint Francis, 300 ... H 7
57373 Saint Lawrence, 249 ... M 4
57779 Saint Onge, 200 ... B 4
57058 Salem⊙, 1,391 ... P 6
† 57730 Sanator, 150 ... B 6
† 57754 Savoy, 15 ... B 5
57780 Scenic, 56 ... D 6
57059 Scotland, 984 ... O 7
57472 Selby⊙, 957 ... J 3
57473 Seneca, 118 ... L 3

57653 Shadehill, 186 ... E 2
57060 Sherman, 82 ... S 6
† 57101 Shindler, 20 ... R 7
57781 Silver City, 40 ... B 5
57061 Sinai, 147 ... P 5
* 57101 Sioux Falls⊙, 72,488 ... R 6
Sioux Falls, ‡95,209 ... R 6
57262 Sisseton⊙, 3,094 ... R 2
57782 Smithwick, 25 ... C 7
57263 South Shore, 199 ... P 3
57783 Spearfish, 4,661 ... B 5
57374 Spencer, 385 ... O 6
† 57010 Spink, 21 ... R 8
57062 Springfield, 1,566 ... N 8
57346 Stephan, 60 ... K 5
57375 Stickney, 421 ... M 6
57264 Stockholm, 116 ... R 3
† 57359 Storla, 75 ... M 6
57265 Strandburg, 98 ... R 3
57474 Stratford, 106 ... N 3
57785 Sturgis⊙, 4,536 ... B 5
57266 Summit, 332 ... P 3
† 57551 Swett, 20 ... E 7
57063 Tabor, 388 ... O 8
† 57433 Tacoma Park, 18 ... N 2
57064 Tea, 302 ... R 7
† 57242 Thomas, 15 ... P 4

57655 Thunder Hawk, 45 ... F 2
† 57769 Tilford, 162 ... C 5
57656 Timber Lake⊙, 625 ... H 3
57475 Tolstoy, 99 ... K 3
57268 Toronto, 216 ... R 4
57657 Trail City, 75 ... H 3
57065 Trent, 177 ... R 6
57376 Tripp, 851 ... N 7
† 57754 Trojan, 25 ... B 5
† 57265 Troy, 13 ... R 3
57476 Tulare, 211 ... N 4
57477 Turton, 121 ... N 3
57574 Tuthill, 73 ... G 7
57269 Twin Brooks, 122 ... R 3
57066 Tyndall⊙, 1,245 ... O 8
57787 Union Center, 50 ... D 4
† 57058 Unityville, 30 ... P 6
57067 Utica, 89 ... P 8
57788 Vale, 89 ... C 4
57068 Valley Springs, 566 ... S 6
57270 Veblen, 377 ... P 2
57478 Verdon, 18 ... N 3
57069 Vermillion⊙, 9,128 ... R 8
57575 Vetal, 17 ... G 7
57070 Viborg, 662 ... P 7
† 57260 Victor, 22 ... R 2
57271 Vienna, 119 ... O 4

† 57349 Vilas, 33 ... O 6
† 57701 Villa Ranchaero 3,171 ... C 5
57379 Virgil, 43 ... N 5
57576 Vivian, 200 ... J 6
57071 Volga, 982 ... R 5
57072 Volin, 157 ... P 8
57380 Wagner, 1,655 ... N 7
57073 Wakonda, 290 ... P 7
57658 Wakpala, 500 ... H 2
57790 Wall, 786 ... E 6
57272 Wallace, 95 ... P 3
57577 Wanblee, 500 ... F 6
57074 Ward, 57 ... R 5
57479 Warner, 175 ... M 3
57791 Wasta, 127 ... D 5
57660 Watauga, 76 ... F 2
57201 Watertown⊙, 13,388 ... P 4
57273 Waubay, 696 ... P 3
57202 Waverly, 40 ... R 3
57274 Webster⊙, 2,252 ... P 3
57480 Wecota, 50 ... L 3
† 57532 Wendte, 20 ... H 5
57075 Wentworth, 196 ... R 6
57881 Wessington, 380 ... M 5
57382 Wessington Springs⊙, 1,300 ... M 5

57481 Westport, 136 ... M 2
57482 Wetonka, 31 ... M 2
57578 Wewela, 16 ... K 7
57276 White, 418 ... R 5
† 57638 White Butte, 15 ... E 2
57661 Whitehorse, 100 ... H 3
57383 White Lake, 395 ... M 6
57579 White River⊙, 617 ... H 6
57277 White Rock, 35 ... R 2
57793 Whitewood, 689 ... B 5
57278 Willow Lake, 353 ... O 4
57279 Wilmot, 518 ... R 3
57076 Winfred, 110 ... P 6
57580 Winner⊙, 3,789 ... K 7
57584 Witten, 140 ... J 7
57384 Wolsey, 436 ... N 5
57585 Wood, 132 ... J 6
57385 Woonsocket⊙, 852 ... N 5
57077 Worthing, 294 ... R 7
57794 Wounded Knee, 500 ... D 7
57386 Yale, 148 ... O 5
57078 Yankton⊙, 11,919 ... P 8
57483 Zell, 87 ... M 4

⊙ County seat.
‡ Population of metropolitan area.
† Zip of nearest p.o.
* Multiple zips

E. C. Werner — Shostal Associates

Beds of fossils await paleontologists in the vast, semi-arid buttes of the Badlands, east of the Black Hills of South Dakota.

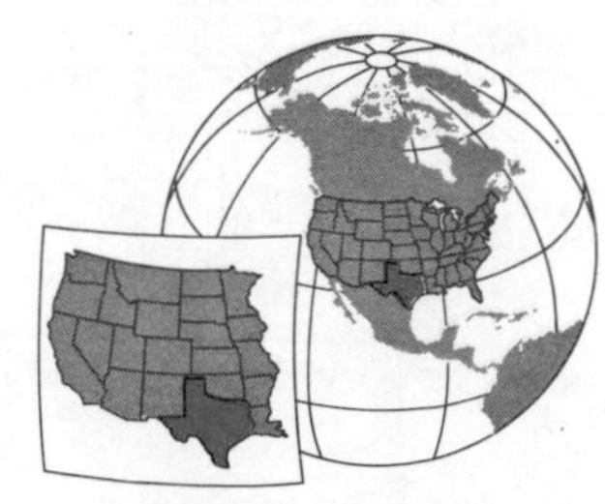

AREA 267,339 sq. mi.
POPULATION 11,196,730
CAPITAL Austin
LARGEST CITY Houston
HIGHEST POINT Guadalupe Pk. 8,751 ft.
SETTLED IN 1686
ADMITTED TO UNION December 29, 1845
POPULAR NAME Lone Star State
STATE FLOWER Bluebonnet
STATE BIRD Mockingbird

COUNTIES

County, Pop.	Key
Anderson, 27,789	J 6
Andrews, 10,372	B 5
Angelina, 49,349	K 6
Aransas, 8,902	H 10
Archer, 5,759	F 4
Armstrong, 1,895	C 3
Atascosa, 18,696	F 9
Austin, 13,831	H 8
Bailey, 8,487	B 3
Bandera, 4,747	E 8
Bastrop, 17,297	G 7
Baylor, 5,221	E 4
Bee, 22,737	G 9
Bell, 124,483	G 6
Bexar, 830,460	F 8
Blanco, 3,567	F 7
Borden, 888	C 5
Bosque, 10,966	G 6
Bowie, 67,813	K 4
Brazoria, 108,312	J 8
Brazos, 57,978	H 7
Brewster, 7,780	A 8
Briscoe, 2,794	C 3
Brooks, 8,005	F 11
Brown, 25,877	F 6
Burleson, 9,999	H 7
Burnet, 11,420	F 7
Caldwell, 21,178	G 8
Calhoun, 17,831	H 9
Callahan, 8,205	E 5
Cameron, 140,368	G 11
Camp, 8,005	K 5
Carson, 6,358	C 2
Cass, 24,133	K 4
Castro, 10,394	B 3
Chambers, 12,187	K 8
Cherokee, 32,008	J 6
Childress, 6,605	D 3
Clay, 8,079	F 4
Cochran, 5,326	B 4
Coke, 3,087	D 6
Coleman, 10,288	E 6
Collin, 66,920	H 4
Collingsworth, 4,755	D 3
Colorado, 17,638	H 8
Comal, 24,165	F 8
Comanche, 11,898	F 5
Concho, 2,937	E 6
Cooke, 23,471	G 4
Coryell, 35,311	G 6
Cottle, 3,204	D 3
Crane, 4,172	B 6
Crockett, 3,885	C 7
Crosby, 9,085	C 4
Culberson, 3,429	C 11
Dallam, 6,012	B 1
Dallas, 1,327,321	H 5
Dawson, 16,604	C 5
Deaf Smith, 18,999	B 3
Delta, 4,927	J 4
Denton, 75,633	G 4
De Witt, 18,660	G 9
Dickens, 3,737	D 4
Dimmit, 9,039	E 9
Donley, 3,641	D 2
Duval, 11,722	F 10
Eastland, 18,092	F 5
Ector, 91,805	B 6
Edwards, 2,107	D 7
Ellis, 46,638	H 5
El Paso, 359,291	A 10
Erath, 18,141	F 5
Falls, 17,300	H 6
Fannin, 22,705	H 4
Fayette, 17,650	H 8
Fisher, 6,344	D 5
Floyd, 11,044	C 3
Foard, 2,211	E 3
Fort Bend, 52,314	J 8
Franklin, 5,291	J 4
Freestone, 11,116	H 6
Frio, 11,159	E 9
Gaines, 11,593	B 5
Galveston, 169,812	K 8
Garza, 5,289	C 4
Gillespie, 10,553	F 7
Glasscock, 1,155	C 6
Goliad, 4,869	G 9
Gonzales, 16,375	G 8
Gray, 26,949	D 2
Grayson, 83,225	H 4
Gregg, 75,929	K 5
Grimes, 11,855	J 7
Guadalupe, 33,554	G 8
Hale, 34,137	C 3
Hall, 6,015	D 3
Hamilton, 7,198	F 6
Hansford, 6,351	C 1
Hardeman, 6,795	E 3
Hardin, 29,996	K 7
Harris, 1,741,912	J 8
Harrison, 44,841	K 5
Hartley, 2,782	B 2
Haskell, 8,512	E 4
Hays, 27,642	F 7
Hemphill, 3,084	D 2
Henderson, 26,466	J 5
Hidalgo, 181,535	F 11
Hill, 22,596	G 5
Hockley, 20,396	B 4
Hood, 6,368	G 5
Hopkins, 20,710	J 4
Houston, 17,855	J 6
Howard, 37,796	C 5
Hudspeth, 2,392	B 10
Hunt, 47,948	H 4
Hutchinson, 24,443	C 2
Irion, 1,070	C 6
Jack, 6,711	F 4
Jackson, 12,975	H 9
Jasper, 24,692	K 7
Jeff Davis, 1,527	C 11
Jefferson, 244,773	K 8
Jim Hogg, 4,654	F 11
Jim Wells, 33,032	F 10
Johnson, 45,769	G 5
Jones, 16,106	E 5
Karnes, 13,462	G 9
Kaufman, 32,392	H 5
Kendall, 6,964	F 8
Kenedy, 678	G 11
Kent, 1,434	D 4
Kerr, 19,454	E 7
Kimble, 3,904	E 7
King, 464	D 4
Kinney, 2,006	D 8
Kleberg, 33,166	G 10
Knox, 5,972	E 4
Lamar, 36,062	J 4
Lamb, 17,770	B 3
Lampasas, 9,323	F 6
La Salle, 5,014	E 9
Lavaca, 17,903	H 8
Lee, 8,048	H 7
Leon, 8,738	J 6
Liberty, 33,014	K 7
Limestone, 18,100	H 6
Lipscomb, 3,486	D 1
Live Oak, 6,697	F 9
Llano, 6,979	F 7
Loving, 164	D 10
Lubbock, 179,295	C 4
Lynn, 9,107	C 4
Madison, 7,693	J 6
Marion, 8,517	K 5
Martin, 4,774	C 5
Mason, 3,356	E 7
Matagorda, 27,913	H 9
Maverick, 18,093	D 9
McCulloch, 8,571	E 6
McLennan, 147,553	G 6
McMullen, 1,095	F 9
Medina, 20,249	E 8
Menard, 2,646	E 7
Midland, 65,433	B 6
Milam, 20,028	H 7
Mills, 4,212	F 6
Mitchell, 9,073	D 5
Montague, 15,326	G 4
Montgomery, 49,479	J 7
Moore, 14,060	C 2
Morris, 12,310	K 4
Motley, 2,178	D 3
Nacogdoches, 36,362	K 6
Navarro, 31,150	H 5
Newton, 11,657	L 7
Nolan, 16,220	D 5
Nueces, 237,544	G 10
Ochiltree, 9,704	D 1
Oldham, 2,258	B 2
Orange, 71,170	L 7
Palo Pinto, 28,962	F 5
Panola, 15,894	K 5
Parker, 33,888	G 5
Parmer, 10,509	B 3
Pecos, 13,748	B 7
Polk, 14,457	K 7
Potter, 90,511	C 2
Presidio, 4,842	C 12
Rains, 3,752	J 5
Randall, 53,885	C 2
Reagan, 3,239	C 6
Real, 2,013	E 8
Red River, 14,298	J 4
Reeves, 16,526	D 11
Refugio, 9,494	G 9
Roberts, 967	D 2
Robertson, 14,389	H 6
Rockwall, 7,046	H 5
Runnels, 12,108	E 6
Rusk, 34,102	K 5
Sabine, 7,187	L 6
San Augustine, 7,858	K 6
San Jacinto, 6,702	J 7
San Patricio, 47,288	G 10
San Saba, 5,540	F 6
Schleicher, 2,277	D 7
Scurry, 15,760	D 5
Shackelford, 3,323	E 5
Shelby, 19,672	K 6
Sherman, 3,657	C 1
Smith, 97,096	J 5
Somervell, 2,793	G 5
Starr, 17,707	F 11
Stephens, 8,414	F 5
Sterling, 1,056	C 6
Stonewall, 2,397	D 4
Sutton, 3,175	D 7
Swisher, 10,373	C 3
Tarrant, 716,317	G 5
Taylor, 97,853	E 5
Terrell, 1,940	B 7
Terry, 14,118	B 4
Throckmorton, 2,205	E 4
Titus, 16,702	K 4
Tom Green, 71,047	D 6
Travis, 295,516	G 7
Trinity, 7,628	J 6
Tyler, 12,417	K 7
Upshur, 20,976	K 5
Upton, 4,697	B 6
Uvalde, 17,348	E 8
Val Verde, 27,471	C 8
Van Zandt, 22,155	J 5
Victoria, 53,766	H 9
Walker, 27,680	J 7
Waller, 14,285	J 8
Ward, 13,019	A 6
Washington, 18,842	H 7
Webb, 72,859	E 10
Wharton, 36,729	H 8
Wheeler, 6,434	D 2
Wichita, 121,862	F 3
Wilbarger, 15,355	E 3
Willacy, 15,570	G 11
Williamson, 37,305	G 7
Wilson, 13,041	F 8
Winkler, 9,640	A 6
Wise, 19,687	G 4
Wood, 18,589	J 5
Yoakum, 7,344	B 4
Young, 15,400	F 4
Zapata, 4,352	E 11
Zavala, 11,370	E 9

CITIES and TOWNS

	Zip	Name/Pop.	Key
	79311	Abernathy, 2,625	B 4
*	79601	Abilene⊙, 89,653	E 5
		Abilene, ‡113,959	E 5
	78516	Alamo, 4,291	F 11
	78209	Alamo Heights, 6,933	F 8
	76430	Albany⊙, 1,978	E 5
	78332	Alice⊙, 20,121	F 10
	79830	Alpine⊙, 5,971	D 11
	77510	Alta Loma, 1,536	K 3
	75925	Alto, 1,045	J 6
	76009	Alvarado, 2,129	G 5
	77511	Alvin, 10,671	J 3
*	79101	Amarillo⊙, 127,010	C 2
		Amarillo, ‡144,396	C 2
	77514	Anahuac⊙, 1,881	K 8
	77830	Anderson⊙, 500	J 7
	79714	Andrews⊙, 8,625	B 5
	77515	Angleton⊙, 9,770	J 8
	79501	Anson⊙, 2,615	E 5
	88021	Anthony, 2,154	A 10
	79313	Anton, 1,034	B 4
	78336	Aransas Pass, 5,813	G 10
	77517	Arcadia, 1,200	K 3
	76351	Archer City⊙, 1,722	F 4
*	76010	Arlington, 90,643	F 2
	78827	Asherton, 1,645	E 9
	79502	Aspermont⊙, 1,198	D 4
	75751	Athens⊙, 9,582	J 5
	75551	Atlanta, 5,007	K 4
*	78701	Austin (cap.)⊙, 251,808	G 7
		Austin, ‡295,516	G 7
	76020	Azle, 4,493	E 1
	77518	Bacliff, 1,900	K 2
	79504	Baird⊙, 1,538	E 5
	75149	Balch Springs, 10,464	H 2
	76821	Ballinger⊙, 4,203	E 6
	78003	Bandera⊙, 891	F 8
	76823	Bangs, 1,214	E 6
	77532	Barrett, 2,750	K 1
	76511	Bartlett, 1,622	G 7
	78602	Bastrop⊙, 3,112	G 7
	77414	Bay City⊙, 11,733	H 9
	77520	Baytown, 43,980	L 2
	77701	Beaumont⊙, 115,919	K 7
		Beaumont-Port Arthur-Orange, ‡315,943	K 7
	76021	Bedford, 10,049	F 2
	78102	Beeville⊙, 13,506	G 9
	77401	Bellaire, 19,009	J 2
	76705	Bellmead, 7,698	H 6
	77418	Bellville⊙, 2,371	H 8
	76513	Belton⊙, 8,696	G 7
	78341	Benavides, 2,112	F 10
	76126	Benbrook, 8,169	E 2
	79505	Benjamin⊙, 308	E 4
	76932	Big Lake⊙, 2,489	C 6
	79720	Big Spring⊙, 28,735	C 5
	78343	Bishop, 3,466	G 10
	77951	Bloomington, 1,676	H 9
	76131	Blue Mound, 1,283	F 1
	78006	Boerne⊙, 2,432	F 8
	75417	Bogata, 1,287	J 4
	75418	Bonham⊙, 7,698	H 4
	79007	Borger, 14,195	C 2
	75557	Boston⊙, 500	K 4
	79009	Bovina, 1,428	A 3
	76230	Bowie, 5,185	G 4
	78832	Brackettville⊙, 1,539	D 8
	76825	Brady⊙, 5,557	E 6
	77422	Brazoria, 1,681	J 9
	76024	Breckenridge⊙, 5,944	F 5
	77833	Brenham⊙, 8,922	H 7
	77611	Bridge City, 8,164	L 7
	76026	Bridgeport, 3,614	G 4
	77423	Brookshire, 1,683	J 8
	77581	Brookside Village, 1,507	J 2
	79316	Brownfield⊙, 9,647	B 4
	78520	Brownsville⊙, 52,522	G 12
		Brownsville-Harlingen-San Benito, ‡140,368	G 12
	76801	Brownwood⊙, 17,368	F 6
	77801	Bryan⊙, 33,719	H 7
		Bryan-College Station, ‡57,978	H 7
	75831	Buffalo, 1,242	J 6
	77612	Buna, 1,649	L 7
†	79007	Bunavista, 1,402	C 2
†	77001	Bunker Hill Village, 3,977	J 1
	76354	Burkburnett, 9,230	F 3
	76028	Burleson, 7,713	F 2
	78611	Burnet⊙, 2,864	F 7
	77836	Caldwell⊙, 2,308	H 7
	77837	Calvert, 2,072	H 7
	76520	Cameron⊙, 5,546	H 7
	79014	Canadian⊙, 2,292	D 2
	75103	Canton⊙, 2,283	J 5
	79835	Canutillo, 1,588	A 10
	79015	Canyon⊙, 8,333	C 3

(continued on following page)

Agriculture, Industry and Resources

DOMINANT LAND USE

- Wheat, Grain Sorghums, Range Livestock
- Cotton, Wheat
- Specialized Cotton
- Cotton, General Farming
- Cotton, Forest Products
- Cotton, Range Livestock
- Rice, General Farming
- Peanuts, General Farming
- General Farming, Livestock, Cash Grain
- General Farming, Forest Products, Truck Farming, Cotton
- Fruit, Truck and Mixed Farming
- Range Livestock
- Forests
- Swampland, Limited Agriculture
- Nonagricultural Land
- Urban Areas

MAJOR MINERAL OCCURRENCES

- At Asphalt
- Cl Clay
- Fe Iron Ore
- G Natural Gas
- Gn Granite
- Gp Gypsum
- Gr Graphite
- He Helium
- Ls Limestone
- Na Salt
- O Petroleum
- S Sulfur
- Tc Talc
- U Uranium

Water Power

Major Industrial Areas

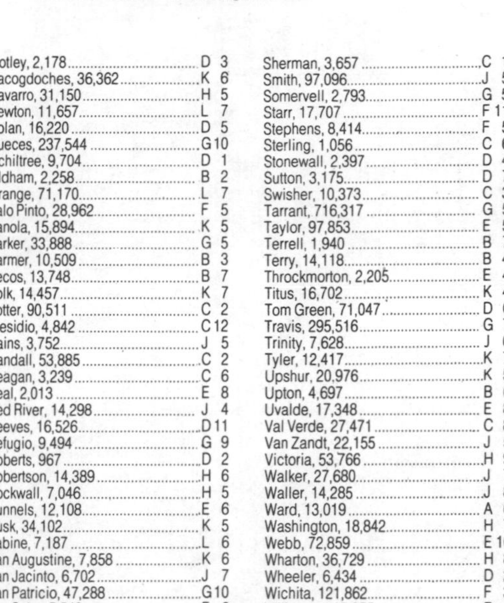

TEXAS
State Capitals
County Seats
© C.S. HAMMOND & Co., N.Y.
Longitude West of Greenwich
NEW MEXICO
OKLAHOMA
ARKANSAS
LOUISIANA
MEXICO
GULF OF MEXICO
FORT WORTH
DALLAS
HOUSTON
WESTERN PART OF TEXAS
Same scale as main map
STOCKTON PLATEAU
BALCONES ESCARPMENT
SERRANIAS DEL BURRO
BIG BEND NATIONAL PARK
PADRE ISLAND NATIONAL SEASHORE
Austin
San Antonio
El Paso
Amarillo
Lubbock
Corpus Christi
Galveston
Beaumont
Wichita Falls
Abilene
San Angelo
Laredo
Brownsville
Waco

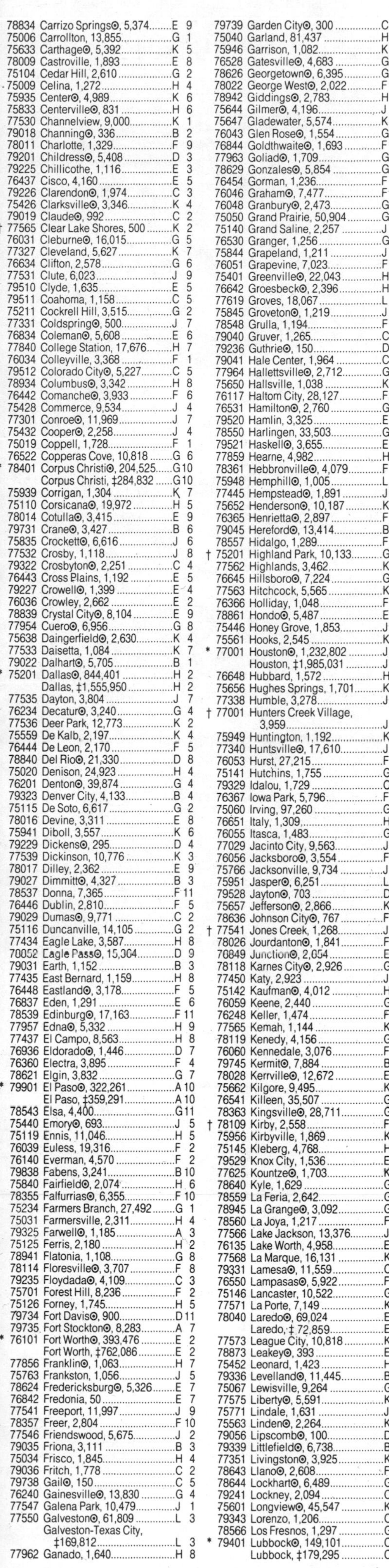

78834 Carrizo Springs⊙, 5,374 E 9
75006 Carrollton, 13,855 G 1
75633 Carthage⊙, 5,392 K 5
78009 Castroville, 1,893 E 8
75104 Cedar Hill, 2,610 G 2
75009 Celina, 1,272 H 4
75935 Center⊙, 4,989 K 6
75833 Centerville⊙, 831 H 6
77530 Channelview, 9,000 K 1
79018 Channing⊙, 336 B 2
78011 Charlotte, 1,329 F 9
79201 Childress⊙, 5,408 D 3
79225 Chillicothe, 1,116 E 3
76437 Cisco, 4,160 E 5
79226 Clarendon⊙, 1,974 C 3
75426 Clarksville⊙, 3,346 K 4
79019 Claude⊙, 992 C 2
† 77565 Clear Lake Shores, 500 K 2
76031 Cleburne⊙, 16,015 G 5
77327 Cleveland, 5,627 K 7
76634 Clifton, 2,578 G 6
77531 Clute, 6,023 J 9
79510 Clyde, 1,635 E 5
79511 Coahoma, 1,158 C 5
75211 Cockrell Hill, 3,515 G 2
77331 Coldspring⊙, 500 J 7
76834 Coleman⊙, 5,608 E 6
77840 College Station, 17,676 H 7
76034 Colleyville, 3,368 F 1
79512 Colorado City⊙, 5,227 C 5
78934 Columbus⊙, 3,342 H 8
76442 Comanche⊙, 3,933 F 6
75428 Commerce, 9,534 J 4
77301 Conroe⊙, 11,969 J 7
75432 Cooper⊙, 2,258 J 4
75019 Coppell, 1,728 F 1
76522 Copperas Cove, 10,818 G 6
* 78401 Corpus Christi⊙, 204,525 G 10
Corpus Christi, ‡284,832 G 10
75939 Corrigan, 1,304 K 7
75110 Corsicana⊙, 19,972 H 5
78014 Cotulla⊙, 3,415 E 9
79731 Crane⊙, 3,427 B 6
75835 Crockett⊙, 6,616 J 6
77532 Crosby, 1,118 J 8
79322 Crosbyton⊙, 2,251 C 4
76443 Cross Plains, 1,192 E 5
79227 Crowell⊙, 1,399 E 4
76036 Crowley, 2,662 E 2
78839 Crystal City⊙, 8,104 E 9
77954 Cuero⊙, 6,956 G 8
75638 Daingerfield⊙, 2,630 K 4
77533 Daisetta, 1,084 K 7
79022 Dalhart⊙, 5,705 B 1
* 75201 Dallas⊙, 844,401 H 2
Dallas, ‡1,555,950 H 2
77535 Dayton, 3,804 J 7
76234 Decatur⊙, 3,240 G 4
77536 Deer Park, 12,773 K 2
75559 De Kalb, 2,197 K 4
76444 De Leon, 2,170 F 5
78840 Del Rio⊙, 21,330 D 8
75020 Denison, 24,923 H 4
76201 Denton⊙, 39,874 G 4
79323 Denver City, 4,133 B 4
75115 De Soto, 6,617 G 2
78016 Devine, 3,311 E 8
75941 Diboll, 3,557 K 6
79229 Dickens⊙, 295 D 4
77539 Dickinson, 10,776 K 3
78017 Dilley, 2,362 E 9
79027 Dimmitt⊙, 4,327 B 3
78537 Donna, 7,365 F 11
76446 Dublin, 2,810 F 5
79029 Dumas⊙, 9,771 C 2
75116 Duncanville, 14,105 G 2
77434 Eagle Lake, 3,587 H 8
78852 Eagle Pass⊙, 15,364 D 9
79031 Earth, 1,152 B 3
77435 East Bernard, 1,159 H 8
76448 Eastland⊙, 3,178 F 5
76837 Eden, 1,291 E 6
78539 Edinburg⊙, 17,163 F 11
77957 Edna⊙, 5,332 H 9
77437 El Campo, 8,563 H 8
76936 Eldorado⊙, 1,446 D 7
76360 Electra, 3,895 F 4
78621 Elgin, 3,832 G 7
* 79901 El Paso⊙, 322,261 A 10
El Paso, ‡359,291 A 10
78543 Elsa, 4,400 G 11
75440 Emory⊙, 693 J 5
75119 Ennis, 11,046 H 5
76039 Euless, 19,316 F 2
76140 Everman, 4,570 F 2
79838 Fabens, 3,241 B 10
75840 Fairfield⊙, 2,074 H 6
78355 Falfurrias⊙, 6,355 F 10
75234 Farmers Branch, 27,492 G 1
75031 Farmersville, 2,311 H 4
79325 Farwell⊙, 1,185 A 3
75125 Ferris, 2,180 H 2
78941 Flatonia, 1,108 G 8
78114 Floresville⊙, 3,707 F 8
79235 Floydada⊙, 4,109 C 3
75701 Forest Hill, 8,236 F 2
75126 Forney, 1,745 H 5
79734 Fort Davis⊙, 900 D 11
79735 Fort Stockton⊙, 8,283 A 7
* 76101 Fort Worth⊙, 393,476 E 2
Fort Worth, ‡762,086 E 2
77856 Franklin⊙, 1,063 H 7
75763 Frankston, 1,056 J 5
78624 Fredericksburg⊙, 5,326 E 7
76842 Fredonia, 50 E 7
77541 Freeport, 11,997 J 9
78357 Freer, 2,804 F 10
77546 Friendswood, 5,675 J 2
79035 Friona, 3,111 B 3
75034 Frisco, 1,845 H 4
79036 Fritch, 1,778 C 2
79738 Gail⊙, 150 C 5
76240 Gainesville⊙, 13,830 G 4
77547 Galena Park, 10,479 J 1
77550 Galveston⊙, 61,809 L 3
Galveston-Texas City, ‡169,812 L 3
77962 Ganado, 1,640 H 8

79739 Garden City⊙, 300 C 6
75040 Garland, 81,437 H 1
75946 Garrison, 1,082 K 6
76528 Gatesville⊙, 4,683 G 6
78626 Georgetown⊙, 6,395 G 7
78022 George West⊙, 2,022 F 9
78942 Giddings⊙, 2,783 H 7
75644 Gilmer⊙, 4,196 J 5
75647 Gladewater, 5,574 K 5
76043 Glen Rose⊙, 1,554 G 5
76844 Goldthwaite⊙, 1,693 F 6
77963 Goliad⊙, 1,709 G 9
78629 Gonzales⊙, 5,854 G 8
76454 Gorman, 1,236 F 5
76046 Graham⊙, 7,477 F 4
76048 Granbury⊙, 2,473 G 5
75050 Grand Prairie, 50,904 G 2
75140 Grand Saline, 2,257 J 5
76530 Granger, 1,256 G 7
75844 Grapeland, 1,211 J 6
76051 Grapevine, 7,023 F 1
75401 Greenville⊙, 22,043 H 4
76642 Groesbeck⊙, 2,396 H 6
77619 Groves, 18,067 L 8
75845 Groveton⊙, 1,219 J 7
78548 Grulla, 1,194 F 11
79040 Gruver, 1,265 C 1
79236 Guthrie⊙, 150 D 4
79041 Hale Center, 1,964 C 3
77964 Hallettsville⊙, 2,712 G 8
75650 Hallsville, 1,038 K 5
76117 Haltom City, 28,127 F 2
76531 Hamilton⊙, 2,760 G 6
79520 Hamlin, 3,325 E 5
78550 Harlingen, 33,503 G 11
79521 Haskell⊙, 3,655 E 4
77859 Hearne, 4,982 H 7
78361 Hebbronville⊙, 4,079 F 10
75948 Hemphill⊙, 1,005 L 6
77445 Hempstead⊙, 1,891 J 7
75652 Henderson⊙, 10,187 K 5
76365 Henrietta⊙, 2,897 F 4
79045 Hereford⊙, 13,414 B 3
78557 Hidalgo, 1,289 F 11
† 75201 Highland Park, 10,133 G 2
77562 Highlands, 3,462 K 1
76645 Hillsboro⊙, 7,224 G 5
77563 Hitchcock, 5,565 K 3
76366 Holliday, 1,048 F 4
78861 Hondo⊙, 5,487 E 8
75446 Honey Grove, 1,853 J 4
75561 Hooks, 2,545 K 4
* 77001 Houston⊙, 1,232,802 J 2
Houston, ‡1,985,031 J 2
76648 Hubbard, 1,572 H 6
75656 Hughes Springs, 1,701 K 5
77338 Humble, 3,278 J 7
† 77001 Hunters Creek Village, 3,959 J 1
75949 Huntington, 1,192 K 6
77340 Huntsville⊙, 17,610 J 7
76053 Hurst, 27,215 F 2
75141 Hutchins, 1,755 G 2
79329 Idalou, 1,729 C 4
76367 Iowa Park, 5,796 F 4
75060 Irving, 97,260 G 2
76651 Italy, 1,309 H 5
76055 Itasca, 1,483 G 5
77029 Jacinto City, 9,563 J 1
76056 Jacksboro⊙, 3,554 F 4
75766 Jacksonville, 9,734 J 5
75951 Jasper⊙, 6,251 L 7
79528 Jayton⊙, 703 D 4
75657 Jefferson⊙, 2,866 K 5
78636 Johnson City⊙, 767 F 7
† 77541 Jones Creek, 1,268 J 9
78026 Jourdanton⊙, 1,841 F 9
76849 Junction⊙, 2,054 E 7
78118 Karnes City⊙, 2,926 G 9
77450 Katy, 2,923 J 8
75142 Kaufman⊙, 4,012 H 5
76059 Keene, 2,440 G 5
76248 Keller, 1,474 F 1
77565 Kemah, 1,144 K 2
78119 Kenedy, 4,156 G 9
76060 Kennedale, 3,076 F 2
79745 Kermit⊙, 7,884 B 6
78028 Kerrville⊙, 12,672 E 7
75662 Kilgore, 9,495 K 5
76541 Killeen, 35,507 G 6
78363 Kingsville⊙, 28,711 G 10
† 78109 Kirby, 2,558 F 8
75956 Kirbyville, 1,869 K 7
75145 Kleberg, 4,768 H 2
79529 Knox City, 1,536 E 4
77625 Kountze⊙, 1,703 K 7
78640 Kyle, 1,629 G 8
78559 La Feria, 2,642 G 11
78945 La Grange⊙, 3,092 G 8
78560 La Joya, 1,217 F 11
77566 Lake Jackson, 13,376 J 8
76135 Lake Worth, 4,958 E 2
77568 La Marque, 16,131 K 3
79331 Lamesa⊙, 11,559 C 5
76550 Lampasas⊙, 5,922 F 6
75146 Lancaster, 10,522 G 2
77571 La Porte, 7,149 K 2
78040 Laredo⊙, 69,024 E 10
Laredo, ‡72,859 E 10
77573 League City, 10,818 K 2
78873 Leakey⊙, 393 E 8
75452 Leonard, 1,423 H 4
79336 Levelland⊙, 11,445 B 4
75067 Lewisville, 9,264 G 5
77575 Liberty⊙, 5,591 K 7
75771 Lindale, 1,631 J 5
75563 Linden⊙, 2,264 K 4
79056 Lipscomb⊙, 100 D 1
79339 Littlefield⊙, 6,738 B 4
77351 Livingston⊙, 3,925 K 7
78643 Llano⊙, 2,608 F 7
78644 Lockhart⊙, 6,489 G 8
79241 Lockney, 2,094 C 3
75601 Longview⊙, 45,547 K 5
79343 Lorenzo, 1,206 C 4
78566 Los Fresnos, 1,297 G 11
* 79401 Lubbock⊙, 149,101 C 4
Lubbock, ‡179,295 C 4

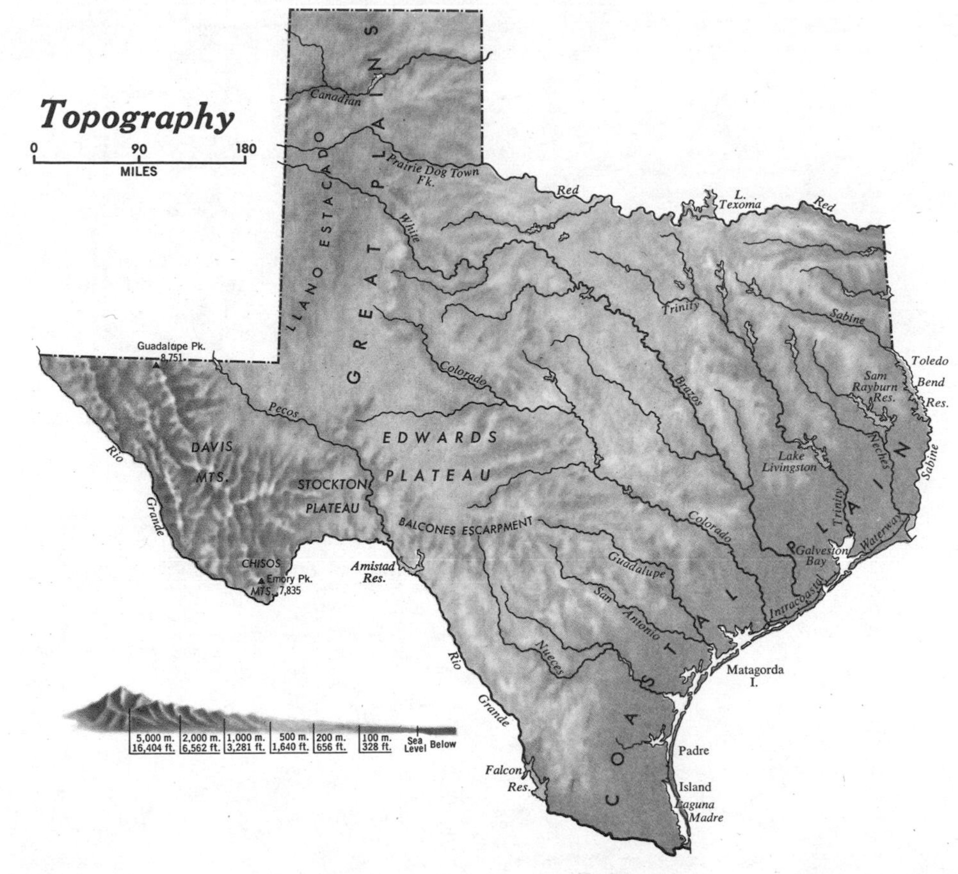

75901 Lufkin⊙, 23,049 K 6
78648 Luling, 4,719 G 8
78569 Lyford, 1,425 G 11
78052 Lytle, 1,271 F 8
75147 Mabank, 1,239 H 5
77864 Madisonville⊙, 2,881 J 7
75148 Malakoff, 2,045 H 5
76063 Mansfield, 3,658 F 2
78654 Marble Falls, 2,209 F 7
79843 Marfa⊙, 2,647 C 12
76661 Marlin⊙, 6,351 H 6
75670 Marshall⊙, 22,937 K 5
76664 Mart, 2,183 H 6
76856 Mason⊙, 1,806 E 7
79244 Matador⊙, 1,091 D 3
78368 Mathis, 5,351 G 9
75567 Maud, 1,107 K 4
78501 McAllen, 37,636 F 11
McAllen-Pharr-Edinburg, ‡181,535 F 11
79752 McCamey, 2,647 B 6
76657 McGregor, 4,365 G 6
75069 McKinney⊙, 15,193 H 4
79057 McLean, 1,183 D 2
77520 McNair, 2,039 K 1
79245 Memphis⊙, 3,227 D 3
76859 Menard⊙, 1,740 E 7
79754 Mentone⊙, 50 D 10
78570 Mercedes, 9,355 F 12
76665 Meridian⊙, 1,162 G 6
79536 Merkel, 2,163 E 5
76941 Mertzon⊙, 513 C 6
75149 Mesquite, 55,131 H 2
76667 Mexia, 5,943 H 6
79059 Miami⊙, 611 D 2
79701 Midland⊙, 59,463 C 6
Midland, ‡65,433 C 6
76065 Midlothian, 2,322 G 5
75773 Mineola, 3,926 J 5
76067 Mineral Wells, 18,411 F 5
78572 Mission, 13,043 F 11
77459 Missouri City, 4,136 J 2
79756 Monahans⊙, 8,333 B 6
76251 Montague⊙, 490 G 4
77580 Mont Belvieu, 1,144 L 1
76557 Moody, 1,286 G 6
79346 Morton⊙, 2,738 B 4
75455 Mount Pleasant⊙, 8,877 K 4
75457 Mount Vernon⊙, 1,806 J 4
76252 Muenster, 1,411 G 4
79347 Muleshoe⊙, 4,525 B 3
76371 Munday, 1,726 E 4
75961 Nacogdoches⊙, 22,544 J 6
75568 Naples, 1,726 K 4
75569 Nash, 1,961 K 4
78059 Natalia, 1,296 F 8
77868 Navasota, 5,111 J 7
77627 Nederland, 16,810 K 8
77461 Needville, 1,024 J 8
75570 New Boston, 3,699 K 4
78130 New Braunfels⊙, 17,859 F 8
75966 Newton⊙, 1,529 L 7
78140 Nixon, 1,925 G 8
76255 Nocona, 2,871 G 4
† 76118 North Richland Hills, 16,514 F 1
79760 Odessa⊙, 78,380 B 6
Odessa, ‡91,805 B 6
79351 O'Donnell, 1,148 C 5
76374 Olney, 3,624 F 4
79064 Olton, 1,782 B 3
77630 Orange⊙, 24,457 L 7
78372 Orange Grove, 1,075 F 10
75684 Overton, 2,084 K 5

76943 Ozona⊙, 2,864 C 7
79248 Paducah⊙, 2,052 D 4
76866 Paint Rock⊙, 193 E 6
77465 Palacios, 3,642 H 9
75801 Palestine⊙, 14,525 J 6
76072 Palo Pinto⊙, 250 F 5
79065 Pampa⊙, 21,726 D 2
79068 Panhandle⊙, 2,141 C 2
75460 Paris⊙, 23,441 J 4
* 77501 Pasadena, 89,277 J 2
77581 Pearland, 6,444 J 2
78061 Pearsall⊙, 5,545 E 9
79772 Pecos⊙, 12,682 D 10
79070 Perryton⊙, 7,810 D 1
79250 Petersburg, 1,300 C 4
78577 Pharr, 15,829 F 11
79071 Phillips, 2,515 C 2
76258 Pilot Point, 1,663 H 4
75968 Pineland, 1,127 L 6
† 77001 Piney Point Village, 2,548 J 1
75686 Pittsburg⊙, 3,844 J 4
79355 Plains⊙, 1,087 B 4
79072 Plainview⊙, 19,096 C 3
75074 Plano, 17,872 H 4
78064 Pleasanton, 5,407 F 9
77978 Point Comfort, 1,446 H 9
78373 Port Aransas, 1,218 H 10
77640 Port Arthur, 57,371 K 8
77365 Porter, 1,900 J 7
78578 Port Isabel, 3,067 G 11
78374 Portland, 7,302 G 10
77979 Port Lavaca⊙, 10,491 H 9
77651 Port Neches, 10,894 K 7
79356 Post⊙, 3,854 C 4
78065 Poteet, 3,013 F 8
78147 Poth, 1,296 F 8
77445 Prairie View, 3,589 J 7
78375 Premont, 3,282 F 10
79845 Presidio, 850 C 12
79252 Quanah⊙, 3,948 E 3
75572 Queen City, 1,227 L 4
75783 Quitman, 1,494 J 5
79357 Ralls, 1,962 C 4
76470 Ranger, 3,094 F 5
79778 Rankin⊙, 1,105 B 6
78580 Raymondville⊙, 7,987 G 11
78377 Refugio⊙, 4,340 G 9
75080 Richardson, 48,582 G 1
76118 Richland Hills, 8,865 F 2
77469 Richmond⊙, 5,777 J 8
78582 Rio Grande City⊙, 5,676 F 11
78583 Rio Hondo, 1,167 G 11
77019 River Oaks, 8,193 E 2
76945 Robert Lee⊙, 1,119 D 6
78380 Robstown, 11,217 G 10
79543 Roby⊙, 784 D 5
76567 Rockdale, 4,655 G 7
78382 Rockport⊙, 3,879 H 9
78880 Rocksprings⊙, 1,221 D 8
75087 Rockwall⊙, 3,121 H 5
76569 Rogers, 1,030 G 7
78584 Roma-Los Saenz, 2,154 E 11
79545 Roscoe, 1,580 D 5
76570 Rosebud, 1,597 G 7
77471 Rosenberg, 12,098 J 8
79546 Rotan, 2,404 D 5
78664 Round Rock, 2,811 G 7
75088 Rowlett, 1,696 H 1
75089 Royse City, 1,535 H 4
78151 Runge, 1,147 G 9
75785 Rusk⊙, 4,914 J 6
78881 Sabinal, 1,554 E 8
76079 Saginaw, 2,382 E 1

76265 Saint Jo, 1,054 G 4
76901 San Angelo⊙, 63,884 D 6
San Angelo, ‡71,047 D 6
* 78201 San Antonio⊙, 654,153 F 8
San Antonio, ‡864,014 F 8
75972 San Augustine⊙, 2,539 K 6
78586 San Benito, 15,176 G 12
79848 Sanderson⊙, 1,229 B 7
78384 San Diego⊙, 4,490 F 10
76266 Sanger, 1,603 G 4
78289 San Juan, 5,070 F 11
77539 San Leon, 1,500 L 2
78666 San Marcos⊙, 18,860 F 8
76877 San Saba⊙, 2,555 F 6
† 76101 Sansom Park Village, 4,771 E 2
76878 Santa Anna, 1,310 E 6
78385 Sarita⊙, 250 G 10
78154 Schertz, 4,061 F 8
78956 Schulenburg, 2,294 H 8
77586 Seabrook, 3,811 K 2
77983 Seadrift, 1,092 H 9
75159 Seagoville, 4,390 H 2
79359 Seagraves, 2,440 D 5
77474 Sealy, 2,685 H 8
78155 Seguin⊙, 15,934 G 8
79360 Seminole⊙, 5,007 B 5
76380 Seymour⊙, 3,469 E 4
79363 Shallowater, 1,339 B 4
79079 Shamrock, 2,644 D 2
† 77001 Sheldon, 1,665 K 1
75090 Sherman⊙, 29,061 H 4
Sherman-Denison, ‡83,225 H 4
77984 Shiner, 2,102 G 8
† 77571 Shore Acres, 1,872 K 2
79851 Sierra Blanca⊙, 900 B 11
77656 Silsbee, 7,271 K 7
79257 Silverton⊙, 1,026 C 3
78387 Sinton⊙, 5,563 G 9
79364 Slaton, 6,583 C 4
78957 Smithville, 2,959 G 7
79549 Snyder⊙, 11,171 D 5
77879 Somerville, 1,250 H 7
76950 Sonora⊙, 2,149 D 7
77659 Sourlake, 1,694 K 7
77587 South Houston, 11,527 J 2
76051 Southlake, 2,031 F 1
† 77001 Southside Place, 1,466 J 2
79081 Spearman⊙, 3,435 C 1
77373 Spring, 1,900 J 7
76082 Springtown, 1,194 G 5
† 77001 Spring Valley, 3,170 J 1
79370 Spur, 1,747 D 4
77477 Stafford, 2,906 J 2
79553 Stamford, 4,558 E 5
79782 Stanton⊙, 2,117 C 5
76401 Stephenville⊙, 9,277 F 5
76951 Sterling City⊙, 780 D 6
79083 Stinnett⊙, 2,014 C 2
78160 Stockdale, 1,132 G 8
79084 Stratford⊙, 2,139 C 1
77478 Sugar Land, 3,318 J 8
75482 Sulphur Springs⊙. 10,642 J 4
79372 Sundown, 1,129 B 4
79086 Sunray, 1,854 C 1
77480 Sweeny, 3,191 J 8
79556 Sweetwater⊙, 12,020 D 5
78390 Taft, 3,274 G 9
79373 Tahoka⊙, 2,956 C 4
76574 Taylor, 9,616 G 7
75860 Teague, 2,867 H 6
76501 Temple, 33,431 G 6
75974 Tenaha, 1,094 K 6
79852 Terlingua, 100 D 12

75160 Terrell, 14,182 H 5
† 78201 Terrell Hills, 5,225 F 8
75501 Texarkana, 30,497 L 4
Texarkana, ‡101,198 L 4
77590 Texas City, 38,908 K 3
73949 Texhoma, 356 C 1
76577 Thorndale, 1,031 G 7
78071 Three Rivers, 1,761 F 9
76083 Throckmorton⊙, 1,105 F 4
78072 Tilden⊙, 600 F 9
75975 Timpson, 1,254 K 6
77375 Tomball, 2,734 J 7
75163 Trinidad, 1,079 J 5
75862 Trinity, 2,512 J 7
75789 Troup, 1,668 J 5
79088 Tulia⊙, 5,294 C 3
75701 Tyler⊙, 57,770 J 5
Tyler, ‡97,096 J 5
78228 University Park, 23,498 H 2
78801 Uvalde⊙, 10,764 E 8
75790 Van, 1,593 J 5
75095 Van Alstyne, 1,981 H 4
79855 Van Horn⊙, 2,240 C 11
79092 Vega⊙, 839 B 2
76384 Vernon⊙, 11,454 E 3
77901 Victoria⊙, 41,349 H 9
77662 Vidor, 9,738 L 7
* 76701 Waco⊙, 95,326 G 6
Waco, ‡147,553 G 6
78959 Waelder, 1,138 G 8
75501 Wake Village, 2,408 K 4
77485 Wallis, 1,028 H 8
75692 Waskom, 1,460 L 5
75165 Waxahachie⊙, 13,452 H 5
76086 Weatherford⊙, 11,750 G 5
77598 Webster, 2,231 K 2
78962 Weimar, 2,104 H 8
79095 Wellington⊙, 2,884 D 3
78596 Weslaco, 15,313 G 11
76691 West, 2,406 G 6
77486 West Columbia, 3,335 J 8
77630 West Orange, 4,787 L 7
† 77001 West University Place, 13,317 J 2
† 76101 Westworth, 4,578 E 2
77488 Wharton⊙, 7,881 J 8
79096 Wheeler⊙, 1,116 D 2
79097 White Deer, 1,092 C 2
76273 Whitesboro, 2,927 H 4
76108 White Settlement, 13,449 E 2
75491 Whitewright, 1,742 H 4
76692 Whitney, 1,371 G 6
* 76301 Wichita Falls⊙, 97,564 F 4
Wichita Falls, ‡127,621 F 4
77378 Willis, 1,577 J 7
75169 Wills Point, 2,636 J 5
75172 Wilmer, 1,922 H 2
77665 Winnie, 1,543 K 8
75494 Winnsboro, 3,064 J 5
79567 Winters, 2,907 E 6
75496 Wolfe City, 1,433 J 4
79382 Wolfforth, 1,090 C 4
78393 Woodsboro, 1,839 G 9
75979 Woodville⊙, 2,662 K 7
76693 Wortham, 1,036 H 6
75098 Wylie, 2,675 H 5
77995 Yoakum, 5,755 G 8
78164 Yorktown, 2,411 G 9
78076 Zapata⊙, 2,102 E 11

⊙ County seat.
‡ Population of metropolitan area.
† Zip of nearest p.o.
* Multiple zips

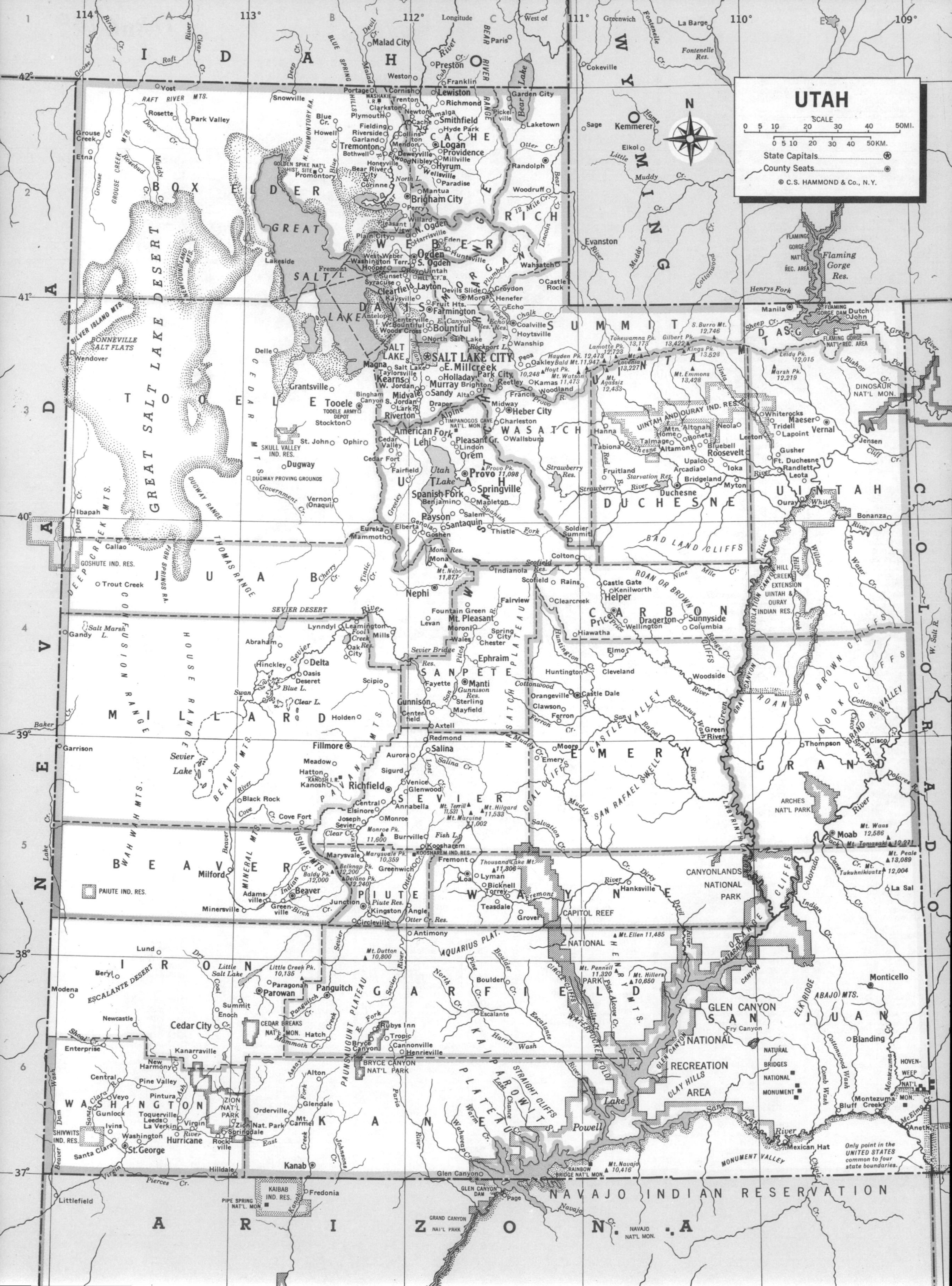

UTAH
SCALE
0 5 10 20 30 40 50MI.
0 5 10 20 30 40 50KM.
State Capitals
County Seats
© C.S. HAMMOND & Co., N.Y.
N
114°
113°
112°
111°
110°
109°
Longitude
West of
Greenwich
42°
41°
40°
39°
38°
37°
IDAHO
WYOMING
COLORADO
NEVADA
ARIZONA
NAVAJO INDIAN RESERVATION
BOX ELDER
CACHE
RICH
WEBER
MORGAN
DAVIS
SUMMIT
DAGGETT
SALT LAKE
TOOELE
UTAH
WASATCH
DUCHESNE
UINTAH
JUAB
CARBON
MILLARD
SANPETE
EMERY
GRAND
SEVIER
BEAVER
PIUTE
WAYNE
IRON
GARFIELD
SAN JUAN
WASHINGTON
KANE
GREAT SALT LAKE
GREAT SALT LAKE DESERT
BONNEVILLE SALT FLATS
SALT LAKE CITY
Ogden
Provo
Logan
Brigham City
Tooele
Heber City
Vernal
Duchesne
Roosevelt
Nephi
Price
Manti
Castle Dale
Fillmore
Richfield
Beaver
Junction
Loa
Parowan
Cedar City
Panguitch
St. George
Kanab
Moab
Monticello
Coalville
Randolph
Farmington
Morgan
Utah Lake
Sevier Lake
Lake Powell
Flaming Gorge Res.
ARCHES NAT'L PARK
CANYONLANDS NATIONAL PARK
CAPITOL REEF NATIONAL
ZION NAT'L PARK
BRYCE CANYON NAT'L PARK
GLEN CANYON NATIONAL RECREATION AREA
NATURAL BRIDGES NATIONAL MONUMENT
DINOSAUR NAT'L MON.
CEDAR BREAKS NAT'L MON.
RAINBOW BRIDGE NAT'L MON.
UINTAH AND OURAY IND. RES.
GOSHUTE IND. RES.
SKULL VALLEY IND. RES.
PAIUTE IND. RES.
SHIVWITS IND. RES.
KAIBAB IND. RES.
DUGWAY PROVING GROUNDS
TOOELE ARMY DEPOT
GOLDEN SPIKE NAT'L HIST. SITE
Kings Pk. 13,528
Mt. Nebo 11,877
Mt. Waas 12,586
Mt. Peale 13,089
Mt. Ellen 11,485
Mt. Navajo 10,416
SEVIER DESERT
ESCALANTE DESERT
MONUMENT VALLEY
SAN RAFAEL SWELL
BOOK CLIFFS
ROAN OR BROWN CLIFFS
WASATCH PLATEAU
KAIPAROWITS PLATEAU
PAUNSAUGUNT PLATEAU
AQUARIUS PLAT.
HENRY MTS.
ABAJO MTS.
UINTA MTS.
Only point in the UNITED STATES common to four state boundaries.

Rising like a Greek amphitheater, the Bingham Open Pit Copper Mine in Utah is constantly changing as giant electric shovels remove seven tons of earth at a time.

AREA 84,916 sq. mi.
POPULATION 1,059,273
CAPITAL Salt Lake City
LARGEST CITY Salt Lake City
HIGHEST POINT Kings Pk. 13,528 ft.
SETTLED IN 1847
ADMITTED TO UNION January 4, 1896
POPULAR NAME Beehive State
STATE FLOWER Sego Lily
STATE BIRD Sea Gull

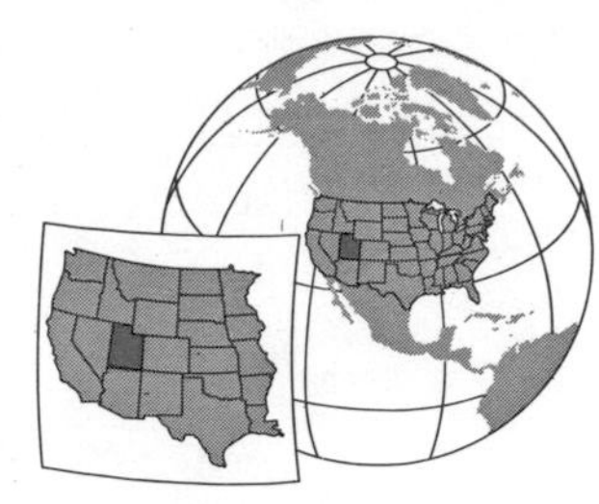

COUNTIES

County	Key
Beaver, 3,800	A 5
Box Elder, 28,129	A 2
Cache, 42,331	C 2
Carbon, 15,647	D 4
Daggett, 666	E 3
Davis, 99,028	B 3
Duchesne, 7,299	D 3
Emery, 5,137	D 4
Garfield, 3,157	C 6
Grand, 6,688	E 5
Iron, 12,177	A 6
Juab, 4,574	A 4
Kane, 2,421	B 6
Millard, 6,988	A 4
Morgan, 3,983	C 2
Piute, 1,164	B 5
Rich, 1,615	C 2
Salt Lake, 458,607	B 3
San Juan, 9,606	E 6
Sanpete, 10,976	C 4
Sevier, 10,103	C 5
Summit, 5,879	D 3
Tooele, 21,545	A 3
Uintah, 12,684	E 3
Utah, 137,776	C 3
Wasatch, 5,863	C 3
Washington, 13,669	A 6
Wayne, 1,483	C 5
Weber, 126,278	B 2

CITIES and TOWNS

Zip	Name/Pop.	Key
† 84003	Alpine, 1,047	C 3
84001	Altamont, 129	D 3
84002	Altonah, 225	D 3
† 84335	Amalga, 207	C 2
84003	American Fork, 7,713	C 3
84510	Aneth, 250	E 6
84711	Annabella, 221	B 5
84712	Antimony, 113	C 5
84005	Arcadia, 150	D 3
84620	Aurora, 493	B 5
84621	Axtell, 150	C 4
84301	Bear River City, 445	B 2
84713	Beaver⊙, 1,453	B 5
† 84660	Benjamin, 503	C 3
84715	Bicknell, 264	C 5
84511	Blanding, 2,250	E 6
84007	Bluebell, 210	D 3
84512	Bluff, 300	E 6
84008	Bonanza, 150	E 3
† 84337	Bothwell, 300	B 2
84716	Boulder, 93	C 6
84010	Bountiful, 27,853	C 3
84012	Bridgeland, 150	D 3
84302	Brigham City⊙, 14,007	C 2
84117	Brighton, 150	C 3
84717	Bryce Canyon, 229	B 6
84718	Cannonville, 113	B 6
84513	Castle Dale⊙, 541	D 4
84514	Castle Gate, 205	D 4
84720	Cedar City, 8,946	A 6
† 84013	Cedar Fort, 188	B 3
84013	Cedar Valley, 290	B 3
84622	Centerfield, 419	C 4
84014	Centerville, 3,268	C 3
84722	Central, 154	B 5
† 84032	Charleston, 196	C 3
84623	Chester, 130	C 4
84723	Circleville, 443	B 5
84305	Clarkston, 420	B 2
84516	Clawson, 95	C 4
84015	Clearfield, 13,316	B 2
84518	Cleveland, 244	D 4
84017	Coalville⊙, 864	C 3
84519	Columbia, 380	D 4
84307	Corinne, 471	B 2
84308	Cornish, 173	B 2
84018	Croydon, 90	C 2
84624	Delta, 1,610	B 4
84625	Deseret, 215	B 4
84309	Deweyville, 248	B 2
84520	Dragerton, 1,614	D 4
84020	Draper, 4,000	C 3
84021	Duchesne⊙, 1,094	D 3
84022	Dugway, 2,357	B 3
84023	Dutch John, 263	E 3
† 84101	East Millcreek, 26,579	C 3
84310	Eden, 421	C 2
84626	Elberta, 325	B 4
84521	Elmo, 141	D 4
84724	Elsinore, 357	B 5
† 84337	Elwood, 294	B 2
84522	Emery, 216	C 5
† 84720	Enoch, 120	A 6
84725	Enterprise, 844	A 6
84627	Ephraim, 2,127	C 4
84726	Escalante, 638	C 6
84628	Eureka, 753	B 4
84629	Fairview, 696	C 4
84025	Farmington⊙, 2,526	C 3
84630	Fayette, 93	C 4
84523	Ferron, 663	C 4
84311	Fielding, 254	B 2
84631	Fillmore⊙, 1,411	B 5
84026	Fort Duchesne, 300	E 3
84632	Fountain Green, 467	C 4
† 84036	Francis, 268	C 3
84727	Fremont, 160	C 5
† 84037	Fruit Heights, 800	C 2
84028	Garden City, 134	C 2
84312	Garland, 1,187	B 2
† 84655	Genola, 424	C 4
84729	Glendale, 200	B 6
84730	Glenwood, 212	C 5
84633	Goshen, 459	C 4
84029	Grantsville, 2,931	B 3
84525	Green River, 1,033	D 4
84731	Greenville, 97	B 5
84313	Grouse Creek, 100	A 2
84733	Gunlock, 93	A 6
84634	Gunnison, 1,073	C 4
84030	Gusher, 125	E 3
84734	Hanksville, 224	D 5
84031	Hanna, 135	D 3
† 84401	Harrisville, 603	C 2
84735	Hatch, 139	B 6
84032	Heber City⊙, 3,245	C 3
84526	Helper, 1,964	D 4
84033	Henefer, 446	C 2
84736	Henrieville, 145	C 6
84527	Hiawatha, 166	D 4
† 84767	Hilldale, 480	B 6
84635	Hinckley, 400	B 4
84636	Holden, 351	B 4
84117	Holladay, 23,014	C 3
84314	Honeyville, 640	B 2
84315	Hooper, 1,705	B 2
84316	Howell, 146	B 2
† 84017	Hoytsville, 500	C 3
84528	Huntington, 857	C 4
84317	Huntsville, 553	C 2
84737	Hurricane, 1,408	A 6
84318	Hyde Park, 1,025	C 2
84319	Hyrum, 2,340	C 2
84034	Ibapah, 135	A 3
† 84052	Ioka, 115	D 3
84738	Ivins, 137	A 6
84035	Jensen, 360	E 3
84739	Joseph, 125	B 5
84740	Junction⊙, 135	B 5
84036	Kamas, 806	C 3
84741	Kanab⊙, 1,381	B 6
84742	Kanarraville, 204	A 6
84637	Kanosh, 319	B 5
84037	Kaysville, 6,192	B 2
84118	Kearns, 17,071	B 3
84529	Kenilworth, 500	D 4
84743	Kingston, 114	B 5
84744	Koosharem, 141	C 5
84038	Laketown, 208	C 2
84039	Lapoint, 335	E 3
84040	Lark, 728	B 3
84530	La Sal, 200	E 5
84745	La Verkin, 463	A 6
84041	Layton, 13,603	C 2
84638	Leamington, 112	B 4
84746	Leeds, 151	A 6
84043	Lehi, 4,659	C 3
84639	Levan, 376	C 4
84320	Lewiston, 1,244	C 2
† 84062	Lindon, 1,644	C 3
84747	Loa⊙, 324	C 5
84321	Logan⊙, 22,333	C 2
84749	Lyman, 180	C 5
84640	Lynndyl, 111	B 4
† 84078	Maeser, 1,248	E 3
84044	Magna, 5,509	B 3
84046	Manila⊙, 226	E 3
84642	Manti⊙, 1,803	C 4
† 84302	Mantua, 413	C 2
† 84663	Mapleton, 1,980	C 3
84750	Marysvale, 289	B 5
84643	Mayfield, 267	C 4
84644	Meadow, 238	B 5
84325	Mendon, 345	B 2
84531	Mexican Hat, 100	E 6
84047	Midvale, 7,840	B 3
84049	Midway, 804	C 3
84751	Milford, 1,304	A 5
84326	Millville, 441	C 2
84752	Minersville, 448	A 5
84532	Moab⊙, 4,793	E 5
84645	Mona, 309	C 4
84754	Monroe, 918	B 5
84534	Montezuma Creek, 500	E 6
84535	Monticello⊙, 1,431	E 6
84050	Morgan⊙, 1,586	C 2
84646	Moroni, 894	C 4
84051	Mountain Home, 140	D 3
84647	Mount Pleasant, 1,516	C 4
84107	Murray, 21,206	C 3
84052	Myton, 322	D 3
84053	Neola, 600	D 3
84648	Nephi⊙, 2,699	C 4
84756	Newcastle, 150	A 6
84327	Newton, 444	C 2
† 84321	Nibley, 367	C 2
† 84401	North Ogden, 5,257	C 2
84054	North Salt Lake, 2,143	C 3
84649	Oak City, 278	B 4
84055	Oakley, 265	C 3
84650	Oasis, 150	B 4
* 84401	Ogden⊙, 69,478	C 2
	Ogden, ‡126,278	C 2
† 84080	Onaqui (Vernon), 541	B 3
84537	Orangeville, 511	C 4
84758	Orderville, 399	B 6
84057	Orem, 25,729	C 3
84059	Ouray, 100	E 3
84759	Panguitch⊙, 1,318	B 6
84328	Paradise, 399	C 2
84760	Paragonah, 275	B 6
84060	Park City, 1,193	C 3
84329	Park Valley, 100	A 2
84761	Parowan⊙, 1,423	B 6
84651	Payson, 4,501	C 3
84061	Peoa, 230	C 3
† 84302	Perry, 909	C 2
† 84028	Pickleville, 106	C 2
† 84401	Plain City, 1,543	B 2
84062	Pleasant Grove, 5,327	C 3
† 84401	Pleasant View, 2,028	B 2
84330	Plymouth, 203	B 2
84331	Portage, 144	B 2
84501	Price⊙, 6,218	D 4
84332	Providence, 1,608	C 2
84601	Provo⊙, 53,131	C 3
	Provo-Orem, ‡137,776	C 3
84063	Randlett, 350	E 3
84064	Randolph⊙, 500	C 2
84652	Redmond, 409	C 4
84701	Richfield⊙, 4,471	B 5
84333	Richmond, 1,000	C 2
84334	Riverside, 290	B 2
84065	Riverton, 2,820	B 3
84763	Rockville, 110	A 6
84066	Roosevelt, 2,005	D 3
84067	Roy, 14,356	C 2
84770	Saint George⊙, 7,097	A 6
84069	Saint John, 200	B 3
84653	Salem, 1,081	C 3
84654	Salina, 1,494	C 5
* 84101	Salt Lake City (cap.)⊙, 175,885	B 3
	Salt Lake City, ‡557,635	B 3
84070	Sandy, 6,438	C 3
84765	Santa Clara, 271	A 6
84655	Santaquin, 1,236	C 4
84656	Scipio, 264	B 4
84657	Sigurd, 291	B 5
84335	Smithfield, 3,342	C 2
84336	Snowville, 174	B 2
† 84065	South Jordan, 2,942	B 3
† 84401	South Ogden, 9,991	C 2
84115	South Salt Lake, 7,810	C 3
84660	Spanish Fork, 7,284	C 3
84662	Spring City, 456	C 4
84767	Springdale, 172	B 6
84663	Springville, 8,790	C 3
84665	Sterling, 144	C 4
84071	Stockton, 469	B 3
84772	Summit, 150	B 6
84539	Sunnyside, 485	D 4
† 84015	Sunset, 6,268	B 2
† 84041	Syracuse, 1,843	B 2
84072	Tabiona, 125	D 3
84073	Talmage, 140	D 3
† 84101	Taylorsville, 12,522	B 3
84773	Teasdale, 160	C 5
84074	Tooele⊙, 12,539	B 3
84774	Toquerville, 185	A 6
84337	Tremonton, 2,794	B 2
84338	Trenton, 390	B 2
84076	Tridell, 212	E 3
84776	Tropic, 329	B 6
† 84401	Uintah, 400	C 2
† 84007	Upalco, 150	D 3
84777	Venice, 220	C 5
84078	Vernal⊙, 3,908	E 3
84080	Vernon, 541	B 3
† 84722	Veyo, 144	A 6
84779	Virgin, 119	A 6
84082	Wallsburg, 211	C 3
† 84017	Wanship, 175	C 3
84780	Washington, 750	A 6
† 84401	Washington Terrace, 7,241	B 2
84542	Wellington, 922	D 4
84339	Wellsville, 1,267	C 2
84083	Wendover, 781	A 3
† 84087	West Bountiful, 1,246	B 3
84084	West Jordan, 4,221	B 3
† 84401	West Weber, 750	B 2
84085	Whiterocks, 600	E 3
84340	Willard, 1,045	C 2
† 84036	Woodland, 190	C 3
84086	Woodruff, 173	C 2
84087	Woods Cross, 3,124	B 3

⊙ County seat.
‡ Population of metropolitan area.
† Zip of nearest p.o.
* Multiple zips

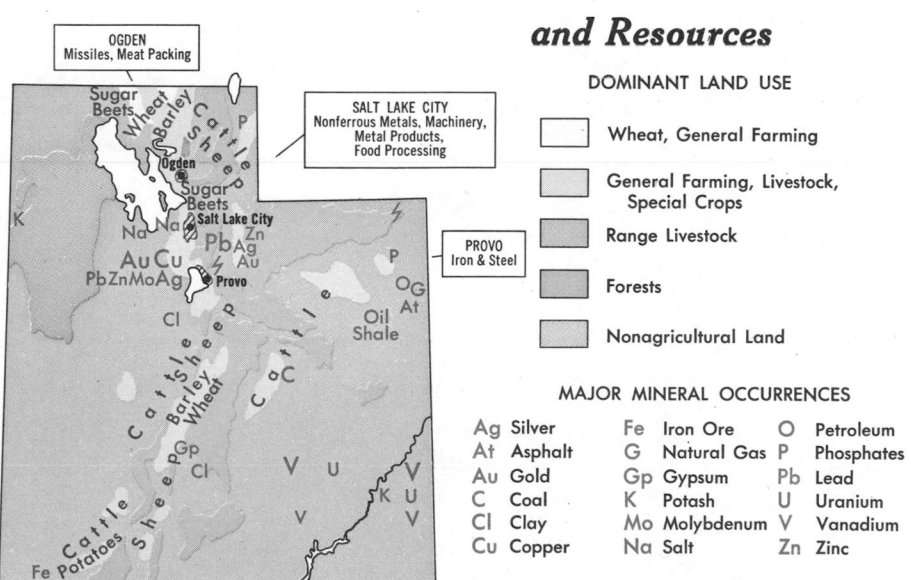

Agriculture, Industry and Resources

OGDEN
Missiles, Meat Packing

SALT LAKE CITY
Nonferrous Metals, Machinery, Metal Products, Food Processing

PROVO
Iron & Steel

Sugar Beets · Wheat · Barley · Cattle · Sheep · Ogden · Salt Lake City · Provo · Oil Shale · Potatoes

DOMINANT LAND USE

- Wheat, General Farming
- General Farming, Livestock, Special Crops
- Range Livestock
- Forests
- Nonagricultural Land

MAJOR MINERAL OCCURRENCES

Ag	Silver	Fe	Iron Ore	O	Petroleum
At	Asphalt	G	Natural Gas	P	Phosphates
Au	Gold	Gp	Gypsum	Pb	Lead
C	Coal	K	Potash	U	Uranium
Cl	Clay	Mo	Molybdenum	V	Vanadium
Cu	Copper	Na	Salt	Zn	Zinc

Water Power

Major Industrial Areas

Topography

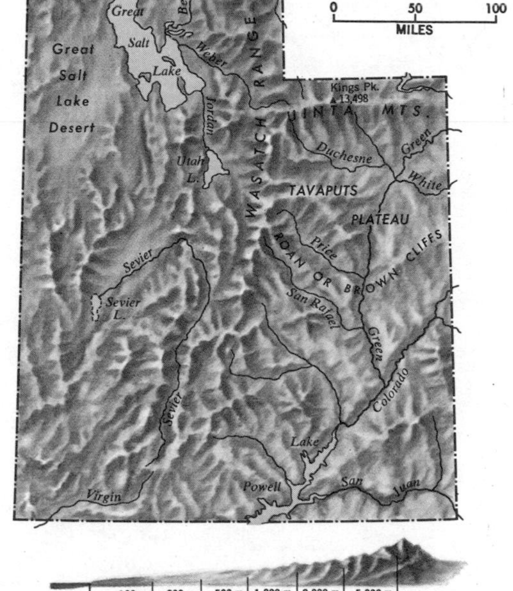

Topography

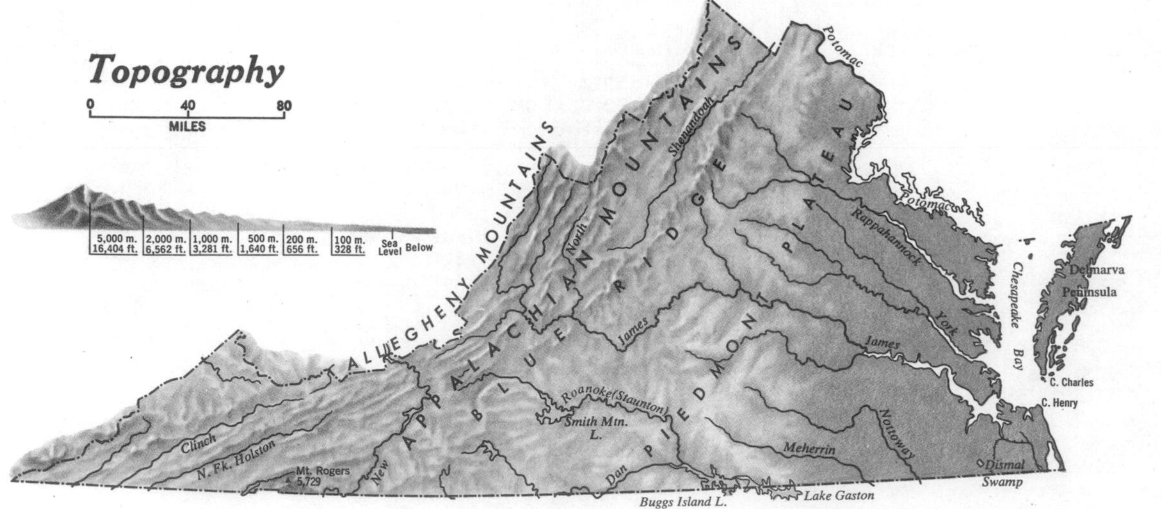

COUNTIES

County	Key
Accomack, 29,004	S 5
Albemarle, 37,780	L 5
Alleghany, 12,461	H 5
Amelia, 7,592	M 6
Amherst, 26,072	K 5
Appomattox, 9,784	L 6
Arlington, 174,284	O 3
Augusta, 44,220	K 4
Bath, 5,192	J 4
Bedford, 26,728	J 6
Bland, 5,423	F 6
Botetourt, 18,193	J 5
Brunswick, 16,172	N 7
Buchanan, 32,071	D 6
Buckingham, 10,597	L 5
Campbell, 43,319	K 6
Caroline, 13,925	O 4
Carroll, 23,092	G 7
Charles City, 6,158	O 6
Charlotte, 11,551	L 6
Chesterfield, 76,855	N 6
Clarke, 8,102	M 2
Craig, 3,524	H 6
Culpeper, 18,218	M 3
Cumberland, 6,179	M 6
Dickenson, 16,077	D 6
Dinwiddie, 25,046	N 6
Essex, 7,099	P 5
Fairfax, 455,021	O 3
Fauquier, 26,375	N 3
Floyd, 9,775	H 7
Fluvanna, 7,621	M 5
Franklin, 26,858	J 6
Frederick, 28,893	M 2
Giles, 16,741	G 6
Gloucester, 14,059	P 6
Goochland, 10,069	N 5
Grayson, 15,439	F 7
Greene, 5,248	M 4
Greensville, 9,604	N 7
Halifax, 30,076	L 7
Hanover, 37,479	N 5
Henrico, 154,364	O 6
Henry, 50,901	J 7
Highland, 2,529	J 4
Isle of Wight, 18,285	P 7
James City, 17,853	P 6
King and Queen, 5,491	P 5
King George, 8,039	O 4
King William, 7,497	O 5
Lancaster, 9,126	R 5
Lee, 20,321	B 7
Loudoun, 37,150	N 2
Louisa, 14,004	N 5
Lunenburg, 11,687	M 7
Madison, 8,638	M 4
Mathews, 7,168	R 6
Mecklenburg, 29,426	M 7
Middlesex, 6,295	R 5
Montgomery, 47,157	H 6
Nansemond, 35,166	P 7
Nelson, 11,702	L 5
New Kent, 5,300	P 5
Northampton, 14,442	S 6
Northumberland, 9,239	R 5
Nottoway, 14,260	M 6
Orange, 13,792	M 4
Page, 16,581	M 3
Patrick, 15,282	H 7
Pittsylvania, 58,789	K 7
Powhatan, 7,696	N 5
Prince Edward, 14,379	M 6
Prince George, 29,092	O 6
Prince William, 111,102	O 3
Pulaski, 29,564	G 6
Rappahannock, 5,199	M 3
Richmond, 5,841	P 5
Roanoke, 67,339	H 6
Rockbridge, 16,637	K 5
Rockingham, 47,890	L 4
Russell, 24,533	D 7
Scott, 24,376	C 7
Shenandoah, 22,852	L 3
Smyth, 31,349	E 7
Southampton, 18,582	O 7
Spotsylvania, 16,424	N 4
Stafford, 24,587	O 4
Surry, 5,882	P 6
Sussex, 11,464	O 7
Tazewell, 39,816	E 6
Warren, 15,301	M 3
Washington, 40,835	D 7
Westmoreland, 12,142	P 4
Wise, 35,947	C 6
Wythe, 22,139	F 7
York, 33,203	P 6

INDEPENDENT CITIES

	Zip	Name/Pop.	Key
*	22301	Alexandria, 110,938	P 3
	24523	Bedford⊙, 6,011	J 6
	24201	Bristol, 14,857	D 7
	24416	Buena Vista, 6,425	K 5
*	22901	Charlottesville⊙, 38,880	M 4
*	23320	Chesapeake, 89,580	R 7
	24422	Clifton Forge, 5,501	J 5
	23834	Colonial Heights, 15,097	O 6
	24426	Covington⊙, 10,060	H 5
	24541	Danville, 46,391	J 7
	23847	Emporia⊙, 5,300	N 7
	22030	Fairfax⊙, 21,970	O 3
*	22040	Falls Church, 10,772	O 3
	23851	Franklin, 6,880	P 7
	22401	Fredericksburg, 14,450	N 4
	24333	Galax, 6,278	G 7
*	23360	Hampton, 120,779	R 6
	22801	Harrisonburg⊙, 14,605	K 4
	23860	Hopewell, 23,471	O 6
	24450	Lexington⊙, 7,597	J 5
*	24501	Lynchburg, 54,083	K 6
	24112	Martinsville⊙, 19,653	J 7
*	23601	Newport News, 138,177	P 6
*	23501	Norfolk, 307,951	R 7
	24273	Norton, 4,001	C 7
	23803	Petersburg, 36,103	N 6
*	23701	Portsmouth⊙, 110,963	R 7
	24141	Radford, 11,596	G 6
*	23201	Richmond (cap.)⊙, 249,621	O 5
*	24001	Roanoke, 92,115	H 6
	24153	Salem⊙, 21,982	H 6
	24592	South Boston, 6,889	L 7
	24401	Staunton⊙, 24,504	K 4
	23434	Suffolk⊙, 9,858	P 7
*	23450	Virginia Beach, 172,106	S 7
	22980	Waynesboro, 16,707	K 4
	23185	Williamsburg⊙, 9,069	P 6
	22601	Winchester⊙, 14,643	M 2

CITIES and TOWNS

	Zip	Name/Pop.	Key
	24210	Abingdon⊙, 4,376	D 7
	23301	Accomac⊙, 373	S 5
	23001	Achilles, 525	R 6
	22920	Afton, 525	L 4
†	22959	Alberene, 200	L 5
	23821	Alberta, 466	N 7
	24310	Allisonia, 325	G 7
	24517	Altavista, 2,708	K 6
	24520	Alton, 250	K 7
	23002	Amelia Court House⊙, 537	N 6
	24521	Amherst⊙, 1,108	K 5
	22002	Amissville, 150	M 3
	24601	Amonate, 500	E 6
	24215	Andover, 300	C 7
	22003	Annandale, 27,428	O 3
	24216	Appalachia, 2,161	C 7
	24522	Appomattox⊙, 1,400	L 6
	24053	Ararat, 500	G 7
*	22201	Arlington⊙, 174,284	P 3
	22922	Arrington, 350	L 5
	23004	Arvonia, 300	M 5
	22011	Ashburn, 345	O 2
	23005	Ashland, 2,934	N 5
	24311	Atkins, 500	F 7
	24411	Augusta Springs, 400	K 4
	24312	Austinville, 750	F 7
	24054	Axton, 540	J 7
	23009	Aylett, 300	O 5
	24602	Bandy, 500	E 6
	24231	Banner, 350	D 7
	22923	Barboursville, 207	M 4
	24313	Barren Springs, 150	G 7
	24055	Bassett, 3,058	J 7
	24314	Bastian, 450	F 6
	22924	Batesville, 450	L 5
	23016	Beaverlett, 178	R 6
†	23201	Bellbluff, 3,900	N 6
	23306	Belle Haven, 504	S 5
	22307	Belleview, 8,299	O 3
	24218	Ben Hur, 300	B 7
	24059	Bent Mountain, 140	H 6
	22610	Bentonville, 700	M 3
	22811	Bergton, 150	L 3
	22611	Berryville⊙, 1,569	M 2
	24526	Big Island, 500	K 5
	24603	Big Rock, 350	D 6
	24219	Big Stone Gap, 4,153	C 7
	24220	Birchleaf, 650	D 6
	23307	Birdsnest, 250	S 6
	24604	Bishop, 400	E 6
	23916	Blackridge, 140	M 7
	24060	Blacksburg, 9,384	H 6
	23824	Blackstone, 3,412	N 6
	24221	Blackwater, 205	B 7
	24527	Blairs, 500	K 7
	24315	Bland⊙, 950	F 6
	23308	Bloxom, 391	S 5
	24605	Bluefield, 5,286	F 6
	22012	Bluemont, 310	N 2
	24064	Blue Ridge, 926	J 6
	24606	Boissevain, 975	F 6
	23235	Bon Air, 10,562	N 5
	24065	Boones Mill, 363	J 6
	22427	Bowling Green⊙, 528	O 4
	22620	Boyce, 378	M 2
	23917	Boydton⊙, 541	M 7
	23827	Boykins, 742	O 7
	23828	Branchville, 189	O 7
	22714	Brandy Station, 530	N 4
	24607	Breaks, 500	D 6
	23022	Bremo Bluff, 200	M 5
	22812	Bridgewater, 2,828	K 4
	22715	Brightwood, 250	M 4
	24316	Broadford, 850	E 7
	22815	Broadway, 887	L 3
	23920	Brodnax, 569	N 7
	22430	Brooke, 275	O 4
	24528	Brookneal, 1,037	L 6
	24415	Brownsburg, 200	K 5
	22610	Browntown, 175	M 3
	22622	Brucetown, 150	M 2
†	22810	Bryce Mountain, 205	L 3
	24066	Buchanan, 1,326	J 5
	23921	Buckingham⊙, 200	L 5
	22432	Burgess, 300	R 5
	24608	Burkes Garden, 275	F 6
	23922	Burkeville, 703	M 6
	24420	Burnsville, 138	J 4
	22435	Callao, 500	P 5
	24067	Callaway, 191	H 7
	22016	Calverton, 200	N 3
	24317	Cana, 168	G 7
	23310	Cape Charles, 1,689	R 6
	23313	Capeville, 300	R 6
	23829	Capron, 314	O 7
†	23039	Cardwell, 200	N 5
	23315	Carrsville, 375	P 7
	23830	Carson, 275	O 6
	22017	Casanova, 200	N 3
	24069	Cascade, 835	J 7
	24224	Castlewood, 799	D 7
	22019	Catlett, 500	N 3
	24609	Cedar Bluff, 1,050	E 6
†	24368	Cedar Springs, 200	F 7
†	22630	Cedarville, 150	M 3
	22437	Center Cross, 360	P 5
	22438	Champlain, 160	O 4
	22021	Chantilly, 620	O 3
	23030	Charles City⊙, 5	O 6
	23923	Charlotte Court House⊙, 539	L 6
	23924	Chase City, 2,909	M 7
	24531	Chatham⊙, 1,801	K 7
	23316	Cheriton, 655	R 6
	23831	Chester, 5,556	O 6
	23832	Chesterfield⊙, 950	N 6
	22623	Chester Gap, 450	M 3
	24319	Chilhowie, 1,317	E 7
	23336	Chincoteague, 1,867	T 5
	24073	Christiansburg⊙, 7,857	H 6
	23339	Chuckatuck, 500	P 7
	23032	Church View, 200	P 5
	24421	Churchville, 250	K 4
	22928	Cismont, 400	M 4
	23899	Claremont, 383	P 6
	23927	Clarksville, 1,641	M 7
	24076	Claudville, 180	H 7
†	23061	Clay Bank, 200	P 6
	24225	Cleveland, 357	D 7
	24533	Clifford, 160	K 5
	24321	Clinchburg, 250	E 7
	24226	Clinchco, 900	D 6
	24227	Clinchport, 286	C 7
	24228	Clintwood⊙, 1,320	D 6

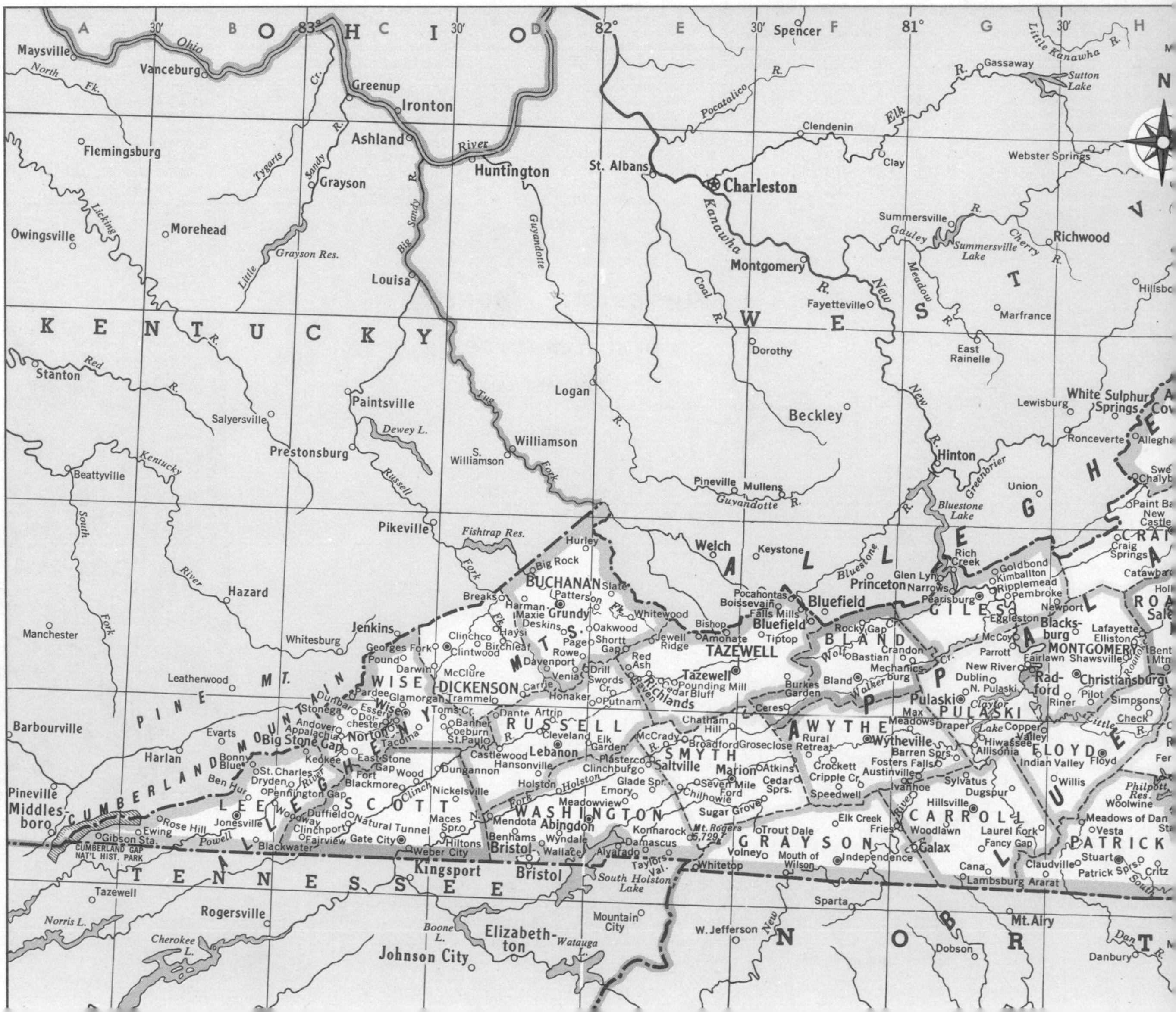

	ZIP	Place	Key
	24534	Clover, 227	L 7
	24077	Cloverdale, 850	J 6
	24535	Cluster Springs, 500	L 7
	23035	Cobbs Creek, 600	R 6
	24230	Coeburn, 2,362	D 7
	24536	Coleman Falls, 250	K 6
	22442	Coles Point, 200	P 4
	24450	Collierstown, 125	J 5
	24078	Collinsville, 6,015	J 7
	22443	Colonial Beach, 2,058	P 4
	23038	Columbia, 125	M 5
	24538	Concord, 400	K 6
	24080	Copper Valley, 425	G 7
	23837	Courtland⊙, 899	O 7
	22931	Covesville, 500	L 5
	24430	Craigsville, 988	J 4
	24315	Crandon, 250	G 6
	23930	Crewe, 1,433	M 6
	24431	Crimora, 450	L 4
	24322	Cripple Creek, 200	F 7
	24082	Critz, 150	H 7
	24323	Crockett, 300	F 7
	22625	Cross Junction, 200	M 2
	22932	Crozet, 1,433	L 4
	23039	Crozier, 300	N 5
	24539	Crystal Hill, 475	L 7
	23934	Cullen, 140	L 6
	22701	Culpeper⊙, 6,056	M 4
	23040	Cumberland⊙, 500	M 6
	22448	Dahlgren, 950	O 4
†	22172	Dale City, 13,857	O 3
	24083	Daleville, 450	J 6
	24236	Damascus, 1,230	E 7
	24237	Dante, 1,153	D 7
	24239	Davenport, 300	D 6
	22821	Dayton, 978	L 4
	24432	Deerfield, 200	K 4
	22025	Delaplane, 164	N 3
	23043	Deltaville, 950	R 5
	23839	Dendron, 336	P 6
	23840	De Witt, 140	N 6
	23936	Dillwyn, 497	M 5
	23841	Dinwiddie⊙, 500	N 6
	23842	Disputanta, 500	O 6
	23047	Doswell, 200	N 5
	23937	Drakes Branch, 702	L 7
	24324	Draper, 276	G 7
	23844	Drewryville, 250	O 7
	24242	Drill, 192	E 6
	23346	Driver, 250	P 7
	24243	Dryden, 400	B 7
	24084	Dublin, 1,653	G 6
	22026	Dumfries, 1,890	O 3
	23938	Dundas, 200	M 7
	24245	Dungannon, 282	D 7
	22454	Dunnsville, 312	P 5
	24085	Eagle Rock, 750	J 5
	22936	Earleysville, 210	M 4
	24246	East Stone Gap, 500	C 7
	23347	Eastville⊙, 203	R 6
	23845	Ebony, 150	N 7
	23349	Eclipse, 295	R 7
†	22485	Edgehill, 225	O 4
	22824	Edinburg, 766	M 3
	24086	Eggleston, 500	G 6
	23846	Elberon, 200	P 6
	22827	Elkton, 1,511	L 4
	24087	Elliston, 700	H 6
	24327	Emory, 458	E 7
	22937	Esmont, 950	L 5
	24274	Esserville, 975	G 2
	23803	Ettrick, 3,950	O 6
	23939	Evergreen, 300	L 6
	24550	Evington, 175	K 6
	24248	Ewing, 700	B 7
	23350	Exmore, 1,421	S 5
	24435	Fairfield, 465	K 5
	24141	Fairlawn, 1,767	G 6
†	22539	Fairport, 175	R 5
	24613	Falls Mills, 500	F 6
	22401	Falmouth, 2,139	O 4
	23901	Farmville⊙, 4,331	M 6
	22460	Farnham, 150	P 5
	24088	Ferrum, 200	H 7
	24089	Fieldale, 1,337	H 7
	24090	Fincastle⊙, 397	J 6
	22939	Fishersville, 975	K 4
	22627	Flint Hill, 200	M 3
	24091	Floyd⊙, 474	H 7
	24551	Forest, 497	K 6
	23055	Fork Union, 350	M 5
	24250	Fort Blackmore, 600	C 7
	22578	Foxwells, 400	R 5
	24330	Fries, 885	F 7
	22630	Front Royal⊙, 8,211	M 3
	22830	Fulks Run, 130	L 3
	22065	Gainesville, 600	N 3
	22463	Garrisonville, 200	N 4
	23857	Gasburg, 150	N 7
	24251	Gate City⊙, 1,914	C 7
†	24228	Georges Fork, 500	C 6
†	24248	Gibson Station, 200	A 7
	24340	Glade Spring, 1,615	E 7
	24554	Gladys, 312	K 6
	24555	Glasgow, 1,304	K 5
	23060	Glen Allen, 985	N 5
	24093	Glen Lyn, 191	G 6
	24438	Glen Wilton, 280	J 5
†	24541	Glenwood, 1,295	K 7
	23061	Gloucester⊙, 700	P 6
	23062	Gloucester Point, 850	R 6
	24094	Goldbond, 250	G 6
	22720	Goldvein, 350	N 4
	23063	Goochland⊙, 800	N 5
	24556	Goode, 200	K 6
	22942	Gordonsville, 1,253	M 4
	22637	Gore, 150	M 2
	23490	Grafton, 500	P 6
	23356	Greenbackville, 300	T 5
	23942	Green Bay, 150	M 6

(continued on following page)

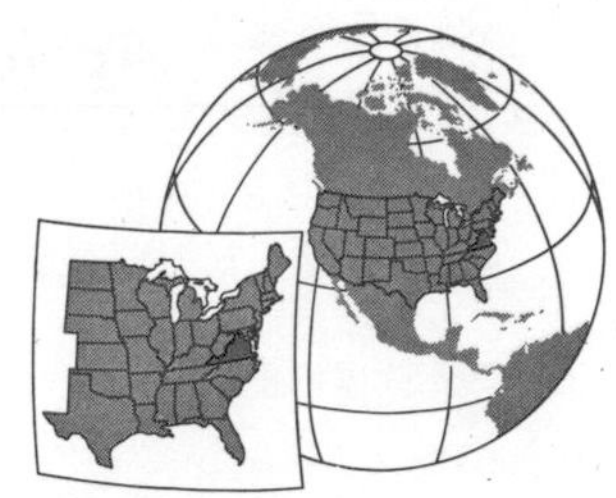

AREA 40,817 sq. mi.
POPULATION 4,648,494
CAPITAL Richmond
LARGEST CITY Norfolk
HIGHEST POINT Mt. Rogers 5,729 ft.
SETTLED IN 1607
ADMITTED TO UNION June 26, 1788
POPULAR NAME Old Dominion
STATE FLOWER Dogwood
STATE BIRD Cardinal

VIRGINIA

SCALE 0 5 10 20 30 40 MI. / 0 5 10 20 30 40 KM.

National Capital
State Capitals
County Seats
Canals

© C.S. HAMMOND & Co., N.Y.

Agriculture, Industry and Resources

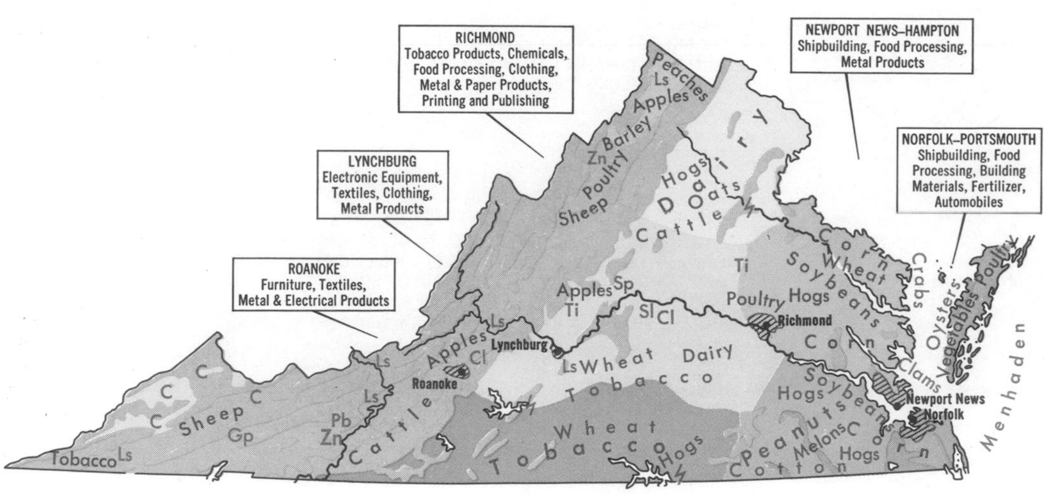

MAJOR MINERAL OCCURRENCES

C	Coal	Sl	Slate
Cl	Clay	Sp	Soapstone
Gp	Gypsum	Ti	Titanium
Ls	Limestone	Zn	Zinc
Pb	Lead		

Water Power
Major Industrial Areas

DOMINANT LAND USE

- Dairy, General Farming
- General Farming, Livestock, Dairy
- General Farming, Livestock, Tobacco
- General Farming, Livestock, Fruit, Tobacco
- General Farming, Truck Farming, Tobacco, Livestock
- Tobacco, General Farming
- Peanuts, General Farming
- Fruit and Mixed Farming
- Truck and Mixed Farming
- Forests
- Swampland, Limited Agriculture

Eric Carle — Shostal Associates

The Governor's Palace in Williamsburg, Virginia, typifies the splendor enjoyed by the royal governors in residence from 1720 to 1780.

	Zip	Place	Key
	23357	Greenbush, 200	S 5
	24440	Greenville, 450	K 5
	22943	Greenwood, 800	L 4
	24557	Gretna, 986	K 7
	24441	Grottoes, 1,166	L 4
†	22301	Groveton, 11,750	O 3
	24614	Grundy⊙, 2,054	D 6
	23065	Gum Spring, 450	N 5
	23066	Gwynn, 438	R 5
	23358	Hacksneck, 200	S 5
	24558	Halifax⊙, 899	L 7
	23359	Hallwood, 254	S 5
	22068	Hamilton, 502	N 2
	23943	Hampden-Sydney, 1,325	L 6
	23069	Hanover⊙, 975	O 5
	23389	Harborton, 200	S 5
	24101	Hardy, 325	J 6
	24618	Harman-Maxie, 925	D 6
	23071	Hartfield, 450	R 5
	22069	Haymarket, 288	N 3
	22472	Haynesville, 500	P 5
	24256	Haysi, 428	D 6
	24442	Head Waters, 250	K 4
	24443	Healing Springs, 175	J 5
	22473	Heathsville⊙, 300	P 5
	24102	Henry, 350	J 7
	22070	Herndon, 4,301	O 3
	23075	Highland Springs, 7,345	O 5
	22132	Hillsboro, 135	N 2
	24343	Hillsville⊙, 1,149	G 7
	24258	Hiltons, 300	D 7
	24347	Hiwassee, 500	G 7
†	22191	Hoadly, 400	O 3
	23390	Hobson, 800	P 7
	23391	Holland, 400	P 7
	24020	Hollins College, 1,082	H 6
	24260	Honaker, 911	D 6
	23395	Horntown, 450	T 5
	24445	Hot Springs, 300	J 4
	24104	Huddleston, 200	K 6
	22639	Hume, 350	N 3
	24620	Hurley, 850	D 6
	24563	Hurt, 1,434	K 6
	24348	Independence⊙, 673	F 7
	24448	Iron Gate, 692	J 5
	22480	Irvington, 504	R 5
	23397	Isle of Wight⊙, 4	P 7
	24350	Ivanhoe, 900	G 7
	23866	Ivor, 444	P 7
	22945	Ivy, 450	L 4
	23081	Jamestown, 12	P 6
	23398	Jamesville, 400	S 5
	23867	Jarratt, 591	O 7
	24565	Java, 160	K 7
	22724	Jeffersonton, 500	N 3
†	23434	Jericho, 2,438	P 7
	24622	Jewell Ridge, 500	E 6
	24263	Jonesville⊙, 700	B 7
	24566	Keeling, 680	K 7
	22832	Keezletown, 210	L 4
	23401	Keller, 235	S 5
	23944	Kenbridge, 1,223	M 7
	23084	Kents Store, 150	M 5
	24265	Keokee, 800	C 7
	22947	Keswick, 300	M 4
	23947	Keysville, 818	M 6
	22482	Kilmarnock, 841	R 5
	24107	Kimballton, 135	G 6
	23085	King and Queen Court House⊙, 100	P 5
	22485	King George⊙, 225	O 4
	23086	King William⊙, 125	O 5
	22488	Kinsale, 250	P 4
†	24236	Konnarock, 300	E 7
	22833	Lacey Spring, 300	L 3
	23950	La Crosse, 674	M 7
	22501	Ladysmith, 300	N 4
	24108	Lafayette, 276	H 6
	23228	Lakeside, 11,137	N 5
	24351	Lambsburg, 650	G 7
	22503	Lancaster⊙, 104	R 5
	23868	Lawrenceville⊙, 1,636	N 7
	24266	Lebanon⊙, 2,272	D 7
	22075	Leesburg⊙, 4,821	N 2
	22505	Lewisetta, 125	R 4
	22642	Linden, 320	M 3
	22834	Linville, 500	L 3
	23091	Little Plymouth, 350	P 5
†	23890	Littleton, 130	O 7
	22507	Lively, 200	P 5
†	23434	Lloyd Place, 2,367	P 7
	22509	Loretto, 200	O 4
	23093	Louisa⊙, 633	M 4
	22080	Lovettsville, 185	N 2
	22949	Lovingston⊙, 350	L 5
	22951	Lowesville, 215	K 5
	24457	Lowmoor, 600	J 5
†	22075	Lucketts, 200	N 2
	23952	Lunenburg⊙, 50	M 7
	22835	Luray⊙, 3,612	M 3
		Lynchburg, ‡123,474	K 6
	24571	Lynch Station, 500	K 6
	23405	Machipongo, 400	S 6
	22727	Madison⊙, 299	M 4
	24572	Madison Heights, 4,900	K 6
	23103	Manakin-Sabot, 200	N 5
	22110	Manassas⊙, 9,164	O 3
	22110	Manassas Park, 6,844	O 3
	23105	Mannboro, 150	N 6
	23106	Manquin, 576	O 5
	23407	Mappsville, 500	T 5
	24354	Marion⊙, 8,158	E 7
	22643	Markham, 300	N 3
	22115	Marshall, 800	N 3
	22954	Massies Mill, 250	K 5
	23109	Mathews⊙, 500	R 6
	23803	Matoaca, 829	N 6
	23110	Mattaponi, 400	P 5
	22644	Maurertown, 158	L 3
	24360	Max Meadows, 782	G 6
	24269	McClure, 250	D 6
	24111	McCoy, 420	G 6
	22840	McGaheysville, 600	L 4
	23872	McKenney, 489	N 7
	22101	McLean, 17,698	O 3
	24120	Meadows of Dan, 150	H 7
	24361	Meadowview, 875	D 7
†	24315	Mechanicsburg, 350	G 6
	23111	Mechanicsville, 5,189	O 5
	23954	Meherrin, 200	M 6
	23410	Melfa, 459	S 5
	24270	Mendota, 375	D 7
	22117	Middleburg, 833	N 3
	22645	Middletown, 507	M 2
	22728	Midland, 180	N 3
	23113	Midlothian, 950	N 6
	22514	Milford, 550	O 4
	24460	Millboro, 300	J 5
	24460	Millboro Springs, 200	J 4
	22646	Millwood, 350	N 2
	23117	Mineral, 397	N 4
	23118	Mobjack, 210	R 6
	23412	Modest Town, 200	T 5
	22517	Mollusk, 400	P 5
	24121	Moneta, 500	J 6
	24574	Monroe, 500	K 6
	24465	Monterey⊙, 223	K 4
	22520	Montross⊙, 419	P 4
	24122	Montvale, 300	J 6
	22523	Morattico, 400	P 5
	23120	Moseley, 200	N 6
	22841	Mount Crawford, 276	L 4
	22524	Mount Holly, 200	P 4
	22842	Mount Jackson, 681	L 3
	24467	Mount Sidney, 950	K 4
	22121	Mount Vernon, 10	O 3
	24468	Mustoe, 150	J 4
	24124	Narrows, 2,421	G 6
	24576	Naruna, 150	L 6
	23413	Nassawadox, 511	S 6
	24577	Nathalie, 225	L 7
	24578	Natural Bridge, 200	J 5
	24579	Natural Bridge Station, 450	K 5
	23122	Naxera, 275	R 6
	22958	Nellysford, 200	L 5
†	22186	New Baltimore, 200	N 3
	23123	New Canton, 200	M 5
	24127	New Castle⊙, 225	H 5
	23415	New Church, 427	S 5
	24469	New Hope, 170	L 4
	23124	New Kent⊙, 25	P 5
	22844	New Market, 718	L 3
	24128	Newport, 600	H 6
		Newport News-Hampton, ‡292,159	P 6
	24129	New River, 700	G 6
	23874	Newsoms, 389	O 7
	24271	Nickelsville, 338	D 7
	22123	Nokesville, 520	N 3
	24272	Nora, 200	D 6
		Norfolk-Portsmouth, ‡680,600	R 7
	23127	Norge, 375	P 6
	22959	North Garden, 200	L 5
†	24301	North Pulaski, 1,315	G 6
	22151	North Springfield, 8,631	O 3
	23955	Nottoway⊙, 170	M 6
	23416	Oak Hall, 350	S 5
	24631	Oakwood, 500	E 6
	22125	Occoquan, 975	O 3
	23417	Onancock, 1,614	S 5
	23418	Onley, 464	S 5
	22960	Orange⊙, 2,768	M 4
†	23077	Owenton, 400	O 5
	23419	Oyster, 225	S 6
	23420	Painter, 363	S 5
	22963	Palmyra⊙, 250	M 5
	23958	Pamplin, 394	L 6
†	24285	Pardee, 190	C 6
	23421	Parksley, 903	S 5
	24132	Parrott, 650	G 6
	24133	Patrick Springs, 800	H 7
	24633	Patterson, 500	D 6
†	23069	Peaks, 500	O 5
	24134	Pearisburg⊙, 2,169	G 6
	24136	Pembroke, 1,095	G 6
	23117	Pendletons, 130	N 5
	24137	Penhook, 150	J 7
	24277	Pennington Gap, 1,886	C 7
†	23072	Perrin, 250	R 6
		Petersburg-Colonial Heights, ‡128,809	N 6
	23959	Phenix, 260	L 6
	22131	Philomont, 250	N 2
	24138	Pilot, 132	H 6
	22964	Piney River, 400	L 5
	24139	Pittsville, 200	K 7
†	23434	Pleasant Hill, 2,277	P 7
	24635	Pocahontas, 891	F 6
	23362	Poquoson, 5,441	R 6
	24471	Port Republic, 150	L 4
	23181	Port Richmond, 130	P 5
	22535	Port Royal, 199	O 4
†	22443	Potomac Beach, 200	P 4
	24279	Pound, 995	C 6
	24637	Pounding Mill, 399	E 6
	23139	Powhatan⊙, 400	N 5
	23875	Prince George⊙, 150	O 6
	23960	Prospect, 275	L 6
	23140	Providence Forge, 500	P 6
	24301	Pulaski⊙, 10,279	G 6
	23422	Pungoteague, 400	S 5
	22132	Purcellville, 1,775	N 2
	23847	Purdy, 350	N 7
	22134	Quantico, 719	O 3
	23423	Quinby, 350	S 5
	22732	Radiant, 250	M 4
	23962	Randolph, 150	L 7
	24472	Raphine, 300	K 5
	22733	Rapidan, 300	M 4
	24639	Raven, 1,819	E 6
	23876	Rawlings, 200	N 7
	22140	Rectortown, 200	N 3
	24640	Red Ash, 800	E 6
	23963	Red House, 200	L 6
	23964	Red Oak, 250	L 7
	22539	Reedville, 400	R 5
	22649	Reliance, 150	M 3
	22734	Remington, 321	N 3
	22070	Reston, 5,723	O 3
	23966	Rice, 194	M 6
	24147	Rich Creek, 729	G 6
	24641	Richlands, 4,843	E 6
		Richmond, ‡518,319	O 5
	24148	Ridgeway, 624	J 7
	24149	Riner, 400	H 6
	24586	Ringgold, 150	K 7
	24150	Ripplemead, 600	G 6
	22651	Riverton, 250	M 3
	22737	Rixeyville, 150	M 3
		Roanoke, ‡181,436	H 6
	23146	Rockville, 290	N 5
	24366	Rocky Gap, 200	F 6
	24151	Rocky Mount⊙, 4,002	J 7
	24280	Rosedale, 200	E 7
	24281	Rose Hill, 700	B 7
	22967	Roseland, 210	K 5
	22141	Round Hill, 581	N 2
	24646	Rowe, 150	D 6
	22545	Ruby, 188	N 3
	24368	Rural Retreat, 872	F 7
	23425	Rushmere, 140	P 6
	24588	Rustburg⊙, 650	K 6
	22546	Ruther Glen, 400	O 5
	23147	Ruthville, 310	P 6
	24282	Saint Charles, 368	B 7
	24283	Saint Paul, 948	D 7
	23148	Saint Stephens Church, 500	O 5
	24370	Saltville, 2,527	E 7
	23149	Saluda⊙, 200	P 5
	23150	Sandston, 8,071	O 5
†	23434	Saratoga Place, 1,245	P 7
	23427	Saxis, 451	S 5
	22969	Schuyler, 375	L 5
	24589	Scottsburg, 157	L 7
	24590	Scottsville, 290	L 5
	23428	Seaford, 2,500	R 6
	22547	Sealston, 200	O 4
†	23837	Sebrell, 200	O 7
	23878	Sedley, 500	P 7
	24474	Selma, 1,058	J 5
	24373	Seven Mile Ford, 342	E 7
	23158	Shanghai, 150	P 5
	24162	Shawsville, 950	H 6
	22849	Shenandoah, 1,714	L 4
	22549	Shiloh, 150	O 4
	22971	Shipman, 500	L 5
	23879	Skippers, 150	O 7
	23430	Smithfield, 2,713	P 7
	22553	Snell, 300	N 4
	22972	Somerset, 240	M 4
	23970	South Hill, 3,858	M 7
	24374	Speedwell, 575	F 8
	24165	Spencer, 500	J 7
	22740	Sperryville, 200	M 3
	22553	Spotsylvania⊙, 350	N 4
*	22150	Springfield, 11,613	O 3
	22554	Stafford⊙, 750	O 4
	22973	Stanardsville⊙, 296	L 4
	22851	Stanley, 1,208	L 3
	24168	Stanleytown, 975	H 7
	22655	Stephens City, 802	M 2
	22170	Sterling, 8,321	O 2
	24285	Stonega, 275	C 7
	23882	Stony Creek, 430	N 7
	22657	Strasburg, 2,431	M 3
	24171	Stuart⊙, 947	H 7
	24477	Stuarts Draft, 750	L 4
	24375	Sugar Grove, 975	E 7
	23883	Surry⊙, 269	P 6
	23163	Susan, 500	R 6
	23884	Sussex⊙, 75	O 7
	24594	Sutherlin, 180	O 7
	24595	Sweet Briar, 875	K 5
	24649	Swords Creek, 315	E 6
	22743	Syria, 325	M 4
	23602	Tabb, 2,500	R 6
	24232	Tacoma, 150	C 7
	23440	Tangier, 814	R 5
	22560	Tappahannock⊙, 1,111	O 5
	24651	Tazewell⊙, 4,168	E 6
	23442	Temperanceville, 300	T 5
	24174	Thaxton, 350	K 6
	22171	The Plains, 418	N 3
	22565	Thornburg, 250	N 4
	22853	Timberville, 959	L 3
	24655	Tiptop, 200	F 6
	23168	Toano, 950	P 6
	22660	Toms Brook, 258	L 3
	23443	Townsend, 500	R 6
	24289	Trammel, 750	D 6
	22172	Triangle, 3,021	O 3
	23886	Triplet, 350	N 7
	24378	Trout Dale, 209	F 7
	24175	Troutville, 522	J 6
	22567	Unionville, 250	N 4
	22176	Upperville, 300	N 2
	23175	Urbanna, 475	P 5
	24656	Vansant, 975	D 6
†	24522	Vera, 200	L 6
	24482	Verona, 1,900	K 4
	24177	Vesta, 200	H 7
	24483	Vesuvius, 385	K 5
	23974	Victoria, 1,408	M 6
	22180	Vienna, 17,152	O 3
	24179	Vinton, 6,347	J 6
	24598	Virgilina, 249	L 7
	24379	Volney, 850	F 7
	23480	Wachapreague, 399	S 5
	23888	Wakefield, 942	O 7
	23177	Walkerton, 175	O 5
	23178	Ware Neck, 500	R 6
	24484	Warm Springs⊙, 300	J 4
	22186	Warrenton⊙, 4,027	N 3
	22572	Warsaw⊙, 511	P 5
	22747	Washington⊙, 189	M 3
	22190	Waterford, 350	N 2
	23180	Water View, 133	P 5
	23890	Waverly, 1,717	O 6
	24251	Weber City, 1,676	C 7
	22576	Weems, 500	P 5
	23181	West Point, 2,600	P 5
	24486	Weyers Cave, 300	L 4
	23485	Whaleyville, 332	P 7
	22663	White Post, 250	M 2
	22578	White Stone, 381	R 5
	24657	Whitewood, 500	E 6
	22579	Wicomico Church, 500	R 5
†	22553	Wilderness, 200	N 4
	23486	Willis Wharf, 400	S 5
	23894	Wilsons, 147	N 6
	23487	Windsor, 685	P 7
†	23832	Winterpock, 150	N 6
	24184	Wirtz, 150	J 6
	24293	Wise⊙, 2,891	C 7
	22748	Wolftown, 300	M 4
	22989	Woodberry Forest, 450	M 4
	22191	Woodbridge, 25,412	O 3
	24381	Woodlawn, 300	G 7
	22664	Woodstock⊙, 2,338	L 3
	22749	Woodville, 200	M 3
	24295	Woodway, 700	C 7
	24185	Woolwine, 150	H 7
	23976	Wylliesburg, 250	L 7
	24382	Wytheville⊙, 6,069	G 7
	22110	Yorkshire, 4,649	O 3
	23490	Yorktown⊙, 350	R 6
	23898	Zuni, 150	P 7

⊙ County seat.
‡ Population of metropolitan area.
† Zip of nearest p.o.
* Multiple zips

Agriculture, Industry and Resources

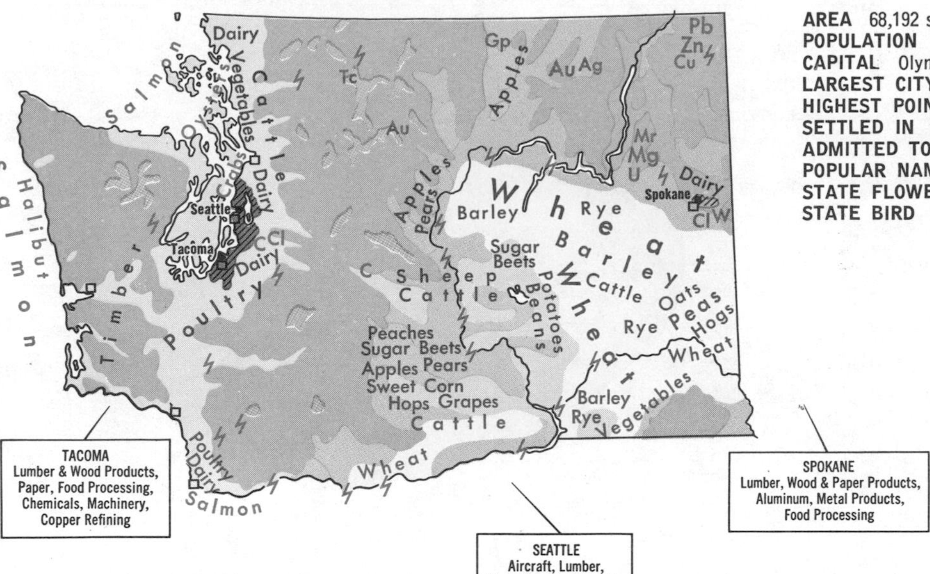

AREA 68,192 sq. mi.
POPULATION 3,409,169
CAPITAL Olympia
LARGEST CITY Seattle
HIGHEST POINT Mt. Rainier 14,410 ft.
SETTLED IN 1811
ADMITTED TO UNION November 11, 1889
POPULAR NAME Evergreen State
STATE FLOWER Coast Rhododendron
STATE BIRD Willow Goldfinch

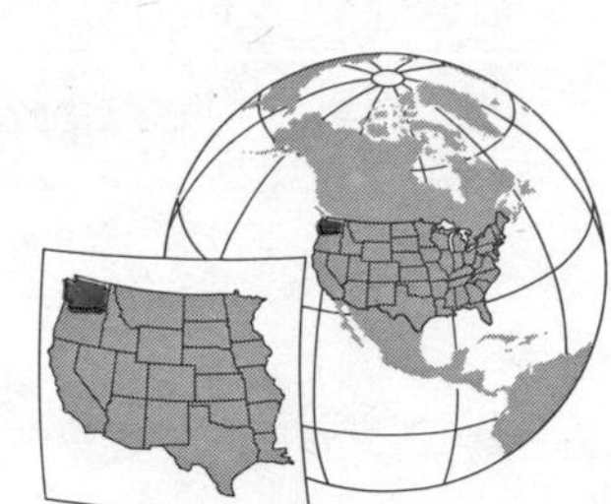

DOMINANT LAND USE

- Specialized Wheat
- Wheat, Peas
- Dairy, Poultry, Mixed Farming
- Fruit and Mixed Farming
- General Farming, Dairy, Range Livestock
- General Farming, Livestock, Special Crops
- Range Livestock
- Forests
- Urban Areas
- Nonagricultural Land

MAJOR MINERAL OCCURRENCES

Ag	Silver	Mr	Marble
Au	Gold	Pb	Lead
C	Coal	Tc	Talc
Cl	Clay	U	Uranium
Cu	Copper	W	Tungsten
Gp	Gypsum	Zn	Zinc
Mg	Magnesium		

- Water Power
- Major Industrial Areas
- Major Sawmilling Centers

Warren Dick — Shostal Associates

Pulpwood being rafted to the mills is a familiar sight in the Northwest, the region which leads the country in lumber production.

COUNTIES

Name/Pop.	Key
Adams, 12,014	G 3
Asotin, 13,799	H 4
Benton, 67,540	F 4
Chelan, 41,355	E 3
Clallam, 34,770	B 2
Clark, 128,454	C 5
Columbia, 4,439	H 4
Cowlitz, 68,616	C 4
Douglas, 16,787	F 3
Ferry, 3,655	G 2
Franklin, 25,816	G 4
Garfield, 2,911	H 4
Grant, 41,881	F 3
Grays Harbor, 59,533	B 3
Island, 27,011	C 2
Jefferson, 10,661	B 3
King, 1,156,633	D 3
Kitsap, 101,732	C 3
Kittitas, 25,039	E 3
Klickitat, 12,138	E 5
Lewis, 45,467	C 4
Lincoln, 9,572	G 3
Mason, 20,918	B 3
Okanogan, 25,867	F 2
Pacific, 15,796	B 4
Pend Oreille, 6,025	H 2
Pierce, 411,027	C 3
San Juan, 3,856	C 2
Skagit, 52,381	D 2
Skamania, 5,845	D 5
Snohomish, 265,236	D 2
Spokane, 287,487	H 3
Stevens, 17,405	H 2
Thurston, 76,894	C 4
Wahkiakum, 3,592	B 4
Walla Walla, 42,176	G 4
Whatcom, 81,950	D 2
Whitman, 37,900	H 4
Yakima, 144,971	E 4

CITIES and TOWNS

	Zip	*Name/Pop.*	*Key*
	98520	Aberdeen, 18,489	B 3
	98220	Acme, 170	C 2
	99101	Addy, 141	H 2
	98522	Adna, 150	B 4
	98810	Aeneas, 85	F 2
	99001	Airway Heights, 744	H 3
	99102	Albion, 687	H 4
	98301	Alder, 300	C 4
	98002	Algona, 1,276	C 3
	98524	Allyn, 850	C 3
	99103	Almira, 376	G 3
	98525	Aloha, 140	A 3
†	98643	Altoona, 66	B 4
	98526	Amanda Park, 495	A 3
	99002	Amber, 32	H 3
	98601	Amboy, 480	C 5
	98221	Anacortes, 7,701	C 2
	99401	Anatone, 70	H 4
	98602	Appleton, 40	D 5
†	99114	Arden, 30	H 2
	98811	Ardenvoir, 350	E 3
	98603	Ariel, 386	C 5
	98223	Arlington, 2,261	C 2
	98304	Ashford, 415	C 4
	99402	Asotin⊙, 637	H 4
	98002	Auburn, 21,817	C 3
†	99348	Ayer, 70	G 4
	98816	Azwell, 152	F 3
	98110	Bainbridge Island-Winslow, 1,461	A 2
	98224	Baring, 75	D 3
	98604	Battle Ground, 1,438	C 5
	98527	Bay Center, 350	A 4
†	98520	Bay City, 58	B 4
†	98004	Beaux Arts, 475	B 2
	98305	Beaver, 450	A 2
	98528	Belfair, 500	C 3
*	98004	Bellevue, 61,102	B 2
	98225	Bellingham⊙, 39,375	C 2
	99104	Belmont, 59	H 3
	99105	Benge, 45	G 4
	99320	Benton City, 1,070	F 4
	99321	Beverly, 86	F 4
	99322	Bickleton, 200	E 5
†	98273	Biglake, 105	C 2
	98605	Bingen, 671	D 5
	98010	Black Diamond, 1,160	D 3
	98230	Blaine, 1,955	C 2
	98231	Blanchard, 200	C 2
	99106	Bluecreek, 40	H 2
†	98382	Blyn, 350	B 3
†	98532	Boistfort, 55	B 4
†	98390	Bonney Lake, 2,313	C 3
†	99126	Bossburg, 66	H 2
	98011	Bothell, 4,883	B 1
	98232	Bow, 975	C 2
	99107	Boyds, 68	G 2
	98310	Bremerton, 35,307	A 2
	98812	Brewster, 1,059	F 2
	98813	Bridgeport, 952	F 3
	98036	Brier, 3,093	C 3
	98320	Brinnon, 500	B 3
†	98537	Brooklyn, 50	B 4
	98920	Brownstown, 80	E 4
†	98310	Brownsville, 50	A 2
	98606	Brush Prairie, 200	C 5
†	98101	Bryn Mawr, 4,589	B 2
	98321	Buckley, 3,446	C 3
	98530	Bucoda, 421	C 4
	98921	Buena, 590	E 4
	99323	Burbank, 800	G 4
	98166	Burien, 2,000	A 2
	98322	Burley, 200	C 3
	98233	Burlington, 3,138	C 2
	98013	Burton, 650	C 3
	98607	Camas, 5,790	C 5
	98323	Carbonado, 394	D 3
	98324	Carlsborg, 500	B 2
	98814	Carlton, 120	F 2
	98014	Carnation, 530	D 3
	98609	Carrolls, 400	C 4
	98610	Carson, 500	D 5
	98815	Cashmere, 1,976	E 3
	98611	Castle Rock, 1,647	B 4
	98612	Cathlamet⊙, 647	B 4
†	98045	Cedar Falls, 200	D 3
	98613	Centerville, 100	D 5
	98531	Centralia, 10,054	C 4
	98520	Central Park, 2,720	B 3
	99003	Chattaroy, 250	H 3
	98532	Chehalis⊙, 5,727	C 4
	98816	Chelan, 2,430	E 3
	98817	Chelan Falls, 200	E 3
	99004	Cheney, 6,358	H 3
	98818	Chesaw, 32	G 2
	99109	Chewelah, 1,365	H 2
	98325	Chimacum, 275	C 3
	98614	Chinook, 445	B 4
	98533	Cinebar, 35	C 4
	98326	Clallam Bay, 750	A 2
	99403	Clarkston, 6,312	H 4
	99110	Clayton, 204	H 3
	98235	Clearlake, 750	C 2
	98399	Clearwater, 155	A 3
	98922	Cle Elum, 1,725	E 3
†	98937	Cliffdell, 50	E 4
	98236	Clinton, 500	C 3
	98244	Clipper, 25	C 2
†	99402	Cloverland, 80	H 4
†	98004	Clyde Hill, 2,987	B 2
†	98055	Coalfield, 500	B 2
	99005	Colbert, 225	H 3
†	98366	Colby, 150	A 2
	99111	Colfax⊙, 2,664	H 4
	99324	College Place, 4,510	G 4
	99113	Colton, 279	H 4
†	98632	Columbia Heights, 1,572	C 4
	99114	Colville⊙, 3,742	H 2
	98819	Conconully, 122	F 2
	98237	Concrete, 573	D 2
	99326	Connell, 1,161	G 4
	98238	Conway, 120	C 2
	98605	Cook, 240	D 5
	98535	Copalis Beach, 481	A 3
	98536	Copalis Crossing, 200	B 3
	98537	Cosmopolis, 1,599	B 4
	98616	Cougar, 76	C 4
	99115	Coulee City, 558	F 3
	99116	Coulee Dam, 1,425	G 3
	98239	Coupeville⊙, 678	C 2
	98923	Cowiche, 150	E 4
	99117	Creston, 325	G 3
	98015	Cumberland, 250	D 3
	99118	Curlew, 200	G 2
	98538	Curtis, 200	B 4
	99119	Cusick, 257	H 2
	98240	Custer, 315	C 2
	98617	Dallesport, 400	D 5
	99121	Danville, 108	G 2
	98241	Darrington, 1,094	D 2
	99122	Davenport⊙, 1,363	G 3
	99328	Dayton⊙, 2,596	H 4
†	99010	Deepcreek, 73	H 3
	98618	Deep River, 500	B 4
	98243	Deer Harbor, 200	B 2
	99006	Deer Park, 1,295	H 3
	98244	Deming, 250	C 2
†	99006	Denison, 100	H 3
	98188	Des Moines, 3,871	B 2
†	98283	Diablo, 200	D 2
†	99111	Diamond, 49	H 4
	99213	Dishman, 9,079	H 3
	99329	Dixie, 200	G 4
†	98279	Doebay, 100	C 2
†	98951	Donald, 100	E 4
	98539	Doty, 210	B 4
†	98858	Douglas, 27	F 3
†	98532	Dryad, 184	B 4
	98821	Dryden, 550	E 3
†	98382	Dungeness, 675	B 2
	98327	Du Pont, 384	C 3
	98019	Duvall, 607	D 3
	98540	East Olympia, 300	B 4
	98925	Easton, 300	D 3
	98245	Eastsound, 800	B 2
	98801	East Wenatchee, 913	E 3
	98328	Eatonville, 2,446	C 4
	98246	Edison, 250	C 2
	98020	Edmonds, 23,998	C 3

(continued on following page)

99008 Edwall, 130 H 3
98330 Elbe, 115 C 4
† 99130 Elberton, 75 H 4
† 98555 Eldon, 60 B 3
99123 Electric City, 651 F 3
† 98360 Electron, 74 C 4
99009 Elk, 100 H 2
98926 Ellensburg⊙, 13,568 E 3
98541 Elma, 2,227 B 4
99124 Elmer City, 324 G 2
99330 Eltopia, 75 G 4
99125 Endicott, 333 H 4
† 98310 Enetai, 2,878 A 2
98822 Entiat, 355 E 3
98022 Enumclaw, 4,703 D 3
98823 Ephrata⊙, 5,255 F 3
† 98310 Erlands Point, 1,017 A 2
99010 Espanola, 75 H 3
98542 Ethel, 100 C 4
† 99348 Eureka, 56 G 4
99126 Evans, 78 H 2
98201 Everett⊙, 53,622 C 3
98247 Everson, 633 C 2
99127 Ewan, 57 H 3
† 98323 Fairfax, 35 C 4
99012 Fairfield, 416 H 3
† 98901 Fairview, 2,111 E 4
98024 Fall City, 1,700 D 3
99128 Farmington, 140 H 3
98248 Ferndale, 2,164 C 2
98424 Fife, 1,458 C 3
99336 Finley, 70 F 4
98466 Fircrest, 5,651 C 3
† 98531 Fords Prairie, 2,250 B 4
98331 Forks, 1,328 A 3
99014 Four Lakes, 200 H 3
98543 Frances, 144 B 4
98249 Freeland, 50 C 2
99015 Freeman, 150 H 3
98250 Friday Harbor⊙, 803 B 2
† 98901 Fruitvale, 3,275 E 4
98544 Galvin, 165 B 4
98334 Gardiner, 80 B 2
99130 Garfield, 610 H 3
† 99362 Garrett, 1,586 G 4
† 98579 Gate, 75 B 4
98824 George, 273 F 3
98335 Gig Harbor, 1,657 C 3
98244 Glacier, 100 D 2
98336 Glenoma, 500 C 4
98619 Glenwood, 500 D 4
98251 Gold Bar, 504 D 3
98620 Goldendale⊙, 2,484 E 5
† 99356 Goodnoe Hills, 40 E 5
98337 Gorst, 750 C 3
99133 Grand Coulee, 1,302 G 3
† 98531 Grand Mound, 100 C 4
98930 Grandview, 3,605 F 4
98932 Granger, 1,567 E 4
98252 Granite Falls, 813 D 2
98546 Grapeview, 250 C 3
98547 Grayland, 750 A 4
98621 Grays River, 400 B 4
99016 Greenacres, 2,324 J 3
98253 Greenbank, 500 C 2
98254 Grotto, 60 D 3
98339 Hadlock, 500 C 2
98255 Hamilton, 196 D 2
98340 Hansville, 250 C 3
98341 Harper, 300 A 2
98933 Harrah, 305 E 4
99134 Harrington, 489 G 3
99135 Hartline, 189 F 3
99332 Hatton, 60 G 4
† 98855 Havillah, 35 F 2
99136 Hay, 55 H 4
98622 Heisson, 70 C 5
98025 Hobart, 500 D 3
† 98648 Home Valley, 120 D 5
98548 Hoodsport, 500 B 3
99333 Hooper, 75 G 4
98550 Hoquiam, 10,466 A 3
98552 Humptulips, 240 A 3
99137 Hunters, 200 G 2
† 99328 Huntsville, 100 G 4
98623 Husum, 200 D 5
98026 Hyak, 50 D 3
98624 Ilwaco, 506 A 4
† 99138 Impach, 44 G 2
99138 Inchelium, 206 G 2
98256 Index, 169 D 3
98342 Indianola, 500 A 1
99139 Ione, 529 H 2
99159 Irby, 30 G 3
98027 Issaquah, 4,313 C 3
98343 Joyce, 375 B 2
98033 Juanita, 9,450 B 1
99335 Kahlotus, 308 G 4
† 98399 Kalaloch, 30 A 3
98625 Kalama, 1,106 C 4
98344 Kapowsin, 450 C 4
99140 Keller, 96 G 2
98626 Kelso⊙, 10,296 C 4
† 98244 Kendall, 100 C 2
98028 Kenmore, 1,400 B 1
99336 Kennewick, 15,212 F 4
98031 Kent, 21,510 C 3
99141 Kettle Falls, 893 H 2
99142 Kewa, 63 G 2
98345 Keyport, 900 A 2
98346 Kingston, 950 C 3
99340 Kiona, 230 F 4
98033 Kirkland, 15,249 B 2
98934 Kittitas, 637 E 4
98628 Klickitat, 700 D 5
† 98832 Krupp (Marlin), 52 F 3
98629 La Center, 300 C 5
98501 Lacey, 9,696 C 3
98257 La Conner, 639 C 2
99143 Lacrosse, 426 H 4
98348 La Grande, 100 C 4
† 98101 Lake Forest Park, 2,530 B 1
98258 Lake Stevens, 1,283 D 3
98259 Lakewood, 950 C 2
99017 Lamont, 88 H 3
98260 Langley, 547 C 2
98350 La Push, 375 A 3
99018 Latah, 169 H 3
98630 Laurel, 100 D 5
99146 Laurier, 50 G 2
98826 Leavenworth, 1,322 E 3
98554 Lebam, 250 B 4
† 98368 Leland, 30 C 3
98035 Lester, 100 D 3
† 98922 Liberty, 25 E 3
99019 Liberty Lake, 300 J 3
98555 Lilliwaup, 80 B 3
99147 Lincoln, 114 G 3
99341 Lind, 622 G 4
98556 Littlerock, 300 B 4
98631 Long Beach, 968 A 4
98351 Longbranch, 400 C 3
98397 Longmire, 60 D 4
98632 Longview, 28,373 B 4
98827 Loomis, 150 F 2
99148 Loon Lake, 500 H 2
98261 Lopez, 100 C 2
98262 Lummi Island, 450 C 2
98635 Lyle, 360 D 5
98263 Lyman, 324 D 2
98264 Lynden, 2,808 C 2
98036 Lynnwood, 16,919 C 3
98935 Mabton, 925 E 4
98828 Malaga, 125 E 3
99149 Malden, 219 H 3
99150 Malo, 25 G 2

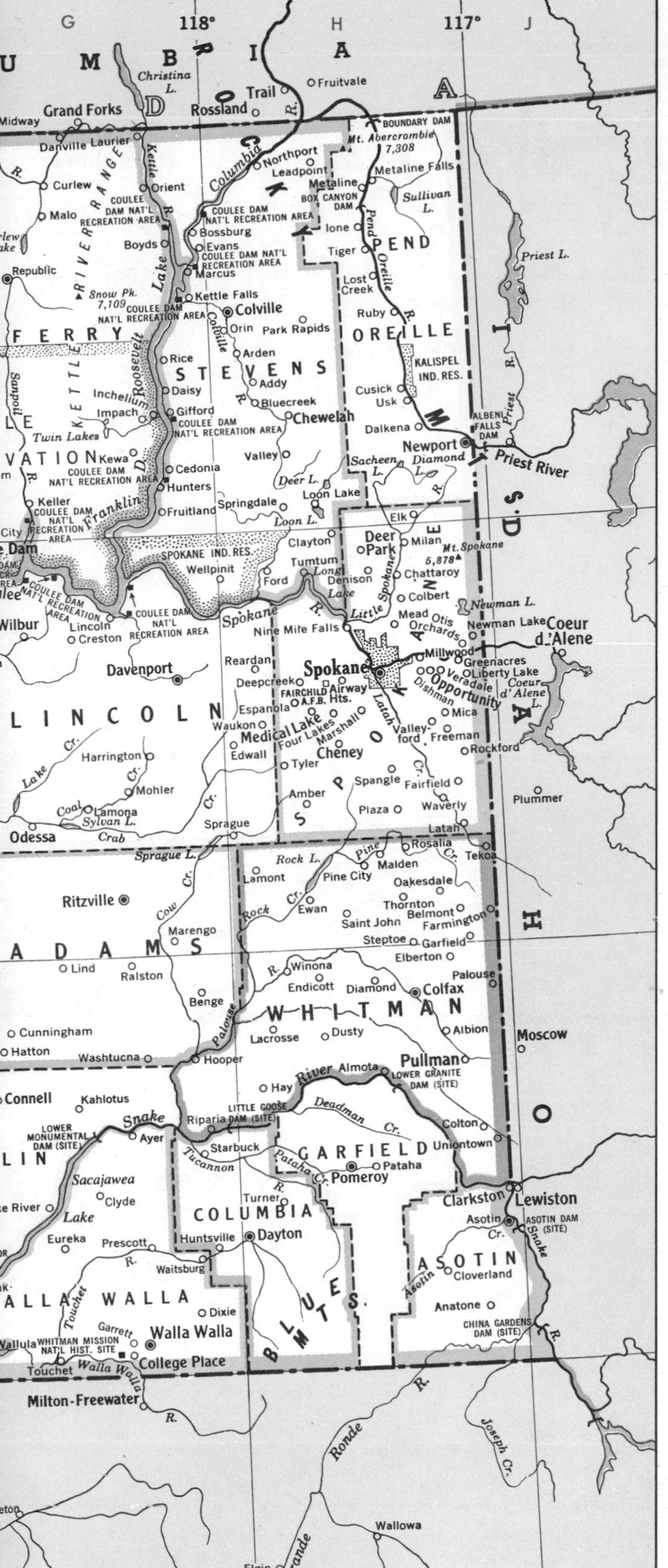

Topography

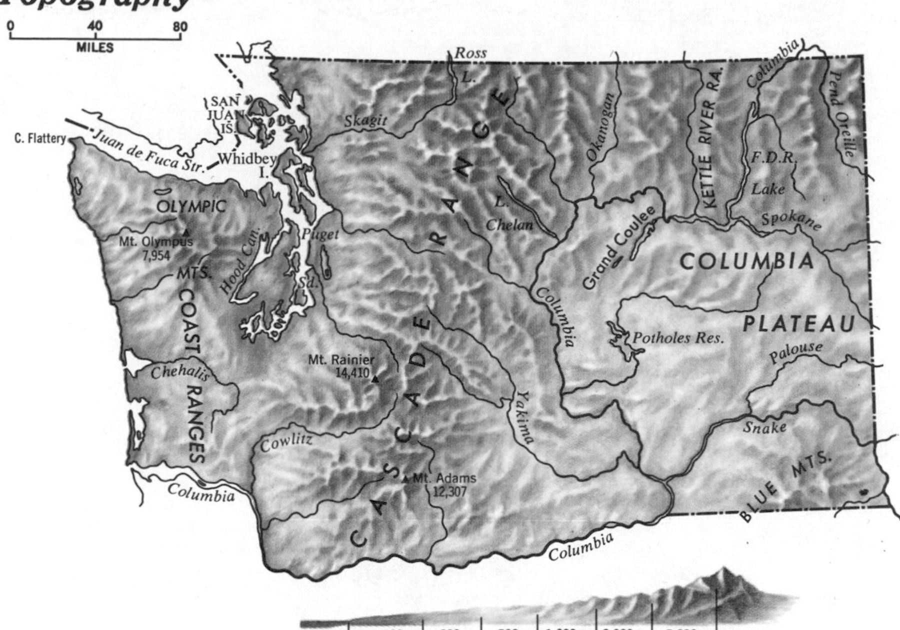

98559 Malone, 175........B 4
98829 Malott, 350........F 2
98353 Manchester, 400........A 2
98830 Mansfield, 273........F 3
98831 Manson, 220........E 3
98266 Maple Falls, 90........D 2
98038 Maple Valley, 2,900........C 3
98267 Marblemount, 387........D 2
99151 Marcus, 142........H 2
98268 Marietta, 300........C 2
98520 Markham, 180........B 4
98832 Marlin, 52........F 3
99020 Marshall, 150........H 3
98620 Maryhill, 90........E 5
98270 Marysville, 4,343........C 2
98560 Matlock, 250........B 3
99344 Mattawa, 180........F 4
98557 McCleary, 1,265........B 3
98558 McKenna, 250........C 4
98273 McMurray, 62........C 2
99021 Mead, 1,099........H 3
99022 Medical Lake, 3,529........H 3
98039 Medina, 3,455........B 2
98563 Melbourne, 200........B 4
98561 Menlo, 200........B 4
98040 Mercer Island (city), 19,047..B 2
† 98826 Merritt, 150........E 3
99343 Mesa, 274........G 4
99152 Metaline, 197........H 2
99153 Metaline Falls, 307........H 2
98834 Methow, 84........E 2
99023 Mica, 130........H 3
99024 Milan, 90........H 3
99212 Millwood, 1,770........H 3
98354 Milton, 2,607........C 3
98355 Mineral, 500........C 4
98562 Moclips, 650........A 3
98836 Monitor, 75........E 3
98272 Monroe, 2,687........D 3
† 98812 Monse, 29........F 2
98563 Montesano⊙, 2,847........B 4
98356 Morton, 1,134........C 4
98837 Moses Lake, 10,310........F 3
98564 Mossyrock, 409........C 4
98043 Mountlake Terrace, 16,600....B 1
98273 Mount Vernon⊙, 8,804........C 2
98936 Moxee City, 600........E 4
98275 Mukilteo, 1,369........C 3
98937 Naches, 666........E 4
98537 Nahcotta, 200........A 4
98565 Napavine, 377........C 4
98638 Naselle, 500........B 4
† 98310 Navy Yard City, 2,827........A 2
98357 Neah Bay, 750........A 2
98566 Neilton, 250........B 3
99155 Nespelem, 323........G 2
† 98283 Newhalem, 350........D 2
99025 Newman Lake, 102........J 3
99156 Newport⊙, 1,418........H 2
99026 Nine Mile Falls, 150........H 3
† 98501 Nisqually, 500........C 3
98276 Nooksack, 322........C 2
98358 Nordland, 500........C 2
† 98100 Normandy Park, 4,208........A 2
98045 North Bend, 1,625........D 3
98639 North Bonneville, 459........C 5
† 98590 North Cove, 50........A 4
99157 Northport, 423........H 2
99158 Oakesdale, 447........H 3
98277 Oak Harbor, 9,167........C 2
98568 Oakville, 460........B 4
98569 Ocean City, 350........A 3
98640 Ocean Park, 918........A 4
† 98520 Ocosta, 300........B 4
99159 Odessa, 1,074........G 3
98840 Okanogan⊙, 2,015........F 2
98359 Olalla, 800........A 2
98279 Olga, 150........C 2
98501 Olympia (cap.)⊙, 23,111........C 3
98841 Omak, 4,164........F 2
98570 Onalaska, 288........C 4
99214 Opportunity, 16,604........H 3
98662 Orchards, 800........C 5
99160 Orient, 200........G 2
98843 Orondo, 130........E 3
98844 Oroville, 1,555........F 2
98360 Orting, 1,643........C 3
98223 Oso, 150........D 2
99344 Othello, 4,122........F 4
99027 Otis Orchards, 900........H 3
98938 Outlook, 300........E 4
98641 Oysterville, 86........A 4
† 98326 Ozette, 50........A 2
98047 Pacific, 1,831........C 3
98571 Pacific Beach, 975........A 3
98361 Packwood, 800........D 4
98845 Palisades, 90........E 3
98048 Palmer, 250........D 3
99161 Palouse, 948........H 4
98398 Paradise Inn, 200........D 4
98939 Parker, 700........E 4
98444 Parkland, 21,012........C 3
99301 Pasco⊙, 13,920........F 4
† 99347 Pataha, 97........H 4
98846 Pateros, 472........E 2
99345 Paterson, 50........F 5
98572 Pe Ell, 582........B 4
98847 Peshastin, 200........E 3
99162 Pine City, 48........H 3
† 98826 Plain, 75........E 3
99028 Plaza, 50........H 3
99346 Plymouth, 89........F 5
98281 Point Roberts, 400........B 2
99347 Pomeroy⊙, 1,823........H 4
98362 Port Angeles⊙, 16,367........B 2
98110 Port Blakely, 600........A 2
98573 Porter, 200........B 4
98364 Port Gamble, 425........C 3
98365 Port Ludlow, 200........C 3
98366 Port Orchard⊙, 3,904........A 2
98368 Port Townsend⊙, 5,241........C 2
98574 Potlatch, 350........B 3
98370 Poulsbo, 1,856........A 1
99348 Prescott, 242........G 4
98050 Preston, 500........D 3
† 98250 Prevost, 25........B 2
99350 Prosser⊙, 2,954........F 4
99163 Pullman, 20,509........H 4
98371 Puyallup, 14,742........C 3
† 98399 Queets, 180........A 3
98376 Quilcene, 900........B 3
98575 Quinault, 340........B 3
98848 Quincy, 3,237........F 3
98576 Rainier, 382........C 4
99165 Ralston, 35........G 4
98377 Randle, 950........D 4
98051 Ravensdale, 400........D 3
98577 Raymond, 3,126........B 4
99029 Reardan, 389........H 3
98052 Redmond, 11,031........B 1
98054 Redondo, 950........C 3
98055 Renton, 25,258........B 2
99166 Republic⊙, 862........G 2
98378 Retsil, 419........A 2
99352 Richland, 26,290........F 4
98160 Richmond Beach, 2,550........A 1
† 98133 Richmond Highlands, 6,854........A 1
98642 Ridgefield, 1,004........C 5
99169 Ritzville⊙, 1,876........G 3
98849 Riverside, 228........F 2
† 98188 Riverton, 23,160........B 2
98188 Riverton Heights, 34,800........B 2
† 98252 Robe, 175........D 2
98250 Roche Harbor, 175........B 2
98579 Rochester, 325........C 4
99030 Rockford, 327........H 3
† 98801 Rock Island, 191........E 3
98283 Rockport, 350........D 2
† 98626 Rocky Point, 1,733........A 2
98061 Rollingbay, 950........A 2
98940 Ronald, 200........E 3
99356 Roosevelt, 60........E 5
99170 Rosalia, 569........H 3
98643 Rosburg, 250........B 4
98941 Roslyn, 1,031........E 3
98580 Roy, 381........C 4
99357 Royal City, 477........F 4
† 98832 Ruff, 40........F 3
† 98401 Ruston, 668........C 3
98581 Ryderwood, 345........B 4
99171 Saint John, 575........H 3
98582 Salkum, 298........C 4
† 98239 San de Fuca, 80........C 2
98379 Sappho, 200........A 2
98583 Satsop, 300........B 3
† 98283 Sauk, 50........D 2
† 98370 Scandia, 75........A 1
† 99321 Schawana, 100........F 4
98380 Seabeck, 200........C 3
† 98110 Seabold, 250........A 1
98062 Seahurst, 3,000........A 2
* 98101 Seattle⊙, 530,831........A 2
Seattle-Everett, ‡1,421,869...A 2
98644 Seaview, 950........A 4
98284 Sedro-Woolley, 4,598........C 2
98381 Sekiu, 500........A 2
98942 Selah, 3,070........E 4
98064 Selleck, 300........D 3
98382 Sequim, 1,549........B 2
98286 Shaw Island, 95........B 2
98584 Shelton⊙, 6,515........B 3
† 98270 Shoultes, 4,754........C 2
98287 Silvana, 300........C 2
98585 Silver Creek, 382........C 4
98383 Silverdale, 950........A 2
98645 Silverlake, 42........C 4
† 98252 Silverton, 65........D 2
98646 Skamania, 250........C 5
98647 Skamokawa, 500........B 4
98288 Skykomish, 283........D 3
† 99357 Smyrna, 70........F 4
98290 Snohomish, 5,174........D 3
98065 Snoqualmie, 1,260........D 3
98066 Snoqualmie Falls, 250........D 3
98851 Soap Lake, 1,064........F 3
98586 South Bend⊙, 1,795........B 4
† 98901 South Broadway, 3,298........E 4
98943 South Cle Elum, 374........D 3
98384 South Colby, 450........A 2
98385 South Prairie, 206........D 3
98386 Southworth, 425........A 2
98387 Spanaway, 5,768........C 3
99031 Spangle, 179........H 3
* 99201 Spokane⊙, 170,516........H 3
Spokane, †287,487........H 3
99032 Sprague, 550........G 3
99173 Springdale, 215........H 2
98292 Stanwood, 1,347........C 2
99359 Starbuck, 216........G 4
98293 Startup, 450........D 3
98852 Stehekin, 40........E 2
98388 Steilacoom, 2,850........C 3
99174 Steptoe, 200........H 3
98648 Stevenson⊙, 916........C 5
98853 Stratford, 160........F 3
98294 Sultan, 1,119........D 3
98295 Sumas, 689........C 2
98390 Sumner, 4,325........C 3
† 98101 Sunnydale, 1,850........B 2
98944 Sunnyside, 6,751........F 4
98392 Suquamish, 950........A 1
* 98401 Tacoma⊙, 154,581........C 3
Tacoma, ‡411,027........C 3
98587 Taholah, 550........A 3
98588 Tahuya, 260........B 3
99033 Tekoa, 808........H 3
† 98826 Telma, 150........E 3
98589 Tenino, 962........C 4
98901 Terrace Heights, 1,033........E 4
99176 Thornton, 97........H 3
98946 Thorp, 350........E 3
98947 Tieton, 415........E 4
99177 Tiger, 69........H 2
98492 Tillicum, 1,900........C 3
98590 Tokeland, 300........A 4
98591 Toledo, 654........C 4
98855 Tonasket, 951........F 2
98948 Toppenish, 5,744........E 4
99360 Touchet, 250........G 4
98649 Toutle, 813........C 4
98393 Tracyton, 1,413........A 2
† 98848 Trinidad, 30........F 3
98650 Trout Lake, 500........D 5
98188 Tukwila, 3,496........B 2
† 98270 Tulalip, 325........C 2
99034 Tumtum, 100........H 3
98501 Tumwater, 5,373........B 3
† 99328 Turner, 25........H 4
98856 Twisp, 756........E 2
99035 Tyler, 69........H 3
98651 Underwood, 500........D 5
98592 Union, 380........B 3
98903 Union Gap, 2,040........E 4
99179 Uniontown, 310........H 4
99180 Usk, 250........H 2
98593 Vader, 387........B 4
99181 Valley, 156........H 2
99036 Valleyford, 250........H 3
* 98660 Vancouver⊙, 42,493........C 5
98950 Vantage, 125........E 4
98244 Van Zandt, 25........C 2
98070 Vashon, 350........A 2
98394 Vaughn, 600........C 3
99037 Veradale, 5,320........H 3
98670 Wahkiacus, 65........D 5
99361 Waitsburg, 953........G 4
98297 Waldron, 75........B 2
99362 Walla Walla⊙, 23,619........G 4
99363 Wallula, 89........G 4
98951 Wapato, 2,841........E 4
98857 Warden, 1,254........F 4
† 98292 Warm Beach, 225........C 2
98671 Washougal, 3,388........C 5
99371 Washtucna, 316........G 4
98858 Waterville⊙, 919........E 3
99038 Waukon, 41........H 3
98395 Wauna, 300........C 3
99039 Waverly, 48........H 3
99040 Wellpinit, 125........G 3
98801 Wenatchee⊙, 16,912........E 3
† 98837 Westlake, 258........F 3
98595 Westport, 1,364........A 4
99352 West Richland, 1,107........F 4
† 98801 West Wenatchee, 2,134........E 3
† 98837 Wheeler, 75........F 3
98146 White Center, 17,300........A 2
† 98541 Whites, 70........B 3
98672 White Salmon, 1,585........D 5
98952 White Swan, 270........E 4
98285 Wickersham, 200........C 2
99185 Wilbur, 1,074........G 3
98906 Wiley City, 250........E 4
98396 Wilkeson, 317........D 3
† 98577 Willapa, 300........B 4
98860 Wilson Creek, 184........F 3
† 98848 Winchester, 70........F 3
98596 Winlock, 890........C 4
99186 Winona, 51........H 4
† 98110 Winslow (Bainbridge Island-Winslow), 1,461........A 2
98862 Winthrop, 371........E 2
98673 Wishram, 575........D 5
98863 Withrow, 30........F 3
98072 Woodinville, 2,900........B 1
98674 Woodland, 1,622........C 5
† 98020 Woodway, 879........C 3
98675 Yacolt, 488........C 5
* 98901 Yakima⊙, 45,588........E 4
† 98004 Yarrow Point, 1,103........B 2
98597 Yelm, 628........C 4
98188 Zenith, 1,900........C 3
98953 Zillah, 1,138........E 4

⊙ County seat.
‡ Population of metropolitan area.
† Zip of nearest p.o.
* Multiple zips

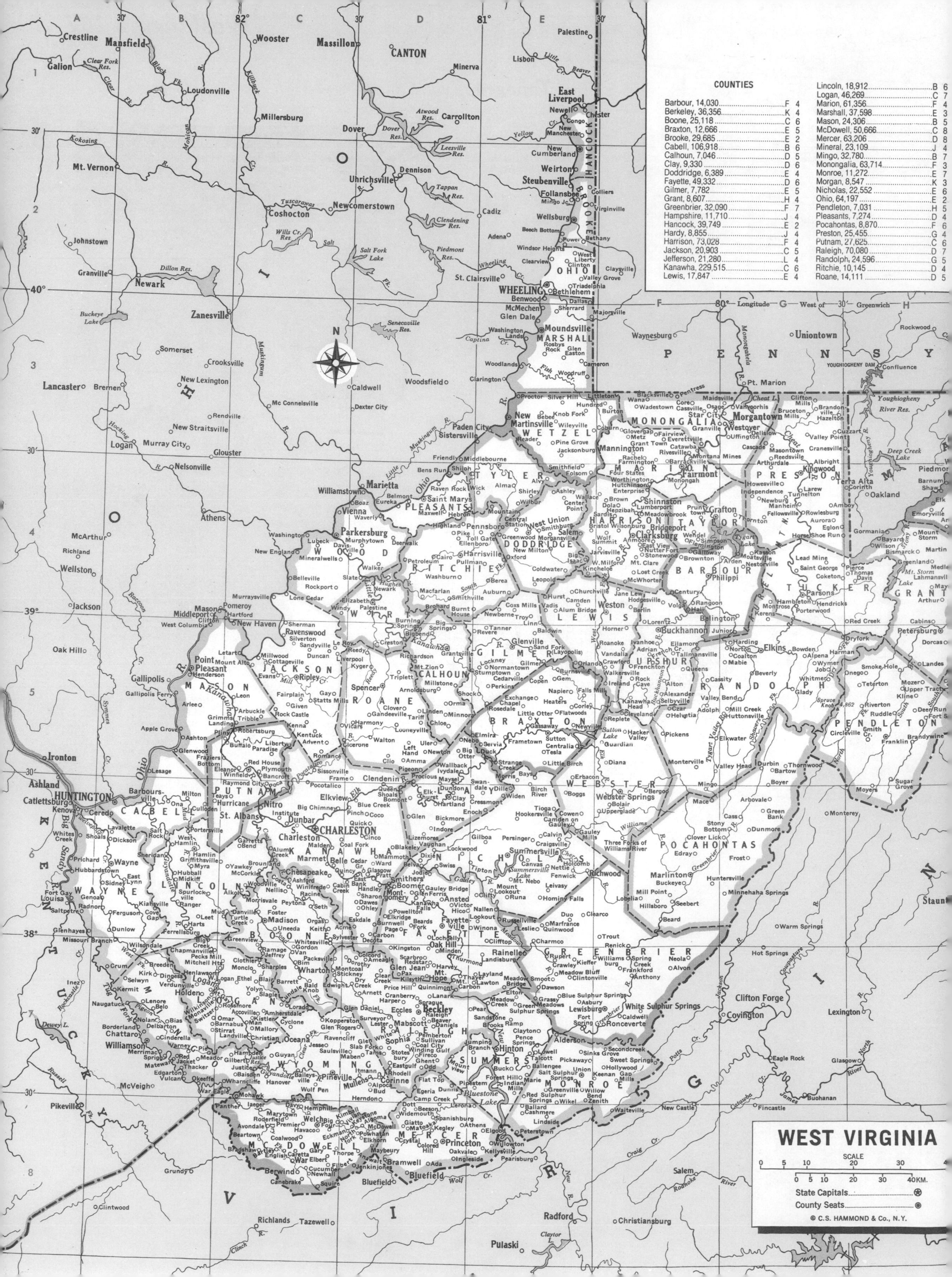
WEST VIRGINIA
COUNTIES
Barbour, 14,030 F 4
Berkeley, 36,356 K 4
Boone, 25,118 C 6
Braxton, 12,666 E 5
Brooke, 29,685 E 2
Cabell, 106,918 B 6
Calhoun, 7,046 D 5
Clay, 9,330 D 6
Doddridge, 6,389 E 4
Fayette, 49,332 D 6
Gilmer, 7,782 E 5
Grant, 8,607 H 4
Greenbrier, 32,090 F 7
Hampshire, 11,710 J 4
Hancock, 39,749 E 2
Hardy, 8,855 J 4
Harrison, 73,028 F 4
Jackson, 20,903 C 5
Jefferson, 21,280 L 4
Kanawha, 229,515 C 6
Lewis, 17,847 E 4
Lincoln, 18,912 B 6
Logan, 46,269 C 7
Marion, 61,356 F 4
Marshall, 37,598 E 3
Mason, 24,306 B 5
McDowell, 50,666 C 8
Mercer, 63,206 D 8
Mineral, 23,109 J 4
Mingo, 32,780 B 7
Monongalia, 63,714 F 3
Monroe, 11,272 E 7
Morgan, 8,547 K 3
Nicholas, 22,552 E 6
Ohio, 64,197 E 2
Pendleton, 7,031 H 5
Pleasants, 7,274 D 4
Pocahontas, 8,870 F 6
Preston, 25,455 G 4
Putnam, 27,625 C 6
Raleigh, 70,080 D 7
Randolph, 24,596 G 5
Ritchie, 10,145 D 4
Roane, 14,111 D 5
SCALE
0 5 10 20 30 40 MI.
0 5 10 20 30 40 KM.
State Capitals
County Seats
© C.S. HAMMOND & Co., N.Y.

Summers, 13,213 E 7
Taylor, 13,878 F 4
Tucker, 7,447 G 4
Tyler, 9,929 E 4
Upshur, 19,092 F 5
Wayne, 37,581 B 6
Webster, 9,809 F 6
Wetzel, 20,314 E 3
Wirt, 4,154 D 4
Wood, 86,818 D 4
Wyoming, 30,095 C 7

CITIES and TOWNS

Zip *Name/Pop.* *Key*
25606 Accoville, 975 C 7
† 24701 Ada, 250 D 8
† 26288 Addison (Webster Springs)⊙, 1,038 F 6
26210 Adrian, 500 F 5
26519 Albright, 319 G 3
24910 Alderson, 1,278 E 7
24807 Algoma, 400 D 8
25501 Alkol, 500 C 6
26320 Alma, 296 E 4
24710 Alpoca, 200 D 7
25003 Alum Creek, 900 C 6
25004 Ameagle, 210 D 7
25607 Amherstdale, 1,602 C 4
24808 Anawalt, 801 D 8
26323 Anmoore, 944 F 4
25812 Ansted, 1,511 D 6
24915 Arbovale, 300 G 6
25006 Arbuckle, 300 C 5
26324 Arden, 200 G 4
25007 Arnett, 300 D 7
25234 Arnoldsburg, 175 D 5
26816 Arthur, 200 H 4
26520 Arthurdale, 950 G 3
24916 Asbury, 280 E 7
24809 Asco, 200 C 8
25009 Ashford, 400 C 6
24712 Athens, 967 E 8
26704 Augusta, 550 J 4
26705 Aurora, 275 G 4
24811 Avondale, 250 C 8
24812 Baileysville, 800 C 7
25608 Baisden, 500 C 7
26801 Baker, 200 J 4
25410 Bakerton, 250 L 4
25010 Bald Knob, 356 C 7
24918 Ballard, 220 E 8
25011 Bancroft, 446 C 5
25504 Barboursville, 2,279 B 6
25609 Barnabus, 750 C 7
26559 Barrackville, 1,596 F 3
25013 Barrett, 950 C 7
24813 Bartley, 600 C 8
† 25411 Bath, 944 K 3
26707 Bayard, 475 H 4
† 26629 Bays, 186 E 5
25014 Beards Fork, 350 D 6
24814 Beartown, 500 C 8
25813 Beaver (Glen Hedrick), 1,711 D 7
25801 Beckley⊙, 19,884 D 7
26030 Beech Bottom, 544 E 2
24714 Beeson, 250 D 8
26250 Belington, 1,567 F 4

AREA 24,181 sq. mi.
POPULATION 1,744,237
CAPITAL Charleston
LARGEST CITY Huntington
HIGHEST POINT Spruce Knob 4,862 ft.
SETTLED IN 1774
ADMITTED TO UNION June 20, 1863
POPULAR NAME Mountain State
STATE FLOWER Rhododendron
STATE BIRD Cardinal

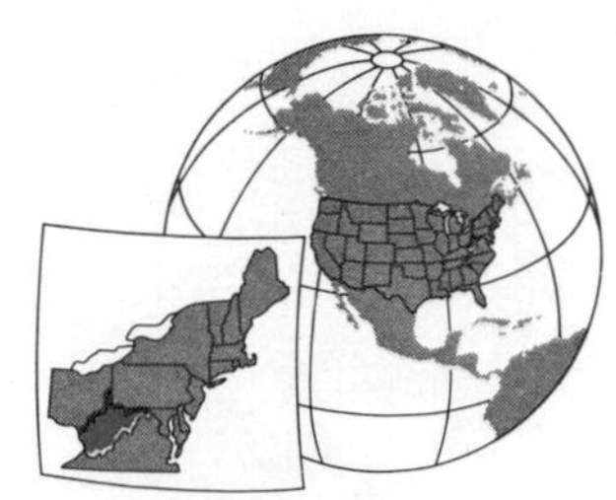

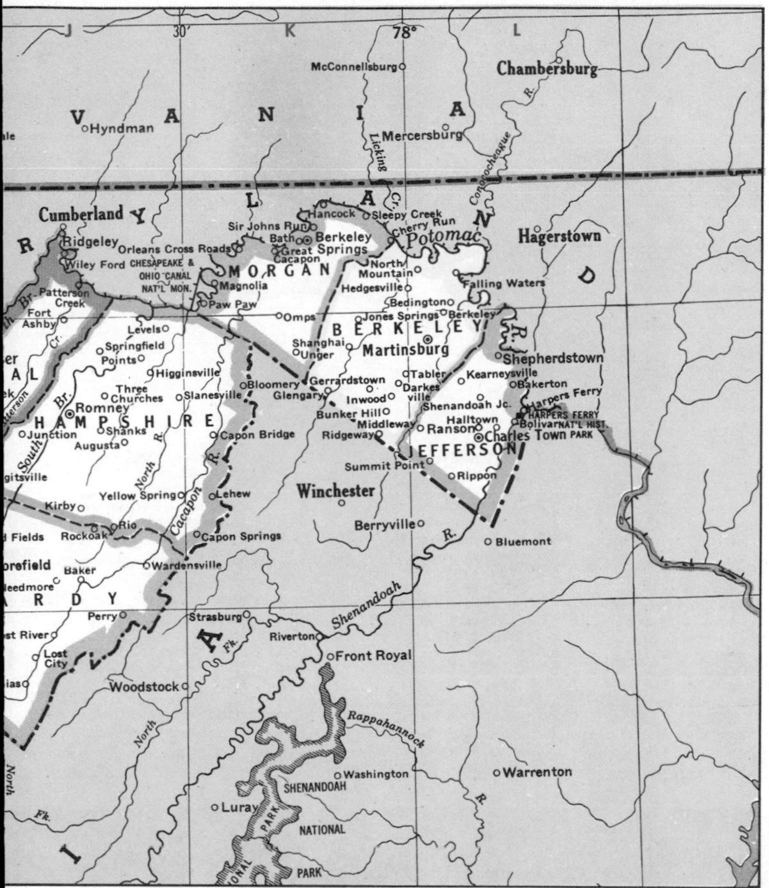

25015 Belle, 1,786 C 6
26134 Belmont, 802 D 4
26656 Belva, 550 D 6
26031 Benwood, 2,737 E 2
26298 Bergoo, 260 F 6
† 25401 Berkeley, 600 L 4
25411 Berkeley Springs⊙, 2,200 K 3
24815 Berwind, 675 C 8
26032 Bethany, 602 E 2
† 26003 Bethlehem, 2,461 E 2
26253 Beverly, 470 G 5
25019 Bickmore, 375 D 6
25302 Big Chimney, 450 C 6
25505 Big Creek, 500 B 7
† 24853 Big Four, 200 C 8
25021 Bim, 395 C 7
26610 Birch River, 650 E 6
26521 Blacksville, 264 F 3
25022 Blair, 700 C 7
25023 Blakeley, 260 D 6
25026 Blue Creek, 300 D 6
24701 Bluefield, 15,921 D 8
26288 Bolair, 450 F 6
25426 Bolivar, 943 L 4
25030 Bomont, 412 D 6
25031 Boomer, 1,261 D 6
25665 Borderland, 250 B 7
24817 Bradshaw, 1,048 C 8
24715 Bramwell, 1,125 D 8
26802 Brandywine, 188 H 5
25666 Breeden, 300 B 7
26330 Bridgeport, 4,777 F 4
† 25314 Brounland, 900 C 6
26334 Brownton, 700 F 4
26525 Bruceton Mills, 209 G 3
26201 Buckhannon⊙, 7,261 F 5
24716 Bud, 400 D 7
25033 Buffalo, 831 C 5
25413 Bunker Hill, 500 K 4
26710 Burlington, 338 J 4
26335 Burnsville, 591 E 5
26562 Burton, 250 F 3
25035 Cabin Creek, 900 C 6
26855 Cabins, 300 H 4
26337 Cairo, 412 D 4
24925 Caldwell, 425 F 7
26660 Calvin, 200 E 6
26208 Camden on Gauley, 243 E 6
26033 Cameron, 1,537 E 3
25820 Camp Creek, 200 D 7
24819 Canebrake, 250 C 8
26662 Canvas, 300 E 6
26711 Capon Bridge, 211 K 4
26823 Capon Springs, 250 K 4
25037 Carbon, 200 D 6
24821 Caretta, 650 C 8
26527 Cassville, 800 F 3
26564 Catawba, 186 F 3
25039 Cedar Grove, 1,275 D 6
26340 Central Station, 275 E 4
26214 Century, 239 F 4
25507 Ceredo, 1,583 B 6
25508 Chapmanville, 1,175 B 7
* 25301 Charleston (cap.)⊙, 71,505 C 6
Charleston, ‡229,515 C 6
25414 Charles Town⊙, 3,023 L 4
25958 Charmco, 900 E 6
25667 Chattaroy, 1,145 B 7
25315 Chesapeake, 2,428 C 6
26034 Chester, 3,614 E 1
25306 Cinco, 500 D 6
26804 Circleville, 180 H 5
26301 Clarksburg⊙, 24,864 F 4
25043 Clay⊙, 479 D 6
25044 Clear Creek, 300 D 7
† 26003 Clearview, 512 E 2
25045 Clendenin, 1,438 D 5
25237 Clifton, 358 B 5
† 25854 Clifty, 250 E 6
† 26058 Clinton, 350 E 2
25046 Clio, 300 D 5
25047 Clothier, 950 C 7
25238 Clover, 350 D 5
24929 Clover Lick, 250 F 6
25823 Coal City, 1,089 D 7
25306 Coal Fork, 950 D 6
26257 Coalton, 234 G 5
24824 Coalwood, 650 C 8
26565 Coburn, 230 F 3
25048 Colcord, 600 D 7
26035 Colliers, 500 E 2
† 24740 Colored Hill, 1,031 D 8
26615 Copen, 312 E 5
25826 Corinne, 1,090 D 7
26713 Corinth, 195 H 4
25051 Costa, 500 C 6
25239 Cottageville, 500 C 5
25509 Cove Gap, 650 B 6
26206 Cowen, 467 E 6
26205 Craigsville, 300 E 6
25828 Cranberry, 297 D 7
25669 Crum, 300 B 7
24826 Cucumber, 275 C 8
25510 Culloden, 1,033 B 6
24827 Cyclone, 500 C 7
25832 Daniels, 950 D 7
25053 Danville, 580 C 6
† 25428 Darkesville, 375 L 4
26260 Davis, 868 H 4
26142 Davisville, 200 C 4
24828 Davy, 993 C 8
25054 Dawes, 800 D 6
24932 Dawson, 200 E 7
25055 Decota, 800 D 6
25670 Delbarton, 903 B 7
26531 Dellslow, 500 G 3
26217 Diana, 600 F 5
† 25535 Dickson, 200 B 6
26617 Dille, 300 E 6
25671 Dingess, 600 B 7
25059 Dixie, 800 D 6
† 26386 Dola, 200 F 4
26835 Dorcas, 250 H 5
25060 Dorothy, 400 D 7
25062 Dry Creek, 290 D 7
26263 Dryfork, 208 H 5
25063 Duck, 500 E 5
25064 Dunbar, 9,151 C 6
24934 Dunmore, 200 G 6
26264 Durbin, 347 G 5
25067 East Bank, 1,025 D 6
25835 Eastgulf, 300 D 7
25512 East Lynn, 500 B 6
† 26301 East View, 1,618 F 4
25836 Eccles, 1,105 D 7
24829 Eckman, 850 C 8
25672 Edgarton, 415 B 7
† 24954 Edray, 175 F 6
24830 Elbert, 400 C 8
25070 Eleanor, 1,035 C 5
26143 Elizabeth⊙, 821 D 4
26717 Elk Garden, 291 H 4
26241 Elkins⊙, 8,287 G 5
† 24868 Elkridge, 500 D 6
25071 Elkview, 1,486 C 6
26267 Ellamore, 400 F 5
26346 Ellenboro, 267 D 4
25965 Elton, 320 E 7
24832 English, 500 C 8
26568 Enterprise, 975 F 4
26203 Erbacon, 350 E 5
25075 Eskdale, 500 D 6
25076 Ethel, 450 C 7
25241 Evans, 400 C 5
26533 Everettville, 200 F 3
26554 Fairmont, 26,093 F 4
† 25271 Fairplain, 200 C 5
26570 Fairview, 640 F 3
† 24966 Falling Springs (Renick), 255 F 6
26571 Farmington, 595 F 3
25840 Fayetteville⊙, 1,712 D 6
26202 Fenwick, 500 E 6
25513 Ferrellsburg, 300 B 6
25823 Fireco, 300 D 7
26818 Fisher, 250 H 4
25841 Flat Top, 550 D 7
26621 Flatwoods, 220 E 5
26347 Flemington, 458 F 4
26037 Follansbee, 3,883 E 2
26348 Folsom, 325 E 4
24935 Forest Hill, 314 E 7
26719 Fort Ashby, 1,225 J 4
25514 Fort Gay, 792 A 6
26806 Fort Seybert, 208 H 5
24936 Fort Spring, 250 E 7
26572 Four States, 300 F 4
25071 Frame, 200 C 5
26623 Frametown, 600 E 5
24938 Frankford, 200 F 7
26807 Franklin⊙, 695 H 5
26218 French Creek 200 F 5
26219 Frenchton, 212 F 5
26146 Friendly, 190 D 3
25515 Gallipolis Ferry, 325 B 5
26349 Galloway, 289 F 4
25243 Gandeeville, 271 D 5
24836 Gary, 850 C 8
26624 Gassaway, 1,253 E 5
25085 Gauley Bridge, 1,800 D 6
25420 Gerrardstown, 258 K 4
25843 Ghent, 450 D 7
† 24736 Giatto, 400 D 8
25621 Gilbert, 778 C 7
26671 Gilboa, 375 E 6
25086 Glasgow, 904 D 6
26038 Glen Dale, 2,150 E 3
25844 Glen Daniel, 300 D 7
25090 Glen Ferris, 275 D 6
† 25813 Glen Hedrick (Beaver), 1,711 D 7
25846 Glen Jean, 1,510 D 7
25848 Glen Rogers, 500 D 7
26351 Glenville⊙, 2,183 E 5
25849 Glen White, 600 D 7
25520 Glenwood, 400 B 5
25093 Gordon, 500 C 7
26720 Gormania, 250 H 4
26354 Grafton⊙, 6,433 G 4
26147 Grantsville⊙, 795 D 5
26574 Grant Town, 946 F 3
26534 Granville, 1,027 F 3
25422 Great Cacapon, 750 K 3
25966 Green Sulphur Springs, 300 E 7
† 25166 Greenview, 250 C 6
26360 Greenwood, 460 E 4
25521 Griffithsville, 300 B 6
25095 Grimms Landing, 350 B 5
26221 Guardian, 200 F 5
24838 Guyan, 250 C 7
25423 Halltown, 325 L 4
26269 Hambleton, 328 G 4
25523 Hamlin⊙, 1,024 B 6
25623 Hampden, 251 C 7
25102 Handley, 500 D 6
24839 Hanover, 300 C 7
† 26250 Harding, 200 G 5
25851 Harper, 300 D 7
25425 Harpers Ferry, 423 L 4
26362 Harrisville⊙, 1,464 E 4
25247 Hartford, 527 C 4
25852 Harvey, 500 D 7
24841 Havaco, 329 C 8
26627 Heaters, 343 E 5
25427 Hedgesville, 274 K 3
26224 Helvetia, 269 F 5
24842 Hemphill, 785 C 8
25106 Henderson, 496 B 5
26271 Hendricks, 317 G 4
25624 Henlawson, 900 B 7
26369 Hepzibah, 600 F 4
24726 Herndon, 500 D 7
25854 Hico, 750 D 6
24946 Hillsboro, 267 F 6
25951 Hinton⊙, 4,503 E 7
26262 Holcomb, 200 E 6
25625 Holden, 2,325 B 7
† 26651 Hookersville, 250 E 6
26575 Hundred, 475 E 3
* 25701 Huntington⊙, 74,315 A 6
Huntington-Ashland, ‡253,743 A 6
25526 Hurricane, 3,491 C 6
24844 Iaeger, 822 C 8
25111 Indore, 200 D 6
25112 Institute, 3,100 C 6
25428 Inwood, 600 K 4
24847 Itmann, 500 D 7
25113 Ivydale, 700 D 5
26377 Jacksonburg, 735 E 3
26378 Jane Lew, 397 F 4
† 26462 Jarvisville, 250 F 4
25114 Jeffrey, 900 C 7
24848 Jenkinjones, 800 D 8
26674 Jodie, 300 D 6
25969 Jumping Branch, 297 E 7
26275 Junior, 513 G 5
24851 Justice, 600 C 7
25430 Kearneysville, 250 L 4
24731 Kegley, 450 D 8
24732 Kellysville, 200 E 8
25248 Kenna, 380 C 5
25530 Kenova, 4,860 A 6
25674 Kermit, 716 B 7
26726 Keyser⊙, 6,586 J 4
24852 Keystone, 1,008 D 8
25859 Kilsyth, 450 D 7
24853 Kimball, 962 C 8
26537 Kingwood⊙, 2,550 G 4
† 25671 Kirk, 400 B 7
25628 Kistler, 750 C 7
24854 Kopperston, 900 C 7
25860 Lanark, 375 D 7
† 25831 Landisburg, 250 E 7
25629 Landville, 250 C 7
25535 Lavalette, 600 B 6
25864 Layland, 455 E 7
† 26430 Layopolis (Sand Fork), 252 E 5
25251 Left Hand, 200 D 5
26676 Leivasy, 450 E 6
25676 Lenore, 800 B 7
25123 Leon, 192 C 5
25971 Lerona, 350 D 8
25537 Lesage, 600 B 5
25972 Leslie, 500 E 6
25865 Lester, 507 D 7
25253 Letart, 250 C 5
24901 Lewisburg⊙, 2,407 E 7
24951 Lindside, 225 E 8
26384 Linn, 212 E 4
26629 Little Birch, 180 E 5
† 26624 Little Otter, 250 E 5
26581 Littleton, 333 F 3
25125 Lizemores, 400 D 6
26677 Lockwood, 300 D 6
25601 Logan⊙, 3,311 B 7
25868 Lookout, 200 E 6
25630 Lorado, 400 C 7
26385 Lost Creek, 571 F 4
† 26101 Lubeck, 500 C 4
26386 Lumberport, 957 F 4
25631 Lundale, 700 C 7
25870 Maben, 200 D 7
26278 Mabie, 366 G 5
25871 Mabscott, 1,254 D 7
25873 MacArthur, 1,614 D 7
25130 Madison⊙, 2,342 C 6
26541 Maidsville, 485 F 3
25306 Malden, 900 C 6
25634 Mallory, 1,240 C 7
25132 Mammoth, 576 D 6
25635 Man, 1,201 C 7
26582 Mannington, 2,747 F 3
25975 Marfrance, 240 E 6
24954 Marlinton⊙, 1,286 F 6
25315 Marmet, 2,339 C 6
25401 Martinsburg⊙, 14,626 K 4
25260 Mason, 1,319 B 4
26542 Masontown, 868 G 3
25678 Matewan, 651 B 7
24736 Matoaka, 608 D 8
24861 Maybeury, 850 D 8

(continued on following page)

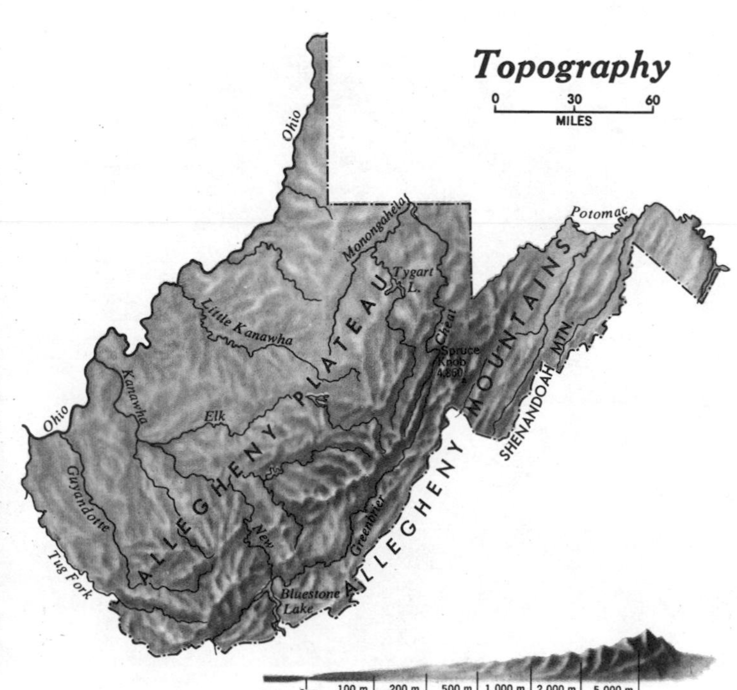

Below | Sea Level | 100 m. 328 ft. | 200 m. 656 ft. | 500 m. 1,640 ft. | 1,000 m. 3,281 ft. | 2,000 m. 6,562 ft. | 5,000 m. 16,404 ft.

(continued)

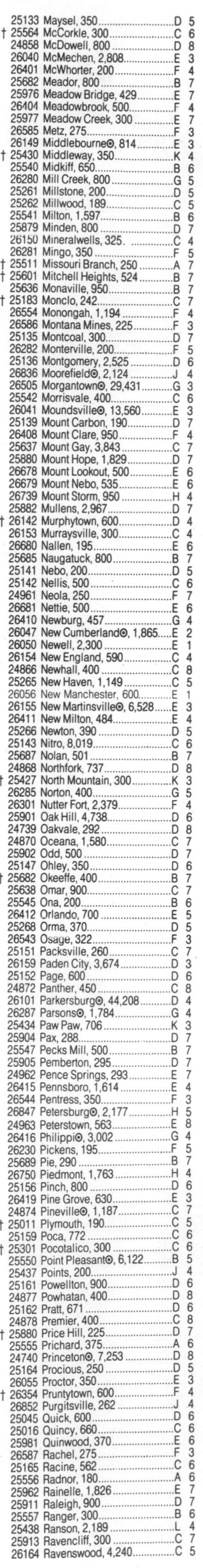

25133 Maysel, 350 .... D 5
† 25564 McCorkle, 300 .... C 6
24858 McDowell, 800 .... D 8
26040 McMechen, 2,808 .... E 3
26401 McWhorter, 200 .... F 4
25682 Meador, 800 .... B 7
25976 Meadow Bridge, 429 .... E 7
26404 Meadowbrook, 500 .... F 4
25977 Meadow Creek, 300 .... E 7
26585 Metz, 275 .... F 3
26149 Middlebourne⊙, 814 .... E 3
† 25430 Middleway, 350 .... K 4
25540 Midkiff, 650 .... B 6
26280 Mill Creek, 800 .... G 5
25261 Millstone, 200 .... D 5
25262 Millwood, 189 .... C 5
25541 Milton, 1,597 .... B 6
25879 Minden, 800 .... D 7
26150 Mineralwells, 325 .... C 4
26281 Mingo, 350 .... F 5
† 25511 Missouri Branch, 250 .... A 7
† 25601 Mitchell Heights, 524 .... B 7
25636 Monaville, 950 .... B 7
† 25183 Monclo, 242 .... C 7
26554 Monongah, 1,194 .... F 4
26586 Montana Mines, 225 .... F 3
25135 Montcoal, 300 .... D 7
26282 Monterville, 200 .... F 5
25136 Montgomery, 2,525 .... D 6
26836 Moorefield⊙, 2,124 .... J 4
26505 Morgantown⊙, 29,431 .... G 3
25542 Morrisvale, 400 .... C 6
26041 Moundsville⊙, 13,560 .... E 3
25139 Mount Carbon, 190 .... D 7
26408 Mount Clare, 950 .... F 4
25637 Mount Gay, 3,843 .... C 7
25880 Mount Hope, 1,829 .... D 7
26678 Mount Lookout, 500 .... E 6
26679 Mount Nebo, 535 .... E 6
26739 Mount Storm, 950 .... H 4
25882 Mullens, 2,967 .... D 7
† 26142 Murphytown, 600 .... D 4
26153 Murraysville, 300 .... C 4
26680 Nallen, 195 .... E 6
25685 Naugatuck, 800 .... B 7
25141 Nebo, 200 .... D 5
25142 Nellis, 500 .... C 6
24961 Neola, 250 .... F 7
26681 Nettie, 500 .... E 6
26410 Newburg, 457 .... G 4
26047 New Cumberland⊙, 1,865 .... E 2
26050 Newell, 2,300 .... E 1
26154 New England, 590 .... C 4
24866 Newhall, 400 .... C 8
25265 New Haven, 1,149 .... C 5
26056 New Manchester, 600 .... E 1
26155 New Martinsville⊙, 6,528 .... E 3
26411 New Milton, 484 .... E 4
25266 Newton, 390 .... D 5
25143 Nitro, 8,019 .... C 6
25687 Nolan, 501 .... B 7
24868 Northfork, 737 .... D 8
† 25427 North Mountain, 300 .... K 3
26285 Norton, 400 .... G 5
26301 Nutter Fort, 2,379 .... F 4
25901 Oak Hill, 4,738 .... D 6
24739 Oakvale, 292 .... D 8
24870 Oceana, 1,580 .... C 7
25902 Odd, 500 .... D 7
25147 Ohley, 350 .... D 6
† 25682 Okeeffe, 400 .... B 7
25638 Omar, 900 .... C 7
25545 Ona, 200 .... B 6
26412 Orlando, 700 .... E 5
25268 Orma, 370 .... D 5
26543 Osage, 322 .... F 3
25151 Packsville, 260 .... C 7
26159 Paden City, 3,674 .... D 3
25152 Page, 600 .... D 6
24872 Panther, 450 .... C 8
26101 Parkersburg⊙, 44,208 .... D 4
26287 Parsons⊙, 1,784 .... G 4
25434 Paw Paw, 706 .... K 3
25904 Pax, 288 .... D 7
25547 Pecks Mill, 500 .... B 7
25905 Pemberton, 295 .... D 7
24962 Pence Springs, 293 .... E 7
26415 Pennsboro, 1,614 .... E 4
26544 Pentress, 350 .... F 3
26847 Petersburg⊙, 2,177 .... H 5
24963 Peterstown, 563 .... E 8
26416 Philippi⊙, 3,002 .... G 4
26230 Pickens, 195 .... F 5
25689 Pie, 290 .... B 7
26750 Piedmont, 1,763 .... H 4
25156 Pinch, 800 .... D 6
26419 Pine Grove, 630 .... E 3
24874 Pineville⊙, 1,187 .... C 7
† 25011 Plymouth, 190 .... C 5
25159 Poca, 772 .... C 6
† 25301 Pocotalico, 300 .... C 6
25550 Point Pleasant⊙, 6,122 .... B 5
25437 Points, 200 .... J 4
25161 Powellton, 900 .... D 6
24877 Powhatan, 400 .... D 8
25162 Pratt, 671 .... D 6
24878 Premier, 400 .... C 8
† 25880 Price Hill, 225 .... D 7
25555 Prichard, 375 .... A 6
24740 Princeton⊙, 7,253 .... D 8
25164 Procious, 250 .... D 5
26055 Proctor, 350 .... E 3
† 26354 Pruntytown, 600 .... F 4
26852 Purgitsville, 262 .... J 4
25045 Quick, 600 .... D 6
25016 Quincy, 660 .... C 6
25981 Quinwood, 370 .... E 6
26587 Rachel, 275 .... F 3
25165 Racine, 562 .... C 6
25556 Radnor, 180 .... A 6
25962 Rainelle, 1,826 .... E 7
25911 Raleigh, 900 .... D 7
25557 Ranger, 300 .... B 6
25438 Ranson, 2,189 .... L 4
25913 Ravencliff, 300 .... C 7
26164 Ravenswood, 4,240 .... C 5

Agriculture, Industry and Resources

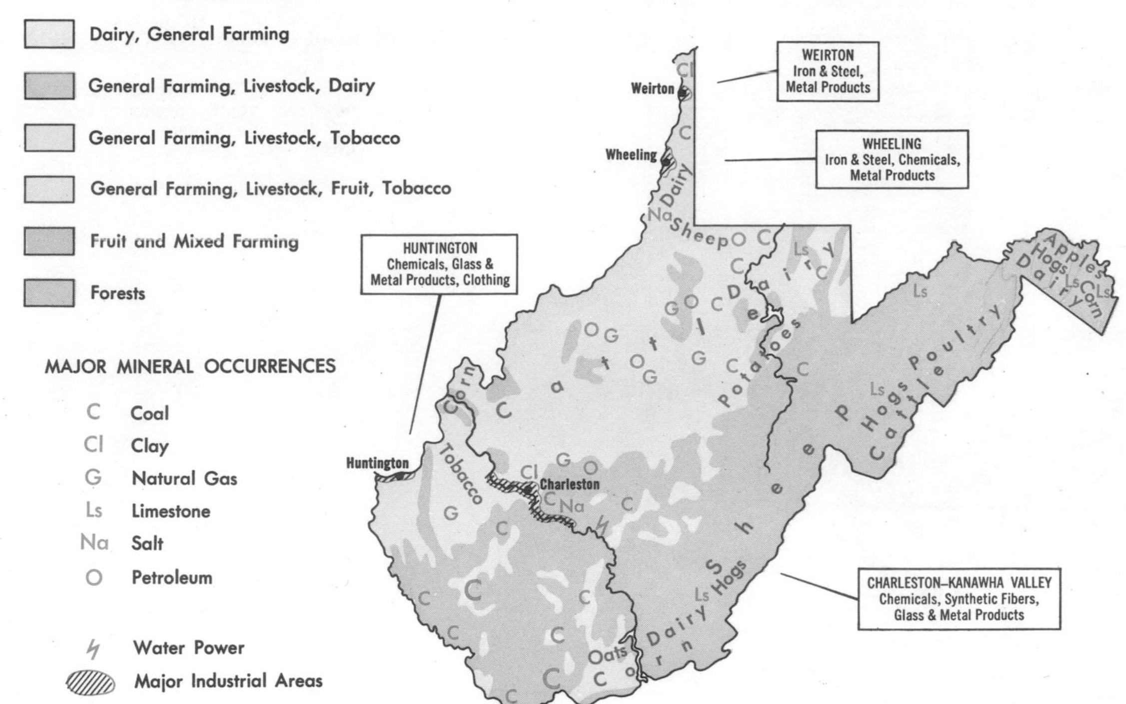

† 25159 Raymond City, 370 .... C 6
26167 Reader, 822 .... E 3
25168 Red House, 600 .... C 5
25692 Red Jacket, 800 .... B 7
25914 Redstar, 200 .... D 7
26547 Reedsville, 379 .... G 3
25270 Reedy, 351 .... D 5
24966 Renick, 255 .... F 6
25915 Rhodell, 500 .... D 7
26261 Richwood, 3,717 .... F 6
26753 Ridgeley, 1,112 .... J 3
25271 Ripley⊙, 3,244 .... C 5
25441 Rippon, 500 .... L 4
26588 Rivesville, 1,108 .... F 3
26234 Rock Cave, 300 .... F 5
24881 Roderfield, 1,161 .... C 8
26757 Romney⊙, 2,364 .... J 4
24970 Ronceverte, 1,981 .... F 7
26636 Rosedale, 234 .... E 5
25643 Rossmore, 400 .... C 7
26425 Rowlesburg, 829 .... G 4
25984 Rupert, 1,027 .... E 7
26689 Russellville, 240 .... E 6
25177 Saint Albans, 14,356 .... C 6
26170 Saint Marys⊙, 2,348 .... D 4
26426 Salem, 2,597 .... E 4
25559 Salt Rock, 350 .... B 6
26430 Sand Fork, 252 .... E 5
25985 Sandstone, 350 .... E 7
25275 Sandyville, 500 .... C 5
25917 Scarbro, 800 .... D 7
† 25674 Selwyn, 500 .... B 7
25181 Seth, 950 .... C 6
† 25427 Shanghai, 200 .... K 4
25182 Sharon, 700 .... D 6
25183 Sharples, 450 .... C 7
25442 Shenandoah Junction, 600 .... L 4
25443 Shepherdstown, 1,688 .... L 4
26057 Sherrard, 400 .... E 3
26431 Shinnston, 2,576 .... F 4
26435 Simpson, 250 .... F 4
25320 Sissonville, 450 .... C 5
26175 Sistersville, 2,246 .... D 3
25920 Slab Fork, 300 .... D 7
† 25654 Slagle, 450 .... C 7
† 26143 Slate, 200 .... D 4
25186 Smithers, 2,020 .... D 6
26437 Smithfield, 294 .... E 4
26178 Smithville, 500 .... D 4
24977 Smoot, 300 .... E 7
25921 Sophia, 1,303 .... D 7
25303 South Charleston, 16,333 .... C 6
25922 Spanishburg, 425 .... D 8
25276 Spencer⊙, 2,271 .... D 5
26763 Springfield, 250 .... J 4
24884 Squire, 900 .... C 8
26505 Star City, 1,312 .... F 3
25188 Stickney, 240 .... D 7
25645 Stirrat, 250 .... C 7
26301 Stonewood, 1,950 .... F 4
25929 Stotesbury, 199 .... D 7
26651 Summersville⊙, 2,429 .... E 6
25446 Summit Point, 455 .... K 4
26601 Sutton⊙, 1,031 .... E 5
24980 Sweet Springs, 500 .... F 7
26690 Swiss, 500 .... D 6
25647 Switzer, 850 .... B 7
25193 Sylvester, 245 .... C 6
† 25428 Tabler, 300 .... L 4
24981 Talcott, 700 .... E 7
26237 Tallmansville, 260 .... F 5
25569 Teays, 200 .... B 6
26764 Terra Alta, 1,474 .... H 4
26640 Tesla, 300 .... E 5
25694 Thacker, 325 .... B 7

26292 Thomas, 713 .... H 4
26440 Thornton, 300 .... G 4
24888 Thorpe, 600 .... D 8
† 26206 Three Forks of Williams River, 375 .... F 6
26691 Tioga, 320 .... E 6
26059 Triadelphia, 547 .... E 2
† 25095 Tribble, 350 .... C 5
26444 Tunnelton, 369 .... G 4
25203 Turtle Creek, 566 .... C 6
25205 Uneeda, 850 .... C 6
24983 Union⊙, 566 .... E 7
26266 Upperglade, 500 .... F 6
26293 Valley Bend, 950 .... F 5
26060 Valley Grove, 509 .... E 2
26294 Valley Head, 600 .... G 5
25206 Van, 800 .... C 7
25696 Varney, 750 .... B 7
25649 Verdunville, 950 .... B 7
26101 Vienna, 11,549 .... D 4

24891 Vivian, 500 .... D 8
26238 Volga, 350 .... F 4
26589 Wadestown, 210 .... F 3
24984 Waiteville, 252 .... F 8
26448 Wallace, 325 .... E 4
25286 Walton, 250 .... D 5
24892 War, 2,004 .... C 8
† 25039 Ward, 850 .... D 6
26851 Wardensville, 288 .... J 4
26181 Washington, 450 .... C 4
† 26041 Washington Lands, 500 .... E 3
26184 Waverly, 407 .... D 4
25570 Wayne⊙, 1,385 .... B 6
26288 Webster Springs⊙, 1,038 .... F 6
26062 Weirton, 27,131 .... E 2
Weirton-Steubenville, ‡165,627 .... E 2
24801 Welch⊙, 4,149 .... C 8
26070 Wellsburg⊙, 4,600 .... E 2
25287 West Columbia, 245 .... B 5

25571 West Hamlin, 715 .... B 6
26074 West Liberty, 975 .... E 2
25601 West Logan, 685 .... C 7
26451 West Milford, 356 .... F 4
26452 Weston⊙, 7,323 .... F 4
26505 Westover, 5,086 .... G 3
26456 West Union⊙, 1,141 .... E 4
25651 Wharncliffe, 1,012 .... C 7
25208 Wharton, 900 .... C 7
26003 Wheeling⊙, 48,188 .... E 2
Wheeling, ‡182,712 .... E 2
24986 White Sulphur Springs, 2,396 .... F 7
25209 Whitesville, 781 .... C 6
26296 Whitmer, 411 .... G 5
25211 Widen, 230 .... E 6
26767 Wiley Ford, 750 .... J 3
26186 Wileyville, 190 .... E 3
25653 Wilkinson, 975 .... B 7
24991 Williamsburg, 225 .... F 7

25661 Williamson⊙, 5,831 .... B 7
26187 Williamstown, 2,743 .... C 4
26461 Wilsonburg, 200 .... F 4
25699 Wilsondale, 200 .... B 7
26075 Windsor Heights, 850 .... E 2
25213 Winfield⊙, 328 .... C 5
25214 Winifrede, 750 .... C 6
25942 Winona, 250 .... E 6
26462 Wolf Summit, 750 .... F 4
† 26257 Womelsdorf (Coalton), 234 .... G 5
† 26055 Woodlands, 200 .... E 3
26591 Worthington, 288 .... F 4
25573 Yawkey, 985 .... C 6
26865 Yellow Spring, 250 .... J 4
25654 Yolyn, 750 .... C 7

⊙ County seat.
‡ Population of metropolitan area
† Zip of nearest p.o.
* Multiple zips

A. D'Arazien — Shostal Associates

At one of Clarksburg, West Virginia's glass plants, liquid glass is poured into a machine and becomes beautifully textured stained-glass panels.

AREA 56,154 sq. mi.
POPULATION 4,417,933
CAPITAL Madison
LARGEST CITY Milwaukee
HIGHEST POINT Timms Hill 1,952 ft.
SETTLED IN 1670
ADMITTED TO UNION May 29, 1848
POPULAR NAME Badger State
STATE FLOWER Wood Violet
STATE BIRD Robin

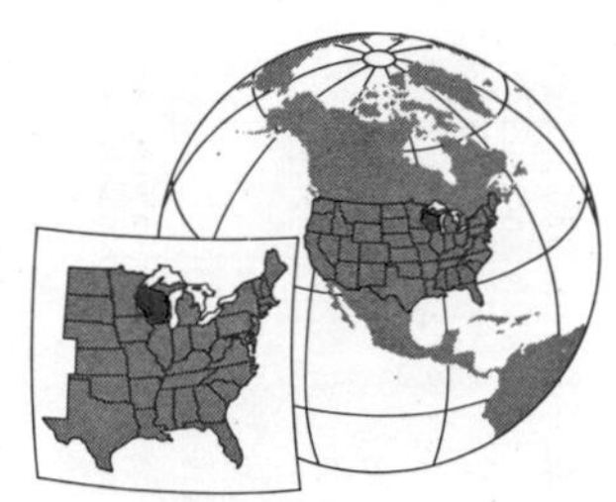

COUNTIES

County, Pop.	Key
Adams, 9,234	G 8
Ashland, 16,743	E 3
Barron, 33,955	C 5
Bayfield, 11,683	D 3
Brown, 158,244	L 7
Buffalo, 13,743	C 7
Burnett, 9,276	B 4
Calumet, 27,604	K 7
Chippewa, 47,717	D 5
Clark, 30,361	E 6
Columbia, 40,150	H 9
Crawford, 15,252	E 9
Dane, 290,272	H 9
Dodge, 69,004	J 9
Door, 20,106	M 6
Douglas, 44,657	C 3
Dunn, 29,154	C 6
Eau Claire, 67,219	D 6
Florence, 3,298	K 4
Fond du Lac, 84,567	K 8
Forest, 7,691	J 4
Grant, 48,398	E 10
Green, 26,714	G 10
Green Lake, 16,878	H 8
Iowa, 19,306	F 9
Iron, 6,533	F 3
Jackson, 15,325	E 7
Jefferson, 60,060	J 9
Juneau, 18,455	F 8
Kenosha, 117,917	K 10
Kewaunee, 18,961	L 6
La Crosse, 80,468	D 8
Lafayette, 17,456	F 10
Langlade, 19,220	H 5
Lincoln, 23,499	G 5
Manitowoc, 82,294	L 7
Marathon, 97,457	G 6
Marinette, 35,810	K 5
Marquette, 8,865	H 8
Menominee, 2,607	J 5
Milwaukee, 1,054,063	L 9
Monroe, 31,610	E 8
Oconto, 25,553	K 6
Oneida, 24,427	G 4
Outagamie, 119,356	K 7
Ozaukee, 54,421	L 9
Pepin, 7,319	C 6
Pierce, 26,652	B 6
Polk, 26,666	B 5
Portage, 47,541	G 6
Price, 14,520	F 4
Racine, 170,838	K 10
Richland, 17,079	F 9
Rock, 131,970	H 10
Rusk, 14,238	D 5
Saint Croix, 34,354	B 5
Sauk, 39,057	G 9
Sawyer, 9,670	D 4
Shawano, 32,650	J 6
Sheboygan, 96,660	L 8
Taylor, 16,958	E 5
Trempealeau, 23,344	D 7
Vernon, 24,557	E 8
Vilas, 10,958	G 3
Walworth, 63,444	J 10
Washburn, 10,601	C 4
Washington, 63,839	K 9
Waukesha, 231,365	K 9
Waupaca, 37,780	J 6
Waushara, 14,795	H 7
Winnebago, 129,931	J 7
Wood, 65,362	F 7

CITIES and TOWNS

Zip	Name/Pop.	Key
54405	Abbotsford, 1,375	F 6
54101	Abrams, 300	L 6
53910	Adams, 1,440	G 8
53001	Adell, 380	L 8
53501	Afton, 250	H 10
53502	Albany, 875	G 10
† 53534	Albion, 250	H 10
54201	Algoma, 4,023	M 6
53002	Allenton, 584	K 9
† 54301	Allouez, 13,753	L 7
54610	Alma⊙, 956	C 7
54611	Alma Center, 495	E 7
54805	Almena, 423	B 5
54909	Almond, 440	G 7
54720	Altoona, 2,842	C 6
49936	Alvin, 160	J 4
54102	Amberg, 711	K 5
54001	Amery, 2,126	B 5
54406	Amherst, 585	H 7
† 54162	Angelica, 200	K 6
54408	Aniwa, 233	H 6
54409	Antigo⊙, 9,005	H 5
54911	Appleton⊙, 57,143	J 7
	Appleton-Oshkosh, ‡276,893	J 7
54510	Arbor Vitae, 950	G 4
54612	Arcadia, 2,159	D 7
53503	Arena, 377	G 9
54511	Argonne, 400	J 4
53504	Argyle, 673	G 10
54721	Arkansaw, 350	B 6
53911	Arlington, 379	H 9
54103	Armstrong Creek, 555	K 4
54410	Arpin, 355	G 6
53003	Ashippun, 400	H 1
54806	Ashland⊙, 9,615	E 2
54304	Ashwaubenon, 9,323	K 7
54411	Athens, 856	G 5
54412	Auburndale, 468	F 6
54722	Augusta, 1,242	D 6
54920	Auroraville, 250	H 7
53506	Avoca, 421	F 9
† 53520	Avon, 600	H 10
54413	Babcock, 260	F 7
53801	Bagley, 271	D 10
54202	Baileys Harbor, 900	M 5
54002	Baldwin, 1,399	B 6
54810	Balsam Lake⊙, 648	B 5
54921	Bancroft, 150	G 7
54614	Bangor, 974	E 8
53913	Baraboo⊙, 7,931	G 9
† 54873	Barnes, 450	D 3
53507	Barneveld, 528	F 10
54812	Barron⊙, 2,337	C 5
† 53001	Batavia, 160	K 8
54723	Bay City, 317	B 6
54814	Bayfield, 874	E 2
† 53201	Bayside, 4,461	M 1
54922	Bear Creek, 520	J 6
53916	Beaver Dam, 14,265	J 9
53802	Beetown, 170	E 10
53004	Belgium, 809	L 8
53508	Belleville, 1,063	G 10
53510	Belmont, 688	F 10
53511	Beloit, 35,729	H 10
54815	Bennett, 350	C 3
53803	Benton, 873	F 10
54923	Berlin, 5,338	H 8
† 53401	Berryville, 150	M 3
† 54410	Bethel, 210	F 6
† 54440	Bevent, 200	H 6
53103	Big Bend, 1,148	K 2
54817	Birchwood, 394	C 4
54414	Birnamwood, 632	H 6
† 54494	Biron, 771	G 7
54106	Black Creek, 921	K 7
53515	Black Earth, 1,114	G 9
54615	Black River Falls⊙, 3,273	E 7
† 54541	Blackwell, 350	J 4
54616	Blair, 1,036	D 7
53516	Blanchardville, 671	G 10
54724	Bloomer, 3,143	D 5
53804	Bloomington, 719	E 10
53517	Blue Mounds, 261	G 9
53518	Blue River, 369	E 9
54107	Bonduel, 995	K 6
53805	Boscobel, 2,510	E 9
54512	Boulder Junction, 500	G 3
54416	Bowler, 272	J 6
54725	Boyceville, 725	C 5
54726	Boyd, 574	E 6
54203	Branch, 225	L 7
53919	Brandon, 872	J 8
54513	Brantwood, 500	F 4
53920	Briggsville, 250	H 8
54110	Brillion, 2,588	L 7
53520	Brodhead, 2,515	G 10
54417	Brokaw, 312	G 5
53005	Brookfield, 32,140	K 1
53521	Brooklyn, 565	H 10
† 53201	Brown Deer, 12,622	L 1
† 53105	Browns Lake, 1,669	K 3
53006	Brownsville, 374	J 8
53522	Browntown, 253	G 10
54819	Bruce, 799	D 5
54820	Brule, 675	C 2
54204	Brussels, 306	L 6
† 54622	Buffalo, 671	C 7
53105	Burlington, 7,479	K 10
53922	Burnett, 241	J 9
53007	Butler, 2,261	K 1
54514	Butternut, 453	E 3
54821	Cable, 281	D 3
54727	Cadott, 977	D 6
53923	Cambria, 631	H 8
53523	Cambridge, 689	H 9
54822	Cameron, 893	C 5
† 53019	Campbellsport, 1,681	K 8
54618	Camp Douglas, 547	F 8
53109	Camp Lake, 1,898	K 10
54928	Caroline, 450	J 6
53011	Cascade, 603	K 8
54205	Casco, 481	L 6
54619	Cashton, 824	E 8
53806	Cassville, 1,343	E 10
54515	Catawba, 215	E 4
53924	Cazenovia, 335	F 8
54111	Cecil, 369	K 6
53012	Cedarburg, 7,697	L 9
53013	Cedar Grove, 1,276	L 8
54824	Centuria, 632	A 5
54621	Chaseburg, 224	D 8
† 53029	Chenequa, 642	J 1
54728	Chetek, 1,630	C 5
54420	Chili, 205	F 6
53014	Chilton⊙, 3,030	K 7
54729	Chippewa Falls⊙, 12,351	D 6
54004	Clayton, 306	B 5
54005	Clear Lake, 721	B 5
54518	Clearwater Lake, 200	H 4
53015	Cleveland, 761	L 8
53525	Clinton, 1,333	J 10
54929	Clintonville, 4,600	J 6
53016	Clyman, 328	J 9
53526	Cobb, 410	F 10
54622	Cochrane, 506	C 7
54421	Colby, 1,178	F 6
54112	Coleman, 683	L 5
54730	Colfax, 1,026	C 6
54930	Coloma, 336	H 7
53925	Columbus, 3,789	H 9
54113	Combined Locks, 2,734	K 7
† 53147	Como, 1,132	K 10
† 53066	Concord, 200	H 1
54519	Conover, 500	H 3
54623	Coon Valley, 596	E 8
54732	Cornell, 1,616	D 5
54827	Cornucopia, 250	D 2
54520	Crandon⊙, 1,582	H 4
54114	Crivitz, 985	L 5
53528	Cross Plains, 1,478	G 9
53807	Cuba City, 1,993	F 10
53110	Cudahy, 22,078	M 2
54829	Cumberland, 1,839	C 4
54931	Dale, 410	J 7
54733	Dallas, 359	C 5
53926	Dalton, 320	H 8
54830	Danbury, 350	B 3
53529	Dane, 486	G 9
53114	Darien, 839	J 10
53530	Darlington⊙, 2,351	F 10
53531	Deerfield, 1,067	H 9
54007	Deer Park, 217	B 5
53532	De Forest, 1,911	H 9
53018	Delafield, 3,182	J 1
53115	Delavan, 5,526	J 10
† 53115	Delavan Lake, 2,124	J 10
54856	Delta, 180	D 3
54208	Denmark, 1,364	L 7
54115	De Pere, 13,309	K 7
† 54663	De Soto, 295	D 9
53808	Dickeyville, 1,057	E 10
54625	Dodge, 204	D 7
53533	Dodgeville⊙, 3,255	F 10
54425	Dorchester, 491	F 5
53118	Dousman, 451	J 1
54734	Downing, 215	B 5
53928	Doylestown, 265	H 9
54009	Dresser, 533	A 5
54736	Durand⊙, 2,103	C 6
† 54217	Dyckesville, 300	L 6
53119	Eagle, 745	H 2
54521	Eagle River⊙, 1,326	H 4
54626	Eastman, 319	D 9
53120	East Troy, 1,711	J 2
54701	Eau Claire⊙, 44,619	D 6
53019	Eden, 376	K 8
54426	Edgar, 928	G 6
53534	Edgerton, 4,118	H 10
54209	Egg Harbor, 184	M 5
54427	Eland, 229	H 6
54428	Elcho, 500	H 5
54429	Elderon, 185	H 6
54932	Eldorado, 200	J 8
54738	Eleva, 574	D 6
53020	Elkhart Lake, 787	L 8
53121	Elkhorn⊙, 3,992	J 10
54739	Elk Mound, 471	C 6
54011	Ellsworth⊙, 1,983	A 6
53122	Elm Grove, 7,201	K 1
54740	Elmwood, 737	B 6
† 53401	Elmwood Park, 456	M 3
53929	Elroy, 1,513	F 8
54430	Elton, 250	J 5
54933	Embarrass, 472	J 6
53930	Endeavor, 328	G 8
54211	Ephraim, 236	M 5
54627	Ettrick, 463	D 7
54934	Eureka, 300	J 7
53536	Evansville, 2,992	H 10
54835	Exeland, 189	D 4
54741	Fairchild, 562	D 6
53931	Fair Water, 373	J 8
54742	Fall Creek, 825	D 6
53932	Fall River, 633	H 9
54120	Fence, 187	K 4
53809	Fennimore, 1,861	E 9
54628	Ferryville, 183	D 9
54524	Fifield, 287	F 4
54212	Fish Creek, 275	M 5
54121	Florence⊙, 800	K 4
54935	Fond du Lac⊙, 35,515	K 8
53125	Fontana, 1,464	J 10
53537	Footville, 698	H 10
54123	Forest Junction, 255	K 7
54213	Forestville, 349	L 6
53538	Fort Atkinson, 9,164	J 10
54629	Fountain City, 1,017	C 7
54836	Foxboro, 950	B 2
53933	Fox Lake, 1,242	J 8
53217	Fox Point, 7,937	M 1
54214	Francis Creek, 492	L 7
53132	Franklin, 12,247	L 2
53126	Franksville, 375	M 3
54837	Frederic, 908	B 4
53021	Fredonia, 1,045	L 8
54940	Fremont, 598	J 7
53934	Friendship⊙, 641	G 8
53935	Friesland, 301	H 8
54630	Galesville, 1,162	D 7
54631	Gays Mills, 623	E 9
† 53127	Genesee, 375	J 2
53127	Genesee Depot, 425	J 2
54632	Genoa, 305	D 8
53128	Genoa City, 1,085	K 11
53022	Germantown, 6,974	K 1
† 53085	Gibbsville, 408	L 8
54525	Gile, 450	F 3
54124	Gillett, 1,288	K 6
54433	Gilman, 328	E 5
54743	Gilmanton, 200	C 7
54435	Gleason, 300	G 5
53023	Glenbeulah, 496	L 8
† 53201	Glendale, 13,436	M 1
53810	Glen Haven, 250	E 10
54013	Glenwood City, 822	B 5
54527	Glidden, 860	E 3
54125	Goodman, 800	K 4
54838	Gordon, 350	C 3
53540	Gotham, 175	F 9
53024	Grafton, 5,998	L 9
53936	Grand Marsh, 200	G 8
54839	Grand View, 350	D 3
54436	Granton, 288	E 6
54840	Grantsburg⊙, 930	A 4
53541	Gratiot, 249	F 10
* 54301	Green Bay⊙, 87,809	K 6
	Green Bay, ‡158,244	K 6
53129	Greendale, 15,089	L 2
53220	Greenfield, 24,424	L 2
54941	Green Lake⊙, 1,109	H 8
54126	Greenleaf, 350	L 7
54942	Greenville, 900	J 7
54437	Greenwood, 1,036	E 6
54128	Gresham, 448	J 6
53130	Hales Corners, 7,771	K 2
† 54729	Hallie, 1,223	D 6
54438	Hamburg, 170	G 5
54015	Hammond, 768	A 6
54943	Hancock, 404	G 7
54529	Harshaw, 200	G 4
53027	Hartford, 6,499	K 9
53029	Hartland, 2,763	J 1
54440	Hatley, 315	H 6
54841	Haugen, 246	C 4
54530	Hawkins, 385	E 4
54843	Hayward⊙, 1,457	D 3
53811	Hazel Green, 982	F 11
54531	Hazelhurst, 334	G 4
† 53538	Hebron, 190	J 10
53137	Helenville, 230	J 10
54844	Herbster, 250	D 2
54441	Hewitt, 300	F 6
53543	Highland, 785	F 9
54129	Hilbert, 896	K 7
54533	Hiles, 260	J 4
54634	Hillsboro, 1,231	F 8
53031	Hingham, 210	K 8
54635	Hixton, 300	E 7
54745	Holcombe, 200	D 5
53544	Hollandale, 256	G 10
54636	Holmen, 1,081	D 8
53138	Honey Creek, 350	J 3
53032	Horicon, 3,356	J 9
54944	Hortonville, 1,524	J 7
† 55082	Houlton, 400	A 5
54303	Howard, 4,911	K 6
† 53081	Howards Grove-Millersville, 998	L 8
53033	Hubertus, 600	K 1
54016	Hudson⊙, 5,049	A 6
54746	Humbird, 219	E 6
54534	Hurley⊙, 2,418	F 3
53034	Hustisford, 789	J 9
54637	Hustler, 190	F 8
† 54450	Hutchins, 409	H 6
54747	Independence, 1,036	D 7
54945	Iola, 900	H 6
54536	Iron Belt, 425	F 3
53035	Iron Ridge, 480	K 9
54847	Iron River, 800	D 2
53938	Ironton, 195	F 8
† 53177	Ives Grove, 250	L 3
53036	Ixonia, 300	H 1
53037	Jackson, 561	K 9
54236	Jacksonport, 180	M 6
53545	Janesville⊙, 46,426	J 10
53549	Jefferson⊙, 5,429	J 10
54748	Jim Falls, 310	D 5
53038	Johnson Creek, 790	J 9
53550	Juda, 500	H 10
54443	Junction City, 396	G 6
53039	Juneau⊙, 2,043	J 9
53139	Kansasville, 300	L 3
54130	Kaukauna, 11,292	K 7
† 53050	Kekoskee, 233	J 8
54215	Kellnersville, 250	L 7
54638	Kendall, 468	F 8
54537	Kennan, 167	F 5
53140	Kenosha⊙, 78,805	M 3
	Kenosha, ‡117,917	M 3
54135	Keshena⊙, 980	J 6
53040	Kewaskum, 1,926	K 8
54216	Kewaunee⊙, 2,901	M 7
53042	Kiel, 2,848	L 8
53812	Kieler, 653	E 10
54136	Kimberly, 6,131	K 7
54946	King, 1,040	H 7
53939	Kingston, 343	H 8
54749	Knapp, 369	B 6
53044	Kohler, 1,738	L 8
53147	Krakow, 315	K 6
54538	Lac du Flambeau, 500	G 4
† 53066	Lac La Belle, 227	H 1
54601	La Crosse⊙, 51,153	D 8
	La Crosse, ‡80,468	D 8
54848	Ladysmith⊙, 3,674	D 5
54639	La Farge, 748	E 8
53940	Lake Delton, 1,059	G 8
53147	Lake Geneva, 4,890	K 10
53551	Lake Mills, 3,556	H 9
54849	Lake Nebagamon, 523	C 3
54539	Lake Tomahawk, 555	H 4
† 54494	Lake Wazeecha, 1,285	G 7
† 54729	Lake Wissota, 1,419	D 6
54138	Lakewood, 300	K 5
† 53065	Lamartine, 190	J 8
53813	Lancaster⊙, 3,756	E 10
54540	Land O'Lakes, 786	H 3
53046	Lannon, 1,056	K 1
54541	Laona, 1,500	J 4
54850	La Pointe, 300	E 2
53941	La Valle, 411	F 8
53047	Lebanon, 250	H 1
54139	Lena, 569	K 6
† 54656	Leon, 160	E 8
† 53190	Lima Center, 175	J 10
53942	Limeridge, 203	F 9
53553	Linden, 408	F 10
54140	Little Chute, 5,365	K 7
54141	Little Suamico, 190	L 6
53554	Livingston, 503	E 10
53555	Lodi, 1,831	G 9
53943	Loganville, 199	F 9
† 54970	Lohrville, 195	H 7
53048	Lomira, 1,084	J 8
† 53523	London, 317	H 9
53556	Lone Rock, 506	F 9
54852	Loretta, 200	E 4
53557	Lowell, 322	J 9
54446	Loyal, 1,126	E 6
54853	Luck, 848	B 4
54217	Luxemburg, 853	L 6
53944	Lyndon Station, 533	F 8
53148	Lyons, 550	K 10
* 53701	Madison (cap.)⊙, 173,258	H 9
	Madison, ‡290,272	H 9
54750	Maiden Rock, 172	B 6
54949	Manawa, 1,105	J 7
54220	Manitowoc⊙, 33,430	L 7
54226	Maplewood, 192	M 6
54448	Marathon, 1,214	G 6
54855	Marengo, 350	E 3
54227	Maribel, 316	L 7
54143	Marinette⊙, 12,696	L 5
54950	Marion, 1,218	J 6
53946	Markesan, 1,378	J 8
53947	Marquette, 161	H 8
53559	Marshall, 1,043	H 9
54449	Marshfield, 15,619	F 6
54450	Mattoon, 377	J 5
53948	Mauston⊙, 3,466	F 8
53050	Mayville, 4,139	K 9
53560	Mazomanie, 1,217	G 9
53558	McFarland, 2,386	H 10
54543	McNaughton, 350	H 4
54451	Medford⊙, 3,454	F 5
54546	Mellen, 1,168	E 3
54642	Melrose, 505	E 7
54952	Menasha, 14,905	J 7
53051	Menomonee Falls, 31,697	K 1
54751	Menomonie⊙, 11,275	C 6
53092	Mequon, 12,110	L 1
54547	Mercer, 1,100	F 3
54452	Merrill⊙, 9,502	G 5
54754	Merrillan, 612	E 7
53561	Merrimac, 376	G 9
53056	Merton, 646	K 1
54148	Middle Inlet, 200	K 5
53562	Middleton, 8,286	G 9
54857	Mikana, 215	C 4
54454	Milladore, 229	G 6
54643	Millston, 200	E 7
54858	Milltown, 634	B 4
53563	Milton, 3,699	J 10
* 53201	Milwaukee⊙, 717,099	M 1
	Milwaukee, ‡1,403,887	M 1
54644	Mindoro, 230	D 7
53565	Mineral Point, 2,305	F 10
54548	Minocqua, 950	G 4
54859	Minong, 420	C 3
54228	Mishicot, 938	L 7
54755	Mondovi, 2,338	C 6
54549	Monico, 285	H 4
53716	Monona, 10,420	H 9
53566	Monroe⊙, 8,654	G 10
53949	Montello⊙, 1,082	H 8
53569	Montfort, 518	E 10
53570	Monticello, 870	G 10
54550	Montreal, 877	F 3

(continued on following page)

A. D'Arazien — Shostal Associates

"America's Dairyland"— Wisconsin cheeses are turned frequently while they age in brine in specially constructed rooms. Temperature and humidity control are vital for proper ripening.

(continued)

53571 Morrisonville, 350 G 9
54455 Mosinee, 2,395 G 6
54149 Mountain, 298 K 5
53057 Mount Calvary, 942 K 8
53816 Mount Hope, 176 D 10
53572 Mount Horeb, 2,402 G 10
54645 Mount Sterling, 181 D 9
† 53572 Mount Vernon, 250 G 10
53149 Mukwonago, 2,367 J 2
53573 Muscoda, 1,099 F 9
53150 Muskego, 11,573 K 2
53058 Nashotah, 410 J 1
54646 Necedah, 740 F 7
54956 Neenah, 22,892 J 7
54456 Neillsville⊙, 2,750 E 6
54457 Nekoosa, 2,409 G 7
54756 Nelson, 272 C 7
54458 Nelsonville, 152 H 7
54150 Neopit, 1,122 J 6
53059 Neosho, 400 J 9
54960 Neshkoro, 385 H 8
54551 Newald, 180 J 4
54757 New Auburn, 368 D 5
53151 New Berlin, 26,937 K 2
53060 Newburg, 425 K 9
† 61075 New Diggings, 224 F 10
54229 New Franken, 250 L 6
53574 New Glarus, 1,454 G 10
53061 New Holstein, 3,012 K 8
53950 New Lisbon, 1,361 F 8
54961 New London, 5,801 J 7
54017 New Richmond, 3,707 A 5
54151 Niagara, 2,347 K 4
54152 Nichols, 207 K 6
† 53401 North Bay, 263 M 3
54935 North Fond du Lac, 3,286 J 8
53951 North Freedom, 596 G 9
† 54016 North Hudson, 1,547 A 5
53064 North Lake, 525 J 1
53153 North Prairie, 669 J 2
54648 Norwalk, 432 E 8
53154 Oak Creek, 13,901 M 2
54649 Oakdale, 300 F 8
53065 Oakfield, 918 J 8
53066 Oconomowoc, 8,741 H 1
† 53066 Oconomowoc Lake, 599 H 1
54153 Oconto⊙, 4,667 L 6
54154 Oconto Falls, 2,517 K 6
54861 Odanah, 442 E 2
54962 Ogdensburg, 206 J 7
54459 Ogema, 280 F 5
53069 Okauchee, 3,134 J 1
† 53555 Okee, 300 H 9
† 54880 Oliver, 210 B 2
54963 Omro, 2,341 J 7
54650 Onalaska, 4,909 D 8
54155 Oneida, 900 K 7
54651 Ontario, 392 E 8
53070 Oostburg, 1,309 L 8
53575 Oregon, 2,553 H 10
53576 Orfordville, 888 H 10
54020 Osceola, 1,152 A 5
54901 Oshkosh⊙, 53,221 J 8
54758 Osseo, 1,356 D 6
54460 Owen, 1,031 F 6
53952 Oxford, 453 H 8
53953 Packwaukee, 250 G 8
† 53168 Paddock Lake, 1,470 K 10
53156 Palmyra, 1,341 H 2
53954 Pardeeville, 1,507 H 8
54552 Park Falls, 2,953 F 4
† 54481 Park Ridge, 817 H 6
53817 Patch Grove, 187 D 10
† 54514 Peeksville, 250 E 3
54156 Pembine, 500 L 4
54553 Pence, 315 F 3
† 54153 Pensaukee, 225 L 6
54759 Pepin, 747 B 7
† 53511 Perrygo Place, 5,912 J 10
54157 Peshtigo, 2,836 L 5
53072 Pewaukee, 3,271 K 1
54554 Phelps, 1,100 H 3
54555 Phillips⊙, 1,511 E 4
54464 Phlox, 235 J 5
54465 Pickerel, 400 J 5
54760 Pigeon Falls, 198 D 7
54466 Pittsville, 708 F 7
53577 Plain, 688 F 9
54966 Plainfield, 642 G 7
53818 Platteville, 9,599 F 10
53158 Pleasant Prairie, 950 L 10
54467 Plover, 1,900 G 7
54761 Plum City, 451 B 6
53073 Plymouth, 5,810 L 8
54864 Poplar, 455 C 2
53901 Portage⊙, 7,821 G 8
54469 Port Edwards, 2,126 G 7
53074 Port Washington⊙, 8,752 L 9
54865 Port Wing, 486 D 2
53820 Potosi, 713 E 10
54160 Potter, 320 K 7
54161 Pound, 284 L 5
53955 Poynette, 1,118 G 9
54967 Poy Sippi, 500 J 7
53821 Prairie du Chien⊙, 5,540 D 9
53578 Prairie du Sac, 1,902 G 9
54762 Prairie Farm, 426 C 5
54556 Prentice, 519 F 4
54021 Prescott, 2,331 A 6
54557 Presque Isle, 251 G 3
54968 Princeton, 1,446 H 8
54162 Pulaski, 1,717 K 6
* 53401 Racine⊙, 95,162 M 3
Racine, ‡170,838 M 3
54867 Radisson, 206 D 4
53956 Randolph, 1,582 H 8
53075 Random Lake, 1,068 K 8
† 53126 Raymond, 300 L 2
54969 Readfield, 200 J 7
54652 Readstown, 395 E 9
† 54814 Red Cliff, 250 E 2
54970 Redgranite, 645 J 7
53959 Reedsburg, 4,585 G 8
54230 Reedsville, 994 L 7
53579 Reeseville, 566 J 9
53580 Rewey, 232 F 10
54501 Rhinelander⊙, 8,218 H 4
54470 Rib Lake, 782 F 5
54868 Rice Lake, 7,278 C 5
53076 Richfield, 247 K 1
53581 Richland Center⊙, 5,086 F 9
54763 Ridgeland, 266 B 5
53582 Ridgeway, 463 F 10
53960 Rio, 792 H 9
54231 Rio Creek, 200 L 6
54971 Ripon, 7,053 J 8
54022 River Falls, 7,238 A 6
† 53201 River Hills, 1,561 M 1
54023 Roberts, 484 A 6
53167 Rochester, 436 K 3
† 53523 Rockdale, 172 J 10
54764 Rock Falls, 200 C 6
53077 Rockfield, 340 L 1
54653 Rockland, 278 D 8
53961 Rock Springs, 432 F 8
† 53178 Rome, 250 H 1
54974 Rosendale, 464 J 8
54473 Rosholt, 466 H 6
54474 Rothschild, 3,141 G 6
† 53583 Roxbury, 220 G 9
54975 Royalton, 200 J 7
53078 Rubicon, 261 K 9
54475 Rudolph, 349 G 7
53079 Saint Cloud, 550 K 8
54024 Saint Croix Falls, 1,425 A 5
† 53201 Saint Francis, 10,489 M 2
† 54601 Saint Joseph Ridge, 250 D 8
54232 Saint Nazianz, 718 L 7
54765 Sand Creek, 200 C 5
53583 Sauk City, 2,385 G 9
53080 Saukville, 1,389 L 9
54559 Saxon, 600 F 3
54560 Sayner, 300 H 4
54977 Scandinavia, 268 H 7
54476 Schofield, 2,577 H 6
† 53042 School Hill, 228 L 8
† 54843 Seeley, 213 D 3
54654 Seneca, 250 E 9
53584 Sextonville, 325 F 9
54165 Seymour, 2,194 K 6
53585 Sharon, 1,216 J 11
54166 Shawano⊙, 6,488 J 6
53081 Sheboygan⊙, 48,484 L 8
53085 Sheboygan Falls, 4,771 L 8
54766 Sheldon, 218 D 5
54871 Shell Lake⊙, 928 C 4
54169 Sherwood, 350 K 7
54170 Shiocton, 830 K 7
† 53525 Shopiere, 350 H 10
53211 Shorewood, 15,576 M 1
† 53701 Shorewood Hills, 2,206 G 9
53586 Shullsburg, 1,376 F 10
53170 Silver Lake, 1,210 K 10
54872 Siren, 639 B 4
54234 Sister Bay, 483 M 5
53086 Slinger, 1,022 K 9

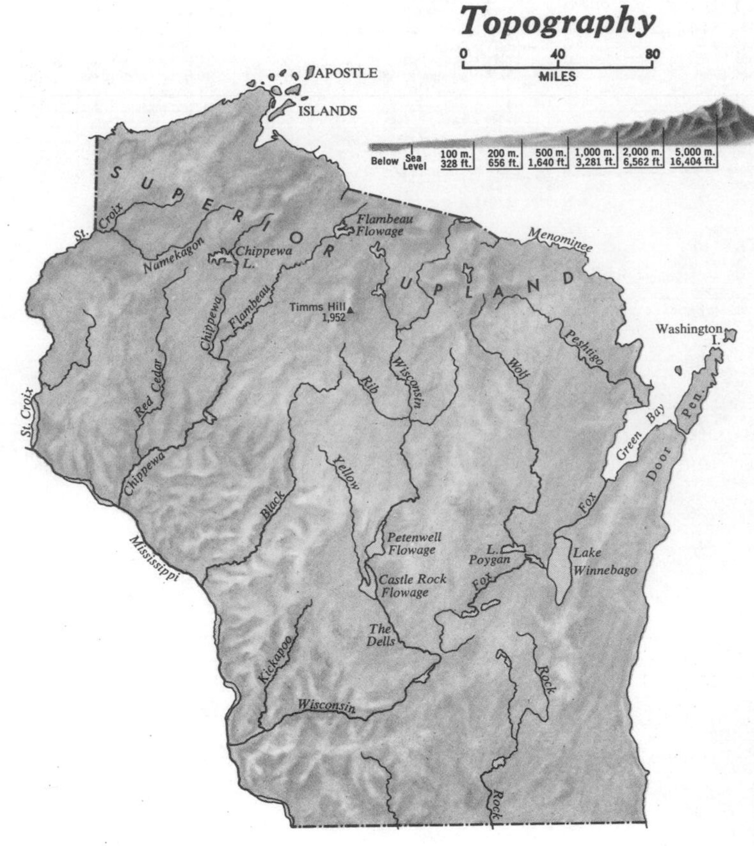

54655 Soldiers Grove, 514 E 9
54873 Solon Springs, 598 C 3
53171 Somers, 400 M 3
54025 Somerset, 778 A 5
53172 South Milwaukee, 23,297 M 2
53587 South Wayne, 436 G 10
54656 Sparta⊙, 6,258 E 8
54479 Spencer, 1,181 F 6
54801 Spooner, 2,444 B 4
53588 Spring Green, 1,199 G 9
54767 Spring Valley, 995 B 6
54768 Stanley, 2,049 E 6
54026 Star Prairie, 362 A 5
54480 Stetsonville, 305 F 5
54657 Steuben, 179 E 9
54481 Stevens Point⊙, 23,479 G 7
54172 Stiles, 300 L 6
53825 Stitzer, 295 E 10
53088 Stockbridge, 582 K 7
54658 Stoddard, 750 D 8
† 53066 Stone Bank, 390 J 1
54876 Stone Lake, 190 C 4
53589 Stoughton, 6,081 H 10
54484 Stratford, 1,239 F 6
54770 Strum, 738 D 6
54235 Sturgeon Bay⊙, 6,776 M 6
53177 Sturtevant, 3,376 M 3
54173 Suamico, 900 K 6
53178 Sullivan, 467 H 1
54485 Summit Lake, 200 H 5
53590 Sun Prairie, 9,935 H 9
54880 Superior (city)⊙, 32,237 C 2
Superior-Duluth, ‡265,350 C 2
† 54880 Superior Village, 476 B 2
54174 Suring, 499 K 5
53089 Sussex, 2,758 K 1
53090 Taycheedah, 600 K 8
54659 Taylor, 322 E 7
† 53820 Tennyson, 402 E 10
53091 Theresa, 611 K 8
53092 Thiensville, 3,182 L 1
54771 Thorp, 1,469 E 6
54562 Three Lakes, 950 H 4
† 53185 Tichigan, 500 K 2
54486 Tigerton, 742 H 6
54240 Tisch Mills, 259 L 7
54660 Tomah, 5,647 F 8
54487 Tomahawk, 3,419 G 5
54175 Townsend, 450 K 5
54888 Trego, 200 C 4
54661 Trempealeau, 743 C 8
53180 Troy Center, 250 J 2
54662 Tunnel City, 226 E 7
54889 Turtle Lake, 637 B 5
53181 Twin Lakes, 2,276 K 11
54241 Two Rivers, 13,553 M 7
53962 Union Center, 205 F 8
53182 Union Grove, 2,703 L 3
54488 Unity, 363 F 6
54245 Valders, 821 L 7
53593 Verona, 2,334 G 9
54489 Vesper, 355 F 7
54664 Viola, 659 E 8
54665 Viroqua⊙, 3,739 D 8
54566 Wabeno, 800 J 5
53093 Waldo, 408 L 8
53183 Wales, 691 J
53184 Walworth, 1,637 J 1
54666 Warrens, 300 E
54890 Wascott, 200 C
54891 Washburn⊙, 1,957 D
54246 Washington Island, 550 M
53185 Waterford, 1,922 K
53594 Waterloo, 2,253 J
53094 Watertown, 15,683 J
53021 Waubeka, 300 L
54980 Waukau, 245 J
53186 Waukesha⊙, 40,258 K
53597 Waunakee, 2,181 G
54981 Waupaca⊙, 4,342 H
53963 Waupun, 7,946 J
54401 Wausau⊙, 32,806 G
54177 Wausaukee, 557 K
54982 Wautoma⊙, 1,624 H
53226 Wauwatosa, 58,676 L
53826 Wauzeka, 437 E
54893 Webster, 502 B
53214 West Allis, 71,723 L
† 53913 West Baraboo, 563 G
53095 West Bend⊙, 16,555 K
54490 Westboro, 950 F
54667 Westby, 1,568 E
53964 Westfield, 884 H
† 54601 West La Crosse, 950 D
† 53201 West Milwaukee, 4,405 L
† 54476 Weston, 3,375 G
54669 West Salem, 2,180 D
54983 Weyauwega, 1,377 H
54895 Weyerhauser, 285 D
54772 Wheeler, 212 C
53217 Whitefisn Bay, 17,394 M
54773 Whitehall⊙, 1,486 D
54491 White Lake, 309 J
54247 Whitelaw, 557 L
53190 Whitewater, 12,038 J
† 54481 Whiting, 1,782 H
54984 Wild Rose, 585 H
53191 Williams Bay, 1,554 J
54670 Wilton, 516 F
54567 Winchester, 230 G
53185 Wind Lake, 900 K
† 53401 Wind Point, 1,251 M
53598 Windsor, 827 H
54985 Winnebago, 1,550 J
54986 Winneconne, 1,608 J
54896 Winter, 450 E
53965 Wisconsin Dells, 2,401 G
54494 Wisconsin Rapids⊙, 18,587 G
54498 Withee, 480 E
54499 Wittenberg, 895 H
53968 Wonewoc, 835 F
54568 Woodruff, 800 G
54028 Woodville, 522 B
54180 Wrightstown, 1,020 K
54671 Wyeville, 203 F
53969 Wyocena, 809 H
54182 Zachow, 160 K

⊙ County seat.
‡ Population of metropolitan area.
† Zip of nearest p.o.
* Multiple zips

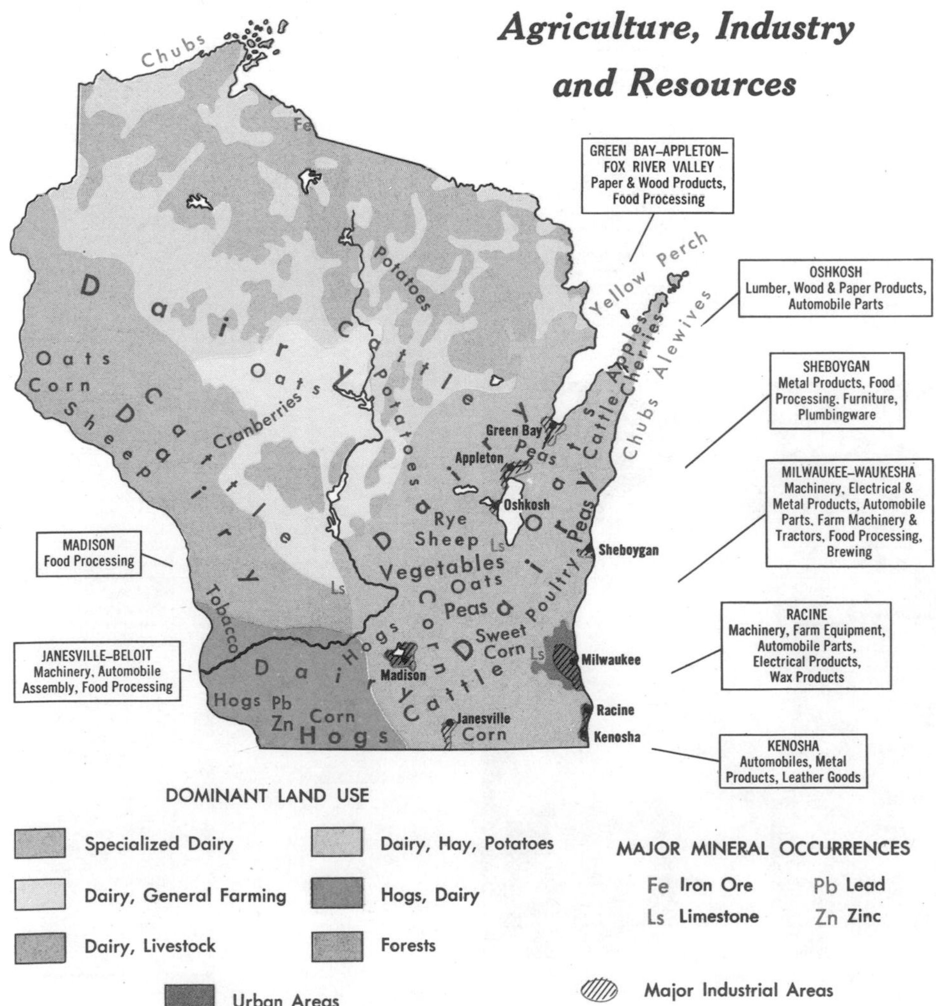

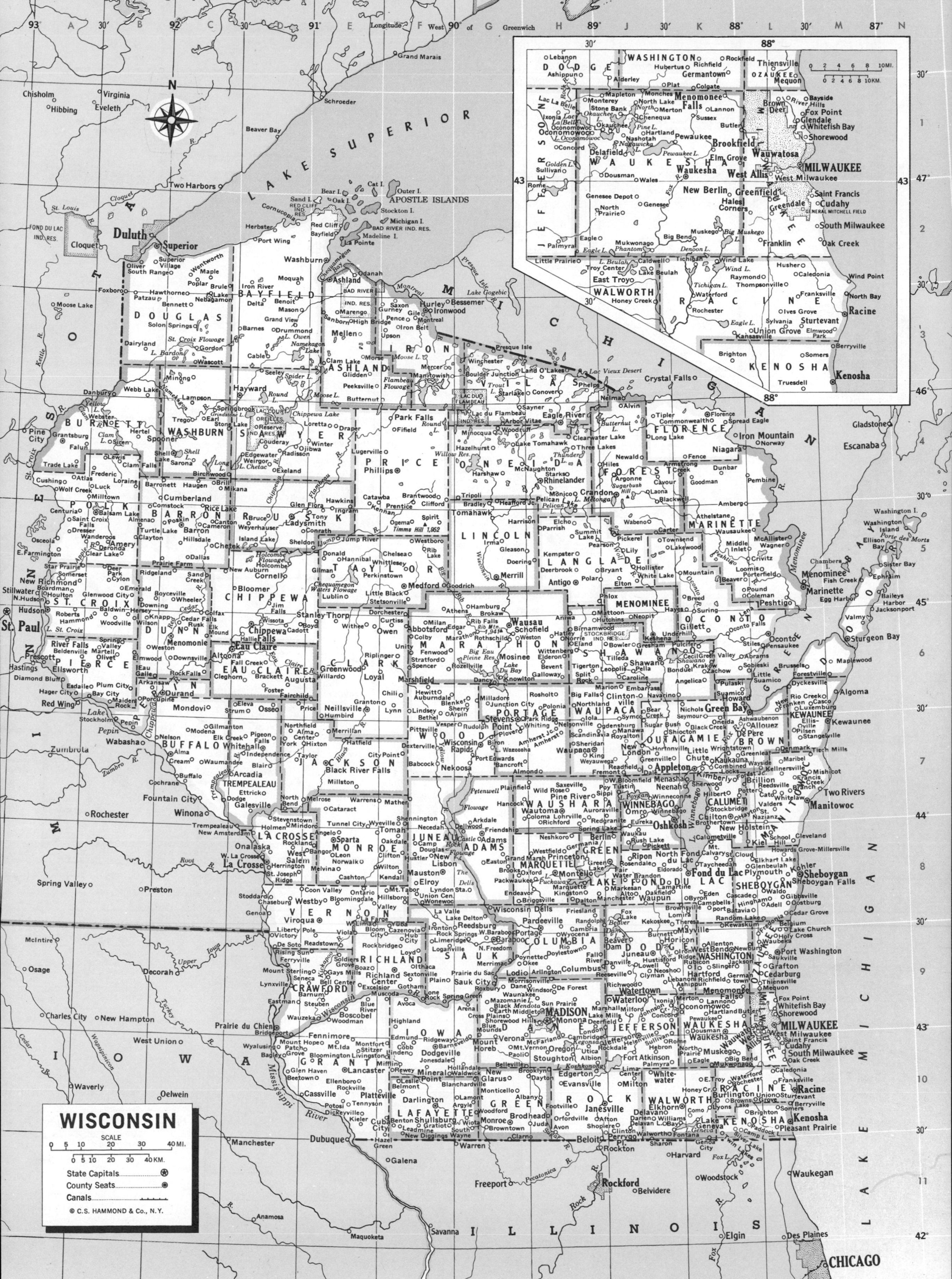

WISCONSIN
SCALE
0 5 10 20 30 40 MI.
0 5 10 20 30 40 KM.
State Capitals
County Seats
Canals
© C.S. HAMMOND & Co., N.Y.
LAKE SUPERIOR
LAKE MICHIGAN
MICHIGAN
MINNESOTA
IOWA
ILLINOIS
GREEN BAY
APOSTLE ISLANDS
Longitude West 90° of Greenwich
MILWAUKEE
MADISON
Green Bay
Duluth
Superior
St. Paul
Chicago
DOUGLAS
BAYFIELD
ASHLAND
IRON
VILAS
BURNETT
WASHBURN
SAWYER
PRICE
ONEIDA
FLORENCE
FOREST
POLK
BARRON
RUSK
TAYLOR
LINCOLN
LANGLADE
MARINETTE
ST. CROIX
DUNN
CHIPPEWA
MARATHON
MENOMINEE
OCONTO
PIERCE
EAU CLAIRE
CLARK
SHAWANO
PEPIN
BUFFALO
WOOD
PORTAGE
WAUPACA
OUTAGAMIE
BROWN
KEWAUNEE
DOOR
TREMPEALEAU
JACKSON
JUNEAU
ADAMS
WAUSHARA
WINNEBAGO
CALUMET
MANITOWOC
LA CROSSE
MONROE
MARQUETTE
GREEN LAKE
FOND DU LAC
SHEBOYGAN
VERNON
SAUK
COLUMBIA
DODGE
WASHINGTON
OZAUKEE
RICHLAND
CRAWFORD
IOWA
DANE
JEFFERSON
WAUKESHA
GRANT
LAFAYETTE
GREEN
ROCK
WALWORTH
RACINE
KENOSHA

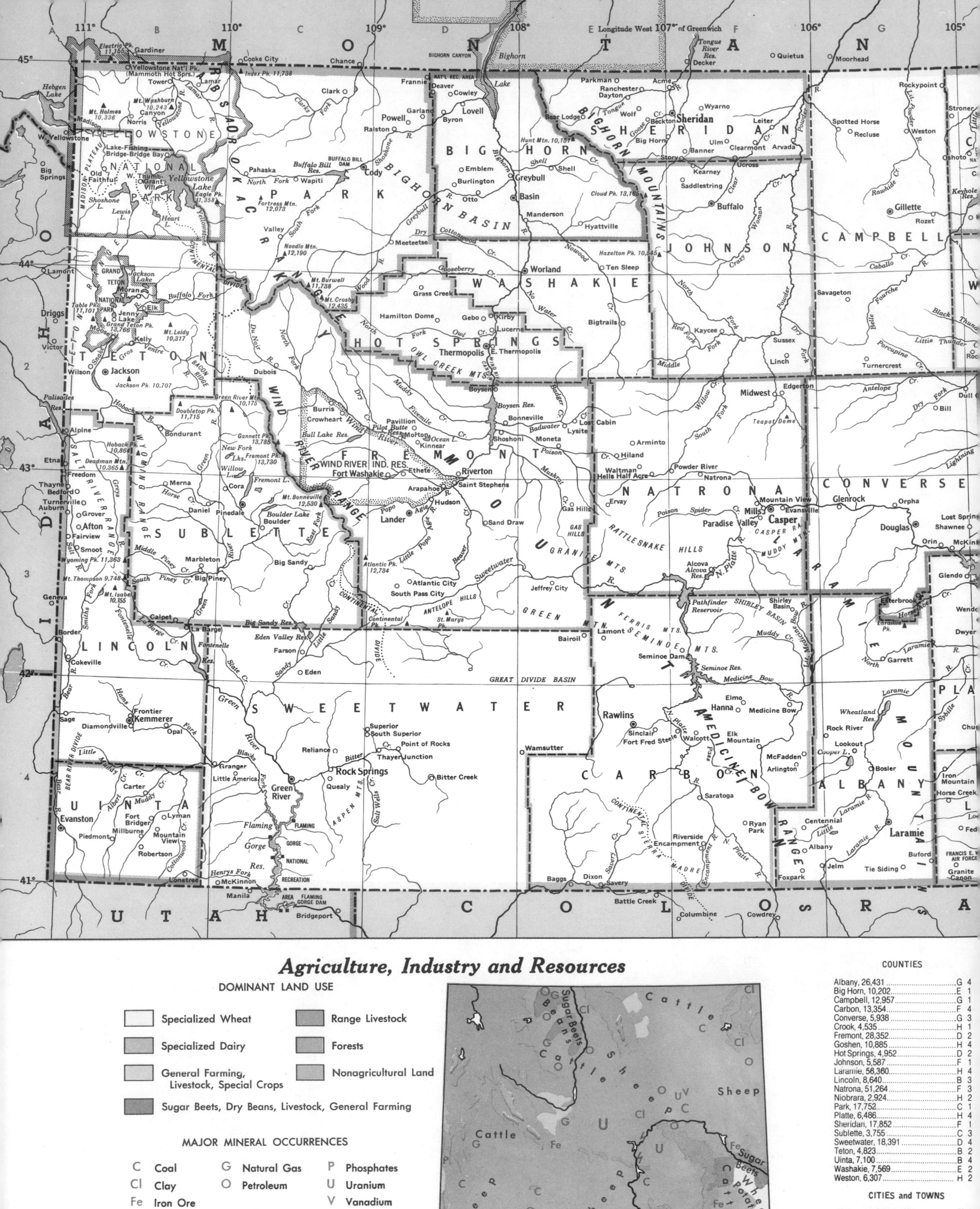

Agriculture, Industry and Resources

DOMINANT LAND USE

- Specialized Wheat
- Specialized Dairy
- General Farming, Livestock, Special Crops
- Sugar Beets, Dry Beans, Livestock, General Farming
- Range Livestock
- Forests
- Nonagricultural Land

MAJOR MINERAL OCCURRENCES

- C Coal
- Cl Clay
- Fe Iron Ore
- G Natural Gas
- O Petroleum
- P Phosphates
- U Uranium
- V Vanadium
- Water Power

COUNTIES

County	Key
Albany, 26,431	G 4
Big Horn, 10,202	E 1
Campbell, 12,957	G 1
Carbon, 13,354	F 4
Converse, 5,938	G 3
Crook, 4,535	H 1
Fremont, 28,352	D 2
Goshen, 10,885	H 4
Hot Springs, 4,952	D 2
Johnson, 5,587	F 1
Laramie, 56,360	H 4
Lincoln, 8,640	B 3
Natrona, 51,264	F 3
Niobrara, 2,924	H 2
Park, 17,752	C 1
Platte, 6,486	H 4
Sheridan, 17,852	F 1
Sublette, 3,755	C 3
Sweetwater, 18,391	D 4
Teton, 4,823	B 2
Uinta, 7,100	B 4
Washakie, 7,569	E 2
Weston, 6,307	H 2

CITIES and TOWNS

Zip	Name/Pop.	Key
82830	Acme, 98	E 1
83110	Afton, 1,290	B 3

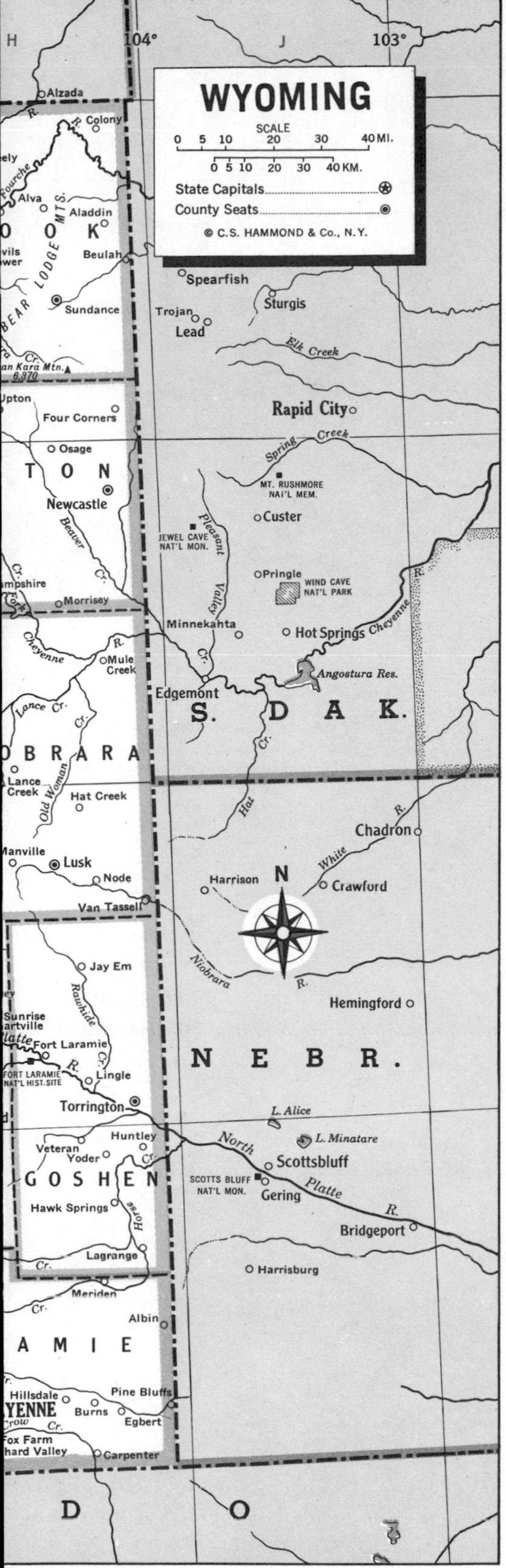

WYOMING

SCALE
0 5 10 20 30 40 MI.
0 5 10 20 30 40 KM.
State Capitals ⊛
County Seats ⊙
© C.S. HAMMOND & Co., N.Y.

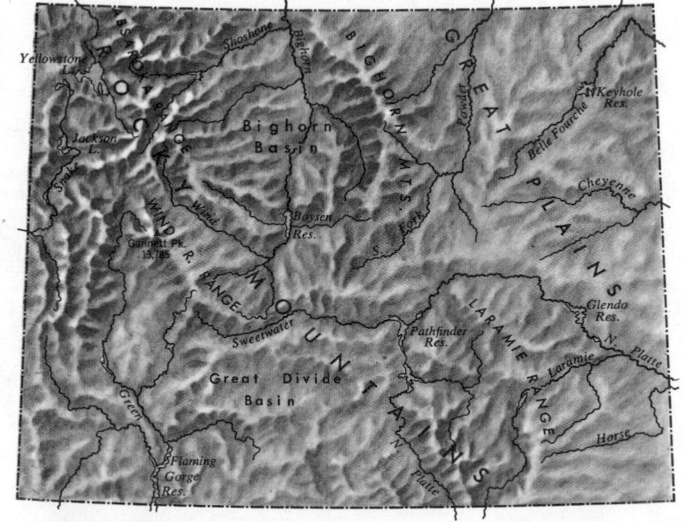

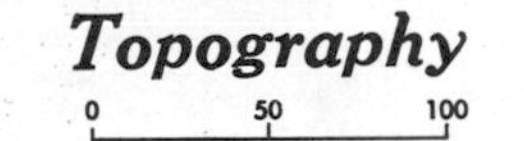

Topography

0 50 100
MILES

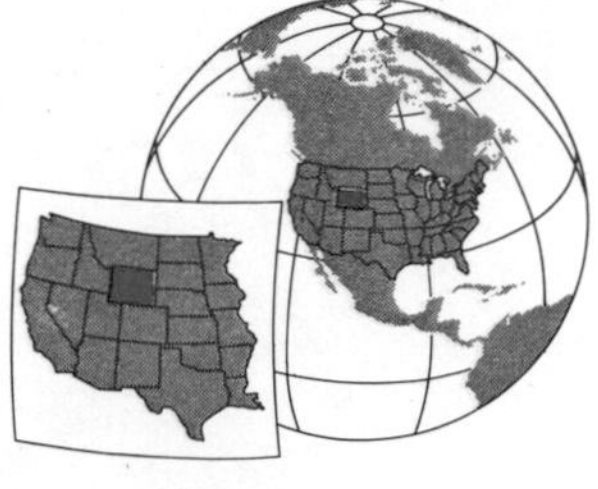

AREA 97,914 sq. mi.
POPULATION 332,416
CAPITAL Cheyenne
LARGEST CITY Cheyenne
HIGHEST POINT Gannett Pk. 13,785 ft.
SETTLED IN 1834
ADMITTED TO UNION July 10, 1890
POPULAR NAME Equality State
STATE FLOWER Indian Paintbrush
STATE BIRD Meadowlark

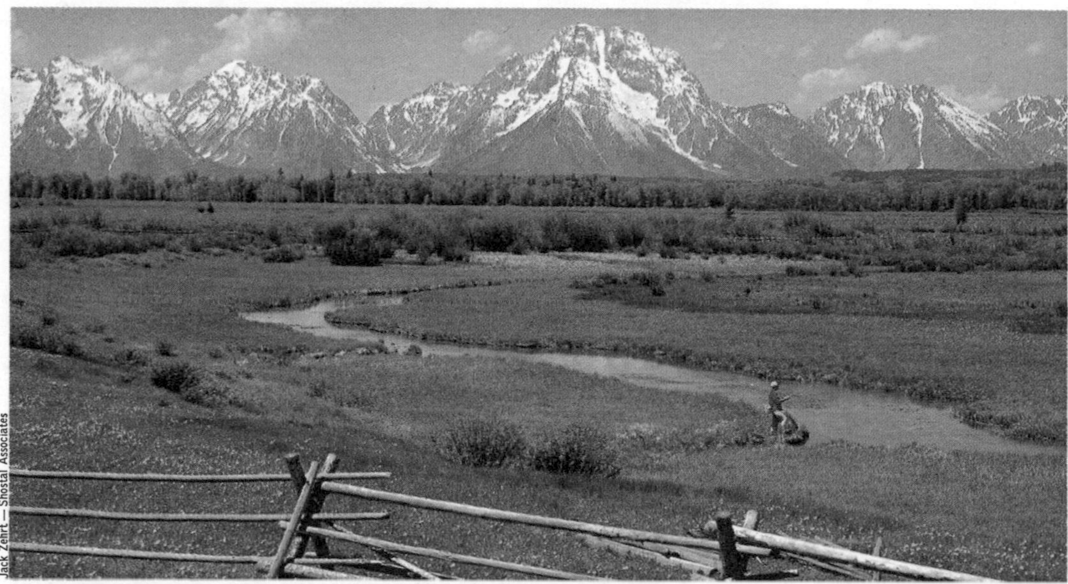

Jack Zehrt—Shostal Associates

Intrepid mountain climbers are challenged by the sheer granite cliffs of Wyoming's Teton Range. Lowland meadows and trails attract less ambitious sportsmen.

82710 Aladdin, 12 H 1
82055 Albany, 50 F 4
82050 Albin, 118 H 4
82620 Alcova, 125 F 3
83127 Alpine, 95 B 2
82711 Alva, 45 H 1
82510 Arapahoe, 682 D 3
82831 Arvada, 50 F 1
82520 Atlantic City, 25 D 3
83111 Auburn, 240 A 3
82321 Baggs, 146 E 4
82322 Bairoil, 150 E 3
82832 Banner, 44 F 1
82410 Basin⊙, 1,145 E 1
82836 Bear Lodge, 25 E 1
82801 Beckton, 110 E 1
83112 Bedford, 290 A 3
82712 Beulah, 63 H 1
82833 Big Horn, 200 E 1
83113 Big Piney, 570 B 3
82923 Big Sandy, 20 C 3
82442 Bigtrails, 25 E 2
82921 Bitter Creek, 20 D 4
82922 Bondurant, 90 B 2
82649 Bonneville, 18 E 2
83114 Border, 25 B 3
82051 Bosler, 80 G 4
82923 Boulder, 30 C 3
82834 Buffalo⊙, 3,394 F 1
82052 Buford, 36 G 4
82411 Burlington, 300 D 1
82053 Burns, 185 H 4
82511 Burris, 30 C 2
82412 Byron, 397 D 1
† 83123 Calpet, 20 B 3
82190 Canyon, 130 B 1
82054 Carpenter, 100 H 4
† 82937 Carter, 33 B 4
82601 Casper⊙, 39,361 F 3
82055 Centennial, 160 F 4
82001 Cheyenne (cap.)⊙, 40,914 H 4
82210 Chugwater, 187 H 4
† 59008 Clark, 25 C 1
82835 Clearmont, 141 F 1
82414 Cody⊙, 5,161 D 1
83114 Cokeville, 440 B 3
† 57717 Colony, 50 H 1
82420 Cowley, 366 D 1
82512 Crowheart, 12 C 2
83115 Daniel, 175 B 3
82836 Dayton, 396 E 1
82421 Deaver, 112 D 1
82714 Devils Tower, 73 H 1
83116 Diamondville, 485 B 4
82323 Dixon, 72 E 4
82633 Douglas⊙, 2,677 G 3
82513 Dubois, 898 C 2
† 82443 East Thermopolis, 316 D 2
82926 Eden, 275 C 3
82635 Edgerton, 350 F 2
† 82053 Egbert, 40 H 4
† 83013 Elk, 10 B 2
82324 Elk Mountain, 127 F 4
† 82327 Elmo, 53 F 4
82422 Emblem, 250 D 1
82325 Encampment, 321 F 4
82520 Ethete, 30 D 2
83118 Etna, 400 A 2
82930 Evanston⊙, 4,462 B 4
82636 Evansville, 832 F 3
83119 Fairview, 245 B 3
82932 Farson, 210 C 3
† 82001 Federal, 15 G 4
82933 Fort Bridger, 150 B 4
† 82301 Fort Fred Steele, 15 E 4
82212 Fort Laramie, 197 H 3
82514 Fort Washakie, 140 C 2
† 82001 Fox Farm, 1,329 H 4
82057 Foxpark, 110 F 4
82423 Frannie, 139 D 1
83120 Freedom, 497 B 3
83121 Frontier, 246 B 4
82424 Garland, 57 D 1
82058 Garrett, 10 G 3
82501 Gas Hills, 200 E 3
† 82430 Gebo, 15 D 2
82716 Gillette⊙, 7,194 G 1
82213 Glendo, 210 G 3
82637 Glenrock, 1,515 G 3
82934 Granger, 137 C 4
82059 Granite Canon, 72 G 4
82425 Grass Creek, 125 D 2
82935 Green River⊙, 4,196 C 4
82426 Greybull, 1,953 E 1
83122 Grover, 120 B 3
82214 Guernsey, 793 H 3
82427 Hamilton Dome, 106 D 2
† 82701 Hampshire, 23 H 2
82327 Hanna, 460 F 4
82215 Hartville, 246 H 3
82217 Hawk Springs, 125 H 4
82060 Hillsdale, 160 H 4
82061 Horse Creek, 225 G 4
82515 Hudson, 381 D 3
82720 Hulett, 318 H 1
82218 Huntley, 50 H 4
82428 Hyattville, 73 E 1
82062 Iron Mountain, 12 G 4
83001 Jackson⊙, 2,101 B 2
82219 Jay Em, 25 H 3
82310 Jeffrey City, 702 E 3
82063 Jelm, 29 G 4
† 83012 Jenny Lake, 10 B 2
82639 Kaycee, 272 F 2
† 82832 Kearney, 49 F 1
82220 Keeline, 30 H 3
83011 Kelly, 35 B 2
83101 Kemmerer⊙, 2,292 B 4
82516 Kinnear, 44 D 2
82430 Kirby, 75 D 2
83123 La Barge, 375 B 3
82221 Lagrange, 189 H 4
† 82190 Lake-Fishing Bridge-Bridge Bay, 167 B 1
† 82190 Lamar, 27 B 1
82328 Lamont, 30 E 3
82222 Lance Creek, 175 H 2
82520 Lander⊙, 7,125 D 3
82070 Laramie⊙, 23,143 G 4
82837 Leiter, 100 F 1
82640 Linch, 185 F 2
82223 Lingle, 446 H 3
82929 Little America, 47 C 4
† 82051 Lookout, 20 G 4
† 82642 Lost Cabin, 25 E 2
82431 Lovell, 2,371 D 1
† 82443 Lucerne, 240 D 2
82225 Lusk⊙, 1,495 H 3
82937 Lyman, 643 B 4
82642 Lysite, 25 E 2
† 82190 Madison, 42 B 1
† 82190 Mammoth Hot Springs (Yellowstone Nat'l Park), 162 B 1
82432 Manderson, 117 E 1
82227 Manville, 92 H 3
† 83113 Marbleton, 223 B 3
82080 McFadden, 150 F 4
82938 McKinnon, 135 C 4
82329 Medicine Bow, 455 F 4
82433 Meeteetse, 459 D 1
† 83115 Merna, 25 B 3
82643 Midwest, 743 F 2
† 82933 Millburne, 54 B 4
82644 Mills, 1,724 F 3
82721 Moorcroft, 981 H 1
83012 Moose, 115 B 2
83013 Moran, 600 B 2
† 82701 Morrisey, 28 H 2
82522 Morton, 35 D 2
82939 Mountain View, 1,641 F 3
82939 Mountain View, 500 B 4
† 57735 Mule Creek, 10 H 2
82701 Newcastle⊙, 3,432 H 2
82722 New Haven, 35 H 1
† 82190 Norris, 20 B 1
82190 Old Faithful, 134 B 1
83124 Opal, 34 B 4
† 82001 Orchard Valley, 1,015 H 4
82652 Orin, 20 G 3
† 82633 Orpha, 12 G 3
82723 Osage, 346 H 2
82434 Otto, 75 D 1
82414 Pahaska, 75 C 1
† 82601 Paradise Valley, 1,764 F 3
82838 Parkman, 30 E 1
82523 Pavillion, 181 D 2
† 82933 Piedmont, 25 B 4
82082 Pine Bluffs, 937 H 4
82941 Pinedale⊙, 948 C 3
82942 Point of Rocks, 20 D 4
82648 Powder River, 75 F 2
82435 Powell, 4,807 D 1
82440 Ralston, 85 D 1
82839 Ranchester, 208 E 1
82301 Rawlins⊙, 7,855 E 4
82725 Recluse, 25 G 1
82943 Reliance, 425 C 4
† 82325 Riverside, 46 F 4
82501 Riverton, 7,995 D 2
82944 Robertson, 39 B 4
† 82701 Rochelle, 23 H 2
82083 Rock River, 344 G 4
82901 Rock Springs, 11,657 C 4
82726 Rockypoint, 22 G 1
82727 Rozet, 50 G 1
82330 Ryan Park, 18 F 4
82840 Saddlestring, 100 F 1
83125 Sage, 45 B 4
82524 Saint Stephens, 100 D 3
82501 Sand Draw, 40 D 3
82331 Saratoga, 1,181 F 4
† 82716 Savageton, 30 G 2
82332 Savery, 29 E 4
† 82720 Seely, 10 H 1
82333 Seminoe Dam, 40 E 3
82229 Shawnee, 11 G 3
82441 Shell, 50 E 1
82801 Sheridan⊙, 10,856 F 1
82601 Shirley Basin, 700 F 3
82649 Shoshoni, 562 D 2
82334 Sinclair, 445 E 4
83126 Smoot, 200 B 3
† 82945 South Superior, 197 D 4
82842 Story, 637 F 1
82729 Sundance⊙, 1,056 H 1
† 82215 Sunrise, 80 H 3
82945 Superior, 2 D 4
† 82639 Sussex, 200 F 2
82442 Ten Sleep, 320 E 1
† 82901 Thayer Junction, 15 D 4
83127 Thayne, 195 A 3
82443 Thermopolis⊙, 3,063 D 2
82240 Torrington⊙, 4,237 H 3
† 82190 Tower, 24 B 1
† 83112 Turnerville, 25 A 3
† 82835 Ucross, 17 F 1
82835 Ulm, 25 F 1
82730 Upton, 987 H 1
82242 Van Tassell, 21 H 3
82243 Veteran, 35 H 4
82335 Walcott, 20 F 4
† 82648 Waltman, 20 E 2
82336 Wamsutter, 139 E 4
82450 Wapiti, 92 C 1
† 82190 West Thumb-Grant Village, 64 B 1
82201 Wheatland⊙, 2,498 H 3
83014 Wilson, 550 B 2
82844 Wolf, 85 E 1
82401 Worland⊙, 5,055 E 1
82845 Wyarno, 12 F 1
82190 Yellowstone Nat'l Park, 162 B 1
82244 Yoder, 101 H 4

⊙ County seat.
† Zip of nearest p.o.

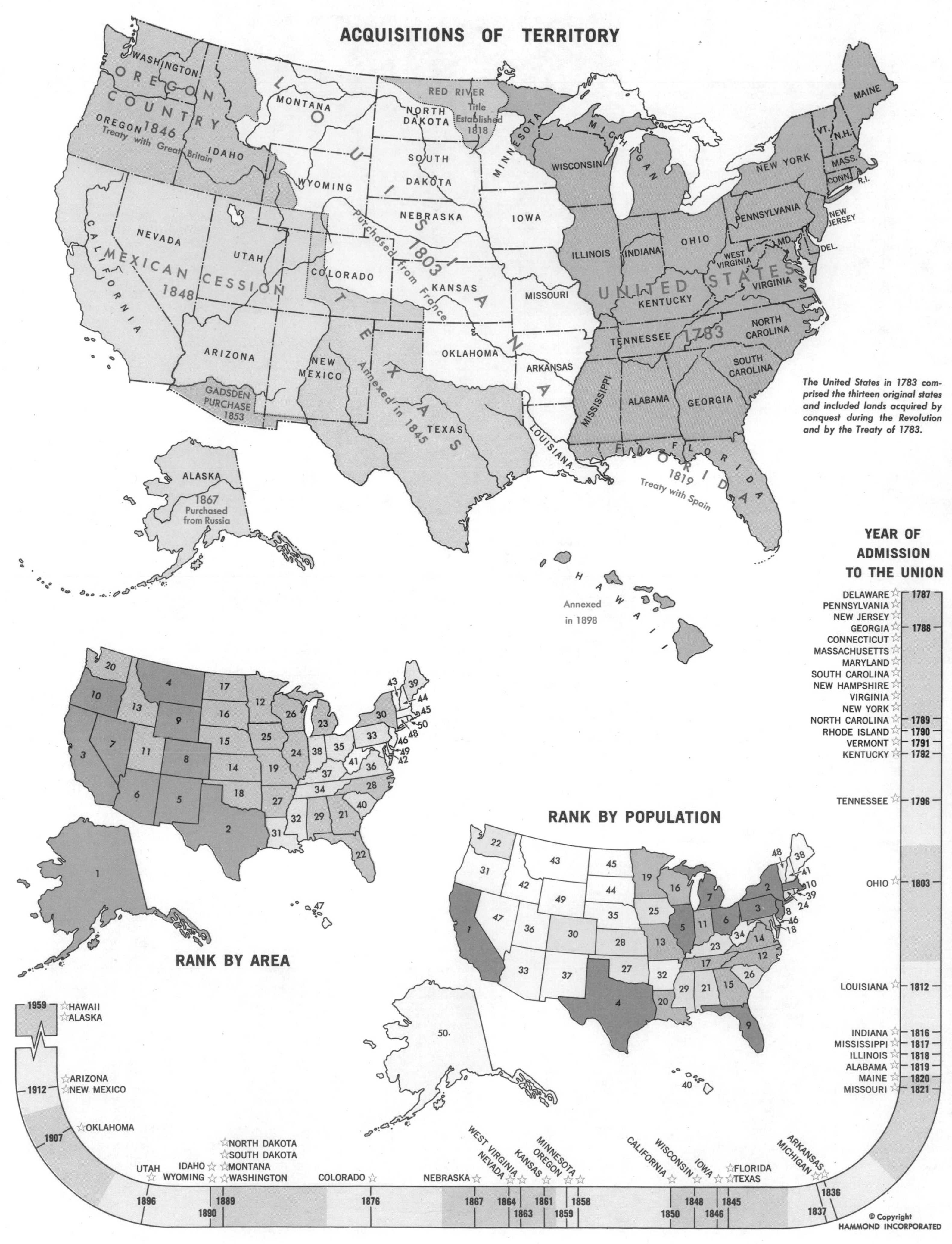
ACQUISITIONS OF TERRITORY
OREGON COUNTRY
OREGON 1846
Treaty with Great Britain
LOUISIANA
1803
Purchased from France
RED RIVER
Title Established 1818
MEXICAN CESSION
1848
TEXAS
Annexed in 1845
GADSDEN PURCHASE
1853
UNITED STATES
1783
FLORIDA
1819
Treaty with Spain
ALASKA
1867
Purchased from Russia
HAWAII
Annexed in 1898
The United States in 1783 comprised the thirteen original states and included lands acquired by conquest during the Revolution and by the Treaty of 1783.
RANK BY AREA
RANK BY POPULATION
YEAR OF ADMISSION TO THE UNION
DELAWARE 1787
PENNSYLVANIA
NEW JERSEY
GEORGIA 1788
CONNECTICUT
MASSACHUSETTS
MARYLAND
SOUTH CAROLINA
NEW HAMPSHIRE
VIRGINIA
NEW YORK
NORTH CAROLINA 1789
RHODE ISLAND 1790
VERMONT 1791
KENTUCKY 1792
TENNESSEE 1796
OHIO 1803
LOUISIANA 1812
INDIANA 1816
MISSISSIPPI 1817
ILLINOIS 1818
ALABAMA 1819
MAINE 1820
MISSOURI 1821
ARKANSAS 1836
MICHIGAN 1837
FLORIDA 1845
TEXAS
IOWA 1846
WISCONSIN 1848
CALIFORNIA 1850
MINNESOTA 1858
OREGON 1859
KANSAS 1861
WEST VIRGINIA 1863
NEVADA 1864
NEBRASKA 1867
COLORADO 1876
NORTH DAKOTA 1889
SOUTH DAKOTA
MONTANA
WASHINGTON
IDAHO 1890
WYOMING
UTAH 1896
OKLAHOMA 1907
ARIZONA 1912
NEW MEXICO
HAWAII 1959
ALASKA

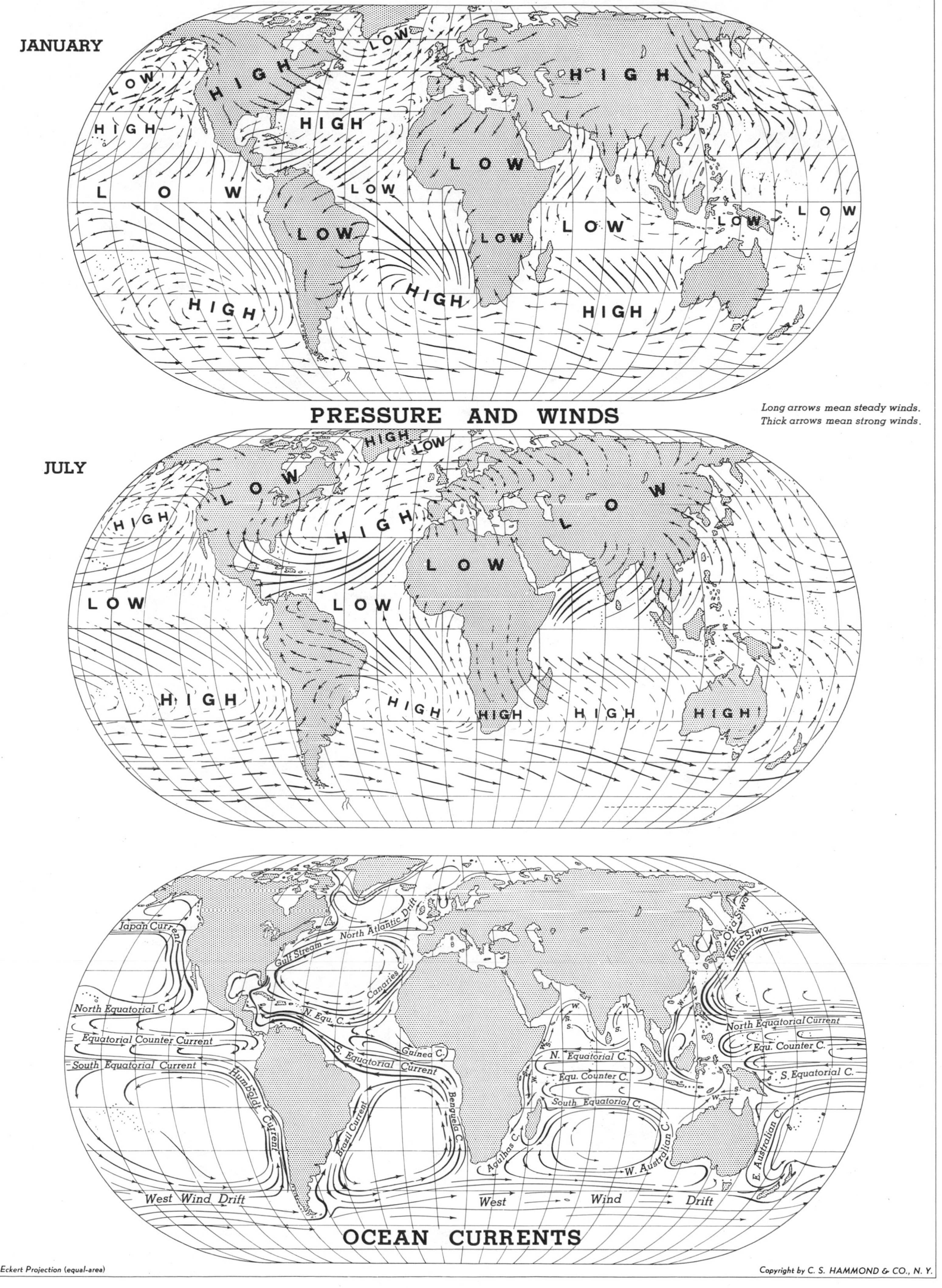
JANUARY
LOW
HIGH
HIGH
HIGH
HIGH
LOW
L O W
LOW
LOW
LOW
LOW
LOW
LOW
LOW
HIGH
HIGH
HIGH
PRESSURE AND WINDS
Long arrows mean steady winds.
Thick arrows mean strong winds.
JULY
HIGH
LOW
LOW
HIGH
HIGH
LOW
LOW
LOW
LOW
HIGH
HIGH
HIGH
HIGH
HIGH
Japan Current
Gulf Stream
North Atlantic Drift
Oya Siwa
Kuro Siwa
Canaries
North Equatorial C.
N. Equ. C.
Equatorial Counter Current
South Equatorial Current
Guinea C.
S. Equatorial Current
North Equatorial Current
Equ. Counter C.
N. Equatorial C.
Equ. Counter C.
S. Equatorial C.
South Equatorial C.
Humboldt Current
Brazil Current
Benguela C.
Agulhas C.
W. Australian C.
E. Australian C.
West Wind Drift
West Wind Drift
OCEAN CURRENTS
Eckert Projection (equal-area)

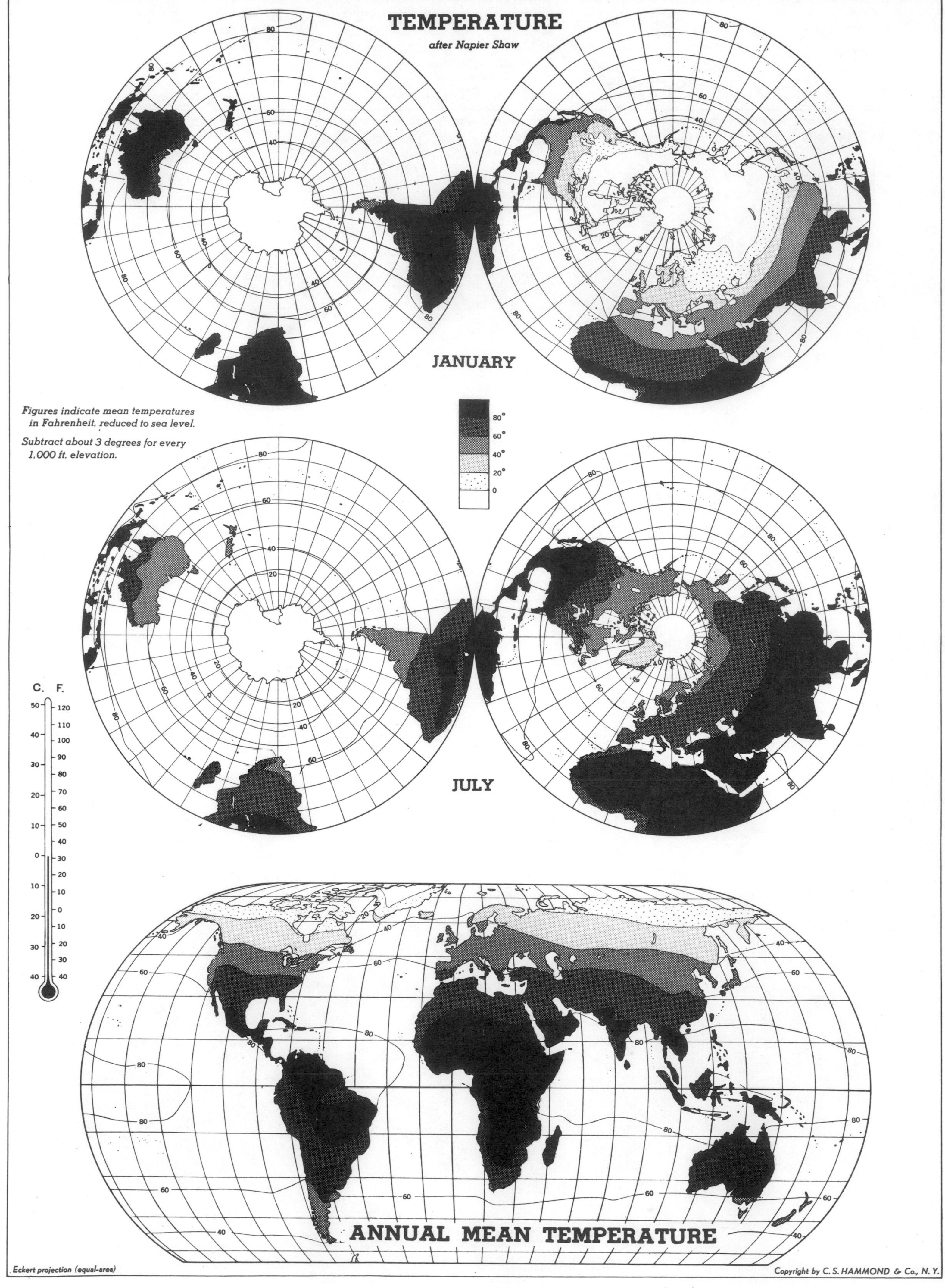

TEMPERATURE
after Napier Shaw
JANUARY
Figures indicate mean temperatures in Fahrenheit, reduced to sea level.
Subtract about 3 degrees for every 1,000 ft. elevation.
80°
60°
40°
20°
0
JULY
C. F.
ANNUAL MEAN TEMPERATURE
Eckert projection (equal-area)
Copyright by C. S. HAMMOND & Co., N. Y.

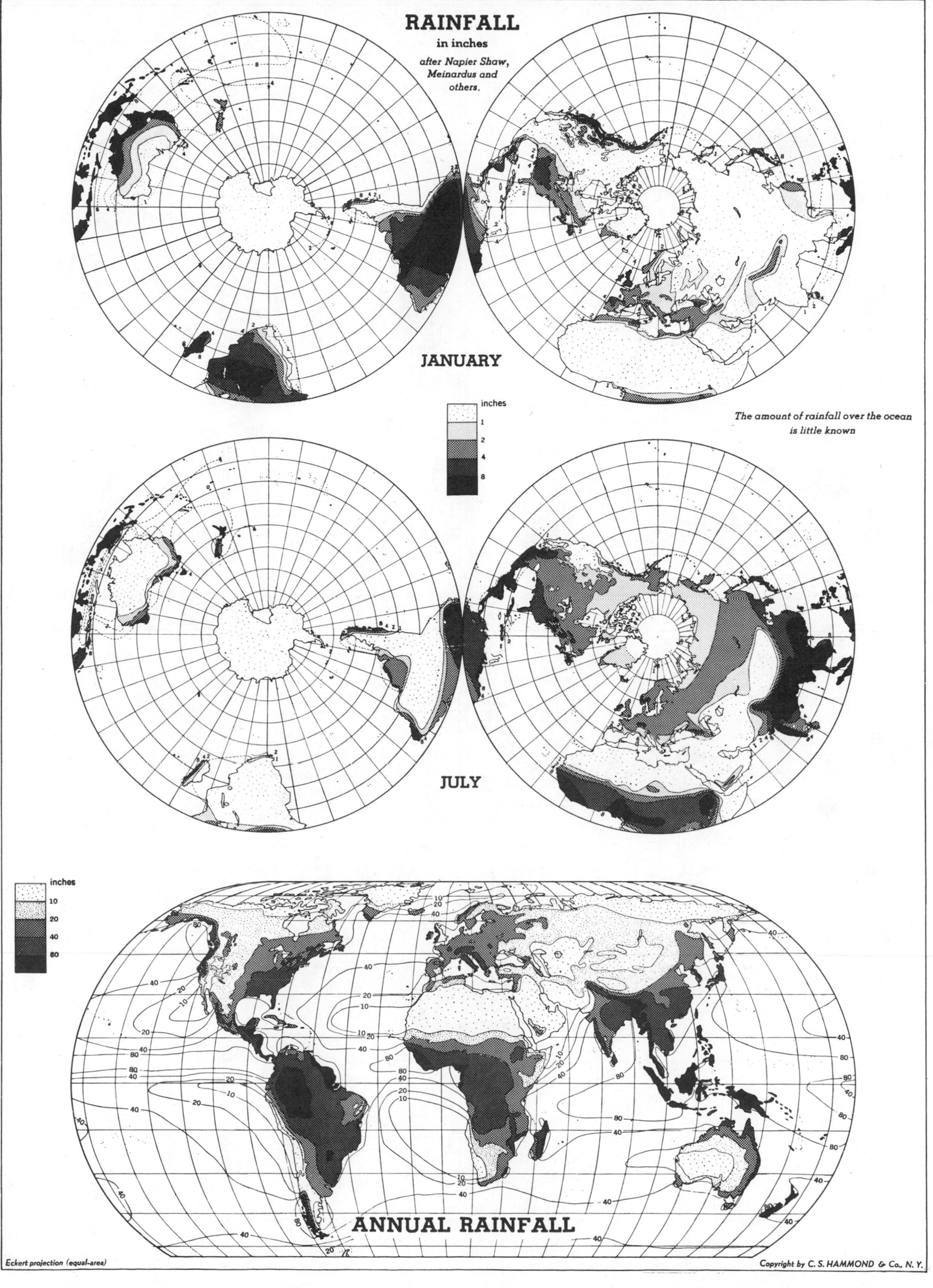
RAINFALL
in inches
after Napier Shaw, Meinardus and others.
JANUARY
inches
1
2
4
8
The amount of rainfall over the ocean is little known
JULY
inches
10
20
40
80
ANNUAL RAINFALL
Eckert projection (equal-area)
Copyright by C. S. HAMMOND & Co., N. Y.

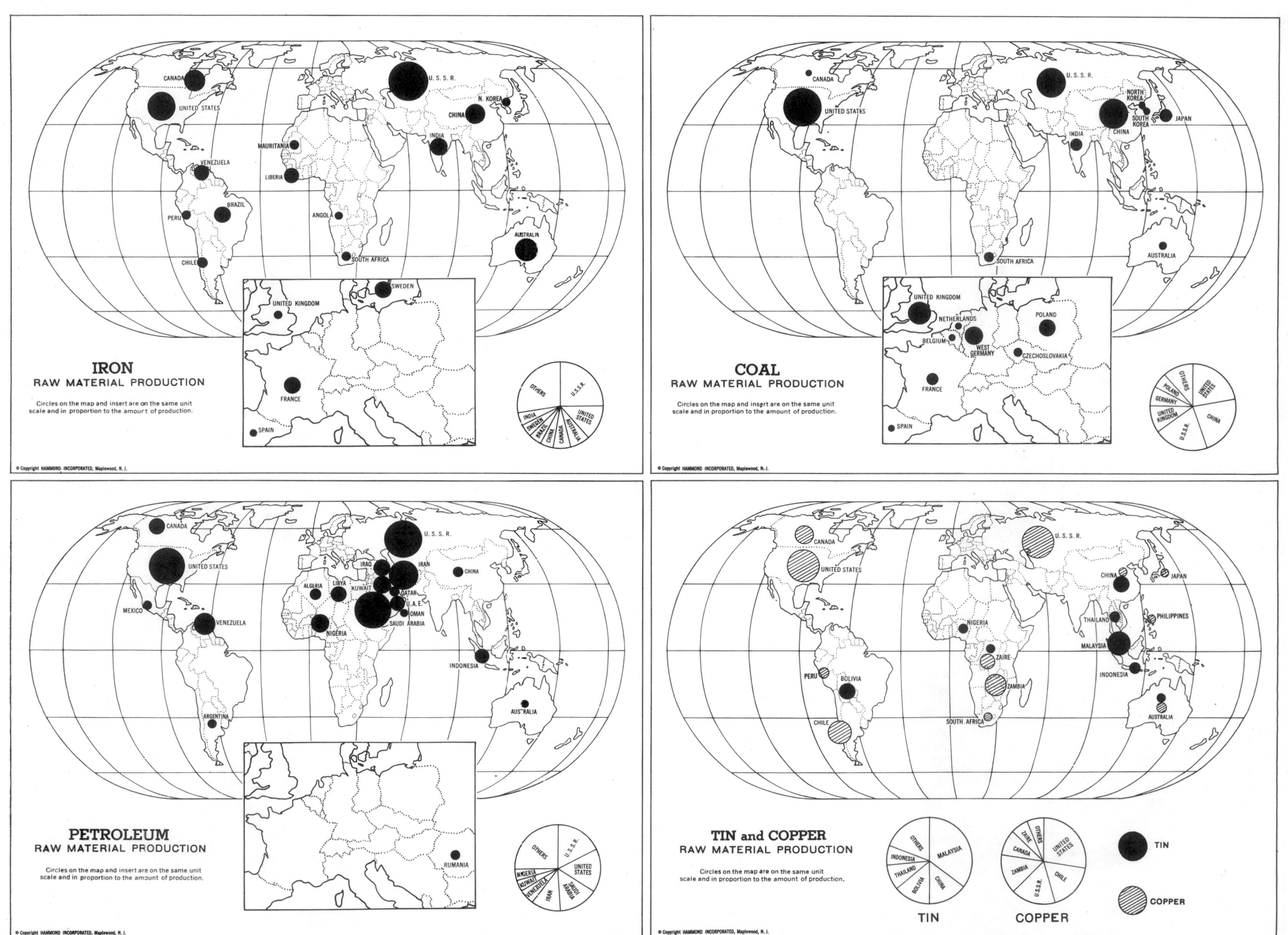
IRON
RAW MATERIAL PRODUCTION
Circles on the map and insert are on the same unit scale and in proportion to the amount of production.
© Copyright HAMMOND INCORPORATED, Maplewood, N.J.
CANADA
UNITED STATES
VENEZUELA
BRAZIL
PERU
CHILE
MAURITANIA
LIBERIA
ANGOLA
SOUTH AFRICA
U.S.S.R.
N. KOREA
CHINA
INDIA
AUSTRALIA
SWEDEN
UNITED KINGDOM
FRANCE
SPAIN
U.S.S.R.
UNITED STATES
AUSTRALIA
CANADA
CHINA
BRAZIL
SWEDEN
INDIA
OTHERS
COAL
RAW MATERIAL PRODUCTION
Circles on the map and insert are on the same unit scale and in proportion to the amount of production.
© Copyright HAMMOND INCORPORATED, Maplewood, N.J.
CANADA
UNITED STATES
U.S.S.R.
NORTH KOREA
SOUTH KOREA
JAPAN
CHINA
INDIA
SOUTH AFRICA
AUSTRALIA
UNITED KINGDOM
NETHERLANDS
BELGIUM
WEST GERMANY
POLAND
CZECHOSLOVAKIA
FRANCE
SPAIN
OTHERS
UNITED STATES
POLAND
GERMANY
UNITED KINGDOM
CHINA
U.S.S.R.
PETROLEUM
RAW MATERIAL PRODUCTION
Circles on the map and insert are on the same unit scale and in proportion to the amount of production.
© Copyright HAMMOND INCORPORATED, Maplewood, N.J.
CANADA
UNITED STATES
MEXICO
VENEZUELA
ARGENTINA
ALGERIA
LIBYA
NIGERIA
IRAQ
KUWAIT
IRAN
QATAR
U.A.E.
OMAN
SAUDI ARABIA
U.S.S.R.
CHINA
INDONESIA
AUSTRALIA
RUMANIA
OTHERS
U.S.S.R.
UNITED STATES
SAUDI ARABIA
IRAN
VENEZUELA
KUWAIT
NIGERIA
TIN and COPPER
RAW MATERIAL PRODUCTION
Circles on the map are on the same unit scale and in proportion to the amount of production.
© Copyright HAMMOND INCORPORATED, Maplewood, N.J.
CANADA
UNITED STATES
PERU
BOLIVIA
CHILE
NIGERIA
ZAIRE
ZAMBIA
SOUTH AFRICA
U.S.S.R.
CHINA
JAPAN
PHILIPPINES
THAILAND
MALAYSIA
INDONESIA
AUSTRALIA
OTHERS
MALAYSIA
INDONESIA
THAILAND
BOLIVIA
CHINA
TIN
OTHERS
ZAIRE
UNITED STATES
CANADA
ZAMBIA
U.S.S.R.
CHILE
COPPER
TIN
COPPER

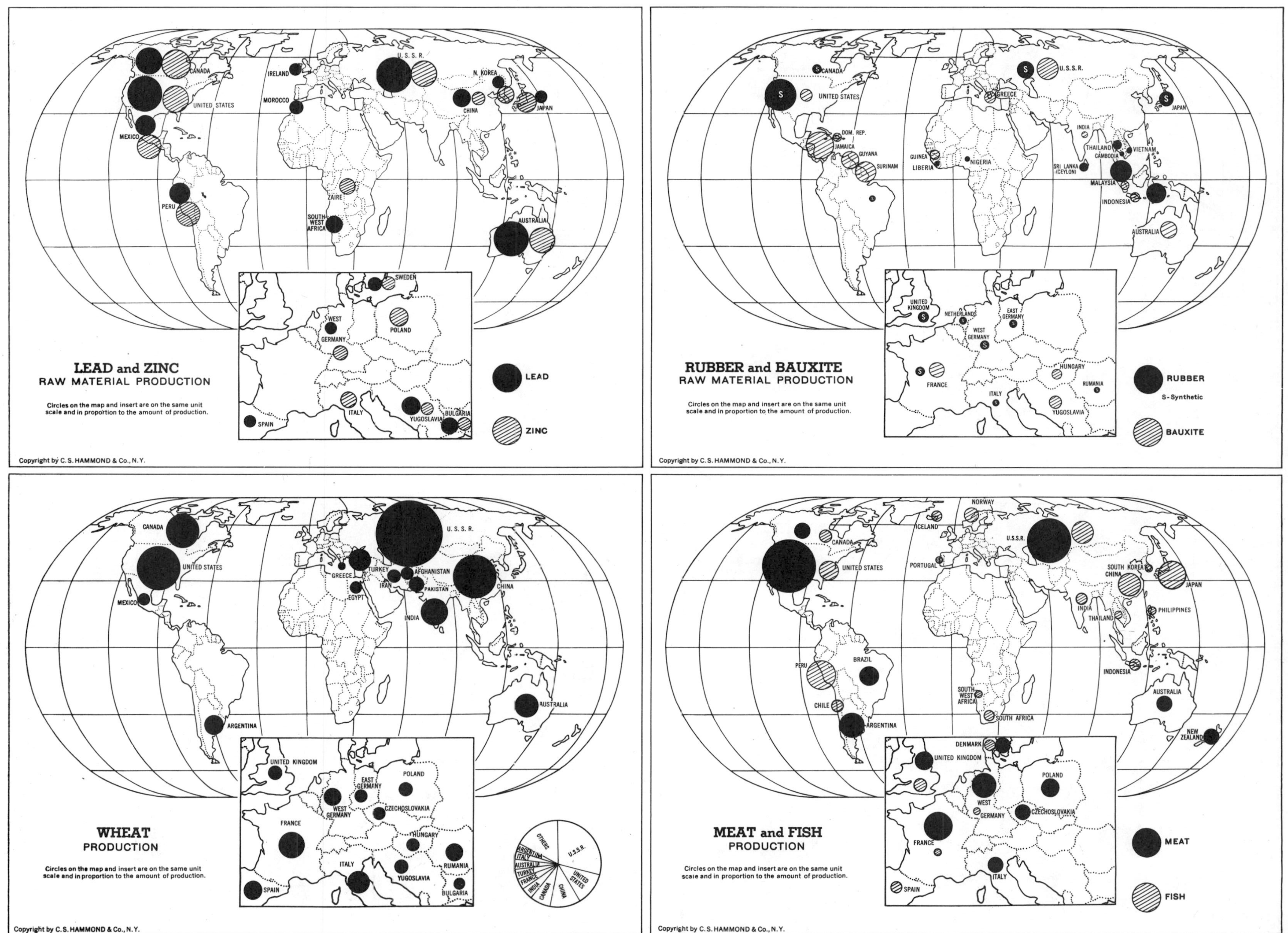
LEAD and ZINC
RAW MATERIAL PRODUCTION
Circles on the map and insert are on the same unit scale and in proportion to the amount of production.
LEAD
ZINC
CANADA
UNITED STATES
MEXICO
PERU
IRELAND
MOROCCO
ZAIRE
SOUTH WEST AFRICA
U. S. S. R.
N. KOREA
CHINA
JAPAN
AUSTRALIA
SWEDEN
WEST GERMANY
POLAND
ITALY
YUGOSLAVIA
BULGARIA
SPAIN
Copyright by C. S. HAMMOND & Co., N. Y.
RUBBER and BAUXITE
RAW MATERIAL PRODUCTION
Circles on the map and insert are on the same unit scale and in proportion to the amount of production.
RUBBER
S-Synthetic
BAUXITE
CANADA
UNITED STATES
DOM. REP.
JAMAICA
GUYANA
SURINAM
GUINEA
LIBERIA
NIGERIA
GREECE
U. S. S. R.
INDIA
SRI LANKA (CEYLON)
THAILAND
CAMBODIA
VIETNAM
MALAYSIA
INDONESIA
JAPAN
AUSTRALIA
UNITED KINGDOM
NETHERLANDS
EAST GERMANY
WEST GERMANY
FRANCE
HUNGARY
RUMANIA
ITALY
YUGOSLAVIA
Copyright by C. S. HAMMOND & Co., N. Y.
WHEAT
PRODUCTION
Circles on the map and insert are on the same unit scale and in proportion to the amount of production.
CANADA
UNITED STATES
MEXICO
ARGENTINA
GREECE
TURKEY
EGYPT
IRAN
AFGHANISTAN
PAKISTAN
INDIA
U. S. S. R.
CHINA
AUSTRALIA
UNITED KINGDOM
EAST GERMANY
WEST GERMANY
POLAND
CZECHOSLOVAKIA
FRANCE
HUNGARY
RUMANIA
ITALY
YUGOSLAVIA
BULGARIA
SPAIN
OTHERS
U.S.S.R.
UNITED STATES
CHINA
CANADA
INDIA
FRANCE
TURKEY
AUSTRALIA
ITALY
ARGENTINA
Copyright by C. S. HAMMOND & Co., N. Y.
MEAT and FISH
PRODUCTION
Circles on the map and insert are on the same unit scale and in proportion to the amount of production.
MEAT
FISH
CANADA
UNITED STATES
PERU
BRAZIL
CHILE
ARGENTINA
ICELAND
NORWAY
PORTUGAL
SOUTH WEST AFRICA
SOUTH AFRICA
U.S.S.R.
SOUTH KOREA
CHINA
JAPAN
INDIA
THAILAND
PHILIPPINES
INDONESIA
AUSTRALIA
NEW ZEALAND
DENMARK
UNITED KINGDOM
WEST GERMANY
POLAND
CZECHOSLOVAKIA
FRANCE
ITALY
SPAIN
Copyright by C. S. HAMMOND & Co., N. Y.

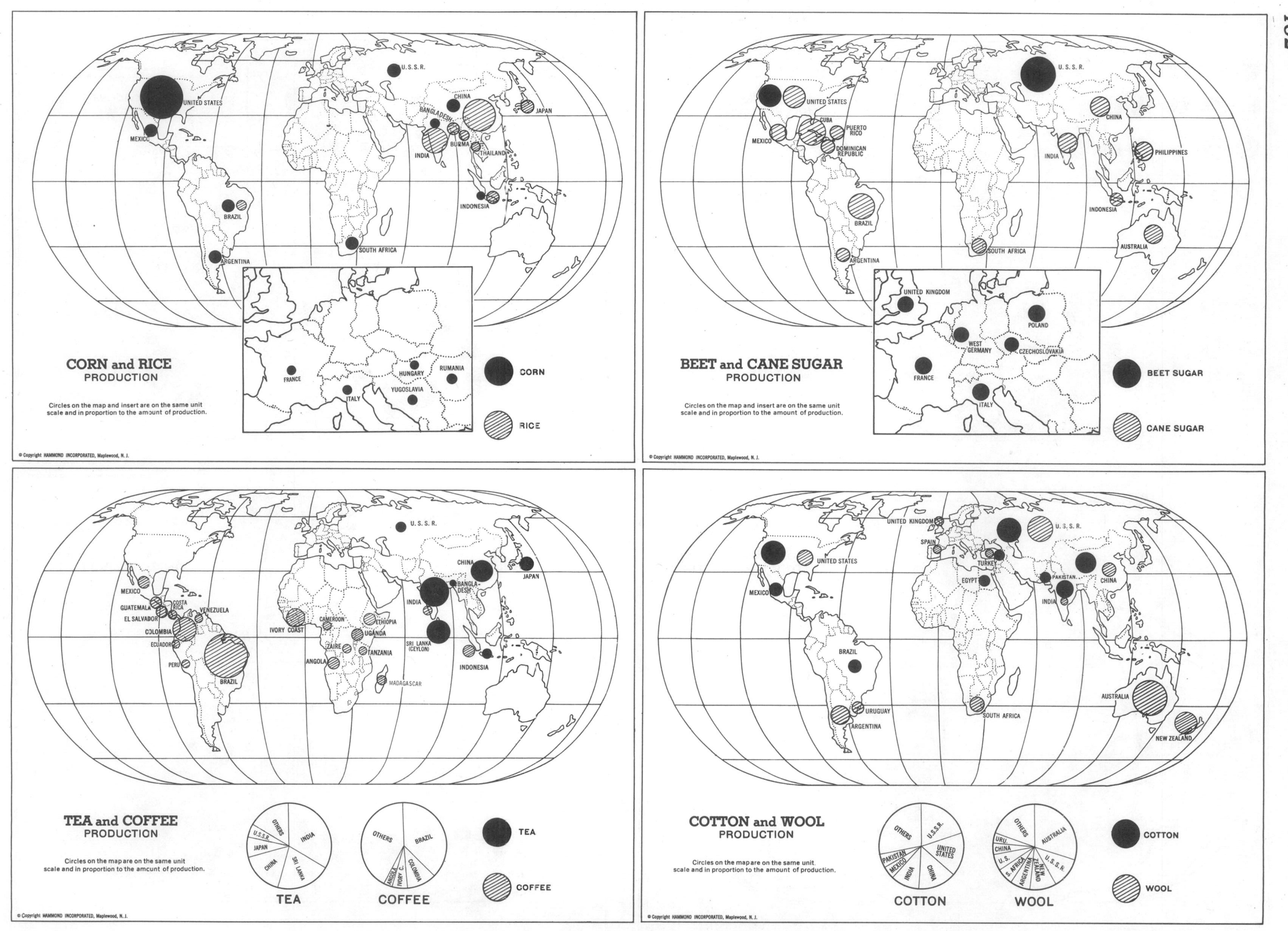
CORN and RICE
PRODUCTION
Circles on the map and insert are on the same unit scale and in proportion to the amount of production.
U.S.S.R.
UNITED STATES
MEXICO
CHINA
BANGLADESH
JAPAN
INDIA
BURMA
THAILAND
BRAZIL
INDONESIA
SOUTH AFRICA
ARGENTINA
FRANCE
HUNGARY
RUMANIA
ITALY
YUGOSLAVIA
CORN
RICE
© Copyright HAMMOND INCORPORATED, Maplewood, N.J.
BEET and CANE SUGAR
PRODUCTION
Circles on the map and insert are on the same unit scale and in proportion to the amount of production.
U.S.S.R.
UNITED STATES
CUBA
PUERTO RICO
MEXICO
DOMINICAN REPUBLIC
CHINA
INDIA
PHILIPPINES
BRAZIL
INDONESIA
AUSTRALIA
SOUTH AFRICA
ARGENTINA
UNITED KINGDOM
POLAND
WEST GERMANY
CZECHOSLOVAKIA
FRANCE
ITALY
BEET SUGAR
CANE SUGAR
© Copyright HAMMOND INCORPORATED, Maplewood, N.J.
TEA and COFFEE
PRODUCTION
Circles on the map are on the same unit scale and in proportion to the amount of production.
U.S.S.R.
CHINA
JAPAN
MEXICO
BANGLA-DESH
INDIA
GUATEMALA
COSTA RICA
VENEZUELA
EL SALVADOR
IVORY COAST
CAMEROON
ETHIOPIA
COLOMBIA
UGANDA
SRI LANKA (CEYLON)
ECUADOR
ZAIRE
TANZANIA
ANGOLA
INDONESIA
PERU
BRAZIL
MADAGASCAR
OTHERS
U.S.S.R.
JAPAN
CHINA
INDIA
SRI LANKA
TEA
OTHERS
BRAZIL
ANGOLA
IVORY C.
COLOMBIA
COFFEE
TEA
COFFEE
© Copyright HAMMOND INCORPORATED, Maplewood, N.J.
COTTON and WOOL
PRODUCTION
Circles on the map are on the same unit scale and in proportion to the amount of production.
UNITED KINGDOM
U.S.S.R.
SPAIN
UNITED STATES
TURKEY
EGYPT
PAKISTAN
CHINA
MEXICO
INDIA
BRAZIL
AUSTRALIA
URUGUAY
SOUTH AFRICA
ARGENTINA
NEW ZEALAND
OTHERS
U.S.S.R.
UNITED STATES
PAKISTAN
MEXICO
INDIA
CHINA
COTTON
OTHERS
AUSTRALIA
URU.
CHINA
U.S.
S. AFRICA
ARGENTINA
NEW ZEALAND
U.S.S.R.
WOOL
COTTON
WOOL
© Copyright HAMMOND INCORPORATED, Maplewood, N.J.

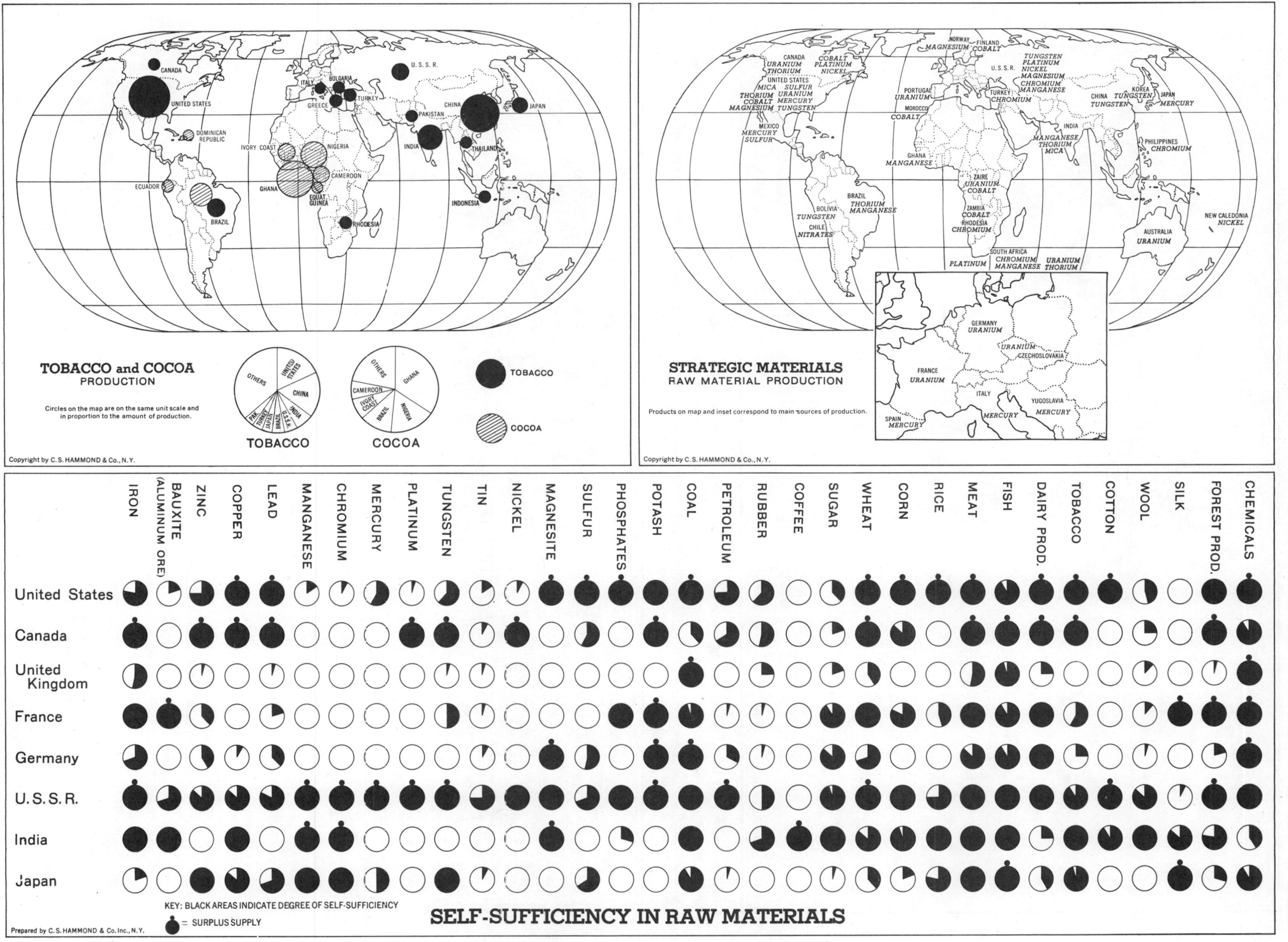
TOBACCO and COCOA
PRODUCTION
Circles on the map are on the same unit scale and in proportion to the amount of production.
TOBACCO
COCOA
Copyright by C. S. HAMMOND & Co., N.Y.
STRATEGIC MATERIALS
RAW MATERIAL PRODUCTION
Products on map and inset correspond to main sources of production.
Copyright by C. S. HAMMOND & Co., N.Y.
IRON
BAUXITE (ALUMINUM ORE)
ZINC
COPPER
LEAD
MANGANESE
CHROMIUM
MERCURY
PLATINUM
TUNGSTEN
TIN
NICKEL
MAGNESITE
SULFUR
PHOSPHATES
POTASH
COAL
PETROLEUM
RUBBER
COFFEE
SUGAR
WHEAT
CORN
RICE
MEAT
FISH
DAIRY PROD.
TOBACCO
COTTON
WOOL
SILK
FOREST PROD.
CHEMICALS
United States
Canada
United Kingdom
France
Germany
U.S.S.R.
India
Japan
KEY: BLACK AREAS INDICATE DEGREE OF SELF-SUFFICIENCY
= SURPLUS SUPPLY
SELF-SUFFICIENCY IN RAW MATERIALS
Prepared by C. S. HAMMOND & Co. Inc., N.Y.

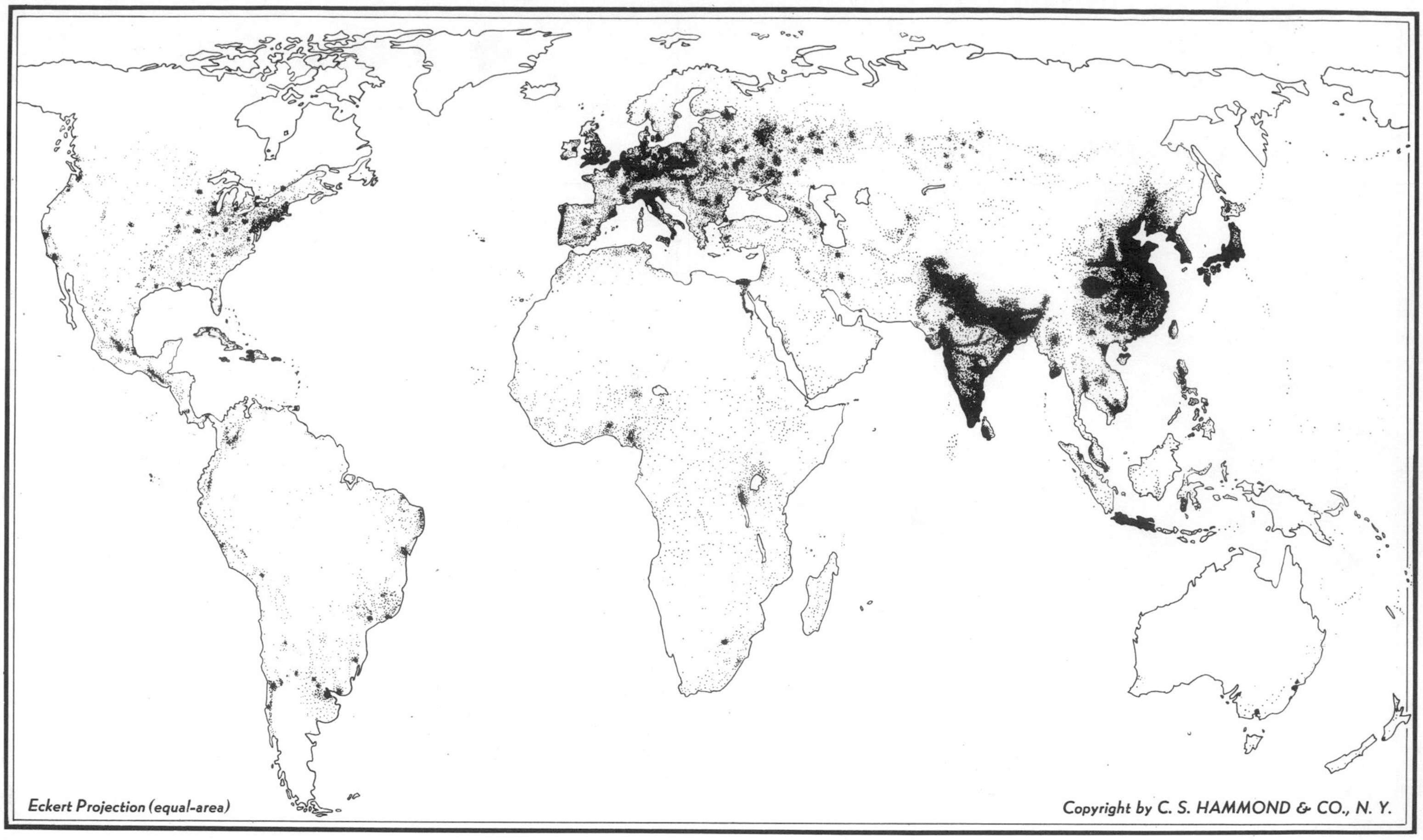

Eckert Projection (equal-area)

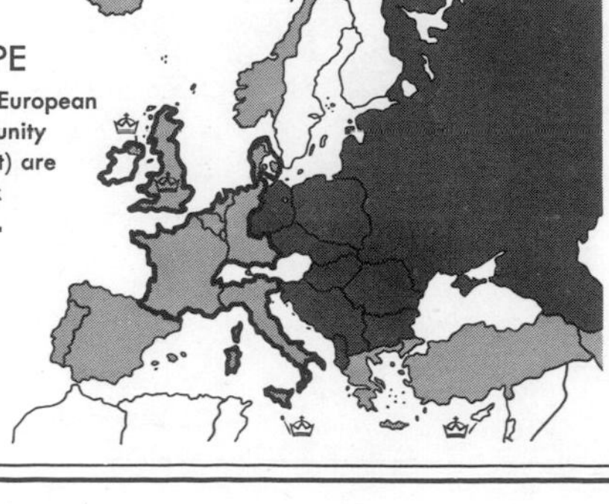

Copyright by C. S. HAMMOND & CO., N. Y.

DENSITY OF POPULATION. *One of the most outstanding facts of human geography is the extremely uneven distribution of people over the Earth. One-half of the Earth's surface has less than 3 people per square mile, while in the lowlands of India, China, Java and Japan rural density reaches the incredible congestion of 2000-3000 per square mile. Three-fourths of the Earth's population live in four relatively small areas; Northeastern United States, North-Central Europe, India and the Far East.*

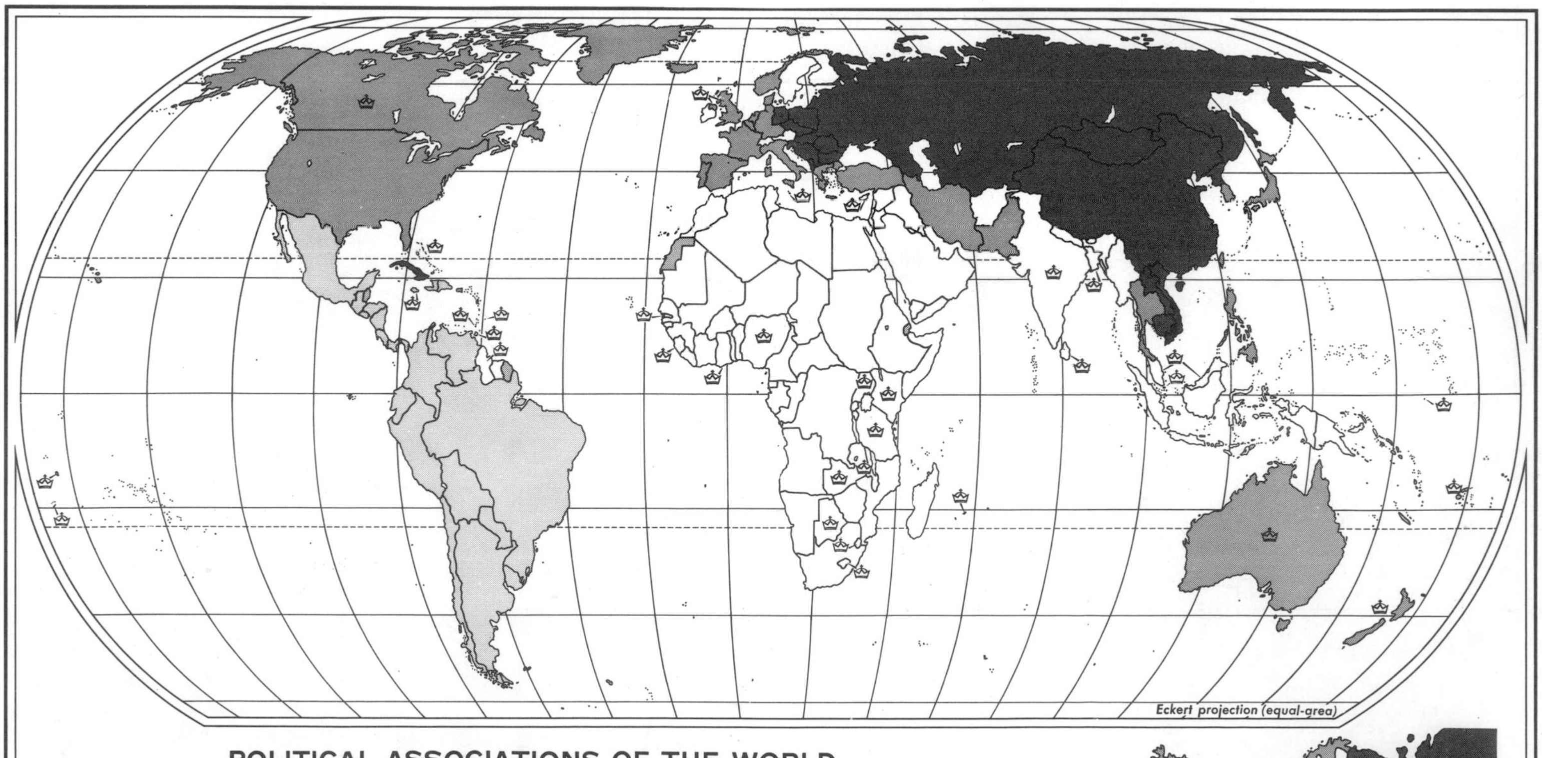

Eckert projection (equal-area)

POLITICAL ASSOCIATIONS OF THE WORLD

- Western powers and associated states
- Colonies and overseas territories of the Western powers
- Members of Organization of American States (OAS) (U.S. also a member)
- Communist states
- Independent members of the British Commonwealth

The present political division of the world into the communist "bloc" and the free nations of the West reflects the ideological conflict that has existed since the close of World War II. The West has sought mutual security pacts such as NATO and SEATO to prevent further communist expansion. A third group, that of the uncommitted or neutral nations has grown in numbers as colonial territories in Africa and Asia have become independent. A regional association, the European Economic Community or Common Market, has made substantial progress in achieving trade and economic cooperation among its members. Further integration along political and social lines is planned.

EUROPE

Members of the European Economic Community (Common Market) are banded by black line thus: ——

MAP PROJECTIONS

by Erwin Raisz

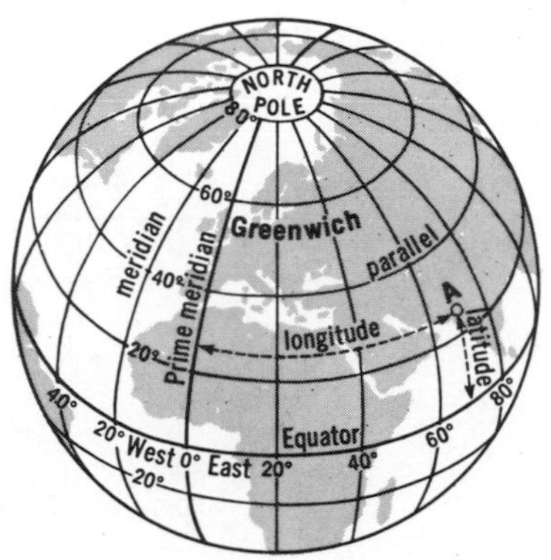

Our earth is rotating around its *axis* once a day. The two end points of its axis are the *poles;* the line circling the earth midway between the poles is the *equator.* The arc from either of the poles to the equator is divided into 90 *degrees.* The distance, expressed in degrees, from the equator to any point is its *latitude* and circles of equal latitude are the *parallels.* On maps it is customary to show parallels of evenly-spaced degrees such as every fifth or every tenth.

The equator is divided into 360 degrees. Lines circling from pole to pole through the degree points on the equator are called *meridians.* They are all equal in length but by international agreement the meridian passing through the Greenwich Observatory in London has been chosen as *prime meridian.* The distance, expressed in degrees, from the prime meridian to any point is its *longitude.* While meridians are all equal in length, parallels become shorter and shorter as they approach the poles. Whereas one degree of latitude represents everywhere approximately 69 miles, one degree of longitude varies from 69 miles at the equator to nothing at the poles.

Each degree is divided into 60 minutes and each minute into 60 seconds. One minute of latitude equals a nautical mile.

The map is flat but the earth is nearly spherical. Neither a rubber ball nor any part of a rubber ball may be flattened without stretching or tearing unless the part is very small. To present the curved surface of the earth on a flat map is not difficult as long as the areas under consideration are small, but the mapping of countries, continents, or the whole earth requires some kind of *projection.* Any regular set of parallels and meridians upon which a map can be drawn makes a map projection. Many systems are used.

In any projection only the parallels or the meridians or some other set of lines can be *true* (the same length as on the globe of corresponding scale); all other lines are too long or too short. Only on a globe is it possible to have both the parallels and the meridians true. The scale given on a flat map cannot be true everywhere. The construction of the various projections begins usually with laying out the parallels or meridians which have true lengths.

Rectangular Projection

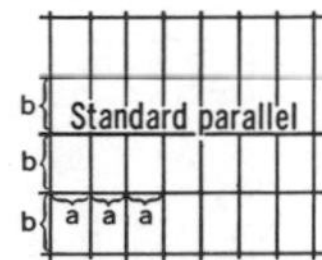

RECTANGULAR PROJECTION — This is a set of evenly-placed meridians and horizontal parallels. The central or *standard parallel* and all meridians are true. All other parallels are either too long or too short. The projection is used for simple maps of small areas, as city plans, etc.

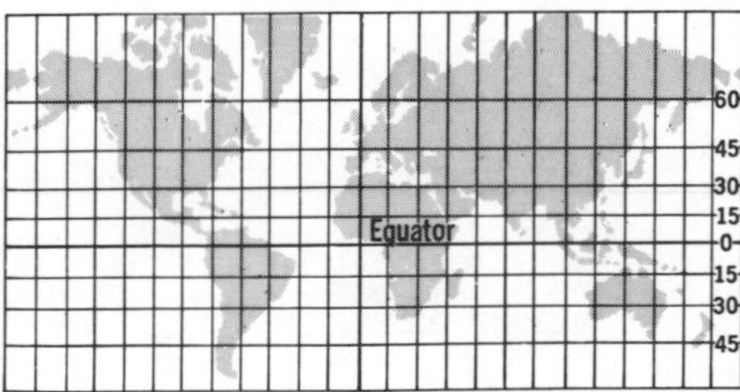

Mercator Projection

MERCATOR PROJECTION — In this projection the meridians are evenly-spaced vertical lines. The parallels are horizontal, spaced so that their length has the same relation to the meridians as on a globe. As the meridians converge at higher latitudes on the globe, while on the map they do not, the parallels have to be drawn also farther and farther apart to maintain the correct relationship. When every very small area has the same shape as on a globe we call the projection *conformal.* The most interesting quality of this projection is that all *compass directions* appear as straight lines. For this reason it is generally used for marine charts. It is also frequently used for world maps in spite of the fact that the high latitudes are very much exaggerated in size. Only the equator is true to scale; all other parallels and meridians are too long. The Mercator projection did *not* derive from projecting a globe upon a cylinder.

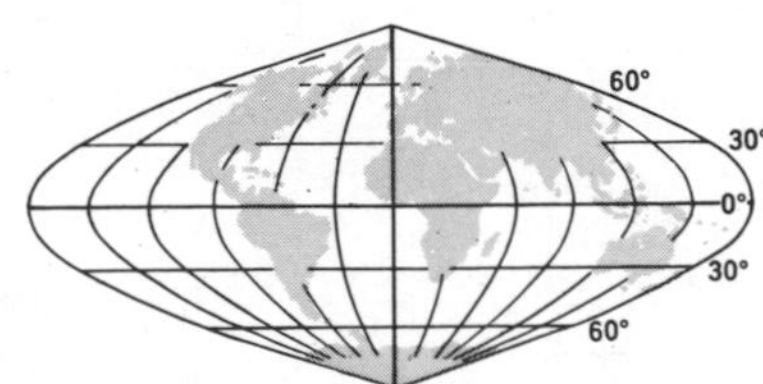

Sinusoidal Projection

SINUSOIDAL PROJECTION — The parallels are truly-spaced horizontal lines. They are divided truly and the connecting curves make the meridians. It does not make a good world map because the outer regions are distorted, but the central portion is good and this part is often used for maps of Africa and South America. Every part of the map has the same area as the corresponding area on the globe. It is an *equal-area* projection.

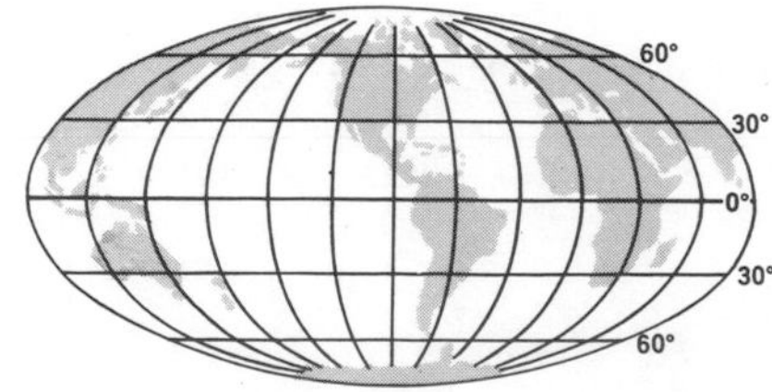

Mollweide Projection

MOLLWEIDE PROJECTION — The meridians are equally-spaced ellipses; the parallels are horizontal lines spaced so that every belt of latitude should have the same area as on a globe. This projection is popular for world maps, especially in European atlases.

GOODE'S INTERRUPTED PROJECTIONS—Only the good central part of the Mollweide or sinusoidal (or both) projection is used and the oceans are cut. This makes an equal-area map with little distortion of shape. It is commonly used for world maps.

Goode's Interrupted Projection

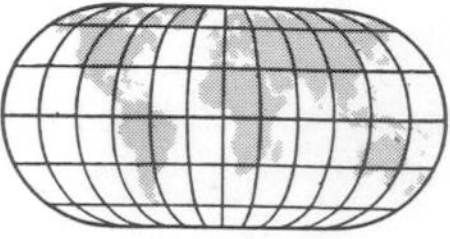
Eckert Projection

ECKERT PROJECTIONS — These are similar to the sinusoidal or the Mollweide projections, but the poles are shown as lines half the length of the equator. There are several variants; the meridians are either sine curves or ellipses; the parallels are horizontal and spaced either evenly or so as to make the projection equal area. Their use for world maps is increasing. The figure shows the elliptical equal-area variant.

CONIC PROJECTION — The original idea of the conic projection is that of capping the globe by a cone upon which both the parallels and meridians are projected from the center of the globe. The cone is then cut open and laid flat. A cone can be made tangent to any chosen *standard parallel*.

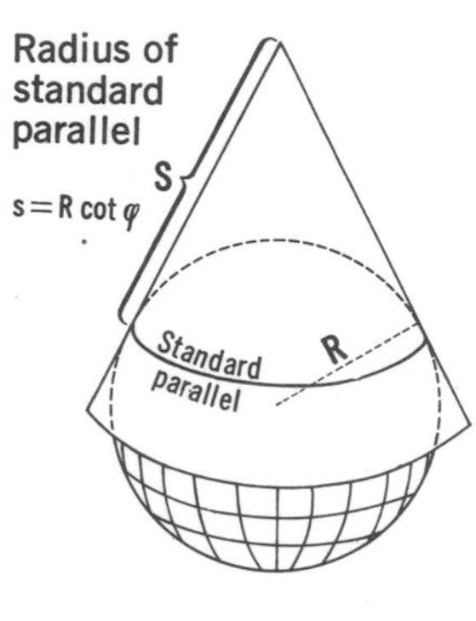

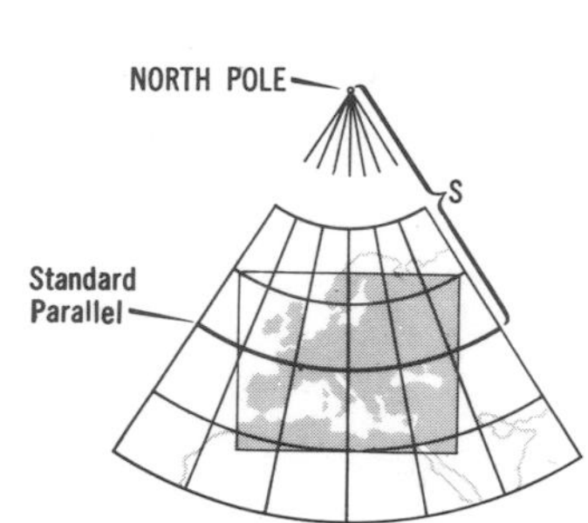

Conic Projection

The actually-used conic projection is a modification of this idea. The radius of the standard parallel is obtained as above. The meridians are straight radiating lines spaced truly on the standard parallel. The parallels are concentric circles spaced at true distances. All parallels except the standard are too long. The projection is used for maps of countries in middle latitudes, as it presents good shapes with small scale error.

There are several variants: The use of *two standard parallels*, one near the top, the other near the bottom of the map, reduces the scale error. In the *Albers projection* the parallels are spaced unevenly, to make the projection equal-area. This is a good projection for the United States. In the *Lambert conformal conic projection* the parallels are spaced so that any small quadrangle of the grid should have the same shape as on the globe. This is the best projection for air-navigation charts as it has relatively straight azimuths.

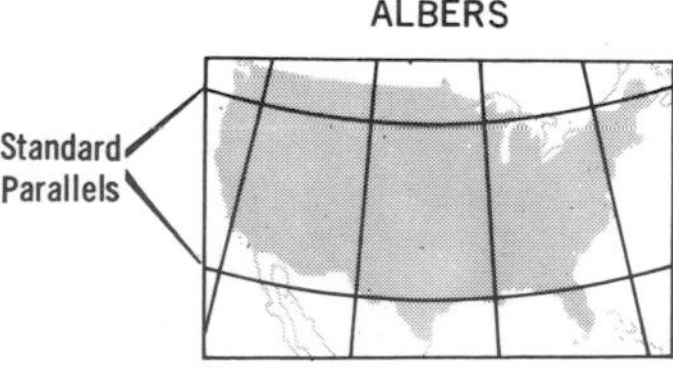

Albers Projection

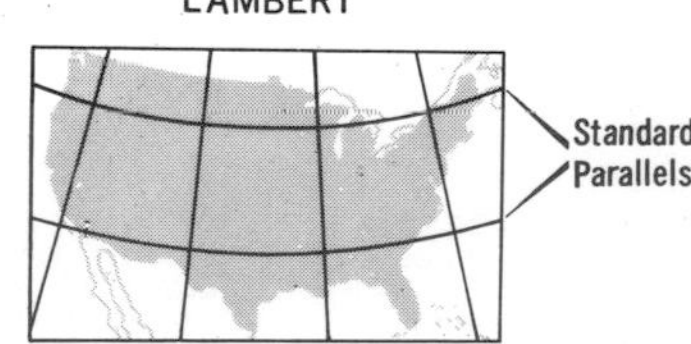

Lambert Conformal Conic Projection

An *azimuth* is a great-circle direction reckoned clockwise from north. A *great-circle direction* points to a place along the shortest line on the earth's surface. This is not the same as compass direction. The center of a great circle is the center of the globe.

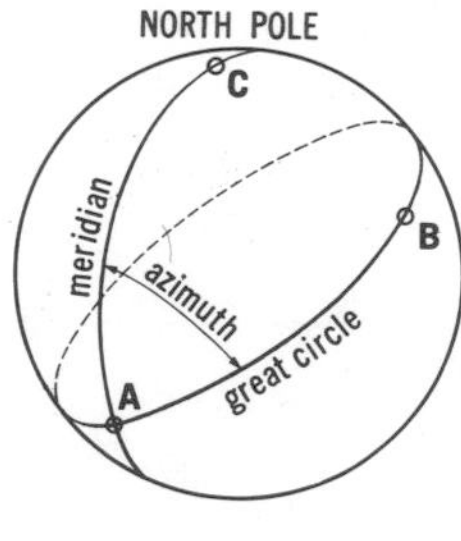

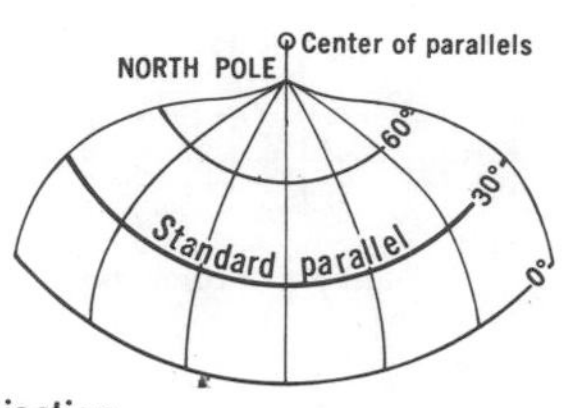

Bonne Projection

BONNE PROJECTION — The parallels are laid out exactly as in the conic projection. All parallels are divided truly and the connecting curves make the meridians. It is an equal-area projection. It is used for maps of the northern continents, as Asia, Europe, and North America.

POLYCONIC PROJECTION — The central meridian is divided truly. The parallels are non-concentric circles, the radii of which are obtained by drawing tangents to the globe as though the globe were covered by several cones rather than by only one. Each parallel is divided truly and the connecting curves make the meridians. All meridians except the central one are too long. This projection is used for large-scale topographic sheets — less often for countries or continents.

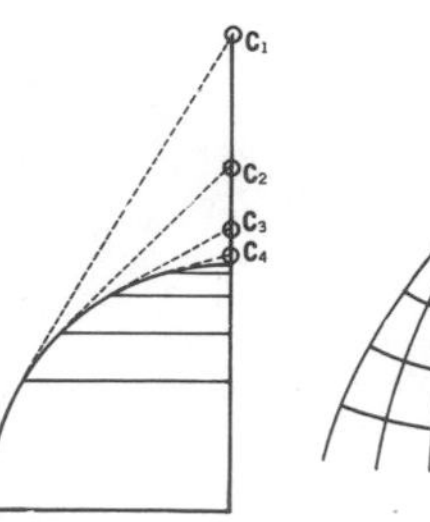

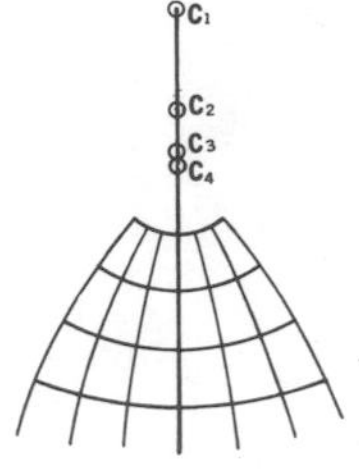

Polyconic Projection

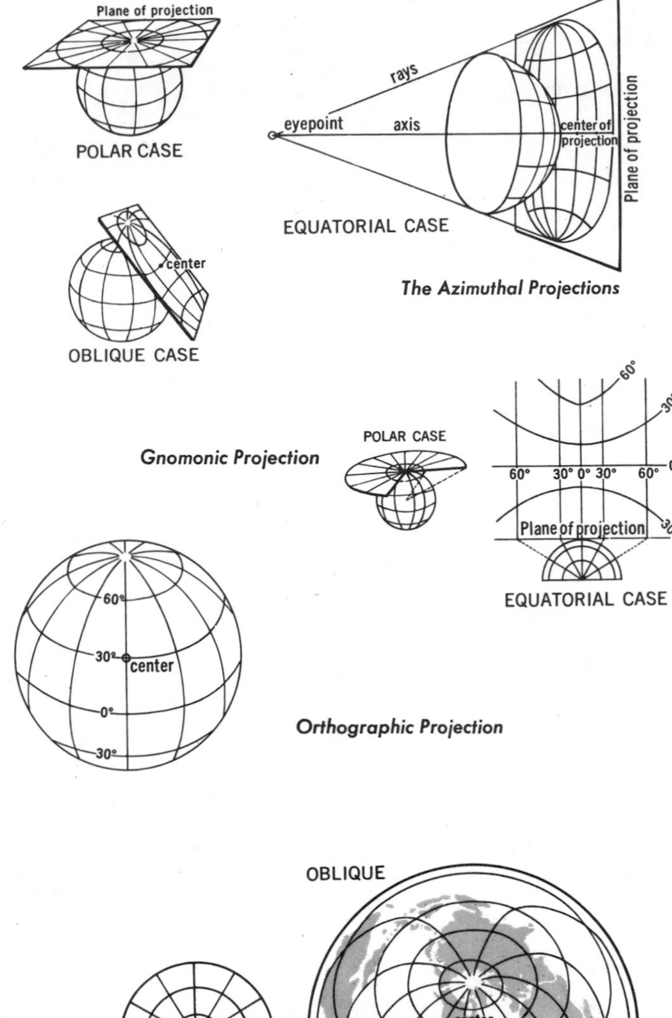

The Azimuthal Projections

Gnomonic Projection

Orthographic Projection

Azimuthal Equidistant Projection

THE AZIMUTHAL PROJECTIONS — In this group a part of the globe is projected from an eyepoint onto a plane. The eyepoint can be at different distances, making different projections. The plane of projection can be tangent at the equator, at a pole, or at any other point on which we want to focus attention. The most important quality of all azimuthal projections is that they show every point at its true direction (azimuth) from the center point, and all points equally distant from the center point will be equally distant on the map also.

GNOMONIC PROJECTION — This projection has the eyepoint at the center of the globe Only the central part is good; the outer regions are badly distorted. Yet the projection has one important quality, all great circles being shown as straight lines. For this reason it is used for laying out the routes for long range flying or trans-oceanic navigation.

ORTHOGRAPHIC PROJECTION — This projection has the eyepoint at infinite distance and the projecting rays are parallel. The polar or equatorial varieties are rare but the oblique case became very popular on account of its visual quality. It looks like a picture of a globe. Although the distortion on the peripheries is extreme, we see it correctly because the eye perceives it not as a map but as a picture of a three-dimensional globe. Obviously only a hemisphere (half globe) can be shown.

Some azimuthal projections do not derive from the actual process of projecting from an eyepoint, but are arrived at by other means:

AZIMUTHAL EQUIDISTANT PROJECTION — This is the only projection in which every point is shown both at true great-circle direction and at true distance from the center point, but all other directions and distances are distorted. The principle of the projection can best be understood from the polar case. Most polar maps are in this projection. The oblique case is used for radio direction finding, for earthquake research, and in long-distance flying. A separate map has to be constructed for each central point selected.

LAMBERT AZIMUTHAL EQUAL-AREA PROJECTION—The construction of this projection can best be understood from the polar case. All three cases are widely used. It makes a good polar map and it is often extended to include the southern continents. It is the most common projection used for maps of the Eastern and Western Hemispheres, and it is a good projection for continents as it shows correct areas with relatively little distortion of shape. Most of the continent maps in this atlas are in this projection.

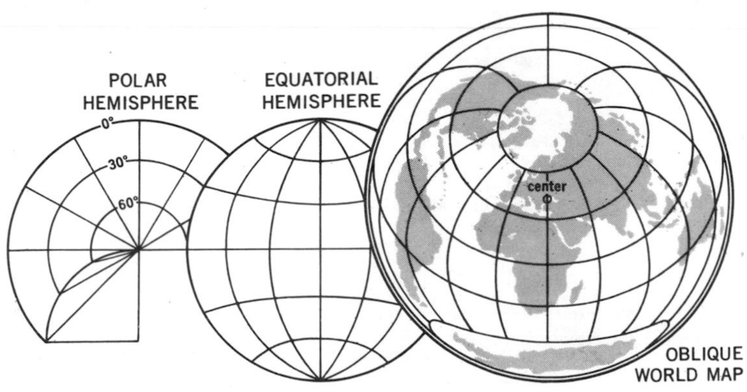

Lambert Azimuthal Equal-Area Projection

IN THIS ATLAS, on almost all maps, parallels and meridians have been marked because they are useful for the following:

(a) They show the north-south and east-west directions which appear on many maps at oblique angles especially near the margins.

(b) With the help of parallels and meridians every place can be exactly located; for instance, New York City is at 41° N and 74° W on any map.

(c) They help to measure distances even in the distorted parts of the map. The scale given on each map is true only along certain lines which are specified in the foregoing discussion for each projection. One degree of latitude equals nearly 69 statute miles or 60 nautical miles. The length of one degree of longitude varies (1° long. = 1° lat. × cos lat.).

WORLD STATISTICAL TABLES

EARTH AND SOLAR SYSTEM

Elements of the Solar System

	Mean Distance From Sun in Miles	Period of Revolution Around Sun	Period of Rotation on Axis	Equatorial Diameter in Miles	Surface Gravity (Earth=1)	Mean Density (Water=1)	Number of Satellites
SUN	....	....	25.4 days	864,000	27.95	1.4	....
MERCURY	36,001,000	87.97 days	59 days (?)	3,100	0.38	5.3	0
VENUS	67,272,000	224.70 days	247 days (?)	7,700	0.88	4.9	0
EARTH	93,003,000	365.26 days	23h 56m	7,927	1.00	5.5	1
MARS	141,708,000	687 days	24h 37m	4,200	0.39	4.0	2
JUPITER	483,880,000	11.86 years	9h 50m	88,698	2.65	1.3	12
SATURN	887,141,000	29.46 years	10h 14m	75,060	1.17	0.7	10
URANUS	1,782,000,000	84.02 years	10h 45m	29,200	1.05	1.3	5
NEPTUNE	2,792,000,000	164.79 years	15h 48m	27,700	1.23	1.6	2
PLUTO	3,664,000,000	247.7 years	6.4 days (?)	8,700 (?)	0.7 (?)	?	0

Dimensions of the Earth

Superficial area	197,272,000	sq. miles
Land surface	57,491,000	" "
North America	9,363,000	" "
South America	6,875,000	" "
Europe	4,063,000	" "
Asia	17,032,000	" "
Africa	11,682,000	" "
Australia	2,967,741	" "
Water surface	139,781,000	" "
Atlantic Ocean	31,862,000	" "
Pacific Ocean	64,186,000	" "
Indian Ocean	28,350,000	" "
Arctic Ocean	3,662,000	" "
Equatorial circumference	24,902	miles
Meridional circumference	24,860	"
Equatorial diameter	7,926.677	"
Polar diameter	7,899.988	"
Equatorial radius	3,963.34	"
Polar radius	3,949.99	"
Volume of the Earth	260,000,000,000	cubic miles
Mass, or weight	6,592,333,000,000,000,000,000	tons
Mean distance from the Sun	93,003,000	miles

The Moon is the Earth's natural satellite. The mean distance which separates the Earth from the Moon is 238,857 miles. The Moon's true period of revolution (sidereal month) is 27⅓ days. The Moon rotates on its own axis once during this time. The phase period or time between new moons (synodic month) is 29½ days. The Moon's diameter is 2,160 miles, its density is 3.3 and its surface gravity is 0.2.

PRINCIPAL LAKES AND INLAND SEAS

	AREA IN SQ. MILES
Caspian Sea	143,550
Lake Superior	31,800
Lake Victoria	26,828
Aral Sea	25,300
Lake Huron	23,000
Lake Michigan	22,400
Lake Tanganyika	12,700
Great Bear Lake	12,275
Lake Baykal	11,780
Lake Nyasa	11,430
Great Slave Lake	10,980
Lake Erie	9,910
Lake Winnipeg	9,464
Lake Ontario	7,600
Lake Ladoga	6,835
Lake Balkhash	6,720
Lake Chad	5,300
Lake Onega	3,710
Lake Titicaca	3,200
Lake Athabasca	3,120
Lake Nicaragua	3,100
Lake Rudolf	2,473
Reindeer Lake	2,467
Issyk-Kul'	2,358
Vänern	2,156
Lake Winnipegosis	2,103
Lake Albert	2,075
Kariba Lake	2,050
Lake Urmia	1,815
Great Salt Lake	1,500
Lake Peipus	1,400
Lake Tana	1,219
Lake Bangweulu . . . Approx.	1,000
Vättern	733
Dead Sea	405
Lake Balaton	266
Lake Geneva	225
Lake of Constance	208
Lake Garda	143
Lake of Neuchâtel	83
Lake Maggiore	82
Lake Como	56
Lake of Lucerne	44.5
Lake of Zürich	34

OCEANS AND SEAS OF THE WORLD

	AREA IN SQ. MILES	GREATEST DEPTH IN FEET	VOLUME IN CUBIC MILES
Pacific Ocean	64,186,000	36,198	167,025,000
Atlantic Ocean	31,862,000	28,374	77,580,000
Indian Ocean	28,350,000	25,344	68,213,000
Arctic Ocean	3,662,000	17,880	3,026,000
Caribbean Sea	970,000	24,720	2,298,400
Mediterranean Sea	960,000	16,896	1,019,400
Bering Sea	875,000	13,422	788,500
Sea of Okhotsk	590,000	11,070	454,700
East China Sea	482,000	10,500	52,700
Hudson Bay	476,000	1,500	37,590
Japan Sea	389,000	13,242	383,200
North Sea	222,000	2,654	12,890
Black Sea	185,000	7,200	....
Red Sea	169,000	7,254	53,700
Baltic Sea	163,000	1,506	5,360

GREAT SHIP CANALS

	LENGTH IN MILES	DEPTH IN FEET
Baltic-White Sea, U.S.S.R.	141	....
Suez, Egypt	100.76	34
Albert, Belgium	81	16.5
Moscow-Volga, U.S.S.R.	80	18
Kiel, West Germany	61	37
Göta, Sweden	54	10
Panama, Canal Zone	50.72	41
Houston Ship, U.S.A.	50	36
Amsterdam-Rhine, Netherlands	45	41
Beaumont-Port Arthur, U.S.A.	40	32
Manchester Ship, England	35.5	28
Chicago Sanitary and Ship, U.S.A.	30	22
Welland, Canada	27.6	30
Juliana, Netherlands	21	11.8
Chesapeake and Delaware, U.S.A.	19	27
Cape Cod, U.S.A.	13	25
Lake Washington, U.S.A.	8	30
Corinth, Greece	4	26.25
Sault Ste. Marie, U.S.A.	1.6	24.5
Sault Ste. Marie, Canada	1.4	18.25

PRINCIPAL ISLANDS OF THE WORLD

	AREA IN SQ. MILES
Greenland	840,000
New Guinea	320,000
Borneo	287,000
Madagascar	226,467
Baffin	183,810
Sumatra	164,148
Philippines	115,707
New Zealand	103,736
Honshu	88,923
England-Scotland-Wales	88,755
Ellesmere	82,119
Victoria	81,930
Celebes	72,986
Java	48,842
Newfoundland	43,359
Cuba	43,038
Luzon	40,420
Iceland	39,768
Mindanao	36,537
Ireland	32,059
Novaya Zemlya	31,900
Hokkaido	30,305
Molucca Islands	30,168
Hispaniola	29,398
Sakhalin	28,215
Tasmania	26,215
Ceylon	25,332
Svalbard	23,958
Banks	23,230
Devon	20,861
Bismarck Arch.	18,770
Tierra del Fuego	18,500
Melville	16,369
Kyushu	16,200
Southampton	15,700
Solomon Islands	15,580
New Britain	14,098
Taiwan (Formosa)	13,948
Hainan	13,000
Prince of Wales	12,830
Vancouver	12,408
Timor	11,527
Sicily	9,926
Somerset	9,370
Sardinia	9,301
New Caledonia	7,335
Shikoku	7,244
Fiji Islands	7,015
New Hebrides	5,700
Kuril Islands	5,700
Falkland Islands	4,618
Bahama Islands	4,404
Jamaica	4,232
Hawaii	4,036
Cape Breton	3,970
New Ireland	3,800
Cyprus	3,473
Puerto Rico	3,435
Corsica	3,368
Crete	3,218
Galápagos Islands	3,042
Hebrides	3,000
Wrangel	2,819
Canary Islands	2,808
Kerguélen	2,700
Prince Edward	2,184
Trinidad and Tobago	1,980
Balearic Islands	1,936
Madura	1,752
South Georgia	1,600
Cape Verde Islands	1,557
Long I., New York	1,401
Socotra	1,400
Gotland	1,225
Isle of Pines	1,180
Samoa	1,173
Réunion	969
Azores	893
Ryukyu Islands	848
Fernando Po	786
Tenerife	785
Maui	728
Mauritius	709
Zanzibar	640
Oahu	604
Guadeloupe	583
Ahvenanmaa (Åland Is.)	564
Kauai	551
Shetland Islands	551
Rhodes	542
Martinique	425
Tahiti	402
Pemba	380
Orkney Islands	376
Madeira Islands	308
Dominica	290
Tonga	270
Caroline Islands	267
Molokai	261
St. Lucia	238
Corfu	229
Bornholm	227
Isle of Man	227
Singapore	226
Guam	212
Isle Royale	210
Virgin Islands	192
Curaçao	182
Barbados	166
St. Vincent	150
Isle of Wight	147
Lanai	141
Grenada	133
Maltese Islands	122
Tobago	116
Seychelles	109
Martha's Vineyard	109
Channel Islands	75
Nantucket	57
St. Helena	47
Ascension	34
Hong Kong	29
Manhattan, New York	22
Bermuda Islands	20

PRINCIPAL MOUNTAINS OF THE WORLD

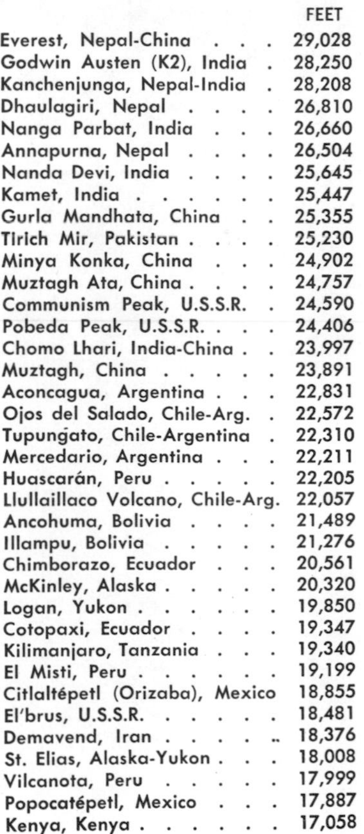

	FEET
Everest, Nepal-China	29,028
Godwin Austen (K2), India	28,250
Kanchenjunga, Nepal-India	28,208
Dhaulagiri, Nepal	26,810
Nanga Parbat, India	26,660
Annapurna, Nepal	26,504
Nanda Devi, India	25,645
Kamet, India	25,447
Gurla Mandhata, China	25,355
Tirich Mir, Pakistan	25,230
Minya Konka, China	24,902
Muztagh Ata, China	24,757
Communism Peak, U.S.S.R.	24,590
Pobeda Peak, U.S.S.R.	24,406
Chomo Lhari, India-China	23,997
Muztagh, China	23,891
Aconcagua, Argentina	22,831
Ojos del Salado, Chile-Arg.	22,572
Tupungato, Chile-Argentina	22,310
Mercedario, Argentina	22,211
Huascarán, Peru	22,205
Llullaillaco Volcano, Chile-Arg.	22,057
Ancohuma, Bolivia	21,489
Illampu, Bolivia	21,276
Chimborazo, Ecuador	20,561
McKinley, Alaska	20,320
Logan, Yukon	19,850
Cotopaxi, Ecuador	19,347
Kilimanjaro, Tanzania	19,340
El Misti, Peru	19,199
Citlaltépetl (Orizaba), Mexico	18,855
El'brus, U.S.S.R.	18,481
Demavend, Iran	18,376
St. Elias, Alaska-Yukon	18,008
Vilcanota, Peru	17,999
Popocatépetl, Mexico	17,887
Kenya, Kenya	17,058
Dykh-Tau, U.S.S.R.	17,054
Ararat, Turkey	16,946
Vinson Massif, Antarctica	16,864
Margherita (Ruwenzori), Africa	16,795
Kazbek, U.S.S.R.	16,558
Djaja, Indonesia	16,503
Blanc, France	15,771
Klyuchevskaya Sopka, U.S.S.R.	15,584
Rosa (Dufourspitze), Italy-Switzerland	15,203
Ras Dashan, Ethiopia	15,157
Matterhorn, Switzerland	14,688
Whitney, California	14,494
Elbert, Colorado	14,433
Rainier, Washington	14,410
Markham, Antarctica	14,272
Shasta, California	14,162
Pikes Peak, Colorado	14,110
Finsteraarhorn, Switzerland	14,022
Tajumulco, Guatemala	13,845
Mauna Kea, Hawaii	13,796
Mauna Loa, Hawaii	13,680
Toubkal, Morocco	13,665
Jungfrau, Switzerland	13,642
Cameroon, Cameroon	13,350
Gran Paradiso, Italy	13,323
Robson, British Columbia	12,972
Grossglockner, Austria	12,461
Fuji, Japan	12,389
Cook, New Zealand	12,349
Pico de Teide, Canary Is.	12,172
Semeru, Java, Indonesia	12,060
Mulhacén, Spain	11,411
Etna, Italy	11,053
Lassen Peak, California	10,457
Kosciusko, Australia	7,316
Mitchell, North Carolina	6,684

LONGEST RIVERS OF THE WORLD

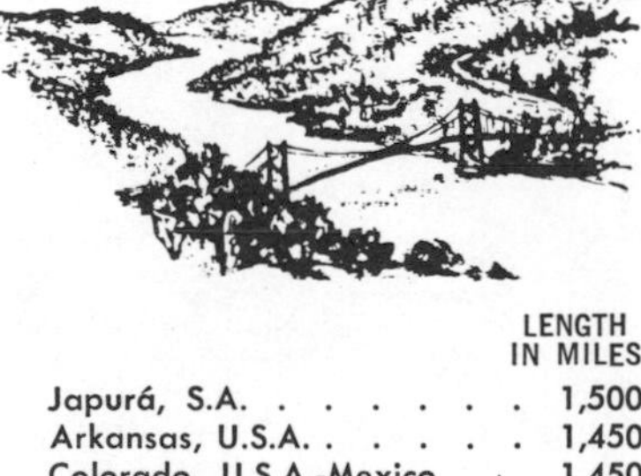

	LENGTH IN MILES
Nile, Africa	4,132
Amazon, S.A.	3,915
Mississippi-Missouri, U.S.A.	3,741
Yangtze, China	3,424
Ob-Irtysh, U.S.S.R.	3,416
Yenisey-Angara, U.S.S.R.	3,100
Hwang (Yellow), China	2,903
Congo, Africa	2,900
Amur, Asia	2,900
Lena, U.S.S.R.	2,650
Mackenzie, Canada	2,635
Mekong, Asia	2,600
Niger, Africa	2,600
Paraná, S.A.	2,450
Murray-Darling, Australia	2,371
Volga, U.S.S.R.	2,292
St. Lawrence, Canada-U.S.A.	2,100
Madeira, S.A.	2,013
Purus, S.A.	1,995
Yukon, Alaska-Canada	1,979
Rio Grande, U.S.A.-Mexico	1,885
São Francisco, Brazil	1,811
Indus, Asia	1,800
Brahmaputra, Asia	1,800
Salween, Asia	1,770
Danube, Europe	1,760
Euphrates, Asia	1,700
Zambezi, Africa	1,700
Tocantins, Brazil	1,700
Syr-Dar'ya, U.S.S.R.	1,660
Saskatchewan, Canada	1,660
Si, China	1,650
Nelson, Canada	1,600
Paraguay, S.A.	1,584
Ural, U.S.S.R.	1,575
Ganges, Asia	1,540
Amu-Dar'ya, Asia	1,500
Japurá, S.A.	1,500
Arkansas, U.S.A.	1,450
Colorado, U.S.A.-Mexico	1,450
Irrawaddy, Burma	1,425
Dnieper, U.S.S.R.	1,420
Negro, S.A.	1,400
Kolyma, U.S.S.R.	1,335
Ohio, U.S.A.	1,306
Orange, Africa	1,300
Kama, U.S.S.R.	1,262
Red, U.S.A.	1,222
Don, U.S.S.R.	1,222
Columbia, U.S.A.-Canada	1,214
Peace, Canada	1,195
Tigris, Asia	1,181
Darling, Australia	1,160
Angara, U.S.S.R.	1,151
Sungari, Asia	1,130
Pechora, U.S.S.R.	1,111
Snake, U.S.A.	1,038
Churchill, Canada	1,000
Pilcomayo, S.A.	1,000
Uruguay, S.A.	1,000
Magdalena, Colombia	1,000
Platte-N. Platte, U.S.A.	990
Oka, U.S.S.R.	918
Canadian, U.S.A.	906
Colorado, Texas, U.S.A.	894
Brazos, U.S.A.	870
Tennessee, U.S.A.	869
South Saskatchewan, Canada	865
Dniester, U.S.S.R.	852
Fraser, Canada	850
Northern Dvina, U.S.S.R.	803
Tisza, Europe	800
North Canadian, U.S.A.	784
Athabasca, Canada	765

GEOGRAPHICAL TERMS

A. = Arabic Camb. = Cambodian Ch. = Chinese Czech. = Czechoslovakian Dan. = Danish Du. = Dutch Finn. = Finnish Fr. = French Ger. = German Ice. = Icelandic It. = Italian Jap. = Japanese Mong. = Mongol Nor. = Norwegian Per. = Persian Port. = Portuguese Russ. = Russian Sp. = Spanish Sw. = Swedish Turk. = Turkish

Å	Nor., Sw.	Stream
Aas	Dan., Nor.	Hills
Abajo	Sp.	Lower
Ada, Adasi	Turk.	Island
Altipiano	It.	Plateau
Altiplano	Sp.	Plateau
Alv, Alf, Elf	Sw.	River
Arrecife	Sp.	Reef
Asa	Nor., Sw.	Hill
Asaga	Turk.	Lower
Austral	Sp.	Southern
Baai	Du.	Bay
Bab	Arabic	Gate or Strait
Bahia	Sp.	Bay
Bahr	Arabic	Marsh, Lake, Sea, River
Baia	Port.	Bay
Baie	Fr.	Bay, Gulf
Baizo	Port.	Low
Bakke	Dan.	Hill
Bana	Jap.	Cape
Bañados	Sp.	Marshes
Band	Per.	Mt. Range
Barra	Sp.	Reef
Bel	Turk.	Pass
Belt	Ger.	Strait
Ben	Gaelic	Mountain
Bera	Du.	Mountain
Berg	Ger., Du.	Mountain
Bir	Arabic	Well
Birket	Arabic	Pond
Boca	Sp.	Gulf, Inlet
Boğhaz	Turk.	Strait
Bolshoi, Bolshaya	Russ.	Big
Bolson	Sp.	Depression
Bong	Korean	Mountain
Boreal	Sp.	Northern
Breen	Nor.	Glacier
Bro	Dan., Nor., Sw.	Bridge
Bucht	Ger.	Bay
Bugt	Dan.	Bay
Bukhta	Russ.	Bay
Bukit	Malay	Hill, Mountain
Bukt	Nor., Sw.	Bay, Gulf
Burnu, Burun	Turk.	Cape, Point
By	Dan., Nor., Sw.	Town
Cabo	Port., Sp.	Cape
Campos	Port.	Plains
Canal	Port., Sp.	Channel
Cap, Capo	Fr., It.	Cape
Cataratas	Sp.	Falls
Catena	It.	Mt. Range
Catingas	Port.	Open Woodlands
Central, Centrale	Fr., It.	Middle
Cerrito, Cerro	Sp.	Hill
Cerros	Sp.	Hills, Mountains
Chai	Turk.	River
Chow	Ch.	Town of the second rank
Ciénaga	Sp.	Swamp
Ciudad	Sp.	City
Col	Fr.	Pass
Cordillera	Sp.	Mt. Range, Mts.
Côte	Fr.	Coast
Csatoria	Magyar	Canal
Cuchilla	Sp.	Mt. Range
Curiche	Sp.	Swamp
Dag, Dagh	Turk.	Mountain
Dağlari	Turk.	Mt. Range
Dal	Nor., Sw.	Valley
Dar	Arabic	Land
Darya	Per.	Salt Lake
Dasht	Per.	Desert, Plain
Deniz, Denizi	Turk.	Sea, Lake
Desierto	Sp.	Desert
Détroit	Fr.	Strait
Djeziret	Arabic, Turk.	Island
Do	Korean	Island
Doi	Thai	Mountain
Eiland	Du.	Island
Elv	Dan., Nor.	River
Embalse	Sp.	Reservoir
Emi	Berber	Mountain
Erg	Arabic	Dune, Desert
Eski	Turk.	Old
Est, Este	Fr., Port., Sp.	East
Estero	Sp.	Estuary, Creek
Estrecho, Estreito	Sp., Port.	Strait
Etang	Fr.	Pond, Lagoon, Lake
Fedja, Feij	Arabic	Pass
Fiume	It.	River
Fjäll	Sw.	Mountain
Fjeld, Fjell	Nor.	Hills, Mountain
Fjord	Dan., Nor., Sw.	Fiord
Fleuve	Fr.	River
Fljót	Icelandic	Stream
Fluss	Ger.	River
Fokani, Fukani	Arabic	Upper
Fors	Sw.	Waterfall
Fos, Foss	Dan., Nor.	Waterfall
Fu	Ch.	Town of importance
Gamla	Nor.	Old
Gamle	Dan.	Old
Gata	Jap.	Lake
Gawa	Jap.	River
Gebel	Arabic	Mountain
Gebergte	Du.	Mt. Range
Gebirge	Ger.	Mt. Range
Ghubbet	Arabic	Bay
Gobi	Mongol	Desert
Goe	Jap.	Pass
Gol	Mongol, Turk.	Lake, Stream
Golf	Ger., Du.	Gulf
Golfe	Fr.	Gulf
Golfo	Sp., It., Port.	Gulf
Gölü	Turk.	Lake
Gora	Russ.	Mountain
Grand, Grande	Fr., Sp.	Big
Groot	Du.	Big
Gross	Ger.	Big
Grosso	It., Port.	Big
Guba	Russ.	Bay, Gulf
Gunto	Jap.	Archipelago
Gunung	Malay	Mountain
Hai	Ch.	Sea
Halbinsel	Ger.	Peninsula
Hamáda, Hammada	Arabic	Rocky Plateau
Hamn	Sw.	Harbor
Hamún	Per.	Marsh
Hanto	Jap.	Peninsula
Has, Hassi	Arabic	Well
Hav	Dan., Nor., Sw.	Sea, Ocean
Havet	Nor.	Bay
Havn	Dan., Nor.	Harbor
Havre	Fr.	Harbor
Higashi, Higasi	Jap.	East
Ho	Ch.	River
Hochebene	Ger.	Plateau
Hoek	Du.	Cape
Hoku	Jap.	North
Holm	Dan., Nor., Sw.	Island
Hory	Czech.	Mountains
Hoved	Dan., Nor.	Cape, Promontory
Hsien	Ch.	Town of the third class
Hu	Ch.	Lake
Huk	Dan., Nor., Sw.	Point
Hus, Huus	Dan., Nor., Sw.	House
Hwang	Ch.	Yellow
Ile	Fr.	Island
Ilet	Fr.	Islet
Ilot	Fr.	Islet
Indre	Dan., Nor.	Inner
Inferieur, Inferiore	Fr., It.	Lower
Inner, Inre	Sw.	Inner
Insel	Ger.	Island
Irmak	Turk.	River
Isla	Sp.	Island
Isola	It.	Island
Jabal, Jebel	Arabic	Mountains
Järvi	Finn.	Lake
Jaure	Sw.	Lake
Jezira	Arabic	Island
Jima	Jap.	Island
Joki	Finn.	River
Kaap	Du.	Cape
Kabir, Kebir	Arabic	Big
Kai	Jap.	Sea
Kaikyo	Jap.	Strait
Kami	Turk.	Upper
Kanaal	Du.	Canal
Kanal	Russ., Ger.	Canal, Channel
Kao	Thai	Mountain
Kap, Kapp	Nor., Sw., Ice.	Cape
Kaupunki	Finn.	Town
Kawa	Jap.	River
Khao	Thai	Mountain
Khrebet	Russ.	Mt. Range
Kiang	Ch.	River
Kiao	Ch.	Point
Kita	Jap.	North
Klein	Du., Ger.	Small
Klint	Dan.	Promontory
Kō	Jap.	Lake
Ko	Thai	Island
Koh	Camb., Khmer	Island
Kong	Ch.	River
Kop	Du.	Peak, Head
Köping	Sw.	Market, Borough
Körfez, Körfezi	Turk.	Gulf
Kosa	Russ.	Spit
Kosui	Jap.	Lake
Kraal	Du.	Native Village
Kuchuk	Turk.	Small
Kuh	Per.	Mountain
Kul	Sinkiang Turki	Lake
Kum	Turk.	Desert
Kuro	Jap.	Black
Laag	Du.	Low
Lac	Fr.	Lake
Lago	Port., Sp., It.	Lake
Lagoa	Port.	Lagoon
Laguna	Sp.	Lagoon
Lagune	Fr.	Lagoon
Lahti	Finn.	Bay, Bight
Län	Sw.	County
Lilla	Sw.	Small
Lille	Dan., Nor.	Small
Ling	Ch.	Mountain
Llanos	Sp.	Plains
Mae Nam	Thai	River
Mali, Malaya	Russ.	Small
Man	Korean	Bay
Mar	Sp., Port.	Sea
Mare	It.	Sea
Medio	Sp.	Middle
Meer	Du.	Lake
Meer	Ger.	Sea
Mer	Fr.	Sea
Meridionale	It.	Southern
Meseta	Sp.	Plateau
Middelst, Midden	Du.	Middle
Minami	Jap.	Southern
Mir	Per.	Mountain
Mis	Russ.	Cape
Misaki	Jap.	Cape
Mittel	Ger.	Middle
Mont	Fr.	Mountain
Montagne	Fr.	Mountain
Montaña	Sp.	Mountains
Monte	Sp., It., Port.	Mountain
More	Russ.	Sea
Morro	Port., Sp.	Mountain, Promontory
Morue	Fr.	Hill
Moyen	Fr.	Middle
Muong	Siamese	Town
Mys	Russ.	Cape
Nada	Jap.	Sea
Naka	Jap.	Middle
Nam	Burm., Lao	River
Nan	Ch., Jap.	South
Nes	Nor.	Cape, Point
Nevado	Sp.	Snow covered peak
Nieder	Ger.	Lower
Nishi, Nisi	Jap.	West
Nizhni, Nizhnyaya	Russ.	Lower
Njarga	Finn.	Peninsula, Promontory
Nong	Thai	Lake
Noord	Du.	North
Nor	Mong.	Lake
Nord	Fr., Ger.	North
Norte	Sp., It., Port.	North
Nos	Russ.	Cape
Novi, Novaya	Russ.	New
Nusa	Malay	Island
Ny, Nya	Nor., Sw.	New
O	Jap.	Big
Ö	Nor., Sw.	Island
Ober	Ger.	Upper
Occidental, Occidentale	Sp., It.	Western
Odde	Dan.	Point
Oeste	Port.	West
Ola	Mong.	Mountains
Ooster	Du.	Eastern
Opper, Over	Du.	Upper
Oriental	Sp., Fr.	Eastern
Orientale	It.	Eastern
Orta	Turk.	Middle
Ost	Ger.	East
Ostrov	Russ.	Island
Ouest	Fr.	West
Öy	Nor.	Island
Ozero	Russ.	Lake
Pampa	Sp.	Plain
Pas	Fr.	Channel, Strait
Paso	Sp.	Pass
Passo	It., Port.	Pass
Peh, Pei	Ch.	North
Peña	Sp.	Rock, Mountain
Penisola	It.	Peninsula
Pequeño	Sp.	Small
Pereval	Russ.	Pass
Peski	Russ.	Desert
Petit	Fr.	Small
Phu	Lao, Annamese	Mtn.
Pic	Fr.	Mountain
Piccolo	It.	Small
Pico	Port., Sp.	Mountain, Peak
Pik	Russ.	Mountain, Peak
Piton	Fr.	Mountain, Peak
Planalto	Port.	Plateau
Plato	Russ.	Plateau
Pointe	Fr.	Point
Poluostrov	Russ.	Peninsula
Ponta	Port.	Point
Presa	Sp.	Reservoir
Presqu'île	Fr.	Peninsula
Proliv	Russ.	Strait
Pulou, Pulo	Malay	Island
Punt	Du.	Point
Punta	Sp., It., Port.	Point
Qum	Turk.	Desert
Rada	Sp.	Inlet
Rade	Fr.	Bay, Inlet
Ras	Arabic	Cape
Reka	Russ.	River
Retto	Jap.	Archipelago
Ria	Sp.	Estuary
Río	Sp.	River
Rivier, Rivière	Du., Fr.	River
Rud	Per.	River
Saghir	Arabic	Small
Sai	Jap.	West
Saki	Jap.	Cape
Salar, Salina	Sp.	Salt Deposit
Salto	Sp., Port.	Falls
San	Ch., Jap., Korean	Hill
Sanmaek	Korean	Mt. Range
Schiereiland	Du.	Peninsula
Se	Camb., Khmer	River
See	Ger.	Sea, Lake
Selvas	Sp., Port.	Woods, Forest
Seno	Sp.	Bay, Gulf
Serra	Port.	Mts.
Serranía	Sp.	Mts.
Seto	Jap.	Strait
Settentrionale	It.	Northern
Severni, Severnaya	Russ.	North
Shan	Ch., Jap.	Hill, Mts.
Shang	Ch.	Upper
Shatt	Arabic	River
Shima	Jap.	Island
Shimo	Jap.	Lower
Shin	Jap.	Land
Shiro	Jap.	White
Shoto	Jap.	Islands
Si	Ch.	West
Siao	Ch.	Small
Sierra	Sp.	Mt. Range, Mts.
Sjö	Nor., Sw.	Lake, Sea
Sok, Suk, Souk	Arabic, Ar. Fr.	Market
Song	Annamese	River
Sopka	Russ.	Volcano
Spitze	Ger.	Mt. Peak
Sredni, Srednyaya	Russ.	Middle
Stad	Dan., Nor., Sw.	City
Stari, Staraya	Russ.	Old
Step	Russ.	Treeless Plain
Straat	Du.	Strait
Strasse	Ger.	Strait
Stretto	It.	Strait
Ström	Dan., Nor., Sw.	Sound
Stung	Camb., Khmer	River
Su	Turk.	River
Sud, Süd	Sp., Fr., Ger.	South
Suido	Jap.	Strait, Channel
Sul	Port.	South
Sund	Dan., Nor., Sw.	Sound
Sungei	Malay	River
Supérieur	Fr.	Upper
Superior, Superiore	Sp., It.	Upper
Sur	Sp.	South
Suyu	Turk.	River
Ta	Ch.	Big
Tafelland	Du.	Plateau
Tagh	Turk.	Mt. Range
Take	Jap.	Peak, Ridge
Takht	Arabic	Lower
Tal	Ger.	Valley
Tandjong, Tanjung	Malay	Cape, Point
Tao	Ch.	Island
Tell	Arabic	Hill
Thale	Thai	Sea, Lake
Tind	Nor.	Peak
Tō	Jap.	East
To	Jap.	Island
Toge	Jap.	Pass
Trask	Finn.	Lake
Tso	Tibetan	Lake
Tugh	Somali	Dry River
Tung	Ch.	Eastern
Udjung	Malay	Point
Umi	Jap.	Bay
Unter	Ger.	Lower
Ura	Jap.	Inlet
Val	Fr.	Valley
Vatn	Nor.	Lake
Vecchio	It.	Old
Veld	Du.	Plain, Field
Velho	Port.	Old
Verkhni	Russ.	Upper
Vesi	Finn.	Lake
Vieho	Sp.	Old
Vik	Nor., Sw.	Bay
Vishni, Vishnyaya	Russ.	High
Vodokhranilishche	Russ.	Reservoir
Volcán	Sp.	Volcano
Vostochni, Vostochnaya	Russ.	East, Eastern
Wadi	Arabic	Dry River
Wald	Ger.	Forest
Wan	Jap.	Bay
Westersch	Du.	Western
Wüste	Ger.	Desert
Yama	Jap.	Mountain
Yarim Ada	Turk.	Peninsula
Yokara	Turk.	Upper
Yug, Yuzhni, Yuzhnaya	Russ.	South, Southern
Zaki	Jap.	Cape
Zaliv	Russ.	Bay, Gulf
Zapadni, Zapadnaya	Russ.	Western
Zee	Du.	Sea
Zemlya	Russ.	Land
Zuid	Du.	South

VOYAGES OF DISCOVERY AND EXPLORATION

Year	Explorer and Nationality	Discovery — Exploration — Journey
B. C.		
500	Himilco (Carthage)	Explores Atlantic Coast of Europe.
470	Hanno (Carthage)	Leads a colonizing expedition to West Africa, as far as Cape Palmas.
330	Pytheas of Massilia (Greek)	Explores coast of Spain, Gaul and Great Britain.
332-326	Alexander the Great (Macedonia)	Enters India in 326.
325	Nearchus (Macedonia)	Sails from the Indus to the Euphrates River.
120	Eudoxus of Cnidus (Greek)	Attempts circumnavigation of Africa.
A. D.		
84	Gnaeus Julius Agricola (Roman)	Circumnavigates Great Britain.
861	Norsemen	Explore Faeroe Islands and Iceland; round north cape of Europe.
876	Gunnbjörn (Norse)	Sights Greenland Coast.
982	Eric the Red (Norse)	Discovers and names Greenland.
1000	Leif Ericson (Norse)	Discovers Newfoundland (Helluland), and Coast of New England (Vinland).
1160	Benjamin of Tudela (Navarre)	Travels in Turkey, Egypt, Assyria and Persia, penetrating to the frontiers of China.
1200	Arabs	Trading merchants discover Siberia.
1253	Jan van Ruysbroek (Dutch)	Reaches Karakorum, the ancient seat of the Mongol Empire.
1271-1295	Marco Polo (Venetian)	Travels in Central Asia, India, Persia. First to travel in China.
1325-1352	Ibn Batuta (Arabian)	Travels through North Africa, East Africa, South Russia, Arabia, India and China.
1487	Bartholomew Dias (Portuguese)	Rounds Cape of Good Hope to a point beyond Algoa Bay.
1492-1494	Christopher Columbus (Genoan)	Discovers the West Indies on Oct. 12, 1492; discovers Dominica, Puerto Rico and several of the Windward Islands on Nov. 3, 1493 during his second voyage; discovers Jamaica on May 3, 1494.
1497	Amerigo Vespucci (Florentine)	Discovers Venezuela and the continent of South America.
1497	John Cabot (Anglo-Venetian)	Sails along the northeast coast of America, discovering Cape Breton Islands and Nova Scotia.
1498	Vasco da Gama (Portuguese)	Takes route to India via Cape of Good Hope.
1498	Sebastian Cabot (English)	Explores American Coast from Gulf of Saint Lawrence to Chesapeake Bay.
1499	Christopher Columbus (Genoan)	Discovers Trinidad on July 31st; enters mouth of Orinoco River on August 1st.
1499	Alonso de Ojeda (Italian)	Discovers Gulf of Venezuela and New Granada.
1500	Vicente Pinzon (Spanish)	Discovers mouth of the Amazon.
1501	Pedro Alvarez Cabral (Portuguese)	Explores Coast of Brazil which he names Santa Cruz.
1502	Amerigo Vespucci (Florentine)	Discovers Bay of Rio de Janeiro.
1502	Christopher Columbus (Genoan)	Visits Central America on his fourth voyage; discovers Martinique.
1513	Ponce de Leon (Spanish)	Discovers Florida and sails up the west coast of the Peninsula.
1513	Vasco Nunez de Balboa (Spanish)	Crosses Isthmus of Panama and discovers the Pacific Ocean.
1518	Juan de Grijalva (Spanish)	Discovers east coast of Mexico.
1519-1521	Hernando Cortez (Spanish)	Conquers Mexico.
1519-1521	Ferdinand Magellan (Spanish) del Cano (after Magellan's death)	First to circumnavigate the globe. Passes thru the Strait of Magellan, crosses the Pacific and discovers the Philippines.
1524	Giovanni Verrazano (Italian)	Explores coast of North Carolina, Maryland, New Jersey and New York.
1524-1535	Jacques Cartier (French)	Explores Gulf of St. Lawrence and ascends river to Montreal.
1534	Francisco Pizarro (Spanish)	Completes the conquest of Peru.
1540-1541	Francisco de Orellana (Spanish)	Crosses Andes east of Quito and descends Amazon River to mouth.
1541	Fernando de Soto (Spanish)	Discovers the Mississippi River.
1576	Sir Martin Frobisher (English)	Explores Labrador and Baffin Bay; discovers Frobisher Bay.
1577-1580	Sir Francis Drake (English)	Second circumnavigation of the globe; explores west coast of North America as far as Oregon.
1592	John Davis (English)	Discovers the Falkland Islands.
1595	Sir Walter Raleigh (English)	Explores Guiana and ascends the Orinoco 400 miles.
1596	William Barents (Dutch)	Discovers Spitzbergen, Nova Zemlya and Barents Sea.
1606	Pedro Fernandez de Queiros (Spanish)	Discovers the New Hebrides.
1608	Samuel de Champlain (French)	Discovers Lake Ontario.
1608	John Smith (English)	Explores Chesapeake Bay and its tributaries.
1609-1610	Henry Hudson (English)	Explores Hudson River and Hudson Bay.
1616	William Baffin (English)	Enters Baffin Bay in quest of Northwest Passage.
1642	Abel Tasman (Dutch)	Discovers Van Dieman's Land (Tasmania) and New Zealand.
1673	Jacques Marquette and Louis Joliet (French)	Explore the Mississippi River from the north.
1681	Renè R. C. La Salle (French)	Explores Lower Mississippi and takes possession for Louis XIV.
1701	Father Kino	Explores California.
1728	Vitus Bering (Dane)	Discovers Bering Strait and proves that Asia and America are not connected.
1768-1775	Capt. James Cook (English)	Circumnavigates the globe and makes hydrographic surveys of the Society Islands, Sandwich Islands, east coast of Australia, Cook Strait in New Zealand.
1789-1793	Alex. Mackenzie (Scotch)	Explores Mackenzie River; first to make overland trip to Pacific Coast.
1792	George Vancouver (English)	Circumnavigates Vancouver Island, explores Gulf of Georgia.
1803-1806	Capt. Meriwether Lewis and Capt. Wm. Clark (U.S.)	Explore northwestern part of U. S. ascending Missouri River, crossing headwaters of Columbia River and following this river to the Pacific.
1819	Sir Wm. E. Parry (English)	Discovers Parry Archipelago.
1821	Fabian von Bellinghausen (Russian)	Explores Antarctic and discovers Peter Island and Alexander Island.
1830	Chas. Sturt (English)	Discovers the Murray River and Lake Alexandrina, Australia.
1841	Sir James C. Ross (English)	Commands expedition to Victoria Land and Volcanoes Erebus and Terror.
1849-1873	David Livingstone (Scotch)	Discovers Lakes Ngami, Shirwa, Nyasa and Victoria Falls.
1850	Sir R. M'Clure (Irish)	Discovers Northwest Passage.
1876	H. M. Stanley (Welsh)	Discovers Lakes Albert and Edward.
1881-1884	Lieut. A. W. Greely (U.S.)	Explores Grinnell Land and N.E. coast of Greenland. Expedition reaches 83° 24½' N. 1882.
1909	Robert E. Peary (U.S.)	Reaches North Pole with Henson and four Eskimos on April 6.
1909	Sir Ernest H. Shackleton (English)	Reaches lat. 88° 23' S.; ascends Mt. Erebus; organizes party which determines the location of the South Magnetic Pole.
1911	Capt. Roald Amundsen (Norwegian)	Discovers the South Pole on December 18.
1911-1914	Sir Douglas Mawson (British)	Explores Antarctic and discovers King George V Land.
1914	Col. Theodore Roosevelt (U.S.)	Discovers Roosevelt River, S. America, a large tributary of the Madera.
1927	C. H. Karius (Australian)	Crosses central New Guinea for first time.
1929	Comm. R. E. Byrd (U.S.)	Makes 1600 mile airplane flight to the South Pole and back, from base at "Little America".
1933-1935	Rear Adm. R. E. Byrd (U.S.)	Discovers Roosevelt Island on Second Antarctic Expedition.
1939-1941	Rear Adm. R. E. Byrd (U.S.)	Explores coast of Palmer Peninsula and adjacent islands.
1946-1947	Rear Adm. R. E. Byrd (U.S.)	Discovers many new mountain peaks and ranges in Antarctica.
1946-1948	Comm. Finn Ronne (U.S.)	Explores area south of Weddell Sea, proving existence of undivided Antarctic continent.
1948	R.C.A.F. fliers (Canadian)	Discover 85 mile long Prince Charles Island in Canadian Arctic.
1949-1952	Capt. John Giaever (Norw.-Swed.-Br.)	Explores Norwegian Antarctic sector in detail.
1951	Maj. Franz Risquez (Venezuela)	Discovers source of Orinoco River.
1953	Col. John Hunt (leader) (British)	Commands expedition making first successful ascent of Mt. Everest; summit reached by Edmond Hillary and Tensing Norkay.
1969	Neil Armstrong and Col. Edwin Aldrin, Jr. (U.S.)	First men to set foot on the moon.

GAZETTEER OF STATES, TERRITORIES AND POSSESSIONS

State or Territory	Land Area (Sq. Mi.)	Population (1970)	Inhabitants per Sq. Mi.	Admitted to the Union	Settled at	Date
Alabama	51,609	3,444,165	66.7	Dec. 14, 1819	Mobile	1702
Alaska	586,412	302,173	0.5	*Aug. 24, 1912	Sitka	1801
Arizona	113,909	1,772,482	15.7	Feb. 14, 1912	Tucson	1580
Arkansas	53,104	1,923,295	36.2	June 15, 1836	Arkansas Post	1685
California	158,693	19,953,134	125.7	Sept. 9, 1850	San Diego	1769
Canal Zone	362	44,198	122.1	*Nov. 18, 1903	....	....
Colorado	104,247	2,207,259	21.2	Aug. 1, 1876	Near Denver	1858
Connecticut	5,009	3,032,217	605.3	Jan. 9, 1788	Windsor	1635
Delaware	2,057	548,104	266.4	Dec. 7, 1787	Cape Henlopen	1627
District of Columbia	67	756,510	11,291.2	** 1790-1791	....	1790
Florida	58,560	6,789,443	115.9	Mar. 3, 1845	St. Augustine	1565
Georgia	58,876	4,589,575	78.0	Jan. 2, 1788	Savannah	1733
Guam	209	84,996	406.7	Dec. 10, 1898	Agana	....
Hawaii	6,450	769,913	119.4	Aug. 21, 1959	....	....
Idaho	83,557	713,008	8.5	July 3, 1890	Coeur d'Alene	1842
Illinois	56,400	11,113,976	197.1	Dec. 3, 1818	Kaskaskia	1720
Indiana	36,291	5,193,669	143.1	Dec. 11, 1816	Vincennes	1730
Iowa	56,290	2,825,041	50.2	Dec. 28, 1846	Burlington	1788
Kansas	82,264	2,249,071	27.3	Jan. 29, 1861	....	1831
Kentucky	40,395	3,219,311	79.7	June 1, 1792	Harrodsburg	1774
Louisiana	48,523	3,643,180	75.1	April 30, 1812	Iberville	1699
Maine	33,215	993,663	29.9	Mar. 15, 1820	Bristol	1624
Maryland	10,577	3,922,399	370.8	April 28, 1788	St. Mary's	1634
Massachusetts	8,257	5,689,170	689.0	Feb. 6, 1788	Plymouth	1620
Michigan	58,216	8,875,083	152.4	Jan. 26, 1837	Near Detroit	1650
Minnesota	84,068	3,805,069	45.3	May 11, 1858	St. Peter's River	1805
Mississippi	47,716	2,216,912	46.5	Dec. 10, 1817	Natchez	1716
Missouri	69,686	4,677,399	67.1	Aug. 10, 1821	St. Louis	1764
Montana	147,138	694,409	4.7	Nov. 8, 1889	....	1809
Nebraska	77,227	1,483,791	19.2	Mar. 1, 1867	Bellevue	1847
Nevada	110,540	488,738	4.4	Oct. 31, 1864	Genoa	1850
New Hampshire	9,304	737,681	79.3	June 21, 1788	Dover and Portsmouth	1623
New Jersey	7,836	7,168,164	914.8	Dec. 18, 1787	Bergen	1617
New Mexico	121,666	1,016,000	8.3	Jan. 6, 1912	Santa Fe	1605
New York	49,576	18,241,266	367.9	July 26, 1788	Manhattan Island	1614
North Carolina	52,586	5,082,059	96.6	Nov. 21, 1789	Albemarle	1650
North Dakota	70,665	617,761	8.7	Nov. 2, 1889	Pembina	1780
Ohio	41,222	10,652,017	258.4	Mar. 1, 1803	Marietta	1788
Oklahoma	69,919	2,559,253	36.6	Nov. 16, 1907	....	1889
Oregon	96,981	2,091,385	21.6	Feb. 14, 1859	Astoria	1810
Pennsylvania	45,333	11,793,909	260.2	Dec. 12, 1787	Delaware River	1682
Puerto Rico	3,435	2,712,033	789.5	Dec. 10, 1898	Caparra	1510
Rhode Island	1,214	949,723	782.3	May 29, 1790	Providence	1636
Samoa	76	27,159	357.4	*Feb. 16, 1900	....	....
South Carolina	31,055	2,590,516	83.4	May 23, 1788	Port Royal	1670
South Dakota	77,047	666,257	8.7	Nov. 2, 1889	Sioux Falls	1856
Tennessee	42,244	3,924,164	92.9	June 1, 1796	Ft. Loudon	1757
Texas	267,339	11,196,730	41.9	Dec. 29, 1845	Matagorda Bay	1686
Utah	84,916	1,059,273	12.5	Jan. 4, 1896	Salt Lake City	1847
Vermont	9,609	444,732	46.2	Mar. 4, 1791	Ft. Dummer	1764
Virgin Islands	132	62,468	473.2	*Mar. 31, 1917	St. Thomas I.	1657
Virginia	40,817	4,648,494	111.1	June 26, 1788	Jamestown	1607
Washington	68,192	3,409,169	50.0	Nov. 11, 1889	Astoria	1811
West Virginia	24,181	1,744,237	72.1	June 20, 1863	Wheeling	1774
Wisconsin	56,154	4,417,933	78.7	May 29, 1848	Green Bay	1670
Wyoming	97,914	332,416	3.4	July 10, 1890	Ft. Laramie	1834

*Date of organization as Territory or acquisition by U. S. **Established under Acts of Congress.

UNITED STATES — POPULATION

Year	Population	Year	Population	Year	Population	Year	Population
1790	3,929,214	1840	17,069,453	1890	62,979,766	1940	132,164,569
1800	5,308,483	1850	23,191,876	1900	76,212,168	1950	151,325,798
1810	7,239,881	1860	31,443,321	1910	92,228,496	1960	179,323,175
1820	9,638,453	1870	38,558,371	1920	106,021,537	1970	203,235,298
1830	12,866,020	1860	50,189,209	1930	123,202,624